Advance Praise for
Integrated Enterprise Excellence,
Volume III—Improvement Project Execution

"**Forrest's books are the industry standard for taking Six Sigma and Lean Six Sigma to its next level.**"
—Bill Wiggenhorn, Retired President of Motorola University, currently Vice Chairman of GEM Global Edu-Tech Management Group

"**[Likely to] become a 'Standard Reference' for Lean Sigma thinking within many Fortune 500 organizations...The book is 'state of the art' in concept and will add greatly to the literature in the Performance Excellence field.**"
—Donald C. Fisher, MSQPC, Executive Director, The Quality Center

"**Other books are light years behind Forrest's 4-book suite, which not only provides senior management with Lean Sigma performance Scorecards, but also a how-to roadmap for Enron-effect avoidance.**"
—Frank Shines, Black Belt, TDLeanSigma, Director, Tech Data Corporation
Author, *The New Science of Success*

"**The book is the most comprehensive one I've found on the tools and specific pathways to achieving excellence. By using a balanced IEE approach a company can leverage their resources to rapidly improve and compete successfully in our 21st century environment.**"
—Bill Baker, Retired Knowledge Management & Benchmarking Champion, Raytheon Company; Principal and Founder, Speed To Excellence

"**An outstanding reference for any serious Lean Six Sigma implementation.**"
—Joseph A Knecht, Operations Manager – Forge Products, *TIMET*

"**An excellent text and valuable reference...accurate, valid, consistent and quite comprehensive, combining the current thinking and integration of traditional Six Sigma and Lean methods.**"
—Mike Jones, Past President, ASQ

Integrated Enterprise Excellence
Volume III—Improvement Project Execution

Integrated Enterprise Excellence Volume III—Improvement Project Execution

A Management and Black Belt Guide for Going Beyond Lean Six Sigma and the Balanced Scorecard

Forrest W. Breyfogle III
Founder and CEO
Smarter Solutions, Inc.

Forrest@SmarterSolutions.com
www.SmarterSolutions.com
Austin, Texas

Integrated Enterprise Excellence, Volume III—Improvement Project
Execution: A Management and Black Belt Guide for Going Beyond Lean
Six Sigma and the Balanced Scorecard

Published by Bridgeway Books in cooperation with Citius Publishing, Inc.
P.O. Box 80107
Austin, TX 78758

For more information about our books, please write to us, call
512.478.2028, or visit our website at www.bridgewaybooks.net.

Library of Congress Control Number: 2008920713

ISBN-13: 978-1-934454-16-9
ISBN-10: 1-934454-16-8

Cover concept design by Priyanka Kodikal.

10 9 8 7 6 5 4 3 2 1

To my beloved wife, Becki, who has made so many sacrifices in support of my work.

Contents

Foreword

Forrest Breyfogle's newest 4-book/volume management guide contains what is unavailable elsewhere, a roadmap for an enduring project management system that establishes achievable goals, prioritizes work efforts and continually improves performance. This series provides a linkage thread between MBA schools and practitioners, which leads to the 3 R's of business: everyone doing the Right things and doing them Right at the Right time.

This volume offers both managers and black belts a project execution process that goes beyond Lean Six Sigma and the Balanced Scorecard. It is the most far-reaching volume of the three-volume series that details Integrated Enterprise Excellence (IEE), a system that is the result of Breyfogle's quarter century of work in the development of a comprehensive set of statistical and non-statistical tools and their integration with each other. IEE stays in place regardless of management continuity, changes in the competitive environment or the economic climate.

IEE is vitally needed to help businesses deal with the extraordinary challenges they are facing today. It enables managers at every level with a power-enhancing dashboard that allows pin-point measurement and ongoing improvement of every function.

This volume analyzes the shortcomings of existing management scorecards and presents a better approach to scorecarding. Breyfogle points out that traditional scorecards capture a picture of the past but do not give insight for the future. In particular, the book describes the weaknesses of the commonly used red-yellow-green scorecard tracking system, which often causes managers to take actions that are counterproductive to meeting both local and corporate goals.

Breyfogle states that most managers focus on creating linkages from strategies to scorecards. Rather, he suggests, strategy should flow from enterprise performance metrics and enterprise financial goals through a wise blending of analytics with innovation. The result is an enterprise-oriented Define-Measure-Analyze-Improve-Control process.

Under this process, Lean Six Sigma projects are selected, which have direct alignment to the enterprise as a whole. This is in contrast to the common practice of selecting projects that at a subsystem level can seem beneficial but can have minimal, if any, impact on the enterprise as a whole.

In an era often characterized by metrics overload, this system measures only what is meaningful. It provides measures on different levels, giving management both the intelligence and tools to make ongoing operational and organizational improvements. Full implementation of the system prevents the unauthorized transfer of assets from one unit to another and thereby gives management the ability to protect the company from financial embarrassment.

At the same time, IEE prevents avoidance of responsibility. Breyfogle's approach offers clarity throughout the organization regarding internal and external requirements and responsibilities. All work is data-driven rather than dependent on whims, instincts and moods of the moment. Every metric has an owner.

The book is invaluable also for its guidance on blending analytics with innovation. True innovation – the kind that creates exciting new products with a definable ready-to-buy market – requires both leaps of the imagination and data-based R&D. Breyfogle points out the critical importance of the voice of the customer and cautions that without wisely blending innovation with analytics, R&D efforts can result in chaos.

This book deserves to become a standard desk reference for everyone in the organization responsible for meeting goals. It makes valuable reading for organization leaders and Six Sigma practitioners. As such, it is the most thorough and detailed reference guide for IEE, expanding upon the work presented in the two earlier published volumes of the series.

Bill Wiggenhorn
Main-captiva, owner
Sr. VP Motorola/President Motorola
University, retired

Keith Moe
Business consultant

Group VP 3M, retired

Preface

Volume 3 of this three-volume series guides both practitioners and organizational leaders through the *execution mechanics of both non-statistical and statistical tools* for enterprise analyses and improvements. This volume can become the day-to-day practitioner and manager reference for project execution and enterprise improvement. This volume illustrates the execution and efficient/effective tool usage for the following challenges:

- Execute improvement projects using a detailed step-by-step roadmap that truly integrates Six Sigma and Lean tools.
- Determine an effective organizational scorecard and metric system so that organizations transition from a firefighting culture to fire prevention.
- Select and effectively utilize the most appropriate statistical and non-statistical data analysis technique at both the project and enterprise level.
- Reduce lead times and inventory through the wise application of Lean and other tools.
- Reduce rework and improve quality through effective use of design of experiments (DOE) and other tools.
- Improve supplier quality and on-time delivery.
- Better meet customer needs in accuracy, performance, consistency, price, and servicing.
- Create and implement innovative ideas into project execution.

This series of three volumes describes how to orchestrate activities, which can provide the highest yields at points where these efforts will have the greatest bottom-line impact. In addition, focus will also be given in this orchestration so that activities will occur at the most opportune times throughout the entire organization.

Simply put, the described system helps an organization move toward the three Rs of business: everyone doing the right things and doing them right at the right time throughout the organization. Rather than seeking out product or service flaws, this system determines whether the process itself is flawed. Rather than force projects where benefits could be questionable, designs and improvements are made that impact the overall systems for doing business. This system elevates every business unit to a new, more productive business way of life.

The ultimate goal for an enterprise management system is to achieve maximum, measurable, predictable, and sustainable bottom-line results for the entire corporation. The volumes in this series describe an Integrated Enterprise Excellence (IEE) business management system, which presents the structure and tools you can use to accomplish these objectives. This IEE methodology provides a power-enhancing performance measurement scorecard/dashboard system that serves as an enterprise-wide route to increase corporate profitability continually.

This series describes how IEE takes Lean Six Sigma and the balanced scorecard to the next level. This system helps organizations overcome some difficulties encountered with previous systems. In IEE, a value chain performance measurement system provides organizations with a no-nonsense metric system that leads to the orchestration of day-to-day value-added activities so that there is true business-needs alignment. Improvement or design projects are created whenever business or operational metrics need betterment. This is in contrast to the search, selection, and creation of Six Sigma/Lean projects that often are not in true alignment with business goals. Organizations can gain a competitive advantage when this system becomes a business way of life.

Businesses that have adopted the Lean Six Sigma methodology have a built-in foundation for implementing this enhanced system. Others will learn how to establish the foundation for this system. For both groups, this series describes an enterprise process roadmap and a project execution roadmap, together with all the tools needed for enterprise excellence.

This volume and other volumes of this series describe the IEE system, which addresses the following example needs:

- Executives want a structured system which can assist them with meeting their financial goals.

- An organizational executive or a change manager is looking for an enterprise management structure that will coordinate, track, enhance, control, and help predict corporate results.
- Leadership wants to become more of a data-driven/data-decision based company so that the right questions are asked before decisions are made.
- Executives want a system that helps them to create a strategy that is more specifically targeted so that everyone has consistent focus toward meeting the organizational goals that they would like to achieve.
- Company leadership wants to reduce the amount of waste that they routinely experience when fighting the problems of the day, which never seem to go away.
- Management wants a no-nonsense measurement and improvement system.
- Leadership wants a streamlined enhancement to their Sarbanes-Oxley (SOX) system so that the company benefits more from its implementation with less effort.
- Lean Six Sigma deployment leaders want to integrate Lean and Six Sigma concepts and tools so that they are using the right tool at the right time.
- Management wants to improve its performance measurement and improvement systems.
- Managers and practitioners want an easy-to-follow roadmap that addresses not only project execution but also enterprise issues as well.
- Organization leaders want a system that can help them to orchestrate people's activities so that everyone is doing the right things and doing them right at the right time.
- Lean Six Sigma deployment leaders want a system that consistently leads to projects that are most beneficial to the overall enterprise.

CEOs benefits from this series include:
- CEOs want to avoid the problem: "Chiefs (CEOs) are being pushed out the door as directors abandon their laissez-faire approach to governance following the prosecutions at Enron Corp., WorldCom Inc., and other companies." (Kelly, 2006)
- CEOs want to create a legacy system of organizational efficiency and effectiveness, which outlives their tenure as company heads.
- CEOs want to create more customers and cash.

Table 0.1 Where to Start?

Where to start?		
Role	*I want to:*	*Source*
Executives, Champions, Managers, MBBs, BBs, GBs, and YBs	Assess the benefits of an IEE measurement and improvement system over other systems (novel format).	Volume 1
Executives, Champions, Managers, and MBBs	Understand the benefits of IEE when compared to other business systems and utilize a roadmap for IEE implemention at the enterprise level.	Volume 2
MBBs, BBs, GBs, and other practitioners	Execute effective process improvement projects, benefit from the project execution roadmap, and effectively utilize tools at both the project and enterprise level.	Volume 3

See Glossary for descriptions.

MBB = Master black belt   BB = Black belt   GB = Green belt   YB = Yellow belt

E-DMAIC (Roadmap): An IEE enterprise define-measure-analyze-improve-control roadmap, which contains among other things a value chain measurement and analysis system where metric improvement needs can pull

P-DMAIC (Roadmap): An IEE project define-measure-analyze-improve-control roadmap for improvement project execution, which contains a true integration of Six Sigma and Lean tools.

Table 0.1 describes how the volumes of this series can address differing readers' needs and interests. The syntax for figure or table references in this volume series is that the first number is the chapter number. A zero was the first number in this table reference since the table is in the preface.

The book, *The Integrated Enterprise Excellence System: An Enhanced, Unified Approach to Balanced Scorecards, Strategic Planning, and Business Improvement*, (Breyfogle, 2008d) introduced new perspectives on what to measure and report; when and how to report it; how to interpret the results; and how to use the results to establish goals, prioritize work efforts and continuously enhance organizational focus and success.

In this three-volume series, *Integrating Enterprise Excellence: Going Beyond Lean Six Sigma and the Balanced Scorecard*, there is both further elaboration on the shortcomings of traditional systems and the details of an IEE implementation. Series volumes make reference to other volumes and *Implementing Six Sigma* (Breyfogle, 2003a) for an expansion of topic(s) or a differing perspective.

A content summary of this volume series is:

- *Integrated Enterprise Excellence Volume I – The Basics: Golfing Buddies Go Beyond Lean Six Sigma and the Balanced Scorecard* – An IEE onset story about four friends who share their experiences while playing golf. They see how they can improve their games in both business and golf using this system that goes beyond Lean Six Sigma and the balanced scorecard. The story compares IEE to other improvement systems.

- *Integrated Enterprise Excellence Volume II – Business Deployment: A Leaders' Guide for Going Beyond Lean Six Sigma and the Balanced Scorecard* – Discusses problems encountered with traditional scorecard, business management, and enterprise improvement systems. Describes how IEE helps organizations overcome these issues utilizing an enterprise process define–measure–analyze–improve–control (E-DMA-IC) system. Systematically walks through the execution of this system.
- *Integrated Enterprise Excellence Volume III – Improvement Project Execution: A Management and Black Belt Guide for Going Beyond Lean Six Sigma and the Balanced Scorecard* – Describes IEE benefits and its measurement techniques. Provides a detailed step-by-step project define–measure–analyze–improve–control (P-DMAIC) roadmap, which has a true integration of Six Sigma and Lean tools.

Volumes of this series build upon each other so that readers develop an appreciation and understanding of IEE benefits and its implementation. These volumes and the previous described book were written to stand alone. Because of this, several concepts and examples are described in more than one book or volume. I felt it was important to repeat key concepts in multiple publications because each book or volume is more than a presentation of tools and examples – that is, focus was given in each book and volume to present IEE so that the reader gains insight to the interconnection of the concepts and determination of how they can benefit from the techniques.

Volume 3 of this series is divided into the following seven parts:

1. Integrated Enterprise Excellence Management System and Enterprise process (E-DMAIC): Define–Measure–Analyze–Improve–Control Phases
2. Improvement Project (P-DMAIC): Define Phase
3. Improvement Project (P-DMAIC): Measure Phase
4. Improvement Project (P-DMAIC): Analyze Phase
5. Improvement Project (P-DMAIC): Improve Phase

6. Improvement Project (P-DMAIC): Control Phase
7. Appendix

Part I

In part one, IEE is described at a high level along with its benefits. Many of the current popular management performance measures, strategic plans, and scorecards (both the red–yellow–green scorecards and the balanced scorecard) are then discussed. Part one also discusses how current management and measurement systems have led to problems such as the collapse of Enron and organizations doing the wrong things – actions that can be detrimental to the system as a whole; for example, Krispy Kreme managers shipping donuts that they knew would be returned so that they would meet short-term financial goals.

An IEE system is described that avoids these common types of management problems. The described enterprise process define–measure–analyze–improve–control (E-DMAIC) system goes beyond Lean Six Sigma and the balanced scorecard. Included in this system are goal setting, a unique/powerful scorecard system, strategic analysis/building, and an improvement system where projects are selected that are in true alignment with business needs. The application of theory of constraints (TOC) to identify enterprise bottlenecks is described and integrated with Lean/Six Sigma tools along with a no-nonsense measurement system.

Parts II–VI

Part II through VI of this volume walks the reader through a detailed P-DMAIC project execution roadmap that utilizes the enhanced measurement/scorecard techniques of IEE. In addition to traditional statistical and non-statistical tools, a true integration of Lean concepts is described for both the Measure and Improve phases with many enhancements over traditional methodologies. Also included is a chapter on team effectiveness, creativity, and the demonstration of project improvement.

Note: Tool complexity typically builds when progressing through a book. The disadvantage of this approach is that the reader can have a difficult time seeing how all the tools interconnect. I believe that the overall big-picture thought process of how everything fits together can be more important and difficult to comprehend than remembering how to apply tools from memory without consulting a book. Because of this, this volume incorporates a basic flow that follows the steps of the E-DMAIC and then the P-DMAIC roadmaps. In this volume, foundation topics are described immediately before they are most applicable. For example, in the P-DMAIC measure phase references are made to hypothesis testing; however, hypothesis test creation details are not described until the P-DMAIC analyze phase. When topics are mention that will be described later in more detail, I reference the future chapter or section that contains the information. Readers who would like an immediate more in depth methodology description can jump ahead in the volume; however, my intent is that the reader simply accepts my explanation of the technique at that point in time, knowing that the topic will have a more in depth description later in the volume.

This volume contains more than 100 examples.

Part VII

The Appendix includes additional concepts that are used in the enterprise process or project execution roadmap steps. These methodologies were placed in the appendix to avoid disruption to the roadmap methodology flow. Included in the appendix are the IEE improvement project execution roadmap with selected drill downs, project execution tollgate check sheets, and reference tables. This volume also has an extensive List of Symbols and Glossary.

Nomenclature and Service Marks

The Glossary and List of Acronyms and Symbols near the back of this volume are a useful reference for the understanding of unfamiliar statistical terms or acronyms/symbols. Book and publication references are also located near the back of this volume and will be referenced using the syntax: Author Name, Publication Date. Referenced examples and exercises use the syntax: Chapter number, exercise (or example) number; (e.g., Example 12.2, where 12 is the chapter number and two is the second exercise in the chapter).

To maximize the clarification of illustrations that span several years, some examples include specific month-year entries. I did this at the risk of making the book appear to be dated in the years to come. Hopefully the reader will understand my reasoning for making this selection and this decision will not deter the reader from benefiting from the book's concepts for many years to come.

Integrated Enterprise Excellence, IEE, satellite-level, 30,000-foot-level, and 50-foot-level are registered service marks of Smarter Solutions, Inc. In implementing the programs or methods identified in this text, you are authorized to refer to these marks in a manner that is consistent with the standards set forth herein by Smarter Solutions, Inc., but any and all use of the marks shall inure to the sole benefit of Smarter Solutions, Inc. Business way of Life and Smarter Solutions are registered service marks of Smarter Solutions, Inc.

Acknowledgments

I want to thank those who helped contribute specific sections of this volume: Rene Kapik contributed Example 28.6, Andy Viswanathan contributed Example 33.3, and David Enck contributed the five-step measurement improvement process in Section 15.20 and Examples 15.5 and 37.1.

I also want to thank others who helped in many ways. Rick Haynes provided many very helpful inputs and great suggestions within areas such as measurement systems analysis, logistic regression, and control plans. Dave Behrendsen work with Rick Haynes to compile exercises from previous publications or training material. Fred Bothwell provided great manuscript and marketing inputs, along with superb publishing and printing coordination. Dorothy Stewart provided editing, while Mallary Musgrove provided many helpful suggestions.

Thanks also need to go to those who gave other helpful improvement suggestions or helped in some other way in the overall process: Jim Alloway, Bob Ashenbrenner, Bill Baker, Don Barber, Bill Bates, Becki Breyfogle, Wes Breyfogle, Alvin Brown, Stephen Craddock, Bob Cheshire, Sonja Cline, Larry Dalton, Daniel Duplessis, Gary Ekstrom, Donn Fisher, Joe Flagherty, Janet Hamil, Jesse Hamilton, John Hannon, Mike Harkins, Robin Hensley, Joe Knecht, Kiran Gurumurthy, Jesse Hamilton, Len Javinet, Bob Jones, Michael Harrington, Cheryl Holden, Arch Holder, Mike Jones, Robert Jones, Rene Kapik, Lally Marwah,

Todd Minnick, Keith Moe, George Nicholas, Dean Norman, Andy Paquet, Tony Perez, Tanya Roberts, Bill Sampson, Janet Shade, Frank Shines, Jeannine Siviy, Wanda Thurm, Alice Toth, John Watson, Stan Wheeler, Gary Wietharn, Bill Wiggenhorn, Brian Winterowd, Johnny Yu, and Brian Zievis.

Statistical analyses were conducted using Minitab. Flowcharts were created using Igrafx.

Solutions Manual (End of Chapter Exercises) and Training

We at Smarter Solutions, Inc. take pride in creating an excellent learning environment for the wise application of tools that will improve organizational business systems. Our IEE approach and workshop handout materials are continually being enhanced and expanded. Our training includes executive, champion, black belt, green belt, yellow belt, master black belt, Lean, and design for integrated enterprise excellence (DFIEE) courses. DFIEE goes beyond Design for Six Sigma (DFSS). Workshops follow the E-DMAIC and P-DMAIC roadmaps, and often contain roadmap drilldowns not included in published books. Many who have already been trained as a black belt or master black belt have found our graduate workshop to be an excellent resource for their continuing education. This 1-week graduate workshop walks through the IEE roadmaps, describing the unique measurements and tool applications described in this volume, with benefits. Public and on-site IEE one-day workshops describe the overall system and its benefits.

Licensing inquiries for training material can be directed through www.smartersolutions.com. Articles, newsletters, and the latest information on how Smarter Solutions, Inc. is working with various organizations and universities are also described at this website. In addition, the availability of a solutions manual to the exercises at the end of chapters is described.

About Smarter Solutions, Inc., Contacting the Author

Your comments and improvement suggestions for this book-volume series are greatly appreciated. For more information about business measurements and improvement strategies, sign up for our newsletter, webinars, or e-mail us for a free initial business consultation.

FORREST W. BREYFOGLE III
Smarter Solutions, Inc.
11044 Research Blvd., Suite B-400
Austin, Texas, 78759, USA
Forrest@SmarterSolutions.com
www.SmarterSolutions.com
512-918-0280

PART I
Integrated Enterprise Excellence Management System and E-DMAIC

1

Background

1.1 Messages in Volume II and Part I of this Volume

Major topics discussed in Volume II and Part I of this volume are:

- **Integrated Enterprise Excellence (IEE) – a system to achieve the three Rs of business:** People can be busy and an organization can be pushing for the creation of improvement projects, but it's still possible to lose sight of the big picture. This can lead to much wasted effort and enterprise system suboptimization. IEE provides a system (see Figure 2.1) for transitioning from firefighting daily or weekly problems to achieving the three Rs of business: everyone doing the Right things and doing them Right at the Right time. In IEE, metrics and goals are created so that there is a pull for project creation (Figures 2.7 and 2.8), where project completion positively impacts the business as a whole.
- **E-DMAIC – a long-lasting enterprise framework for measurements and improvement that is refinement over time:** Organizations can be very successful through the directives and insight of a few key individuals. However, things

can quickly degrade if these individuals are no longer with the company. The E-DMAIC system process (see Figure 2.5) provides a foundation for an enhanced enterprise performance measurement, analysis, and improvement system that is systematically refined over time and remains stable with leadership and organizational changes.

- **Improved analytics and innovation – better strategy building:** IEE is a business system which includes the use of analytics and innovation for more effective focused strategies building. This leads to targeted improvement and design projects which benefit the business as a whole, and avoid suboptimization. Often organizations build their year-to-year efforts around a strategy that was developed in an executive retreat (see Figure 1.4). With this approach, functions in the organization create plans to execute these strategies, which can change from year-to-year or with leadership transitions. In addition, opinion-based strategy statements that rely solely on intuition and insight by the leadership may not lead to the best efforts throughout the organization. If the strategies are set after a thorough understanding of the enterprise performance and constraints, they are more effective in driving change and improving the business as a whole. The ability to support a strategic plan with performance data improves the buy-in and acceptance across the organization. In the E-DMAIC process, strategies are formulated (see step 5 in Figure 2.5) around the use of analytics and innovation to create an enterprise improvement plan (see Figure 3.7).
- **Building from the Define and Measure steps of E-DMAIC – a consistent over-time enterprise foundation:** Instead of building from a retreat-developed strategy, IEE leads through the E-DMAIC define and measure phase (see Sections 3.2–3.5), which include the creation of an enterprise value chain (see Figure 3.1) that has 30,000-foot-level and satellite-level metric reporting. This 30,000-foot-level and satellite-level metric view provides an enterprise-wide measurement system offering predictive statements (see Figures 3.3 and 3.4). This is unlike common tabular and graphic metric reporting (see Table 1.1, Figures 1.1–1.3) that provide stories of what has happened in the past and provide little, if any, insight to what can be expected in the future unless something changes.

- **The right business metrics and presentation method –
  the right behavior and better business performance:**
  The selection of the right enterprise business metrics can
  lead to improved performance, while some business metrics will not lead to the right behavior. Even with the right
  enterprise business metrics, the method to display or present such dashboards and scorecards may not lead to the
  right behavior (see Figure 3.4). The IEE system for metric
  creation and posting improves organizational resource utilization since common-cause variability will not be treated
  as though it were a special-cause condition (i.e., IEE is a
  means of implementing a fire-prevention system, as opposed to firefighting the problems of the day).
- **Analyzing the enterprise as a whole in E-DMAIC –
  business constraint removal and true enterprise improvement:** Resolving business problems and issues that
  are not constraining throughput, profit, or other satellite-
  level business metrics does not generally return the savings
  that are expected. In E-DMAIC, analyses identify enterprise-
  wide business performance constraints for exploitation. This
  effort in IEE results in improved resource utilization and
  true overall enterprise benefits, which is accompanied by a
  system for maintaining the gains (see Chapter 3).

1.2   Messages in Part II–VI of this Volume

Major topics discussed in Part II–Part VI of this volume are:

- **P-DMAIC roadmap – true integration of Six Sigma and Lean
  tools:** The format of the project execution roadmap shows how
  to effectively integrate Six Sigma and Lean tools. The roadmap
  provides the details to improve the efficiency and effectiveness
  of problem resolutions (see Appendix Section D.2). Lean tools
  are integrated into this roadmap in both measure phase drill
  down and the improve phase of the roadmap.
- **Metric roadmap tree diagrams – effective metric tracking:** It is not only important to determine what to measure
  but also how to report and assess the metrics (see Section
  1.7 and Figure 1.1). These metrics are applicable not only
  in the P-DMAIC roadmap but as part of the E-DMAIC value chain as well. Tree diagrams provide guidance for the

selection of the most appropriate metric for a variety of situations (see Figures D.2 and D.3).

- **Analyze phase tree diagrams – effective tool selection:** In the analyze phase, both visualization and analytical tool selection is very important. Erroneous conclusions can result when an inappropriate tool is used. Tree diagrams provide guidance for analytical and visual-representation tool selection (see Figures D.4 and D.5).
- **Detailed tool description – effective tool usage for both E-DMAIC and P-DMAIC roadmaps:** The presented tools describe not only tool execution but also the thought process for problem definition and tool selection in P-DMAIC. Many of these tools (Chapters 6–39) are also very useful in E-DMAIC execution.
- **Sequence of topic presentation – better P-DMAIC understanding and roadmap execution:** This volume presents tools as they would be executed or considered for execution in the P-DMAIC roadmap. This volume-topic sequence conveys the overall thought process of the roadmap. In addition, many chapters begin with an illustration of the roadmap and what roadmap steps will be covered in the chapter (Chapters 6–39).
- **Project roadmap toll gate check sheets – better project execution:** Check sheets (see Figures E1–E9) help with the overall project execution thought process, ensuring that all steps are satisfactorily executed. These check sheets can become a communication tool between the project reviewers and project execution practitioners.

1.3   Volume Layout

The purpose of this section is to provide the reader insight to this volume's layout. This understanding can help readers determine where they should start their reading.

Another book, *Integrated Enterprise Excellence: Going Beyond Lean Six Sigma and the Balanced Scorecard* (Breyfogle, 2008d) provides a high-level view of the IEE system and its benefits. *Integrated Enterprise Excellence Volume I – The Basics: Golfing Buddies Go Beyond Lean Six Sigma and the Balanced Scorecard* (Breyfogle, 2008a) contrasts several measurement and improvement systems in a novel format, illustrating the benefit of IEE.

Integrated Enterprise Excellence Volume II – Business Deployment: A Leaders' Guide for Going Beyond Lean Six Sigma and the Balanced Scorecard describes the building of an E-DMAIC framework.

This volume is not a quick-read book that has no future usefulness. My intent is that this how-to volume will be frequently referenced by practitioners and management to gain insight to improvement project and tool execution at both the E-DMAIC and P-DMAIC level. Since I am not sure about the reader's background relative to their understanding of key points in the previously described books (Breyfogle, 2008a, b, and d), Part I of this volume reiterates important fundamental concepts that were described in these books.

Part II–VI of this volume provides a step-by-step execution sequencing of the P-DMAIC process steps. For readers who want to immediately proceed to a description of the framework and execution of the overall P-DMAIC system, Part II is the place to start. Since readers have various needs and backgrounds, I thought it was important to provide a foundation so that everyone would begin reading the P-DMAIC roadmap portion of this book with a similar understanding about management systems and the shortcomings of commonly used metrics and improvement strategies.

I addressed these reader needs in Part I. Readers can choose the sections of the following chapters that best address their specific needs:

- Chapter 1: Background
- Chapter 2: Creating an IEE system
- Chapter 3: Enterprise-DMAIC system

The appendix Part VII material was positioned in this volume so that there was no reader flow disruption (e.g., P-DMAIC roadmap description).

1.4 The IEE System

Everyone within a business should be focusing his/her efforts toward creating **M**ore **C**ustomers and **C**ash. The **E**xistence and **Ex**cellence of organizations depend on it (i.e., $E=MC^2$) the same formula as Albert Einstein's famous equation. However, in reality, people can often be very busy and are far from achieving the three Rs of business: everyone doing the right things and doing them right at the right time throughout the organization, from an enterprise process point of view. Organizations can have a very difficult time orchestrating activities so that all personnel are in step to the rhythm that is necessary to obtain their business objectives and goals.

When we think about accomplishing activities in the workplace, we might immediately think of the phrase "What you measure is what you get" as being the cornerstone for this organizational orchestration. However, we must be careful. Data collection procedures and report-out formats can stimulate the wrong activities. I prefer to paraphrase this statement as "What and how you measure can stimulate what you get."

> Data collection procedures and report-out formats can stimulate the wrong activities.

Traditional management metrics often include tabular reporting and perhaps classic trend and bar charts. Management can also use a scorecard system to monitor and track both financial and non-financial areas of the business against measurement goals established for each of these metrics. With this scorecard approach, metric owners are tracked against and are responsible for achieving established goals for their metrics. These goals might be a part of the balanced scorecard (Kaplan and Norton, 1992) system, where the four perspectives of financial, customer, internal business process, and learning and growth are to be addressed throughout the organization.

Scorecard balance is important because if there is no balance one metric could be getting more focus than another. However, the natural balance described later in this volume is much more powerful than forcing a structure throughout the business via an organizational chart, which can change over time. In addition, the balanced scorecard system can lead to the suboptimization of processes, which can be detrimental to the enterprise as a whole.

Volumes in this series reference the system for enhancing scorecards and more as Integrated Enterprise Excellence or IEE. IEE goes beyond Lean Six Sigma and the balanced scorecard. In these volumes, tools and the overall thought process are presented in a step-by-step format that begins with the enterprise process and leads to the specifics of selecting and executing process improvement projects that are in true alignment with business goals.

IEE provides an enhanced scorecard and improvement project execution roadmap system. Included roadmaps provide a true integration of Lean and Six Sigma tools within the traditional define–measure–analyze–improve–control (DMAIC) roadmap. These roadmap steps are not only followed at the project execution level but the enterprise level as well. This volume focuses on applying the DMAIC roadmap at the project execution level. Volume 2 focuses on applying the DMAIC roadmap at the enterprise level. In this volume, the reader is referred to Volume 2, when appropriate, for more details on enterprise execution steps. In this volume, the reader is also referred to *Implementing Six Sigma*, when appropriate, for more details on a topic or additional topics that might be helpful but is not directly linked to the overall roadmap. In addition, Appendix E summarizes additional topics from the *Implementing Six Sigma* that might interest the reader.

Figure 2.1 illustrates the overall IEE system roadmap. In this system, an **E**nterprise (process) E-DMAIC roadmap (center figure 5-step sequence) has linkage in the improve phase to the improvement **P**roject P-DMAIC roadmap (bottom 5-step sequence) or design project define–measure–analyze–design–verify (DMADV) roadmap (top 5-step sequence).

In IEE, the value chain (see Figure 3.1) describes in flowchart fashion both primary and support organizational activities and their accompanying 30,000-foot-level or satellite-level metrics, which have no calendar boundaries. Example primary activity flow is develop product–market product–sell product–produce product–invoice/collect payments–report satellite-level metrics. Example support activities include IT, finance, HR, labor relations, safety and environment, and legal.

In this system, organizational value chain metrics improvement needs *pull for project creation* for either process improvement or design projects that are in true alignment with business needs (see Glossary "pull for project creation" and Figure 3.37). This volume describes the advantage of this enterprise process measurement pull system for project selection over traditional Lean Six Sigma implementations where there is a *push for project creation* (i.e., let's list potential projects and decide which project to work on first (see Glossary "push for project creation")).

In this series, Volume 2 followed the overall thought process of evaluating the enterprise process (E-DMAIC) to the mechanics of selecting improvement or design projects. This volume follows the sequence of executing a specific improvement project (P-DMAIC), as illustrated in Figure 2.1. I will highlight the benefits of Six Sigma and Lean tools that are most applicable and challenge some of the traditional Six Sigma/Lean Six Sigma techniques that can lead to questionable results. I will expand on other techniques that are beyond the boundaries of these methodologies.

In this series, Volume 2 described how to select and track the right measures within a company so that Lean/Six Sigma efforts best meet the strategic needs of the business and reduce day-to-day firefighting activities of the organization. In this volume, the described P-DMAIC project execution roadmap illustrates how to execute Lean/Six Sigma projects wisely so that the most appropriate Lean or Six Sigma tool is used when executing both manufacturing and transactional projects. All size organizations can reap very large benefits from this pragmatic approach to implementing Six Sigma/Lean Six Sigma, no matter if the organization is in the manufacturing, service, or development area.

Volume 2 describes the infrastructure for selecting and managing projects in an organization. This volume describes the tools and roadmap for both executing process improvement/re-engineering projects and conducting the enterprise analyses referenced in Volume 2. Many practical examples and application exercises are included. In addition, this series offers a classroom structure through which students can learn practical tools and a roadmap for immediate application.

The strategies and techniques described in the volumes of this series are consistent and aligned with the philosophies of such quality authorities as W. Edwards Deming (see Volume 2), J. M. Juran, Walter Shewhart, Genichi Taguchi, Kaoru Ishikawa, and others. *Implementing Six Sigma*, 2nd edition (Breyfogle, 2003a) described the integration of these methods with initiatives such as ISO-9000, Malcolm Baldrige award, Shingo prize, and GE Work-Out.

1.5   Six Sigma and Lean Six Sigma

Unlike IEE, Six Sigma and Lean Six Sigma are not an enterprise business management system. Six Sigma and Lean Six Sigma are a statistical quality performance measurement and management system that focuses on creating/completing projects which reduce the frequency of errors. These projects utilize both statistical and non-statistical tools to improve processes, where emphasis is given to creating projects that have validated financial benefits.

Six Sigma also addresses process improvement relative to voice of the customer (VOC) needs. The success of Six Sigma deployments is typically touted as a financial project savings total; however, as discussed later, claims from these finance-validated projects can often be challenged as to whether they truly impacted the bottom-line organizational benefits positively.

The term *sigma* (σ), in the name *Six Sigma*, is a letter in the Greek alphabet used to describe variability (i.e., standard deviation). The classical Six Sigma unit of measure is defects per opportunity. Sigma quality level offers an indicator of how often defects are likely to occur, where a higher sigma quality level indicates a process that is less likely to create defects. A six sigma quality level is said to equate to 3.4 defects per million opportunities (DPMO). Appendix Section B.1 describes the determination of this number and other sigma quality level performance level numbers (e.g., 4 sigma quality level equates to 6210 DPMO. A 3.4 ppm process defect rate is often considered near perfection; hence, a six sigma quality level is often considered a goal.

Lean has typically been associated with manufacturing, but the techniques apply to all business areas. In Lean, focus is given to process speed and efficiency. Lean focus has been given to the reduction of waste. The seven types of waste frequently referenced with Lean are overproduction, waiting, transportation, inventory, over-processing, motion, and defects. More recently some have added people utilization to this list; however, we can expand the list even further to include wasted space, wasted effort, wasted energy, and so forth.

Lean methods assess the operation of the factory and supply chain with an emphasis on the reduction of wasteful activities. Lean emphasizes the reduction of inconsistencies associated with manufacturing routings, material handling, storage, lack of communication, batch production, and so forth. As described in Volume 2, the Toyota production system (TPS) is usually considered the benchmark for Lean implementation.

Lean waste-elimination efforts give focus to pull scheduling, takt time, and flow production. With pull scheduling, production builds address what the customer is currently buying, as opposed to long-range forecasts. Takt is customer-demand rate. Processes should be changed so that they run at the customer-demand rate. Flow production involves the elimination of operational movement and waiting with an emphasis on eliminating batch products/transactions processing.

Lean can reduce inventory value by reducing work in progress (WIP). This can be accomplished by focusing on smaller job sizes and quicker processing times. By decreasing WIP on the floor, inventory is turned over more rapidly (i.e., inventory turns are increased).

Both Lean and Six Sigma have very powerful tools; however, deployments that don't equally consider Lean and Six Sigma methodologies are missing out on the benefits of having a complete tool set. This situation is analogous to someone using a wrench instead of a hammer to drive a nail into a board. Yes, one could complete the nailing task; however, the job would be more difficult than if a hammer were used. Similarly, a Lean improvement effort to reduce machine defects might not consider the power of design of experiments (DOE) techniques as a viable tool for defect reduction if this tool is not a part of the practitioner's tool set.

At the beginning of the 21st century, Six Sigma and Lean evolved into Lean Six Sigma. Lean Six Sigma integrates the concepts of Lean and Six Sigma; however, organizations often still have both Lean and Six Sigma camps, where each camp describes its preference or priority of one of the techniques over the other. Volume 3 in this series describes the E-DMAIC system where measurements pull for the right tool, whether the tool is Lean or Six Sigma. Lean Six Sigma basically combines the tools, methods, and infrastructure of Six Sigma and Lean. Companies have reported billions in financial benefits from executing Six Sigma and Lean Six Sigma projects.

The IEE strategy does not suggest that Six Sigma be implemented before Lean or Lean be implemented before Six Sigma in an organization. In this strategy, the preference is to implement Lean and Six Sigma methodologies at the same time.

Companies who are implementing Lean Six Sigma create an infrastructure that supports the completion of projects and delivers significant reported financial benefits. This cannot be accomplished effectively if there is not a mixture of both core people who are 100% time dedicated to the effort and others who receive these responsibilities as part of their current assignments.

In a company-wide deployment, the CEO and other executives decide whether the company will adopt Lean Six Sigma. They are responsible for shaping the deployment, regularly monitoring its success, and guiding the use of resources. Champions are executive-level managers who are responsible for managing and guiding the Lean Six Sigma deployment and its projects.

Practitioner role titles are typically based upon a martial arts belting structure, where the color of an individual's belt is dependent upon his/her skill mastery. Black belts are process improvement practitioners who typically receive 4 weeks of training over 4 months. It is most desirable that black belts are dedicated resources; however, many organizations utilize part-time resources. During training, black belt trainees lead the execution of a project that has in-class report-outs and critiques. Between training sessions, black belt trainees should receive project coaching, which is very important for their success. They are expected to deliver high-quality report-outs to peers, champions, and executives. Upon course completion, black belts are expected to continue delivering financial beneficial projects (e.g., 4–6 projects per year with financial benefits of $500,000–$1,000,000). Black belts can mentor green belts (described later).

Master black belts are black belts who have undertaken 2 weeks of advanced training and have a proven track record of delivering results through various projects and project teams. They should be a dedicated resource to the deployment. Before they train, master black belts need to be certified in the material that they are to deliver. Their responsibilities include coaching black belts, monitoring team progress, and assisting teams when needed.

Green belts are part-time practitioners who typically receive 2 weeks of training over 2 months. Their primary focus is on projects that are in their functional area. The inference that someone becomes a green belt before a black belt should not be made. Business and personal needs/requirements should influence the decision whether someone becomes a black belt or green belt. If someone's job requires a more in-depth skill set, such as the use of design of experiments (DOE), then the person should be trained as a black belt. Also, at deployment initiation, black belt training should be conducted first so that this additional skill set can be used when coaching others.

Yellow belts are team members who typically receive 3 days of training, which helps them in the effectiveness of their participation in project execution such as data collection, identifying voice of the customer, and team meetings.

1.6 Traditional Performance Metrics can Stimulate the Wrong Behavior

The book *Lean Thinking* (Womack and Jones, 1996) describes companies that successfully implemented the Toyota Production System. Two companies featured in this book were Wiremold Company and Lantech, Inc. Two executives from these companies, Jean Cunningham and Orest Fiume, later wrote *Real Numbers: Management Accounting in a Lean Organization* (Cunningham and Fiume, 2003).

> Complex accounting created a kind of funhouse mirror, where a skinny man could look fat by simply shifting his position.

When *Real Numbers* was published, Jean Cunningham was chief financial officer and vice president of Company Services for Lantech, Inc., and was a leader in the company's transformation to Lean. Orest Fiume had retired as vice president of Finance and Administration and director of Wiremold Company.

These financial executives from two highly regarded companies make many insightful statements regarding existing accounting departments and systems. I highly recommend this book and periodically will reference statements from it. Readers need to keep in mind that these statements are from financial executives in their fields of expertise.

Cunningham and Fiume (2003) make the following points:

- Information must... be easily understood and actionable. Over the years, however, managers have been forced to understand their own departments, not in terms of income and cost, but as variances and percentages that bear little relationship to reality (i.e., where variances mean the differences between what is expected and what actually occurs).
- Those same managers learned that variances could be nudged up or down to present a better picture of the operation – for instance, by using labor hours to make a million pieces of plastic that were not actually needed, even if that meant damaging the real business interests.
- Complex accounting created a kind of funhouse mirror, where a skinny man could look fat by simply shifting his position.

It is not uncommon for newspaper articles to make statements similar to the following (Petruno, 2006):

There is a sinking feeling among technology stock investors this summer – a feeling of history repeating.

At the start of 2002, the bear market of that era had been raging for nearly two years. Then came a wave of corporate scandals that showed the Enron Corp. debacle of late 2001 was no one-off affair.

As shares of Tyco International Ltd., Adelphia Communications Corp. and WorldCom Inc. collapsed in the first half of 2002 amid allegations of massive financial fraud by executives, demoralized investors began wondering whether they could trust any number on balance sheets and income statements.

The scandals helped fuel a last burst of panicked selling, driving down the Standard & Poor's 500 index nearly 30 percent in the first nine months of 2002 and the Nasdaq composite index by 40 percent.

Now, investors' faith in corporate accounting again is under siege. Over the past few months more than 65 companies, most of them technology companies, have disclosed that they were under scrutiny or investigation by federal authorities for possibly manipulating executives' stock option grants to boost the potential payoffs.

In another article, "CEO firings at a record pace so far this year" (Kelly, 2006), it is stated that "chiefs are being pushed out the door as directors abandon their laissez-faire approach to governance following the prosecutions at Enron Corp., WorldCom, Inc. and other companies."

These high-profile illustrations highlight only the tip of the iceberg relative to how organizational metric reporting can lead to the wrong behaviors. Organizations need a leadership system to overcome a "laissez-faire approach to governance." I will later describe how the no-nonsense IEE approach addresses these issues.

The next section will describe characteristics of a good metric. This section will be followed by sections that describe how commonly used organizational internal functional metric tracking and reporting can stimulate the wrong behavior throughout the organization.

1.7   Characteristics of a Good Metric

We have all heard the clichés:

- You get what you measure.
- What you measure is what you get.
- If you don't measure it, you can't manage it.
- Tell me how I'm going to be measured and I'll tell you how I'll perform.
- You cannot improve what you can't measure.
- Garbage in, garbage out.
- If you don't measure it, it's just a hobby.

These clichés are true! Measurements need to convey the voice of the process, which stimulate the most appropriate behavior. Measurements need to provide an unbiased process performance assessment. When process output performance is not accurately seen and reported relative to a desired result, there is not much hope for making improvements. Generic measures for any process are quality, cost, and delivery. Most processes need a balance measurement set to prevent optimizing one metric at the expense of overall process health. Metrics can also drive the wrong behavior if conducted in isolation from the overall enterprise needs. When appropriate, the addition of a people measure assures balance between task and people management.

As an illustration, consider the last customer-satisfaction survey form that you received. Do you think that a summary of responses from this survey truly provides an accurate assessment of what you experienced in your purchase process? My guess is that your response is no. It seems that often surveys are conducted so that the responses will be satisfactory but don't truly provide insight into what actually happens in a process.

Writing an effective survey and then evaluating the responses is not easy. What we would like to receive from a survey is an honest picture of what is currently happening in the process, along with providing improvement direction. A comment section in a hotel guest survey might provide insight to a specific actionable issue or improvement possibility.

> COMMON CAUSE: natural or random variation that is inherent in a process or its inputs.

Good metrics provide decision-making insight that leads into the most appropriate conclusion and action or non-action. The objective is the creation of an entity that is measurable, auditable, sustainable, and consistent. Effective and reliable metrics require the following characteristics:

- *Business alignment*: Metrics consume resources for both data collection and analyses. Metrics need to provide insight to business performance, its issues, and its needs. Metrics surrounding your business alignment can be found by looking at your value chain.
- *Honest assessment*: Creating metrics so that the performance of someone or an organization will appear good has

no value and can be detrimental to the organization. Metrics need to be able to provide an honest assessment, whether good, bad, or ugly.

- *Consistency*: Identified components in any metric need to be defined at the outset and remain constant. Criteria and calculations need to be consistent with respect to time.
- *Repeatability and reproducibility*: Measurements should have little or no subjectivity. We would like for a recorded measurement response to have little or no dependence on who and when someone recorded the response.

> SPECIAL CAUSE: Variation in a process from a cause that is not an inherent part of the current process or its inputs.

- *Actionability*: Often measures are created for the sake of measuring, without any thought as to what would be done if the metric were lower or higher. Include only those metrics that you will act on; that is, either remove a degradation problem or hold the gain. When the metrics response is unsatisfactory, organizations need to be prepared to conduct root-cause analysis and corrective or preventive actions.
- *Time-series tracking*: Metrics should be captured in time-series format, not as a snapshot of a point-in-time activity. Time-series tracking can describe trends and separate special-cause from common-cause variability in predictable processes.

> PREDICTABLE PROCESS: A stable, controlled process where variation in outputs is only caused by natural or random variation in the inputs or in the process itself.

- *Predictability*: A predictability statement should be made when time-series tracking indicates that a process is predictable.
- *Peer comparability*: In addition to internal performance measurements, benefits are achieved when comparisons can be made between peer groups in another business or company. A good peer comparison provides additional analysis opportunities, which can identify improvement possibilities.

Metric utilization requires commitment and resource allotments; hence, it is important to do it right. When organizations strive to become more metric driven, it is important to avoid metric-design and metric-usage errors. Common mistakes include the following:

- Creating metrics for the sake of metrics. Lloyd S. Nelson, director of Statistical Methods for the Nashua Corporation, stated: "The most important figures needed for management of any organization are unknown or unknowable" (Deming, 1986).
- Formulating too many metrics, resulting in no actions.
- Lacking metric follow-up.
- Describing metrics that do not result in the intended action.
- Creating metrics that can have subjective manipulation.

If not exercised effectively, metrics can become a dark force where good energy is absorbed by bad stuff – a black hole where good resources are lost.

1.8   Traditional Scorecards, Dashboards, and Performance Metrics Reporting

A scorecard helps manage an organization's performance through the optimization and alignment of organizational units, business processes, and individuals. A scorecard can also provide goals and targets, helping individuals understand their organizational contribution. Scorecards can span the operational, tactical, and strategic business aspects and decisions of any business. A dashboard displays information so that an enterprise can be run effectively. A dashboard organizes and presents information in a format that is easy to read and interpret.

A performance metric is a performance-related measurement of activity or resource utilization. Year-to-date metric statements are one form of performance metric reporting, while other formats involve tables or charts.

> Performance-measure report-out formats can have a dramatic influence on behaviors. Many situations can have numerous report-out options.

Performance-measure report-out formats can have a dramatic influence on behaviors. Many situations can have numerous report-out options. Much unproductive work can be generated if the best scorecard/dashboard metric is not chosen.

This section describes some frequently used performance metrics and scorecard/dashboard reporting formats, which can create detrimental organizational behavior. Later sections of this chapter will introduce an alternative IEE scorecard/dashboard performance-measurement system that allows organizational enterprise management systems to react more quickly to favorable or unfavorable circumstances.

Table 1.1 exemplifies one commonly used performance measure report-out. This report format has calendar boundaries that reflect only quarterly and annual results. This type of chart does not present response data as though it were a result of internal processes that inherently have variability. In addition, this chart cannot identify trends, detect unusual events in a timely fashion, or provide a prediction statement.

Is there a consistent message presented in Table 1.1? Invariably you will get stories that cannot be verified in the chart.

Look at the third line. You might hear something like "We staffed up in 2002 to prepare for annexations, but they did not happen as quickly as expected. This drove our cost per call up. As we annexed in 2003, you can see it coming down. We are on track."

It may be a true story, but is it the whole cause as it is represented? It is a good bet that the presenter will describe many of the ups and downs in the table in a story format, where in reality much of this motion is the result of common-cause variability. Have you seen tables like this before?

This form of performance reporting and of other year-to-date metric statements typically leads to *stories*. This means that someone presenting this scorecard/dashboard will typically give an explanation for the up-and-down movements of the previous quarter or year. This is not dissimilar to a nightly stock market report of the previous day's activity, where the television or radio reporter gives a specific reason for even small market movements. This form of reporting provides little, if any, value when it comes to making business decisions.

Whether in a business performance measure or a stock market report, these reported causal events may or may not have affected the output. The individual measurement value may cause an alarm that triggers some corrective action, or the numbers may be viewed only as a simple report. In either case, most measurement variability is typically the result of the system's common-cause variations.

An alternative to table presentations for a data-driven company is chart presentations. For example, user guidelines from Quick-Base (2006) state: "What information do you want to show? This is always the first question you must ask yourself when creating a chart. For example, if you want to show what percentage each salesperson contributes to the bottom line, try a pie chart, which is great for showing how parts relate to a whole. Or maybe you'd prefer to show how each salesperson has been doing over the course of the year. In that case, a line chart might work best. That way you could plot each person's sales numbers through time and see who is improving."

This frequently followed charting advice could lead to a Figure 1.1 report-out. Other frequent report-out formats for this type of data are shown in Figures 1.2 and 1.3.

Similar to summarizing data through a table, the chart report formats in Figures 1.1–1.3 typically lead to *stories* about the past. The chart presentation format will dictate the presented *story* type. For example, the calendar boundaries in the bar-chart reporting format in Figure 1.3 will surely lead to adjacent month and previous year–month comparisons. This type of chart, like the other charts, can be difficult to interpret. This interpretation difficulty often leads to inconsistencies and erroneous conclusions in the stories generated by different presenters.

> Reporting individual up-and-down historical movement or arbitrary time-based comparisons does not provide insight to future process-output expectations.

Consider which interests us the most: the past or the future? Most often the response to this question is "the future." Reporting individual up-and-down historical movement or arbitrary time-based comparisons does not provide insight to future process-output expectations, assuming that the process experiences no dramatic positive or negative change. However, if we could somehow estimate the future and didn't like the resulting prediction, we gain insight to improvement focus opportunities; that is, the metric improvement needs pull for creating a process-improvement project.

Report charts need to lead to activities that are beneficial to the organization. Traditional tabular and chart reporting leads to *stories* about the past without any formal system that describes

Table 1.1: Traditional Performance Measures: Tabular Reporting
(Austin, 2004)

Performance Measure	FY 2001 Actual	FY 2002 Actual	FY 2003 Actual	FY 2003 Amended	FY 2004 Amended
Percentage of customers satisfied with dispatch staff	99.99%	100%	99.99%	98%	98%
Percentage of priority one calls dispatched to field crews within 80 minutes of receipt	99.99%	99%	99.99%	95%	95%
Labor cost per customer call taken in Dispatch Operations	$4.20	$5.31	$5.09	$4.88	$5.09
Number of calls taken through Dispatch Operations	62,054	59,828	63,046	60,000	60,000
Number of priority one calls dispatched to field crews	5,797	4,828	6,686	5,000	6,500
Number of work orders and component parts (segments) created in database	8,226	4,724	7,742	5,500	6,700

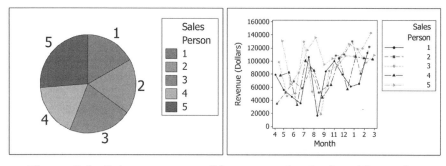

Figure 1.1: Salesperson monthly revenue for the last 12 months
presented as pie chart and line chart.

what might be expected in the future. Later I will discuss an IEE alternative data reporting system that provides increased insight as to where improvement efforts would be most beneficial.

Consider how accurate is this year-based reporting if something has changed during the year? For example, if there was a fundamental sales process change in August, then we would be including old information with the latest information when examining annualized data in a pie chart. Wouldn't it be better to first identify if and when a change occurred and then either compare new to old process responses, or describe what is happening most recently?

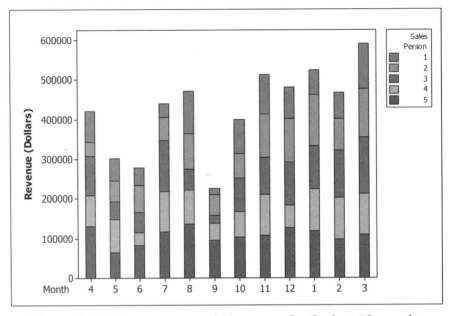

Figure 1.2: Salesperson monthly revenue for the last 12 months presented as stacked bar chart.

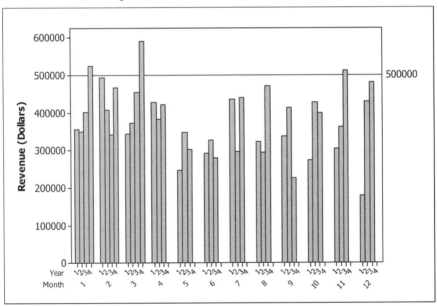

Figure 1.3: Year-to-year monthly revenue chart tracking against a mean monthly goal of $500,000. Years are designated as 0, 1, 2, and 3; e.g., 0 = 2000 and 1 = 2001. The figure indicates that the data was compiled at the end of March, since there are four bars for months 1 (January), 2 (February), and 3 (March).

Later in this chapter, I will discuss an IEE alternative data reporting system that provides increased insight to where improvement efforts would be most beneficial. Example 37.2 revisits this data using an IEE analysis approach.

1.9 Strategic Planning

Business leaders must have a strategy to meet their objectives. Without a strategy, time and resources can be wasted on piecemeal, disparate activities. Without a strategy, mid-level managers will fill the void with their interpretation of what the business should be doing, typically resulting in a disjointed set of activities.

However, "strategy has become a catchall term used to mean whatever one wants it to mean. Executives now talk about their "service strategy," their "branding strategy," their "acquisition strategy," or whatever kind of strategy that is on their mind at a particular moment." (Hambrick and Fredrickson, 2001)

Consider the company strategy in Figure 1.4, which typifies other companies' strategies. An organization can spend much time creating such a strategic listing; however, it can often have difficulty in interpreting what it should do relative to addressing the passed-down strategy.

In addition, what data analyses were conducted ahead of time, which influenced the creation of the corporate strategy? Even if there were good pre-strategy build data analyses, can the direction of the entire company rest on a few statements, which can change when there is leadership change?

Figure 2.5 will describe an E-DMAIC alternative that leads to specific actionable items with goals. In this process, create strategies is step 5, not step 1 or 2. An E-DMAIC process for strategy development is described in Section 3.7. Figure 3.7 illustrates a drill-down from organization goals through strategies to specific actionable projects.

Consider the strategy shown in Figure 1.4, which typifies other companies' strategies. An organization can spend much time creating such a strategic listing; however, an organization can often have difficulty interpreting what it should do relative to addressing the passed-down strategy. An IEE alternative that leads to specific actionable items with goals is described later. Figure 3.7 illustrates a drill-down from organization goals through strategies to specific actionable projects.

Figure 2.4 Corporate Strategy Example (Foxconn 2006).

Foxconn's objective is to maintain its position as one of the leading manufacturers of connectors, PC enclosures, and other precision components, and to successfully develop products and market its products for use in network communication and consumer electronic products. A number of strategies have been developed to attain this objective:

Develop strategic relationship with industry leaders — By working closely with top-tier PC and IC companies, Foxconn is able to predict market trends accurately and introduce new products ahead of its competitors.

Focus on the development of global logistic capabilities — This enables Foxconn to respond quickly and efficiently to the customer's requirements around the world.

Expansion of production capacity — Foxconn currently has production facilities in Asia, Europe, and the United States. Expanding its existing production capacity increases economics of scale.

Achieve further vertical integration — Further integration of the production process allows Foxconn to exercise better control over the quality of its products.

Maintain technologically advanced and flexible production capabilities — This increases Foxconn's competitiveness relative to its peers and allows it to stay one step ahead of the opposition.

New products — Foxconn will leverage off its manufacturing expertise and continue to move tirelessly into new areas of related business.

Figure 1.4: Corporate strategy example (Foxconn, 2006).

1.10   The Balanced Scorecard

The balanced scorecard, as presented by Kaplan and Norton (1992), tracks the business in the areas of financial, customer, internal processes, and learning and growth. In this model, each area is to address one of the following questions:

- *Financial*: To succeed financially, how should we appear to our shareholders?
- *Customer*: To achieve our vision, how should we appear to our customers?
- *Internal business process*: To satisfy our shareholders and customers, what business processes must we excel at?
- *Learning and growth*: To achieve our vision, how will we sustain our ability to change and improve?

> ... it seems to me that it would be very difficult for an organization to create a level five system when the primary guiding light for the organization is its strategy, which can change with new leadership.

Figure 1.5 illustrates how these metrics are to align with the business vision and strategy. Each category is to have objectives, measures, targets, and initiatives.

Scorecard balance is important because if you don't have balance you could be giving one metric more focus than another, which can lead to problems. For example, when focus is given to only on-time delivery, product quality could suffer dramatically to meet ship dates. However care needs to be given in how this balance is achieved. A natural balance is much more powerful than forcing balance through the organizational chart using a scorecard structure of financial, customer, internal business process, and learning and growth that may not be directly appropriate to all business areas. In addition, a scorecard structure that is closely tied to the organization chart has an additional disadvantage in that it will need to be changed whenever significant reorganizations occur.

In IEE, natural scorecard balance is achieved throughout the business via the enterprise value chain (see Figure 3.1), noting that overall learning and growth would typically be assigned to HR but, when appropriate, can also be assigned to other functional performance. Metrics are assigned an owner who is accountable for the metric's performance. These metrics can be cascaded downward to lower organization functions, where these metrics also are assigned owners who have performance accountability. With this IEE system whenever there is an organizational change the basic value chain metrics will not change, only metric ownership will change.

When creating these metrics it is not only important to determine *what to measure* but it is also very important to also focus

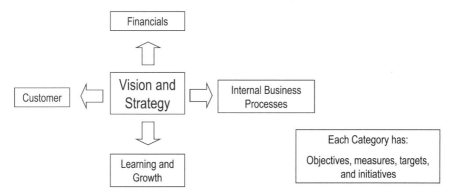

Original article: "The Balanced Scorecard – measures that drive performance," by Robert Kaplan and David Norton, 1992

Figure 1.5: Traditional performance measures: The balanced scorecard.

on the *how to report* so that this metric performance tracking leads to the most appropriate action, which maybe to do nothing. Later a system to accomplish this is described.

Figure 1.5 describes how the balanced scorecard (Kaplan and Norton, 1992) system is to have a created vision and strategy from which functional objectives, measures, targets, and initiatives are cascaded throughout the organization chart.

Jim Collins describes in *Good to Great* (2001) a level five leader as someone who is great while leading an organization and whose affect remains after the person is no longer affiliated with the organization. I describe the level-five-leader-created legacy as being a *Level Five System.*

In my workshops, I often ask, "Do you think your organization's strategy would change if there were different leadership?" A vast majority give a positive response to this question. Because of this, it seems to me that it would be very difficult for an organization to create a Level Five System when the primary guiding light for the organization is its strategy, which can change with new leadership.

I don't mean to imply that organizational strategies are bad, but I do believe that strategies created without structurally evaluating the overall organizational value chain and its metrics can lead to unhealthy behavior. To illustrate this, consider the following example.

Parameters for a global service corporation dashboard were defined by the following underlying strategic executive goals for the year:

> Grow revenue 25 percent per year, earn minimum of 20 percent net profit, achieve 60 percent of revenue with repeat customers, balance regional growth, fill open positions corresponding with growth, ensure that all employees are competent and high performers, realize projects within time and cost targets, limit ratio of overhead to productive time to 20 percent, and satisfy customers 100 percent.

These objectives, measures, targets, and initiatives were then set up to be monitored, as shown in Figure 1.6, where each metric is to have an owner. Color-coding is used to help clearly identify actual performance versus targets and forecasts. The exclamation

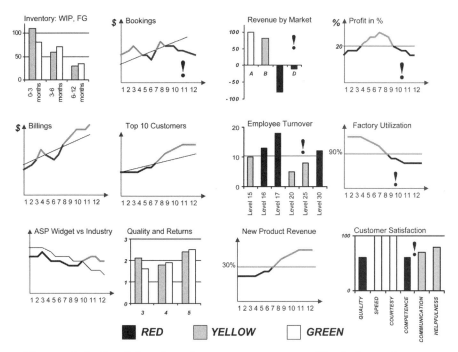

Figure 1.6: Traditional performance measures: The balanced score-card executive dashboard. WIP: Work in progress, FG: finished goods.

marks indicate red flags, where objectives are not being met and attention is needed.

These executive dashboard metrics can then be drilled down further, as shown in 1.7. Would you like to sign up to own this metric and its achievement? The strategic objectives described previously set a customer-satisfaction metric goal of 100%. Not a bad target; however, meeting this number is not easy. Simply setting this goal will not make it happen, at least not as the team setting the goal would like it to happen. One might wonder how this goal was determined. Do you think this goal is SMART; that is, specific, measurable, actionable, relevant, time based?

For this metric type, an unachieved goal earns an exclamation mark, indicating that the metric's owner may need reminding that his or her job-performance rating depends on achievement of this goal. What kind of activity might this type of pressure create, especially when improvement detection is immediately needed? We might initially think that the owner would, as soon as possible, start an investigation into where quality improvements need to be made. But we need to be realistic. Immediate improvements are needed to make this scorecard look better. Might there be other ways to make this happen?

Before we react, let's step back to see the bigger picture. A customer-satisfaction goal is not being met; however, is this level of customer satisfaction really a problem? What were the scores from previous reporting periods? If the scores are better now, this would be good since improvements are being demonstrated – even though the strategic goal is not being met. Without a historical time-dependent reference, could there be disagreements for what is good or bad?

Keeping in mind the type of metric described in Figure 1.7, consider the following situation:

A few years ago, when my wife and I were buying a new car, negotiating the price of the car with the sales associate got to be a game with me. After we closed the deal, the sales associate pointed to a survey that was facing us under his Plexiglas desktop. This survey had all 5s checked. He told us that we would be getting a survey in the mail. Then he said that he always gets 5s on his survey. He pointed to my wife and said that he wanted her, not me, to fill out the survey.

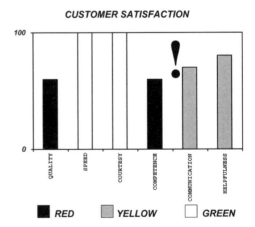

Figure 1.7: Traditional performance measures: The balanced scorecard/dashboard customer satisfaction drill-down.

Consider the following points:

- The salesman said we would receive a survey in the mail.
- He pointed out that he always gets 5s, as noted on the survey form on his desk.
- He wanted my wife, not me, to fill out the survey.

Do you think he might be trying to bias the survey in his favor – perhaps a bonus is riding on these results? Do you think this type of behavior is what the metric should be creating? This is one form of trying to manage the output of the metric process, rather than systematically working to change the process, or the inputs to the process, so that an improved response occurs. Simply setting high-level goals and then managing to those goals, can lead to the wrong behavior. Making true long-lasting gains in customer satisfaction is more involved than working to get satisfactory scores on evaluation sheets. Attaining long-lasting customer satisfaction involves improving the process and the inputs to the process.

Let's next examine the profit scorecard in Figure 1.8. Notice that the *x*-axis units are 1–12. What do you think this indicates? Months is a good bet since the metric starts with 1, which is probably the first month after the company's fiscal year. Notice, also, how this tracking is made only against the goal with no indication of what kind of performance has been experienced in

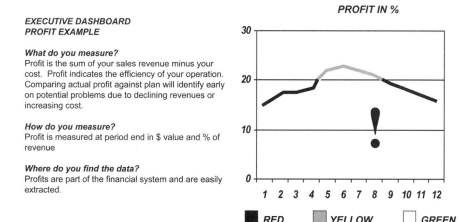

Figure 1.8: Traditional performance measures: The balanced scorecard/dashboard profit drill-down.

the past. Since the goals are annualized, the target line is drawn beginning the first month of the year, but there is no record of performance the previous year, nor whether the goal is reasonable or simply a pie-in-the-sky objective.

If people are really held accountable for achieving this metric objective, very undesirable behavior can result. Since there is an exclamation point, the owner of this metric would need to take immediate action to drive these numbers in the right direction. A high-level metric such as this could lead to the Enron effect, where money could be simply shifted from one area to the next to make things look better. Or the metric could lead to immediate cost-cutting measures that might significantly damage the company's future outlook. You can cut costs to improve profitability for only so long. At some point in time you will see diminishing returns and possible increase in fixed costs due to inefficiencies created by a lack of resources. This form of metric reporting can also lead to the previously described behavior, where Krispy Kreme shipped donuts that they knew would be returned so that quarterly expectations would be met.

Metric reporting, where focus is given only to whether output-type goals are met, can cause behavioral problems lower in the organization as well. Consider the following:

A prison representative purchased a commodity item only at the end of the supplier's quarterly financial reporting period. Near the end of every quarter, the salesperson for the supplier called, offering the prison a price incentive for immediate purchase. Because of the type of product sold, there was no reason for this cyclic behavior. Since manufacturing personnel were on overtime and were under pressure to increase production volume, quality problems were more prevalent during this period than others.

This odd behavior was eventually noticed and an investigation conducted. Asked why the prison waited until the end of the quarter to purchase the product, the representative responded that the salesperson called at the end of the quarter with a discounted price.

Additional company investigation revealed that the salesperson typically had difficulty meeting his quarterly target objective. Near the end of every quarter, the salesperson would ask his manager for approval to give customer discounts, which would help their department meet its targeted goals. If these goals were not met, there would be no personal or departmental bonuses. The manager routinely complied.

What makes this situation even worse is that the salesperson was getting paid off the top line (total products sold), while the company was taking a significant impact at the bottom line. That is, the salesperson was getting rewarded for total products sold, while the company's true profit from the transaction was reduced by the sales commission as well as additional overtime costs due to demand spike.

All these negative corporate-profitability behaviors originated with the company's salesperson commission policy. Rather than someone noticing and investigating, this type of situation could be readily identified in an E-DMAIC structure during the analyze phase. In this structure, a project could have been created that later resolved the undesirable behavior of the sales department through changing either the reward policy or discounting policy so that these demand spikes would no longer occur.

The shortcomings of many traditional performance metrics are that they often reflect only fiscal year metrics, make comparisons to a point estimate from a previous month or year, and don't have a procedure for improving the process so that gains occur and are maintained. These traditional methods don't view the enterprise process as a system of processes, where the performance metric is the result of these processes along with the variability that occurs within them. Long-lasting change is a result of systematic improvement to these processes.

> The shortcomings of many traditional performance metrics are that these metrics often reflect only fiscal year metrics, make comparisons to a point estimate from a previous month or a previous year, and don't have a procedure for improving the process so that gains occur and are maintained.

This form of metric reporting is always after-the-fact reporting and not predictive. Imagine if a customer said, "Based on past experience, our products will have a consumer half-life of only _____ years. If innovations and improvements are not sustained, our revenues will decline by _____ percent over the next _____ years." This type of data-driven statement leads to long-term thinking that can have long-lasting results.

1.11   Red–Yellow–Green Scorecards

The previously described balance scorecards and other scorecards that are not balanced often use red, yellow, and green to
show whether actions are needed relative to meeting established
objectives. The Office of Planning and Performance Management
of the U.S. Department of Interior uses these metrics in the following way (US Dept. of Interior, 2003):

> Office of Management and Budget (OMB) has established an
> Executive Branch Management Scorecard to track how well depart-
> ments and agencies are executing the five President's Management
> Agenda (PMA) components. The Scorecard also strengthens the sense
> of accountability on the part of these agencies. The Scorecard pres-
> ents an updated assessment of the status and progress being made
> to address each of the President's Management Agenda (PMA) goals.
>
> Status is assessed against the standards for success that have
> been developed for each initiative and are published in the 2003
> Budget. They are defined as follows:
>
> - Green: Meets all of the standards for success.
> - Yellow: Achieved some, but not all, of the criteria.
> - Red: Has any one of a number of serious flaws.
>
> Progress is assessed on a case-by-case basis against the deliver-
> ables and timelines that each agency has established for the five
> PMA components. They are defined as:
>
> - Green: Implementation is proceeding according to plans.
> - Yellow: Some slippage or other issues requiring adjustment by
>   the agency in order to achieve the initiative objectives in a time-
>   ly manner.
> - Red: Initiative [is] in serious jeopardy and is unlikely to realize
>   objectives absent significant management intervention.
>
> The President reviews each agency scorecard with the respective
> cabinet member.

Interior is using the Scorecard approach to assist in monitoring progress toward achieving the PMA goals at a departmental level. Criteria specific to Interior and its bureaus were developed through a collaborative, cross-departmental effort. The
criteria were combined with rating scales from 0–10 using color

rating bars that visually indicate progress and status scores. Interior bureaus and offices are asked to conduct a self-assessment of their status and progress in realizing PMA goals every six months, with the first of these self-assessments conducted in May 2002. Based on the self-assessment, the Department identifies the next actions that need to be taken by specific bureaus and offices to "get to green." Actions are entered into the Department's PMA tracking system so that they can be monitored along with the Citizen-Centered Governance Plan activities to assess the Department's progress as a whole in meeting the PMA goals.

When it is conducted throughout an organization, do you think that this form of goal setting and managing to these goals will lead to the right behavior? Goals are important; however, metric targets need to be SMART. Arbitrary goal setting and management to these goals can lead to the wrong behavior!

> SMART goals are specific, measurable, actionable; relevant, time-based

Let's now discuss the presentation of red–yellow–green scorecards, which can have different presentation formats. Figure 1.9 and Table 1.2 illustrate two possible formats.

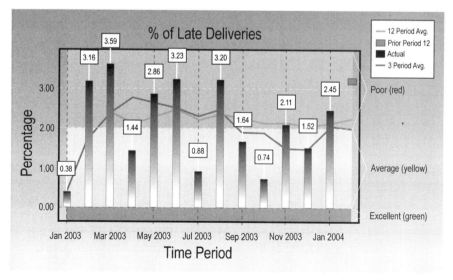

Figure 1.9: Red–yellow–green graphical reporting.

Table 1.2: Red–Yellow–Green Tabular Scorecard Example

RED

YELLOW

GREEN

Monthly SCORECARD
Business Unit Name

Measurement	Targets	Aug'04	Sep'04	Oct'04	Nov'04	Dec'04
FINANCE						
Finance Metric A		3.387525	2.965966	3.042505	2.891057	3.485847
Yellow if equal to or higher than	3.05	3.05	3.05	3.05	3.05	3.05
Green if equal to or higher than	3.1	3.1	3.1	3.1	3.1	3.1
Finance Metric B		2.09819	2.254758	2.345674	2.207099	2.316309
Yellow if equal to or higher than	2.2	2.2	2.2	2.2	2.2	2.2
Green if equal to or higher than	2.25	2.25	2.25	2.25	2.25	2.25
Finance Metric C		0.762611	0.958071	1.051227	0.867969	1.158351
Yellow if equal to or higher than	0.9	0.9	0.9	0.9	0.9	0.9
Green if equal to or higher than	0.95	0.95	0.95	0.95	0.95	0.95

CUSTOMER

FINANCE

INTERNAL BUSINESS OPS

LEARNING & GROWTH

Let's further examine a scorecard like Table 1.2. When creating this type of scorecard, metrics are established throughout the organization, along with goals for the metrics. When a metric goal is being met, all is well and the color is green. When measurements are close to not being met, the color is yellow. The metric is colored red when the goal is not being met and corrective action needs to be taken.

What do you see in this scorecard? There are a lot of metrics grouped by business area. Also, many measurements are colored red and metrics even transition from red to green and back. Finally, there are a lot of metrics for one scorecard. One rule of thumb is that most scorecards should include 7–10 metrics. Anything more than that and a person will struggle monitoring and acting on them.

How can you have a metric that is red for the entire reporting period? Is no one monitoring it? Is it based on an arbitrary target and just ignored? Who knows, but all are possible.

Since red–yellow–green scorecard reporting is now readily available on many ERP systems, cascading this type of scorecard throughout the organization can initially seem very appealing. However, with this form of reporting, some companies might be experiencing many, if not all, green metrics. While in other companies red-triggered events can be creating much work; however, when the metrics are examined collectively over time there does not seem to be much, if any, individual metric improvement.

When assessing these two types of company scorecard situations, one might think that there would be a big difference in how well the organizations are performing. However, this is not necessarily true.

Perhaps the first company is a supplier to a company or government agency that requires red–yellow–green scorecard reporting and includes in their agreement a penalty if the color is not green. What kind of goal-setting activity would result from this type of policy, especially if the customer is not actively involved in all goal-setting metrics?

People in the second organization are expending a lot of effort trying to improve their many metrics when they are red. It would seem like these organizations might start lobbying for lower goals when they are set for the next fiscal year.

How well red–yellow–green scorecards are performing depend upon established goals, which may not be realistic and/or lead process suboptimization effort throughout the organization chart.

Metric tracking against this type of goals can lead to ineffective firefighting activities or playing games with the numbers.

Game playing to meet calendar goals can also impact bonuses. This form of activity can occur not only at the executive level or in the sales department. The following example illustrates how the wrong activity can be stimulated at an employee level by a goal-driven metric.

All employees in a company were given a bonus if they met a calendar-based revenue goal. This company's business service involved managing large amounts of customer money. Large checks could flow to the company from its customer even though the company kept only a small portion of the money. A company goal had been set at one level for many years, so employees became accustomed to receiving this periodic bonus compensation.

A major customer was to make an unusually large payment. The payment size required signature approval by the customer's CEO. The customer asked if they could pay in smaller amounts spread over a longer period so that they could avoid the hassle of having CEO approval. The service company agreed since it wanted to be customer driven but later determined that this agreement negated the periodic bonus.

In an attempt to resolve this employee bonus unfairness, an administrator took it upon himself to adjust the compensation internally so it appeared that the company was paid in the period the service was performed. However, this accounting adjustment negatively impacted the customer and caused havoc.

Have you experienced any organization that has had similar issues with a goal-driven metric? A final example follows:

A salesperson calls customers who have committed to purchasing products in the next quarter, asking them if they would move up their order to the current quarter. He then offers a discount for this order shift. The salesperson's motivation for doing this was that he was having trouble meeting his quarterly numbers, which would negatively impact his pay for this quarter. The consequence of this practice is similar to the previous illustration.

Employee incentive plans are not bad; however, care needs to be exercised or the wrong activities can prevail. An alternative scorecard style to red–yellow–green metrics is described in Examples 3.1 and 3.2.

1.12   Example 1.1: Tabular Red–Yellow–Green Scorecard Reporting Alternative

Table 1.2 presented a red–yellow–green graphic scorecard/dashboard report out for a continuous response that has a criterion. The following observations were made from the chart for finance metric B, which had a target of 2.25 or higher. There were five red, two yellow, and six green occurrences:

	Targets	Aug'04	Sep'04	Oct'04	Nov'04	Dec'04	Jan'05	Feb'05	Mar'05	Apr'05	May'05	Jun'05	Jul'05	Aug'05
Finance Metric B		2.10	2.25	2.35	2.21	2.32	2.21	2.16	2.49	2.51	2.16	2.17	2.29	2.14
Yellow if equal to or higher than	2.20	2.20	2.20	2.20	2.20	2.20	2.20	2.20	2.20	2.20	2.20	2.20	2.20	2.20
Green if equal to or higher than	2.25	2.25	2.25	2.25	2.25	2.25	2.25	2.25	2.25	2.25	2.25	2.25	2.25	2.25

The following IEE scorecard/dashboard metric reporting process will be used when analyzing the data:

1. Assess process predictability.
2. When the process is considered predictable, formulate a prediction statement for the latest region of stability. The usual reporting format for this statement is the following:
   (a) When there is a specification requirement: nonconformance percentage or DPMO
   (b) When there is no specification requirement: median response and 80% frequency of occurrence rate

Applying the IEE scorecard/dashboard metric reporting process to this data set yields:

1. As previously stated, the purpose of red–yellow–green charting is to stimulate improvements. Figure 1.10 provides an IEE assessment of how well this is accomplished (see Chapters 12 and 13 for chart-creation methods). This figure contains a control chart, probability plot, and histogram. As noted in the previous example, when there are no occurrences beyond the two horizontal lines (i.e., upper and lower control limits), no patterns or data shifts, the process is said to be in control. Again, when this occurs, we have no reason to not believe that the up-and-down monthly variability is the result of common-cause variability (i.e., the process is predictable. Since the process is predictable, we can consider past data from the region of stability to be a random sample of the future.
2. The histogram shown in Figure 1.10 is a traditional tool that describes the distribution of random data from a

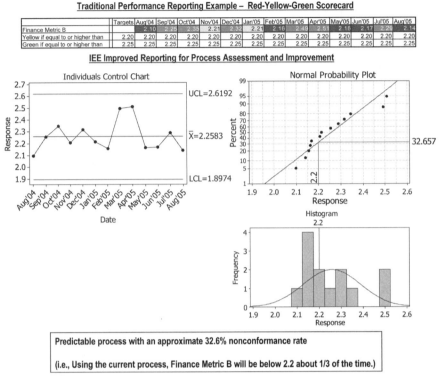

Traditional Performance Reporting Example – Red-Yellow-Green Scorecard

	Targets	Aug'04	Sep'04	Oct'04	Nov'04	Dec'04	Jan'05	Feb'05	Mar'05	Apr'05	May'05	Jun'05	Jul'05	Aug'05
Finance Metric B		2.10	2.25	2.35	2.21	2.32	2.21	2.16	2.49	2.51	2.16	2.17	2.29	2.14
Yellow if equal to or higher than	2.20	2.20	2.20	2.20	2.20	2.20	2.20	2.20	2.20	2.20	2.20	2.20	2.20	2.20
Green if equal to or higher than	2.25	2.25	2.25	2.25	2.25	2.25	2.25	2.25	2.25	2.25	2.25	2.25	2.25	2.25

Figure 1.10: Illustration of IEE-improved finance metric B continuous-response reporting: Red–yellow–green (see Table 1.2) scorecard versus IEE reporting (histogram included for illustrative purposes only).

population that has a continuous response. However, it is difficult to determine from a histogram the expected percentage beyond a criterion. A probability plot is a better tool to determine the nonconformance percentage. In a probability plot, actual data values are plotted on a coordinate system where percentage *less than* is on the *y*-axis. The probability plot in Figure 1.10 provides an estimate that approximately 32.6% of future monthly reporting will be less than the lower-bound criterion, unless a fundamental process improvement is made or something else external to the process occurs. From this figure, we also observe that this percentage value is consistent with an estimated proportion below the 2.2 reference line in the histogram graph. This percentage is also similar to the percentage of red occurrences (i.e., 5 out of 13). If this nonconformance percentage of 32.6% is undesirable, this metric would pull for project creation.

> Effective long-lasting improvements to processes are not made by firefighting individual time-line conditions that are beyond a desired objective. Process improvements are made by collectively examining process data over the period of stability so that insight might be gained to determine what should be done differently overall. This can be accomplished through the execution of a P-DMAIC project.

2

Creating an Integrated Enterprise Excellence System

The previous chapter described problems with traditional business metrics and how conventional strategic planning can lead to activities that are not in the best interest of the business as a whole. This chapter provides a high-level description of how Integrated Enterprise Excellence (IEE) can create a culture that transitions organizations from firefighting to an orchestrated governance system that moves toward the three Rs of business: everyone doing the Right things and doing them Right at the Right time.

> IEE can create a culture that transitions organizations from firefighting to an orchestrated system that moves toward the three Rs of business.

In a company, a governance model might define the composition of the cross-organizational or cross-functional teams who will monitor the processes, the metrics, the meeting frequency, and so on. Organizations can have governance models for key strategic areas like total customer experience, warranty, and so on. Rather than targeting key strategies, which can change over time, the IEE system focus is on the enterprise value chain, its metrics, and targeted improvement efforts. The overall governance system for this focus can be achieved through enterprise process define–measure–analyze–improve–control (E-DMAIC), which can be orchestrated by the enterprise process management (EPM) organization (see Section 3.2).

As business competition gets tougher, there is much pressure on product development, manufacturing, and service organizations to become more productive and efficient. Developers need to create innovative products in less time, even though the products may be more complex, while at the same time addressing business risks. Manufacturing organizations feel growing pressure to improve quality while decreasing costs and to increase production volumes with fewer resources. Service organizations must reduce lead times and improve customer satisfaction. Organizations can address these issues by adopting an implementation strategy that has direct linkage to both customer needs and bottom-line benefits. One might summarize this process as the following:

> IEE is a sustainable business management governance system, which integrates business scorecards, strategies, and process improvement so that organizations move toward the three Rs of business (everyone is doing the Right things and doing them Right at the Right time). IEE provides the framework for innovation and continual improvement, which goes beyond Lean Six Sigma's project-based defect- and waste-reduction methods. The existence and excellence of a business depends on more customers and cash; or, $E = MC^2$. As a business way of life, IEE provides the organizational orchestration to achieve more customer and cash.

The word *quality* often carries excess baggage with some people and therefore does not appear in this definition. For example, it is often difficult to get buy in throughout an organization when a program is viewed as a quality program that is run by the quality department. IEE is to be viewed as a methodology that applies to all functions within every organization. This system can become the framework for overcoming communication barriers and building an organizational cultural norm for continuous improvement. The wise application of statistical and non-statistical tools, including business metrics such as satellite-level and 30,000-foot-level metrics, occurs at all levels. Organizations benefit considerably when these scorecard/dashboard metrics and improvement techniques become a business way of life; however, there can be initial resistance to adopting the overall system.

The performance and improvement system of IEE basically lowers the water level in an organization, which can show some ugly rocks. People who have been hiding behind an ineffective organizational measurement and improvement system could initially be very concern by the increased visibility to their functional performance. However, an advantage of the IEE system is that the system not only can show ugly rocks but also has a very effective step-by-step system for remove the rocks – one by one starting with the largest rocks first.

2.1 Overview of IEE

Management needs to ask the right questions; the right questions lead to the wise use of statistical and non-statistical techniques for the purpose of obtaining knowledge from facts and data. Management needs to encourage the *wise* application of statistical techniques. Management needs to operate using the bromide In God we trust; all others bring data.

This series volume suggests periodic process reviews and projects based on assessments leading to a knowledge-centered activity (KCA) focus in all aspects of the business, where KCA describes efforts for wisely obtaining knowledge and then wisely using this knowledge within organizations and processes. KCA can redirect the focus of business so that efforts are more productive.

When implemented at GE, Six Sigma had evolved to a project-based system where emphasis was given to defect reduction. In this deployment, the quantification of project success was an improved process sigma quality level (see Appendix Section B.1) and with a quantifiable financial benefit.

Because Six Sigma projects begin with a problem statement, it is only natural that Six Sigma is considered to be a problem-solving system. The evolution from Six Sigma to Lean Six Sigma resulted in the expansion of problem statement opportunities to include the gambit of considering waste in traditional Lean deployments; that is, overproduction, waiting, transportation, inventory, over-processing, motion, defects, and people utilization.

However, often project deployments that center on the use of Lean or Six Sigma tools do not significantly impact the organization's big picture. Organizations may not pick the best projects to work on, which could result in sub-optimization that makes the system as a whole worse. In addition, Lean Six Sigma is a

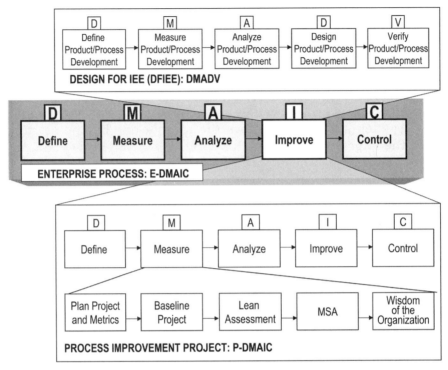

Figure 2.1: IEE high-level enterprise process roadmap with P-DMAIC process improvement and DMADV design project roadmaps (MSA: measurement systems analysis).

project-driven system, not a business system. IEE is an encompassing business system that addresses these issues, and more.

Lean Six Sigma curriculums typically don't address organizational measurements and the building of a business strategy that targets the system as a whole. DMAIC is the traditional roadmap for executing and managing Six Sigma process-improvement projects. DMAIC is used in IEE not only to describe process-improvement project execution steps, but also to establish the framework for the overall enterprise process.

Figure 2.1 shows how the IEE *enterprise process* DMAIC roadmap has linkage in the *enterprise process* improve phase to the *improvement project* DMAIC roadmap and *design project* define–measure–analyze–design–verify (DMADV) roadmap. The measure phase of the improvement project DMAIC roadmap has the additional noted drill-downs.

I refer to the enterprise-process DMAIC roadmap as E-DMAIC and to the project DMAIC roadmap as P-DMAIC.

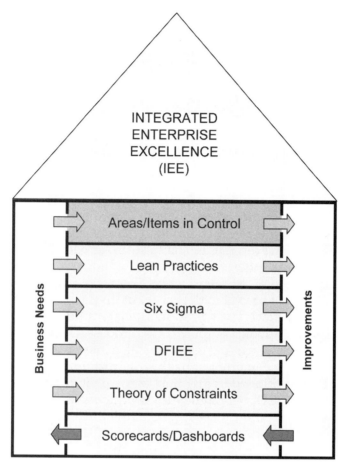

Figure 2.2: Integration of tools and methodologies.

As noted earlier, I refer to the enterprise-process DMAIC road-map as E-DMAIC and to the project DMAIC roadmap as P-DMAIC. Volume 2 sequentially describes the steps of the E-DMAIC roadmap. This volume sequentially describes execution of the P-DMAIC project roadmap (see Appendix D).

Figure 2.2 illustrates the IEE integration of Lean, Six Sigma, and other tools and techniques at both the enterprise and process-improvement project level. In the E-DMAIC roadmap, Lean tools are specifically described in the analyze phase. In the P-DMAIC roadmap, Lean tools are specifically described in the measure and improve phases.

Excessive measurement system error can lead to firefighting behavior and make it difficult to develop correlations that help determine what inputs drive the outputs. The focus tends to be on improving the process, when the needed effort should be on improving the measurement system. Measurement systems analysis (MSA) addresses these issues (see Chapter 15), which are applicable as both enterprise performance metrics and project metrics.

This volume walks through the process improvement project (P-DMAIC) roadmap. However, many Six Sigma and Lean tools also apply to the design project DMADV process, which is often called Design for Six Sigma (DFSS). In IEE, DFSS projects are referenced as design for Integrated Enterprise Excellence (DFIEE).

DFIEE projects can take the form of product design, process design, or (Information Technology) IT projects. In IEE, these three DFIEE forms follow a similar DMADV roadmap, as noted in Figure 2.1; however, the tool emphasis for each of these situations can be quite different.

In product DFIEE, Six Sigma and Lean tools are linked to address new types of products that build upon the knowledge gained from previously developed products (e.g., the development of a new vintage notebook computer). In process DFIEE, Six Sigma tools are linked to the development of a new process that has never previously been created by the organization (e.g., creation of a call center within a company that in the past did not have a call center). In IT DFIEE, Six Sigma and Lean tools are integrated into the overall development process. Example benefits from this are structure systems for capturing the voice of the customer (VOC), identifying risks, and perhaps significantly improving/reducing test times with DOE strategies.

Figure 2.1 illustrates the integration of DFIEE within the overall IEE process, while Breyfogle (2003a) provides additional discussion about the tools and thought process of DFSS.

The E-DMAIC system provides an infrastructure for linking high-level enterprise process performance measurements, analyses, improvements, and controls. This framework can lead to the development of specific improvement strategies that are in true alignment with business goals.

From these created strategies, targeted functional value chain metric improvement needs can be developed, which are in alignment with business measurement goals (see Figure 3.6). Positive change in functional baseline 30,000-foot-level performance scorecard/dashboard metrics is the measure of success relative to achieving targets. Each functional business measurement goal is to have an owner whose personal performance is measured against achieving his/her metric goal.

> Long-lasting improvements in the 30,000-foot-level scorecard/dashboard metrics are the result of systematic process improvement and design projects. This IEE improvement metric system creates a stimulus, or pull, for the creation of these improvement and design projects.

Long-lasting improvements in the 30,000-foot-level scorecard/dashboard metrics are the result of systematic process improvement and design projects. This IEE improvement metric system creates a stimulus, or pull, for the creation of these improvement and design projects.

From this system, projects are created that are in true alignment to business needs. In addition, this system framework leads to the creation and execution of a long-lasting business measurement and improvement organizational system.

This offering provides many more benefits than the push for the creation and execution of Lean Six Sigma projects from a list of potential projects and then quantifying the success by how much money was saved through these projects. This policy can lead to projects that have little, if any, value to the true bottom line of the organization or to multiple projects claiming the same savings.

As noted earlier, the flow of Volume 2 followed the overall thought process of evaluating the enterprise process (E-DMAIC). This Volume 3 addresses the mechanics of executing a specific improvement project (P-DMAIC), as illustrated in Figure 2.1. I will highlight the benefits of Six Sigma and Lean tools that are most applicable and challenge some of the traditional Six Sigma/Lean Six Sigma techniques that can lead to questionable results. I will expand on other techniques that are beyond the boundaries of these methodologies. The reader can reference *Implementing Six Sigma*, 2nd edition for more elaboration on the traditional methodologies of Six Sigma and Lean.

The described approach in this series of volumes goes beyond traditional techniques so that there is a pull for project creation by enterprise process measurements. A traditional Six Sigma model can lead to all levels of management asking for the creation of Six Sigma projects that improve the numbers against which they are measured. These projects often are not as beneficial as one might think since this project selection approach does not focus on identifying and resolving enterprise process constraint issues. We have had people come back to us saying that another Six Sigma provider is claiming that they have saved 100 million dollars in a company; however, no one can seem to find the money.

This IEE approach can help sustain Six Sigma or Lean Six Sigma activities, a problem which many companies who have previously implemented Six Sigma or Lean Six Sigma are now confronting. In addition, this system focuses on downplaying a traditional Six Sigma policy that all Six Sigma projects must have a defined defect. I have found that this policy can lead to many non-productive activities, playing games with the numbers, and overall frustration. This practice of not defining a defect makes this strategy much more conducive to a true integration with general workflow improvement tools that use Lean thinking methods.

To achieve success, organizations must wisely address metrics and their infrastructure. The success of deployment is linked to a set of cross-functional metrics that lead to significant improvements in customer-satisfaction and bottom-line benefits. Companies experiencing success have created an infrastructure to support the strategy.

An IEE business strategy involves the measurement of how well business processes meet organizational goals and offers strategies to make needed improvements. The application of the techniques to all functions results in a very high level of quality at reduced costs with a reduction in lead times, resulting in improved profitability and a competitive advantage. It is most important to choose the best set of measurements for a particular situation and to focus on the wise integration of statistical and other improvement tools offered by an IEE implementation.

Volume 2 of this series described the IEE business strategy: executive ownership and leadership, a support infrastructure, projects with bottom-line results, full-time black belts, part-time green belts, reward/motivation considerations, finance engagement, and training in all roles, both "hard" and "soft" skills.

Organizations create strategic plans and policies. They also create organizational goals that describe the intent of the organization. These goals should have measurable results, which are attained through defined action plans. The question of concern is: How effective and aligned are these management system practices within an organization? An improvement to this system can dramatically impact an organization's bottom line.

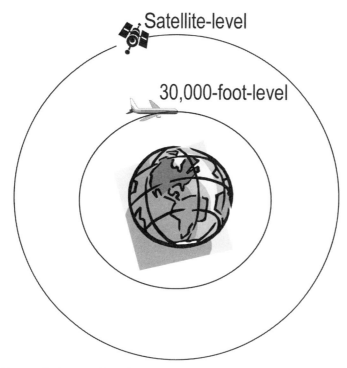

Figure 2.3: Satellite-level and 30,000-foot-level scorecard/
dashboard metrics.

An IEE system measures the overall organization using score-cards/dashboards metrics that report at the satellite-level and 30,000-foot-level metrics, as illustrated in Figure 2.3. Physically, these metrics can take on many responses, as illustrated in Figure 2.4. Traditional business metrics that could be classified as satellite-level metrics are gross revenue, profit, net profit margin, earnings before interest, depreciation and amortization (EBIDA), and VOC. Satellite-level metrics are not to replace existing financial metrics but provide a time-series financial view of the enterprise as a whole over time. This view can provide insight that is needed to make process improvements that have a long-lasting positive impact on the business as a whole.

Traditional operational metrics at the 30,000-foot-level are defective/defect rates, lead time, waste, days sales outstanding (DSO), on-time delivery, number of days from promise date, number of days from customer-requested date, dimensional property, inventory, and head count. Example 9.1 of Volume 2 describes

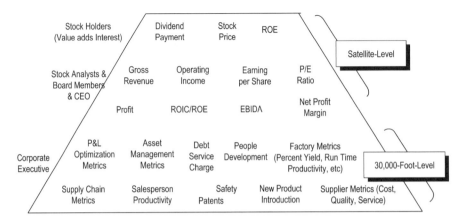

ROE = Return on Equity; OI = Operating Income; P/E = Price to Earnings; ROIC = Return on Invested Capital
P&L = Profit & Loss; EBIDA = Earnings Before Interest Depreciation, and Amortization; VOC = Voice of the Customer

Figure 2.4: Example satellite-level and 30,000-foot-level metrics.

an enterprise process financial analysis linkage of these metrics to process improvement projects.

> Both satellite-level and 30,000-foot-level metrics are tracked over time and do not have calendar year boundaries. If nothing has changed in ten years, satellite-level and 30,000-foot-level charts would present how the system performed over the past ten years.

Both satellite-level and 30,000-foot-level metrics are tracked over time and do not have calendar year boundaries. If nothing has changed in 10 years, satellite-level and 30,000-foot-level charts would present how the system performed over the past 10 years. Organizations can find it to be very beneficial when they align project selection with satellite-level theory of constraint (TOC) metrics (i.e., TOC throughput (see Glossary), investment/inventory, and operating expense).

Data presented in the satellite-level and 30,000-foot-level scorecard/dashboard format provide additional business insight when, for example, compared to tabular quarterly format reporting. Satellite-level and 30,000-foot-level reporting involves the creation of scorecards/dashboard metrics throughout the organization's value chain. An enterprise cascading measurement methodology (ECMM) is a system that cascades and aligns important value chain metrics throughout the organization so that meaningful measurements are statistically tracked over time at various business functional levels.

ECMM tracking cascades satellite-level business metrics down to high-level key process output variable (KPOV) operational metrics. These high-level KPOV metrics might have a 30,000-foot-level, 20,000-foot-level, and 10,000-foot-level metric reporting, where all these high-level metrics are tracked using infrequent subgrouping/sampling techniques. This cascading can further progress down to 50-foot-level key process input variable (KPIV) metrics, where frequent sampling feedback is used to determine when timely adjustments are needed to a process.

High-level KPOV metrics provide voice of the process (VOP) views at various organizational levels, while low-level KPIV metrics provide the trigger for when timely process adjustments are needed so that high-level KPOV performance is maintained. For example, in popular grocery stores, a high-level KPOV-cascaded metric from an overall customer satisfaction metric could be grocery store check-out time. A related low-level KPIV to this high-level check-out-time metric would the number of people in line, which could provide a timely decision point for determining whether grocery store checkers should be added, reduced, or remain the same.

High-level ECMM metrics in conjunction with an effective process improvement system can transition a business from a culture of firefighting to one of fire prevention. Within this fire-prevention culture, business performance metric improvement needs pull for the creation of projects that lead to long-lasting, beneficial process change. The result from this is that there are less future fires to fight.

An illustration of how an organizational metric cascading environment can create a fire-prevention culture is:

> An enterprise's 30,000-foot-level on-time-shipment tracking could consist of weekly random selecting 100 product shipments and then comparing how well each shipment performed relative to its due date. For this reporting, each product shipment could be viewed as an attribute (i.e., it was received on time or not). This data would then be combined to create a weekly cumulated non-conformance rate for deliveries relative to due dates.
>
> For this reporting format, a shipment that is 1 day late would carry the same delinquency severity level as a shipment that is twenty days late. Typically the reporting of these two

non-compliance deliveries would not be viewed with an equivalent level of dissatisfaction. Hence, if at all possible, it would be better to convert this form of attribute conformance reporting to continuous data (e.g., a 3.0 would indicate three days late, while –1.0 would indicate one day early).

This data format could then be tracked over time using the basic IEE scorecard/dashboard metric reporting process described below. There should be ownership for each 30,000-foot-level metric. This owner would be responsible for achieving assigned future process improvement goals for his/her 30,000-foot-level performance metric(s).

During an E-DMAIC study, this metric could have been determined to be a high potential area for improvement. This volume will later show how an enterprise improvement plan (EIP) can be used to drill down from a goal to high potential areas for improvement (see Figure 3.6).

This 30,000-foot-level metric could also be cascaded downward as a 20,000-foot-level metric, 10,000-foot-level metric, etc. throughout the organization. This could be accomplished by using a similar sampling procedure to the one described above for product delivery times by sites and perhaps individual part numbers. The assignment of deliver metric ownership for the 20,000-foot-level and other components of the 30,000-foot-level organizational metrics can provide the focus needed for process measurement and improvement opportunities.

If an improvement is desired for this enterprise 30,000-foot-level metric, a Pareto chart could be useful to determine which sites and part numbers should be given focus for improving the 30,000-foot-level metric as a whole (i.e., creation of targeted projects that are pulled for creation by metric improvement needs).

The reader should note how this approach is quite different than passing down an across the board goal of "improving on-time shipments" for all sites through an organizational chart or other means. With the above approach, sites that are performing well need to only maintain their performance, while other sites that are not performing well would get the needed attention focus for determining what to do to improve their performance. In the sites that are not doing well, one or more projects would be pulled for creation by this metric improvement need.

The above described high-level measurement cascading report tracking (e.g., 30,000-foot-level, 20,000-foot-level, and

10,000-foot-level) is accomplished through the IEE scorecard/ dashboard metric reporting process:

1. Assess process predictability.
2. When the process is considered predictable, formulate a prediction statement for the latest region of stability. The usual reporting format for this statement is:
   (a) When there is a specification requirement: non-conformance percentage or defects per million opportunities (DPMO)
   (b) When there are no specification requirements: median response and 80% frequency of occurrence rate

In IEE, prediction statements are referred to as a process capability/performance metric. Reiterating, if there is a specification or requirement, IEE prediction statements usually are reported as a non-conformance proportion rate; e.g., out-of-specification percentage or defects per million opportunities (DPMO). In IEE, both continuous and attribute pass/fail response data utilize this reporting format. Again, if there are no specific specification(s) or requirement(s) for a continuous response, then a median response and 80% frequency of occurrence rate is reported. An 80% frequency of occurrence rate is typically used for this situation, since this percentage value provides an easy to understand picture of what variability around the median can be expected from the process.

It needs to be highlighted that prediction statements provide a best estimate of how the process is currently performing and what performance could be expected from the process in the future unless something changes either positively or negatively.

Predictive processes can shift either positively or negatively at any point of time. For example, a process improvement could occur in any month or day of the year. When a process shifts between two stable/predictable regions, the quantification of the before and after change predictive statements difference is a best estimate statement for the project's benefit.

This metric tracking approach assesses the organization as a system, which can lead to focused improvement efforts and a reduction of firefighting activities. Data presented in this format can be useful for executives as an input to the creation of their strategic plans and then to tracking the results from the execution of these strategic plans. With this strategy, action plans to achieve organizational goals center around the creation and implementation of projects in the E-DMAIC system, as illustrated in Figure 2.5.

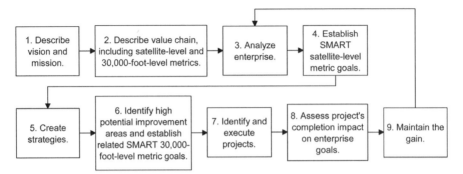

Figure 2.5: Aligning projects with business needs through E-DMAIC roadmap for project selection and P-DMAIC or DMADV roadmap for project execution.

The following describes the basic thought process of an E-DMAIC execution using the steps of Figure 4.7.

- Step 1 (Define phase)
  - Define vision and mission.
- Step 2 (Define phase (value-chain steps) and measure phase (value-chain measurements))
  - Describe value chain, including 30,000-foot-level metrics.
  - Create satellite-level metrics for the past 3–10 years. We want to ensure that the selected time is long enough that multiple business cycles are captured.
  - Compile 30,000-foot-level value-chain metrics.
- Step 3 (Analyze phase)
  - Analyze satellite-level and 30,000-foot-level metrics looking for improvement opportunities.
  - Analyze the enterprise as a whole looking for constraints, improvement opportunities, and new product opportunities, which could include acquisitions or selling portions of the business.
- Step 4 (Analyze phase)
  - Establish SMART goals that are consistent with the work from step 3.
- Step 5 (Analyze phase)
  - Create strategies from analyses described in step 3.
- Step 6 (Analyze phase)
  - Identify high potential areas and related 30,000-foot-level scorecard/dashboard metrics for focusing improvement efforts using goals and the value-chain process map to help guide the selection process.

  - Establish 30,000-foot-level value-chain metric goals with agree-to ownership and time for achievement. The project champion should be the owner of the metric that is to be improved.
  - Identify potential projects that are in alignment with determined business needs.
- Step 7 (Improve phase)
  - Select and assign well-scoped projects that are not too large or too small.
  - Work for timely project completion of process using resource of champion and black belt or green belt with coaching.
- Step 8 (Improve phase)
  - Assess project completion impact on enterprise goals.
- Step 9 (Control phase)
  - Maintain the gains.
  - Repeat.

IEE 30,000-foot-level scorecard/dashboard metrics are high-level operational or project metrics. The right metrics are needed for the orchestration of the right activities. The E-DMAIC process just described accomplishes this by linking improvement activities to business goals and to strategies that are aligned with these goals through the use of analytics.

This strategy can also be used with other types of improvement projects such as reliability excellence and behavior-based safety. People in organizations often feel overwhelmed when facing multiple improvement activities and when resources are in competition between associated projects. This system can tie all the improvement practices together and prioritize the resources where needed. It can help organizations understand and improve the key drivers that affect the metrics and enterprise process scorecards.

2.2   IEE as a Business Strategy

In a work environment, tasks are completed. These tasks can lead to a response even though the procedures to perform them are not formally documented. Lead time is one potential response for the completion of a series of tasks. Another is the quality of the completed work. Reference will be made to important responses from a process as key process output variables (KPOVs), sometimes called the *Y*s of the process.

Sometimes the things that are completed within a work environment cause a problem to customers or create a great deal of waste; that is, overproduction, waiting, transportation, inventory, overprocessing, motion, defects, and people utilization, which can be very expensive to an organization. Attempts to solve waste do not always address these problems from an overall system viewpoint. The organization might also have a variety of KPOVs, such as a critical dimension, overall lead time, a DPMO rate that could expose a hidden-factory rework issue currently not reported, customer satisfaction, and so on.

For this type of situation, organizations often react to the up-and-down movements of the KPOV level over time in a firefighting mode, fixing the problems of the day. Frequent arbitrary tweaks to controllable process variables and noise (e.g., material differences, operator-to-operator differences, machine-to-machine differences, and measurement imprecision) can cause excess variability and yield a large non-conforming proportion for the KPOV. Practitioners and management might think that their day-to-day problem-fixing activities are making improvements to the system. In reality, these activities often expend many resources without making any improvements to the process. Unless long-lasting process changes are made, the proportion of non-compliance will remain approximately the same.

When we manage simply toward goals and targets throughout the organization chart, we are managing to the Ys in the mathematical relationship $Y = f(X)$. This can lead to the wrong behavior, that is, the Enron effect. The way to make long-lasting improvements is through process changes or improving the management of the Xs that are shown in Figure 2.6.

> When we manage simply toward goals and targets throughout the organization chart, we are managing to the Ys in the mathematical relationship $Y = f(X)$. This can lead to the wrong behavior, that is, the Enron effect. The way to make long-lasting improvements is through process changes or improving the management of the Xs.

Organizations that frequently encounter this type of situation have much to gain from the implementation of an IEE business strategy. They can better appreciate this potential gain when they consider all the direct and indirect costs associated with their current level of non-conformance.

The described methodology is a deployment system that uses both statistical and non-statistical tools. As Figure 2.1 illustrates,

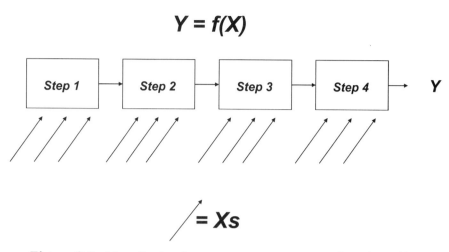

Figure 2.6: Magnitude of a process response as a function of its input levels.

an E-DMAIC system can lead to an improvement project that follows the P-DMAIC roadmap. P-DMAIC is an enhanced version of the traditional Six Sigma DMAIC roadmap. The P-DMAIC roadmap offers additional component breakdown in the measure phase and true Lean tool integration.

In this business strategy, a practitioner applies the P-DMAIC roadmap either during a workshop or as a project after a workshop. The baseline for a created project would be determined through the IEE scorecard/dashboard metric-reporting process:

1. Assess process predictability.
2. When the process is considered predictable, formulate a prediction statement for the latest region of stability. The usual reporting format for this statement is the following:
   (a) When there is a specification requirement: non-conformance percentage or DPMO
   (b) When there is no specification requirement: median response and 80% frequency of occurrence rate

Figure 2.7 illustrates for continuous data the pull for project creation and benefit from the project as demonstrated in the 30,000-foot-level metric change. Figure 2.8 illustrates the same for an attribute response. It should be noted for continuous data that all individual values from the stable region of the process are used to create a voice of the process (VOP) distribution. The

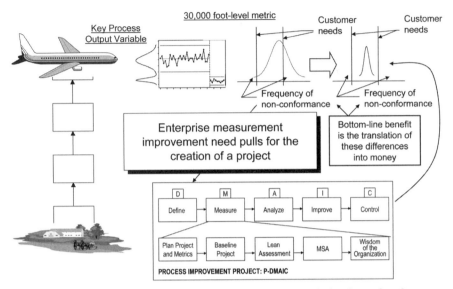

Figure 2.7: IEE project creation, execution, and the benefits for a continuous response.

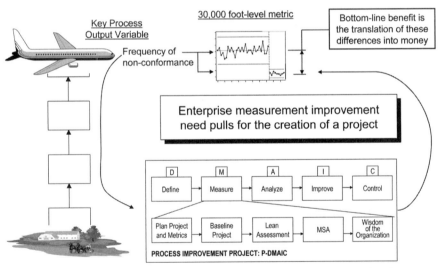

Figure 2.8: IEE project creation, execution, and the benefits for an attribute response.

placements of specifications on this distribution provide an assessment of how well the process is performing relative to customer requirements, for example, a form of voice of the customer (VOC). While for attribute data, no distribution plot is needed since the centerline is a direct nonconformance rate estimate.

A resulting change process can have less waste and be more robust or indifferent to process noise variables. This effort can result in an improved-process mean shift or reduced variability or both, which leads to quantifiable bottom-line monetary benefits.

The success of IEE is a function of management commitment and an infrastructure that supports this commitment. However, this commitment does not need to come from the CEO level. This infrastructure can start anywhere. It can then spread throughout the company when system benefits materialize and can be shown to others.

2.3 Applying IEE

Care needs to be exercised in an organization. Otherwise policies or standard operating procedures can lead to *unintended consequences.*

Consider the following questions:

1. Does your organization have metrics that drive the wrong kind of behavior?
2. Does your organization have excessive firefighting?
3. Does your organization have projects that sound beneficial that are even validated by finance but have questionable benefits?
4. Is your organization not meeting its financial goals?

Organizations that have any of these issues can benefit from an IEE implementation. Volume 2 describes the enterprise-level execution system (i.e., through E-DMAIC). This volume describes the project-level execution system (i.e., through P-DMAIC).

What can organizations do to be most effective in improving their measurement, analysis, and improvement system? What should individuals do to increase their application knowledge and grow in how they utilize tools and help their organization improve? In addition to initial workshop training and continual sharpen-the-saw follow-up training, coaching needs to be structurally blended into the system. In addition to learning at a peer level, it is important for everyone to have a skilled-mentor relationship with one or more people. This coaching no only benefits individuals but the overall organizational enterprise system.

Volume 2 describes the creation of an IEE deployment where a week-long workout kicks off the creation of an E-DMAIC system. Both organizational infrastructure-creation and individual project-execution coaching is included in this deployment model as part of the ongoing building and refinement process.

3

Enterprise Define–Measure–Analyze–Improve–Control

3.1 E-DMAIC – Roadmap

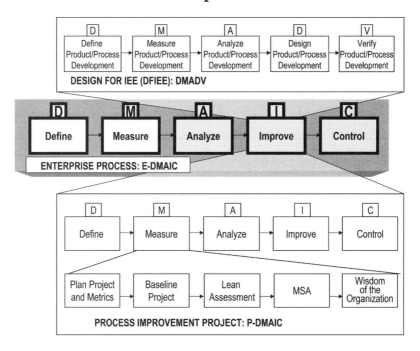

The previous chapter described the Integrated Enterprise Excellence (IEE) system. This chapter provides E-DMAIC highlights from Volume 2 of this series.

3.2 E-DMAIC – Define and Measure Phase: Enterprise Process Value Chain

Most organizations create an organizational chart and then manage through that organizational chart. However, the enterprise process customer can experience something quite different; that is, the impact from the fundamental flow of what is being done. The steps of the value chain capture at a high level what we do and how we measure what is done. The metrics that are aligned to steps of the value chain (see Section 16.2 for flowchart creation) are to be tracked and reported at the satellite-level or 30,000-foot-level (see Chapters 12 and 13 for a description of how to create these scorecard/dashboard metrics). Metrics described throughout this volume could be tracked in the value chain at the 30,000-foot-level. For example, the total productive maintenance (TPM) metrics described later, could be an organizational 30,000-foot-level metric. The shaded functional steps in the value chain are an indication of drill-down procedures, as described in the next section.

> Most organizations create an organizational chart and then manage through that organizational chart. However, the enterprise process customer can experience something quite different; i.e., the impact from the fundamental flow of what is being done.

An organizational value chain can begin at the corporate level, site level, or other levels throughout the company. This value chain can also become the linkage to all standard operating procedures and processes. An example of a partially constructed value chain is shown in Figure 3.1. Notice how the main flow describes at a high level what the organization does, where separate functions such as HR and IT could be described as separate entities. Figure 3.2 includes an Enterprise Process Management (EPM) function value chain drill down, which coordinates the execution of the E-DMAIC measurement, analysis, and improvement organizational system. In all cases, created metrics describe what is important to the business and where these metrics should address Lean E-DMAIC issues such as quality, waste, lead time, and total costs.

The following figures illustrate various aspects of the value chain (Volume 2 includes additional examples):

- Figure 3.1 illustrates an organizational value chain, which includes satellite-level and 30,000-foot-level metrics.
- Figure 3.2 illustrates an organizational value chain where the overall E-DMAIC process management orchestration can reside, noting that this is where current enterprise process analysis and improvement procedures could reside.
- Figure 3.3 exemplifies value chain linkage with organization's satellite-level metrics.
- Figure 3.4 exemplifies value chain linkage with a 30,000-foot-level functional performance metric.

3.3   E-DMAIC – Technical Aspects of Satellite-Level and 30,000-Foot-Level Charting

The primary intent of traditional control charting is to timely identify when a special cause condition occurs and take appropriate action. This is not the case with satellite-level and 30,000-foot-level control charting. Because of this, there are several technical

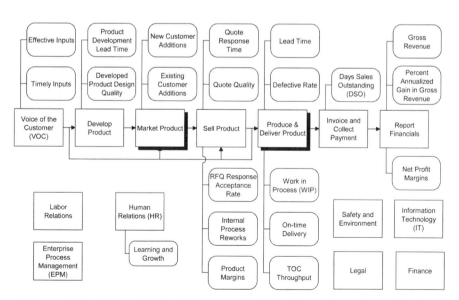

Figure 3.1: Value chain with scorecard/dashboard metrics. Shaded areas designate processes that have sub-process drill-downs.

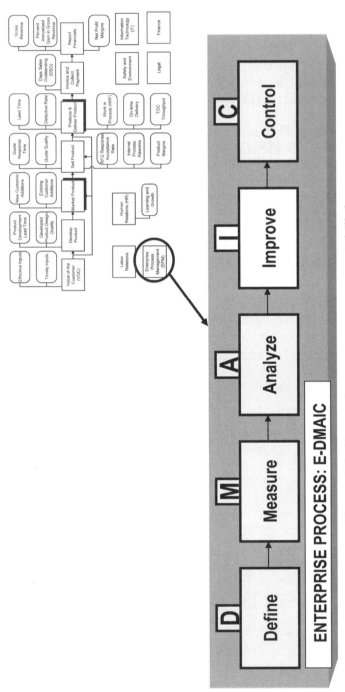

Figure 3.2: Enterprise process management drill-down.

issues to address when creating these charts. The purpose of this section is to provide chart-creation highlights.

Satellite-level and 30,000-foot-level charting focus is the providing of a high-level view for what the internal or external customer of the process is expected to experience. As noted earlier, the two basic objectives for satellite-level and 30,000-foot-level performance metric reporting is:

1. Assess process predictability.
2. When the process is considered predictable, formulate a prediction statement for the latest region of stability. The usual reporting format for this statement is as follows:
   (a) When there is a specification requirement: nonconformance percentage or defects per million opportunities (DPMO).
   (b) When there is no specification requirement: median response and 80% frequency of occurrence rate.

Because of these charting objectives, the mechanics to create these charts is often different than traditional control charting (Breyfogle, 2003b, 2004b, 2005b, and 2006). Later there will be more elaboration on the details of this statement and the chart-creation details for various situations. Highlights of issues that need addressing when creating satellite-level and 30,000-foot-level charts are as follows:

- The reporting and use of probability plots is different for attribute and continuous data (see Section 8.1), as demonstrated in the following examples.
- Control charting subgroups are created using infrequent subgrouping/sampling techniques so that short-term variations, which might be caused by typical variation in input levels, will result in charts that view these perturbations as common-cause variability sources.
- Individuals control charts can trigger false special-cause conditions when plotted data are from a distribution that is not normally distributed (see Appendix Section B.2).

3.4   E-DMAIC – Example 3.1: Satellite-Level Metrics

This example gives focus to the interpretation and use of satellite-level metrics. The mechanics of creating these charts is described in Example 12.8.

We want to satisfy stakeholders with our products and services. To accomplish this, we need to define and observe key metrics and indicators. Let's start with the financials, which provide a business-health picture of how well objectives and stockholder expectations are being met.

Organizations often establish annual gross-revenue growth-and-profit-margin objectives. Earlier it was illustrated how simply focusing on quarterly numbers often leads to the wrong activities. This example provides an alternative system-focused methodology that can provide more timely information on how good performance is relative to business goals.

Consider that the satellite-level metrics for Acme Medical are gross revenue (GR), percentage annual gain in GR, and net-profit margins. The report-out of these satellite-level metrics in Figure 3.3 shows a time-series plot of monthly GR. The reader should note that no curve has been fitted to this line for making future-revenue projections. Time-series projections can be very dangerous. Building an accurate time-series model requires a great deal of data. Because it would take 1 year to capture only 12 data points, this analysis could easily miss a timely statement about nonlinearity or a flattening of a growth curve. Because no statement was made relative to predictability, extrapolations could be very deceiving.

One might ask: why not simply report total revenue growth for each month, instead of including percent gain in gross revenue, which the figure includes? For one thing, a total revenue plot does not directly address a common organizational goal; i.e., to grow the business by a certain percentage year over year. Also, a simple monthly total revenue growth report-out offers no statement about future output expectations from the current processes.

In the IEE satellite-level report-out in Figure 3.3, the 12-month percentage gain in GR (monthly reporting) is determined by calculating the annual percentage gain as if the yearly financial statements were closing that month. For example, a March 2008 percentage-gain point would be determined as:

$$\frac{\text{GR \% annual gain}}{\text{plot point for 3/08}} = \frac{GR_{[4/1/07 \text{ to } 3/31/08]} - GR_{[4/1/06 \text{ to } 3/31/07]}}{GR_{[4/1/06 \text{ to } 3/31/07]}}(100)$$

If a goal is to increase annual gross-revenue growth, detecting a process shift can take some time. However, this tracking procedure is in true alignment with the organizational annual-revenue-growth goal statement and can provide a monthly feedback assessment on the impact of efforts to achieve this goal.

With this form of reporting, management should not be reacting to the up-and-down control chart variability as though it were special cause. This does not mean that one should ignore the variation and simply talk it away as common-cause variability. What it does mean is that we do not react either positively or negatively to individual common-cause datum points (i.e., we would examine the data collectively). If the numbers were down below what is desired, focus would be given to process-improvement effort, as opposed to spending a lot of time explaining what happened last month.

The results from an interpretation of the annualized percentage gain in GR and profit margins plots shown in Figure 3.3 using the IEE scorecard/dashboard metric reporting process:

1. Assess process predictability.
2. When the process is considered predictable, formulate a prediction statement for the latest region of stability. The usual reporting format for this statement is the following:
   (a) When there is a specification requirement: nonconformance percentage or DPMO
   (b) When there is no specification requirement: median response and 80% frequency of occurrence rate

An interpretation of the *annual-gross-revenue-growth plots* shown in Figure 3.3 using this process is as follows:

1. A control chart test on the annual-gross-revenue data indicated a shift about June 00. Perhaps another company was acquired at this time. Since then, the process has experienced only common-cause variability. Even though the control chart appears to have some trends from this point in time, the rules of control charting would have us conclude that the process is now predictable.
2. From the probability plot, we estimate that since June 00 a monthly median of 27.2% and an 80% occurrence frequency of 25.2–29.3% has occurred; that is, we expect that 80% of the future monthly reporting will be between these two percentages.

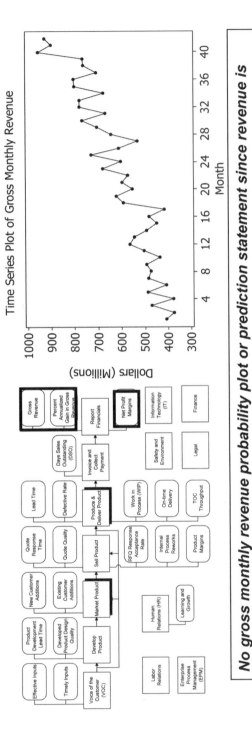

Figure 3.3: (Part A) Comparison of traditional performance reporting with an IEE value-chain satellite-level scorecard/dashboard report.

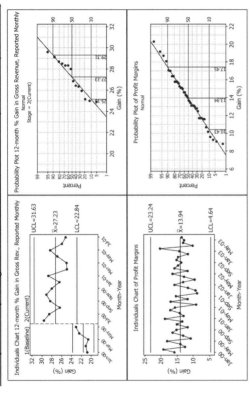

Figure 3.3: (Part B) Comparison of traditional performance reporting with an IEE value-chain satellite-level scorecard/dashboard report. Stage 1 (baseline) and Stage 2 (new) process levels are designated are at the top of the graphs.

An interpretation of *profit-margin plots* shown in Figure 3.3 using this process is as follows:

1. Even though the control chart of profit appears to have trends, the rules of control charting would have us conclude that the process was predictable.
2. From the probability plot, we estimate a monthly median of 13.9% and an 80% monthly occurrence frequency of 10.4 to 17.4%; that is, we expect that 80% of the future monthly reporting will be between these percentages.

After all value-chain metrics are collectively examined, realistic goals can be set to improve the satellite-level metrics. A strategy could then be created to improve these metrics, which is part of the E-DMAIC process analyze phase. As part of this enterprise decision-making process, areas thought to drive higher net-profit margins might be the reduction of defects and the creation of a new product line.

Specific goals can be established for improvements to the 30,000-foot-level scorecard/dashboard metrics. The 30,000-foot-level metric's owners would be responsible for making targeted improvements in the allotted time frame; for example, shift the process mean to the desired goal in 6 months. For the 30,000-foot-level metric to improve its level of performance, a fundamental improvement is needed in the process.

These metric improvement needs would pull for P-DMAIC project creation. Managers would then assign black belts or green belts to these projects who would follow the IEE project-execution roadmap described in this volume. Since these managers are measured against the success of the metric shift, they will want to have frequent updates about the status of the project. The overall system that accomplishes this is part of the E-DMAIC analyze and improve phases.

One should note how this form of management focuses on improving the systems of doing things, as opposed to firefighting the process common-cause ups and downs or targeting tabular outputs that do not meet expectations (e.g., red–yellow–green metric reporting).

This E-DMAIC reporting at the satellite-level and 30,000-foot-level can lead to a very positive governance model that moves organizations toward achieving the three Rs of business: everyone doing the Right things and doing them Right at the Right time. This is in contrast to a business governance model that encourages the executive team to do whatever it takes to achieve the next calendar-based financial target; that is, trying to manage the *Y* output of a process rather than giving focus to improving the process or its *X* inputs, which either positively or negatively impact the *Y* output.

Many practitioners would be hesitant to present this type of satellite-level and 30,000-foot-level (later examples in this chapter) metric report-out to their management. This is understandable since this report-out is probably quite different than what has been previously presented and requested.

For those readers who see the benefit in this type of reporting and do not know how to get their management's interest, I suggest using advocacy selling and stealth training techniques. For the advocacy selling portion of this strategy, you could describe the charts off-line to a leading thinking influential person, who is on the executive team. After taking the time to understand the IEE reporting methodology off-line, he/she could then support the creation of an opportunity where you give a short presentation to the executive team. In this presentation, you could select data sets from your business where you compare your current methods with the described IEE methodology.

Now comes the stealth training. During the meeting you should give focus to the prediction statement, which is highlighted at the bottom of the presentation slide. You should not make any statement about the graphs per se, which is the stealth training portion of this presentation. What you want is someone to ask a question about the charts and variation swings. In most of these type meetings, someone will ask about the data variability that is conveyed in the charts.

When responding to this and other initial questions, don't try to give too much initial explanation – more detailed information can come in another presentation. You might simply say that all the up and down motion in the control chart is common-cause variability, which indicates that the process is predictable. Pointing now to the probability plot you could then show how the prediction statement was determined.

I suggest that you also have a slide that compares this IEE report-out methodology to your traditional reporting methodology, which makes no prediction statement. During this presentation you might be able to demonstrate that your organization's many firefighting skirmishes have not really fixing much, if anything, long term.

I have had practitioners say that there is no way that their management would ever accept satellite-level and 30,000-foot-level reporting. However, these practitioners did try and now they say that their management is requesting this form of reporting.

3.5   E-DMAIC – Example 3.2: 30,000-Foot-level Metric with Specifications

This example focuses on the interpretation and use of 30,000-foot-level metrics. The mechanics of creating these charts is described in Example 12.9.

Let's say that on-time delivery is considered one of the greatest customer satisfiers to sales of products and services in Acme Medical's business value chain. This example provides a high-level view of the output from IEE 30,000-foot-level scorecard/dashboard metric reporting. For the purpose of illustration, the following data were randomly generated from a normal distribution.

In Acme Medical's value chain, the on-time delivery 30,000-foot-level scorecard/dashboard metric performance was tracked by randomly selecting one shipment weekly. Results from this analysis are shown in Figure 3.4, where +1 indicates 1 day late and −1 indicates 1 day early.

The following IEE scorecard/dashboard metric reporting process will be used when analyzing the data:

1.   Assess process predictability.
2.   When the process is considered predictable, formulate a prediction statement for the latest region of stability. The usual reporting format for this statement is the following:
     (a)   When there is a specification requirement: nonconformance percentage or DPMO.
     (b)   When there is no specification requirement: median response and 80% frequency of occurrence rate.

Interpretation of Figure 3.4 using this process is as follows:

1.   Even though the control chart in Figure 3.4 appears to have trends, the rules of control charting would have us conclude that the process was predictable. As a reminder, these data were randomly generated and all variability was due to chance.
2.   The agreed-to shipping requirement was that shipments were not to be late (i.e., >+1.0) and no earlier than 5 days

Traditional Performance Reporting Example – Red-Yellow-Green Scorecard

Week Number	65	66	67	68	69	70	71	72	73	74	75
Days Late	-2.16	-1.12	0.07	1.13	-1.88	-0.82	-4.78	-3.29	-1.67	-0.41	0.09
No greater than	1	1	1	1	1	1	1	1	1	1	
No less than	5	5	5	5	5	5	5	5	5	5	

IEE Improved Reporting for Process Assessment and Improvement

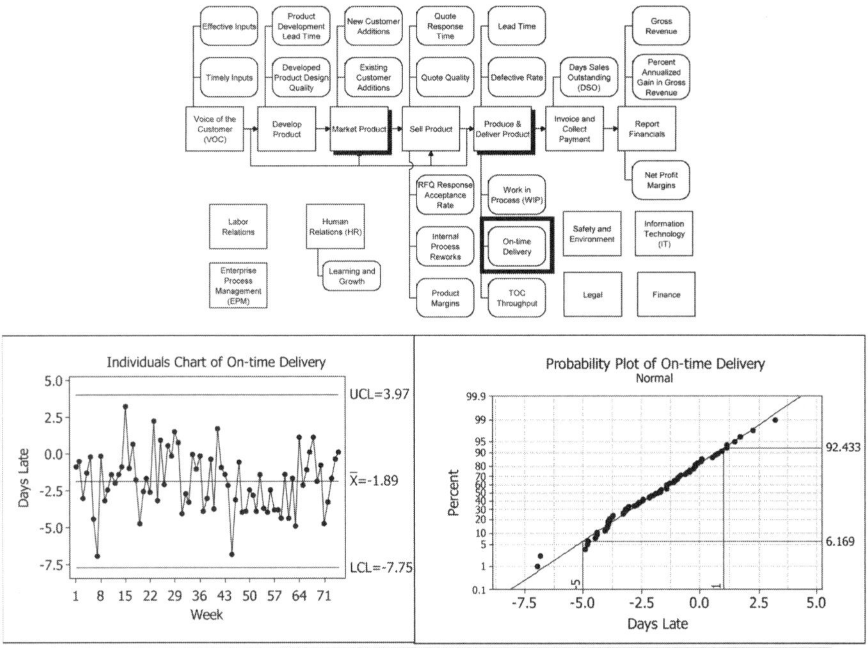

Predictable process with approximately 13.7% nonconformance

(i.e., Using the current process, deliveries are not on time about 14% of the time.)

Figure 3.4: Comparison of traditional performance reporting with an IEE value chain 30,000-foot-level on-time delivery performance scorecard/dashboard report. The traditional performance reporting example contains the most recent eleven data points.

(i.e., –5.0) from their due date. The value-chain manager responsible for producing and delivering the product is responsible for this metric relative to current level of performance maintenance and any desired improvements. Acme's current performance and predicted future performance is that about 6.1% of all shipments will be earlier than the agreed-to date and about 7.6% of all shipments will be later than the agreed-to date (100–92.433 = 7.567 rounded off). This leads to the expectation that about 13.7% (6.1+7.6) will be either earlier or later than the agree-to delivery date.

Often, on-time-delivery metrics are reported as attribute data; that is, each shipment was received within the agreed-to time interval or not. It is hoped that the reader will appreciate the value of using the above continuous-response data-analysis approach over attribute reporting. With continuous data, much more insight is gained with a significantly smaller sample size. As illustrated in the example above, we not only estimate the proportion of shipments that are both early and late, but also describe the distribution of delivery times.

Using control charting rules, we have no reason to infer that the apparent short-term trends in the 30,000-foot-level control chart were from chance and should not be reacted to as individual values. Long-lasting improvements to this metric can be made through fundamental process changes.

> When all value chain metrics are collectively examined in the E-DMAIC analyze phase, this metric could be chosen as one that needs improvement because of its anticipated impact upon gross revenue and net profit improvement goals. If this were the case, this metric would be pulling for an improvement project creation.

When all value-chain metrics are collectively examined in the E-DMAIC analyze phase, this metric could be chosen as one that needs improvement because of its anticipated impact on gross-revenue goals, net-profit improvement goals, or customer retention. If this were the case, this metric would be creating a pull for project creation. The owner of this "produce and deliver product" metric would be responsible for making the targeted improvements in the allotted time frame; for example, shifting the process mean to the desired goal in 6 months. This manager would then assign a black belt or green belt to the project, where he would follow the IEE project-execution roadmap described later in this volume. Since this manager is measured against the success of the metric shift, he will want to have frequent updates about the status of the project.

Note how this form of management focuses on improving the systems of doing things, as opposed to firefighting the common-cause ups and downs of processes or point tabular values that do not meet expectations, such as red–yellow–green metric reporting.

3.6 E-DMAIC – Analyze Phase: Enterprise Process Goal Setting

Vince Lombardi changed the National Football League (NFL) Green Bay Packers, who were perpetually losing at the time, into an NFL dynasty. Coach Lombardi said, "If you are not keeping score, you are just practicing."

Dr. Deming states (Deming, 1986), "If you have a stable system, then there is no use to specify a goal. You will get whatever the system will deliver. A goal beyond the capability of the system will not be reached .... If you do not have a stable system, then there is again no point in setting a goal. There is no way to know what the system will produce: it has no capability."

Dr. Lloyd S. Nelson stated, "If you can improve productivity, or sales, or quality, or anything else, by, for example, 5% next year without a rational plan for improvement, then why were you not doing it last year?"

When organizations establish scorecard goals, much care needs to be exercised. Goals should be SMART. However, these guidelines are often violated. Arbitrary goals set for individuals or organizations can be very counterproductive and costly.

The implication of Dr. Deming's statement is that simple goal setting alone will not yield an improved output. For an improved output, organizations need to give due diligence to bettering the process. This series of volumes focuses on the creation of more customers and cash (MC^2), not the simple creation of arbitrary goals throughout the organization, which can lead to the wrong activities or strategies that often lead to interpretation and action-item inconsistencies.

> The implication of Dr. Deming's statement is that simple goal setting alone will not yield an improved output. For an improved output, organizations need to give due diligence to bettering the process.

In E-DMAIC, satellite-level and 30,000-foot-level scorecard/dashboard metrics are examined over time before financial goals are established. The assessment of these non-calendar bounded metrics helps with the creation of SMART goals. This assessment could lead to the following mean monthly satellite-level metric goals:

- Sales growth: 10%
- Operating margins: 20%
- ROCE: 20%

Other organizational goals that could be tracked at the 30,000-foot-level scorecard/dashboard metric level are as follows:

- Environmental: Energy cost reductions of at least 25% over 3 years.
- New products: 30% of products sold are products that have been available 5 years or less.

Section 3.12 later describes the drill down process from these satellite-level enterprise process goals to 30,000-foot-level goals and then specific projects that facilitate the process of achieving these goals.

3.7   E-DMAIC – Analyze Phase: Strategic Analyses and Development

Strategic thinking is important to the business. A strategic analysis includes (Hambrick and Fredrickson, 2001):

- Industrial analysis
- Customer/marketplace trends
- Environmental forecast
- Competitor analysis
- Assessment of internal strengths, weaknesses, resources

A strategy needs to be dynamic so that it can address timely changes, flexible so that it can address multiple options if they should arise, and able to form an effective assessment of current conditions for the creation of a meaningful 2–3-year plan. Most strategic plans emphasize one or two components of what is truly needed in a strategy.

> ... what is missing is guidance as to what constitutes a strategy and what should be the outcome.

In the article "Are you sure you have a strategy?" (Hambrick and Fredrickson, 2001) Donald Hambrick and James Fredrickson describe shortcomings with developed frameworks for strategic analysis. They point out that what is missing is guidance as to what constitutes a strategy and what should be the outcome.

"Strategy has become a catchall term used to mean whatever one wants it to mean. Executives now talk about their "service strategy," their "branding strategy," their "acquisition strategy," or whatever kind of strategy that is on their mind at a particular moment. But strategists – whether they are chiefs (CEOs) of established firms, division presidents, or entrepreneurs – must have a strategy, an integrated, overarching concept of how the business will achieve its objectives." (Hambrick and Fredrickson, 2001)

"Consider these statements of strategy drawn from actual documents and announcements of several companies:"

- 'Our strategy is to be the low-cost provider.'
- 'We're pursuing a global strategy.'
- 'The company's strategy is to integrate a set of regional acquisitions.'
- 'Our strategy is to provide unrivaled customer service.'
- 'Our strategic intent is to always be the first mover.'
- 'Our strategy is to move from defense to industrial applications.'

"What do these declarations have in common? Only that none of them is a strategy. They are strategic threads, mere elements of strategy. But they are no more strategies than Dell Computer's strategy can be summed up as selling direct to customers, or than Hannibal's strategy was to use elephants to cross the Alps. And their use reflects an increasingly common syndrome – the catchall fragmentation of strategy." These described strategic elements are not inconsistent with the previously referenced example strategy (see Figure 1.4), which a corporation stated on the Internet.

"Executives then communicate these strategic threads to their organizations in the mistaken belief that doing so will help managers make tough choices. But how does knowing that their firm is pursuing an "acquisition strategy or a first-mover strategy" help the vast majority of managers do their job or set priorities?"

Business leaders must have a strategy to meet their objectives. Without a strategy, time and resources can be wasted on piecemeal, disparate activities. Without a strategy, mid-level managers will fill the void with their interpretation of what the business should be doing, typically resulting in a disjointed set of activities.

The define phase of E-DMAIC is to include the company's vision, mission, values, and Jim Collins' three circles questions (Collins, 2001), which are as follows:

1. What you can be the best in the world at (and, equally important, at what can you not be the best in the world)?
2. What drives your economic engine?
3. What are you deeply passionate about?

The organization's value chain along with satellite-level and 30,000-foot-level scorecard/dashboard metrics is created in the measure phase of E-DMAIC.

In the IEE, organizations are now in a position to assess the current state of the high-level value chain metrics to determine the most appropriate goals for an organization. These goals, blended with a strategic analysis, can then provide inputs to a strategy, which is a centrally integrated, externally oriented concept on how the objectives can be achieved.

Volume 2 describes a process that organizations can walk through to execute the five critical elements for strategy development.

3.8   E-DMAIC – Analyze Phase: Theory of Constraints

The outputs of a system are a function of the whole system, not just individual processes. When we view our system as a whole, we realize that the output is a function of the weakest link. The weakest link of the system is the constraint. If care is not exercised, we can be focusing on a subsystem that, even though improved, does not impact the overall system output. We need to focus on the orchestration of efforts so that we optimize the overall system, not individual pieces. Unfortunately, organization charts lead to workflow by function, which can result in competing forces within the organization. With TOC, systems are viewed as a whole, and work activities are directed so that the whole system performance measures are improved. To illustrate this, consider the system that is shown in Figure 3.5. Similar to water flow through a garden hose, the squeezing of one portion of the hose reduces water flow volume (i.e., step 5 in the figure).

Without considering the whole system, we might be spending a great deal of time and effort working on process step 2 because this step is not meeting its localized-created target objectives

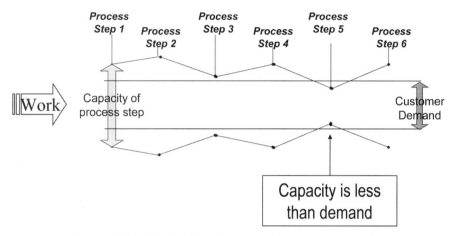

Figure 3.5: Identifying the overall system constraint.

relative to operating efficiencies, equipment utilization, etc. From this figure, we note that improvements to process step 2 would not significantly impact the overall system and could actually degrade the overall metrics if additional work in progress (WIP) is created from the improvements.

The TOC system chain extends from market demand through the organization chain to suppliers. Let's consider an example when this high-level view of the overall system is not addressed. An organization works at improving internal process efficiencies. Capacity then increases. Excess inventory is then created because there is not sufficient demand. Discovery is then made that the constraint is really the sales and marketing process.

Within an organization, there are often constraints that we may or may not consider. Types of constraints that exist are market, resource, material, supplier, financial, and knowledge/competency. We need to look at the rules (i.e., policies) that drive the constraints.

The implementation of Total Quality Management (TQM) has often been implemented by dividing the system into processes and then optimizing the quality of each process. This approach is preferable to chasing symptoms, but new problems can be created if the individual process is not considered in concert with other processes that it affects.

The theory of constraints presented by Goldratt (1992) focuses on reducing system bottlenecks as a means to continually improve the performance of the entire system. Rather than viewing the system in terms of discrete processes, TOC addresses the larger systematic picture as a chain or grid of interlinked chains. The performance of the weakest link determines the performance of the whole chain. According to Goldratt, the vast majority of constraints results from policies (e.g., rules, training, and other measures), while few constraints are physical (e.g., machines, facilities, people, and other tangible resources). For example, a large portion of highway road repair seems initially to be physically constrained by traffic flow. But the real constraint could also be government acquisition policy, which mandates the award of contracts to the lowest bidder. This drives contractors to the use of low-quality materials with shorter life in an effort to keep costs down and remain competitive.

> The theory of constraints presented focuses on reducing system bottlenecks as a means to continually improve the performance of the entire system. Rather than viewing the system in terms of discrete processes, TOC addresses the larger systematic picture as a chain or grid of interlinked chains.

TOC considers three dimensions of system performance in the following order: throughput (total sales revenues minus the total variable costs for producing a product or service), inventory (all the money a company invests in items it sells), and operating expense (money a company spends transforming inventory into throughput). Focus on these dimensions can lead a company to abandon traditional management cost accounting while at the same time causing an improvement in competitive price advantage.

3.9   E-DMAIC – Example 3.3: Theory of Constraints

In this example, I will use terms typically associated with manufacturing; however, the concepts apply equally to transactional processes.

A simple system is shown in Figure 3.6. Raw materials are processed through four component steps to produce a finished product. Each process step is an overall value stream link. The capacity of each step is described in the figure along with the market demand of 105 units per day. The goal is to make as much money as possible from the process.

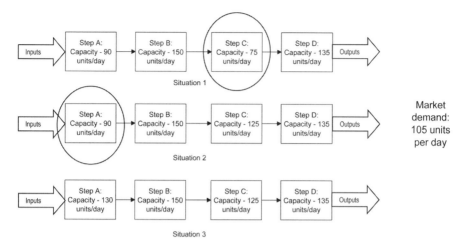

Figure 3.6: System constraint identification and resolution.

From the examination of situation 1 in the figure, it is noted that the capacity of Step C is 75, which is less than the market demand of 105. Even though other steps in our value stream process may not be performing up to their equipment utilization and efficiency goals, focus should be given first to increasing the capacity of Step C. From this E-DMAIC analysis, Step C would be an opportunity for a P-DMAIC project.

Upon completion of the P-DMAIC project for Step C, the process then exhibited the characteristics of situation 2 shown in the figure. An analysis of this situation indicates that the constraint is now at Step A. From this E-DMAIC analysis, it would now be appropriate for a P-DMAIC project to focus on Step A.

Upon completion of a P-DMAIC project of Step A, the process then started exhibiting the characteristics of situation 3. An analysis of this situation indicates that all four steps of the process have enough capacity to meet the market demand. The internal system constraints relative to satisfying a market demand of 115 units per day have been removed. The constraint has moved outside the system to the market place. The next P-DMAIC project should focus on determining what can be done to increase product demand through improvements in the marketing and sales processes.

This example illustrated the importance of starting by analyzing the big picture to determine where efforts should focus when creating P-DMAIC projects. Loosing sight of the big picture can lead to the ineffective utilization of resources and the sub-optimization of processes.

3.10   E-DMAIC – Analyze Phase: Lean Tools and Assessments

Womack *et al.* (1996) states that lean thinking can be summarized in five principles: precisely specify *value* by specific product, identify the *value stream* for each product, make value *flow* without interruptions, let the customer pull value from the producer, and pursue perfection. The intent of this chapter is to stimulate Lean enterprise-system improvement thinking for both manufacturing and transactional processes.

The four goals of a Lean Enterprise process are to improve quality, eliminate waste, reduce lead time, and reduce total costs (MacInnes, 2002), where:

- Quality examines how well products and/or services address the wants and needs of customers.
- Waste includes activities that consume resources, time, or space but has no value add relative to meeting customer requirements. The seven types of waste discussed later in this chapter are overproduction, waiting, transportation, inventory, over-processing, motion, and defects.
- Lead time is the total time for completion of a series of process steps (e.g., customer order receipt to customer payment). Lead time consists of the cycle time, which is the task time completion of a single transaction; batch delay time, which is the wait time for other transactions within a batch; and process delay time, which is the time batches wait from the completion of one operation to the start of another operation.
- Both direct and indirect costs comprise total costs. The balance of product pricing and of operating costs is essential for an organization's success. Cost reduction involves focusing on the reduction of organizational waste and lead times.

All these measures need to be an integral part of the value chain and its performance metrics. Lean techniques are applicable not only in the E-DMAIC analyze phase for project identification but also P-DMAIC.

3.11　E-DMAIC – Analyze Phase: Identification of Project Opportunities

As described earlier, traditional Six Sigma and Lean Six Sigma deployments could be viewed as push for project creation system. Consider the following:

- The success of a Six Sigma or Lean Six Sigma deployment is often measured by the total reported financial benefits of the projects. However, an honest assessment, as noted earlier, can often yield a statement like, "We have supposedly saved 100 million dollars, but no one can seem to find the money." This may sound absurd, but I have heard this comment and similar comments many times.
- It is not uncommon for organizations to report the training of many people (e.g., over 500 green belts), where perhaps only 10% of those trained have completed even one project. This type of report tells me that the planned projects are not really important to management.

IEE is more of a business system than traditional Six Sigma and Lean Six Sigma deployments. With this approach, we focus on a system that has measures and goals so that there is a pull for project creation as a means to meet these goals systematically. In this system, emphasis is given to creating financial benefits that are felt by the entire company, not just at the individual subprocess measurement level. It is also important that expectations and developed strategies are consistent with the "laws of physics," as described earlier (e.g., Enron problem avoidance).

> From this analysis, an enterprise improvement plan (EIP) can be created to identify potential project opportunities that are in direct alignment with business goals and voice of the customer inputs.

Volume 2 of his series described various analysis techniques that indicate where improvement efforts should focus. In the E-DMAIC analyze phase, risks versus benefits assessments need to be made for the creation of organizational strategies and specific actionable improvement items. Figure 3.2 illustrates the management and orchestration of this effort by an Enterprise Process Management (EPM) function.

From this analysis, an enterprise improvement plan (EIP) can be created to identify potential project opportunities that are in direct alignment with business goals and voice of the customer inputs (see Figure 3.7). These identified projects are important to the process owner who understands that the only way for him/her to meet his/her specific measurement goals is by completing identified projects that impact these metric.

In the E-DMAIC improve phase, EIP results orchestrates project selection.

3.12   E-DMAIC – Improve Phase

Dr. Lloyd S. Nelson stated, "In the state of statistical control, action initiated on appearance of a defect will be ineffective and will cause more trouble. What is needed is improvement of the process, by reduction of variation, or by change of level, or both. Study of the sources of product, upstream, gives powerful leverage on improvement" (Deming, 1986).

> From the E-DMAIC analyze phase, the improve phase takes information to develop specific action plans for the purpose of improving the overall business with not only financial savings but also customer relations.

From the E-DMAIC analyze phase, the improve phase takes information to develop specific action plans for the purpose of improving the overall business not only with financial savings but also with customer relations. These action plan types can be subdivided into three categories:

1. Design projects (i.e., product, process, or IT)
2. Process improvement projects
3. Business process improvement events (BPIEs)

Organizations need a system to identify and resolve simple re-occurring problems in a timely fashion. The resolution for these issues could involve a simple agree-to procedure change where the process change could have procedural documentation in a value chain drill down, and people who would be impacted would receive process change notification. Or, the solution might involve

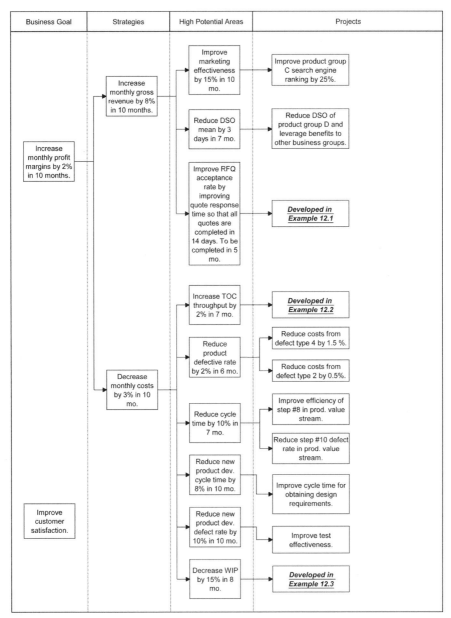

Figure 3.7: EIP illustration (see Volume 2 for referenced examples).

an IT implementation to mistake-proof a process (i.e., a design project creation).

I refer to the activities to accomplish these improvements as business process improvement events (BPIEs). Unlike projects that go through the full P-DMAIC process, BPIEs do not need to undergo the rigor of a formal project; e.g., demonstrate a beneficial shift in the 30,000-foot-level scorecard/dashboard metric and describe the financial project benefit).

> This IEE DMADV design-project approach is appropriate for product, process, or information technology (IT) projects.

For DFIEE, the basic thought process differs from the process improvement roadmap. The process used in IEE is called DMADV (define-measure-analyze-design-verify), as illustrated in Figure 2.1. This IEE DMADV design-project approach is appropriate for product, process, or IT projects.

For companies who develop new products, such as a new computer or insurance policy, there is typically a development process. However, much of the responsibility specifics for executing the process still reside with the product development manager. One might ask the question whether they think that the execution of a product development cycle and success of the developed product could differ dramatically if there were different product managers. The typical response to this question is affirmative.

What we would like is a product development process that is efficient, effective, and more robust to differences between product development managers. Implementation of the IEE DMADV roadmap addresses this by providing the opportunity for the wise integration of Lean and Six Sigma tools such as design of experiments (DOE) with existing development process requirements. This system can provide a more effective product-to-product development process learning-bridge framework so that products can be developed better, faster, and more in alignment to customer needs. This system can enhance product development and at the same time yield a system that is more robust to product manager-to-manager differences.

Another application of the fundamental IEE DMADV roadmap is new process development. This same basic IEE DMADV roadmap can be applied to the creation of a process or system that the organization has never done before or has not done recently (e.g., building of a new call center, acquiring a company, or setting up a new facility). This system can complement a project manager's skills for the task at hand. This is done through tool applications that help, among other things, mitigate risks, improve workflows, and increase systems' test effectiveness. The result is a system that helps meet expected objectives.

Lastly, the IEE DMADV roadmap is also applicable to IT projects. This system can complement existing IT development processes by providing, among other things, a system for capturing end-user customer needs and a system for testing the effectiveness of the newly developed product before going live.

For simple improvements where there is no need for specific quantification of the amount of improvement from the project, a BPIE can be sufficient. However, for more complicated processes where the solution is not obvious, a formal roadmap system can be invaluable for describing the overall thought and data collection/analysis process.

How does a team determine whether an improvement idea could be a quick win, whether it is a BPIE or a P-DMAIC project? Use the following five criteria to determine its quick-win viability: easy to implement, fast to implement, cheap to implement, within the team's control, and reversible.

> The P-DMAIC roadmap provides a work breakdown structure where a project can be subdivided into a plan that has easily digestible parts. This methodology systematically maps out the detail of paths and tasks needed to accomplish a project.

The P-DMAIC roadmap (see Appendix D) provides a work breakdown structure where a project can be subdivided into a plan that has easily digestible parts. This methodology systematically maps out the detail of paths and tasks needed to accomplish a project. This work breakdown structure flow can reveal the real level of complexity involved to achieve the project's goal. Potentially overwhelming projects can then become manageable, as well as uncovering unknown complexity. Planning teams move from theory to the real world relative to project scope and due dates. In addition, this project execution breakdown structure gives both participants and reviewers outside the team a presentation structure that can be checked for logical links and completeness at each level of the detailed plan. Much of the remainder of this volume will be walking through this roadmap.

The E-DMAIC analyze phase includes an EIP system for potential projects identification (see Figure 3.7). Table 3.1 illustrates how a project selection matrix can establish a project prioritization using differently weighted criteria. Projects with the largest total score have the highest perceived priority and would be assigned to the appropriate black belts or green belts.

3.13   E-DMAIC – Control Phase

Organizations need a system to control IEE execution as described in Figure 2.1. Corporate strategy needs to address how the business intends to engage in its environment. Compensation policies, information systems, or training policies are critically important and should reinforce/support strategy (Hambrick and Fredrickson, 2001). However, these internal organizational arrangement choices are not a part of strategy.

In IEE, these systems are to be described and executed as part of the organization's value chain (see Figure 3.2). The controls that ensure key processes' execution are to be described in an enterprise control plan. This control plan can become the single repository for the documentation of existing controls such as financial audits and equipment calibrations. The AIAG control plan format described later in this volume is most conducive to manufacturing and process-level control scenarios. The following generic control plan creation system is applicable to both transactional and manufacturing situations.

Table 3.2 illustrates the collection of the following steps for nine examples (Ex. a–Ex. i) as part of an enterprise control plan. Individual entries can be linked to a high-level value chain step, a sub-process step, an attached document, internet web page linkage, referenced document, etc.

1.   Identify a value chain process output or input to monitor/control.
     • Ex. a: Customer order lead time
     • Ex. b: Part flatness
     • Ex. c: Telephone response time
     • Ex. d: Process temperature
     • Ex. e: Number of people in grocery check-out line
     • Ex. f: Defective rate
     • Ex. g: Internet domain name reapplication

Table 3.1: EIP Project Selection Matrix

EIP Project Selection Matrix

	Potential impact to business strategy/goals	30,000-foot-level metric data available	Smaller amount of resources needed for project	Available personnel for team	Time to complete < 6 months	Input (cause) data available	Champion has authority to implement changes	<<<Process Outputs	Training — Total	Standard — Total
Training*	5	10	9	6	8	9	8	<<<Importance - Training Project	8	0
Standard	10	8	9	6	2	2	7	<<<Importance - Standard Project	7	0
								Correlation of input to output		
Project 1									0	0
Project 2									0	0

* Training -- First project assigned to coincide with a training course

Table 3.2: E-DMAIC Control Plan Illustration

	1	2	3	4	5	6	7	8	9	10	11	12	13
	Location and ownership		Metric description							Metric evaluation and reactions			
	Value chain process output or input to monitor/control	Owner	Input or output measurement description	IEE Tracking methodology	Select subgrouping/ sampling period	Sample size	Tracking process to determine whether predictable process or not	Prediction methodology, if applicable	Process capability/ performance measurement spec. or report-out statement	Device or individual making measurement	Metric report-out destination	Metric assessment	Reaction plan
a	Customer order lead time	Operations manager	Hours from order init. To fulfillment	30,000-foot-level	Weekly	All	Mean and standard deviation	Normal prob. Plot of all data from stable region	Median and 80% freq. of occurrence	Computer	Value chain and monthly exec. Meeting	1	2
b	Part flatness	Process owner	Inches in thousandsths	30,000-foot-level	Daily	Five	Mean and log standard deviation	Log-normal probability plot of all data from stable region	± 0.001 in.	Dial indicator	Customer	1	2
c	Telephone response time	Call center manager	Seconds	30,000-foot-level	Weekly	All	Mean and standard deviation	Normal prob. Plot of all data in stable region	60 sec. or less	Computer	Value chain and monthly exec. Meeting	1	2
d	Process temperature	Operator	Degrees Centigrade	50-foot-level pre-control chart	About 30 min., pre per-control rules	One	Individual value	N/A	50 °C ± 2 °C	Thermocouple	Operator	Determine if an adjustment is needed, per pre-control chart rules.	Adjust temperature per pre-control chart rules.
e	No. of people in grocery check-out line	Check-out supervisor	Number of people	50-foot-level pre-control chart	About 5 min., per pre-control rules	All	Mean	Total non-conformances divided by units produced in stable region	Between 2 and 4	Visual computer sensor	Store check-out supervisor	Determine if an adjustment is needed, per pre-control chart rules.	Add or reassign checkers per pre-control chart rules.
f	Defective rate	Oeprations manager	Percent non-conformance	30,000-foot-level	Weekly	All	Mean	N/A	1.50%	Visual inspection	Value chain and monthly exec. Meeting	1	2
g	Internet domain name reapplication	Internet manager	Currently need to apply or not	50-foot-level signal within 90 days of due date, Jan 1 checkout	N/A examine yearly	N/A	N/A	N/A	Loss of service is less than 90 days	Manual assessment	Internet manager	Determine if it is time for reapplication.	Domain reapplication is initiated when signal is presented.
h	Profit margins	President	Corporate profit margins	Satellite-level	Monthly	One	Individual value	Normal prob. Plot of all data in stable region	Median and 80% freq. of occurrence	Financial system	Value chain and monthly exec. Meeting	1	3
i	Number of days to report financials	CFO	Days	30,000-foot-level	Monthly	One	Individual value	Normal prob. Plot of all data in stable region	10 days is upper spec. limit	Manual time stamp	Value chain and monthly exec. Meeting	1	2

1. Determine if process is predictable. If process is predictable, determine process capability/performance metric.
2. If process is predictable and the response is not satisfactory, pull for project creation or continue/expedite existing project's completion. Investigate special cause conditions and take necessary actions.
3. If processes are predictable and the response is not satisfactory relative to meeting business goals, reassess EIP work, project selection, and project execution. Investigate special cause conditions and take necessary actions.

- Ex. h: Profit margins
- Ex. i: Number of days to report financials
2. Assign ownership
   - Ex. a (lead time): Operations manager
   - Ex. b (part flatness): Process owner
   - Ex. c (telephone response time): Call center manager
   - Ex. d (process temperature): Operator
   - Ex. e (number of people in check-out line): Check-out supervisor
   - Ex. f (defective rate): Operations manager
   - Ex. g (domain reapplication): Internet manager
   - Ex. h (profit margins): President
   - Ex. i (days to report financials): Chief financial officer (CFO)
3. Describe input or output measurement
   - Ex. a (lead time): Hours from order initiation to fulfillment
   - Ex. b (part flatness): Inches in thousandths
   - Ex. c (telephone response time): Seconds
   - Ex. d (process temperature): Degrees centigrade
   - Ex. e (Number of people in check-out line): Number of people
   - Ex. f (defective rate): Percent non-conformance
   - Ex. g (domain reapplication): Currently need to apply or not
   - Ex. h (profit margins): Corporate profit margins
   - Ex. i (days to report financials): Days
4. Describe response tracking (i.e., with engineering process control, if applicable)
   - Ex. a (lead time): 30,000-foot-level (i.e., high-level output tracking)
   - Ex. b (part flatness): 30,000-foot-level (i.e., high-level output tracking)
   - Ex. c (telephone response time): 30,000-foot-level (i.e., high-level output tracking)
   - Ex. d (process temperature): 50-foot-level pre-control chart
   - Ex. e (number of people in check-out line): 50-foot-level pre-control chart
   - Ex. f (defective rate): 30,000-foot-level (i.e., high-level output tracking)
   - Ex. g (domain reapplication): 50-foot-level signal within 90 days of due date; on January 1, check to ensure signal is properly set for activation during the year
   - Ex. h (profit margins): Satellite-level (i.e., business-level output tracking)

- Ex. i (days to report financials): 30,000-foot-level (i.e., high-level output tracking)

5. Select subgrouping/sampling period, if appropriate
   - Ex. a (lead time): Weekly
   - Ex. b (part flatness): Daily
   - Ex. c (telephone response time): Weekly
   - Ex. d (process temperature): About 30 min, per pre-control chart rules
   - Ex. e (number of people in check-out line): About 5 min, per pre-control chart rules
   - Ex. f (defective rate): Weekly
   - Ex. g (domain reapplication): N/A, examine yearly
   - Ex. h (profit margins): Monthly
   - Ex. i (days to report financials): Monthly

6. Determine sample size
   - Ex. a (lead time): All
   - Ex. b (part flatness): Five
   - Ex. c (telephone response time): All
   - Ex. d (process temperature): One
   - Ex. e (number of people in check-out line): All
   - Ex. f (defective rate): All
   - Ex. g (domain reapplication): N/A
   - Ex. h (profit margins): One
   - Ex. i (days to report financials): One

7. Describing tracking process to assess whether predictable process or not
   - Ex. a (lead time): Mean and standard deviation
   - Ex. b (part flatness): Mean and log standard deviation
   - Ex. c (telephone response time): Mean and standard deviation
   - Ex. d (process temperature): Individual value
   - Ex. e (number of people in check-out line): Mean
   - Ex. f (defective rate): Mean
   - Ex. g (domain reapplication): N/A
   - Ex. h (profit margins): Individual value
   - Ex. i (days to report financials): Individual value

8. Determine prediction methodology, if applicable
   - Ex. a (lead time): Normal probability plot of all data in stable/predictable region
   - Ex. b (part flatness): Lognormal probability plot of all data in stable/predictable region
   - Ex. c (telephone response time): Normal probability plot of all data in stable/predictable region

- Ex. d (process temperature): N/A
- Ex. e (number of people in check-out line): N/A
- Ex. f (defective rate): Total non-conformances divided by units produced in stable/predictable region
- Ex. g (domain reapplication): N/A
- Ex. h (profit margins): Normal probability plot of all data in stable/predictable region
- Ex. i (days to report financials): Normal probability plot of all data in stable/predictable region

9. Established measurement criterion or objective
   - Ex. a (lead time): 80% frequency of occurrence
   - Ex. b (part flatness): ± 0.001 in.
   - Ex. c (telephone response time): 1 min or less
   - Ex. d (process temperature): 50 ± 2°C
   - Ex. e (number of people in check-out line): Between 2 and 4 people
   - Ex. f (defective rate): 1.5%
   - Ex. g (domain reapplication): Loss of service is less than 90 days
   - Ex. h (profit margins): 80% frequency of occurrence
   - Ex. i (days to report financials): 10 days is upper specification limit

10. Describe device or individual making measurement
    - Ex. a (lead time): Computer
    - Ex. b (part flatness): Dial indicator
    - Ex. c (telephone response time): Computer
    - Ex. d (process temperature): Thermocouple
    - Ex. e (number of people in check-out line): Visual computer sensor
    - Ex. f (defective rate): Visual inspection
    - Ex. g (domain reapplication): Manual assessment
    - Ex. h (profit margins): Financial system
    - Ex. i (days to report financials): Manual time stamp

11. Describe metric report-out destination
    - Ex. a (lead time): Value chain and monthly executive meeting
    - Ex. b (part flatness): Customer
    - Ex. c (telephone response time): Value chain and monthly executive meeting
    - Ex. d (process temperature): Operator
    - Ex. e (number of people in check-out line): Store check-out supervisor

- Ex. f (defective rate): Value chain and monthly executive meeting
- Ex. g (domain reapplication): Internet manager
- Ex. h (profit margins): Value chain and monthly executive meeting
- Ex. i (days to report financials): Value chain and monthly executive meeting

12. Assess measurement response
    - Ex. a (lead time): Determine if process is predictable. If process is predictable, determine process capability/performance metric.
    - Ex. b (part flatness): Determine if process is predictable. If process is predictable, determine process capability/performance metric.
    - Ex. c (telephone response time): Determine if process is predictable. If process is predictable, determine process capability/performance metric.
    - Ex. d (process temperature): Determine if an adjustment is needed, per pre-control chart rules.
    - Ex. e (number of people in check-out line): Determine if an adjustment is needed, per pre-control chart rules.
    - Ex. f (defective rate): Determine if process is predictable. If process is predictable, determine process capability/performance metric.
    - Ex. g (domain reapplication): Determine if it is time for reapplication.
    - Ex. h (profit margins): Determine if process is predictable. If process is predictable, determine process capability/performance metric.
    - Ex. i (days to report financials): Determine if process is predictable. If process is predictable, determine process capability/performance metric.

13. Create action reaction plan
    - Ex. a (lead time): If process is predictable and the response is not satisfactory, pull for project creation or continue/expedite existing project's completion. Investigate special cause conditions and take necessary actions.
    - Ex. b (part flatness): If process is predictable and the response is not satisfactory, pull for project creation or continue/expedite existing project's completion. Investigate special cause conditions and take necessary actions.

- Ex. c (telephone response time): If process is predictable and the response is not satisfactory, pull for project creation or continue/expedite existing project's completion. Investigate special-cause conditions and take necessary actions.
- Ex. d (process temperature): Adjust temperature per pre-control chart rules.
- Ex. e (number of people in check-out line): Add or reassign checkers per pre-control chart rules.
- Ex. f (defective rate): If process is predictable and the response is not satisfactory, pull for project creation or continue/expedite existing project's completion. Investigate special-cause conditions and take necessary actions.
- Ex. g (domain reapplication): Domain reapplication is initiated when signal is presented.
- Ex. h (profit margins): If processes are predictable and the response is not satisfactory relative to meeting business goals, reassess EIP work, project selection, and project execution. Investigate special-cause conditions and take necessary actions.
- Ex. i (days to report financials): If process is predictable and the response is not satisfactory, pull for project creation or continue/expedite existing project's completion. Investigate special-cause conditions and take necessary actions.

The success of E-DMAIC improve phase initiated projects is very dependent upon management's project reviews. These regular review meetings and their effectiveness are a part of the E-DMAIC control phase. Techniques to utilize during these presentations are described in Appendix C.

Regular reviews are essential to keep focus and direction toward the successful completion of individual projects and the collection of EIP projects that benefit the enterprise as a whole. A targeted report-out frequency is:

- Weekly: To champion from black belts/green belts
- Monthly: To business/function leadership from champions
- Quarterly: To executives from business/function leadership

Meetings with example agendas and topics are:

- Weekly 30-min champion-black belt meeting agenda: Activities, recent accomplishments, issues/needs, and next-week plan. The project master black belt can also attend this meeting, along with other separate black belt meetings to resolve technical or other issues.
- Monthly business/function leadership meeting agenda: Description of projects with anticipated financial gains, 30,000-foot-level scorecard/dashboard metrics report-out progression with goal, recent accomplishments, issues/needs, and next-month plans. All current projects need regular review for the purpose of maintaining schedules, results, and the resolution of problem/road blocks.
- Quarterly executive meeting agenda: Satellite-level metrics with improvement goals, value chain with key 30,000-foot-level scorecard/dashboard metrics, EIP, summary of projects, recent accomplishments, issues/needs, and next-month plan.

During weekly project reviews, management's use of the P-DMAIC check sheets provided in the appendix can expedite meetings and help build a consistent thought process between management and black belts/green belts. As a communication tool, this roadmap helps ensure that nothing gets overlooked. During the meeting, management needs to ask open-ended questions so that insight is gained to the methodologies, logic, and data used in the decision-making process.

In addition to process improvement and design project report-outs, BPIE activity should also be reported in status meetings.

Organizations need to have a system for project tracking. Initially, when there are not many projects, this system could be a simple Excel™ spreadsheet. In time, organizations need to migrate to a computer system that can roll up project status and report-outs across functions and business units. This system needs to be able to drill down to project specifics and offer a repository for leveraging project success to other business areas, in addition to providing lessons learned. This system can be part of a company's becoming a learning organization (Senge, 1990).

In this system, a decision support system (DSS) could be the database repository for the process and/or system solutions. When someone's problem is similar to a previously solved problem, he/she can gain access to a potential solution through a DSS keyword or problem description search entry. This system could also provide a financial project repository tracking system.

The EPM (see Figure 3.2) functional assessment of 30,000-foot-level scorecard/dashboard metrics can provide a system of control for the effectiveness of project selection and execution in the E-DMAIC improve phase. In addition, these metrics can provide insight to what should be done to the overall project implementation process.

In the final P-DMAIC roadmap step, a control plan documents how project gains are to be maintained. Section 39.5 describes a traditional AIAG control plan for this documentation; however, specifics for the entries will vary between companies. In IEE, resulting control plans should be part of the overall organization value chain as described earlier in this section. Similarly, an E-DMAIC control plan addresses enterprise controls.

When there is a pull for project creation IEE system, resulting project control metrics should be placed in the enterprise control plan. To illustrate this, let's consider that an improvement is to be made in order lead time. Upon project completion, management needs to require a scorecard format that includes a control chart with a process capability/performance metric statement (i.e., is the process predictable and what is predicted). This could be a very different form of reporting from current procedures.

3.14   E-DMAIC – Summary

In IEE an enterprise scorecard or dashboard system is created through the value chain and customer needs. Differences between the E-DMAIC scorecard/dashboard system and traditional scorecard systems include:

- The reporting of numbers in a table against goals, which do not have SMART characteristics, can lead to the wrong behavior (e.g., Enron effect).
- The reporting of numbers, which do not have the characteristics of a good metric (see Section 1.4), can lead to wasted effort, misdirected activities, and playing games with the numbers.
- Traditional scorecard systems do not highlight the need for improving the Xs and/or process to get improvements in the Y (i.e., $Y = f(X)$). For a metric to improve, typically a focused project effort is needed, which requires a commitment of people resource. This resource commitment is often lacking

when sole focus is given to meeting next period's numbers (e.g., arbitrarily set goals).

- Traditional scorecard system goals typically have not been determined by analyzing the enterprise as a whole, which can lead to sub-optimization and no true benefit for the enterprise as a whole.

The IEE measurement and improvement system can transition an organization from a firefighting mode to a system where organizational improvements impact the business as a whole.

Improved behaviors can result when owned metrics have a 30,000-foot-level reporting style during periodic (e.g., monthly) management status meetings. Cascading metric report-outs in this format from CEO/president/board room downward throughout the organization can lead to a reduction in firefighting and wasted efforts for the whole enterprise. During this status meeting, some metrics would be reported to demonstrate continued stability/predictability, while other metrics that were to be improved toward a SMART goal would lead to process improvement project status reporting. This form of metric reporting can lead to more constructive status meeting discussions and less need for micromanagement, which some managers have a tendency to do.

Spear and Bowen (1999) articulated four Lean DNA rules and their view of the Toyota reasoning process. Jackson (2006) added a fifth rule with some rewording of the original rules. To expand the DNA definition to an IEE system, I added four additional rules with some rewording of previous rules. The IEE DNA rules are:

Rule 1: *Standardize processes and work* (i.e., create efficient and effective processes that have reduced variability and improved quality).

Rule 2: *Zero ambiguity* (i.e., internal and external customer requirements are perfectly clear).

Rule 3: *Flow the process* (i.e., material and information flow directly with minimal waste and variation).

Rule 4: *Speak with data* (i.e., compile and present the most appropriate data so that the right question is answered, and both statistical and visualization tools are used effectively).

Rule 5: *Develop leaders who are teachers* (i.e., leaders need to truly understand and then coach employees in E-DMAIC and P-DMAIC execution).

Rule 6: *Align work to the value chain* (i.e., align and document processes in the value chain so that information is readily accessible to fulfill employee and supplier needs).

Rule 7: *Report metrics at the 30,000-foot-level* (i.e., avoid scorecard systems that track against goals or calendar point performance metric reporting, which often leads to wasted resources through firefighting. Metrics need to be created so that there are no playing games with the numbers).

Rule 8: *Build strategies after analyzing the value chain, its metrics, and goals* (i.e., avoid creating strategies in isolation and aligning work activities to these strategies. Execution possibilities for strategy statements such as those in Section 1.6 are very team dependent and can lead to detrimental activities for the enterprise as a whole).

Rule 9: *Let metric improvement needs pull for project creation* (i.e., a push for project creation system can lead to the suboptimization of processes that don't favorably impact the business as a whole).

From the E-DMAIC portion of this volume, the reader will see how his/her organization can benefit from KCA in an IEE system. The EPM function (see Figure 3.2) can become the repository for this long-lasting organizational governance system that contains meaningful enterprise scorecards/dashboard metrics and an improvement system that helps organizations get out of the firefighting mode. Additional articles/information about IEE and the creation of a level 5 system are at www.SmarterSolutions.com.

The next chapters of this volume provide the P-DMAIC details to execute an improvement project, which in IEE would initiate from the improve phase of the E-DMAIC roadmap.

PART II
Improvement Project Roadmap: Define Phase

The next parts of this volume follow the steps of the DMAIC process improvement project. This roadmap describes the thought process and application of both Six Sigma and Lean tools to improve a 30,000-foot-level metric scorecard/dashboard that is important to the business.

4

P-DMAIC – Define Phase

4.1   P-DMAIC Roadmap Component

Volume 2 described the selection of projects in the E-DMAIC improve phase. This chapter is the first in a series that describes the improvement project or P-DMAIC steps.

The graphic in this section highlights the P-DMAIC roadmap steps (see Appendix Section D.1) that are described in this chapter. Appendix E contains the tollgate check sheets for this and other phases. This chapter provides guidelines for effectively initiating a project as part of the define phase.

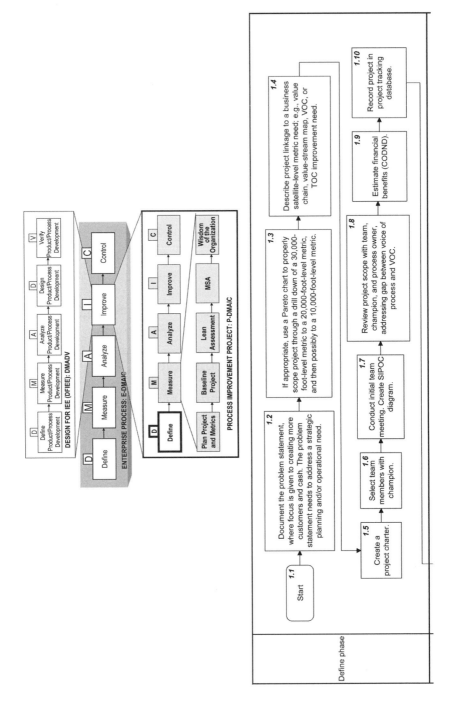

Note
Many of the following chapters will have a lead-in section like the one shown in this section. The purpose of this graphic is to aid the reader in determining how the upcoming chapter's content fits into the improvement project execution portion of the overall IEE roadmap (see Figure 2.1).
Appendix Section D.1 shows the overall IEE project execution roadmap. The reader should note that the flowchart shown in this section is the same as the "Define phase" swim lane of the project execution roadmap shown in Section D.1.
Some future chapters that provide background information for an upcoming roadmap concept but do not tie directly to the project execution roadmap will not have this type of graphic at the chapter's beginning.

4.2 Processes and Metrics

We encounter devices that have an input and an output. For example, the simple movement of a light switch causes a light to turn on. An input to this process is the movement of the switch. Within the switch, a process is executed whereby internal electrical connections are made, and the output is a light turning on. This is just one example of an input-process-out (IPO), which is illustrated in Figure 4.1.

As users of a light switch, toaster, or a radio, we are not typically interested in the mechanical details of how the process is executed. We typically view these processes like a black box. However, there are other processes with which we are more involved. For example, the process we use when preparing for and traveling to work/school. For this process, there can be multiple outputs such as arrival time at work/school, whether we experienced an

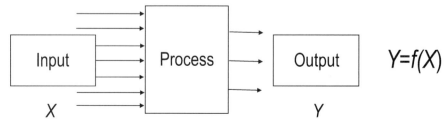

Figure 4.1: Input-process-output.

automobile accident or other problems, and perhaps whether your children/spouse also arrived at school on time. The important outputs to processes can be called as key process output variables (KPOVs), critical to quality (CTQ) characteristics, or *Y*s.

There is always a process, even though it cannot be seen or is not standardized. Manufacturing processes are easy to see. We can simply follow the product. Processes are much more difficult to see in other business areas such as legal and finance. There are also processes that are beyond the scope of producing, distributing, or selling a product or service. These managerial processes include budgeting, business planning, rewards/recognition, and process reporting. Middle management typically owns the responsibilities for the design and management of these processes. These processes should help orchestrate the business toward efficiency and effectiveness, where everyone is going in the same direction toward meeting business objectives. When these processes are poor, the organization can become dysfunctional, which can result in much wasted effort and even business failure. Since the means to making improvement is through the process, understanding the process is crucial for making improvements.

For both a black box process and other processes, we can track output over time to examine the performance of the system. Inputs to processes can take the form of *inherent process inputs* (e.g., raw material), *controlled variables* (e.g., process temperature), and *uncontrolled noise variables* (e.g., raw material lots). For our go-to-work/school process, consider that we daily quantified the difference between our arrival time and our planned arrival time and then tracked this metric over time. For this measure, we might see much variability in the output of our process. We might then wish to examine why there is so much variability by consciously trying to identify the inputs to the process that can affect the process output. For reducing the variability of commuting time, we might list inputs to our process as departure time from home, time we got out of bed, traffic congestion during the commute, and whether someone had an accident along our route to work or school.

> ...we might see much variability in the output of our process. We might then wish to examine why there is so much variability by consciously trying to identify the inputs to the process that can affect the process output.

Inputs to processes can take the form of inherent process inputs (e.g., raw material), controlled variables' (e.g., process temperature), and uncontrollable noise variables (e.g., raw material lots). For our go-to-work/school process a controllable input might be setting the alarm clock, while an uncontrollable input is whether someone had an accident on our route that affected travel time. By examining our arrival times as a function of the time departing home, we might find that if we left the house 5 minutes earlier we could reduce our commute time by 25 minutes. For this situation, departure time is a key process input variable (KPIV) that is an important X, which affects our arrival time. When this KPIV is controlled in our go-to-work/school process, we can reduce the amount of variability in our arrival time at work or school (KPOV).

Another tactic to reduce the variability of our arrival time is to change our process so that we can reduce the commute time or make our process robust to uncontrollable/noise input variables. For example, we might change our travel route to work/school so that our travel time is reduced during the high-traffic hours of the day. This change could also reduce the likelihood of lengthy delays from accidents, that is, we made our process robust to the occurrence of accidents, which was a noise input variable.

Similarly, in business and other organizations we have processes or systems. For the go-to-work/school process, the identification of inputs and of potential process changes that positively impact our process output is not too difficult. Easy fixes can also occur within business processes when we view our process systematically through an IEE strategy. However, the identification and improvement systems for some business processes can be more involved. For these more complex situations, I view this search for KPIVs and process improvement strategies as a murder mystery where we use a structured approach for the uncovering of clues that lead us to how we can improve our process outputs.

Let's now consider Table 4.1 as example, which illustrates KPOVs (Ys) that a company could experience along with one, of perhaps many, KPIV (Xs) for each of these processes.

These Ys are at various levels within an organization's overall system of doing business. One should note that the input to one process can be the output from another. For example, a described input for expense is work in progress (WIP), which is a high-level output from other processes.

Table 4.1: KPOVs (*Y*s) with a KPIV (*X*) for Each

	*Y*s or KPOVs	*X*s or KPIVs
1	Profits	Identification and exploitation of enterprise constraint
2	Customer satisfaction	Out of stock items
3	Enterprise goal	Development of improvement strategies from enterprise analysis
4	Expense	Amount of WIP
5	Production cycle time	Amount of internal rework
6	Defect rate	Invoices returned because they were sent to the wrong department
7	Critical dimension on a part	Process temperature

For processes, there are both customers and suppliers. This relationship to a process is often expressed using a supplier–input–process–output–customer (SIPOC) diagram, as illustrated in the next section.

In IEE, a cascading measurement system can be created, which aligns metrics throughout the organization to the overall needs of the organization. The tracking of these measurements over time can then pull for P-DMAIC or DFIEE project creation, which addresses common-cause variability improvement needs for the process output. Through this pragmatic approach, where no games are played with the numbers, organizations have a systematic way to improve both customer satisfaction and their bottom line. This system is much more than a quality initiative; it is a business way of life.

This system utilizes a 30,000-foot-level scorecard/dashboard metric terminology to describe a high-level view for KPOV, CTQ, or *Y* variable responses. This high-level, "in-flight airplane view" for operational and project metrics has infrequent subgrouping/sampling so that short-term variations, which might be caused by KPIVs, will result in charts that view these perturbations as common-cause issues. A 30,000-foot-level individuals control chart (see Chapters 12 and 13) can reduce the amount of organizational firefighting when used to report operational metrics.

In this system, there can be an alignment and management of metrics throughout the organization so that there is an orchestration of the right activity being done at the correct time. Meaningful measurements are statistically tracked over time at various functional levels of the business. This leads to an enterprise cascading measurement methodology where meaningful measurements are statistically tracked over time at various functional levels of the business. In this system, there is an alignment of important metrics throughout the organization. This alignment extends from the satellite-level business metrics to high-level KPOV operational metrics, which can be at the 30,000-foot-level, 20,000-foot-level, or 10,000-foot-level (infrequent subgrouping/sampling), to KPIVs at the 50-foot-level (frequent subgrouping/sampling). This metric system helps organizations run the business so that there is less firefighting and a pull for project creation and execution system whenever operational metric improvements are needed.

4.3   Supplier–Input–Process–Output–Customer

Most performed work involves a process. The output of a process is the product or service produced. As described earlier, important process variables that describe the output lead time or defective rates level are called key process output variables or KPOVs (Ys). Key process input variables or KPIVs (Xs) are the inputs that affect the process KPOVs. IEE provides the roadmap for identifying and then controlling KPIVs that affect the KPOVs, or change the process so that the KPOVs improve.

Project scope should be aligned with improvement needs of its high-level value chain. A SIPOC (suppliers-inputs-process-outputs-customers) diagram adds supplier and customer to the IPO as described earlier. SIPOC can be useful as a communication tool, which helps team members view the project the same way and helps management know where the team is focusing its efforts.

The purpose of the SIPOC is to show all the components of the work process flow and to show how these components are related to one another. The SIPOC is a high-level flow diagram used to delineate the following:

- Suppliers (providers of resources required)
- Inputs (resources required by the process)
- Activities or process steps
- Outputs (deliverables from the process, including known defects)
- Customer (anyone who receives an output)

For each SIPOC category, the team creates a list. For example, the input portion of SIPOC would have a list of inputs to the process, while the process steps portion of SIPOC should be high level, containing only 4–7 high-level steps (see flowcharting in Section 16.2). In a SIPOC:

- Inputs don't need to line up in rows
- Inputs and outputs should be nouns

- Process steps should be verbs
- The scope of the project is defined as improving the process step activities and improving the quality of the inputs
- Outputs from intermediate steps that are inputs for other intermediate steps are not listed as outputs at the SIPOC level of detail

An example of SIPOC for a project that is to improve service and reduce inventory is illustrated in Figure 4.2.

A SIPOC is important to the project, in that it is the first concrete description of the project scope. A project scope will include only improvements in the *"P"* process columns steps and the quality of the *"I"* input column inputs. If there are other areas being considered in the project, the SIPOC is not properly defined, and should be adjusted.

The SIPOC should be revisited at each phase of the project. Doing so ensures that the project remains focused on the scope as originally defined or that scope changes are deliberate. The SIPOC also reveals hidden partners in the process as KPIVs, KPOVs, and their sources are identified. Finally, the SIPOC is a useful check for the adequacy and completeness of the control plan.

4.4   Project Valuation, Cost of Poor Quality, and Cost of Doing Nothing Differently

Volume 2 of this series discussed in the E-DMAIC roadmap analyze phase some basic enterprise process financial analysis concepts. This section will focus on assessing the business value of a project.

As discussed earlier, one way in which a Six Sigma deployment differs from many prior business improvement efforts is its focus on rigorous calculation and on tracking of financial benefits

Suppliers	Inputs	Process	Outputs	Customers
AOM system	Flat data files	Receive flat files from system.	Reports	PPMs
QAD system	Orders/invoices	Execute programs to create reports.	Report files	Site Managers
	Inventory	Transmit reports to their destinations.	Data files	Executives
		Process report data to create finshed service reports.		
		Publish the final reports.		

Figure 4.2: SIPOC diagram illustration.

delivered by projects. To measure the benefits of IEE projects consistently, a uniform set of guidelines must be developed by each business, in alignment with internal finance policies. Procedures need to be established so that multiple projects do not claim the same savings. System credibility is lost when every project is reporting millions of dollars in savings, when as a company we know that it is not possible to have all of these savings.

Often, existing financial systems are not structured to quantify project value easily for its validation. It is important to establish a baseline measurement of the process before starting to improve the process and for the IEE measurement and improvement function to work closely with finance to determine the validation strategy.

Organizations have financial analysis standards. The black belt may need to ask their financial organization for:

- Standard employee labor rates; e.g., hourly, salary, and management categories
- Actual and as-sold value of a transaction or item
- Typical floor space charges; e.g., dollars per square-foot
- Cost of money percentage used to value working capital changes
- Organizational overhead rate; i.e., the added overhead organizational burden as a percentage of direct labor costs
- Additional possible information
  - Time based pricing factors; e.g., is there financial benefits for faster process execution
  - Financial incentives or penalties related to project area performance

Traditional cost of poor quality (COPQ) calculations look at costs across the entire company using the categories of prevention, appraisal, internal failure, and external failure, as described in Table 4.2. Organizations often do not disagree with these categories, but they typically do not expend the effort to determine this costing for their particular situations.

Organizations need to determine how they are going to cost out projects. The procedure that they use can affect how projects are selected and executed. I think that other categories need to be considered when making these assessments.

I prefer the term Cost of Doing Nothing Differently (CODND) to the COPQ term. The reason I have included the term differently is that organizations often are doing something under the banner of process improvements. These activities could include Lean

Table 4.2: Traditional Quality Cost Categories and Examples

PREVENTION
Training
Capability Studies
Vendor Surveys
Quality Design
APPRAISAL
Inspection and Test
Test Equipment and Maintenance
Inspection and Test Reporting
Other Expense Reviews
INTERNAL FAILURE
Scrap and Rework
Design Changes
Retyping Letters
Late Time Cards
Excess Inventory Cost
EXTERNAL FAILURE
Warranty Costs
Customer Complaint Visits
Field Service Training Costs
Returns and Recalls
Liability Suits

manufacturing, TQM, ISO9000, and so on. The term "Cost of Doing Nothing" is not really broad enough since the organizations are doing something. Because of this, I added the word differently to form the acronym CODND.

A mission of Six Sigma has been the reduction of cost of poor quality (COPQ). In Six Sigma, the interpretation for COPQ has a less rigid interpretation than traditional quality cost categories and perhaps a broader scope; however, its calculation centers around costs associated with defects or perhaps targets that have been established since no specification exist.

I prefer to base project financial benefits from the CODND, which has broader costing implications than COPQ. In a traditional Six Sigma implementation, a defect needs to be defined, which impacts COPQ calculations. In transactional and other environments when there are no natural specifications, this can be difficult to accomplish.

Defect definition is not a requirement within an IEE implementation or a CODND calculation. Not requiring a defect definition for financial calculations has advantages since the nonconformance criteria placed on many transactional processes and metrics such as inventory and cycle times are often arbitrary in that criteria can differ between people who are creating the metric.

In an IEE implementation, if a defect definition is clear and more appropriate than CODND then it could equal a COPQ calculation. However, when there is no obvious defect definition, we can determine a CODND from which the project would give focus to reduce (e.g., reducing WIP and its current CODND carrying cost). In this series of volumes, I will use the nomenclature CODND.

Quality cost issues can dramatically affect a business, but very important issues are often hidden from view. Organizations can be missing the largest issues when they focus only on the tip of the iceberg, as shown in Figure 4.3. It is important for organizations to direct their efforts so that these hidden issues, which are often more important than the readily visible issues, are uncovered. IEE techniques can help flatten many of the issues that affect overall cost. However, management needs to ask the right questions so that these issues are effectively addressed. Success is a function of a need, vision, and plan.

Project benefits are usually classified as hard or soft savings. Hard savings are either above or below the operating profit line. Above the operating profit line examples are cost reduction and revenue enhancement. Below the operating profit line examples are working capital reductions and cost avoidance. The quantification of these benefits is typically expressed as CODND. Soft savings, as described below, have indirect benefits.

Categories of hard savings are:

- Revenue increase (collections, sales, capacity, lead time)
- Labor reduction (salary, wages, overtime, benefits)
- Material savings
- Reduction or elimination of contracts with outside vendors

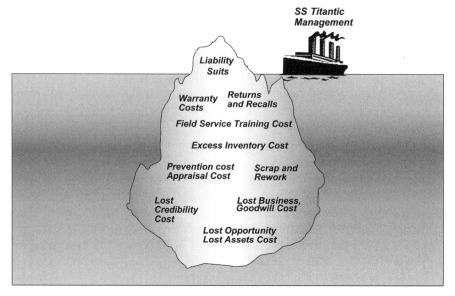

Figure 4.3: Cost of poor quality or Cost of doing nothing differently.

- Reduction in warranty claims (errors, write-offs, services, leases)
- Other fixed savings (travel, communications, pagers, cell phones, shipping, utilities).

Working capital benefit improvements produce real money, but below the operating profit line. Generally, project benefits are calculated using a cost of money approach that utilizes a cost of debt calculation, with the concept being that improvement in these areas equates to financing that is avoided. The financial analysis can tell the black belt the appropriate cost of capital for their company.

Inventory reduction addresses the following:

- Finished goods: Completed product or service that is available for purchase.
- WIP: Products which are not yet available to the customer for purchase.
- Parts: Items which are available to be used in the production of a product or service.
- Maintenance and repair – equipment spares: Items that are available to be used in repair or maintenance.

- Accounts receivable reduction.
- Money due to the firm from its customers.

Soft benefits are less tangible. It is often difficult to assign specific monetary value to them. Examples of soft benefits are:

- Customer satisfaction
- Employee morale
- Reputation of the company or brand
- Regulatory compliance
- Legal exposure
- Safety

Some companies attempt to evaluate and track soft benefits because they feel that soft benefits are as important as the hard benefits.

An organization could consider a further breakdown of hard and soft project benefits into the following categories that were used at IOMEGA (APQC, 2001):

Bottom-line hard dollar
- Decreases existing business costs.
- Example: defects, warranty, maintenance, labor, freight.
- Takes cost off the books or adds revenue to the books.

Cost avoidance
- Avoids incremental costs that have not been incurred, but would have occurred if project were not performed.
- Example: Enhanced material or changes that would affect warranty work.

Lost profit avoidance
- Avoids lost sales that have not been incurred, but would have occurred if project had not occurred.
- Example: A project reduces frequency of line shutdowns.

Productivity
- Increases in productivity which improves utilization of existing resources.
- Example: Redeployment of labor or assets to better use.

Profit enhancement
- Potential sales increase, which would increase gross profit.
- Example: Change that was justifiable through a survey, pilots, or assumptions.

Intangible
- Improvements to operations of business which can be necessary to control, protect, and/or enhance company assets but are not quantifiable.
- Example: Administrative control process that could result in high legal liability expense if not addressed.

Let's use a days sales outstanding (DSO) IEE project example to illustrate two options for conducting a project benefit analysis. DSO is typically the average number of days it takes to collect revenue after a sale has been made. For purposes of this study we defined DSO as the number of days before or after the due date that a payment is to be received. A +1 would indicate that an invoice receipt was one day after the due date, while a –1 would indicate that receipt was one day before the due date.

For an individual invoice, its DSO would be from the time the invoice was created until payment was received. CODND considerations could include the monetary implications of not getting paid immediately; for example, costs associated with interest charges on the money due and additional paperwork charges. COPQ calculations typically involve the monetary implications beyond a criterion; for example, costs associated with interest charges on the money due after the due date for the invoice and additional paperwork/activity charges beyond the due date.

One might take the position that incurred costs should not be considered until the due date of an invoice since this is the cost of doing business. This could be done. However, consider that some computer companies actually get paid before products are built for their internet on-line purchases and that their suppliers are paid much later for the parts that are part of the product assembly process. If we look at the total CODND opportunity costs, this could lead to out-of-the-box thinking. For example, we might be able to change our sales and production process so that we too could receive payment at the time of an order.

Finally, it needs to be highlighted that if all the product produced from a process can be sold and if the project improved the overall capacity of the process (i.e., improved the capacity of the process bottleneck), the project financial credit should be total additional revenue for the additional product sold less cost of goods sold. That is, all current fixed costs are already covered and should not be spread across the new production capacity resulting from the project.

4.5 Define Phase Objectives

The objective of the project define phase is to describe the CTQ/ business issue, the customer, and the involved core business process. During the define phase, a problem statement is formulated. Customer requirements are gathered, and a project charter is created, where the project scope is determined by the team with the support of management. Other activities during this phase include: definition of the 30,000-foot-level metric (Six Sigma deployments could refer to this as a CTQ); identification of both internal and external customers; identification and definition of what is to be improved (e.g., defect or lead time); estimation of CODND; development of high-level process map; initiation of a SIPOC.

The success of a project depends also on communication. The project charter and periodic report-outs provide an effective means for communication so that there is no misunderstanding of the objectives and status of a project.

The following list describes the focus areas for the define phase of an IEE project:

- Projects should be aligned with the improvement needs of its high-level value chain and business goals. Constraints and assumptions should be included.
- A two-to-three sentence problem statement needs to focus on the symptoms and not the possible solution. Customer and business impact information should be included along with current DPMO or other baseline information, data sources for problem analysis, and a CODND estimate.

  Example: Companies are dissatisfied with the customer service call wait time in our XYZ office. Our service records show an estimated median wait time of 80 seconds with 80% of wait times between 25 and 237 seconds. *Note*: This example illustrates how a 30,000-foot-level operational metric within an IEE enterprise can pull project creation.

- Stakeholders (finance, managers, people who are working in the process, upstream/downstream departments, suppliers, and customers) need to agree to the usefulness of the project and its problem statement.

- The financial liaison person should work closely with the project leader and champion to create a cost benefit analysis for the project. This could include expense reduction, revenue enhancements, loss avoidance, reduced costs, or other CODND benefits.
- The project scope needs to be sized correctly and documented in a project charter format. All involved need to agree to the objectives, scope, boundaries, resources, project transition, and closure of the project charter. The details on this charter should be updated as the project proceeds through the overall IEE execution roadmap.
- Projects should be large enough to justify the investment of resources but small enough to ensure problem understanding and development of sustainable solutions. The scope should accurately define the bounds of the project so that project creep, a major cause for missed deadlines, is avoided.

   Example: Reduce the hold time of calls at the XYZ office with the intention of leveraging success to other call centers.
- Targeted improvement goals should be measurable. These goals should be tied to CODND benefits when appropriate.

   Example: Reduce the median call wait time to 40 seconds or less, yielding a $200,000 per year benefit at the XYZ office.
- Measurements should be described. If defects are the 30,000-foot-level metric, what constitutes a defect and how it will be tracked should be described. If lead time is the metric, the plans for lead time quantification and tracking should be described. *Note*: Some organizations may choose to report a sigma quality level metric; however, this is not recommended within an IEE implementation.
- The categories of a SIPOC should have been addressed, where the process portion of SIPOC is at high level, containing only 4–7 high-level steps. How the SIPOC aligns with the high-level supply chain map and its needs should be demonstrated along with the gap between voice of the process (VOP) and voice of the customer (VOC).
- Team members should be selected by the champion and project leader (e.g., black belt), so that they provide different insights and skills (e.g., self-facilitation, technical/subject-matter expertise) needed for the successful completion of the project in a timely fashion. Names, roles, and amount

of time for project dedication should be addressed for each team member.

- The champion needs to work with the project leader so that the project status is sufficiently documented within a corporate database that can be conveniently accessed by others.

4.6 Primary Project Metric

Each process improvement project has a problem statement. This statement needs to be written so that the business is compelled to support the problem resolution. An important aspect of the problem statement is project metric selection.

Since many organizational metrics are interdependent, it is not uncommon for a problem statement to identify more than one 30,000-foot-level metric as being impacted by the issue. Multiple metrics typically address differing problem aspects in cost, quality, and time. Even though this is okay, it does not mean that the project statement should target all listed 30,000-foot-level metrics.

Projects should be chartered with a single primary metric and have a goal to improve this measurement. This practice ensures that the upcoming numerical analyses and decision-making steps will be relatively straightforward. Multiple metrics can make these steps confusing.

This strategy is consistent with the principles of Dr. Deming, who stated that cost savings will follow fixing the quality. A generalization of this position is that if you fix any aspect of a process, improvements in other areas will follow. For example, a reduction in lead time leads to a reduction in overall costs and possible improved quality.

To illustrate the creation of project metrics that have interdependencies, consider the following. The performance of a process is a function of three aspects: cost, quality, and time. Fix one of the three performance aspects and you should see improvements in the other two. In projects, we can track these other two measurement aspects as secondary project metrics. Secondary project metrics are chosen to ensure that a black belt does not improve a primary metric to the detriment of secondary metrics.

One final point is that project primary and/or project metrics can be a metric such as defects per million opportunities (DPMO) or rolled throughput yield (RTY). These hidden factory or in-process metrics are described in Chapter 6.

4.7   Problem Statement

Each project has stakeholders. A project could have stakeholders from finance, managers, and people who are working in the process, upstream/downstream departments, suppliers, and customers.

Upon completing the decision that a project will be undertaken, it is critical that the stakeholders agree to a project problem statement. The documentation of this agreement is part of the project define phase. In addition to containing a baseline statement with improvement goals, the problem statement should be compelling reason for the organization to assign time and resources to correct the problem.

A problem statement should reflect the current state of the problem. The problem statement needs to provide a complete, but concise, description of the problem relative to how often, when, and process location. The problem statement needs to include the data's source. A future state or solution should not be proposed. Impact estimate should address cost, customer satisfaction, and employee satisfaction. The problem statement is dynamic and can change over time.

Key parts of a problem statement are:

1. Current performance as a function of the 30,000-foot-level metric.
2. Expected performance as a function of the 30,000-foot-level metric.
3. Impact of the existing problem to the organization.
   (a) As stated in the 30,000-foot-level metric.
   (b) In dollars or other business metric.
4. Time period that the baseline problem was determined.
5. Objective of the project
   (a) Usually a percentage gap between the current and expected performance; i.e., part 1 and 2 noted above.
   (b) An organizational benefit quantification in dollars or another metric, which is an improvement project staffing resource justification.
   (c) Target completion date.

The following problem statement template and objective statement templates are not intended to be a recipe. The purpose of these templates is to aid in problem and objective statements' formulation.

Problem statement template:

In (*time period*) the (*process name*) produced (*performance level*), which was (___) percent of the expected performance of (*target performance*), resulting in a (*value of the problem in dollars, man-hours, or other unit*) impact to the (*business metric*).

Objective statement template:

Improve (*process name*) performance gap of (*current – expected above*) by (___) percent to (*project goal*) by (*planned completion date*) resulting in a benefit of (*same units as problem statement*).

A problem statement:

- Is clearly aligned with the goals and strategic objectives of the business.
- Focuses on a core issue; for example, TOC bottleneck system operation that can lead to more customers and cash.
- Addresses a chronic issue which is not well understood and has caused past difficulties.
- Is large enough to justify the investment of project resources.
- Is small enough to be completed in 6 months or less.
- Can be summarized in several short sentences that clearly communicate the problem and its estimated impact on the customer or the business.
- Is a mechanism that creates a laser sharp focus for the team effort and helps avoid going into tangential issues.
- Is a document acceptable to the champion, core team members, process owner(s), sponsors, and other concerned executives.
- Is a living statement and captures the best understanding of the issue at the time.

A problem statement is not:

- An easily developed or quick statement that was developed by someone without team discussion.
- A plan to implement a predetermined solution (i.e., a "just do it" project).
- A way to get the organization to address a pet peeve.
- A list of potential root causes of the problem or a summary of potential solution(s).
- A place to capture the background and/or past, recent, or future events about the issue.
- Set in concrete.

Problem statement creation steps are as follows:

- Black belt/green belt creates a draft based on the best understanding of the project and conducts initial review with the champion and the process owner.
- Black belt/green belt shares the revised draft with the core team and invites full discussion on it. They incorporate their ideas and changes.
- Black belt/green belt again reviews the statement with the champion and process owner, not for semantics but for general concept.
- As better understanding is developed or the business needs change, black belt/green belt reflects the changes and starts the process again (i.e., there is flexibility).

Example of problem statement:

- On-time deliveries of product ABC ordered from our website are averaging 70%, as measured from shipping reports, where on-time shipment is defined as arriving on the date requested by the customer.
  - This resulted in increased customer complaints and shipping costs, along with lost sales.
  - Shipping penalties totaled $120,000 in the last 6 months; lost sales have not yet been quantified but are thought to exceed $1 million.

Pareto charts (See Chapter 8) can help prioritize drill-down opportunities, which often occur with project scoping. For example, a Pareto chart of identified failure categories in a 30,000-foot-level scorecard/dashboard value chain metric could lead to focusing on reduction of the largest failure type that would be tracked at a 20,000-foot-level for the project (see Example 13.5).

Theory of constraints (TOC) techniques in E-DMAIC analyze phase could also help identify constraint improvement opportunities, which can dramatically affect the overall system output.

As described earlier, IEE emphasizes the pull for project creation that address true business needs at the entire system level. A visual demonstration of a project's alignment to these needs is achieved through the identification of the impacted metric in the value chain along with the identification of the project in the EIP, which describes the organization's goals and strategy alignment.

4.8 Secondary Project Metrics

To reiterate, project focus should be given to improve one 30,000-foot-level metric (i.e., the primary KPOV metric). Secondary metrics have been called an insurance policy that protects the company from the black belt; i.e., improving a project's 30,000-foot-level metric, while degrading another metric. In the previous described call center hold-time example a secondary metric might be drop rate. This secondary metric provides company protection from a proposed solution that simply instructs the operator to quickly answer the call asking the caller if they could please hold. Another example is that a project improved on-time delivery but sacrificed overall product or service quality.

The reason for secondary-metric protection is that often seemingly positive process improvements can result in a net organizational loss, caused by negative change effects in areas not targeted by the improvement project. The goal for all secondary metrics is to ensure that their performance does not degrade; however, in many, if not most, cases these performance metrics will also demonstrate improvements at project completion.

A simplistic view is that every improvement project targets one of three performance aspects; i.e., costs, quality, or time. This implies that the primary focus of a project is to improve quality, reduce cost, or shorten lead times. One of these three is to be molded into the problem statement. The other two performance metrics can become secondary metrics. For example, if a project focus is to reduce the time to process a customer order, one appropriate secondary metric would be a quality aspect such as delivery-error or incomplete-delivery rate. Another appropriate secondary metric would be costs such as staffing costs or customer credits. These metrics are selected to ensure that a demonstrated reduction in customer order processing time has not been achieved at the expense of an increase in errors from cutting corners to go faster or an increased business cost by adding people to solve the process problem. A secondary project charter metric inclusion demonstrates to the business leadership that the improvement leader is addressing the project from a big-picture point of view.

4.9 Project Charter

The project charter is a contract with the team and the business where the team takes ownership. An example of IEE DMAIC

IEE Project Charter	
Project Title and Type (e.g. Black or Green Belt)	
Project Description	
Start Date	
Completion Date	
Primary KPOV Metric	
Project Goal (in terms of the KPOV & $)	
Secondary Metrics	
Non-quantified Benefits	**Customer**	
	Financial	
	Internal Productivity	
Phase Milestones (Start and stop dates)	**Define**	
	Plan Projects & Metrics	
	Baseline Project	
	Consider Lean Tools	
	MSA	
	Wisdom of the Org.	
	Analyze Phase	
	Improve Phase	
	Control	
Team Support	
Team Members	

Figure 4.4: IEE project charter.

project charter format is shown in Figure 4.4. All involved must agree to the objectives, scope, boundaries, resources, project transition, and closure. The details on this charter should be updated as the project proceeds within the overall project execution roadmap. The champion needs to work with the black belt so that the project status can be sufficiently documented within a corporate database that can be conveniently accessed by others.

At the beginning stages of an IEE project, the champion needs to work with the black belt and process owner so that the right people are on the team. Team selection should result in team members being able to provide different insights and skills (e.g., self-facilitation, technical/subject-matter expertise) needed to the completion of the project in a timely fashion.

In the project charter there is a section for non-quantified benefits. This section lists potential project organizational benefits less tangible than the primary and secondary metrics. For example, this section can include anticipated soft savings project benefits such as morale or lead time improvements. These statements will not impact any initial ROI estimate; however, these statements can provide compelling project execution support.

In the project execution roadmap, a SIPOC provides both project scope boundaries and direction for making process improvements.

4.10   Applying IEE

The financial quantification of projects is very important within the IEE infrastructure of an organization. However, organizations should not overlook the value from soft savings and improved customer satisfaction. Also, organizations should consider TOC methodologies within the overall financial measurement strategy of an organization.

The financial liaison person should work closely with the project leader and champion to create a cost benefit analysis for the project. This could include expense reduction, revenue enhancements, loss avoidance, reduced costs, or other CODND benefits.

To reiterate:

- Projects should be large enough to justify the investment of resources, but small enough to ensure problem understanding and development of sustainable solutions. The

scope should accurately define the bounds of the project so that project creep, a major cause for missed deadlines, is avoided.
- *Example*: Reduce the hold time of calls at the XYZ office with the intention of leveraging success to other call centers.
- Targeted improvement goals should be measurable. These goals should be tied to CODND benefits when appropriate.
- *Example*: Reduce the median call wait time to 40 seconds or less, yielding a $200,000 per year benefit at the XYZ office.
- Measurements should be described. If defects are the 30,000-foot-level metric, what constitutes a defect and how it will be tracked should be described. If lead time is the metric, the plans for lead time quantification and tracking should be described. *Note*: Some organizations may choose to report a sigma quality level metric; however, this is not recommended in an IEE implementation.

Presentation effectiveness is essential to convey project status, analyses, and result to others. Appendix C highlights four presentation focus areas: be in earnest, employ vocal variety, make it persuasive, and speak with knowledge.

4.11   Exercises

1. Describe the differences and similarities between your company's project selection process and the EIP (see Figure 3.7) process. State the benefits and detriments of each system. If desired, you may change the wording in the first sentence from "your company's project" to "a company's project."
2. After reading the following problem statement, answer the questions and create a new problem statement.
   The amount of money in accounts receivable is too high and customers pay too slowly. A new computer system which tracks payments will increase our ability to track payment performance by customer and cut working capital by 50%, resulting in $2 MM in savings for the business.

- Describe the KPOV for this process.
- Describe the customer requirements and business goals.
- Note whether potential causes are included.
- Note whether the business already has a solution.
- Note whether background is included.
- Describe the real pain.
- Note whether the opportunity is quantified, including any investment cost.

3. Demonstrate a possible alignment of the project described in Exercise 2 to the value chain and EIP (see Figure 3.7).
4. Create a project charter for the problem statement created in Exercise 2
5. Create the SIPOC for the project described in Exercise 2.
6. Brainstorm potential CODND categories for the project described in Exercise 2. Estimate the percentage of the revenue lost from problem categories identified within your (company's) project.
7. Develop a list of next steps project action items.
8. Repeat Exercises 1–7 for a project in your organization.

5

P-DMAIC – Team Effectiveness

5.1 P-DMAIC Roadmap Component

The previous chapter described project initiation. A major factor for project success is how well teams work together. This chapter describes some team-development concepts. The graphic in this section highlights the P-DMAIC roadmap steps (see Appendix Section D.1) that are described in this chapter. Appendix E contains the tollgate check sheets for this and other phases. The next chapter covers project planning and in-process metrics in our progression through the P-DMAIC roadmap.

During a project's execution, teams are created in the define phase. Teams are also used for IEE infrastructure building and management. The success of these tasks depends upon transforming a group of diverse individuals into a team that is productive and highly functional. This chapter describes the characteristics of teams and what could be done to improve their effectiveness.

The range of commitment levels that stakeholders can have during project definition is: enthusiastic, will lend support, compliant, hesitant, indifferent, uncooperative, opposed, or hostile. An expectation for enthusiastic support by all team members for all projects is not realistic. However, team leaders can do a

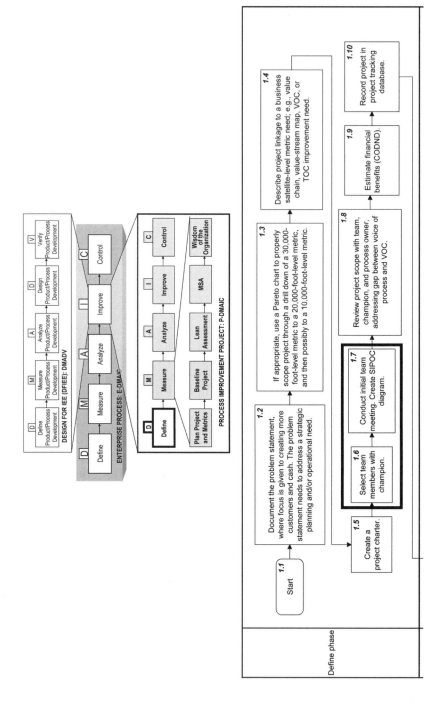

stakeholder analysis, quantify where each member is in the described scale above, keeping in mind the importance of moving team members toward the enthusiastic level.

The next section describes a commonly used and easy-to-follow model that can improve team effectiveness.

5.2 Orming Model

It is commonly agreed that teams go through stages to become a highly effective team. In addition, it is generally agreed that teams can improve the quality of their interactions when each member of the team is aware of these stages. Tuckman (1965) described four stages of team development as f*orming,* st*orming,* n*orming,* and perf*orming.* These team stages are often collectively referenced as the orming model. Successful teams are those who transition back and forth between these stages when circumstances change. Adjourning and recognition can be considered as the final stages of the team stages.

In the forming stage, the team leader needs to provide structure for the team, clarifying expectations about the initiation of team processes. The work that needs to be accomplished is: team member introduction, team resource assessment, and objective definition. Issues that need to be overcome are the team leader's taking on most of the work, team members not organized around a common objective, and team not taking advantage of all the team resources. The status of the team execution process at this stage is a wait and see attitude, where the team process is usually noticed but avoided.

In the storming stage, the team leader coaches the team in maintaining focus on the goals and expectations, managing the team process and conflict resolution, generating ideas, and explaining decisions. The work that needs to be accomplished is: identifying team member expectations, discussing differences, and conflict management. Issues that surface are team members feeling unsatisfied and/or overburdened, and lack of contribution. The status of the team execution process at this stage is the formation of cliques because the general perception is that the effort does not require teamwork.

In the norming stage, the team leader primarily acts as a facilitator who provides encouragement, helps with consensus building, and gives feedback. Attention needs to be given to resolving differences through establishing ground rules, developing trust, and discussing directly how better to work together. Issues that arise are ongoing disagreements between team members and team members' working at cross-purposes. The status of the team execution process at this stage is general support for leadership, with the sharing of leadership among the team.

In the performing stage, the team leader facilitates the team process, where there is a delegation of tasks and objectives. Attention needs to be given to objective achievement, team member satisfaction, and collaboration. Issues that surface are unfinished work and not celebrating success. The status of the team execution process at this stage is that members are not dependent on the designated leaders, where everyone shares the responsibility for initiating and discussing team process issues.

To illustrate this concept, consider each of the following resulting orming model behaviors when a team member misses a meeting.

- Send replacement – may move team down to forming
- Leader represent missing member – a norming or storming phase behavior
- Other members share responsibility – performing phase behavior

5.3   Interaction Styles

Teams are made up of individuals who have different styles. Individuals may be more task-oriented or people-oriented. Some team members prefer to focus more on the job at hand, while others focus on relationships. People also tend to be thinkers and doers. Thinkers reflect on their work, while doers tend to discuss their work more openly. Everybody strikes his or her balance between these characteristics. This yields a distinctive profile for each individual on a team and the team as a whole.

The inherent dynamics can be quite different between teams since the styles for members of the team can be quite different. The success of a team is dependent upon how well the differences between individuals are understood and capitalized upon. Teams need to have profile diversity, but the team also needs to be able to work together.

The question of concern is: What should be done to make the teams within an IEE implementation most effective? Those who are involved in creating the team should consider the interaction styles of people and how well these people's skills and styles would complement each other toward the common team goal. Secondly, after the team is formed, it is important that each team member understand and consider the difference in interaction styles between the team members so that each knows how best to interface with the team as a whole and with individuals within the team.

There are many tests that assess the personality of individuals (e.g., Myers–Briggs). It can be advantageous to take such a test and study the results to determine what each member of the team needs to do to interact better with the team as a whole or with other individuals who have a personality style that can easily conflict with their own.

One model describes the interaction styles of people as they relate to teams. These styles are driver, enthusiast, analyzer, or affiliator, where the characteristics for these styles are (Teamwork, 2002):

- *Driver*: Someone who takes charge. Drivers focus on results. They exert a strong influence to get things done.
- *Enthusiast*: Someone who is a social specialist. Enthusiasts express opinions and emotions easily. They prefer a strong interaction with people.
- *Analyzer*: Someone who likes to be well organized, thinking things out. Analyzers prefer specific projects and activities. They enjoy putting structure into ideas.
- *Affiliator*: Someone who is an adaptive specialist. Affiliators have a high concern for good relationships. They seek stability and predictability. They want to be a part of the bigger picture.

The potential strengths and potential weaknesses of each style are noted in Table 5.1.

5.4 Making a Successful Team

When initiating teams, it is important to have members who have the appropriate skill sets (e.g., self-facilitation and technical/subject-matter expertise). The teams should have an appropriate

Table 5.1: Potential Strengths and Potential Weaknesses of Styles

Style	Streng	ths	Weaknesses	
Driver	*Determined *Decisive *Direct	*Thorough *Efficient	*Dominating *Demanding *Impatient	*Unsympathetic *Critical
Enthusiast	*Personable *Enthusiastic	*Stimulating *Innovative	*Opinionated *Reactionary	*Undependable
Analyzer	*Industrious *Serious *Orderly	*Persistent *Methodical	*Indecisive *Critical	*Uncommunicative
Affiliator	*Cooperative *Dependable	*Supportive *Helpful	*Conforming *Hides true feelings	*Uncommitted

number of members and representation. When launching a team, it is important to have a clear purpose, goals, commitment, ground rules, roles, and responsibilities set for the team members. Schedules, support from management, and team empowerment issues must also be addressed.

Team dynamics and performance issues must also be addressed, such as:

1. Team-building techniques that address goals, roles, responsibilities, introductions, and stated/hidden agenda.
2. Team facilitation techniques that include applying coaching, mentoring, and facilitation techniques that guide a team to overcome problems (e.g., overbearing, dominant, or reluctant participants). In addition, the unquestioned acceptances of opinions as facts, feuding, floundering, rush to accomplishment, attribution, digressions, tangents, etc.
3. Measurement of team performance in relationship to goals, objectives, and metrics.
4. Use of team tools such as nominal group technique, force-field analysis, and other team tools are described in Chapter 16.

Ten ingredients for a successful team have been described as (Scholtes, 1988):

1. Clarity in team goals
2. An improvement plan
3. Clearly defined roles
4. Clear communication
5. Beneficial team behaviors
6. Well-defined decision procedures

   7. Balanced participation
   8. Established ground rules
   9. Awareness of the group process
 10. Use of the scientific approach

I will address each of these ten points as they apply to the execution of a project within IEE. However, these ingredients also apply to the executive team and steering team.

1. *Clarity of team goals*: All team members should understand and maintain focus on the goals of the project as expressed within the IEE team charter. During the execution of projects, there will be times when it is best to redirect or re-scope a project. There will be other times when new project opportunities arise, or it appears that it would be best to abort further work on the project. All of these situations can occur during a project's execution. In IEE, it is important for the team lead to inform the project champion and others about these issues. Until formal alterations are made to the project charter, it is important that the team maintain focus on the current project chart definition.

2. *An improvement plan*: A project execution plan should be made from the IEE project execution roadmap. This plan guides the team to determine schedules and identify mileposts. Reference is made to these documents when there are discussions about what direction to take next and about resource/training needs.

3. *Clearly defined roles*: The efficiency and effectiveness of teams are dependent upon how well everyone's talents are tapped. It is also important for members to understand what they are to do and who is responsible for various issues and tasks. Ideally, there are designated roles for all team members. The chain of command of an organization should not dictate the roles and duty assignments within a team.

4. *Clear communication*: The effectiveness of discussions is based upon how well information is transferred between members of the team. Team members need to speak with clarity and directness. Team members need to listen to others proactively, avoiding both interruptions and talking when someone else is speaking.

5. *Beneficial team behaviors*: Within teams there should be encouragement to use the skills and methodologies that make discussions and meetings more effective. Each team meeting should use an agenda. There should be a facilitator who is responsible for keeping the meeting focused and moving. Someone should take minutes for each meeting. There should be a draft of

the next agenda and evaluation of the meeting. Everyone should give his or her full attention to the meeting. No one should leave the meeting unless there is truly an emergency. During a meeting, members should initiate discussions, seek information, and clarify/elaborate on ideas. There should be focused discussions, avoiding digressions.

6. *Well-defined decision procedures*: A team should be aware and flexible in order to execute the different ways to reach a decision. Discussions should determine when a poll or consensus is most appropriate. Many of the decision-making procedures are part of the IEE project execution roadmap.

7. *Balanced participation*: Every team member should participate in discussions and in decisions. Team members should share their contribution of talents and be committed to the success of the project. Ideally, there should be balanced participation with the building of the styles offered by each team member.

8. *Established ground rules*: Every team should establish ground rules that address how meetings will be run. Norms should be set for how members are to interact and what kind of behavior is acceptable. Some important ground rules for meetings are: high priority on attendance, promptness for meeting start/stop times with full attendance, clear indications of meeting place and time along with how this notification is communicated.

9. *Awareness of the group process*: Team members should be aware of how the team works together where attention is given to the content of the meeting. Members should be sensitive to non-verbal communication and to the group dynamics. They should feel free to comment and intervene when appropriate to correct a process problem of the group.

10. *Use of the scientific approach*: Teams need to focus on how they can best use the IEE project execution roadmap for their particular situation. They should focus on the when and how to implement the best tool for every given situation.

5.5   Team Member Feedback

Teams need to work both smart and hard at completing their tasks. However, the team needs to support the needs of individual members. To understand the needs of team members, there has to be feedback. The most common form of this feedback is a one-on-one conversation.

We want feedback to be constructive. For this to happen, we must acknowledge the need for both positive and negative feedback, know when and how to both give and receive feedback, and understand the context (Scholtes, 1988).

Feedback should be descriptive, relating objectively to the situation, giving examples whenever possible. The basic format for such a statement follows, where descriptive words could be changed for the particular situation.

> "When you are late for meetings, I get angry because I think it is wasting the time of all the other team members, and we are never able to get through our agenda items. I would like you to consider finding some way to plan your schedule that lets you get to these meetings on time. That way we can be more productive at the meetings, and we can all keep to our tight schedules."

Additional guidelines for giving feedback are: don't use labels such as immature, don't exaggerate, don't be judgmental, speak for yourself, and talk about yourself, not about the other person. In addition, phrase the issue as a statement rather than a question, restrict feedback to things you know for certain, and help people hear/accept your compliments when positive feedback is given.

Guidelines for receiving feedback are: breathe to relax, listen carefully, ask questions for clarification, acknowledge the understanding of the feedback, acknowledge the validity of points, and, when appropriate, take time out to sort what you heard before responding.

Within a team, it is best to anticipate and prevent problems whenever possible. However, whenever a problem occurs, it should be thought of as a team problem. It is important to neither under- nor overreact to problems. Typical decisions that need to be made by the team leader for problems are: do nothing, off-line conversation, impersonal group time (e.g., start of meeting describing the problem with no mention of name), off-line confrontation, in-group confrontation, and expulsion from the group, an option that should not be used. These options are listed in order of preference and sequence of execution. That is, off-line confrontation would typically be used only if a less forceful off-line conversation earlier did not work.

5.6   Reacting to Common Team Problems

Ten common group problems have been described as (Scholtes, 1988):

1. Floundering
2. Overbearing participants
3. Dominating participants
4. Reluctant participants
5. Unquestioned acceptance of opinions as facts
6. Rush to accomplishment
7. Attribution
8. Discounted values
9. Wanderlust: digression and tangents
10. Feuding members

1. *Floundering*: Teams often experience trouble starting or ending a project, and/or addressing various stages of the project. Problems occurring at the beginning of a project can indicate that the team is unclear or overwhelmed by its task. When this occurs, specific questions should be asked and addressed by the team such as: "Let's review our project charter and make sure that it's clear to everyone." "What do we need to do so that we can move on?"

2. *Overbearing participants*: Because of their position of authority or area of expertise, some members wield a disproportionate amount of influence. This can be detrimental to the team when they discourage discussion in their area. When this occurs, the team leader can reinforce the agreement that no area is sacred and a team policy of "In God we trust. All others must have data!"

3. *Dominating participants*: Some team members talk too much, using long anecdotes when a concise statement would do. These members may or may not have any authority or expertise. When this occurs, the leader can structure discussions that encourage equal participation using such tools as nominal group technique. The leader may need to practice gate-keeping using such statements as "Paul, we've heard from you on this. I'd like to hear what others have to say."

4. *Reluctant participants*: Some team members rarely speak. A group can have problems when there are no built-in activities that encourage introverts to participate and extroverts to listen.

When this occurs, the leader may need to divide the tasks into individual assignments with reports. A gate-keeping approach would be to ask the silent person a direct question about his experience in the area under consideration.

5. *Unquestioned acceptance of opinions as facts*: Team members sometime express a personal belief with such confidence that listeners assume that what they are hearing is fact. When this occurs, the leader may ask a question such as, "Is your statement an opinion or fact? Do you have data?"

6. *Rush to accomplishment*: Often, teams will have at least one member who is either impatient or sensitive to the outside pressures to such a level that he/she feels that the team must do something now. If this pressure gets too great, the team can be led to unsystematic efforts to make improvements that lead to chaos. When this occurs, the leader can remind the members of the team that they are to follow the systematic IEE roadmap, which allows for the possibility of executing quick "low-hanging fruit fixes" when these fixes are appropriate for a project.

7. *Attribution*: There is a tendency to attribute motives to people when we don't understand or disagree with their behavior. Statements such as "They won't get involved since they are waiting their time out to collect their pension" can lead to hostility when aimed at another team member or someone outside the team. When this occurs, the leader could respond by saying, "That might well explain why this is occurring. But, how do we know for sure? Has anyone seen or heard something that indicates this is true? Is there any data that supports this statement?"

8. *Discounted values*: We all have certain values and perspectives which may consciously or unconsciously be important to us. When these values are ignored or ridiculed, we feel discounted. A discounted statement "plop" occurs when someone makes a statement that no one acknowledges, and discussion picks up on a subject totally irrelevant to the statement. The speaker then wonders why there was no response. The speaker needs feedback whether such a statement is or is not relevant to the conversation. When this occurs, the leader can interject conversation that supports the discounted person's statement. If a team member frequently discounts people, the leader might give off-line constructive feedback.

9. *Wanderlust: digression and tangents*: Meetings that have unfocused conversations are examples of wanderlust conversation. When this happens, team members can wonder where the time went for the meeting. To deal with this problem, the team leader can

write an agenda that has time estimates for each item, referencing the time when discussions deviate too far from the current topic.

10. *Feuding members*: Within a team, sometimes there are members who have been having feuds long before the team creation. Their behavior can disrupt a team. Interaction by other team members could be viewed as taking sides with one of the combatants. It is best that feuding members not be placed on the same team. When this is not possible, the leader may need to have off-line discussions with both individuals at the onset of the team's creation.

5.7   Applying IEE

It is important to keep team focus so that everyone is going in the right direction for timely project execution. The chapter after the next chapter discusses the project execution plan. The described P-DMAIC project execution roadmap steps in this volume can be used as a guideline for creating this plan and providing overall project direction. The project check sheet in the appendix can be used during meetings to provide project status against roadmap steps execution.

5.8   Exercises

1. Consider the following meeting dynamics of a team in the P-DMAIC analyze phase.
   - The team is behind schedule and has a presentation to upper management due next week. An agenda has been set to determine where to focus improvements and to calculate the CODND.
   - The last few meetings have seemed like re-runs with no clear direction on where to drill down and focus low-hanging fruit improvements.
   - During the meeting, various group members share conflicting opinions about what area of the process should be the point of focus for improvements.
   - Team members are complaining that nothing is getting done and are losing momentum to work on the project.

- The team leader will not budge on the direction in which he or she thinks the team should go, although most members are in disagreement with his or her perception.

Discuss and record what went wrong, how the facilitator could have acted differently in order to gain team consensus, and what tools/actions are most appropriate for this scenario.

2. Consider the orming model of team development and compare the three methods in dealing with a team member missing a meeting and how it may affect a team which is in the performing state.
   (a) The missing member sends a replacement from the same organization to the team meeting who has never participated with the team.
   (b) The missing member sends their material to the team leader to be presented to the team.
   (c) The missing member sends their material to a fellow team member to be presented to the team.

PART III
Improvement Project Roadmap: Measure Phase

An objective of the measure phase is the development of a reliable and valid measurement system of the business process identified in the define phase.

6

P-DMAIC – Measure Phase (Plan Project and Metrics): Voice of the Customer and In-Process Metrics

6.1   P-DMAIC Roadmap Component

The last chapter described the aspects of creating the project execution team. This chapter initiates the next step in the P-DMA-IC roadmap (i.e., plan project and in-process metrics). The graphic in this section highlights the P-DMAIC roadmap steps (see Appendix Section D.1) that are described in this chapter. Appendix E contains the tollgate check sheets for this and other phases.

This chapter provides guidelines for effectively initiating a project as part of the define phase with focus on capturing project voice of the customer (VOC) and any in-process metrics that may be appropriate. The next chapter describes project management aspects of this roadmap phase.

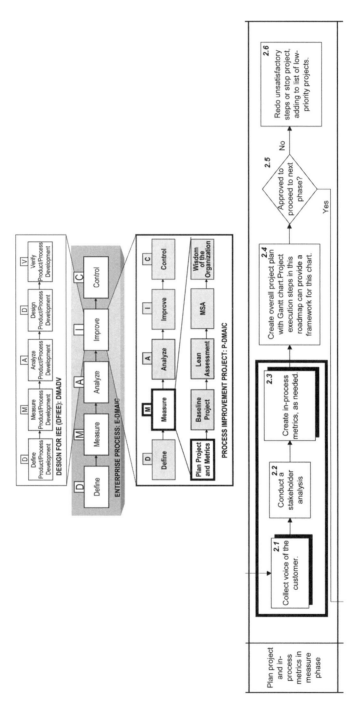

6.2 Project Customer and Stakeholder Definition and Information Sources

In a SIPOC, suppliers of a customer focus on what they do in a process; i.e., lead time, cost, and defects. Customers focus on their needs; i.e., delivery, price, and quality.

Process output variables provide a voice of the process quantification. Process output specifications are a quantification of the VOC needs. The overlay of specifications on process output distributions quantifies customer do/need gap.

Customer satisfaction is achieved by minimizing the do/need gap. A VOC system can identify and close this gap at both the enterprise and project level, where many of the E-DMAIC VOC concepts described in Volume 2 are also applicable at the project level.

VOC can originate from many sources, as illustrated in Figure 6.1. A step-by-step process to obtain project VOC input is:

1. Define your customer.
2. Obtain customer's wants, needs, and desires.
3. Assure that project is meeting customer needs.

Process stakeholders are individuals or functions that are either directly or indirectly impacted by the process. Customers are a stakeholder; however, there are others. Potential stakeholders in a process include:

- Process customer
- Process supplier
- Prior internal operation
- Next internal operation
- Regulators
- Intermediate processors (Shipping companies, resellers,etc.)
- Community (environmental issues)

The above three-step procedure can be used to also determine if there are any project stakeholder need gaps.

Stakeholders can have the following classifications:

- Direct – Concerned about the process output and how the process performs relative to meeting their requirements. They may perform process audits and conduct reviews.

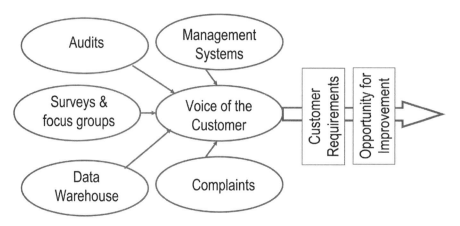

Figure 6.1: VOC sources.

- Indirect – Concern only with the process output. They are satisfied with periodic reports showing how their needs are being met.
- Internal – Groups that are in the same organization as the existing process and report to the same leadership. They can have an impact on changes so that their expectations are better met.
- External – Groups that are outside the organization's sphere of influence; e.g., a division that has different leadership. They have limited ability to impact the process relative to expectations.

An example stakeholder analysis is shown in Table 6.1.

Direct customers/stakeholders are the primary source for active collection of VOC information. The indirect customer/stakeholder will typically have provided their VOC through requirement documents.

6.3   Example 6.1: Project Customer Identification

A 30,000-foot-level performance metric for the Division Controller is days sales outstanding (DSO). An EIP for the company targeted a working capital reduction for the company, which led to a DSO reduction project (see Glossary for DSO definition). Accounting assembled a team which described its project customers as:

Table 6.1: Stakeholder Analysis Example

Stakeholder	Direct/ Indirect	Internal/ External	Requirements/ Expectations	How measured or reported	Gaps	Information/ Feedback method	Possible project/ process concerns	Communication plan
Supplier	Direct	External	To accept all in spec materials	Supplier quality rating	3%	Monthly 30,000-foot-level reports & rejected material	Might change acceptance criteria	Notify of project goal. Request contact point
Worker	Direct	Internal	Execute process procedure correctly	Performance review	?	Yearly review. Weekly meetings.	Lose or change job expectations	Communicate project goal, select representative to keep up with progress, and have management deal with fears
Next process step	Direct	Internal	100% good	Defect reports	?	None	Lose or change job expectations	Communicate project goal, select representative to keep up with progress, and have management deal with fears
Shipping Company	Indirect	External	Shipping documents correct. Ready as promised	None	?	None	None	None
Regulator	Indirect	External	Reporting on time and requirements met	Quarterly reports	None	Quarterly reporting	Unknown	Notify of project intent
End User	Indirect	External	Functionality, price, and quality	Production metrics,	Too many complaints	VOC efforts	May lose customers	Consider advertising campaign after completion

- Accounting, since their procedures would be changed
- Division controller, since he/she needs the improvement in their 30,000-foot-level scorecard/dashboard metric
- Functions of company that would be impacted by procedural changes

6.4 Project VOC

Quality function deployment (QFD) or the "house of quality," a term coined in QFD because of the shape of its matrix, is a tool that can aid in meeting the needs of the customer/stakeholder and in-translating these requirements into basic requirements that have direction (see Breyfogle, 2003a). An overall product QFD implementation strategy involves first listing the customer expectations (VOC). These "whats" are then tabulated along with the list of design requirements ("hows") related to meeting these customer expectations.

Most IEE project work does not require the rigors of QFD creation; however, the concepts are still applicable at the project level (i.e., we need to start with the "whats" of the customer). Whether we are at the enterprise level or project level, we still have customers who have:

- *Needs*: Basic expectations that they will purchase.
- *Wants*: Performance features that they might be willing to purchase.
- *Desires*: Features that they want to have but may or may not be willing to purchase. Features include function or deliverables that they would not think would be included or do not know exist.

To reiterate, the end product user is not the only customer. For example, a supplier that produces a component part/transaction of a larger assembly/service has a customer relationship with the company responsible for the larger assembly/service. A process to determine the needs of customers can also be useful to define such business procedural tasks as office physical layout, accounting procedures, product testing procedures, and internal organizational structure. Focusing on the needs of customers goes hand in hand with "answering the right question" and with the IEE assessment sections described at the end of many chapters.

For a project VOC assessment, consider whether the project scope description is specific enough to indicate what questions should be asked and whether it includes the customer. Consider what is known, the sources for this knowledge, and its validity. Dated historical information, one-source information, and purely technical knowledge can be misleading.

Consider alternative internal and external sources for information before interacting with the project's customer. Internal sources include: company policies, employee suggestions, technical reports/experts, specifications, product development data, and strategic goals. External sources include: customer complaints, industrial benchmarking, government regulations, and academic reports.

For the previously described DSO project example, potential sources for initial information prior to customer interaction include: company policies, benchmarking of other division and/or company payment policies, and assessment of expectations from accounts payable group (i.e., expectations from customers of this process).

Proactive data collection opportunities are: customer surveys, market studies, and customer interviews. I will focus on interviews since interviews can be very useful to gain project insight.

A customer selection matrix is useful to decide who should be interviewed. As illustrated in Table 6.2, this matrix provides an overview of all potential customer titles or roles that have product requirements. The "*Y*," or yes, in the matrix indicates that someone in that organization would be interviewed.

Deciding whether to interview someone for each matrix juncture depends upon many factors, including knowledge, willingness, and availability of the interviewee. When time is short, a priority ranking can help decide who should be interviewed.

Developed customer-specific interview questions should help determine wants and both emotional and rational needs. Insight is to be sought for product/process characteristics relative to its look, feel, smell, and critical parameters/tolerances. Other information to quantify is: end user requirements relative to usage environ-

Table 6.2: Defining Project VOC Contacts ("*Y*" represents "yes" that someone in that organization would be interviewed)

	Manufacturing Eng	*New Prod. Eng*	*Marketing*	*Line Worker*	*Order Entry*
Customer A	Y		Y		Y
Customer B	Y				Y
Customer C	Y	Y	Y	Y	Y
Your Company	Y		Y		Y

ment, service, and component interaction. Any manufacturing/supplier process and timing issues should also be identified.

6.5   In-Process Metrics: Overview

The following two sections describe the calculation defects per million opportunities (DPMO) and rolled throughput yield (RTY). The Six Sigma metric, sigma quality level, is described in Section B.1 of Appendix B.

Six Sigma deployments have traditionally emphasized the quantification of DPMO for all projects. Selecting the proper project metrics is critical to driving the right behavior. Business metrics should make sense, be easy to understand, and be independent of who is compiling the metrics. Organizations that require a DPMO rate or sigma-quality-level metric for every project will find that this metric can often be very subjective. For example, what is a defect when the 30,000-foot-level metric is inventory level? There is none. Whenever there is not a true specification, organizations that make DPMO/sigma-quality-level requirement typically establish a goal in lieu of having a specification (e.g., a DSO defect occurs if an invoice is beyond 10 days late). However, this goal is not the same as a mechanical specification where the parts will not function properly if they are not made within a certain tolerance. A specification needs to be a customer requirement that is not dependent upon the individual who happens to be creating the goal.

However, there are instances when a DPMO metric or RTY is an appropriate in-process project metric, as described in the Appendix D Figure D.1 decision tree.

6.6   In-Process Metrics: Defects Per Million Opportunities

I will use the example shown in Figure 6.2 to illustrate the calculation of DPMO. In this illustration, a sales contract is completed in four process steps, where defects may or may not be reworked. A total of 40 random contracts were recorded over a stable/predictable period of time in the 30,000-foot-level control chart. From these 40 samples, 20 contracts were Type A and another 20 were Type B. The number of defects in these contracts was 112, which yielded an estimate for the process DPMO rate of 169,696. Some

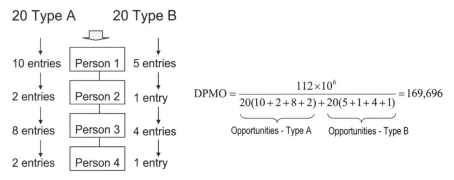

Figure 6.2: DPMO calculations.

organizations might then convert this DPMO rate to a sigma quality level of 2.4–2.5 using Table L.

6.7 In-Process Metrics: RTY

Reworks within an organization that have no value and are often not considered within the metrics of a factory are often referred to as the hidden factory. The Six Sigma metric rolled throughput yield (RTY) is a metric that includes the hidden factory impact. RTY measures the percent of product that goes through the process without being scrapped or reworked. Process yield is not the same as RTY since this scrapped product yield metric ignores rework. Process yield is the percentage of units that are not scrapped. RTY measures how well products or services are processed by organizations.

Figure 6.3 compares the two metrics, where Y is the yield at each of the three process steps. In this illustration:

- 64.3% (0.90*0.84*0.85 = 0.643) of the units completed the process without being reworked or scrapped.
- Rework expenses = 21.4% (214 units)
- Scrap expenses = 14.3% (143 units)

6.8 In-Process Metrics: Applications

Figure D.1 in Appendix D contains the drill down of Step 2.2 of the project execution roadmap; however, the tools are also applicable in the enterprise analyze phase.

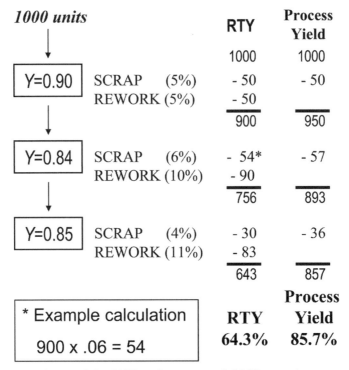

Figure 6.3: RTY and process yield illustration.

To high-level managers, the Six Sigma quality level metric (see Appendix B Section B.1) might sound very attractive since they could create a system where all organizations have the same scorecard; that is they could compare the sigma quality level of manufacturing with business office processes. However, in reality, the sigma quality level calculation is very dependent upon the definition of opportunity. One function within a company could make their sigma quality level number look better by decreasing their opportunity size. Because of this, among other issues, IEE discourages the use of sigma quality level metrics.

However, DPMO rates and RTY can be beneficial in enterprise analyses for drilling down a process to targeted project improvement areas and some project metric reporting. Both DPMO and RTY quantify the hidden factory, whether the process is manufacturing or transactional. In addition, when several products experience one process, these metrics can become the bridge from product to process metrics.

An illustration of the bridge from product to process is printed circuit board manufacturing, where many product types can go through one manufacturing line. Defining an opportunity for failure as the sum of the number of solder joints and printed circuit board components could lead to the weekly 30,000-foot-level scorecard/dashboard tracking of the ratio of defects to the number of opportunities.

The benefit of this measurement technique is that improvements for future product production are really achieved through improving the overall system that produces all products, not a specific product; that is improving the metrics that measure the process, which are independent of product type. This same thought process also applies to transactional processes such as insurance claim error rates, where opportunity size would compensate for differing complexity of individual insurance claims.

The components of an RTY yield analysis can also be very beneficial at both the enterprise analyze phase or project execution phase. A Pareto chart of yield for each process step gives insight to where targeted improvement efforts could have the most overall system benefit (i.e., the step that has the lowest yield).

The IEE logic for utilizing in-process metrics for various situations is shown in Figure D.1. In the decision tree, IEE non-discrete event tracking is defects per a common unit of measure (e.g., defects per square foot (or meters) of titanium sheet metal). It is important to see how this situation differs from the discrete event printed circuit board illustration, where, for example, a joint was either satisfactorily soldered or it wasn't.

6.9 Exercises

1. Describe customers for a project. Create a strategy for capturing voice of the customer and tracking how well his/her needs are fulfilled.
2. List initial sources of information that should be consulted prior to interacting with the customers identified in Exercise 1.
3. A process has 10 steps with yields:

Y1	Y2	Y3	Y4	Y5	Y6	Y7	Y8	Y9	Y10
0.82	0.81	0.85	0.78	0.87	0.80	0.88	0.83	0.89	0.90

Create a table that shows operation step yields and cumulative RTYs. Determine the overall process RTY. Describe manufacturing, business process, and/or project situations for this type of data. Include example operation steps to monitor.

4. A process has ten steps with the following data:

Operation	Defects	Units
1	12	380
2	72	943
3	22	220
4	85	1505
5	23	155
6	23	255
7	102	1023
8	93	843
9	55	285
10	68	1132

Calculate operation yields for each step. Determine the rolled throughput yield and total defects per unit. Describe manufacturing, business process, and/or project situations for the origination of this type of data. Include example operation steps to monitor.

5. A process produces a total of 300 units and has a total of 80 defective units failed. Determine the number of units it would take to produce 100 conforming units.

7

P-DMAIC – Measure Phase (Plan Project and Metrics): Project Plan

7.1 P-DMAIC Roadmap Component

The previous chapter initiated the plan project and in-process metrics P-DMAIC step, along with describing voice of the customer collection. This chapter further elaborates on this roadmap step by providing project management highlights for consideration during the overall project execution plan development. The graphic in this section highlights the P-DMAIC roadmap steps (see Appendix Section D.1) that are described in this chapter. Appendix E contains the tollgate check sheets for this and other phases.

It is important that focus be given to creating and executing a plan that leads to timely project closure with enterprise benefits.

7.2 Project Management

Project management is the management, allocation, and timely use of resources for the purpose of achieving a specific goal. Focus

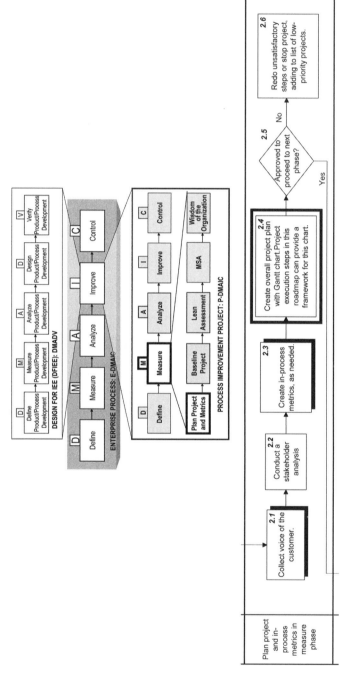

in project management should be given to the efficient utilization of resources and minimization of execution time. To meet schedule requirements and objectives, project managers need to integrate and balance technical, financial, and human resources.

Successful projects begin with an initial definition and charter that has good scope. Then the black belt needs to work with the champion and process owner to create due dates for the various project phases and activities. The black belt works with the project champion to create a plan to check on the status of the project. This team also needs to create a plan to report the progress of the project to various levels of management and to project stakeholders, including personnel within the operations of the process. Names, roles, and amount of time for project dedication should be addressed for each team member.

Project management is very important when executing projects. However, the efficient completion of tasks should not be overlooked when managing the project tasks. For example, consider the creation of a process flowchart for a project. It can be much more efficient to use a computer projector with a flowcharting program to create dynamically a process flowchart during a team meeting, rather than positioning sticky notes on the wall to represent process steps.

The chapter describes briefly some basic project management tools. These tools are applicable to both project executions and IEE infrastructure management.

7.3   Project Management: Planning

The three pillars of project management are: project objectives, resources, and time. Project management involves the balancing of these pillars. For example, a team could increase resources in order to reduce the time it takes to meet objectives, or the team could extend the time for project completion to reduce resources and still meet objectives. The champion and team need to understand the flexibility that a project has for each pillar.

A project flexibility matrix helps management and teams decide upon and then communicate the prioritization of these pillars to others. Table 7.1 shows a project flexibility matrix. It is important for teams to discuss these issues with management prior to the initiation of a project so that a team will know the needs and priorities of the organization. If the project falls behind schedule, the most flexible category provides guidance on what should be done; for example, add resources for the Table 7.1 scenario.

Management needs to realize that it cannot have it all. Sometimes trade-off needs to occur. It is good to include a project flexibility matrix signed off by management within the project charter.

Errors in estimating costs or time allocations can cause projects to fail. Vital tasks that are forgotten or have no owner or completion date can result in project failure. These pitfalls are avoided when project tasks follow a work breakdown structure that is aligned with the IEE 9-step DMAIC project execution roadmap.

Within a work breakdown structure, a project is broken down into easily digestible parts. This methodology systematically maps out the detail of paths and tasks needed to accomplish a project. A work breakdown structure can reveal the real level of complexity involved in the achievement of any goal. Potentially overwhelming projects can then become manageable, and unknown complexity can be discovered. Planning teams move from theory to the real world relative to project scope and due dates. In addition, a work breakdown structure gives both participants and reviewers outside the team a presentation structure that can be checked for logical links and completeness at each level of the detailed plan. Figure 7.1 shows an example project work breakdown structure.

Resources for a project need to be determined and then managed. Project managers need to consider the skills and time commitments of personnel who are needed for a project; for example statistics, people skills, process, and technical writing. A work–breakdown-activity and team-member matrix, as illustrated in Table 7.2, pictorially describes how each team member fulfills activities needed for project completion. This matrix also can include time estimates for the task, where O is optimistic time, R

Table 7.1: Project Flexibility Matrix

	Most Flexible	*Moderately Flexible*	*Least Flexible*
Time			X
Resource	X		
Project Objectives		X	

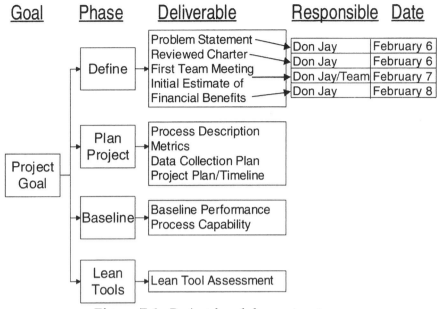

Figure 7.1: Project breakdown structure.

is realistic time, and P is pessimistic time, along with a weighted average (WA) of these numbers. Project managers sometimes determine WA from the relationship:

$$WA = \frac{O + 4R + P}{6}$$

Historical information should be used whenever possible when estimating recorded time commitments; however, wisdom of the organization techniques can also be used to determine the estimates. These estimates should be refined as the project work progresses. Before an IEE project is begun, the black belt and champion should agree on resource needs and investment expenditures. The needs list and budget have to be approved. Costs should be tracked throughout the project.

7.4 Project Management: Measures

A simple Gantt chart, as illustrated in Figure 7.2, can show the planned and actual start and completion dates/times for a project.

Table 7.2: Example, Project Resource Needs: *O* is optimistic time, *R* is realistic time, and *P* is pessimistic time, along with an overall weighted average (WA) that some project managers use for these estimates.

WB Activity	Person				Totals			
	John	Jill	Max	Mary	Time	Estimates	Time	Estimates
	Time needed	Time needed	Time needed	Time needed	Optimistic	Realistic	Pessimistic	Weighted Avg
								(O+4*R+P)/6
Design forms	(4,5,6)	0	0	(1,1,2)	5	6	8	6.2
Train Operators	(1,1,2)	(4,5,6)	(1,1,2)	0	6	7	10	7.3
Gather data	(1,1,2)	0	(5,7,10)	(1,1,3)	7	9	15	9.7
Analyze data	(7,10,12)	(1,1,1)	(2,3,3)	(2,3,4)	12	18	20	17.3

Gantt charts are easy to understand and simple to change. Gantt charts can track progress versus goals and checkpoints. The Figure 7.2 output format does not show interdependencies and no details of activities; however, project management software does offer these capabilities.

The success of large projects depends upon rigorous planning and coordination. Formal procedures to accomplish these strategies are based on networks. Program evaluation and review technique (PERT) and critical path method (CPM) procedures offer the structure for this network analysis. Historically, the differences were that activity time estimates in PERT were probabilistic, while they were assumed deterministic in CPM. Today, CPM and PERT are typically considered as one approach.

A PERT–CPM chart can give insight to the chronological sequence of tasks that require the greatest expected accomplishment time and can identify the critical path. The CPM can provide valuable information to the early forecasting of problems, interrelationships, responsibility identification, and the allocation leveling of resources. An arrow diagram, as shown in Figure 7.3,

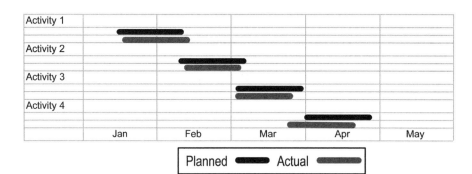

Figure 7.2: Gantt chart with planned and actual start dates.

can be used to describe PERT–CPM activity relationships, where activities are displayed as arrows, while nodes represent the start and finish of activities. The arrows can have the activity described along with its schedule completion time. A dashed arrow describes a dummy activity, which is the situation where one activity must wait for another activity with no intervention of any other activity.

When boxes are used within a PERT–CPM analysis, the activity is noted within the box. Figure 7.4 illustrates how tasks that can be done at the same time are listed together and numbered the same. Also, time estimates for each task can be included ES: estimated start, EF: estimated finish, and the actual dates: AS: actual start, AF: actual finish. This diagram can indicate what is possible and which tasks can be adapted to fit available resources. For example, we can offer completion times that depend upon how many workers are cleaning the garage.

The completion time for each activity is assumed to follow a beta distribution, while, because of the central limit theorem, the duration for the entire project follows a normal distribution. As noted earlier, each activity is to have an estimate for the optimistic time (O), pessimistic time (P), and most likely time (R). The estimated duration for each activity is

$$\mu = (O + 4R + P)/6$$

The estimated standard deviation for each activity is

$$\sigma = (P - O)/6$$

The estimated duration for the project is the sum of the durations for the activities on the critical path. The estimated variance for the project is the sum of the variances for the activities on the critical path.

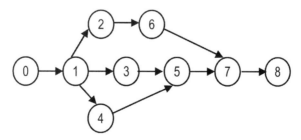

Figure 7.3: Arrow diagram.

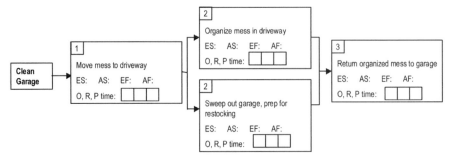

Figure 7.4: Example network diagram with boxes.

PERT–CPM project scheduling consists of planning, scheduling, improving, and controlling. Within the planning phase, the project is segmented into activities along with completion times. Activities are then linked through a network diagram. Within the schedule phase, the start and completion times for activities are assessed, along with any critical activities that must be completed on time to keep the project on schedule. Within the improving phase, activities that are considered critical should be highlighted as implementation improvement opportunities. Within the control phase, the network diagram and Gantt chart give timely feedback and allow for timely adjustments.

Controlling a project involves tracking costs, expected savings, and schedule, noting any gaps. The alignment of team members and their skills with project goals is important. Risk analysis should be conducted at all steps. The project manager needs to stay in the proactive mode, providing honest and meaningful feedback to team, sponsor, and management.

7.5   Example 7.1: CPM/PERT

Given the data in Table 7.3, determine the critical path, project duration, probability of completing the project in 10 units of time or less, and the probability of completing the project in 14 or more units of time. (Six Sigma Study Guide, 2002).

From the arrow diagram that is shown in Figure 7.5 we observe that there are two paths in this project: ABD and ACE. The duration for path ABD is 12.33, and the duration for path ACE is 9. Thus, ABD is the critical path, and the project duration is

12.33. The estimated variance for the critical path is 0.11 + 0.44 + 0.11 = 0.66. The estimated standard deviation for the critical path is the square root of the variance, which is 0.81.

To determine the probability of completing the project in 10 or fewer time units, we need to calculate the area under this normal probability density function (PDF) to the left of 10 (See Chapter 8). To do this, we can calculate Z from the relationship:

$$Z = \frac{X - \mu}{\sigma} = \frac{10 - 12.5}{0.81} = -3.09$$

For this Z value, an approximate probability of 0.001 is then determined from Table A (Appendix G).

To determine the probability of completing the project in 14 or more time units, we need to determine the area under the normal PDF to the right of 14. To do this, we can first calculate Z from the relationship:

$$Z = \frac{X - \mu}{\sigma} = \frac{14 - 12.5}{0.81} = 1.85$$

Table 7.3: CPM/PERT Example

Activity	Predecessor	Optimistic Time	Most Likely Time	Pessimistic Time
A	None	2	3	4
B	A	4	5	8
C	A	2	4	5
D	B	3	4	5
E	C	1	2	4

The duration, standard deviation, and variance for each activity are

Activity	Predecessor	Optimistic Time	Most Likely Time	Pessimistic Time	Estimated Mean	Estimated Standard Deviation	Estimated Variance
A	None	2	3	4	3.00	0.33	0.11
B	A	4	5	8	5.33	0.66	0.44
C	A	2	4	5	3.83	0.50	0.25
D	B	3	4	5	4.00	0.33	0.11
E	C	1	2	4	2.17	0.50	0.25

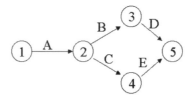

Figure 7.5: Example arrow diagram.

For this Z value, a probability of 0.032 is then determined from Table A (Appendix G).

The project execution roadmap check sheet shown in Appendix E can be viewed as project management tasks that need to be addressed or considered for timely project completion. Upon project completion, the champion needs to work with the black belt to get a final project report that is posted in a timely fashion in their organization's project tracking data base.

7.6 Applying IEE

As noted earlier, it is important to keep team focus so that everyone is going in the right direction for timely project execution. The described P-DMAIC project execution roadmap steps can be used as a guideline for creating the Gantt chart plan and providing overall project direction. The provided project check sheets can be used during meetings to provide project status against roadmap steps execution.

This chapter presented only a high-level view of project management. The reader can find more information about project management and its certifications at www.pmi.org.

7.7 Exercises

1. Create a project management flexibility table for your project.
2. Create a work breakdown structure for your project, laying out the 9-step DMAIC.
3. Construct a Gantt chart for your project showing your project activities planned start and end dates.

4. Create an arrow chart for your project. Discuss how to establish reasonable time estimates for activities. Discuss how historical data could be used to determine time ranges.

5. Given the data below, determine the critical path, project duration, and slack time, where slack time is the amount of time an activity can be delayed without delaying the project.

Activity	Predecessor	Duration
A	None	3
B	A	5
C	A	4
D	B	4
E	C	2

6. For the activities below, determine the probability of completing the project in 48 or more time units.

Activity	Preceded By	Optimistic Time	Expected Time	Pessimistic Time
A	None	10.17	12.06	15.42
B	None	14.81	15.84	18.53
C	A and B	12.45	15.31	16.72
D	C	11.79	14.54	17.74
E	C	10.63	12.56	15.34

7. For the activities below, determine the probability of completing the project in 28.3 or more time units.

Activity	Preceded By	Optimistic Time	Expected Time	Pessimistic Time
A	None	14.27	16.69	18.81
B	None	11.93	13.47	14.52
C	A and B	10.07	11.09	12.11
D	A and B	11.17	12.86	14.84

8. Create a project flexibility matrix for a project. This could be a work or home project.

9. Create a work breakdown structure for a project. This could be a work or home project.

10. Create a flexibility matrix for your project.
    (a) Discuss project priorities with your champion when creating your project flexibility matrix.

11. Create a work breakdown structure for your project's define and measure phase.
    (a) With the aid of your champion and team create a work breakdown structure plan for your project.

12. Create an elevator speech that describes the benefits of IEE to executives within 20 seconds.

(a) Have others critique your speech.
(b) Improve your speech and practice it so that it becomes second nature.
(c) Be prepared to present your speech at the next training session.

8

Response Statistics, Graphical Representations, and Data Analyses

The next four chapters provide the foundation for understanding the P-DMAIC project base-lining concepts described in Chapters 12 and 13. The presented concepts in these chapters also provide the foundation for creating value-chain 30,000-foot-level and satellite-level scorecard/dashboard performance metrics.

8.1 Continuous versus Attribute Response

Continuous or variables data can assume a range of numerical responses on a continuous scale, as opposed to data that can assume only discrete levels. Data are said to be continuous when there are no boundaries between adjacent values. For example, a process response might be 2.0, 2.0001, or 3.00005.

Attribute, or discrete, data have the presence or absence of some characteristic in each transaction; e.g., proportion nonconforming in a pass/fail test. Binary attribute data can take a pass/fail or on-time/not-on-time syntax. For example, 1 out of 1000 transactions is *defective*. This situation is often modeled by the binomial distribution.

Another attribute situation occurs when a transaction can have multiple failures, or *defects*. For example, on the average there may be 3 *defects* out of 1000 transactions. For this situation, we would count the total number of defects for the 1000 transactions. This situation can often be modeled by the Poisson distribution.

Percentage can be either continuous or attribute based on the type of data used in the calculation. If attributes are used in the calculation, the response is attribute, while if a continuous response is used in the calculation, the response is considered continuous. An illustration of each is:

- *Attribute response*: Last week 10,000 transactions were executed and there were 100 defective transactions. This 1% [(100/10,000)*100] would be an attribute since the numerator and denominator are attribute.
- *Continuous response*: A batch contained 500 pounds before processing. After processing 475 pounds remained. The process yield of 95% [(475/500)*(100)] could be considered a continuous response output.

If data can be presented in either continuous or attribute format, the continuous format is preferred.

8.2   Time-Series Plot

A run chart or time-series plot permits the study of data over time for trends or patterns, where the x-axis is time and the y-axis is the measured variable. Generally 20–25 points are needed to establish patterns and baselines. Example trend charts are:

- The S&P 500 daily closing prices as shown in Figure 8.1.
- An organization's KPOV reported hourly as shown in Figure 8.2; e.g., dimension of a part or time to fill an order (see Table 12.2 for data).
- A company's gross revenue, as shown in Figure 8.3.

Often a problem exists with the interpretation of run charts. There is a tendency to over-examine individual KPOV responses without enough consideration given to the process variability that created the responses. For example, individuals often react

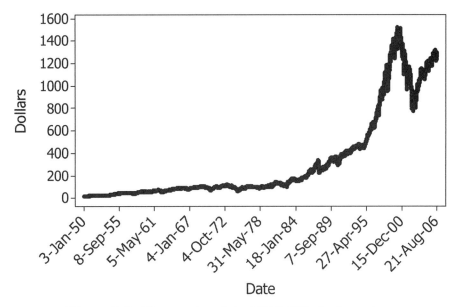

Figure 8.1: Time-series plot of S&P 500 closing price.

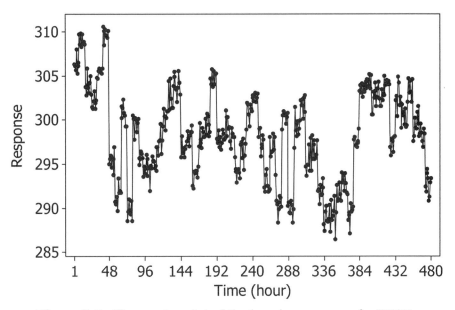

Figure 8.2: Time-series plot of the hourly response of a KPOV.

to a point as though it were a special cause when it did not meet a specification condition, or concluding that a trend is occurring in time-series data when there were only a few supporting observations.

End-of-day stock market reports are an example of this type thinking. The nightly news often provides a crisp, defined reason as to why the stock market moved either up or down that day, even when there is only a very small amount of change.

When there is correlation between the values of a time series and previous values of the same series, data are said to be auto-correlated. This occurs in the stock market. This type of response lacks stability, which implies that there are predictability issues. Because of this, traditional control chart analyses are not useful for stock market analyses.

Control charts offer simple tests that identify special cause oc-currences from common-cause variability through the compari-son of datum points and trends to an upper control limit (UCL) and a lower control limit (LCL), as described in this and in the next several chapters. Processes that are not stable/predictable will exhibit out-of-control signals when tracked on a control chart.

However, the decision about whether a process is stable/predictable or not is not a sole function of the process response. How we collect data and then examine process data can impact our decision about whether a process is stable or not. Example 12.4 will later illustrate this point.

8.3   Example 8.1: Time-Series Plot of Gross Revenue

This example shows the creation of a time-series plot for a satellite-level metric shown in:

- Breyfogle (2008d) – Figure 7.9
- Volume 2 – Figure 7.7
- This volume – Figure 3.3.

Example 12.8 will show the computation methods of the other satellite-level metric plots shown in these figures.

The gross revenue for a company is shown in Table 8.1 and presented as a time-series plot in Figure 8.3.

8.4   Example 8.2: Culture Firefighting or Fire Prevention?

In this example, a traditional approach will be used initially to address nonconformance issues. A high-level IEE alternative

Table 8.1: Value Chain Satellite-level Gross Revenue Metric
(Millions of Dollars)

Mon.	Rev.		Mon.	Rev.		Mon.	Rev.		Mon.	Rev.		Mon.	Rev.		Mon.	Rev.
1	406		8	474		15	449		22	572		29	705		36	805
2	373		9	493		16	481		23	681		30	768		37	709
3	470		10	435		17	414		24	604		31	670		38	762
4	377		11	505		18	592		25	730		32	780		39	765
5	486		12	564		19	623		26	611		33	781		40	956
6	406		13	546		20	554		27	531		34	677		41	900
7	483		14	494		21	598		28	644		35	803		42	929

Mon. = month
Rev. = revenue

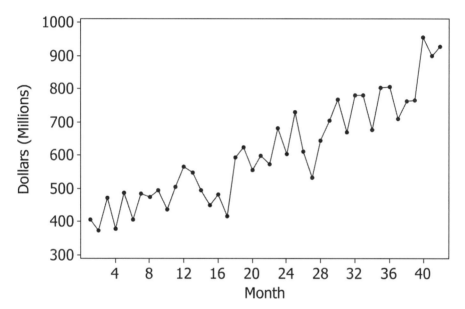

Figure 8.3: Time-series plot of gross revenue.

approach will then be presented, along with its benefits. Chapter 12 describes for continuous data the mechanics of creating this alternative metric-reporting format, while Chapter 13 addresses attribute data.

An organization collects data and reacts whenever an out-of-specification condition occurs or a goal is not met. The following example dialog is what could happen when attempts are made to fix all out-of-specification problems whenever they occur in a manufacturing or service environment. This scenario could apply equally to a business service process whenever the goals of an organization are not being met.

Consider a product that has specification limits of 72–78. An organization might react to collected data in the following manner:

- First datum: 76.2
  - Everything is OK.
- Second datum: 78.2
  - Joe, go fix the problem.
- Data: 74.1, 74.1, 75.0, 74.5, 75.0, 75.0
  - Everything OK; Joe must have done a good job!
- Next datum: 71.8
  - Mary, fix the problem.
- Data: 76.7, 77.8, 77.1, 75.9, 76.3, 75.9, 77.5, 77.0, 77.6, 77.1, 75.2, 76.9
  - Everything OK; Mary must have done a good job!
- Next datum: 78.3
  - Harry, fix the problem.
- Next data: 72.7, 76.3
  - Everything OK; Harry must have fixed the problem.
- Next datum: 78.5
  - Harry, seems like there still is a problem.
- Next data: 76.0, 76.8, 73.2
  - Everything OK; the problem must be fixed now.
- Next datum: 78.8
  - Sue, please fix the problem that Harry could not fix.
- Next data: 77.6, 75.2, 76.8, 73.8, 75.6, 77.7, 76.9, 76.2, 75.1, 76.6, 76.6, 75.1, 75.4, 73.0, 74.6, 76.1
  - Everything is great; give Sue an award!
- Next datum: 79.3
  - Get Sue out there again. She is the only one who knows how to fix the problem.
- Next data: 75.9, 75.7, 77.9, 78
  - Everything is great again!

> Reaction to the out-of-specification conditions individually did not improve the process or prevent the likelihood of having problems in the future. The firefighters did not fix anything.

A plot of this information is shown in Figure 8.4. From this plot, we see that the previously described reaction to the out-of-specification conditions individually did not improve the process or prevent the likelihood of having problems in the future. The firefighters did not fix anything.

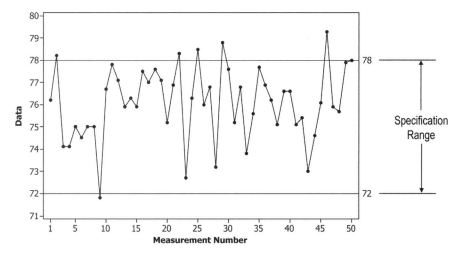

Figure 8.4: Reacting to common-cause variability as though it were special cause.

Figure 8.5 shows a re-plot of the data as an individuals control chart. The control limits in this figure are calculated from the data. Specifications in no way affect the control limits. This chart is a statement of the VOP relative to whether the process is considered in statistical control or not, stable or not. Since people often have difficulty in understanding what *in control* means, I prefer to use the term *predictable*.

These lower and upper control limits (LCL and UCL, respectively) represent a ±3 sampling standard deviation around the mean $(\overline{x})$. For this type of chart, the ±3 sampling standard deviation is usually considered to be 2.66 times the mean of the adjacent-time-value moving range (see Chapter 12). Since the up-and-down movements are within the UCL and LCL and there are no unusual patterns, we would conclude that there are no special-cause data conditions and that the source of process variability is common cause. The process is predictable.

Some readers might think that the control limits seem too wide and wonder about tightening up the control limits. My response to that is this:

The control limits are considered the VOP and are directly calculated from the data. In some cases the control limits could be too wide. This occurrence is typically a function of data-collection

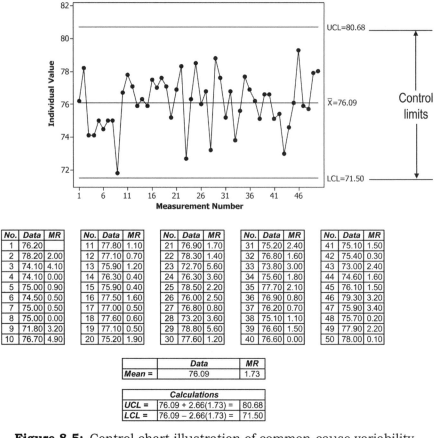

Figure 8.5: Control chart illustration of common-cause variability.

procedures or a special-cause condition. When this occurs, you would work these issues instead of changing the control limits. For this data set, this is not the case.

Most think action limits (i.e., VOC), when they decide to tighten control limits. This may seem to be a good thing, but is *not*. If you tighten the control limits to be narrower than the VOP, the result is most certainly an increase in firefighting.

This organization had been reacting to the out-of-specification conditions as though they were special cause. The focus on fixing out-of-specification conditions often leads to firefighting. When firefighting activities involve tweaking the process, additional variability can be introduced, degrading the process rather than improving it.

Deming noted the following:

- "A fault in the interpretation of observations, seen everywhere, is to suppose that every event (defect, mistake, accident) is attributable to someone (usually the nearest at hand), or is related to some special event."
- "We shall speak of faults of the system as common causes of trouble, and faults from fleeting events as special causes."
- "Confusion between common causes and special causes leads to frustration of everyone, and leads to greater variability and to higher costs, exactly contrary to what is needed."
- "I should estimate that in my experience most troubles and most possibilities for improvement add up to proportions something like this: 94% belong to the system (responsibility of management), 6% [are] special."

Let's revisit the data using a Deming approach. When data are in statistical control, we can say that the process is predictable. The next obvious question is: What do you predict? When a process control chart has recently shown stability, we can lump all data in this stable region and consider that these data are a random sample of the future, assuming that nothing either positively or negatively changes the system.

Using this approach, we could create the dot plot shown in Figure 8.6.

An attribute assessment (pass or fail) for this data would yield a 12% (6/50) defective rate. However, some of these failures or non-failures are borderline and, if we reran this experiment, we could

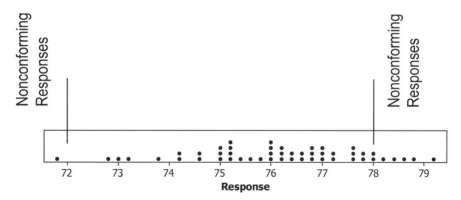

Figure 8.6: Dot plot attribute estimation of process percentage nonconformance rate.

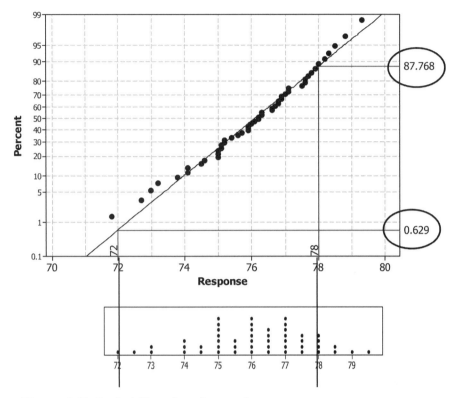

Figure 8.7: Probability plot of a continuous process output response from a stable process, with nonconformance rate estimation.

get a significantly different response. Also, the overall response distribution, which considers the magnitude of all responses, has no impact on our statement relative to nonconformance.

A better approach would be to create a probability plot of the data from this stable control chart region. Figure 8.7 shows the results, where a probability plot is an estimated cumulative percent-less-than distribution plot. For example, a best estimate for this population is that about 0.629% will be below 72 and 87.768% will be less than 78. Chapter 12 describes the application of probability plotting in more detail.

From this analysis, we conclude that the process has an approximate 13% common-cause, nonconformance rate both now and in the future, unless something either negatively or positively impacts the *overall* process. If the financial impact of this nonconformance rate is unsatisfactory, this measurement could pull for the creation of a project to improve the process.

Note, the 13% determination from the probability plot is the following:

- 0.629 + [100 − 87.768] = 12.861, rounded to 13%
- 0.629 is estimated percentile below the specification limit
- [100 − 87.768] is estimated percentile above the specification limit.

Inconsistent and ineffective organizational metric reporting can lead to much waste. The methodology described above is a consistent process, which can lead to fewer firefighting activities:

Reiterating, the IEE scorecard/dashboard metric reporting process:

1. Assess process predictability.
2. When the process is considered predictable, formulate a prediction statement for the latest region of stability. The usual reporting format for this statement is the following:
   (a) When there is a specification requirement: nonconformance percentage or DPMO
   (b) When there is no specification requirement: median response and 80 percent frequency of occurrence rate.

The described satellite-level and 30,000-foot-level control charts and process capability/performance metric statements can be created for a variety of situations. A process capability/performance metric statement can quantify the magnitude of disconnection between VOP and VOC.

It is important to note that this described prediction analysis applies to stable processes. In the stable region of processes, data need to be analyzed collectively for the purpose of gaining insight to improvement opportunities. This is in contrast to attempting to explain why one datum point is up and another point is down.

For nonpredictable processes, understanding is gained through data examination. For example, a process change could have resulted in a shift in the process response to a new region of stability. For this situation, each region of stability needs to be examined separately. Another example is when distinct multiple distributions are prevalent; for example, the holiday season needs to be examined separately from the rest of the year. A final example is when one point occurs beyond the control limits. For this situation, it could be appropriate to assess that one occurrence as an individual special-cause condition while collectively analyzing all the other points from the region of stability.

Later the IEE scorecard/dashboard metric reporting process will be described in more detail. Example 37.3 compares the IEE scorecard/dashboard creation thought process to traditional scorecard/dashboard annual or quarter calendar-based statement reporting.

Chapters 12 and 13 describe the mechanics of creating the described satellite-level/30,000-foot-level control charts and of formulating process capability/performance metric statements for a variety of situations, where a process capability/performance metric statement is a quantification of the magnitude of disconnection between voice of the process and voice of the customer.

8.5   Measurement Scales

How measurements are examined at both the KPOV and KPIV level are important. Four measurement data scales are nominal, ordinal, interval, and ratio.

- *Nominal data* examines whether datum equals a particular value; e.g., male and female counts. There is no ordering; e.g., it makes no sense to state female>male or male>female.
- *Ordinal data* has ordering but value differences are not important; e.g., Likert satisfaction scale ranking of 1 to 5 where 5 is satisfied and 1 is dissatisfied. Ordinal data can be ranked but the differences between ordinal values cannot be quantified.
- *Interval data* has ordering with a constant scale but no natural zero. Differences make sense but ratios make no sense. For example, 40°–30°=10° makes sense, but 0° is arbitrary; hence, 20°/10° does not mean that 20° is twice as hot as 10°.
- *Ratio scale* is ordered with a constant scale and has a natural zero; e.g., height, age, weight, and length. It is meaningful to state that 20 feet is twice as long as 10 feet.

8.6   Variability and Process Improvements

Variability is everywhere. Consider a person who parks his/her car inside his/her garage. The final position of the car is not the same exact place day after day. The driver has variability when parking the car. Variability in parking position can be measured over time. When nothing unusual occurs, the sources of variability in parking position are considered common cause. However, if a cat were to jump in front of the car during parking, this might distract the driver and cause additional variability, i.e., special cause.

If his/her variability, either common or special cause, when parking the care is too large from the center parking position in the garage, he/she could hit the garage-door frame. If parking variability is too large because of special causes, e.g., the cat, attempts need to be made to avoid the source of special cause. If parking variability is too large from common cause, the process of parking needs to be changed.

For the purpose of illustration, consider a person who wants to determine his/her average parking position and the consistency he/she has in parking his/her car inside the garage. It is not reasonable to expect that he/she would need to make measurements every time that the car is parked. During some period of time, e.g., one month, he/she could periodically take measurements of the parked position of the car. These measurements would then be used to estimate, for example, an average parking position for that period of time.

Similarly, all automobiles from a manufacturing line will not be manufactured in exactly the same way. Automobiles will exhibit variability in many different ways. Manufacturers have many criteria or specifications that must be achieved consistently. These criteria can range from dimensions of parts in the automobile to various performance specifications. An example criterion is the stopping distance of the automobile at a certain speed. To test this criterion, the automobile manufacturer cannot test every vehicle under actual operating conditions to determine whether it meets this criterion. In lieu of this, the manufacturer could test against this criterion using a sample from the population of automobiles manufactured.

8.7 Sampling

A sample is a portion of a larger aggregate or population from which information is desired. The sample is observed and examined, but information is desired about the population from which the sample is taken. A sample can provide predictive population characteristics; however, beginning experimenters often misconceive some test performance details. These practitioners might consider taking a ten-unit sample from today's production, making a measurement, determining some statistical properties of the sample, and then reporting these statistics to management for decision-making purposes.

Arbitrary sampling plans such as this can yield erroneous conclusions. One problem with this form of sampling is that the test sample may not accurately represent the population of interest. A sample that is not randomly selected from the interested population can give experimental bias, yielding a statement that is not representative for the population.

For example, a sample of automobiles to assess a criterion characteristic should be taken over some period of time with the consideration of such parameters as production shifts, workers, and differing manufacturing lines that may affect the measured response; i.e., a random sample without bias. A response *(x)* from random population samples is said to be a random variable.

If there is a great deal of variability in a population, there may not be much confidence in reported statistical metrics; e.g., average or mean response. A confidence interval statement quantifies estimate uncertainty since the width of the interval is a function of both sample size and sample variability. When a population characteristic such as the mean is contained in a confidence interval, the likelihood of the true value being outside this range is a quantifiable value (see confidence intervals in Chapter 19).

Still another point not to overlook when evaluating data is that there are other estimates besides the mean that can be a very important part of expressing the characteristic of a population. One of these considerations is the standard deviation of a population, which quantifies the variability of a population. Another consideration is the process capability/performance metric or a population-percentage value compliance statement.

This chapter describes some basic data statistics and graphical techniques, which provide the foundation for many of the later described topics.

8.8   Simple Graphic Presentations

It can be meaningful to present data in a form that visually illustrates the frequency of occurrence of values. This display of data could be accomplished using a dot plot or histogram.

A dot plot is a simple procedure to illustrate data positioning and its variability. Along a numbered line, a dot plot displays a dot for each observation. Dots are stacked when data are close together. When too many points exist vertically, each dot may represent more than one point. Figure 18.3 shows dot plots within a marginal plot.

A histogram is another form of plot to make such illustrations. To create a histogram when the response only takes on certain discrete values, a tally is made each time a discrete value occurs. After a number of responses is taken, the tally for the grouping of occurrences can then be plotted in histogram form. For example, Figure 8.8 shows a histogram of 200 rolls of two dice, in which the sum of the dice for eight of these rolls was two.

However, when making a histogram of response data that are continuous, the data need to be placed into classes (i.e., groups or cells). For example, in a set of data there might be six measurements that fall between the numbers of 0.501 and 1.500; these measurements can be grouped into a class that has a center value of 1. Many computer programs internally handle this grouping. Breyfogle (2003a) discusses a manual approach for determining histogram cell width. A stem-and-leaf diagram is constructed much

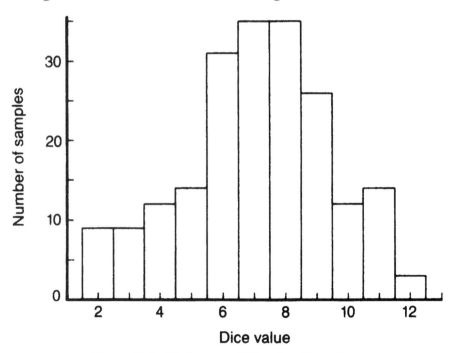

Figure 8.8: Histogram: 200 rolls of two dice.

like a tally column for creating a histogram, except that the last digit of the data value is recorded in the plot instead of a tally mark.

It should be noted that, even though histograms are commonly used to illustrate data, the probability plotting techniques described later in this chapter typically give much more visual information about the population from which the data are sampled.

8.9   Example 8.3: Histogram and Dot Plot

A sample yields the following 24 data points, ranked low to high value:

2.2   2.6   3.0   4.3   4.7   5.2   5.2   5.3   5.4   5.7   5.8   5.8   5.9   6.3
6.7   7.1   7.3   7.6   7.6   7.8   7.9   9.3   10.0   10.1

A computer generated histogram plot of this data is shown in Figure 8.9. A dot plot is shown in Figure 8.10.

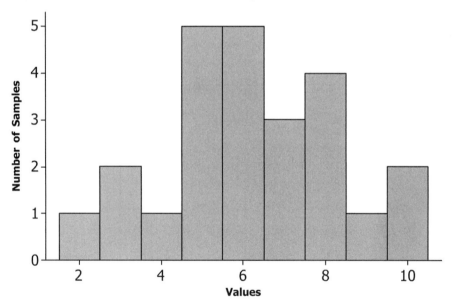

Figure 8.9: Histogram of the data.

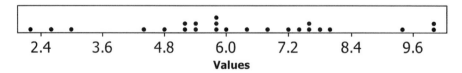

Figure 8.10: Dot plot of the data.

8.10 Sample Statistics (Mean, Range, Standard Deviation, and Median)

A well-known statistic for a sample is the mean $(\overline{x})$. The mean is the arithmetic average of the data values $(x_1, x_2, x_3, ..., x_i)$, which is mathematically expressed in the following equation using a summation sign Σ for sample size (n) as:

$$\overline{x} = \frac{\sum\limits_{i=1}^{n} x_i}{n}$$

A sample provides an estimate $\overline{x}$ for the true mean of a population μ from which the sample is randomly drawn. Consider, for example, the time it takes to respond to a telephone inquiry. Six randomly selected phone conversations were closely monitored, where the duration of the phone conversation was 6, 2, 3, 3, 4, and 5 minutes. An estimate for the mean duration of phone inquiries is:

$$\overline{x} = \frac{6+2+3+3+4+5}{6} = 3.83$$

Range is a statistic that describes data dispersion. It is simply the difference between the highest and lowest value of a set of data. The range for the previous set of data is 4 (i.e., 6–2 = 4). Range values can give a quick assessment of data variability; however, values are dependent upon the sample size and outlier data can give distorted results. A better measure of data variability is standard deviation.

Standard deviation is a statistic that quantifies the data dispersion. A manager would be interested not only in the mean conversation duration but also in conversation length variability. One equation form to determine standard deviation from sampled data is:

$$s = \left[\frac{\sum\limits_{i=1}^{n} (x_i - \overline{x})^2}{n-1} \right]^{1/2}$$

A sample yields an estimate s for the true population standard deviation σ. When data have a bell-shape distribution (i.e., are normally distributed), approximately 68.26% of the data is expected to be within a plus or minus one standard deviation range of the mean. For this example, the standard deviation estimate for the above phone conversation duration is:

$$s = \left[\frac{(6 - 3.83)^2 + ...}{6 - 1} \right]^{1/2} = 1.472$$

It should be noted that the standard deviation of a population when all the data are available is calculated using a denominator term n, not $n-1$. Some calculators offer both standard deviation calculation options. The $n-1$ term in the denominator of the previous equation is commonly called *degrees of freedom*. This term will be used throughout this volume and is assigned the Greek letter v (pronounced nu). The number of degrees of freedom is a function of the sample size and is a tabular input value often needed to make various statistical calculations.

Variance is the square of the standard deviation. Variance is equivalent to moment of inertia, a term encountered in engineering. For this illustration, the sample variance s^2 is:

$$s^2 = 1.472^2 = 2.167$$

The curves shown in Figure 8.11 have a frequency distribution shape that is often encountered when smoothing histogram data. The mathematical model corresponding to the frequency distribution is the probability density function (PDF). Each of these density function curves is bell-shaped and is called a *normal PDF*, where height of the plot is related to probability; i.e., prob(x).

For a given sample size, a smaller standard deviation yields more confidence in data-analysis results. This is pictorially illustrated in Figure 8.11, which shows that case 2 has more variability than case 1, which will cause more uncertainty in any estimated population parameter mean. Calculation of the confidence interval that quantifies this uncertainty will be discussed in later chapters.

The sample median is the number in the middle of all the data. It can be represented as x_{50} or $\bar{x}$. The 50 denotes that 50% of the measurements are lower than the x value. Similarly, x_{30} indicates the 30th percentile. To determine the median of data, the data

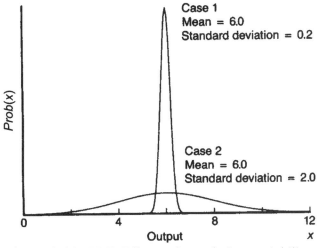

Figure 8.11: PDF: Effects of population variability.

first need to be ranked. For the preceding data set, the median is the mean of the two middle values, because there is an even number of data points, which is

$$2\ 3\ 3\ 4\ 5\ 6 : \text{median} \;=\; \frac{3+4}{2} \;=\; 3.5$$

However, if the data were 1 2 4 5 6, the sample median would be 4, the middle of an odd number of data points.

As described, the mean and median quantify the central tendency of measurements, while the range and standard deviation describe variability of measurements. Throughout this series of volumes, mean and standard deviation metrics will have various applications. For example, we can use these metrics collectively in a process to determine estimates for percentage nonconformance beyond specification limits. Another application is statistical tests for equality of the mean and standard deviation of input parameters (e.g., machines or raw material), which could affect the desirability of a KPOV).

One important point that is often not formally considered is whether the sample is truly from the population of interest. For example, a sample of the first production lots from a supplier can be very different from a random sample of future products that experiences more over-time variability from process settings changes, operator differentiators, and raw material lot-to-lot differences.

8.11   Descriptive Statistics

IEE Application Examples
- *Random sample invoices from last 17 month region of process predictability (See Chapter 12); i.e., days sales outstanding (DSO), where the number of days beyond the due date was measured and reported*
- *Random sample of parts manufactured over the last five months (time when the process changed to an improved level of stability/predictability), where the diameter of the parts was measured and reported*

A tabular output of descriptive statistics calculated from data summarizes information about the data set. The following computer output shows a summary for the 14 samples described in Example 22.1. In this dataset, values designated as x_1, x_2, x_3, ..., x_{14}, were taken from both a current product design and new product design. Lower numbers are better.

Descriptive Statistics

Variable:	n	Mean	Median	TrMean	SD	SE Mean
Current:	14	0.9551	0.8970	0.9424	0.1952	0.0522
New:	14	0.6313	0.6160	0.6199	0.1024	0.0274

Variable:	Minimum	Maximum	Q1	Q3
Current:	0.7370	1.3250	0.7700	1.1453
New:	0.5250	0.8740	0.5403	0.6868

This output has tabular values for the following:

- *Mean*: Arithmetic average of the data values $(x_1, x_2, x_3, ..., x_n)$, which is mathematically expressed in the following equation using a summation sign Σ for sample size (n): $\bar{x} = \sum_{i=1}^{n} x_i / n$

- *Median*: The data of n observations are ordered from smallest to largest. For an odd sample size, median is the ordered value at $(n+1)/2$. For an even sample size, median is the mean of the two middle ordered values.

- *TrMean (trimmed mean)*: Average of the values remaining after both 5% of the largest and smallest values, rounded to the nearest integer, are removed.
- *Standard deviation*: Sample standard deviation of data, which can be mathematically expressed as $\sqrt{\sum(x - \bar{x})^2/(n-1)}$
- *SE mean (standard error of mean)*: $StDev/\sqrt{n}$.
- *Minimum*: Lowest number in data set.
- *Maximum*: Largest number in data set.
- *Q1 and Q3*: The data of n observations are ordered from smallest to largest. The observation at position $(n + 1)/4$ is the first quartile (Q1). The observation at position $3(n + 1)/4$ is the third quartile (Q3).

8.12 Pareto Charts

The Pareto principle states that 80% of the trouble comes from 20% of the problems, i.e., the vital few problems. A Pareto chart is a graphical technique used to quantify problems so that effort can be expended in fixing the "vital few" causes, as opposed to the "trivial many." The chart is named after Vilfredo Pareto (born, 1848), an Italian economist.

A procedure to construct a Pareto chart is as follows:

1. Define the problem and process characteristics to use in the diagram.
2. Define the period of time for the diagram. This time period can be a region of predictability in an attribute 30,000-foot-level control chart, which can be much better than creating a stacked Pareto bar chart that tracks over time defect types by week or day. A stacked Pareto bar chart often leads to firefighting the current problems without getting to a root cause correction so that the defect type is less likely to occur in the future.
3. Total the number of times each characteristic occurred.
4. Rank the characteristics according to the totals from step 3.
5. Plot the number of occurrences of each characteristic in descending order in a bar graph form along with a cumulative plot of the magnitudes from the bars. Some-

times, however, Pareto charts do not have a cumulative percentage overlay.

6. Trivial columns can be lumped under one column designation; however, care must be exercised not to forget a small but important item.

Much insight can often be gained for process improvement opportunities by displaying a Pareto chart of the total number of each defect-category occurrence in the latest predictability region of an attribute 30,000-foot-level control chart. From this categorization, much benefit can be gained through quality improvements efforts by creating and executing a project that targets the defect type that provides the most opportunity for overall process improvement; i.e., a pull for project creation.

Pareto chart can consider data from different perspectives. For example, a Pareto chart of defects by machine may not be informative, while a Pareto chart of defects by manufacturing shifts could illustrate a problem source. Figures 8.12, 13.15, 32.2, and 33.6 illustrate Pareto chart usage.

Pareto charts are also useful in other situations such as time pacing, which is the undertaking of events such as new product introduction, factory re-layout, or regular interval staff training (Bicheno, 2004). In timing pacing, a product quantity analysis would have the following two Pareto charts: value of products sold by product type and number of products manufactured by product type. In timing pacing, a contribution analysis would have the following two Pareto charts: total TOC throughput by product type and unit TOC throughput per bottleneck minute by product type.

Care must be exercised when using a Pareto chart to identify where focus efforts should target. A Pareto bar might appear taller than other bars simply by chance. A statistical significance test is useful in conjunction with a Pareto chart to determine if bar-height differences are statistically significant.

8.13   Example 8.4: Improving a Process that has Defects

As noted earlier, process control charts are useful to monitor the process stability and identify the point at which special cause situations occur. A process is generally considered to be in control/

predictable whenever it is sampled periodically and the measurements from the samples are within the UCL and LCL, which are positioned around a centerline (CL). Note that these control limits are independent of any specification limits.

Consider that the final test of a complex printed circuit-board assembly in a manufacturing facility yielded the fraction nonconforming control chart shown in Figure 8.12 (See Chapter 13 for the creation of this type of control chart). This chart, which describes the output of this process, could also be presented in percent nonconforming units. A run chart without control limits could cause the organization to react to the individual ups and down of the chart as special cause.

In addition, organizations can react to limited data and draw erroneous conclusions. Consider at what conclusion an organization might arrive after collecting only the first four points on the chart if the x-axis and y-axis data were considered continuous. Someone might conclude from a time-series plot that the downward trend was significant with this limited data. However, further analyses could indicate that there was not enough information to reject a zero slope null hypothesis (see Chapter 25).

In the process control chart it is noted that sample number 1 had a defect rate approximately equal to 0.18, while overall mean defect rate was 0.244. This process is in control/predictable; i.e., no special causes are noted. However, the defect rate needs to be reduced so that there will be less rework and scrap; i.e., reduce the magnitude of common causes. A team was then formed. The team noted the following types of production defects for the 3200 manufactured printed circuit boards (Messina, 1987):

440	Insufficient solder
120	Blow holes
80	Unwetted
64	Unsoldered
56	Pinholes
40	Shorts
800	

From the Pareto chart of the solder defects shown in Figure 8.12, it becomes obvious that focus should first be given to the insufficient solder characteristic. A brainstorming session with experts in the field, i.e., engineers, technicians, manufacturing workers, chemists, management, etc., could then be conducted to create a cause-and-effect diagram for the purpose of identifying

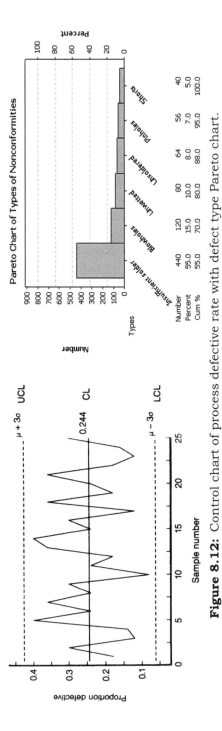

Figure 8.12: Control chart of process defective rate with defect type Pareto chart.

the most likely sources of the defects. Regression analysis followed by a DOE might then be most appropriate to determine which of the factors has the most impact on the defect rate. This group of technical individuals can perhaps also determine a continuous data response to use in addition to or in lieu of the preceding attribute response consideration. One can expect that a continuous data response output would require a much smaller sample size.

After changes are made to the process and improvements are demonstrated on the control charts, a new Pareto chart can then be created. Perhaps the improvements will be large enough to the insufficient solder characteristic that blow holes may now be the largest of the vital few to be attacked next. Process control charts could also be used to track insufficient solder individually so that process degradation from the fix level can be identified quickly.

Changes should then be made to the manufacturing process after a confirmation experiment verifies the changes suggested by the experiments. The data pattern of the control chart should now shift downward in time to another region of stability. As part of a continuing process improvement program, the preceding steps can be repeated to identify other areas to improve.

8.14 Population Distribution: Continuous Response

A histogram or dot plot process-output representation and its statistics can be useful; however, often a more structured approach is needed to characterize how well a process is performing relative to customer needs. To make this estimate, a population distribution model is needed.

When a PDF indicates that a normal, Weibull, or lognormal distribution is an adequate fit (described later in this chapter), nonconformance percentages can be directly estimated relative to customer needs. These modeling distributions are sometimes referenced as parent distributions. Child distributions will be discussed in the hypothesis test chapter of this volume.

For an independent variable x, the height of a PDF curve relates to the probability of an occurrence x or $p(x)$. The mathematical nomenclature for PDF is $f(x)$, which has an equation format that is dependent upon the distribution type.

The nomenclature for a cumulative probability density function is CDF, which has a mathematical nomenclature of $F(x)$. The CDF cumulates probability as a function of x. The equation format for this accumulation is again dependent upon distribution type.

8.15 Normal Distribution

The normal distribution is a frequently encountered PDF. This distribution is characterized by the bell-shaped Gaussian curve. The normal distribution is a model that can be used to describe the common cause response of many processes.

The following two scenarios exemplify data that follow a normal distribution:

1. A dimension on a part is critical. This critical dimension is measured daily on a random sample of parts from a large production process. The measurements on any given day are noted to follow a normal distribution.
2. A customer orders a product. The time it takes to fill the order was noted to follow a normal distribution.

Figure 8.13 illustrates the characteristic bell shape of the normal PDF, while Figure 8.14 shows the corresponding S shape of the normal cumulative distribution function (CDF).

The normal PDF is

$$f(x) = \frac{1}{\sigma\sqrt{2\pi}} \exp\left[-\frac{(x - \mu)^2}{2\sigma^2}\right] \quad -\infty \leq x \leq +\infty$$

where μ = mean and σ = standard deviation. The CDF is

$$F(x) = \int_{-\infty}^{x} \frac{1}{\sigma\sqrt{2\pi}} \exp\left[-\frac{(x - \mu)^2}{2\sigma^2}\right] dx$$

The reason that these relationships are now included in this volume is to mathematically illustrate the relationship of $f(x)$ and $F(x)$. Values from distributions can easily be determined from tables or computer programs. Later in this volume, I will present distribution equations only when the relationships are simple to calculate; e.g., Weibull. Breyfogle (2003a) includes the mathematical relationships for distributions described in this volume.

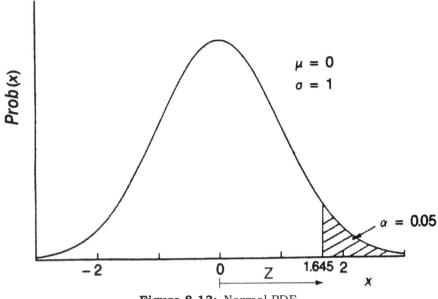

Figure 8.13: Normal PDF.

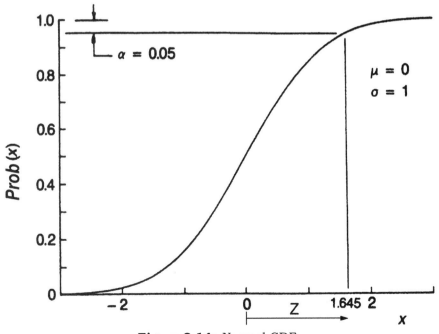

Figure 8.14: Normal CDF.

These curves were generated for $\mu = 0$ and $\sigma = 1$. The area shown under the PDF corresponds to the ordinate value of the CDF. Any normal X variable governed by $X{\sim}N(\mu;\ \sigma^2)$, a short-hand notation for a normally distributed random variable x with mean μ and variance σ^2, can be converted into variable $Z \sim N(0; 1)$ using the relationship:

$$Z = \frac{X - \mu}{\sigma}$$

CDF is dependent only on the mean μ and standard deviation σ. A commonly applied characteristic of the normal distribution is the relationship of percent of population to the standard deviation. Figure 8.15 pictorially quantifies the percent of population as a function of standard deviation.

Areas under this standardized normal curve are shown in Tables A, B, and C in the Appendix G. To illustrate conceptually the origin of these tables, the reader can note from Table B that $U_\alpha = U_{0.05} = 1.645$, which is the area shaded in Figure 8.13. Also the quantity for U_α is noted to equal the double-sided value in Table C when $\alpha = 0.10$; i.e., the single-sided probability is multiplied by 2. In

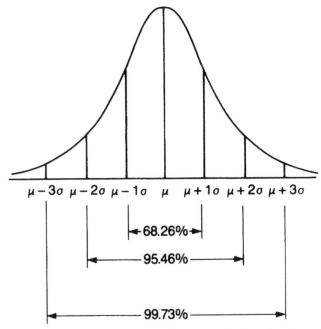

Figure 8.15: Properties of a normal distribution.

addition, the single-sided value equates to the value that can be determined from Table A for $Z_\alpha = Z_{0.05}$; i.e., a more typical table format.

As an additional point to illustrate the preceding concept, the reader can also note that the 2σ value of 95.46% from Figure 8.13 equates to a double-tail (α) area of approximately 0.05; i.e., $(100-95.46)/100 \approx 0.05$. For an $\alpha = 0.05$, Table C yields a value of 1.960, which equates approximately to the σ value of 2.0 shown in Figure 8.13; i.e., $\pm 2\sigma$ contains approximately 95% of the population.

The importance of this to the reader is that we would expect 68.26% of observations to all within $\pm 1\sigma$ of the mean, μ; 95% within $\pm 2\sigma$, and so on. There is always a probability that observations will fall outside these limits.

As a side note, most books consider only one type of table for each distribution. The other table forms were included in this book so that the practitioner can more readily understand single- and double-tail probability relationships and determine the correct tabular value to use when solving the types of problems addressed later.

The reader should be aware of the methods that a book or computer program uses to compute a Z statistic. The area for a Z value is sometimes computed from the center of the distribution.

8.16   Example 8.5: Normal Distribution

The number of emails received in one day may be characterized as:

- *Shape*: mound shaped (most observations clustered near the center)
- *Center*: μ = 50 emails (population mean)
- *Spread*: σ = 10 emails (standard deviation)

The proportion of days for which there are 57 or more emails can be mathematically expressed as $P(X \geq 57)$. The Z value for determining this probability is:

$$Z = \frac{X - \mu}{\sigma} = \frac{57 - 50}{10} = 0.7$$

Table A yields $P(X \geq 57) = P(Z \geq 0.7) = 0.2420$, i.e., 24.20%.

Many computer statistical programs provide a function that would yield a similar result.

8.17   Probability Plotting

Percent characteristics of a population can be determined from the cumulative distribution function, CDF, which is the integration of the probability density function, PDF. Probability plots are useful in visually assessing how well data follow distributions and in estimating from data the unknown parameters of a PDF/CDF. These plots can also be used to estimate the percent less than (or greater than) a population criteria; e.g., nonconformance beyond specification limits.

A basic concept behind probability plotting is that if data plotted on a probability distribution scale follow a straight line, then the population from which the samples are drawn can be represented by that distribution. After a process response distribution is identified, statements can be made about percentage values of the population, which can often be more enlightening than the mean and standard deviation statistics.

There are many different types of probability coordinate systems to address data from differing distributions; e.g., normal PDF lognormal or Weibull PDF. Some computer programs can generate probability plots conveniently and yield precise parameter estimations. However, manual plots can also be generated using probability paper (see Breyfogle, 2003a). This series of volumes contains only computer-generated probability plots.

When creating a histogram, data are grouped into intervals. A PDF can describe the shape of a histogram, in which the area under the PDF is equal to 100% of the population. The median of the variable described by a PDF, for example, is the value where the area under the curve is split 50/50; i.e., 50% of the population is less than or greater than the median value. Other percentiles of population values can similarly be determined; however, because this percentage value is the area under a curve, it is difficult to get an accurate value for any given value of the variable on the abscissa of a PDF.

As noted earlier, the PDF is integrated to yield the CDF, which graphically yields population percentile (less than or greater than) values on one axis of the plot. However, drawing a line through test data to determine population characteristics is not accurate because the data do not typically follow a straight line on commonly used x–y coordinates; e.g., linear and lognormal.

A probability plot addresses this nonlinear plotting phenomenon through the transformation of the axes so that a particular CDF shape will appear as a straight line. The data are adequately fit by that distribution.

8.18   Interpretation of Probability Plots

One axis of the probability plot is the percentage or proportion of the population, while the other axis is the metric response. For example, a straight line on a probability plot intersecting a point having the coordinates 30% (less than) and 2.2 can be read as "30% of the population is estimated to have values equal to or less than 2.2." Note that this could mean that 30% of the devices exhibit failure before a usage of 2.2 or that a measurement is expected to be less than 2.2 for 30% of the time.

Probability plots have many distribution alternatives. If a distribution is not known, data can be plotted on different coordinate systems in an attempt to find the probability distribution that best fits the data. This series of volumes will only illustrate computer-generated probability plots; however, manual plots are an alternative (Breyfogle, 2003a).

Probability plots have many applications. These plots are an excellent tool to gain better insight into what may be happening physically in a process. A probability plot tells a story. For example, a straight line indicates that a particular distribution may adequately represent a population, while a "knee" can indicate that the data are from two (or more) distributions. One data point that deviates significantly from an otherwise straight line on a probability plot could be an outlier that is caused, for example, by an erroneous reading.

8.19   Example 8.6: PDF, CDF, and then a Probability Plot

Consider that a population had a specification of 6 ± 2. The following twenty-five random samples from the population were ranked low to high:

3.8 4.6 4.6 4.9 5.2 5.3 5.3 5.4 5.6 5.6 5.7 5.8 5.9
6.0 6.1 6.1 6.3 6.3 6.4 6.5 6.6 6.8 7.0 7.4 7.6

In these data there is, for example, one output response between 3.6 and 4.5, while there are seven between 4.6 and 5.5. These ranked values can be grouped into cells as shown in Table 8.2 and then be plotted to create the histogram shown in Figure 8.16. These measurements form a bell-shaped PDF that is characteristic of a normal distribution. Figure 8.17 illustrates an integration plot of the data, which yields the characteristic S-shaped curve of the normal CDF.

We would now like to determine the estimated percentage beyond specification limits. This is difficult to accomplish using a histogram or cumulative distribution plot. Having percentage less than values on the y-axis, as is done in the CDF, is beneficial; however the y-axis coordinate system needs an appropriate transformation if plotted data from a distribution are to follow a straight line.

This is what probability paper (see Breyfogle, 2003a) and computer-generated probability plots can provide. That is, probability paper and computer-generated plots adjust the percentage less than coordinate system so that, if data are from that distribution, plotted data follow a straight line.

For the purpose of probability plot understanding, let's consider the plotting of data on a probability plot, understanding that computer statistical software will do this automatically. As with any coordinate-system plot we need to have both an x-axis and y-axis value. However, with sampled data from a distribution we have only one data point. What is needs is the pairing up of each datum point with a percent less value. Table H provides values for

Table 8.2: Data Groupings

Response	Test Data[a] (number of items)	Test Data[b] Integration (number of items less than or equal to a value)
3.6–4.5	1	1
4.6–5.5	7	8
5.6–6.5	12	20
6.6–7.5	4	24
7.6–8.5	1	25

[a] For Figure 8.16
[b] For Figure 8.17

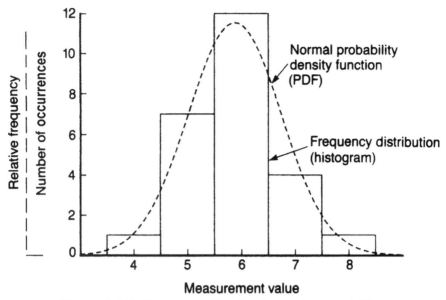

Figure 8.16: Frequency distribution and normal PDF.

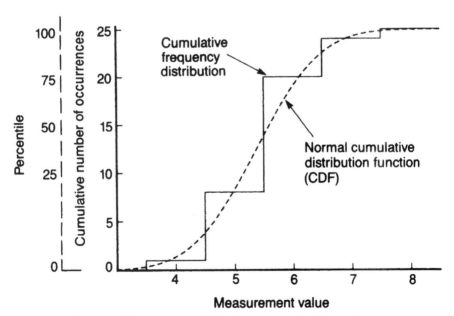

Figure 8.17: Cumulative frequency distribution.

ranked low-to-high sampled data pairing, where the sample size varies between one and twenty-six. From this table the pairing for this example would be:

Data point:	3.8	4.6	4.6	4.9	5.2	5.3	5.3	5.4	5.6	5.6
Plot position:	2.0	6.0	10.0	14.0	18.0	22.0	26.0	30.0	34.0	38.0

Data point:	5.7	5.8	5.9	6.0	6.1	6.1	6.3	6.3	6.4	6.5
Plot position:	42.0	46.0	50.0	54.0	58.0	62.0	66.0	70.0	74.0	78.0

Data point:	6.6	6.8	7.0	7.4	7.6
Plot position:	82.0	86.0	90.0	94.0	98.0

The P value this plot tests the null hypothesis that the data are from the distribution plotted. Hypothesis testing will be covered later in this volume; however, since the reported P value not equal to or less than 0.05, we for now will simply state that we have no reason to believe that the data are not from a normal distribution.

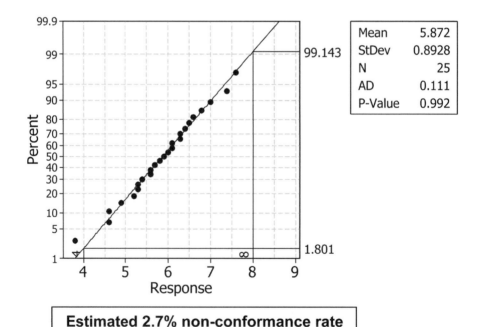

Estimated 2.7% non-conformance rate

Figure 8.18: Normal probability plot of the measurement response, showing the best percentage estimates for the sampled population non-conformance.

From Figure 8.18, we note that the data fit well to a normal distribution since the data follow a straight line and there is a best-estimate nonconformance rate of 2.7% [Rounded value from (100–99.143) + 1.801 = 2.658]. Since this estimate is from an extrapolation, we would like more data to provide a better estimate and ensure that nothing different occurs relative to the distribution shape near the tolerance boundaries.

Because a normal distribution plot was used to make this determination, a similar answer could have been determined by using the previously described z statistic. The determined nonconformance percentages may be slightly different, since the population mean and standard deviation from a probability plot is typically determined using a different procedure; e.g., maximum likelihood estimates. However, unlike the z statistic method, the above probability plot procedure has easy-to-use flexibility beyond the normal distribution.

The probability plot can also offer easy-to-understand insight to the overall expected response of the process when there are no specifications. In IEE, we often express the process capability/ performance metric for these process-response situations as an estimated median response and 80% frequency of occurrence, as illustrated in Figure 8.19.

8.20   Probability Plotting Censored Data

Consider an evaluation in which components were to be tested to failure, however, some of the samples had not yet experienced a failure at test termination time. Only measured data such as failure times can be plotted on a probability plot. Individual censored datum points, i.e., times when components were removed from test without failure cannot be plotted. When there are censored data, these data affect the percentage value plot considerations of the uncensored data. Data entry into a statistical analysis program describes this censoring. Statistical analysis programs then use an algorithm to adjust the plot positions that were described in the previous section using Table H. Breyfogle (2003a) provides censored data application illustrations.

8.21   Weibull and Exponential Distribution

As illustrated in Figure 8.20, the Weibull distribution has shape flexibility; hence, this distribution can be used to fit many types

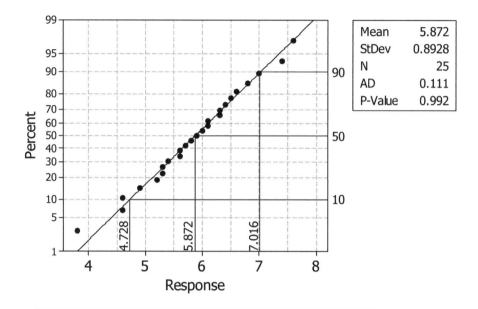

Figure 8.19: Normal probability plot of the measurement response, showing the best estimate for the median response and 80% frequency of occurrence.

of data. The shape parameter (*b*) in the Weibull equation defines the PDF shape. If the plotted response is time to failure for a non-repairable device, *b* = 1 equates to a constant failure rate over time, *b* > 1 indicates a wear-out mode, and *b* < 1 indicates early-life failures.

Another parameter is *k* (scale parameter or characteristic life), which describes conceptually the magnitude of the *x*-axis scale. The *k* scale parameter equates to the 63.2% less than value of the plot (see Breyfogle, 2003a). The exponential distribution is a special case of the Weibull distribution where *b* equates to one and *k* is the mean of the distribution.

The other parameter contained in the three-parameter model is the location parameter (x_0), which is the *x*-axis intercept equating to the value where there is zero probability of lesser values.

When x_0 equals zero, the proportion of failures $F(x)$ at a certain time reduces to simply

$$F(x) = 1 - \exp\left[-\left(\frac{x}{k}\right)^b\right]$$

At one extreme, the two-parameter Weibull distribution asymptotically approaches zero. A third parameter in the three-parameter Weibull distribution describes an alternative asymptotic boundary. The 2-parameter Weibull distribution is very useful in describing component reliability characteristics since the shape parameter property of the Weibull distribution describes the failure rate characteristic of the component; i.e., early life, constant failure rate, and wear-out mode (see Breyfogle, 2003a).

8.22   Lognormal Distribution

Like the Weibull distribution, the lognormal distribution exhibits many PDF shapes, as illustrated in Figure 8.21. This distribution is often useful in the analysis of economic, dimensional, and cycle-time data where there is a natural lower boundary.

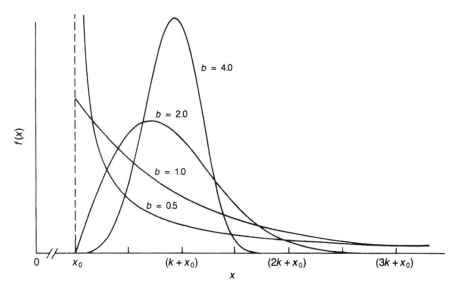

Figure 8.20: Weibull PDF.

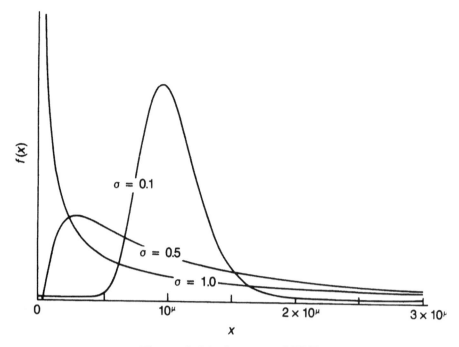

Figure 8.21: Lognormal PDF.

The logarithm of data from this distribution is normally distributed; hence, with this transformation, data can be analyzed as if they came from a normal distribution.

The tails of the normal distribution asymptotically approach zero at plus and minus infinity. The two-parameter lognormal distribution is very useful in describing situations that asymptotically approach a lower boundary of zero. The third parameter in a three-parameter lognormal distribution offers the flexibility of having an asymptotic boundary that is not zero.

8.23   Example 8.7: Comparing Distributions

The following data were randomly generated from a lognormal distribution. Figure 8.22 shows the data distribution identification plot with a 95% plotted confidence interval for percent of population.

11.8872	0.3486	0.1610	5.3783	0.9413	1.9138
0.7113	2.9990	2.5720	2.4191	1.7611	3.36390

0.9349	0.1613	2.2085	0.2602	1.1408	0.4859
2.8852	1.9183	0.2045	1.1757	12.2797	0.1873
0.3752	4.1532	1.4062	0.5663	2.6464	1.0056

When comparing distributions for data fit, the lowest Anderson-Darling (AD) statistic value is used to indicate the best mathematical fit; i.e., lognormal distribution in this case. However, the selected distribution needs also to make sense for the modeled process. Something else to look for is whether the *P* value is not smaller than the desired hypothesis test cut-off. However, we need also to examine visually how well the probability plot fits the data. Much can be gained from this examination.

A process which is by nature lognormal distributed can have what appear to be outliers or special-cause conditions in an individuals control chart (will later be described in control chart chapters), if the data were only analyzed as though it was from a normal distribution. This phenomenon can be observed in this figure's normal probability plot where two points are significantly removed to the right from a straight-line fit. A lognormal distribution is often a good fit when data have a natural boundary such as zero; e.g., duration of hold time in a call center.

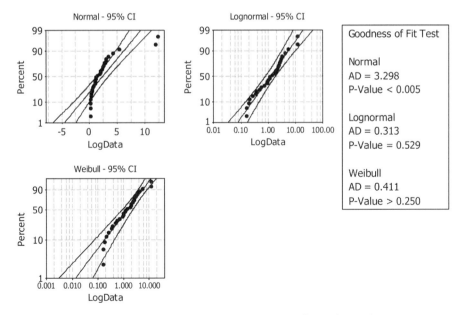

Figure 8.22: Comparing distribution data fits where data were randomly generated from a lognormal distribution.

8.24   Distribution Applications and Approximations

The next chapter discusses distribution applications and approximations for both continuous- and attribute-response distributions.

8.25   Applying IEE

It is important that management ask questions encouraging the collection and analyses of data so that much can be gained from the efforts of employees. If care is not exercised, a practitioner may simply collect data, compile the data using traditional statistical techniques, and then report the results in a form that leads to firefighting or one-at-a-time fix attempts. For example, the direction of management might lead an experimenter to collect data and make a report with no suggestions on what steps should be taken to improve unfavorable results.

When unfavorable results exist, there are many other issues that should be considered. These issues can be more important to consider than the simple reporting of the results from randomly collected data. Unfortunately, these issues can involve how the data are initially collected. Many resources can be wasted if forethought is not given to the best approach to take when working to resolve an unsatisfactory situation.

For example, understanding the source of the variability in measurements may be more beneficial. A random effects model or variance components analysis (see Chapter 24) could be used in an experiment design having such considerations. Or perhaps there should be an emphasis on understanding what factors affect the mean experimental output.

A high-level view, e.g., daily defect rate, might help us see that most of our day-to-day problems are common causes. With this knowledge, we can then create a team that leads the effort toward quantifiable results. At a lower-level view, perhaps temperature was identified through DOE to be a key process input variable (KPIV). When temperature transitions to an unacceptable level (See pre-control charts in Chapter 38), the process should be shut down for problem resolution immediately before many poor-quality production parts are manufactured.

For a given situation, defining the best problem to solve and convincing others that this is the best problem to solve can be much more difficult than the analytical portion of the problem. It is hoped that the described examples can be used as a model to help define and convince others of the best problem to solve for a specific situation.

8.26 Exercises

1. Describe a situation in which you or your organization exhibits variability.
2. Determine the mean, standard deviation, variance, median, and number of degrees of freedom for the following sampled sequential data: 9.46, 10.61, 8.07, 12.21, 9.02, 8.99 10.03, 11.73, 10.99, 10.56.
3. Manually calculate the mean, standard deviation, variance, and median of the following four data sets. Comment on the results.

(a)	100	100	100	100	100
(b)	50	75	100	125	150
(c)	50	100	100	100	150
(d)	75	75	75	100	175

4. Describe the source of measurement variability of a manufactured plastic part if the parts were made from a multi-cavity tool and there were many injecting molding machines.
5. A potential functional problem exists with machines that are stored in a large warehouse, where the shipping boxes are stacked high and packed close together. Management wants to collect a test sample of the product to assess the problem's magnitude. Describe a major physical problem with implementing the task.
6. Describe the type of product variability, i.e., common or special cause, which is consistent but at an undesirable high level of 10%.
7. Describe a situation in which a process exhibits a special cause problem.
8. Over time, a process has experienced consistent variability, but a larger amount than desired. Should management be told that the process is out of control? Explain.
9. A new operator did not completely understand his job tasks in manufacturing. The first day of employment he made more mistakes than other first-day operators who per-

formed a similar task. Describe the type of cause for recent problems in this process.

10. Describe the type of reporting problem that exists when a reporter gives a reason at the end of each day as to why the stock market either went up or down.

11. For the data set shown determine the overall sample mean and standard deviation. Determine also the sample mean and standard deviation for each of the machines. Comment on results:

Response	Machine	Response	Machine
109.4	A	126.12	A
83.03	A	119.45	B
120.75	B	84.65	A
89.2	A	102.22	A
121.26	A	135.68	B
121.47	B	98.47	A
85.77	A	116.39	A
84.22	A	118.55	B
111.3	B	103.39	A
99.7	A	89.52	A
135.74	A	101.22	B
151.01	B	107.78	A
135.18	A	119.43	A
130.88	A	78.53	A
108.8	B	84.47	A
120.56	A	106.84	A

12. Given a normally distributed population with mean 225 and standard deviation 35. Determine the value where the probability is .90 being less than the value.

13. Given that the following data were selected from a lognormal distribution, determine the value where the probability is 0.20 of being less than this value.

    1.64, 1.31, 5.52, 4.24, 3.11, 8.46, and 3.42

14. Given an exponentially distributed population with mean 216.24. Determine the probability of a randomly selected item having a value between 461.1 and 485.8.

15. Determine the probability that a randomly selected item from a population having a Weibull distribution with shape parameter of 1.6 and a scale parameter of 117.1 has a value between 98.1 and 99.8.

16. Consider that the 31 observations shown below were a random sample from a population. Determine the estimated 80% frequency of occurrence range. Determine the estimated proportion below a lower specification limit of 120 and an upper specification limit of 150.

141.9   124.8 131.7 126.5 129.0 136.0 134.3 144.9
140.5   134.1 137.0 147.1 126.6 155.5 133.4 120.7
138.8   125.0 133.0 142.4 146.0 137.4 120.8 145.2
125.0   127.0 118.3 137.1 136.5 105.8 136.9

17. Consider that the 48 observations shown below were a random sample from a population. Determine the estimate for 80% frequency of occurrence range. Determine the expected proportion below a lower specification limit of 95 and an upper specification limit of 130.

125.3   100.9 90.5   106.0 117.8 100.5 100.0 126.3
106.9   110.2 101.0 115.7 108.8 93.4   121.2 115.3
108.9   126.9 107.2 114.0 111.3 101.8 117.2 105.2
109.4   123.7 102.8 118.9 127.8 114.3 113.9 112.3
109.8   103.1 105.6 97.0   105.2 111.3 97.2   105.8
121.5   101.1 103.7 94.2   109.5 116.9 105.9 125.2

18. Create a probability plot of the overall data shown in Exercise 8.11. Create also probability plots of the data for each machine. Comment on results.

19. The diameter of a shaft has m μ = 75 mm with a standard deviation of σ = 8 mm. Determine the proportion of the population of bushings that has a diameter less than 65 mm.

20. Determine the proportion of the population described in the previous exercise that has a diameter between 55 mm and 95 mm.

21. Consider a situation where a response equal to or greater than 12.5 was undesirable. The collection of data was very expensive and time-consuming; however, a team was able to collect the following set of random measurements: 9.46, 10.61, 8.07, 12.21, 9.02, 8.99, 10.03, 11.73, 10.99, and 10.56.

    (a) Conduct an attribute assessment; i.e., state whether all measurements are in specification or not.

    (b) Make a visual assessment of data normality using a histogram. From the plot, estimate the mean and percentage of time the response is estimated to be 12.5 or larger.

(c) Make a visual assessment of data normality using a normal probability plot. From this plot, estimate the median and percentage of time 12.5 or larger. Estimate the response level where 10% is below. Estimate the response level that 10% of the population does not exceed. Estimate the range of response exhibited by 80%; i.e. ± 40% from the median, of the population.

(d) Use the Z table, i.e., Table A, to refine these estimates from part c of this exercise.

22. List the important parameters for each of the following: Normal distribution (e.g., mean and standard deviation), exponential distribution, two-parameter Weibull distribution, and lognormal distribution.

23. Describe a business process application of a normal probability plot that can improve the explanation and understanding of a process output; e.g., 80% of invoice payments are between 5 and 120 days delinquent.

24. Collect and compile data from your work/personal life for analysis by a statistical program. The response is to be continuous with time-series reporting. Key process input levels are to be noted for each response output. For each entry include both continuous and discrete input levels.

(a) Document your continuous output variable.

(b) Document your discrete input variable(s).

(c) Document your continuous input variables(s).

9

Attribute Response Statistics

This is the second of four chapters that describe the foundation for the creation of IEE performance and project metrics; i.e., the project's baseline. The last chapter described the background for describing a continuous response population's characteristics. This chapter extends the previous chapter content to attribute response statistics.

Suppose a one hundred transaction sample from a process experienced two transaction failures. The question of concern is how you feel reporting to management that the process will deliver a *defective rate* that is no more than 3%. This *defective* transaction failure rate question can be addressed using a binomial distribution.

Consider that a transaction in the above illustration can experience *more* than one failure and the total number of failures from the one hundred samples is reported. The question of concern could then be changed to how you feel reporting to management that the process will deliver a *defect rate* that is no more than 3%. This *defect* transaction failure rate question can be addressed using a Poisson distribution.

Background is provided for describing an attribute-response population's characteristics. These techniques are applicable to both project-response base-lining and enterprise satellite-level/ 30,000-foot-level scorecard/dashboard metrics.

This chapter describes the binomial and Poisson distribution. The binomial distribution is used to describe an attribute pass/ fail response that is analogous to a flip of the coin (one chance in two of passing) or a roll of a die (one chance in six of rolling a particular number). The Poisson distribution can address count data for example, multiple defects that can occur on one sample.

Again, defective response data can be modeled using the binomial distribution, while defect response data can be modeled using the Poisson distribution.

9.1   Attribute versus Continuous Data Response

The data discussed in the previous chapter were continuous, or variable, data. Continuous data can assume a range of numerical responses on a continuous scale, as opposed to data that can assume only discrete levels, whereas attribute data have the presence or absence of some characteristic in each device under test; for example, proportion nonconforming in a pass/fail test.

An example of continuous data is the micrometer readings of a sample of parts. Still another example of attribute data is the output of an inspection process in which parts are either passed or failed (as opposed to measuring and recording the dimension of the part). Another example of attribute data is the number of defects on a part recorded by an inspector.

Percentage can be either continuous or attribute based on the numerator and denominator of the percent calculation being either attribute or continuous; for example, percent profit is continuous but percent defective is attribute. One should strive for continuous data information over attribute information whenever possible, since continuous data provides more information using a smaller sample size. Deployments that focus on having a ppm and DPMO metric for all projects can lose site of this because these measurements are attribute.

9.2   Visual Inspections

Visual inspections still often remain a very large single form of inspection activity to determine if a product is satisfactory; that is an attribute pass/fail response. However, characteristics often do not completely describe what is needed, and inspectors need to make their own judgment. When inspections are required, standards need to be set up so that consistent decisions are made. The general consensus is that visual inspections are no more than 80% effective.

Another problem that can occur is that a visual inspection does not address the real desires of the customer. A classified defect found within a manufacturing organization may or may not be a typical customer issue. Also, there can be issues that a customer thinks are important which are not considered by the test.

Visual inspections often lead to the thinking that quality can be inspected into a product. This can be a very expensive approach. In addition, people typically believe that a test does better at capturing defects than it really does. An exercise at the end of this chapter and also the measurement systems analysis chapter (Chapter 15) illustrates the typical ineffectiveness of these tests.

Whether the inspections are visual or not, the frequency of defects and types of defects need to be communicated to the appropriate area for process improvement considerations. The later described techniques can improve the effectiveness of these tests and reduce the frequency of when they are needed.

9.3 Binomial Distribution

As noted earlier, a binomial distribution is useful for attribute data when there are only two possible response outputs; that is pass or failure, compliance or noncompliance, yes or no, present or absent. Altering a previously discussed normal distribution scenario to a binomial distribution scenario yields the following:

A dimension on a part is critical. This critical dimension is measured daily on a random sample of parts from a large production process. To expedite the inspection process, a tool is designed to either pass or fail a part that is tested. The output now is no longer continuous. The output is now binary; pass or fail for each part; hence, the binomial distribution can be used to develop an attribute sampling plan.

Other application examples are:

- Product either passes or fails test; determine the number of defective units.

- Light bulbs work or do not work; determine the number of defective light bulbs.
- People respond yes or no to a survey question; determine the proportion of people who answer yes to the question.
- Purchase order forms are filled out either incorrectly or correctly; determine the number of transactional errors.
- The appearance of a car door is acceptable or unacceptable; determine the number of parts of unacceptable appearance.

The following binomial equation could be expressed using either of the following two expressions:

- The probability of exactly x defects in n binomial trials with probability of defect equal to p is (see $P(X=x)$ relationship).
- For a random experiment of sample size n in which there are two categories of events, the probability of success of the condition x in one category, while there is $n-x$ in the other category, is:

$$P(X = x) = \binom{n}{x} p^x (q)^{n-x} \quad x = 0, 1, 2, \ldots, n$$

where $(q = 1 - p)$ is the probability that the event will not occur. Also, the binomial coefficient gives the number of possible combinations respect to the number of occurrences, which equates to

$$\binom{n}{x} = {}_nC_x = \frac{n!}{x!(n-x)!}$$

From the binomial equation it is noted that the shape of a binomial distribution is dependent on the sample size (n) and proportion of the population having a characteristic (p); for example, proportion of the population that is not in compliance. For an n of 8 and various P values, that is, 0.1, 0.5, 0.7, and 0.9, Figure 9.1 illustrates these four binomial distributions, for the probability of an occurrence P.

The normal parameter approximation for the binomial is:

$$\bar{x} = p$$
$$s = \sqrt{\frac{p(1-p)}{n}}$$

when $np > 5$ and $n(1-p) > 5$

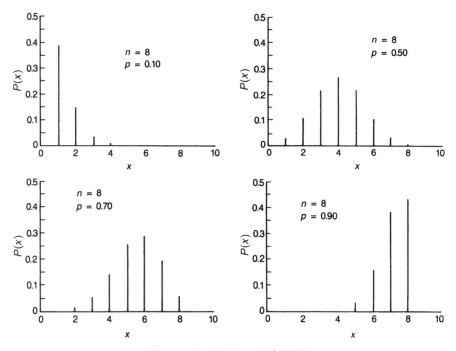

Figure 9.1: Binomial PDF.

When the number of occurrences of the event is zero ($x = 0$), the binomial equation becomes

$$P(X = 0) = \frac{n!}{x!(n-x)!} p^x q^{n-x} = q^n = (1-p)^n$$

9.4 Example 9.1: Binomial Distribution – Number of Combinations and Rolls of Die

The number of possible combinations of three letters from the letters of the word *quality*; (i.e., $n = 7$ and $x = 3$), is

$$_nC_r = \frac{n!}{x!(n-x)!} = \frac{7!}{3! \times 4!} = \frac{7 \times 6 \times 5 \times 4 \times 3 \times 2}{3 \times 2 \times 4 \times 3 \times 2} = 35$$

Consider now that the probability of having the number 2 appear exactly 3 times in 7 rolls of a six sided die is

$$P(X = 3) = \binom{n}{x} p^x (1-p)^{n-x} = (35)(0.167)^3 (1-0.167)^{7-3} = 0.0784$$

where the number 35 was determined previously under a similar set of numeric values, and 0.167 is the probability of a roll of "2" occurring (i.e., 1/6=0.167). Hence, the probability of getting the number 2 to occur exactly three times in seven rolls of a die is 0.0784.

Similarly, we could calculate the probability of 2 occurring for other frequencies besides 3 out of 7. A summary of these probabilities, for example, probability of rolling a 2 one time is 0.390557, is as follows:

$$P(X=0) = 0.278301$$
$$P(X=1) = 0.390557$$
$$P(X=2) = 0.234897$$
$$P(X=3) = 0.078487$$
$$P(X=4) = 0.015735$$
$$P(X=5) = 0.001893$$
$$P(X=6) = 0.000126$$
$$P(X=7) = 3.62E\text{-}06$$

The probabilities from this table sum to one. From this summary, we note that the probability, for example, of rolling the number 2 two, three, four, five, six, or seven times is 0.096245: 0.078487 + 0.015735+0.001893+0.000126+3.62256E-06.

9.5   Example 9.2: Binomial – Probability of Failure

A part is said to be defective if a hole that is drilled into it is less or greater than specifications. A supplier claims a failure rate of 1 in 100. If this failure rate were true, the probability of observing exactly one defective part in 10 samples is:

$$P(X = 1) = \frac{n!}{x!(n - x)!} p^x q^{n-x} = \frac{10!}{1!(10 - 1)!}(0.01)^1 (0.99)^{10-1} = 0.091$$

The probability of having exactly one defect in the test is only 0.091.

This exercise has other implications. An organization might choose a sample of 10 to assess a criterion failure rate of 1 in 100. The effectiveness of this test is questionable because the failure rate of the population would need to be much larger than

1/100 for there to be a good chance of having a defective test sample. That is, the test sample size is not large enough to do an effective job. When making sample size calculations we need to include the chance of having zero failures and other frequencies of failures. The sample size calculations shown in Chapter 21 address this need.

9.6 Hypergeometric Distribution

Use of the hypergeometric distribution in sampling is similar to that of the binomial distribution except that the sample size is large relative to the population size. To illustrate this difference, consider that the first 100 parts of a new manufacturing process were given a pass/fail test in which one part failed. A later chapter shows how a confidence interval for the proportion of defects within a process can be determined given the one failure in a sample of 100. However, in reality the complete population was tested; hence, there is no confidence interval. The experimenter is 100% confident that the failure rate for the population that was sampled, that is, 1/100 is 0.01 for the 100 sampled parts. This illustration considers the extreme situation where the sample size equals the population size. The hypergeometric distribution should be considered whenever the sample size is larger than approximately 10% of the population. Appendix Section B3 in Breyfogle (2003) shows the mathematics of this distribution.

9.7 Poisson Distribution

A random experiment of a discrete variable can have several events and the probability of each event is low. This random experiment can follow the Poisson distribution. The following scenarios exemplify data that can follow a Poisson distribution.

> There are a large number of critical dimensions on a part. Dimensions are measured on a random sample of parts from a large production process. The number of out-of-specification conditions is noted on each sample. This collective number-of-failures information from the samples can often be modeled using a Poisson distribution.

Other application examples are estimating the number of cosmetic nonconformities when painting an automobile, projecting the number of industrial accidents for next year, and estimating the number of un-popped kernels in a batch of popcorn.

The probability of observing exactly x events in the Poisson situation is given by the Poisson PDF:

$$P(X = x) = \frac{e^{-\lambda}\lambda^x}{x!} = \frac{e^{-np}(np)^x}{x!} \quad x = 0, 1, 2, 3, \cdots$$

where e is a constant of 2.71828, x is the number of occurrences, and λ can equate to a sample size multiplied by the probability of occurrence, that is, np.

The probability of observing a or fewer events is

$$P(X \le a) = \sum_{x=0}^{a} P(X = x)$$

The Poisson distribution is dependent only on one parameter, the mean (μ) of the distribution. Figure 9.2 shows Poisson distributions, or the probability of an occurrence P, for the mean values of 1, 5, 8, and 10.

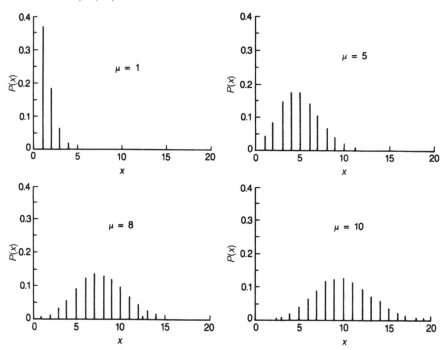

Figure 9.2: Poisson PDF.

9.8 Example 9.3: Poisson Distribution

A company observed that over several years they had a mean manufacturing line shutdown rate of 0.10 per day. Assuming a Poisson distribution, determine the probability of two shutdowns occurring on the same day.

For the Poisson distribution, $\lambda = 0.10$ occurrences/day and $x = 2$ results in the probability

$$P(X = 2) = \frac{e^{-\lambda}\lambda^{x}}{x!} = \frac{e^{-0.1}0.1^{2}}{2!} = 0.004524$$

9.9 Population Distributions: Applications, Approximations, and Normalizing Transformations

The last chapter and this chapter have shown density functions for continuous and attribute responses. Table 9.1 summarizes the application of distributions to a variety of situations.

The equation forms for the discrete distributions (see Breyfogle, 2003a) are rather simple to solve even though they might initially look complex. By knowing the sample size and the percentage of good parts, the mechanics of determining the probability or chance of getting a *bad* or *good* individual sample involves only simple algebraic substitution. Unfortunately, in reality, the percent of good parts is the unknown quantity, which cannot be determined from these equations without using an iterative-solution approach.

An alternative approach to this binomial criterion validation dilemma is the use of another distribution that closely approximates the shape of the binomial distribution. The Poisson distribution is applicable to address not only exponential distribution problems but it can also be used for some binomial problems. The method can be better understood by noting how the binomial distribution shape skews toward the shape of the exponential distribution when the proportion defective (p) is a low number. However, when the proportions of good parts approach 0.5, the normal distribution can be utilized.

Table 9.2 provides some rules of thumb to determine when the preceding approximations can be used, along with determining whether the binomial distribution is applicable in lieu of the hypergeometric distribution.

Table 9.1: Distribution/Process Application Overview

Distribution or Process	Applications	Examples
Normal distribution	Can be used to descriptive various physical, mechanical, electrical, and chemical properties	Part dimensions Voltage outputs Chemical composition level
Binomial Distribution	Can be used to describe the situation where an observation can either pass or fail	Part sampling plan where the part meets or fails to meet a specification criterion
Hypergeometric distribution	Similar to the binomial distribution; however, the sample size is large relative to the population size	Binomial sampling where a sample of 50 is randomly chosen from a population of size 100
Lognormal distribution (two parameter)	Shape flexibility of density function yields an adequate fit to many types of data Normal distribution equations can be used with the logarithm of the original data	Describes repair times of equipment Describes cycle or lead time data when a natural lower limit of 0.0 exists
Lognormal distribution (three parameter)	Shape flexibility of the two parameter distribution with the added flexibility that the zero probability point can take on values that are other than zero	Describes cycle or lead time data when there is a natural lower limit other than zero Deliver times where it must take at least one hour
Weibull distribution (two parameter)	Shape flexibility of density function conveniently describes increasing, constant, and decreasing failure rates as a function of usage (age)	Life of mechanical and electrical components Data which has a natural lower limit of 0.0 exists, such as thickness of metal removed in a grinding operation
Weibull distribution (three parameter)	Shape flexibility of the two parameter distribution with the added flexibility that the zero probability point can take on values that are other than zero	Mechanical part tensile strength The difference in the thickness of metal removed from a target value in a grinding operation.
Exponential distribution	Shape can be used to describe device system failure rates that are constant as a function of usage	MTBF or constant failure rate of a system
Poisson distribution	Convenient distribution to use when designing test that assume that the underlying distribution is exponential	Accidents per week in an intersection, Count of defects found per unit or batch
Homogeneous Poisson Process (HPP)	Model that describes occurrences that happen randomly in time	Modeling of constant system failure rate
Non- Homogeneous Poisson Process (NHPP)	Model that describes occurrences that either decrease or increase in frequency with time	System failure rate modeling when the rate increases or decreases with time

The distributions previously discussed are a few of the many possible alternatives. However, these distributions are, in general, sufficient to solve most industrial engineering problems. An exception to this statement is the multinomial distribution,

Table 9.2: Distribution Approximations

Distribution	Approximate Distribution	Situation
Hypergeometric	Binomial	$10n \leq$ population size (Miller and Freund 1965)
Binomial	Poisson	$n \geq 20$ and $p \leq 0.05$. If $n \geq 100$, the approximation is excellent as long as $np \leq 10$ (Miller and Freund 1965)
Binomial	Normal	np and $n(1 - p)$ are at least 5 (Dixon and Massey 1969)

n = sample size; p proportion (e.g., rate of defective parts)

Table 9.3: Data Normalizing Transformations

Data Characteristics	**Data (x_i) Transformation**
$\alpha \propto$ constant	None
$\sigma \propto \mu^2$	$1/x_i$
$\sigma \propto \mu^{3/2}$	$1/\sqrt{x_i}$
$\sigma \propto \mu$	$\text{Log } x_i$
$\sigma \propto \sqrt{\mu}$, Poisson (count) data or binomial proportions where Poisson approximation is appropriate	$\sqrt{x_i}$ or $\sqrt{x_i + 1}$
Upper- and lower-bounded data (e.g., 0–1 probability of failure) (logit transformation)	$\log \dfrac{x_i - \text{lower limit}}{\text{upper limit} - x_i}$

in which the population can best be described with more than one distribution, for example, bimodal distribution. This type of distribution can occur, for example, when a supplier sorts and distributes parts that have a small plus or minus tolerance at an elevated piece price. The population of parts that are distributed to the larger plus or minus tolerance will probably have a bimodal distribution.

A specific example of this situation is the distribution of resistance values for resistors that have a ±10% tolerance. A manufacturer may sort and remove the ±1% parts that are manufactured, thereby creating a bimodal situation for the parts that have the larger tolerance.

A summary of common normalizing transformations is given in Table 9.3. As an alternative to the transformations included in the table, Box (1988) describes a method for eliminating unnecessary coupling of dispersion effects and location effects by determining an approximate transformation using a lambda plot. Montgomery (1997) and Box *et al.* (1978) discuss transformations in greater depth. With transformations, one should note that the conclusions of the analysis apply to the transformed populations.

9.10 Applying IEE

Consider the following situations: A practitioner compiles data that tracks the proportion of product that passes or fails a specification, makes a process failure rate confidence statement comparing two machine failure rates. In these cases, it is often easy for a practitioner to overlook how he/she could have benefited by changing from traditionally reported attribute statistics to a continuous-response assessment. If this transition can be made, much more process insight can typically be made with less effort.

9.11 Exercises

1. A complex software system averages 7 errors per 5000 lines of code. Determine the probability of exactly 2 errors in 5000 lines of randomly-selected lines of code.
2. The probability of a salesperson making a successful sales call is 0.2 when 8 sales calls are made in a day. Determine the probability of making exactly 3 successful sales calls in a day. Determine the probability of making more than 2 successful sales calls in a day.
3. A complex software system averages 6 errors per 5000 lines of code. Determine the probability of less than 3 errors in 2500 lines of randomly selected lines of code. Determine the probability of more than 2 errors in 2500 lines of randomly selected lines of code.
4. Fifty items are submitted for acceptance. If it is known that there are 4 defective items in the lot, determine the probability of finding exactly 1 defective item in a sample of 5. Determine the probability of finding less than 2 defective items in a sample of 5.
5. List visual inspections which can yield questionable results in organizations.
6. An electronic manufacturer observed a mean of 0.20 defects per board. Assuming a Poisson distribution, determine the probability of three defects occurring on the same board.

7. Give an example application of how each of the following distributions could be applicable to your personal life: normal, binomial, hypergeometric, Poisson, exponential, Weibull, and lognormal.

8. Count the number of times the sixth letter of the alphabet occurs in the following paragraph and compare to others within the workshop. Save the results from the counts of all members of the workshop:

> *The farmer found that his field of alfalfa had a certain type of fungus on it. The fungus was part of a family of parasitic microbes. The only answer that the farmer had found to fight the feisty fungus was spraying his fields with a toxic chemical that was not certified. It was the only method that offered him any hope of success. Unfortunately, when the farmer began to spray his fields, the federal agent from the FDA was in the area. The federal agent's opinion of the fungus was that it was not at a stage of significant concern. He offered the farmer a choice: Stop the contamination of the flora of the region or face a fine of substantial amount. The farmer halted the spraying of his alfalfa fields.*

9. Collect and compile data from your work/personal life for analysis by a statistical program. The response is to be discrete with time-series reporting; for example, failure rate. Create a table that describes the source of failures:
   a. Document your discrete output variable.
   b. Document your discrete input variable.

10

Traditional Control Charting and IEE Implementation

This is the third of four chapters that describe the foundation for the creation of IEE performance and project metrics; i.e., the project's baseline. The last two chapters described continuous response and attribute population's characteristics. This chapter describes the application of time-series plots and traditional control charting options, along with a description of why traditional control charts can lead to the wrong activities. Chapters 12 and 13 will later describe the IEE system for control chart selection and process capability/performance metric determination, which is significantly different from traditional control charting and process capability assessments.

What does the next four-chapter content mean to projects? The previous two chapters described different types of project and enterprise data. The concepts presented in these two chapters provide a foundation for determining the current project or operational baseline performance, from which process improvement activities can be evaluated.

To determine this baseline, we first need to establish whether the process is stable or predictable. To make this assessment we need to determine:

- Whether the process is consistent over time or whether the process is cyclic or has experienced one or more performance shifts
- Length of time that the process has performed at its current level

For processes that are stable/predictable, we then want to know how capable the process is relative to meeting specifications or expectations. The next two chapters address the traditional approach to answer these questions, while Chapters 12 and 13 describe the IEE approach.

I often get the comment: why do you present traditional control charting instead of focusing solely on the IEE 30,000-foot-level control charting methodology. My response is that readers have varying backgrounds. For those readers who are familiar with traditional control charting they need to understand the potential shortcomings of traditional control charting techniques. Other readers might encounter specific requests for charts that are not suggested as an IEE control charting option. These readers will need to supply their requester information on why the requested methodology can be deceiving, referencing this series of volumes (or referenced articles) for an explanation and suggested alternative approach.

10.1   Monitoring Processes

This chapter describes both the traditional selection methods for various control charts, as illustrated in Figure 10.1. Chapters 12 and 13 provide some alternative approaches that can lead to better sampling and chart-selection decisions.

A process is said to be in statistical control when special causes don't exist. Figure 10.2 illustrates both an out-of-control (unpredictable) and an in-control process (predictable) condition. When a process is in statistical control, this does not imply that the process is producing the desired quality of products relative to specification limits. The overall output of a process can be in statistical control and still be producing defects at a rate of 20%. This high-defective rate is considered to be a process capability/performance metric issue, not a process control issue, as illustrated in Figure 10.3.

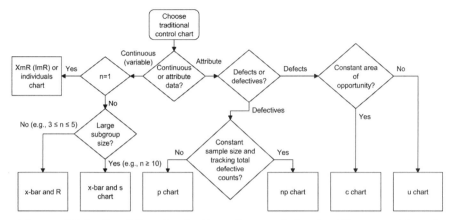

Figure 10.1: Traditional selection of control charts. *Chapters 12 and 13 describe alternative control charting alternatives that can be much more beneficial.*

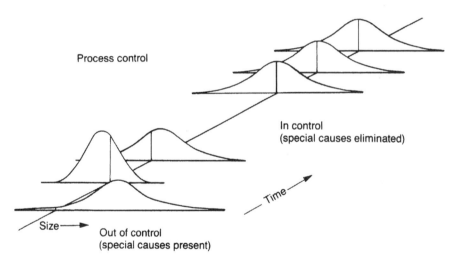

Figure 10.2: Process control [*Continuing Process Control and Process Capability Improvement,* Ford Corporate Quality Education and Training Center, 1987.]

Nonconformance can occur because the process mean is shifted excessively from the nominal target value and/or because variability is excessive. Process capability/performance metric studies are to describe the current process output in a control chart region that has stability/predictability. When a process capability/performance metric statement is unsatisfactory in a region of

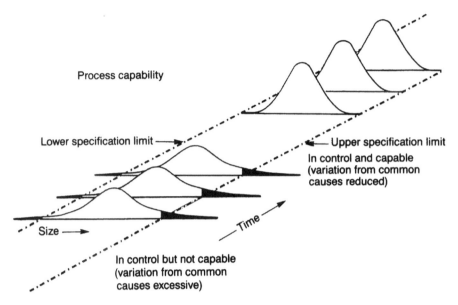

Figure 10.3: Process capability [*Continuing Process Control and Process Capability Improvement*, Ford Corporate Quality Education and Training Center, 1987.]

process stability, this type of problem is a fault of the system and needs to be addressed as a common cause problem.

10.2   Statistical Process Control Charts

Shewhart control charts (Shewhart, 1931) track processes by plotting data over time in the form shown in Figure 10.4. This chart can track either variables or attribute process parameters. The types of variable charts described are process mean ($\bar{x}$), range (R), standard deviation (s), and individual values (X). The attribute types discussed are proportion nonconforming (p), number of nonconforming items (np), number of nonconformities (c), and nonconformities per unit (u). Figure 10.1 described the traditional application of these charts.

The typical control limits are plus and minus three sampling standard deviation limits, where the standard deviation value is a function of the sampling plan. Traditionally we have strived for at least 20 data points; however, IEE high-level tracking does not *require* as many metric subgroupings. When a point falls outside

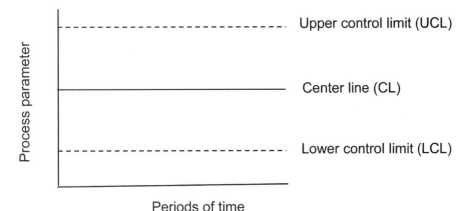

Figure 10.4: Control chart format.

these limits, the process is said to be out of control (i.e., the process is unpredictable). Interpretations of other control chart patterns are discussed in the next section. It should be emphasized that the process, not the specification, determines the process control limits noted in the following sections.

The terms *variables data* and *continuous data* describe the same situation. These situations involve measurements such as lead time, weight, temperature, and size. A rough rule of thumb is to consider data as continuous if at least 10 different values occur and no more than 20% of the data sets are repeat values.

10.3   Interpretation of Control Chart Patterns

When a process is in control/predictable, the control chart pattern should exhibit *natural characteristics* as if it were from random data. Unnatural patterns involve the absence of one or more of the characteristics of a natural pattern. Some examples of natural patterns are: mixture, stratification, and/or instability.

Unnatural patterns classified as mixture have an absence of points near the centerline. These patterns can be the combination of two different patterns on one chart: one at a high level and one at a low level. Unnatural patterns classified as stratification have up-and-down variations that are very small in comparison to the control limits. This pattern can occur when samples are taken consistently from widely different distributions. Unnatural patterns classified as instability have points outside the control limits. This pattern indicates that something, either *goodness* or *badness*, has changed within the process.

Consider further the analysis approach to determine whether there is instability in the process. It should be remembered that whenever the process is stated to be out of control/unpredictable, the statement might have been made in error because there is a chance that either abnormally *good* or *bad* samples were drawn. This chance of error increases with the introduction of more criteria when analyzing the charts. When using the following pattern criteria, this chance of error should be considered before making a process out-of-control statement.

Because the upper control limit (UCL) and lower control limit (LCL) each are 3σ (sampling standard deviation), consider a control chart that is subdivided into three 3σ regions, as noted in Figure 10.5. While statistical computer analysis programs may offer other tests, four rules for out-of-control conditions relative to these zones are as follows:

1. One point beyond zone A
2. Two out of three points in zone A or beyond
3. Four out of five points in zone B or beyond
4. Nine points in zone C or beyond

In Figure 10.6 the out-of-control data points are identified with the applicable condition number. Calculated probabilities for each of the four conditions are also shown in the figure (see Breyfogle (2003a) for probability equations). The probabilities used in these

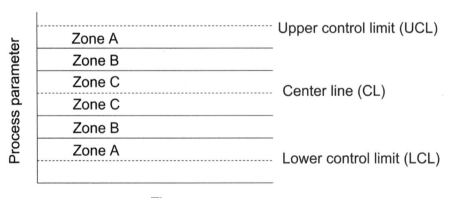

Figure 10.5: Control chart zones.

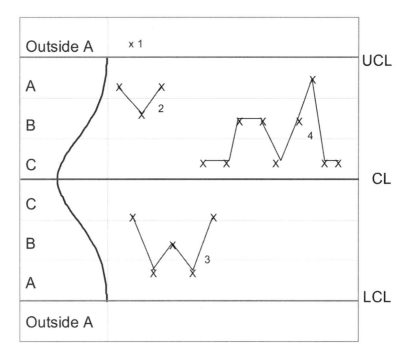

Rule1 P(rule1)=0.0014

Rule2 P(rule2)=(.021)² *(1–0.21)=0.000432

Rule3 P(rule3)=(.0014+.021+.136)⁴ *(1–.0014–.21–.136)=.000530

Rule4 P(rule4)=(.0014+.021+.136+.341)⁹ =(.5)⁹ =.001932

Figure 10.6: Control charts: zone tests.

calculations were determined from normal distribution percentile values (see Figure 8.15) to be:

$$P(\text{Region A}) = \frac{99.73 - 95.46}{2 \times 100} = 0.021$$

$$P(\text{Region B}) = \frac{95.46 - 68.26}{2 \times 100} = 0.136$$

$$P(\text{Region C}) = \frac{68.26}{2 \times 100} = 0.341$$

Another test is the runs test, which indicates that the process has shifted. Sequential data are evaluated relative to the centerline. A shift has occurred if:

- At least 10 out of 11 sequential data points are on the same side of the centerline.
- At least 12 out of 14 sequential data points are on the same side of the centerline.
- At least 14 out of 17 sequential data points are on the same side of the centerline.
- At least 16 out of 20 sequential data points are on the same side of the centerline.

Other patterns within a control chart can tell a story. For example, a cyclic pattern that has large amplitude relative to the control limits may indicate that samples are being taken from two different distributions. This could occur because of operator or equipment differences.

The above battery of runs test is commonly suggested in books; however, there is a cost in terms of decreasing the average run length (ARL) of the chart. Lloyd Nelson has noted that he prefers to use nine consecutive points all on the same side of the center-line as the only test of this type (Nelson, 1993).

10.4 $\bar{x}$ and R and $\bar{x}$ and s Charts: Mean and Variability Measurements

These Shewhart control charts assume that any subgroup range or standard deviation is an estimate of a single, unchanging over-all process standard deviation.

Consider that a rational subgrouping of m samples of size n is taken over some period of time. The number of m samples should be at least 20 to 25, where n will often be smaller and either 4, 5, or 6. For each sample of size n, a mean and range can be de-termined, where range is the difference between high and low readings.

For a process variable to be in statistical control, both the mean and range (or standard deviation) of the process must be in control. Typically, for a new process, the process mean ($\bar{x}$) is not known; hence, it has to be calculated using the equation:

$$\bar{\bar{x}} = \frac{\bar{x}_1 + \bar{x}_2 + \ldots \bar{x}_m}{m}$$

Similarly the mean range value (R) of the m subgroups is:

$$\overline{R} = \frac{R_1 + R_2 + \cdots + R_m}{m}$$

For small sample sizes, a relatively good estimate for the population standard deviation $(\hat{\sigma})$ is (see Table J for factor d_2):

$$\hat{\sigma} = \frac{\overline{R}}{d_2}$$

Standard deviation, s, is not an unbiased population standard deviation estimate. The unbiased estimate for standard deviation is s/c_4, where c_4 values are noted in Table J. For small samples such as $n = 4$ or $n = 5$ the efficiency of the range estimate is good and little is lost by using $\overline{R}$ in a control chart.

When the sample size n for the subgroup is moderately large, say $(n > 10$ to $12)$, the range method for estimating σ loses efficiency. In these situations, it is best to consider using $\overline{x}$ and s charts, where s, the sample standard deviation, can be determined using the relationship:

$$s = \left[\frac{\sum_{i=1}^{n}(x_i - \overline{x})^2}{n-1} \right]^{1/2}$$

For m subgroups, $\overline{s}$ can then be determined using the equation:

$$\overline{s} = \frac{s_1 + s_2 + \cdots + s_m}{m}$$

The upper control limit (UCL) and lower control limit (LCL) around a centerline (CL) for $\overline{x}$ and $(R$ or $s)$ can be determined from the following equations, where the constants (e.g., A_2 and D_3) are to be determined from Table J in the back of this volume:

$$LCL = \overline{\overline{x}} - A_2 \overline{R} \qquad\qquad UCL = \overline{\overline{x}} + A_2 \overline{R}$$

$$\overline{x}: CL = \overline{\overline{x}} \qquad\qquad \text{or}$$

$$LCL = \overline{\overline{x}} - A_3 \overline{s} \qquad\qquad UCL = \overline{\overline{x}} + A_3 \overline{s}$$

$$R: \quad CL = \bar{R} \qquad LCL = D_3\bar{R} \qquad UCL = D_4\bar{R}$$

$$s: \bar{s} \qquad LCL = B_3\bar{s} \qquad UCL = B_4\bar{s}$$

If successive group values plotted on the s or R charts are in control, control statements can then be made relative to a $\bar{x}$ chart.

When it is possible to specify the standard values for the process mean (μ) and standard deviation (σ), these standards could be used to establish the control charts without the analysis of past data. For this situation, the following equations are used, where the constants are again taken from Table J:

$$\bar{x}: \quad CL = \mu \qquad LCL = \mu - A\sigma \qquad UCL = \mu + A\sigma$$

$$R: \quad CL = d_2\sigma \qquad LCL = D_1\sigma \qquad UCL = D_2\sigma$$

$$s: \quad CL = c_4 c \qquad LCL = B_5\sigma \qquad UCL = B_6\sigma$$

Care must be exercised when using this approach because the standards may not be applicable to the process, which can result in many out-of-control signals.

10.5   Example 10.1: $\bar{x}$ and R Chart

A grinding machine produces treads for a hydraulic system of an aircraft to a diameter of 0.4037 ± 0.0013 in. Go/no-go thread ring gages are currently used in a 100% test plan to reject parts that are not within the tolerance interval specification. In an attempt to understand better the process variability so that the process can be improved, variables data were taken for the process. Measurements were taken every hour on five samples using a visual comparator that had an accuracy of 0.0001. The averages and ranges from this test are noted in table 10.1, where only the last two digits of the measurements are analyzed (Grant and Leavenworth, 1980).

The $\bar{x}$ and R chart parameters are (values are expressed in units of 0.0001 inch in excess of 0.4000 inch) as follows:

Table 10.1: $\bar{x}$ and R Chart Data. (last two digits of measurements; e.g., 36=0.4036 in.)

Sample Number	Subgroup Measurements					Mean $\bar{x}$	Range (R)
1	36	35	34	33	32	34.0	4
2	31	31	34	32	30	31.6	4
3	30	30	32	30	32	30.8	2
4	32	33	33	32	35	33.0	3
5	32	34	37	37	35	35.0	5
6	32	32	31	33	33	32.2	2
7	33	33	36	32	31	33.0	5
8	23	33	36	35	36	32.6	13
9	43	36	35	24	31	33.8	19
10	36	35	36	41	41	37.8	6
11	34	38	35	34	38	35.8	4
12	36	38	39	39	40	38.4	4
13	36	40	35	26	33	34.0	14
14	36	35	37	34	33	35.0	4
15	30	37	33	34	35	33.8	7
16	28	31	33	33	33	31.6	5
17	33	30	34	33	35	33.0	5
18	27	28	29	27	30	28.2	3
19	35	36	29	27	32	31.8	9
20	33	35	35	39	36	35.6	6
						$\bar{\bar{x}} = 33.55$	$\bar{R} = 6.2$

For $\bar{x}$ chart (top chart in Figure 10.7):

$$\text{UCL} = \bar{\bar{x}} + A_2\bar{R} = 33.55 + 0.577(6.2) = 37.13$$

$$\text{CL} = \bar{\bar{x}} = 33.55$$

$$\text{LCL} = \bar{\bar{x}} - A_2\bar{R} = 33.55 - 0.577(6.2) = 29.97$$

For R chart (bottom chart in Figure 10.7):

$$\text{UCL} = D_4\bar{R} = 2.114(6.2) = 13.11$$

$$\text{CL} = \bar{R} = 6.2$$

$$\text{LCL} = D_3\bar{R} = 0(6.2) = 0$$

A statistical-program-generated $\bar{x}$ and R control chart is shown in Figure 10.7. The control limits in this chart are slightly different from

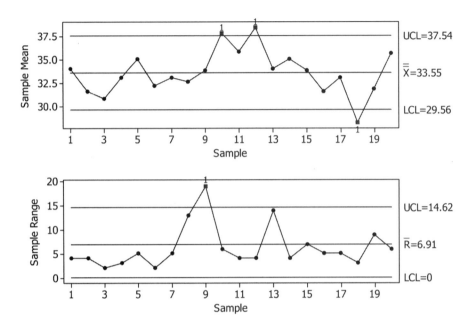

Figure 10.7: $\bar{x}$ and R control chart example (3.0 sample standard
deviation limits).

the manual calculations. The reason for this is that the statistical-
program-generated chart limits were determined using a pooled
standard deviation that had an unbiasing constant. This statistical-
program procedure is more difficult to calculate manually but provides better control chart limits for detecting out-of-control signals.
The pooled standard deviation with an unbiasing constant procedure will be used for the $\bar{x}$ and R charts that are presented in this
volume.

Both the $\bar{x}$ (points 10, 12, and 18) and R (points 9 and 13)
charts show lack of control. These points should have an assignable cause for being outside the control limits. However, in general, determining the real cause after some period of time may be
impossible. In addition, often not much can be done about these
past causes besides creating some awareness of trying to prevent
a certain type of problem in the future. However, this chart gives
evidence that there is opportunity to reduce the variability of the
current process. For this example, the previously noted abnormal
variation in the mean was determined to be from the machine
setting, while abnormal variation in the range was determined
to be from operator carelessness. After isolating special causes,
these points should then, in general, be removed from the data to
create new control charts with new limits.

If we assume an average range value of 0.0006, the tolerance of ± 0.0013 could be consistently obtainable with a stable/ predictable process that is centered within the specification, if there are no operator and machine problems. However, the $\bar{x}$ chart indicates that the process mean is shifted from the nominal specification. An example in Chapter 11 quantifies the measurement of this process capability/performance metric.

Whenever natural tolerances are found to be consistently within specification limits, consideration should be given to replacing a 100% inspection plan with periodic variable measurements of samples. For this example, this can mean that the replacement of the 100% go/no-go test with periodic measurements and control charting of the actual dimensions of five samples, as long as the control chart is in control/predictable and has an acceptable process capability/performance metric. Often this change can yield both a significant savings and improvement in quality, because the process is better understood.

A practitioner might have chosen a different approach to setup this control chart plan. For example, someone might have chosen to use a single value rather than a subgroup size of five. The resulting control chart would then be an *XmR* or individuals control chart, as described in the next section. The creation of *XmR* or individuals control charts from this data is an exercise at the end of this chapter.

10.6   *XmR* and Individuals Control Chart: Individual Measurements

A control chart of individual values is often referred to as an *I* chart or an *X* chart. A moving range chart often accompanies these charts; hence, the designation *ImR* or *XmR* chart. I will use the *XmR* nomenclature in this chapter. Note:

> The moving range chart of the *XmR* charting pair tracks data transition magnitudes, typically between adjacent time-series values. One should note that these reported transitions are already visually shown in the individuals control chart. Reporting only an individuals control chart, without the moving range chart pair, simplifies and can cause less reader confusion. Because of this I later suggest only using an individuals chart when making a 30,000-foot-level report out. This suggestion does not restrict a practitioner from examining a moving range chart for improved process understanding.

The criteria of $\bar{x}$ and R charts consider sample sizes greater than one within the sampling groups. For some situations, such as chemical batch processes, only a sample size of one is achievable. Individual measurements of this type can be monitored using X charts. For other situations, someone can choose which type of chart to use.

For an individual-measurement control chart, the process average is simply the mean of the n data points, which is:

$$\bar{x} = \frac{\sum_{i=1}^{n} x_i}{n}$$

Most frequently, adjacent values are used to determine the moving range; however, someone could use a larger duration when making this calculation. The constants shown would need to be adjusted accordingly. When using adjacent values, moving ranges ($\overline{MR}$s) are determined from the data, using the equations:

$$MR_1 = |x_2 - x_1| \quad MR_2 = |x_3 - x_2| ,\ldots$$

The average moving range (MR) is the average MR value for the n values described by

$$\overline{MR} = \frac{\sum_{i=1}^{m} MR_i}{m} = \frac{(MR_1) + (MR_2) + (MR_3), \ldots, (MR_m)}{m}$$

Charting parameters for the individual values chart are as follows:

$$CL = \bar{x} \qquad LCL = \bar{x} - \frac{3(\overline{MR})}{d_2} = \bar{x} - 2.66(\overline{MR})$$

$$UCL = \bar{x} + \frac{3(\overline{MR})}{d_2} = \bar{x} + 2.66(\overline{MR})$$

The 2.66 factor is $3/d_2$, where 3 is for three standard deviations and d_2 is from Appendix Table J for a sample size of 2 (i.e., $3/1.128 = 2.66$). This relationship can be used when the moving range is selected to expand beyond the adjacent samples. For this situation, the value for d_2 would be adjusted accordingly.

When using two adjacent values to determine moving range, the charting parameters for the moving range chart are

$$\text{CL} = \overline{MR} \qquad \text{UCL} = D_4\,\overline{MR} = 3.267(\overline{MR})$$

The 3.267 factor D_4 is from Table J for a sample size of 2.

As was implied earlier in this section, some practitioners prefer not to construct moving range charts because any information that can be obtained from the moving range is contained in the X chart, and the moving ranges are correlated, which can induce patterns of runs or cycles (ASTM STP15D). Because of this artificial autocorrelation, the assessment of moving range charts (when they are used) should not involve the use of run tests for out-of-control conditions.

In IEE, control charting has extensive use not only for process analyses but also for report-outs that have visibility to all levels of management. To re-emphasize, I personally prefer the individuals control chart over the *XmR* chart for this reporting since the report-out is simplified and easier to explain. In this series of Volumes, I will primarily use an individuals control chart instead of an *XmR* chart.

10.7   Example 10.2: *XmR* Charts

The viscosity of a chemical mixing process has the centipoise (cP) measurements as noted in Table 10.2 for 20 batches (Messina, 1987). Within a service organization, these data could be thought of as the time it takes to complete a process such as a purchase order request, where this execution time was reported for one weekly random sample.

The *MR*s are determined from the relationship:

$$MR_1 = |x_2 - x_1| = |70.10 - 75.20| = 5.10$$

$$MR_2 = |x_3 - x_2| = |74.40 - 75.20| = 0.80 ,...$$

The process mean and moving range mean are calculated and used to determine the individual-measurement control chart parameters of:

Table 10.2: *XmR* Chart Data

Batch Number	Viscosity (cP)	Moving Range (*MR*)
1	70.10	—
2	75.20	5.10
3	74.40	0.80
4	72.07	2.33
5	74.70	2.63
6	73.80	0.90
7	72.77	1.03
8	78.17	5.40
9	70.77	7.40
10	74.30	3.53
11	72.90	1.40
12	72.50	0.40
13	74.60	2.10
14	75.43	0.83
15	75.30	0.13
16	78.17	2.87
17	76.00	2.17
18	73.50	2.50
19	74.27	0.77
20	75.05	0.78
	$\bar{x} = 74.200$	$\overline{MR} = 2.267$

$$CL = \bar{x} \qquad LCL = \bar{x} - 2.66(\overline{MR}) \qquad UCL = \bar{x} + 2.66(\overline{MR})$$
$$CL = 74.200 \quad LCL = 74.200 - 2.66(2.267) \quad UCL = 74.200 + 2.66(2.267)$$
$$LCL = 68.170 \qquad\qquad UCL = 80.230$$

The moving range chart parameters are:

$$CL = \overline{MR} = 2.267 \quad UCL = 3.267(\overline{MR}) = 3.267(2.267) = 7.406$$

The *XmR* computer plots shown in Figure 10.8 indicate no out-of-control condition for this data (i.e., a predictable process). If we consider that the 20 batch readings are a random sample of the process, we could make a probability plot of the raw data to determine the expected range of viscosities that will be experienced by the customer. We also could make process capability/performance metric assessment.

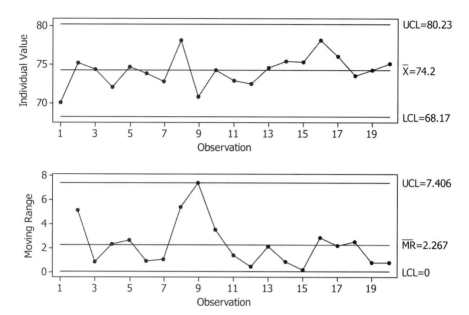

Figure 10.8: *XmR* control chart example.

10.8 *p* Chart: Proportion Nonconforming Measurements

This section describes the creation of the proportion chart (i.e., *p* chart). This Shewhart control chart is sometimes call percentage chart or attribute chart, which assumes any sample which is an estimate of a single overall fraction nonconforming.

Consider *m* rational subgroups where each subgroup has *n* samples with *x* nonconformities or defective units. The nonconforming proportion (*p*) for a subgroup is:

$$p = \frac{x}{n}$$

When the sample size for each subgroup is equal, the process mean nonconforming proportion $\bar{p}$ for the *m* subgroups is:

$$\bar{p} = \frac{\sum_{i=1}^{m} p_i}{m}$$

where in general m should be at least 20–25. The chart parameters for this binomial scenario are:

$$CL = \bar{p} \qquad LCL = \bar{p} - 3\sqrt{\frac{\bar{p}(1 - \bar{p})}{n}}$$

$$UCL = \bar{p} + 3\sqrt{\frac{\bar{p}(1 - \bar{p})}{n}}$$

A LCL cannot be less than zero; hence, this limit is set to zero whenever a limit is calculated below zero.

One of the problems that occur with this type of chart is that sample sizes are often not equal. One approach to solve this problem is to use the average sample size with a p value that is most typically determined as the total number of defects from all the samples divided by the total number of samples that are taken. These charts are easy to interpret since the control limits are at the same level for all samples. However, this approach is not very satisfactory when there are large differences in sample sizes. A better way to create this chart, but resulting in a more difficult chart to interpret, is to adjust the control chart limits for each sample. For this chart we have:

$$\bar{p} = \frac{\sum\limits_{i=1}^{m} D_i}{\sum\limits_{i=1}^{m} n_i}$$

where D_i is the number of nonconformances within the ith sample of m total samples. Control limits for the ith sample is then:

$$CL = \bar{p} \qquad LCL = \bar{p} - 3\sqrt{\frac{\bar{p}(1 - \bar{p})}{n_i}}$$

$$UCL = \bar{p} + 3\sqrt{\frac{\bar{p}(1 - \bar{p})}{n_i}}$$

10.9   Example 10.3: p Chart

A machine manufactures the cardboard container used to package frozen orange juice. Cans are then inspected to determine

Table 10.3: Data for p Chart Example

Sample Number	Number of Nonconformances	Sample Nonconforming Fraction
1	12	0.24
2	15	0.30
3	8	0.16
4	10	0.20
5	4	0.08
6	7	0.14
7	16	0.32
8	9	0.18
9	14	0.28
10	10	0.20
11	5	0.10
12	6	0.12
13	17	0.34
14	12	0.24
15	22	0.44
16	8	0.16
17	10	0.20
18	5	0.10
19	13	0.26
20	11	0.22
21	20	0.40
22	18	0.36
23	24	0.48
24	15	0.30
25	9	0.18
26	12	0.24
27	7	0.14
28	13	0.26
29	9	0.18
30	6	0.12

whether they will leak when filled with orange juice. A p chart is initially established by taking 30 samples of 50 cans at half-hour intervals within the manufacturing process, as summarized in Table 10.3 (Montgomery, 1985).

Within a service organization, this data could be considered defective rates for the completion of a form, such as whether a purchase order request was filled out correctly. Note that in this example there was no assessment of the number of errors that might be on an individual form (this would involve a *c* or *u* chart). An alternative analysis approach for this data is described in Example 13.2.

The process average is:

$$\bar{p} = \sum_{i=1}^{m} \frac{p_i}{m} = \frac{0.24 + 0.30 + 0.16, \ldots}{30} = 0.2313$$

The chart parameters are then:

$$CL = 0.2313 \quad LCL = 0.2313 - 3\sqrt{\frac{0.2313(1 - 0.2313)}{50}} = 0.0524$$

$$UCL = 0.2313 + 3\sqrt{\frac{0.2313(1 - 0.2313)}{50}} = 0.4102$$

The *p* chart of the data is shown in Figure 10.9. Samples 15 and 23 are beyond the limits in the control chart; hence, the process is considered to have out-of-control conditions or is unpredictable. If investigation indicates that these two points were caused by an

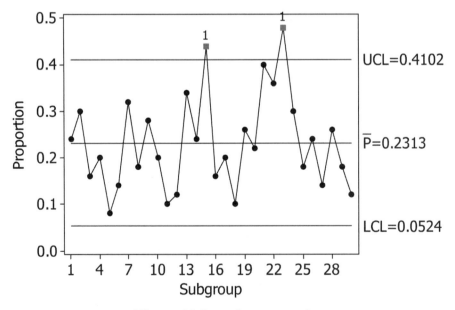

Figure 10.9: *p* chart example.

adverse condition, for example, a new batch of raw material or an inexperienced operator, the process control limits can be recalculated without the data points. Whenever out-of-control conditions exist that cannot be explained, these data points should typically not be removed from the control limit computations. If this initial process control chart also does not have any abnormal patterns, the control limits are used to monitor the current production on a continuing basis.

For an in-control/predictable process the magnitude of the average failure rate should be examined for acceptability. A reduction in the overall average typically requires a more involved overall process or design change (i.e., a common-cause issue). Pareto charts and DOE techniques can be a powerful approach to aid in determining which changes are beneficial to improving the process.

This chapter described the traditional control chart analysis approach for this type of problem. Chapter 13 describes the IEE alternative data analysis approach.

10.10   *np* Chart: Number of Nonconforming Items

An alternative to the *p* chart when the sample size (*n*) is constant is an *np* chart. In this chart, the number of nonconforming items is plotted instead of the fraction nonconforming (*p*). The chart parameters are:

$$\text{CL} = n\bar{p} \qquad \text{LCL} = n\bar{p} - 3\sqrt{n\bar{p}(1-\bar{p})} \qquad \text{UCL} = n\bar{p} + 3\sqrt{n\bar{p}(1-\bar{p})}$$

where $\bar{p}$ is determined similar to a *p* chart. Chapter 13 describes the IEE alternative data analysis approach.

10.11   *c* Chart: Number of Nonconformities

In some cases the number of nonconformities or defects per unit is a more appropriate unit of measure than the fraction nonconforming. An example of this situation is one in which a printed circuit board is tested. If the inspection process considered the board as a pass/fail entity, then a *p* chart or *np* chart would be appropriate. However, a given printed circuit board can have multiple failures; hence, it may be better to track the total number of defects per unit of measure. For a printed circuit board, the unit of measure could be the number of solder joints in 100 cards, while the unit of measure when manufacturing cloth could be the number of blemishes per 100 square yards.

The c chart can be used to monitor these processes if the Poisson distribution is an appropriate model. As noted earlier, the Poisson distribution can be used for various analysis considerations if the number of opportunities for nonconformities is sufficiently large and the probability of occurrence of a nonconformity at a location is small and constant. The chart parameters for the c chart are:

$$\text{CL} = \bar{c} \qquad \text{LCL} = \bar{c} - 3\sqrt{\bar{c}} \qquad \text{UCL} = \bar{c} + 3\sqrt{\bar{c}}$$

where $\bar{c}$ is the mean of the occurrences and the LCL is set to zero if the calculations yield a negative number.

As an IEE alternative, Chapter 13 describes the advantages of using an individuals control chart for tracking this type of data. Example 13.4 describes another approach when failures are infrequent.

10.12   *u* Chart: Nonconformities Per Unit

A u chart plot of defects can be used in lieu of a c chart when the rationale subgroup size is not constant. This occurs, for example, when defects are tracked daily and production volume has daily variation. For a sample size n that has a total number of nonconformities c, u equates to:

$$u = c/n$$

The control chart parameters for the u chart are then:

$$\text{CL} = \bar{u} \qquad \text{LCL} = \bar{u} - 3\sqrt{\bar{u}/n} \qquad \text{UCL} = \bar{u} + 3\sqrt{\bar{u}/n}$$

where $\bar{u}$ is the mean of the occurrences.

Like the c chart, Chapter 13 describes the advantages of using an individuals control chart for tracking this type of data. Example 13.4 describes another approach when failures are infrequent.

10.13   Notes on the Shewhart Control Chart

Nelson (1999) noted that the following statements are incorrect. In this section, I will summarize some of the thoughts presented in this article.

Incorrect Statements:

- Shewhart charts are a graphical way of applying a sequential statistical significance test for an out-of-control condition.
- Control limits are confidence limits on the true process mean.
- Shewhart charts are based on probabilistic models.
- Normality is required for the correct application of an $\bar{x}$ chart.
- The theoretical basis for the Shewhart control chart has some obscurities that are difficult to teach.

Shewhart control charts are to indicate the presence of causes that produce deviations from a stable process operation. Shewhart (1931) called these causes "assignable," while Dr. Deming (1986) called these causes "special" causes. When special causes are no longer indicated, the process is said to be "in-statistical control," noting that an in-control or stable process does not mean that the process provides the desired output.

Many of Shewhart's control charting procedures inherently have a short-term view for sampling variation imbedded in their control chart limit calculations, which basically defines how stability is to be viewed. Later in this volume it is shown how some traditional Shewhart control charting procedures can lead to firefighting. An alternative IEE approach is then presented, which overcomes this problem. With the IEE approach, stability is determined from a long-term sampling variation point of view, which impacts calculated control chart limits.

> Shewhart control charts are to indicate the presence of causes that produce deviations from a stable process operation... Many of Shewhart's control charting procedures inherently have a short-term view for sampling variation imbedded in their control chart limit calculations, which basically defines how stability is to be viewed ... some traditional Shewhart control charting procedures can lead to firefighting. An alternative IEE approach ... overcomes this problem. With the IEE approach, stability is determined from a long-term sampling variation point of view, which impacts calculated control chart limits.

   Wheeler (1997) makes a nomenclature point, which I have adopted in this series of volumes: "As long as people see Shewhart chart as a manual process-control algorithm, they will be blinded to its use for continual improvement. In keeping with this I have been using 'predictable process' and 'unpredictable process' rather than the more loaded phrases 'in-control process' and 'out-of-control process.' I find this helpful in two ways; predictability is what it is all about, and many people use 'in control' as a synonym for 'conforming'."

   Tukey (1946) points out that the Shewhart control chart is not a method for detecting deviations from randomness. He wrote, "This was not Shewhart's purpose, and it is easy to construct artificial examples where non-randomness is in control or randomness is out of control. A state of control, in Shewhart's basic sense, is reached when it is *uneconomic* to look for assignable causes, and experience has shown that the compactness of the distribution associated with a good control chart implies this sort of control." A control chart tests for the practical significance of an effect, which is different from a statistical significance despite the fact that the word significance can be used for both. Shewhart charts are not based on any particular probabilistic model. He did not base his choice of the 3σ limit on any particular statistical distribution.

   It is sometimes suggested that data can be improved by transforming the data, so that they behave as though they came from a normal distribution. This can be appropriated if the non-normal distribution to be transformed is known (Nelson, 1994). However, there could be problems if the distribution has to be estimated from preliminary data. Many skewed distributions can be traced from two normally distributed sources with different parameters.

   If one were to view the control chart as a statistical significance test for each point in succession, the question would then become: What is the significance of the test? This calculation does not make sense for a situation where the test is continued repeatedly until a significant result is obtained, even though there are no special causes present. Similarly, when a control chart is not a statistical significance test, the upper and lower limits do not form a confidence interval. The control chart was developed empirically by Shewhart. Its applicability has withstood the test of time.

10.14   Rational Subgroup Sampling and IEE

The effective use of control charts is dependent upon both rational sampling and subgrouping. Rational sampling involves the best selection of the best what, where, how, and when for measurements. Other issues include the creation of both product and process measurements that either directly or indirectly affect internal/external customer satisfaction. Sampling plans should lead to analyses that give insight, not just present numbers.

Traditionally, rational subgrouping issues involve the selection of samples that yield relatively homogeneous conditions within the subgroup for a small region of time or space, perhaps five in a row. For the $\bar{x}$ and R chart described in this chapter, the within-subgroup variation defines the limits of the control chart on how much variation should exist between the subgroups. For a given situation, differing subgrouping methodologies can dramatically affect the measured variation within subgroups, which in turn affects the width of the control limits.

Traditionally sampling frequency has been considered rational if it is frequent enough to monitor process changes; however, Chapter 12 will address other issues to consider when creating an IEE satellite-level and 30,000-foot-level control chart sampling plan.

10.15 Applying IEE

Subgrouping can affect the output and resulting decisions from $\bar{x}$ and R charts. Average charts identify differences between subgroups, while the range charts identify inconsistency within the subgroups. The variation within subgroups determines the sensitivity of the control charts. Because of this, it is important to consider the sources of variation for the measurement and then organize the subgroups accordingly.

Consider the hourly sampling of five parts created one after another from a single cavity mold. This subgroup size is five and the frequency of sampling is hourly. Sources of variability are cycle-to-cycle and hour-to-hour. A process could have low variability between cycles in conjunction with raw material variability that affects the hour-to-hour measurements. The measurement of five consecutive pieces for this process yields control limits that are small. Concerns for immediate investigation can then result from many apparent out-of-control conditions (i.e., an unpredictable process indication).

Sometimes the decisions for sampling and subgrouping are more involved. Consider, for example, a four-cavity molding process, which has an hourly sampling frequency of five parts. Depending upon the data, a traditional control charting strategy could lead to many out-of-control signals, where firefighting activities did not fix anything long term. Unlike traditional control charting, an IEE sampling plan to create a control chart for this situation considers any typical cavity-to-cavity, cycle-to-cycle, and hour-to-hour differences as potential sources of common-cause variability. Inappropriate actions can result when these sources are not considered collectively within sampling plans. Chapter 12 describes subgrouping sampling alternative for this situation.

One object of the IEE 30,000-foot-level and satellite-level scorecard/dashboard metrics is to get out of the firefighting mode, where common-cause issues cause reaction as though they were special-cause events. If, for example, daily raw material changes impact our process, within IEE we view this as a process problem, not a special-cause event. With an IEE strategy, this type of variability should be reflected within the control limits.

For the high-level metrics of IEE, we want infrequent subgrouping/sampling so that short-term variations caused by KPIV perturbations are viewed as common-cause issues. A 30,000-foot-level individuals control chart created with infrequent subgrouping/sampling can reduce the amount of firefighting in an organization. However, this does not mean that a problem does not exist within the process. Chapter 11 describes some approaches to view the process capability/performance metric, or how well the process meets customer specifications or overall business needs. When process capability/performance metric improvements are needed, we can initiate an IEE project; i.e., IEE projects are pulled into the system, by metric improvement needs.

10.16   Exercises

1. Create a run chart and control chart for the following data set: 9.46, 10.61, 8.07, 12.21, 9.02, 8.99 10.03, 11.73, 10.99, 10.56.

2. Given the historical nonconformance proportion of 0.77 and a subgroup sample size of 21, determine the upper control limit for a *p* chart. Determine whether this limit is a function of the variability between subgroups and the implication of this issue.

3. Given that the historical average for number of nonconformities per unit has been 2.13, determine the upper control limit for a *c* chart. Determine whether this limit is a function

of the variability between subgroups and the implication of this issue.

4. Create a control chart of the data that is in the chart below (AIAG, 1995b). Comment.

Subgroup	Measurement				
	1	2	3	4	5
1	0.65	0.70	0.65	0.65	0.85
2	0.75	0.85	0.75	0.85	0.65
3	0.75	0.80	0.80	0.70	0.75
4	0.60	0.70	0.70	0.75	0.65
5	0.70	0.75	0.65	0.85	0.80
6	0.60	0.75	0.75	0.85	0.70
7	0.75	0.80	0.65	0.75	0.70
8	0.60	0.70	0.80	0.75	0.75
9	0.65	0.80	0.85	0.85	0.75
10	0.60	0.70	0.60	0.80	0.65
11	0.80	0.75	0.90	0.50	0.80
12	0.85	0.75	0.85	0.65	0.70
13	0.70	0.70	0.75	0.75	0.70
14	0.65	0.70	0.85	0.75	0.60
15	0.90	0.80	0.80	0.75	0.85
16	0.75	0.80	0.75	0.80	0.65

5. Make an assessment of the statistical control of a process using an individuals control chart: 3.40, 8.57, 2.42, 5.59, 9.92, 4.63, 7.48, 8.55, 6.10, 6.42, 4.46, 7.02, 5.86, 4.80, 9.60, 5.92.

6. Make an assessment of the below data using the standard $\bar{x}$ and R strategy. Consider that someone decided to use an individuals control charting strategy in lieu of the $\bar{x}$ and R strategy. Consider five scenarios for the resulting data as the five columns below. That is, one set of individuals data would be 36, 31, 30, ..., 35, 33, while another data set would be 35, 31, 30, ..., 36, 35. Compare and describe result differences.

Sample number	Number 1	Number 2	Number 3	Number 4	Number 5
1	36	35	34	33	32
2	31	31	34	32	30
3	30	30	32	30	32
4	32	33	33	32	35

5	32	34	37	37	35
6	32	32	31	33	33
7	33	33	36	32	31
8	23	33	36	35	36
9	43	36	35	24	31
10	36	35	36	41	41
11	34	38	35	34	38
12	36	38	39	39	40
13	36	40	35	26	33
14	36	35	37	34	33
15	30	37	33	34	35
16	28	31	33	33	33
17	33	30	34	33	35
18	27	28	29	27	30
19	35	36	29	27	32
20	33	35	35	39	36

7. Discuss the concepts of special and common cause relative to Shewhart charts. Describe the statistical meaning of the term *in control*. Describe a non-manufacturing application of control charts.

8. A process produces an output that is measured as a continuous response. The process is consistent from day to day.
   (a) Given only this information, comment on what can be said, if anything, about the process capability/performance metric.
   (b) Give an example of a service, manufacturing, and personal process where this might apply.

9. Control chart the following data set. Conduct a process capability/performance metric assessment for the process. Comment on the results. Offer improvement suggestions for the data reporting and analysis procedure.
   (a) Create a *p*-chart.
   (b) Create an individuals control chart.
   (c) From the control charts estimate the process capability/ performance metric level.
   (d) Comment on whether useful information can be obtained from these plots.
   (e) Determine what could be done different to track this process.

Day	Number of failures	Transactions
1	1	100
2	0	100
3	0	100
4	2	100
5	0	100
6	1	100
7	0	100
8	1	100
9	0	100
10	1	100

10. An organization produced the same number of transactions daily, reporting the total number of transactional defects daily.

Day	Defects	Day	Defects
1	102	16	98
2	76	17	86
3	82	18	90
4	121	19	119
5	90	20	137
6	119	21	97
7	87	22	115
8	60	23	70
9	165	24	83
10	67	25	69
11	144	26	72
12	73	27	136
13	95	28	105
14	81	29	78
15	107	30	137

(a) Create a *c* chart of the data and assess whether the plot is in-control/predictable.

(b) Create an individuals control chart of the data and assess whether the plot is in-control/predictable.

(c) Explain results.

11

Traditional Process Capability and Process Performance Metrics

This is the fourth of four chapters that describe the foundation for creating IEE performance and project metrics (i.e., the project's baseline). The first two chapters in this series described continuous response and attribute population's characteristics. The third chapter described time series plots and traditional control charting options, along with a description of why traditional control charts can lead to the wrong activities. This chapter describes traditional process capability and performance studies.

It is important to highlight that process capability metric statements are applicable for in-control or stable/predictable processes. For many situations, this limitation is not applicable. For example, a stock market process capability statement is not appropriate. Another example is the monthly tracking of corporate gross revenue, which usually is not from a stable/predictable process (e.g., gross revenue is growing at an erratic rate), which is not necessarily a bad thing.

Chapter 12 will show how a particular region of a control chart can indicate stability using IEE 30,000-foot-level analysis techniques; while, traditional control charting techniques would indicate that the same control charting period is out of control. This would mean that for this time period a process capability/performance metric statement is an appropriate part of an IEE analysis but is not for a traditional analysis.

In Six Sigma and elsewhere, process capability and process performance studies often utilize indices to describe how a process is performing relative to specification criteria. Statisticians often challenge how well these indices accomplish this. However, the fact remains that customers often request these indices when communicating with their suppliers. A customer might set process capability and/or process performance indices targets, and then ask the suppliers to report on how well they meet these targets.

In this chapter I will describe some traditional process–capability–reporting metrics and summarize the issues that are prevalent with this type of reporting. Appendix Section B.1 describes the sigma quality level metric, another type of process capability reporting.

A couple of issues that are often not addressed adequately in process-capability-metric reporting is if/how process stability is determined before the calculation and if/how normality or lack-of-normality is addressed when making the calculation. Chapter 12 will describe an IEE alternative to overcome the deficiencies of indices and other process capability reporting.

As with control charting, I often get the comment: why do you present traditional process capability reporting techniques instead of focusing solely on the IEE 30,000-foot-level reporting methodology. Similar to my response for control charting, my response is that readers have varying backgrounds. For those readers who are familiar with process capability index reporting, they need to understand the shortcomings of these traditional reporting techniques. Other readers might encounter specific requests for report-outs that are not suggested as an IEE process capability/performance metric option. These readers will need to supply their requester information on why the requested methodology can be deceiving, referencing this series of volumes (or referenced articles) for an explanation and suggested alternative approach.

11.1   Process Capability Indices for Continuous Data

Process capability and process performance indices are an integral part of the original Six Sigma measurement system. These metrics are closely related to the calculation of sigma quality level (Breyfogle, 2003a).

AIAG (1995b) provides the following definitions:

- C_p: This is the capability index, defined as the tolerance width divided by the process capability, irrespective of process centering.
- C_{pk}: This is the capability index, which accounts for process centering. It relates the scaled distance between the process mean and the closest specification limit to half the total process spread.
- P_p: This is the performance index, defined as the tolerance width divided by the process performance, irrespective of process centering. Typically, it is expressed as the tolerance width divided by six times the sample standard deviation. It should be used only to compare to C_p and C_{pk} and to measure and prioritize improvement over time.
- P_{pk}: This is the performance index, which accounts for process centering. It should be used only to compare to or with C_p and C_{pk} and to measure and prioritize improvement over time.

It is important to understand that these definitions are not followed by all organizations.

- Some organizations interpret process capability as how well a product performs relative to customer needs (i.e., specification). This interpretation is closer to the definition given as above for process performance.
- Some organizations require/assume that processes are in control before conducting process capability/performance assessments. Other organizations lump all data together, resulting in special-cause data increasing the value for long-term variability.
- The term *process performance* is not always used to describe P_p and P_{pk}.

The equations for process capability/performance indices are quite simple but very sensitive to the input value for standard deviation (σ). There are various opinions on how to determine standard deviation in a given situation. AIAG (1995b) provides its interpretation of how to calculate variability. It is important to note that organizations do use other approaches.

Inherent Process Variation: The portion of process variation is due to common causes only. This variation can be estimated from control charts by $\bar{R}/d_2$, among other things (e.g., $\bar{s}/c_4$).

Total Process Variation: Process variation is due to both common and special causes. This variation may be estimated by s, the sample standard deviation, using all of the individual readings obtained from either a detailed control chart or a process study; that is:

$$s = \sqrt{\sum_{i=1}^{n} \frac{(x_i - \bar{x})^2}{n-1}} = \hat{\sigma}_s$$

where x_i is an individual reading, $\bar{x}$ is the average of individual readings, and n is the total number of all of the individual readings.

Process Capability: The 6σ range of a process's inherent variation; for statistically stable processes only, where σ is usually estimated by $\bar{R}/d_2$.

Process Performance: The 6σ range of a process's total variation, where σ is usually estimated by s, the sample standard deviation.

The equations presented in this chapter apply to normally distributed data. Computer programs can often address data, which do not originate from a normally distributed population.

11.2   Process Capability Indices: C_p and C_{pk}

The process capability index C_p represents the allowable tolerance interval spread in relation to the actual spread of the data when the data follow a normal distribution. This equation is as follows:

$$C_p = \frac{\text{USL} - \text{LSL}}{6\sigma}$$

where USL and LSL are the upper specification limit (USL) and lower specification limit (LSL), respectively, and 6σ describes the range or spread of the process. Data centering is not taken into account in this equation. Options for standard deviation (σ) are given later in this section.

Figure 11.1 illustrates graphically various C_p values relative to specification limits; C_p addresses only the spread of the process; C_{pk} is used concurrently to consider the spread and mean shift of the process, as graphically illustrated in Figure 11.2. Mathematically, C_{pk} can be represented as the minimum value of the two quantities:

$$C_{pk} = \min \left[\frac{\text{USL} - \mu}{3\sigma}, \frac{\mu - \text{LSL}}{3\sigma} \right]$$

The relationship of C_{pk} to C_p is:

$$C_{pk} = C_p(1 - k)$$

Computer programs can offer appropriate options for the methods discussed above. Strategies for estimating standard deviation (σ) for these equations include the following:

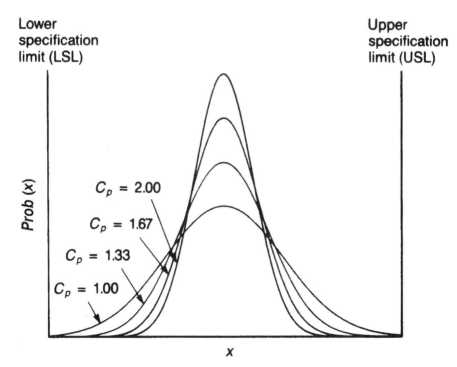

Figure 11.1: C_p illustrations.

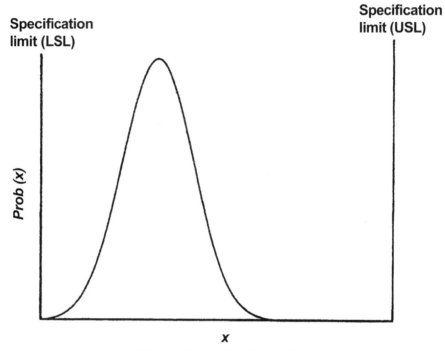

Figure 11.2: C_{pk} illustration.

- *Short-term view for σ*: From an $\bar{x}$ and R chart the following estimates are made: $\hat{\sigma} = s = \bar{R}/d_2$, $\hat{\mu} = \bar{\bar{x}}$ (AIAG, 1995b).
- *Long-term view for σ*: In 1998, total standard deviation from a variance components analysis (see Chapter 24) was used in the Motorola University's Continuous Improvement Curriculum (CIC) training program (Spagon, 1998).

A minimum acceptable process capability index often recommended (Juran, *et al.*, 1976) is 1.33 (4σ); however, Motorola, in its Six Sigma program, proposes striving to obtain a minimum individual process step C_p value of 2.0 and a C_{pk} value of 1.5.

11.3   Process Capability/Performance Indices: P_p and P_{pk}

These indices are sometimes referred to as long-term capability/ performance indices. Not all organizations report information as

P_p and P_{pk}. Some organizations calculate C_p and C_{pk}, so that they report information that is similar to P_p and P_{pk}.

The relationship between P_p and P_{pk} is similar to that between C_p and C_{pk}. The process capability index P_p represents the allowable tolerance spread relative to the actual spread of the data when the data follow a normal distribution. This equation is

$$P_p = \frac{\text{USL} - \text{LSL}}{6\sigma}$$

where USL and LSL are the upper specification limit and lower specification limit. No quantification for data centering is described within this P_p relationship. Calculation alternatives for σ are given below. Pictorially the relationship between P_p and P_{pk} is similar to that between C_p and C_{pk} relative to specification limits. Differences can be the spread of the distribution for given process.

Mathematically, P_{pk} can be represented as the minimum value of the two quantities:

$$P_{pk} = \min\left[\frac{\text{USL} - \mu}{3\sigma}, \frac{\mu - \text{LSL}}{3\sigma}\right]$$

Computer programs offer appropriate options from the methods presented here. Suggested strategies to estimate standard deviation (σ) for these equations include the following:

From an $\bar{x}$ and R chart the following estimates are made (AIAG, 1995b): $\hat{\mu} = \bar{\bar{x}}$ and:

$$\hat{\sigma} = \sqrt{\sum_{i=1}^{n} \frac{(x_i - \bar{\bar{x}})^2}{n-1}} \cdot x$$

where x_i are individual readings from a process that has n total samples (including subgroup samples), and $\bar{\bar{x}}$ is the process mean from the control chart.

11.4   Process Capability/Performance Misunderstandings

Practitioners need to be very careful about the methods they use to calculate and report process capability/performance indices. I have seen a customer asking for C_p and C_{pk} metrics when the documentation really stipulated the use of a long-term estimate for standard deviation. The supplier was initially operating under the assumption that C_p and C_{pk} measure short-term variability. A misunderstanding of this type between customer and supplier could be very costly.

Another possible source of confusion is the statistical computer program package used to calculate these indices. I have seen a supplier enter randomly collected data into a computer program, thinking that the usual sampling standard deviation formula would be the source of the standard deviation value used in the capability computations. The computer program presumed by default that the data were collected sequentially. The computer program estimated a short-term standard deviation by calculating the average moving range of the sequential entries and then converting this moving range value to a standard deviation.

The program then listed the response as C_p and C_{pk}. The practitioner thought that he had used the program correctly because the output (C_p and C_{pk}) was consistent with the customer's request. However, the data were not generated in sequence. If he had re-entered the same data in a different sequence, a different C_p and C_{pk} metric would probably result. For non-sequentially generated data, the practitioner should limit his/her calculations to options of this program that lead to a P_p and P_{pk} type computation. The underlying assumption with this approach is that the data are collected randomly over a long period of time and accurately describe the population of interest.

Process capability/performance index metrics require good communication and agreement on the techniques used for calculation. These agreements should also include sample size and measurement considerations. Within IEE strategy, we can avoid many of these issues by reporting in process/capability noncompliance rate units for both continuous and attribute data.

11.5 Confusion: Short-Term versus Long-Term Variability

A great deal of confusion and difference of opinion exists relative to the terms short-term and long-term variability. The following summarizes the basic differences in two main categories.

Opinion 1

Process capability describes the "capability" or the best a process could currently be expected to work. It does not address directly how well a process is running relative to the needs of the customer. Rather, it considers short-term variability. A long-term variability assessment attempts to address directly how well the process is performing relative to the needs of the customer. Typically, analysis focuses on determining short-term variability with an assumed adjustment of 1.5σ to compensate for drifts to get long-term variability. Special causes, which have the most impact on long-term variability estimates, from a control chart might be included in the analyses. Some might object that predictions couldn't be made without process stability. Processes can appear to be out of control from day-to-day variability effects such as raw material, which, they would argue, is common-cause variability.

Standard deviation input to process capability and process performance equations can originate from short-term or long-term considerations. In determining process capability indices from $\bar{x}$ and R control chart data, the standard deviation within subgroups is said to give an estimate of the short-term variability of the process, while the standard deviation of all the data combined is said to give an estimate of its long-term variability.

In a manufacturing process, short-term variability typically does not include, for example, raw material lot-to-lot variability and operator-to-operator variability. Within a business process, short-term variability might not include, for example, day-to-day variability or department-to-department variability. Depending upon the situation, these long-term variability sources might be considered special causes and not common causes.

Process capability indices C_p and C_{pk} typically assess the potential short-term capability by using a short-term standard deviation estimate, while P_p and P_{pk} typically assess overall long-term capability by using a long-term standard deviation estimate. Sometimes the relationship P_p and P_{pk} is referred to as process performance.

Some organizations require or assume that processes are in control before conducting process capability/performance index assessments. Other organizations lump all data together, which results in special-cause data increasing the estimates of long-term variability. These organizations might try to restrict the application of control charts to monitoring process inputs.

Opinion 2

Process capability describes how well a process is executing relative to customer needs. The terms short term and long term are not typically considered separately as part of a process capability assessment.

The quantification for the standard deviation term within process capability calculations describes the overall variability of a process. When determining process capability indices from $\bar{x}$ and R control chart data, an overall standard deviation estimate would be used in the process capability equations. Calculation procedures for standard deviations differ from one practitioner to another, ranging from lumping all data together to determining total standard deviation from a variance components model.

This opinion takes a more long-term view of variability. It involves a different view of factors in an in-control process. In manufacturing, raw material lot-to-lot variability and operator-to-operator variability are more likely considered common causes. In a business process, day-to-day variability or department-to-department variability are more likely considered as common causes.

The described mathematics of the process capability indices C_p and C_{pk} does not give direct focus to customer needs. P_p and P_{pk} indices are more suited for making assessments relative to this opinion's stated needs, as illustrated in the next section.

11.6   Calculating Standard Deviation

This section addresses the confusion encountered with regard to the calculation of the seemingly simple statistic, standard deviation. Though standard deviation is an integral part of the calculation of process capability, the method used to calculate it is rarely adequately scrutinized. In some cases, it is impossible to get a specific desired result if data are not collected in the appropriate fashion. Consider the following three sources of continuous data (Method 6 gives other alternatives for data collection and analyses):

- *Situation 1*: An $\bar{x}$ and R control chart with subgroups of sample size of 5.

- *Situation 2*: An individuals chart (X chart) with individual measurements.
- *Situation 3*: A random sample of measurements from a population.

All three are real possible sources of information, but no one method is correct for obtaining an estimate of standard deviation σ in all three scenarios. Pyzedek (1998) presents five methods of calculating standard deviation. Figure 11.3 illustrates six approaches to make this calculation, while the following elaborates more on each of these techniques.

Method 1

Long-term estimate of σ. One approach for calculating the standard deviation of a sample (s) is to use the formula :

$$\hat{\sigma} = \sqrt{\sum_{i=1}^{n} \frac{(x_i - \bar{x})^2}{n - 1}}$$

where $\bar{x}$ is the average of all data, x_i are the data values, and n is the overall sample size.

Sometimes computer programs apply an unbiasing term to this estimate, dividing the above by $c_4(n-1)$ (Minitab, 2007). Tabulated values for c_4 at n–1 can be determined from Table J or by using a mathematical relationship (Breyfogle, 2003).

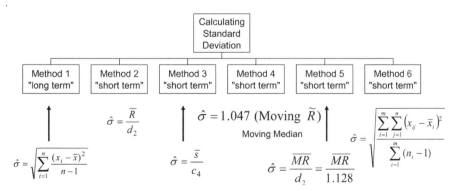

Figure 11.3: Various ways to calculate process standard deviation.

- *Situation 1*: When data come from an $\bar{x}$ and R chart, this traditional estimate of standard deviation is only valid when a process is stable, though some use this method even when processes are not stable. Shewhart shows that this method overestimates scatter if the process is influenced by a special cause. This estimate should never be used to calculate control limits. Control limits are calculated using sampling distributions.
- *Situation 2*: When data are from an individuals control chart, this approach can give an estimate of process variability from the customer's point of view.
- *Situation 3*: For a random sample of data from a population, this is the only method that makes sense, because the methods presented below all require the sequence of part creation.

Method 2

Short-term estimate of σ: A standard method for estimating standard deviation from $\bar{x}$ and R control chart data is:

$$\hat{\sigma} = \frac{\bar{R}}{d_2}$$

where $\bar{R}$ is the average of the subgroup range values from a control chart, and d_2 is a value from Table J which depends upon subgroup sample size.

- *Situation 1*: When data come from an $\bar{x}$ and R chart, this estimator alleviates the problem of the standard deviation being inflated by special causes because it does not include variation between time periods. Shewhart proposed using a rational subgroup to achieve this, where the subgroup sample is chosen so that the opportunity for special causes is minimized. Often this is accomplished by selecting consecutively produced units from a process. The method of analysis is inefficient when range is used to estimate standard deviation because only two data values are used from each subgroup. This inefficiency increases as the subgroup size increases. Efficiency increases when subgroup standard deviation is used.

- *Situation 2*: When data are from an individuals control chart, this calculation is not directly possible because the calculation of $\bar{R}$ for a subgroup size of one is not possible.
- *Situation 3*: For a random sample of data from a population, this calculation is not possible because the sequence of unit creation is not known.

Method 3

Short-term estimate of σ: The following equation derives from the equation used to determine the centerline of a control chart when the process standard deviation is known:

$$\hat{\sigma} = \frac{\bar{s}}{c_4}$$

where $\bar{s}$ is the average of the subgroup standard deviation values from a control chart, and c_4 is a value from Table J which depends upon subgroup sample size. Subgroup standard deviation values are determined by the formula shown in Method 1.

- *Situation 1*: When data are from an $\bar{x}$ and R or s chart, the comments relative to this situation are similar to the comments in Method 2. In comparison to Method 2, this approach is more involved but more efficient.
- *Situation 2*: When data are from an individuals control chart, this calculation is not possible because the calculation of $\bar{s}$ for a subgroup size of one is not possible.
- *Situation 3*: For a random sample of data from a population, this calculation is not possible since the sequence of unit creation is not known.

Method 4

Short-term estimate of σ: The following relationship is taken from one of the equation options used to determine the centerline of an individual control chart

$$\hat{\sigma} = 1.047 \text{ (Moving } \tilde{R})$$

where a correction factor of 1.047 is multiplied by the median of the moving range (Moving $\tilde{R}$).

- *Situation 1*: When data are from an $\bar{x}$ and R chart, this approach is not directly applicable.
- *Situation 2*: When data are from an individuals control chart, this calculation is an alternative. If the individuals control chart values are samples from a process, we would expect a higher value if there is less variability from consecutively created units when compared to the overall variability experienced by the process between sampling periods of the individuals control chart. Research has recently indicated that this approach gives good results for a wide variety of out-of-control patterns.
- *Situation 3*: For a random sample of data from a population, this calculation is not possible because the sequence of unit creation is not known.

Method 5

Short-term estimate of σ: The following equation derives from one of the equations used to determine the centerline of an individual control chart:

$$\hat{\sigma} = \frac{\overline{MR}}{d_2} = \frac{\overline{MR}}{1.128}$$

where $\overline{MR}$ is the moving range between two consecutively produced units and d_2 is a value from the table of factors for constructing control charts using a sample size of two.

- *Situation 1*: When data are from an $\bar{x}$ and R chart, this approach is not directly applicable.
- *Situation 2*: When data are from an individuals control chart, this calculation is an alternative. Most of the Method 4 comments for this situation are similarly applicable. This is the method suggested in AIAG (1995b). Some practitioners prefer Method 4 over Method 5 (Pyzedek, 1998).
- *Situation 3*: For a random sample of data from a population this calculation is not possible because the sequence of unit creation is not known.

Method 6

Short-Term estimate of σ: The following relationship is sometimes used by computer programs to pool standard deviations when there are m subgroups of sample size n.

$$\hat{\sigma} = \frac{S_p}{c_4(d)}$$

where
$c_4(d)$ is a value that can be determined from Table J and,

$$S_p = \sqrt{\frac{\sum\limits_{i=1}^{m}\sum\limits_{j=1}^{n}\left(x_{ij} - \bar{x}_i\right)^2}{\sum\limits_{i=1}^{m}(n_i - 1)}}$$

and

$$d = \left(\sum\limits_{i=1}^{m} n_i\right) - m + 1$$

The purpose of using $c_4(d)$ when calculating $\hat{\sigma}$ is to reduce bias to this estimate. Values for c_4 are given in Table J.

- *Situation 1*: When data come from an $\bar{x}$ and R or s chart, the comments relative to this situation are similar to the comments in Methods 2 and 3. If all groups are to be weighed the same regardless of the number of observations, the $\bar{s}$ (or $\bar{R}$) approach is preferred. If the variation is to be weighted according to subgroup size, the pooled approach is appropriate.
- *Situation 2*: When data are from an individuals control chart, this calculation is not directly possible because the calculation of $\bar{R}$ for subgroup size of one is not possible.
- *Situation 3*: For a random sample of data from a population, this calculation is not possible because the sequence of unit creation is not known.

11.7   Example 11.1: Process Capability/Performance Indices

The process data from Example 10.1 was shown in Table 10.1. An $\bar{x}$ and R control chart concluded that the data were from an out-of-control/unpredictable process, while a later IEE analysis (see Example 12.3) indicates that the process is in control or predictable.

Specifications for this process are 0.4037 ± 0.0013 (i.e., 0.4024–0.4050). Tabular and calculated values are in units of 0.0001 (i.e., the specification limits will be considered as 24–50).

Breyfogle (2003) shows the manual calculation procedures for this data set. A statistical program analysis is presented in Figure 11.4, which utilizes average moving range estimates for C_p and C_{pk} calculations and a pooled standard deviation estimate for P_p and P_{pk}. The calculated process capability and process performance indices from this figure are: C_p=1.46, C_{pk}=1.07, P_p=1.23, and P_{pk}=0.90.

Chapter 12 will later describe the advantages of only communicating a 3403 ppm total or 0.3% IEE process capability/

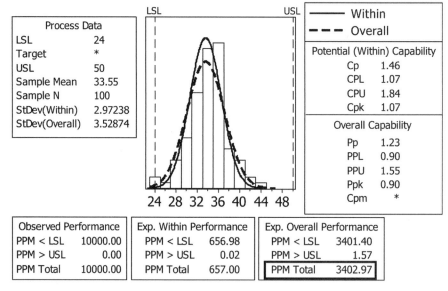

Figure 11.4: Process capability using average moving range estimates for C_p and C_{pk} calculations and a pooled standard deviation estimate for P_p and P_{pk}.

performance metric, as shown in the lower right hand corner of the output.

11.8 Process Capability/Performance for Attribute Data

The *p* chart and other attribute control charts are different from variables data in that each point can be directly related to a proportion or percentage of nonconformance relative to customer requirements, while points on a variables chart indicate a response irrespective of specification needs.

AIAG (1995b) defines capability as follows: "For attribute charts, capability is defined simply as the average proportion or rate of nonconforming product, whereas capability for variables charts refers to the total (inherent) variation ($6\hat{\sigma}_{\bar{R}/d_2}$) yielded by the (stable) process, with and/or without adjustments for process centering to specification targets."

AIAG (1995b) also states: "If desired, this can be expressed as the proportion conforming to specification (i.e., $1-\bar{p}$). For a preliminary estimate of process capability, use historical data, but exclude data points associated with special causes. For a formal process capability study, new data should be run, preferably for 25 or more periods, with the points all reflecting statistical control. The $\bar{p}$ for these consecutive in-control periods is a better estimate of the process's current capability."

Attribute assessments are not only applicable to pass/fail tests at the end of a manufacturing line. They can also be used to measure the "hidden factory," (see Glossary), using a DPMO scale.

11.9 Exercises

1. The example $\bar{x}$ and R chart in Chapter 10 (Figure 10.7) indicated that samples numbered 9, 10, 12, 13, and 18 were out of control (i.e., an unpredictable process). The process specifications are 0.4037 ± 0.0013 (i.e., 0.4024–0.4050). Tabular and calculated values will be in units of 0.0001 (i.e., the specification limits will be considered as 24–50). Assume that for each of these data points, circumstances for an out-of-control response were identified and will be avoided in future production. Determine the process

capability/performance indices of the remaining 14 subgroups, which are as follows:

------------ Measurements -------------

Subgroup	Obs 1	Obs 2	Obs 3	Obs 4	Obs 5
1	36	35	34	33	32
2	31	31	34	32	30
3	30	30	32	30	32
4	32	33	33	32	35
5	32	34	37	37	35
6	32	32	31	33	33
7	33	33	36	32	31
11	34	38	35	34	38
14	36	35	37	34	33
15	30	37	33	34	35
16	28	31	33	33	33
17	33	30	34	33	35
19	35	36	29	27	32
20	33	35	35	39	36

2. Determine the process capability and process performance measures of the following sequentially collected sampled data that had a lower specification of 2 and an upper specification of 16 with responses: 3.40, 8.57, 2.42, 5.59, 9.92, 4.63, 7.48, 8.55, 6.10, 6.42, 4.46, 7.02, 5.86, 4.80, 9.60, and 5.92.

3. A company is incorporating a Six Sigma program. A process is said to be capable of producing a response of 36 ±12. Someone compiled the following responses from the process, which were not collected in time sequence: 41.3, 30.8, 38.9, 33.7, 34.7, 20.4, 28.3, 35.1, 37.9, and 32.6. Determine best estimate for the process capability and process performance indices to report. List any concerns or questions you have about the data.

4. Using the same data in Exercise 11.2, determine the capability and process performance measures considering that there is only an upper specification of 10.

12

P-DMAIC – Measure Phase (Baseline Project): IEE Process Predictability and Process Capability/Performance Metric Assessments (Continuous Response)

12.1 P-DMAIC Roadmap Component

The previous four chapters described the foundation for creating IEE performance and project metrics; i.e., the project's baseline. The first two chapters of this series described continuous response and attribute population's characteristics. The third chapter described time-series plots and traditional control charting options, along with a description of why traditional control charts can lead to the wrong activities. The fourth chapter described traditional process capability and performance studies.

The graphic in this section highlights the P-DMAIC project baseline roadmap steps (see Appendix Section D.1) that are described in this chapter. Appendix E contains the tollgate check sheets for this and other phases.

Previously the scorecard/dashboard reporting of IEE satellite-level and 30,000-foot-level metrics was illustrated. Example 1.1 compared a red–yellow–green scorecard to IEE metric reporting.

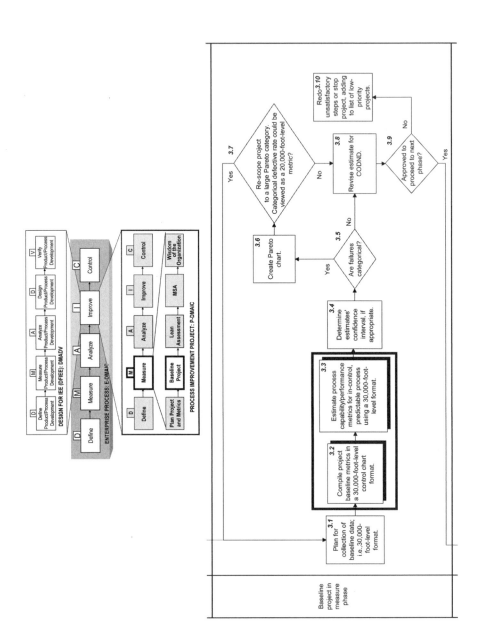

This chapter and the next chapter elaborate more on the IEE scorecard/dashboard two-step creation process:

1. Assess process predictability.
2. When the process is considered predictable, formulate a prediction statement for the latest region of stability. The usual reporting format for this statement is:
   (a) When there is a specification requirement: nonconformance percentage or defects per million opportunities (DPMO).
   (b) When there are no specification requirements; median response and 80% frequency of occurrence rate.

This chapter describes the execution of this process for a variety of continuous-output charting situations; i.e., this chapter will illustrate how to create the:

- Satellite-level scorecard/dashboard profit margin plot in Figure 3.3.
- 30,000-foot-level on-time delivery performance scorecard/ dashboard metric statement in Figure 3.4.

In this assessment, the initial data compiling describes the voice of the process (VOP), while a gap assessment is the comparison of the VOP to voice of the customer (VOC) expectations (e.g., specifications). This chapter will describe how to accomplish this using 30,000-foot-level control charting to assess predictability and a process capability/performance metric statement to address how well the VOP meets VOC desires.

The next chapter will extend the IEE satellite-level and 30,000-foot-level scorecard/dashboard reporting to attribute-output situations; for example, the next chapter will illustrate how to create the 30,000-foot-level defective rate performance scorecard/dashboard metric statement in Figure 7.10 of Volume 2.

The baseline project in the measure phase 3.2 and 3.3 drilldown steps provides the decision trees for 30,000-foot-level control charting and process capability/performance metric selection process. Figures 12.1 and 12.2 describe these drill downs, highlighting the continuous-data branch. This chapter describes the IEE use of these drill downs for continuous process output data, while the next chapter describes the use of these drill downs for attribute data.

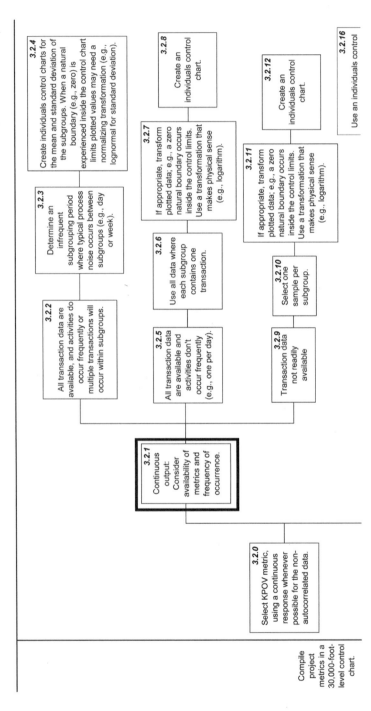

Figure 12.1: IEE 30,000-foot-level control chart decision tree. Drill down of step 3.2 of project execution roadmap (see Appendix D Section D.3) with continuous output option highlighted.

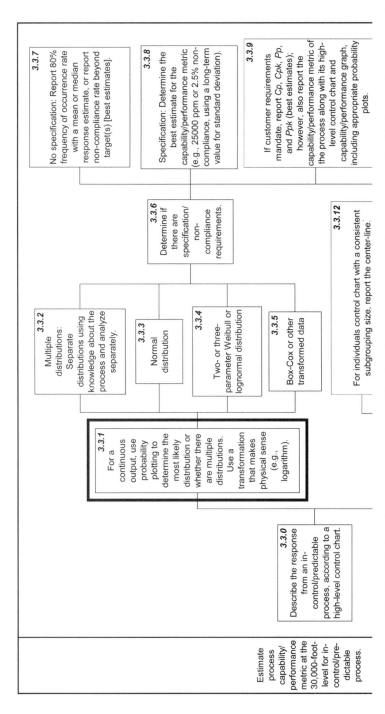

Figure 12.1: IEE 30,000-foot-level process capability/performance metric decision tree. Drill down of step 3.3 of project execution roadmap (See Appendix D Section D.3) with continuous output option highlighted.

12.2   Satellite-Level View of the Organization

Organizations often evaluate their business by comparing their currently quarterly profit or another business measure to the quarterly figures from a previous year or a previous month. From this comparison, one often describes whether the business is either up or down to the compared time frame. Within this type of analysis, business metrics from previous fiscal years are not typically carried over to the current year in a time-series chart. Action plans might be created from these simple monthly or quarterly comparisons, which are not dissimilar from the firefighting activities which were described in Example 8.2.

Measurements should lead to the right activity. However, the procedure of evaluating a current response without systematically looking at previous responses in a time-series chart, which separates common cause from special cause, can lead to activities that are very costly and not effective. The monthly or quarterly comparison tracking procedure that was initially described is not looking at the organization as a system that can have ups and downs in its metrics caused by common-cause variability. The magnitude of these fluctuations is a function of the business and how the business is run. Changes to these perturbations need to be resolved by looking at the system as a whole, not by reacting to individual monthly or quarterly comparisons.

With the IEE approach, we create satellite-level metrics that view the organization as a system. Over time we expect to see variation within this system (e.g., month-to-month). To assess whether our system is experiencing any special-cause events or trends, we will use an individuals control chart. This chart can give us a very different view of the business when we compare quarters or some other period of time.

With the satellite-level metric we are viewing the organization as a system or a process. From this view, we can make projections when there is common-cause variability, where we expect the next month to be within a range, unless something differently occurs, either positive or negative. This charting technique can also be modified to address trending or seasonal issues. We can also plot the data from common-cause variability to describe the expected variability from the system at the satellite-level; for example, 80% of the months we are experiencing a Return on investment (ROI) annualized rate between 5% and 12%.

Within an IEE deployment, a common-cause response improvement need can pull for the creation and execution of a project. This approach to business management helps create a learning organization, as described by Senge (1990). This approach for data analyses provides the framework for creating a long-lasting system that reduces organizational firefighting. With this system, improvement projects are undertaken which have true alignment to business needs.

12.3   30,000-Foot-Level, 20,000-Foot-Level, and 50-Foot-Level Operational and Project Metrics

Consider the view from an airplane. When the airplane is at an elevation of 30,000 feet, passengers can see a big picture view of the landscape. However, when the airplane is at 50 feet during landing, passengers view a much smaller portion of the landscape. Similarly a 30,000-foot-level control chart gives a macro view of a process KPOV or Y, while a 50-foot-level control chart gives more of a micro view of some aspect of the process (i.e., Key Process Input Variable (KPIV) or X of the process). In an IEE organization, we might also describe the drill down of 30,000-foot-level Key Process Output Variables (KPOVs) measures to other high-levels such as 20,000-foot-level, 15,000-foot-level, and 10,000-foot-level, noting that the 50-foot-level is reserved for the KPIV designation.

In training sessions, control charts are typically taught to identify in a timely fashion special causes within the control of a process at a low level; within IEE I would describe this as the 50-foot-level. An example of this form of control in IEE is to identify in a timely way when temperature changes to an unacceptable, predetermined level. When this occurs the process is adjusted so that the temperature variable problem is fixed before a large amount of product with unsatisfactory characteristics is produced. In IEE, pre-control charts, which are discussed later, are often a better charting choice than traditional control charts to identify when a timely process adjustment needs to be made so that the 30,000-foot-level metric remains satisfactory. These 50-foot KPIVs that need close monitoring and their allowed tolerances could have been determined from an IEE project.

In IEE, control charts are used as part of a high level scorecard/dashboard, where this emphasis can lead to a reduction in firefighting the problems of the day. These charts can change the culture so that there is less common-cause variation issues attacked as though they were special cause. IEE can create a measurement system scorecard/dashboard so that fire preventive actions are created to address common-cause issues where products do not consistently meet specification needs, in lieu of the day-to-day firefighting of non-compliance issues. The IEE roadmap provides a structured approach for fire prevention through the wise use and integration of process improvement/re-engineering tools as needed within process improvement activities.

Unlike 50-foot-level control charts, the IEE measurements at a high level suggest infrequent subgrouping/sampling to capture how the process is performing relatively to overall customer needs. When the sampling frequency is long enough to span all short-term process noise inputs such as raw material differences between days or daily cycle differences, I call this a high-level control chart (e.g., a 30,000-foot-level control chart). At this sampling frequency, we might examine only one sample or a culmination of process output data, plotting the response on an individuals control chart.

When someone is first introduced to this concept of infrequent subgrouping/sampling, a concern typically expressed is that this measurement does not give any insight to what we should do to improve. This observation is true; the purpose of this measurement is not to determine what should be done to improve. The two intents for this infrequent subgrouping/sample approach are:

- To determine if we have special-cause or common-cause conditions from a 30,000-foot-level vantage point.
- To compile and analyze data so that they provide a long-term view of the process capability/performance metric of our process relative to meeting the needs of customers.

At the initial state of evaluating a situation, the IEE approach does not suggest that practitioners get bogged down trying to collect a lot of data with the intent of identifying a cause-and-effect relation that can fix their problem. The IEE approach does suggest that this form of data collection should occur after a problem has been identified relative to meeting either an internal or external customer requirement KPOV, where the improvement team identifies the prioritization of effort for further evaluation.

Teams identify focus items for further investigation during brainstorming activities within the IEE project measure phase. These items can be monitored with the intent of determining if there is a cause-and-effect relationship. In IEE this gathering of wisdom of the organization includes activities such as process mapping, cause-and-effect diagram, cause-and-effect matrix, and failure mode and effects analysis (FMEA).

To reiterate, when selecting a rational subgroup to create a 30,000-foot-level control chart, the practitioner needs to create a sampling plan that will give a long-term view of process variability. The project execution roadmap provides selection direction for the IEE control charting procedure that is most appropriate for a variety of situations. A sampling plan to create a baseline of a process might be to select randomly one daily KPOV response from a historical data set during the last one and half years. An individuals control chart could then identify whether the process has exhibited common-cause or special-cause conditions.

If there are many special-cause conditions spread throughout the time frame of the chart, it might be appropriate to see what the chart would look like when examined at a less frequent rate. If the chart now consists of common-cause variability, we might conclude that the previous subgrouping had variability between the subgroups, which should later be investigated by the team for the purpose of gaining insight to what might be done to improve the overall process.

When many special-cause conditions appear on a control chart with too frequent sampling, these special-cause conditions could be viewed as noise to the system when examined using a less frequent sampling approach. I believe that long-term regular perturbations (e.g., day of the week effect on duration of calls in the call center) should typically be viewed as a source for common-cause variability of the system/process. They should be dealt with accordingly from a process point of view, if they adversely impact KPOV voice of the customer relative to specification limits or other business needs. That is, they should be addressed looking at the process inputs/outputs collectively rather than as individual special-cause conditions.

For processes that exhibit common-cause variability, the next step is to assess the KPOV relative to the needs of customers. This assessment is most typically made relative to specification requirements or other desired outcomes. One example of this is that the process capability and process performance indices such as C_p, C_{pk}, P_p, and P_{pk} do not directly addresses the customer requirements, noting that these types of indices can be deceiving. Performance targets are not specifications and should not be used to measure process capability.

A probability plot of the data can be a good supplementary tool to understand and describe better pictorially expected variability. This form of output can also be very beneficial in describing the process capability/performance metric as a median along with a percent frequency of occurrence range. A probability plot for this instance might indicate for the current process an estimated median of 20 days and 80% frequency of occurrence between 2 and 42 days to fill orders. For an IEE project in this area, someone might then estimate the cost impact of this process variability on an organization and/or general customer dissatisfaction level. These values could then be the baseline against which IEE projects are measured.

When this measurement and process improvement strategy is implemented, a statistical alteration to the 30,000-foot-level control chart appearance serves as an indicator that change occurred. We want to monitor this chart as time proceeds with the intent of detecting a shift or change in the control chart pattern toward the better as a result of implemented IEE changes.

In addition, the 30,000-foot-level control chart could be considered as a useful part of the control phase on project completion. After project completion, something new could happen within the process to cause the control chart to go out of control (unpredictable process). The 30,000-foot-level control chart could identify that this change occurred, which might lead to the reinvestigation of a particular process. This information could be very useful to an organization, even though its feedback might not be timely.

12.4 IEE Application Examples: Process Predictability and Process Capability/Performance Metric

- *Satellite-level metric*: The last 3-year ROI for a company was reported monthly in a control chart. No special causes or trends were identified. Monthly ROIs were plotted on a normal probability plot, where a null hypothesis for normality was not rejected (see Chapter 19). The process capability/performance metric of the system was reported on a probability plot as a best-estimate median monthly value with 80% frequency of occurrence. Organizational goals were set to improve the common-cause measurement response. A strategic plan was created and was in alignment with the organizational goal to improve this metric. 30,000-foot-level operational metrics were then chosen that would be the focus of improvement efforts. IEE projects were then chosen to improve these metrics.

- *Transactional 30,000-foot-level metric*: One randomly selected, paid invoice was selected each day from the last 15 months of invoices (i.e., days sales outstanding (DSO)), where the number of days beyond the due date was measured and reported. The difference in payment date from its scheduled date for each sample was reported in an individuals control chart, where no reason was identified for a couple special-cause data points. This data were plotted on a normal probability plot, where a null hypothesis (see Chapter 19) for normality was rejected. A lognormal plot fit the data well. An individuals control chart of the lognormal data did not indicate any special-cause conditions. The lognormal probability plot was used to estimate the proportion of invoices beyond 30, 60, and 90 days late. An IEE project was initiated to improve the DSO metric.

- *Transactional 30,000-foot-level metric*: The mean and standard deviation of all DSOs were tracked, using a weekly subgrouping in two individuals control charts. No special causes were identified. The long-term process capability/performance metric of the process was reported as percentage of individual transaction nonconformance beyond 30, 60, and/or 90 days.

- *Manufacturing 30,000-foot-level metric (KPOV)*: One random sample of a manufactured part was selected each day over the last year. The diameter of the part was measured and plotted in an individuals control chart. No special causes were identified. A null hypothesis for normality could not be rejected. The long-term process capability/performance metric was reported as the estimated parts-per-million (ppm) rate beyond the specification limits.

- *Transactional and Manufacturing 30,000-foot-level lead time metric (a Lean metric)*: One transaction was randomly selected each day over the last year, where the time from order entry to fulfillment was measured. The differences between these times relative to their due date were reported in an individuals control chart. No special causes were identified. The null hypothesis for normality could not be rejected. The long-term process capability/performance metric was reported as the estimated ppm rate beyond the due date for the transactions.

- *Transactional and Manufacturing 30,000-foot-level inventory metric or satellite-level TOC metric (a Lean metric)*: Inventory was tracked monthly using an individuals control chart. No special causes were identified. A null hypothesis for normality could not be rejected. The long-term process capability/ performance metric was reported as the expected median inventory levels with 80% month-to-month frequency of occurrence and the associated monetary implications.

- Manufacturing 30,000-foot-level quality metric: The number of printed circuit boards produced weekly for a high-volume manufacturing company is similar. The process experiences multiple products that have differing degrees of complexity. It was decided to track DPMOs, where the number of opportunities at the end of the week was defined as the total number of solder joints plus the number of soldered components. The weekly DPMO rate is tracked on an individuals control chart. No special causes were identified. The total number of defects in the predictable region of the control chart was divided by the number of opportunities to determine the reported process capability/performance metric.

- *Product DFIEE*: An IEE product design project was to increase 30,000-foot-level product MTBF (Mean Time Between Failures); for example, laptop computer MTBF rate by vintage of the computer. An individuals control chart tracked the product MTBF by product vintage. The process capability/performance metric of the system was reported on the probability plot as a median with 80% frequency of occurrence interval. This reporting described common-cause variability and what might be expected for MTBF rates in the future unless something were done differently to change the design process. Frequencies of problem categories were compiled in the predictable region of the control chart as a Pareto chart to identify improvement opportunities for newly developed products.

12.5   Traditional versus 30,000-Foot-Level Control Charts and Process Capability/Performance Metric Assessments

In the second half of the 1920s when Dr. Walter A. Shewhart of Bell Telephone Laboratories developed a theory of statistical quality control, he concluded that there were two components to variations that were displayed in all manufacturing processes. The first component was a steady component, that is, random variation that appeared to be inherent in the process. The second component was an intermittent variation to assignable causes. He concluded that assignable causes could be economically discovered and removed with an effective diagnostic program, but that random causes could not be removed without making basic process changes. Dr. Shewhart is credited with developing the standard control chart test based on 3σ limits to separate the steady component of variation from assignable causes. Shewhart control charts came into wide use in the 1940s because of war production efforts. Western Electric is credited with the addition of other tests based on sequences or runs (Western Electric, 1956).

Deming notes (Deming, 1986): "A fault in the interpretation of observations, seen everywhere, is to suppose that every event (defect, mistake, accident) is attributable to someone (usually the one nearest at hand), or is related to some special event. The fact is that most troubles with service and production lie in the system." Dr. Deming adds: "We shall speak of faults of the system as common causes of trouble, and faults from fleeting events as special causes." Dr. Deming elaborates further: "Confusion between common causes and special causes leads to frustration of everyone, and leads to greater variability and to higher costs, exactly contrary to what is needed. I should estimate that in my experience most troubles and most possibilities for improvement add up to proportions something like this: 94% belong to the system (responsibility of management), 6% special."

Control charts offer the study of variation and its source over time. Control charts can provide not only monitoring and control, but also the time-stamp identification of improvements. Control charts can be constructed from either a Shewhart or Deming point of view, which are as follows:

- *Shewhart* control charts can identify assignable causes that could be internal or external to the system.
- *Deming* control charts can separate a process's special from common-cause issues, where special causes originate from fleeting events experienced by the system and common causes originate from the natural variation of the process that is both internal and external to the system.

It is important to highlight that for a given process there can be very significant differences in the identification of out-of-control conditions for these two charting approaches. This is very important, since reacting to fix the problem of the day when it is a common-cause issue as though it were a special cause adds little, if any, value to the long-term performance of the process. The IEE 30,000-foot-level control chart creation approach is in alignment with the philosophy of Dr. Deming.

A traditional Shewhart explanation of the value for control charts is that control charts can give early identification of special causes so that issues can be resolved in a timely fashion, before many poor-quality parts/transactions are produced. This can be a benefit; however, organizations often focus only on the output of a process when applying control charts. This type of measurement is not really controlling the process and may not offer timely problem identification. To control a process using control charts, we would prefer to monitor the key process input variables, where the process flow is stopped for timely resolution when the variable goes out of control or at an undesirable level (see pre-control charts in Chapter 38).

IEE discourages the use of sigma quality level metrics. In addition, there can be much confusion about traditional process capability and process performance indices such as C_p, C_{pk}, P_p, and P_{pk}. Sometimes I am asked bizarre questions about how to calculate, transform, or interpret a process capability or process performance indices. I typically then ask the person how long he/she has been involved with these metrics. This person might give a response of 3 years. I then reply, "I know that you are confused and I have no reason to doubt your intelligence. If you are confused by these indices and you have been working to understanding them, what do you think is the level of understanding for these metrics at the line-worker and CEO level?" The response that I always get is that they are confused too. I then respond that he/she should use alternative metrics for this reporting.

This chapter describes the implementation of the following IEE alternative high-level measurement system process for various situations, as summarized in Figures 12.1 and 12.2. Individual measurement report tracking is accomplished through IEE scorecard/dashboard metric reporting process as follows:

1. An infrequent subgrouping/sampling plan is determined so that the typical variability from process input factors occurs between subgroups; e.g., subgroup by day, week, or month.
2. The process is analyzed for predictability using control charts.

3. When the process is considered predictable, formulate a prediction statement for the latest region of stability. The usual reporting format for this prediction statement is:
    (a) When there is a specification requirement: nonconformance percentage or DPMO.
    (b) When there are no specification requirements: median response and 80% frequency of occurrence rate

The techniques covered in this chapter are normally associated with manufacturing processes. However, these analysis techniques are very useful to also assess parameters in other areas of the business (e.g., the time required to process an invoice).

IEE uses the term process capability/performance metric to describe a process' predictive output in terms that everyone can easily understand (i.e., step 3 in the above process). It is important to note that this metric reporting format is consistent for both continuous and attribute responses. This consistency is unlike traditional reporting where continuous response outputs lead to the reporting of process capability and process performance indices (see Chapter 11) and attribute responses lead to the reporting of proportion nonconformance.

I realize that customers often ask for process capability and process performance indices; hence, these metrics can be calculated and supplied to customers. However, organizations should strongly consider the methods described in this chapter as the approach that they use for their own measurement reporting system. In addition, consideration should also be given to any stealth training (see Glossary) that they could do to educate their customers on the value of this alternative metric reporting methodology.

To reiterate, IEE utilizes control charts to examine processes from a higher viewpoint, which is consistent with Dr. Deming's philosophy. In my opinion, this application may offer more value to an organization than using process control charts as they are currently used in most organizations. As noted earlier, Dr. Deming made the statement that 94% of the troubles in a process belong to the system (common cause); only 6% are special cause. With this approach, an individuals control chart might illustrate to management and others that past firefighting activities have been the result of common-cause issues. Because most of these issues were not special-cause issues, this expensive approach to issue resolution had no lasting value.

This IEE approach will not view short-term typical process shifts as special-cause excursion control chart issues but as noise to the overall process response. If the process is shown to be predictable and the process overall does not yield a desired response, there is a pull for project creation. Within the improvement projects, inputs and their levels are examined collectively over the process' stable/predictable period of time to determine opportunities for process improvement.

12.6   Traditional Control Charting Problems

Chapters 10 and 11 focused on the general concepts of traditional control charting and process capability. This chapter describes inherent risks of many traditional control charting techniques and process capability assessments.

In IEE, we focus on the creation of control charts where we can separate special-cause occurrence from common-cause variability. The question of concern is whether for a given process one person might setup a control charting strategy which indicates that the system is out of control/unpredictable, while another person sets up a control charting strategy that indicates that the system is predictable.

The answer is an affirmative one. Think about the significance of this. For a given process, one control charting planner could be spending much energy trying to resolve reported special-cause issues, which could lead to much firefighting. While, another person, who examines the same process, is working to understand what process improvements should be made to address common-cause issues that are leading to an overall unsatisfactory process nonconformance rate.

To illustrate how this could happen, consider a manufacturing process that produces a widget, although the same methodology would apply to business processes (e.g., call center or grocery checkout line). There is one dimension on this widget that is considered very important and needs to be monitored by way of a control chart. However, the measurement can only be made in a laboratory environment, which results in a large per sample cost and the desire to minimize the number of collected samples. Consider also that new raw material is supplied daily and, unknown to the experimenter, is that this between-lot variability dramatically affects the measured response to such an extent that raw material lot-to-lot variability is a KPIV driver that can lead to much non-compliant product.

Using a traditional sampling approach, one person might choose to daily collect a sample of five parts, where the parts are manufactured consecutively. Another person might choose to create a sampling plan where five parts are selected every week, where one sample is collected randomly each day. In each case, a more frequent sampling plan was thought to be too expensive.

Both of these people plotted information on an $\bar{x}$ and R chart using a subgroup size of five, where one person had daily sub-grouping and the other had weekly subgrouping. For the above described scenario, the person with the daily subgrouping would conclude that the process was out of control, while the person who selected the weekly subgrouping plan would conclude that the process was in control.

The upper and lower control chart limits that are to identify special-cause and common-cause variability are determined through process variability calculations, not tolerances. For the above de-scribed scenario, the daily sampling of five consecutive parts would have a lower control limit calculated standard deviation than the sampling of five parts throughout the week (i.e., one part daily).

Because of this, the $\bar{x}$ and R chart that was created using five consecutive parts would indicate an out-of-control condition be-cause of the large daily raw material lot-to-lot variability, which has no impact on the upper and lower control chart limits calcula-tion. For this daily subgrouping scenario, there could be frequent panic because, when an out-of-control condition occurs, the pro-duction line is supposed to stop until the problem is resolved. In addition, the next obvious question is: What should be done with the production parts from the previous day's non-compliant inspection? Do we need to institute a sorting plan for that daily production lot? On the next day, since the material changed, the process might now be within the control limits. Everybody heaves a sigh of relief that the problem is now fixed – until another batch of material arrives that adversely affects the widget.

The sampling plan of five parts weekly would not indicate an out-of-control condition (i.e., predictable process) because the day-to-day raw material variability would increase the spread of the upper and lower control chart limits. However, this does not mean that a problem does not exist. A process capability/performance metric nonconformance rate study would be unsat-isfactory, indicating that a common-cause problem exists. This process study might indicate that there is an overall 10% noncon-formance problem; that is 10% of the widgets produced overall from the process are not conforming to specification.

This problem then could be translated into monetary and customer satisfaction terms that everyone can understand. A team could then tackle this problem by collecting data that provides more insight into what could cause the problem (i.e., metrics improvement needs pull for project creation). During this investigation many ideas could be mentioned, one of which is raw material lot-to-lot variability. The collection of data and subsequent analysis using the techniques described later in this volume would indicate that there is a process problem with raw material. A quick fix might be to sort for satisfactory raw material and work with the supplier to tighten tolerances.

A more desirable solution might be to conduct a design of experiments (DOE) to determine whether there are process settings that would make the process more robust to the variability of raw material characteristics. Perhaps through this experiment we would find that if process temperature were increased, raw material variability would no longer affect widget quality. Through a DOE we could gain knowledge about our process, in which temperature could be monitored as a KPIV at the 50-foot level. A frequent sampling plan should be considered when monitoring temperature because the quality of the process output depends on the performance of this KPIV. When this upstream KPIV is not performing satisfactory relative to its calculated tolerance for high-quality product, immediate adjustments needs to be made to this KPIV.

Consider how control charts were used initially in the above illustration. For the sampling plan of five parts weekly, the overall within subgroup measurement variability was high. This tracking resulted in the consideration of raw material lot-to-lot variability as common-cause variability to the system. The more frequent daily sampling plan viewed raw material day-to-day variability as a special cause. Not everyone in the statistical community agrees as to whether material variability for this example should be considered special or common cause. When making this decision for yourself, consider that Dr. Deming described problems to be common cause when they are system problems that needed to be addressed by management. The question is whether you consider the typical day-to-day variability of raw material as a system problem or not. In IEE, this day-to-day raw material variability would be considered as a potential source for common-cause variability, before the charting process is begun.

In this illustration, we compared the results from the two sampling plans using $\bar{x}$ and R charts. This example illustrated how results using this chart can be very dependent upon the sampling plan. For an IEE strategy, we typically use an individuals control chart when making in-control/predictability assessments, with an appropriate data normalizing transformation when the underlying plotted data type plotted cannot be represented by a normal distribution, for example, count data, failure rates, and many transactional environments that have a lognormal distribution. The reason for this is that with individuals control charts the variability that occurs between subgroups affects the control limits.

This chapter will later describe how it is generally more desirable to track the mean and standard deviation or log standard deviation as an individuals charts when assessing whether a process is in control/predictable. The reason for this is that with individuals control charts between the subgroup variability affects the control limits calculation. This chapter will show how this control chart selection process is a part of the IEE roadmap.

In IEE, identified process KPIVs through such techniques as DOE need to be controlled through either mistake-proofing or frequent 50-foot-level monitoring using techniques such as pre-control charts, which are described later. It needs to be highlighted that this low-level temperature process measurement should not be chosen arbitrary by someone implementing an overall statistical process control (SPC) system throughout the company. Because of this approach, where data was used to determine the KPIV, we should take it seriously when the temperature tracking chart indicates adjustments are needed.

As earlier described, the above scenario is applicable to transactional processes as well as manufacturing situations. For example, a transactional situation could be DSO, where we are assessing the difference between payment time and due date. A developed KPIV that could be identified through a project might be the timeliness of reminder calls to customers that have a history of late payments.

12.7 Discussion of Process Control Charting at the Satellite-Level and 30,000-Foot-Level

The 30,000-foot-level control chart is an important consideration when implementing an IEE strategy; however, some readers may feel uncomfortable with the approach since it has some differences from traditional control charting techniques. Because of this concern, this section will *reiterate* and further elaborate on the technique.

Classically, it is stated that when creating control charts, subgroups should be chosen so that opportunities for variation among the units within a subgroup are small. The thought is that if variation within a subgroup represents the piece-to-piece variability over a very short period of time, then any unusual variation between subgroups would reflect changes in the process that should be investigated for appropriate action. The following will discuss the logic of this approach.

Let's elaborate on a previously described scenario. A process has one operator per shift and batch-to-batch raw material changes occur daily. Consider also that there are some slight operator-to-operator differences and raw material differences from batch-to-batch, but raw material is always within specification limits. If a control chart is established where five pieces are taken in a row for each shift, the variability used to calculate $\bar{x}$ and R control chart limits does not consider operator-to-operator and batch-to-batch raw material variability. If the variability between operators and batch-to-batch is large relative to five pieces in a row, the process could frequently appear to be going out of control (i.e., an unpredictable process). We are often taught that when a process goes out of control (becomes unpredictable) we should "stop the presses" and fix the special-cause problem. Much frustration can occur in manufacturing when time is spent to no avail trying to fix a problem over which operators may have little, if any, control.

One question that someone might ask is whether the manufacturing line should be shut down because of such a special cause. Someone could even challenge whether out-of-control conditions caused by raw material should be classified as special cause. *Note*: This point does not say that raw material is not a problem to the process even though it is within tolerance. The point is whether the variability between raw material lots should be treated as a special cause. It seems that there is a very good argument to treat this type of variability as common cause. If this were the case, control limits should then be created to include this variability.

To address this, we could track the measurement from only one unit on an individuals control chart, noting that a data normalizing transformation may be appropriate if the type of data do not follow a normal distribution. To address whether the batch-to-batch variability or other variability sources are causing a problem, the long-term variability of the process could then be compared to specification needs as illustrated in Figure 12.3.

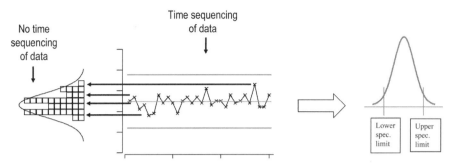

Figure 12.3: Illustration of control charting and process capability/ performance metric assessment at the 30,000-foot-level.

Mathematically, this comparison could be expressed in process capability and process performance units such as C_p, C_{pk}, P_p, P_{pk} (see Chapter 11 for why these units can cause confusion and problems). In addition, this variability could be described as percent beyond specification or in parts-per-million (ppm) defect rates. If there is no specification, as might be the case in transactional or service processes, variability could be expressed as a median and in percent of occurrence. An example of this application is that the median time to process an order is 30 days, while 80% of the time a purchase order takes between 10 and 50 days to fill.

If the process is not capable of meeting specification needs, a project can be created. Further analysis of the process using the other tools would show that the process is not robust to raw material batch-to-batch variations, as illustrated in Figure 12.4. The graphical tools described later can give insight to these differences (e.g., multi-vari charts, box plots, and marginal plots). Analytical tools described later mathematically examine the significance of these observed differences, for example, variance components analysis, Analysis of Variance (ANOVA), and Analysis of Means (ANOM).

When we react to the problem of the day, we are not structurally assessing this type of problem. Noting that every step is not required for all projects, an IEE project improvement strategy involves the following:

- Baseline the current process 30,000-foot-level metrics.
- Structural brainstorming for improvements using techniques such as process flowcharting, cause-and-effect diagram, cause-and-effect matrix, and FMEA.
- Utilize passive analyses to help gain insight to improvement opportunities (e.g., multi-vari analysis, ANOVA, regression analysis).

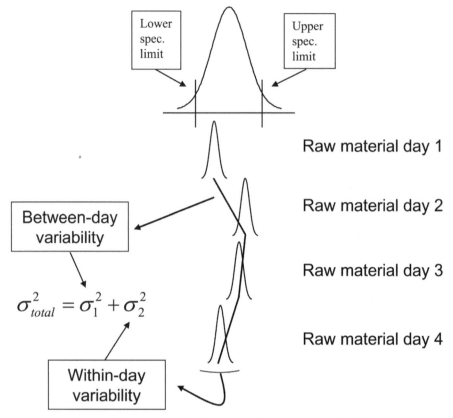

Figure 12.4: Potential sources for output variability.

- Conduct proactive testing/experimentation to identify procedural change opportunities, if appropriate (i.e., DOE).
- Conduct kaizen event to determine what could be done to improve process workflow, when appropriate.
- Implement procedural improvements; for example, work flow improvements, machine settings, and mistake proofing (error proofing).
- Demonstrate 30,000-foot-level metrics improvement.
- Maintain the gain through a control plan that can include active process control procedures.

One final note is that in traditional control charting it is preferable to have 25–30 subgroups when creating a control chart. However, sometimes history data are not available and we need to start collecting new data at the 30,000-foot-level. Waiting for the collection of 25–30 samples before making a decision may not be practical.

For example, with a daily infrequent subgrouping/sampling plan, this would mean that someone could not start to make a decision for perhaps 5–6 weeks. For traditional control charting, the primary focus is to identify special-cause conditions. This would equate to the IEE 50-foot-level view of a KPIV. For these situations, a minimum number of 25–30 samples would be needed so that "more confidence" is achieved for the calculated control limits values.

However, typically at the 30,000-foot-level most problems are common cause (i.e., process issues); hence, if we error on the side of identifying a special-cause condition as a common-cause condition, it is not as important from an IEE perspective as it would be from a traditional control charting perspective.

With an IEE approach it is preferable, when no historical data is available, to start taking data immediately using an infrequent subgrouping/sampling data collection plan. Even thought things are not perfect the control chart limits can then be calculated. Using traditional control chart limit calculation techniques, the calculated limits can be theoretically challenged for small data sets; however, this approach still gives us a quick snapshot of our process.

If the 30,000-foot-level control chart is considered in control we would state that the process is predictable. The uncertainty in the process capability/performance metric from the small sample size can readily be quantified from the available data using confidence limit calculations. With an IEE approach, we are perhaps more cognizant of whether the sample being analyzed is representative of the true population of interest than its pure size.

12.8　IEE Process Predictability and Process Capability/Performance Metric: Individual Samples with Specifications

The methodologies described in this section are applicable to the creation of 30,000-foot-level metrics for the following process assessments that have specification requirements:

- One sample per chemical batch where there are upper and lower tolerances.
- DSO when there is an upper criterion for number of days late beyond due date.

- Duration of all infrequent equipment changeover times when there is an upper criterion for task completion time.
- Duration of hold time in a call center when there is an upper criterion for the time to complete the task.
- Duration of time in the checkout line at a store when there is a lower and upper time criterion.
- One sampled part/process measurement daily, where the part has an upper and lower tolerance.
- The fill time for one sampled customer order is measured weekly.

The roadmap steps for this IEE application are the following:

1. Control chart creation steps (Figure 12.1):
   - Continuous output [3.2.1] – All transaction data are available and activities don't occur frequently (e.g., one per day) [3.2.5] – Use all data where each subgroup contains one transaction [3.2.6] – If appropriate, transform the data [3.2.7] – Create an individuals control chart [3.2.8]
   - Continuous output [3.2.1] – Not readily available transaction data [3.2.9] – Select one sample per subgroup [3.2.10] – If appropriate, transform the data [3.2.11] – Create an individuals control chart [3.2.12]
2. Process capability/performance metric creation steps for predictable processes (Figure 12.2):
   - For a continuous output, use probability plotting to determine the most likely distribution or whether there are multiple distributions [3.3.1] – Normal distribution [3.3.3] – Determine if there are specification/non-compliance requirements [3.3.6] – Specification: Determine the best estimate for the capability/performance metric (e.g., 25,000 ppm or 2.5% non-compliance, using a long-term value for standard deviation) [3.3.8]

12.9   Example 12.1: IEE Process Predictability and Process Capability/Performance Metric: Individual Samples with Specifications

IEE Application Examples
- *Transactional: One paid invoices were randomly selected each week. The number of days past the invoice due date was tracked over time to determine if the process was predictable.*

> *For regions of predictability, a process capability/performance metric was made relative to specification limits.*
> - *Lead Time (Manufacturing and Transactional): Every week one transaction was randomly selected. Lead times for completing the transactions were tracked over time to determine if the process was predictable. For regions of predictability, a process capability/performance metric was made relative to specification limits.*

The methodology described in this example applies to the scenarios described in the previous section.

Consider that the time-series chemical-mixing process viscosity data presented in Example 10.2 were collected using an infrequently subgrouping/sampling plan. Consider also that there was a 72 to 78 specification.

When specifications exist for a stable/predictable process, we would like to make a statement as to how the process is performing relative to these specifications. Within traditional Six Sigma programs, this quantification for a continuous response is typically expressed using process capability indices (C_p and C_{pk}) and/or process performance indices (P_p and P_{pk}) and/or a sigma quality level. However, there is much confusion with these metrics (see Chapter 11).

The alternative IEE reporting methodology provides a very good, easier-to-understand estimate of what the process customer experiences. For data collected using an infrequent subgrouping/sampling plan, the process capability/performance metric would simply be the estimated defective/defect percentage/proportion rate or ppm failure rate. A probability plot is useful to estimate the process capability/performance metric for this process.

Using this approach, the 30,000-foot-level process metric assessment is described in Figure 12.5, where the process is concluded to be predictable with an estimated process capability/performance metric of 17.4% nonconformance [(100 − 96.793) + 14.192 = 17.399].

12.10 IEE Process Predictability and Process Capability/Performance Metric: Multiple Samples in Subgroups Where There Are Specification Requirements

The methodologies described in this section are applicable to the creation of 30,000-foot-level metrics for the following process assessments that have specification requirements:

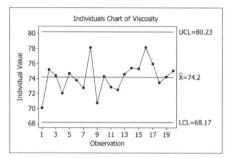 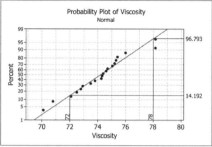

Predictable process with an approximate 17.4% non-conformance rate

Figure 12.5: Individuals control chart and normal probability plot to estimate process capability/performance metric.

- DSO when there are multiple subgroup samples and there is upper criterion for number of days late beyond due date.
- Duration of hold time in a call center when there are multiple subgroup samples and there is an upper criterion for the time to complete the task.
- Duration of time in the checkout line at a store when there are multiple subgroup samples and there is a lower and upper time criterion.
- Multiple sampled part/process measurements daily, where the part has an upper and lower tolerance.
- The fill time for multiple sampled customer orders is measured weekly.

The complete population could be analyzed within each subgroup in lieu of selecting samples for each subgroup. When this occurs, we are considering that the data are a random sample of the process.

Infrequent subgrouping/sampling of one datum point from a process for each subgroup has an advantage in separating process common-cause variability from special-cause variability when compared to an $\bar{x}$ and R strategy. The reason for this is that the control chart limits for the individuals control chart considers between subgroup variability, while the $\bar{x}$ and R control chart limits do not. However, when a great deal of data is readily available for each subgroup (e.g., ERP system that captures days sales outstanding (DSO) for all invoices), we have the flexibility to use more data, thereby improving our decision-making process.

An alternative procedure to implement is an infrequent sub-grouping/sampling approach where multiple samples are analyzed for each subgroup. This sample size for each subgroup should be approximately the same. Since there are multiple samples in the subgroups, two control charts are needed to assess within subgroup changeover time. One control chart assesses whether within subgroup mean response changes over time, while the other control chart address whether within subgroup variability changes over time. Often it is better to track the logarithm of the standard deviation, especially when the subgroup size is less than 10, because standard deviations data lack robustness to normality; that is, an individuals control chart assumes the underlying distribution is normal. Data in this format can lead to a variance components analysis for the source of variability, as described later.

It should be emphasized that this control charting procedure can lead to a very different set of control limits than an $\bar{x}$ and s chart. Control limits for the above-described procedure are calculated by quantifying between subgroup variability, as opposed to the $\bar{x}$ and s or $\bar{x}$ and R procedure, which calculates limits from within subgroup variability.

The process capability/performance metric calculation could be determined by combining all data and creating a probability plot, as described in the previous section. However, this approach does not directly address the differing variability that could occur between and within subgroups, which is described in Figure 12.6. The following two examples consider the overall variability calculation when making the process capability/performance metric calculation, which is mathematically described as (see Chapter 24):

$$\sigma_{Overall}{}^2 = \sigma_{Within\text{-}subgroupvariability}{}^2 + \sigma_{Between\text{-}subgroupvariability}{}^2$$

The roadmap steps for this IEE application are:

1. Control chart creation steps (Figure 12.1):
   - Continuous output [3.2.1] – All transaction data are available and activities do occur frequently or multiple transactions will occur within subgroups [3.2.2] – Determine an infrequent subgrouping period where typical process noise occurs between subgroups (e.g., day or week) [3.2.3] – Create individuals control charts for the mean and standard deviation of the subgroups. For a subgroup size less than 10, a normal distribution approximation for standard deviation may not suffice; that

Overall variability

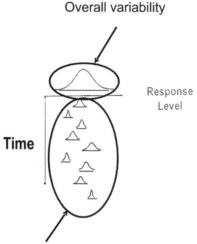

Within and between subgroup variability

Figure 12.6: Within subgroup (short-term variability) and overall variability (long-term variability) of a process' output.

Table 12.1: Process Time-Series Data

Subgroup	Sample One	Sample Two	Sample Three	Sample Four	Sample Five
1	102.7	102.2	102.7	103.3	103.6
2	108.2	108.8	106.7	106.6	109.1
3	101.9	103.0	100.6	101.4	101.3
4	103.9	105.5	104.3	104.5	104.5
5	97.2	99.0	96.5	94.9	96.5
6	94.4	93.0	93.0	95.2	93.6
7	104.7	103.6	103.7	104.7	104.5
8	102.5	102.7	101.2	100.6	103.1
9	101.9	103.1	101.0	101.2	101.4
10	95.0	95.3	95.3	94.4	94.2

is, a logarithm transformation of standard deviation may be necessary.

2. Process capability/performance metric creation steps for predictable processes (Figure 12.2):
    *   For a continuous output, use probability plotting to determine the most likely distribution or whether there are multiple distributions [3.3.1] – Normal distribution [3.3.3] – Determine if there are specification/

non-compliance requirements [3.3.6] – Specification: Determine the best estimate for the capability/performance metric (e.g., 25,000 ppm or 2.5% non-compliance, using a long-term value for standard deviation) [3.3.8]

12.11   Example 12.2: IEE Process Predictability and Process Capability/Performance Metric: Multiple Samples in Subgroups Where There Are Specification Requirements

IEE Application Examples
- *Transactional: One hundred paid invoices were randomly selected each week. The number of days past the invoice due date was tracked over time to determine if the process was predictable. For regions of predictability, a process capability/ performance metric was made relative to specification limits.*
- *Lead time (Manufacturing and Transactional): Every week 25 transactions were randomly selected. Lead times for completing the transactions were tracked over time to determine if the process was predictable. For regions of predictability, a process capability/performance metric was made relative to specification limits.*

The methodology described in this example applies to the scenarios described in the previous section.

A process predictability statement along with a process capability/performance metric statement relative to the customer specifications of 95–105 is desired for the sample process data shown in Table 12.1. This example not only uses the IEE process for determining the 30,000-foot-level metrics but also will illustrate why $\bar{x}$ and R control chart analysis can be deceptive.

This type of data traditionally leads to $\bar{x}$ and R control charts, as shown in Figure 12.7.

Whenever a measurement on a control chart is beyond the upper control limit (UCL) or lower control limit (LCL), this process is said to be out of control. Out-of-control conditions are considered special-cause conditions, and out-of-control conditions can trigger a causal problem investigation. Since so many out-of-control conditions are apparent in this, many causal investigations could have been initiated. But out-of-control processes are not

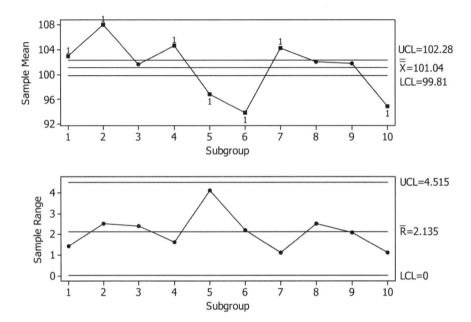

Figure 12.7: $\bar{x}$ and R control chart.

predictable, and no process capability/performance metric statement should be made about how the process is expected to perform in the future relative to its specification limits.

When creating a sampling plan, we may select only one sample
instead of several samples for each subgroup. Let's say that this
is what happened and only the first measurement was observed
for each of the 10 subgroups. For this situation, we would create
an individuals control chart like the one shown in Figure 12.8.

This control chart is very different from the previously shown
$\bar{x}$ and R charts. Since the plotted values are within the control
limits, we can conclude only common-cause variability exists and
the process should be considered to be in control or predictable.

The dramatic difference between the limits of these two control charts is caused by the differing approaches to determining
sampling standard deviation, which is a control limit calculation
term. To illustrate this, let's examine how these two control chart
limit calculations are made.

As previously described, for $\bar{x}$ charts, the UCL and LCL are
calculated from the relationship:

$$LCL = \bar{\bar{x}} - A_2\bar{R} \qquad UCL = \bar{\bar{x}} + A_2\bar{R}$$

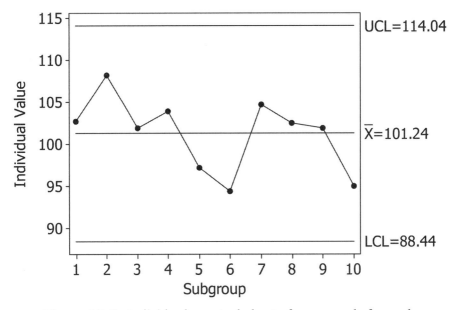

Figure 12.8: Individuals control chart of one sample for each subgroup.

where $\bar{\bar{x}}$ is the overall average of the subgroups, A_2 is a constant depending upon subgroup size (see Table J) and $\bar{R}$ is the average range within subgroups.

For the individuals or X chart calculation the UCL and LCL are determined from the relationships:

$$\text{LCL} = \bar{x} - 2.66(\overline{MR}) \qquad \text{UCL} = \bar{x} + 2.66\,(\overline{MR})$$

where $\overline{MR}$ is the average moving range between subgroups.

The limits for the $\bar{x}$ chart are derived from within-subgroup variability $(\bar{R})$, while sampling standard deviations for an individuals control chart is calculated from between-subgroup variability $(\overline{MR})$.

Which control charting technique is most appropriate? It depends on how you categorize the source of variability relative to common and special causes, as previously described. IEE considers that the variability between subgroups should affect the control limits. For this to occur, we need a sampling plan where the impact from this type of noise variable occurs between subgroupings. When creating control charts at the 30,000-foot-level, we need to include between-subgroup variability within our control chart limit calculations, as was achieved in the earlier individuals control chart procedure.

In this situation, the subgroup mean and log standard deviation are tracked using two individuals control charts to assess whether the process is predictable. When a process is predictable, the overall process capability/performance metric can be determined by collectively analyzing the data, as shown in Figure 12.9.

We can conclude from this analysis that the process is predictable. Rather than report process capability in C_p, C_{pk}, P_p and P_{pk} units, it is more meaningful to report a process capability and performance metric of expected overall performance parts per million. In this case, it's 268,525.98 or 27% nonconformance. This prediction is based on the assumption there will be no overall change in future process response levels. This assumption will be continually assessed as we monitor the 30,000-foot-level control chart.

We then need to calculate the cost of poor quality (COPQ) or the cost of doing nothing different (CODND) for this process. If this was an enterprise 30,000-foot-level scorecard/dashboard metric and the CODND amounts are unsatisfactory, we could pull for creating an IEE project. With this overall approach, the entire system is assessed when process improvements are addressed. This differs from the use of Figure 12.7 which could lead you to create unstructured activity that is unproductive if you are trying to understand the cause of isolated events, which are really common cause, as per the previously described definition.

Note, Figure 12.9 illustrates how someone can get a similar answer using either a raw-data probability plot or a statistical software process capability analysis. I will be illustrating this point by including both plots in this and several figures to follow; however, only one of these plots should be included in a report-out.

One should also note that when creating a large-amount-of-data probability plot it is unlikely that the data will fit a distribution well enough so that a null hypothesis of distribution fit is not rejected (see Chapter 19). Rather than solely evaluating distribution fit by looking at a hypothesis-test p-value, I like to visually examine the plot to see if the fit is close enough for quantifying an approximate process capability/performance metric and see if there is something that can be learned from the plot. For example, someone might gain insight from a plot to potential outliers or multiple distributions, which could give direction on process improvement opportunities.

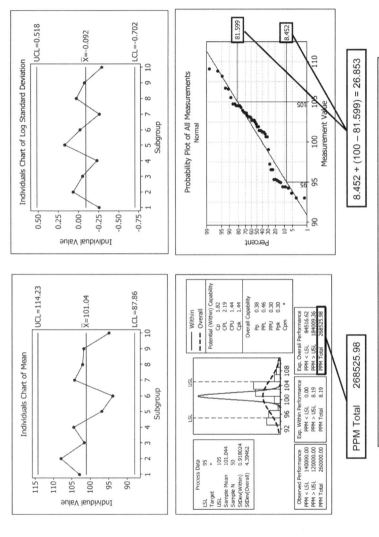

Figure 12.9: IEE 30,000-foot-level report-out, where there are multiple samples in each subgroup. The only reason that a probability plot and a process capability analysis are both included in this figure is to illustrate that the two approaches yield similar results. Only one should be included in a typical report-out.

12.12   Example 12.3: IEE Individuals Control Chart of Subgroup Means and Standard Deviation as an Alternative to Traditional $\bar{x}$ and R Chart

The data analysis in Example 10.1 used an $\bar{x}$ and R control chart to conclude that the process from which samples were collected was out of control. In this example we will re-analyze the measured diameter data using the IEE suggested alternative procedure; i.e., an individuals control chart of the mean and individuals control chart of the logarithm of standard deviation. The process capability/performance metric will then be calculated against a specification of 0.4024 to 0.4050 example value (24 to 50 as expressed in ten thousands of an inch).

Unlike the $\bar{x}$ and R chart approach, this analysis result shown in Figure 12.10 indicates that the process is in control/predictable. The process capability/performance metric is estimated to be 0.3% (rounded and converted 3402.97 ppm total to a percentage).

12.13   Example 12.4: The Implication of Subgrouping Period Selection on Process Stability Statements

Figure 8.2 illustrated the application of a time-series plot to hourly collected data, where this data could be the dimension on a sample part or a transaction time. If there were an upper specification limit of 305 and the company policy was to work on the process any time a sampled response was above the specification limit, there would be much generated activity (i.e., firefighting).

The data to create this hourly time-series plot are shown in Table 12.2, along with the day, shift, and hour of the day for each product/transaction response produced. If one were to examine this time-series data in an individuals control chart, as shown in Figure 12.11, the conclusion would be that the process is out of control (i.e., not predictable). However, now let's examine the process at the 30,000-foot-level using an IEE approach.

From the project execution roadmap drill down shown in Figure 12.1, we note from the step sequence of 3.2.1>3.2.2>3.2.3 that we need initially to: "Determine an infrequent subgrouping/sampling period where typical process noise occurs between subgroups." After a discussion with personnel familiar with the process, it was concluded that there could be differences in process

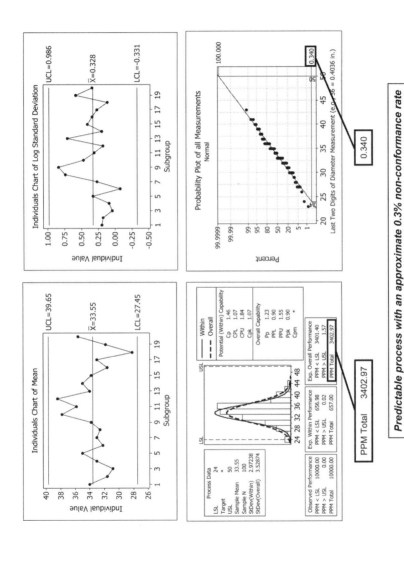

Figure 12.10: IEE 30,000-foot-level report-out, where there are multiple samples in each subgroup. The only reason that a probability plot and a process capability analysis are both included in this figure is to illustrate that the two approaches yield similar results. Only one should be included in a typical report-out.

Table 12.2: Hourly Sampling

Seq	Day	Shift	Hour	Response	Seq	Day	Shift	Hour	Response	Seq	Day	Shift	Hour	Response	Seq	Day	Shift	Hour	Response	Seq	Day	Shift	Hour	Response
1	1	1	1	306.35	97	5	1	1	294.55	193	9	1	1	297.38	289	13	1	1	290.59	385	17	1	1	303.92
2	1	1	2	306.15	98	5	1	2	296.00	194	9	1	2	297.68	290	13	1	2	289.49	386	17	1	2	303.09
3	1	1	3	305.69	99	5	1	3	293.67	195	9	1	3	298.79	291	13	1	3	289.39	387	17	1	3	304.15
4	1	1	4	308.07	100	5	1	4	295.58	196	9	1	4	296.89	292	13	1	4	290.77	388	17	1	4	302.60
5	1	1	5	305.26	101	5	1	5	294.64	197	9	1	5	298.07	293	13	1	5	290.30	389	17	1	5	303.90
6	1	1	6	306.47	102	5	1	6	294.48	198	9	1	6	296.63	294	13	1	6	288.31	390	17	1	6	303.19
7	1	1	7	306.09	103	5	1	7	291.97	199	9	1	7	297.39	295	13	1	7	289.87	391	17	1	7	304.03
8	1	1	8	309.77	104	5	1	8	294.79	200	9	1	8	298.94	296	13	1	8	296.78	392	17	1	8	304.35
9	1	2	9	308.57	105	5	2	9	294.47	201	9	2	9	298.46	297	13	2	9	301.49	393	17	2	9	303.56
10	1	2	10	309.80	106	5	2	10	295.87	202	9	2	10	297.73	298	13	2	10	298.81	394	17	2	10	304.59
11	1	2	11	308.29	107	5	2	11	295.40	203	9	2	11	297.98	299	13	2	11	298.18	395	17	2	11	304.54
12	1	2	12	309.76	108	5	2	12	295.26	204	9	2	12	301.09	300	13	2	12	299.60	396	17	2	12	303.83
13	1	2	13	308.71	109	5	2	13	294.55	205	9	2	13	298.11	301	13	2	13	299.82	397	17	2	13	305.16
14	1	2	14	308.86	110	5	2	14	294.84	206	9	2	14	300.34	302	13	2	14	298.35	398	17	2	14	303.56
15	1	2	15	308.63	111	5	2	15	294.26	207	9	2	15	300.31	303	13	2	15	299.00	399	17	2	15	305.10
16	1	2	16	303.74	112	5	2	16	296.88	208	9	2	16	298.99	304	13	2	16	299.98	400	17	2	16	300.62
17	1	3	17	302.79	113	5	3	17	296.89	209	9	3	17	299.14	305	13	3	17	302.24	401	17	3	17	300.63
18	1	3	18	303.94	114	5	3	18	295.96	210	9	3	18	297.59	306	13	3	18	301.68	402	17	3	18	303.18
19	1	3	19	305.80	115	5	3	19	297.58	211	9	3	19	296.68	307	13	3	19	302.30	403	17	3	19	302.49
20	1	3	20	303.61	116	5	3	20	297.68	212	9	3	20	299.11	308	13	3	20	300.14	404	17	3	20	303.31
21	1	3	21	303.11	117	5	3	21	299.58	213	9	3	21	298.40	309	13	3	21	302.56	405	17	3	21	304.25
22	1	3	22	304.19	118	5	3	22	296.13	214	9	3	22	298.01	310	13	3	22	300.88	406	17	3	22	301.58
23	1	3	23	304.95	119	5	3	23	297.62	215	9	3	23	298.08	311	13	3	23	302.82	407	17	3	23	302.62
24	1	3	24	302.90	120	5	3	24	299.27	216	9	3	24	295.78	312	13	3	24	294.75	408	17	3	24	303.56
25	2	1	1	301.42	121	6	1	1	301.29	217	10	1	1	294.09	313	14	1	1	293.62	409	18	1	1	304.36
26	2	1	2	301.25	122	6	1	2	300.44	218	10	1	2	294.42	314	14	1	2	294.86	410	18	1	2	302.41
27	2	1	3	302.10	123	6	1	3	298.84	219	10	1	3	292.88	315	14	1	3	294.89	411	18	1	3	301.57
28	2	1	4	303.24	124	6	1	4	300.34	220	10	1	4	294.33	316	14	1	4	297.16	412	18	1	4	301.54
29	2	1	5	301.98	125	6	1	5	300.27	221	10	1	5	294.44	317	14	1	5	294.19	413	18	1	5	303.51
30	2	1	6	301.23	126	6	1	6	300.97	222	10	1	6	294.04	318	14	1	6	297.99	414	18	1	6	302.20
31	2	1	7	302.26	127	6	1	7	300.97	223	10	1	7	293.40	319	14	1	7	294.24	415	18	1	7	302.96
32	2	1	8	304.84	128	6	1	8	304.42	224	10	1	8	297.19	320	14	1	8	298.25	416	18	1	8	305.02
33	2	2	9	304.70	129	6	2	9	301.21	225	10	2	9	297.51	321	14	2	9	295.61	417	18	2	9	302.82
34	2	2	10	305.53	130	6	2	10	304.68	226	10	2	10	295.65	322	14	2	10	297.18	418	18	2	10	303.90
35	2	2	11	305.83	131	6	2	11	302.41	227	10	2	11	297.89	323	14	2	11	297.62	419	18	2	11	304.11
36	2	2	12	305.72	132	6	2	12	301.41	228	10	2	12	294.28	324	14	2	12	295.61	420	18	2	12	304.50
37	2	2	13	305.36	133	6	2	13	301.33	229	10	2	13	295.85	325	14	2	13	295.65	421	18	2	13	304.07
38	2	2	14	305.23	134	6	2	14	303.86	230	10	2	14	295.97	326	14	2	14	296.08	422	18	2	14	304.40
39	2	2	15	305.85	135	6	2	15	304.87	231	10	2	15	297.28	327	14	2	15	297.68	423	18	2	15	304.06
40	2	2	16	310.59	136	6	2	16	305.45	232	10	2	16	298.93	328	14	2	16	291.92	424	18	2	16	296.90
41	2	3	17	310.18	137	6	3	17	303.68	233	10	3	17	301.93	329	14	3	17	292.17	425	18	3	17	295.90
42	2	3	18	308.52	138	6	3	18	303.48	234	10	3	18	301.73	330	14	3	18	290.42	426	18	3	18	297.89
43	2	3	19	310.34	139	6	3	19	302.02	235	10	3	19	300.61	331	14	3	19	292.59	427	18	3	19	297.57
44	2	3	20	309.64	140	6	3	20	303.65	236	10	3	20	299.27	332	14	3	20	291.44	428	18	3	20	297.53
45	2	3	21	309.54	141	6	3	21	305.56	237	10	3	21	301.80	333	14	3	21	291.59	429	18	3	21	296.36
46	2	3	22	309.34	142	6	3	22	304.19	238	10	3	22	301.31	334	14	3	22	293.37	430	18	3	22	298.06
47	2	3	23	310.17	143	6	3	23	302.90	239	10	3	23	300.98	335	14	3	23	292.30	431	18	3	23	298.09
48	2	3	24	295.00	144	6	3	24	295.79	240	10	3	24	302.77	336	14	3	24	288.13	432	18	3	24	302.20
49	3	1	1	295.53	145	7	1	1	298.16	241	11	1	1	302.54	337	15	1	1	287.37	433	19	1	1	302.74
50	3	1	2	295.95	146	7	1	2	296.27	242	11	1	2	302.18	338	15	1	2	289.58	434	19	1	2	300.45
51	3	1	3	294.63	147	7	1	3	296.78	243	11	1	3	302.84	339	15	1	3	290.23	435	19	1	3	304.94
52	3	1	4	295.62	148	7	1	4	296.65	244	11	1	4	303.06	340	15	1	4	288.49	436	19	1	4	304.22
53	3	1	5	295.53	149	7	1	5	295.72	245	11	1	5	302.08	341	15	1	5	288.42	437	19	1	5	301.69
54	3	1	6	293.78	150	7	1	6	296.74	246	11	1	6	302.52	342	15	1	6	288.69	438	19	1	6	302.61
55	3	1	7	296.85	151	7	1	7	297.00	247	11	1	7	303.03	343	15	1	7	290.36	439	19	1	7	301.82
56	3	1	8	290.66	152	7	1	8	297.60	248	11	1	8	298.08	344	15	1	8	287.32	440	19	1	8	299.08
57	3	2	9	290.40	153	7	2	9	298.74	249	11	2	9	298.97	345	15	2	9	288.68	441	19	2	9	301.76
58	3	2	10	291.29	154	7	2	10	297.90	250	11	2	10	299.11	346	15	2	10	290.90	442	19	2	10	300.51
59	3	2	11	289.67	155	7	2	11	296.96	251	11	2	11	295.84	347	15	2	11	288.57	443	19	2	11	300.91
60	3	2	12	293.33	156	7	2	12	298.25	252	11	2	12	297.23	348	15	2	12	289.05	444	19	2	12	299.50
61	3	2	13	291.75	157	7	2	13	298.64	253	11	2	13	296.83	349	15	2	13	289.68	445	19	2	13	301.24
62	3	2	14	291.94	158	7	2	14	298.58	254	11	2	14	298.24	350	15	2	14	291.38	446	19	2	14	299.17
63	3	2	15	291.75	159	7	2	15	299.34	255	11	2	15	297.71	351	15	2	15	286.47	447	19	2	15	299.41
64	3	2	16	301.59	160	7	2	16	292.49	256	11	2	16	292.35	352	15	2	16	289.47	448	19	2	16	302.04
65	3	3	17	300.23	161	7	3	17	292.23	257	11	3	17	291.82	353	15	3	17	292.58	449	19	3	17	304.73
66	3	3	18	301.33	162	7	3	18	294.11	258	11	3	18	293.73	354	15	3	18	290.81	450	19	3	18	303.08
67	3	3	19	302.33	163	7	3	19	293.98	259	11	3	19	294.38	355	15	3	19	291.04	451	19	3	19	304.54
68	3	3	20	300.77	164	7	3	20	294.22	260	11	3	20	292.55	356	15	3	20	292.88	452	19	3	20	304.46
69	3	3	21	300.53	165	7	3	21	294.26	261	11	3	21	291.88	357	15	3	21	291.59	453	19	3	21	303.21
70	3	3	22	299.23	166	7	3	22	293.46	262	11	3	22	291.99	358	15	3	22	291.57	454	19	3	22	302.03
71	3	3	23	299.31	167	7	3	23	294.67	263	11	3	23	292.16	359	15	3	23	290.76	455	19	3	23	304.61
72	3	3	24	288.52	168	7	3	24	296.95	264	11	3	24	298.08	360	15	3	24	294.06	456	19	3	24	297.61
73	4	1	1	289.54	169	8	1	1	299.67	265	12	1	1	295.88	361	16	1	1	292.88	457	20	1	1	298.18
74	4	1	2	291.02	170	8	1	2	297.41	266	12	1	2	296.36	362	16	1	2	293.78	458	20	1	2	300.27
75	4	1	3	289.77	171	8	1	3	297.79	267	12	1	3	296.43	363	16	1	3	291.93	459	20	1	3	299.11
76	4	1	4	289.58	172	8	1	4	296.78	268	12	1	4	298.43	364	16	1	4	293.99	460	20	1	4	298.95
77	4	1	5	289.29	173	8	1	5	299.09	269	12	1	5	296.65	365	16	1	5	292.82	461	20	1	5	300.90
78	4	1	6	290.82	174	8	1	6	298.63	270	12	1	6	298.06	366	16	1	6	291.77	462	20	1	6	299.57
79	4	1	7	288.52	175	8	1	7	298.08	271	12	1	7	293.78	367	16	1	7	291.58	463	20	1	7	301.56
80	4	1	8	300.53	176	8	1	8	298.14	272	12	1	8	290.77	368	16	1	8	288.64	464	20	1	8	298.14
81	4	2	9	300.12	177	8	2	9	300.14	273	12	2	9	290.38	369	16	2	9	289.17	465	20	2	9	298.46
82	4	2	10	297.76	178	8	2	10	298.29	274	12	2	10	288.35	370	16	2	10	289.43	466	20	2	10	299.53
83	4	2	11	300.24	179	8	2	11	300.74	275	12	2	11	289.85	371	16	2	11	287.07	467	20	2	11	298.50
84	4	2	12	300.07	180	8	2	12	300.40	276	12	2	12	290.62	372	16	2	12	290.51	468	20	2	12	297.56
85	4	2	13	298.62	181	8	2	13	299.44	277	12	2	13	291.33	373	16	2	13	289.60	469	20	2	13	296.92
86	4	2	14	299.64	182	8	2	14	298.11	278	12	2	14	291.19	374	16	2	14	289.80	470	20	2	14	299.03
87	4	2	15	300.16	183	8	2	15	298.58	279	12	2	15	290.09	375	16	2	15	290.11	471	20	2	15	298.41
88	4	2	16	295.67	184	8	2	16	304.66	280	12	2	16	298.94	376	16	2	16	297.77	472	20	2	16	292.40
89	4	3	17	294.88	185	8	3	17	304.04	281	12	3	17	300.52	377	16	3	17	298.01	473	20	3	17	291.87
90	4	3	18	295.53	186	8	3	18	305.77	282	12	3	18	300.95	378	16	3	18	297.04	474	20	3	18	293.92
91	4	3	19	296.46	187	8	3	19	303.73	283	12	3	19	300.81	379	16	3	19	297.02	475	20	3	19	294.39
92	4	3	20	296.15	188	8	3	20	305.54	284	12	3	20	300.52	380	16	3	20	296.88	476	20	3	20	293.38
93	4	3	21	295.66	189	8	3	21	304.05	285	12	3	21	299.61	381	16	3	21	297.36	477	20	3	21	290.81
94	4	3	22	293.57	190	8	3	22	305.22	286	12	3	22	300.30	382	16	3	22	297.53	478	20	3	22	291.31
95	4	3	23	294.66	191	8	3	23	305.28	287	12	3	23	300.77	383	16	3	23	298.98	479	20	3	23	292.92
96	4	3	24	293.90	192	8	3	24	297.86	288	12	3	24	290.19	384	16	3	24	303.28	480	20	3	24	293.41

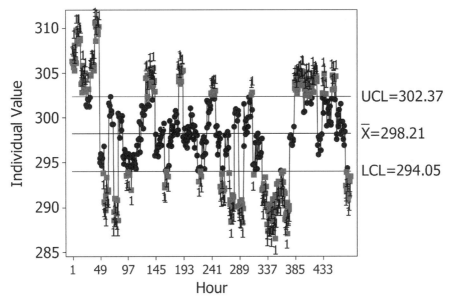

Figure 12.11: Individuals control chart of hourly sampled data.

output by hour of the day and operator shifts. Because of this, a daily subgrouping/sampling period was chosen, which led to the 30,000-foot-level report-out shown in Figure 12.12, indicating that the process is predictable with an estimated process capability/ performance metric rate of 9.4% nonconformance (e.g., ppm 94,147.07 response rounded and converted to a percentage).

A technical note is that the control chart data are to be independent. The data in Figure 8.2 are not independent and is said to have autocorrelation. An infrequent subgrouping/sampling breaks up autocorrelation.

Using an IEE approach, we would not firefight the problems of the day using either a time-series plot where the response is compared to the upper specification limit of 305 or an individuals control chart of an hourly response that had many out-of-control signals (which needed to be addressed in a timely fashion). Instead, the 30,000-foot-level metric report-out would lead to the pull for an IEE project, which is to improve the process so that the common-cause 9.4% nonconformance rate is reduced.

Note, in Figure 12.12 the 30,000-foot-level standard deviation control chart had no logarithm transformation (reference step 3.2.4 in Figure 12.1). A hypothesis test (see Chapter 19) for standard deviation normality was not rejected; hence, no transformation was made. However, one could establish a rule that they

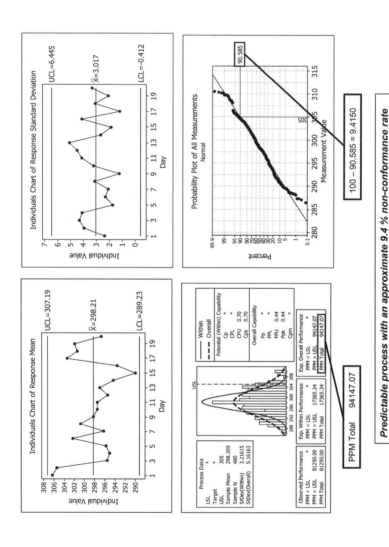

Figure 12.12: Individuals control chart of daily mean and standard deviation of hourly sampled data, along with process capability/performance metric estimate. The only reason that a probability plot and a process capability analysis are both included in this figure is to illustrate that the two approaches yield similar results. Only one should be included in a typical report-out.

always utilize a logarithm transformation when creating this type of standard deviation control chart.

Note also how Figure 12.12 probability plot tails do not have a good fit with the overall-best-estimate straight line. This plot-shape situation can be caused by the presence of multiple distributions. When this occurs, I suggest making a pragmatic decision relative to reporting a process capability/performance metric estimate. For this case, I believe that the fit is good enough to provide a good overall estimate; however, in other cases, it may be appropriate to analyze distributions separately and combine the individual results before reporting the collective estimate.

12.14   Describing a Predictable Process Output When No Specification Exists

The methodologies described in this section are applicable to the creation of satellite-level and 30,000-foot-level metrics for the following process assessments, which do not have specification requirements. Consider that a satellite-level or 30,000-foot-level control chart is predictable. The next step would be to make a prediction statement. However, specification requirements are needed to describe this prediction in terms of percentage non-conformance, C_p, C_{pk}, P_p, P_{pk}, or sigma quality level. The complete population could be analyzed within each subgroup in lieu of selecting samples for each subgroup.

This situation occurs frequently in business and service processes (e.g., lead time, costs, lead time, and inventory). Sometimes organizations create targets and analyze them as if they are specifications. This practice can yield deceptive results since targets are subjective and there may be game playing with the targets so that the presented results are what someone wishes to convey.

An approach that I have found useful for this type of situation is to describe an overall 30,000-foot-level response as an estimated median and 80% frequency of occurrence. This percentage value can be determined mathematically using a Z table (Table A) or a statistical computer program. A computer-generated IEE analysis is graphically shown in Figure 12.13. In Part 1 of this figure, an individuals control chart shows predictability and how time-sequenced data can be conceptually accumulated to create a distribution of non-sequenced data.

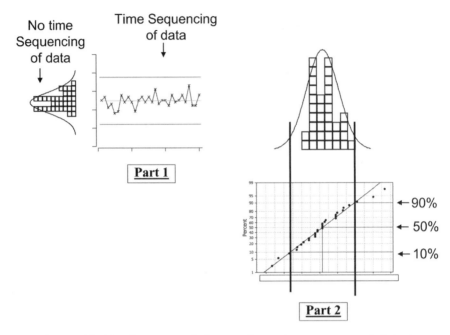

Figure 12.13: Conceptual change from time-sequenced data to no time-sequencing of data and reporting out 80% frequency of occurrence.

Since the process is predictable, we can considered the data from the 30,000-foot-level control chart to be a random sample of the future, unless something changes in the process. It is difficult to determine percentage of the population from a histogram. Part 2 of this figure illustrates the reporting of a median and 80% frequency of occurrence rate.

This approach is applicable to non-normal distributions as well. The only difference is that an individuals control chart for single readings would need a normalizing transformation, and the appropriate probability distribution would be needed to reflect this transformation (e.g., lognormal). This type of presentation provides a good process baseline from which desired improvements can be assessed. From this plot, quick estimations are also available for differing percentage and response levels.

The roadmap steps for this IEE application are:

1. Control chart creation steps (Figure 12.1):
    *   Continuous output [3.2.1] – All transaction data are available and activities don't occur frequently (e.g., one

per day) [3.2.5] – Use all data where each subgroup contains one transaction [3.2.6] – If appropriate, transform the data [3.2.7] – Create an individuals control chart [3.2.8]

- Continuous output [3.2.1] – Not readily available transaction data [3.2.9] – Select one sample per subgroup [3.2.10] – If appropriate, transform the data [3.2.11] – Create an individuals control chart [3.2.12]

2. Process capability/performance metric creation steps for predictable processes (Figure 12.2):
   - For a continuous output, use probability plotting to determine the most likely distribution or whether there are multiple distributions [3.3.1] – Normal distribution [3.3.3 (or 3.3.2, 3.3.4, 3.3.5)] – Determine if there are specification/non-compliance requirements [3.3.6] – No specification: Report 80% frequency of occurrence rate with a mean or median response estimate, or report non-compliance rate beyond target(s) [best estimates] [3.3.7]

12.15 Example 12.5: Describing a Predictable Process' Output When No Specification Exists

People's busy schedules and other factors can make it very difficult to get good attendance at professional society meetings. An average monthly attendance of 10% of the membership is considered to be very good. As the new local ASQ section chair in Austin, Texas, I thought attendance was important and chose this metric as a measure of success for my term. My stretch goal was to double average monthly attendance from the level experienced during the previous 6 years.

The process of setting-up and of conducting a professional society session meeting with program is more involved than one might initially think. Steps in this process include guest speaker/topic selection, meeting room arrangements, meeting announcements, and many other issues. I wanted to create a baseline that would indicate expected results if nothing were done differently from our previous meeting creation process. Later, I also wanted to test the two process means to see if there was a significant difference of the processes at an α level of 0.05.

This situation does not differ much from a metric that might be expected from business or service processes. A process exists and a goal has been set, but there are no real specification limits. Setting a goal or soft target as a specification limit for the purpose of determining process capability/performance indices could yield very questionable results. Table 12.3 summarizes our previous section meeting attendance. The section does not meet during the summer months and a chair's term is from July 1 to June 30.

The 30,000-foot-level assessment shown in Figure 12.14 indicates that the process is predictable. The process capability/performance metric statement for the process is that the estimated median attendance of the section is 45 with an 80% attendance frequency of occurrence between 34 and 57. Note that other population percentage estimates or less than percentages for specific responses can easily be determined from this plot.

If a larger attendance is desired than what is predicted from this process, improvements are needed. Example 22.7 describes improvements that were made to the process and the statistical test to assess the impact of these improvements.

Table 12.3: ASQ Austin Section Meeting Attendance

Date	9/9/1993	10/14/1993	11/11/1993	12/9/1993	1/13/1994	2/17/1994	3/10/1994	4/14/1994	5/12/1994
Attendance	66	45	61	36	42	41	46	44	47

Date	9/8/1994	10/13/1994	11/10/1994	12/8/1994	1/12/1995	2/16/1995	3/9/1995	4/3/1995	5/16/1995
Attendance	46	51	42	42	61	57	47	46	28

Date	9/14/1995	10/12/1995	11/9/1995	12/14/1995	1/11/1996	2/8/1996	3/14/1996	4/11/1996	5/9/1996
Attendance	45	37	45	42	58	49	39	53	58

Date	9/12/1996	10/10/1996	11/14/1996	12/12/1996	1/9/1997	2/13/1997	3/13/1997	4/10/1997	5/8/1997
Attendance	44	37	52	33	43	45	35	29	33

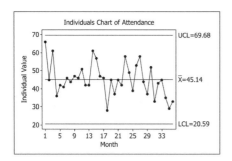
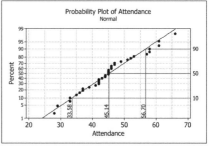

Predictable process with an approximate median attendance of 45 and 80% frequency of occurrence between 34 and 57

Figure 12.14: Individuals control chart of previous attendance and process capability/performance metric.

12.16   Non-Normal Distribution Prediction Plot and Process Capability/Performance Metric Reporting

A population is considered normally distributed when plotted data plot follow the characteristic bell-shaped curve. We note that the tails of a normal distribution approach plus and minus infinity. When data fit a normal distribution, percentage of population statements can be made for various x-values using analytical techniques.

However, for many situations data do not follow a normal distribution. Consider the company that is tracking the difference between the time payment was received and the invoice's due date. A normal distribution in general does not fit this situation well since there is a lower boundary. To illustrate this natural boundary, consider how we would not expect to pay for a product before we decided to purchase it; that is, there is a natural lower boundary and the distribution curve would tend to be skewed to the right.

The individual control chart can give false special-cause signals when data are not inherently from a normal distribution. Because of this, certain type of data may need a normalizing transformation before the creation of an individuals chart (see Appendix B Section B.2). In addition, this inherent distribution needs to be addressed in the formulation of a process capability/performance metric (e.g., probability plot).

It should be noted that a normal distribution might still fit a data set even though we would expect that the underlying characteristic of the population to be from another distribution. This occurs, for example, when the data are distantly removed from the lowest natural boundary.

Non-normality is common for measurements such as flatness, roundness, and particle contamination. The process capability/performance metric described previously have focused on the normal distributions. A normalizing transformation can be appropriate if the non-normal distribution to be transformed is known (Nelson, 1994). Statistical software can expedite this calculation where distribution parameter estimates originate from the maximum likelihood or least squares estimate (e.g., 2- or 3-parameter lognormal, 2- or 3-parameter Weibull distribution).

However, there could be problems if the distribution has to be estimated from preliminary data. Many skewed distributions can be traced to two normally distributed sources with different parameters (Nelson, 1999). Table 9.3 describes normalizing transformations for various situations.

The methodologies described in this section are applicable to the creation of 30,000-foot-level metrics for the following process assessments, which tend to be non-normal because they have a natural lower boundary. For example, we do not expect invoices to be paid before purchased and the flatness of a part to be less than perfectly flat (i.e., a boundary of 0.000 flatness). In these situations time-based metrics (e.g. cycle time) can often be modeled as a lognormal distribution.

A general approach for transforming data to a normal distribution is a Box–Cox transformation (Box, *et al.*, 1978), where values (*Y*) are transformed to the power of λ (i.e., Y^λ). This relationship has the following characteristics:

$\lambda = -2$ *Y* transformed = $1/Y^2$
$\lambda = -0.5$ *Y* transformed = $1/\sqrt{Y}$
$\lambda = 0$ *Y* transformed = $\ln(Y)$
$\lambda = 0.5$ *Y* transformed = $\sqrt{Y}$
$\lambda = 2$ *Y* transformed = Y^2

Care needs to be exercised when transforming data since an unnatural transformation can cause special-cause data to appear as common-cause occurrence in an individuals control chart and provide an erroneous process capability/performance metric statement.

The most frequent encountered normalizing transformations in IEE are:

- Logarithm transformation (Box–Cox: λ = 0) (e.g., cycle time or lead time).
- Square root transformation (Box–Cox: λ = 0.5) (e.g., defect counts and defective rates).

Satellite-level and 30,000-foot-level chart reporting, which utilized normalizing transformations should note this transformation in the control chart and probability plot header. Data transformations should be transparent to the readers of the report-out.

Maximum likelihood value for λ is when the residual sum of squares from the fitted model is minimized, as shown in Example 12.6.

The roadmap steps for this IEE application are:

1. Control chart creation steps (Figure 12.1):
   - Continuous output [3.2.1] – All transaction data are available and activities do not occur frequently (e.g., one

per day) [3.2.5] – Use all data where each subgroup contains one transaction [3.2.6] – If appropriate, transform the data [3.2.7] – Create an individuals control chart [3.2.8]

- Continuous output [3.2.1] – Not readily available transaction data [3.2.9] – Select one sample per subgroup [3.2.10] – If appropriate, transform the data [3.2.11] – Create an individuals control chart [3.2.12]

2. Process capability/performance metric creation steps for predictable processes (Figure 12.2):
   - For a continuous output, use probability plotting to determine the most likely distribution or whether there are multiple distributions [3.3.1] – Two- or three-parameter Weibull or lognormal distribution [3.3.4] – Determine if there are specification/non-compliance requirements [3.3.6] – Specification: Determine the best estimate for the capability/performance metric (e.g., 2500 ppm or 2.5% non-compliance, using a long-term value for standard deviation) [3.3.8].
   - For a continuous output, use probability plotting to determine the most likely distribution or whether there are multiple distributions [3.3.1] – Box–Cox or other transformed data [3.3.5] – Determine if there are specification/non-compliance requirements [3.3.6] – Specification: Determine the best estimate for the capability/performance metric (e.g., 2500 ppm or 2.5% non-compliance, using a long-term value for standard deviation) [3.3.8].

12.17   Example 12.6: IEE Process Predictability and Process Capability/Performance Metric – Non-Normal Distribution Using Box–Cox Transformation

A chemical process has residue, as shown in Table 12.4, with a specification upper limit of 0.02. There is no lower limit; however, there is a natural bound of zero.

The following describes a progression of this analysis:

- Figure 12.15 shows an individuals control chart of the data with no transformation. No reason was identified for the special-cause points identified in the plot.
- Figure 12.16 shows a process capability/performance metric estimate using a normal distribution. Note how the curve extends beyond zero, which is not physically possible; that

Table 12.4: Amount of Residue by Period

Period	Residue	Period	Residue	Period	Residue	Period	Residue
1	0.027	26	0.015	51	0.018	76	0.010
2	0.027	27	0.013	52	0.034	77	0.041
3	0.064	28	0.011	53	0.014	78	0.015
4	0.042	29	0.009	54	0.013	79	0.029
5	0.019	30	0.011	55	0.011	80	0.028
6	0.019	31	0.015	56	0.025	81	0.024
7	0.019	32	0.027	57	0.016	82	0.011
8	0.016	33	0.016	58	0.091	83	0.030
9	0.024	34	0.019	59	0.018	84	0.052
10	0.032	35	0.016	60	0.025	85	0.019
11	0.015	36	0.017	61	0.015	86	0.016
12	0.025	37	0.027	62	0.012	87	0.022
13	0.007	38	0.018	63	0.012	88	0.024
14	0.072	39	0.010	64	0.029	89	0.046
15	0.023	40	0.013	65	0.015	90	0.024
16	0.018	41	0.021	66	0.012	91	0.012
17	0.019	42	0.015	67	0.013	92	0.023
18	0.019	43	0.015	68	0.026	93	0.016
19	0.016	44	0.021	69	0.013	94	0.031
20	0.019	45	0.013	70	0.010	95	0.025
21	0.035	46	0.035	71	0.011	96	0.018
22	0.021	47	0.012	72	0.028	97	0.013
23	0.015	48	0.011	73	0.035		
24	0.019	49	0.021	74	0.016		
25	0.012	50	0.014	75	0.023		

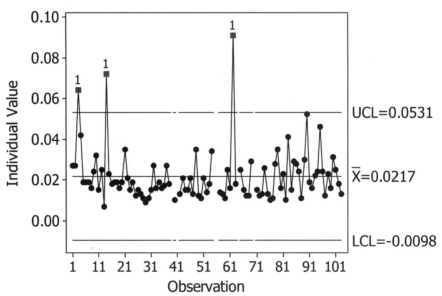

Figure 12.15: Individuals control chart for amount of residue, without transformation.

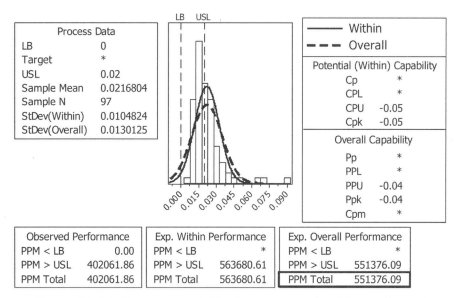

Figure 12.16: Process capability for amount of residue estimated using a normal distribution (shown for reference).

is the process capability/performance metric estimates are not accurate. The process capability/performance metric from this analysis was circled; however, because of the lack of normality this process capability/performance metric is not valid. This value will be later compared to transformed analyses.

- Figure 12.17 shows a normal probability plot. From this plot, it is no surprise that the null hypothesis of normality is rejected (see Chapter 19) since the process has a physical boundary of 0.
- Figure 12.18 shows a Box–Cox plot with a rounded value for λ of −0.50.
- Figure 12.19 shows a normal probability plot of the transformed data. The transformed data closely follows a straight line on a probability plot.
- Figure 12.20 shows an individuals control chart of the transformed data, indicating that the process is predictable.
- Figure 12.21 shows the process capability/performance metric. To create this plot, the lower bound was adjusted a very small distance of 0.001, since zero or negative values are not permissible with this modeling (in general we might need to off-set our data so that there are no zero or negative

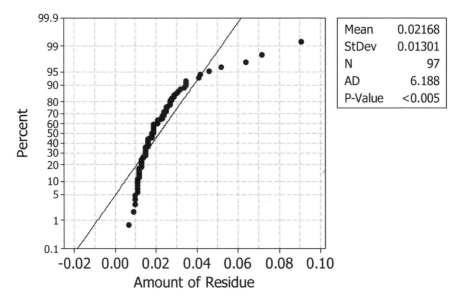

Figure 12.17: Normal probability plot of amount of residue.

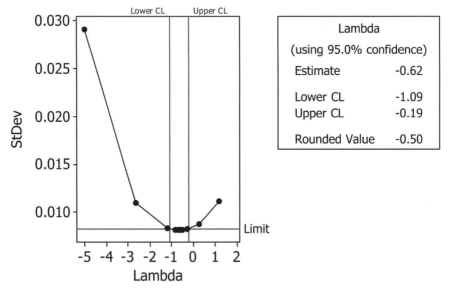

Figure 12.18: Box–Cox plot of amount of residue to determine
transforming constant.

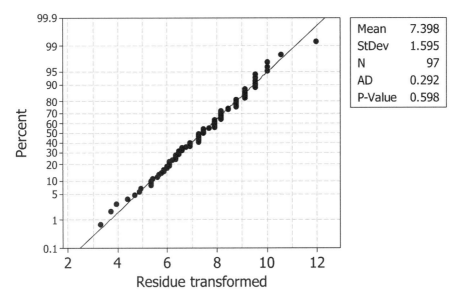

Figure 12.19: Normal probability plot of transformed residue data, Box–Cox $\lambda = -0.50$

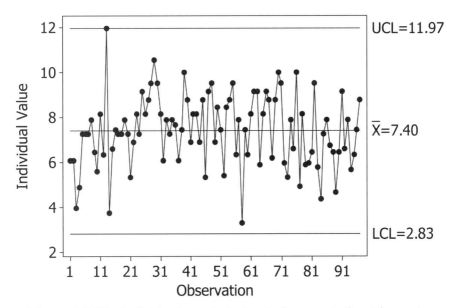

Figure 12.20: Individuals control chart of amount of residue using Box–Cox transformation with $\lambda = -0.50$

values). In this plot, the data normalizing transformation caused the upper and lower specification limits to switch.

For most people, the process capability/performance metric estimate of approximately 42% nonconformance (rounded 418,866.61 ppm value which was converted to percentage) is a far easier metric to understand for long-term process predictability than the other traditionally reported values of 0.07 for C_{pk} and P_{pk}, noting that C_p and P_p values cannot be determined since the specification is one-sided.

The plot in the upper left corner of Figure 12.21 shows a histogram of the non-transformed data. This plot is consistent with Figure 12.16 which yielded an estimated nonconformance of 55% (rounded 551,376.09 ppm value which was converted to percentage) for the non-transformed data. The 42% transformed nonconformance estimate is a better prediction than the 55% non-transformed estimate.

12.18   Example 12.7: IEE Process Predictability and Process Capability/Performance Metric – Non-Normal Distribution with Zero and/or Negative Values

The prompt payment of invoices is critical to a company's cash flow. Consider that a days' sales outstanding (DSO) metric, which tracks the difference between the date an invoice payment was received and its due date, follows the underlying distribution shown in Figure 12.22. Consider also that some invoices have 90-day terms; hence, it is not unreasonable that some invoices could be paid 30 days early.

This randomly generated data from a three-parameter lognormal distribution is to simulate a real situation, where 0 days represent the situation where a payment was received precisely on its due date. By simple observation, we note that this distribution does not have a bell-shaped curve appearance where tails extend equally on both sides of its median value and approach a theoretically infinite value. This distribution has a long tail to the right.

The difference in invoice payment durations, which affects the spread of this distribution, could originate from differences in payment practices between the companies invoiced, invoice amounts (larger invoice amounts may take longer to be paid), day of the week invoiced, invoicing department, etc. With IEE methodology, any impact by these input variables on payment duration is considered as a source for common-cause variability.

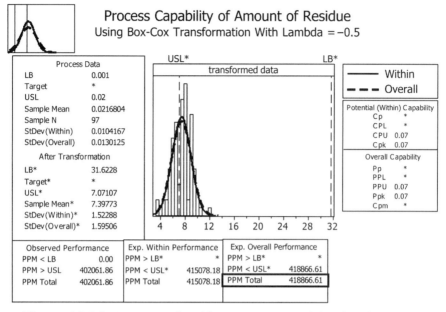

Figure 12.21: Amount of residue process capability/performance metric estimate.

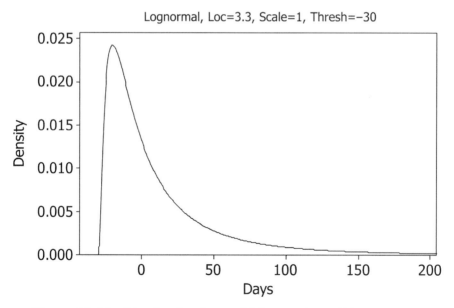

Figure 12.22: Distribution from which samples will be randomly selected in the example simulation.

Consider that over time nothing has changed within this process. We want next to simulate what might be expected if we were to track a process sample over time. Let's simulate what might be expected if only one paid invoice were randomly selected weekly; that is, consider that only one sample per subgroup was collected, since it is hard to collect the data.

Relative to the decision for weekly versus more frequent subgrouping/sampling, we decided not to have a daily subgrouping/sampling since we thought that there might be a difference by day of the week; hence, the decision to select weekly subgrouping/sampling. One random weekly sample payment yielded the following relative to its due date:

Week	DSO	Week	DSO	Week	DSO	Week	DSO	Week	DSO
1	9.99	8	-2.56	15	59.27	22	55.69	29	46.19
2	-1.44	9	-18.91	16	48.69	23	-19.37	30	160.79
3	10.38	10	-13.96	17	88.19	24	3.56	31	12.46
4	-12.36	11	-7.96	18	-12.83	25	56.13	32	-6.45
5	-23.23	12	3.84	19	-22.74	26	88.08	33	-26.12
6	31.55	13	22.34	20	24.02	27	-6.08	34	25.40
7	-22.41	14	-9.73	21	98.12	28	-21.65	35	-14.86

An individuals control chart plot of this data is shown in Figure 12.23. Since these data are randomly selected, we would expect that the control chart would have a random scatter within the upper and lower control chart boundaries. This chart doesn't have this appearance. The data in this chart seem to exhibit a lower boundary condition about −25 days. In addition, although through chance we could experience an out-of-control condition for this random data, we would not expect to experience this with only 35 tracked subgroupings.

The individuals control chart is not robust to non-normal data (see Appendix B.2); therefore, for some situations such as this one, data need to be transformed when creating the control chart.

As we can see in Figure 12.24, the normal distribution does not fit well. Both the three-parameter Weibull and three-parameter lognormal distribution fit well, while the two-parameter lognormal and Weibull distributions could not be considered, since these distributions cannot accept zero or negative values.

I prefer the Weibull distribution, in general, for reliability analyses and the lognormal for transactional situations. Because of this, the individuals control chart shown in Figure 12.25 is created through a logarithm normalizing transformation, after adjusting the data set

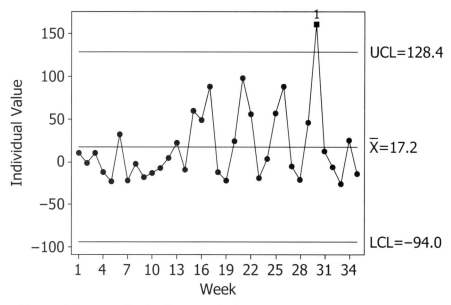

Figure 12.23: Individuals control chart of DSO metric; that is difference between invoice payment date and due date.

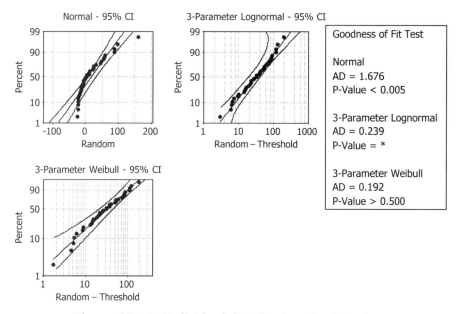

Figure 12.24: Individual distribution identification.

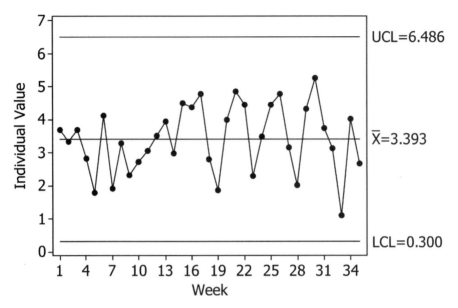

Figure 12.25: Individuals control chart of transformed data (natural log).

by subtracting the three-parameter-lognormal threshold estimate (i.e., datum point value − (Thresh)), where Figure 12.26 "Thresh" estimate is −29.08.

This transformed individuals plot indicates that the process is predictable. The next appropriate question to answer is: What is predicted?

We could simply estimate from a probability plot the reported percentage that is not paid on time or is paid beyond a certain number of days late. However, this form of reporting does not give us a picture of the amount of variability that exists within the current process. A median response value with an 80% frequency of occurrence gives us a much more descriptive picture of the expectations from our process, which is easy to understand from the CEO to the line operator level.

From Figure 12.26, we conclude that three-parameter lognormal distribution fits well and seems appropriate for the modeled situation. From Figure 12.27, which does not consider the three-parameter threshold adjustment, we estimate the process capability/performance metric to be a median of 0.7 days with 80% frequency of occurrence of −20.9 to 78.8 days. The logarithmic *x*-axis in the "with threshold" plot (Figure 12.26) resulted in

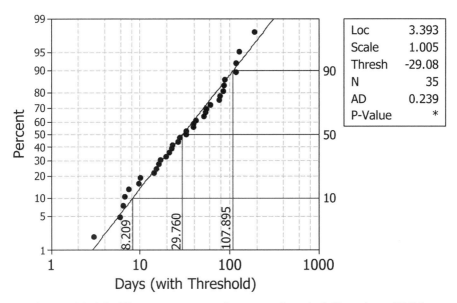

Figure 12.26: Three-parameter lognormal probability plot of DSO, with threshold adjustment.

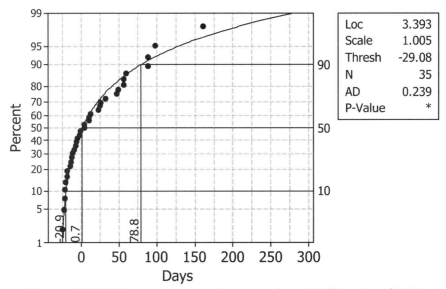

Figure 12.27: Three-parameter lognormal probability plot of DSO, without threshold adjustment.

a straight-line probability plot, which is used to assess model fit. The linear *x*-axis in the "without threshold" plot (Figure 12.27) has a curved probability plot, which is used to describe the process capability/performance metric in easy-to-understand terms.

The reason there is no *P* value provided in the statistical output is that the software compares a three-parameter to a two-parameter distribution and provides a *P* value for it being a better fit; that is basically a hypothesis test for a threshold value of zero.

12.19   Non-Predictability Charts and Seasonality

In IEE, we strive to provide high-level insight to what the process customer experiences; i.e., at the 30,000-foot-level. When a process contains a bi-modal characteristic we can split the distribution when creating a 30,000-foot-level control chart. For other situations such as DSO when there can be major differences among the many customers invoiced, a process capability/performance metric probability plot would probably not be a straight line, even with a normalizing transformation. For this situation, a simply practical assessment can be made of whether the best estimate median and 80% frequency of occurrence statement are close enough for either making an on-going value chain performance statement and/or a process improvement project base-line metric.

Seven reasons that a created 30,000-foot-level or satellite-level control chart might not indicate predictability are:

1. Subgrouping/sampling frequency
2. Non-normality of plotted data
3. Multiple distributions
4. Business policy
5. Seasonality
6. Infrequent special-cause occurrences
7. Fundamental process non-predictability

The following discussion addresses each of these items:

1. *Subgrouping/sampling frequency*: A 30,000-foot-level control chart could indicate non-predictability because not all common-cause input variation occurred between adjacent subgroups. This situation occurs in the daily subgrouping/sampling of call center activity when differences occur between days of the week (i.e., would be better to subgroup by week).

2. *Non-normality of plotted data*: The individuals control chart is not robust to non-normality. A normalizing transformation may be applicable. If there is a natural boundary, a lognormal transformation is often useful. Data normalizing transformations need to make physical sense for the specific situation (e.g., as noted in Table 9.3).

3. *Multiple distributions*: Technically control charts are applicable for situations where there is one source of variability (i.e., one distribution). In the real world this infrequently occurs. Processes often have many inputs that can affect the output. The question is whether a single distribution is close enough so that process performance expectations can be gained.

4. *Business policy*: Non-predictable organizational 30,000-foot-level control charts can have an underlying business-nature cause. If the cause for this non-predictability is a business policy, consideration should be given to changing the business policy. For example, a business noted that sales spiked near the end of the every quarter. Upon investigation, it was noted that a sales-commission bonus policy was dependent upon the achievement of total quarterly gross sales goals. It was noted that the sales people were offering discounted prices at the end of every quarter so that they could meet their bonus-driven objectives. This policy dramatically increased quarterly demand, which lead to additional over-time manufacturing expense, missed order delivery dates, and higher defective rates for these orders. For this situation, a revised sales-commission policy could lead to more predictable processes, which would benefit the bottom-line of the business as a whole.

5. *Seasonality*: Bar-chart metrics such as that shown in Figure 1.3 lead us to make seasonal-type metric statements even when seasonality-time issues are not present (e.g., this metric is down compared to the same month last year). Organizations can experience natural seasonality differences; however, an IEE focus is to create metrics that provide insight to what should be done differently to improve the overall system. Simple year-to-year monthly or quarterly reports do not provide this insight.

When an organization has natural season variation such as holiday season versus non-holiday season, multiple processes often exist. For this situation, two 30,000-foot-level charts can be created. One chart is for the holiday season, while the other is for the non-holiday season. Data presented in this format can lead to different behavior. For example, this form of data presentation could more directly lead to an investigation of what can be done to improve profits during off-peak demand. This investigation could lead to a company purchase another company that has the opposite demand cycle or an expansion of their business model. A business purchase example is Clorox, owner of Kingsford charcoal briquettes, buying the Duraflame log business, while a business expansion model is that grass-cutting crews could install holiday lights during their off season.

6. *Infrequent special-cause occurrences*: To illustrate this situation, consider that a 30,000-foot-level control chart indicated that once every 3 to 5 months a plant experienced less power usage. It was also noted that an electrical storm occurred at each one of these occurrences, resulting in a power outage that decreases consumption. For this situation, the organization could make a 30,000-foot-level power-usage statement when an electrical storm did not occur. The electrical storm situation would then be made as a separate statement, noting that an investigation or project should be considered to determine what could be done to reduce the risk of plant disruption during electrical storms.

7. *Fundamental process non-predictability*: One previously described situation when a process is typically not predictable is corporate gross revenue. Another illustration when predictability is not expected is a company's daily stock closing price. For these situations and other similar occurrences, 30,000-foot-level and satellite-level metrics are typically better presented using a time-series plot without making any prediction statement.

12.20   Value Chain Satellite-Level and 30,000-Foot-Level Example Metrics

Satellite-level and 30,000-foot-level value chain metric interpretation were presented as examples in Breyfogle (2008d), Volume 2, and previously in this volume. The next remaining examples in this chapter and the last example in the next chapter will present the data and computation methods to create these charts.

12.21   Example 12.8: Value Chain Metric Computations – Satellite-Level Metric Reporting

Example 8.1 showed the creation of a time-series plot for a satellite-level metric. This example shows the computation of other satellite-level metric plots shown in:

- Breyfogle (2008d) – Figure 7.9
- Volume 2 – Figure 7.7
- This volume – Figure 3.3

As noted earlier, organizations often establish annual gross revenue growth and profit margin objectives. Earlier it was illustrated how simply focusing on quarterly numbers often leads to the wrong activities. This example provides an alternative system-focused methodology that can provide more timely information on how good performance is relative to business goals.

Table 12.5 contains monthly reporting of Acme Medical's gross revenue, percent annual gain in gross revenue, and net profit margins. The 12-month percent gain in gross revenue (monthly reporting) is determined by calculating the annual percentage gain as if the yearly financial statements were closing that month.

A detailed interpretation of the percent annualized gain in gross revenue and profit margins plots is shown in Figures 12.28 and 12.29 using the IEE scorecard/dashboard metric reporting process:

1. Assess process predictability.
2. When the process is considered predictable, formulate a prediction statement for the latest region of stability. The usual reporting format for this statement is:
    (a) When there is a specification requirement: nonconformance percentage or defects per million opportunities (DPMO).
    (b) When there are no specification requirements: median response and 80% frequency of occurrence rate.

Interpretation of *annual gross revenue growth plots* shown in Figure 12.28 using this process:

1. An individuals control chart test on the annual gross revenue data indicated a shift about June 00. At this point

Table 12.5: Value Chain Satellite-level Data

Month-Year	Profit Margins (%)	Gross Monthly Revenue (Millions)	Gross 12 Month Revenue (Millions)	Gross Historical 12 Month Revenue to Compare	Gross Revenue Percent Annual Gain *
Jan-00	15.8	406			
Feb-00	19.2	373			
Mar-00	12.5	470			
Apr-00	14.0	377			
May-00	18.1	486			
Jun-00	10.7	406			
Jul-00	13.1	483			
Aug-00	16.4	474			
Sep-00	15.1	493			
Oct-00	11.7	435			
Nov-00	15.0	505			
Dec-00	13.4	564	5472		
Jan-01	18.7	546	5612		
Feb-01	13.0	494	5733		
Mar-01	14.2	449	5712		
Apr-01	17.1	481	5816		
May-01	15.6	414	5744		
Jun-01	9.1	592	5930		
Jul-01	17.0	623	6070		
Aug-01	11.7	554	6150		
Sep-01	15.3	598	6255		
Oct-01	8.8	572	6392		
Nov-01	9.3	681	6568		
Dec-01	11.6	604	6608	5472	20.8
Jan-02	15.8	730	6792	5612	21.0
Feb-02	13.1	611	6909	5733	20.5
Mar-02	9.6	531	6991	5712	22.4
Apr-02	12.8	644	7154	5816	23.0
May-02	16.4	705	7445	5744	29.6
Jun-02	11.7	768	7621	5930	28.5
Jul-02	15.8	670	7668	6070	26.3
Aug-02	14.6	780	7894	6150	28.4
Sep-02	13.7	781	8077	6255	29.1
Oct-02	15.1	677	8182	6392	28.0
Nov-02	14.6	803	8304	6568	26.4
Dec-02	11.6	805	8505	6608	28.7
Jan-03	14.3	709	8484	6792	24.9
Feb-03	20.3	762	8635	6909	25.0
Mar-03	10.2	765	8869	6991	26.9
Apr-03	13.1	956	9181	7154	28.3
May-03	12.8	900	9376	7445	25.9
Jun-03	13.6	929	9537	7621	25.1

$$* \text{ GR \% annual gain } 3/08 = \frac{\text{GR[From } 4/1/07 \text{ to } 3/31/08] - \text{GR}[4/1/06 \text{ to } 3/31/07]}{\text{GR}[4/1/06 \text{ to } 3/31/07]} (100)$$

where GR = gross revenue

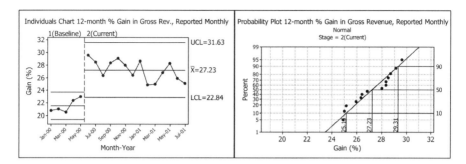

> **Percent 12-month gain in gross revenue: Predictable process since Jun 00 with an estimated monthly median of 27.2% and 80% occurrence frequency of 25.2% to 29.3%**

Figure 12.28: Value chain satellite-level reporting of 12-month percent gain in gross revenue, monthly reporting.

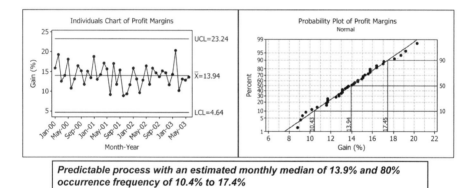

> **Predictable process with an estimated monthly median of 13.9% and 80% occurrence frequency of 10.4% to 17.4%**

Figure 12.29: Value chain satellite-level reporting of profit margins.

in time another company could have been acquired. Since this point in time, the process has experienced only common-cause variability. Even though the control chart appears to have some trends from this point in time, the rules of control charting would have us conclude that the process is now predictable.

2. From the probability plot, we estimate since June 00 an approximate monthly median of 27.2% and 80% occurrence frequency of 25.2% to 29.3%; that is, we estimate that 80% of the future monthly reporting will be between these two percentage values.

Interpretation of *profit margins plots* shown in Figure 12.29 using this process:

1. Even though the control chart of profit appears to have trends, the rules of control charting would have us conclude that the process was predictable.
2. From the probability plot we estimate a monthly median of 13.9% and 80% monthly occurrence frequency of 10.4% to 17.4%; that is, we estimate that 80% of the future monthly reporting will be between these two percentages.

If this response is not consistent with business goals, projects would be pulled for creation.

12.22   Example 12.9: Value Chain Metric Computations – 30,000-Foot-Level Metric with Specifications

This example shows computation of the 30,000-foot-level value chain metric, on-time delivery, shown in:

- Breyfogle (2008d) – Figure 7.10
- Volume 2 – Figure 7.8
- This volume – Figure 3.4

In Acme Medical's value chain, the on-time delivery 30,000-foot-level scorecard/dashboard metric performance was tracked by randomly selecting one shipment weekly. Shipment deliveries were considered non-compliant relative to delivery shipment time if they were received greater than 1 day late or 5 days early. Recent data results are shown in Table 12.6, where +1 indicates 1 day late and −1 indicates 1 day early.

The following IEE scorecard/dashboard metric reporting process will be used when analyzing the data:

1. Assess process predictability.
2. When the process is considered predictable, formulate a prediction statement for the latest region of stability. The usual reporting format for this statement is:
   (a) When there is a specification requirement: nonconformance percentage or DPMO.

Table 12.6: Value Chain 30,000-Foot-Level On-time Delivery Data;
that is, 1.0 is 1 day late and −3.0 is 3 days early

Week	Delivery	Week	Delivery	Week	Delivery
1	-0.93	26	-2.09	51	-2.81
2	-0.55	27	0.54	52	-3.92
3	-3.04	28	-0.18	53	-1.43
4	-1.30	29	1.47	54	-3.71
5	-0.24	30	0.76	55	-3.99
6	-4.45	31	-4.06	56	-2.45
7	-6.94	32	-2.71	57	-3.85
8	-0.20	33	-3.28	58	-3.84
9	-3.18	34	-0.07	59	-4.38
10	-2.46	35	-1.09	60	-1.42
11	-1.44	36	-0.19	61	-4.38
12	-2.00	37	-3.93	62	-1.69
13	-1.42	38	-3.06	63	-4.91
14	-0.89	39	-0.41	64	1.14
15	3.22	40	-3.76	65	-2.16
16	-1.01	41	1.71	66	-1.12
17	0.65	42	-0.96	67	0.07
18	-1.80	43	-1.42	68	1.13
19	-4.76	44	-2.16	69	-1.88
20	-2.60	45	-6.82	70	-0.82
21	-1.68	46	-3.17	71	-4.78
22	-2.64	47	-0.61	72	-3.29
23	2.24	48	-3.96	73	-1.67
24	-3.21	49	-3.91	74	-0.41
25	0.93	50	-2.45	75	0.09

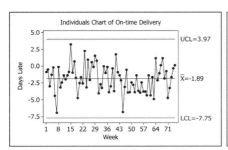 

Predictable process with approximately 13.7% nonconformance

Figure 12.30: Value chain 30,000-foot-level on-time delivery performance scorecard/dashboard metric statement.

(b) When there are no specification requirements: median response and 80% frequency of occurrence rate.

Interpretation of Figure 12.30 using this process:

1. From Figure 12.30, it is concluded that the process is predictable.
2. Current performance and predicted future performance is that about 6.1% of all shipments will be earlier than the agreed-to date and about 7.6% of all shipments will be later than the agreed-to date (100 − 92.433 = 7.567, rounded-off). This leads to the expectation that about 13.7% (6.1 + 7.6) will be either earlier or later than the agree-to delivery date.

12.23   Example 12.10: Value Chain Metric Computations – 30,000-Foot-Level Continuous Response Metric with No Specifications

The fabricated data in this example is for illustrative purposes only. The data in Table 12.7 were randomly generated from a normal distribution; however, DSO data are more typically better modeled as a lognormal distribution, since there is a lower boundary; for example, we don't expect to receive payment before the invoice is created.

For this example, consider that invoice terms are 90 days. If an invoice were paid on the due date, this DSO transaction datum

Table 12.7: Value Chain 30,000-Foot-Level DSO Data

Week	DSO	Week	DSO	Week	DSO	Week	DSO	Week	DSO	Week	DSO
1	29.8	16	-18.4	31	-25.7	46	21.3	61	-3.5	76	-16.4
2	5.0	17	14.3	32	17.7	47	13.0	62	17.5	77	8.7
3	-14.2	18	-2.7	33	21.6	48	-3.7	63	-0.3	78	8.6
4	30.1	19	-6.1	34	38.6	49	14.4	64	4.5	79	-44.6
5	-7.7	20	-19.2	35	0.0	50	22.7	65	22.3	80	-31.5
6	28.8	21	-1.1	36	-2.0	51	-1.6	66	41.7	81	-1.1
7	9.3	22	8.7	37	10.7	52	0.9	67	19.2	82	11.4
8	-8.9	23	-16.8	38	36.9	53	21.8	68	-6.1	83	-39.3
9	-8.1	24	-2.4	39	13.3	54	27.4	69	28.8	84	-29.5
10	-5.5	25	-31.8	40	22.7	55	10.5	70	-2.2	85	-23.1
11	-1.2	26	-2.7	41	8.3	56	35.9	71	26.1	86	21.7
12	19.8	27	3.3	42	6.5	57	-11.5	72	-15.0	87	-5.0
13	13.0	28	-10.2	43	-0.9	58	3.9	73	18.8	88	24.1
14	-15.9	29	1.9	44	4.5	59	5.7	74	27.6	89	9.5
15	2.9	30	18.3	45	-4.0	60	20.1	75	28.0	90	-7.7

would be 0. If a DSO transaction were paid 10 days late, this datum DSO transaction would be 10, while if an invoice were paid 40 days early, this datum DSO transaction would be a −40. We would not expect to receive any transaction payments below −90, since 90 days was the term provided.

The following IEE scorecard/dashboard metric reporting process will be used when analyzing the data:

1. Assess process predictability.
2. When the process is considered predictable, formulate a prediction statement for the latest region of stability. The usual reporting format for this statement is:
    (a) When there is a specification requirement: nonconformance percentage or DPMO.
    (b) When there are no specification requirements: median response and 80% frequency of occurrence rate.

Interpretation of Figure 12.31 using this process:

1. The rules of control charting would have us to conclude that the process was predictable.
2. Since there are no true specification requirements, 50% and 80% frequency of occurrence reporting gives a good feel for what to expect from the process, including its variability. For this process, we estimate a median (50% frequency of occurrence) of about 4.8 days late with an 80% frequency of occurrence of 18.2 days early to 27.9 days late.

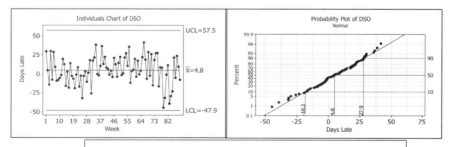

Predictable process with an approximate median of 4.8 days late and 80% occurrence frequency of 18 days early to 28 days late

Figure 12.31: Value chain 30,000-foot-level DSO performance scorecard/dashboard metric statement.

12.24 IEE Difference

Figure 12.12 shows the output of a process where within-day variability is less than between-day variability. If someone were to sample from this process and then create an $\bar{x}$ and R chart, the process could have many out-of-control signals (unpredictable process indication) since the control limits are calculated from within-day variability. From this sampling plan, C_p and C_{pk} indices, using a statistical software program such as Minitab, would be determined from a within-day standard deviation, while P_p and P_{pk} would be determined from an overall standard deviation. In addition, for this type of situation, there are typically other within day variance components that could dramatically affect the results, depending upon how someone chose to sample from the process.

Minitab statistical software uses the above procedure to differentiate between short-term and long-term variability. However, other statistical software packages and calculation procedures do not necessarily make this differentiation. This confusion gets amplified when we consider the differences that can result from how frequently a process is sampled to make the calculation. Because of these differences, a company can make a wrong decision through the determination, interpretation, and comparison of these indices.

Another issue that compounds this confusion is that the described equations are for normally distributed data. Some computer programs can address situations where data are not from a normal distribution; however, this is often not done in practice, and the omission can affect the accuracy of the reported metrics. In addition, sample size, confidence intervals, and not having samples taken from the time period of interest can distort results. Finally, these indices are not appropriate when data are attribute, which is typically expressed as a ppm defect rate or a percent defective rate.

It is important for organizations to build awareness of the exposures when using these metrics within their training and coaching. I have found that most people find it much easier to visualize and interpret an estimated ppm rate (or percentage of nonconformance) beyond customer objectives/specifications than a process capability/performance index value. Because of this, within IEE, I encourage organizations to use this metric with appropriate data normalizing transformations, in lieu of C_p, C_{pk}, P_p, and P_{pk} process metrics. Another benefit of this approach is that there can now be a single unit of measure for both attribute and continuous situations within manufacturing, development, and transactional processes.

Many times people have asked me for a procedure to convert the failure rate of an attribute process into a C_{pk} metric. This conversion makes no physical sense. Apparently, these people are confronted with a policy that they must report a single metric – C_{pk}. Note that if a process had a continuous response and there were upper and lower specification limits, we would also need to report C_p. It is hoped that you see how the policy of using the process capability/performance indices of C_p, C_{pk}, P_p, and P_{pk} can cause confusion within an organization and between suppliers/customers. This is another argument to use an estimated ppm rate or nonconformance percentage rate as a single metric for both attribute and continuous data. When reported out in the format show in Figures 7.7 to 7.10 in Volume 2, even high-level transformed satellite-level and 30,000-foot-level metrics can become second nature for easy interpretation and understanding (i.e., keep it simple for the reader).

One last point about this set of metrics: I have been asked $C_p/C_{pk}/P_p/P_{pk}$ questions by many who have a very solid statistical background. Often I respond to them by asking: If you are confused, what do you think is the level of understanding of others who have less statistical background? He/she invariably responds that the metric does create a great deal of confusion. I believe that we should report metrics that all understand and can picture in their minds. People can picture a metric that relates to a nonconformance rate. With this approach, even though our estimates may not be perfect for many reasons, the reporting of a nonconformance rate gives us a picture of relative conformance to criteria.

Within IEE, an infrequent subgrouping/sampling strategy for the creation of a 30,000-foot-level control chart avoids these problems. This chart offers a time-series baseline from which a process capability/performance metric can be determined. These metrics can be used for both operational metrics and to establish a baseline for IEE projects. From this capability/performance measure, the CODND can be established. The CODND metric along with any customer satisfaction issues can then be assessed to determine whether improvement efforts are warranted.

Some Six Sigma programs have a standard practice where black belts compare short-term process capability to long-term process performance directly for all projects, where short-term variability is considered as the entitlement of a process. Since these differences would be fallout from our IEE project execution road-map if this difference had statistical significance, there is nothing to gain by making such a routine comparison, which can be very costly and depends much on the sampling procedure that was used to determine the metrics.

Finally, with the IEE approach, I also do not recommend con-verting ppm rates to sigma quality levels because the results lead to confusion. The 1.5 standard deviation shift that is buried within a sigma quality level metric is confusing to many and distorts interpretations and comparisons between other process metrics. In addition, this conversion can become a very large issue when organizations must fabricate specification requirements in order to determine their sigma quality levels for various processes (e.g., transactional processes).

IEE can help organizations improve their bottom-line and customer satisfaction; however, its effectiveness is a function of how wisely the metrics and project execution strategy are imple-mented.

12.25 Additional Control Charting and Process Capability Alternatives

Breyfogle (2003a) also describes the following control charting and process capability calculation options:

- Cumulative sum (CUSUM) control chart
- Exponential weighted moving average (EWMA) with engi-neering process control (EPC)
- Zone control chart
- 3-way control chart
- Target or nominal control chart
- Z control chart
- Confidence interval on process capability indices
- Statistical tolerancing

12.26 Applying IEE

Both continuous and attribute process predictability and process capability/performance metric data assessments are addressed at the end of Chapter 13.

12.27 Exercises

1. Determine the upper and lower control limits for the following 31 daily observations; (i.e., data). Determine UCL and LCL and make a statement about whether the process is in-control/predictable.

141.9	124.8	131.7	126.5	129.0	136.0	134.3	144.9	140.5	134.1	137.0	147.1
126.6	155.5	133.4	120.7	138.8	125.0	133.0	142.4	146.0	137.4	120.8	145.2
125.0	127.0	118.3	137.1	136.5	105.8	136.9					

2. Determine the UCL and LCL for the following 48 once daily observations (i.e., 30,000-foot-level data). Determine UCL and LCL and make a statement about whether the process is in-control/predictable.

125.3	100.9	90.5	106.0	117.8	100.5	100.0	126.3	106.9	110.2	101.0	115.7
108.8	93.4	121.2	115.3	108.9	126.9	107.2	114.0	111.3	101.8	117.2	105.2
109.4	123.7	102.8	118.9	127.8	114.3	113.9	112.3	109.8	103.1	105.6	97.0
105.2	111.3	97.2	105.8	121.5	101.1	103.7	94.2	109.5	116.9	105.9	125.2

3. The output of a process is produced by two machines. Create a 30,000-foot-level response for the overall output of this process, which does not consider the effect of machine.

Response	Machine	Response	Machine
109.40	A	126.12	A
83.03	A	119.45	B
120.75	B	84.65	A
89.20	A	102.22	A
121.26	A	135.68	B
121.47	B	98.47	A
85.77	A	116.39	A
84.22	A	118.55	B
111.30	B	103.39	A
99.70	A	89.52	A
135.74	A	101.22	B
151.01	B	107.78	A
135.18	A	119.43	A
130.88	A	78.53	A
108.80	B	84.47	A
120.56	A	106.84	A

4. The KPOV from a process yielded the following:

Subgroup	Sample 1	Sample 2	Sample 3	Sample 4	Sample 5
1	98.731	98.943	97.712	107.912	97.266
2	87.394	96.018	98.764	100.563	98.305
3	113.910	109.791	115.205	116.298	116.837
4	120.052	111.994	110.041	119.676	119.242
5	107.035	105.492	111.519	114.119	100.468
6	98.436	102.282	92.957	100.247	107.214
7	89.928	90.444	98.230	89.860	88.137
8	104.424	102.700	97.119	101.723	102.168
9	93.209	98.536	102.683	111.545	105.954
10	89.059	91.914	91.172	95.646	105.608
11	106.586	100.760	106.271	108.019	105.288
12	103.583	122.339	110.341	107.661	111.157
13	103.785	100.825	95.790	104.117	108.512
14	109.769	109.791	110.307	106.365	99.336
15	112.115	111.952	109.979	124.777	110.935
16	88.464	95.487	91.104	100.842	85.606
17	110.206	103.991	110.982	109.633	113.925
18	94.751	102.563	101.663	98.483	88.963
19	103.387	108.197	105.230	103.677	95.469
20	96.668	97.482	102.466	101.277	103.000

Conduct a CODND assessment relative to a one-sided upper specification limit of 115 considering the following current policies within the company:
- Whenever a response greater than 115 is encountered, it costs the business $50.00.
- Next year's annual volume is 1,000,000 units for the 220 days of production. Assume that the 20 days in the data set are representative of the entire year.
- The current procedure for tracking this metric is to test five samples per day. If any one of the five samples is beyond 115, a root-cause investigation team is assembled to fix the problem. On average, the costs for this fixing activity are $50,000 per occurrence, which considers people's time and lost output.

5. For the data in Exercise 8.11, determine the overall expected process capability/performance metric and then the expected process capability/performance metric by machine type. Comment on results.

6. A chemical process has a specification upper limit of 0.16 and physical lower limit of 0.10 for the level of contaminant. Determine the estimated process capability/performance metric, which had the following output:

Period	Level	Period	Level	Period	Level
1	0.125	40	0.135	81	0.14
2	0.18	41	0.125	82	0.13
3	0.173	42	0.12	83	0.132
4	0.1215	43	0.135	84	0.141
5	0.1515	44	0.1195	85	0.1325
6	0.139	45	0.1265	86	0.21
7	0.144	46	0.115	87	0.135
8	0.205	47	0.115	88	0.135
9	0.1785	48	0.12	89	0.1445
10	0.1625	49	0.12	90	0.155
11	0.17	50	0.13	91	0.166
12	0.13	51	0.16	92	0.1475
13	0.18	52	0.17	93	0.1415
14	0.11	53	0.12	94	0.133
15	0.14	54	0.16	95	0.126
16	0.14	55	0.14	96	0.111
17	0.14	56	0.115	97	0.13
18	0.1365	57	0.225	98	0.13
19	0.1385	58	0.154	99	0.135
20	0.1365	59	0.126	100	0.135
21	0.1395	60	0.1075	101	0.13
22	0.135	61	0.128	102	0.1265
23	0.135	62	0.13	103	0.14
24	0.135	63	0.13	104	0.157
25	0.14	64	0.121	105	0.17
26	0.1525	65	0.1145	106	0.195
27	0.155	66	0.14	107	0.16
28	0.18	67	0.142	108	0.175
29	0.184	68	0.135	109	0.14
30	0.1625	69	0.115	110	0.135
31	0.18	70	0.1115	111	0.119
32	0.175	71	0.115	112	0.1
33	0.17	72	0.12	113	0.128
34	0.184	73	0.115	114	0.135
35	0.165	74	0.1025	115	0.125
36	0.1525	75	0.1215	116	0.125
37	0.1535	76	0.1335	117	0.1285
38	0.1355	77	0.165	118	0.1215
39	0.135	78	0.14	119	0.1185
40	0.135	79	0.15		
41	0.125	80	0.14		

7. At the 30,000-foot-level, a process had time-series responses of 25, 27, 23, 30, 18, 35, and 22. Determine the process capability/performance metric estimate relative to a one-sided upper specification limit of 36.

8. A process with a one-sided specification has a C_{pk} of 0.86. Determine the proportion of production that is expected to fall beyond the specification limit. Assume that long-term standard deviation was used when calculating the process capability index.

9. Given a mean of 86.4 and an upper specification limit of 94.4, determine the maximum standard deviation if a C_{pk} greater than 1.67 is required. Assume that long-term standard deviation was used when calculating the process capability index.

10. Determine the expected process capability/performance indices of a process that had the 30,000-foot-level data determined in Exercise 8.16, where the lower and upper specifications were 120 and 150. Determine from these indices the expected proportion beyond the upper and lower specification limits for the process. Compare these results to the results from a probability plot. Calculate sigma quality level and comment on this metric relative to the other process capability metrics.

11. Determine the expected process capability/performance indices of a process that had the 30,000-foot-level data determined in Exercise 8.17, where the lower and upper specifications were 95 and 130. Determine from these indices the proportion beyond the upper and lower specification limits. Compare these results to the results from a probability plot. Calculate sigma quality level and comment on this metric relative to the other process capability metrics.

12. A sales force had an 11-step process, where each step tracked the success to input ratio. Consider that the values below were the number of weekly successes for a sub-process step, where there were approximately 1000 weekly leads. Consider the cost of each unsuccessful lead was $500. Estimate the CODND. Comment on your results.

Sample number	Number of successes	Successful fraction	Sample number	Number of successes	Successful fraction
1	12	0.012	16	8	0.008
2	15	0.015	17	10	0.010
3	8	0.008	18	5	0.005
4	10	0.010	19	13	0.013
5	4	0.004	20	11	0.011
6	7	0.007	21	20	0.020
7	16	0.016	22	18	0.018
8	9	0.009	23	24	0.024
9	14	0.014	24	15	0.015
10	10	0.010	25	9	0.009
11	5	0.005	26	12	0.012
12	6	0.006	27	7	0.007
13	17	0.017	28	13	0.013
14	12	0.012	29	9	0.009
15	22	0.022	30	6	0.006

13. The number of weekly product Dead on Arrival (DOA) units is noted below. Approximately 50 products are shipped weekly. Estimate the CODND, considering that each DOA unit costs the business about $500.

Sample number	Number of successes	Successful fraction	Sample number	Number of successes	Successful fraction
1	12	0.24	16	8	0.16
2	15	0.30	17	10	0.20
3	8	0.16	18	5	0.10
4	10	0.20	19	13	0.26
5	4	0.08	20	11	0.22
6	7	0.14	21	20	0.40
7	16	0.32	22	18	0.36
8	9	0.18	23	24	0.48
9	14	0.28	24	15	0.30
10	10	0.20	25	9	0.18
11	5	0.10	26	12	0.24
12	6	0.12	27	7	0.14
13	17	0.34	28	13	0.26
14	12	0.24	29	9	0.18
15	22	0.44	30	6	0.12

14. Account receivables were considered late if payment was not received within 75 days. Consider that the viscosity column in Table 10.2 were the DSO for a daily randomly-sampled invoice. Determine if the process has any special causes. Determine the estimate for percentage of invoices that are beyond 75 days. Estimate the CODND if the average invoices were $10,000 and the interest rate that could be achieved on money is 6% for the 1000 invoices made per year.

Invoice	DSO	Invoice	DSO
1	70.1	11	72.9
2	75.2	12	72.5
3	74.4	13	74.6
4	72.07	14	75.43
5	74.7	15	75.3
6	73.8	16	78.17
7	72.77	17	76
8	78.17	18	73.5
9	70.77	19	74.27
10	74.3	20	75.05

15. Often customers ask for a C_p or C_{pk} value for their new product from a supplier. Discuss alternatives, confusion, and what could better address their underlying need.

16. A supplier was requested by a customer to produce information concerning their C_{pk} level. They were to estimate the expected percentage of failures that would occur if C_{pk} falls below 1.33. Consider how you would answer this question, assuming that there are both upper and lower specification limits.

17. The following time-series registration data were obtained for a device:

0.1003	0.0990	0.0986	0.1009	0.0983	0.0995
0.0994	0.0998	0.0990	0.1000	0.1010	0.0977
0.0999	0.0998	0.0991	0.0988	0.0990	0.0989
0.0996	0.0996	0.0996	0.0986	0.1002	0.0979
0.1008	0.1005	0.0982	0.1004	0.0982	0.0994
0.1008	0.0984	0.0996	0.0993	0.1008	0.0977
0.0998	0.0991	0.0988	0.0999	0.0991	0.0996
0.0993	0.0991	0.0999			

Determine whether the process appears predictable. Describe how well the process is doing relative to a specification of 0.1000 in. +/−0.003

18. A machine measures the peel-back force necessary to remove the packaging for electrical components. A tester records an output force that changes as the packaging is separated. Currently, one random sample is taken from three shifts and compared to a ± specification limit that reflects the customer needs for a maximum and minimum peel-back force range. Whenever a measurement exceeds the specification limits, the cause is investigated.
    (a) Evaluate the current plan and create a sampling plan utilizing control charts.
    (b) Assume that the peel-back force measurements are in-control/predictable. Create a plan to determine if the process is capable of meeting the ± specifications.
    (c) Discuss alternative sampling considerations.

19. Select the traditional and IEE suggested control charting methodology for the following set of DSO data, where one sample was taken every day for the last 50 days. Conduct a process capability/performance metric assessment.
    (a) Create a traditional control chart for this type of data, stating whether the chart indicates that the process is in control or not.
    (b) Create an IEE control chart for this type of data, stating whether the chart indicates that the process is in control or not.
    (c) Comment on the differences between the traditional and IEE results.
    (d) What process capability/performance metric statement can be made for each chart?

Day	DSO	Day	DSO	Day	DSO
1	1	18	3.2	35	6.9
2	12	19	7.4	36	2.5
3	7	20	0.4	37	7.6
4	0.1	21	248.8	38	0.4
5	3.1	22	0.1	39	0.5
6	145.6	23	0.9	40	20
7	2.8	24	1.1	41	4.1
8	1	25	0.1	42	19
9	0.6	26	70.8	43	18.1

10	0.1	27	2.6	44	0.2
11	0.5	28	5	45	1.2
12	19.7	29	0.7	46	10.3
13	0.1	30	0.8	47	3.3
14	24.3	31	6.7	48	73.6
15	704	32	4.8	49	5.9
16	3.3	33	4.1	50	0.3
17	1.9	34	9.9		

20. For the following days sales outstanding (DSO) conduct a process stability assessment and then make a process capability/performance metric statement when the process is predictable and the data are non-normal.

(a) Create an individuals chart of the data and comment.

(b) Examine several probability plots together to select a normalizing transformation (see hint before selecting distributions to consider). State the normalizing transformation that will be used.

(c) Create a probability plot of the data, documenting the parameters of the distribution.

(d) Transform each data point by first shifting all data points by the magnitude of the threshold value so that all data points will be positive. For the lognormal distribution, a 30,000-foot-level control chart can then easily be created by specifying a Box–Cox transformation with a lambda of zero. State whether the process is predictable or not.

(e) Determine and document a process capability/performance statement using a probability plot of the non-transformed data set.

Hint: A normalizing transformation will be needed that can address the minus numbers in the data set. This normalizing transformation would be used to assess whether a process is predictable and then be a part of the statement about the capability/performance metric. The threshold parameter in a three-parameter lognormal and three-parameter Weibull distribution adds flexibility so that the lognormal and Weibull distribution can address negative data points.

Week	DSO	Week	DSO	Week	DSO	Week	DSO
1	-3.340	26	-0.239	51	71.875	76	2.310
2	34.165	27	8.831	52	23.621	77	37.931
3	-5.886	28	-12.341	53	-25.530	78	24.174
4	-21.898	29	94.103	54	18.929	79	-24.706
5	9.248	30	57.791	55	27.003	80	-13.303
6	1.393	31	69.886	56	-10.538	81	192.627
7	52.070	32	-19.761	57	45.714	82	-11.922
8	1.035	33	90.780	58	110.190	83	39.755
9	-6.770	34	39.971	59	57.046	84	55.883
10	20.779	35	50.901	60	77.286	85	-24.101
11	87.154	36	1.861	61	12.501	86	-9.915
12	12.822	37	50.602	62	-21.321	87	23.700
13	-11.230	38	46.732	63	9.724	88	-9.804
14	-14.700	39	8.931	64	3.448	89	8.148
15	35.368	40	93.270	65	-3.446	90	17.550
16	-2.067	41	10.053	66	0.193	91	28.981
17	32.261	42	48.735	67	4.172	92	12.514
18	45.297	43	-3.316	68	-0.427	93	48.334
19	12.850	44	37.561	69	4.052	94	12.223
20	19.861	45	-20.879	70	27.613	95	139.733
21	65.448	46	57.469	71	2.305	96	7.318
22	28.507	47	-4.189	72	-19.986	97	89.320
23	63.427	48	13.317	73	-9.966	98	78.195
24	33.741	49	35.019	74	-3.385	99	15.282
25	29.727	50	-30.092	75	8.878	100	-30.315

13

P-DMAIC – Measure Phase (Baseline Project): IEE Process Predictability and Process Capability/Performance Metric Assessments (Attribute Response)

13.1   P-DMAIC Roadmap Component

Chapters 10 and 11 focused on the general concepts of traditional control charting and process capability. The last chapter illustrated the creation of a project's baseline using 30,000-foot-level control charting and process capability/performance metric techniques for continuous data. This chapter extends the concepts to attribute data.

The graphic in this section highlights the P-DMAIC roadmap steps (see Appendix Section D.1) that are described in this chapter. Appendix E contains the tollgate check sheets for this and other phases. The techniques described in this chapter are a portion of the decision tree for 30,000-foot-level control charting and process capability/performance metric selection; that is, Figures 13.1 and 13.2 show drill-downs to the project-execution-roadmap steps 3.2 and 3.3, highlighting an attribute response.

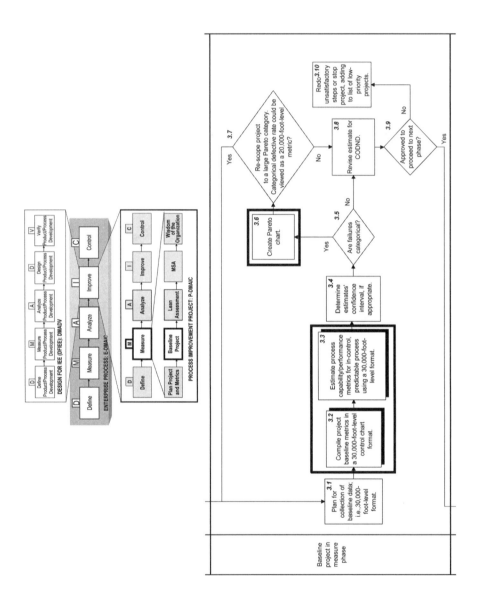

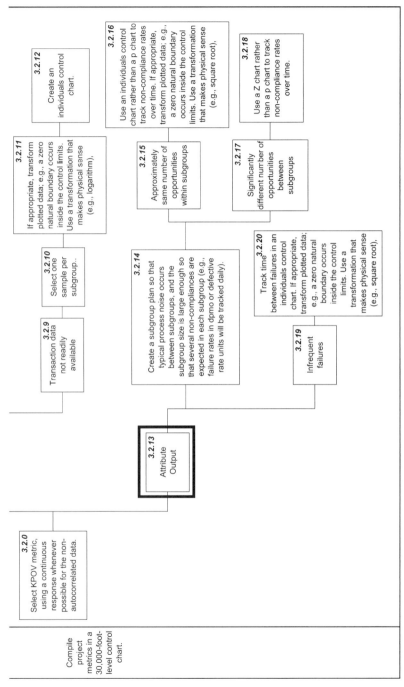

Figure 13.1: IEE 30,000-foot-level control chart decision tree. Drill down of step 3.2 of project execution roadmap with attribute output option highlighted.

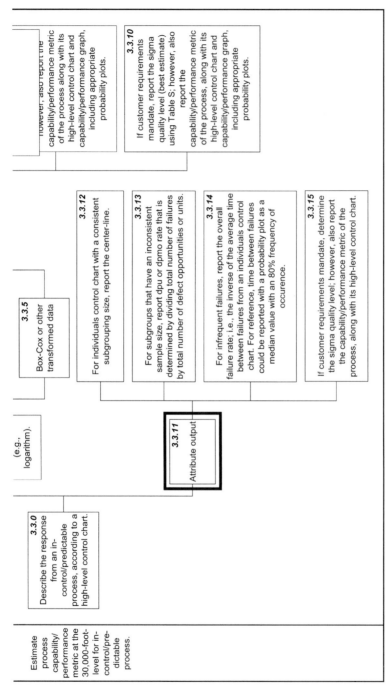

Figure 13.2: IEE 30,000-foot-level process capability/performance metric decision tree. Drill down of step 3.3 of project execution roadmap with attribute output option highlighted.

13.2 IEE Process Predictability and Process Capability/ Performance Metric: Attribute Pass/Fail Output

The methodologies described in this section are applicable to the creation of 30,000-foot-level metrics for the following process assessments:

- The daily defective rate for transactions (e.g., insurance claims or manufactured parts).
- The daily process of defects per million opportunities (DPMO) rate when there are multiple defect opportunities when completing a variety of transactions (e.g., completing an invoice or manufacturing a printed circuit board).

The standard deviation used to calculate control chart limits for variables data is computed from the data. However, if one examines the binomial and Poisson distribution equations (see Breyfogle, 2003a), he/she will find that the standard deviation is dependent on the mean of the data (not data dispersion as with variables data). Because of this, the standard deviation for an attribute control that uses the binomial or Poisson distribution will be derived from a formula based on the mean.

For the binomial-distribution-based and Poisson-distribution-based control charts, we assume that when a process is in statistical control the underlying probabilities remain fixed over time. This does not happen very often and can have a dramatic impact on the binomial-distribution-based and Poisson-distribution-based control chart limits when the sample size gets large. For large sample sizes, batch-to-batch variation can be greater than the prediction of traditional theory because of the violation of an underlying assumption. This assumption is that the sum of one or more binomial-distributed random variables will follow a binomial distribution. This is not true if these random variables have differing values (Wheeler, 1995a). The implication of this is that with very large sample sizes, classical control chart formulas squeeze limits toward the centerline of the charts and can result in many points falling outside the control limits. The implication is that the process is out of control most of the time (unpredictable process) when in reality the control limits do not reflect the true common-cause variability of the process.

The usual remedy for this problem is to plot the attribute failure rates as individual measurements. One problem with this approach is that the failure rate for the time of interest can be very low. For this situation, the control chart limit might be less than zero, which is not physically possible. One approach to get around this problem is to use an individuals control chart to track time between failures and/or to make an appropriate normalization transformation for the data.

Another problem with plotting failure rates directly as individual measurements is that there can be a difference in batch sample size. A way to address this problem is to use a *Z* chart. However, this has the same problem previously described relative to variability being just a function of the mean. Laney (1997) suggests combining the approaches of using an *XmR* chart with a *Z* chart to create *Z&MR* charts for this situation. I prefer not to use the *Z* transformation if at all possible. To accomplish this when sample sizes differ dramatically between subgroups is to select random samples from the subgroups so that the sample sizes are approximately the same. Example 13.2 illustrates the creation of this *Z* chart type.

The steps to perform this IEE analysis under various situations are:

1. Control chart creation steps (see Figure 13.1):
   - *Attribute output [3.2.13]*: Create a subgroup plan so that typical process noise occurs between subgroups, and the subgroup size is large enough so that at a minimum several non-compliances are expected in each subgroup (e.g., failure rates in DPMO or defective rate units will be tracked daily [3.2.14]. Approximately same number of opportunities within subgroups [3.2.15]. Use an individuals control chart rather than a *p* chart to track non-compliance rates over time, where the data may need an appropriate normalizing transformation [3.2.16].
   - *Attribute output [3.2.13]*: Create a subgroup plan so that typical process noise occurs between subgroups, and the subgroup size is large enough so that at a minimum several non-compliances are expected in each subgroup (e.g., failure rates in DPMO or defective rate units will be tracked daily) [3.2.14]. Significantly different number of opportunities between subgroups [3.2.17]. Use a *Z* chart rather than a *p* chart to track non-compliance rates over time [3.2.18].
2. Process capability/performance metric creation steps for predictable processes (Figure 13.2):

- *Attribute output [3.3.11]*: For individuals control chart with a consistent subgrouping size, report the centerline nonconformance rate [3.3.12].
- *Attribute output [3.3.11]*: For infrequent failures or subgroups that have an inconsistent sample size, report DPU or DPMO rate that is determined by dividing total number of failures by total number of defect opportunities or unit [3.3.13].

13.3   Example 13.1: IEE Process Predictability and Process Capability/Performance Metric: Attribute Pass/Fail Output

IEE Application Examples
- *Transactional workflow metric (could similarly apply to manufacturing; e.g., inventory or time to complete a manufacturing process): The number of days beyond the due date was measured and reported for all invoices, where the number of transactions in each subgroup was approximately the same. If an invoice was beyond 30 days late, it was considered a failure or defective transaction. The proportion of invoices not paid within the prescribed criterion was tracked over time to determine if the process was predictable. For regions of predictability, a process capability/performance metric was made relative to specification limits. Note: it would be much better for the data in this scenario to be tracked as continuous response, as noted in the previous chapter.*
- *Transactional quality metric: The number of defective recorded invoices was measured and reported, where the number of transactions in each subgroup was approximately the same. The proportion of invoices not paid within the prescribed criterion was tracked over time to determine if the process was predictable. For regions of predictability, a process capability/performance metric was made relative to specification limits.*

The methodology described in this example applies to the scenarios described in the previous section. This example not only uses the IEE process for determining the 30,000-foot-level metrics but will also illustrate why *p* chart results can be deceptive.

Table 13.1: Process Time Series Data

Day	Failures	Subgroup Size	Failure Rate	Day	Failures	Subgroup Size	Failure Rate
1	287	10,000	0.0287	11	155	10,000	0.0155
2	311	10,000	0.0311	12	160	10,000	0.016
3	222	10,000	0.0222	13	224	10,000	0.0224
4	135	10,000	0.0135	14	245	10,000	0.0245
5	188	10,000	0.0188	15	103	10,000	0.0103
6	175	10,000	0.0175	16	273	10,000	0.0273
7	142	10,000	0.0142	17	294	10,000	0.0294
8	215	10,000	0.0215	18	217	10,000	0.0217
9	272	10,000	0.0272	19	210	10,000	0.021
10	165	10,000	0.0165	20	241	10,000	0.0241

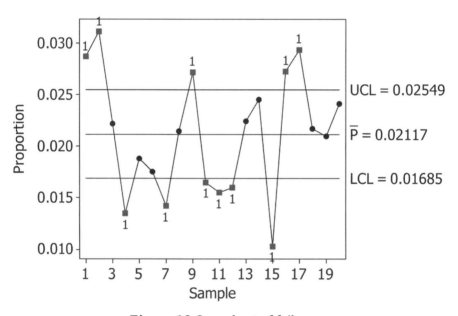

Figure 13.3: *p* chart of failures.

The daily transactions shown in Table 13.1 have the noted failures and calculated failure rate for each period. This type of data traditionally leads to a *p* chart, as shown in Figure 13.3.

On a control chart whenever a measurement is beyond the lower control limit (LCL) or the upper control limit (UCL), the process is said to be out of control. Out-of-control conditions are special-cause conditions, which can trigger causal problem investigations. This is the traditional approach using a Shewhart strategy.

For the control chart in Figure 13.3, many causal investigations could have been initiated since there are many out-of-control signals. Out-of-control processes are not predictable; hence, no process capability claim should be made.

For *p* charts, the lower control limit (LCL) and upper control limit (UCL) are as follows:

$$\text{LCL} = \bar{p} - 3\sqrt{\frac{\bar{p}(1-\bar{p})}{n}} \qquad \text{UCL} = \bar{p} + 3\sqrt{\frac{\bar{p}(1-\bar{p})}{n}}$$

From these equations, we note that the UCL and LCL limits are determined from the average failure rate ($\bar{p}$) and subgroup size (n). When the subgroup size is large, as it can be in many business situations, the distance between the UCL and LCL can become quite small. Variability from day-to-day material lot differences or day-to-day transaction differences can create the type of out-of-control signals as shown in Figure 13.1.

An individuals control chart is a control chart that captures between-subgroup variability. When adjacent subgroups are used to determine average moving range ($\overline{MR}$), the individuals control chart has LCL and UCL of:

$$\text{LCL} = \bar{x} - 2.66(\overline{MR}) \qquad \text{UCL} = \bar{x} + 2.66(\overline{MR})$$

The control limits are a function of the average moving range between adjacent subgroups. The individuals control chart is not robust to non-normal data; hence, for some situations, data need to be transformed when creating the control chart.

When attribute control chart subgroup sizes are similar, an individuals control chart can often be used in lieu of a *p* chart. The advantage of this approach is that between-subgroup variability will impact control chart limit calculations. An individuals control chart of the failure rate in Table 13.1 is shown in Figure 13.4.

This control chart indicates that the process is predictable; quite different from the conclusion drawn from the *p* chart. As previously discussed, when a process is predictable, we can not only make a statement about the past but also use historical data to make a statement about what we might expect in the future, assuming that things stay the same.

The process capability/performance metric for this process can then said to be a defective rate about 0.021. That is, since

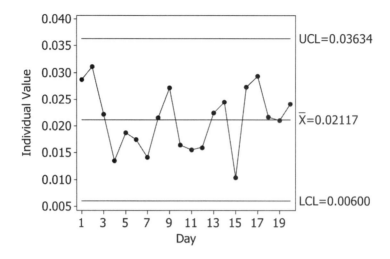

Predictable process with an approximate 2.1% non-conformance rate

Figure 13.4: Individuals control chart of failure rate.

the process is in control/predictable, we estimate that the future failure rate will be about 0.021, unless a significant change is made to the process or something else happens that either positively or negatively affects the overall response. This situation also implies that band-aid or firefighting efforts can waste many resources, when the real need is for fundamental business process improvements.

If improvement is needed for this 30,000-foot-level metric, a Pareto chart of defect reasons can give insight to where improvement efforts should focus. The most frequent defect type could be the focus of a new IEE project. For this IEE implementation strategy, we could say common-cause measurement improvement needs are pulling for the creation of an IEE project.

A subtle, but important, distinction between the two approaches is the customer view of the process. In the example above, the Shewhart approach (*p* chart) encourages a firefighting response for each instance outside of the control limits, while the IEE approach encourages looking at the issue as an organic whole (i.e., an issue of capability rather than of stability). If the problem is an ongoing one, then the IEE view is more aligned with the customer view (whether internal or external) of process performance. The above process is stable/predictable, though perhaps not satisfactory, from the customer perspective.

13.4   Example 13.2: IEE Individuals Control Chart as an Alternative to Traditional *p* Chart

The *p* chart data analysis in Example 10.3 indicated that the process was out of control. In this example, the data will be analyzed using the IEE suggested alternative procedure (i.e., an individuals control chart of the failure rate). The results from the two control charts will be compared. A z-chart analysis will also be illustrated.

Unlike the *p* chart approach, the individuals control chart analysis shown in Figure 13.5 indicate that the process is predictable, where the estimated process capability/performance metric is a non-compliance rate of 23.1%.

We note that the results of this individuals control chart analysis of the Table 13.1 data are very different from the previous *p* chart analysis. This analysis shows no out-of-control points. With this analysis we would now consider the out-of-control points determined in the *p* chart analysis to be common cause, not special cause. As noted earlier, the reason for differing results between these two analytical approaches is that the individuals control chart analysis considers variability between samples when determining control limits. A *p* chart analysis (also for *np* chart, *c* chart, and *u* chart analysis) assumes that dispersion is a function of location

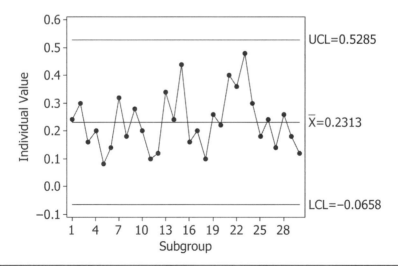

Predictable process with an approximate 23% non-conformance rate

Figure 13.5: *p* chart alternative example - individuals control chart.

and uses theoretical limits. The individuals control chart makes no such assumption and uses empirical limits. Wheeler (1995a) states that theoretical limits only offer a larger number of degrees of freedom. However, if the theory is correct, an *XmR* chart will be about the same. However, if the theory is wrong, the theoretical limits will be wrong, yet the empirical limits will still be correct.

As noted earlier, some issues often need to be addressed when conducting an individuals control chart analysis for this type of situation. First, an individuals control chart analysis is not bound by physical restraints that might be present. For example, the individuals control chart computer program analysis has a lower control limit below zero, which is not physically possible. Hence, this limit needs to be adjusted to zero. Sometimes this problem can be overcome by reassessing our subgrouping/sampling, or by viewing the data differently. We might also consider plotting the total number of failures (i.e., an *np* chart alternative) or the reciprocal of the failure rate instead of failure rate itself.

Another potential issue with the individuals control chart analysis approach for this situation is that this analysis does not consider that there could be differing subgroup sample sizes. If these differences are not large, this issue might not be important; however, if the differences are large, they can adversely affect the analysis.

To address the differing sample size issue for an individuals control chart analysis of this situation, we could sample a subgroup fixed number that we knew would occur. I like this approach. An alternative is to analyze the data using a *Z&MR* chart, where a *Z* transformation is made of the nonconformance rates (Laney, 1997). This transformation is then analyzed as an individual measurement. For this procedure:

$$Z_i = \frac{p_i - \bar{p}}{\hat{\sigma}_{p_i}} \qquad \text{for example: } Z_1 = \frac{p_1 - \bar{p}}{\hat{\sigma}_{p_1}} = \frac{0.24 - 0.2313}{0.05963} = 0.145$$

where p_i is the nonconformance proportion at the *i*th sample and the value for $\hat{\sigma}_{p_i}$ is determined from the relationship:

$$\hat{\sigma}_{p_i} = \sqrt{\frac{\bar{p}(1-\bar{p})}{n_i}} \qquad \text{for example: } \hat{\sigma}_{p_1} = \sqrt{\frac{0.2313(1-0.2313)}{50}} = 0.05963$$

A *Z* chart could be created from these calculations where the centerline would be zero and the UCL and LCL would be +/−3 standard

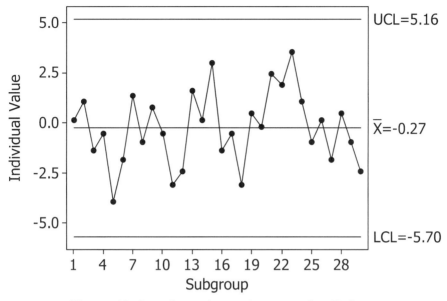

Figure 13.6: *p* chart alternative example - Z chart.

deviations. However, this does not resolve the previously discussed problem of limits being calculated from dispersion of the mean. The solution to this dilemma is to analyze the *Z*-score transformed data as though they were individual measurements. This *Z&MR* chart has limits that are calculated the same as *XmR* charts, except *Z* values replace the original data values. Figure 13.6 shows the results of this analysis. We note that this control chart is very similar in appearance to Figure 13.5; however, we do not have the problem of having a zero bound with this chart. We should note that in general there could be large differences between these two plots when there are sample size differences between subgroups.

13.5   IEE Process Predictability and Process Capability/Performance Metric: Infrequent Failures

The methodologies described in this section are applicable to the creation of 30,000-foot-level metrics for the following infrequent failure or rare event assessments:

- An organization has an occasional safety problem such as a spill or an injury. The number of defects is currently tracked monthly and reported in a c chart, where the reporting for most months is zero. Much effort has been spent to eliminate the problems, but problems still occur on the average once every seven months.

- Daily 30 customers were contacted by phone and asked if their shipment was complete. A daily p chart of the response frequently bounced off zero and was not very informative.
- A company requires that a supplier conducts an ongoing reliability test (ORT) of an electronic product that the supplier manufactures. The company later integrates this product into a larger system in its manufacturing facility. An ORT plan was created where every week a sample of newly manufactured units would experience a week-long customer-simulated test. The number of failures would then to be tracked weekly in a c chart to assess manufacturing process degradation; however, because the expected product failure rate is low, no failures are expected during most reporting periods.

These scenarios involve count data, which can often be modeled by a Poisson distribution using a c chart or a binomial distribution using a p chart. If the time between subgrouping/sampling is small relative to the frequency of failure, the plot points for most data can be zero. When one rare problem or failure occurs during the grouped time period, the plot will shift (i.e., shifts from zero to one in a c chart). This occasional shift for low failure rates (e.g., 1/7 failures per month, provides little information).

A better alternative to these scenarios is using an individuals control chart to track time between failures or the failure rate between failure occurrences. With this strategy, the above scenario could be restated to:

- An organization has an occasional safety problem such as a spill or an injury. Whenever a problem occurs, the time since the last occurrence will be noted. This time could be calendar hours or man-months. A plot will then be made on an individuals control chart that reflects the time since the last failure or a calculated failure rate since the last failure.
- Daily 30 customers were contacted by phone and asked if their shipment was complete. Whenever a problem is described, the number of calls since the last occurrence is noted. A plot will then be made on an individuals control chart that reflects the time since the last described shipment problem or a calculated failure rate since the last shipment problem.

An alternative to this process is to record the serial number of the failure and track the time between documented serial number failures, where the report-out would take into account the sample proportion relative to production volume.

- A company requires that a supplier conduct an ongoing-reliability test (ORT) of an electronic product that the supplier manufacturers. The supplier will sample products each week and submit the products to a customer-environment simulated test, where these sampled products will be exercised for 5 weeks. Whenever a failure occurs, the total test time of machines will be recorded since the last failure. A plot will then be made on an individuals control chart that reflects the total machine usage since the last failure or a calculated failure rate since the last failure.

The roadmap steps for this IEE application are as follows:

1. Control chart creation steps (Figure 13.1):
   - Attribute output [3.2.13] – Infrequent failures [3.2.19] – Track time between failures in an individuals control chart, where a normalizing transformation may be needed [3.2.20].
2. Process capability/performance metric creation steps for predictable processes (Figure 13.2):
   - Attribute output [3.3.11] – For infrequent failures report DPU or DPMO rate that is determined by dividing total number of failures by total number of defect opportunities. [3.3.13].

13.6 Example 13.3: IEE Process Predictability and Process Capability/Performance Metric – Infrequent Failures Output

Infrequent failures in a company could appear as accidents or service outages. Failures of this type might be reported in a format similar to Table 13.2, where No. is the number of failures that occurred during the month.

Since we are counting the number of monthly defects, the traditional approach would be to track the number of monthly defects using a *c* chart, as illustrated in Figure 13.7. This control chart,

Table 13.2: Number of Monthly Incidents

Month	No.	Month	No.	Month	No.	Month	No.	Month	No.	Month	No.
1	0	11	0	21	0	31	0	41	1	51	0
2	0	12	1	22	1	32	0	42	1	52	0
3	1	13	0	23	0	33	1	43	0	53	1
4	1	14	0	24	0	34	0	44	1	54	0
5	0	15	0	25	1	35	1	45	0	55	0
6	0	16	1	26	0	36	0	46	1	56	1
7	0	17	0	27	1	37	0	47	0		
8	0	18	0	28	0	38	1	48	0		
9	1	19	0	29	0	39	0	49	0		
10	0	20	1	30	1	40	0	50	1		

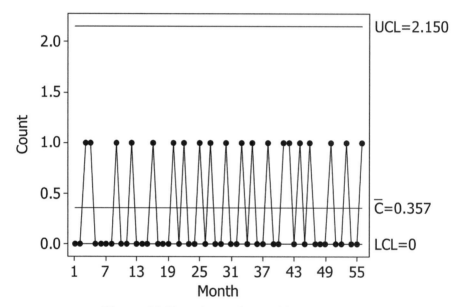

Figure 13.7: c chart of monthly instances.

which tracks the failure counts per month, is not very useful. Many months are zero, and it would be very difficult to determine if the process improved or degraded.

Instead of the above format, consider now that the times between failures were recorded and presented in the format shown in Table 13.3. An individuals control chart of this data is shown in Figure 13.8.

This chart indicates that our process is predictable. It needs to be highlighted that in general a normal distribution may not adequately represent the distribution of times between failure data that is being analyzed. A data normalizing transformation may be appropriate before creating an individuals control chart.

Table 13.3: Time Between Each Incident

Failure Number	Days since Last Failure	Failure Number	Days since Last Failure	Failure Number	Days since Last Failure
2	73	9	71	16	34
3	45	10	65	17	50
4	126	11	90	18	60
5	96	12	89	19	112
6	117	13	74	20	105
7	128	14	84	21	98
8	74	15	89		

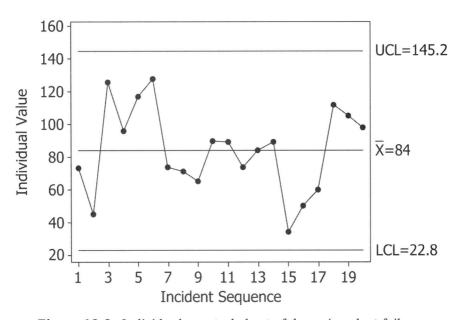

Figure 13.8: Individuals control chart of days since last failure.

Since this process is in control/predictable, we would estimate that that the future mean time between failure (MTBF) rate would be about 84 days. This centerline of 84 could be converted into an average annual or monthly failure rate.

This type of situation also lends itself to including an 80% frequency of occurrence value. This value should be used only to help others better understand the natural variability that we can expect from the current process (i.e., 1/MTBF is a failure rate), which is targeted process capability/performance metric. The

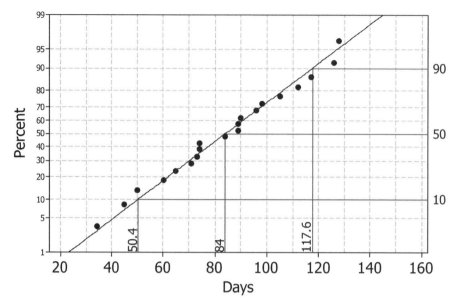

Figure 13.9: Probability plot of days since previous incident.

probability plot in Figure 13.9 indicates a median of 84 days with an 80% frequency of occurrence from about 50 (50.4 rounded off) days to 118 (117.6 rounded off) days.

Consider that a cost analysis of these failures indicated that improvement was needed. This would be the 30,000-foot-level metric pulling for an IEE project creation. Consider that a project change was implemented, which resulted in the following incident data:

Failure Number	Days since Last Failure
22	119
23	106
24	112
25	107
26	119
27	117

Plotting this data on 30,000-foot-level chart and process capability/performance metric are shown in Figures 13.10 and 13.11.

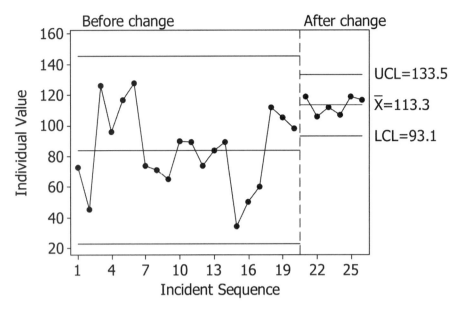

Figure 13.10: Individuals control chart, before and after change.

This figure indicates that the process has reached a new stability/ predictability level, where the new process capability/performance metric estimate has a median of 113 (113.3 rounded off) and frequency of occurrence of 106 (105.8 rounded off) to 121 (120.9 rounded off). In time, when more data becomes available, this prediction estimate would be refined.

This reporting provides much more insight than the c chart report. This IEE reporting can lead to less firefighting, fewer activities that lead to the wrong behavior (shifting numbers to or from a current quarter to meet objectives), and less playing games with the numbers in general, for whatever reason, and quicker identification when something either positively or negatively occurred in the process.

One final point to consider is that we often start monitoring failure because of a high frequency of complaints. Because of this, we might start with counts of complaints or failures per day, week or month, and then transition to the above MTBF assessment. Where, it is important to keep in mind that the time scale does not need to calendar-based. For instance, the unit of time could be the number of transactions between failures.

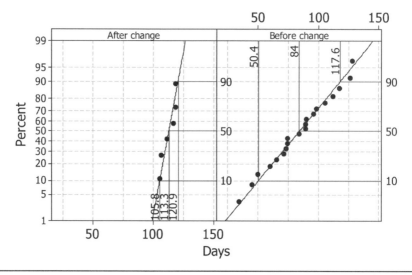

Predictable process before and after change (see Figure 13.10)

Before change prediction: median 84 days and 80% frequency of occurrence between 50 and 118 days

After change prediction: median 113 days and 80% frequency of occurrence between 106 and 121 days

Figure 13.11: Probability plot for process capability/performance metric estimate, before and after change.

13.7 Example 13.4: IEE Process Predictability and Process Capability/Performance Metric – Rare Spills

A department occasionally experiences a spill, which is undesirable (Wheeler, 1996). Everything possible is done to prevent spills; however, over the last few years a spill occurs on the average about once every 7 months. The following describes two methods to analyze infrequent occurrences.

The first spill occurred on February 23 of year 1. The second occurred on January 11 of year 2. The third occurred on September 15 of year 2. The number of days between the first and second spill is 322 days. The number of days between the second

Table 13.4: Spill Data

Date of Occurrence	Time Between Spills
2/23/1990	
1/11/1991	322
9/15/1991	247
7/5/1992	294
2/17/1993	227
9/28/1993	223
3/19/1994	172
7/12/1994	115

spill and third spill is 247 days. Dates of occurrence and time between spills for these and other occurrences are summarized in Table 13.4.

Figure 13.12 shows the c chart analysis of this data, where the number of failures were determined and plotted for each month. This chart shows no out-of-control condition; however, since there are so many plotted zeros, this charting format is not conducive to effective decision making. A better approach is to track time-between-failures on an individuals chart, as shown in Figure 13.13.

Using this IEE control charting method, it appears in the chart that there could a gradual decrease in the time between failures. However, since no special cause condition is shown in the 30,000-foot-level control chart, we conclude that this pattern could have occurred by chance from a process that has not experienced any change. A current process performance/capability statement assessment for this currently-concluded predictable process is that on the average there is about 229 days between incidents or 1.6 incidents per year (i.e., 365(1/229) = 1.6)

We need to highlight that just because the control chart is not indicating any special-cause condition does not mean that we should ignore the situation. We need to be cognizant that the "jury is out" in that we do not have enough evidence to state with confidence that safety incident frequency is getting worse. For this type of situation, someone might do a quick assessment to make sure there is nothing obviously degrading in the frequency of safety incidents from a process point of view.

As noted earlier, the individuals control chart is not robust to data that are not normally distributed (see Appendix Section B.2).

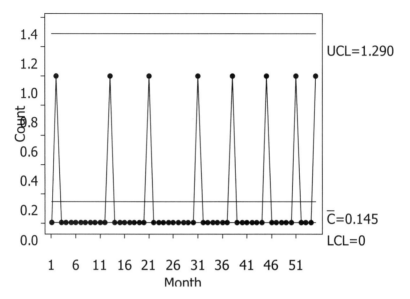

Figure 13.12: *c* chart analysis.

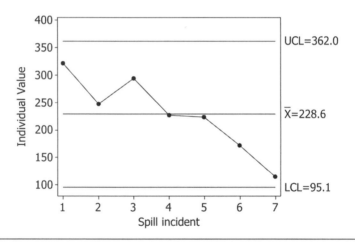

Conclusions: Don't have enough evidence to say that the process is not predictable; however, the plot indicates that there could be a decrease in time between spill incidents; i.e., more data is needed for a determination.

Current best-estimate prediction statement for the process is 229 days between incidents or 1.6 incidents per year.

Figure 13.13: Individuals control chart analysis of time between failures, an alternative to *c* chart.

The implication of this is that out-of-control signals can occur if the data are from a process that has an underlying distribution that is not normal.

In the original source for this data, the failure rate rather than time between failures was plotted. This method provides an average failure rate, but rate-value-data values can have a natural skew to the point that the individual chart produces false out-of-control signals.

Time-between-failure data tends to follow a Poisson distribution. Failure rate data will generally follow an inverse Poisson distribution $(1/x)$. When the time between failures exceeds around 40 to 50, the failure rate data begins to approach normality to an extent that failure rate can be tracked using an individuals control chart.

There are cases where an individuals control chart of the time between failures indicates that the data needs transformation. This is more common when the mean time between failures is small; e.g., 5 or less. When this occurs, a square-root data transformation is appropriate.

13.8   Direction for Improving an Attribute Response

IEE focuses on creating control charts so that control limits are determined by the variability that occurs between subgroups. Previously it was illustrated how an individuals control chart can often be more appropriate than a traditional *p* chart, noting that a normalizing transformation of the data may be appropriate if the type of data does not follow a normal distribution.

Figure 8.12 illustrates a situation where the best estimate to describe the failure rate capability/performance metric of the process at the 30,000-foot-level is the mean of the control chart (where the subgroup size is equal), which could be expressed in parts-per-million (ppm) units. If the process capability/performance metric level is unsatisfactory, a project can be created. The Pareto chart shown in this figure can provide insight to where improvement efforts would be most beneficial (see Appendix Section D.1, steps 3.5, 3.6, and 3.7 of the project execution roadmap). It is most preferable that this project scoping occurs at the enterprise before project definition; however, this drill down may need to occur after a project is started.

The Pareto chart can give us direction; however, we need to exercise care when making decisions solely from such graphical tools. Statistical significance such as a chi-square test and binomial analysis of means (ANOM) (see Chapter 23) should be used to test for a statistical significant difference in the data that were used to determine the Pareto bar heights.

It should note that the proper statistical name for the above referenced chi-square test is chi-square test of independence. This is different from the chi-square goodness of fit test, which has a different purpose. The only similarity is that the chi-square statistic is used for estimating significance. This volume will make reference to the chi-square test of independence as a chi-square test.

A significantly large Pareto chart bar can target process improvement efforts. When this occurs, the 30,000-foot-level tracking metric can be drilled down to focus on largest defect/defective cause. This defect/defective type tracing over time would be a 20,000-foot-level.

13.9   Example 13.5: Value Chain Metric Computation – 30,000-Foot-Level Attribute Assessment with Pareto Chart

This example contains computation of the 30,000-foot-level defective rate value chain metric, which is shown in:

- Breyfogle (2008d) – Figure 7.12
- Volume 2 – Figure 7.10

The produce and deliver value chain performance defective rate metric of Acme Medical is presented in Table 13.5. The defective rate 30,000-foot-level metric performance was tracked over time. Results from this analysis are shown in Figure 13.14.

The following IEE scorecard/dashboard metric reporting process will be used when analyzing the data:

1.   Assess process predictability.
2.   When the process is considered predictable, formulate a prediction statement for the latest region of stability. The usual reporting format for this statement is:
     (a)   When there is a specification requirement: nonconformance percentage or defects per million opportunities (DPMO).
     (b)   When there are no specification requirements: median response and 80% frequency of occurrence rate.

Table 13.5: Data for Value Chain 30,000-Foot-Level Defective Rate Performance Scorecard/Dashboard Metric. Stg: Stage; Def. Rate: Defective Rate (percent)

Day	Def. Rate	Stg	Day	Def. Rate	Stg	Day	Def. Rate	Stg	Day	Def. Rate	Stg	Day	Def. Rate	Stg	Day	Def. Rate	Stg
1	5.19846	1	26	6.100565	2	51	4.346701	2	76	5.352003	2	101	5.394805	2	126	5.664226	2
2	5.956555	1	27	5.146287	2	52	4.968625	2	77	4.856142	2	102	5.801384	2	127	4.425392	2
3	5.407518	1	28	5.267146	2	53	5.550502	2	78	5.458213	2	103	3.820133	2	128	4.717576	2
4	6.077013	1	29	4.575449	2	54	4.999145	2	79	4.752013	2	104	4.95071	2	129	5.192633	2
5	6.611962	1	30	5.372643	2	55	4.692636	2	80	4.200684	2	105	4.968329	2	130	5.18763	2
6	5.996385	1	31	4.499022	2	56	6.014419	2	81	5.655548	2	106	5.102664	2	131	6.143957	2
7	5.093956	1	32	5.066897	2	57	4.780758	2	82	4.845902	2	107	5.639803	2	132	4.127662	2
8	7.292982	1	33	5.73376	2	58	4.606171	2	83	6.176916	2	108	3.933291	2	133	5.100236	2
9	6.608044	1	34	4.724755	2	59	5.224966	2	84	4.37932	2	109	4.644831	2	134	4.041317	2
10	5.938893	1	35	5.36565	2	60	4.681968	2	85	5.115276	2	110	4.744277	2	135	4.730249	2
11	6.44066	1	36	6.167346	2	61	5.294173	2	86	4.569488	2	111	4.145019	2	136	5.161066	2
12	6.224348	1	37	4.045009	2	62	5.44789	2	87	5.175913	2	112	5.014803	2	137	3.86566	2
13	6.398748	1	38	4.468197	2	63	4.310641	2	88	5.456215	2	113	4.321917	2	138	5.862742	2
14	6.028732	1	39	4.910757	2	64	5.39652	2	89	5.441361	2	114	5.10123	2	139	5.011175	2
15	5.913832	1	40	4.519564	2	65	5.737691	2	90	4.95427	2	115	5.253219	2	140	5.161649	2
16	5.866364	1	41	4.72765	2	66	4.201294	2	91	4.656219	2	116	5.764662	2	141	5.934573	2
17	4.85115	2	42	4.586522	2	67	4.550172	2	92	4.692823	2	117	5.385868	2	142	5.536779	2
18	5.194891	2	43	5.018425	2	68	4.794158	2	93	6.157623	2	118	4.520019	2	143	4.284331	2
19	5.1991	2	44	4.646411	2	69	5.367154	2	94	4.688412	2	119	5.037036	2	144	4.204961	2
20	4.93468	2	45	4.646941	2	70	5.473898	2	95	4.737247	2	120	5.230441	2	145	5.151822	2
21	5.251173	2	46	5.308056	2	71	5.447196	2	96	4.651656	2	121	4.402522	2	146	5.571977	2
22	6.333642	2	47	5.718089	2	72	5.823504	2	97	4.153137	2	122	5.270059	2			
23	4.881219	2	48	5.823684	2	73	5.102458	2	98	4.436168	2	123	4.853369	2			
24	4.457135	2	49	4.386983	2	74	5.036417	2	99	4.24643	2	124	5.829311	2			
25	4.73857	2	50	5.187427	2	75	4.991851	2	100	4.792832	2	125	4.780916	2			

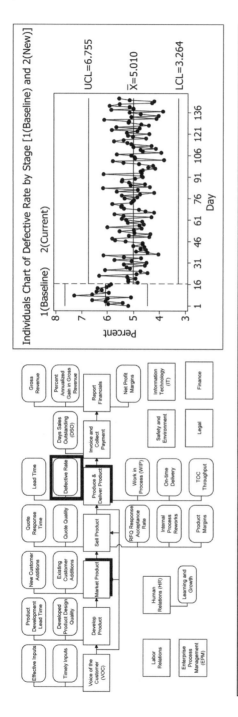

Figure 13.14: Value chain with 30,000-foot-level defective rate performance scorecard/dashboard metric statement. Stage 1 and 2 are denoted by the numbers at the top of the graph.

Interpretation of Figure 13.14 using this process:

1. The individuals control chart of defective rate by stage indicates a process shift on day 16 establishing a new level of predictive performance. Consider that a hypothesis test of the data from stage two of the control chart, when compared to stage one, indicated that an improvement was made (see Chapter 21). The control chart was constructed to denote this shift, where the process has stabilized and has now a new process capability/performance metric.

2. Since these data are attribute and the subgroup sizes are equal, the centerline of the stable/predictable process region is the estimated future defective rate. The current performance and predicted future defective rate is about 5% (5.01 rounded-off). The centerline shift of 1% is an estimate of the process improvement on day 16.

Since day 16, this process has been experiencing common-cause variability. These are best estimates of the performance of this process. If this process response is not satisfactory, something needs to be done to improve the process (i.e., a pull for project creation).

It is important to reiterate that the apparent short-term trends in the 30,000-foot-level control chart were all from chance and should not be reacted to as an individual value. Long-lasting improvements to this metric can be made through fundamental changes to the process.

When all value chain metrics are collectively examined in the E-DMAIC analyze phase, this metric could still be chosen as one that needs improvement because of its anticipated impact upon gross revenue and net profit business goals. If this were the case, this metric would pull for project creation. The owner of this "Produce and Deliver Product" metric would be responsible for making the targeted improvements in the allotted time frame (e.g., shift process mean to the desired goal in six months). A Pareto analysis was conducted to determine whether there were one or more opportunities for IEE projects.

Two Pareto charts of the transaction failure types since the improvement are shown in Figure 13.15, where one Pareto addresses the frequency of occurrence by type of transaction failure and the other by cost of doing nothing different (CODND) impact for each transaction failure type. Even though the type 3 defect had the largest frequency of occurrence, the financial impacts from types 4 and 2 transaction defects impact the financial bottom

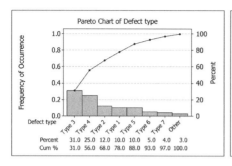
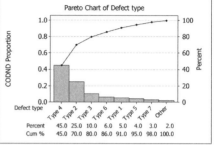

Figure 13.15: Pareto charts of defect type by occurrence frequency and CODND impact.

line the most. Hence, a reduction of type 4 and 2 failures would be likely candidates for projects. These projects should be considered along with other projects when putting together a plan for executing the projects in the E-DMAIC improve phase.

13.10 Applying IEE

Metrics drive behavior; however, it is important to sure to use the most appropriate sampling and control charting techniques. The 30,000-foot-level control and corresponding process capability/performance metrics give a high-level view of what the customer is feeling with the highlight that a process must be predictable before a process capability/performance metric statement is made.

The intent in this big picture is not the timely identification and resolution of process problems. Its purpose is to separate common-cause process variability from special-cause conditions, which may require immediate attention because something changed, perhaps dramatically.

If variability is greater than desired, consider the impact of the measurement system (see Chapter 15). One customer of mine had a situation where the contribution from measurement uncertainty was one-half of the total variability of the product output that he/she was using to determine whether he should ship a product or not.

A variance components analysis is another analysis alternative that can give direction on where to focus variability reduction efforts. A variance components analysis approach can not only quantify a standard deviation to use within process capability/performance metric calculations, but can also suggest where to focus process improvement efforts. It can also be used whenever time series data are limited.

Consider the impact of forcing a specification where one does not exist. I have seen some organizations spend much time creating a very questionable metric by arbitrarily adding a specification value where one was not really appropriate – so that they could make a C_{pk} metric. This situation can often occur in business and service processes. Consider using the described probability plotting reporting procedure for this situation.

Organizations often evaluate the success of a Six Sigma deployment as the collective financial benefit from project completions, where there is a push for project creation; for example, brainstorm for projects and rank these projects to see which projects to work on first. However, when we step back to the collective enterprise view, we do not often see the project financial benefits within the overall organization's return-on investment (ROI) or profit margins. With a Lean Six Sigma push for project creation system, organizations could even be sub-optimizing processes to the detriment of the overall enterprise.

In IEE, the collective examination of responses from an organization's 30,000-foot-level metrics, along with an enterprise analysis, can provide insight into which metrics need improvement. This approach ensures that the project definition and completion is in alignment with the overall enterprise satellite-level metrics improvement goals. That is, in IEE enterprise metric improvement needs stimulate a pull for project creation.

13.11 Exercises

1. Consider that an airplane's departure time is classified late if its entry door is not closed within 15 minutes of its scheduled departure time. Discuss whether this type of airline data is attribute or continuous/variables data and what might be done differently to better describe departure time of flights relative to customer expectations.
2. Weekly, 100,000 transactions were made, where the number of defective units by week for the last 30 weeks was:

883	900	858	611	763	754	737	643	683	613
867	554	593	663	757	475	865	771	855	978
961	837	640	976	840	739	731	648	955	670

Create an individuals control chart to track the output of this process at the 30,000-foot-level. Determine whether the process is predictable. If it is predictable, determine the process capability/performance metric. Your customer required the calculation of a sigma quality level for the process. Estimate the process sigma quality level. Comment on the results and analyses.

3. Estimate the proportion defective rate assuming only the first four points in Figure 13.3 had been collected and a management decision was being requested. Using only these first four points, project what the failure rate would be in 10 days. Comment on your results.

4. Management initially wanted the evaluation of a random sample to assess a process that is considered a problem whenever the response is larger than 100. Management believes that an unsatisfactory rate of 2% is tolerable, but would like a rate not to exceed 3%. Describe control charting alternatives that could have been used earlier within the process to give the requested response. Describe the advantages of the alternative strategies over the currently proposed single-sample approach.

5. A manufacturing company was conducting a go/no-go test on a critical dimension that had a specification of 0.100 ± 0.002 inch. The company thought that they were getting a reject rate of 10%. Describe what, if anything, could be done differently within the sampling plan to understand the process better.

6. Further investigation into the process output that was described in Exercise 10.9, led to the following, where units are produced sequentially. Create a control chart and conduct a process capability/performance metric assessment for the process. Comment on the differences between this time-between-failure reporting using an individuals control chart and the p-chart failure reporting in Exercise 10.9.
    (a) Create an individuals control chart of the failure rate.
    (b) Conduct a process capability/performance metric assessment for the process.
    (c) Comment on the differences between this time-between-failure reporting and the reporting in exercise 10.9 with a p-chart.

Failure number	Unit number that failed
1	99
2	402
3	490
4	550
5	725
6	930

7. Create a traditional control chart and an IEE control chart for the following data. Conduct a process capability/performance metric assessment.

   (a) Create a traditional control chart for this type of data stating whether the chart indicates that the process is in control or not.

   (b) Create an IEE control chart for this type of data, stating whether the chart indicates that the process is in control or not.

   (c) Comment on the differences between the traditional and IEE results.

   (d) What process capability/performance metric statement can be made for each chart?

Day	Defective units	Subgroup size	Failure rate
1	200	20000	0.01
2	150	20000	0.0075
3	180	20000	0.009
4	250	20000	0.0125
5	300	20000	0.015
6	140	20000	0.007
7	270	20000	0.0135
8	320	20000	0.016
9	150	20000	0.0075
10	200	20000	0.01

14

P-DMAIC – Measure Phase (Lean Assessment)

14.1   P-DMAIC Roadmap Component

The last two chapters described the creation of value chain performance and project metrics at the 30,000-foot-level. This chapter progresses to the next P-DMAIC step, Lean assessment. The graphic in this section highlights the P-DMAIC roadmap steps (see Appendix Section D.1) that are described in this chapter. Appendix E contains the tollgate check sheets for this and other phases.

Whenever the primary project 30,000-foot-level metric is lead time or work in progress (WIP) reduction, the project team should give high application consideration to Lean tools. Volume 2 describes the application of Lean tools in the analyze phase of E-DMAIC. This chapter describes how many of these Lean tools are applicable in the Lean assessment portion of the P-DMAIC roadmap.

This chapter describes both the current and future state value stream map; however, quantifiable benefits from the future state map show up in the P-DMAIC improve phase.

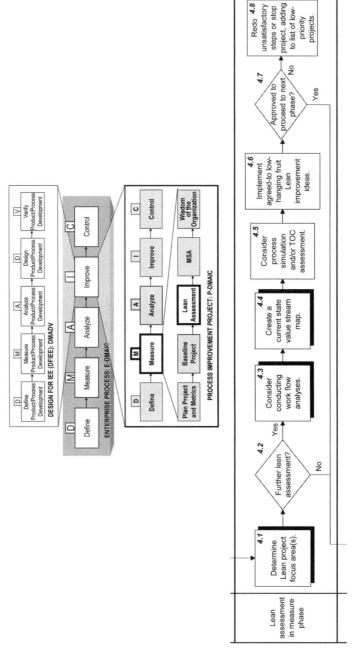

14.2   Waste Identification and Prevention

If we consider that waste is being generated anywhere work is accomplished, we can create a vehicle through which organizations can identify and reduce it. The goal is total elimination of waste through the process of defining waste, identifying its source, planning for its elimination, and establishing permanent control to prevent reoccurrence.

Muda is the Japanese term for waste. Seven elements to consider for the elimination of muda are correction, overproduction, processing, conveyance, inventory, motion, and waiting. Initiatives to consider for reducing waste include the 5S method that focuses on improvements through sorting (cleaning up), storage (organizing), shining (cleaning), standardize (standardizing), and sustaining (training and discipline). Since 5S is a Lean improvement vehicle, it is described in more detail as part of the P-DMAIC improvement phase.

In the financials of a business, inventory appears as an asset, which can lead to the wrong activities. In practice, however, inventory is a detriment to business interests for the following reasons:

- *Space*: Wasted space and hidden cost for area maintenance
- *Material handling*: Moving stock around or sorting to get the right part/transaction
- *Investment*: Investment cost that does not earn interest
- *Hidden operations*: Difficult to see what is being produced because of the stacking of parts
- *Quality*: Hidden rejects in inventory
- *Batched parts*: Promote further excessive production batching
- *Equipment*: Large inventories hide frequent maintenance emergencies

14.3   Principles of Lean

The principles of Lean are: (1) define customer value, (2) focus on the value stream, (3) make value flow, (4) let the customer pull product, and (5) pursue perfection relentlessly. Lean is an answer to a customer need or desire. The product or service is provided in a timely manner and at an appropriate price. You or I don't determine value; value is in the eyes of the customer.

Within Lean, we identify the value stream. This might be a process or series of process steps from concept to launch to production, order to delivery to disposition, or raw materials (RMs) to customer receipt to disposal. It consists of steps that add value to a product. Within Lean, we eliminate steps that do not add value, where a product can be tangible or intangible.

When working on the product/service, we start at receipt of customer request and end at delivery to customer. We strive for no interruptions. That is, we strive for no muda. We work to avoid batch processing and strive for one-piece flow. We want a pattern of processing that accomplishes smooth flow through the process without stacking of material between process steps. We want to minimize WIP and develop standard work processes.

We strive to have just-in-time workflow, which yields exactly the right product in exactly the right place at exactly the right time. With this approach, nothing is produced until the downstream customer requests it. An application example is a made-to-order sandwich shop versus a fast food hamburger shop that makes a batch of hamburgers in anticipation of customer demand.

> Waste is anything other than the minimum number of people, the minimum amount of effort, material, information, and equipment necessary to add value to the product.

Waste is anything other than the minimum number of people, the minimum amount of effort, material, information, and equipment necessary to add value to the product. We will now consider the following attributes of waste: value added, required non-value added, manufacturing waste, waste in design, and waste in administration. We will also consider what we might do to hunt for waste.

When there is a value-added activity, the customer recognizes its importance and is willing to pay for it. Value-add actions transform the product in form, fit, or function, where the product could be information or physical product. Work is done right the first time. Required non-value-added activities do not increase customer-defined value. However, the activity may be a required business necessity (e.g., accounting), employee necessity (e.g., payroll), or process necessity (e.g., inspection).

Manufacturing waste includes:

- *Overproduction*: Making more than you need
- *Waiting*: People or product waiting

- *Transportation*: Moving materials
- *Inventory*: Having more than you need
- *Overprocessing*: Taking unnecessary steps
- *Motion*: People moving
- *Defects*: Making it wrong, fixing it

Waste in design includes:

- *Overproduction*: Un-launched designs
- *Waiting*: Waiting for signatures, approvals, data
- *Transportation*: Handoffs to other organizations
- *Inventory*: Backlogs, outdated designs
- *Overprocessing*: Approval routings, excessive analysis
- *Motion*: Obtaining forms, paperwork
- *Defects*: Incorrect drawings, data

Waste in administration and transactional processes include:

- *Overproduction*: Excessive reporting
- *Waiting*: Waiting for signatures, approvals, data
- *Transportation*: Handoffs to other organizations
- *Inventory*: backlogs
- *Overprocessing*: Approval routings, signature requirements
- *Motion*: Obtaining forms, paperwork
- *Defects*: Incorrect data, missing data

Traditionally within Lean, an organization might form hunting parties to identify waste. With this approach, an individual can use a notepad to identify and record waste in his/her assigned area, sharing the findings with the team. In Integrated Enterprise Excellence (IEE), the following Lean metrics, when tracked at the 30,000-foot-level, can give insight to where the overall enterprise can best target its improvement efforts:

- Inventory
  - Finished Goods (FG)
  - WIP
  - Raw Material (RM)
- Scrap
- Headcount
- Product changeover time
- Setup time
- Distance Traveled

- Yield
- Cycle Time (C/T): In Lean, C/T is considered to be how often a part or transaction is completed (time for one piece). Also, duration of operator time for the completion of work before repeating the steps.
- Average Completion Rate (ACR): Number of things completed per unit of time.
- Takt Time: Customer demand rate (your available work time per shift divided by customer demand rate per shift). Metric is expressed in units of time to produce one unit of product.
- Lead Time (L/T): Time for one piece or transaction to move completely through a process or value stream to the customer
- Value-added time (VA): Work that a customer is willing to pay for
- Inventory turns: Annual cost of goods sold/average value of inventories during the year
- Little's Law: Lead time = WIP (# units)/ACR (# units/time)
- Process cycle efficiency = value-added time divided by lead time

Another aspect of Lean is the visual factory, which involves management by sight. The creation of a visual factory involves the collection and display of real-time information to the entire workforce at all times. Work cell bulletin boards and other easily seen media might report information about orders, production schedules, quality, delivery performance, and financial health of business.

Within an IEE roadmap, Lean tools should be considered if the 30,000-foot-level scorecard/dashboard metric (Y variable or KPOV) implies the need for improved workflow; for example, the time it takes to complete a task or reduce WIP.

Continuous flow manufacturing (CFM) within Lean consists of the efficient utilization of operations and machines to build parts. Non-value-added activities in the operation are eliminated. Flexibility is a substitute for work-in-process inventory. A product focus is established in all areas of operation. Through CFM, organizations have simplified manufacturing operation into product or process flows, organized operations so that there is similarity between days, and established flow or lead times.

Within an IEE roadmap, Lean tools should be considered if the 30,000-foot-level scorecard/dashboard metric (Y variable or key process output variable (KPOV)) implies the need for improved workflow; for example, the time it takes to complete a task or reduce WIP. The Lean tools described next in this chapter can be used in both the enterprise analyze phase assessment and process improvement project execution.

14.4 Example 14.1: Takt Time

As noted earlier, takt time is customer demand rate. That is, the available work time per shift divided by customer demand rate per shift. This metric is expressed in units of time to produce one unit of product.

Determine the takt time, given the following:

- 1000 parts or transactions per day (i.e., customer requirements, not capability)
- 8 h shifts
- Two 15 min breaks per shift
- Two shifts per day

$$\text{Takt time} = \frac{(8.0 \text{ hr.} - .50 \text{ hr.}) \times 60 \text{ min./hr.} \times 60 \text{ sec./min.} \times 2 \text{ shifts/day}}{1000 \text{ transactions/day}}$$

$$= 54 \text{ sec. per transaction}$$

The comparison of takt time to production capacity can highlight when either excess or insufficient process capacity exists. Takt time is important since it should be used to set the tempo of the organization.

14.5 Little's Law

Little's law is:

$$\text{Lead time} = \frac{\text{WIP}}{\text{ACR}}$$

where ACR = Average Completion Rate.

This equation quantifies the average length of time it takes to complete any work item or work items (lead time) from the amount of work that is waiting to be completed (WIP) and the ACR (transactions per day or week completed).

This relationship is more useful than one might initially think. Consider that we would like to get the lead time or average delivery time, but often it is very difficult to track individual transactions through all the process steps and then average these values.

For example, the average duration to compete an insurance claim could be determined by dividing the number of claims in the overall system (WIP) by the ACR (i.e., average number of claims completed in a given period of time).

14.6   Example 14.2: Little's Law

Determine the average wait time at a call center when, for a given day at 10 random times, the number of people observed waiting on hold averaged 12. For the same 24-h day, 1000 calls were received.

$$ACR = 1000/24 = 41.67 \text{ calls/hour}$$

$$\text{Lead time} = WIP/ACR = 12/41.67 = .288 \text{ hours or } 17.3 \text{ minutes}$$

14.7   Identification of Process Improvement Focus Areas for Projects

Examine the E-DMAIC 30,000-foot-level scorecard/dashboard value chain metrics collectively to gain insight to project improvement opportunity areas for quality improvement, waste elimination, lead time reduction, and/or total costs reduction. For waste elimination, overproduction focus can be a most beneficial starting point, since this is often the largest waste source.

Quality improvement assessment

1. Report-out 30,000-foot-level scorecard/dashboard metric from the value chain that is being assessed for improvement opportunities.
2. Describe both internal and external customer wants and needs (i.e., expectations and requirements).

3. Conduct a gap analysis of differences between products and services offerings relative to customer wants and needs. This assessment can address the 30,000-foot-level process capability/performance metric relative to desired levels along with product/process design effectiveness.
4. Identify high impact areas of the business that have the most leverage for reducing the gap between performance and customer needs.
5. Compile and prioritize process improvement opportunities using a cause-and-effect matrix (See Chapter 16).
6. Combine the cause-and-effect matrix items from this business area with other business areas.
7. Determine a potential improvement goal for the 30,000-foot-level scorecard/dashboard metric.
8. Describe resulting IEE process improvement quality projects along with other IEE projects.

Waste elimination assessment

1. Within IEE, general waste reduction areas are created through the initialization and institutionalized system, where individuals propose a business process improvement event (BPIE) when waste removal opportunities are identified in real time. This is different from the search for waste removal activities. The other improvement area opportunities described in this section involve the pull for project creation from 30,000-foot-level scorecard/dashboard metric improvement needs.

Lead time assessment

1. Report-out 30,000-foot-level scorecard/dashboard metric from the value chain that is being assessed for improvement opportunities.
2. Initiate the construction of a value stream map or time value diagram of the business area.
3. Use Little's law to determine lead times for each step
4. Calculate value-added time for each process step.
5. Determine the total value-added time for the overall process.
6. Determine overall process cycle efficiency (value-added time divided by lead time)
7. Determine the process cycle efficiencies for each step. Use a Pareto chart to describe the results.

8. Consider process simulation to model process variability for the purpose of exposing waste and testing proposed changes.
9. Brainstorm for improvement opportunities to improve cycle efficiencies, targeting a ratio of 1 (i.e., 100% efficiency), considering that lead time consists of the three components: cycle time, batch delay, and process delay. In product design, one opportunity for improvement is the simplification of products or services so that there is more direct alignment with customer wants and needs. In supply, one opportunity for improvement is that an upstream/downstream analysis of the demand/supply-chain indicates that logistic practices create waste in the form of inventory. In manufacturing, potential process improvement opportunities are standardizing best practices, reducing changeover time (expedites build-to-customer-order fulfillments), one-piece/continuous flow (eliminates both process and batch delays), technology (hardware and software implementations can reduce cycle time and error frequency), and product customization earlier within overall process (which can improve implementation efficiency).
10. Identify process constraints.
11. Establish appropriate in-process metrics.
12. Compile and prioritize process improvement opportunities using a cause-and-effect matrix.
13. Combine the cause-and-effect matrix items from this business area with other business areas.
14. Determine a potential improvement goal for the 30,000-foot-level scorecard/dashboard metric.
15. Describe resulting IEE process improvement lead time projects along with other IEE projects.

WIP reduction assessment

1. Report out 30,000-foot-level scorecard/dashboard metric from the value chain that is being assessed for improvement opportunities.
2. Initiate the construction of a value stream map of the business area.
3. Determine takt time.
4. Determine mean WIP for each process step.
5. Determine mean WIP for the overall process.
6. Pareto chart WIP by process step.

7. Consider process simulation to model process variability for the purpose of exposing waste and testing proposed changes.
8. Brainstorm for improvement opportunities to reduce WIP, targeting a value of zero.
9. Identify process constraints.
10. Establish appropriate in-process metrics.
11. Compile and prioritize process improvement opportunities using a cause-and-effect matrix.
12. Combine the cause-and-effect matrix items from this business area with other business areas.
13. Determine a potential improvement goal for the 30,000-foot-level scorecard/dashboard metric.
14. Describe resulting IEE process improvement WIP projects along with other IEE projects.

Total cost reduction

1. Report out 30,000-foot-level scorecard/dashboard metric from the value chain that is being assessed for improvement opportunities.
2. For established services/products, initiate with high-cost products and processes, where an ABC and cost maintenance may be beneficial. For new services/products, consider process improvement efforts relative to target pricing, target costing, and value engineering.

14.8   Lean Assessment

As Yogi Berra, retired baseball player and later team manager, said, "You can observe a lot by watching." A first step to understand a process is to observe it. Process observation involves walking the actual process while taking notes to describe what is actually occurring. This step-by-step documentation includes a description, distance from last step, estimated task time, observations, and return rate. Both the observation worksheet and the standardized work chart (or standard work sheet) described below can become the template for this documentation. A link in the overall enterprise value chain is a potential repository for standardized work charts (see Figure 16.5).

Table 14.1: Lean Principles

Workplace	People	Systems
◆ Workplace organization	◆ People effectiveness	◆ Workstation tool reliability
◆ Standardized work	◆ Quality at the source	◆ Cellular flow
◆ Visual controls		◆ Batch reduction or elimination
		◆ Pull versus push systems
		◆ Point of use systems

Table 14.2: Lean Assessment Matrix Example

Lean Area		Project Importance		
Category	Principle	None	Some	Major
Workplace	Organization	x		
Workplace	Standardized work		x	
Workplace	Visual controls		x	
People	Effectiveness			x
People	Quality at source		x	
System	Tool reliability	x		
System	Cellular flow		x	
System	Batch reduction or elimination			x
System	Pull vs. push system			x
System	Point of use systems	x		

Instructions: Describe the level of project importance for each Lean principle by entering an "X" in the appropriate box

Table 14.1 summarizes Lean focus opportunities for the identification of targeted areas to improve the value chain performance metrics. Upon completion of this observation, the Lean assessment matrix shown in Table 14.2 can provide a prioritization of improvement focus area opportunities. I will now elaborate on each Lean principle area described in the table.

Workplace

The workplace should be organized. It should be a neat, clean, and safe environment with an arrangement that provides specific locations for everything with the elimination of anything that is not required. Materials should be stored close to where they are used.

The workplace should have standardized work. Everyone in operations should follow the best known sequence. This best known sequence involves deviation detection from standards with timely resolution, ideally in real time. These deviations include product defects (e.g., quality, cost, delivery, inventory, and regulatory compliance), human errors, and abnormal conditions (e.g., equipment, safety, or general business conditions). Standardization is not easy. Organizations often have difficulty allotting the time to standardize, and even if they do, sustaining the standardization can be very difficult. Utilization of standardization work charts such as the one described later is this chapter can be beneficial in describing what is being done and in giving insight to what should be done to improve.

In the workplace, visual controls signals provide immediate understanding of situations and/or conditions. These controls need to be simple, efficient, self-regulated, and worker-managed. Examples include schedule/status boards, color-coded files, and good directional signals.

People

People are important ingredient to the success of an organization. The effective use of people and of their talent is essential. For this to occur, highly specific jobs need the flexibility of team-task rotation. Team members need to be cross-trained and multi-skilled so that they can work many operations in multiple areas. People need to be given high responsibility and authority.

Organizations need to create a quality-at-the-source discipline. People need to be certain that high-quality information and/or products are passed on to the next area. Adequate inspection tools need to be provided, along with visual tools that demonstrate acceptable standards. Systems need to have workstation tool reliability. Operations' tools and equipment need to be efficient and effective. Computer system response time needs to be good, and tool down time needs to be minimal.

Systems

Systems that have cellular flow can be very beneficial (see Chapter 36). The physical linkage of people and of supporting hardware/software in the most efficient and effective combination minimizes waste and maximizes value-add activities.

Batch systems can cause a large amount of WIP. Procedures that reduce or eliminate batching can be very beneficial. Pull systems can yield very large benefits over push systems. Pull systems control the flow of resources over time based on rules and system status. Push systems that are based on schedules, forecasts, or when time is available to perform activities should be avoided. It is also very desirable to create systems that are available where needed (i.e., point-of-use systems). For example, a layout requires locating a number of point-of-use stores on the factory floor, where work center demands are allocated to these stores, including the setting of inventory levels.

Another approach to identify improvement opportunities is to videotape an operation, play back the recording, and document sequence times through work element. This document could follow the combination work table format, which is illustrated later in this chapter. Analysis of these work times can lead to effective focused improvement efforts.

14.9   Workflow Analysis: Observation Worksheet

Before suggesting or implementing changes, existing processes need to be understood. This is accomplished by walking and observing the current process in action. This activity to improve current conditions understanding applies not only to manufacturing but also to transactional processes, where, for example, we might walk through user application sequences in a computer menu.

When walking the process, a form should be used to summarize all observations. An example worksheet template is shown in Table 14.3. This step-by-step documentation describes activities,

Table 14.3: Observation Worksheet

Value Stream Observation Worksheet

Process #	Description	Inventory	Estimated Cycle Time for Task	Observations	Return Rate

distance from last step, estimated task time, observations, and return rate.

This tool can be used in both the E-DMAIC analyze phase and the P-DMAIC measure phase. When lead time, defect/defective rates, or WIP is a 30,000-foot-level scorecard/dashboard enterprise value chain or project metric, the observation worksheet provides information that can identify waste in overproduction, waiting, transportation, inventory, overprocessing, motion, and defects. This description can help identify where targeted improvement efforts should focus.

14.10 Workflow Analysis: Standardized Work Chart

The posting of a standardized work chart or a standard work sheet at each work station becomes a means of visual control. Table 14.4 illustrates an example layout, which includes a spaghetti diagram (see Figure 14.2). A link in the overall enterprise value chain (see Figure 3.1) is a potential repository for these charts.

As part of Toyota production system (TPS), the standard work sheet includes lead time, work sequence, and standard inventory (Ohno, 1988). Ohno states, "A proper work procedure, however, cannot be written from a desk. It must be tried and revisited many times in the production plan. Furthermore, it must be a procedure that anybody can understand on sight."

As a tool, the standardized work chart can be used in both the E-DMAIC analyze phase and the P-DMAIC measure phase. When lead time or defective/defect rates is a 30,000-foot-level scorecard/dashboard enterprise value chain or project metric, the standard sheet provides a picture of activities that can identify waste in waiting, transportation, overprocessing, and motion. This picture can help identify where targeted improvement efforts should focus.

14.11 Workflow Analysis: Combination Work Table

Table 14.5 illustrates the layout of a combination work table. This tool can be used in both the E-DMAIC and the P-DMAIC measure phase. When lead time or defective/defect rates are a 30,000-foot-level scorecard/dashboard enterprise value chain or project

Table 14.4: Standardized Work Chart (or Standard Work Sheet), Example

Standardized Work Chart

Part No:			Part Name:		Revision & Date:
Process Name:					
Takt Time =		Cycle time =		Other:	

Seq	Work Element	Observation
1	Issue Material	Issues faster than usage
2	Step 1	
3	Step 2	Seems to take longer than others
4	Step 3	Other room makes travel difficult
5	Step 4	
5	Deliver	Long walk to Shipping
6		
7		
8		
9		
10		

Work Layout

Supplier   Step 2   Shipping   Step 4   Step 1   Step 3

Table 14.5: Combination Work Table, Example

Combination Work Table							

Department/Operation: Hand Work ———   Machine time ········ Walking ⌒Wait ▭▭▭

Qty per shift: Takt time: Revision/date:

Seq-uence	Work Element	Wait	Hand Wk.	Walking	Machine	Time (seconds) 2 4 6 8 10 12 14 16 18 20 22 24 26 28 30 32 34 36 38 40 42 44 46 48 50 52 54
1	Issue Material				0	
2	Draw 1		6.04	1	0	
3	Draw 2	1.00	9.14	1	0	
4	Draw 3		3.88	1	0	
5	Draw 4		6.86	1	0	
6	Deliver				0	

Consider a cellular work layout where there are multiple cells which are staffed based on work load. Each has two operators and they all share a shipping clerk.

Draw 3   Draw 4   Customer

Ship to cust.

Draw2   Mat. Issue

Draw 1   Material Supplier

Oper 2   Oper 1   Shipping Clerk

metric, the combination work table provides a picture of activities that can identify waste in waiting, transportation, overprocessing, and motion. This picture can help identify where targeted improvement efforts should focus.

14.12 Workflow Analysis: Logic Flow Diagram

Figure 14.1 illustrates a logic flow diagram. This tool is sometimes combined with a process flow chart. The methodology can be used in both the E-DMAIC analyze phase and the P-DMAIC measure phase. When lead time or WIP is a 30,000-foot-level scorecard/dashboard enterprise value chain or project metric, the logic flow map can provide insight to the identification of waste in overproduction, waiting, transportation, and inventory. This insight can help direct improvement efforts.

The logic flow map provides a snapshot of process activities in terms of value added, non-value added but necessary, and waste (non-value added). Symbols describe activities such as work delay, inspection, operation activity, transportation, and storage.

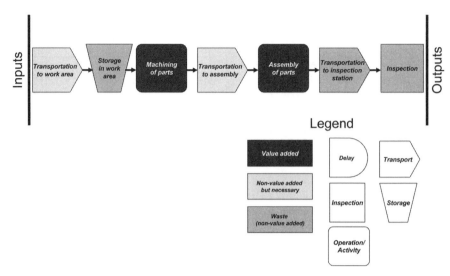

Figure 14.1: Logic flow map.

These tools, along with a cause-and-effect diagram and the value stream mapping method described in a later section, can help a black belt gain insight to the process and to opportunities for improvement.

14.13   Workflow Analysis: Spaghetti Diagram or Physical Process Flow

Figure 14.2 illustrates a spaghetti diagram. This tool can be used in both the E-DMAIC analyze phase and the P-DMAIC measure phase. When lead time is a 30,000-foot-level scorecard/dashboard enterprise value chain or project metric, the spaghetti diagram provides a picture of activities that can identify waste in transportation and motion. This picture can help identify where targeted improvement efforts should focus. This tool can be a part of the standardized work chart.

14.14   Why–Why or Five Whys Diagram

A simple problem-solving tool is the why–why or five whys. Insight can be gained into why a particular procedure is followed

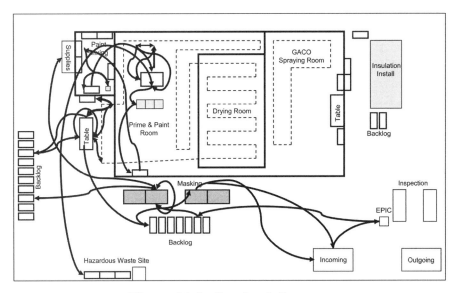

Figure 14.2: Spaghetti diagram.

or why a problem exists by asking "why" repeatedly, where five is a good rule of thumb. An example why–why fault tree analysis is shown in Figure 14.3.

14.15   Time-Value Diagram

I will first discuss the time-value diagram; however, a given situation may benefit more from a value stream map, which will be discussed later in this chapter.

In a time-value diagram, times for process steps can be considered as calendar time, work time, and value-added time. With this information, effort is focused on what changes should be made to reduce non-value-added times, which result in an improvement in the overall lead time.

Figure 14.4 shows one format of a time-value diagram. Steps to create such a diagram are:

1. Determine total lead time.
2. Determine queue times between steps.
3. Create step segments proportional to the task times.

Figure 14.3: Why–why diagram or five whys (three whys shown)
(modified from Higgins (1994)).

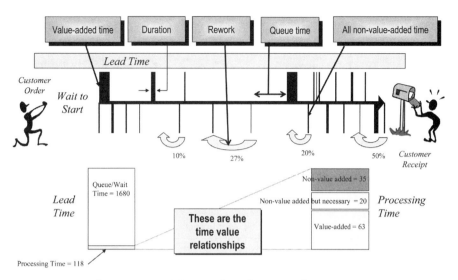

Figure 14.4: Time-value diagram illustration.

4. Place steps and queues along the line segment in the order they happen.
    (a) Place value add steps above the line.
    (b) Place non-value adding steps below the line.
    (c) Separate with queue times.
5. Draw in rework loops and label with rework percentage (items sent back/items that reach that step).
6. Indicate percentage of time in queue versus time in activity.
7. Indicate percentage of activity time that is value added versus non-value added.

When a time-value diagram includes the distribution of times for each step, simulation models can be built to understand better the impact of various process conditions on the overall output. This information can help determine where improvement efforts should be made.

14.16   Example 14.3: Development of a Bowling Ball

This example shows both the integration of Lean and Six Sigma tools, along with an application of product design for Integrated Enterprise Excellence (DFIEE).

Part A: Before Change

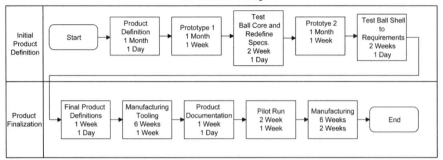

Part B: After Change

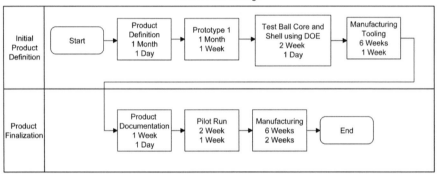

Figure 14.5: Simplified time-value diagram for developing a bowling ball, before change and after change.

An 8-month development process of bowling balls is to be reduced. A time-value diagram with calendar times and work times is shown in Figure 14.5 (Part A). In such a figure one might also indicate value-added activities with a "VA" designation.

From Figure 14.5 (Part B), we note that the IEE team reduced the development lead time by 1.75 months. (i.e., 8 months – 6.25 months = 1.75 months). The team combined two prototype definition steps through design of experiments (DOE) statistical techniques. This DOE step optimized the bowling ball core and shell requirements simultaneously. By considering manufacturing factors within this development DOE, we can also expect to produce a ball that has less variability. If the development process cycle time needs further reduction, one should then assess other non-value-added steps or steps that have a large discrepancy between calendar and work time.

Example 37.1 illustrates another application of the simplified time-value diagram, as part a sales quoting improvement project report-out.

14.17 Value Stream Mapping

When the 30,000-foot-level scorecard/dashboard measures for lead time and other Lean metrics are not satisfactory, the value stream mapping approach can create insight to where efforts should be placed to improve the overall enterprise process. Focused IEE projects can result from this activity. Example 37.2 describes the application of value stream mapping for a transactional process.

In Toyota, value stream mapping is known as "material and information flow mapping." In the Toyota production system, current and future states/ideal states are depicted by practitioners when they are developing plans to install Lean systems. Much attention is given to establishing flow, eliminating waste, and adding value. Toyota views manufacturing flows as material, information, and people/process. The value stream mapping methodology described in this section covers the first two of these three items (Rother and Shook, 1999). This section is an overview of the methodology described in this reference.

A value stream map can trace both product and information flow across organizational boundaries of a company. This mapping tool can describes how a high level process is executed. Value stream maps show the sequential flow of transactions or items along with the information flow such as ordering and customer feedback. A well created value stream map will show the process from the raw material supplier through the customer delivery along with the information flow from the customer to the business and to the raw material (RM) suppliers. In a transactional process, the customer and the supplier may be one in the same, but either way the map shows both the transaction flow and the information flow.

A value stream manager, who is responsible for the entire value stream and reports to senior management, can be a great asset to an organization. This person can take ownership of the overall system 30,000-foot-level scorecard/dashboard metric and lead a focus effort to improving the overall system to avoid the suboptimization of individual processes. The value stream manager can be responsible for the prioritization and orchestration of IEE projects, which have a specific focus to improve the overall value stream.

Material Icons	**Represents**	**Notes**
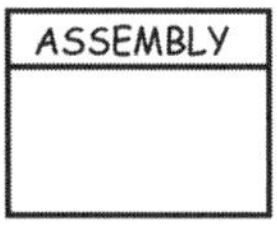 ASSEMBLY	Manufacturing Process	One process box equals an area of flow. All processes should be labeled. Also used for departments, such as Production Control.
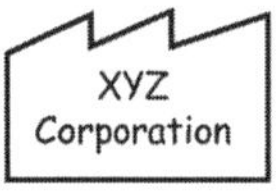 XYZ Corporation	Outside Sources	Used to show customers, suppliers, and outside manufacturing processes.
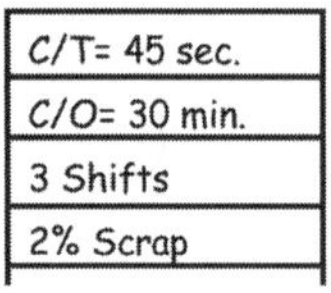 C/T= 45 sec. C/O= 30 min. 3 Shifts 2% Scrap	Data Box	Used to record information concerning a manufacturing process, department, customer, etc.
 I 300 pieces 1 Day	Inventory	Count and time should be noted.
 Mon. & Wed.	Truck Shipment	Note frequency of shipments.
 →	Movement of production material by PUSH	Material that is produced and moved forward before the next process needs it, usually based on a schedule.
 ⇒	Movement of finished goods to the customer	
 ⊐	Supermarket	A controlled inventory of parts that is used to schedule production at an upstream process.

Figure 14.6: Material flow, information flow, and general icons (Part 1 of 3) (from Rother and Shook (1999), with permission.)

Material Icons	Represents	Notes
 ↻	Withdrawal	Pull of materials, usually from a supermarket.
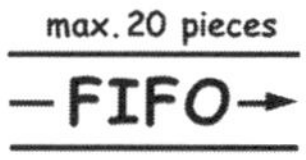 max. 20 pieces —FIFO→	Transfer of controlled quantities of material between processes in a "First-In-First-Out" sequence.	Indicates a device to limit quantity and ensure FIFO flow of material between processes. Maximum quantity should be noted.

Information Icons	Represents	Notes
 ←	Manual information flow	For example: production schedule or shipping schedule.
 ←	Electronic Information flow	For example via electronic data interchange.
 Weekly Schedule	Information	Describes an information flow.
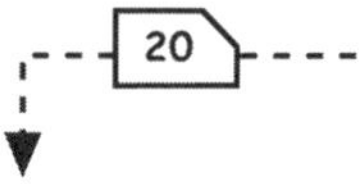 20	Production Kanban (dotted line indicates kanban path)	The "one-per-container" kanban. Card or device that tells a process how many of what can be produced and gives permission to do so.
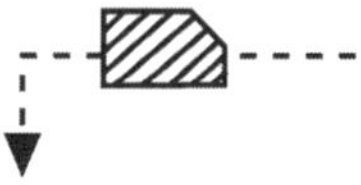 ▨	Withdrawal Kanban	Card or device that instructs the material handler to get and transfer parts (i.e. from a supermarket to the consuming process).
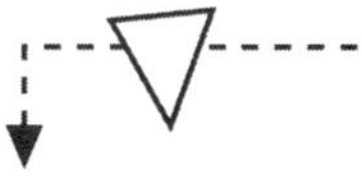 ▽	Signal Kanban	The "one-per-batch" kanban. Signals when a reorder point is reached and another batch needs to be produced. Used where supplying process much produce in batches because changeovers are required.

Figure 14.6: (Part 2 of 3)

Information Icons	**Represents**	**Notes**
	Sequenced-Pull Ball	Gives instruction to immediately produce a predetermined type and quantity, typically one unit. A pull system for subassembly processes without using a supermarket.
	Kanban Post	Place where kanban are collected and held for conveyance.
	Kanban Arriving in Batches	
 **OXOX**	Load Leveling	Tool to intercept batches of kanban and level the volume and mix of them over a period of time.
	"Go See" Production Scheduling	Adjusting schedules based on checking inventory levels.

General Icons	**Represents**	**Notes**
	"Kaizen Lightening Burst"	Highlights improvement needs at specific processes that are critical to achieving the value stream vision. Can be used to plan kaizen workshops.
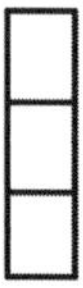	Buffer or Safety Stock	"Buffer" or "Safety Stock" must be noted.
	Operator	Represents a person viewed from above.

Figure 14.6: (Part 3 of 3)

The type of value stream map described in this section utilizes symbols such as those illustrated in Figure 14.6. These symbols represent various activities when conducting value stream mapping.

Those who create a current-state map, such as that shown in Figure 14.7, need to walk the actual pathways of material and information flow beginning with a quick walk of the entire value stream. One should start at the end and work upstream, mapping the entire value stream, using a pencil and paper for documentation and a stopwatch to record times that were personally observed. The template described earlier can be used to record observations. The investigation results are then documented in a current-state value stream map.

Things to consider when creating a value stream map:

- Team members individually create a value stream map. The most accurate map is then created through consensus after collectively examining all maps.
- The value stream map creation tools are paper, pencil, eraser, and stop watch.
- After describing typical customers, compile 30,000-foot-level data that address order quantities, delivery frequency, and product mix.
- Before beginning a detailed study, initially walk the process quickly to gain high-level insight to the overall value stream steps.
- When creating the value stream, each person should interview all shift workers, verify observations against document procedures, and record all as-is observations.

A value stream creation process:

1. Position customer icon in the upper right corner with customer requirements.
   - Insert the customer name in an "outside sources" (factory) icon that is placed at the upper right corner of the sheet of paper.
   - Below the "outside sources" box, draw a data box, recording customer requirements (e.g., number of pieces weekly of each product type, batch/tray size, number of shifts).
2. Create process boxes, moving from left to right, documenting below each process relevant data within data boxes.
   - Document process name in process box.

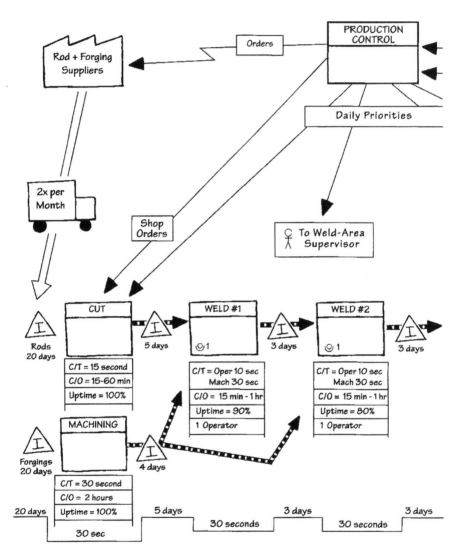

Figure 14.7: Current state value stream example (from Rother and Shook (1999), with permission).

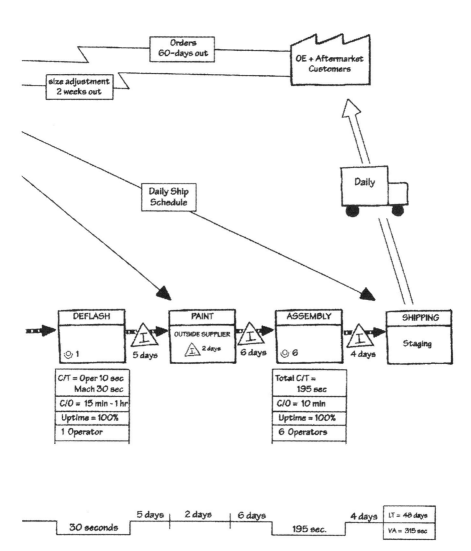

Figure 14.7: (Part 2), current state

- Create a process box wherever there is a disconnection of the process, and material flow stops.
- Example recordings are C/T, C/O, number of people, available work time in seconds (minus time for meetings, breaks, and cleanup) and EPE.
- When multiple flows merge, draw one flow over another. When there are many branches, initially focus on key components.

3. Record inventory and its position, using a triangle icon.
   - Document amount of inventory and duration of time for a part/transaction.
4. Describe transportation to the customer and from suppliers using a truck or airplane icon, describing material quantity or number of transactions in a data box and movement with a broad arrow.
   - Do not draw map for every purchased part. Draw flow for one or two main RMs.
5. Place production control department icon at the top center of the diagram, including any notes where systems such as Materials Requirements Planning (MRP) exist.
   - Use go see icon, if appropriate.
6. Describe manual or electronic information flows with straight/lightning bolt arrows.
   - Separate line for forecasts and daily orders.
7. Describe material flow, using either a push arrow or pull arrow.
   - *Push arrow*: process produces independent of needs of downstream customer.
   - *Pull arrow*: parts produced as specified by the kanban.
8. Draw a timeline that takes one part/transaction throughout its value stream.
9. Record inventory lead times, which are calculated as inventory quantity divided by daily customer requirements.
10. Record process times.
11. Estimate total production lead time by adding the lead times through each process and inventory triangle.
12. Add up the value-adding times or the processing times for all processes in the value stream.
13. Compare value-added to total lead time. Process cycle efficiency is defined as the amount of value-added process time divided by total lead time.

When creating a future state map for a value stream (and to improve phase action), one should keep in mind some important Lean principles. Overproduction can be created with a batch-and-push mass production system. This can occur when production is created by commands from production control instead of needs by the downstream customer of the process. Defects can remain as part of the hidden factory until discovered downstream in the process. This can result in a very long total time for a part to get through the production process, while value-added time for producing the product is very small. The most significant source of waste is overproduction, which can cause various types of waste from part storages, additional part handling, additional sorting, and rework to shortages at some production steps because the factory needs to produce parts to maintain its efficiency, even though no parts are needed. Mass production thinking implies that it is cheaper to produce if you produce more and at a faster rate. However, this is true from traditional accounting practices only where there is a direct-cost-per-item perspective that ignores all other real costs associated with direct and indirect production costs.

A Lean value stream strives for the following characteristics:

1. Produce to takt time. For industries such as distribution, customer products, and process industries, a unit of customer demand for a takt time calculation could be the amount of work that can be accomplished by the process bottleneck during a fixed time interval (e.g., 1 h).

2. Whenever possible, develop continuous flow, where continuous flow refers to the production of one piece at a time and the immediate passing of this part to the next step. It might be best to have a combination of continuous flow with a FIFO (first-in-first-out) pull system.

3. A supermarket is an inventory of parts that are controlled for the production scheduling of an upstream process. When continuous flow does not extend upstream, use supermarkets to control production. This might be needed when a machine creates several part numbers, supplier's location is distant, or there is a long lead time or unreliable process interface. Control by scheduling to downstream needs, as opposed to an independent scheduling function. A production kanban (described later and see Glossary) should trigger the production of parts, while a withdrawal kanban instructs the material handler to transfer parts downstream.

4. Attempt customer scheduling to only one production process or subprocess in the overall production process (i.e., the pacemaker process) (see Glossary). Frequently, this process is the most downstream continuous flow process in the value stream.
5. Use load leveling at the pacemaker process so that there is an even distribution of production of different products over time. This improves the flexibility of the overall process to have a short lead time when responding to different customer requirements, while keeping finished goods inventory and upstream supermarkets low.
6. Release and withdraw small consistent work increments at the pacemaker process. This creates a predictable production flow, which can yield to quick problem identification and resolution. When a large amount of work is released to the shop floor, each process can shuffle orders, which results in increased lead time and the need for expediting.
7. In fabrication processes that are upstream to the pacemaker process, create the ability to make every part every day; i.e., EPE day. We would then like to reduce EPE to shorter durations; e.g., shift. This can be accomplished by the shortening of changeover times and running smaller batches in upstream fabrication processes. An approach to determining initial batch size at fabrication processes is by determining how much time remains in a day to make changeovers. A typical target is that there is 10% of the time available for changeovers.

A future-state value stream map minimizes waste by addressing the above issues. An example future-state map is shown in Figure 14.8. From this future-state value stream map, an implementation plan is then created.

14.18   Value Stream Considerations

Everyone in the entire value stream should be aware of rate of customer consumption at end of value stream. For value stream creation and analysis, consider:

*   *Market and customers*: Nimbleness to respond to market changes

- *Flexibility*: Low times for changeover/setup times and computer system changeovers
- *Activities*: Avoidance of time traps (e.g., many products flow through a single step)
- *Cost and complexity*: Reduced complexity and number of offerings reduce cost and WIP
- *Little's Law (i.e., speed of process is inversely related to amount of WIP)*: Reduction of WIP

14.19   Additional Enterprise Process Lean Tools, Concepts, and Examples

The following Lean tools described in Chapter 14 have applicability not only in the P-DMAIC improve phase but also in the E-DMAIC analyze phase: learning by doing, standard work, one-piece flow, poka-yoke, visual management, 5S, kaizen event, kanban, demand management, level production, continuous flow, changeover reduction, and total productive maintenance.

Additional transactional Lean examples are:

- Example 37.1 (sales quoting process)
- Example 37.2 (sales quote project)

Chapter 36 illustrates 5S application of Lean concepts to situations that could be considered transactional (i.e., inventory, suppliers, computer systems, and costing systems).

> Lean methodologies are very powerful concepts; however, care must be given to where improvement efforts should focus. Most Lean deployments don't seem to view the overall enterprise system systematically as a whole to determine what should be done to improve the overall business metrics.

14.20   Applying IEE

Lean methodologies are very powerful concepts; however, care must be given to where improvement efforts should focus. Most Lean deployments don't seem to view the overall enterprise system

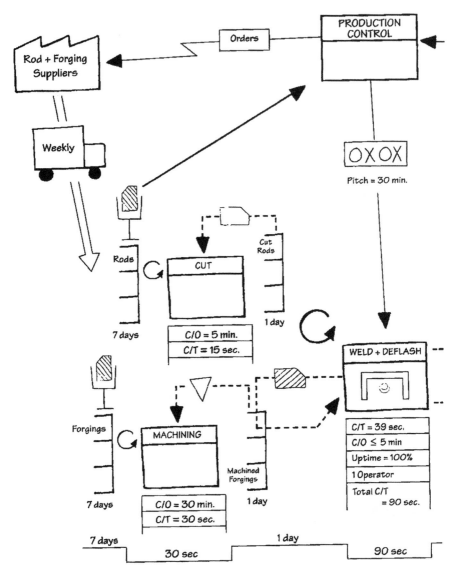

Figure 14.8: Future state value stream example (from Rother and Shook (1999), with permission).

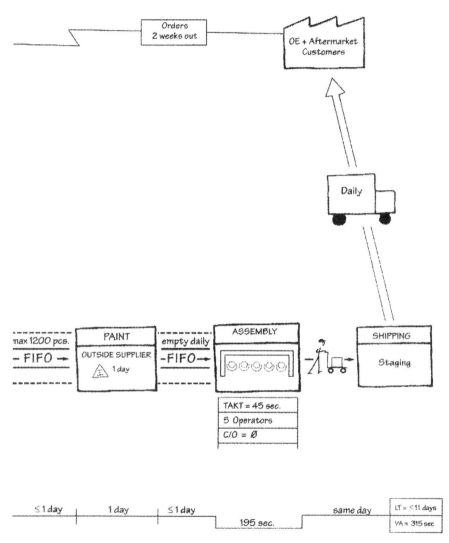

Figure 14.8: (Continued).

systematically as a whole to determine what should be done to improve the overall business metrics. I have heard organizations boast that they do one kaizen event every week. One of the main principles of Lean is creating a customer pull system. When an organization sets a goal for the number of kaizen events for a period of time, I think that a tool is being pushed into the system.

In IEE, satellite-level metric goals are to lead to 30,000-foot-level scorecard/dashboard goals. The needs of a project to achieve measurement goals then pull for use of the right tool. If the goal is a reduction in lead time or inventory, then Lean tools need to be considered. A kaizen event could be an excellent tool for obtaining timely results.

As noted earlier, a paper and pencil approach is typically suggested for the collection and analysis of information for the above procedure. Better information can be gained by walking the process, rather than just examining database information in an "ivory tower." However, when a value stream map includes the distribution of times for each activity, simulation models can be very useful to understand better the impact of changing conditions on the overall output and the impact of various "what-if's" on the process. This information can lead to better focused improvement efforts.

Viewing the enterprise as a whole can lead to a different behaviors. For example, one supplier of automobile parts described to me how one of its customers routinely required tightly toleranced parts, which often leaded to scrap and tooling breakages. This supplier described how a second customer visited his facility and asked him to make some sample parts. This customer took the parts and then designed his products around the tolerance capabilities of their processes. Interestingly, the second supplier is typically considered to have higher automobile product quality. Viewing the enterprise as a whole can lead to activities where suppliers and their processes are considered to be a partnership for overall business success.

The techniques described in this chapter can be used as part of P-DMAIC. Likewise, the Lean tools described in the project execution roadmap can be used at the E-DMAIC level.

14.21 Exercises

1. Describe an application of Lean in your everyday processes.

2. Describe how a company is claiming that they have a Lean program; however, the company is not seeing the benefits from the deployment. If desired, you may change the previous sentence wording from "company is claiming" to "company could be claiming."

3. Within a 24-hour period, an emergency room treats an average of 100 patients. From 30 random observation times, an average number of people in the waiting room was determined to be five. Determine the takt time and how long on average people spend in the waiting room.

4. Describe your project. Complete a Lean focus assessment matrix for the project.

Lean Area		Improvement Importance		
Category	Principle	None	Some	Major
Workplace	Organization			
Workplace	Standardized work			
Workplace	Visual controls			
People	Effectiveness			
People	Quality at source			
System	Tool reliability			
System	Cellular flow			
System	Batch reduction or elimination			
System	Pull vs. push system			
System	Point of use systems			

Instructions: Describe the level of importance for each Lean principle by entering an "X" in the appropriate box

5. An organization has the workflow described in Figure 14.1. A manufacturing organization is described; however, the same flow could exist within a transactional environment. Consider that all seven steps had a mean time to completion of 30 minutes with a standard deviation of 7 minutes, where their completion time was normally distributed. Create the IEE metrics that contain 50 simulated events with the current process. Consider that an IEE project was conducted which lead to all waste being removed from the process. Demonstrate this change by creating 50 more simulated events. Illustrate the change and benefits using IEE metrics and tools.

(a) Create 50 rows of random numbers from a normal distribution random for each of the seven steps (mean =30, standard deviation = 7). Create another column that contains the summation of these process steps (i.e., by rows). Each row in this new column represents the total time for completion of the overall process.

(b) Create a 30,000-foot-level control chart for the combined data from the process steps. Report the mean completion duration time.

(c) Determine the process capability/performance metric in 80% frequency of occurrence units. Report this interval.

(d) Create another analysis column that contains the summation of the process steps that were not considered waste. Combine this data with the initial data. Create a 30,000-foot-level control chart for this data, showing the process change. Report the new mean.

(e) Demonstrate the difference between the two process outputs in one normal probability plot. Describe the difference.

(f) Create a probability plot that shows only the new process capability/performance level in 80% frequency of occurrence units. Report the 80% frequency of occurrence units.

(g) Conduct an appropriate analysis that test for significance between the means and describes the mean amount of improvement with confidence intervals. Describe tools used and results.

(h) Conduct an appropriate analysis that tests for difference between output variability between the before and after change scenarios. Describe tools used and results.

(i) Show the impact of the change using a visualization of data tool that everybody is familiar with (i.e., dot plot). Describe tools used and results.

6. Within a 24-hour period, an emergency room treats an average of 100 patients. From thirty random observation times, an average number of people in the waiting room were determined to be five.

(a) Determine takt time.

(b) Determine cycle time.

(c) Determine throughput (average time people spend in the waiting room).

15

P-DMAIC – Measure Phase: Measurement Systems Analysis

15.1 IEE Project Execution Roadmap

Chapters 12 and 13 described the baseline of 30,000-foot-level metrics. The last chapter described Lean tools consideration for improving the 30,000-foot-level metric. The graphic in this section highlights the P-DMAIC roadmap steps (see Appendix Section D.1) that are described in this chapter. Appendix E contains the tollgate check sheets for this and other phases. This chapter describes the assessment of the measurement system on the 30,000-foot-level metric.

15.2 Data Integrity and Background

As part of executing an Integrated Enterprise Excellence (IEE) project, data integrity needs to be addressed. Data integrity assessments can be considered a part of measurement systems analysis (MSA) studies. Within this activity we should first consider whether we are measuring the right thing. For example, a customer might require delivery within 1 week of placing an order; however, we

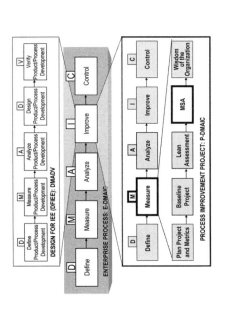

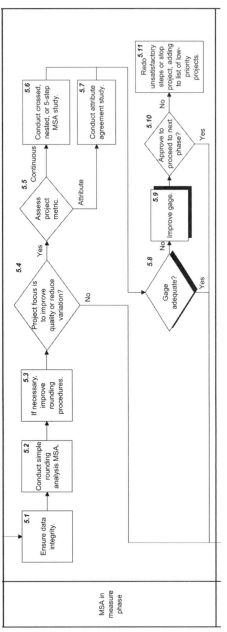

track when the order was received by the service group to when the transaction was shipped. For this case, we did not consider all the time it took for all steps of the process relative to customer needs (e.g., time from shipment to customer receipt). Another example of the lack of data integrity: A wrong number is recorded into a database that is used by others for analyses. For example, because of the layout of a facility, people might not have time to walk the distance required to record an accurate time relative to when a product was actually received at the receiving dock.

Data integrity/validity can cause project failures. This can occur when the available data do not represent what the business believes they represent. For example, there can be:

- Incomplete inclusion or missed categorization of events.
- Operational definition conflicts.
- Data entry errors.
- Rounding or truncating data prior to recording values.

Actions to verify integrity/validity include:

- Compare data sheets to electronic data files for accuracy.
- Ask if all events are captured in the data.
- Ask how similar events are recorded.
- Observe or follow the data collection process.
- Verify all automated efficiencies and formulas with manual calculations

After any data integrity issues are resolved within an IEE project, the next step in MSA is the evaluation of the measuring device. The remaining portion of this chapter will focus on this evaluation.

Manufacturing uses many forms of measuring systems when making decisions about how well a product or process conforms to specifications requirements (Definitions for the following terms are in the glossary). An organization might create an attribute screen that assesses every part or system produced and ships only those that meet conformance requirements. Organizations may routinely use gage blocks, calipers, micrometers, optical comparators, or other devices as part of their measurement system. Through the use of various measurement devices, organizations make decisions about the dimensions or tensile strength of a part or the titration of a chemical process.

However, organizations sometimes do not even consider that their measurements might not be exact. Such presumptions and inadequate considerations can lead to questionable analyses and conclusions. Organizations need to consider the impact of not having a quality measurement system.

Measurement system issues are not unique to manufacturing. Transactional or service processes can have MSA issues. Consider that a document is reviewed for completeness and accuracy at several points in a process. Each decision step is a measurement step, where some documents may be erroneously rejected and others erroneously accepted.

As part of metrology, organizations need to understand the implication of measurement error on decisions make about their products and processes. To ensure the integrity of the responses given by measurement systems, organizations need to have effective calibration standards and systems. Organizations need also to have processes in place that result in good control and integrity of calibration standards and measurement devices.

Organizations frequently overlook the impact of not having quality measurement systems. Organizations sometimes do not even consider that their measurements might not be exact. Such presumptions and inadequate considerations can lead to questionable analyses and conclusions.

When appraisers/operators do not measure a part consistently, the expense to a company can be very great: satisfactory parts are rejected and unsatisfactory are accepted. In addition, a poor measurement system can make the process capability/performance metric assessment of a satisfactory process appear unsatisfactory. Sales are lost and unnecessary expenses incurred in trying to fix a manufacturing or business process when the primary source of variability is from the measurement system.

Traditionally, the tool to address the appraiser/operator consistency is a gage repeatability and reproducibility (R&R) study, which is the evaluation of measuring instruments to determine capability to yield a precise response. Gage repeatability is the variation in measurements considering one part and one operator. Gage reproducibility is the variation between operators' measuring one part.

This chapter presents procedural guidelines for assessing the quality of a measurement system for both nondestructive testing and destructive testing, where AIAG (2002) refers to destructive testing as nonreplicable testing. Gage R&R and other issues that affect an overall MSA system are discussed.

15.3   IEE Application Examples: MSA

- *Satellite-level metric*: Focus was to be given to create IEE projects that improved a company's Return on investment (ROI). As part of a MSA assessment, the team decided that effort needed to be given initially to how the satellite-level metric was calculated. It was thought that there might be some month-to-month inconsistencies in how this metric was being calculated and reported.
- *Satellite-level metric*: IEE projects were to be created that improved the company's customer satisfaction. Focus was given to ensure that the process for measuring customer satisfaction gave an accurate response.
- *Transactional 30,000-foot-level metric*: Days sales outstanding (DSO) reduction was chosen as an IEE project. Focus was given to ensure that DSO entries accurately represent process execution times.
- *Manufacturing 30,000-foot-level metric (key process output variable (KPOV))*: An IEE project was to improve the process capability/performance metric for the diameter for a manufactured product (i.e., reduce the number of parts beyond the specification limits). A MSA was conducted of the measurement gage to ensure that they were rejecting the correct parts.
- *Transactional and manufacturing 30,000-foot-level lead time metric (a Lean metric)*: An IEE project to improve the time from order entry to fulfillment was measured. Focus was given to ensure that the lead time entries accurately represented processing times.
- *Transactional and manufacturing 30,000-foot-level inventory metric or satellite-level theory of constraints (TOC) metric (a Lean metric)*: An IEE project was to reduce inventory. Focus was given to ensure that entries accurately represented what happened within the process.
- *Manufacturing 30,000-foot-level quality metric*: An IEE project was to reduce the number of defects in a printed circuit board manufacturing process. A MSA was conducted to determine if defects were both identified and recorded correctly into the company's database.
- *Transactional 50-foot-level metric (key process input variable (KPIV))*: An IEE project to improve the 30,000-foot-level metrics for DSOs identified a KPIV to the process. A MSA was

conducted to determine that the metric was reported accurately.
- *Product DFIEE*: It was discovered that many design test activities were not aligned with the problem types typically experienced by customers. An IEE project was created to ensure that the test process was able to efficiently detect typical customer problems.

15.4   Initial MSA Considerations

When initiating an MSA, it is important to select the best course for action. Some guidelines are:

- Continuous response data MSA?
  - Quality decisions (pass/fail) are made with a continuous measurement and the project is focused on improving quality or reducing rework/repair costs.
  - Process control decisions are made with a continuous measurement and the project is focused on process capability/performance metric issues.
- Attribute data MSA?
  - Quality decisions (pass/fail or accept/rework) are made by appraisers/people and there is a difference in performance by person.
  - Process control decisions are made based on appraisers'/people's individual decisions and there is a performance difference by person.
- Simple MSA
  - When you do not need the traditional MSA analysis.

15.5   Simple MSA Assessment

When making a simple MSA assessment, compare the rounding error of the measurement system to the expected current and future process variation.

- If the project focus is on the process capability/performance metric, rounding error should be less than or equal to 20% of the expected process variation.
- If the project focus is on quality, rounding error should be less than or equal to 20% of the current and future process tolerance.

To illustrate the application of this technique, consider that a goal was set to improve a process' mean process lead time to 4 days. Expected variability was that most occurrences would be between 2 and 6 days. If the data are recorded as day started and day completed, the error would be +/−1 day on each recorded value or 2 days overall.

When we compare this 2-day overall uncertainty to our overall expected variability of 4 days, we would have 50% uncertainty or error due to the measurement system, that is, $\{[1 - (-1)]/[6-2]\} \times 100 = 50\%$. According to the above rules, this measurement system would not be satisfactory since 50% is not less than or equal to 20%.

To improve our measurement system, we would like to develop a methodology where entries and exit transaction times are stamped so that total transaction entry rounding discrimination reduces from daily to hourly or even minute increments.

15.6   Variability Sources in a 30,000-Foot-Level Metric

Consider that excess variability in a 30,000-foot-level continuous-response metric result in an unsatisfactory process capability/performance metric, as illustrated in Figure 15.1.

Mathematically, measurement systems analysis involves the understanding and quantification of measurement variance, as described in the following equation, in relation to process variability and tolerance spread:

$$\sigma_T^2 = \sigma_P^2 + \sigma_m^2$$

where
σ_T^2 = Total Variance
σ_P^2 = Process Variance
σ_m^2 = Measurement Variance

Pictorial representation of 40% measurement error is shown in Figure 15.2.

This variability (σ_T^2) can have many components such as those illustrated in Figure 15.3. Most of this chapter will be dedicated to the quantification of measurement systems component to this variability.

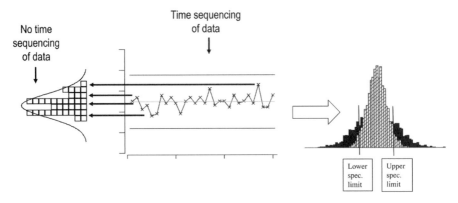

Figure 15.1: Source for measurement error. Histogram with measurement error is dark area. Histogram without measurement error is light area.

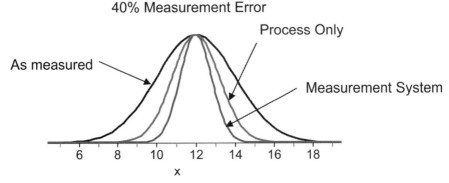

Figure 15.2: Pictorial representation of 40% measurement error.

Graphically, accuracy and precision are described in Figures 15.4 and 15.5. Accuracy is the degree of agreement of individual or average measurements with an accepted reference value or level (i.e. bias). Precision is the degree of mutual agreement among individual measurements made under prescribed like conditions (ASTM, 1977).

MSA assesses the statistical properties of repeatability, reproducibility, bias, stability, and linearity. Gage R&R studies address the variability of the measurement system, while bias, stability, and linearity studies address the accuracy of the measurement system.

This chapter focuses on measurement systems in which readings can be repeated on each part, but includes destructive test

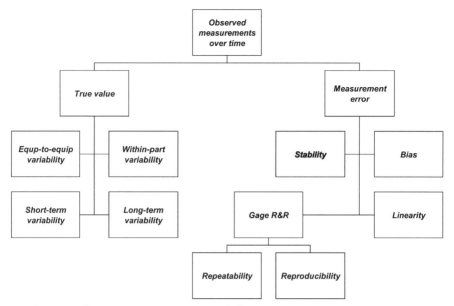

Figure 15.3: Measurement variability sources. Equip: equipment.

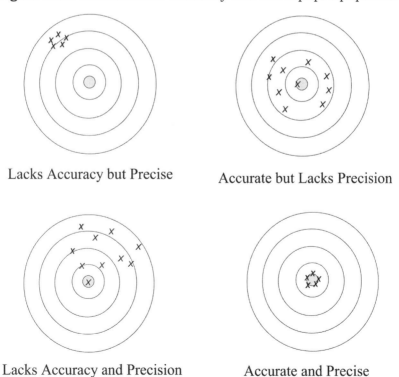

Lacks Accuracy but Precise

Accurate but Lacks Precision

Lacks Accuracy and Precision

Accurate and Precise

Figure 15.4: Measurement accuracy and precision.

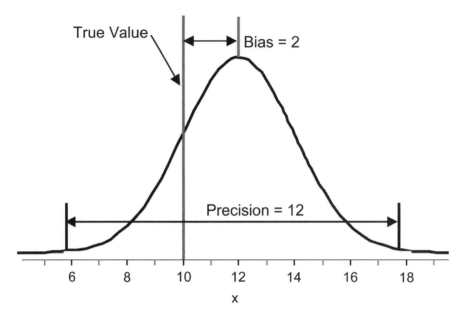

Figure 15.5: Measurement precision and bias.

situations as well. The gage R&R (repeatability and reproducibility) methodologies presented are applicable to both initial gage assessments and studies that help determine whether a measurement system is contributing a large amount to an unsatisfactory reported process capability/performance index.

15.7 Three Uses of Measurments

Three measurement uses are descriptive, enumerative, and analytical.

1. *Part Quality*: Descriptive measurements compare a parameter to a tolerance. For example, a part's lead bent must be less than 0.0002 in. Descriptive statistics do not draw conclusions about the process, but just whether the part being measured is within or outside of specification limits.
2. *Batch Quality*: Enumerative measurements characterize a given batch or product lot using a sample from the batch or lot. With this measurement, a sample is taken from a batch and a decision is made whether to release the product for shipment.

3. *Process Capability*: Analytic measurements utilizing process or product measurements can establish whether the process is in control/predictable and describe its process capability/performance metric. An example is the monitoring of a developer solvent concentration.

Figure 15.6 illustrates the impact from precision relative to part-tolerance decisions. The gray area around the specification limit is where measurements cannot be trusted relative to lower specification limit (LSL) and the upper specification limit (USL) decisions. If the P/T value (described later in this chapter) is 30%, 15% on either side of the specification limits is suspect.

Figure 15.7 illustrates the impact from precision relative to statement about the natural process variability. The histogram below depicts a P/NPV = 25%.

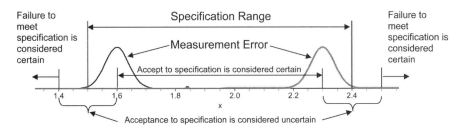

Figure 15.6: Measurement error impact on quality decisions.

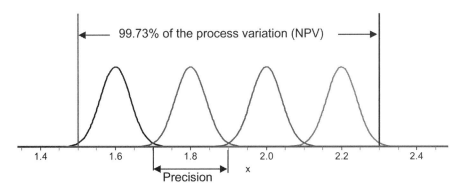

Figure 15.7: Precision's relationship to natural process variation.

15.8 Terminology

There are inconsistencies in MSA terminology AIAG (2002). I will utilize the following definitions:

- Accuracy is the closeness of agreement between an observed value and the accepted reference value.
- Precision is the net effect of discrimination, sensitivity, and repeatability over the operating range (size, range, and time) of the measurement system. Precision, or measurement system variation, can be broken down into the components, R&R.
- Part variation (PV) is the part-to-part component in the MSA study. The magnitude of this study's component depends upon the true part-to-part variability of the selected samples.
- Measurement system error is the combined variation due to gage bias, repeatability, reproducibility, stability and linearity.
- Bias is the difference between the observed average of measurements (trials under repeatability conditions) and a reference value, historically referred to as accuracy. Bias is evaluated and expressed at a single point with the operating range of the measurement system.
- Repeatability is the variability resulting from successive trials under identically defined conditions of measurement; often referred to as equipment variation (EV), which could be a misleading term. The best term for repeatability is within-system variation when the conditions of measurement are fixed and defined (i.e., fixed part, instrument, standard, method, operator, environment, and assumptions). In addition to within-equipment variation, repeatability will include all within variation from the conditions in the measurement error model. Repeatability is the variation due to the measuring device, which results from the variation observed when the same operator measures the same part repeatedly with the same device. This is the minimum possible variation with the current system.
- Reproducibility is the variation in the average of measurements caused by normal different conditions of change in the measurement process. Typically, it has been defined as the variation in average measurements of the same part (measured) between different appraisers (operators) using the same measurement instrument and method in a stable environment. This is often true for manual instruments influenced by the skill of the operator. It is not true, however,

for measurement processes (i.e., automated systems) where the operator is not a major source of variation. For this reason, reproducibility is referred to as the average variation between-systems or between-conditions of measurement (i.e., the variation due to the measurement system). It is the variation observed when different operators measure the same parts using the same device.

- Appraiser variation (AV) is the average measurements of the same part between different appraisers using the same measuring instrument and method in a stable environment. AV is one of the common sources of measurement system variation that results from difference in operator skill or technique, using the same measurement system. Appraiser variation is commonly assumed to be the reproducibility error associated with a measurement, this is not always true (as described under reproducibility). Within a gage R&R analysis, this will sometimes be listed in a crossed analysis as operator variance.

- Stability refers to both statistical stability of measurement process and measurement stability over time. Both are vital for a measurement system to be adequate for its intended purpose. Statistical stability implies a predictable, underlying measurement process operating within common cause variation. Measurement (alias drift) addresses the necessary conformance to the measurement standard or reference over the operating life (time) of the measurement system.

15.9 Gage R&R Considerations

In a gage R&R study, the following characteristics are essential:

- The measurement must be in statistical control, which is referred to as statistical stability. This means that variation from the measurement system is from common causes only and not special causes.

- Increments of measurement must be small relative to both process variability and specification limits. A common rule of thumb is that we would like to see the increments be no greater than one-tenth of the smaller of either the 99.7% spread of process variability or the specification limit spread; however, this is often very difficult.

The purpose of a measurement system is to understand better the sources of variation that can influence the results produced by the system. A measurement is characterized by location and spread, which are impacted by the following metrics:

- *Location*: bias, stability, and linearity metrics
- *Spread*: repeatability and reproducibility

Bias assessments need an accepted reference value for a part. This can usually be done with tool room or layout inspection equipment. A reference value is derived from readings and compared with appraisers' observed averages. The following describes such an implementation method:

- Measure one part in a tool room.
- Instruct one appraiser to measure the same part 10 times, using the gage being evaluated.
- Determine measurement system bias using the difference between the reference value and observed average.
- Express percent of process variation for bias as a ratio of bias to process variation multiplied by 100.
- Express percent of tolerance for bias as a ratio of bias to tolerance multiplied by 100.

Measurement system stability is the amount of total variation in a system's bias over time on a given part or master part. One method of study is to plot the average and range of repeated master or master part readings on a regular basis. Care must be given to ensure that the master samples taken are representative (e.g., not just after morning calibration).

Linearity graphs are a plot of bias values throughout the expected operating range of the gage. Later sections of this chapter describe how to implement this gage assessment method.

Various measures of evaluating the acceptability of the measurement system spread are as follows:

- Percent of tolerance
- Percent of process variation
- Number of distinct data categories, percent of study, and percent of variance components (as described later, all of these results are a function of the gage R&R study's samples part-to-part variability)

The equations to calculate percent of tolerance, process, and study include a multiple of the study's gage R&R standard deviation. This multiple converts standard deviation to a normal distribution spread. This volume uses a multiple of 6.00, which translates to a 99.73% normal distribution spread; however, companies sometime use a 5.15 multiple, which translates to a 99% normal distribution spread.

When selecting or analyzing a measurement system, a primary concern is discrimination. Discrimination or resolution of a measurement system is its capability to detect and faithfully indicate even small changes in the measured characteristic. Because of economic and physical limitations, measurement systems cannot perceive infinitesimal separate or different measured characteristics of parts or a process distribution. Measured values of a measured characteristic are instead grouped into data categories. For example, the incremental data categories using a rule might be 0.1 in., while a micrometer might be 0.001 in. Parts in the same data category have the same value for the measured characteristic. The difference or resolution of a measurement system is illustrated in Figure 15.8.

When the discrimination of a measurement system is not adequate, the identification of process variation or individual part characteristic values is questionable. This situation warrants the investigation of improved measurement techniques. The recommended discrimination is at most one-tenth of six times the total

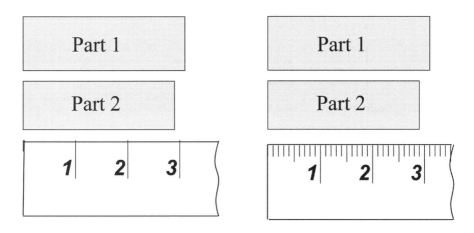

Initial Rounding   Improved Rounding

Figure 15.8: Implication of rounding to MSA.

process standard deviation or about one-half of the process standard deviation.

Discrimination needs to be at an acceptable level for analysis and control. Discrimination needs to be able both to detect the process variation for analysis and to control for the occurrence of special causes. The number of distinct data categories determined from a gage R&R study can be used for this assessment. Figure 15.9 illustrates how the number of categories affects conclusions about control and analysis, where the result of the gage R&R analysis is dependent upon the variability of the study's samples.

Unacceptable discrimination symptoms can also appear in a range chart, which describes the repeatability of operators within a gage R&R study. When, for example, the range chart shows only one, two, or three possible values for the range within the control limits, the discrimination for the measurements is inadequate. Another situation of inadequate discrimination is one in which the range chart shows four possible values for the range within control limits, and more than one-fourth of the ranges are zero.

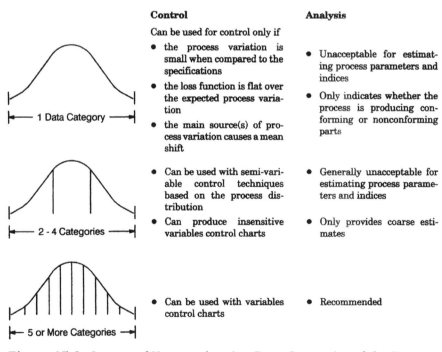

Figure 15.9: Impact of Non-overlapping Data Categories of the Process Distribution on Control and Analysis Activities (Measurement Systems Analysis Reference Manual, Chrysler Corp., Ford Motor Company, General Motors Corp. 1995).

15.10 Gage R&R Relationships

For illustration, let's consider a manual gage used by operators. A measurement process is said to be consistent when the results for operators are repeatable and the results between operators are reproducible. A gage is able to detect part-to-part variation whenever the variability of operator measurements is small relative to process variability. The percent of process variation consumed by the measurement (% R&R) is then determined once the measurement process is consistent and can detect part-to-part variation.

Gage R&R studies yield an estimate for the measurement system standard deviation with the components:

$$\sigma_m = \sqrt{\sigma_r^2 + \sigma_R^2}$$

where

σ_m = Measurement System Standard Deviation

σ_r = Gage Standard Deviation or Repeatability

σ_R = Appraiser Standard Deviation or Reproducibility

Whenever possible, gage R&R study inputs should include the tolerance and a historical standard deviation, which can be estimated from a process' 30,000-foot-level metric. Given these additional inputs, the effectiveness of the gage can be described from the five perspectives discussed below. However, comparing σ_m functions to tolerance and historical standard deviation quantities is the most useful perspective when assessing gage effectiveness for a particular operational set of conditions.

From a gage R&R study, the study's total variation σ_{ST} consists of components originating from the study's part-to-part variability σ_{sp} and the measurement system standard deviation σ_m, as described by the equation

$$\sigma_{ST}^2 = \sigma_{sp}^2 + \sigma_m^2$$

A variance component response in a gage R&R study is the quantification of these terms.

Assessment 1: Variance Component Percentage

The total gage R&R variance component percentage comparison to the total study variance component is calculated using the equation:

$$\text{Study's \% R\&R variance components contribution} = \frac{\sigma_m^{\ 2}}{\sigma_{ST}^{\ 2}} \times 100$$

Purpose: Describes how much the gage variance component contributes to the total study variance.

Assessment 2: Percent of Study Variation

The total gage R&R percentage to total study variation is calculated using the following equation. The number six was included in both the numerator and denominator to illustrate that the relationship is really between the spreads of the two distributions, even though six cancels out in the algebraic relationship.

$$\text{Study variation \% R\&R contribution} = \frac{6 \times \sigma_m}{6 \times \sigma_{ST}} \times 100$$

Purpose: A description of total gage variability to the total variability of the study.

Assessment 3: Number of Distinct Categories

The number of distinct categories, as illustrated in Figure 15.9, is based on study variability and is calculated using the equation:

$$\text{Number of Distinct Categories} = \left[\frac{\sigma_{sp}}{\sigma_m}\right] \times 1.41$$

If the number of distinct categories is fewer than two, the measurement system is of no value in controlling the process. If the number of categories is two, the data can be divided into high and low groups, but this is equivalent to attribute data. The number of categories must be at least five, and preferably more, for the measurement system to perform in an acceptable analysis of the process.

Purpose: A description for the ability of the gage to discriminate between parts in the study.

Assessment 4: Percent of Tolerance

The total gage R&R percentage of tolerance is calculated using the equation

$$\%\text{R\&R contribution to tolerance} = \frac{6\sigma_m}{\text{tolerance}} \times 100$$

where tolerance is the upper specification limit (USL) minus the lower specification limit (LSL). This metric could be considered a measure of precision-to-tolerance (P/T) for each component.

Purpose: Describes the ability of the gage to judge parts relative to their tolerance.

Assessment 5: Percent of Process

The total gage R&R percentage of process variability is calculated using the following equation. The number six was included in both the numerator and denominator to illustrate that the relationship is really between the spreads of the two distributions, even though six cancels out in the algebraic relationship.

$$\%\text{R\&R contribution to Process} = \frac{6\sigma_m}{6 \times \text{Historical Standard Deviation}} \times 100$$

where tolerance is the USL minus the LSL. This is basically a measure of precision to natural process variability (P/NPV).

Purpose: Describes the ability of the gage to judge part-to-part process differences.

Table 15.1 summarizes an important facet that is often overlooked in gage R&R studies. We must remember that standard

Table 15.1: Gage R&R Report-Out Perspectives

Perspective	Approach	Advantages	Disadvantages
1	% contribution as ratio to total variance	Percentages add to 100%	Standard deviation is determined from distribution of test samples
2	% study	Easy to visualize	Standard deviation is determined from distribution of test samples
			Source percentages don't have a sum of 100%
3	Number of categories	Single number	Standard deviation is determined from distribution of test samples
		Easy to visualize	Does not have much discrimination
4	% tolerance	Easy to visualize	Source percentages don't have a sum of 100%
		Response measured against customer needs	
5	% process	Easy to visualize	Source percentages don't have a sum of 100%
		Compared to demonstrated process standard deviation that should originate from a large sample representative of the population	

deviation calculations for the calculations of number of categories, percent contribution as ratio to variance, and percent study are dependent upon the variability of the samples selected for the study. That is, if one person were to have five samples that had much less sample-to-sample variability than someone else, the gage R&R results could be quite different. For this reason, I suggest, when making a decision about gage acceptability, using percent of process and percent of tolerance, not the other gage R&R outputs.

Gage R&R analyses typically offer several different outputs and options that help with the understanding of the sources of gage R&R issues. Output graphs can describe differences by part, operator, operator*part interaction, and the components of variation. Traditionally, practitioners used manual techniques for gage R&R studies. Computer gage R&R programs now offer additional options such as analysis of variance (ANOVA) for significance tests. Because of procedural differences, ANOVA result outputs may differ from manual computations.

The output from a gage R&R analysis typically includes $\bar{x}$ and R charts. Confusion sometimes occurs in the interpretation of these charts. Unlike control charts, time is not the scale for the horizontal axis. On these charts, the x-axis is segmented into regions for the various operators and their measurements of the samples. This leads to a very different method of interpretation from traditional control charts.

The following equations that determine the control limits of a gage R&R $\bar{x}$ chart are similar to those that hold for normal control charts:

$$\text{UCL}_{\bar{x}} = \bar{\bar{x}} + A_2\bar{R}$$
$$\text{LCL}_{\bar{x}} = \bar{\bar{x}} - A_2\bar{R}$$

In this equation, $\bar{\bar{x}}$ is the overall average (between and within operator), $\bar{R}$ is an estimate of within operator variability, and A_2 is determined from Table J. Out-of-control conditions in an $\bar{x}$ chart indicate that part variability is high compared to R&R, which is desirable. If the part averages fall within the control limits, the measurement system cannot discriminate the differences of the study's parts, which indicates that the measurement is inadequate, given the underlying assumption that the distribution of sampled parts is similar to the historical process standard deviation.

The methods to construct an R chart are similar. The inconsistencies of appraisers appear as out-of-control (unpredictable process) conditions in the R chart.

15.11 Preparation for a Measurement System Study

Sufficient planning and preparation should be done prior to conducting a measurement system study. Typical preparation prior to study includes the following steps:

1. Use traceable standards if accuracy and linearity are required.
2. Plan the approach. For instance, determine by engineering judgment, visual observations, or gage study if there is appraiser influence in calibrating or using the instrument. Reproducibility can sometimes be considered negligible, for example, when pushing a button.
3. Select number of appraisers, number of sample of parts, and number of repeat reading. Consider requiring more parts and/or trials for circle dimensions. Bulky or heavy parts may dictate fewer samples. Consider using at least two operators and ten samples, each operator measuring each sample at least twice (all using the same device). Select appraisers who normally operate the instruments.

4. Select sample parts from the process that represent its entire operating range (e.g., six times the historical standard deviation of the process). Number each part.
5. Ensure that the instrument has a discrimination that is at least one-tenth of the expected process variation of the characteristic to be read. For example, if the characteristic's variation is 0.001, the equipment should be able to read a change of 0.0001.

Ensure that the measuring methods of the appraiser and instrument follow the defined procedure. It is important to conduct the study properly. All analyses assume statistical independence of all readings. To reduce the possibility of misleading results, do the following:

1. Execute measurements in random order to ensure that drift or changes that occur will be spread randomly throughout the study.
2. Record readings to the nearest number obtained. When possible, make readings to nearest one-half of the smallest graduation (e.g., 0.00005 for 0.0001 graduations).
3. Use an observer who recognizes the importance of using caution when conducting the study.
4. Ensure that each appraiser uses the same procedure when taking measurements.

Most studies involve multiple samples, measured by multiple appraisers, multiple times. The size of the test is a function of the allowed time as measurement costs.

15.12 Measurement Systems Improvement Needs and Possible Improvement Sources

General guidelines for determining an improvement need the following:

- Continuous measurement system
  - Always if percent of tolerance or process is greater than 30%
  - Usually if percent of tolerance or process is greater than 20%
  - Possibly if a bias is detected or there is an instability or linearity issue with the measurement system

- Attribute measurement system, which is described in more depth later in this chapter
  - Always if agreement confidence interval with the standard (known value) does not include 100%
  - Always if the appraiser agreements differ significantly

General guidelines for improvement opportunities
- Continuous measurement system
  - Gage R&R issues
    - Excessive reproducibility is addressed through a standardization of the procedures and measurement conditions
    - Excessive repeatability is addressed by material improvements to the measurement system equipment or environment, possibly with a gauge replacement
  - Accuracy issues
    - Perform a calibration
    - Correct result by removing bias from reported value
    - Replace gage
  - Linearity issues
    - Perform a calibration
    - Correct result with an equation that removes the changing bias from reported value
    - Replace gage
- Attribute measurement system
  - Improvements in the decision criteria to remove ambiguity
  - Development of a more quantitative gauge

15.13   Example 15.1: Gage R&R

IEE Application Example
- *Manufacturing 30,000-foot-level Metric (KPOV): An IEE project was to improve the process capability/performance of the diameter for a manufactured product. A MSA was conducted of the measurement gage.*

A 30,000-foot-level process capability/performance metric needed improvement. An IEE project to improve this metric had the following MSA analysis:

Five samples selected from a manufacturing process are to represent the normal spread of the process. Two appraisers who

Table 15.2: Measurements for Gage R&R Example

| Trials | Appraiser 1 | | | | |
	Part 1	Part 2	Part 3	Part 4	Part 5
1	217	220	217	214	216
2	216	216	216	212	219
3	216	218	216	212	220
Avg.	216.3	218.0	216.3	212.7	218.3
Range	1.0	4.0	1.0	2.0	4.0

Average of averages = 216.3

| Trials | Appraiser 2 | | | | |
	Part 1	Part 2	Part 3	Part 4	Part 5
1	216	216	216	216	220
2	219	216	215	212	220
3	220	220	216	212	220
Avg.	218.3	217.3	215.7	213.3	220.0
Range	4.0	4.0	1.0	4.0	0.0

Average of averages = 216.9

normally do the measurements are chosen to participate in the study. Each part is measured three times by each appraiser. Results of the test are shown in Table 15.2 (AIAG, 1995a).

The product specification was 100 +/−15 (i.e., process tolerance is 30). Historical standard deviation was estimated to be 3.5. The following output and Figure 15.10 is the result of a gage R&R computer analysis.

Gage R&R Study – ANOVA Method

Two-way ANOVA Table with Interaction

```
Source              DF        SS        MS         F        P
Part                 4   129.467   32.3667   13.6761   0.013
Appraiser            1     2.700    2.7000    1.1408   0.346
Part * Appraiser     4     9.467    2.3667    0.9221   0.471
Repeatability       20    51.333    2.5667
Total               29   192.967


Alpha to remove interaction term = 0.25
```

Gage R&R (ANOVA) for Resp

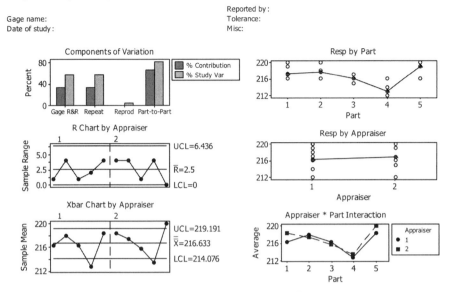

Figure 15.10: Gage R&R analysis.

Two-Way ANOVA Table without Interaction

Source	DF	SS	MS	F	P
Part	4	129.467	32.3667	12.7763	0.000
Appraiser	1	2.700	2.7000	1.0658	0.312
Repeatability	24	60.800	2.5333		
Total	29	192.967			

Gage R&R

Source	VarComp	%Contribution (of VarComp)
Total Gage R&R	2.54444	33.85
Repeatability	2.53333	33.70
Reproducibility	0.01111	0.15
Appraiser	0.01111	0.15
Part-To-Part	4.97222	66.15
Total Variation	7.51667	100.00

Process tolerance = 30
Historical standard deviation = 3.5

		Study Var	%Study Var	%Tolerance	%Process
Source	StdDev (SD)	(6 * SD)	(%SV)	(SV/Toler)	(SV/Proc)
Total Gage R&R	1.59513	9.5708	58.18	31.90	45.58
Repeatability	1.59164	9.5499	58.05	31.83	45.48
Reproducibility	0.10541	0.6325	3.84	2.11	3.01
Appraiser	0.10541	0.6325	3.84	2.11	3.01
Part-To-Part	2.22985	13.3791	81.33	44.60	63.71
Total Variation	2.74165	16.4499	100.00	54.83	78.33

Number of Distinct Categories = 1

The first two-way ANOVA (see Chapter 27) of the study's data considered both appraiser and part–appraiser interaction. The second two-way ANOVA did not consider the appraiser*part interaction. From this analysis, appraiser and part–appraiser interaction were not found statistically significant because the probability of significance values (P) for appraiser or part–appraiser interaction were not small (e.g., not less than 0.05).

A summary of the gage R&R from the five perspectives is:

No.	Perspective	Response
1	Variance Component Percentage	33.85
2	Percent of Study Variation	58.18
3	Number of Distinct Categories	1
4	Percent of Tolerance	31.90
5	Percent of Process	45.58

As noted earlier, the first three responses are dependent upon the part-to-part evaluation sample variability. A reiteration of the importance of this is that evaluation samples that have large part-to-part differences will on the average have a better response (i.e., items numbered 1 and 2 will be lower and item number 3 will be higher) than when the evaluation samples have small part-to-part differences.

The previously described guidelines lead us to conclude that improvement is needed since both percent of tolerance and percent of process (i.e., items numbered 4 and 5) are beyond 30%.

Graphical outputs associated with a gage R&R study can give additional insight into a gage and opportunities for improvement. In a gage R&R study, the $\bar{x}$ control chart addresses measurement variability relative to part-to-part variation. The limits for a control chart in a gage R&R study relate to part-to-part variation.

The control limits for these charts are based on repeatability inconsistencies, not part-to-part variation. For this study, the $\bar{x}$ chart by operator plot had only 30%, or less than half, of the averages outside the limits. The measurement system in this example is concluded to be inadequate to detect part-to-part variations, assuming that the parts used in the study truly represent the total process variation. An adequate measurement system is present when a majority of part averages fall outside the limits and appraisers agree on which parts fall outside the limits.

When the R chart of a gage R&R study is in control/predictable, the inspection process by appraisers is similar. If one appraiser has an out-of-control condition, his/her method could differ significantly from the others. If all appraisers have some out-of-control ranges, the measurement system is apparently sensitive to appraiser technique and needs improvement to obtain useful data. For this example, there does not appear to be any inconsistency within and between operators.

Other output graphs from a gage R&R study can give additional insight to sources of variability (e.g., part-to-part, operator, operator–part interaction, and components of variance). These charts, for this example, do not appear to contain any additional information that was already determined through other means.

From this analysis, we would recommend either improving or replacing the existing measurement system.

15.14   Linearity

Linearity is the difference in the bias values through the expected operating range of the gage. For a linearity evaluation, one or more operators measure parts selected throughout the operating range of the measurement instrument. For each of the chosen parts, the average difference between the reference value and the observed average measurement is the estimated bias. Sources for reference values of the parts include tool room or layout inspection equipment.

If a graph between bias and reference values follows a straight line throughout the operating rate, a regression line slope describes the best fit of bias versus reference values. This slope value is then multiplied by the process variation (or tolerance) of the parts to determine an index that represents the linearity of the gage. Gage linearity is converted to a percentage of process variation (or tolerance) when multiplied by 100 and divided by process variation (or tolerance). A scatter plot of the best-fit line using graphical techniques can give additional insight to linearity issues.

15.15   Example 15.2: Linearity

The five parts selected for the evaluation represent the operating range of the measurement system based upon the process variation. Layout inspection determined the part reference values. Appraisers measured each part 12 times in a random sequence. Results are shown in Table 15.3 (AIAG, 2002).

Figure 15.11 shows the results of a computer analysis of the data. The difference between the part reference value and the part average yielded bias. Inferences of linear association between the biases (accuracy measurements) and reference value (master part measurement) use the goodness-of-fit (R^2) value. Conclusions are then drawn from this to determine if there is a linear relationship. Linearity is determined by the slope of the best-fit line, not the goodness-of-fit (R^2). If there is a linear relationship, a decision needs to be made to determine if the amount is acceptable. Generally a lower slope indicates better gage linearity.

Table 15.3: Measurements for Linearity Example

Part	Reference Value 2	3	6	8	10
1	2.7	5.1	5.8	7.6	9.1
2	2.5	3.9	5.7	7.7	9.3
3	2.4	4.2	5.9	7.8	9.5
4	2.5	5.0	5.9	7.7	9.3
5	2.7	3.8	6.0	7.8	9.4
6	2.3	3.9	6.1	7.8	9.5
7	2.5	3.9	6.0	7.8	9.5
8	2.5	3.9	6.1	7.7	9.5
9	2.4	3.9	6.4	7.8	9.6
10	2.4	4.0	6.3	7.5	9.2
11	2.6	4.1	6.0	7.6	9.3
12	2.4	3.8	6.1	7.7	9.4
Part Avg.	2.49	4.13	6.03	7.7	9.4
Reference	2	4	6	8	10
Bias	-0.5	-0.1	-0	0.3	0.6
Range	0.4	1.3	0.7	0.3	0.5

Gage Linearity and Bias Study for Resp

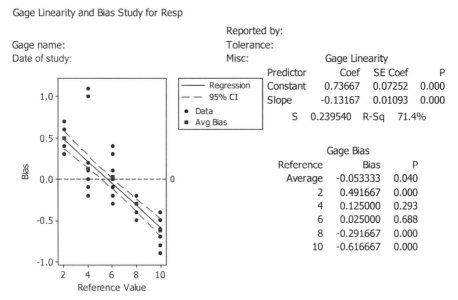

Figure 15.11: Gage linearity plot analysis.

15.16 Attribute Agreement Analysis

The following is a short method for conducting an attribute gage study. An attribute gage either accepts or rejects a part after comparison to a set of limits. Unlike a gage that reports a continuous response measurement, an attribute gage cannot quantify the degree to which a part is good or bad.

A short attribute gage study can be conducted by first selecting 20 parts. Choose parts, if possible, so that some parts are slightly below and some above specification limits. Use two appraisers and conduct the study in a manner to prevent appraiser bias. Appraisers inspect each part twice, deciding whether the part is acceptable or not.

If all measurements agree (four per part), the gage is accepted. Gage needs improvement or reevaluation if measurement decisions do not agree or are not consistent with an established standard or correct answer relative to the master part. Choose an alternative measurement system if gage cannot be improved since the measurement system is unacceptable (AIAG, 2002).

Some statistical programs offer an analysis approach for an attribute agreement analysis. Kappa and Kendall's correlation statistics are used to evaluate the agreement. Kendall's correlation is used when there is ordering of the attribute data categories.

When conducting an agreement analysis, the kappa result considers the binomial condition. For the Kendall correlation of ordered responses, a lower correlation effect will be achieved the further the result is from the standard or the appraiser. To illustrate this situation, consider the situation where there is a 1 to 5 score, where the relationship has order as in 1>2>3>4>5 or 1<2<3<4<5. For situations like this, the Kendall correlation term is most appropriate to evaluate the gage agreement.

In a binomial case, these two methods are similar. In an ordered attribute response, as the following example, the Kendall coefficient takes into account that the adjacent values show more correlation than do the ones that are farther away.

15.17   Example 15.3: Attribute Agreement Analysis

A company is training five new appraisers for the written portion of a standardized essay test. The ability of the appraiser to rate essays relative to standards needs to be assessed; 15 essays were rated by each appraiser on a five-point scale (–2, –1, 0, 1, 2). Table 15.4 shows the results of the test.

A statistical computer MSA analysis yielded: (Minitab, 2007)

Table 15.4: Example 24.3: Attribute Gauge Study Data
(Minitab, 2007)

Appraiser	Sample	Rating	Attribute	Appraiser	Sample	Rating	Attribute	Appraiser	Sample	Rating	Attribute
Simpson	1	2	2	Simpson	6	1	1	Simpson	11	-2	-2
Montgome	1	2	2	Montgome	6	1	1	Montgome	11	-2	-2
Holmes	1	2	2	Holmes	6	1	1	Holmes	11	-2	-2
Duncan	1	1	2	Duncan	6	1	1	Duncan	11	-2	-2
Hayes	1	2	2	Hayes	6	1	1	Hayes	11	-1	-2
Simpson	2	-1	-1	Simpson	7	2	2	Simpson	12	0	0
Montgome	2	-1	-1	Montgome	7	2	2	Montgome	12	0	0
Holmes	2	-1	-1	Holmes	7	2	2	Holmes	12	0	0
Duncan	2	-2	-1	Duncan	7	1	2	Duncan	12	-1	0
Hayes	2	-1	-1	Hayes	7	2	2	Hayes	12	0	0
Simpson	3	1	0	Simpson	8	0	0	Simpson	13	2	2
Montgome	3	0	0	Montgome	8	0	0	Montgome	13	2	2
Holmes	3	0	0	Holmes	8	0	0	Holmes	13	2	2
Duncan	3	0	0	Duncan	8	0	0	Duncan	13	2	2
Hayes	3	0	0	Hayes	8	0	0	Hayes	13	2	2
Simpson	4	-2	-2	Simpson	9	-1	-1	Simpson	14	-1	-1
Montgome	4	-2	-2	Montgome	9	-1	-1	Montgome	14	-1	-1
Holmes	4	-2	-2	Holmes	9	-1	-1	Holmes	14	-1	-1
Duncan	4	-2	-2	Duncan	9	-2	-1	Duncan	14	-1	-1
Hayes	4	-2	-2	Hayes	9	-1	-1	Hayes	14	-1	-1
Simpson	5	0	0	Simpson	10	1	1	Simpson	15	1	1
Montgome	5	0	0	Montgome	10	1	1	Montgome	15	1	1
Holmes	5	0	0	Holmes	10	1	1	Holmes	15	1	1
Duncan	5	-1	0	Duncan	10	0	1	Duncan	15	1	1
Hayes	5	0	0	Hayes	10	2	1	Hayes	15	1	1

Attribute Agreement Analysis for Rating

Each Appraiser versus Standard

```
Assessment Agreement

Appraiser    # Inspected   # Matched   Percent         95 % CI
Duncan                15           8     53.33   (26.59, 78.73)
Hayes                 15          13     86.67   (59.54, 98.34)
Holmes                15          15    100.00   (81.90, 100.00)
Montgomery            15          15    100.00   (81.90, 100.00)
Simpson               15          14     93.33   (68.05, 99.83)


# Matched: Appraiser's assessment across trials agrees with
the known standard.


Fleiss' Kappa Statistics

Appraiser    Response     Kappa   SE Kappa          Z    P(vs > 0)
Duncan       -2         0.58333   0.258199    2.25924       0.0119
             -1         0.16667   0.258199    0.64550       0.2593
             0          0.44099   0.258199    1.70796       0.0438
             1          0.44099   0.258199    1.70796       0.0438
             2          0.42308   0.258199    1.63857       0.0507
             Overall    0.41176   0.130924    3.14508       0.0008
Hayes        -2         0.62963   0.258199    2.43855       0.0074
             -1         0.81366   0.258199    3.15131       0.0008
             0          1.00000   0.258199    3.87298       0.0001
             1          0.76000   0.258199    2.94347       0.0016
             2          0.81366   0.258199    3.15131       0.0008
             Overall    0.82955   0.134164    6.18307       0.0000
Holmes       -2         1.00000   0.258199    3.87298       0.0001
             -1         1.00000   0.258199    3.87298       0.0001
             0          1.00000   0.258199    3.87298       0.0001
             1          1.00000   0.258199    3.87298       0.0001
             2          1.00000   0.258199    3.87298       0.0001
             Overall    1.00000   0.131305    7.61584       0.0000
Montgomery   -2         1.00000   0.258199    3.87298       0.0001
             -1         1.00000   0.258199    3.87298       0.0001
             0          1.00000   0.258199    3.87298       0.0001
```

```
              1            1.00000   0.258199   3.87298      0.0001
              2            1.00000   0.258199   3.87298      0.0001
              Overall      1.00000   0.131305   7.61584      0.0000
Simpson      -2            1.00000   0.258199   3.87298      0.0001
             -1            1.00000   0.258199   3.87298      0.0001
              0            0.81366   0.258199   3.15131      0.0008
              1            0.81366   0.258199   3.15131      0.0008
              2            1.00000   0.258199   3.87298      0.0001
              Overall      0.91597   0.130924   6.99619      0.0000
```

Kendall's Correlation Coefficient

Appraiser	Coef	SE Coef	Z	P
Duncan	0.87506	0.192450	4.49744	0.0000
Hayes	0.94871	0.192450	4.88016	0.0000
Holmes	1.00000	0.192450	5.14667	0.0000
Montgomery	1.00000	0.192450	5.14667	0.0000
Simpson	0.96629	0.192450	4.97151	0.0000

Between Appraisers

Assessment Agreement

# Inspected	# Matched	Percent	95 % CI
15	6	40.00	(16.34, 67.71)

Matched: All appraisers' assessments agree with each other.

Fleiss' Kappa Statistics

Response	Kappa	SE Kappa	Z	P(vs > 0)
-2	0.680398	0.0816497	8.3331	0.0000
-1	0.602754	0.0816497	7.3822	0.0000
0	0.707602	0.0816497	8.6663	0.0000
1	0.642479	0.0816497	7.8687	0.0000
2	0.736534	0.0816497	9.0207	0.0000
Overall	0.672965	0.0412331	16.3210	0.0000

Kendall's Coefficient of Concordance

Coef	Chi - Sq	DF	P
0.966317	67.6422	14	0.0000

All Appraisers Versus Standard

```
Assessment Agreement

# Inspected   # Matched    Percent           95 % CI
     15            6         40.00        (16.34, 67.71)
# Matched: All appraisers' assessments agree with
the known standard.
Fleiss' Kappa Statistics

Response        Kappa     SE Kappa          Z    P(vs > 0)
-2           0.842593    0.115470      7.2971       0.0000
-1           0.796066    0.115470      6.8941       0.0000
0            0.850932    0.115470      7.3693       0.0000
1            0.802932    0.115470      6.9536       0.0000
2            0.847348    0.115470      7.3383       0.0000
Overall      0.831455    0.058911     14.1136       0.0000

Kendall's Correlation Coefficient

Coef             SE Coef             Z                     P
0.958012    0.0860663       11.1090      0.0000

* NOTE * Single trial within each appraiser. No
percentage of assessment agreement within appraiser
is plotted.
```

Attribute Agreement Analysis

The following three assessment agreement tables were displayed, accompanied by Kappa and Kendall's statistics:

- Appraiser versus standard
- Between appraisers
- All appraisers versus standard

The significance ($p=0.0000$) of Kendall's coefficient for both between appraisers and appraisers versus the standard leads us to a further examination where we note that Duncan's and Hayes's assessments have a poor standards' match. However, Holmes and Montgomery have a perfect 100% match, noting that there is a confidence interval associated with each match as graphically illustrated in Figure 15.12. From this data analysis we conclude that additional training is needed for Duncan, Hayes, and Simpson.

Assessment Agreement   Date of study:
                                           Reported by:
                                           Name of product:

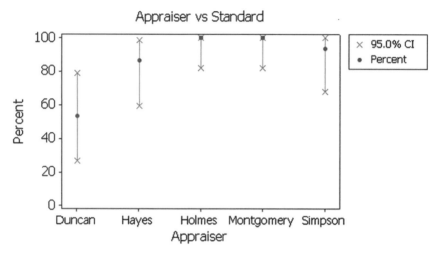

Figure 15.12: MSA assessment agreement.

We should note that we could have assessed within appraiser variability if each appraiser had multiple trials for each test condition.

From this analysis we would recommend to improving the measurement process criteria or operational definitions for scoring.

15.18   Gage Study of Destructive Testing

Unlike non-destructive tests, destructive tests cannot test the same unit repeatedly to obtain an estimate for pure measurement error. However, an upper bound on measurement error for destructive tests is determinable using the control chart technique described (Wheeler, 1990).

When testing is destructive, it is impossible to separate the variation of the measurements themselves from the variation of the product being measured. However, it is often possible to minimize the product variation between pairs of measurements through the careful choice of the material that is to be measured. Through repeated duplicate measurements on material that is thought to minimize product variation between the two measurements, an upper bound is obtainable for the variation due to the measurement process. The simple control chart method illustrated in the following example shows the application of this procedure.

15.19 Example 15.4: Gage Study of Destructive Testing

The data in Table 15.5 are viscosity measurements by lot (Wheelcr, 1990). For this MSA study, consider that the readings for the samples represent duplicate measurements because they were obtained using the same methods, personnel, and instruments. Because each lot is separate, it is reasonable to interpret the difference between the two viscosity measurements as the primary component of measurement error.

To illustrate the broader application of this approach, consider that these data could also represent a continuous process where the measurements are destructive. If this were the case, measurements need to be taken so that the samples are as similar as possible. This selection often involves obtaining samples as close together as possible from the continuous process.

Figure 15.13 shows a range chart for these data. These duplicate readings show consistency because no range exceeds the control limit of 0.2007. An estimate for the standard deviation of the measurement process is:

$$\sigma_m = \frac{\bar{R}}{d_2} = \frac{0.0614}{1.128} = 0.054$$

where $\bar{R}$ is average range and d_2 is from Table J where $n = 2$.

These calculated ranges do not reflect batch-to-batch variation and should not be used in the construction of the control limits for average viscosity. When tracking the consistency of the process, it is best to use the average of the duplicate readings with an individuals control chart and a moving range chart (i.e., individu-

Table 15.5: Destructive Testing Example – Calculations for Range Chart

Lot	1	2	3	4	5	6	7
Sample 1	20.48	19.37	20.35	19.87	20.36	19.32	20.58
Sample 2	20.43	19.23	20.39	19.93	20.34	19.30	20.68
Range	0.05	0.14	0.04	0.06	0.02	0.02	0.10

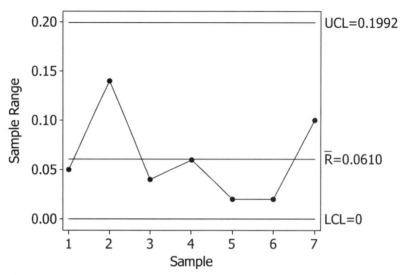

Figure 15.13: Range chart of difference between two samples for destructive test.

als control chart, as in Table 15.6). The grand average is 20.045, and the average moving range is 0.918. The individuals control chart in Figure 15.14 indicates no inconsistency in the process.

Both types of control charts are needed. The range chart checks for consistency within the measurement process, while the individuals control chart checks for consistency of the production process.

From the individual control chart, an estimate for the standard deviation of the product measurements is:

$$\sigma_p = \frac{\bar{R}}{d_2} = \frac{0.918}{1.128} = 0.814$$

where $\bar{R}$ is average range and d_2 is from Table J where $n = 2$.

The estimated number of distinct categories is then:

$$\text{Number of Distinct Categories} = \left[\frac{\sigma_p}{\sigma_m}\right] \times 1.41 = \frac{0.814}{0.054} \times 1.41 = 21.2$$

The magnitude for number of distinct categories suggests that the measurement process adequately detects product variation.

In summary, the pairing of units so that sample-to-sample variation is minimized can give a reasonable estimate of the

Table 15.6: Destructive Testing Example – Calculations for Individuals Control Chart

Lot	1	2	3	4	5	6	7
Sample 1	20.48	19.37	20.35	19.87	20.36	19.32	20.58
Sample 2	20.43	19.23	20.39	19.93	20.34	19.30	20.68
$\bar{x}$	20.46	19.30	20.37	19.90	20.35	19.31	20.63
MR		1.16	1.07	0.47	0.45	1.04	1.32

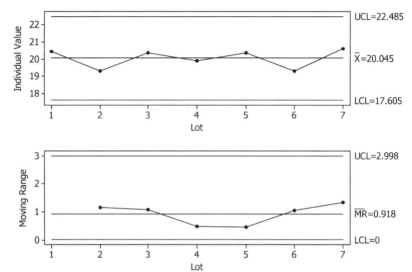

Figure 15.14: *XmR* of mean of two samples for destructive test.

measurement process using a simple control chart approach. Estimates from these calculations are useful to then determine an estimate for the number of distinct categories for the measurement process.

Although it was not done in this example, comparison of measurement variability to historical process variability and tolerance is a good practice. This could be accomplished using the previously described assessments of:

Assessment 4: Percent of Tolerance

The total gage R&R percentage of tolerance is calculated using the equation:

$$\%\text{R\&R contribution to tolerance} = \frac{6\sigma_m}{\text{tolerance}} \times 100$$

where tolerance is USL minus LSL. This metric could be considered a measure of precision-to-tolerance (P/T) for each component, where the purpose is to provide the ability of the gage to judge parts relative to their tolerance.

Assessment 5: Percent of Process

The total gage R&R percentage of process variability is calculated using the following equation. The number six was included in both the numerator and denominator to illustrate that the relationship is really between the spreads of the two distributions, even though six cancels out in the algebraic relationship.

$$\%\text{R\&R contribution to Process} = \frac{6\sigma_m}{6 \times \text{Historical Standard Deviation}} \times 100$$

where tolerance is USL minus LSL. This is basically a measure of P/NPV.

15.20   5-Step Measurement Improvement Process

The described methodology can provide very good insight to the quantification of the various aspects of an overall measurement system. This understanding can lead to an improved targeting of improvement efforts. This is especially useful if there is an indication that the measurement system is a very significant contributor to process capability/performance metric issues.

Gage R&R studies are useful for quantifying the variation in a measurement system; however this is only part of the problem (Enck, 2002). The team needs a method to reduce the variation, once it is identified. In addition, for a complete assessment of the measurement system, teams need to address the important issues of accuracy and long term stability. This section provides an overview of a 5-step MSA and improvement process that addresses these measurement system issues. This methodology has been successfully used in a variety of industries, from semiconductor to medical device manufacturing, to improve and control their measurement systems.

Previously, the standard breakdown of the measurement variance for a gage R&R study was described as the variance of the gage plus the variance of the operator. In order to reduce the measurement variation, this general breakdown needs to be further refined so that specific sources of variation can be identified and removed. The described approach provides a simple and effective method for identifying and helping the practitioner reduce measurement variation.

The following 5-step method assesses sources of variation in stages. At each stage the practitioner is responsible for hypothesizing the potential sources of variation and developing methods to remove the source if the measurement system variation for that stage is too large. The following provides an applied view of the 5-step methodology. Each step has the purpose, acceptance criteria, method to conduct the test and comments. Documentation is an important part of the analysis. Documentation should be maintained so that practitioners conducting future studies will know: the measurement relevance, what equipment was used, what measurements were taken, and the procedure used to make those measurements.

Terminology and relationships used in the 5-step measurement improvement process sections are as follows:

- NPV: natural process variation, T: tolerance, P: precision
- S_{MS}: standard deviation of measurement system
- S_{Total}: standard deviation of total variability of measurements over time from true value variabilities and from measurement error
- P/T: $(6.00 \times S_{MS})/$tolerance
- P/NPV: $(6.00 \times S_{MS})/(6.00 \times S_{Total}) = S_{MS}/S_{Total}$

1. Machine Variation

This step tries to reduce the impact of external sources of variation on the measurement system so that the experimenter can study variation due only to gage variables, short-term environmental variables, and possibly some operator variables.

Sources of Variation: Machine variation, short term environmental, possible operator variables and unstable fixture

How to Conduct This Test

1. Take 20 to 30 sequential measurements of a typical part.

2. Do not touch the part or adjust the gage during the measurements.
3. Use one operator.

Acceptance Criteria

1. Plot the observations on a control chart and determine that there are no significant out-of-control patterns.
2. If there are fewer than five distinct measurement values, the control limits will be slightly narrow due to rounding
   - This needs to be considered for any control chart patterns run test.
   - If an observation is outside the control limits, but within one resolution increment, the process may not be out of control (i.e., a predictable process).
3. The P/T (P/NPV) ratio is less than 5% (10%) unless operator decisions are involved in the measurement, in which case it may go as high as 10% (15%).

Comments

1. Twenty to thirty measurements were used because the machine variation measurements are typically easy to collect; if the measurements are difficult to obtain, a minimum is usually 16.
2. The ratio targets are typical standards and may be modified based on circumstances.
3. Conduct a blind study.
   - An operator measures the part, but is not allowed to see or hear the final measured value.
   - A second person records the measurements.

2. Fixture Study

This step evaluates the variation added due to the part being re-fixtured. For measurement systems that are manual, variation seen in the fixture study impacts between operator differences as well as that any improvements to the measurement process can impact reproducibility as well as repeatability. Rather than running the whole gage R&R study and finding that the fixture method adds a lot of variation, this step allows a shorter test to be used to fix any problems that you find prior to conducting the larger gage R&R study.

Sources of Variation: Same as machine variation, with re-fixturing included.

How to Conduct This Test

1. Take 16 measurements of a typical part.
2. Remove the part from the gage and replace it for each measurement.
3. Use one operator.

Acceptance Criteria

1. Plot the observations on a control chart and determine that there are no significant out-of-control patterns.
2. The P/T (P/NPV) ratio is less than 15–20% (20–25%). This is flexible and depends on what the final goal is; however, the larger the values, the less likely it is to reach the final goal.

Comments

1. If the results are unacceptable, use technical knowledge and organizational wisdom to change the system and retest. Once the variation in this stage is satisfactory, move on to the next test.

3. Accuracy (Linearity)

This step determines whether the measurement system is *biased* across the tolerance range of the parameter being measured.

How to Conduct This Test

1. Take 16 measurements of a traceable standard.
2. Do not adjust the gage during the measurements.
3. Remove the standard from the gage and replace it for each measurement.
4. Repeat this for three standards (low, middle, high) across the range of the natural process variation of the parts.
5. Use one operator.

Acceptance Criteria

1. Plot the observations on a control chart and that there are no significant out-of-control patterns.
2. 95% confidence intervals contain the certified standard value for each of the three standards.
3. Regression analysis shows an insignificant slope from a practical point of view (e.g., the bias may be increasing; however, the largest bias is less than 5% of the specification range. You should also compare the bias to the natural process variation.)
4. The P/T ratio for an accuracy study will be close to the P/T for the fixture variation study. Since the measurements are on standards which may be different from the parts being measured, this metric is not critical.

4. Repeatability and Reproducibility

This step (the traditional "R&R") will use additional experiments to quantify the total variation of the measurement system. Further, we will be able to isolate between operator, part, and within operator variation. If the total variation for the measurement system is unacceptable, the isolated sources of variation will provide a guide as to where the best opportunities for improvement lie.

Sources of Variation. Same as re-fixturing with time, operator, and operator by part variation included

How to Conduct This Test

1. Develop a measurement plan based on the sources of variation to be studied and the hypothesized importance of each source of variation. Below are some possible ranges to use when selecting the measurement plan:
   - 4–6 operators
   - 4–6 parts
   - 3–4 measurements per day
   - 3–5 days
2. Do not adjust the gage during the measurements. If it is known that the gage is incapable of remaining stable over

time, fix this source of variation prior to conducting the gage R&R. If it is not possible, use the standard preparation method during the gage R&R stage.

3. Setup a measurement schedule that randomizes the order of the operators and the order in which the parts are measured. This is used to try to spread the effects of any unknown factors equally between all assignable sources of variation.

4. Have the operators' record factors that may affect the measurements, such as: temperature, gage settings, condition of part, and observations about anything unusual. These can be written down on the data sheets.

5. Analyze the data as described previously.

Acceptance Criteria

1. Refer to gage R&R section.
2. P/T and P/NPV are less than the targets.

5. Long-Term Stability

This step will monitor the measurement system on an ongoing basis in order to verify that the system is operating in the same manner (i.e., stable and consistent) over time. This can also be used to provide information on when a gage may need to be calibrated.

How to Conduct This Test

1. Obtain 1 to 2 parts that can be used as an internal reference part.
2. Meet with the operators and discuss the importance of this part of the MCA. With the operators' input, create a measurement plan that covers all shifts and all operators. This sampling plan is important in that it will provide information about the whole measurement system.
3. Measure the parts at least once a day over a 20 to 30 day period for a minimum of 20 to 30 measurements.
4. After taking the initial measurements, implement a sampling plan to monitor the measurement system continually as long

as it is being used. Based on the results of the initial measurements, the sampling plan may be reduced if the process is stable. Even with a reduced sampling plan, the philosophy of complete system coverage should be maintained.

5. Document the conditions during the measurements. Document variables that are thought to be important:
   - Operator
   - Any important gage settings
   - Any important environmental conditions

Acceptance Criteria

1. Plot the observations on a control chart and determine that there are no significant out-of-control patterns.
2. The P/T and P/NPV ratios are satisfactory (meet the previously specified criteria).

Comment

1. If the process goes out of control and cannot be brought back so that it is in control/predictable, the measurement system needs to be recalibrated.
2. As long as the process is in control/predictable, the variation and calibration have not changed.
3. Consider using this control process as part of the calibration process.

15.21 Uncertainty Due to Data Rounding

Rounding can create a large amount of measurement uncertainty. To illustrate this, consider that a quote process response is about 3 days, where reported quote time is averaged to the nearest day. From the Figure 15.15 visual representation of this situation, we note that a reported duration of 3 days could actually take between 2 ½ (3 − ½) and 3 ½ (3 + ½) days. Dividing the difference of 2 days (4 days minus 2 days, as illustrated in the figure) by the 3-day duration yields a potential measurement discrepancy of 67%.

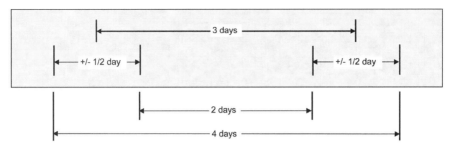

Figure 15.15: Uncertainty due to data rounding.

Measurements need to have small enough rounding increments so that reported metrics provide an accurate representation of performance.

15.22   Example 15.5: 5-Step Measurement Improvement Process

The following example will provide a brief description of the machine variation, fixture variation, linearity, gage R&R, and long term stability studies for an optical microscope (Enck, 2002).

A company used an optical microscope to measure part widths. A total of 30 operators used the measurement technique on a daily basis. A team was working on reducing the defect rate for this particular KPOV. After base lining and calculating the process capability for this parameter, they conducted a 5-step MSA. Organizational wisdom indicated that the measurement system had a lot of variation; however it had never been quantified using a P/T ratio. In order to keep the project on track, the objective of the MSA was to develop a test method that had a P/T and P/NPV ratio that was less than 30%. Any further improvements would be handled by another team at a later date. The part tolerance was 1.2 mils, and the historical process standard deviation was 0.21 mils.

The measurement process consisted of aligning the part with the centerline of the screen, zeroing out the micrometer, rolling the stage until the centerline was aligned with the opposite side of the part, and recording the measurement. Figure 15.16 shows the optical microscope screen.

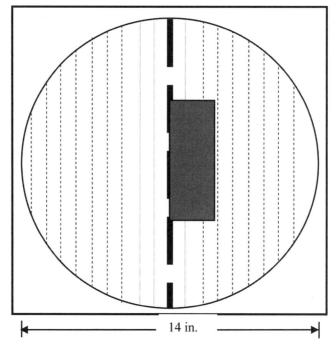

14 in.

Figure 15.16: Optical microscope screen.

1. Machine Variation

The machine variation phase consisted of placing a part on the microscope stage and measuring it 30 times without touching the part. An individuals control chart and P/T ratio were used to analyze the results. Figure 15.17 shows the control chart.

All measurements collected in this 5-step study were taken in a blind manner. A piece of paper was placed over the gage display and the operator conducted the measurement as stated in the standard operating procedure (SOP). When the measurement was completed, a second person looked under the paper and recorded the measurement without telling the operator the result.

The measurements were in control/predictable; however, the P/T ratio was 15.8%. When operators make decisions about where to start and stop measurements, the measurement variation tends to be high. The team wanted to reduce the variation so that when more operators were included the P/T ratio would remain acceptable.

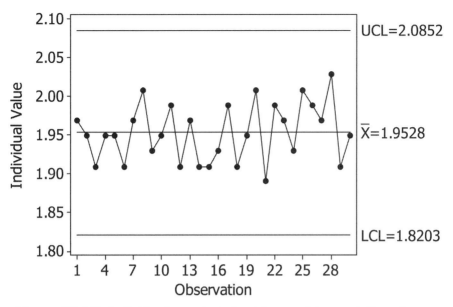

Figure 15.17: Individuals control chart for machine variation phase.

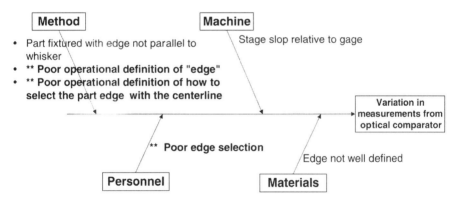

Figure 15.18: Highlights from a cause-and-effect diagram to identify potential causes of excess variation.

Figure 15.18 highlights the results from a cause-and-effect diagram, which was used to identify potential causes of excess variation in the optical microscope measurement process. Edge selection was chosen as having the largest potential impact on the measurement variation. An improved edge selection process was then developed, which used the left side of the centerline as the starting point and ending point for the measurement.

The 30 measurements for the machine variation study were repeated with the new process. An individuals control chart indicated that the process was in control/predictable and that the P/T ratio had been reduced to 7.08%. A statistical test that compared the initial process variance to the new process variance showed a significant difference with a *P* value less than 0.001. The measurement variation at this stage was deemed acceptable so that the team proceeded to the fixture variation study.

2. Fixture Variation

The fixture variation study consisted of picking the part up, placing it on the stage, measuring the part and repeating the process. This procedure was repeated 16 times. An individual's control chart was generated and P/T ratio was determined. The control chart was in control/predictable with a P/T ratio of 15.46%. Part orientation was considered the most likely candidate for the increase in variation. The SOP for the measurement was then modified to improve part alignment. The team believed that most of the variation of the measurement process was represented by the fixture variation study and that difference between operators would be small. Because of this, the team felt comfortable moving to the next step of the 5-step MSA with the improved SOP.

3. Linearity Study

The linearity study assessed the bias across the range of part widths of interest. There was a concern that if a single operator were used, any bias would reflect bias of the operator and that this would differ between operators. It was decided to pick the most experienced operator and assume that any bias observed would be from the gage rather than from the operator. If there was a difference between operators, it would show up in the gage R&R study as excessive variation from differences between operators.

Standards were selected at the low, medium, and high levels of the range of interest. Figure 15.19 shows the regression analysis of the deviation from target for 16 measurements that were taken for each standard versus the stated value of the National Institute of Standards and Technology (NIST) standard. The relationship is statistically significant; however, when using the average deviation from target, the maximum bias for the three standards was

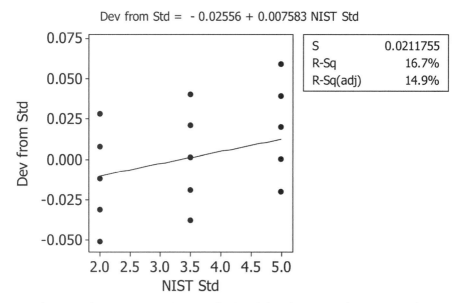

Figure 15.19: Regression analysis of the deviation from target for 16 measurements that were taken for each standard versus the stated standard value.

less than 5% of the specification range. Given the relatively small bias over the range of interest, the bias was considered not to have practical significance.

4.   Repeatability and Reproducibility

The gage R&R study consisted of three operators measuring each of three parts three times a day for 4 days. The SOPs developed during the machine and fixture variation studies were used for this study. Each operator was trained on the SOP and was required to conduct a 16 run fixture study achieving a 20% P/T ratio prior to being certified for the measurement system. Once the operators were certified, the gage R&R study was conducted. The analysis, as seen in Table 15.7 and Figure 15.20, follows from the previous discussion on gage R&R studies. There were statistical differences observed between operators; however, the differences were not of practical importance to the team's goal. The P/T ratio was 20.13%, and the P/NPV was 22.83%. These results met the stated goals so that the team moved on to the next phase of the 5-step MSA.

Table 15.7: Gage R&R Study

Two-Way ANOVA Table With Interaction

```
Source                    DF        SS        MS        F       P
Sample R                   2   20.3591   10.1795  4602.35   0.000
Operator R                 2    0.0612    0.0306    13.84   0.016
Sample R * Operator R      4    0.0088    0.0022     1.65   0.167
Repeatability             99    0.1325    0.0013
Total                    107   20.5616
```

Alpha to remove interaction term = 0.25

Gage R&R

```
                                        %Contribution
Source                    VarComp       (of VarComp)
Total Gage R&R            0.002200           0.77
  Repeatability          0.001338           0.47
  Reproducibility        0.000862           0.30
    Operator R           0.000789           0.28
    Operator R*Sample R  0.000073           0.03
Part-To-Part             0.282704          99.23
Total Variation          0.284903         100.00
```

Process tolerance = 1.2
Historical standard deviation = 0.21

```
                                     Study Var   %Study Var   %Tolerance
Source                  StdDev (SD)   (6 * SD)       (%SV)    (SV/Toler)
Total Gage R&R           0.046901     0.28141        8.79        23.45
  Repeatability          0.036579     0.21947        6.85        18.29
  Reproducibility        0.029355     0.17613        5.50        14.68
    Operator R           0.028087     0.16852        5.26        14.04
    Operator R*Sample R  0.008533     0.05120        1.60         4.27
Part-To-Part             0.531699     3.19019       99.61       265.85
Total Variation          0.533763     3.20258      100.00       266.88
```

```
                         %Process
Source                  (SV/Proc)
Total Gage R&R             22.33
  Repeatability            17.42
  Reproducibility          13.98
    Operator R             13.37
    Operator R*Sample R     4.06
Part-To-Part             253.19
Total Variation          254.17
```

Number of Distinct Categories = 15

Gage R&R (ANOVA) for Data Run Order

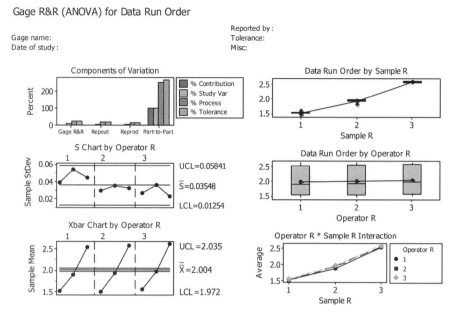

Figure 15.20: Gage R&R graphical analysis.

The objective of this team was to develop a test method that had a P/T ratio and P/NPV ratio that were less than 30%. The change that they made early in the MSA study helped them achieve this objective.

If they had wanted to quantify the improvement in the measurement system, they would have conducted a gage R&R study prior to starting the 5-step MSA so that they would have had a baseline with which to compare their results.

5. Long Term Stability

The team selected a single part for the long-term stability control chart. A baseline of 20 days was established with the part being measured once a day. The shift and operator were randomly selected and recorded. The part that was measured was called the golden part and it was kept in a nitrogen box next to the measurement gage. The long-term stability control chart was used to detect any change in the measurement process that might cause an increase in the measurement system variation or a change in the accuracy.

Summary

This section provided a 5-step MSA and a simple example. This method can be used as part of an IEE project or as an integrated part of how measurement systems are setup in either a manufacturing plant or research and development lab.

15.23   Applying IEE

Organizations often overlook the importance of conducting a MSA. Much money can be wasted trying to fix a process when the major source of variability is the measurement system. Practitioners often need to give more consideration to the measurement system before beginning experimentation work. To illustrate the importance of pretest MSA, consider a design of experiments (DOE). When the measurement system is poor, significance tests can detect only factors with very large effects. There might be no detection of important smaller factor effects. The importance of a measurement system is also not often considered when making sample size and confidence interval calculations. An unsatisfactory measurement system can affect these calculations dramatically.

This chapter describes procedures to determine whether a measurement system is satisfactory. The measurement system is only one source of variability found when a product or process is measured. Other possible sources of variability are differences between raw material, manufacturing lines, and test equipment. In some experiments, it is advantageous to consider these other sources of variability in addition to operator variability within the experiment. The techniques described in Chapter 24 use a nested design structure that can quantify the variance components not only of a process but also of measurement system parameters. Knowing and then improving the sources of variability for a measurement system improve the bottom line in an expedient manner. Note that a MSA may need re-analysis as the process capability/performance metric improves.

15.24   Exercises

1. In an exercise in Chapter 9, a paragraph was examined. The times the sixth character occurs were counted. Discuss

this visual inspection process. What do you think should be done to increase awareness of any deficiencies and approaches for making process improvements?

2. Conduct a gage R &R study of the following data, where five parts are evaluated twice by three appraisers.

	Appraiser A					Appraiser B					Appraiser C				
Part	1	2	3	4	5	1	2	3	4	5	1	2	3	4	5
1	113	113	71	101	113	112	117	82	98	110	107	115	103	110	131
2	114	106	73	97	130	112	107	83	99	108	109	122	86	108	90

3. For the following data, conduct a gage R&R study to assess whether the gage is acceptable, may be acceptable, or is unacceptable. A specification tolerance is 0.004 (i.e., for a specification of 0.375 + 0.002, where measurement unit is 0.0001). A table value of 56, for example, equates to a measurement of 0.3700 + (56 × 0.0001) = 0.3756 (IBM, 1984).

Appraiser	1			2			3		
Sample No.	1st Trial	2nd Trial	3rd Trial	1st Trial	2nd Trial	3rd Trial	1st Trial	2nd Trial	3rd Trial
1	56	55	57	57	58	56	56	57	56
2	63	62	62	64	64	64	62	64	64
3	56	54	55	57	55	56	55	55	55
4	57	55	56	56	57	55	56	57	55
5	58	58	57	59	60	60	57	60	60
6	56	55	54	60	59	57	55	57	56
7	56	55	56	58	56	56	55	55	57
8	57	57	56	57	58	57	57	58	57
9	65	65	64	64	64	65	65	64	65
10	58	57	57	61	60	60	58	59	60

4. Determine an estimate for bias given the following set of measurements and a reference value of 19.919: 20.5513, 20.1528, 20.6246, 19.9609, and 20.7493

5. Conduct a MSA of the following data. State the level of significance of the interaction between part and appraiser. Describe equipment variation as a percentage of process variation. Describe appraiser variation as a percentage of process variation.

Part	Appraiser	Trial	Measurement	Part	Appraiser	Trial	Measurement
1	1	1	7.783	8	2	1	22.625
1	1	2	8.012	8	2	2	22.845
1	1	3	7.718	8	2	3	22.409
1	1	4	7.955	8	2	4	22.027
1	2	1	8.582	9	1	1	19.385
1	2	2	8.192	9	1	2	19.272
1	2	3	8.438	9	1	3	18.746
1	2	4	8.205	9	1	4	18.941
2	1	1	12.362	9	2	1	20.387
2	1	2	12.327	9	2	2	20.024
2	1	3	12.578	9	2	3	20.507
2	1	4	12.692	9	2	4	20.283
2	2	1	13.366	10	1	1	24.282
2	2	2	13.657	10	1	2	24.973
2	2	3	13.262	10	1	3	24.731
2	2	4	13.364	10	1	4	24.796
3	1	1	9.724	10	2	1	26.631
3	1	2	9.93	10	2	2	26.395
3	1	3	9.203	10	2	3	26.577
3	1	4	10.107	10	2	4	26.753
3	2	1	10.182	11	1	1	24.486
3	2	2	10.46	11	1	2	24.175
3	2	3	10.36	11	1	3	24.364
3	2	4	10.71	11	1	4	23.616
4	1	1	15.734	11	2	1	24.352
4	1	2	14.979	11	2	2	24.464
4	1	3	14.817	11	2	3	24.451
4	1	4	14.489	11	2	4	24.497
4	2	1	15.421	12	1	1	29.092
4	2	2	15.622	12	1	2	28.365
4	2	3	15.789	12	1	3	29.243
4	2	4	15.661	12	1	4	29.156
5	1	1	11.22	12	2	1	29.207
5	1	2	12.355	12	2	2	30.033
5	1	3	11.837	12	2	3	30.022
5	1	4	12.126	12	2	4	30.175
5	2	1	12.148	13	1	1	27.283
5	2	2	12.508	13	1	2	26.861
5	2	3	13.193	13	1	3	27.273
5	2	4	11.986	13	1	4	26.717

Part	Appraiser	Trial	Measurement	Part	Appraiser	Trial	Measurement
6	1	1	17.123	13	2	1	29.742
6	1	2	17.191	13	2	2	29.246
6	1	3	17.731	13	2	3	29.808
6	1	4	17.079	13	2	4	29.605
6	2	1	18.805	14	1	1	35.693
6	2	2	18.948	14	1	2	35.951
6	2	3	19.57	14	1	3	35.65
6	2	4	19.244	14	1	4	35.789
7	1	1	15.643	14	2	1	35.616
7	1	2	16.294	14	2	2	35.832
7	1	3	16.255	14	2	3	35.958
7	1	4	16.161	14	2	4	35.973
7	2	1	17.211	15	1	1	34.374
7	2	2	17.159	15	1	2	34.278
7	2	3	17.43	15	1	3	34.25
7	2	4	17.699	15	1	4	34.478
8	1	1	22.317	15	2	1	37.093
8	1	2	22.114	15	2	2	38.1
8	1	3	22.163	15	2	3	37.271
8	1	4	22.548	15	2	4	37.706

6. Conduct a MSA of the following data, where the historical process standard deviation was 4, while the tolerance range was 15. State the level of significance of the interaction between part and appraiser. Describe equipment variation as a percentage of study variation. Describe appraiser variation as a percentage of study variation. Determine the variance components estimates. Report the number of distinct categories. Describe total gage R&R as percentage of study, process variation, and tolerance. Note any other major observations.

   (a) Conduct a MSA of the data.

   (b) State the level of significance of the interaction between part and appraiser.

   (c) Describe equipment variation as a percentage of study variation.

   (d) Describe appraiser variation as a percentage of study variation.

   (e) Describe the variance components estimates.

   (f) Report the number of distinct categories.

   (g) Report total gage R&R as six times standard deviation.

   (h) Describe total gage R&R as percentage of study.

(i) Describe total gage R&R as percentage tolerance.
(j) Describe total gage R&R as percentage process variation.
(k) Any other major observations?

Part	Appraiser	Trial 1	Trial 2	Trial 3	Trial 4
1	1	9.621	9.549	9.502	9.526
1	2	10.416	10.271	10.103	10.398
1	3	10.405	10.748	10.382	10.355
2	1	14.393	14.271	14.338	14.229
2	2	15.348	15.123	15.785	15.666
2	3	15.453	15.501	15.82	15.644
3	1	12.124	12.073	11.852	11.833
3	2	12.228	12.332	12.332	12.899
3	3	13.005	13.116	13.07	12.782
4	1	17.356	17.5	17.737	17.496
4	2	19.129	18.837	18.775	18.804
4	3	18.921	18.532	18.645	18.443
5	1	15.32	15.046	15.27	15.118
5	2	15.91	15.701	15.578	15.778
5	3	16.804	16.645	16.957	16.734
6	1	20.443	20.469	20.475	20.511
6	2	22.907	22.651	22.718	22.512
6	3	22.974	23.008	23.121	22.967
7	1	20.118	19.769	19.872	19.998
7	2	20.986	20.995	21.064	20.955
7	3	21.577	21.284	21.383	21.381
8	1	25.774	25.969	25.852	25.463
8	2	28.047	27.857	27.84	28.166
8	3	29.669	29.833	29.624	29.692
9	1	25.552	25.65	25.607	25.662
9	2	26.178	26.16	26.594	26.141
9	3	26.739	26.407	26.044	26.358

16

P-DMAIC – Measure Phase (Wisdom of the Organization)

16.1 P-DMAIC Roadmap Component

The previous chapter described measurement systems analysis (MSA) assessment on the 30,000-foot-level metric. The graphic in this section highlights the P-DMAIC roadmap steps (see Appendix Section D.1) that are described in this chapter. Appendix E contains the tollgate check sheets for this and other phases. This chapter initiates the capturing of wisdom of the organization improvement thoughts.

Projects have a 30,000-foot-level response (Y) that needs improvement. This Y can be significantly affected by the Xs within the process (i.e., $Y=f(x)$). In the wisdom of the organization project execution phase, we want to gain insight to where to look for improvements opportunities.

One Integrated Enterprise Excellence (IEE) aspect is the use of data to gain insight to what might be done differently to improve. This is analogous to a murder mystery where information is gathered that can generate insightful clues to help determine "who dunnit". Similarly, during the execution of a project, we want to gain insight to where focus efforts and data collection should concentrate.

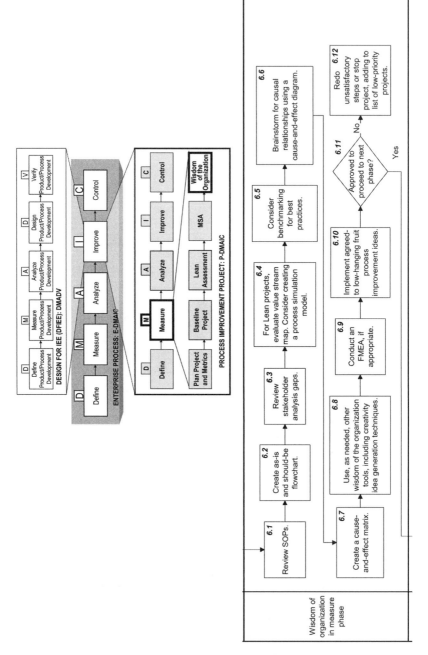

Often when starting a project, the team lead has biases, which can hinder effectiveness in finding a solution. Rather than the project lead immediately starting the collecting-data process upon project initiation, it is much more effective to create a system for using teams to help gain this insight. This is accomplished using the wisdom of the organization drill down process.

The basic suggested tool flow to capture the team's wisdom of the organization inputs is as follows:

- Flow chart the as-is process (i.e., the detailed steps described in the supplier–input–process–output–customer (SIPOC))
- Create a cause-and-effect diagram
- Create a cause-and-effect matrix
- Conduct a failure mode and effects analysis (FMEA)

The purpose of initiating with flowcharting is that the documentation and examination of current process activities. This assessment often surprises many, since the team thought that something else was being done. Other brainstorming tools such as affinity diagramming, as described later in this chapter, could also be added, when appropriate, to the above 4-step process.

This wisdom of the organization assessment could lead to some obvious beneficial process changes (e.g., standardized work practices). These agree-to changes need not have formal statistical analyses to prove their worth. This type of change should be implemented when most appropriate. If these changes truly improve the process, the 30,000-foot-level metric will change to a new, improved level.

However, often it is not clear whether some brainstormed "Xs" currently impact or would impact the overall process. We create from the wisdom of the organization effort hypotheses that can be tested in the project execution analyze phase. The result of these analyses can then lead to process changes during the improve phase roadmap step.

16.2 Flowcharting

We are not typically concern about processes until there is an unacceptable output such as quality, speed, service, or cost. Often there is a tendency to use a band aid or create a work around that patches the problem. Patches eventually fail. In addition, when work around is frequently used with suppliers and this conveys a message that the experienced issue is okay.

Deming stated, "If you can't describe what you are doing as a process, then you don't know what you are doing." In both E-DMAIC analyze phase and measure phase of the project execution roadmap, it is system structure and relationships is presented using flowcharts. A flowchart provides a picture of the steps that are needed to create a deliverable. The process flowchart document can maintain consistency of application, identify opportunities for improvement, and identify key process input variables (KPIVs). It can also be very useful to train new personnel and to describe activities expediently during audits.

A flowchart provides a complete pictorial sequence of a procedure to show what happens from start to finish. Applications include procedure documentation, manufacturing processes, work instructions, and product-development steps. Flowcharting can minimize the volume of documentation, including ISO 9000 documentation.

We would like to have a feedback and feed forward loop between suppliers and the process, along with similar loops between the customer and the process; however, these loops often either do not exist or are not very effective. Feedback loops can cutoff potential problems at the input level. For example Federal Express will not deliver to post office boxes since they do not own the boxes and the recipient is not there; for example, they would not know there was a problem if there was an address error. While, the US postal service will deliver to post office boxes since they own the boxes.

Flowcharts should be at a level of detail that is appropriate for the background and experience of the intended audience. Display flowcharts on the web so that they have computer-click drill downs (described later in this section) which can address multiple audience needs, where the details presented in the low-level computer-click sub-process steps are only viewed by those executing these steps.

Figure 16.1 exemplifies the form of a process flowchart and includes frequently used symbols to describe the activities associated with a process chart.

An arrowhead on the line segment that connects symbols shows the direction of flow. The conventional direction of a flowchart is top to bottom or left to right. Usually the return-loop flow is left and up. When a loop feeds into a box, the arrowhead may terminate at the top of the box, at the side of the symbol, or at the

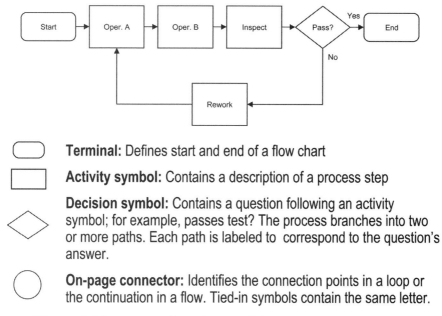

Terminal: Defines start and end of a flow chart

Activity symbol: Contains a description of a process step

Decision symbol: Contains a question following an activity symbol; for example, passes test? The process branches into two or more paths. Each path is labeled to correspond to the question's answer.

On-page connector: Identifies the connection points in a loop or the continuation in a flow. Tied-in symbols contain the same letter.

Figure 16.1: Process flow chart and frequently used symbols.

line connecting the previous box. The use of on-page connectors can simplify a flowchart by reducing the number of interconnection lines.

An illustration of a process can proceed down the left side of a page, have a line or on-page connector that connects the last box of the left column with the first box of the right column, and continue down the right side of a page. Boxes should be large enough to contain all necessary information to describe who does what. Notes can contain nondirective information.

When creating a flowchart, consider and describe the purpose and the process to be evaluated. Define all steps to create a product or service deliverable. This can be done in several different ways. One common approach is to conduct a meeting for those familiar with a process. The team then describes the sequence of steps on a wall or poster chart using one self-stick removable note for each process step. With this approach, the team can easily add or rearrange process steps. After the meeting, one person typically documents and distributes the results.

Another approach when documenting or defining new processes in a team meeting is to use a process-flowcharting computer program directly in conjunction with a projector, which displays the computer's image on a screen. A facilitator would enter and adjust the process steps at the team's direction. This approach can significantly reduce time, greatly improve accuracy, and dramatically diminish the reworking of process description. Process-flowcharting programs offer the additional benefit of easy creation and access to sub-processes. These highlighted sub-processes can be shown by double-clicking with a mouse.

Figures 16.2 and 16.3 illustrate a couple flowcharting process layout options, which can be a drill down from the organizational value chain. In Figure 16.3, swim lanes describe the placement of activities in distinct marketing strategies. However, the parallel rectangular regions in swim lane flowcharting are often used to describe task-completion activities within and cross functional boundaries; e.g., departments in an organizational.

One option to the creation of a swim lane functional flowchart is to start by using sticky notes on a wall to describe the high-level process steps. Under each high-level step, additional sticky notes are then used to create a column listing of sequential sub-process steps. After all process steps are documented on the wall with sticky notes, the high-level process steps are repositioned so that they become "department" listings for horizontally displayed swim lanes. The subprocess sticky-note steps are then re-positioned on the wall to the right of their corresponding high-level swim lane header. As-is, should-be, and could-be swim lane process steps along with their interconnections can be assessed to determine what might be done, for example, to reduce the overall process cycle time.

Figure 16.4 shows the linkage of value stream mapping (VSM) to the value chain, where VSM addresses both product and information flow, along with the reporting of lead time versus value-added time. From this model, we can also run simulations to address "what if" possibilities. The customer value stream is very important since it is a basis for organizational improvements. Figure 16.5 shows how a simple value chain click can lead to a procedural document and URL site option linkage.

With an IEE project, we want to get to the root cause so that the issue does not reoccur. Determined process gaps at process boundary conditions are either a deployment or design issues. Deployment issues are when the design is not executed effectively relative to skills, policy, materials, etc. If there is a design failure, then execution improvements will not fix the problem.

Within the overall DMAIC project execution process we want to create an as-is flowchart at a level of detail that gives additional insight to what is actually happening in the process so that

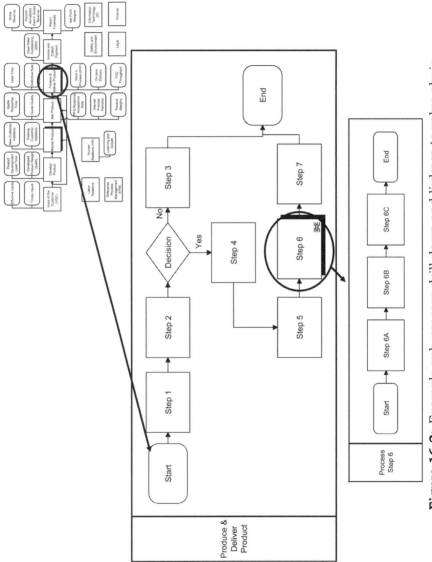

Figure 16.2: Example sub-process drill down and linkage to value chain.

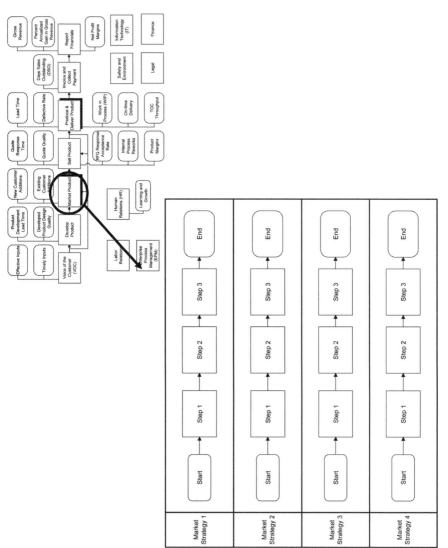

Figure 16.3: Example sub-process swim lane drill down.

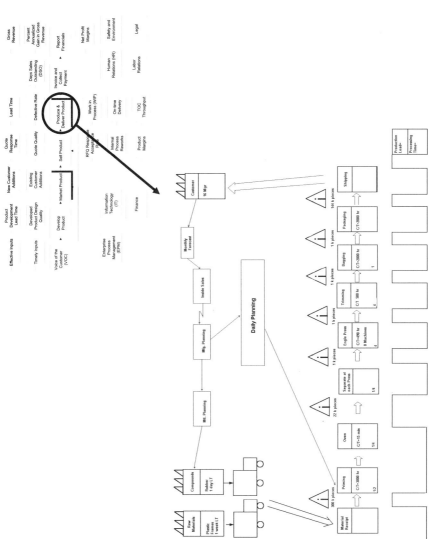

Figure 16.4: Example sub-process value stream map drill down.

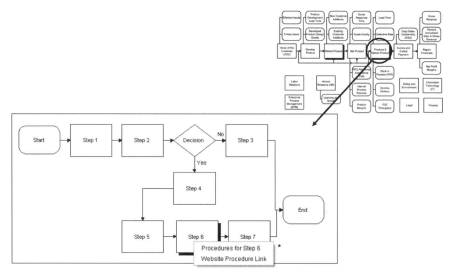

* Options after clicking on Step 6

Figure 16.5: Example link in a process step.

brainstorming improvement sessions become more effective (e.g., cause-and-effect diagram creation as the next step of the overall IEE roadmap). Steps to accomplish this are:

1. Create should-be process flowchart.
2. As a team create an as-is process flowchart.
3. Identify gaps between should-be and as-is processes.
4. Identify execution variation within the as-is process.
5. Review stakeholder analysis gaps for opportunities.
6. Create could-be process flowchart, which may later be determined unfeasible because of non-existent technology, too expensive implementation, not a socially acceptable solution, or not legal allowed.
7. List and categorize potential low-hanging fruit process improvement opportunities. Look for:
   (a) Non-value added delays, transportation, rejects, and storage.
   (b) Activities that could be performed in unison.
   (c) Lack of inspection and decision points.
   (d) No feedback loops.

Within this assessment, process steps can be classified as value-add or non-value-add. Within this assignment, steps such as inspection would be given an assignment of non-value-add. These assessments can provide insight to where to focus improvement efforts.

Flowcharting of key processes for IEE projects can lead to the establishment and documentation of a standard operating procedure (SOP) that is used by all. Such documented organizational procedures within the value chain can dramatically reduce variability and lead time, along with improving the product quality. In addition, a flowchart can give insight to other process improvement focus areas and measurement needs that are beyond the scope of the current project.

An alternative or supplement to a detailed process flow chart is a high-level process map that shows only a few major process steps as activity symbols. For each of these symbols, KPIVs to the activity are listed on one side of the symbol, while key process output variables (KPOVs) to the activity are listed on the other side of the symbol. These KPIVs and KPOVs can then be used as inputs to a cause-and-effects matrix, which is described later in this chapter.

In the end, this work can lead to significant improvements so that the project's 30,000-foot-level metric is positively impacted by workflow and/or operating instructions enhancements.

16.3   Process Modeling and Simulation

Process modeling and computer simulation programs can be built around the flow charts and value stream maps described in the previous sections. These models can be used to gain insight to what can be done to improve existing processes addressed in a P-DMAIC roadmap or through process optimization initiation within DFIEE/DFSS.

These models can consider process input variation, resource utilization, cost, and other parameters (see Figure 37.1). Models can be used to gain insight to what can be done to improve. A step-by-step process to create a simulation is:

1. Establish objectives and constraints.
2. Gather, analyze, and validate data.
3. Build an accurate model.
4. Conduct simulation experiments.
5. Document and present results.

16.4 Benchmarking

With benchmarking, we learn from others. Benchmarking involves the search of an organization for the best practices, adaptation of the practices to its processes, and improving with the focus of becoming the best in class. Benchmarking can involve comparisons of products, processes, methods, and strategies. Internal benchmarking makes comparisons between similar operations within an organization. Competitive benchmarking makes comparisons with the best direct competitor. Functional benchmarking makes comparisons of similar process methodologies. Generic benchmarking makes comparisons of processes with exemplary and innovative processes of other companies. Sources of information for benchmarking include the internet, in-house published material, professional associations, universities, advertising, and customer feedback.

16.5 Brainstorming

A brainstorming session is a very valuable means of generating new ideas and involving a group. There are many ways both to conduct a brainstorming session and to compile the information from the session. The generation of ideas can take place formally or informally. Flexibility should exist when choosing an approach because each team and group seems to take on a personality of its own. Described next is a formal process, which can be modified to suit specific needs.

To begin this process of gathering information by brainstorming, a group of people is assembled in a room with tables positioned in a manner to encourage discussion, in the shape of a U, for example. The participants should have different perspectives on the topic to be addressed. The problem or question is written down so that everyone can see it. The following basic rules of the exercise are followed by the facilitator and explained to the members.

1. Ask each member in rotation for one idea. This continues until all ideas are exhausted. It is acceptable for a member to pass a round.
2. Rule out all evaluations or critical judgments.
3. Encourage wild ideas. It may be difficult to generate them; hence, wild ideas should not be discouraged because they

encourage other wild ideas. They can always be tamed down later.

4. Encourage good-natured laughter and informality.
5. Target for quantity, not quality. When there are many ideas, there is more chance of a good idea surfacing.
6. Look for improvements and combinations of ideas. Participants should feel free to modify or add to the suggestions of others.

For the most effective meeting, the leader should consider the following guidelines:

1. The problem needs to be simply stated.
2. Two or more people should document the ideas in plain sight so that the participants can see the proposed ideas and build on the concepts.
3. The name of the participant who suggested the idea should be placed next to it.
4. Ideas typically start slowly and build speed. Change in speed often occurs after someone proposes an off-beat idea. This change typically encourages others to try to surpass it.
5. A single session can produce over 100 ideas, but many will not be practical.
6. Many innovative ideas can occur after a day or two has passed.

A follow-up session can be used to sort the ideas into categories and rank them. When ranking ideas, members vote on each idea that they think has value. For some idea considerations, it is beneficial to have a discussion of the pros and cons about the idea before the vote. A circle is drawn around the ideas that receive the most votes. Through sorting and ranking, many ideas can be combined and others eliminated.

Brainstorming can be a useful tool for a range of questions, from defining the right question to ask to determine the factors to consider within a design of experiments (DOE). Brainstorming sessions can be used to determine, for example, a more effective general test strategy that considers a blend of reliability testing and DOE. The cause-and-effect diagramming tool, as discussed later in this chapter, can be used to assemble thoughts from the sessions. I like to facilitate brainstorming sessions using a computer projector system. This approach can expedite the recording of ideas and dissemination of information after the session.

Computers with specialized network software are now sometimes utilized in administering brainstorming sessions. This tool
can be a very effective means to gather honest opinions whenever
participants might be hesitant to share their views when management or some influential peers are present in the room.

16.6 Cause-and-Effect Diagram

An effective tool as part of a problem-solving process is the cause-
and-effect diagram, also known as an Ishikawa diagram, after its
originator Karoru Ishikawa, or fishbone diagram. This technique
is useful to trigger ideas and promote a balanced approach in
group brainstorming sessions in which individuals list the perceived sources or causes of a problem (i.e., effect). The technique
can be useful, for example, to determine the factors to consider
within a regression analysis or DOE.

A cause-and-effect diagram provides a means for teams to
focus on the creation of a list of process input variables that could
affect KPOVs. With this strategy, we can address strata issues
based on key characteristics (e.g., who, what, where, and when).
The analysis of this stratification later through both graphical
and analytical techniques can provide needed insight for pattern
detection, providing an opportunity for focused improvement
efforts.

When constructing a cause-and-effect diagram, it is often appropriate to consider six areas or causes that can contribute to
a characteristic response or effect: materials, machine, method,
personnel, measurement, and environment. Each one of these
characteristics is then investigated for sub-causes. Sub-causes
are specific items or difficulties that are identified as factual or
potential causes to the problem (i.e., effect).

There are variations to creating a cause-and-effect diagram. A
team may choose to emphasize the most likely causes by circling
them. These causes could, for example, be used as initial factor
considerations within a DOE. Besides the identification of experimental factors within the cause-and-effect diagram, it can also
be beneficial to identify noise factors (n), for example, ambient
room temperature and a raw material characteristic that cannot
be controlled, and factors that can be controlled (c), such as process temperature or speed, by placing the letter n or c next to the
named effect. Figure 16.6 shows another option where focus was

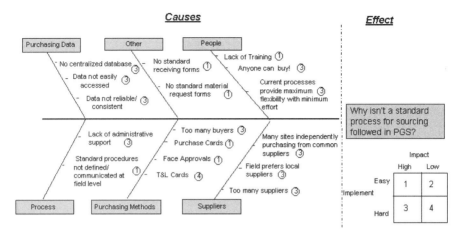

Figure 16.6: Completed cause-and-effect diagram.

given to targeted categories for the effect, and an importance and ease-of-resolution matrix were included.

16.7   Cause-and-Effect Matrix and Analytical Hierarchy Process

A matrix diagram is useful to discover relationships between two groups of ideas. The typical layout is a two-dimensional matrix. A cause-and-effect matrix is sometimes called a prioritization matrix or characteristic selection matrix. This matrix prioritizes items within a matrix diagram.

Cause-and-effect matrices are used to help decide upon the order of importance of a list of items. This list could be activities, goals, or characteristics that were compiled through a cause-and-effect diagram, tree diagram, or other means. Through prioritization, matrices teams have a structured procedure to narrow focus to key issues and opinions that are most important to the organization. The prioritization matrix provides the means to make relative comparisons, presenting information in an organized manner. A quality function deployment (QFD) matrix is an example application of a characteristic selection matrix format (see Breyfogle, 2003a).

Within a cause-and-effect matrix, we can assign relative importance to weights responses. Sometimes these weights are simply assigned by the organization or team. However, there are several

	B: Soft skills	C: Project management	D: Analytic skills	E: Statistical knowledge
A: Fire in the belly	B2	A2	A2	A3
	B: Soft skills	B1	B2	B3
		C: Project management	C1	C3
			D: Analytic skills	D2

1	Low	Low
2	Medium	Medium
3	High	High

Description	Score	Percent
B: Soft skills	8	38
A: Fire in the belly	7	33
C: Project management	4	19
D: Analytic skills	2	10
E: Statistical knowledge	0	0

For example: Tabled B values are B2, B1, B2, and B3, which yields a score of: 2 + 1 + 2 + 3 = 8

Figure 16.7: Illustration of AHP for categories within prioritization matrix: Black belt selection process.

techniques for more objectively establishing these prioritization criteria. The analytical hierarchy process (AHP) is one of these techniques (Canada and Sullivan, 1989). Within the AHP app roach, a number of decision-makers can integrate their priorities into a single priority matrix using a pairwise fashion. This result of this matrix is a prioritization of the factors.

Figure 16.7 shows the result of a paired comparison of all characteristics that are being considered within the selection of black belts. Within this AHP, for example, the cell response of B2 when comparing factor "A: Fire in the belly" with factor "B: Soft skills" would indicate that the team thought factor B was more important than factor A at a medium level. After completing the matrix, the team sums values for all factors and then normalizes these values to a scale, for example 100. An AHP could be used to quantify the importance category used in the creation of a cause-and-effect matrix (i.e., the top numeric row shown in Table 16.1).

The cause-and-effect matrix, or characteristic selection matrix, is a tool that can aid in the prioritization of importance of process input variables. This relational matrix prioritization by a team can help with the selection of what will be monitored to determine if there is a cause-and-effect relationship and whether key process input controls are necessary. The results of a cause-and effect matrix can lead to other activities such as FMEA, multi-vari charts, correlation analysis, and DOE.

Table 16.1: Cause-and-Effect Matrix or Characteristic Selection Matrix Example

		Key process output variables (with prioritization)						Results	Percentage
		A	B	C	D	E	F		
		5	3	10	8	7	6		
	1	4	3		3			53	5.56%
	2	10		4	6		6	174	18.24%
Key	3		4					0	0.00%
process	4			9	5	9	8	241	25.26%
input	5	4				6		62	6.50%
variables	6		6		5		2	52	5.45%
	7	5		4		5		100	10.48%
	8		3		4		5	62	6.50%
	9	6		3		2		74	7.76%
	10		2	4				40	4.19%
	11	4			4	2	5	96	10.06%

To construct a cause-and-effect matrix, do the following:

1. List horizontally the KPOVs that were identified when documenting the process. These variables are to represent what the customer of the process considers important and essential.
2. Assign a prioritization number for each KPOV, where higher numbers have a larger priority (e.g., using values from 1 to 10). These values do not need to be sequential. Figure 16.7 shows the result of a paired comparison of all characteristics that are being considered in the selection of black belts. This procedure could be used to quantify the importance category used in the creation of a cause-and-effect matrix.
3. List vertically on the left side of the cause-and-effect matrix all KPIVs that may cause variability or nonconformance to one or more of the KPOVs.
4. Reach by consensus the amount of effect each KPIV has on each KPOV. Rather than use values from 1 to 10, where 10 indicates the largest effect, consider a scale using levels "0, 1, 3, and 5" or "0, 1, 3, and 9".
5. Determine the result for each process input variable by first multiplying the key process output priority (step 2) by the consensus of the effect for the KPIV (step 4) and then summing up these products.
6. The KPIVs can then be prioritized by the results from step 5 and/or a percentage of total calculation.

Additional cause-and-effect matrix considerations are as follows:

1. Do not duplicate weight values. Try to spread them from 10 to 1.
2. Try to limit the columns from 2 to 5. More than 5 causes too much averaging and the tool loses some power in discrimination.
3. All columns must be independent (e.g., you should not use overall defect rate with another column being a specific defect rate because an improvement to the specific defect will create gains in both columns identically).
4. Two methods in selecting the column measures:
    a) The primary process metric is first and weighted 10. Secondary metrics are then included with weight <5.
    b) If the primary metric has segments (as overall component can be broken into the subcomponents for each major process step, where all step times = total time), then you would use the segment of the primary metric by step on the top of the matrix. In this case, you might weight them based on relative fraction of the primary metric in each category.
5. Considering the Kano model for customer needs, all the column categories should be in the same Kano type. Mixing Kano types is a common problem which causes weighting issues. This could happen if a defect rate column is used (performance metric) along with safety (basic metric) since who could not rate safety as a 10, which would make it equal in weight to the primary project metric. You should just assume all the basic issues are to be considered, but not in the matrix.
6. Keep the number of causes (rows) from 5 to 15. If you get much greater than 15, the tool loses some power of discrimination.
7. Always state the direction of goodness for the column cha racteristics such as reduces cost or improves yields. Stating the column title with a direction of goodness reduces the confusion when scoring the relationship between the columns and rows, where a strong negative relationship and a strong positive relationship may both be scored equally.

The example cause-and-effect matrix shown in Table 16.1 indicates a consensus that focus should be given to KPIVs numbered 2 and 4.

The results from a cause-and effect matrix can give direction for:

- The listing and evaluation of KPIVs in a control plan summary
- The listing and exploration of KPIVs in an FMEA.

16.8 Affinity Diagram

Using an affinity diagram, a team can organize and summarize the natural grouping from a large number of ideas and issues that could have been created during a brainstorming session. From this summary, teams can better understand the essence of problems and breakthrough solution alternatives.

To create an affinity diagram, record each brainstorming idea individually on a self-stick removable note, using at a minimum a noun and verb to describe each item. An affinity diagram often addresses 40–60 items but can assess 100–200 ideas. Next, place the self-stick removable note on a wall and ask everyone, without talking, to move the notes to the place where they think the issue best fits. Upon completion of this sorting, create a summary or header sentence for each grouping. Create subgroups for large groupings as needed with a subhead description. Connect all finalized headers with their groupings by drawing lines around the groupings, as illustrated in Figure 16.8.

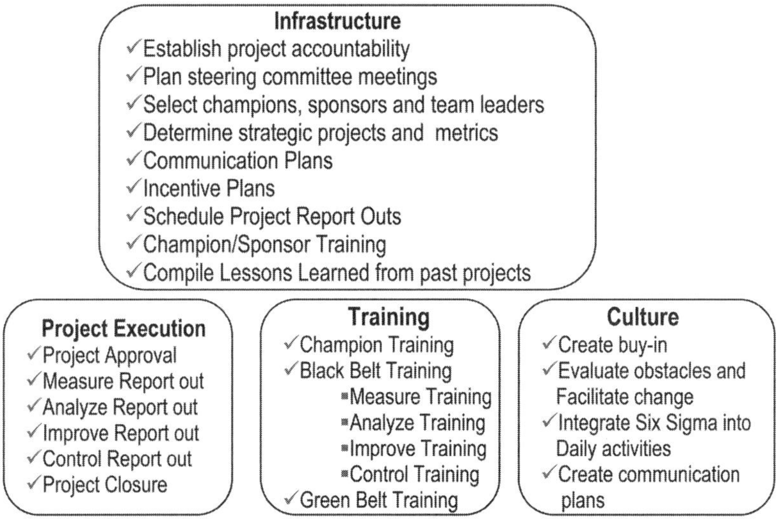

Infrastructure
- ✓ Establish project accountability
- ✓ Plan steering committee meetings
- ✓ Select champions, sponsors and team leaders
- ✓ Determine strategic projects and metrics
- ✓ Communication Plans
- ✓ Incentive Plans
- ✓ Schedule Project Report Outs
- ✓ Champion/Sponsor Training
- ✓ Compile Lessons Learned from past projects

Project Execution
- ✓ Project Approval
- ✓ Measure Report out
- ✓ Analyze Report out
- ✓ Improve Report out
- ✓ Control Report out
- ✓ Project Closure

Training
- ✓ Champion Training
- ✓ Black Belt Training
  - ▪ Measure Training
  - ▪ Analyze Training
  - ▪ Improve Training
  - ▪ Control Training
- ✓ Green Belt Training

Culture
- ✓ Create buy-in
- ✓ Evaluate obstacles and Facilitate change
- ✓ Integrate Six Sigma into Daily activities
- ✓ Create communication plans

Figure 16.8: Affinity diagram: An organizations description of what are the essential elements of a Six Sigma implementation.

16.9   Nominal Group Technique

Nominal group technique (NGT) expedites team consensus on relative importance of problems, issues, or solutions. A basic procedure for conducting an NGT session is described below; however, voting procedures can differ depending upon team preferences and the situation.

An NGT is conducted by displaying a generated list of items, perhaps from a brainstorming session, on a flipchart or board. A final list is then created by eliminating duplications and making clarifications. The new final list of statements is then prominently displayed, and each item is assigned a letter, A, B, ..., Z. On a sheet of paper, each person ranks the statements, assigning the most important a number equal to the number of statements with the least important assigned the value of one. Results from the individual sheets are combined to create a total overall prioritization number for each statement.

16.10   Force Field Analysis

Force field analysis can be used to analyze what forces in an organization are supporting and driving toward a solution and which are restraining progress. The technique forces people to think together about the positives and negatives of a situation and the various aspects of making a change permanent.

After an issue or problem is identified, a brainstorming session is conducted to create a list of driving forces and then a list of restraining forces. A prioritization is then conducted of the driving forces that could be strengthened. There is then a prioritization of the restraining forces that could be reduced to better achieve the desired result. An example presentation format for this information is shown in Figure 16.9, which employs the weight of the line to indicate the importance of a force. Table 16.2 shows example action plans that could be created for restraining forces identified in a force field analysis.

16.11   FMEA

The previous section of this chapter initiated the wisdom of the organization P-DMAIC phase. The following sections of this

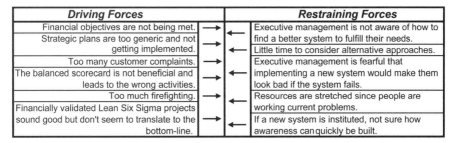

Driving Forces		Restraining Forces
Financial objectives are not being met.	→ ←	Executive management is not aware of how to find a better system to fulfill their needs.
Strategic plans are too generic and not getting implemented.	→	
	←	Little time to consider alternative approaches.
Too many customer complaints.	→	Executive management is fearful that implementing a new system would make them look bad if the system fails.
The balanced scorecard is not beneficial and leads to the wrong activities.	→ ←	
Too much firefighting.	→	Resources are stretched since people are working current problems.
Financially validated Lean Six Sigma projects sound good but don't seem to translate to the bottom-line.	→ ←	
	←	If a new system is instituted, not sure how awareness can quickly be built.

Figure 16.9: Force field analysis for identifying and executing an enhanced system for measurements and improvements.

Table 16.2: Action Items for Restraining Forces for Identifying and Executing an Enhanced System for Measurements and Improvements

Restraining Forces	Action Items
Executive management is not aware of how to find a better system to fulfill their needs.	Dedicate someone to search the Internet for articles and books about improved business systems that aligns business metrics, strategies, and improvement; i.e., more than a just-do-project system. This system is to have a metric reporting system that gets the organization out of the firefighting mode. This information is to be analyzed by a steering committee, which is to provide recommendations for further investigation.
Little time to consider alternative approaches.	Allocate 50% of a leading thinking, influencer person's time to conduct a search for alternative business-system approaches. This person is to investigate opportunities and attend public one-day overview sessions from various providers to see which offering best fits their needs.
Executive management is fearful that implementing a new system would make them look bad if the system fails.	Train a couple Black Belts and then conduct an on-site workout that creates the structure for a business measurement, analysis, and improvement system. With this start small and grow large implementation the downside risks are minimal, while the upside potential is huge.
Resources are stretched since people are working current problems.	Identify a business system that truly gets people out of the firefighting mode, not just do projects that may or may not be truly aligned to business needs.
If a new system is instituted, not sure how awareness can quickly be built.	Identify a business system that has easy-to-read books that can be disseminated to not only employees but suppliers and customers as well. These books and articles need to enhance an understanding of the techniques at various reader's needs and level of understanding.

chapter continue wisdom on the organization application concepts with the failure mode and effects analysis (FMEA) tool.

To be competitive, organizations must continually improve. Potential FMEA is a method that facilitates process improvement. Using FMEAs, organizations can identify and eliminate concerns early in the development of a process or design and provide a form of risk analysis. The quality of procured parts or services can improve when organizations work with their suppliers to implement

FMEAs within their organization. Properly executed FMEAs can improve internal and external customer satisfaction in addition to the bottom line of organizations.

Process FMEAs (PFMEAs) are illustrated in this chapter; however, when executing improvement projects highly ranked cause-and-effect matrix items are typically assessed, as opposed to process steps. PFMEA applications include assembly, machines, work stations, gages, procurement, training of operators, and tests. Design FMEA (DFMEA) applications include component, subsystem, and main system are discussed in Breyfogle (2003a).

Benefits of a properly-executed FMEA include:

* Improved product functionality and robustness
* Reduced warranty costs
* Reduced day-to-day manufacturing problems
* Improved safety of products and implementation processes
* Reduced business process problems

16.12   IEE Application Examples: FMEA

* *Transactional 30,000-foot-level metric*: DSO reduction was chosen as an IEE project. The team used a cause-and-effect matrix to prioritize items from a cause-and-effect diagram. A FMEA was conducted of the process steps and/or highest categories from the cause-and-effect matrix.
* *Manufacturing 30,000-foot-level metric (KPOV)*: An IEE project was to improve the capability/performance metric for the diameter of a manufactured product (i.e., reduce the number of parts beyond the specification limits). The team used a cause-and-effect matrix to prioritize items from a cause-and-effect diagram. A FMEA was conducted of the process steps and/or highest categories from the cause-and-effect matrix.
* *Transactional and manufacturing 30,000-foot-level lead time metric (a Lean metric)*: An IEE project to improve the time from order entry to fulfillment was measured. The team used a cause-and-effect matrix to prioritize items from a cause-and-effect diagram. A FMEA was conducted of the process steps and/or highest categories from the cause-and-effect matrix.
* *Transactional and Manufacturing 30,000-foot-level inventory metric or satellite-level TOC metric (a Lean metric)*: An IEE

project was to reduce inventory. The team used a cause-and-effect matrix to prioritize items from a cause-and-effect diagram. A FMEA was conducted of the process steps and/or highest categories from the cause-and-effect matrix.

- *Manufacturing 30,000-foot-level quality metric*: An IEE project was to reduce the number of defects in a printed circuit board manufacturing process. The team used a cause-and-effect matrix to prioritize items from a cause-and-effect diagram. A FMEA was conducted of the process steps and/or highest categories from the cause-and-effect matrix.

16.13　FMEA Implementation

Timeliness and usefulness as a living document are important aspects of a successful FMEA. To achieve maximum benefit, organizations need to conduct FMEAs before a failure is unknowingly instituted into a process or design.

FMEA input is a team effort, but one individual typically is responsible, by necessity, for its preparation. It is the role of the responsible facilitator to orchestrate the active involvement of representatives from all affected areas. FMEAs should be part of design or process concept finalization that acts as a catalyst for the stimulation and interchange of ideas between functions. A FMEA should be a living document that is updated for design changes and the addition of new information.

Important FMEA implementation issues include the following:

- Use as a living document with periodic review and updates.
- Conduct early enough in development cycle to
  - design potential failure modes out by eliminating root causes.
  - reduce seriousness of failure mode if elimination is not possible.
  - reduce occurrence of the failure mode.

Implementation benefits of a FMEA include the following:

- Early actions in the design cycle save time and money.
- Thorough analysis with teams creates better designs and processes.
- Complete analysis provides possible legal evidence.
- Previous FMEAs provide knowledge leading to current design or product FMEAs.

Team interaction is an important part of creating a FMEA. Organizations should consider using outside suppliers in a FMEA and creating the team so that it consists of five to seven knowledgeable, active members. When executing a FMEA, teams work to identify potential failure modes for design functions or process requirements. They then assign a severity to the effect of this failure mode. They also assign a frequency of occurrence to the potential cause of failure and likelihood of detection. Organizations can differ in approach to assigning numbers to these factors (i.e., severity, frequency of occurrence, and likelihood of detection – sometimes called SOD values), with the restriction that higher numbers are worse. After these numbers are determined, teams calculate a risk priority number (RPN) which is the product of these three numbers. Teams use the ranking of RPNs to focus process improvement efforts.

An effective road map to create FMEA entries is as follows:

- Note an input to a process or design (e.g., process step, key input identified in a cause-and-effect matrix, or design function).
- List two or three ways input/function can go wrong.
- List at least one effect of failure.
- For each failure mode, list one or more causes of input going wrong.
- For each cause, list at least one method of preventing or detecting cause.
- Enter SOD values.

16.14 Development of a Process FMEA

For a process or assembly FMEA, design engineering input is important to ensure the appropriate focus on important design needs. Team effort should include knowledgeable representation from design, manufacturing/process, quality, reliability, tooling, and operators.

A process FMEA presumes that the product meets the intent of the design. A process FMEA does not need to include potential failure modes, causes, and mechanisms originating from the design, though a process FMEA team may choose to include some design issues. The design FMEA covers the effect and avoidance of these issues. A process FMEA can originate from a flowchart that identifies the characteristics of the product/process

Table 16.3: Blank FMEA Form

POTENTIAL
FAILURE MODE AND EFFECTS ANALYSIS

FMEA Type (Design or Process):					Project Name/Description:								Date (Orig.):			
Responsibility:								Prepared By:					Date (Rev.):			
Core Team:													Date (Key):			
Design FMEA (Item /Function) Process FMEA (Function/Requir ements)	Potential Failure Mode	Potential Effect(s) of Failure	S e v	C l a s s	Potential Cause(s) / Mechanism(s) of Failure	O c c u r	Current Controls	D e t e c	R P N	Recommended Actions	Responsibility & Target Completion Date	Actions Taken	S e v	O c c u r	D e t e c	R P N

associated with each operation. Included are appropriate product effects from available design FMEA. The documentation for a FMEA should include its flowchart.

Table 16.3 shows a blank FMEA form. A team determines the process FMEA tabular entries following the guidelines presented in the next section.

16.15 Process FMEA Tabular Entries

A process FMEA in the format of Table 16.3 contains the following:

- *Header Information.* Documents the process description and supplies other information about when and who created the FMEA.
- *Process Function/Requirements from a Process FMEA.* Contains a simple description of the process or operation analyzed. Example processes include assembly, soldering, and drilling. Concisely indicates the purpose of the analyzed process or operation. When numeric assembly operations exist with differing potential failure modes, the operations may be listed as separate processes.
- *Potential failure mode*: Describes how the process could potentially fail to conform to process requirements and/or design intent at a specific operation. Contains for each operation or item/function a list of each potential failure mode in terms of the component, subsystem, system, or process characteristic. Consider how the process/part fails to meet specifications and/or customer expectations. Subsequent or previous operations can cause these failure modes; however, teams should assume the correctness of incoming parts and materials. Items considered are previous problems and new issues foreseen by brainstorming. Includes failure modes

such as broken, incorrect part placement, and electrical short-circuited.

- *Potential effect(s) of failure*: Describes the effects of the failure mode on the function from an internal or external customer point of view. Considers what the customer experiences or the ramifications of this failure mode either from the end-user point of view or from subsequent operation steps. Example end-user effects are poor performance, intermittent failure, and poor appearance. Example subsequent operation effects are "does not fit," "cannot mount," and "fails to open."

- *Severity*: Assesses the seriousness of the effect of the potential failure mode to the customer. Estimation is typically based on a 1 to 10 scale where the team agrees to a specific evaluation criterion for each ranking value. Table 16.4 shows example evaluation criteria for the automotive industry.

- *Classification*: Includes optional information that classifies special process characteristics that may require additional process controls. Applies when government regulations, safety, and engineering specification concerns exist for the product and/or process. An appropriate character or symbol in this column indicates the need for an entry in the recommended action column to address special controls in the control plan.

- *Potential causes(s) of failure*: Describes how failure could occur in terms of a correctable or controllable item. Contains a concise, descriptive, and comprehensive list of all root causes (not symptoms) of failure. The resolution of some causes directly affects the failure mode. In other situations, a DOE determines the major and most-easily-controlled root causes. Includes causes such as human error, improper cure time, and missing part.

- *Occurrence*: Estimates the frequency of occurrence of fai lure without consideration of detecting measures. Gives the number of anticipated failures during the process execution. Consideration of statistical data from similar processes improves the accuracy of ranking values. Alternative subjective assessments use descriptive words to describe rankings. Table 16.5 shows example occurrence criteria.

- *Current process controls*: Describes controls that can prevent failure mode from occurring or detect occurrence of the failure mode. In an update to their booklet, AIAG (2001) changed this from a one-column category to a two-column category, where one column is for prevention, while the other

Table 16.4: Severity Evaluation Criteria Example for Process FMEA

Criteria: Severity of Effect

This ranking results when a potential failure mode results in a final customer and/or a manufacturing/assembly plant defect. The final customer should always be considered first. If both occur, use the higher of the two severities.

Effect	Customer Effect	Manufacturing/Assembly Effect	Ranking
Hazardous without warning	Very high severity ranking when a potential failure mode affects safe vehicle operation and/or involves noncompliance with government regulation without warning.	Or may endanger operator (machine or assembly) without warning.	10
Hazardous with warning	Very high severity ranking when a potential failure mode affects safe vehicle operation and/or involves noncompliance with government regulation with warning.	Or may endanger operator (machine or assembly) with warning.	9
Very high	Vehicle/item inoperable (loss of primary function).	Or 100% of product may have to be scrapped, or vehicle/item repaired in repair department with a repair time greater than one hour.	8
High	Vehicle/item operable but at a reduced level of performance. Customer very dissatisfied.	Or product may have to be sorted and a portion (less than 100%) scrapped, or vehicle/item repaired in repair department with a repair time between a half-hour and an hour.	7
Moderate	Vehicle/item operable but comfort/convenience item(s) inoperable. Customer dissatisfied.	Or a portion (less than 100%) of the product may have to be scrapped with no sorting, or vehicle/item repaired in repair department with a repair time less than a half-hour.	6
Low	Vehicle/item operable but comfort/convenience item(s) operable at reduced level of performance.	Or 100% of product may have to be reworked, or vehicle/item repaired off-line but does not go to repair department.	5
Very low	Fit and finish/squeak and rattle item does not conform. Defect noticed by most customers (greater than 75%).	Or the product may have to be sorted, with no scrap, and a portion (less than 100%) reworked.	4
Minor	Fit and finish/squeak and rattle item does not conform. Defect noticed by 50% of customers.	Or a portion (less than 100%) of the product may have to be reworked, with no scrap, on-line but out-of-station.	3
Very minor	Fit and finish/squeak and rattle item does not conform. Defect noticed by discriminating customers (less than 25%).	Or a portion (less than 100%) of the product may have to be reworked, with no scrap, on-line but in-station.	2
None	No discernible effect.	Or slight inconvenience to operation or operator, or no effect.	1

Source: Reprinted with permission from the *FMEA Manual* (DaimlerChrysler, Ford Motor Company, General Motors Supplier Quality Requirements Task Force).

Table 16.5: Occurrence Evaluation Criteria Example for Process
FMEA.

Probability	Likely Failure Rates	Ranking
Very high: Persistent failures	≥100 per thousand pieces	10
	50 per thousand pieces	9
High: Frequent failures	20 per thousand pieces	8
	10 per thousand pieces	7
Moderate: Occasional failures	5 per thousand pieces	6
	2 per thousand pieces	5
	1 per thousand pieces	4
Low: Relatively few failures	0.5 per thousand pieces	3
	0.1 per thousand pieces	2
Remote: Failure unlikely	≤0.01 per thousand pieces	1

Source: Reprinted with permission from the *FMEA Manual* (DaimlerChrysler, Ford Motor Company, General Motors Supplier Quality Requirements Task Force).

column is for detection. Process controls include control methods such as inspection and poke-yoke (fixture mistake proofing) at the subject or subsequent operations. The preferred method of control is prevention or reduction in the frequency of the cause/mechanism to the failure mode/effect. The next preferred method of control is detection of the cause/mechanism, which leads to corrective actions. The least preferred method of control is detection of the failure mode.

- *Detection*: Assesses the probability of detecting a potential cause/mechanism from process weakness or the subsequent failure mode before the part/component leaves the manufacturing operation. Ranking values consider the probability of detection when failure occurs. Table 16.6 shows example detection evaluation criteria.

- *Risk priority number (RPN).* Product of severity, occurrence, and detection rankings. The ranking of RPN prioritizes design concerns; however, problems with a low RPN still deserve special attention if the severity ranking is high.

- *Recommended Action(s)*: This entry is proposed actions intended to lower the occurrence, severity, and/or detection rankings of the highest RPN failure modes. Example actions include DOE to improve the understanding of causes and control charts to improve the focus of defect prevention/continuous improvement activities. Teams should focus on activities that lead to the prevention of defects (i.e., occurrence ranking reduction) rather than improvement of detection methodologies

Table 16.6: Detection Evaluation Criteria Example for Process FMEA

Detection	Criteria	Inspection Type A	B	C	Suggestion Range of Detection Methods	Ranking
Almost impossible	Absolute certainty of nondetection.			X	Cannot detect or is not checked.	10
Very remote	Controls will probably not detect.			X	Control is achieved with indirect or random checks only.	9
Remote	Controls have poor chance of detection.			X	Control is achieved with visual inspection only.	8
Very low	Controls have poor chance of detection.			X	Control is achieved with double visual inspection only.	7
Low	Controls may detect.		X	X	Control is achieved with charting methods, such as SPC (Statistical Process Control).	6
Moderate	Controls may detect.		X		Control is based on variable gauging after parts have left the station, or Go/No Go gauging performed on 100% of the parts after parts have left the station.	5
Moderately high	Controls have a good chance to detect.	X	X		Error detection in subsequent operations, OR gauging performed on setup and first-piece check (for setup causes only).	4
High	Controls have a good chance to detect.	X	X		Error detection in-station, or error detection in subsequent operations by multiple layers of acceptance: supply, select, install, verify. Cannot accept discrepant part.	3
Very high	Controls almost certain to detect.	X	X		Error detection in-station (automatic gauging with automatic stop feature). Cannot pass discrepant part.	2
Very high	Controls certain to detect.	X			Discrepant parts cannot be made because item has been error-proofed by process/product design.	1

Inspection Types: A. Error-proofed; B. Gauging; C. Manual Inspection.

Source: Reprinted with permission from the *FMEA Manual* (DaimlerChrysler, Ford Motor Company, General Motors Supplier Quality Requirements Task Force).

(i.e., detection ranking reduction). Teams should implement corrective action to identified potential failure modes where the effect is a hazard to manufacturing/assembly personnel. Severity reduction requires a revision in the design and/or process. "None" indicates that there are no recommended actions.

- *Responsibility for recommended action*: Documents the organization and individual responsible for recommended action and target completion date.
- *Actions taken*: Describes implementation of recommended action and effective date.
- *Resulting RPN*: Contains the recalculated RPN resulting from corrective actions that affected previous severity, occurrence, and detection rankings. Blanks indicate no action taken.

The responsible process engineer follows up to ensure the adequate implementation of all recommended actions. A FMEA should include design changes and other relevant actions even after the start of production. Table 16.7 provides an example of a completed process FMEA that has an RPN trigger number of 150, along with a severity trigger number of 7. Table 16.8 is another example of a completed FMEA with an action RPN trigger number of 130.

16.16   Generating a FMEA

Before beginning the discussion on generating a failure mode and effects analysis (FMEA), I want to highlight two philosophies on severity scoring.

One philosophy is that a score of 10 is reserved for death or measurable mortality, no matter what the process. This philosophy makes the point that this is the only way that corporations can look across multiple products and processes to compare that risk aspect. With this process, 7 or 8 might be complete loss of intended business function and 3 or 4 might indicate the realm of non-critical loss.

In another philosophy, it is not considered necessary to make evaluations across multiple products and processes. With this philosophy, the full 1–10 span can be sized to address expected process situation extremes.

Table 16.7: Example – Potential Failure Mode and Effects Analysis (Process FMEA)

FMEA Type (Design or Process): Process	Project Name/Description: Cheetah/Change surface finish of part			Date (Orig.): 4/14
Responsibility: Paula Hinkel	Prepared By: Paula Hinkel			Date (Rev.): 6/15
Core Team: Sam Smith, Harry Adams, Hilton Dean, Harry Hawkins, Sue Watkins				Date (Key):

Design FMEA (Item/Function)/ Process FMEA (Function/Requirements)	Potential Failure Mode	Potential Effect(s) of Failure	S e v	C l a s s	Potential Cause(s)/Mechanism(s) of Failure	O c c u r	Current Controls	D e t e c	R P N	Recommended Actions	Responsibility and Target Completion Date	Actions Taken	S e v	O c c u r	D e t e c	R P N
Solder dipping	Excessive solder/solder wire protrusion	Short to shield cover	9		Flux wire termination	6	100% inspection	3	162	Automation/DOE/ 100% chk with go/no go gage	Sam Smith 6/4	Done	9	4	2	72
	Interlock base damage	Visual defects	7		Long solder time	8	Automatic solder tool	3	168	Automation/DOE/ define visual criteria	Harry Adams 5/15	Done	7	4	2	56
			7		High temp	8	Automatic solder tool/ SPC	3	168	Automation/DOE	Hilton Dean 5/15	Done	7	4	2	56
	Delamination of interlock base	Visual defects	7		See interlock base damage	8	Automatic solder tool/ SPC	3	168	Automation/DOE	Sue Watkins 5/15	Done	7	4	2	56
	Oxidization of golden plating pins	Contact problem/no signal	7		Moisture in interlock base	5	No	7	245	Inform supplier to control molding cond.	Harry Hawkins 5/15	Done	7	2	7	98
			8		Not being cleaned in time	7	Clean in 30 minutes after solder dip	5	280	Improve quality of plating define criteria with customer	Sam Smith 5/15	Done	8	2	5	80
Marking	Marking permanency test	Legible marking/ customer unsatisfaction	6		Marking ink	4	SPC	2	48	None						
			6		Curing	5	UV energy and SPC	3	90	None						
			6		Smooth marking surface	8	None	6	288	Rough surface	Sam Smith 5/15	Change interlock texture surface	6	3	6	108

Source: Pulse, a Technitrol Company, San Diego, CA (Jim Fish and Mary McDonald).

Table 16.8: Example – Potential Failure Mode and Effects Analysis (PFMEA)

FMEA Type (Design or Process):		Project Name/Description: Business operations of A to Z imports									Date (Orig.): 6/11				
Responsibility:		Prepared By: KC									Date (Rev.): 7/31				
Core Team: KC, JG, LM											Date (Key):				
Design FMEA (Item/Function) Process FMEA (Function/Requirements)	Potential Failure Mode	Potential Effect(s) of Failure	C l a s s / S e v	Potential Cause(s)/Mechanism(s) of Failure	O c c u r	Current Controls	D e t e c	R P N	Recommended Actions	Responsibility and Target Completion Date	Actions Taken	S e v	O c c u r	D e t e c	R P N
Business Operations	Shut down	Loss of income/bankruptcy	9	Tornado hits location	3	None	10	270	Install weather channel radio in store, and keep on during store hours	JG 7/8	Installed and tested	9	3	2	54
			9	Law suit by visitor hurt in store during visit	3	Insurance coverage against accidents in store	2	54	None						
			9	Law suit by visitor owing to faulty merchandise	5	Warning labels on merchandise	2	90	None						
			9	Electrical fire burns down store	2	Fire extinguishers and sprinklers	10	180	Install ground fault interruptors, and overload/thermal protection on all high wattage fixtures	LM 6/28	Installed GFIs and thermal protection	9	2	1	18
			9	IRS audit shows misreporting of finances	5	CPA audits accounts at tax time	4	180	Change procedure to allow closing of books every 6 months, and CPA to audit the same	KC 7/15	Procedure changed, accounting personnel and CPA informed	9	2	2	36
			9	Excessive competition	5	Agreement with property owners on limiting number of import stores	2	90	None						

Table 16.8: (Continued)

Potential Failure Mode	Potential Effects	SEV	Potential Causes	OCC	Current Controls	DET	RPN	Recommended Actions	Resp. / Date	Actions Taken	SEV	OCC	DET	RPN
Earnings growth does not meet targets	Delayed loan repayments	9	Loss of lease	10	Rental agreement on month to month basis, automatically renews	10	900	Negotiate with leasing company to change lease agreement to yearly	KC 7/19	Talked matter over with property owners, obtained verbal assurance, but lease stays month to month	9	10	10	900
		6	Sales staff impolite	4	Job interview at time of hiring	5	120	Institute sales training of new hires for half day in addition to existing training. Do not assign to floor if candidate's performance in sales training is suspect	KC 8/2	Sales training module added to existing training package	6	2	2	24
		6	Excessive competition	5	Agreement with property owners on limiting number of import stores	2	60	None						
		6	Supplier delays owing to late payments	3	None	10	180	Conduct FMEA on this cause, treating it as a failure mode itself						
		6	Local economy slows	5	None	10	300	Monitor area growth thru quarterly checks with the local Chamber of Commerce	JG 7/15	Obtained population growth for city, and income statistics for quarter ending March 31st.	6	5	2	60
		6	Store untidy	9	Employees have standing orders to attend customers first; and upkeep of store second.	1	54	None						

I can see the advantage of each philosophy. A company should decide what best works for them. The following illustration utilizes the second philosophy.

The following describes FMEA generation management to minimize team time and improve success rate.

1	2	3	4	5	6	7	8	9		← Column
Design FMEA (Item /Function) Process FMEA (Function/Requirements)	Potential Failure Mode	Potential Effect(s) of Failure	S e v	C l a s s	Potential Cause(s) / Mechanism(s) of Failure	O c c u r	Current Controls	D e t e c	R P N	Recommended Actions	Responsibility & Target Completion Date	Actions Taken	S e v	O c c u r	D e t e c	R P N

1. The black belt project leader determines the FMEA format based on. (column 1).
    a. Process steps.
    b. Key items from the cause-and-effect analysis that require further development.
    c. Participating organizations or business units (e.g., what are the risks of a problem occurring in procurement, engineering, and sales).
2. Initiate the FMEA with only the black belt and the process subject matter expert (SME), who is preferably the current process owner (columns 2, 3).
    a. Use the SME knowledge to identify the current process failure modes and effects.
        i.   Failure mode is how the process failed.
        ii. Failure effect is how the failure is recognized in the process.
    b. Avoid it could happen failures unless they are catastrophic in nature, such as items considered in a safety analysis or that there is a risk interrupting business operations.
3. Convene the team to work the cause and controls columns (columns 6, 8).
    (a) First review the failure mode and effects columns. Discuss with the SME if any common issues were not included. Add entries, if appropriate; however, avoid it could happen issues.
    (b) Ask the team for potential causes for each failure mode. Each failure cause is entered on a new line, where prior columns entries are copied down to the new line.
    (c) If a cause is identified that is really the effect of prior causes, consider adding this to the potential failure mode column and continuing.

(d) The team lists the current in-place controls that are to detect or avoid the occurrence of the cause listed in the same column. The described control should not be what could be done but what is currently being done.

(e) Adjourn for the day so that everyone can think about what was done. Provide each participant with a hard or electronic copy of the developed FMEA.

4. Convene the team to perform the scoring.

(a) Start with severity (column 4). The severity code is for the identified failure effect in the same row.

   (i) Review one of the default severity scoring tables (e.g., Table 16.4).

   (ii) Determine the most severe failure effect for this project, consider it as 10.

   (iii) Determine the least severe failure effect for this project, consider it a 1.

   (iv) As a group determine a few intermediate conditions of severity and provide them with numeric values from 2 to 9.

   (v) For each failure effect (column 3 entry) score its severity. Every repeated failure effect should have the same score. If the team wants to score them differently, the effect is probably not adequately defined. For example, there might be two defective part entries that should be scored with different severities. This difference might occur because one defective situation involves scrapping defective units, while another defective situation involves reworking defective units. For this situation, two failure effects could be generated where one is defective part-scrapped and another is defective part – reworked.

   (vi) Review all the severity scores to ensure the values are all appropriate, which is defined only to each other. "Are they in the right order of severity?".

(b) Score occurrence rate (column 7). This is the occurrence rate of the identified cause in the same row.

   (i) Review one of the default occurrence rate scoring tables (e.g., Table 16.5).

   (ii) Determine the most frequent occurrence rate of the causes for this project, consider it a 10.

   (iii) Determine the least frequent occurrence rate effect for this project, consider it a 1.

(iv) As a group determine a few intermediate conditions of occurrence rate and provide them with
numeric values from 2 to 9.

(v) For each cause (column 6 entry) score its occurrence rate. Every repeated cause should have the
same score. If the team wants to score them differently, they are probably not adequately defined.

(vi) Review all the occurrence rate scores to ensure ap-
propriateness of the assigned values. In this assessment focus on how well they are assigned to
each other (i.e, are they in the right rating order?).

(c) Score the current controls (column 9). This is the controls for the cause listed in the same line. The detec-
tability of the cause at its source or point of occurrence
can be considered in place of a control system.

(i) Review one of the default controls scoring tables
(e.g., Table 16.6).

(ii) Set the condition where there are no controls as a 10.

(iii) Determine the best set of controls for the causes in
this project, consider it a 1. This is the case where
the cause is virtually 100% avoided.

(iv) Now as a group determine a few intermediate conditions of controls/detectability and provide them
with numeric values ranging from 2 to 9.

(v) For each listed control (column 8 entry) score the
ability to identify and avoid the cause in the same
row. Every repeated control should have the same
score. If the team wants to score them differently, they are probably not adequately defined. This
may come where the control is a review or approval
step. It may need to be modified to be a review of
xxx (i.e., describe review step) or approval of xxxx
(i.e., describe approval step) so that different control scores may be used.

(vi) Review all the control scores to ensure the values
are all appropriate relative to each (i.e., Are they in
the right order of effectiveness?).

16.17 Exercises

1. Create a process flowchart that describes your early morning activities. Consider the day of the week in the process

flowchart. List KPIVs and KPOVs. Identify steps that add value and steps that do not add value. Consider what could be done to improve the process.

2. Create a process flowchart that describes the preparation and conducting of a regular meeting that you attend. List KPIVs and KPOVs. Identify steps that add value and steps that do not add value. Consider what could be done to improve the process.

3. List a process that impacts you personally at school or work. Consider what metrics could be created to get focus on how much the process needs improvement.

4. Document and/or research a process in work, school, community, or personal life. List KPIVs, KPOVs, and appropriate metrics. Examples include the criminal conviction process, your investment strategy, a manufacturing process, and college admission process.

5. Describe how you are going to document a process for your IEE project.

6. Create a more detailed process flow chart from the SIPOC described in an earlier exercise.

7. Create a cause-and-effect diagram of improvement opportunities for the previously identified project.

8. Describe tools that can help initiate breakthrough change.

9. Even when all brainstorming rules are followed, what is a common execution problem when preparing and executing a brainstorming session?

10. Describe past instances when an existing process exhibited a breakthrough for process improvement.

11. Conduct a FMEA of a pencil. Consider that the function is to make a black mark. Requirements could include that it is to make a mark, it marks a black color, and it intermittently fails to mark. Failure modes would then be that it makes no mark at all, mark is not black in color, and it marks intermittently.

12. Conduct a FMEA on implementing Lean Six Sigma within an organization where there is a "push for project creation" implementation.

13. For your project create a cause-and-effect diagram where causes are identified as either noise (n) or controllable (c) factors.

    (a) Use Minitab to create the cause-and-effect diagram, where a "c" is place in front of the word if the cause is controllable and an "n" if the cause is noise.

(b) How many noise and controllable factors did you create?

(c) Comment on the procedure to create the diagram using a software program versus using sticky-pad notes to input a thought to a cause-and-effect diagram that is created on the wall.

PART IV
Improvement Project Roadmap: Analyze Phase

Starting with the process map in conjunction with the cause-and-effect diagram, cause-and-effect matrix, and FMEA, we can look for information systems that have the data for testing relationships. This data can be transformed into information through the reviewing of reports and data analysis. When appropriate data sources are not present, we can interview subject matter experts (SMEs) and/or collect our own data.

The chapters in this part of this volume address the analysis of data for the purpose of learning about causal relationships. Information gained from this analysis can provide insight into the sources of variability and unsatisfactory performance, and help improve processes. The tools in this phase are primarily passive. The reason for this is that within this phase the level of input variables from the wisdom of the organization are observed passively to see whether a relationship can be detected between them. If there is an observed relationship, this knowledge can help focus improvement efforts. When data are not readily available, it may be appropriate in the analyze phase to start conducting proactive design of experiments (DOE) tests immediately (see Chapter 29).

Tools included in this section include visualization of data, inference testing, variance components, regression, and analysis of variance (ANOVA). Improvements can be made in any phase of DMAIC. Tools in this phase can be used at the E-DMAIC level and later to quantify statistically and describe pictorially project improvements.

17

P-DMAIC – Analyze Phase: Data Collection Plan and Experimentation Traps

17.1 P-DMAIC Roadmap Component

The graphic in this section highlights the P-DMAIC roadmap steps (see Appendix Section D) that are described in this chapter. Appendix Section E contains the tollgate check sheets for this and other phases.

Among other things the define phase described the project and the measure phase created the 30,000-foot-level baseline metric. In addition, another measure phase output from a project execution's wisdom of the organization phase yield theories about what potential KPIVs could impact the response levels. Starting with the process map in conjunction with the cause-and-effect diagram, cause-and-effect matrix, and FMEA, we can look for information systems that currently collect desired data. This data can be transformed into information through the reviewing of reports and data analysis. When appropriate data sources are not present, we can interview subject matter experts and/or collect our own data.

Changes are appropriate when there is general consensus that one or more changes will benefit the process. If these changes did provide an improved process response, the 30,000-foot-level chart

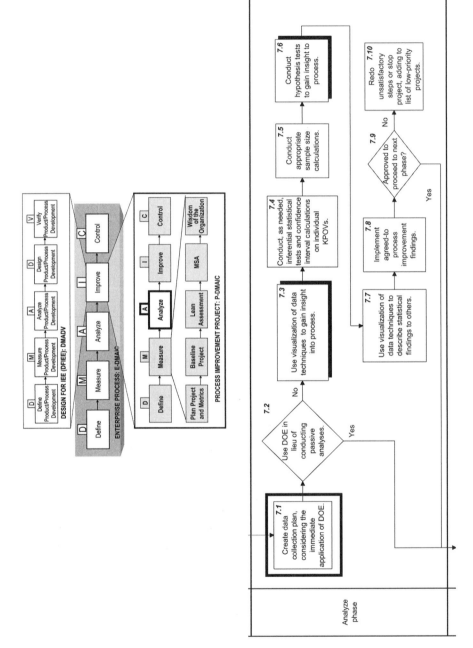

would statistically shift to a new, improved region of stability/predictability.

Within the overall project execution roadmap, we typically should react as though we are not sure whether there is any merit to the wisdom of the organization theory or hypothesis, until there are supporting data analyses. In addition, for theories that have merit, we typically would like a statistical estimate for how much the factor's input level is expected to impact the process response's level.

Lastly, there are situations in which an input factor's level is found to impact significantly the output response level; however, there are no obvious solutions as to what process change can be implemented to reduce its overall response-output-level impact (e.g., differences between machines or people). This type of situation can lead to the creation of new systems that originate from creative problem-solving techniques or DOEs, providing additional insight to solution alternatives.

In the analyze phase, passive analysis techniques act like a funnel where many potential key process input variable (KPIV) factors are reduced to a few KPIV factors. The end result of this factor funneling is the knowledge gained to where targeted focusing efforts should be made for process improvements efforts.

17.2 Solution Determination Process

Project solutions are to improve a key process output variable (KPOV) or Y variable in the relationship $Y = f(X)$, where X is a KPIV. A solution to a project problem might be the control of one or more Xs or a fundamental process change. In projects, we want to bridge from tribal knowledge, which was captured in the wisdom of the organization roadmap phase, to a solution implementation. If a solution is obvious after capturing wisdom-of-the-organization inputs and the solution is easily implemented, the impact from a just-do-it implementation can be assessed at the 30,000-foot-level.

However, if a solution is not obvious, a "who dunnit" investigation facilitated through the identification and examination of clues can lead to a solution. The creation of an environment for generating insightful clues is accomplished through data examination. In the analyze phase, data are passively assessed against hypotheses, using both visualization and statistical tools.

Table 17.1: Example Solution Determination Table for HR
On-Boarding Process

Identified KPIV	Problem		Potential Causes
	Condition	Severity	
Job levels	High job grades is larger	12 days	Relocation
			Additional interviews
			Negotiations
Site	Site B is larger	8 days	Using different process

A solution determination table can help with the visualization of this thought process. Consider that in the Human Relations (HR) process an identified problem was that the length of time to on-board people was too long. Table 17.1 illustrates a solution determination procession for two identified analyze phase KPIVs, which during the analyze phase were found to be have a statistically significant impact on the KPOV.

To have the opportunity to undergo this thought process we need to compile data in a format that can be analyzed. This will be discussed in the next session.

17.3   Data Collection Plan Needs, Source, and Types

Data collection is the execution of a systematic plan for taking measurements of key variables in an efficient and effective manner. Data collection is the foundation of analyzing and understanding processes. An operational definition for the collection of data is an easy-to-follow procedural translation for the measurements and their discussion. A data collection plan (DCP) that accomplishes operational definition needs addresses:

- what to measure
- how to measure it
- when and where to measure it
- how many measurements to make
- how to record the data
- determine if customers and suppliers use the same measurement procedures, when appropriate
- a method to assess the variation of the data collection process

Populations are often too large to analyze in their entirety. A random sample of data from the population can be used to estimate characteristics of the population, as illustrated in Figure 17.1.

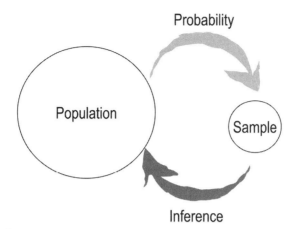

Figure 17.1: Sample's relationship to population.

The following describes the various types of population sample data, while Table 17.2 lists data origination sources which are:

- Numerical
  - Can perform arithmetic operations on the data
  - Can be continuous data (e.g., a measurement of salary, weight, volume, length)
  - Can be discrete (e.g. number of children, number of defects)
  - Can be attribute (e.g., percent yield or percent defective)
- Categorical
  - Cannot perform arithmetic operations on the data
  - Classify the data (e.g. color, gender)

Sources for data in a process include historical data, current process data, new process measurement, and experimentation. Each source of data has pros and cons.

17.4   Data Collection Tools

Data collection tools, which are described in more detail below, include:

- Check Sheets
  - Basic
  - Confirmation

Table 17.2: Data Source Options with Pros and Cons

Data Source	Pros	Cons
Historical	Cheap, Quick, Available, Familiar, Quantity	Accuracy, Relevance, Misleading, Outdated, May not be right variable
Current Process	Current Data, Relevant, Knowledge of Accuracy, No Additional Cost, Available	May be Long Collection Time, Data Collection tied to Process Cycle, Process May Change, May Not be Right Variable
New Process Measurement	Current Data, Right Variable, Knowledge of accuracy, New information, May be short term	Costs Money and Time, Process May Change, Impacts Process
Experimentation	Efficient, Effective, Economic, Provides New Process Knowledge (data)	Costs Money and Time, Requires Expertise, Could interfere with process or production

- Frequency plot
- Location
- Traveler
• Automated data collection
• Sampling
  - Random
  - Stratified
  - Systematic
• Surveys
  - Questionnaires
  - Interviews
• Infrequent sampling
• Design of experiments (DOE)

It can save time to format data collection sheets to match the format that would be entered into analysis software. For analyses, data typically needs to be in columns, where each row is an observation.

It is a good practice to add dummy data into the newly created data collection sheets. An analysis of this data as though it were real could identify issues with the sheets. This check can lead to the avoidance of time and money collecting data that is not in a format conducive to analyses.

Check sheets provide a simple standardized recording methodology for data collection from historical or current observations.

Effort needs to be given to making the collection process as mistake proof as possible. Information from check sheets can indicate patterns and trends. After agreement is reached on the definition of events or conditions, data are collected over a period of time and then summarized.

The format of a basic check sheet is shown in Table 17.3. The use and format for a confirmation check sheet, frequency plot check sheet, location check sheet, and traveler check sheet are described below.

Confirmation check sheet incorporates checking off process steps to confirm that they have been completed.

In the frequency plot check sheet, event or items are captured over time in an operational process. For example, to create a frequency check sheet that captures type of defects observed over time, adjust the Table 17.3 format so that the "week" column is replaced by "completed repairs" and the rows labeled "defect" are replaced by "date."

Data collectors use a location check sheet to describe physically where on a part defects occur. This check sheet can provide insight to where to target improvement efforts.

A traveler check sheet travels with the transaction or work item. Sequential entries and time stamps are made at all process operations. Traveler sheets can be a good vehicle for determining lead times, value-add times, work delays, etc.

Automated data collection utilizes electronic computerized systems to monitor events through software (e.g., the time stamping of a transaction flow). The benefit of this type of data collection is that KPIVs and KPOVs can be monitored with improved data quality and collection time, providing real time process analysis opportunities. Problems include the expense and time to create the system, which might have limited change flexibility. In addition, frequent sampled data can be auto-correlated, which can lead to phantom special cause signals, if care is not exercised.

Table 17.3: Basic Check Sheet Format

Defect	Week			Total
	1	2	3	
A	III	IIIII	II	10
B	I	II	II	5
C	IIII	I	I	6

Sampling can be:

- Random
    - Taken using a procedure to ensure there is no bias in the order in which items are selected
    - A random number statistical function generator can be used to plan random sampling
- Stratified
    - Divides the population into groups of interest (strata)
    - Then usually applies random sampling within the group
- Systematic
    - Sets a regular schedule for sampling based on frequency (every 10th item is selected), or based on time (every hour)

Current Enterprise Resource Planning (ERP) systems can provide access to all data in the business process transactional world. When capturing over time orders, invoices, inventory adjustments, etc., there can be millions of data points. Sampling effectively from these populations can be a challenge.

If we want to capture all forms of variation, an approach that could be used is to load the million records into an Access database. A random sample of 20,000 records during period of time could then be selected and analyzed. Or we might randomly select and compile 1000 records for each subgroup period/strata, noting the other variable settings for each record.

Another form of data collection is surveys. The purpose of surveys is to obtain opinions, reactions, knowledge or ideas about an issue. Within surveys it is important that error associated with non-response bias and with non-truthful responses is minimized.

Surveys contain a group of carefully worded questions so that responses are not biased. Often a Likert scale of 1–5 represents category codes. Surveys can be conducted as questionnaires or interviews. Expertise is required to develop and administer surveys, which can involve a marketing research department or the services of an independent survey firm.

Infrequent subgrouping/sampling provide a big picture view of processes, which can involve a smaller number of samples than alternative methods. This sampling captures and quantifies the overall impact of KPIV variability without the intent of developing a full understanding of the contribution from each. As an illustration, suppose that potential KPIVs are machine, time of day, and raw material that changed daily. For this situation, we could test whether the process is in control/predictable with one daily sample. For the in-control/predictable region of a process, the data collectively can be analyzed to describe the process customer experience.

DOE (see Chapters 29–34) is typically included as an improvement tool in Six Sigma roadmaps. This approach can be very beneficial in that the analysis of existing data can give insight to what factors and level of factors should be considered in a DOE. However, sometimes there are no current data or the current data is sketchy. In addition, there are other times when it is believed that nothing can be gained by taking the time to compile and analyzing historical data. For these situations, it can be most appropriate to bypass passive analysis tools and go directly to a DOE.

17.5   Sampling Error Sources

Sampling error can be measured with probability theory, as described in later chapters. Non-sampling error must be controlled by using appropriate sampling procedures (e.g., well designed survey instruments). Non-response bias occurs in surveys when only a portion of the samples respond. Non-truthful responses usually result when sensitive questions are asked. Measurement error occurs when we are not answering the right question.

When collecting data, sample size trade-offs need consideration. The amount of required data depends on the specific project and improvement goals and is a function of the desired confidence level and sample variability. Other factors that need to be considered are sample costs, timely data collection, and control of non-sampling error.

The technical details of the sampling will be covered in later modules; however, it is important to reiterate that the sample needs to be a random sample of the population. This is often not easy to do (e.g., a large sample of today's transactions is not a random sample of future transactions). If a random sample cannot be obtained for passive analyses, a DOE may be more appropriate to gain process understanding.

17.6   Experimentation Traps

Randomization is used in experiments and in data collection when attempting to avoid experimental bias. However, there are other traps that can similarly yield erroneous conclusions. For example, erroneous statements can result from not considering measurement error, poor experiment design strategy, erroneous assumptions, and/or data analysis errors.

Invalid conclusions can easily result when good statistical experimentation techniques are not followed. Perhaps more erroneous conclusions occur because of this than from inherent risks associated with the probability of getting a sample that is a typical. The next four sections illustrate examples associated with poor experiment methodology. These problems emphasize the risks associated with not considering measurement error, lack of randomization, confused effects, and not tracking the details of the implementation of an experiment design.

17.7   Example 17.1: Experimentation Trap – Measurement Error and Other Sources of Variability

Consider that the data in Table 17.4 are the readings (in 0.001 of a centimeter (cm)) of a functional gap measured between two mechanical parts. The design specifications for this gap were 0.008 ± 0.002 cm. This type of data could be expected from the measurements in a manufacturing line, when the 16 random samples were taken over a long period of time.

However, there are two areas that are often not considered in enough detail when making such an evaluation: first, how samples are selected when making such an assessment of the capability/performance of the response; second, the precision and accuracy of the measurement system are often overlooked.

Relative to sampling methodology, consider the experimenter who is being pressed for the characterization of a process. He/she may take the first product parts from a process and consider them to be a random sample of future process builds. This type of assumption is not valid because it does not consider the many other variability sources associated with processes (e.g., raw material lot-to-lot variability that might occur over several days).

In regard to the measurement systems analysis, it is often assumed that gages are more precise than they really are. It is

Table 17.4: Ten Random Samplings from a Normal PDF with Mean 6 and Standard Deviation 2

Within-Group Sample Number	Sampling Group Numbers									
	1	2	3	4	5	6	7	8	9	10
1	2.99	7.88	9.80	6.86	4.55	4.87	5.31	7.17	8.95	3.40
2	6.29	6.72	4.04	4.76	5.19	8.03	7.73	5.04	4.58	8.57
3	2.65	5.88	4.82	6.14	8.75	9.14	8.90	4.64	5.77	2.42
4	10.11	7.65	5.07	3.24	4.52	5.71	6.90	2.42	6.77	5.59
5	5.31	7.76	2.18	8.55	3.18	6.80	4.64	10.36	6.15	9.92
6	5.84	7.61	6.91	3.35	2.45	5.03	6.65	4.17	6.11	4.63
7	2.17	7.07	4.18	4.08	7.95	7.52	2.86	6.87	5.74	7.48
8	4.13	5.67	8.96	7.48	7.28	9.29	8.15	8.28	4.91	8.55
9	7.29	8.93	8.89	5.32	3.42	7.91	8.26	6.60	6.36	6.10
10	5.20	4.94	7.09	3.82	7.43	5.96	6.31	4.46	5.27	6.42
11	5.80	7.17	7.09	5.79	5.80	6.98	8.64	7.08	5.26	4.46
12	5.39	2.33	3.90	4.45	6.45	6.94	1.67	6.97	5.37	7.02
13	10.00	3.62	5.68	5.19	7.72	7.77	7.49	4.06	2.54	5.86
14	9.29	7.16	7.18	5.57	3.53	7.12	6.14	10.01	6.69	4.80
15	4.74	9.39	7.14	4.42	7.69	3.71	2.98	2.20	7.89	9.60
16	5.19	7.98	2.36	7.74	5.98	9.91	7.11	5.18	5.67	5.92
$\bar{x}$	5.77	6.74	5.96	5.42	5.74	7.04	6.23	5.97	5.88	6.30
s	2.41	1.86	2.30	1.59	1.97	1.69	2.19	2.38	1.42	2.14

typically desirable to have a measurement system that is at least ten times better than the range of the response that is of interest. Measurement error can cause ambiguities during data analysis. The basic sources for error need to be understood to manage and reduce their magnitude and to obtain clear and valid conclusions. The variability from a measurement tool can be a large term in this equation, leading to erroneous conclusions about what should be done to reduce process variability.

The measured variability of parts can have many sources such as repeatability, the variability associated with the ability of an appraisers' getting a similar reading when given the same part again (σ_1^2); reproducibility, the variability associated with the ability of differing appraisers obtaining a similar reading for the same part (σ_2^2); and measurement tool-to-tool (σ_3^2), within lots (σ_4^2), and between lots (σ_5^2). The total variability (σ_T^2) for this example would be equal to the sum of the variance components, which are

$$\sigma_T^2 = \sigma_1^2 + \sigma_2^2 + \sigma_3^2 + \sigma_4^2 + \sigma_5^2$$

Measurements will include all these sources of variability. The precision of the measurements of parts is dependent on $\sigma_T{}^2$. In addition, the accuracy depends upon any bias that occurs during the measurements.

Someone in manufacturing could be confronted with the question of whether to reject initial product parts, given the information from any column of Table 17.4. With no knowledge about the measurement system, a large reproducibility term, for example, can cause good parts to be rejected and bad parts to be accepted. Variance components and measurement systems analysis (see Chapter 24) can provide an estimate of the parameters in this equation.

17.8   Example 17.2: Experimentation Trap – Lack of Randomization

Table 17.5 shows measurements that were made sequentially to assess the effect of pressure duration on product strength.

From the data plot of Figure 17.2, strength appears to have increased with duration; however, from the preceding table it is noted that the magnitude of pressure duration was not randomized relative to the test number.

The collection of data was repeated in a random fashion to yield the data shown in Table 17.6. From the data plot in Figure 17.3, strength does not now appear to increase with duration. For an unknown reason, the initial data indicate that strength increases with the test number. Often such unknown phenomena can cloud test results. Perhaps the first two samples of the initial experiment were taken when the machine was cold, and this was the real reason that the strength was lower. Randomization reduces the risk of an unknown phenomenon affecting a response, leading to an erroneous conclusion.

Table 17.5 Sequential Measurements to Determine Pressure Duration on Product Strength

Test Number	Duration of Pressure (sec)	Strength (lb.)
1	10	100
2	20	148
3	30	192
4	40	204
5	50	212
6	60	208

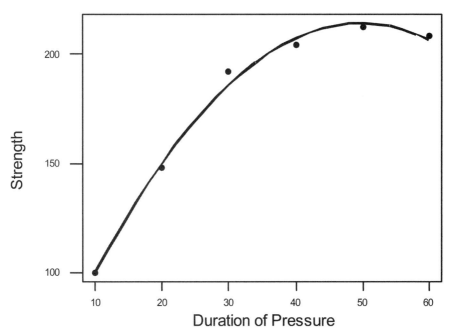

Figure 17.2: Plot of the first set of experimental data.

Table 17.6: Randomized Measurements to Determine Pressure Duration on Product Strength

Test Number	Duration of Pressure mean(sec)	Strength (lb.)
1	30	96
2	50	151
3	10	190
4	60	200
5	40	210
6	20	212

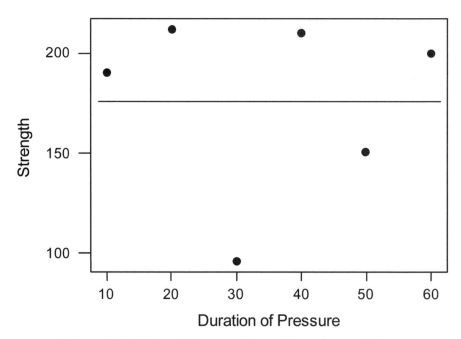

Figure 17.3: Plot of the second set of experimental data.

17.9   Example 17.3: Experimentation Trap – Confounded Effects

The following strategy was used to determine if resistance readings on wafers are different when taken with two types of probes and/or between automatic and manual readings. Wafers were selected from 12 separate part numbers G_1 through G_{12}, as shown in Table 17.7.

However, with this experiment design, the differences between probes are confused with the differences between part numbers. For example, wafer G_1 is never tested with probe type 2; hence, this part number could affect our decision whether probe type significantly affects the resistance readings. Table 17.8 indicates a full factorial design that removes this confusing effect. Note that future chapters will illustrate other test alternatives to full factorial experiment designs that can reduce experiment time dramatically.

17.10   Example 17.4: Experimentation Trap – Independently Designing and Conducting an Experiment

A system under development had three different functional areas. In each of these areas, there were two different designs that could be used in production.

Table 17.7 Initial Experiment Strategy for Example: Wafers are represented by "G" numbers

Automatic
Probe type 1   G1, G2, G3, G4
Probe type 2   G5, G6, G7, G8, G9, G10, G11, G12

Manual
Probe type 1   G1, G2, G3, G4
Probe type 2   G5, G6, G7, G8, G9, G10, G11, G12

Table 17.8: Revised Experiment Strategy for Example: A dash indicates the tabular position of a datum point

	------------ Auto ---------------		----------- Manual --------	
	Probe 1	Probe 2	Probe 1	Probe 2
G1	--	--	--	--
G2	--	--	--	--
.	.	.	.	.
.	.	.	.	.
.	.	.	.	.
G11	--	--	--	--
G12	--	--	--	--

To evaluate the designs, an engineer built eight special systems, which contained all combinations of the design considerations (i.e., a full factorial DOE). The systems were built according to the matrix shown in Table 17.9, in which the functional areas are designated as *A, B,* and *C,* and the design considerations within these areas are designated either as plus mean (+) or minus mean (–).

The engineer then gave the eight systems to a technician to perform an accelerated reliability test. The engineer told the technician to note the time when each system failed and to call him after all the systems had failed. The engineer did not tell the technician that there were major differences between each of the test systems. The technician did not note any difference because the external appearance of the systems was similar.

After running the systems for 1 day, the technician accidentally knocked one of the systems off the table. There was no visible damage; however, the system now made a different sound when operating. The technician chose not to mention this incident because of the fear that the incident might affect his work performance rating. At the end of the test, the technician called the engineer to give the failure times for the eight systems.

During the analysis, the engineer did not note that one of the systems had an early failure time with an unexpected mode of failure. Because of schedule pressures from management, the engineer's decision was based only on "quick and dirty" statistical analysis of the mean effects of the factors without conducting a residual analysis (see Chapter 25). Unknown to the engineer, the analytical results from this experiment led to an erroneous and very costly decision.

Table 17.9: Full Factorial DOE Trials

Functional Area

System Number	A	B	C
1	+	+	+
2	+	+	–
3	+	–	+
4	+	–	–
5	–	+	+
6	–	+	–
7	–	–	+
8	–	–	–

This type of experiment trap can occur in industry in many forms. It is important for the person who designs a test to have some involvement in the details of the test activity. When breaking down the communication barrier that exists in this example, the test designer may also find some other unknown characteristic of the design/process that is important. This knowledge along with some interdepartmental brainstorming can yield a better overall basic test strategy.

Wisely applied DOE techniques can be very beneficial to improve the bottom line. A DOE does not have to investigate all possible combinations of the factor levels. Later it will be described how seven two-level factors can be assessed in only eight trials.

17.11   Sampling Considerations

Readers might state that it is hard to believe that they could ever fall into one or more of the preceding example traps. However, within an individual experiment these traps can be masked; they may not be readily identifiable to individuals who are not aware of the potential pitfalls.

The reader may conclude from the previous examples that it will suggest that all combinations of the parameters or factors need direct experimental assessment during test. This is not usually true; experimental design techniques are suggested that are manageable within the constraints of industry. This objective is achieved by using design matrices that yield much information for each test trial.

Random sampling plans are based on the assumption that errors are independent and normally distributed. In real data, this independence assumption is often invalid, yielding serious inaccuracies. If appropriate, randomization is introduced as an approximation alternative when conducting an experiment. The adoption of the randomization approach has the advantage that it does not require information about the nature of dependence. However, there are situations where randomization is not appropriate. To illustrate this, consider stock market prices. The magnitude of the closing price on a given day is dependent on its closing price the previous day.

One approach to this data-dependence issue is that of a specific model for dependence. If such a model is valid, it is possible to develop procedures that are more sensitive than those that depend only on randomization. Box *et al.* (1978) illustrates with elementary examples that the ability to model dependence using time series can lead to problem solutions in the areas of forecasting, feedback control, and intervention analysis.

The sampling plans described later assume that the process is stable/predictable. If the measurements are not from a stable/predictable process, the test methodology and confidence statements can be questionable. Even if an experiment strategy is good, the lack of stability can result in erroneous conclusions.

17.12 Example 17.5: Continuous Response Data Collection

One 30,000-foot-level corporate metric for a company is on-time product delivery. The company has several facilities that ship product. The corporate on-time metric is the compilation of a similar metric from each facility.

In the past, on time delivery was viewed as an attribute pass/fail output (i.e., was the product was received on time or not); 9 months ago the organization started examining the response as a continuous output, since more information could be gleaned from the data using this format. Agreement was reached that a product delivery response of 1.7 would indicate that a product shipment was received 1.7 days late, while a response of –3.2 would indicate that the product was received 3.2 days early.

It was believed that day of the week for product shipment could impact the output; hence, weekly subgrouping/sampling was selected for the 30,000-foot-level metric tracking. Each week 20 shipments were randomly selected by facility (i.e., four random samples per day). The mean and log standard deviation of weekly delivery time from all sites were each tracked using an individuals control chart.

Since the on-time product delivery 30,000-foot-level control chart tracking showed a process shift 14 weeks ago, data will be compiled from this point in time. Wisdom of the organization thoughts are that on-time delivery could be influenced by product shipped, day of the week shipped, facility shipping the product, and delivery distance.

The team believed that an understanding of which parameters that affected the output would give them insight to what could be done to improve the process. Data entries would be made using the spreadsheet format:

Shipment Number	Days Late	Product Shipped	Day of the Week Shipped	Site Shipped	Delivery Distance

17.13 Example 17.6: Attribute Response Data Collection

One 30,000-foot-level metric for a distribution company is the number of shipments that have overage, shorts, or damage. Since shipments contain multiple items, the rate for both defective shipments and defective items within the shipments are tracked. The company delivers 7 days a week. It is believed that the failure rate could differ by the day of the week; hence, the 30,000-foot-level control chart has weekly subgrouping/sampling.

Wisdom of the organization thoughts are that there could be a difference in the frequency of defective shipments or defective items in the shipments by operator, area, type of failure, shift, and day of the week. Since there are data integrity concerns with the current data, a data collection sheet needs to be created so that the data can later be easily compiled for analyses. Since the output is attribute pass/fail, the data will need to be reduced for each analysis (e.g., shipment defective rate by shift) into a format such as that shown in Table 17.10, which illustrates a weekly example data collection sheet.

Since the 30,000-foot-level control chart showed a process shift 14 weeks ago, the compiled data will be from this point in time.

Table 17.10: Example Weekly Data Collection Sheet, Pass/Fail Output

Day	Operator name*	Area	Shift	Part Count				
				Pass	Fail over	Fail short	Fail damaged	Total Parts

* Every operator has one row. Can later be easily reformated for analyses in statistical software.

17.14 Exercises

1. What are the benefits and disadvantages of the different sources of data?
2. What are the considerations for determining sample size?
3. In a data collection sheet intending to collect information on the type of defect in a production or transaction, you have the choice to have the person pick the defect name from a list or to write it in a blank space on the form. Which choice would you choose? Why?

18

P-DMAIC – Analyze Phase: Visualization of Data

18.1 P-DMAIC Roadmap Component

Chapter 16 described techniques for consensus determination of potential key process input variables (KPIVs). The previous chapter described data-collection considerations when compiling information to test wisdom of the organization generated theories (i.e., conduct hypothesis tests). The graphic in this section highlights the P-DMAIC roadmap steps (see Appendix Section D.1) that are described in this chapter. Appendix E contains the tollgate check sheets for this and other phases.

The importance of getting to know your data and graphing is essential. When analyzing collected data we strive to both create a visual representation of the situation and conduct a hypothesis test. It can be deceiving to just look at hypothesis test results.

Previous chapters presented some graphical techniques that could describe information visually. These techniques included histograms, time series plots, probability plotting, control charts, cause-and-effect diagrams, and Pareto charts. This chapter describes additional visualization techniques, while Chapters 20–28 describe various hypothesis tests.

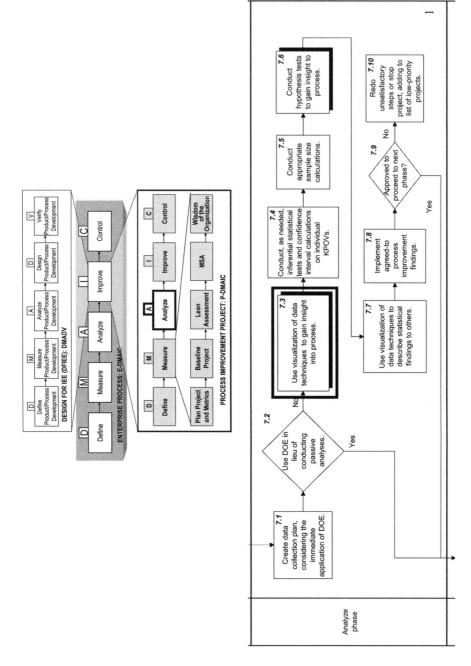

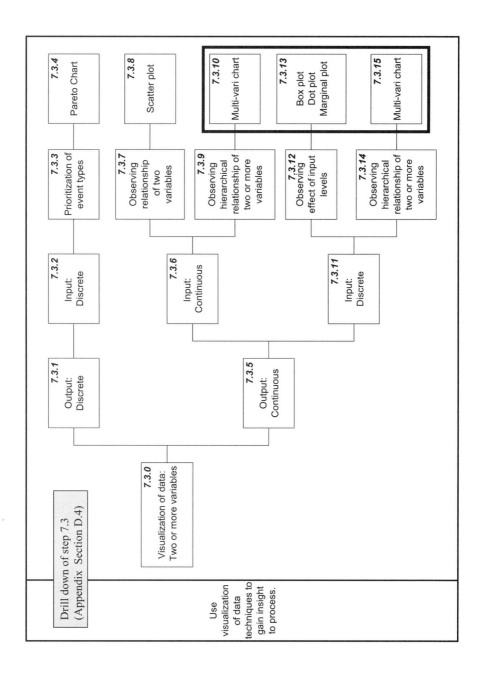

Through these exploratory data analysis (EDA) tools, we can compile data into groups or strata based on key character- istics (e.g., who, what, where, and when). The visualization of this stratification can help detect a pattern which provides an opportunity for improvement efforts focus (i.e., provide visual insight into KPIVs to KPOVs (key process output variables) rela- tionships). The visualization offered by these techniques allows us to assess a great deal of information about the process with- out modifying it and to determine where to focus improvement efforts.

With these tools, we can both visually and statistically look for differences between samples, interrelationships between vari- ables, and changeover time. Knowledge gained from these tests can suggest process modifications, KPIV control needs, or design of experiments (DOE) opportunities.

18.2 IEE Application Examples: Visualization of Data

- *Transactional 30,000-foot-level metric*: days sales outstand- ing (DSO) reduction was chosen as an Integrated Enterprise Excellence (IEE) project. A cause-and-effect matrix ranked company as an important input that could affect the DSO response (i.e., the team thought that some companies were more delinquent in payments than other companies). A box plot and marginal plot were created from sampled data to show visually the similarities and differences in DSO response times by company.
- *Manufacturing 30,000-foot-level metric*: An IEE project was to improve the process capability/performance metric of a manufactured product diameter (i.e., reduce the number of parts beyond the specification limits). A cause-and-effect matrix ranked cavity of the mold as an important input that could be yielding different part diameters. A box plot and marginal plot were created from the sampled data to show visually the similarities and differences in part diameter by cavity.
- *Transactional and Manufacturing 30,000-foot-level lead time metric (a Lean metric)*: An IEE project to improve the time from order entry to fulfillment was measured. A cause-and- effect matrix ranked department as an important input that could affect the overall order entry time response (i.e., the

team thought that some departments did not process orders as quickly as others). A box-plot and marginal plot were created from sampled data to show visually the similarities and differences in order entry times by department.

- *Transactional and Manufacturing 30,000-foot-level inventory metric or satellite-level* theory of constraints *(TOC) metric (a Lean metric)*: An IEE project was to reduce inventory. A cause-and-effect matrix ranked work in progress (WIP) by production line as an input that could affect the overall inventory response. A box plot and marginal plot were created from sampled data to show visually the similarities and differences in WIP by production line.
- *Transactional 30,000-foot-level metric*: An IEE project was to reduce wait time for incoming calls in a call center. A cause-and-effect matrix ranked time of call as an important input that could affect the overall wait time. Sampled hierarchical data were collected and presented in a multi-vari chart. This chart showed variability within hours of a 12-h workday, between hours, between days of the week, and between weeks of the month. The multi-vari chart showed a consistently large wait time around noon on Fridays.

18.3 Box Plot

A box plot (or box-and-whisker plot) is useful for describing various aspects of data pictorially. Box plots can visually show differences between characteristics of a data set.

Figure 18.1 shows the common characteristics of a box plot. The box displays the lower and upper quartiles (the 25th and 75th percentiles), and the median (the 50th percentile) appears as a horizontal line within the box. The whiskers are then often extended to:

Lower limit: $Q_1 - 1.5(Q_3 - Q_1)$
Upper limit: $Q_3 + 1.5(Q_3 - Q_1)$

In this case, points outside the lower and upper limits are considered to be outliers and are designated with asterisks (*). The whisker length rule is set so that a small sample from a normal distribution will capture all points in the whiskers. No asterisks are seen until the sample sizes get large.

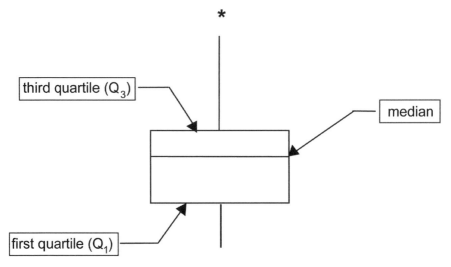

Figure 18.1: Box plot characteristics.

18.4   Example 18.1: Plots of Injection-Molding Data – Box Plot, Marginal Plot, Main Effects Plot, and Interaction Plot

An injection-molding process made plastic cylindrical connectors (Taylor, 1991). Every hour for 3 hours, two parts were selected from each of four mold cavities. Measurements were made at each end and in the middle. The data are shown in Table 18.1.

Techniques applied in this example are box plot, marginal plot, main effects plot, and interaction plot. The box plot in Figure 18.2 shows the differences in the sample by cavity. The marginal plot of the data stratification in Figure 18.3 permits the visualization of the distribution of data in both the x and y direction. The main effects plot in Figure 18.4 quantifies the average difference noted between cavities.

From the interaction plot in Figure 18.5 it appears that there is an interaction between cavity and position (i.e., lines are not parallel) (see Figure 29.1). Parts from cavities 2, 3, and 4 were wider at the ends, while cavity number one had a taper. That is, the center dimension is lowest for cavities 2, 3, and 4, while the center measurement in cavity 1 is midway. From this plot we get a pictorial quantification of the average difference between these three cavities as a function of position.

Table 18.1: Multi-vari Chart Injection-Molding Data

Part	Location	Time 1 Cavity 1	2	3	4	Time 2 Cavity 1	2	3	4	Time 3 Cavity 1	2	3	4
1	Top	0.2522	0.2501	0.2510	0.2489	0.2518	0.2498	0.2516	0.2494	0.2524	0.2488	0.2511	0.2490
	Middle	0.2523	0.2497	0.2507	0.2481	0.2512	0.2484	0.2496	0.2485	0.2518	0.2486	0.2504	0.2479
	Bottom	0.2518	0.2501	0.2516	0.2485	0.2501	0.2492	0.2507	0.2492	0.2512	0.2497	0.2503	0.2488
2	Top	0.2514	0.2501	0.2508	0.2485	0.2520	0.2499	0.2503	0.2483	0.2517	0.2496	0.2503	0.2485
	Middle	0.2513	0.2494	0.2495	0.2478	0.2514	0.2495	0.2501	0.2482	0.2509	0.2487	0.2497	0.2483
	Bottom	0.2505	0.2495	0.2507	0.2484	0.2513	0.2501	0.2504	0.2491	0.2513	0.2500	0.2492	0.2495
	avg	0.25158	0.24982	0.25072	0.24837	0.25130	0.24948	0.25045	0.24878	0.25155	0.24923	0.25017	0.24867

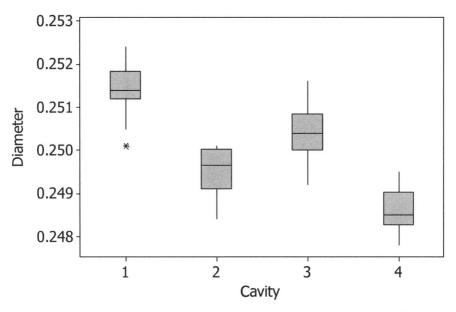

Figure 18.2: Box plot of diameter versus cavity.

Personally I do not like to use a main effects plot for this type of analysis since only the mean is plotted and the graph gives no indication about variability and sample size. I like to use a main effects plot in DOE to describe the amount of factor significance.

The box plot does not give an indication of sample size. A large sample size box plot can look very similar to a small sample size box plot. When the sample size is not large I like to get a picture that provides a feel for the sample size in the same plot. For small sample sizes, I think that it is important to have sample size visual when mentally quantifying differences and variability. Because of this, I prefer to use a dot plot or marginal plot when there are not many samples.

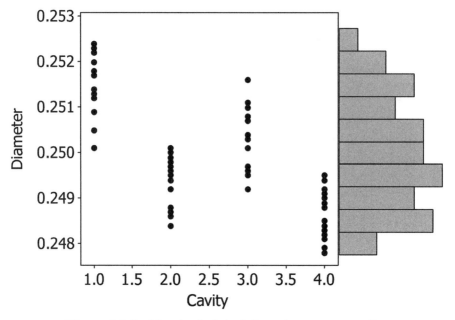

Figure 18.3: Marginal plot of diameter versus cavity.

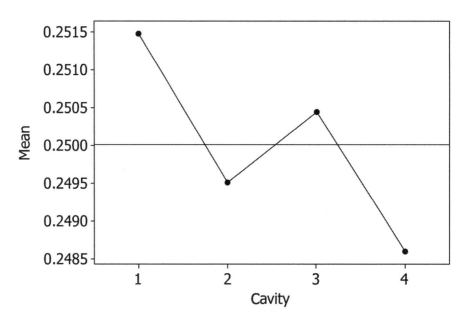

Figure 18.4: Main effects plot of mean cavity differences.

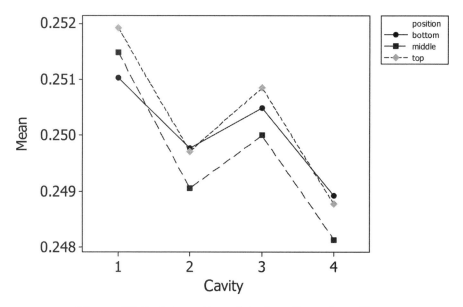

Figure 18.5: Interaction plot of cavity and position.

18.5   Multi-Vari Charts

Leonard Seder (1950) can be given credit for introducing the multi-vari chart, which is described in this section.

Within a discrete manufacturing environment, contributing factors to overall variability of a response include differences between time periods, production tool differences, part-to-part variations, and within-part variability. Within a continuous flow manufacturing process, contributing factors to overall variability include within shifts, across shifts, and across days/weeks/months. Multi-vari charts allow visual decomposition into components and the identification of the component that affects variability the most.

Considerations when constructing a multi-vari chart are as follows:

- If there are many measurements within a part, the average, highest, and lowest values could be used.
- Reconstruction of the chart using various arrangements for the axes can aid in the detection of patterns and relationships.
- Connecting mean values on the chart can aid the visual representation.

Visual observations can lead to the use of other analytical tools that test hypotheses. These techniques include variance component analysis and analysis of means (discussed in Chapters 24 and 26). Information gained from these analyses can lead to effective targeting of process improvement efforts.

18.6   Example 18.2: Multi-Vari Chart of Injection-Molding Data

This example expands upon the previous chart analysis of data in Table 18.1. The technique applied in this example is the multi-vari chart, which is shown in Figure 18.6.

From the observation of the multi-vari chart it appears that:

- Any difference between time periods appears to be small.
- Differences occur between cavities for a given time period (largest variation source).

Cavities 2, 3, and 4 appear to have thicker ends, while cavity 1 has a slight taper; 16 of the 18 parts from cavities 2, 3, and 4 exhibit a "V" pattern.

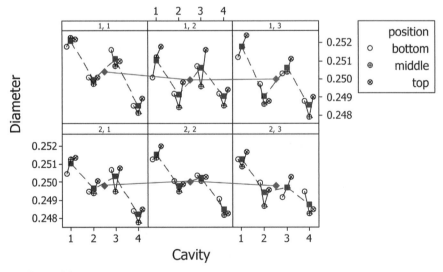

Panel variables: part, time

Figure 18.6: Multi-vari chart for diameter by position within part.

Another option for presentation of multi-vari information is to use a mean effects plot of each variable source consideration. These data will later be analyzed in Chapters 26 and 24 as a statistical hypothesis using analysis of means and variance components techniques.

18.7 Applying IEE

Presenting information in the form of graphs and charts can be very enlightening. Visual representation of data can alert the analyst to erroneous data points or the invalidity of some statistical tests. It can give information that leads to the discovery and implementation of important process improvements. In addition, visual representations can be used to present information in a form quickly understood by others.

However, visual representations of data should not be used alone to formulate conclusions. What appears to be an important observation in a visual representation could simply be something that has a relatively high chance of occurring. Hence, it is important to test observation theories using hypothesis techniques before formulating conclusions and action plans. We need to blend statistical analysis with pictures of the data so that we can maximize our insight to information that can be gleaned from the data.

Another factor should be considered when attempting to formulate conclusions from observed data. Consider the situation in which temperature was monitored within a process and not found to be a statistically significant factor affecting a KPOV. One might then disregard the possibility of changing the temperature of a process to improve the response of the KPOV. We need to remember that the visual and analytical tools described typically consider only the current operating range of the KPIVs. In other words, changing the temperature of a process to a value either higher or lower than its current operating value could prove to be a statistically significant improvement. DOE techniques can complement these visual techniques by offering a means to extend the knowledge gained to other factors and levels of factors beyond normal operating conditions.

The *wise* implementation of graphical techniques, hypothesis tests, DOE techniques, and other statistical tools can be a very powerful combination, yielding very beneficial process measurement and improvement activity.

18.8 Exercises

1. An experiment was conducted where each student recorded his/her height, weight, gender, smoking preference, usual activity level, and resting pulse. Then they all flipped coins, and those whose coins came up heads ran in place for 1 min. Then the entire class recorded their pulses once more (Minitab, 2007).

   Create a multi-vari chart that provides insight into the effect of factors.

Column	Name	Count	Description
C1	Pulse2	92	Second pulse rate
C2	Ran	92	1 = ran in place 2 = did not run in place
C3	Smokes	92	1 = smokes regularly
			2 = does not smoke regularly
C4	Gender	92	1 = male 2 = female

Pulse2	Ran	Smokes	Gender		Pulse2	Activity	Smokes	Gender
88	1	2	1		64	2	2	1
70	1	2	1		84	2	1	1
76	1	1	1		62	2	2	1
78	1	1	1		58	2	2	1
80	1	2	1		50	2	2	1
84	1	2	1		62	2	1	1
84	1	2	1		68	2	1	1
72	1	2	1		54	2	1	1
75	1	2	1		76	2	2	1
118	1	2	1		84	2	2	1
94	1	1	1		70	2	2	1
96	1	2	1		88	2	1	1
84	1	1	1		76	2	2	1
76	1	2	1		66	2	1	1
76	1	2	1		90	2	2	1
58	1	2	1		94	2	1	1
82	1	1	1		70	2	1	1
72	1	1	1		70	2	2	1
76	1	1	1		68	2	2	1
80	1	2	1		84	2	2	1
106	1	2	1		76	2	2	1

Pulse2	Ran	Smokes	Gender	Pulse2	Activity	Smokes	Gender
76	1	2	1	66	2	2	1
102	1	2	1	84	2	2	2
94	1	1	1	70	2	2	2
140	1	2	2	60	2	2	2
100	1	2	2	92	2	1	2
104	1	1	2	66	2	2	2
100	1	2	2	70	2	2	2
115	1	1	2	56	2	2	2
112	1	2	2	74	2	1	2
116	1	2	2	72	2	2	2
118	1	2	2	80	2	2	2
110	1	1	2	66	2	2	2
98	1	1	2	76	2	2	2
128	1	2	2	74	2	2	2
62	2	2	1	78	2	2	2
62	2	2	1	68	2	2	2
74	2	1	1	68	2	2	2
66	2	2	1	80	2	2	2
76	2	2	1	76	2	1	2
66	2	1	1	84	2	2	2
56	2	1	1	92	2	1	2
70	2	2	1	80	2	2	2
74	2	2	1	68	2	2	2
68	2	2	1	84	2	2	2
74	2	1	1	76	2	2	2

2. Create a box plot of the previous data set with pulse 2 as the response and gender as the category.

3. Discuss the value of the techniques presented in this chapter and explain how they can be applied to IEE projects.

4. Select various tools to describe visually the data from the two machines that are in Exercise 8.11. Comment on results.

5. The CODND for the situation described in Exercise 12.4 was excessive. A wisdom of the organization study for this improvement project yields potential KPIVs as inspector, machine, process temperature, material lot, and day-to-day variability relative to within day variability. The data below were collected to assess these relationships. Use visualization of data techniques to describe differences

between inspectors, machines, material lot, and day-to-day variability relative to within-day variability.

Sub-group	Within Subgroup	KPOV	Temperature	Machines	Inspector Lot No.	Material
1	1	98.731	88.3954	1	1	21
1	2	98.943	81.4335	2	2	21
1	3	97.712	74.9126	3	1	21
1	4	107.912	79.0657	1	2	21
1	5	97.266	76.5458	2	1	21
2	1	87.394	74.9122	3	2	55
2	2	96.018	72.1005	1	1	55
2	3	98.764	82.7171	2	2	55
2	4	100.563	77.0318	3	1	55
2	5	98.305	86.3016	1	2	55
3	1	113.91	81.3605	2	1	10
3	2	109.791	90.9656	3	2	10
3	3	115.205	80.8889	1	1	10
3	4	116.298	78.649	2	2	10
3	5	116.837	81.4751	3	1	10
4	1	120.052	78.3577	1	2	33
4	2	111.994	73.9516	2	1	33
4	3	110.041	71.0141	3	2	33
4	4	119.676	87.6358	1	1	33
4	5	119.242	78.8888	2	2	33
5	1	107.035	83.6368	3	1	26
5	2	105.492	81.9133	1	2	26
5	3	111.519	73.8307	2	1	26
5	4	114.119	80.4301	3	2	26
5	5	100.468	77.4916	1	1	26
6	1	98.436	84.3751	2	2	29
6	2	102.282	82.0356	3	1	29
6	3	92.957	80.1013	1	2	29
6	4	100.247	80.5547	2	1	29
6	5	107.214	78.7169	3	2	29
7	1	89.928	81.3302	1	1	45
7	2	90.444	77.6414	2	2	45
7	3	98.23	78.9692	3	1	45
7	4	89.86	80.3613	1	2	45
7	5	88.137	80.282	2	1	45
8	1	104.424	82.6526	3	2	22

Sub-group	Within Subgroup	KPOV	Temperature	Machines	Inspector Lot No.	Material
8	2	102.7	88.0823	1	1	22
8	3	97.119	74.2354	2	2	22
8	4	101.723	78.962	3	1	22
8	5	102.168	75.926	1	2	22
9	1	93.209	86.1496	2	1	67
9	2	98.536	73.1816	3	2	67
9	3	102.683	82.8007	1	1	67
9	4	111.545	79.6613	2	2	67
9	5	105.954	81.8933	3	1	67
10	1	89.059	80.1729	1	2	8
10	2	91.914	83.8426	2	1	8
10	3	91.172	82.3181	3	2	8
10	4	95.646	80.6746	1	1	8
10	5	105.608	81.7851	2	2	8
11	1	106.586	85.6406	3	1	102
11	2	100.76	80.5955	1	2	102
11	3	106.271	84.1347	2	1	102
11	4	108.019	82.5592	3	2	102
11	5	105.288	81.927	1	1	102
12	1	103.583	90.0957	2	2	3
12	2	122.339	86.0469	3	1	3
12	3	110.341	88.5115	1	2	3
12	4	107.661	81.2703	2	1	3
12	5	111.157	72.8305	3	2	3
13	1	103.785	82.6283	1	1	88
13	2	100.825	81.2085	2	2	88
13	3	95.79	81.2694	3	1	88
13	4	104.117	75.9062	1	2	88
13	5	108.512	89.9129	2	1	88
14	1	109.769	85.4022	3	2	67
14	2	109.791	87.6654	1	1	67
14	3	110.307	83.7251	2	2	67
14	4	106.365	78.1496	3	1	67
14	5	99.336	88.5317	1	2	67
15	1	112.115	81.8326	2	1	76
15	2	111.952	83.8367	3	2	76
15	3	109.979	90.6023	1	1	76
15	4	124.777	78.7755	2	2	76
15	5	110.935	80.0546	3	1	76

Sub-group	Within Subgroup	KPOV	Temperature	Machines	Inspector Lot No.	Material
16	1	88.464	79.3654	1	2	55
16	2	95.487	74.0516	2	1	55
16	3	91.104	86.9088	3	2	55
16	4	100.842	82.2633	1	1	55
16	5	85.606	85.141	2	2	55
17	1	110.206	96.0845	3	1	90
17	2	103.991	75.3364	1	2	90
17	3	110.982	86.5558	2	1	90
17	4	109.633	83.5594	3	2	90
17	5	113.925	67.5415	1	1	90
18	1	94.751	80.982	2	2	87
18	2	102.563	77.4577	3	1	87
18	3	101.663	88.3292	1	2	87
18	4	98.483	83.6419	2	1	87
18	5	88.963	86.0019	3	2	87
19	1	103.387	77.5763	1	1	65
19	2	108.197	82.1948	2	2	65
19	3	105.23	78.6831	3	1	65
19	4	103.677	75.5058	1	2	65
19	5	95.469	88.4383	2	1	65
20	1	96.668	75.6825	3	2	13
20	2	97.482	84.6413	1	1	13
20	3	102.466	72.9894	2	2	13
20	4	101.277	78.5712	3	1	13
20	5	103.000	82.8468	1	2	13

19

Confidence Intervals and Hypothesis Tests

The last chapter described visualization tools. This chapter provides the foundation of conducting statistical tests, which can be used both in the project analyze and improve phases. This foundation also applies to analyses at the enterprise level.

Statistically a population is a group of data from a single distribution. In a practical sense, a population could also be considered to be a segment or a group of data from a single source or category. In the process of explaining tools and techniques, multiple populations may be discussed as originating from different sources, locations, or machines.

Descriptive statistics help to pull useful information from data, whereas probability provides among other things a basis for inferential statistics and sampling plans. In this chapter, focus will be given to inferential statistics where we will bridge from sample data to statements about the population. That is, properties of the population are inferred from the analysis of sample.

Samples can have random sampling with replacement and random sampling without replacement. In addition, there are more complex forms of sampling such as stratified random sampling. For this form of sampling a certain number of random samples are drawn and analyzed from divisions of the population space.

We can also have systematic sampling where a sample might be taken after 20 parts are manufactured. We can also have subgroup sampling where five units might be drawn every hour.

From a random sample of a population, we can estimate characteristics of the population. For example, the mean of a sample ($\bar{x}$) is a point estimate of the population mean (μ). This chapter introduces the topic of confidence intervals that give probabilistic ranges of values for true population characteristics from sampled data. Application of the central limit theorem to this situation will also be illustrated.

Hypothesis tests address the situation of making a selection between two choices from sampled data (or information). Because we are dealing with sampled data, there is always the possibility that our sample was not an accurate representation of the population. Hypothesis tests address this risk. The techniques described in this chapter provide the basis for statistical significance tests of stratifications that were thought important by teams when executing IEE projects.

One thing we need to keep in mind is that something can be statistically significant but have no practical importance. For example, a study of 10,000 transactions determined that a new procedure reduced the time to complete a transaction from 90 minutes to 89 minutes and 59 seconds. The difference of 1 second may be statistically significant but have no practical importance to the process. Note that a difference can be found to be statistically significant if the sample size is large enough. This is one of the reasons we need to blend statistical analyses with pictures of the data so we can maximize our insight to information that can be gleaned from the data.

When a parametric distribution is assumed during analyses, parametric estimates result. When no parametric distribution is assumed during analyses, nonparametric estimates result. Focus in this volume is given to parametric estimates; however, nonparametric estimates are also discussed.

19.1   Sampling Distributions

Distributions are applicable for both populations and sampling. Previously population distributions, sometimes called parent distributions, were discussed. The described distributions for a continuous response were normal, lognormal, and Weibull. For an attribute response, the binomial distribution was applied to pass/fail situations and the Poisson distribution was utilized for count data. This section describes sampling distributions.

From a population, samples can be taken with the objective of characterizing a parameter of the population (e.g., population-mean confidence interval). A distribution that describes the characteristic of this sampling is called the sampling distribution or child distribution. These distributions are used in hypothesis tests.

The shape of the distribution of a population does not usually need to be considered when making confidence interval statements about the population mean (see Chapter 20) because the sampling distribution of the mean tends to be normally distributed; that is the central limit theorem, which is described later in this chapter.

19.2 Confidence Interval Statements

As noted earlier, the mean of a sample does not normally equate exactly to the mean of the population from which the sample is taken. An experimenter has more confidence that a sample mean is close to the population mean when the sample size is large and less confidence when the sample size is small. Statistical procedures quantify the uncertainty of a sample through a confidence interval statement.

A confidence interval can be single-sided or double-sided. A confidence interval statement can also relate to other characteristics besides mean values (e.g., population variance). The following statements are examples of single- and double-sided confidence interval statements about the mean.

$$\mu \leq 8.0 \qquad \text{with 95\% confidence}$$
$$2.0 \leq \mu \leq 8.0 \qquad \text{with 90\% confidence}$$

Similar statements can be made about standard deviation and other population characteristics. The mechanics of determining confidence intervals for various situations are discussed in Chapters 20 and 22. An application of this methodology is completion of Steps 3.4 and 8.24 of the improvement project execution roadmap, which is shown in Appendix Section D.1.

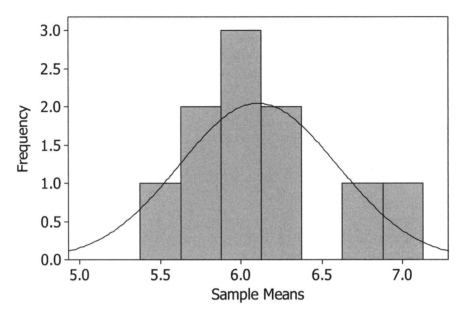

Figure 19.1: Plot of sample mean values.

19.3   Central Limit Theorem

The central limit theorem is an important theoretical basis of many statistical procedures, such as calculation of the confidence interval of a sample mean. It states that a plot of *sampled mean values* from a population tends to be normally distributed. Figure 19.1 indicates that a plot of the 10 sample mean values from Table 17.4 has the shape of a normal distribution. The distribution of mean values taken from a population will tend to be normal even when the underlying distribution is not normal. The standard deviation of this sampling distribution is $s/\sqrt{n}$, where s is the sample standard deviation and n is the sample size. For a given standard deviation, the spread of the sampling distribution decreases when sample size increases; that is we have more confidence in our results when sample size is large.

19.4   Hypothesis Testing

In industrial situations, we frequently want to decide whether the parameters of a distribution have particular values or relationships.

That is, we may wish to test a hypothesis that the mean or standard deviation of a distribution has a certain value or that the difference between two means is zero. Hypothesis testing procedures are used for these tests. Here are some practical examples:

1. A manufacturer wishes to introduce a new product. In order to make a profit, he needs to be able to manufacture 1200 items during the 200 work hours available for the workforce in the next 5 weeks. The product can be successfully manufactured if the mean time that is required to manufacture an item is no more than six labor hours per part. The manufacturer can evaluate manufacturability by testing the hypothesis that the mean time for manufacture is equal to 6 hours.
2. The same manufacturer is planning to modify the process to decrease the mean time required to manufacture another type of product. The manufacturer can evaluate the effectiveness of the change by testing the hypothesis that the mean manufacturing time is the same before and after the process change.

Both of these situations involve tests on the mean values of populations. Hypothesis tests may also involve the standard deviations or other parameters.

A statistical hypothesis has the following elements:

-   A null hypothesis (H_0) that describes the value or relationship being tested.
-   An alternative hypothesis (H_a).
-   A test statistic, or rule, used to decide whether to reject the null hypothesis.
-   A specified probability value (noted as α) that defines the maximum allowable probability that the null hypothesis will be rejected when it is true.
-   The power of the test, which is the probability (noted as $[1-\beta]$) that a null hypothesis will be rejected when it is false.
-   A sample of observations to be used for testing the hypothesis.

The null and alternative hypotheses arise from the problem being addressed. In Example 1, the null hypothesis is that the mean time to manufacture an item is equal to six. The item cannot be successfully manufactured if the mean time is larger than six, so that the alternative hypothesis is that the mean is greater than six. The mean time to manufacture is noted as μ, and the shorthand notation for the null and alternative hypotheses can be expressed as:

$$H_0: \mu = \mu_0 \text{ and } H_a: \mu > \mu_0$$

where $\mu_0 = 6$. This is the nomenclature I will use in this volume; however, the null hypothesis for this type of situation is sometimes expressed as $\mu \leq \mu_0$.

The hypothesis in the second example concerns the relationship between two mean values. The null hypothesis is that the mean time to manufacture the item is the same before and after the change. Because the manufacturer wishes to establish the effectiveness of the change, the alternative hypothesis is that the mean time is shorter after the change. If the mean time to manufacture before the change is μ_1 and the mean time to manufacture after the change is μ_2, the shorthand notation is:

$$H_0: \mu_1 = \mu_2 \text{ and } H_a: \mu_1 > \mu_2$$

where no values need to be specified for μ_1 and μ_2. Table 19.1 gives examples of various hypothesis formats.

The rule used to test the hypothesis depends on the type of hypothesis being tested. Consider Example 1, where the usual rule is to reject the null hypothesis if the average of an appropriate sample of manufacturing times is sufficiently larger than six; how much larger depends on the allowable probability of making an error.

The result of a hypothesis test is a decision either to reject or not reject the null hypothesis; that is, the hypothesis is either rejected or we reserve judgment about it. In practice, we may act as though the null hypothesis is accepted if it is not rejected. Because we do

Table 19.1: Hypothesis Testing: *Single-* and *Double-Sided* Tests on Population Mean

Single Sided

$H_0: \mu = \mu_0$		$H_0: \mu = \mu_0$
$H_a: \mu > \mu_0$	or	$H_a: \mu < \mu_0$

Double Sided

$H_0: \mu = \mu_0$		$H_0: \mu_1 = \mu_2$
$H_a: \mu \neq \mu_0$	or	$H_a: \mu_1 \neq \mu_2$

not know the truth, we can make one of the following two possible errors when running a hypothesis test:

1. We can reject a null hypothesis that is in fact true.
2. We can fail to reject a null hypothesis that is false.

The first error is called a type I error, and the second is called a type II error. This relationship is shown in Table 19.2. Hypothesis tests are designed to control the probabilities of making either of these errors; we do not know that the result is correct, but we can be assured that the probability of making an error is within acceptable limits. The probability of making a type I error is controlled by establishing a maximum allowable value of the probability, called the level of the test, usually noted as α. The specific rule used to govern the decision reject or fail to reject the null hypothesis (H_0) is determined by selecting a particular value for α. A statistical analysis provides a calculated probability value or P value. This P value is compare to the α criterion value. When the P value is lower than the α criterion the null hypothesis is rejected. An often quoted statement for this condition is: if P is low, ho (i.e., H_0) must go.

Selecting an appropriate sample size usually controls the probability of making a type II error. Consider Example 1 again. If the true mean time to manufacture an item is not six, it can have one of any number of possible values. It could be 6.01, 6.1, 7, 20, 100, etc. To design the hypothesis test properly, the manufacturer selects a possible value that is to be protected against and specifies the probability that the hypothesis should be rejected if the true mean equals the selected value. For example, the manufacturer may decide that the hypothesized mean is 6 and should be rejected with probability 0.85 if the true mean time is 8 or with

Table 19.2: Hypothesis Testing Error Types

		True state of nature	
		H_0	H_a
Conclusion made	H_0	Correct conclusion	Type II error
	H_a	Type I error	Correct conclusion

probability 0.98 if the true time is 9 hours. In common notation, these differences of 2 (i.e., 8 − 6 = 2) and 3 (i.e., 9 − 6 = 3) correspond to values for δ. The probability of rejecting for a given value of μ is called the power of the test at μ, and it is one minus the probability of making a type II error (β) at μ. The manufacturer designs the test by selecting a sample size that ensures the desired power at the specified alternative value. Sample size selection is discussed at near the beginning of Chapters 20, 21, 22, and 23.

After a rule for rejecting the null hypothesis and a sample size is selected, a random sample is selected and used to run the test. Statistical statements about population means are robust to the data not being normally distributed, while statistical evaluations about population standard deviations may not be robust to a lack of normality.

One question that is often asked is what value should be selected for α and β? Without any prior knowledge or input 0.05 is a conventional response. A 0.05 probability translates to a 1 in 20 chance. These parameters could be much lower with critical issues such as safety. See Section 19.7 for more discussion on this topic.

The parameters α, β, and δ are sometimes referred to as producer's risk, consumer's risk, and acceptable amount of uncertainty, respectively.

19.5   Example 19.1: Hypothesis Testing

Consider that someone is on trial in a court of law for murder. The person either committed the crime or did not commit the crime. This situation takes the form of a hypothesis test where the null hypothesis is that the person is innocent (i.e., not guilty) and the alternative hypothesis is that he is guilty.

Evidence (information) is presented to the jury. The jury then deliberates to decide whether the person is guilty or not. If the jury makes the decision that the person is innocent, there is β risk of error; that is the jury is failing to reject the null hypothesis that the person is innocent. If the jury makes the decision that the person is guilty, there is α risk of error; that is the jury rejects the null hypothesis that the person is innocent.

To quantify these two risks conceptually within the current court of legal system of a country, consider a random selection of 10,000 murder cases in which the suspect was found innocent and 10,000 murder cases in which the suspect was found guilty. If we could determine the real truth (whether they did in fact commit murder or not), the risks associated with our current judicial system would be:

$$\alpha = \frac{u}{10,000} \qquad \beta = \frac{v}{10,000}$$

where u is the number of people found guilty who were in fact innocent and v is the number of people not found guilty who were in fact guilty.

19.6   Example 19.2: Probability Plot Hypothesis Test

Example 8.6 described the creation of the probability plot shown in Figure 8.18, which had a p-value of 0.992. Since this p-value is not less than 0.05, we would fail to reject the null hypothesis that the data are normally distributed at a level of 0.05. That is, we would behave as though the data are from a normal distribution, keeping in mind that if we had more data from the population our conclusion could change.

19.7   Choosing Alpha

Often the practitioners simply selects an α of 0.05; however, often other considerations should be given to this selection. An α level of risk choice in hypothesis testing should depend on type I and/or type II error consequences (John, 1990). Consider that a change was developed that was thought to improve the 80% current process yield. A test hypothesis for assessing this process change is:

$$H_0: \mu = 80 \quad H_a: \mu > 80$$

The null hypothesis would be rejected if the new process average is significantly larger than 80. If this occurs, a pilot plant test would be conducted for further investigation. For this initial assessment, type I error cost would be only a few weeks work, while type II error cost could be the lost of a new exciting financially attractive process enhancement. This stage warrants a fairly large alpha value and a small beta value.

The consequences at the next stage are different. The hypothesis test stated above is the same; however, null hypothesis rejection consequences are different whenever the new process implementation is expensive. For an expensive implementation, we want to be sure that we do not implement the new process at much expense to only find that there was no improvement. Because of this, we want a conservative test; hence a small α. We would also like to have a small β. if there is sufficient time and budget to run a lengthy evaluation.

Consider another example where a pharmaceutical company is proposing a new product that is to alleviate an illness symptom. Usual procedure is to select two groups of patients where one group is given the product and the other group is given a placebo without their awareness. Patient responses are noted and tested against a null hypothesis that the new drug is not beneficial and an alternate hypothesis that the drug is beneficial with no harmful effects. Drug approval would occur whenever the drug is shown to be beneficial (i.e., rejecting the null hypothesis, approving the drug for use). This approval step is very serious, which leads to a low value for α.

19.8   Nonparametric Estimates: Runs Test for Randomization

When conducting hypothesis tests, it is important that data are random. A runs test assesses whether the sequence of collected data is in random order.

A run is defined as a group of consecutive observations either all greater than or less than some value. To assess whether data are in random order using a runs test, data are evaluated in terms of the number of runs above and below the median. Within this nonparametric test, no assumption is required about the population distribution parameters.

19.9   Example 19.3: Nonparametric Runs Test for Randomization

Forty people are selected randomly. Each person is asked a question, which has five possible answers that are coded 1–5. A gradual bias in the question phrasing or a lack of randomization when selecting people would cause non-randomization of the responses. The responses were:

```
1    1    2    1    1    1    1    1    1    2    3    3
     2    0    0    0    0    1    1    3    3    4    4
     5    5    5    5    2    1    1    2    2    2    1
     1    3    3    3    3    2
```

The following statistical analysis indicates that the null hypothesis of a random response is rejected at a *P*-level less than 0.0000.

Runs Test: Response

```
Runs test for Response

Runs above and below K = 2.05

The observed number of runs = 7
The expected number of runs = 19.2
14 observations above K, 26 below
P-value = 0.000
```

The null hypothesis of the data sequence being random is rejected.

19.10   Applying IEE

It is good practice to visualize the data in conjunction with making mathematical computations. Probability plotting is a good tool to use when making such an observation. After looking at the data, the analyst might determine that the wrong question was initially asked; for example, a statement about the percentage of population would be more meaningful than a statement about the mean of a population.

It is unfortunate (Hoerl, 1995) that the vast majority of works in statistical books and papers focuses almost exclusively on deduction; that is testing hypothesis or an estimation of parameters in an assumed model. Very little exists in print on how to use induction to revise subject matter theory based on statistical analysis. Deductive reasoning begins with premises (theory) and infers through analysis what should be seen in practice, whereas induction is reasoning from particulars to the general.

While both types of reasoning are required by scientific methods, statistical education focuses primarily on deduction because it lends itself more to mathematics. As a result, most books teach rigorous adherence to preset rules for decision making when covering hypothesis testing. For example, if the null hypothesis is rejected, the possibility of questioning the original assumptions based on what is seen in the data is never mentioned. However, the primary needs of engineers and scientists are inductive. They need to use data to create general rules and statements. This requirement explains why statistical techniques are not more widely used in these disciplines.

This volume suggests various approaches to creating hypotheses. The Applying IEE sections at the end of the subsequent chapters challenge the underlying assumptions of many planned hypothesis tests (i.e., are we trying to answer the best question). When analyzing data and integrating the statistical techniques described here, practitioners should not lose sight of the need to challenge the underlying assumptions of hypothesis tests. It is very important to ask the right question before expending effort to answer the query. Answering the wrong question is sometimes referred to as a type III error. This might seem humorous; however, it happens more than one might initially think.

19.11 Exercises

1. Is the null hypothesis one-sided or two-sided in a test to evaluate whether the product quality of two suppliers is equal?
2. Describe a decision that you make within your personal life that could be phrased as a hypothesis test.
3. Discuss the usefulness of the techniques presented in this chapter and explain how they can be applied to IEE projects.

20

Inferences: Continuous Response

The hypothesis and confidence interval techniques discussed in the last chapter provide the foundation for this and many of the following chapters of this volume.

I have included this and the next chapter near the beginning the P-DMAIC roadmap analyze phase tools description to provide a foundation for the introduction of other analyze tools. However, the described techniques are applicable in other roadmap phases such as the measure phase in both P-DMAIC and E-DMAIC.

This and the next chapter describe inferences for a one-sample population. The current chapter provides analyses for a continuous response, while the next chapter addresses an attribute response. An example continuous-output application is the amount of tire tread that exists after 40,000 kilometers (km) of automobile usage. One tire might, for example, have 6.0 millimeters (mm) of remaining tread, while another tire might measure 5.5 mm.

In this chapter, the estimation of population mean and of standard deviation from sampled data is discussed in conjunction with probability plotting.

20.1   Summarizing Sampled Data

The classic analysis of sampled data taken from a continuous response population has focused on determining a sample mean ($\bar{x}$)
and standard deviation (s), along with confidence interval statements that can relate both of these sampled characteristics to
the actual population values (μ and σ, respectively). Experimental
considerations of this type answer some basic questions about the
sample and population. However, analysts responsible for either
generating a criterion specification or making a pass/fail decision
often do not consider the other information that data analyses
can convey. For example, an experiment might be able to indicate
that 90% of the automobiles using a certain type of tire will have
at least 4.9 mm of tire tread after 40,000 km. Such a statement
might be more informative than a statement that relates only to
the mean tire tread after 40,000 km.

20.2   Sample Size: Hypothesis Test of a Mean
Criterion for Continuous Data Response

One of the most common questions asked of a statistical consultant is: "What sample size do I need (to verify this mean criterion)?" The following equation (Diamond, 1989) can be used to
determine the sample size (*n*) necessary to evaluate a hypothesis
test criterion at given values for α, β, and δ (i.e., producer's risk,
consumer's risk, and an acceptable amount of uncertainty, re-
spectively). Sometimes the population standard deviation (σ) is
known from previous test activity; however, this is not generally
the case. For this second situation, δ can be conveniently expressed in terms of σ.

$$n = (U_\alpha + U_\beta)^2 \; \frac{\sigma^2}{\delta^2}$$

In this equation, U_β is determined from the single-sided Table B
in the Appendix B. If the alternative hypothesis is single-sided
(e.g., μ < criterion), U_α is also determined from Table B; however, if
the alternative hypothesis is double-sided (e.g., μ < or > criterion),
U_α is determined from Table C.

If the standard deviation is not known, the sample size should be adjusted using the following equation (Diamond, 1989):

$$n = (t_\alpha + t_\beta)^2 \; \frac{s^2}{\delta^2}$$

In this equation, t_β is determined from the single-sided Table D. If the alternative hypothesis is single-sided (e.g., μ < criterion), t_α is also determined from Table D; however, if the alternative hypothesis is double-sided (e.g., μ < or > criterion), t_α is determined from Table E.

An alternative approach for sample size calculations is described later in this chapter.

20.3   Example 20.1: Sample Size Determination for a Mean Criterion Test

A stereo amplifier output power level is desired to be at least 100 watts (W) per channel on average. Determine the sample size that is needed to verify this criterion given the following:

α = 0.1, which from Table B yields U_α = 1.282.
β = 0.05, which from Table B yields U_β = 1.645.
δ = 0.5σ.

Substitution yields:

$$n = (1.282 + 1.645)^2 \; \frac{\sigma^2}{(0.5\sigma)^2} = 34.26$$

Rounding up to a whole number yields a sample size of 35.

If the standard deviation is not known, this sample size needs to be adjusted. Given that the number of degrees of freedom for the t-table value equals 34 (i.e., 35−1), interpolation in Table D yields $t_{0.1;34}$ = 1.307 and $t_{0.05; 34}$ = 1.692; hence:

$$n = (1.692 + 1.307)^2 \; \frac{s^2}{(0.5s)^2} = 35.95$$

Rounding up to a whole number yields a sample of 36.

The following statistical analysis program yielded a similar result:

Power and Sample Size

```
1-Sample t Test

Testing mean = null (versus > null)
Calculating power for mean = null + difference
Alpha = 0.1 Assumed standard deviation = 1
```

	Sample	Target	
Difference	Size	Power	Actual Power
0.5	36	0.95	0.953784

Because individuals want to make sure that they are making the correct decision, they often specify very low α and β values, along with a low δ value. This can lead to a sample size that is unrealistically large with normal test time and resource constraints. When this happens, the experimenter may need to accept more risk than he or she was originally willing to tolerate. The sample size can then be recalculated permitting the larger risks (a higher α and/or β value) and/or an increase in uncertainty (a higher δ value).

20.4   Confidence Intervals on the Mean and Hypothesis Test Criteria Alternatives

An IEE organization uses data whenever possible to make decisions; however, care must be exercised. Sample-data observation analyses without a statistical assessment can be deceiving. For example, a sample-data relationship might lead someone to take action because they believe something is true, when, in fact, the relationship occurred because of not unlikely chance. That is, the simple observation of a characteristic from sample data may not be representative of what is expected from the true population's characteristics. Business reduces the risks of this occurring when they have a true understanding and appreciation of confidence intervals and hypothesis test in their decision-making process.

Table 20.1: Mean Confidence Interval Equations

	Single-Sided	Double-Sided
σ Known	$\mu \leq \bar{x} + \dfrac{U_\alpha \sigma}{\sqrt{n}}$ or $\mu \geq \bar{x} - \dfrac{U_\alpha \sigma}{\sqrt{n}}$	$\bar{x} - \dfrac{U_\alpha \sigma}{\sqrt{n}} \leq \mu \leq \bar{x} + \dfrac{U_\alpha \sigma}{\sqrt{n}}$
σ Unknown	$\mu \leq \bar{x} + \dfrac{t_\alpha s}{\sqrt{n}}$ or $\mu \geq \bar{x} - \dfrac{t_\alpha s}{\sqrt{n}}$	$\bar{x} - \dfrac{t_\alpha s}{\sqrt{n}} \leq \mu \leq \bar{x} + \dfrac{t_\alpha s}{\sqrt{n}}$
Using reference tables	U_α: Table B t_α: Table D[a]	U_α: Table C t_α: Table E[a]

[a] $\nu = n - 1$ (i.e., the number of degrees of freedom used in the t table is equal to one less than the sample size).

After sample mean ($\bar{x}$) and standard deviation (s) are determined from the data, Table 20.1 summarizes the equations used to determine from these population estimates the intervals that contain the true mean (μ) at a confidence level of $[(1-\alpha)100]$. The equations in this table use the t tables (as opposed to the U tables) whenever the population standard deviation is not known. Because of the central limit theorem, the equations noted in this table are robust even when data are not from a normal distribution.

If a sample size is calculated before conducting the experiment using desired values for α, β, and δ, the null hypothesis is not rejected if the criterion is contained within the appropriate confidence interval for μ. This decision is made with the β risk of error that was used in calculating the sample size (given the underlying δ input level of uncertainty). However, if the criterion is not contained within the interval, then the null hypothesis is rejected. This decision is made with α risk of error.

Other methods can be used when setting up a hypothesis test criterion. Consider, for example, the alternative hypothesis (H_a) of $\mu > \mu_a$, where μ_a is a product specification criterion. From Table 20.1 it can be determined that:

$$\bar{x}_{\text{criterion}} = \mu_a + \frac{t_\alpha s}{\sqrt{n}}$$

When $\bar{x}$ is greater than the test $\bar{x}_{criterion}$, the null hypothesis is rejected. When $\bar{x}$ is less than $\bar{x}_{criterion}$, the null hypothesis is not rejected. An alternative approach for this problem is to use the equation form as:

$$t_0 = \frac{(\bar{x} - \mu_a)\sqrt{n}}{s}$$

where the null hypothesis is rejected if $t_0 > t_\alpha$.

The equations above apply to planned statistical hypothesis testing, where prior to testing itself α, β, and δ were chosen. However, in reality, data are often taken without making these pretest decisions. The equations presented here are still useful in making an assessment of the population, as seen in the following example.

20.5   Example 20.2: Confidence Intervals on the Mean

Consider the 16 data points from sample 1 of Table 17.4, which had a sample mean of 5.77 and a sample standard deviation of 2.41. Determine the various 90% confidence statements that can be made relative to the true population mean, first assuming that the standard deviation is 2.0 and then treating it as an unknown parameter.

Given that σ is 2.0, the single-sided and double-sided 90% confidence (i.e., $\alpha = 0.1$) interval equations are as shown below. The U_α value of 1.282 is from the single-sided Table B, given $\alpha = 0.1$. The U_α value of 1.645 is from the double-sided Table C, given $\alpha = 0.1$.

Single-Sided Scenarios:

$$\mu \le \bar{x} + \frac{U_\alpha \sigma}{\sqrt{n}}$$

$$\mu \ge \bar{x} - \frac{U_\alpha \sigma}{\sqrt{n}}$$

$$\mu \le 5.77 + \frac{1.282(2.0)}{\sqrt{16}}$$

$$\mu \ge 5.77 - \frac{1.282(2.0)}{\sqrt{16}}$$

$$\mu \le 5.77 + 0.64$$

$$\mu \ge 5.77 - 0.64$$

$$\mu \le 6.41$$

$$\mu \ge 5.13$$

Double-Sided Scenario:

$$\bar{x} - \frac{U_\alpha \sigma}{\sqrt{n}} \leq \mu \leq \bar{x} + \frac{U_\alpha \sigma}{\sqrt{n}}$$

$$5.77 - \frac{1.645(2.0)}{\sqrt{16}} \leq \mu \leq 5.77 + \frac{1.645(2.0)}{\sqrt{16}}$$

$$5.77 - 0.82 \leq \mu \leq 5.77 + 0.82$$

$$4.95 \leq \mu \leq 6.59$$

If the standard deviation is not known, the resulting equations for single-sided and double-sided 90% confidence intervals are the following. The t_α value of 1.341 is from the single-sided Table D, given $\alpha = 0.1$ and $\nu = 16 - 1 = 15$. The t_α value of 1.753 is from the double-sided Table E, given $\alpha = 0.1$ and $\nu = 16 - 1 = 15$.

Single-Sided Scenarios:

$$\mu \leq \bar{x} + \frac{t_\alpha s}{\sqrt{n}}$$

$$\mu \leq 5.77 + \frac{(1.341)(2.41)}{\sqrt{16}}$$

$$\mu \leq 5.77 + 0.81$$

$$\mu \leq 6.58$$

$$\mu \geq \bar{x} - \frac{t_\alpha s}{\sqrt{n}}$$

$$\mu \geq 5.77 - \frac{(1.341)(2.41)}{\sqrt{16}}$$

$$\mu \geq 5.77 - 0.81$$

$$\mu \geq 4.96$$

Double-Sided Scenario:

$$\bar{x} - \frac{t_\alpha s}{\sqrt{n}} \leq \mu \leq \bar{x} + \frac{t_\alpha s}{\sqrt{n}}$$

$$5.77 - \frac{1.753(2.41)}{\sqrt{16}} \leq \mu \leq 5.77 + \frac{1.753(2.41)}{\sqrt{16}}$$

$$5.77 - 1.06 \leq \mu \leq 5.77 + 1.06$$

$$4.71 \leq \mu \leq 6.83$$

   Computer programs can provide confidence intervals for continuous response data. In addition, these computer programs can test null hypotheses. For the double-sided interval calculated above, where 6 is the mean criterion, a computer analysis yielded.

One-Sample T: Sampling 1

```
Test of mu = 6 vs mu not = 6

Variable      N                    Mean    StDev    SE Mean
Sampling 1    16                   5.774   2.407    0.602

Variable      90.0% CI        T        P
Sampling 1    (4.720, 6.829) -0.307   0.713
```

   This confidence interval is similar to the above manual calculations, where differences are from round-off error. For a hypothesis risk criterion of 0.05, the *P* value of 0.713 indicates that we would fail to reject the null hypothesis that the mean is equal to 6.
   The mean and standard deviation used in the preceding calculations were randomly created from a normal distribution where $\mu = 6.0$. Note that this true mean value is contained in these confidence intervals. When the confidence interval is 90%, we expect the interval to contain the true value 90% of the time that we take random samples and analyze the data.

20.6   Example 20.3: Sample Size – An Alternative Approach

The equation given above for sample size included the risk levels for both α and β. An alternative approach can be used if we want to determine a mean value within a certain ± value and level of confidence (e.g., ±4 at 95% confidence). To determine the sample size for this situation, consider the equation

$$\mu = \bar{x} \pm \frac{U_\alpha \sigma}{\sqrt{n}}$$

It then follows that:

$$4 = \frac{U_\alpha \sigma}{\sqrt{n}} = \frac{1.96\sigma}{\sqrt{n}}$$

or

$$n = \frac{(1.96)^2 \sigma^2}{4^2} = 0.24\sigma^2$$

20.7   Standard Deviation Confidence Interval

When a sample of size n is taken from a population that is normally distributed, the double-sided confidence interval equation for the population's standard deviation (σ) is:

$$\left[\frac{(n-1)s^2}{\chi^2_{\alpha/2;\nu}}\right]^{1/2} \leq \sigma \leq \left[\frac{(n-1)s^2}{\chi^2_{(1-\alpha/2;\nu)}}\right]^{1/2}$$

where s is the standard deviation of the sample and the χ^2 values are taken from Table G with $\alpha/2$ risk and ν degrees of freedom equal to the sample size minus 1. This relationship is not robust to data not being from a normal distribution.

20.8   Example 20.4: Standard Deviation Confidence Statement

Consider again the 16 data points from Sample 1 of Table 17.4, which had a mean of 5.77 and a standard deviation of 2.41. Given that the standard deviation was not known, the 90% confidence interval for the standard deviation of the population would then be:

$$\left[\frac{(16-1)(2.41)^2}{\chi^2_{(0.1/2;[16-1])}}\right]^{1/2} \leq \sigma \leq \left[\frac{(16-1)(2.41)^2}{\chi^2_{(1-[0.1/2];[16-1])}}\right]^{1/2}$$

$$\left[\frac{87.12}{25.00}\right]^{1/2} \leq \sigma \leq \left[\frac{87.12}{7.26}\right]^{1/2}$$

$$1.87 \leq \sigma \leq 3.46$$

The standard deviation used in this calculation was from a random sample taken from a normal distribution, where $\sigma = 2.0$. Note that this true standard deviation value is contained in this confidence interval. When the confidence interval is 90%, we expect the interval to contain the true value 90% of the time that we take random samples and analyze the data.

20.9   Percentage of the Population Assessments

Criteria are sometimes thought to apply to the mean response of the product's population with no regard to the variability of the product response. Often what is really needed is that all of the product should have a response that is less than or greater than a criterion.

For example, a specification may exist that a product should be able to withstand an electrostatic discharge (ESD) level of 700 volts (V). Is the intent of this specification that the mean of the population (if tested to failure) should be above 700 V? Or, should all products built be able to resist a voltage level of 700 V?

It is impossible to be 100% certain that every product will meet such a criterion without testing every product that is manufactured. For criteria that require much certainty and a 100% population requirement, 100% testing to a level that anticipates field performance degradation may be required. However, a reduced confidence level may be acceptable with a lower percent confidence requirement (e.g., 95% of the population). Depending on the situation, the initial criterion may need adjustment to reflect the basic test strategy.

Other books present approaches to this situation such as K factors (Natrella, 1966) using tables and equations that consider both the mean and standard deviation of the sample. However, with this approach, the assumption of normality is very important and the sample size requirements may often be too large.

Another possible approach is a "best estimate" probability plot, which can give visual indications to population characteristics that may not otherwise be apparent. A probability plot may indicate, for example, that data outliers are present or that a normal distribution assumption is not appropriate. In addition, some computer software packages include confidence intervals in their probability plots.

20.10   Example 20.5: Percentage of the Population Statements

Consider again the first sample from Table 17.4 that yielded a mean value of 5.77 and a standard deviation of 2.41. Figure 20.1 is a computer-generated normal probability plot of the data.

From this plot, one notes that evaluating only the mean value for this sample may yield deceiving conclusions because the standard deviation is rather large compared to the reading values. In addition, the normal distribution can be used to represent the population, because the data tend to follow a straight line. If a criterion of 20 was specified for 95% of the population (given that a low number indicates goodness), an individual would probably feel comfortable that the specification was met because the "best estimate" plot estimates that 95% of the population is less than 9.5. However, if the criterion were 10 for this percentage of the

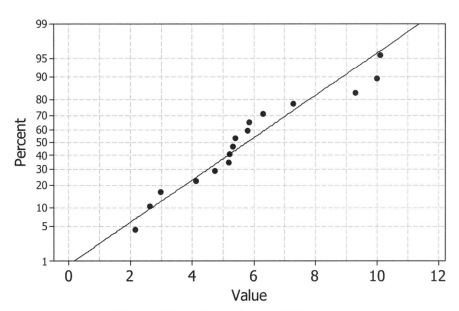

Figure 20.1: Normal probability plot.

population, we would probably conclude that the manufacturing process might need to be examined for possible improvements. Regression and/or design of experiments (DOE) might be appropriate to assess which of those parameters considered, perhaps from a brainstorming session, are statistically significant in reducing the mean and/or standard deviation of the process.

Probability plots of data can often be enlightening. From these plots one may find, for example, that the data are not normally distributed. If there is a knee in the curve, this may indicate that there are two distributions in the process (i.e., a bimodal distribution). In this case it might be beneficial to try to determine why one sample is from one distribution while another sample is from another distribution. This may happen, for example, because one of two suppliers produces a better part than the other. Another possibility is that the normal probability plot has curvature and may be better fitted to some other distribution (e.g., a three-parameter Weibull distribution).

As a minimum, when choosing a sample size for making a decision about the percentage of population, extrapolation should be avoided to reach the desired percentage value. In this example, one could use Table H to determine the approximate percentage plot positions for various sample sizes. Table 20.2 shows the results from a ranking of the data with these percentages for this data set.

One notes from the tabulated values that the percentage plot position extremes are 3.1% and 96%. This means that a probability plot of the 16 data points has no extrapolation when single-sided (high value) statements are made about 95% of the population. The percentage plot positions in Table H indicate that 26 data points are needed to yield non-extrapolated single-sided statements about 98% of the population.

Another valid concern can emerge from this type of experiment. If the sample is drawn from a process over a short period of time, this sample does not necessarily represent what the process will do in the future. DOE techniques again can be used as a guide to adjust parameters used to manufacture the parts. The procedure described within this example could then still be applied to get a "big picture spatial representation" of what could be expected of the process in the future; that is, the data are from the factorial trials and are not a true random sample of a population (See, Breyfogle (2003), Example 43.3). In addition, any statistically significant parameters could then be focused upon, perhaps to improve the process mean and/or reduce the process variability. The process

Table 20.2: Ranked Data and Plot Positions

Original Sample Number	Ranked Sample Value	Percentage Plot Position
7	2.17	3.1
3	2.65	9.4
1	2.99	15.6
8	4.13	21.9
15	4.74	28.1
16	5.19	34.4
10	5.20	40.6
5	5.31	46.9
12	5.39	53.1
11	5.80	59.4
6	5.84	65.6
2	6.29	71.9
9	7.29	78.1
14	9.29	84.4
13	10.00	90.6
4	10.11	96.9

then could be continually monitored via individuals control charts for drifts of the process mean and standard deviation.

20.11 Example 20.6: Base-Lining a 30,000-Foot-Level Continuous-Response Metric and Determining Process Confidence Interval Statements

A project was to reduce process lead time, where data were not readily available. An infrequent subgrouping/sampling frequency was selected with one daily random sample.

From Appendix Section D.1, the step for selecting the appropriate control chart is noted to be step 3.2.12 (i.e., create an individuals control chart). From this same book section, the roadmap step for selecting the appropriate process capability/performance metric statement is step 3.3.7; that is no specification report 80% frequency of occurrence rate with a mean or median response estimate, or report noncompliance rate beyond target(s).

Table 20.3 shows historical lead-time data and Figure 20.2 shows an individuals control chart of the data.

It appears from this figure that there was a shift in the process response output. An investigation revealed a significant change

Table 20.3: Historical Lead Times

Day	Time	Day	Time	Day	Time	Day	Time	Day	Time	Day	Time
1	107.22	27	115.77	53	113.00	79	102.55	105	112.96	131	108.93
2	111.49	28	108.94	54	101.11	80	104.52	106	113.75	132	104.11
3	115.45	29	111.61	55	113.81	81	107.86	107	111.64	133	102.02
4	106.71	30	103.15	56	108.34	82	96.34	108	110.77	134	101.24
5	103.65	31	114.55	57	111.24	83	108.92	109	110.02	135	102.57
6	101.91	32	102.13	58	119.31	84	116.01	110	102.55	136	108.74
7	107.35	33	114.90	59	106.48	85	110.76	111	92.46	137	90.29
8	113.30	34	114.09	60	122.06	86	115.20	112	106.24	138	99.15
9	111.47	35	116.61	61	103.96	87	109.11	113	117.44	139	103.24
10	95.76	36	111.24	62	116.18	88	107.97	114	108.12	140	97.41
11	109.16	37	108.27	63	115.71	89	118.01	115	104.75	141	105.90
12	115.08	38	110.08	64	105.44	90	101.72	116	109.01	142	94.70
13	102.78	39	100.28	65	112.30	91	107.09	117	115.34	143	94.73
14	108.95	40	115.43	66	108.57	92	107.98	118	113.63	144	96.27
15	107.10	41	112.32	67	113.68	93	107.68	119	104.25	145	96.11
16	110.39	42	105.30	68	112.13	94	107.15	120	110.88	146	96.76
17	120.41	43	114.34	69	113.98	95	107.74	121	114.55	147	97.84
18	110.18	44	108.94	70	109.41	96	110.48	122	113.46	148	108.94
19	108.55	45	109.55	71	112.35	97	114.51	123	109.10	149	101.52
20	108.82	46	114.67	72	113.96	98	109.44	124	102.30	150	93.93
21	115.71	47	105.98	73	110.69	99	108.80	125	103.24	151	103.64
22	119.45	48	112.47	74	114.64	100	115.21	126	102.75	152	90.79
23	111.94	49	112.33	75	111.42	101	111.27	127	104.68	153	96.63
24	119.64	50	112.30	76	111.40	102	110.09	128	97.48	154	99.30
25	107.13	51	111.81	77	106.96	103	116.20	129	98.44	155	102.19
26	112.94	52	115.63	78	110.62	104	118.99	130	100.80		

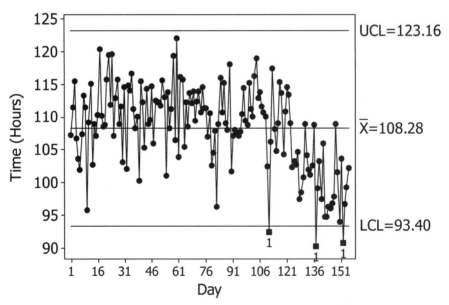

Figure 20.2: Individuals control chart of historical lead times.

was made to the process at day 124. Because of this, an individuals control chart stage was set at this point in time; that is the control chart limits were determined separately for the stages.

From the staged control chart shown in Figure 20.3 we have no reason to believe that the process is not predictable. Considering that data from day 124 to 155 are a random sample of the future, the tools described in this chapter can be used to calculate the confidence interval for the process population mean and standard deviation. A computer generated analysis of the data yielded.

One-Sample T: Mean – Days 124–155

```
Variable          N  Mean    StDev SE Mean  95% CI
Mean Days124-155 32 100.207 4.816  0.851     98.471, 101.944)
```

One-Sample: Standard Deviation – Days 124–155

```
StDev   95%   CI
4.816  (3.86,    6.40)
```

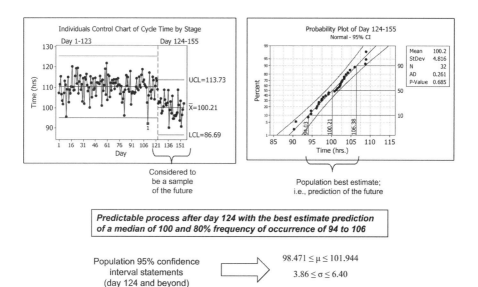

Figure 20.3: Individuals control chart of lead time with process capability/performance metric statement.

It should be noted that even when a control chart contains all the data during a period of time I consider that this data are still a sample of the process. The logic for this is that if you could go back in time and repeat the process measurements, you would probably get different responses (i.e., response data are a sample of the process).

Also shown in Figure 20.3 is the process capability/performance metric with confidence intervals. The special-cause signal on day 111 was investigated. Nothing was found abnormal; hence, it was concluded that this special-cause signal was a chance occurrence.

From the computer-generated statistical analysis, the confidence intervals for the 10%, 50%, and 90% figure values are:

Percent	Best estimate	Lower bound	Upper bound
10	94.0337	91.7692	96.2983
50	100.2080	98.5384	101.8770
90	106.3810	104.1170	108.6460

The CODND is determined by quantifying the annualized financial impact from the current process level.

This example demonstrates a confidence interval calculation for percent of population. Statistical software packages can also determine the percent confidence intervals at x-values (e.g., specifications). This confidence interval procedure can be used for project execution roadmap step 3.4 in Appendix Section D.1.

When examining the previous individuals control chart one might conclude that data trends were present. It should be noted that the data for this example were randomly generated, with a process shift at the staged time. Random data often, if not typically, exhibits the phenomenon where trends can be read into the data. The point is that this type of inference often occurs with real data; that is reacting to trends even though the apparent trends often are the result of chance common-cause variability.

20.12   Applying IEE

This chapter illustrates techniques in which random samples are used for hypothesis testing or confidence interval statements. This type of assessment might be suggested during initial problem definition; however, one might consider the following questions to determine if there is an IEE alternative.

1. Is the sample really taken from the population of interest? If, for example, a sample is taken from the start-up of a manufacturing process, the sample output will not necessarily represent future machine builds. Hence, a machine failure rate test during this early phase of production may not yield a failure rate similar to later experience by the customer.
2. Is the process that is being sampled stable/predictable? If it is not, then the test methods and confidence statements cannot be interpreted with much precision. Process control charting techniques can be used to determine the stability of a process.
3. What is going to be done if the process does not meet a test criterion? Are the parts going to be shipped anyway, as long as the output is "reasonable"?
4. Would a DOE be more useful than a random sample taken at some point in time? A DOE test strategy can yield information indicating where the process/design may be improved.

Let's not play games with the numbers. Future chapters will illustrate approaches that can be more helpful in answering the real questions: How can we design, build, or test this product smarter to give the customer the best possible product at the lowest possible price?

20.13 Exercises

1. From sampled data, state the distribution used to calculate the confidence interval on the mean. Also, state the distribution that is used to calculate the confidence interval on the standard deviation.
2. The following data give the difference between actual arrival time and scheduled arrival time for the 12 monthly flights someone made into his/her resident city during the previous year; plus values indicate the number of minutes the flight was late. The traveler was always scheduled to arrive at the same time on the last Wednesday of the month.

June	July	Aug	Sep	Oct	Nov	Dec	Jan	Feb	Mar	Apr	May
0.1	3.2	18.4	2.5	15.6	90.9	102.1	.8		20.2	31.3	1.4	21.9

(a) Determine the sample mean and standard deviation.

(b) Estimate the 95% confidence intervals for the population mean and standard deviation. Note any assumptions.

(c) Display data in a histogram format.

(d) Create a normal probability plot of the data.

(e) Estimate arrival time range for 90% of the flights (using normal probability plot and Z table (Table A). Comment on analysis.

(f) Interpret the plots and describe any further investigation.

(g) If someone were to make a general inference about the arrival times of all passengers into the airport, state a key underlying assumption that is violated.

(h) Explain the potential problem with making inferences about next year's arrival times from the current year's arrival times.

3. A random sample yielded the measurements 9.4, 10.6, 8.1, 12.2, 15.9, 9.0, 9.1, 10.0, 11.7, 11.0.

(a) Determine the sample mean and the 95% confidence interval for the population mean.

(b) Determine the sample standard deviation and the 95% confidence interval for the population standard deviation.

(c) Display the data using a histogram and normal probability plots.

(d) Estimate the response that is exceeded 10% of the time (using probability plot and Z table (Table A). Comment on the validity of the analysis and results.

(e) Estimate process capability/performance metric for a specification of 10.0 ± 4.0. Comment on the validity of the analysis and results.

4. The following randomly sampled data were submitted for analysis: 33.4, 42.2, 37.1, 44.2, 46.0, 34.0, 32.6, 42.7, 32, and 39.5.

(a) Determine the sample mean and the 95% confidence interval for the population mean.

(b) Determine the sample standard deviation and the 95% confidence interval for the population standard deviation.

    (c) Display the data using a histogram and normal probability plots.

    (d) Using the plots and Z table (i.e., Table A), estimate the range of responses expected 90% of the time. Comment on the validity of the analysis and results.

    (e) Estimate the process capability/performance metrics for a specification of 40.0 ± 7.0. Comment on the validity of the analysis and results.

    (f) List possible sources for this data.

5. A 10 random-sample evaluation of the specification 75 ± 3 yielded readings of 77.1, 76.8, 76.3, 75.9, 76.1, 77.7, 76.7, 75.7, 76.9, 77.4.

    (a) Determine the sample mean and the 95% confidence interval for the population mean.

    (b) Determine the sample standard deviation and the 95% confidence interval for the population standard deviation.

    (c) Display the data using a histogram and normal probability plots.

    (d) Using plots and Z table (Table A), estimate the proportion beyond the specification limits. Determine the process capability/performance indices. Comment on the validity of the analysis and results.

    (e) Determine where emphasis should be given to make the process more capable of meeting specifications (reducing variability or shifting mean).

    (f) Give an example from manufacturing, development, and service where these data might have originated.

6. A sample of 10 was taken from an in-control/predictable process. A variance of 4.2 and a mean of 23.2 were calculated. Determine the 95% confidence interval on the mean and standard deviation. Explain any potential problems with this analysis.

7. A sample of 10 from an in-control/predictable process had a variance of 4.2 and a mean of 23.2. Determine the 90% lower confidence bound on the mean and standard deviation? Describe any potential problems with this analysis.

8. To address some customer problem reports, management wants a random sample evaluation to assess the products currently produced. Determine the sample size needed to assess a mean response criterion of 75 if risks are at a level

of 0.05. Consider that δ equals the standard deviation of the process response. State the test hypothesis. Discuss how well the basic test strategy will probably assess the needs of the customer.

9. A product design consists of five components that collectively affect a response. Four of the component dimensions are 4.0 ± 0.1, 3.0 ± 0.1, 6.0 ± 0.1, and 2.0 ± 0.1 mm. If the dimensions for each component follow a normal distribution, determine the dimension and specification needed for the fifth component given a final $\pm 3\sigma$ sigma statistical dimension of 20.00 ± 0.25 mm. Explain practical difficulties with the results of this type of analysis.

10. A company designs and assembles the five components described in the previous exercise, which are manufactured by different suppliers. Create a strategy for meeting the overall specification requirement of the assembled product.

    (a) Create a preproduction plan that assesses assumptions and how the process is producing relative to meeting specification requirements.

    (b) State needs during production start-up.

    (c) State alternatives for out-sourcing the component parts that could lead to improved quality.

11. Weekly the 30,000-foot-level sample measurements from a new process were 22, 23, 19, 17, 29 and 25. Create an appropriate time-series reporting system for this process. Determine the confidence interval for the mean and variance. If a computer program is used for the computation, also show the appropriate equations. Comment on the results.

12. Determine the critical value of the appropriate statistic when testing the estimated bias for the data given below, using a one-sided test and a 0.05 significance level given a reference value of 23.915. Determine whether the hypothesis that there is no bias can be rejected. Data: 23.4827, 24.7000, 23.6387, 23.7676, 24.2380, and 23.4773.

13. Use a statistical program that tests the null hypothesis that the data in Exercise 8.16 are from a population that is normally distributed.

14. Use a statistical program that tests the null hypothesis that the data in Exercise 8.17 are from a population that is normally distributed.

15. Calculate the confidence intervals for the mean and standard deviation for each machine from the data described in Exercise 22.10. Create a probability plot of the data for each machine. Test the hypothesis that each machine has output that is normally distributed.

16. Determine the sample statistic value and note the table(s) that is appropriate when determining the confidence interval on the mean when the standard deviation is not known.

21

Inferences: Attribute (Pass/Fail) Response

This chapter and the previous chapter describe inferences for a one-sample population. The last chapter provides analyses for a continuous response, while this chapter addresses an attribute response.

Described is the evaluation of defective count data (go/no-go attribute information). An example attribute (pass/fail or pass/nonconformance) situation is a copier fed or failed to feed individual sheets of paper satisfactorily; that is, a copier may feed 999 sheets out of 1000 sheets of paper on the average without a jam. The purpose of these experiments may be to assess with a confidence interval an attribute criterion or evaluate the proportion of parts beyond a continuous criterion value; for example, 20% of the electrical measurements are less than 100,000 ohms.

Samples are evaluated to determine whether they will either pass or fail a requirement (a binary response). Experiments of this type can assess the proportion of a population that is defective through either a confidence interval statement or a hypothesis test of a criterion.

As illustrated later, tests of pass/fail attribute information can require a much larger sample size than tests of a continuous response. For this reason, this chapter also includes suggestions on how to change an original attribute test approach to a continuous response test alternative, often allowing more relevant information to be obtained with greatly reduced sample size requirements.

The binomial distribution is used for this type of analysis, given that the sample size is small relative to the size of the population, for example, less than 10% of the population size. A hypergeometric distribution, as described earlier, can be used when this assumption is not valid.

21.1   Attribute Response Situations

The equation forms for the binomial distributions might initially look complex; however, they are rather mathematically simple to apply. Simply by knowing the sample size and the percentage of "good" parts, it is easy to determine the probability (chance) of getting a "bad" or "good" sample part.

However, a typical desired response is to determine whether a criterion is met with a manageable risk of making the wrong decision. For example, the experimenter may desire to state that at least 99% of the parts are satisfactory with a risk of only 0.10 of making the wrong decision. Or, an experimenter may desire the 90% confidence interval for the defective proportion of the population.

The binomial equation can be used to assess this situation using an iterative computer routine. The Poisson or the normal distribution can be used to approximate the binomial distribution under the situations noted in Table 9.2. Because failure rates typically found in industry are low, the Poisson distribution is often a viable alternative for these attribute tests.

21.2   Sample Size: Hypothesis Test of an Attribute Criterion

The following equation is a simple approximation of the sample size needed to make a hypothesis test using the binomial distribution with α and β risks (Diamond, 1989), where the failure rate at which α applies is ρ_α, while the failure rate at which β applies is ρ_β.

$$n = \left(\frac{(U_\alpha)[(\rho_\alpha)(1-\rho_\alpha)]^{1/2} + (U_\beta)[(\rho_\beta)(1-\rho_\beta)]^{1/2}}{\rho_\beta - \rho_\alpha} \right)^2$$

U_α is the value from Table B or C (Appendix G), depending on whether H_a is single- or double-sided, and U_β is from the single-sided Table B(Appendix G). After the test, if the failure rate falls within the confidence bounds, the null hypothesis is not rejected with β risk of error.

For readers who are interested, this sample size equation assumes that a normality approximation to the binomial equation is appropriate. In general, this is valid because the sample size required for typical α and β level risks is high enough to approximate normality, even though the failure criterion is low. The example in the next section illustrates this point. Alternative approaches for sample size calculations are presented later in this chapter.

21.3 Example 21.1: Sample Size – A Hypothesis Test of an Attribute Criterion

A supplier manufactures a component that is not to have more than 1 defect every 1000 parts (i.e., a 0.001 failure rate criterion). The supplier wants to determine a test sample size for assessing this criterion.

The failure rate criterion is to be 1/1000 (0.001); however, the sample size requires two failure rates (ρ_β and ρ_α). To determine values for ρ_β and ρ_α, assume that a shift of 200 was thought to be a minimal "important increment" from the above 1000-part criterion, along with $\alpha = \beta = 0.05$. The value for ρ_β would then be 0.00125, i.e., 1/(1000 – 200), while the value for ρ_α would be 0.000833, i.e., 1/(1000 + 200). For this single-sided problem, the values are determined from Table B (Appendix G). Substitution yields

$$n = \left(\frac{(1.645)[(0.000833)(1 - 0.000833)]^{1/2} + (1.645)[(0.00125)(1 - 0.00125)]^{1/2}}{0.00125 - 0.000833} \right)^2$$

$$n = 64,106$$

A statistical computer analysis program yields a similar result:

Power and Sample Size

```
Test for One Proportion

Testing proportion = 0.000833 (versus > 0.000833)
Alpha = 0.05

Alternative   Sample     Target
Proportion     Size      Power     Actual Power
  0.00125      64095      0.95        0.950001
```

Are you ready to suggest this to your management? There goes your next raise! This is not atypical of sample size problems encountered when developing an attribute sampling plan. These calculations could be repeated for relaxed test considerations for α, β, ρ_β, and/or ρ_α. If these alternatives still do not appeal to you, consider the reduced sample size testing alternative and the Applying IEE section for better alternatives described later in this chapter.

As stated above, the sample size equation that we used was based on a normal distribution approximation. To illustrate why this approximation is reasonable for this test situation, first note from Table 9.2 that normality is often assumed if $np > 5$ and $n(1-P) > 5$. In the example, $\rho = 0.001$ and $N = 64,106$, which yields a np value of 64.106 [64,106 × 0.001], which is greater than 5, and $n(1-P)$ value of 64,042 [64,106 × 0.999], which is also greater than 5.

21.4   Confidence Intervals for Attribute Evaluations and Alternative Sample Size Considerations

In lieu of using a computer algorithm to determine the confidence interval, the Poisson distribution can often be used to yield a satisfactory approximation. Given this assumption and given a small number of failures, Table K (Appendix G) can be used to calculate a confidence interval for the population failure rate more simply. A rule of thumb is that we should have at least five failures before determining attribute confidence intervals.

If a normal distribution approximation can be made, for example, a large sample size, the confidence interval for the population proportion (ρ) can be determined from the equation

$$p - U_\alpha \sqrt{\frac{pq}{n}} \leq \rho \leq p + U_\alpha \sqrt{\frac{pq}{n}}$$

where $p = r/n$, $q = 1 - p$, and U_α is taken from a two-sided U table (i.e., Table C of Appendix G). As in the approach mentioned earlier for continuous data, a sample size may be determined from this equation. To do this we can rearrange the equation as

$$\rho = p \pm U_\alpha \sqrt{\frac{pq}{n}}$$

For a desired proportion $\pm$ confidence interval of Δp and a proportion rate of $\bar{p}$, we note

$$\Delta p = U_\alpha \sqrt{\frac{\bar{p}(1 - \bar{p})}{n}}$$

Solving for n yields

$$n = \left(\frac{U_\alpha}{\Delta p}\right)^2 (\bar{p})(1 - \bar{p})$$

Computer programs can provide attribute confidence intervals that require no approximating distributions. In addition, these computer programs can test a null hypothesis.

For example, if we had an upper failure rate criterion of 0.01 units and encounter 8 defective transactions out of a random sample of 1000 transactions, our sample failure rate would be 0.008 (8/1000). A one-sided confidence interval failure rate and hypothesis test from a computer program yielded:

Test and CI for One Proportion

```
Test of p = 0.01 vs p < 0.01

                                                    Exact
Sample   X      N  Sample p  95.0% Upper Bound  P-Value
1        8  1000  0.008000            0.014388    0.332
```

If we chose an $\alpha = 0.05$ decision criterion, we would fail to reject the null hypothesis that the failure rate is equal to 0.01. Our 95% upper bound confidence interval is 0.014, which is larger than our criterion.

21.5   Reduced Sample Size Testing for Attribute Situations

The previously presented sample size calculation protects both the customer and the producer. A reduced sample size may be used for a criterion verification test when the sample size is chosen so that the criterion is set to a confidence interval limit with a given number of allowed failures; that is, the failure rate criterion will be equal to or less than the limit at the desired confidence level.

The example in the next section illustrates the simple procedure to use when designing such a test; it also shows that in order to pass a test of this type the sample may be required to perform at a failure rate that is much better than the population criterion. This method also applies to the certification of a reparable system failure rate.

If the Poisson distribution is an appropriate approximation for this binomial test situation, sample size requirements can be determined from Table K (Appendix G). A tabular value (B) can be determined for the chosen number of permissible failures (r) and desired confidence value (c). This value is then substituted with the failure rate criterion (ρ_a) into the following equation to yield a value for T, the necessary test sample size where T symbolizes time. T is used in this equation for consistency with the reliability application equation discussed in Breyfogle (2003).

$$T = B_{r;c} / \rho_a$$

21.6 Example 21.2: Reduced Sample Size Testing – Attribute Response Situations

Given the failure rate criterion (ρ_a) of 0.001 (1/1000) from the previous example, determine a zero failure test sample size such that a 95% confidence interval bound will have

$$\rho \le 0.001$$

From Table 9.2 it is noted that the Poisson approximation seems to be a reasonable simplification because the failure rate criterion of 0.001 is much less than 0.05 and the test will surely require a sample size larger than 20.

From Table K, $B_{0;0.95}$ equals 2.996. The sample size is then

$$T = B_{0;0.95}/\rho_a = 2.996/0.001 = 2996$$

The sample size for this example is much less than that calculated in the previous example, i.e., 64,106; however, this example does not consider both α and β risks. With a zero failure test strategy, there is a good chance that the samples will not perform well enough to pass the test objectives, unless the actual failure rate, which is unknown to the experimenter, is much better than the criterion.

To see this, consider, for example, that only one failure occurred while testing the sample of 2996. For this sample, the failure rate is lower than the 0.001 criterion (i.e., 1/2996 = 0.00033). However, from Table K (Appendix G), $B_{1;0.95}$ equals 4.744 for one failure and a level equal to 0.95. The single-sided 95% confidence interval for the failure rate, given information from this test using the relationship shown at the bottom of Table K, is

$$\rho \le B_{1;095}/T = 4.744/2996 = 0.00158 \quad (\text{i.e.,} \rho \le 0.00158)$$

The 0.001 failure rate criterion value is contained in the above 95% confidence bounds. The original test objectives were not met (i.e., a failure occurred during test); hence, from a technical point of view the product did not pass the test. However, from a practical point of view, the experimenter may want to determine (for reference only) a lesser confidence interval, for example, 80% confidence, that would have allowed the test to pass had this value been chosen initially.

From Table K, the single-sided 80% confidence for the failure rate is

$$\rho \le B_{1;0..95}/T = 2.994/2996 = 0.0009993 \quad (\text{i.e., } \rho \le 0.0009993)$$

The 0.001 criterion is now outside the single-sided 80% confidence interval. A major business decision may rest on the outcome of this test. From a practical point of view, it seems wise for the experimenter to report this lower confidence interval information to management and others along with the cause of the failure and a corrective action strategy; that is, don't we really want to have zero failures experienced by the customer? The experimenter might also state that a DOE is being planned to determine the changes that should be made to improve the manufacturing process so that there is less chance that this type of failure will occur again. From this information, it may be decided that a limited shipment plan is appropriate for the current product. Note that the same general method could be used if more than one failure occurred during the test. Other confidence statements that might also be appropriate under certain situations are a double-sided confidence interval statement or a single-sided statement where $\rho \ge$ a value.

The experimenter may be surprised to find that one failure technically means that the test done was not passed, even though the sample failure rate was much better than the criterion. Breyfogle (2003) illustrates how a test performance ratio can be used to create pretest graphical information that can be an aid when choosing the number of permissible failures and test confidence interval level. A lower level than initially desired may be needed in order to create a reasonable test.

21.7   Example 21.3: Sampling Does Not Fix Common-Cause Problems

Often it seems that organizations do not truly appreciate that sampling does not fix problems. This example describes two actual situations where there was a misperception about the value of sampling.

Situation 1

A company's security department regularly conducts after-hours random audits to determine if employees' desks where locked and no confident information was unsecured. A 30,000-foot-level assessment of this metric revealed that the process was predictable and there was a 7% non-conformance rate, which was unacceptable relative to expectations. The data analyzer told the security department that something fundamentally different needed to be done to improve this non-conformance rate.

The intent of the statement "something fundamentally different needed to be done" was that somehow the day-to-day actions of employees would need to be changed. That is, when departing for the day, employee behavior would need to be changed so that they were less likely to forget to lock their desk and secure confidential information.

The security department misunderstood the statement. The security department increased their sample size, which did nothing to change behavior. The only benefit from this increased sample size action was a tightened 7% non-conformance rate confidence interval.

Another independent question that one might ask is whether the right question was being asked. Perhaps more company proprietary information is truly lost through executive employee turn-over, idle employee-to-employee conversations at restaurants/bars, or unsecured notebook computers that have sensitive information. Perhaps more focus should be given to these areas, rather than the easy-to-measure metric of desk audits.

Perhaps the security desk-audit sample size should be reduced to decrease auditing expense and the 30,000-foot-level control chart be posted in an attempt to build awareness to the issue; that is, with the hope/intent that the metric does not at least degrade.

Situation 2

An audit of 1500 call center representatives five times a month resulted in 7500 monthly samples. A 90% pass rate was desired; however, the observed pass rate was 10%. A black belt advised reducing the sample size and putting these resources into improving the process until a 50% rate was achieved. A monthly sample size of 7500 is not really needed to realize a 10% conformance rate does not equal a desired 90% conformance rate.

One should also note that in a 30,000-foot-level control chart sample size builds over time when there is common-cause variability. That is, for this example a predictable process over 5 months can be considered to have a sample size of 37,500 (i.e., 5 × 7500)

21.8   Example 21.4: Base-Lining a 30,000-Foot-Level Attribute-Response Metric and Determining Process Confidence Interval Statement

A project was to reduce a process defective rate. Belief was that the defective rate could differ by day of the week; hence, a weekly infrequent subgrouping/sampling frequency was selected. All weekly transactions have been recorded as either pass or fail and the number of transactions in each subgroup is similar but not exactly the same.

From Appendix Section D.1, the step for selecting the appropriate control chart is noted to be step 3.2.14; that is, create a subgroup plan so that typical process noise occurs between subgroups, and the subgroup size is large enough so that several non-compliances are expected in each subgroup (e.g., failure rates in DPMO or defective rate units will be tracked daily). From this same volume section, the roadmap step for selecting the appropriate process capability/performance metric statement is step 3.3.13; that is for infrequent failures or subgroups that have an inconsistent sample size, report DPU or DPMO rate that is determined by dividing total number of failures by total number of defect opportunities or units.

Table 21.1 contains historical defective data. The data's defective rate individuals control chart shown in Figure 21.1 indicates a process shift. Further investigation led to the conclusion that general process degradation began on week 18.

Figure 21.2 includes staging of the defective rate for the individuals control chart, where week 18 is the transition point. From this chart, we have no reason to not believe that the process has future predictability.

Since the process has differing subgroup sizes, the project execution roadmap step 3.3.13 suggests estimating the defective proportion from the raw data over the most current 30,000-foot-level control chart's region of stability. This results in an estimated defective rate of

$$\text{Defective Rate (Week 18 – 39)} = \frac{3072}{108795} = 0.0282$$

For this process, we could then simply state that the process is predictable with an estimated defective rate of 0.0282; that is, as shown in Figure 21.2. For this situation, there was not much

Table 21.1: Summary Report of Defective Units by Week

Week	Subgroup Size	Defectives	Week	Subgroup Size	Defectives	Week	Subgroup Size	Defectives
1	4357	76	14	5368	96	27	4416	150
2	5931	92	15	4477	31	28	5490	142
3	4898	99	16	5274	98	29	4615	114
4	5749	74	17	4801	69	30	4642	149
5	4189	121	18	4256	118	31	5028	140
6	5114	41	19	4861	109	32	4556	111
7	5009	77	20	4156	129	33	5736	174
8	5233	144	21	5584	155	34	4557	182
9	5483	74	22	5291	142	35	4866	111
10	4948	100	23	4604	121	36	5402	157
11	5301	94	24	5333	181	37	5034	127
12	5112	75	25	4658	139	38	5059	149
13	4257	84	26	5583	111	39	5068	161

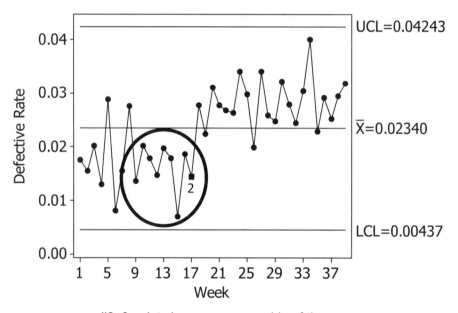

#2: 9 points in a row on one side of the
center line special cause test

Figure 21.1: Individuals control chart of defective rate.

difference in averaging the failure rates, which would be the centerline of the non-transformed control chart. However, for other situations these defective rate estimation procedures could yield much larger differences.

Even though we have captured all pass/fail data that went through this process we can still consider the data from the latest region of

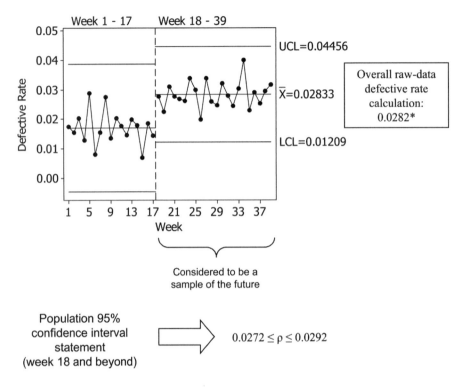

* Better estimating procedure because of differing sample sizes

Figure 21.2: Individuals control chart of defective rate by stage.

stability to be a sample of the future. If the magnitude of this estimate is undesirable something needs to be done to improve the process.

The tools described in this chapter can be used to determine the overall process population defective rate confidence interval. This calculation is made by analyzing the raw data totals for the 30,000-foot-level control chart's region of stability; that is, a total of 3072 defective occurrences out of 108,795 transactions. A statistical program output for this is:

Test and CI for One Proportion

```
Sample      X         N    Sample p              95% CI
1        3072   108795    0.028237   (0.027260, 0.029238)
```

A hypothesis could also be made that the failure rate is equal to the failure rate from transactions prior to week 18. To make this assessment, the following estimate for the overall week 1–17 failure rate could be used. Note, a later chapter will describe how to compare two proportions, which would be a better procedure for this situation:

$$\text{Defective Rate (Week } 1-17) = \frac{1445}{85501} = 0.017$$

A statistical program using 0.017 as a test criterion yielded the output:

Test and CI for One Proportion

```
Test of p = 0.017 vs p not = 0.017
                                                    Exact
Sample     X       N Sample p         95% CI        P-Value
1       3072 108795 0.028237 (0.027260, 0.029238)  0.000
```

From the previous control chart analysis, it was concluded that there was degradation in the process defective rate. This analysis supports that conclusion, since the *P* value is less than 0.05 and the 0.017 defective rate is below the population defective rate confidence interval.

From our overall analysis, it could be stated that our process is now predictable with a best-estimate defective rate of 0.28, which has a 95% confidence interval of 0.027 to 0.029. This confidence interval procedure can be used for project execution roadmap step 3.4 shown in Appendix Section D.1.

21.9   Attribute Sample Plan Alternatives

The preceding discussion assumes that the sample size is small relative to the population size. If the sample size is greater than one-tenth of the population size, the hypergeometric distribution should be considered.

It is important to emphasize that the sample must be randomly selected from the population and that the outcome of the experiment only characterizes the population from which the sample is taken. For example, a sample taken from an initial production process may be very different from the characteristics of production parts manufactured in the future and sent to the customer.

American National Standards Institute (ANSI) document could be used to select an alternative approach to choosing an attribute-sampling plan. For example,

- ANSI/ASQC Z1.4-1993 (Cancelled MIL-STD-105): Sampling procedures and tables for inspection by attributes
- ANSI/ASQC Z1.9-1993 (canceled MIL-STD-414): Sampling procedures and tables for inspection by variables for percent nonconforming

Still another approach is to consider sequential binomial test plans, which are similar in form to those shown in Breyfogle (2003) for the Poisson distribution. Ireson (1966) gives the equations necessary for the application of this method, originally developed by Wald (1947). However, with the low failure rate criteria of today, this sequential test approach is not usually a realistic alternative.

21.10   Acceptable Quality Level Sampling Can Be Deceptive

The intent of this section is not to give instruction on how to create an acceptable quality level (AQL) sampling plan. There are many other sources for this type of information. The intent of this section is, rather to show how an AQL pass/fail sample lot test strategy for product is not effective. A more effective approach is to monitor the process, using techniques such as control charts.

With AQL sampling plans, a lot is inspected to determine if it should be accepted or rejected. Sampling plans are typically determined from tables as a function of an AQL criterion and other characteristics of the lot. Pass/fail decisions for an AQL evaluated lot are based only on the lot's performance, not on previous product performance from the process. AQL sampling plans do not give a picture of how a process is performing.

AQL sampling plans are inefficient and can be very costly, especially when high levels of quality are needed. Often, organizations think that they will achieve better quality with AQL sampling plans than they really can. The trend is that organizations are moving away from AQL sampling plans; however, many organizations are slow to make the transition. The following describes the concepts and shortcomings of AQL sampling plans.

When setting up an AQL sampling plan, much care needs to be exercised in choosing samples. Samples must be a random sample from the lot. This can be difficult to accomplish. Neither sampling nor 100% inspection guarantees that every defect will be found. Studies have shown that 100% inspection is at most 80% effective.

There are two kinds of sampling risks:

1. Good lots can be rejected.
2. Bad lots can be accepted.

The operating characteristic (OC) curve for sampling plans quantifies these risks. Figure 21.3 shows an ideal operating curve. Because we cannot achieve an *ideal* OC curve, we describe OC curves using the following terms:

Acceptable Quality Level (AQL)

- AQL is typically considered to be the worst quality level that is still considered satisfactory. It is the maximum percent defective that for purposes of sampling inspection can be considered satisfactory as a process average.

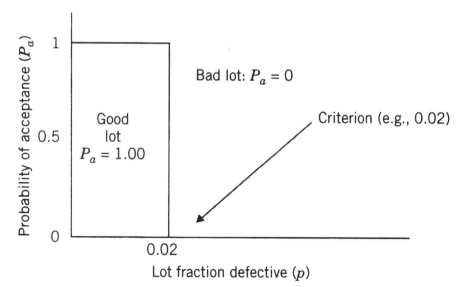

Figure 21.3: Ideal operating curve.

- The probability of accepting an AQL lot should be high. A probability of 0.95 translates to an α risk of 0.05.

Rejectable Quality Level (RQL)

- This is considered to be unsatisfactory quality level.
- This is sometimes called *lot tolerance percent defective* (LTPD).
- This consumer's risk has been standardized in some tables as 0.1.
- The probability of accepting an RQL lot should be low.

Indifference Quality Level (IQL)

- Quality level is somewhere between AQL and RQL.
- This is frequently defined as quality level having probability of acceptance of 0.5 for a sampling plan.

An OC curve describes the probability of acceptance for various values of incoming quality. P_a is the probability that the number of defectives in the sample is equal to or less than the acceptance number for the sampling plan. The hypergeometric, binomial, and Poisson distributions describe the probability of acceptance for various situations.

The Poisson distribution is the easiest to use when calculating probabilities. The Poisson distribution can often be used as an approximation for the other distributions. The probability of exactly x defects ($P(x)$) in n samples is

$$P(x) = \frac{e^{-np}(np)^x}{x!}$$

For "*a*" allowed failures, $P(x \le a)$ is the sum of $P(x)$ for $x = 0$ to $x = a$.

Figure 21.4 shows an AQL OC curve for an AQL level of 0.9%. Someone who is not familiar with the OC curves of AQL would probably think that passage of this AQL 0.9% test would indicate goodness. Well this is not exactly true because from this OC curve it can be seen that the failure rate would have to be actually about 2.5% to have a 50%/50% chance of rejection.

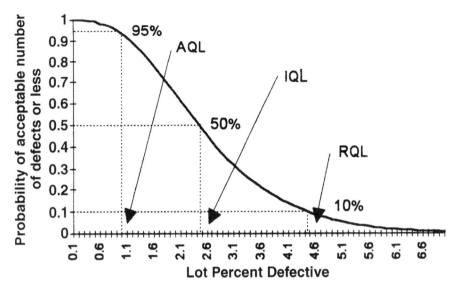

Figure 21.4: An OC curve. N =150, c =3.

AQL sampling often leads to activities that are associated with attempts to test quality into a product. AQL sampling can reject lots that are a result of common-cause process variability. When a process output is examined as AQL lots and a lot is rejected because of common cause variability, customer quality does not improve.

In lieu of using AQL sampling plans to periodically inspect the output of a process, more useful information can be obtained by using control charts first to identify special cause issues. Process capability/performance studies can then be used to quantify the common cause of the process. If a process is not capable, something needs to be done differently to the process to make it more capable.

21.11 Example 21.5: AQL

For N (lot size) = 75 and AQL = 4.0%, ANSI/ASQC Z1.4-1993 (Cancelled MIL-STD-105) yields for a general inspection level II a test plan in which

- Sample size = 13
- Acceptance number = 1
- Rejection number = 2

From this plan we can see how AQL sampling protects the producer. The failure rate at the acceptance number is 7.6% (i.e., $(1/13)(100) = 7.6\%$), while the failure rate at the rejection number is 15.4% (i.e., $(2/13)(100) = 15.4\%$).

Usually a sample size is considered small relative to the population size if the sample is less than ten percent of the population size. In this case, the population size is 75 and the sample size is 13; that is, 13 is greater than 10% of the population size. However, for the sake of illustration let's determine the confidence interval for the failure rate for the above two scenarios as though the sample size relative to population size were small. This calculation yielded:

Test and CI for One Proportion

```
Test of p = 0.04 vs p < 0.04
                                      95% Upper          Exact
Sample     X      N     Sample p        Bound         P-Value
1          1      13    0.076923       0.316340         0.907
```

Test and CI for One Proportion

```
Test of p = 0.04 vs p < 0.04

                                      95% Upper          Exact
Sample     X      N     Sample p        Bound         P-Value
1          2      13    0.153846       0.410099         0.986
```

For this AQL test of 4% the 95% confidence bound for one failure is 31.6% and or two failures is 41.0%. Practitioners often don't realize how these AQL assessments do not protect the customer as much as they might think. To reiterate, a test that samples and makes statements about the process at the 30,000-foot-level can provide more insight with less effort.

21.12   Applying IEE

When determining a test strategy, the analyst needs to address the question of process stability. If a process is not stable/predictable, the test methods and confidence statements cannot be interpreted with much precision. Process control charting techniques can be used to determine the stability of a process.

Consider also what actions will be taken when a failure occurs in a particular attribute-sampling plan. Will the failure be "talked away"? Often no knowledge is obtained about the "good" parts. Are these "good parts" close to "failure"? What direction can be given to fixing the source of failure so that failure will not occur in a customer environment? One should not play games with numbers! Only tests that give useful information for continually improving the manufacturing process should be considered.

The examples in this chapter illustrate that test sample size can often become very large when verifying low failure criteria. To make matters worse, large sample sizes may actually be needed for each lot that is produced.

Fortunately, however, many problems that are initially defined as attribute tests can be redefined to continuous response output tests. For example, a tester may reject an electronic panel if the electrical resistance of any circuit is below a certain resistance value. In this example, more benefit could be derived from the test if actual resistance values are evaluated. With this information, percent of population projections for failure at the resistance threshold could then be made using probability plotting techniques. After an acceptable level of resistance is established in the process, resistance could then be monitored using control chart techniques for variables. These charts then indicate when the resistance mean and standard deviation are decreasing or increasing with time, an expected indicator of an increase in the percentage builds that are beyond the threshold requirement.

Additionally, DOE techniques could be used as a guide to manufacture test samples that represent the limits of the process. This test could perhaps yield parts that are more representative of future builds and future process variability. These samples will not be "random" from the process, but this technique can potentially identify future process problems that a random sample from an initial "batch" lot would miss.

With the typical low failure rates of today, AQL sampling is not an effective approach to identify lot defect problems. However, often it can be difficult to convince others that AQL does not add much value and should be replaced by a better process monitoring system.

If AQL testing is commonplace in an organization, consider viewing the AQL's department activity as a process where input to the process is various types of batches that enter this process. The output to this process is whether the lot failed or not. Next calculate *P* for some period of time, for example, weekly, by dividing the number of lots that failed by the number of lots that were tested. Next plot these *P* values on an individuals control chart and assess the frequency of lots. A Pareto chart could then be created to summarize overall the types of failure captured within the AQL department. To better grasp how many unacceptable lots that are perhaps missed by the AQL department because of a low sample size, resampling of some lots that failed can give valuable insight. I would suspect that many of the failed lots would pass the second time. If this is the case, one would suspect that many of the lots that passed might fail if they were re-tested). This information collectively could be very valuable in obtaining a better overall picture of the value of the department and in determining where improvements could be made.

21.13   Exercises

1. Determine the 95% confidence interval for a population defective rate given a sample of 60 with 5 defectives.
2. A 10 random-sample evaluation of the specification 75 ± 3 yielded readings of 77.1, 76.8, 76.3, 75.9, 76.1, 77.7, 76.7, 75.7, 76.9, 77.4. Make a best estimate attribute assessment of the population relative to the specification limits. Suggest an IEE analysis approach.
3. The following data give the difference between actual arrival time and the scheduled arrival time for the 12 monthly flights that someone made into his/her resident city during the last year; positive values indicate the number of minutes the flight was late. The traveler always used the same airline and was scheduled to arrive at the same time on the last Wednesday of the month.

June	July	Aug	Sep	Oct	Nov	Dec	Jan	Feb	Mar	Apr	May
0.1	3.2	18.4	2.5	15.6	90.9	102.1	0.8	20.2	31.3	1.4	21.9

   (a) Give conclusions if a flight is considered "on-time" when it arrives within 20 minutes.
   (b) Give IEE consideration.
4. A process is considered to have an unsatisfactory response whenever the output is greater than 100. A defective rate

of 2% is considered tolerable; however, a rate of 3% is not considered tolerable.

(a) Calculate a sample size if all risk levels are 0.05.

(b) Give examples from manufacturing, development, and service where this type of question might have originated.

(c) Explain potential implementation problems and IEE considerations.

5. A part is not to exceed a failure rate of 3.4 failures in one million.

(a) Determine the sample size needed for a hypothesis test of the equality of this failure rate to a 3.4 parts per million failure rate. Use risks of 0.05 and an uncertainty of $\pm$ 10% of the failure rate target.

(b) Determine the sample size if one failure were permitted with a 95% confidence statement. using a reduced sample size testing approach.

(c) Determine the failure rate of the sample if two failures occurred during the test, using a reduced sample size testing approach.

(d) Comment on your results and implementation challenges. List IEE opportunities.

6. A random sample of 100 units was selected from a manufacturing process. These units either passed or failed a tester in the course of the manufacturing process. A record was kept so that each unit could later be identified as to whether it passed or failed the manufacturing test. Each unit was then thoroughly tested in the laboratory to determine whether it should have passed or failed. The result of this laboratory evaluation was that a correct assessment was performed in manufacturing of 90 out of the 100 samples tested. Determine the 95% confidence interval for the test's effectiveness.

22

P-DMAIC – Analyze Phase: Continuous Response Comparison Tests

22.1 P-DMAIC Roadmap Component

The previous two chapters described inferences from continuous and attribute population samples. This chapter and the next chapter extend these concepts to inferences when comparing more than one population.

The graphic in this section highlights the P-DMAIC roadmap steps (see Appendix Section D.1) that are described in this chapter. Appendix E contains the tollgate check sheets for this and other phases. This chapter focuses on continuous response situations; e.g., do two machines manufacture, on average, shaft diameter to the same dimension? The next chapter focuses on attribute response situations; for example, is the failure frequencies of completing a purchase order correctly the same between two departments?

In the P-DMAIC and E-DMAIC analyze phases, these tools can provide insight to inputs that can affect an output; that is, the Xs in the equation $Y = f(X)$. This insight can then lead to improvement opportunities. In the improve phase of the P-DMAIC roadmap, these tools can also statistically assess change impact on a process output.

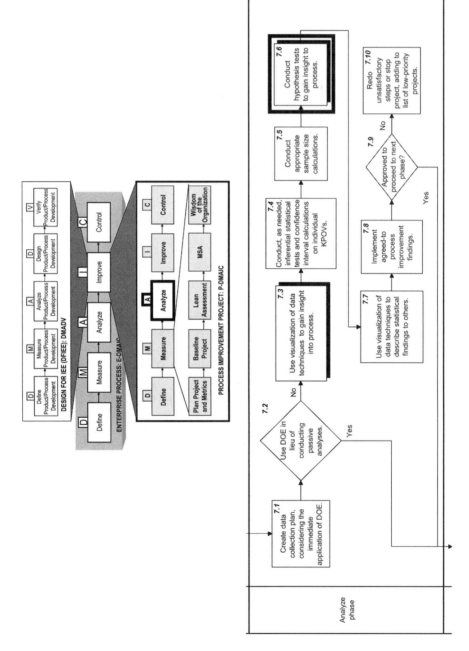

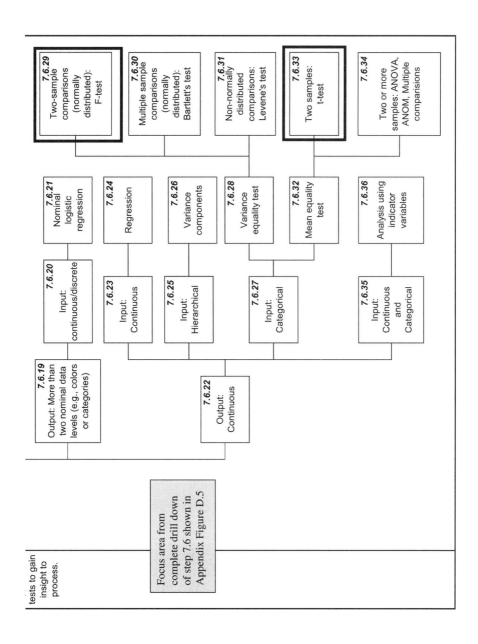

22.2   IEE Application Examples: Comparison Tests

- *Transactional 30,000-foot-level metric*: DSO reduction was chosen as an IEE project. A cause-and-effect matrix ranked company as an important input that could affect the DSO response; that is, the team thought that Company A was more delinquent in payments than other companies. From randomly sampled data, a *t*-test was conducted to test the hypothesis of equality of mean DSO of Company A to the other companies.

- *Manufacturing 30,000-foot-level metric (KPOV)*: An IEE project was to improve the process capability/performance of the diameter of a manufactured product; that is, reduce the number of parts beyond the specification limits. A cause-and-effect matrix ranked cavity of the two-cavity mold as an important input that could be yielding different part diameters. From randomly sampled data, a *t*-test was conducted to test the hypothesis of mean diameter equality for cavity 1 and cavity 2. An *F*-test was conducted to test the hypothesis of variability equality for cavity 1 and cavity 2.

- *Transactional and Manufacturing 30,000-foot-level lead time metric (a Lean metric)*: An IEE project to improve the time from order entry to fulfillment was measured. A low-hanging fruit change was made to the process. Using the 30,000-foot-level control chart data, a confidence interval was created to describe the impact of the change in mean system's lead time.

22.3   Comparing Continuous Data Responses

The methods discussed in this chapter can be used, for example, to compare two production machines or suppliers. Both mean and standard deviation output can be compared between the samples to determine whether a difference is large enough to be statistically significant. The comparison test of means is robust to the shape of the underlying distribution not being normal; however, this is not true when comparing standard deviations. Nonparametric statistical comparisons may be used when underlying distribution issues are of concern.

The null hypothesis for the comparison test is that there is no difference, while the alternative hypothesis is that there is a difference. The basic comparison test equations apply also to the DOE and ANOVA analyses, which are treated in more detail later.

22.4   Sample Size: Comparing Means

Brush (1988) gives graphs that can be used to aid with the selection of sample sizes. Diamond (1989) multiplies the appropriate single sampled population equation by 2 to determine a sample size for each of the two populations.

22.5   Comparing Two Means

When comparing the means of two samples, the null hypothesis is that there is no difference between the population means, while the alternative hypothesis is that there is a difference between the population means. A difference between two means could be single-sided, that is, $\mu_1 > \mu_2$ or $\mu_1 < \mu_2$, or double-sided, i.e., $\mu_1 \neq \mu_2$. Table 22.1 summarizes the equations and tables to use when making these comparisons to determine whether there is a statistically significant difference at the desired level of risk. The null hypothesis rejection criterion is noted for each of the tabulated scenarios.

22.6   Example 22.1: Comparing the Means of Two Samples

IEE Application Examples

- *Transactional 30,000-foot-level metric: Hypothesis test of equality of mean DSO of Company A to Company B.*
- *Manufacturing 30,000-foot-level metric (KPOV): Hypothesis test of equality of diameters from the two cavities of a plastic injection mold.*

A problem existed in manufacturing where the voice quality of a portable dictating machine was unsatisfactory. It was decided to use off-line DOEs to assess the benefit of design and process changes before implementation, rather than using the common

Table 22.1: Significance Tests for the Difference between the Means
of Two Samples

$\sigma_1^2 = \sigma_2^2$	$\sigma_1^2 \neq \sigma_2^2$

σ Known

$$U_0 = \frac{|\bar{x}_1 - \bar{x}_2|}{\sigma \sqrt{\dfrac{1}{n_1} + \dfrac{1}{n_2}}}$$

$$U_0 = \frac{|\bar{x}_1 - \bar{x}_2|}{\sqrt{\dfrac{\sigma_1^2}{n_1} + \dfrac{\sigma_2^2}{n_2}}}$$

Reject H_0 if $U_0 > U_\alpha$ Reject H_0 if $U_0 > U_\alpha$

σ Unknown

$$t_0 = \frac{|\bar{x}_1 - \bar{x}_2|}{s \sqrt{\dfrac{1}{n_1} + \dfrac{1}{n_2}}}$$

$$t_0 = \frac{|\bar{x}_1 - \bar{x}_2|}{\sqrt{\dfrac{s_1^2}{n_1} + \dfrac{s_2^2}{n_2}}}$$

$$s = \sqrt{\frac{(n_1 - 1)s_1^2 + (n_2 - 1)s_2^2}{n_1 + n_2 - 2}}$$

Reject H_0 if $t_0 > t_\alpha$ where

$$\nu = \frac{[(s_1^2/n_1) + (s_2^2/n_2)]^2}{\dfrac{(s_1^2/n_1)^2}{n_1 + 1} + \dfrac{(s_2^2/n_2)^2}{n_2 + 1}} - 2$$

Reject H_0 if $t_0 > t_\alpha$ where
$$\nu = n_1 + n_2 - 2$$

Reference Tables

H_a	U_α	t_α
$\mu_1 \neq \mu_2$	Table C	Table E
$\mu_1 > \mu_2$ (if $\bar{x}_1 > \bar{x}_2$)		
or	Table B	Table D
$\mu_1 < \mu_2$ (if $\bar{x}_1 < \bar{x}_2$)		

strategy of implementing changes and examining the results using a one-at-a-time strategy.

Over 20 changes were considered in multiple DOEs, but only three design changes were found beneficial. A comparison experiment was conducted to confirm and quantify the benefit of these three design changes. The results from the test were as follows; a lower number indicates that a machine has better voice quality:

Sample Number	Current Design (Voice Quality Measurement)	New Design (Voice Quality Measurement)
1	1.034	0.556
2	0.913	0.874
3	0.881	0.673
4	1.185	0.632
5	0.930	0.543
6	0.880	0.748
7	1.132	0.532
8	0.745	0.530
9	0.737	0.678
10	1.233	0.676
11	0.778	0.558
12	1.325	0.600
13	0.746	0.713
14	0.852	0.525

The mean ($\bar{x}$) and standard deviation (s) of the 14 samples are

	Current Design	New Design
	$\bar{x}_1 = 0.955$	$\bar{x}_2 = 0.631$
	$s_1 = 0.195$	$s_2 = 0.102$

From the sample data, the mean level from the new design is better than that of the current design; however, the question of concern is whether the difference is large enough to be considered statistically significant. Because the standard deviations are unknown and are thought to be different, it follows that

$$t_0 = \frac{|\bar{x}_1 - \bar{x}_2|}{\sqrt{\dfrac{s_1^2}{n_1} + \dfrac{s_2^2}{n_2}}} = \frac{|0.955 - 0.631|}{\sqrt{\dfrac{(0.195)^2}{14} + \dfrac{(0.102)^2}{14}}} = 5.51$$

Reject H_0 if $t_0 > t_\alpha$, where the degrees of freedom for t_α are

$$v = \frac{[(s_1^2 / n_1) + (s_2^2 / n_2)]^2}{\frac{(s_1^2 / n_1)^2}{n_1 + 1} + \frac{(s_2^2 / n_2)^2}{n_2 + 1}} - 2$$

$$= \frac{[(0.195^2 / 14) + (0.102^2 / 14)]^2}{\frac{(0.195^2 / 14)^2}{14 + 1} + \frac{(0.102^2 / 14)^2}{14 + 1}} - 2 = 20.6$$

Assume that the changes will be made if this confirmation experiment shows significance at a level of 0.05. For 21 degrees of freedom, Table D yields a $t_\alpha = t_{0.05}$ value of 1.721.

The test question is single-sided; i.e., whether the new design is better than the old design. It does not make sense for this situation to address whether the samples are equal, i.e., a double-sided scenario. Money should only be spent to make the change if the design changes show an improvement in voice quality. Because 5.51 > 1.721, i.e., $t_0 > t_\alpha$, the design changes should be made.

A statistical computer program analysis of this data yielded:

Two-Sample T-Test and CI: Current Design, New Design

```
Two-sample T for Current Design vs New Design
```

	N	Mean	St Dev	SE Mean
Current Design	14	0.955	0.195	0.052
New Design	14	0.631	0.102	0.027

```
Difference = mu (Current Design) - mu (New Design)
Estimate for difference: 0.323786
95% CI for difference: (0.200473, 0.447099)
T-Test of difference = 0 (vs not =): T-Value = 5.50
P-Value = 0.000 DF = 19
```

The computer output shows 19 degrees of freedom, while the manual approach was 21. The computer analysis used a different approach to determine degrees of freedom; however, this difference should not have much impact on our results.

We notice that this output's *t*-value is approximately the same as the manual calculation. For an α decision level of 0.05, we would declare significance since the *P* value of 0.000 is less than the 0.05 criteria.

This output additionally provides the best estimate for the difference of 0.323786 and a 95% confidence interval of 0.200473 to 0.447099 for this difference. Note that this confidence interval did not contain zero. An additional point to make is that if one of the confidence interval boundaries equals zero, then the *P* value would equal 0.05.

22.7   Comparing Variances of Two Samples

A statistical significance test methodology to determine whether a sample variance (s_1^2) is larger than another sample variance (s_2^2) is first to determine

$$F_0 = \frac{s_1^2}{s_2^2} \quad s_1^2 > s_2^2$$

For significance this ratio needs to be larger than the appropriate tabular value of the *F* distribution noted in Table F. From this one-sided table is taken $F_{\alpha;\nu1;\nu2}$, where ν_1 is the number of degrees of freedom, that is, sample size minus one, of the sample with the largest variance, while ν_2 is the number of degrees of freedom of the smallest variance. A variance ratio that is larger than the tabular value for a indicates that there is a statistically significant difference between the variances at the level of α.

Without a prior reason to anticipate inequality of variance, the alternative to the null hypothesis is two-sided. The same equation applies; however, the value from Table F would now be $F_{\alpha/2;\nu1;\nu2}$ (Snedecor and Cochran, 1980).

Unlike the test for differing means, this test is sensitive to the data's being from a normal distribution. Care must be exercised when doing a variance comparison test because a statistically significant difference may in reality result from a violation of the underlying assumption of normality. A probability plot of the data can yield information useful for making this assessment. Some statistical computer programs offer the Levene's test for the analysis if data are not normally distributed.

22.8   Example 22.2: Comparing the Variance of Two Samples

IEE Application Examples

- *Transactional 30,000-foot-level metric: Hypothesis test of equality of DSO variance of Company A to Company B.*
- *Manufacturing 30,000-foot-level metric (KPOV): Hypothesis test of equality of diameter variance from the two cavities of a plastic injection mold.*

The standard deviations of the two samples of 14 in Example 22.1 were 0.195 for the current design and 0.102 for the new design. The designers had hoped that the new design would produce less variability. Is there reason to believe, at the 0.05 significance level, that the variance of the new design is less?

$$F_0 = \frac{s_1^2}{s_2^2} = \frac{0.195^2}{0.102^2} = 3.633$$

The number of degrees of freedom are

$$\nu_1 = 14-1 = 13 \qquad \nu_2 = 14-1 = 13$$

With these degrees of freedom, interpolation in Table F yields

$$F_{\alpha;\nu 1;\nu 2} = F_{0.05;\ 13;\ 13} = 2.58$$

Because $3.633 > 2.58$ (i.e., $F_0 > F_{\alpha;\nu 1;\nu 2}$), we conclude that the variability of the new design is less than the old design at a significance level of 0.05, if each of the distributions are normally distributed. From the probability plots shown in Figure 22.1, we fail to reject the null hypothesis of normality since each distribution has a *P* value greater than 0.05. That is, from this analysis we have no reason to believe that each data set is not normally distributed; hence, the *F*-test statistical variance comparison analysis is appropriate.

A statistical program analysis for testing the hypothesis of variance equality is shown in Figure 22.2. Since the *F*-test *P* value in this figure is 0.027, which is less than 0.05, we can reject the null hypothesis of normality. That is, we believe that the variability of the new process is smaller than the old process. The Levene's

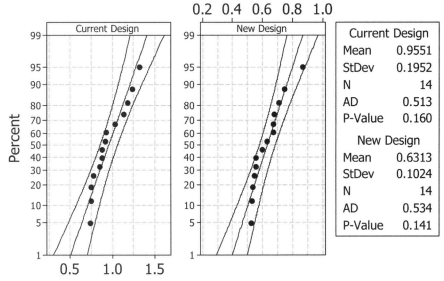

Figure 22.1: Normal probability plot of current and new design with 95% confidence interval.

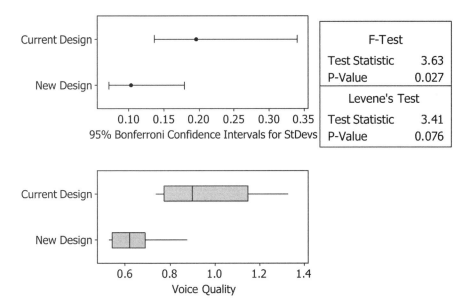

Figure 22.2: Test for equal variances of current design and new design.

test would be used for the test statistic of variance equality if either of the two distribution's normality hypothesis tests were rejected.

22.9   Comparing Populations Using a Probability Plot

Probability plots of experimental data can supplement traditional comparison tests. These plots can show information that may yield a better basic understanding of the differences between the samples. Two probability plots on one set of axes can indicate graphically the differences in means, variances, and possible outliers; i.e., data points that are "different" from the other values. There may have been an error when recording some of the data. This type of understanding can often be used to help improve the manufacturing processes.

22.10   Example 22.3: Comparing Responses Using a Probability Plot

Consider the data presented in Example 22.1. The normal probability plots of these data in Figure 22.3 without confidence intervals show graphically the improvement in mean and standard deviation; i.e., increased slope with new design. The data tend to follow a straight line on the normal probability plot.

However, when further root-cause understanding is desired, the experimenter might choose to investigate outlier points from a distribution that seems most appropriate.

Additional information can be obtained from the normal probability plot. If, for example, a final test criterion of 1.0 exists, the current design would experience a rejection rate of approximately 40%, while the new design would be close to zero.

The probability plot is a powerful tool, but management may not be familiar with the interpretation of the graph. Because the data seem to follow a normal distribution, a final presentation format could use the sample means and standard deviations to draw the estimated PDFs in order to convey the results in an easily understood manner. These graphs can then be illustrated together as shown in Figure 22.4 for comparative purposes.

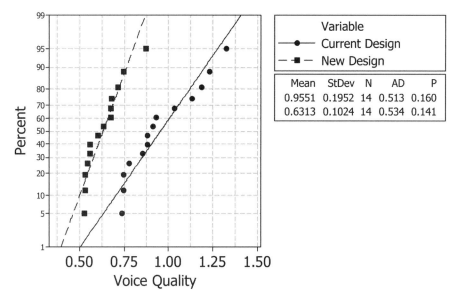

Figure 22.3: Normal probability plot comparison.

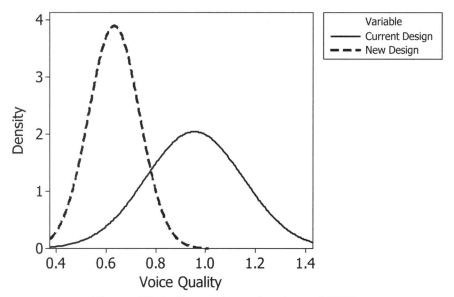

Figure 22.4: Comparison of estimated PDFs.

22.11   Example 22.4: IEE Demonstration of Process Improvement for a Continuous Response

A project was to reduce process lead time, where data were not readily available. An infrequent subgrouping/sampling frequency was selected with one daily random sample.

For this project, Example 20.6 described the 30,000-foot-level continuous response baseline metric and the determination of the process response confidence interval statements. This example will describe the demonstration of project benefits at the 30,000-foot-level, where the before/after process change measurements are shown in Table 22.2. The process change was implemented on day 211.

The Appendix Section D.1 P-DMAIC project execution roadmap steps for demonstrating project benefits are:

- Step 8.19: Show impact of change in the 30,000-foot-level control chart.
- Step 8.20: Show visually the estimated process capability/ performance metric improvement.
- Step 8.21: Describe statistically the magnitude of improvements.
- Step 8.22: Describe project benefit; e.g., CODND impact.

Table 22.2: Lead Times Before and After Change

Day	Time	Day	Time	Day	Time	Day	Time	Day	Time
124	102.30	144	96.27	164	102.02	184	95.14	204	107.66
125	103.24	145	96.11	165	102.03	185	102.27	205	95.18
126	102.75	146	96.76	166	100.43	186	106.21	206	100.12
127	104.68	147	97.84	167	111.41	187	99.00	207	104.55
128	97.48	148	108.94	168	106.96	188	104.62	208	102.14
129	98.44	149	101.52	169	90.71	189	90.19	209	102.70
130	100.80	150	93.93	170	98.35	190	97.92	210	109.49
131	108.93	151	103.64	171	108.45	191	105.29	211	84.16
132	104.11	152	90.79	172	97.90	192	104.61	212	90.84
133	102.02	153	96.63	173	101.17	193	98.23	213	87.58
134	101.24	154	99.30	174	99.63	194	103.87	214	89.91
135	102.57	155	102.19	175	99.26	195	100.05	215	93.35
136	108.74	156	101.24	176	99.24	196	101.99	216	90.97
137	90.29	157	103.55	177	100.11	197	108.63	217	89.85
138	99.15	158	92.99	178	95.99	198	104.17	218	91.65
139	103.24	159	96.41	179	101.38	199	96.61	219	90.40
140	97.41	160	107.83	180	96.20	200	98.14	220	91.38
141	105.90	161	113.03	181	92.64	201	112.05		
142	94.70	162	98.44	182	92.17	202	96.82		
143	94.73	163	105.04	183	104.29	203	100.84		

Figure 22.5 shows the 30,000-foot-level metric before and after the process change; i.e., P-DMAIC project execution roadmap Steps 8.22 and 8.23. In addition, this figure shows the determination of the two sample boundaries and the associated hypothesis tests for a population mean shift and variance change; i.e., the statistics for project execution roadmap Step 8.24. The procedures to conduct these statistical tests were described in this chapter.

The following statistical computer program output indicates a significant reduction in the mean lead time response at a level of 0.05. The best estimate for amount of improvement is 10.84 hours with a 95% confidence interval of 8.80 to 12.88 hours.

Two-Sample T-Test and CI: Lead Time

Two-sample T for Lead Time

Stage	N	Mean	StDev	SE Mean
Day 124-210	87	100.85	5.11	0.55
Day 211-220	10	90.01	2.53	0.80

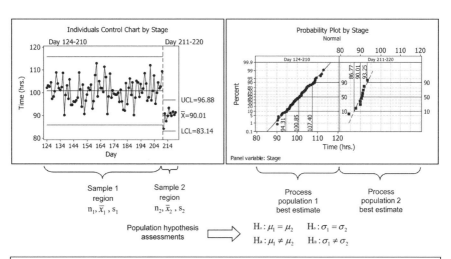

Predictable process experienced on day 211 a significant standard deviation response reduction and a mean lead time reduction of approximately 10.8 hours. Process currently is experiencing a median lead time of approximately 90.0 hours with an 80% occurrence frequency of 86.8 to 93.2 hours.

Figure 22.5: The 30,000-foot-level lead time metric, before and after process change.

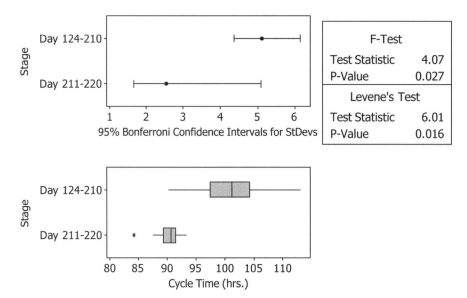

Figure 22.6: Test for equal variances, before and after change.

```
Difference = mu (Day 124-210) - mu (Day 211-220)
Estimate for difference: 10.8416
95% CI for difference: (8.8044, 12.8788)
T-Test of difference=0 (vs not=): T-Value=11.18
P-Value=0.000 DF=18
```

Since both the *F*-test and Levene's test in Figure 22.6 show a significant difference at a level of 0.05, it was not necessary to test for normality of each population. Our conclusion is that the project reduced both the mean and variability of the lead-time response.

The benefit from the project would be the difference in the CODND before and after the process shift. Typically best-estimated financial values are reported, along with other intangible benefits; i.e., project execution roadmap Step 8.25.

22.12   Paired Comparison Testing

When possible, it is usually advantageous to pair samples during a comparison test. In a paired comparison test, a reduction in experimental variability can permit the detection of smaller data shift, even though the total number of degrees of freedom is reduced since the sample size now is the number of comparisons.

An example of this type of test is the evaluation of two pieces of inspection equipment to determine whether there is a statistically-significant difference between the equipment. With this technique, products could be inspected on each piece of equipment. The differences between the paired trials are statistically tested against a value of zero using the equations noted in Table 20.1. Note that the sample size now becomes the number of comparisons, and the degrees of freedom are minus one the number of comparisons.

22.13 Example 22.5: Paired Comparison Testing for New Design

The data in Example 22.3 were previously considered as two separate experiments. However, the data were really collected in a paired comparison fashion. Fourteen existing drive mechanisms were labeled 1 through 14. The voice quality was measured in a machine using each of these drives. The drives were then rebuilt with the new design changes. The voice quality was noted again for each drive, as shown in Table 22.3.

For the alternative hypothesis that the new design is better than the existing design, we need to conduct a one-sided test. Noting that $t_{0.05} = 1.771$ in the single-sided Table D for $\nu = 13$ (i.e., $n-1$) degrees of freedom, the change in voice quality for each drive sample for this single-sided 95% confidence interval is the following:

$$\mu \le \bar{x} - \frac{t_\alpha s}{\sqrt{n}}$$

$$\mu \le 0.324 - \frac{1.771(0.229)}{\sqrt{14}} = 0.216$$

The lower side of the single-sided 95% confidence interval is greater than zero, which indicates that the new design is better than the current design. Another way to determine whether there is a statistically-significant difference is to consider

$$\text{Test criterion} = \frac{t_\alpha s}{\sqrt{n}} = \frac{1.771(0.216)}{\sqrt{14}} = 0.102$$

Table 22.3: Current Design to New Design Response Change

Sample Number	Current Design	New Design	Change (Current - New)
1	1.034	0.556	0.478
2	0.913	0.874	0.039
3	0.881	0.673	0.208
4	1.185	0.632	0.553
5	0.930	0.543	0.387
6	0.880	0.748	0.132
7	1.132	0.532	0.600
8	0.745	0.530	0.215
9	0.737	0.678	0.059
10	1.233	0.676	0.557
11	0.778	0.558	0.220
12	1.325	0.600	0.725
13	0.746	0.713	0.033
14	0.852	0.525	0.327

$$\bar{x} = 0.324$$
$$s = 0.229$$

Because $0.324 > 0.102$, there is a statistically-significant difference in the population means at the 0.05 level; i.e., the new design is concluded to be better than the old design.

A statistical program computer analysis of this data yields

Paired T-Test and CI: Current Design, New Design

```
Paired T for Current Design - New Design

                  N        Mean        StDev      SE Mean
Current Design   14     0.955071     0.195209     0.052172
New Design       14     0.631286     0.102416     0.027372
Difference       14     0.323786     0.228801     0.061150

95% CI for mean difference: (0.191680, 0.455891)
T-Test of mean difference = 0 (vs not = 0): T-Value =
5.29 P-Value = 0.000
```

Since the *P* value is less that 0.05, we reject the null hypothesis that the two populations have equal means. From this analysis, we also note a 95% confidence interval for the mean difference is 0.19 to 0.46.

The normal probability plot of the change data, as shown in Figure 22.7, can help show the magnitude of improvement as it relates to percent of population. In addition, a best estimate of the PDF describing the expected change, as shown in Figure 22.8, can serve as a useful pictorial presentation to management. This PDF was created using the $\bar{x}$ and s estimates for the change be- cause the normal probability plot followed a straight line.

This real example does not illustrate the benefit of paired testing. Paired testing is most beneficial when means vary a lot; for exam- ple, comparing the weight loss from a diet or gasoline performance in a variety of both compact and full-size vehicles, as illustrated in the next example. The means did not vary much in this example.

22.14 Example 22.6: Paired Comparison Testing for Improved Gas Mileage

A new brand (B) of gasoline is being marketed that claims to pro- vide better gas mileage than the other brands (A). Ten coworkers agree to participate in the test and drive with the new gasoline for a month and one of the other brands for a month. Each person records their gas mileage at the end of each month. Can brand B support their claim of better gas mileage with 95% confidence?

Car	Brand A	Brand B
A	22.2	23
B	17.2	17.8
C	19.9	20.2
D	23.3	23.2
E	19.7	20.8
F	15.6	15.4
G	18.5	18.8
H	19.8	20.3
I	17.8	18.3
J	22.3	22.6

The analysis below shows the results of both a standard *t*-test and a paired *t*-test. The paired *t*-test indicates significance at

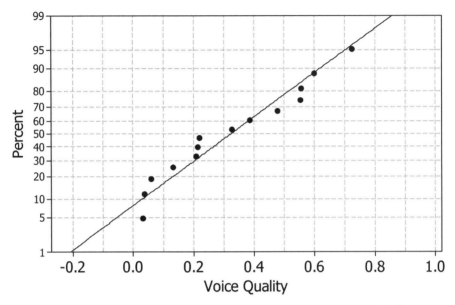

Figure 22.7: Normal probability plot indicating the expected difference
between the new and old design.

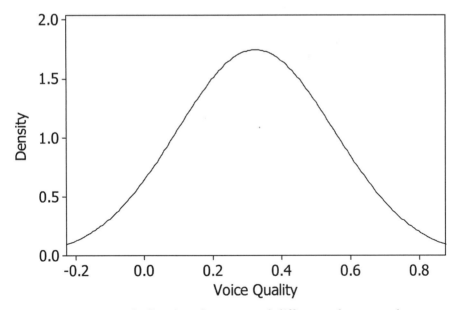

Figure 22.8: PDF indicating the expected difference between the new
and old design.

a level of 0.05, while the standard *t*-test does not. In the paired *t*-test, fundamental differences between the driving behaviors of people and their cars do not impact significance calculations as it does in the non-paired *t*-test.

Two-Sample T-Test and CI: Brand A, Brand B

```
Two-sample T for Brand A vs Brand B

                N        Mean       StDev     SE Mean
Brand A        10       19.63        2.45        0.78
Brand B        10       20.04        2.52        0.80

Difference = mu (Brand A) - mu (Brand B)
Estimate for difference: -0.41
95% CI for difference: (-2.75, 1.93)
T-Test of difference = 0 (vs not =) : T-Value = -0.37
P-Value = 0.717 DF = 17
```

Paired T-Test and CI: Brand A, Brand B

```
Paired T for Brand A - Brand B

                N        Mean      St Dev     SE Mean
Brand A        10      19.630       2.451       0.775
Brand B        10      20.040       2.518       0.796
Difference     10      -0.410       0.387       0.122

95% CI for mean difference: (-0.687, -0.133)
T-Test of mean difference = 0 (vs not = 0) : T-Value = -3.35
P-Value = 0.009
```

22.15   Comparing More Than Two Samples

Subsequent chapters will discuss techniques for comparing the means of more than two populations. ANOVA techniques can assess the overall differences between factor level or treatments. ANOM can test each factor level or treatment against a grand mean.

Some computer programs offer Bartlett's test for comparing multiple variances if the data are normal. If the data are not normal, a Levene's test can be used.

22.16   Example 22.7: Comparing Means to Determine if Process Improved

Example 12.5 described a situation where I was the newly-elected chair of an ASQ section and wanted to increase monthly meeting attendance during my term. The example illustrated what attendance should be expected if nothing were done differently. This example lists the process changes that were made in an attempt to improve attendance. It also shows the resulting attendance and analyses to see whether the objective was met.

I set a stretch goal to double attendance at our monthly meeting, but I would have been happy with a 50% increase in attendance. I knew that the stretch goal was going to be exceptionally difficult to meet since we had to reduce the frequency of our newsletter to every other month because of recent cash flow problems. My focus was not trying to drive improved attendance through the output measurement; i.e., do better since attendance is not meeting our goal. Instead I worked with our executive committee on implementing the following process changes that were thought to improve attendance. Note that I had some control over the implementation of process changes, but I had no control over how many people would actually decide to attend the meeting. The process changes that I focused on implementing with the executive committee team were as follows:

- Work with program chair to define interesting programs and get commitments from all presenters before the September meeting.
- Create an email distribution list for ASQ members and others. Send notice out the weekend before the meeting.
- Create a website.
- Submit meeting notices to newspaper and other public media.
- Videotape programs for playing on cable TV.
- Add door prizes to meeting.
- Send welcome letters to visitors and new members.

- Post job openings on website and email notices to those who might be interested.
- Submit "from the chair" article to the newsletter chair on time so newsletter is mailed on time.

The term of a section chair is July 1 to June 30. There are no June, July, and August meetings. My term encompassed meetings from September 1997 to May 1998. The attendance from September 1992 to May 1998 is shown in Table 22.4.

Figure 22.9 shows an individuals control chart of these data. For this control chart, the control limits were calculated from data

Table 22.4: Attendance Data

9/9/1993	10/14/1993	11/11/1993	12/9/1993	1/13/1994	2/17/1994	3/10/1994	4/14/1994	5/12/1994
66	45	61	36	42	41	46	44	47
9/8/1994	10/13/1994	11/10/1994	12/8/1994	1/12/1995	2/16/1995	3/9/1995	4/3/1995	5/16/1995
46	51	42	42	61	57	47	46	28
9/14/1995	10/12/1995	11/9/1995	12/14/1995	1/11/1996	2/8/1996	3/14/1996	4/11/1996	5/9/1996
45	37	45	42	58	49	39	53	58
9/12/1996	10/10/1996	11/14/1996	12/12/1996	1/9/1997	2/13/1997	3/13/1997	4/10/1997	5/8/1997
44	37	52	33	43	45	35	29	33
9/11/1997	10/16/1997	11/13/1997	12/11/1997	1/8/1997	2/12/1998	3/12/1998	4/9/1998	5/13/1998
108	59	51	49	68	60	51	48	60

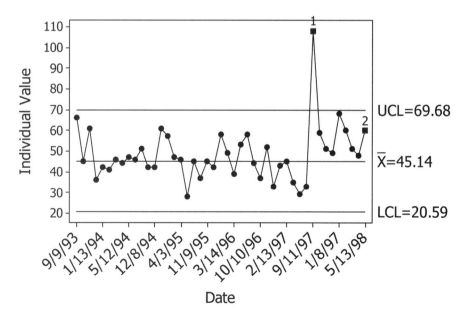

Figure 22.9: Individuals control chart.

up to the beginning of my term; i.e., from 9/9/93 to 5/8/97. This chart shows two out-of-control conditions during my term, i.e., to the better. The designation "1" indicated that one point was more than 3 sigma limits from the centerline. This was the first meeting of my term as chair where we had a panel discussion concerning information for consideration when setting up future meetings. The designation "2" indicated nine points in a row on the same point of the centerline; i.e., zone test of the statistical software that was used.

Let's now compare the variance in attendance and mean attendance between 9/92-5/97 and 9/97-5/98 as a hypothesis test using statistical software. Figure 22.10 shows a test of the homogeneity of the two variances. The *F*-test shows a statistically-significant difference because the probability is less than 0.05; however, Levene's test does not. Levene's test is more appropriate for this situation because we did not remove the extreme data point, shown as an asterisk in the box plot, because we had no justification for removal. A test for mean difference yielded the following:

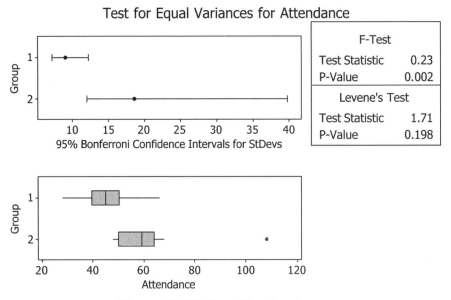

Figure 22.10: Equality of variance.

Two Sample T-Test and Confidence Interval

```
Two sample T for attend1 vs attend2

                    N      Mean      StDev     SE Mean
attend1 (9/92-5/97)  36    45.14      9.02        1.5
attend2 (9/97-5/98)   9    61.6      18.6         6.2

95% CI for mu attend1 - mu attend2: (-31.1, -1.7)
T-Test mu attend1 = mu attend2 (vs <) : T = -2.57
P = 0.017 DF = 8
```

For this test, the null hypothesis was that the two means were equal, while the alternative hypothesis was that there was an improvement in attendance, i.e., one-sided *t*-test. Because the 95% confidence interval did not contain zero (also $P = 0.017$, which is less than 0.05), we can choose to reject the null hypothesis because α is less than 0.05.

From this output, we are also 95% confident that our process changes improved mean attendance between 2 and 31 people per meeting. Our best estimate for percentage improvement is

$$\text{Best Estimate for Percent Improvement in Attendance} = \frac{61.6 - 45.14}{45.14}(100) = 36.5\%$$

My stretch goal of doubling meeting attendance was not met; however, attendance was shown, at a significance level of 0.05, to improve during my term as chair with a best estimate of 36.5%. I felt good about the results of the executive team's effort to improve attendance. I am confident that the results would have been even better had we been able to print our newsletter at our previous frequency rate of once monthly.

An additional observation from the attendance plot is that attendance may have been on the decline immediately preceding my term. An exercise at the end of this chapter addresses the null hypothesis that there was no change between my term and the previous year.

22.17   Applying IEE

Whenever conducting a comparison test, consider whether the test could be conducted using paired comparison techniques. In general, fewer samples are required if the test objective can be met in this way, as opposed to comparison tests between samples. In addition, probability plotting techniques can be a tool for understanding the data. A probability plot of the data may reveal something worth investigating which was not obvious from a comparison of mean or standard deviation values.

Problems may occur when making comparisons. For example, the quality of parts supplied by two sources may be compared. A problem with this type of test is that the samples that are drawn do not necessarily represent parts to be manufactured in the future. Also, the samples need to be taken from processes that are stable/predictable. If the processes are not stable/predictable, the test conclusion may not be valid.

For this situation an IEE consideration might be to have the supplier manufacture, and label, specially-made parts that reflect normal boundaries experienced in their processes. A DOE design structure can be used to describe how these specially-built parts are to be manufactured, where one of the factors under consideration might be supplier A versus supplier B. Other factors to consider are new versus experienced operator, first shift versus second shift, raw material supply source A versus B, high versus low machine tolerance limits, manufacturing line A versus B, tester A versus B, and so forth. This comparison test build strategy can also indicate what factors are causing a degraded response so that these problems can get fixed.

For added insight into the range of variability that might be expected from the current process, a probability plot could be made of all the DOE trial data. Care should be taken in interpreting this type of plot because the data are not random.

After a supplier is qualified using the procedure above, process control charts should be implemented for the purpose of tracking and stopping the process should degradation later occur. A DOE strategy may again be needed in the future to discover the source of any degradation.

22.18 Exercises

1. From sampled data, note the distribution used when
    (a) Calculating the confidence interval on the mean.
    (b) Calculating the confidence interval on the standard deviation.

    (c)   Comparing two sampled variances.

2.   Using additional information found in Chapter 22 (Table 22.4) compare the attendance of my term as ASQ chair to the previous year, as opposed to attendance since 1992.

3.   The difference between the actual arrival time and scheduled arrival time for 20 trips made into Dallas were noted. The flights were on the same airline at approximately the same time of day; however, half of the flights were from St. Louis (denoted as S) while the other half were from New York (denoted as N). Plus values indicate the number of minutes the flight was late. The times were:

City	Time	City	Time
(N)	14.3	(S)	11.1
(N)	10.4	(S)	8.7
(N)	6.4	(S)	11.1
(N)	6.3	(S)	11.2
(N)	8.9	(S)	13.3
(N)	8.5	(S)	11.0
(N)	10.2	(S)	9.4
(N)	10.0	(S)	8.7
(N)	13.2	(S)	9.1
(N)	16.5	(S)	9.6

    (a)   Determine at a significance level of 0.05 whether the variability in arrival times were longer for the New York flight.

    (b)   Determine at a significance level of 0.05 whether on the average the arrival time from New York was longer than that from St. Louis.

    (c)   To save parking fees, estimate when a friend should meet the traveler at the pickup/drop-off area. Assume that the distribution of these arrival times is representative of future flights. Consider that it takes 10 minutes to walk from the gate to the load zone and that the friend should wait only 5% of the times.

4.   It is important that the mean response from a manufacturing process be increased, but any change to the process is expensive to implement. A team listed some changes that it thought would be beneficial. Team members conducted a test with the current process settings and the new settings. They wanted to be certain that the change would be beneficial

before implementing it. For this reason, they decided to keep the current process unless they could prove that the new process would be beneficial at a level of significance of 0.01. Discuss results and assess what should be done.

Current process readings: 98.1, 102.3, 98.5, 101.6, 97.7, 100.0, 103.1, 99.1, 97.7, 98.5

New process readings: 100.9, 101.1, 103.4, 85.0, 103.4, 103.6, 100.0, 99.7, 106.4, 101.2

5. In 1985, a manufacturing company produced televisions in both Japan and the United States. A very large random sample of products was taken to evaluate the quality of picture relative to a standard, which was a good measurement for picture quality. It was found that all the US-manufactured products had no defects, while the Japanese-built products had some defects. However, customers typically preferred the picture quality of Japanese-manufactured televisions. Explain this phenomenon.

6. A manufacturer wants to determine if two testers yield a similar response. Ten parts were measured on machine A and another ten parts were measured on machine B.

    Machine A: 147.3, 153.0, 140.3, 161.0, 145.1, 145.0, 150.1, 158.7, 154.9, 152.8

    Machine B: 149.6, 155.5, 141.3, 162.1, 146.7, 145.5, 151.6, 159.3, 154.8, 152.7

    (a) Determine if there is a statistically-significant difference in the mean response at a level of 0.05.

    (b) Consider that the data were collected so that the 10 parts had two-machine measurement pairing; for example, the first part yielded a value of 147.3 on machine A, while it yielded 149.6 on machine B. Determine if there is a statistically-significant difference in the mean.

    (c) For the paired evaluation, use a normal probability plot to quantify pictorially the best estimate for the difference that would be expected 80% of the time. Determine the value using a Z table (i.e. Table A in the appendix).

7. Given the data sets:

    Data set A: 35.8, 40.4, 30.3, 46.8, 34.1, 34.0, 38.1, 45.0, 41.9, 40.2

    Data set B: 40.9, 35.7, 36.7, 37.3, 41.8, 39.9, 34.6, 38.8, 35.8, 35.6

(a) Determine if there is a difference in the means at a level of 0.05 for the data.
(b) Determine if the variability of data set A is larger.
(c) Describe manufacturing, development, and service examples from which the data could have originated.

8. Given the data below, determine if there is a significant difference between Scale A and B. Report the value of the computed statistic in the hypothesis test.

Part	Scale A	Scale B
1	256.93	256.84
2	208.78	208.82
3	245.66	245.61
4	214.67	214.75
5	249.59	249.69
6	226.65	226.57
7	176.57	176.49

9. Test for a significant difference between sample 1 and sample 2. Comment.

Sample 1: 10, 15, 12, 19
Sample 2: 15, 19, 18, 22

10. Compare the mean and variance of the Machine A and B. State the test statistics and their values that were used in making these comparisons. (Six Sigma Test Guide, 2002). These are the same data as those shown in Exercise 8.11. Comment on the results.

Machine A	Machine B
109.4	120.75
83.03	121.47
89.2	111.3
121.26	151.01
85.77	108.8
84.22	119.45
99.7	135.68
135.74	118.55
135.18	101.22
130.88	
120.56	
126.12	
84.65	

102.22
98.47
116.39
103.39
89.52
107.78
119.43
78.53
84.47
106.84

11. Exercise 18.5 showed data that were collected passively for the purpose of understanding better what might be done to improve the KPOV. Test for a significant difference in measured response between inspectors.

23

P-DMAIC – Analyze Phase: Comparison Tests for Attribute Response

23.1   P-DMAIC Roadmap Component

The last chapter and this chapter extend the single-population inference concepts described in Chapters 20 and 21 to inferences when comparing more than one population. The last chapter focused on continuous response situations, while this chapter addresses attribute response situations; e.g., does the failure frequencies of completing a purchase order differ between departments? The graphic in this section highlights the P-DMAIC roadmap steps (see Appendix D) that are described in this chapter. Appendix E contains the tollgate check sheets for this and other phases.

23.2   IEE Application Examples: Attribute Comparison Tests

- *Manufacturing 30,000-foot-level quality metric*: An IEE project is to reduce the number of defects in a printed circuit board manufacturing process. A highly ranked input from the cause-and-effect matrix was inspector; i.e., the team

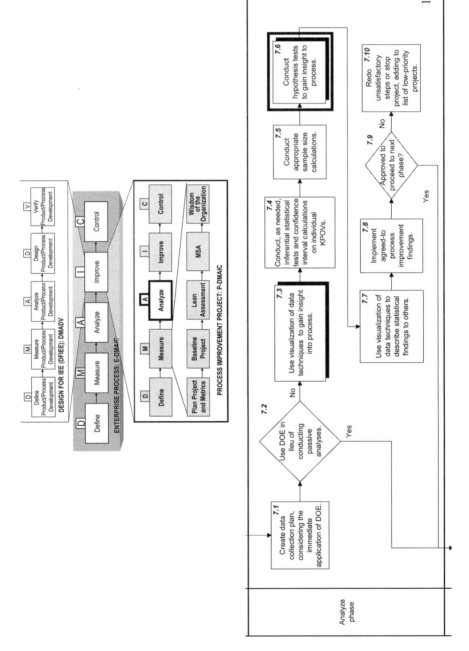

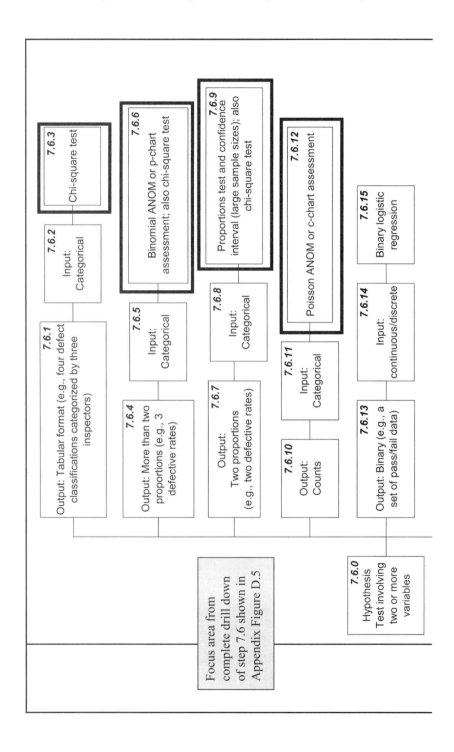

7.6.3 Chi-square test

7.6.2 Input: Categorical

7.6.1 Output: Tabular format (e.g., four defect classifications categorized by three inspectors)

7.6.6 Binomial ANOM or p-chart assessment; also chi-square test

7.6.5 Input: Categorical

7.6.4 Output: More than two proportions (e.g., 3 defective rates)

7.6.9 Proportions test and confidence interval (large sample sizes); also chi-square test

7.6.8 Input: Categorical

7.6.7 Output: Two proportions (e.g., two defective rates)

7.6.12 Poisson ANOM or c-chart assessment

7.6.11 Input: Categorical

7.6.10 Output: Counts

7.6.15 Binary logistic regression

7.6.14 Input: continuous/discrete

7.6.13 Output: Binary (e.g., a set of pass/fail data)

7.6.0 Hypothesis Test involving two or more variables

Focus area from complete drill down of step 7.6 shown in Appendix Figure D.5

thought that inspectors could be classifying failures differently. A null hypothesis test of equality of defective rates reported by inspector indicated that the difference was statistically significant.

- *Transactional 30,000-foot-level metric:* DSO reduction was chosen as an IEE project. A cause-and-effect matrix ranked as a possible important input was that there was a difference between companies in the number of defective invoices reported or lost. The null hypothesis test of equality of defective invoices by company indicated that there was a statistically significant difference.

- *Manufacturing 30,000-foot-level quality metric:* The number of printed circuit boards produced weekly for a high-volume manufacturing company is similar. Printed circuit board failure rate reduction was chosen as an IEE project. A cause-and-effect matrix ranked product type as an important input that could affect the overall failure rate. A chi-square test was conducted of the null hypothesis of equality of failure rate by product type.

23.3   Comparing Attribute Data

The methods presented in this chapter can be used, for example, to compare the frequency of failure of two production machines or suppliers. The null hypothesis for the comparison tests is that there is no difference, while the alternative hypothesis is that there is a difference.

23.4   Sample Size: Comparing Proportions

Natrella (1966) gives tables for sample size selection when comparing the attribute response of two populations. Brush (1988) gives graphs that can be used to aid with the selection of sample sizes. Diamond (1989) multiplies the appropriate single-sampled population calculation by 2 to determine a sample size for each of two populations. Statistical software programs can calculate sample size alternatives given the experimental risk levels and magnitude of difference desired to detect from the test.

One rule of thumb that does not structurally assess α and β levels is that there should be at least five failures for each category.

23.5 Comparing Proportions

The chi-square distribution can be used to compare the frequency of occurrence for categorical variables. Within this test, often called a χ^2 goodness-of-fit test, we compare an observed frequency distribution with a theoretical distribution. An example application is that a company wants to determine if inspectors categorize failure similarly. Consider that inspectors are described as A_1, A_2, and so forth, while types of failures are B_1, B_2, and so forth. The chi-square test assesses the association or lack of independency in a two-way classification. This procedure is used when testing to see if the probabilities of items or subjects being classified for one variable depend on the classification of the other variable.

Data compilation and analysis are in the form of the following *contingency table*, in which observations are designated as O_{ij} and expected values are calculated to be E_{ij}. Expected counts are printed below observed counts. The column totals are the sum of the observations in the columns; the row totals are the sum of the observations in the rows.

	A_1	A_2	A_3	A_n	Total
B_1	O_{11}	O_{12}	O_{13}	O_{1t}	$T_{\text{row 1}} = O_{11} + O_{12} + O_{13} + \ldots + O_{1t}$
	E_{11}	E_{12}	E_{13}	E_{1t}	
B_2	O_{21}	O_{22}	O_{23}	O_{2t}	$T_{\text{row 2}} = O_{21} + O_{22} + O_{23} + \ldots + O_{2t}$
	E_{21}	E_{22}	E_{23}	E_{2t}	
B_3	O_{31}	O_{32}	O_{33}	O_{3t}	$T_{\text{row 3}} = O_{31} + O_{32} + O_{33} + \ldots + O_{3t}$
	E_{31}	E_{32}	E_{33}	E_{3t}	
B_s	O_{s1}	O_{s2}	O_{s3}	O_{st}	$T_{\text{row s}} = O_{31} + O_{32} + O_{33} + \ldots + O_{st}$
	E_{s1}	E_{s2}	E_{s3}	E_{st}	
Total	$T_{\text{col 1}}$	$T_{\text{col 2}}$	$T_{\text{col 3}}$	$T_{\text{col t}}$	$T = T_{\text{row 1}} + T_{\text{row 2}} + T_{\text{row 3}} + \ldots + T_{\text{row s}}$

The expected values are calculated using the equation

$$E_{st} = \frac{T_{\text{row s}} \times T_{\text{col t}}}{T} \quad \text{yielding for example} \quad E_{11} = \frac{T_{\text{row 1}} \times T_{\text{col 1}}}{T}$$

The null hypothesis might be worded as follows: The detection rate is equal for all inspectors.. The alternative hypothesis is that at least one detection proportion is different. The chi-square statistic (see Table G) could be used when assessing this hypothesis, where the number of degrees of freedom (ν) is the (number of rows: 1) (number of columns: 1) and α is the table value. If the following χ^2_{cal} is larger than this chi-square criterion ($\chi^2_{v,\alpha}$), the null hypothesis is rejected at α risk.

$$\chi^2_{cal} = \sum_{i=1}^{s} \sum_{j=1}^{t} \frac{(O_{ij} - E_{ij})^2}{E_{ij}}$$

23.6   Example 23.1: Comparing Proportions

IEE Application Examples

- *Manufacturing 30,000-foot-level quality metric: The null hypothesis of equality of defective rates by inspector was tested.*
- *Transactional 30,000-foot-level metric: The null hypothesis test of equality of defective invoices by company invoiced was tested.*

The abilities of three x-ray inspectors at an airport were evaluated on the detection of key items. A test was devised in which 90 pieces of luggage were "bugged" with a device that they should question. Each inspector was exposed to exactly 30 of the "bugged" items in random fashion. The null hypothesis is that there is no difference between inspectors. The alternative hypothesis is that at least one of the proportions is different (Wortman, 1990).

	Insp 1	Insp 2	Insp 3	Treatment Total
Detected	27	25	22	74
Undetected	3	5	8	16
Sample total	30	30	30	90

A computer analysis of these data yielded the following:

Chi-Square Test: Insp 1, Insp 2, Insp 3

```
Expected counts are printed below observed counts.
Chi-Square contributions are printed below expected
counts.
```

	Insp 1	Insp 2	Insp 3	Total
1	27	25	22	74
	24.67	24.67	24.67	
	0.221	0.005	0.288	
2	3	5	8	16
	5.33	5.33	5.33	
	1.021	0.021	1.333	
Total	30	30	30	90

Chi-Sq = 2.889, DF = 2, P-Value = 0.236

The value for χ^2_{cal} was 2.889, which is not larger than $\chi^2_{v,\alpha} = \chi^2_{2,0.05} =$ 5.99; hence, there is not sufficient evidence to reject the null hypothesis at $\alpha = 0.05$. Similarly, we can see from the computer output that the P value of 0.236 is not less than a α criterion of 0.05.

23.7   Comparing Nonconformance Proportions and Count Frequencies

Consider the situation in which an organization wants to evaluate the nonconformance rates of several suppliers to determine if there are differences. The chi-square approach just explained could assess this situation from an overall point of view; however, the methodology does not identify which supplier(s) might be worse than the overall mean.

A simple approach to address this problem is to plot the nonconformance data in a P chart format, where each supplier would replace the typical P chart time-series subgroupings. Zone tests would not be applicable because the order sequence of plotting the supplier information is arbitrary. The only applicable test occurs when a supplier exceeds either the upper or lower control limit, i.e., decision level for the test. Similarly a u chart could be used when there are count data. These tests are not technically a hypothesis test since decision levels are calculated using control charting methods.

For this analysis, there are some statistical programs that contain a methodology similar to the Analysis of Means (ANOM) procedure for continuous data described in Chapter 26, for both proportion and count data when the sample size between categories is the same. This method provides statistical significance-based decision levels for the above binomial (comparing proportions) and

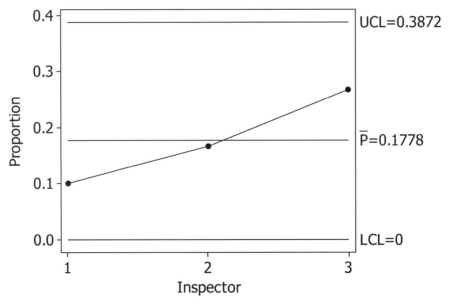

Figure 23.1: *P* chart comparison test.

Poisson (comparing count frequency) situations. The null hypothesis statement for these tests is that the rate from each category equates to the overall mean.

23.8   Example 23.2: Comparing Nonconformance Proportions

For the data in Example 23.1, compare each inspector nonconformance rate to the overall mean non-conformance rate using a *p* chart procedure and a binomial ANOM statistical significance test.

Figure 23.1 shows the results from a *p* chart analysis procedure, while Figure 23.2 shows the one-way binomial ANOM statistical significance test procedure. In both cases we do not have enough information to suggest that there is a difference in individual inspector rates to the overall mean. Note that decision bounds are wider for the *p* chart, which does not consider the number of comparisons that are being made to the overall mean when creating the decision levels.

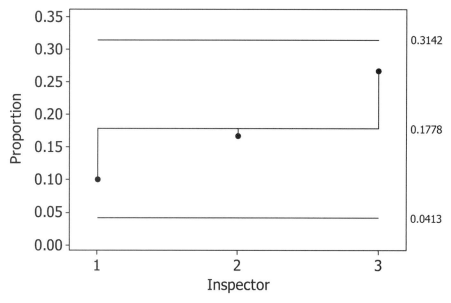

Figure 23.2: One-way binomial ANOM. Decision limits alpha equals 0.05.

23.9 Example 23.3: Comparing Counts

Ten inspectors evaluated the same number of samples from a process during the last month. Inspections were visual, where multiple defects could occur on one unit. The number of logged defects was

Inspector	1	2	3	4	5	6	7	8	9	10
Defects	330	350	285	320	315	390	320	270	310	318

Figure 23.3 shows the results of a one-way Poisson ANOM, where the hypothesis of equality of the defect rate to the overall average was rejected for inspectors six and eight. An IEE project team could use the information from this analysis to address next why there appeared to be difference in inspection results; perhaps inspectors were using a different inspection criterion for their decisions.

23.10 Example 23.4: Difference in Two Proportions

A team believed that they had made improvements to a process. They needed to test this hypothesis statistically and wanted to

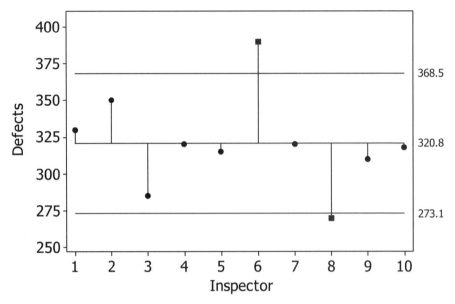

Figure 23.3: One-way Poisson ANOM. Decision limits alpha equals 0.05.

determine the 95% confidence interval for the improvement in PPM rate, given the following data.

Before improvement: 6290 defects out of 620000
After improvement: 4661 defects out of 490000

A computer analysis yielded.

Test and CI for Two Proportions

```
Sample       X              N        Sample p

1          6290         620000        0.010145
2          4661         490000        0.009512


Difference = p (1) - p (2)
Estimate for difference: 0.000632916
95% CI for difference: (0.000264020, 0.00100181)
Test for difference = 0 (vs not = 0): Z = 3.36 P-Value
= 0.001

Fisher's exact test: P-Value = 0.001
```

This analysis included a Fisher's exact test response. In a Fisher's exact test, assessment is made as to whether two binary variables are independent. For this test, an exact *P* value results from the analysis of a 2×2 contingency table of the following hypotheses:

H_0: row and column variables are independent
H_a: row and column variables are dependent

When cell counts are small, the *P* value from a chi-square test may be inaccurate; however, the Fisher's exact test *P* value is accurate for all sample sizes.

From this analysis, we can reject the null hypothesis that no improvement was made. The 95 percent confidence interval for the PPM improvement rate is 264 to 1001.

23.11   Example 23.5: IEE Demonstration of Process Improvement for an Attribute Response

A project was to reduce a process defective rate. Belief was that the defective rate could differ by day of the week; hence, a weekly infrequent subgrouping/sampling frequency was selected. All weekly transactions have been recorded as either pass or fail and the number of transactions in each subgroup is similar but not exactly the same. Example 21.4 created a 30,000-foot-level attribute response baseline metric and the determination of the process response confidence interval statement.

This example will describe the demonstration of project benefits at the 30,000-foot-level, where the before/after process change measurements are shown in Table 23.1.

During the wisdom of the organization phase of the project execution roadmap, one cause-and-effect diagram item was difference between test fixtures. A hypothesis test assessment of this relationship indicated that there was a significant difference between reported fixture failure rates even though the fixture input failure rate was approximately the same. The project team worked with the process implementers to resolve fixture differences along with improving the overall gage measurement accuracy. This process change was implemented on week 40.

Figure 23.4 shows a 30,000-foot-level control chart using the origination time for the process baseline as it was determined in Example 21.4. Since this figure indicates a process shift, a

Table 23.1: Subgroup Size and Defectives Before and After Change

Week	Subgroup Size	Defectives	Week	Subgroup Size	Defectives	Week	Subgroup Size	Defectives	Week	Subgroup Size	Defectives
18	4256	118	26	5583	111	34	4557	182	42	4581	54
19	4861	109	27	4416	150	35	4866	111	43	4239	69
20	4156	129	28	5490	142	36	5402	157	44	4221	79
21	5584	155	29	4615	114	37	5034	127	45	5381	80
22	5291	142	30	4642	149	38	5059	149	46	5429	69
23	4604	121	31	5028	140	39	5068	161	47	4407	52
24	5333	181	32	4556	111	40	5201	48	48	4762	57
25	4658	139	33	5736	174	41	5587	65			

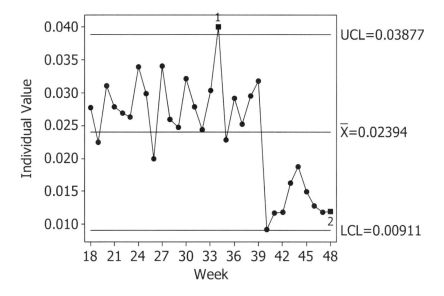

#1: 1 point > 3.0 standard deviations from center line
#2: 9 points in a row on one side of the center line special cause test

Figure 23.4: The 30,000-foot-level lead time metric, before and after process change, with no staging.

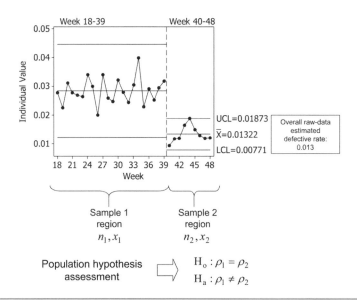

Figure 23.5: The 30,000-foot-level lead time metric with staging before and after process change on week 40.

week-40-staged 30,000-foot-level control chart was created. This control chart, as shown in Figure 23.5, indicates that after the change the process has reached a new process stability/predictability level.

A null hypothesis testing the equality of the defective rate before change to the defective rate after change is $p_1 = p_2$. Inputs to this analysis are n and x for each process sample, which respectively are the total number of transactions and defectives. The statistical analysis results from this assessment are:

Test and CI for Two Proportions

```
Sample      X            N        Sample p

1         3072       108759       0.028246
2          573        43808       0.013080


Difference = p (1) - p (2)
Estimate for difference: 0.0151661
95% CI for difference: (0.0137165, 0.0166158)
Test for difference = 0 (vs not = 0): Z = 20.51 P-Value
= 0.000
```

Relative to project benefits, we could state that a best estimate for project failure rate reduction 0.0151 with a 95% confidence interval of 0.0137 to 0.0166.

23.12 Applying IEE

The methods included in this chapter are traditionally used to compare suppliers, machines, and so forth by taking samples from the populations. In general, when designing a test, the analyst attempts to use a continuous response output, as opposed to an attribute response, whenever possible. For example, a particular part may be considered a failure when it tests beyond a certain level. Instead of analyzing what proportion of parts is beyond this level, fewer samples are required if the actual measurement data are recorded.

Let's revisit the example where a test was conducted to see if there was a difference between inspectors. If we assessed only the results of our hypothesis test deductively, we would stop our investigation because the null hypothesis could not be rejected.

However, if we used inductive reasoning, we would learn from these data to challenge previous understandings or create a new hypothesis. Using inductive reasoning, we should probably be concerned that the overall detection rate for the "bugs" we applied for the x-ray inspectors was only 82% (i.e., [74/90] × 100). From a practical point of view, the overall detection process needs to be investigated and improved. Perhaps a control chart program should be implemented as a means to track progress, where "bugs" are periodically applied and monitored for detection.

23.13   Exercises

1. A manufacturer wants to select only one supplier of a key part that is used in the manufacturing process. The cost for parts from supplier A is greater than that for supplier B. A random sample of 1000 parts was taken from each of the supplier's processes. The output from each sample was compared to the specification. Supplier A had 10 parts beyond the specification limits, while supplier B had 15.
    (a)   Determine if there is a significant difference at a level of 0.1.
    (b)   Comment on findings and make recommendations.
2. Assess whether a difference can be claimed in the following supplier non-conformance rates. Comment on results and the applicability to other situations within business.

Supplier 1	Supplier 2	Supplier 3	Supplier 4
20%	40%	60%	20%

3. Assess whether a difference can be claimed in the following supplier non-conformance rates. Compare the results to exercise 2 and comment on the use of statistical analyses to make decisions.

	Supplier 1	Supplier 2	Supplier 3	Supplier 4
Defectives	1	2	3	1
Sample Size	5	5	5	5

4. Assess whether a difference can be claimed in the following supplier non-conformance rates. Compare the results to the assessments in exercises 2 and 3 and comment on the use of statistical analyses to make decisions.

	Supplier 1	Supplier 2	Supplier 3	Supplier 4
Defectives	10	20	30	10
Sample Size	50	50	50	50

5. A team believed that they had made improvements to a process. They needed to test this hypothesis statistically and wanted to determine the 95% confidence interval for the improvement in PPM rate for the following data.

    Before improvement: 6,290 defects out of 620,000
    After improvement: 4,661 defects out of 490,000

    Comment on the results relative to the difference if the after sample size was reduced with results being 466 defects out of 49,000. Note the same percent maintained.

6. In Exercise 19.4, the difference between the actual arrival times and the scheduled arrival times for 20 trips into Dallas was noted. Consider that flights are considered on time if they arrive no later than 15 minutes after their scheduled arrival time, as compiled in the following table.

Origination	number of flights on time	number of flights late
N	9	1
S	10	0

    Determine if there is a significant difference between the arrival times for flights from St. Louis (S designation) and New York (N designation). Comment on the analysis.

7. Using the drill-down in Appendix D, determine the tools that could be used to assess a potential KPIV for a visual inspection process where parts are either accepted or rejected. If all operators made a similar judgment for a part, their rejection rates should be approximately the same. Suggest a strategy to make a passive analysis which tests for differences between appraisers. Create a dummy set of data and make such an analysis.

8. Every day an operations department reported the number of observed defects so that they could react on the biggest problem of the day, noting that there can be more than one defect type on a transaction. The department plotted the daily distribution of failures in a time-series chart as stacked colored

bars, where each color represented a failure type. Yesterday they experienced the following frequency of failures:

Failure Type	Failures	Non-failures
ReasonA	6	14
ReasonB	4	16
ReasonC	3	17
ReasonD	3	17
ReasonE	3	17
ReasonF	2	18

How should they react to this data? If an overall significant difference cannot be detected at a level of 0.05 between failure types, increase number of failures and non-failures of each failure type using multiples of 2, 3, 4, etc. times until an overall significant difference can be detected; report the number of failures and non-failures of each failure type with the accompanying *P* value along and the appropriate visual describing the overall distribution frequency. Repeat the above increase in failure frequency, analyzing the data using the appropriate ANOM technique. Note failure frequency when significance can be stated at a level of 0.05 for one or more failure types; note the significant failure type(s). Describe problems with the overall approach used by the operations department and an IEE alternative approach.

9. The types of defects from the previous day's transactions were presented in a meeting using a pie chart. After the meeting you asked for and received the raw data. You found that 1000 transactions were completed during the previous day with the following defects:

Type A defect: 1
Type B defect: 3
Type C defect: 4
Type D defect: 5

(a) Use a chi-square test to assess the equality of failure rate by defect type.
(b) Use a binomial ANOM test to assess the equality of each failure rate type to the overall failure rate
(c) Comment on what might be done different within the reporting process

Re-examine the data. Offer suggestions for reporting this type of information.

24

P-DMAIC – Analyze Phase: Variance Components

24.1 P-DMAIC Roadmap Component

Chapter 22 described two population equality comparisons, where the response was continuous. The last chapter extended population equality comparison tests to attribute outputs. The next five chapters will extend the response assessment of a population as a function of multiple input situations. In the P-DMAIC and E-DMAIC analyze phases, these tools can provide insight to inputs that can be affecting an output; i.e., the Xs in the equation $Y = f(X)$. This insight can then lead to improvement opportunities. The graphic in this section highlights the P-DMAIC roadmap steps (see Appendix Section D.1) that are described in this chapter. Appendix E contains the tollgate check lists for this and other phases.

The methodology described in this chapter is a random effects model or components of variance model, as opposed to a fixed-effects model as described in Chapter 26. The statistical model for this hierarchical model or fully nested ANOVA is similar to that of the fixed effects model. The difference is that in the random effects model the levels (or treatments) could be a random sample from a larger population of levels. For this situation we would like

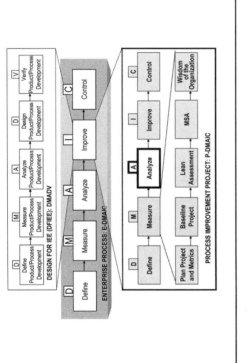

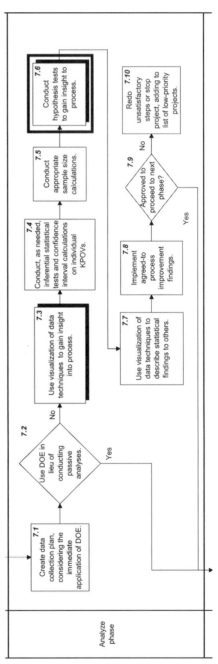

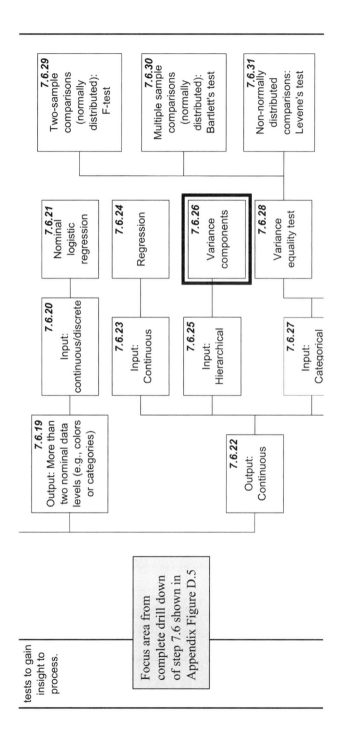

7.6.29 Two-sample comparisons (normally distributed): F-test

7.6.30 Multiple sample comparisons (normally distributed): Bartlett's test

7.6.31 Non-normally distributed comparisons: Levene's test

7.6.21 Nominal logistic regression

7.6.24 Regression

7.6.26 Variance components

7.6.28 Variance equality test

7.6.20 Input: continuous/discrete

7.6.23 Input: Continuous

7.6.25 Input: Hierarchical

7.6.27 Input: Categorical

7.6.19 Output: More than two nominal data levels (e.g., colors or categories)

7.6.22 Output: Continuous

tests to gain insight to process.

Focus area from complete drill down of step 7.6 shown in Appendix Figure D.5

to extend conclusions, based on samples of levels, to all population levels, whether explicitly considered or not. In this situation, the test attempts to quantify the variability from factor levels.

24.2   IEE Application Examples: Variance Components

- *Manufacturing 30,000-foot-level metric (KPOV)*: An IEE project was to improve the process capability/performance of a manufactured product diameter; i.e., reduce the number of parts beyond the specification limits. A cause-and-effect matrix ranked the variability of diameter within a part and between the four-cavity molds as important inputs that could be affecting the overall 30,000-part-diameter metric. A variance component analysis was conducted to test significance and estimate the components.
- *Transactional 30,000-foot-level metric*: DSO reduction was chosen as an IEE project. A cause-and-effect matrix ranked company as an important input that could affect the DSO response. The team wanted to estimate the variability in DSO between and within companies. A variance component analysis was conducted to test significance and estimate the components.

24.3   Description

Earlier, we discussed the impact that key process input variables can have on the output of a process. A fixed-effects model assesses how the level of key process input variables affects the mean response of key process outputs, while a random effects model assesses how the key process input variables affect the variability of key process outputs.

A key process output of a manufacturing process could be the dimension or characteristic of a product. A key process output of a service or business process could be time from initiation to delivery. The total affect of n variance components on a key process output can be expressed as the sum of the variances of each of the components:

$$\sigma^2_{\text{total}} = \sigma^2_1 + \sigma^2_2 + \sigma^2_3 + \ldots + \sigma^2_n$$

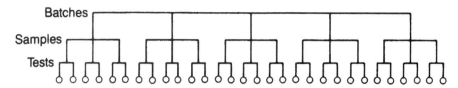

Figure 24.1: A 5 × 3 × 2 hierarchical design. (G. E. P. Box, W. Hunter, and S. Hunter *Statistics for Experimenters*, John Wiley and Sons, 1978.)

The components of variance within a manufacturing process could be material, machines, operators, and the measurement system. In service or business processes, the variance components can be the day of the month the request was initiated, department-to-department variations when handling a request, and the quality of the input request. An important use of variance components is the isolation of different sources of variability that affect product or system variability. This problem of product variability frequently arises in quality assurance, where the isolation of the sources of variability can be very difficult.

A test to determine these variance components often has the nesting structure seen in Figure 24.1. Other books describe in detail the analysis of variance method for estimating variance components. In this procedure, the expected mean squares of the analysis of variance table are equated to their observed value in the analysis of variance (ANOVA) table and then solved for the variance components. In this series of volumes, a statistical analysis computer program will be used for computations.

Occasionally, variance components analyses yield negative estimates. Negative estimates are viewed with concern because it is obvious that, by definition, variance components cannot be negative. For these situations, it has intuitive appeal to accept the negative estimate and to use it as evidence that the true value is zero. This approach suffers from theoretical difficulties because using a zero in place of the negative estimates can affect the statistical properties of the other estimates. Another approach is to use an alternative calculating technique that yields a nonnegative estimate. Still another approach is to consider that this is evidence that the linear model is incorrect and that the problem needs to be reexamined.

An output often included with a computer variance component analysis is the expected mean-square values. Although not discussed in this volume, these values can be used to determine confidence intervals for variance components or percent contribution.

24.4 Example 24.1: Variance Components of Pigment Paste

Consider that numerous batches of a pigment paste are sampled and tested once. We would like to understand that the variation of the resulting moisture content is that shown pictorially in Figure 24.2 (Box *et al.*, 1978).

In this figure, η is the long-run process mean for moisture content. Process variation is the distribution of batch means about this process mean, sampling variation is the distribution of samples about the batch mean, and analytical variation is the distribution of analytical test results about the sample mean.

The overall error ($\varepsilon = y - \eta$) will contain the three separate error components (i.e., $\varepsilon = \varepsilon_t + \varepsilon_s + \varepsilon_b$), where ε_t is the analytical test error, ε_s is the error made in taking the samples, and ε_b is the batch-to-batch error. By these definitions, the error components

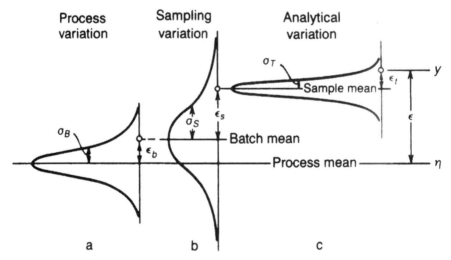

Figure 24.2: Three components of variance in the final moisture reading. (a) Distribution of batch means about the process mean η. (b) Distribution of sample means about the batch mean. (c) Distribution of analytical test results about sample mean.
(G. E. P. Box, W. Hunter, and S. Hunter *Statistics for Experimenters*, John Wiley and Sons, 1978.)

ε_t, ε_s, and ε_b have zero means. The assumption is made that the samples are random (independent) from normal distributions with fixed variances σ_t^2, σ_s^2 and σ_b^2.

Consider now the following data that were collected using the hierarchical design shown in Figure 24.1:

		Batch														
Sample	Sub-sample	1	2	3	4	5	6	7	8	9	10	11	12	13	14	15
1	1	40	26	29	30	19	33	23	34	27	13	25	29	19	23	39
	2	39	28	28	31	20	32	24	34	27	16	23	29	20	24	37
2	1	30	25	14	24	17	26	32	29	31	27	25	31	29	25	26
	2	30	26	15	24	17	24	33	29	31	24	27	32	30	25	28

A variance components analysis for this set of experimental data is shown below. For now let's concentrate only on the outputs from this table as described below. Chapter 26 describes the mathematical relationships from a single-factor ANOVA table. However, one major difference between the ANOVA table calculations in Chapter 26 and this ANOVA table is that the probability calculations for a variance components analysis are dependent upon the design hierarchy; for example, the probability calculation for "Batch" is the statistical comparison of "Sample" to "Batch," not "Error" to "Batch."

```
Fully Nested Analysis of Variance

Analysis of Variance for Moisture
```

Source	DF	SS	MS	F	P
Batch	14	1210.9333	86.4952	1.492	0.226
Sample	15	869.7500	57.9833	63.255	0.000
Error	30	27.5000	0.9167		
Total	59	2108.1833			

```
Variance Components
```

Source	Var Comp.	% of Total	StDev
Batch	7.128	19.49	2.670
Sample	28.533	78.01	5.342
Error	0.917	2.51	0.957
Total	36.578		6.048

Example mathematical relationships in this analysis are

- MSBatch = 1210.9333/14 = 86.4952
- F_{Batch} = 86.4952/57.9833 = 1.492

For this analysis, the "sample" is nested in "batch." The variance components estimated from the model are

Analytical test variance = 0.92
(standard deviation = 0.96)

Sample variance (within batches) = 28.5
(standard deviation = 5.3)

Process variance (between batches) = 7.1
(standard deviation = 2.6)

The square roots of these variances are estimates of the standard deviations, which are compared pictorially in Figure 24.3. These results indicate that the largest individual source for variation was the error arising in chemical sampling. Investigators given this information then discovered and resolved the problem of operators' not being aware of the correct sampling procedure.

24.5   Example 24.2: Variance Components of a Manufactured Door Including Measurement System Components

When a door is closed, it needs to seal well with its mating surface. Some twist of the manufactured door can be tolerated because of a seal that is attached to the door. However, a large degree of twist cannot be tolerated because the seal would not be effective, excessive force would be required to close the door, and excessive load on the door-latching mechanism could in time cause failure.

Let's consider this situation from the point of view of the supplier of the door. The burden of how well a door latches due to twist does not lie completely with the supplier of the door. If the mating doorframe is twisted, there can be a customer problem, no matter how well the door is manufactured. The supplier of the door never sees the doorframe; hence, they cannot check the quality of the overall assembly. Also, the doors are supposed to be interchangeable between frames.

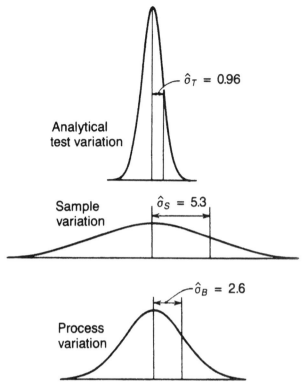

Figure 24.3: Diagrammatic summary of results of experiment to determine components of variance. (G. E. P. Box, W. Hunter, and S. Hunter Statistics for Experimenters, John Wiley and Sons, 1978.)

The customer of the door supplier often rejects doors. The supplier of the door can only manufacture to the specification. The question of how to measure the door twist then arises. Drawing specifications indicate that the area where the door is to seal has a 0.031-in. tolerance. Currently, this dimension is measured in the fixture that manufactures the door. However, it has been noticed that the door tends to spring into a different position after leaving the fixture. Because of this, it was concluded that there needed to be built a measurement fixture for checking the door which simulated where the door would be mounted on hinges in taking the measurements that assess how it seals.

A nested experiment was then planned where other issues of concern were also included (e.g., measurement system). There was only one manufacturing jig and one inspection jig. The following sources of variability were considered: week-to-week, shift-to-shift, operator-to-operator, within-part variability, in-spector measurement repeatability, and inspector measurement reproducibility.

24.6 Example 24.3: Determining Process Capability/Performance Metric Using Variance Components

The following set of data (AIAG, 1995b) was presented initially as Exercise 4 in Chapter 10 on control charts. Example 11.1 described a procedure used to calculate process capability/performance metric for this in-control/predictable process. This chapter gives an additional calculation procedure for determining standard deviations from the process.

		Subgroups									
		1	2	3	4	5	6	7	8	9	10
	1	0.65	0.75	0.75	0.60	0.70	0.60	0.75	0.60	0.65	0.60
	2	0.70	0.85	0.80	0.70	0.75	0.75	0.80	0.70	0.80	0.70
Samples	3	0.65	0.75	0.80	0.70	0.65	0.75	0.65	0.80	0.85	0.60
	4	0.65	0.85	0.70	0.75	0.85	0.85	0.75	0.75	0.85	0.80
	5	0.85	0.65	0.75	0.65	0.80	0.70	0.70	0.75	0.75	0.65

		Subgroups					
		11	12	13	14	15	16
	1	0.80	0.85	0.70	0.65	0.90	0.75
	2	0.75	0.75	0.70	0.70	0.80	0.80
Samples	3	0.90	0.85	0.75	0.85	0.80	0.75
	4	0.50	0.65	0.75	0.75	0.75	0.80
	5	0.80	0.70	0.70	0.60	0.85	0.65

These control chart data have samples nested within the subgroups. A random-effects model would yield the following computer analysis results:

```
Fully Nested Analysis of Variance

Analysis of Variance for Data

Source     DF         SS          MS          F         P

Subgrp     15      0.1095      0.0073      1.118     0.360
Error      64      0.4180      0.0065
Total      79      0.5275
```

```
Variance Components

Source      Var Comp.    % of Total      StDev

Subgrp        0.000         2.30         0.012
Error         0.007        97.70         0.081
Total         0.007                      0.082
```

An interpretation of this output is the following: The long-term standard deviation would be the total component of 0.082, while the short-term standard deviation component would be the error component of 0.081. These values for standard deviation are very similar to the values determined using the approach presented in Chapter 11.

Variance components technique can be useful for determining the process capability/performance metric when a hierarchy of sources affects process variability. The strategy will not only describe the variability of the process for process capability/performance calculations, but it will also indicate where process improvement should focus to reduce the magnitude of component variation.

24.7   Example 24.4: Variance Components Analysis of Injection-Molding Data

From the multi-vari analysis in Example 18.1 of the injection molding data given in Table 18.1, it was thought that differences between cavities affected the diameter of parts. A variance components analysis of the factors yielded the following results, where the raw data were multiplied by 10,000 so that the magnitude of the variance components would be large enough to be quantified on the computer output.

```
Fully Nested Analysis of Variance

Analysis of Variance for Diameter

Source     DF          SS          MS        F        P

Time        2      56.4444     28.2222    0.030    0.970
Cavity      9    8437.3750    937.4861   17.957    0.000
Part       12     626.5000     52.2083    1.772    0.081
Position   48    1414.0000     29.4583
Total      71   10534.3194
```

```
Variance Components

Source     Var Comp.    % of Total        StDev

Time        -37.886*         0.00         0.000
Cavity      147.546         79.93        12.147
Part          7.583          4.11         2.754
Position     29.458         15.96         5.428
Total       184.588                      13.586
```

In this analysis, variability between positions was used to estimate error. Using position measurements to estimate error, the probability value for cavity is the only factor less than 0.05. We estimate that the variability between cavities is the largest contributor, at most 80% of total variability. We also note that the percentage value for position has a fairly high value relative to time. This could indicate that, consistent with our observation from the multivari chart, there are statistically-significant differences in measurements across the parts. Variance component factors need to be adjusted by the 10,000 multiple made initially to the raw data.

24.8   Example 24.5: Project Analysis for Variance Components of an Hourly Response That Had an Unsatisfactory Process Capability/Performance Metric

Example 12.4 identified a process as predictable but had an unsatisfactory process capability/performance metric. An IEE project was created to reduce the frequency of non-conformance. The wisdom of the organization created cause-and-effect matrix indicated high-ranked beliefs that differences between hours of the day and work-shifts could affect the response's variability.

A variance components analysis of the data presented in the original example (Table 12.2) yielded:

Nested ANOVA: Response Versus Day, Shift, Hour

```
Analysis of Variance for Response

Source    DF          SS         MS          F         P

Day       19    8008.8039   421.5160      5.798     0.000
Shift     40    2907.9931    72.6998     16.550     0.000
```

```
Hour      420    1844.9079      4.3926
Total     479   12761.7049
```

Variance Components

Source	Var Comp.	% of Total	StDev
Day	14.534	52.92	3.812
Shift	8.538	31.09	2.922
Hour	4.393	15.99	2.096
Total	27.465		5.241

Since the *P* values for both day and shift are significant, the hypothesis relative to the variability between days and between shifts affecting the response was supported. From these analyses, the project team has evidence that something is happening in these process areas.

The team should now spend time observing and perhaps videotaping the process to gain understanding of what is causing these significant variability sources, with the end goal of determining what could be done to reduce the magnitude of the effect from these process input variables.

24.9   Applying IEE

Variability is often the elusive enemy of manufacturing and transactional processes. Variance components analysis can aid in the identification of the major contributors to this variability.

As noted earlier, variance components techniques can be used for process capability/performance metric assessments. When variability in a product or process is too large and the source of this variability is understood, a few simple changes may be all that is necessary to reduce its magnitude and improve quality.

In other cases, it may not be clear how a large detrimental variance component can be reduced. In this case, it may be appropriate to use a DOE strategy that considers various factors that could contribute to the largest amount of variability in the area of concern. Output from this experiment could better indicate what changes should be made to the process in order to reduce variability. Perhaps this analysis can lead to the development of a process that is more robust to the variability of raw material.

Before conducting a gage R&R study, as discussed in Chapter 15, consider replacing the study with a variance components analysis, which can give more insight into the sources of variability for process improvement efforts. This analysis may show that the measurement procedure is causing much variability and needs to be improved.

24.10 Exercises

1. Fabric is woven on a large number of looms (Montgomery, 1997). It is suspected that variation can occur both within samples from fabric from the same loom and between different looms. To investigate this, four looms were randomly selected and four strength determinations were made on the fabric that was produced. Conduct a variance-of-components analysis of the data:

   | | | Observations | | |
Looms	*1*	*2*	*3*	*4*
1	98	97	99	96
2	91	90	93	92
3	96	95	97	95
4	95	96	99	98

2. Example 24.2 described a variance components strategy to measure the twist of a door. Build a plan to execute this strategy. Include the number of samples for each factor considered.

25

P-DMAIC – Analyze Phase: Correlation and Simple Linear Regression

25.1 P-DMAIC Roadmap Component

This is the second chapter of five chapters for assessing a population response as a function of multiple input situations. The last chapter described a hierarchical structure. While this chapter will describe the regression of two continuous variables; e.g., temperature versus a product dimension or invoice size versus Days sales outstanding (DSO) days beyond due date. The graphic in this section highlights the P-DMAIC roadmap steps (see Appendix Section D.1) that are described in this chapter. Appendix E contains the tollgate check sheets for this and other phases.

When conducting an analysis in the P-DMAIC and E-DMAIC phases, there is often a direct relationship between two variables. If a strong relationship between a process input variable is correlated with a key process output variable, the input variable could then be considered a key process input variable. The equation $Y = f(x)$ can express this relationship for continuous variables, where Y is the dependent variable and x is the independent variable. Parameters of this equation can be determined using regression techniques. The techniques described in this chapter will describe hypothesis relationship testing so that organizations avoid the extreme problem of "jumping to a conclusion on a trend of one."

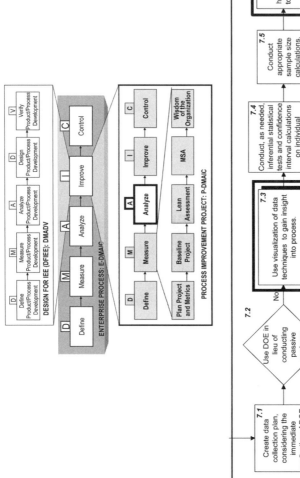

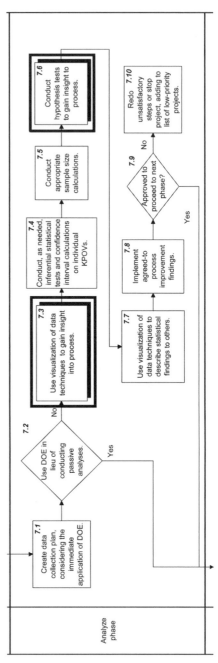

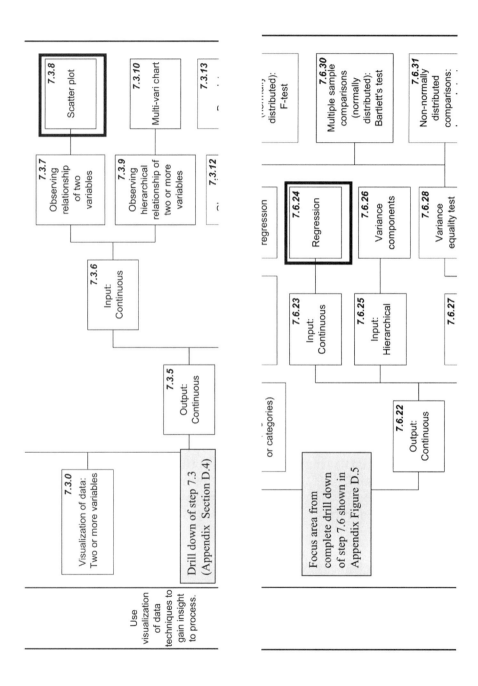

After the establishment of a relationship, an appropriate course of action would depend upon the particulars of the situation. If the overall process is not capable of meeting the needs of the customer consistently, it may be appropriate to initiate tighter specifications or to initiate control charts for this key process input variable. However, if the variability of a key process input variable represents the normal variability of raw material, an alternative course of action might be more appropriate. For this case, it could be beneficial to conduct a DOE with the objective of determining other factor settings that would improve the process output robustness to normal variability of this key process input variable.

The mathematical equations presented in this chapter focus on linear relationships. Correlation between two variables can be quadratic or even cubic. When investigating data, it is important to plot the data. If the relationship repeats to be non-linear, other models can be investigated for a fit using a commercially-available statistical analysis program.

25.2   IEE Application Examples: Regression

- *Transactional 30,000-foot-level metric*: An IEE project was created to improve DSO. One input that surfaced from a cause-and-effect matrix was the size of the invoice. A scatter plot and regression analysis of DSO versus size of invoice was created.
- *Manufacturing 30,000-foot-level metric*: An IEE project was created to reduce the non-conformance rate of a manufactured part's diameter. One input that surfaced from a cause-and-effect matrix was the temperature of the manufacturing process. A scatter plot and regression analysis of part diameter versus process temperature was created.

25.3   Scatter Plot (Dispersion Graph)

A scatter plot or dispersion graph shows the relationship between two variables pictorially. It gives a simple illustration of how one variable can influence the other. Care must be exercised when interpreting dispersion graphs. A plot that shows a relationship does not prove a true cause-and-effect relationship; i.e., it does not prove causation. Happenstance data can cause the appearance of a relationship. For example, the phase of the moon could appear to affect a process that has a monthly cycle.

When constructing a dispersion graph, first define clearly the variables that are to be evaluated. Next, collect at least 30 data pairs (50 or 100 pairs are better). When creating a scatter plot, data pairs should be plotted so that the independent variable is on the *x*-axis, while the dependent variable is on the *y*-axis. The plot illustrates the potential strength of the relationship between two variables, which may be linear, quadratic, or some other mathematical relationship.

25.4 Correlation

A statistic that represents the strength of a linear relationship between two variables is the sample correlation coefficient (*r*). A correlation coefficient can take values between −1 and +1. A−1 indicates perfect negative correlation, while a +1 indicates perfect positive correlation. Zero indicates no correlation. The equation for the sample correlation coefficient (*r*) of two variables is

$$r = \frac{\sum(x_i - \bar{x})(y_i - \bar{y})}{\sqrt{\sum(x_i - \bar{x})^2 \sum(y_i - \bar{y})^2}}$$

where (x_i, y_i) are the coordinate pairs of evaluated values and $\bar{x}$ and $\bar{y}$ are the averages of the *x* and *y* values respectively. Figure 25.1 shows four plots with various correlation characteristics. It is important to plot the analyzed data. Two data variables may show no linear correlation but may still have a quadratic relationship.

The hypothesis test for the correlation coefficient (ρ) to equal zero is

$$H_0: \rho = 0$$
$$H_A: \rho \neq 0$$

If the *x* and *y* relationships are jointly normally distributed, the test statistic for this hypothesis is

$$t_0 = \frac{r\sqrt{n-2}}{\sqrt{1-r^2}}$$

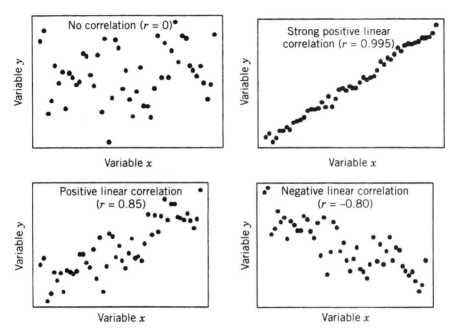

Figure 25.1: Correlation coefficients.

Table 25.1: Delivery Time Data

Number of cases (x)	Delivery Time (y)	Number of cases (x)	Delivery Time (y)	Number of cases (x)	Delivery Time (y)	Number of cases (x)	Delivery Time (y)	Number of cases (x)	Delivery Time (y)
7	16.68	7	18.11	16	40.33	10	29	10	17.9
3	11.5	2	8	10	21	6	15.35	26	52.32
3	12.03	7	17.83	4	13.5	7	19	9	18.75
4	14.88	30	79.24	6	19.75	3	9.5	8	19.83
6	13.75	5	21.5	9	24	17	35.1	4	10.75

where the null hypothesis is rejected if $\mid t_0 \mid > t_{\alpha/2,n\text{-}2}$ using a one-sided t-table value.

Coefficient of determination (R^2) is simply the square of the correlation coefficient. Values for R^2 represent the percentage of variability accounted for by the model. For example, $R^2 = 0.8$ indicates that 80% of the variability in the data is accounted for by the model.

25.5   Example 25.1: Correlation

The times for 25 soft drink deliveries (*y*) monitored as a function of delivery volume (*x*) are shown in Table 25.1. (Montgomery and

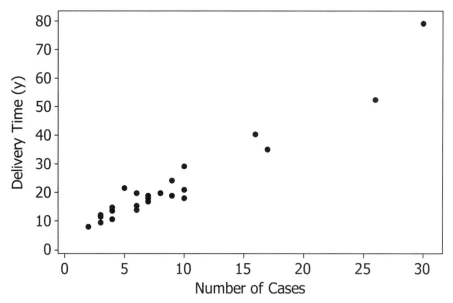

Figure 25.2: Plot of number of cases versus delivery time.

Peck, 1982) The scatter plot of these data shown in Figure 25.2 indicates that there probably is a strong correlation between the two variables. The sample correlation coefficient between delivery time and delivery volume is determined using a computer program or equation to be

$$r = \frac{\sum (x_i - \bar{x})(y_i - \bar{y})}{\sqrt{\sum (x_i - \bar{x})^2 \sum (y_i - \bar{y})^2}} = \frac{2473.34}{\sqrt{(1136.57)(5784.54)}} = 0.96$$

Testing the null hypothesis that the correlation coefficient equals zero yields

$$t_0 = \frac{r\sqrt{n-2}}{\sqrt{1-r^2}} = \frac{0.96\sqrt{25-2}}{\sqrt{1-0.96^2}} = 17.56$$

Using a single-sided t-table (i.e., Table D) at $\alpha/2$, we can reject H_0 since $\mid t_0 \mid > t_{\alpha/2,n-2}$, where $t_{0.05/2,23} = 2.069$. Or, we can use a two-sided t-table (i.e., Table E) at α. These data are discussed again in Example 25.2.

A computer statistical program analysis yielded:

Correlations: Delivery Time (y), Cases

```
Pearson correlation of Delivery Time (y) and Cases =
0.965
P-Value = 0.000
```

For the *P* value of 0.000, we can declare significance for a test criterion of 0.05.

25.6   Simple Linear Regression

Correlation only measures association, while regression model methods serve to develop quantitative variable relationships that are useful for estimation and prediction. In regression equations, the independent variable is variable *x*, while the dependent variable is *y*. This section focuses on regression models that contain linear variables; however, regression models can also include quadratic and cubic terms; i.e., model contains non-linear parameters.

The simple linear regression model (i.e., with a single regressor *x*) takes the form

$$Y = \beta_0 + \beta_1 x + \varepsilon$$

where β_0 is the intercept, β_0 is the slope, and ε is the error term. All data points do not typically fall exactly on the regression model line. The error term σ^2 makes up for these differences from other variables such as measurement errors, material variations in a manufacturing operation, and personnel. Errors are assumed to have mean zero and unknown variance σ^2, and they are not correlated. When the magnitude of the coefficient of determination (R^2) is large, the error term is relatively small, and the model has a good fit.

When a linear regression model contains only one independent (regressor or predictor) variable, it is called *simple linear regression*. When a regression model contains more than one independent variable, it is called a *multiple linear regression model*. The focus of this chapter is simple linear regression.

The primary purpose of regression analysis is to determine the unknown regression model parameters. We determine these regression coefficients through the method of least squares. Least squares minimize the sum of squares of the residuals, which are described below. The fitted simple linear regression model that gives a point estimate of the mean of y for a particular x is

$$\hat{y} = \hat{\beta}_0 + \hat{\beta}_1 x$$

where the regression coefficients are

$$\hat{\beta}_1 = \frac{S_{xy}}{S_{xx}} = \frac{\sum\limits_{i=1}^{n} y_i x_i - \dfrac{\left(\sum\limits_{i=1}^{n} y_i\right)\left(\sum\limits_{i=1}^{n} x_i\right)}{n}}{\sum\limits_{i=1}^{n} x_i^2 - \dfrac{\left(\sum\limits_{i=1}^{n} x_i\right)^2}{n}} = \frac{\sum\limits_{i=1}^{n} y_i(x_i - \bar{x})}{\sum\limits_{i=1}^{n} (x_i - \bar{x})^2}$$

$$\hat{\beta}_0 = \bar{y} - \hat{\beta}_1 \bar{x}$$

The difference between the observed value y_i and the corresponding fitted value $\hat{y}_i$ is a residual. The ith residual is

$$e_i = y_i - \hat{y}_i$$

Residuals are important for investigating the adequacy of the fitted model and detecting the departure from underlying assumptions. Residual analysis techniques are discussed in the next section.

Statistical regression programs can calculate the model and plot the least-square estimates. Programs can also generate a table of coefficients and conduct an analysis of variance. Significance tests of the regression coefficients involve either the t-distribution for the table of coefficients or the F-distribution for analysis of variance. One null hypothesis is that β_0 is constant, and the alternative hypothesis is that it is not constant. Another null hypothesis is that β_1 is zero, and the alternative hypothesis is that it is not zero. In both cases, $\alpha = 0.05$ corresponds to a computer probability P value of 0.05, which practitioners often use as a level of significance to reject the null hypothesis.

For the analysis of variance table, total variation is broken down into the pieces described by the sum of squares (SS):

$$SS_{total} = SS_{regression} + SS_{error}$$

where

$$SS_{\text{total}} = \sum (y_i - \bar{y})^2$$

$$SS_{\text{regression}} = \sum (\hat{y}_i - \bar{y})^2$$

$$SS_{\text{error}} = \sum (y_i - \hat{y}_i)^2$$

Each sum of square has an associated number of degrees of freedom equal to

Sum of Squares	Degrees of Freedom
SS_{total}	n–1
$SS_{\text{regression}}$	1
SS_{error}	n–2

When divided by the appropriate number of degrees of freedom, the sums of squares give good estimates of the source of variability, i.e., total, regression, and error). This variability is analogous to a variance calculation and is called *mean square*. If there is no difference in treatment means, the two estimates are presumed to be similar. If there is a difference, we suspect that the regressor causes the observed difference. Calculating the *F*-test statistic tests the null hypothesis that there is no difference because of the regressor:

$$F_0 = \frac{MS_{\text{regression}}}{MS_{\text{error}}}$$

Using an *F*-table, we should reject the null hypothesis and conclude that the regressor causes a difference, at the significance level of α, if

$$F_0 > F_{\alpha,1,n-2}$$

Alternatively, a probability value could be calculated for F_0 and compared to a criterion; e.g., $\alpha = 0.05$. The null hypothesis is rejected if the calculated value is less than the criterion. This approach is most appropriate when a computer program makes the computations. This test procedure is summarized in an analysis of variance table, as shown in Table 25.2.

The coefficient of determination (R^2) is a ratio of the explained variation to total variation, which equates to

Table 25.2: The Analysis of Variance Table for Simple Regression

Source of Variation	Sum of Squares	Degrees of Freedom	Mean Square	F_0
Regression	$SS_{regression}$	1	$MS_{regression}$	$F_0 = \dfrac{MS_{regression}}{MS_{error}}$
Error	SS_{error}	$n-2$	MS_{error}	
Total	SS_{total}	$n-1$		

$$R^2 = 1 - \frac{SS_{error}}{SS_{total}} = \frac{SS_{regression}}{SS_{total}} = \frac{\sum (\hat{y}_i - \bar{y})^2}{\sum (y_i - \bar{y})^2}$$

The multiplication of this coefficient by 100 yields the percentage variation explained by the least-squares method. A higher percentage indicates a better least-squares predictor.

If a variable is added to a model equation, R^2 will increase even if the variable has no real value. A compensation for this is an adjusted value, $R^2(adj)$, which has an approximate unbiased estimate for the population R^2 of

$$R^2(adj) = 1 - \frac{SS_{error}/(n-p)}{SS_{total}/(n-1)}$$

where p is the number of terms in the regression equation and n is the total number of degrees of freedom.

The correlation coefficient of the population, ρ, and its sample estimate r are connected intimately with a bivariate population known as the bivariate normal distribution. This distribution is created from the joint frequency distributions of the modeled variables. The frequencies have an elliptical concentration.

25.7 Analysis of Residuals

For our analysis, modeling errors are assumed to be normally and independently distributed with mean zero and a constant but unknown variance. An abbreviation for this assumption is NID(0, σ^2).

An important method for testing the assumption of an experiment is residual analysis, where a residual is the difference between the observed value and the corresponding fitted value. Residual analyses play an important role in investigating the adequacy of the fitted model and in detecting departures from the model.

Residual analysis techniques include the following:

- Checking the normality assumption through a normal probability plot and/or histogram of the residuals.
- Checking for correlation between residuals by plotting residuals in time sequence.
- Checking for correctness of the model by plotting residuals versus fitted values.

The assumptions for a valid regression or ANOVA are unique to all earlier tests. In regression and ANOVA you check the assumptions after the test rather than before. This is because you are validating the assumptions on the model not the data.

25.8   Analysis of Residuals: Normality Assessment

If the NID(0, σ^2) assumption is valid, a histogram plot of the residuals should look like a sample from a normal distribution. Expect considerable departures from a normality appearance when the sample size is small. A normal probability plot of the residuals can similarly be conducted. If the underlying error distribution is normal, the plot will resemble a straight line.

Commonly, a residual plot will show one point that is much larger or smaller than the others. This residual is typically called an *outlier*. One or more outliers can distort the analysis. Frequently, outliers are caused by the erroneous recording of information. If this is not the case, further analysis should be conducted. This data point may give additional insight into what could be done to improve a process dramatically.

To perform a rough check for outliers, substitute residual error e_{ij} values into

$$d_{ij} = \frac{e_{ij}}{\sqrt{MS_E}}$$

and examine the standardized residuals values. About 68% of the standardized residuals should fall within a d_{ij} value of ± 1. About 95% of the standardized residuals should fall within a d_{ij} value of ± 2. Almost all (99%) of the standardized residuals should fall within a d_{ij} value of ± 3.

25.9   Analysis of Residuals: Time Sequence

A plot of residuals in time order of data collection helps detect correlation between residuals. A tendency for positive or negative runs of residuals indicates positive correlation. This implies a violation of the independence assumption. An individuals control chart of residuals in chronological order by observation number can verify the independence of errors. Positive autocorrelation occurs when residuals don't change signs as frequently as should be expected, while negative autocorrelation is indicated when the residuals frequently change signs. This problem can be very serious and difficult to correct. It should be avoided initially. An important step in obtaining independence is conducting proper randomization initially.

25.10   Analysis of Residuals: Fitted Values

For a good model fit, this plot should show a random scatter and have no pattern. Common discrepancies include the following:

- Outliers, which appear as points that are either much higher or lower than normal residual values. These points should be investigated. Perhaps someone recorded a number incorrectly. Perhaps an evaluation of this sample provides additional knowledge that leads to a major process improvement breakthrough.
- Non-constant variance, where the difference between the lowest and highest residual values either increases or decreases for an increase in the fitted values. A measurement instrument could cause this where error is proportional to the measured value.
- Poor model fit, where, for example, residual values seem to increase and then decrease with an increase in the fitted value. For the described situation, a quadratic model might possibly be a better fit than a linear model.

Normalizing transformations (See Table 9.3) are sometimes very useful for addressing these problems mentioned above.

25.11   Example 25.2: Simple Linear Regression

IEE Application Examples

- *Regression analysis of DSO versus size of invoice.*
- *Regression analysis of part diameter versus processing temperature.*

Consider the data shown in Table 25.1 that were used for the correlation Example 35.1. The output from a regression analysis of this data is:

```
Regression Analysis

The regression equation is
Delivery Time (y) = 3.32 + 2.18 Cases

Predictor     Coef      StDev         T         P
Constant     3.321     1.371      2.42     0.024
Cases        2.1762    0.1240     17.55    0.000

S = 4.181   R-Sq = 93.0%      R-Sq(adj) = 92.7%

Analysis of Variance
Source              DF       SS       MS         F       P
Regression           1    5382.4   5382.4    307.85   0.000
Residual Error      23     402.1     17.5
Total               24    5784.5

Unusual Observations
Obs Cases Delivery    Fit  StDev Fit Residual St Resid
 9    30.0   79.240 68.606     2.764    10.634    3.39RX
22    26.0   52.320 59.901     2.296    -7.581   -2.17RX

R denotes an observation with a large standardized
residual
X denotes an observation whose X value gives it large
influence.
```

Figure 25.3 shows a plot of this model along with the 95% prediction interval (PI) bands and confidence interval (CI) bands. The confidence bands reflect the confidence intervals on the equation coefficients. The prediction bands reflect the CI for the PI percentage of population responses at any given level of the independent variable. Figure 25.4 shows various residual analysis plots.

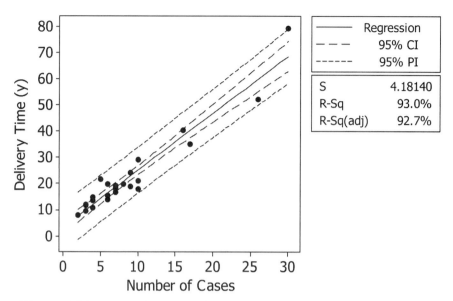

Figure 25.3: Regression plot of number of cases versus delivery time. $Y = 3.32 + 2.18X$; R2 = 93.0%. CI: confidence interval; PI: prediction interval.

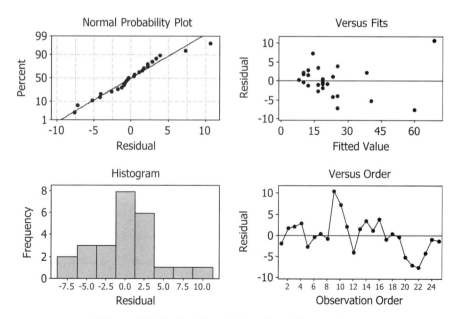

Figure 25.4: Residual plots for delivery time.

The tabular value of 92.7% for R^2 would initially give us a good feeling about our analysis. However, when we examine the data we notice that most readings were between 0 and 10 cases. The values beyond 10 could almost be considered an extrapolation to the majority of data used fitting this model. In addition, the plots indicate that these values do not fit the general model very well. The residuals versus fitted plot indicate that there could also be an increase in the variability of delivery time with an increase in the number of cases.

At this point, the practitioner needs to stop to reflect on the real purpose of the analysis. The model does not fit very well, and Montogmery and Peck [1982] discuss further analysis such as the number of cases versus distance. This type of analysis may be appropriate, and there could be additional factors to consider, such as operator, time of day of delivery, and weather.

However, let's not forget that data collection and analysis take time, and our time is valuable. If the general model response meets the needs of customers and is economically satisfactory, perhaps we should do no further analysis and move on to some other problem. However, if we need to reduce delivery time, then our actions need to reflect this objective.

25.12 Applying IEE

Correlation and regression techniques can be very valuable; however, care needs to be exercised when using these methods. Some things to consider are the following:

- The regression model describes the region on which it is based and may not accurately represent extrapolated values.
- It is difficult to detect a cause-and-effect relationship if measurement error is large.
- A true cause-and-effect relationship does not necessarily exist when two variables are correlated.
- A process may be affected by a third variable so that the two variables vary simultaneously.
- Least-squares predictions are based on historical data, which may not represent future relationships accurately.
- An important independent variable for process improvement may be disregarded for further considerations because a study did not show correlation between this variable and the response that needed improvement. However, this

variable might be shown to be important in a DOE if it was set outside its normal operating range.

25.13 Exercises

1. Two variables within a process are thought to be correlated. Generate a scatter plot, determine the value of the coefficient of correlation, conduct a significance test on the coefficient of correlation, and estimate the variability in y thought to be caused by x.

X	Y	X	Y	X	Y
27.02	50.17	43.09	50.09	57.07	49.80
30.01	49.84	43.96	49.77	59.07	49.91
33.10	50.00	46.14	49.61	59.96	50.20
34.04	49.79	46.99	49.86	61.05	49.97
35.09	49.99	48.20	50.18	61.88	50.16
35.99	49.97	49.87	49.90	63.08	49.97
36.86	49.93	51.92	49.84	63.87	50.12
37.83	49.94	53.97	49.89	66.10	50.05
39.13	50.10	55.02	50.02	67.17	50.20
39.98	50.09	55.97	49.81	68.01	50.19

2. The strength of a part was monitored as function of process temperature. Generate a scatter plot, determine the value of the coefficient of correlation, conduct a significance test on the coefficient of correlation, determine the regression equation, generate a residual diagnostic plot, and estimate the percentage of variability in strength caused by temperature.

Temp.	Strength	Temp.	Strength	Temp.	Strength
140.6	7.38	140.5	6.95	142.1	3.67
140.9	6.65	139.7	8.58	141.1	6.58
141.0	6.43	140.6	7.17	140.6	7.42
140.8	6.85	140.1	8.55	140.5	7.53
141.6	5.08	141.1	6.23	141.2	6.28
142.0	3.80	140.9	6.27	142.2	3.46
141.6	4.93	140.6	7.54	140.0	8.67
140.6	7.12	140.2	8.27	141.7	4.42
141.6	4.74	139.9	8.85	141.5	4.25
140.2	8.70	140.2	7.43	140.7	7.06

3. The dependent variable y was monitored as a function of an independent variable x. Conduct a regression analysis and comment.

X	Y	X	Y	X	Y
2.19	47.17	10.45	48.93	47.17	10.45
0.73	47.43	11.38	49.14	47.43	11.38
3.95	47.16	10.72	49.50	47.16	10.72
6.85	47.44	13.42	49.69	47.44	13.42
1.81	47.83	12.35	49.78	47.83	12.35
4.49	47.94	13.91	49.92	47.94	13.91
3.71	48.20	9.43	50.29	48.20	9.43
11.21	48.19	21.76	50.17	48.19	21.76
6.02	48.59	19.92	50.78	48.59	19.92
8.42	48.77	19.45	50.41	48.77	19.45

X	Y	X	Y
31.2	52.8	40.46	55.20
28.83	52.95	44.29	55.39
35.64	53.31	36.68	55.44
34.5	53.8	50.75	55.61
29.35	53.77	37.99	55.77
33.87	54.16	49.02	56.03
40.08	54.17	45.66	56.14
38.72	54.52	43.55	56.25
34.86	54.88	48.00	56.53
38.47	54.85	49.00	57.01

4. Estimate the proportion defective rate for the first four points in Figure 8.12. Using only these four points as a continuous response, project what the response would be in 10 days using simple regression analysis techniques. Comment on this response. Describe a null hypothesis to test the whether change occurred over time. Conduct a test of this null hypothesis. Comment on your results.

5. Analyze and comment on the following data relationship

Input (X):	2	4	1	5	1.5	6
Output (Y):	18	20	15	20	17	50

6. Conduct a regression analysis of the following data. Determine the expected value for Y given $X = 93.1$.

X	Y	X	Y
78.4	-9	62.7	-8.7
89.9	-18.2	81.9	-5.5
54.2	-33.5	88	-14.9
58.3	-25.6	60.9	-19.8
98.3	-1.5	60.7	0.9
57.8	-9	70.1	-38.5
66	-35.2	86.7	-5.8
67.1	-20.3	94.4	-33.7
97.3	-40.3	61.5	-38.4
76.5	0.3	72.4	-26.2
86.1	-16.1	63.9	-3.1
63.7	4.1	97.4	-43.6

7. Create a linear model. Determine the lower 80% CI (one-sided) for the predicted value of y when $x=100$.

X	Y
84.4	307.03
88	304.74
71.5	276.05
59.9	225.88

8. The lead time of an accounts receivable process is a 30,000-foot-level metric. Twelve random samples from invoices were selected over the year, one random sample selected for each month. One of two invoicing departments was noted for each invoice. The monetary value for each invoice was also noted. Determine the CI for the mean lead time and conduct other appropriate analyses.

Sample	Lead time (days)	Department	Value for invoice
1	47	1	24000
2	28	2	12000
3	45	1	22000
4	51	1	30000
5	47	1	23000
6	56	1	28000
7	55	1	75000
8	54	1	22000
9	59	1	33000
10	48	1	78000
11	33	2	24000

9. Create a scatter plot and conduct a regression analysis of the following data. Describe the results.

Temp.	Strength	Temp.	Strength	Temp.	Strength
140.6	7.38	140.5	6.95	142.1	3.67
140.9	6.65	139.7	8.58	141.1	6.58
141.0	6.43	140.6	7.17	140.6	7.42
140.8	6.85	140.1	8.55	140.5	7.53
141.6	5.08	141.1	6.23	141.2	6.28
142.0	3.80	140.9	6.27	142.2	3.46
141.6	4.93	140.6	7.54	140.0	8.67
140.6	7.12	140.2	8.27	141.7	4.42
141.6	4.74	139.9	8.85	141.5	4.25
140.2	8.70	140.2	7.43	140.7	7.06

10. Conduct a simple linear regression for each of the four following data sets (XA, YA), (XB,YB), (XC, YC), and (XD, YD).
    (a) Describe your regression analysis conclusions.
    (b) Create a scatter plot of each data set pair.
    (c) Describe your analysis conclusions.

XA	YA	XB	YB	XC	YC	XD	YD
10	8.04	10	9.14	10	7.46	8	6.58
14	9.96	14	8.10	14	8.84	8	5.76
5	5.68	5	4.74	5	5.73	8	7.71
8	6.95	8	8.14	8	6.77	8	8.84
9	8.81	9	8.77	9	7.11	8	8.47
12	10.84	12	9.13	12	8.15	8	7.04
4	4.26	4	3.10	4	5.39	8	5.25
7	4.82	7	7.26	7	6.42	19	12.50
11	8.33	11	9.26	11	7.81	8	5.56
13	7.58	13	8.74	13	12.74	8	7.91
6	7.24	6	6.13	6	6.08	8	6.89

26

P-DMAIC – Analyze Phase: Single-factor (One-way) Analysis of Variance and Analysis of Means

26.1 P-DMAIC Roadmap Component

This is the third chapter of five chapters for assessing a population response as a function of multiple input situations. The first chapter of this series of chapters described a hierarchical structure, while the last chapter described the regression of two continuous variables; e.g., methods for comparing two conditions or treatments. For example, the voice quality of a portable recording machine involved two different designs.

This chapter describes single-factor analysis of variance (ANOVA) experiments (completely randomized design) with two or more levels or treatments. This method is based on a fixed-effects model (as opposed to a random-effects model or components-of-variance model) and tests the null hypothesis that the different processes give an equal response. The graphic in this section highlights the P-DMAIC roadmap steps (see Appendix Section D.1) that are described in this chapter. Appendix E contains the tollgate check sheets for this and other phases. These techniques are not only applicable in the analyze phase of P-DMAIC but also E-DMAIC.

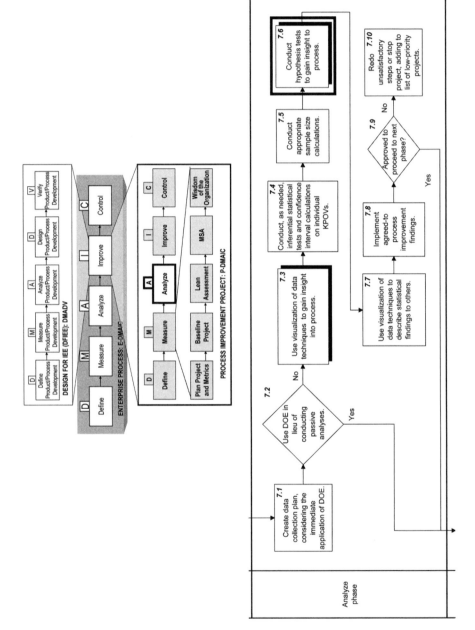

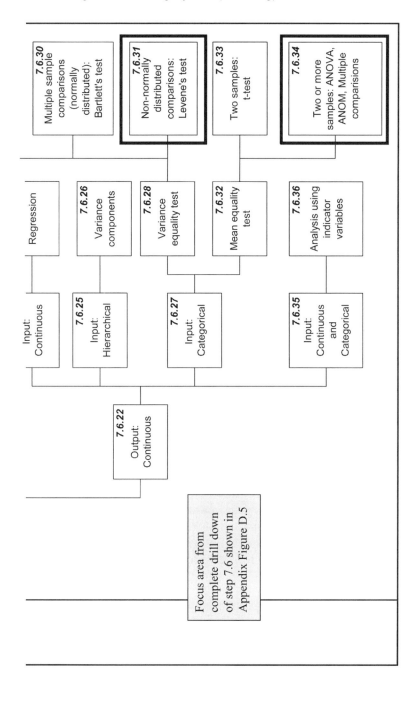

The statistical model for the fixed-effects model is similar to that of the random-effects model or components-of-variance model. The difference is that with the fixed-effects model, the levels are specifically chosen by the experimenter. For this situation, the test hypothesis is about the mean response effects due to factor levels, and conclusions apply only to the factor levels considered in the analysis.

Conclusions cannot be extended to similar levels not explicitly considered. The term analysis of variance originates from a partitioning of total variability into its component parts for the analysis; however, for fixed-effects model, this partitioning of variability (or variance) is only a method for assessing mean effects of the factor levels.

26.2   IEE Application Examples: ANOVA and ANOM

- *Transactional 30,000-foot-level metric*: An IEE project was to reduce DSO. A cause-and-effect matrix ranked company as an important input that could affect the DSO response; i.e., the team thought that some companies were more delinquent in payments than other companies. From randomly-sampled data, a statistical evaluation was conducted to test the hypothesis of equality of means for the DSOs by company.
- *Manufacturing 30,000-foot-level metric*: An IEE project was to improve the process capability/performance metric of a manufactured product diameter; i.e., reduce the rate of specification noncompliance. A cause-and-effect matrix ranked cavity as an input that could affect this noncompliance since there could be a significant difference in the mean part diameter from the cavities. From randomly-sampled data, statistical tests were conducted to test the hypotheses of mean diameter equality and equality of variances for the cavities.
- *Transactional and Manufacturing 30,000-foot-level lead time metric (a Lean metric)*: An IEE project was to improve the time from order entry to fulfillment. Over a region of process stability/predictability, for ten days end-of-day WIP was recorded for each process step. Little's law could then be used to convert this WIP data to cycle time data. The hypothesis of step mean and variance cycle time equality was then tested.

26.3   Application Steps

1. Describe the problem in terms of the KPOV. For example:
    (a) Lead time needs to be reduced ten percent.
    (b) A part dimension is non-compliant five percent of the time.
2. Describe the analysis. For example:
    (a) Determine if there is a significant difference in the mean delivery time of five company sites.
    (b) Determine if there is a significant difference in the mean diameter of plastic-injected parts from the five mold cavities.
3. Choose a large enough sample and randomly conduct the experiment.
4. Conduct an ANOVA.
5. Conduct a multiple-comparison test.
6. Conduct an ANOM.
7. Conduct a test for data normality test and equality of variance.
8. Translate conclusions from the experiment into terms relevant to the problem statement or process question.

Table 26.1 summarizes these various hypothesis tests, which are described in this chapter.

Table 26.1: ANOVA, ANOM, and Other Hypotheses

- ◆ Mean Significance Test
  - ■ ANOVA
    - ➢ $H_0: \mu_1 = \mu_2 = \mu_3 = \mu_4 = \mu_5$
    - ➢ $H_a: \mu_i \neq \mu_j$ for at least one pair (i, j), where, for example, μ_x is the mean delivery time of department x
  - ■ Multiple Comparisons
    - ➢ $H_0: \mu_1 = \mu_2, \mu_1 = \mu_3, \mu_2 = \mu_3 \dots$
    - ➢ $H_a: \mu_1 \neq \mu_2, \mu_1 \neq \mu_3, \mu_2 \neq \mu_3 \dots$
  - ■ ANOM
    - ➢ $H_0: \mu_1 = \mu_{\text{average of treatments}} \quad \mu_2 = \mu_{\text{average of treatments}} \dots$
    - ➢ $H_a: \mu_1 \neq \mu_{\text{average of treatments}} \quad \mu_2 \neq \mu_{\text{average of treatments}} \dots$
- ◆ Variance Significance Test
  - ➢ $H_0: \sigma_1^2 = \sigma_2^2 = \sigma_3^2 = \sigma_4^2 = \sigma_5^2$
  - ➢ $H_a: \sigma_i^2 \neq \sigma_j^2$ for at least one pair (i, j), where, for example, σ_x^2 is the variance in delivery time of department x

26.4   Single-factor ANOVA Hypothesis Test

The levels of in single-factor ANOVA problem can be pictorially compared using a box plot, dot plot, marginal plot, and/or mean effects plot. ANOVA tests for a significance difference in the mean factor-level response.

For a single-factor ANOVA, a linear statistical model can describe the observations of a level with j observations taken under level i (i = 1, 2,..., a; j = 1, 2,...n):

$$y_{ij} = \mu + \tau_i + \varepsilon_{ij}$$

where y_{ij} is the (ij)th observation, μ is the overall mean, τ is the ith level effect, and ε_{ij} is random error.

In an ANOVA hypothesis test, model errors are assumed to be normally- and independently-distributed random variables with mean zero and variance σ^2. In the analysis, this variance is assumed constant for all factor levels.

An expression for the hypothesis test of means is

$$H_0: \mu_1 = \mu_2 = \ldots = \mu_a$$
$$H_A: \mu_i \neq \mu_j \quad \text{for at least one pair } (i, j)$$

When H_0 is true, all levels have a common mean, μ, which leads to an equivalent expression in terms of τ:

$$H_0: \tau_1 = \tau_2 = \ldots \tau_a = 0$$
$$H_A: \tau_i \neq 0 \text{ (for at least one } i)$$

Hence, we can describe a single-factor ANOVA test as assessing the equality of level means or whether the level effects (τ_i) are zero.

26.5   Single-factor ANOVA Table Calculations

The total sum of squares of deviations about the grand average $\bar{y}$ (sometimes referred to as the total corrected sum of squares) represents the overall variability of the data:

$$SS_{\text{total}} = \sum_{i=1}^{a} \sum_{j=1}^{n} (y_{ij} - \bar{y})^2$$

This equation is intuitively appealing because a division of SS_{total} by the appropriate number of degrees of freedom would yield a sample variance of y's. For this situation, the overall number of degrees of freedom is $an - 1 = N - 1$.

Total variability in data as measured by the total corrected sum of squares can be partitioned into a sum of two elements. The first element is the sum of squares for differences between factor level averages and the grand average. The second element is the sum of squares of the differences of observations within factor levels from the average of factorial levels. The first element is a measure of the differences between the means of the levels, whereas the second element is due to random error. Symbolically, this relationship is

$$SS_{total} = SS_{factor\ levels} + SS_{error}$$

where $SS_{factor\ levels}$ is called the sum of squares due to factor levels, i.e., between factor levels or treatments, and SS_{error} is called the sum of squares due to error, i.e., within factor levels or treatments:

$$SS_{factor\ levels} = n\sum_{i=1}^{a}(\bar{y}_i - \bar{y})^2$$

$$SS_{error} = \sum_{i=1}^{a}\sum_{j=1}^{n}(y_{ij} - \bar{y}_i)^2$$

When divided by the appropriate number of degrees of freedom, these sums of squares give good estimates of the total variability, the variability between factor levels, and the variability within factor levels (or error). Expressions for the mean square are

$$MS_{factor\ levels} = \frac{SS_{factorlevels}}{a - 1}$$

$$MS_{error} = \frac{SS_{error}}{n - a}$$

If there is no difference in treatment means, the two estimates are presumed to be similar. If there is a difference, we suspect that the observed difference is caused by differences in the treatment

Table 26.2: ANOVA Table for Single-Factor, Fixed-Effects Model

Source of Variation	Sum of Squares	Degrees of Freedom	Mean Square	F_0
Between-factor levels	$SS_{\text{factor levels}}$	$a - 1$	$MS_{\text{factor levels}}$	$F_0 = \dfrac{MS_{\text{factor levels}}}{MS_{\text{error}}}$
Error (within-factor levels)	SS_{error}	$N - a$	MS_{error}	
Total	SS_{total}	$N - 1$		

factor levels. Calculating the F-test statistic tests the null hypothesis that there is no difference in factor levels:

$$F_0 = \frac{MS_{\text{factor levels}}}{MS_{\text{error}}}$$

Using an *F*-table, we should reject the null hypothesis and conclude that there are differences in treatment means if

$$F_0 > F_{\alpha, a-1, n-a}$$

Alternatively, a probability value could be calculated for F_0 and compared to a criterion; e.g., $\alpha = 0.05$. The null hypothesis is rejected if the calculated value is less than the criterion. This approach is most appropriate when a computer program makes the computations. This test procedure is summarized in an ANOVA table, as shown in Table 26.2.

26.6   Estimation of Model Parameters

In addition to factor-level significance, it can be useful to estimate the parameters of the single-factor model and the confidence intervals on the factor-level means. For the single factor model

$$y_{ij} = \mu + \tau_i + \varepsilon_{ij}$$

estimates for the overall mean and factor-level effects are

$$\hat{\mu} = \overline{y}$$
$$\hat{\tau}_i = \overline{y}_i - \overline{y}, \quad i = 1, 2, \ldots, a$$

P-DMAIC – Analyze Phase: Single-factor (One-way)   701

These estimators have intuitive appeal. The grand average of observations estimates the overall mean and the difference between the factor levels and the overall mean estimates the factor-level effect.

A $100(1 - \alpha)$ percent confidence interval estimate on the ith factor level is

$$\bar{y}_i \pm t_{\alpha,N-a}\sqrt{MS_E/n}$$

where t-values for α are from a two-sided t-table.

26.7   Unbalanced Data

A design is considered unbalanced when the number of observations in the factor levels is different. For this situation, ANOVA equations needs only slight modifications. For an unbalanced design, the formula for $SS_{\text{factor levels}}$ becomes

$$SS_{\text{factor levels}} = \sum_{i=1}^{a} n_i(\bar{y}_i - \bar{y})^2$$

A balanced design is preferable to an unbalanced design. With a balanced design, the power of the test is maximized and the test statistic is robust to small departures from the assumption of equal variances. This is not the case for an unbalanced design.

26.8   Model Adequacy

Valid ANOVA results require that certain assumptions be satisfied. As experimenters, we collect and then statistically analyze data. Whether we think about it or not, model building is often the center of statistical analysis. The validity of an analysis also depends on basic assumptions. One typical assumption is that errors are normally and independently distributed with mean zero and constant but unknown variance NID(0, σ^2).

To help with meeting the independence and normal distribution requirement, an experimenter needs to select an adequate sample size and randomly conduct the trials. After data are collected, computer programs offer routines to test the assumptions. Generally, in a fixed-effect ANOVA, moderate departures from normality of the residuals are of little concern. Because the *F*-test is only slighted affected, ANOVA and related procedures of fixed effects are said to be robust to the normality assumption. Non-normality affects the random-effects model more severely.

In addition to an analysis of residuals, there is also a direct statistical test for equality of variance. An expression for this hypothesis is

$$H_0 : \sigma_1^2 = \sigma_2^2 = \ldots = \sigma_a^2$$
$$H_A : \text{ at least one variance is different}$$

Bartlett's test is frequently used to test this hypothesis when the normality assumption is valid. Levene's test can be used when the normality assumption is questionable. An example later in this chapter includes a computer output using these test statistics.

26.9   Analysis of Residuals: Fitted Value Plots and Data Normalizing Transformations

Residual plots should show no structure relative to any factor included in the fitted response; however, trends in the data may occur for various reasons. One phenomenon that may occur is inconsistent variance. One example of this situation is that the error of an instrument may increase with larger readings because the error is a percentage of the scale reading. If this is the case, the residuals will increase as a function of scale reading.

Fortunately, a balanced fixed-effects model is robust to variance's not being homogeneous. The problem becomes more serious for unbalanced designs, situations in which one variance is much larger than others, and for the random-effects model. A data normalizing transformation may then be used to reduce this phenomenon in the residuals, which would yield a more precise significance test.

Another situation occurs when the output is count data, where a square root transformation may be appropriate, while a log-normal transformation is often appropriate if the trial outputs are standard deviation values and a logit transformation might be helpful when there are upper and lower limits. A summary of common normalizing transformations is described in Table 9.3.

26.10   Comparing Pairs of Treatment Means

The rejection of the null hypothesis in an ANOVA indicates that there is believed to be difference between the factor levels (treatments). However, no information is given to determine which means are different. It can often be useful to make further comparisons and analysis among groups of factor level means. Multiple comparison methods assess differences between treatment means in either the factor level totals or the factor level averages. Methods include those of Tukey and Fisher. Montgomery (1997) describes several methods of making these comparisons.

Later in this chapter, the analysis of means (ANOM) approach is shown to compare individual means to a grand mean.

26.11   Example 26.1: Single-factor ANOVA

IEE Application Examples

- *Hypothesis test for the equality of the mean delivery time relative to due date for five departments*
- *Hypothesis test that the mean dimension of a part is equal for three machines*

The bursting strengths of diaphragms were determined in an experiment. Use ANOVA techniques to determine if there is a statistically significant difference at a level of 0.05.

Type 1	Type 2	Type 3	Type 4	Type 5	Type 6	Type 7
59.0	65.7	65.3	67.9	60.6	73.1	59.4
62.3	62.8	63.7	67.4	65.0	71.9	61.6
65.2	59.1	68.9	62.9	68.2	67.8	56.3
65.5	60.2	70.0	61.7	66.0	67.4	62.7

These data could also be measurements from
- Parts manufactured by 7 different operators
- Parts manufactured on 7 different machines
- Time for purchase order requests from 7 different sites
- Delivery time of 7 different suppliers

The box plot and dot plot shown in Figure 26.1 and Figure 26.2 indicate that there could be differences between the factor levels

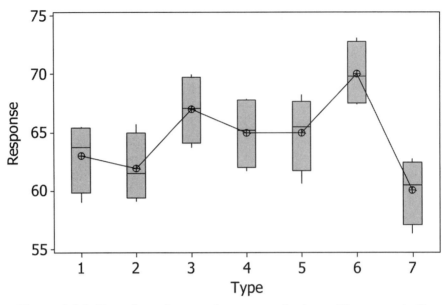

Figure 26.1: Box plots of strength response by type. Means are indicated by solid circles and connected with lines.

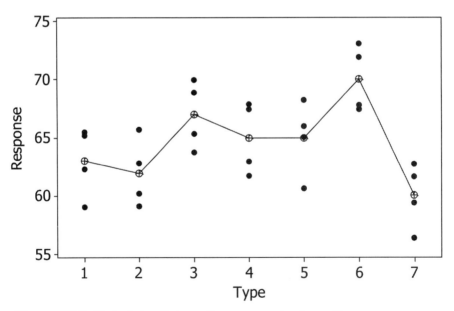

Figure 26.2: Dot plots of strength response by type. Group means are connected with lines.

(or treatments). However, these plots do not address the question statistically.

An ANOVA tests the hypothesis for equality of treatment means; i.e., that the treatment effects are zero, which is expressed as

$$H_0: \tau_1 = \tau_2 = \dots \tau_a = 0$$

$$H_A: \tau_i \neq 0 \text{ (for at least one } i\text{)}$$

The resulting ANOVA table is as follows:

One-Way ANOVA: Response versus Type

```
Source    DF        SS        MS        F         P
Type       6    265.34     44.22      4.92     0.003
Error     21    188.71      8.99
Total     27    454.05


S = 2.998      R-Sq = 58.44%      R-Sq(adj) = 46.57%

                              Individual 95% CIs For Mean Based on
                              Pooled StDev
Level  N     Mean   StDev   ------+---------+---------+---------+---
1      4   63.000   3.032           (-----*-----)
2      4   61.950   2.942        (-----*-----)
3      4   66.975   2.966                (-----*-----)
4      4   64.975   3.134            (-----*-----)
5      4   64.950   3.193            (-----*-----)
6      4   70.050   2.876                    (-----*-----)
7      4   60.000   2.823   (-----*-----)
                           ------+---------+---------+---------+---
                             60.0      65.0      70.0      75.0

Pooled StDev = 2.998

Tukey 95% Simultaneous Confidence Intervals

All Pairwise Comparisons among Levels of Type

Individual confidence level = 99.62%


Type = 1 subtracted from:

Type  Lower  Center  Upper  -------+---------+---------+---------+--
2    -7.945  -1.050  5.845              (------*------)
3    -2.920   3.975 10.870                 (------*------)
4    -4.920   1.975  8.870               (------*------)
5    -4.945   1.950  8.845               (------*------)
```

```
6     0.155   7.050 13.945                      (------*------)
7    -9.895  -3.000  3.895          (------*------)
                                -------+---------+---------+---------+--
                                     -10         0        10        20

Type = 2 subtracted from:

Type Lower Center  Upper -------+---------+---------+---------+--
3    -1.870   5.025 11.920                (------*------)
4    -3.870   3.025  9.920          (------*------)
5    -3.895   3.000  9.895          (------*------)
6     1.205   8.100 14.995                (------*------)
7    -8.845  -1.950  4.945          (------*------)
                                -------+---------+---------+---------+--
                                     -10         0        10        20

Type = 3 subtracted from:

Type Lower Center  Upper -------+---------+---------+---------+--
4    -8.895  -2.000  4.895          (------*------)
5    -8.920  -2.025  4.870          (------*------)
6    -3.820   3.075  9.970              (------*------)
7   -13.870  -6.975 -0.080      (------*------)
                                -------+---------+---------+---------+--
                                     -10         0        10        20

Type = 4 subtracted from:

Type Lower Center  Upper -------+---------+---------+---------+--
5    -6.920  -0.025  6.870              (------*------)
6    -1.820   5.075 11.970                  (------*------)
7   -11.870  -4.975  1.920      (------*------)
                                -------+---------+---------+---------+--
                                     -10         0        10        20

Type = 5 subtracted from:

Type Lower Center  Upper -------+---------+---------+---------+--
6    -1.795   5.100 11.995                  (------*------)
7   -11.845  -4.950  1.945      (------*------)
                                -------+---------+---------+---------+--
                                     -10         0        10        20

Type = 6 subtracted from:

Type Lower Center  Upper -------+---------+---------+---------+--
7   -16.945-10.050 -3.155 (------*------)
                                -------+---------+---------+---------+--
                                     -10         0        10        20
```

This ANOVA indicates that rejection of the null hypothesis is appropriate because the *P* value is lower than a predetermined 0.05 value; however, this statistic gives us no indication which material types are different from the other. With the Tukey multiple comparison model, we examine each of the comparisons to see which interval plot does not contain zero. For example, type 6 subtracted from type 7 does not contain zero; hence, we conclude that there is a significant difference between type 6 and type 7.

Figure 26.3 shows tests of the model assumptions. No pattern or outlier data are apparent in either the "residuals versus order of the data" or "residuals versus fitted values." The normal probability plot and histogram indicate that the residuals may not be normally distributed. A transformation of the data might improve this fit, but it is doubtful that any difference would be large enough to be of practical importance. These data will be further analyzed as an ANOM example.

26.12   Analysis of Means (ANOM)

ANOM is a statistical test procedure in a graphical format, which compares *k* groups of size *n*. Consider the following x_{ij} data format where there are *j* observations in *k* groups.

		Groups		
1	2	3	...	*K*
		Observations		
x_{11}	x_{21}	x_{31}	...	x_{k1}
x_{12}	x_{22}	x_{32}	...	x_{k2}
x_{13}	x_{23}	x_{33}	...	x_{k3}
⋮	⋮	⋮	⋮	⋮
x_{1j}	x_{2j}	x_{3j}	...	x_{kj}
$\bar{x}_1$	$\bar{x}_2$	$\bar{x}_3$	...	$\bar{x}_i$
s_1	s_2	s_3	...	s_i

The grand mean $\bar{\bar{x}}$ of the group means ($\bar{x}_i$) is simply the average of these mean values, which is written

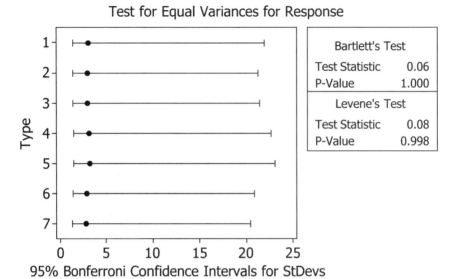

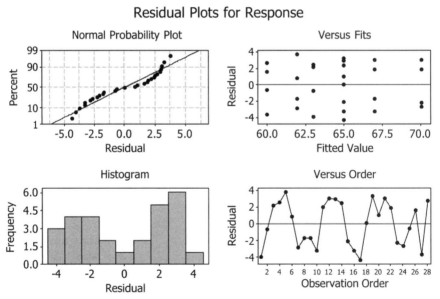

Figure 26.3: Single factor ANOVA model tests.

$$\bar{\bar{x}} = \frac{\sum\limits_{i=1}^{k} \bar{x}_i}{k}$$

The pooled estimate for the standard deviation is the square root of the average of the variances for the individual observations.

$$s = \sqrt{\frac{\sum\limits_{i=1}^{k} s_i^2}{k}}$$

The lower and upper decision lines (LDL and UDL) are

$$\text{LDL} = \bar{\bar{x}} - h_\alpha s \sqrt{\frac{k-1}{kn}} \qquad \text{UDL} = \bar{\bar{x}} + h_\alpha s \sqrt{\frac{k-1}{kn}}$$

where h_α is from Table I for risk level α, number of means k, and degrees of freedom $[(n-1)k]$. The means are then plotted against the decision lines. If any mean falls outside the decision lines, there is a statistically-significant difference for this mean from the grand mean.

If normality can be assumed, ANOM is also directly applicable to attribute data. It is reasonable to consider a normality approximation if both np and $n(1-p)$ are at least 5. For a probability level p of 0.01, this would require a sample size of 500; i.e., $500(0.01) = 5$.

26.13   Example 26.2: ANOM

The ANOVA example above indicated that there was a statistically significant difference in the bursting strengths of seven different types of rubber diaphragms *(k = 7)*. We will now determine which diaphragms differ from the grand mean. A data summary of the mean and variance for each rubber type, each having four observations *(n = 4)*, is

	*i*th Sample Number						
	1	2	3	4	5	6	7
$\bar{x}_i$	63.0	62.0	67.0	65.0	65.0	70.0	60.0
s_i^2	9.2	8.7	8.8	9.8	10.2	8.3	8.0

The overall mean is

$$\bar{\bar{x}} = \frac{\sum_{i=1}^{k} \bar{x}_i}{k} = \frac{63 + 62 + 67 + 65 + 65 + 70 + 60}{7} = 64.57$$

The pooled estimate for the standard deviation is

$$s = \sqrt{\frac{\sum_{i=1}^{k} s_i^2}{k}}$$

$$= \left(\frac{9.2 + 8.7 + 8.8 + 9.8 + 10.2 + 8.3 + 8.0}{7}\right)^{1/2}$$

$$= 3.0$$

The number of degrees of freedom is $(n - 1)k = (4 - 1)(7) = 21$. For a significance level of 0.05 with 7 means and 21 degrees of freedom, it is determined by interpolation from Table I that $h_{0.05} = 2.94$. The upper and lower decision lines are then

$$\text{UDL} = \bar{\bar{x}} + h_\alpha s \sqrt{\frac{k-1}{kn}} = 64.57 + (2.94)(3.0)\sqrt{\frac{7-1}{7(4)}} = 68.65$$

$$\text{LDL} = \bar{\bar{x}} + h_\alpha s \sqrt{\frac{k-1}{kn}} = 64.57 - (2.94)(3.0)\sqrt{\frac{7-1}{7(4)}} = 60.49$$

A computer generated ANOM chart with the limits and measurements is shown in Figure 26.4. Note that the limits are similar to those calculated manually. This plot graphically illustrates that μ_6 and μ_7 are statistically significant different from the grand mean.

26.14 Example 26.3: ANOM of Injection-Molding Data

From the Example 18.2 multi-vari analysis and the Example 24.4 variance components analysis of the injection molding data

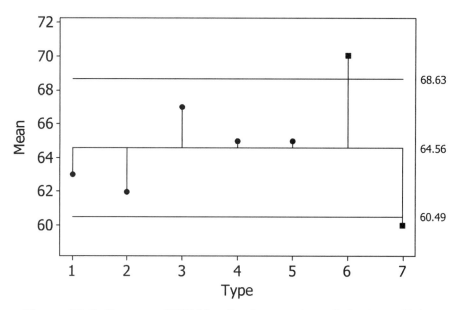

Figure 26.4: One-way ANOM for diaphragm strength by type. Alpha equals 0.05.

described in Table 18.1, it was concluded that differences between cavities affected the diameter of the part. However, the variance components analysis did not indicate how the cavities differed. The computer ANOM output shown in Figure 26.5 for cavities addresses these needs, where the level of significance for the decision lines is 0.05.

We note how the ANOM decision lines in Figure 26.5 are much closer than the previous analysis plot shown in Figure 26.4. When examining the ANOM decision level calculation formulas, it is noted how the decision limits are only a function of within-factor-level variability. For this molding example, it is not surprising that the within-cavity variation is small relative to between cavity variability. This phenomena result in a small distance between the decision levels and all cavities appearing different from the overall mean.

For this type of situation, it can be useful to examine how much different each cavity mean is from the overall value. It can also be useful to examine how each cavity is performing relative to specification needs.

From this overall analysis, we conclude that the differences between cavity 1 and 4 are the main contributors to this source of variability.

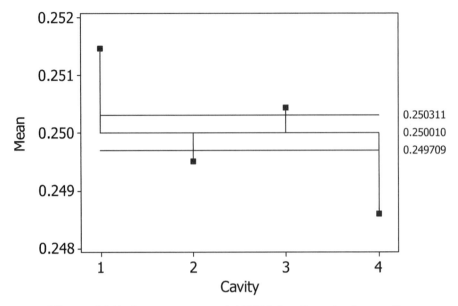

Figure 26.5: One-way normal ANOM for diameter by cavity.

26.15   General Linear Modeling

The General Linear Model (GLM) is an additional analysis method that exists in most statistical software packages. GLM is useful for performing ANOVA on ill-conditioned data; i.e., data that is not balanced or does not have observations in all combinations.

The GLM algorithm is the same as that used for regression and ANOVA. ANOVA and regression methods are special cases of GLM. GLM should be considered when it is required to analyze more than two attribute Xs or a mixture of attributes and continuous Xs and it is important to assess their combined effect on Y.

In GLM, the output will be text based with ANOVA and coefficient tables, where significance is determined without reference to any plots or charts. Software packages that include a GLM analysis have differing implementations. Because of these differences, users should initial conduct an analysis on a known data set to learn how the software works.

26.16   Nonparametric Estimate: Kruskal-Wallis Test

A Kruskal-Wallis test provides an alternative to a one-way ANOVA. This test is a generalization of Mann-Whitney test procedure. The null hypothesis is that all medians are equal. The alternative hypothesis is that the medians are not all equal. For this test, it is assumed that independent random samples taken from different populations have a continuous distribution with the same shape. For many distributions, the Kruskal-Wallis test is more powerful than Mood's median test (described later), but it is less robust against outliers.

26.17   Example 26.4: Nonparametric Kruskal-Wallis Test

The yield per acre for four methods of growing corn was Conover, 1980

Method			
1	2	3	4
83	91	101	78
91	90	100	82
94	81	91	81
89	83	93	77
89	84	96	79
96	83	95	81
91	88	94	80
92	91		81
90	89		
	84		

The following computer output indicates the difference to be statistically significant.

```
Kruskal-Wallis Test on Yield Per Acre versus Method

Method        N      Median        Ave Rank        Z

Method 1      9      91.00          21.8          1.52
Method 2     10      86.00          15.3         -0.83
Method 3      7      95.00          29.6          3.60
Method 4      8      80.50           4.8         -4.12
Overall      34                     17.5

H = 25.46   DF = 3   P = 0.000
H = 25.63   DF = 3   P = 0.000 (adjusted for ties)
```

26.18 Nonparametric Estimate: Mood's Median Test

A Mood's median test is sometimes called a median test or sign scores test. Like the Kruskal-Wallis test, a Mood's median test is a nonparametric alternative to ANOVA. In this chi-square test, the null hypothesis is that the population medians are equal. The alternative hypothesis is that the medians are not all equal.

For this test, it is assumed that independent random samples taken from different populations have a continuous distribution with the same shape. The Mood's median test is more robust to outliers than the Kruskal-Wallis test. The Mood's median is less powerful than the Kruskal-Wallis for data from many distributions.

26.19 Example 26.5: Nonparametric Mood's Median Test

Examine the data from Example 26.4 using Mood's Median Test procedure instead of a Kruskal-Wallis test.

The following computer program response had a slightly different significance level along with a different output format.

```
Mood median test for Yield Per Acre versus Method

Chi-Square = 17.54  DF = 3 P = 0.001

                                 Individual 95.0% CIs
Method    N<= N>  Median  Q3-Q1  ---------+---------+---------+-------
Method 1   3   6   91.0    4.0                     (--+---)
Method 2   7   3   86.0    7.3             (---+-----)
Method 3   0   7   95.0    7.0                        (---+------)
Method 4   8   0   80.5    2.8   (---+)
                                 ---------+---------+---------+-------
                                     84.0      91.0      98.0

Overall median = 89.0
```

26.20 Other Considerations

Variability in an experiment can be caused by nuisance factors in which we have no interest. These nuisance factors are sometimes unknown and not controlled. Randomization guards against this type of factor affecting results. In other situations, the nuisance factor is known but not controlled. When we observe the value of a factor, it can be compensated for by using analysis-of-covariance techniques. In yet another situation, the nuisance factor is both known and controllable. We can systematically eliminate the effect on comparisons among factor level considerations (i.e., treatments) by using a randomized block design.

Experiment results can often be improved dramatically through the wise management of nuisance factors. Statistical software can offer blocking and covariance analysis options. Statistical books such as Montgomery (1997) discuss the mechanics of these computations.

26.21 Applying IEE

Factors involved in a single-factor ANOVA can be quantitative or qualitative. Quantitative factors are those levels that can be expressed as a numeric scale such as time or temperature. Qualitative factors such as machine or operator cannot be expressed in a numerical scale.

When there are several levels of a factor and the factors are quantitative, the experimenter is often interested in developing an empirical model equation for the response variable of the process that is being studied. When starting this investigation, it is good practice first to create a scatter plot of the data. This plot can give insight into the relationship between the response and factor levels. Perhaps this relationship is nonlinear. The fit of the model then could be conducted using regression analysis. This procedure makes no sense when the factor levels are qualitative.

Important aspects of the described techniques that are often not addressed are sample size and method of selection. First, the sample must be a random sample of the population of interest. Second, the sample size must be large enough to give adequate confidence in the metric. Neither of these needs is easy to achieve. Making supplier and other comparative decisions on the value of a metric alone can cause problems. When an organization reports a Six Sigma metric or process capability/performance index, consider how it determined the value. Consider also asking the organization about the details of the process measurement and improvement program. This second query may provide more insight than any Six Sigma metric.

26.22 Exercises

1. For the following data, conduct an ANOVA and ANOM. Assess significance levels at 0.05.

Machine Number	Samples									
1.0	35.8	40.4	30.3	46.8	34.1	34.0	38.1	45.0	41.9	40.2
2.0	40.9	35.7	36.7	37.3	41.8	39.9	34.6	38.8	35.8	35.6
3.0	36.0	38.3	47.9	35.9	38.1	35.8	31.5	37.4	40.3	44.0
4.0	44.8	40.0	43.9	43.3	38.8	44.9	42.3	51.8	44.1	45.2
5.0	37.5	40.4	37.6	34.6	38.9	37.4	35.9	41.0	39.4	28.9
6.0	33.1	43.4	43.4	43.3	44.3	38.4	33.9	34.5	40.1	33.7
7.0	37.5	41.9	43.7	38.6	33.2	42.7	40.5	36.1	38.3	38.0

2. The normal probability plot of residuals for the ANOVA exercise in this chapter had some curvature. Repeat the analysis using a natural logarithm transformation of the data. Give the results and explain whether the normalizing transformation leads to any change in conclusion.

3. When conducting an ANOM, determine the value to use if a significance level of 0.05 is desired. There are 5 levels, where each has 7 samples.

4. Wisdom of the organization thought operator could affect a response. Conduct an analysis and comment.

Oper1	Oper2	Oper3
50	58	49
45	52	55
47	53	28
53	59	35
52	60	25

5. Given the factor level output below, analyze the data for significance

Level 1	Level 2	Level 3	Level 4
34.6	90.1	124.4	71.8
103.1	82.1	75.4	35.8
102.9	61.8	112.8	61.9
31.2	24.3	47.9	47.6
31.7	26.0	45.0	42.6
68.1	72.4	115.1	70.2
64.3	67.6	114.0	43.2
102.8	104.7	108.4	75.7

75.2	101.6	95.6	66.9
96.9	80.1	91.9	96.2
40.9	56.0	123.1	93.6
52.4	82.3	87.9	64.4
81.4	104.9	61.4	106.8
22.9	31.5	106.3	83.7
56.4	37.2	69.5	34.9
50.5	58.1	104.6	54.0
78.3	100.1	91.5	122.5

6. Given the factor level output below, analyze the data for significance

Level 1	Level 2	Level 3	Level 4	Level 5
51.9	46.5	44.9	115.2	33.6
120.2	82.7	68.1	26.7	43.9
42.4	79.6	90.9	27.7	48.7
62.9	91.4	88.7	86.6	45.6
34.0	92.0	65.6	118.1	65.1
42.1	50.9	57.2	118.3	44.5
97.3	85.8	45.3	77.3	63.2
62.1	65.2	26.0	89.9	42.2
70.1	118.5	42.6	77.3	76.2
56.9	53.1	35.2	58.4	33.7
108.1	59.1	73.4	28.6	76.4
89.1	30.3	79.8	46.1	45.2
36.0	93.2	91.3	103.2	79.2
43.8	41.4	84.1	122.5	48.3
118.6	101.8	67.4	96.9	98.3
68.9	35.9	100.6	94.7	54.8
87.6	81.5	45.6	109.7	62.3
41.4		95.9		
94.1		32.6		
62.0		28.6		
74.8		116.1		
105.8		45.4		

7. Exercise 18.5 showed data that were collected passively for the purpose of understanding better what might be done to improve a KPOV. Using the appropriate statistical tools, test for statistically-significant differences between inspector, machines, process temperature, material lot, and day-to-day variability relative to within-day variability. Compare these results to a graphical assessment.

27

P-DMAIC – Two-Factor (Two-Way) Analysis of Variance

27.1 P-DMAIC Roadmap Component

This is the fourth chapter of five chapters for assessing a population response as a function of multiple input situations. The first chapter of this series of chapters described a hierarchical structure. The second chapter described the regression of two continuous variables; e.g., methods for comparing two conditions or treatments. The last chapter described analysis of variance (ANOVA).

Experiments often involve the study of more than one factor. Factorial designs are most efficient for the situation in which combinations of levels of factors are investigated. These designs evaluate the change in response caused by different levels of factors and the interaction of factors.

This chapter focuses on two-factor ANOVA or two-way ANOVA of fixed effects. The graphic in this section highlights the P-DMAIC roadmap steps (see Appendix Section D.1) that are described in this chapter. Appendix E contains the tollgate check sheets for this and other phases.

The next chapters describe factorial experiments in which there are more than two factors.

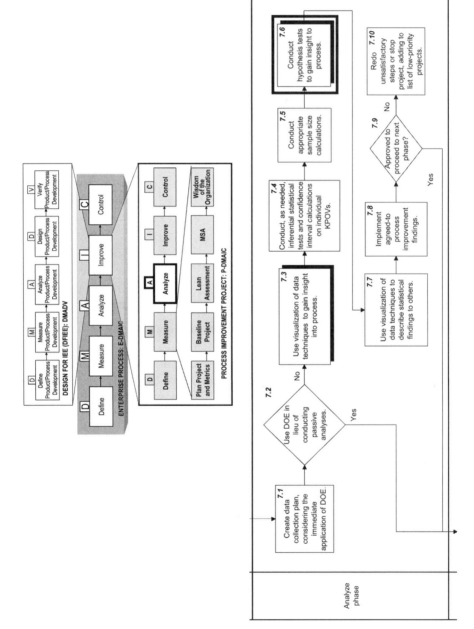

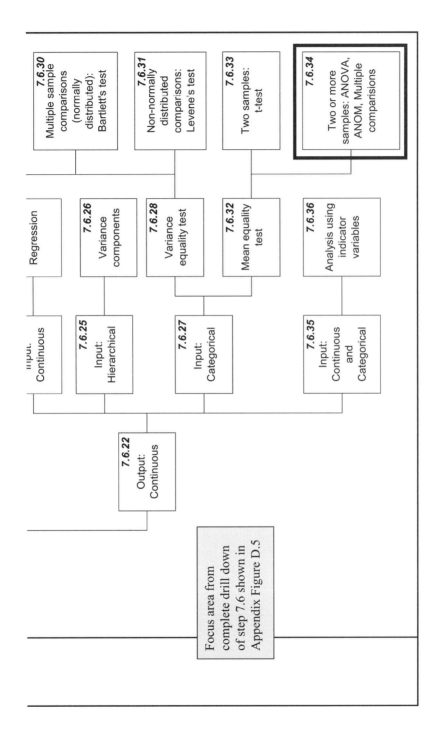

7.6.30 Multiple sample comparisons (normally distributed): Bartlett's test

7.6.31 Non-normally distributed comparisons: Levene's test

7.6.33 Two samples: t-test

7.6.34 Two or more samples: ANOVA, ANOM, Multiple comparisons

Regression

7.6.26 Variance components

7.6.28 Variance equality test

7.6.32 Mean equality test

7.6.36 Analysis using indicator variables

Input: Continuous

7.6.25 Input: Hierarchical

7.6.27 Input: Categorical

7.6.35 Input: Continuous and Categorical

7.6.22 Output: Continuous

Focus area from complete drill down of step 7.6 shown in Appendix Figure D.5

27.2   Two-Factor Factorial Design

The general two-factor factorial experiment takes the form shown in Table 27.1, in which design is considered completely randomized because observations are taken randomly. In this table response, factor A has levels ranging from 1 to a, while factor B has levels ranging from 1 to b, and the replications have replicates 1 to n. Responses for the various combinations of factor A with factor B take the form y_{ijk} where i denotes the level of factor A, j notes the level of factor B, and k represents the replicate number. The total number of observations is then abn.

A description of the fixed linear two-factor model is then

$$y_{ijk} = \mu + \tau_i + \beta_j + (\tau\beta)_{ij} + \varepsilon_{ijk}$$

where μ is the overall mean effect, τ_i is the effect of the ith level of A (row factor), β_j is the effect for the jth level of B (column factor), $(\tau\beta)_{ij}$ is the effect of the interaction, and ε_{ijk} is random error.

For a two-factor factorial, row and column factors or treatments are of equal interest. The test hypothesis for row factor effects is

$$H_0{:}\tau_1 = \tau_2 = \ldots = \tau_a = 0$$

$$H_A{:} \text{ at least one } \tau_i \neq 0$$

The test hypothesis for column factor effects is

$$H_0{:} \beta_1 = \beta_2 = \ldots = \beta_b = 0$$

$$H_A{:} \text{ at least one } \beta_j \neq 0$$

The test hypothesis for the interaction of row and column factor effects is

$$H_0{:} (\tau\beta)_{ij} = 0 \quad \text{for all values of } i, j$$

$$H_A{:} \text{ at least one } (\tau\beta)_{ij} \neq 0$$

Table 27.1: General Arrangement for a Two-Factor Factorial Design

		Factor B			
		1	2	. . .	b
Factor A	1				
	2				
	.				
	a				

As in one-factor ANOVA, the total variability can be partitioned into the sum of the sum of squares from the elements of the experiment, which can be represented as

$$SS_T = SS_A + SS_B + SS_{AB} + SS_e$$

where SS_T is the total sum of squares, SS_A is the sum of squares from factor A, SS_B is the sum of squares from factor B, SS_{AB} is the sum of squares from the interaction of factor A with factor B, and SS_e is the sum of squares from error. These sums of squares have the following degrees of freedom:

Effect	Degrees of Freedom
A	$a - 1$
B	$b - 1$
AB interaction	$(a - 1)(b - 1)$
Error	$ab(n - 1)$
Total	$abn - 1$

Mean-square and F_0 calculations are also similar to one-factor ANOVA. These equations for the two-factor factorial are given in Table 27.2.

The difference between a two-factor ANOVA approach and a randomized block design on one of the factors is that the randomized block design would not have the interaction consideration.

Table 27.2: Two-Factor Factorial ANOVA Table for Fixed-Effects Model

Source	Sum of Squares	Degrees of Freedom	Mean Square	F_0
Factor A	SS_A	$a - 1$	$MS_A = \dfrac{SS_A}{a - 1}$	$F_0 = \dfrac{MS_A}{MS_E}$
Factor B	SS_B	$b - 1$	$MS_B = \dfrac{SS_B}{b - 1}$	$F_0 = \dfrac{MS_B}{MS_E}$
Interaction	SS_{AB}	$(a - 1)(b - 1)$	$MS_{AB} = \dfrac{SS_{AB}}{(a - 1)(b - 1)}$	$F_0 = \dfrac{MS_{AB}}{MS_E}$
Error	SS_E	$ab(n - 1)$	$MS_E = \dfrac{SS_E}{ab(n - 1)}$	
Total	SS_T	$abn - 1$		

Table 27.3: Life Data, in hours, for Battery Two-Factorial Design

Material Type	Temperature (Degrees F)					
	15		70		125	
1	130	155	34	40	20	70
	74	180	80	75	82	58
2	150	188	136	122	25	70
	159	126	106	115	58	45
3	138	110	174	120	96	104
	168	160	150	139	82	60

27.3   Example 27.1: Two-Factor Factorial Design

A battery is to be used in a device subjected to extreme temperature variations. At some time during development, an engineer can select one of only three plate material types. After product shipment, the engineer has no control over temperature; however, he/she believes that temperature could degrade the effective life of the battery. The engineer would like to determine if one of the material types is robust to temperature variations. Table 27.3 gives the observed effective life, in hours, of the battery at controlled temperatures in the laboratory (Montgomery, 1997).

The two-factor ANOVA output is

```
Two-Way Analysis of Variance

Analysis of Variance for Response

Source        DF      SS        MS        F        P

Material      2      10684     5342      7.91     0.002
Temp          2      39119     19559     28.97    0.000
Interaction   4       9614     2403      3.56     0.019
Error         27     18231     675
Total         35     77647
```

Using an $\alpha = 0.05$ criterion, we conclude that there is a statistically-significant interaction between material types and temperature because the interaction probability value is less than 0.05 [and $F_0 > (F_{0.05,4,27} = 2.73)$]. We also conclude that the main effects of material type and temperature are also statistically-significant because each of their probabilities are less than 0.05 [and $F_0 > (F_{0.05,2,27} = 3.35)$].

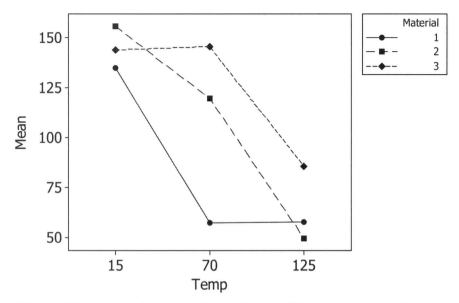

Figure 27.1 Interaction plot of mean battery life as a function of material and temperature.

A plot of the average response at each factor level is shown in Figure 27.1, which aids in the interpretation of experimental results. The significance of the interaction term in our model shows up as the lack of parallelism of these lines. From this plot we note degradation in life with an increase in temperature regardless of material type. If it is desirable for this battery to experience less loss of life at elevated temperature, type 3 material seems to be the best choice of the three materials.

Whenever there is a difference in the rows' or columns' means, it can be useful to make additional comparisons. This analysis shows these differences, but the significance of the interaction can obscure comparison tests. One approach to address this situation is to apply the test at only one level of a factor at a time.

Using this strategy, let us examine the data for statistically-significant differences at 70 degrees (i.e., level 2 of temperature). We can use analysis of means (ANOM) techniques to determine factor levels relative to the grand mean. The ANOM output shown in Figure 27.2 indicates that material types 1 and 3 differ from the grand mean. The residual plot in Figure 27.3 seems well behaved.

Some statistical computer programs also offer options for making multiple comparisons of the means. Tukey's multiple

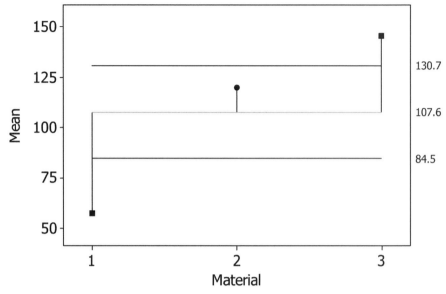

Figure 27.2 One-way normal ANOM for life at 70 degrees.
Alpha decision levels equal 0.05.

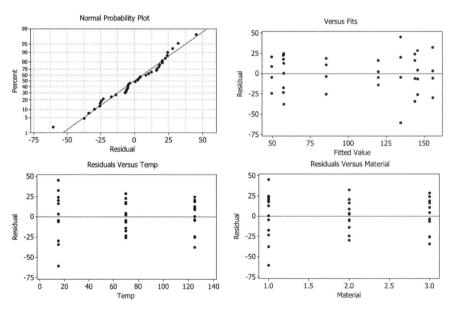

Figure 27.3 Residual plots for ANOVA results of battery life.

comparison test shown below indicates that for a temperature level of 70 degrees the mean battery life cannot be shown as different between material types 2 and 3. In addition, the mean battery life for material type 1 is statistically significantly lower than that for both battery types 2 and 3.

```
Tukey Simultaneous Tests (For Temperature = 70 degrees)
Response Variable Response
All Pairwise Comparisons among Levels of Material

Material = 1 subtracted from:
Level     Difference        SE of                    Adjusted
Material   of Means     Difference    T-Value        P-Value
2             62.50         14.29      4.373          0.0046
3             88.50         14.29      6.193          0.0004

Material = 2 subtracted from:
Level     Difference        SE of                    Adjusted
Material   of Means     Difference    T-Value        P-Value
3             26.00         14.29      1.819          0.2178
```

The coefficient of determination (R^2) can help describe the amount of variability in battery life explained by battery material, temperature, and the interaction of material with temperature. From the ANOVA output, we note

$$SS_{\text{Model}} = SS_{\text{Material}} + SS_{\text{Temperature}} + SS_{\text{Interaction}}$$
$$= 10,683 + 39,118 + 9613$$
$$= 59,414$$

which results in

$$R^2 = \frac{SS_{\text{Model}}}{SS_{\text{Total}}} = \frac{59,414}{77,647} = 0.77$$

From this, we conclude that about 77% of the variability is represented by our model factors.

The adequacy of the underlying model should be checked before adopting conclusions. Figure 27.3 provides a normal plot of the residuals and a plot of residuals versus the fitted values for the ANOVA.

The normal probability plot of the residuals does not reveal anything of particular concern. The residual plot of residuals versus fitted values seems to indicate a mild tendency for the variance of the residuals to increase as battery life increases. The residual plots of battery type and temperature seem to indicate that material type 1 and low temperature might have more variability. However, these problems do not appear large enough to have a dramatic impact on the analysis and conclusions.

27.4 Nonparametric Estimate: Friedman Test

A Friedman test is a nonparametric analysis of a randomized block experiment. This test, which is a generalization of the paired sign test, provides an alternative to the two-way ANOVA. The null hypothesis is that all treatment effects are zero. The alternative hypothesis is that not all treatment effects are zero.

Additivity is the sum of treatment and block effects. ANOVA possesses additivity. That is, the fit of the model is the sum of treatment and block effects. Within the Friedman test, additivity is not required for the test; however, it is required when estimating the treatment effects.

27.5 Example 27.2: Nonparametric Friedman Test

The effect of a drug treatment on enzyme activity was evaluated within a randomized block experiment. Three different drug therapies were given to four animals, where each animal belonged to a different litter. The null hypothesis was that all treatment effects are zero. The alternative hypothesis was that not all treatment effects are zero (Minitab, 2007).

		Therapy		
		1	2	3
	1	0.15	0.55	0.55
	2	0.26	0.26	0.66
	3	0.23	-0.22	0.77
Litter	4	0.99	0.99	0.99

From the following computer output, we could not reject the null hypotheses at a level of 0.05.

```
Friedman test for Enzyme Activity by Therapy blocked
by Litter

S = 2.38   DF = 2   P = 0.305
S = 3.80   DF = 2   P = 0.150 (adjusted for ties)

                   Est      Sum of
Therapy    N     Median      Ranks
1          4     0.2450        6.5
2          4     0.3117        7.0
3          4     0.5783       10.5

Grand median = 0.3783
```

27.6 Applying IEE

Two-factor factorial experiments offer more information than one-factor experiments. The two-factor factorial experiment is often the best approach for a given situation. The method gives information about interactions and can apply to both manufacturing and business processes. However, in some situations the experiment can be very costly because it requires many test trials. In addition, it does not address other factors that may significantly affect a process. The normal approach for dealing with other process factors not considered in the experiment is either to hold them constant or let them exhibit "normal" variability. In many situations, neither of these alternatives is very desirable.

Before conducting a two-factor factorial, it is best to reflect on the objective of the experiment and on important aspects of the situation. Often it is best to execute this reflection in a team setting in which attendees have different perspectives on the situation. Initially, the situation should be crisply defined, and what is desired from the experimental analysis should be determined. Next, the group should use brainstorming techniques to create a list of all factors that can affect the situation. The group can then prioritize these factors and list any test constraints.

Reflection on the issues in this team meeting may indicate that a two-factor factorial approach is the best for the particular situation, but, if there are many factors, then a DOE approach, discussed in Chapters 29–33, may be a better alternative.

27.7 Exercises

1. The breaking strength of a fiber is studied as a function
    of four machines and three operators using fiber from one
    batch. Using computer software, analyze the following data
    and draw conclusions. Comment on how these variables
    could be related to a transactional process (Montgomery,
    1997).

Operator	Machine			
	1	2	3	4
1	109	110	108	110
1	110	115	109	108
2	110	110	111	114
2	112	111	109	112
3	116	112	114	120
3	114	115	119	117

28

P-DMAIC – Analyze Phase: Multiple Regression, Logistic Regression, and Indicator Variables

28.1 P-DMAIC Roadmap Component

This is the final chapter of five chapters for assessing a population response as a function of multiple input situations. The first chapter of this series of chapters described a hierarchical structure. The second chapter described the regression of two continuous variables. The third chapter described ANOVA, while the last chapter described two-way ANOVA.

Chapter 26 presented the simple regression model, used to estimate a response as a function of the magnitude of one regressor variable. This chapter discusses using multiple regressor variables to build a multiple regression model. In addition, categorical data such as location, operator, and color are modeled using indicator or dummy variables. The graphic in this section highlights the P-DMAIC roadmap steps (see Appendix Section D.1) that are described in this chapter. Appendix E contains the tollgate check sheets for this and other phases.

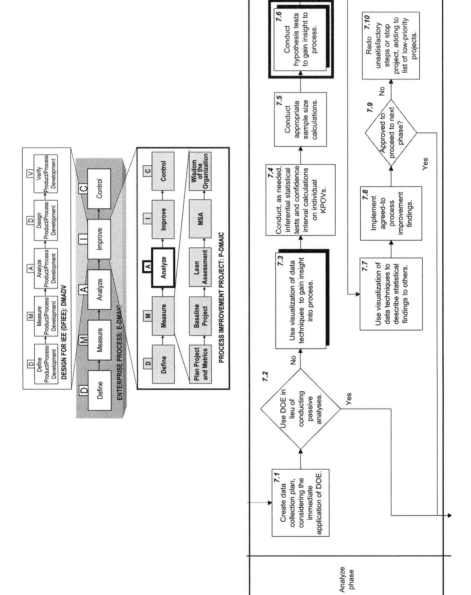

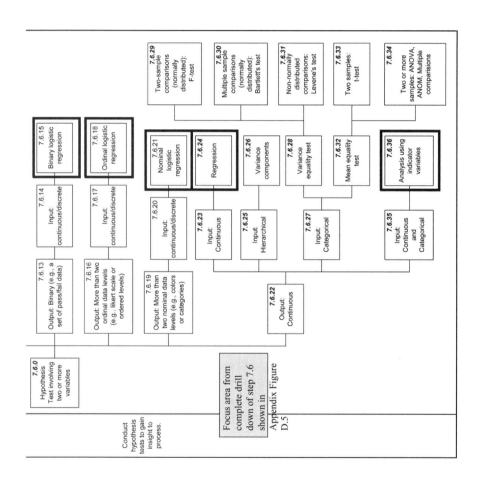

7.6.0 Hypothesis Test involving two or more variables

Conduct hypothesis tests to gain insight to process.

Focus area from complete drill down of step 7.6 shown in Appendix Figure D.5

7.6.15 Binary logistic regression

7.6.14 Input: continuous/discrete

7.6.13 Output: Binary (e.g., a set of pass/fail data)

7.6.18 Ordinal logistic regression

7.6.17 Input: continuous/discrete

7.6.16 Output: More than two ordinal data levels (e.g., likert scale or ordered levels)

7.6.21 Nominal logistic regression

7.6.20 Input: continuous/discrete

7.6.19 Output: More than two nominal data levels (e.g., colors or categories)

7.6.24 Regression

7.6.23 Input: Continuous

7.6.22 Output: Continuous

7.6.26 Variance components

7.6.25 Input: Hierarchical

7.6.28 Variance equality test

7.6.27 Input: Categorical

7.6.32 Mean equality test

7.6.36 Analysis using indicator variables

7.6.35 Input: Continuous and Categorical

7.6.29 Two-sample comparisons (normally distributed): F-test

7.6.30 Multiple sample comparisons (normally distributed): Bartlett's test

7.6.31 Non-normally distributed comparisons: Levene's test

7.6.33 Two samples: t-test

7.6.34 Two or more samples: ANOVA, ANOM, Multiple comparisions

28.2 IEE Application Examples: Multiple Regression

- *Transactional 30,000-foot-level metric*: An IEE project was
  created to improve DSO. Two inputs that surfaced from a
  cause-and-effect matrix were the size of the invoice and the
  number of line items included within the invoice. A multiple regression analysis was conducted for DSO versus
  size of invoice and the number of line items included in the
  invoice.
- *Manufacturing 30,000-foot-level metric*: An IEE project was
  created to reduce the non-conformance rate of a manufactured part's diameter. Input that surfaced from a cause-and-
  effect matrix were the temperature, pressure , and speed of
  the manufacturing process. A multiple regression analysis
  of part diameter versus process temperature, pressure, and
  speed was conducted.

28.3 Description

A general model includes polynomial terms in one or more variables such as:

$$Y = \beta_0 + \beta_1 x_1 + \beta_2 x_2 + \beta_3 x_1^2 + \beta_4 x_2^2 + \beta_5 x_1 x_2 + \varepsilon$$

where β's are unknown parameters and ε is random error. This
full quadratic model of Y on x_1 and x_2 is of great use in DOE.

For the situation without polynomial terms where there are k
predictor variables, the general model reduces to the form:

$$Y = \beta_0 + \beta_1 x_1 + \ldots + \beta_k x_k + \varepsilon$$

The object is to determine from data the least-squares esti-
mates $(b_0, b_1, \ldots, b_k)$ of the unknown parameters $(\beta_0, \beta_{1, \ldots,} \beta_k)$ for
the prediction equation:

$$\hat{Y} = b_0 + b_1 x_1 + \ldots + b_k x_1$$

where $\hat{Y}$ is the predicted value of Y for given values of $x_1, \ldots, x_k$.
Many statistical software packages can perform these calcula-
tions. The following example illustrates this type of analysis.

28.4   Example 28.1: Multiple Regression

IEE Application Examples

- *Analysis of DSO versus invoice amount and the number of line items in the invoice.*
- *Analysis of part diameter versus temperature, pressure, and speed of a manufacturing process.*

An investigator wants to determine the relationship of a key process output variable (KPOV), product strength, to two key process input variables (KPIVs), hydraulic pressure during a forming process and acid concentration. The data are given in Table 28.1 (Juran, 1988), which resulted in the following analysis:

```
Regression Analysis

The regression equation is
strength = 16.3 + 1.57 pressure + 4.16 concentration
```

Table 28.1: Data for Multiple Regression Model of Product Strength

Strength	Pressure	Concentration
665	110	116
618	119	104
620	138	94
578	130	86
682	143	110
594	133	87
722	147	114
700	142	106
681	125	107
695	135	106
664	152	98
548	118	86
620	155	87
595	128	96
740	146	120
670	132	108
640	130	104
590	112	91
570	113	92
640	120	100

```
Predictor           Coef        StDev          T          P
Constant           16.28        44.30        0.37      0.718
pressure            1.5718       0.2606       6.03      0.000
concentration       4.1629       0.3340      12.47      0.000

S = 15.10   R-Sq = 92.8%   R-Sq(adj) = 92.0%

Analysis of Variance

Source              DF          SS          MS           F          P

Regression           2        50101       25050      109.87      0.000
Residual Error      17         3876         228
Total               19        53977

Source              DF      Seq SS
pressure             1       14673
concentration        1       35428
```

Some of the entries in this output are more important than other entries. I will now highlight some of the more important aspects of this table. The predictor and coefficient (coeff.) describe the prediction model: strength = $16.3 + 1.57$ pressure + 4.16 concentration. The P columns give the significance level for each model term. Typically, if a P value is less than or equal to 0.05, the variable is considered statistically significant (i.e., null hypothesis is rejected). If a P value is greater than 0.10, the term is removed from the model. A practitioner might leave the term in the model if the P value lies in the gray region between these two probability levels. Note that these probability values for the model parameters are determined from the t-statistic values shown in the output.

The coefficient of determination (R^2) is presented as R-Sq and R-Sq(adj) in the output. This value represents the proportion of the variability accounted for by the model, where the R^2 (adj) adjusts for the degrees of freedom. When a variable is added to an equation, the coefficient of determination will get larger, even if the added variable has no real value. R^2 (adj) is an approximate unbiased estimate that compensates for this. In this case, the model accounts for a very large percentage of the variability because the R^2 (adj) value is 92%.

In the ANOVA portion of this output, the F value is used to determine an overall P value for the model fit. In this case the resulting P value of 0.000 indicates a very high level of significance. The regression and residual sum of squares (SS) and mean-square (MS) values are interim steps toward determining the F value. Standard error is the square root of the mean square.

No unusual patterns were apparent in the residual analysis plots. Also, no correlation was shown between hydraulic pressure and acid concentration.

28.5 Other Considerations

Regressor variables should be independent within a model: They should be completely uncorrelated. Multicollinearity occurs when variables are dependent. A measure of the magnitude of multicollinearity that is often available in statistical software is the variance inflation factor (VIF). VIF quantifies how much the variance of an estimated regression coefficient increases if the predictors are correlated. Regression coefficients can be considered poorly estimated when VIF exceeds 5 or 10 (Montgomery and Peck, 1982). Strategies for breaking up multicollinearity include collecting additional data or using different predictors.

Another approach to data analysis is the use of stepwise regression (Draper and Smith, 1966) or of all possible regressions of the data when selecting the number of terms to include in a model. This approach can be most useful when data derive from an experiment that does not have experiment structure. However, experimenters should be aware of the potential pitfalls resulting from happenstance data (Box *et al.*, 1978).

A multiple regression best subset analysis is another alternative analysis. Consider an analysis of all possible regressions for the data shown in Table 32.3. Table 28.2 illustrates a computer output with all possible regressions. This approach first considers only one factor in a model, then two, and so forth (Table 28.2, *Notes* 1 and 2). The R^2 value is then considered for each of the

Table 28.2: Summary from all Possible Regressions Analysis

N = 16	Regression Models for Dependent Variable: Timing Model: Model 1		
Number in Model ①	R-Square ③	C(P) ④	Variables in Model ②
1	0.33350061	75.246939	MOT_ADJ
1	0.57739025	43.320991	ALGOR
2	0.58342362	44.531203	ALGOR EXT_ADJ
2	0.91009086	1.664676	ALGOR MOT_ADJ
3	0.91500815	3.125709	ALGOR MOT_ADJ SUP_VOLT
3	0.91692423	2.874888	ALGOR MOT_ADJ EXT_ADJ
4	0.91949041	4.538967	ALGOR MOT_ADJ EXT_ADJ MOT_TEMP
4	0.92104153	4.335921	ALGOR MOT_ADJ EXT_ADJ SUP_VOLT
5	0.92360771	6.000000	ALGOR MOT_ADJ EXT_ADJ SUP_VOLT MOT_TEMP

models (Table 28.2, *Note* 3); only factor combinations containing the highest two R^2 values are shown in Table 28.2. For example, if one were to consider a model containing only one factor, the factor to consider would be algor. Likewise, if one were to consider a model containing only two factors, the factors to consider would be algor with mot_adj.

The Mallows' C_p statistic [$C(P)$ in Table 28.2, *Note* 4] is useful for determining the minimum number of parameters that best fits the model. Technically, this statistic measures the sum of the squared biases plus the squared random errors in Y at all n data points (Daniel and Wood, 1980).

The minimum number of factors needed in the model occurs when the Mallows' C_p statistic is a minimum. From this output, the pertinent Mallows' C_p statistic values under consideration as a function of a number of factors in this model are:

Number in model	Mallows' C_p [a]
1	43.32
2	1.67
3	2.87
4	4.33
5	6.00

[a]The Mallows' C_p is not related to the process indices C_p.

From this summary it is noted that the Mallows' C_p statistic is minimized whenever there are two parameters in the model. The corresponding factors are algor and mot_adj. This conclusion is consistent with the analysis in Example 32.1.

28.6 Example 28.2: Multiple Regression Best Subset Analysis

The results from a cause-and-effect matrix lead to a passive analysis of factors A, B, C, and D on Thruput. In a plastic molding process, for example, the throughput response might be shrinkage as a function of the input factors temperature 1, temperature 2, pressure 1, and hold time.

A	B	C	D	Throughput
7.13	3.34	3.20	146.74	19.25
7.36	3.31	3.17	147.89	19.32

8.05	3.06	3.15	144.67	19.34
7.13	2.92	3.17	153.87	19.37
6.90	3.06	3.20	160.31	19.41
7.13	3.08	3.50	161.00	20.33
8.05	2.81	3.43	166.06	20.56
7.13	2.81	3.52	169.97	20.72
8.05	2.97	3.50	160.08	20.75
8.28	2.81	3.40	166.52	20.82
8.05	2.92	3.70	149.27	21.39
8.28	2.92	3.66	170.89	21.41
8.28	2.83	3.57	172.04	21.46

A best subset computer regression analysis of the collected data assessing the four factors yielded:

Vars	R-Sq	Adj. R-Sq	Cp	S	A	B	C	D
1	92.1	91.4	38.3	0.25631			X	
1	49.2	44.6	294.2	0.64905		X		
2	96.3	95.6	14.9	0.18282	X		X	
2	95.2	94.3	21.5	0.20867		X	X	
3	98.5	98.0	4.1	0.12454	X		X	X
3	97.9	97.1	7.8	0.14723	X	X	X	
4	98.7	98.0	5.0	0.12363	X	X	X	X

For this computer output format, an "*X*" is placed in the column(s) for the variable(s) considered in the model.

We would like to create a model that provides a good estimate with the fewest number of terms. From this output we note that:

- *R-Sq*: Look for the highest value when comparing models with the same number of predictors (vars)
- *Adj. R-Sq*: Look for the highest value when comparing models with different number of predictors
- C_p: Look for models where C_p is small and close to the number of parameters in the model; for example, look for a model with C_p close to four for a three-predictor model that has an intercept constant. Often we just look for the lowest C_p value

- *s*: We want *s*, the estimate of the standard deviation about the regression, to be as small as possible

The regression equation for a three-parameter model from a computer program is:

```
Throughput = 3.87 + 0.393 A + 3.19 C + 0.0162 D
```

Predictor	Coef	SE Coef	T	P	VIF
Constant	3.8702	0.7127	5.43	0.000	
A	0.39333	0.07734	5.09	0.001	1.4
C	3.1935	0.2523	12.66	0.000	1.9
D	0.016189	0.004570	3.54	0.006	1.5

```
S = 0.1245   R-Sq = 98.5%   R-Sq(adj) = 98.0%
```

The magnitude of the VIFs is satisfactory, i.e., not larger than 5–10. In addition, there were no observed problems with the residual analysis.

28.7 Indicator Variables (Dummy Variables) to Analyze Categorical Data

Categorical data such as location, operator, and color can also be modeled using simple and multiple linear regressions. It is not generally correct to use numerical code when analyzing this type of data within regression since the fitted values within the model will be dependent upon the assignment of the numerical values. The correct approach is through the use of indicator variables or dummy variables, which indicate whether a factor should or should not be included in the model.

If we are given information about two variables, we can calculate the third. Hence, only two variables are needed for a model that has three variables, where it does not matter which variable is left out of the model. After indicator or dummy variables are created, indicator variables are analyzed using regression to create a cell means model.

If the intercept is left out of the regression equation, a no intercept cell means model is created. For the case where there are three indicator variables, a no intercept model would then have three terms where the coefficients are the cell means.

28.8   Example 28.3: Indicator Variables

Revenue for Arizona, Florida, and Texas is shown in Table 28.3 (Bower, 2001). This table also contains indicator variables that were created to represent these states. One computer analysis possibility is:

```
The regression equation is
Revenue = 48.7 - 24.1 AZ - 16.0 FL

Predictor        Coef       SE Coef           T           P
Constant      48.7325        0.4437      109.83       0.000
AZ           -24.0826        0.6275      -38.38       0.000
FL           -15.9923        0.6275      -25.49       0.000

S = 3.137    R-Sq = 91.2%    R-Sq(adj) = 91.1%
```

Calculations for various revenues would be:
Texas Revenue = 48.7−24.1(0)−16.0(0) = 48.7
Arizona Revenue = 48.7−24.1(1)−16.0(0) = 24.6
Florida Revenue = 48.7−24.1(0)−16.0(1) = 32.7
   A created no intercept cell means model from a computer analysis would be:

```
The regression equation is
Revenue = 24.6 AZ + 32.7 FL + 48.7 TX

Predictor      Coef       SE Coef        T         P
Noconstant
AZ          24.6499        0.4437     55.56     0.000
FL          32.7402        0.4437     73.79     0.000
TX          48.7325        0.4437    109.83     0.000

S = 3.137
```

Note how the coefficients when rounded off equate to the previously calculated revenues.

28.9   Example 28.4: Indicator Variables with Covariate

Consider the following data set that has created indicator variables and a covariate. This covariate might be a continuous response variable such as process temperature or dollar amount for an invoice.

Table 28.3: Revenue by State

Revenue	Location	AZ	FL	TX	Revenue	Location	AZ	FL	TX	Revenue	Location	AZ	FL	TX
23.487	AZ	1	0	0	35.775	FL	0	1	0	48.792	TX	0	0	1
20.650	AZ	1	0	0	33.978	FL	0	1	0	52.829	TX	0	0	1
22.500	AZ	1	0	0	30.985	FL	0	1	0	48.591	TX	0	0	1
24.179	AZ	1	0	0	30.575	FL	0	1	0	49.826	TX	0	0	1
26.313	AZ	1	0	0	34.700	FL	0	1	0	52.484	TX	0	0	1
23.849	AZ	1	0	0	34.107	FL	0	1	0	43.418	TX	0	0	1
25.052	AZ	1	0	0	31.244	FL	0	1	0	44.406	TX	0	0	1
25.647	AZ	1	0	0	32.769	FL	0	1	0	45.899	TX	0	0	1
25.014	AZ	1	0	0	31.073	FL	0	1	0	53.997	TX	0	0	1
21.443	AZ	1	0	0	29.655	FL	0	1	0	42.590	TX	0	0	1
25.690	AZ	1	0	0	32.161	FL	0	1	0	48.041	TX	0	0	1
31.274	AZ	1	0	0	26.651	FL	0	1	0	48.988	TX	0	0	1
26.238	AZ	1	0	0	32.825	FL	0	1	0	47.548	TX	0	0	1
23.253	AZ	1	0	0	30.567	FL	0	1	0	44.999	TX	0	0	1
22.084	AZ	1	0	0	34.424	FL	0	1	0	44.212	TX	0	0	1
21.565	AZ	1	0	0	29.600	FL	0	1	0	48.615	TX	0	0	1
29.800	AZ	1	0	0	25.149	FL	0	1	0	41.634	TX	0	0	1
23.248	AZ	1	0	0	34.342	FL	0	1	0	47.562	TX	0	0	1
29.785	AZ	1	0	0	28.557	FL	0	1	0	44.616	TX	0	0	1
28.076	AZ	1	0	0	31.490	FL	0	1	0	47.660	TX	0	0	1
18.606	AZ	1	0	0	38.966	FL	0	1	0	50.278	TX	0	0	1
22.876	AZ	1	0	0	31.129	FL	0	1	0	48.802	TX	0	0	1
26.688	AZ	1	0	0	36.983	FL	0	1	0	51.430	TX	0	0	1
25.910	AZ	1	0	0	36.940	FL	0	1	0	46.852	TX	0	0	1
28.320	AZ	1	0	0	36.318	FL	0	1	0	48.704	TX	0	0	1
22.192	AZ	1	0	0	32.802	FL	0	1	0	53.269	TX	0	0	1
25.048	AZ	1	0	0	28.994	FL	0	1	0	43.165	TX	0	0	1
27.056	AZ	1	0	0	31.236	FL	0	1	0	53.987	TX	0	0	1
25.312	AZ	1	0	0	35.703	FL	0	1	0	51.484	TX	0	0	1
29.996	AZ	1	0	0	38.738	FL	0	1	0	49.923	TX	0	0	1
22.902	AZ	1	0	0	35.032	FL	0	1	0	49.618	TX	0	0	1
26.942	AZ	1	0	0	27.430	FL	0	1	0	46.043	TX	0	0	1
21.384	AZ	1	0	0	29.046	FL	0	1	0	47.716	TX	0	0	1
23.952	AZ	1	0	0	34.942	FL	0	1	0	46.465	TX	0	0	1
21.793	AZ	1	0	0	36.624	FL	0	1	0	54.701	TX	0	0	1
26.664	AZ	1	0	0	34.198	FL	0	1	0	48.776	TX	0	0	1
23.886	AZ	1	0	0	33.307	FL	0	1	0	47.817	TX	0	0	1
23.242	AZ	1	0	0	33.644	FL	0	1	0	54.188	TX	0	0	1
22.764	AZ	1	0	0	34.063	FL	0	1	0	51.947	TX	0	0	1
29.126	AZ	1	0	0	33.558	FL	0	1	0	54.657	TX	0	0	1
23.734	AZ	1	0	0	35.538	FL	0	1	0	50.777	TX	0	0	1
18.814	AZ	1	0	0	31.162	FL	0	1	0	53.390	TX	0	0	1
24.544	AZ	1	0	0	30.260	FL	0	1	0	51.147	TX	0	0	1
22.632	AZ	1	0	0	27.638	FL	0	1	0	44.404	TX	0	0	1
25.184	AZ	1	0	0	32.833	FL	0	1	0	45.515	TX	0	0	1
22.869	AZ	1	0	0	35.859	FL	0	1	0	49.694	TX	0	0	1
26.900	AZ	1	0	0	38.767	FL	0	1	0	49.716	TX	0	0	1
24.870	AZ	1	0	0	34.535	FL	0	1	0	48.896	TX	0	0	1
25.490	AZ	1	0	0	28.816	FL	0	1	0	45.447	TX	0	0	1
23.652	AZ	1	0	0	31.324	FL	0	1	0	51.111	TX	0	0	1

Response	Factor1	Factor2	A	B	High	Covariate
1	A	High	1	0	1	11
3	A	Low	1	0	−1	7
2	A	High	1	0	1	5
2	A	Low	1	0	1	6
4	B	High	0	1	1	6
6	B	Low	0	1	−1	3
3	B	High	0	1	1	14
5	B	Low	0	1	−1	20
8	C	High	0	0	1	2
9	C	Low	0	0	−1	17
7	C	High	0	0	1	19
10	C	Low	0	0	−1	14

```
A regression analysis yields:

The regression equation is

Response = 9.28 - 6.84 A - 4.13 B - 0.883 High - 0.0598
Covariate
Predictor       Coef        SE Coef         T           P
Constant        9.2773      0.4904         18.92       0.000
A              -6.8438      0.4463        -15.33       0.000
B              -4.1345      0.4163         -9.93       0.000
High           -0.8832      0.1696         -5.21       0.001
Covariate      -0.05979     0.03039        -1.97       0.090

S = 0.580794   R-Sq = 97.6%   R-Sq(adj) = 96.2%
```

Similar to Example 28.3, an estimated response can be calculated for various categorical variable situations.

28.10   Binary Logistic Regression

Binary logistic regression is applicable when the response is binary, such as pass or fail, and inputs are continuous or attribute variables. Logistic regression uses a transformation or link function to convert the binary or binomial data into continuous variable. There are a number of link functions used for this transformation. For our purposes we will only discuss the logit link function because of its general applicability and the simplicity of the function.

The logit function is:

$$Logit(p) = \ln\left(\frac{p}{1-p}\right)$$

This relationship is the logarithm of the ratio of the pass and fails probabilities. The ratio of probabilities ranges from 0 to infinity, where the logarithm transforms the data so that it ranges from negative to positive infinity, as shown in Figure 28.1. It is these infinite tails that allow the data to meet the requirements for the regression algorithm.

Logistic regression is actually a special case of the general linear model (GLM) algorithm, in that it is robust to unbalanced data and its ability to process mixtures of continuous and discrete predictors or *X*s as a typical GLM method.

Most logistical regression statistical analysis software includes methods to analyze attribute data such as nominal or ordinal data. These methods are not included in this volume but are just extensions of the binary logistic regression discussed below.

To illustrate the application, let's consider the following example.

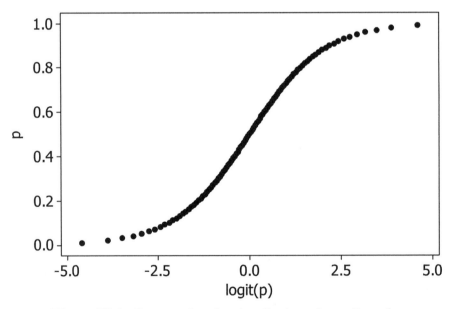

Figure 28.1: Scatter plot showing the transformation of p with a logit function.

28.11   Example 28.5: Binary Logistic Regression for Ingot Preparation

Ingots prepared with different heating and soaking times are tested for readiness to be rolled:

Sample	Heat	Soak	ready	not ready	Trials	Sample	Heat	Soak	ready	not ready	Trials
1	7	1	10	0	10	11	27	1	55	1	56
2	7	1.7	17	0	17	12	27	1.7	40	4	44
3	7	2.2	7	0	7	13	27	2.2	21	0	21
4	7	2.8	12	0	12	14	27	2.8	21	1	22
5	7	4	9	0	9	15	27	4	15	1	16
6	14	1	31	0	31	16	51	1	10	3	13
7	14	1.7	43	0	43	17	51	1.7	1	0	1
8	14	2.2	31	2	33	18	51	2.2	1	0	1
9	14	2.8	31	0	31	19	51	4	1	0	1
10	14	4	19	0	19						

The results of a statistical analysis program are:

```
Link Function: Logit

Response Information

Variable        Value          Count

not ready       Event             12
                Non-event        375
Trials          Total            387


Logistic Regression Table

                                            Odds    95% CI
Predictor    Coef       SE Coef    Z     P  Ratio Lower Upper

Constant  -5.55917    1.11969-4.96 0.000
Heat       0.0820308 0.0237344 3.46 0.001  1.09  1.04  1.14
Soak       0.0567713  0.331212 0.17 0.864  1.06  0.55  2.03


Log-Likelihood = -47.673
Test that all slopes are zero: G = 11.643, DF = 2, P-
Value = 0.003


Goodness-of-Fit Tests

Method            Chi-Square        DF        P

Pearson             13.5431         16     0.633
Deviance            13.7526         16     0.617
Hosmer-Lemeshow      7.3812          6     0.287
```

By convention the logit(p) being predicted is the lesser event, where $p < (1-p)$. Even if your input data is the higher percent binomial case, where $p > 0.5$, the software predicts the lower percentage case, where $p < 0.5$.

There are two ways to determine significance. The primary method is to consider the P value provided for each predictor. In this example they are heat and soak. Examination of the P values shows that only heat is significant.

A second output, odds ratio, is available when using binary output data, which is a measure of the change in the odds with a unit change in the predictor. For a binary predictor, such as gender, the odds ratio represents the change in odds between the two predictor levels. The odds are defined as the ratio of pass to fail.

$$\text{Odds}_{male} = \frac{P(\text{male \& passing})}{P(\text{male \& failing})} \qquad \text{Odds}_{female} = \frac{P(\text{female \& passing})}{P(\text{female \& failing})}$$

$$\text{OddsRatio} = \frac{\text{Odds}_{male}}{\text{Odds}_{female}}$$

In the prior example, the predictor is a continuous variable; the odds ratio is defined as the ratio of the odds for a one unit change in the predictor. For the soak term, the odds ratio will tell you how the odds change with a 1 minute change in the soak time.

In all cases, an odds ratio of 1.0 indicates there is no change in the odds when the predictor value changes. As the ratio deviates from 1.0 there is more of a change. There is no clear odds ratio that defines significance although you can judge significance using the confidence interval. In this example, the soak has an odds ratio of 1.06, which can be interpreted to mean that every minute of added soak time, the odds of being "ready" is increased by 6% (a factor of 1.06).

The next step is to verify that the regression assumptions were met. In a traditional GLM analysis you would perform an analysis of the residuals. For logistic regression, a number of other methods are used for the same purpose. For this example, we will use two of the methods, a goodness of fit test and a delta chi-square versus probability.

There is a number of goodness of fit tests that can be used; each has its own benefits. We will use the Pearson chi-square goodness of fit test for this example. This method uses a chi-square test which is commonly used in Lean Six Sigma work. In practice, the passing of any of the provided goodness-of-fit tests, with a *P* value > 0.05, indicates the model has an adequate fit.

Figure 28.2 is a delta chi-square versus probability analysis, which is an equivalent to a residual analysis look for outliers. This chart uses the predicted probability, as the *x*-axis, and the delta chi-square value on the *y*-axis. The delta chi-square value is the magnitude of change in the chi-square goodness-of-fit test when that observation is removed from the data set. A high value indicates an observation that does not fit the regression model well, and it should be treated like an unusual observation identified in a standard regression. The observation should be investigated, removed if it is found to be an errant observation or kept if it is not found to have any assignable special causes.

The final step in a logistic regression is the generation of the predictive model. This can be performed manually or using the functionality of an analysis software. Manually, the regression output provides the predicted logit value for each observation. This value is then transformed back to a binary percentage. The event probability (EPRO) is the estimated EPRO value for that observation, which is the reverse transform of the logit equation. The regression coefficients provided by the analysis are used as

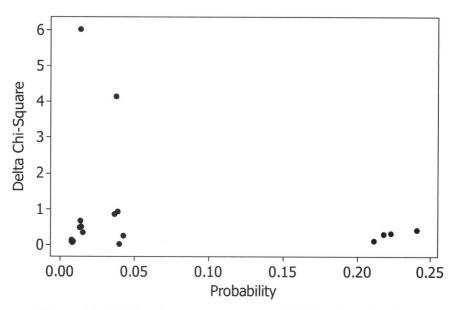

Figure 28.2: Delta chi-square versus probability chart for heat and soak model.

a standard regression output, except that they estimate the logit which is transformed into the estimate probability.

$$\hat{p} = \frac{1}{1 + e^{-\text{logit}(\hat{p})}} = EPRO$$

$$\text{where } \text{logit}(p) = \ln\left(\frac{p}{1-p}\right) = constant + coef_1 * x_1 + coef_2 * x_2 + \dots$$

From the Logistic Regression output:
```
Constant = -5.55917, Heat = coef1 = 0.0820308, Soak =
coef2 = 0.0567713
```

Using the predicted probabilities for each observation in this example, a surface plot can be created, as illustrated in Figure 28.3. In the surface plot you will recognize the significance of the heat with the increasing percentage along with the minor effect of the soak in the other axis.

Since this example has only one significant factor, and it is evaluated at four discrete levels, we can use a second method to examine the effects, a *p* chart. Rearranging the data by heat only we get:

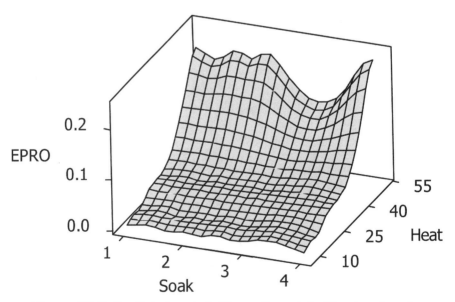

Figure 28.3: Predicted probability surface plot of heat and soak.

Heat	Not Ready by Heat	Sample Size
7	0	55
14	3	157
27	6	159
51	3	13

Examining the data in a *p* chart format, as shown in Figure 28.4, leads us to conclude that the heat at the 51 level causes a larger portion of not reads.

28.12   Example 28.6: Binary Logistic Regression for Coating Test

Determine the best organic coating addition to pass a standard-ized pencil test method for film hardness (modified-ISO 1518). The goal is to apply the lowest amount of organic coating to a non-woven substrate that is used to wrap and protect high-end automotive chrome parts from damage. (Kapik, 2006)

The coating must not be visibly scratched when tested per ISO 1518's three pencil hardness and three pressure loadings

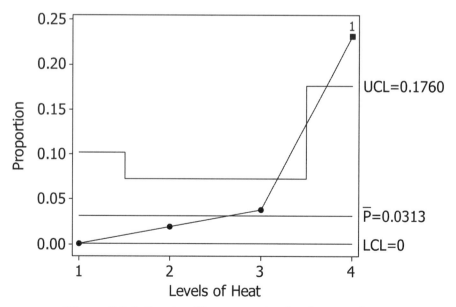

Figure 28.4: Levels of heat examined using a p chart.

specification. The coated specimen is considered failed if there is a visible scratch with a magnification of $20x$ or if penetration through the sample occurs during the standardized test method.

Three variables at three levels were evaluated:

1. Organic coating: 0, 6, and 12%
2. Pencil harnesses: 1 (Hard), 2, and 3 (Soft)
3. Pencil pressures: 80, 120, and 160 psig

Results from the experiment are shown in Table 28.4.

The following binary logistic regression analysis performs logistic regression on a binary response variable, where the binary variable has only two possible values (e.g., pass or fail). To build a model, one or more predictors are fitted using an iterative re-weighted least squares algorithm for the purpose of obtaining the maximum likelihood estimates of the parameters.

Table 28.4: Binary logistic regression coating test data and calculated EPRO.

Trial	Organic Coating (%)	Pencil Lead Hardness	Pressure	Pass	Trials	EPRO	Trial	Organic Coating (%)	Pencil Lead Hardness	Pressure	Pass	Trials	EPRO
1	0	1	80	10	10	0.95076	15	6	2	160	1	10	0.04988
2	0	1	120	0	10	0.00856	16	6	3	80	10	10	1
3	0	1	160	0	10	0	17	6	3	120	10	10	1
4	0	2	80	10	10	0.99911	18	6	3	160	10	10	0.99719
5	0	2	120	2	10	0.33469	19	12	1	80	10	10	1
6	0	2	160	0	10	0.00022	20	12	1	120	10	10	0.99788
7	0	3	80	10	10	1	21	12	1	160	0	10	0.17377
8	0	3	120	9	10	0.99971	22	12	2	80	10	10	1
9	0	3	160	7	10	0.60312	23	12	2	120	10	10	0.99996
10	6	1	80	10	10	0.99978	24	12	2	160	10	10	0.92458
11	6	1	120	8	10	0.66835	25	12	3	80	10	10	1
12	6	1	160	0	10	0.0009	26	12	3	120	10	10	1
13	6	2	80	10	10	1	27	12	3	160	10	10	0.99999
14	6	2	120	10	10	0.99156							

The odds of a reference event are the ratio of P(event) to P(not event). The estimated coefficient of a factor or covariate predictor is the estimated change in the log of P(event)/P(not event) for each unit change in the predictor, assuming the other predictors remain constant. The estimated coefficients can also be used to calculate the odds ratio, or the ratio between two odds. Through exponentiation the estimated coefficient of a factor yields the ratio of P(event)/P(not event) for a certain factor level compared to the reference level. (Minitab, 2007)

Results from a logit regression analysis are:

Binary Logistic Regression: Pass, Trials versus Organic Coat, Pencil Lead

```
Link Function: Logit

Response Information

Variable        Value        Count
Pass            Event          197
                Non-event       73
Trials          Total          270


Logistic Regression Table

                                                              95%
                                                     Odds     CI
Predictor        Coef      SE Coef      Z      P     Ratio   Lower
Constant       9.49013    1.90126    4.99   0.000
Organic        0.741914   0.172730   4.30   0.000    2.10    1.50
Coating, %
Pencil Lead    5.04984    1.08652    4.65   0.000  156.00   18.55
Hardness
Pressure      -0.157819   0.0294851 -5.35   0.000    0.85    0.81


Predictor                        Upper
Constant
Organic Coating, %                2.95
Pencil Lead Hardness           1312.16
Pressure                          0.90


Log-Likelihood = -38.219
Test that all slopes are zero: G = 238.720, DF = 3,
P-Value = 0.000
```

Goodness-of-Fit Tests

Method	Chi-Square	DF	P
Pearson	51.1004	23	0.001
Deviance	31.2020	23	0.118
Hosmer-Lemeshow	8.0441	7	0.329

The delta chi-square plot in Figure 28.5 shows no unusual observations. Since at least one of the goodness-of-fit tests shows a non-significant *P* value (two of the three in this case – Deviance and Hosmer-Lemeshow), we can continue to evaluate the model.

For this binary logistic regression the EPRO or predicted probability is the probability that the response for *i*th factor is one or a success. Surface plots for a given set of data can differ because of interpolation methods used by the software. One of these software surface plot options yielded the calculated EPRO versus organic coating and pressure plot shown in Figure 28.6. Similarly a plot of calculated EPRO versus organic coating and pencil lead hardness is shown in Figure 28.7.

Analysis conclusions are:

1. As pencil hardness increased from 1 (hard) to 3 (soft), the probability of passing the test improved.

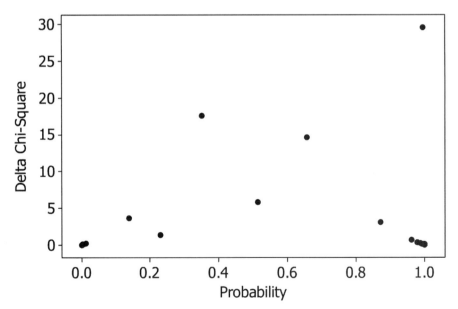

Figure 28.5: Delta chi-square vs. probability chart for coating model.

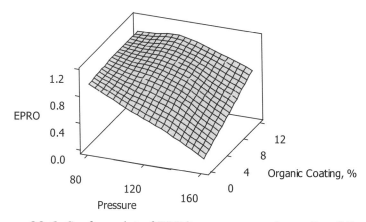

Figure 28.6: Surface plot of EPRO versus organic coating (%), pressure.

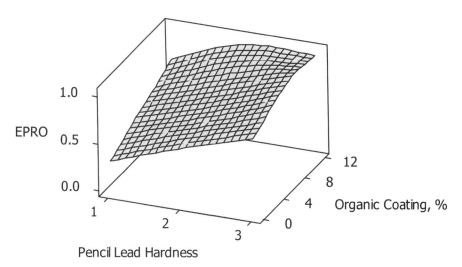

Figure 28.7: Surface plot of EPRO verses organic coating (%), pencil lead hardness.

2. As the organic coating level increased from 0% to 12%, the probability of passing the test improved.
3. As the pressure increased from 80 to 160 psig, the probability of failing the test increased.
4. Even at the highest level of coating, there was a high probability of scratching the coating using pencil hardness 1 at 160 psig (~83%).

5. The decision was to use 10% organic coating as this had a probability of passing the test of 67% using pencil hardness 2 and a probability of passing the test of 100% using pencil hardness 3 at 160 psig.

28.13   Other Logistic Regression Methods

Logistic regression methods are available for most attribute data formats. These are categorized as either nominal or ordinal data. Nominal data is where there are three or more attributes that have no specific order or ranking, such as color (red, blue, green....) or process location (cities, states....). Nominal logistic regression is used for this data type.

Ordinal logistic regression is used in cases where there are three or more attribute levels that have a natural order or ranking. This ordering does not have to be in equal differences between the attributes. An example of this is likert scale data (e.g., very negative, negative, neutral, positive, very positive). This type of data provides more information than the nominal case because of the group ordering.

Both of these methods, as in the binary logistic regression, will work with both continuous and categorical predictors. The continuous predictors are typically called covariates, while the categorical predictors are called factors. Software packages that provide a logistic regression function may have slightly different conventions for the terms and functionality, so one should review the instructions prior to use.

28.14   Exercises

1. Conduct a multiple regression analysis of the continuous input pulse data previously presented as Exercise 1 at the end of chapter 18. Comment on the results.
2. Analyze Example 28.3 run with a constant and the three possible combinations or the two indicator variables. Demonstrate how the same results are obtained for the three analyses.
3. Conduct a multiple regression analysis of the four factors on lead time. Comment on the results.

A	B	C	D	Lead time
63.8	30.13	26.11	25.60	442.75
64.3	30.36	26.10	25.36	444.36
62.9	31.05	26.02	25.20	444.82
66.9	30.13	25.97	25.36	445.51
69.7	29.90	26.02	25.60	446.43
70.0	30.13	26.03	28.00	467.59
72.2	31.05	25.94	27.44	472.88
73.9	30.13	25.94	28.16	476.56
69.6	31.05	25.99	28.00	477.25
72.4	31.28	25.94	27.20	478.86
64.9	31.05	25.97	29.60	491.97
74.3	31.28	25.97	29.28	492.43
74.8	31.28	25.94	28.56	493.58

4. Conduct a multiple regression analysis of the five factors on the response. Replace the final reading for E of 1443.3 with 14433.0 and reanalyze. Comment on the results.

A	B	C	D	E	Result
144.1	124.6	124.3	150.0	81.6	2416.9
122.8	51.1	71.9	104.0	50.2	1422.6
130.3	80.4	146.6	125.2	129.2	1842.9
82.5	71.4	105.6	66.9	149.0	1276.7
117.0	138.1	63.9	65.0	148.3	1795.9
108.4	92.3	79.5	107.1	91.5	1777.8
125.8	55.7	61.5	101.2	89.7	1437.5
120.7	56.4	140.5	110.8	115.9	1526.4
63.1	51.5	67.4	146.5	129.5	1796.2
65.2	139.5	132.0	130.0	51.8	2365.1
58.5	55.7	115.6	70.7	57.6	1174.6
115.2	64.1	119.9	121.3	72.2	1683.6
129.4	87.0	135.8	102.1	92.4	1704.3
98.2	138.8	144.7	110.2	69.2	2190.8
69.8	53.7	66.8	54.4	119.5	1016.7
147.0	122.5	97.4	80.3	56.5	1798.6
64.4	81.0	96.3	78.1	55.8	1447.1
76.7	113.1	121.9	87.0	95.5	1784.8
127.7	61.8	124.5	137.2	138.8	1801.4
86.0	61.6	140.7	96.6	146.8	1443.3

5. Assess the significance of the five factors (A–E) on the response in data set below.
   (a) Conduct a multi-regression analysis using all factors with VIF for the factors.

(b) Note the probability levels for the factors B and D.
(c) Examine the regression analysis to see if any other fac-
     tors are significant at a level of 0.05.
(d) Conduct a best subset analysis.
(e) Conduct a residual analysis.
(f)   Describe an IEE scenario where such a data set could
     have been encountered in your business.

FactorA	FactorB	FactorC	FactorD	FactorE	Resp
42.8472	60.288	74.8574	61.42	111.381	82.714
42.6425	81.497	71.094	109.194	88.419	88.952
37.552	69.356	69.8057	65.789	110.485	68.93
42.3507	134.812	75.6542	145.354	156.396	127.299
38.1677	100.69	78.6435	113.673	129.705	107.407
42.4722	105.589	66.1241	102.36	109.474	113.371
48.1279	117.746	63.2013	144.351	121.031	128.809
44.4346	100.689	75.8793	72.267	169.448	102.457
46.1869	102.86	72.2666	112.989	92.453	105.881
38.1336	71.658	66.4661	67.484	155.651	83.228
39.1405	83.732	73.9306	79.194	109.908	84.993
37.2787	88.559	74.9014	116.534	86.517	94.819
45.7326	112.803	76.8157	119.852	135.044	111.306
35.5554	84.428	73.3119	107.774	109.894	100.248
41.2271	111.734	73.5397	140.337	60.893	111.851
41.3331	114.892	80.6737	140.073	143.648	114.015
34.8684	86.538	76.2678	64.641	110.26	85.485
43.6079	105.482	78.5142	102.841	113.295	112.521
38.586	87.224	72.4421	44.817	126.575	79.382
49.4884	105.78	74.9155	105.689	140.349	106.396
41.2136	96.009	70.2389	85.398	132.353	100.704
39.4794	100.618	64.0437	113.511	156.171	102.37
30.7306	75.478	69.4136	89.801	164.71	76.191
43.0078	110.102	78.2802	102.364	112.201	93.707
44.1159	115.805	75.2305	121.736	144.741	108.485

6. Using the below data set, assess whether the four loca-
    tions equally generate revenue. Assess whether generated
    revenue is a function of the number of daily sales call con-
    tacts. Create an indicator variable analysis that contains
    both location and number of daily sales call contacts.
    (a) Conduct an ANOVA analysis of revenue by location.
         Document F value and P value. Make a test hypothesis
         conclusion statement.
    (b) Conduct an ANOM analysis of revenue by location.
         Make a test hypothesis conclusion statement.
    (c) Conduct a regression analysis of revenue by number of
         daily sales call contacts. Document the best-estimate
         equation. Document test statistic and P value. Make a
         test hypothesis conclusion statement.
    (d) Conduct indicator variables regression analysis with-
         out a constant. Document the modeling equation.

Revenue	Location	Daily call contacts	Revenue	Location	Daily call contacts
8.0761	LocationA	260	−12.0745	LocationB	130
−2.6372	LocationA	210	40.5657	LocationB	350
0.6917	LocationA	190	−13.074	LocationB	90
2.3224	LocationA	230	22.1015	LocationB	310
22.117	LocationA	250	30.9986	LocationB	270
16.0591	LocationA	210	12.2945	LocationB	250
−10.544	LocationA	170	27.2024	LocationB	290
36.8964	LocationA	280	33.1342	LocationB	310
24.2957	LocationA	320	47.6009	LocationB	310
24.2657	LocationA	240	7.8176	LocationB	210
3.5748	LocationA	240	16.8641	LocationB	250
−15.7055	LocationA	100	19.8095	LocationB	290
10.2706	LocationA	230	20.3152	LocationB	240
22.2315	LocationA	280	13.9763	LocationB	220
−6.3884	LocationA	150	−7.7602	LocationB	190
−19.9718	LocationA	110	36.2805	LocationB	260
2.9379	LocationA	220	3.9896	LocationB	180
−13.5559	LocationA	140	−21.6434	LocationB	70
18.6596	LocationA	260	57.5398	LocationB	360
29.3213	LocationA	230	30.3677	LocationB	330
1.6742	LocationA	190	12.6677	LocationB	220
−53.7004	LocationA	50	2.4706	LocationB	210
6.5414	LocationA	200	14.0351	LocationB	280
−8.7237	LocationA	140	34.5144	LocationB	310
1.8213	LocationA	200	7.3757	LocationB	220
0.7115	LocationC	220	−29.7567	LocationD	50
−31.8664	LocationC	60	−2.5342	LocationD	150
14.5462	LocationC	250	2.7842	LocationD	170
−7.9462	LocationC	110	−8.2622	LocationD	150
−1.0772	LocationC	160	−12.706	LocationD	90
−10.7956	LocationC	130	−53.69	LocationD	60
4.6414	LocationC	230	−21.9711	LocationD	100
−23.7047	LocationC	80	16.7867	LocationD	290
27.0274	LocationC	280	−11.5566	LocationD	160
−2.8039	LocationC	160	−24.8011	LocationD	60
7.3445	LocationC	230	−39.5116	LocationD	70
−30.2219	LocationC	80	−4.607	LocationD	150
13.1078	LocationC	230	−7.447	LocationD	120
19.3735	LocationC	300	−10.2162	LocationD	120

1.1095	LocationC	160		-5.9291	LocationD	170
-9.0635	LocationC	180		15.7499	LocationD	280
18.7002	LocationC	210		9.8421	LocationD	200
11.6017	LocationC	270		-12.9319	LocationD	150
-9.5929	LocationC	150		7.1461	LocationD	250
11.2543	LocationC	210		-20.398	LocationD	60
41.5753	LocationC	320		-50.948	LocationD	50
-2.7188	LocationC	190		-5.3185	LocationD	200
34.1	LocationC	340		-50.6212	LocationD	40
2.3438	LocationC	220		-17.794	LocationD	60
24.556	LocationC	250		20.6997	LocationD	280

7. A call center randomly selects and monitors five calls daily. They monitor the duration of the call, the employee who responded to the call (number 1–12), and the dollar amount of product sales that was affected by the call. The organization wanted to create the most appropriate control charting methodology for their situation, report process capability against an upper specification of 175 seconds, and then gain insight to what might be done to improve their response time.

   (a) Create an $\bar{x}$ and R chart. Note whether the charts are in-control, and comment on the plusses and minuses of using this methodology along with any process capability statement that could be made.

   (b) (Optional) Create a 3-way control chart (See Breyfogle 2003 for methodology). Note whether the charts are in-control, and comment on the plusses and minuses of using this methodology along with any process capability statement that could be made.

   (c) Create and individuals chart of the subgroup mean and log its standard deviation. Note whether the charts are in-control, and comment on the plusses and minuses of using this methodology along with any process capability statement that could be made.

   (d) Make a process capability/performance metric statement.

   (e) State and apply a visualization tool that is appropriate when assessing within and between day variability. Comment on conclusions from the analysis.

   (f) State and apply a hypothesis analytical tool that is appropriate when assessing within and between day variability. Comment on conclusions from the analysis.

(g) State and apply a visualization tool that is appropriate when assessing differences between employees. Comment on conclusions from the analysis.

(h) State and apply a hypothesis test tool that is appropriate when assessing differences between the mean responses from employees collectively. Comment on conclusions from the analysis.

(i) State and apply a hypothesis test tool that is appropriate when assessing differences between the mean responses of each employee. Comment on conclusions from the analysis.

(j) State and apply a hypothesis test tool that is appropriate when assessing differences between the mean response from each employee and the overall mean. Comment on conclusions from the analysis.

(k) State and apply a hypothesis test tool that is appropriate when assessing differences between the variance response from each employee. Comment on conclusions from the analysis.

(l) State and apply a visualization tool that describes amount of product sales as a function of call duration. Comment on conclusions from the analysis.

(m) State and apply a hypothesis test tool that describes amount of product sales as a function of call duration.

(n) Comment on conclusions from the analysis.

The collected data are:

Day	Sample	Duration	Employee	SizeOrder	Day	Sample	Duration	Employee	SizeOrder
1	Sample1	129.366	4	162612	22	Sample1	96.095	2	87693
1	Sample2	130.668	9	29669	22	Sample2	108.261	10	73372
1	Sample3	132.261	11	73484	22	Sample3	99.224	5	81185
1	Sample4	143.449	6	83479	22	Sample4	83.321	5	72451
1	Sample5	137.431	9	93858	22	Sample5	77.937	2	105279
2	Sample1	155.466	12	97250	23	Sample1	91.777	5	95465
2	Sample2	131.876	8	135142	23	Sample2	87.851	2	62550
2	Sample3	157.514	8	129326	23	Sample3	111.84	1	193302
2	Sample4	152.987	4	104459	23	Sample4	101.006	5	113610
2	Sample5	166.951	8	81765	23	Sample5	86.673	5	32814
3	Sample1	119.142	11	45241	24	Sample1	151.203	6	84397
3	Sample2	114.724	10	120604	24	Sample2	145.147	7	178032
3	Sample3	126.954	6	134207	24	Sample3	129.718	3	96799
3	Sample4	136.343	3	108883	24	Sample4	130.467	4	152662
3	Sample5	124.569	7	97697	24	Sample5	138.601	7	20186
4	Sample1	105.672	3	120603	25	Sample1	138.164	4	136424
4	Sample2	130.933	3	135372	25	Sample2	127.35	8	99035
4	Sample3	119.522	11	117597	25	Sample3	165.92	8	117146
4	Sample4	119.826	3	104866	25	Sample4	118.492	7	79914
4	Sample5	138.701	11	108323	25	Sample5	126.662	3	100175
5	Sample1	57.94	5	149542	26	Sample1	128.754	6	70055
5	Sample2	86.753	1	115451	26	Sample2	110.944	10	109188
5	Sample3	106.76	1	59659	26	Sample3	132.195	4	136081
5	Sample4	84.081	1	101774	26	Sample4	121.679	3	-25497

Day	Sample	Duration	Employee	SizeOrder	Day	Sample	Duration	Employee	SizeOrder
5	Sample5	80.776	1	115256	26	Sample5	135.691	9	68884
6	Sample1	90.685	1	117680	27	Sample1	167.897	9	140703
6	Sample2	97.265	5	63472	27	Sample2	188.83	8	104962
6	Sample3	102.751	1	145701	27	Sample3	187.734	4	117081
6	Sample4	99.598	1	92113	27	Sample4	176.402	6	125002
6	Sample5	114.666	6	110302	27	Sample5	205.357	6	107542
7	Sample1	122.728	7	151281	28	Sample1	171.947	4	108833
7	Sample2	143.246	12	101075	28	Sample2	191.591	12	20004
7	Sample3	96.958	2	124590	28	Sample3	160.853	7	158523
7	Sample4	116.454	3	53703	28	Sample4	166.871	12	96363
7	Sample5	105.127	1	110061	28	Sample5	180.103	12	131143
8	Sample1	136.263	8	140136	29	Sample1	108.13	2	143962
8	Sample2	135.997	6	81907	29	Sample2	78.017	1	39779
8	Sample3	140.682	3	92143	29	Sample3	90.939	5	141781
8	Sample4	144.995	12	75571	29	Sample4	68.686	5	109613
8	Sample5	137.464	8	107562	29	Sample5	57.205	2	123787
9	Sample1	122.78	6	96498	30	Sample1	87.125	6	89704
9	Sample2	132.875	6	139075	30	Sample2	115.732	10	116480
9	Sample3	118.088	6	144278	30	Sample3	101.492	1	20263
9	Sample4	159.836	8	155761	30	Sample4	93.001	1	110522
9	Sample5	151.587	12	97489	30	Sample5	80.529	6	109234
10	Sample1	138.419	8	112632	31	Sample1	178.807	12	46657
10	Sample2	130.72	3	120110	31	Sample2	196.3	4	101881
10	Sample3	138.914	3	-2768	31	Sample3	211.181	8	76481

Day	Sample	Duration	Employee	SizeOrder	Day	Sample	Duration	Employee	SizeOrder
10	Sample4	136.082	4	64125	31	Sample4	196.003	12	113776
10	Sample5	119.831	9	190656	31	Sample5	226.245	3	30038
11	Sample1	117.167	4	53408	32	Sample1	109.438	2	116116
11	Sample2	133.389	11	128739	32	Sample2	124.427	9	98218
11	Sample3	111.272	10	80735	32	Sample3	123.466	3	186594
11	Sample4	125.388	3	103314	32	Sample4	118.463	10	61244
11	Sample5	85.639	5	177900	32	Sample5	128.814	4	113718
12	Sample1	130.569	7	55544	33	Sample1	146.395	4	57208
12	Sample2	117.396	9	100861	33	Sample2	128.32	11	104340
12	Sample3	135.106	8	111763	33	Sample3	136.608	9	79928
12	Sample4	126.644	7	118991	33	Sample4	106.817	10	110696
12	Sample5	124.622	10	96224	33	Sample5	157.345	8	98644
13	Sample1	102.691	5	99268	34	Sample1	142.411	4	137599
13	Sample2	71.914	5	124436	34	Sample2	153.816	9	29805
13	Sample3	52.36	1	163480	34	Sample3	131.905	11	115291
13	Sample4	90.462	5	114593	34	Sample4	113.73	2	136956
13	Sample5	56.735	5	110180	34	Sample5	127.512	11	48876
14	Sample1	57.282	5	107766	35	Sample1	191.742	7	81623
14	Sample2	68.997	4	53086	35	Sample2	200.052	8	67106
14	Sample3	60.113	6	83170	35	Sample3	192.407	8	61710
14	Sample4	38.821	5	82170	35	Sample4	181.916	7	139807
14	Sample5	65.419	1	105288	35	Sample5	195.399	8	124285
15	Sample1	117.002	11	53877	36	Sample1	102.701	10	123937
15	Sample2	135.377	4	123551	36	Sample2	119.137	9	119059

Day	Sample	Duration	Employee	SizeOrder
15	Sample3	127.018	9	122866
15	Sample4	123.12	10	65363
15	Sample5	125.551	6	220649
16	Sample1	105.045	2	72380
16	Sample2	143.751	12	109310
16	Sample3	125.39	9	69085
16	Sample4	133.213	3	108608
16	Sample5	94.924	5	102880
17	Sample1	137.094	6	79341
17	Sample2	127.929	6	130131
17	Sample3	136.902	3	140279
17	Sample4	122.567	4	138740
17	Sample5	128.582	3	46337
18	Sample1	127.095	4	82915
18	Sample2	142.833	8	66788
18	Sample3	127.896	4	136343
18	Sample4	90.982	2	51940
18	Sample5	108.865	3	75241
19	Sample1	84.78	2	63672
19	Sample2	80.035	5	125564
19	Sample3	98.437	10	132551
19	Sample4	90.828	6	123263
19	Sample5	99.457	2	118704
20	Sample1	104.231	5	113866

Day	Sample	Duration	Employee	SizeOrder
36	Sample3	101.614	3	129182
36	Sample4	141.902	12	207007
36	Sample5	112.661	10	94982
37	Sample1	175.702	12	128663
37	Sample2	179.718	8	74514
37	Sample3	165.77	12	126302
37	Sample4	180.437	3	111177
37	Sample5	183.465	6	51320
38	Sample1	136.684	7	135163
38	Sample2	134.958	9	110583
38	Sample3	119.841	10	111059
38	Sample4	128.88	6	114417
38	Sample5	120.835	11	108467
39	Sample1	109.887	1	62303
39	Sample2	130.427	11	96287
39	Sample3	138.022	11	84002
39	Sample4	148.968	12	132248
39	Sample5	99.53	5	82678
40	Sample1	111.652	3	153617
40	Sample2	84.571	6	100873
40	Sample3	107.647	2	128008
40	Sample4	126.045	4	65053
40	Sample5	110.36	7	121897
41	Sample1	160.312	12	50404

Day	Sample	Duration	Employee	SizeOrder
20	Sample2	71.781	6	120059
20	Sample3	70.577	10	42855
20	Sample4	122.215	11	102744
20	Sample5	79.657	1	115660
21	Sample1	144.43	8	92079
21	Sample2	118.021	11	34707
21	Sample3	136.272	11	140843
21	Sample4	124.482	6	165047
21	Sample5	108.136	1	76159

Day	Sample	Duration	Employee	SizeOrder
41	Sample2	158.666	3	134062
41	Sample3	146.845	9	131391
41	Sample4	135.076	3	98795
41	Sample5	141.182	8	92260
42	Sample1	193.121	6	138891
42	Sample2	171.185	12	139507
42	Sample3	178.808	3	64650
42	Sample4	174.542	12	128064
42	Sample5	147.034	8	92583

PART V
Improvement Project Roadmap: Improve Phase

This IEE improve phase includes the mechanics of conducting a design of experiments (DOE). However, the IEE project execution roadmap includes DOE as a possible tool in the early part of the analyze phase.

The Lean tool, future state value stream mapping, is also considered a part of the project improve phase IEE roadmap. However, to aid with the description of the tool, this methodology was described with current state value stream mapping in Chapter 14. Lean improvement tools such as kaizen events, 5S, and total productive maintenance (TPM) are included in Chapter 36.

TRIZ (see List of Symbols and Acronyms) and other creativity approaches are described in Chapter 35. These tools can provide the vehicle for stimulating thought on what should be done to improve the system.

This chapter also describes how project improvements are to be reported.

29

Benefiting from Design of Experiments

The last five chapters described passive analysis tools that are useful in the analyze phase of project define–measure–analyze–improve–control (P-DMAIC) and enterprise define–measure–analyze–improve–control (E-DMAIC). Analysis of variance (ANOVA) and regression techniques described in these chapters are useful for determining if there is a statistically significant difference between treatments and levels of variables. For example, ANOVA assessments include tests for differences between departments, suppliers, or machines. Regression techniques are useful for describing the effects of temperature, pressure, delays, and other key process inputs on key process outputs such as lead time and dimensions on a production part.

ANOVA and regression techniques help determine the source of differences without making changes to the process. However, ANOVA and regression results sometimes do not describe the most effective process improvement activities. For example, a regression analysis might not indicate that temperature affects the output of a process. Because of this analysis, a practitioner might choose not to investigate further a change in temperature setting to improve the response of a process. The deception can occur because the normal variability of temperature in the process is not large enough to be detected as a statistically significant effect. This limitation is overcome with design of experiments (DOE).

George Box has a statement that is often quoted: "To find out what happens to a system when you interfere with it you have to interfere with it (not just passively observe it)" (Box, 1966). DOE techniques are useful when a practitioner needs to "kick" a process so that it can give us insight into possible improvements. DOE techniques offer a structured approach for changing many factor settings within a process at once and observing the data collectively for improvements/degradations. DOE analyses not only yield a significance test of the factor levels but also give a prediction model for the response. These experiments can address all possible combinations of a set of input factors (a full factorial) or a subset of all combinations (a fractional factorial).

A Forbes article written by Koselka (1996) refers to this concept as multivariable testing (MVT). DOE techniques yield an efficient strategy for a wide range of applications. In DOE, the effects of several independent factors (variables) can be considered simultaneously in one experiment without evaluating all possible combinations of factor levels.

I believe you should consider DOE in the improve phase of P-DMAIC, DFIEE, or elsewhere whenever you want to try something. In the following five chapters, a background for DOE is described along with the basic structure of various experiment design alternatives, with emphasis on two-level fractional factorial designs; that is, as opposed to full factorial designs that consider all possible combinations of factor levels. After these five chapters, Chapter 34 will then describe response surface methodology (RSM) as part of DOE.

Also this chapter provides: (a) a simple illustration of why two-level DOE works and (b) the mechanics of setting up and conducting an experiment. The focus is on continuous response designs; attribute data are also discussed. This chapter provides a background for the benefits of DOE, while the following chapter provides additional insight to benefits from using the IEE approach to implementing DOE.

As described in Chapters 31 and 32, DOE techniques offer an efficient, structured approach for assessing the mean effects between factor levels for a response. However, often the real need is the reduction of variability. Chapter 33 addresses the use of DOE for variability reduction.

DOE P-DMAIC roadmap linkages are described in Appendix Section D.1.

29.1 Terminology and Benefits

There are many benefits to DOE. Koselka (1996) lists the following applications:

- Reducing the rejection rate of a touch-sensitive computer screen from 25% to less then 1% within months.
- Maintaining paper quality at a mill while switching to a cheaper grade of wood.
- Reducing the risks of misusing a drug in a hospital by incorporating a standardized instruction sheet with patient–pharmacist discussion.
- Reducing the defect rate of the carbon-impregnated urethane foam used in bombs from 85% to 0%.
- Improving the sales of shoes by using an inexpensive arrangement of shoes by color in a showcase, rather than an expensive, flashy alternative.
- Reducing errors on service orders while at the same time improving response time on service calls.
- Improving bearing durability by a factor of five.

29.2 Example 29.1: Traditional Experimentation

A one-at-a-time experiment was conducted when there was interest in reducing the photoconductor speed of a process. Bake temperature and percent additive were the factors under consideration, and each experimental trial was expensive.

The experimenter first chose to set bake temperature and percent additive to their lowest level setting because this was the cheapest manufacturing alternative. The percent additive was then increased while the bake temperature remained constant. Because the photoconductor speed degraded (i.e., a higher number resulted), the bake temperature was next increased while the percent additive was set to its original level. This combination

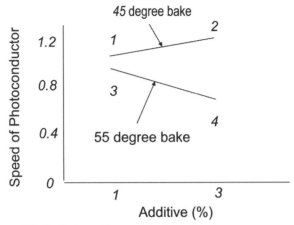

Figure 29.1: Interaction of factors (test sequence noted).

yielded the lowest results; hence, the experimenter suggested this combination to management as the "optimum combination." A summary of this sequence is as follows:

Test Results as a Function of Factor Levels			
Sequence Number	Bake Temperature (°C)	Percent Additive (%)	Speed of Photoconductor
1	45	1	1.1
2	45	3	1.2
3	55	1	1.0

From this summary of results, it is obvious that one combination of bake temperature with additive percentage was not evaluated. Consider now that another trial was added to address this combination of parameters and that the resulting photoconductor speed was measured as 0.6. The two factors, bake temperature and percent additive, interact to affect the output level. Figure 29.1 shows an interaction plot of these data where the lowest (best) speed of conductor is obtained by adjusting both parameters concurrently.

The straight line interconnecting the points assumes a linear relationship between the test point combinations, which may not be precise. However, this is surely a better initial test evaluation than using the original one-at-a-time approach.

As an example of a two-factor interaction, consider how copiers might have a higher failure rate when both temperature and humidity are high. The failure rate was not higher because of increased temperature or increased humidity levels alone. Temperature and humidity interacted to cause an increase in the failure rate. Failure rate models must consider temperature and humidity collectively. A one-at-a-time approach evaluating the failure of a copier could miss this point if the factors were not considered collectively.

29.3   Need for DOE

To be competitive in today's markets, companies need to execute design, manufacturing, and business processes with aggressive cost and schedule constraints. To meet these challenges, organizations need efficient experimentation techniques that provide useful information. DOE techniques are tools that can help satisfy these needs.

In manufacturing and design verification, it is natural because of time constraints to focus experiment evaluations on nominal operating conditions. However, customers rarely receive a "nominally" built machine or use a product under "nominal operating conditions." Similarly, a manufacturing process rarely produces products under nominal tolerance conditions. DOE techniques can aid in the development of quality products that meet the needs of customers even though they might have a variety of different applications. DOE techniques can also help manufacturing with process parameters and other considerations so that they create quality products on a continuing basis.

Factors to consider in an experiment to determine whether a product will perform satisfactorily in a customer environment include such considerations as environmental conditions, external loads, product tolerances, and general human factors. Factors for experimental consideration in the manufacturing process are part tolerances, process parameter tolerances, supplier sources, and manufacturing personnel. Factors to consider in a business process include departments, time of day, days of the week, and personnel.

If factors such as part tolerances and environmental conditions are assessed, it is natural to setup an experiment that monitors change in an output as a function of factors changed individually while holding all other factors constant. However, experiments performed at nominal conditions and then at other conditions using a one-at-a-time assessment for factor levels are inefficient and can lead to erroneous conclusions. It is important to understand the effect that factors have collectively on a product so that appropriate changes can be made to reduce variability and to deliver a price-competitive product.

In product development, a test strategy needs to give early problem detection and isolation while promoting a reduced product development lead time along with a low-cost basic design. In manufacturing, quick problem detection and resolution are most important. In addition, efficient techniques are needed to help maintain and continually improve the manufacturing process. In transactional or business processes, the identification and quantification of process improvement opportunities can help weigh the monetary tradeoffs between savings of implementation and cost of implementation. DOE techniques can provide major benefits to development, manufacturing, and business/transactional processes.

Traditional one-at-a-time approaches can miss interactions and are inefficient. However, much effort can be wasted if two-factor interactions are not investigated *wisely*. For example, consider the number of trials needed to assess all combinations of seven two-level factors. There would be 128 trials (i.e., $2^7 = 128$). Such tests can become very expensive. *Wisely* applied DOE techniques can require only a small subset of all possible combinations and still give information about two-factor interactions.

As mentioned, DOE techniques are often associated with manufacturing processes. For example, the setting of 15 knobs could initially be assessed in 16 trials. However, the techniques are also applicable to development tests. For example, an improved development test strategy could reduce the amount of no trouble found (NTF) encountered from field returns. The techniques are also applicable to service processes; for example, reducing absenteeism of students in high school.

29.4   Common Excuses for Not Using DOE

I believe that DOEs can be very powerful. However, not everybody agrees with me. The following are actual responses to the question of why an individual does not use DOE.

- Fifteen minutes with a statistician never helped before.
- Do not use statistical techniques because of schedules.
- Statistically designed experiments take too much time.
- We only have one or two more experiments to run.
- Statistically designed experiments take too many samples.

- It is only applicable where rigid specs are already defined.
- It is only applicable when nothing is defined.
- We already know all the variables and interactions from previous experiments.
- Intuition gets quicker results.
- It takes away the creative ability of the engineer.
- What do you mean variance? One microinch is one microinch.
- It may be good for simple systems, but not for multiparametric ones.
- My project has too many variables to use statistics.
- We tried it once and nothing was significant.
- Statistical tests do not tell you anything about variables not measured.
- Statistics is a method to use when all else fails.

29.5 DOE Application Examples

I have been involved in the creation and analysis of many DOEs. The following list contains some of these additional DOEs, which are described in *Implementing Six Sigma* (Breyfogle, 2003), where many of these designs had unique twists for either the design and/or analyses:

- *Example 43.2*: A quality function deployment (QFD) evaluation with DOE—improving the quality of a plasma display with design for manufacturability issues being addressed.
- *Example 43.3*: A reliability and functional test of an assembly—created a unique reliability assessment that required a lot less samples and uncovered issues that a traditional reliability test would not have probably uncovered.
- *Example 43.4*: A development strategy for a chemical product—created a DOE design that addressed the results from a mixture design with process and customer usage parameters.
- *Example 42.3*: A pass/fail hardware/software system functional test—describe how DOE matrices could efficiently detect combinational design problems.

Other DOE experiments that addressed many factors in only a few trials; for example, 10–15 factors in 16 trials include:

- Reducing the crumbliness of biscuits that sandwiched egg and sausage in a fast-food chain.
- Eliminating an aluminum extrusion die-breakage problem that was approximately equal to the total revenue for a manufactured part.
- Identifying factors that affected product warp.

The DOE basics described in the next few chapters is not complex. However, the details of creating and appropriately analyzing a DOE can lead to many problems that impact the quality of the experiment and its results. I highly suggest that a person get help from someone who is experienced with the DOE execution philosophy that they desire to apply; that is, not all DOE strategies are created equal with respect to experimental effectiveness.

29.6   Exercises

1. Create a two-factor interaction plot of the following data:

Temperature	Pressure	Response
100	250	275
100	300	285
120	250	270
120	300	325

(a) Determine what parameter settings yield the highest response.

(b) Determine what parameter settings of pressure would be best if it were important to reduce the response variability that results from frequent temperature variations between the two extremes.

2. Early in development, two prototype automobiles were tested to estimate the fuel consumption (i.e., average miles per gallon). The net average of the three vehicles over 20,000 miles was reported to management. Describe what could be done differently to this test if we wanted to understand better the characteristics that affect fuel consumption.

3. Describe a nonmanufacturing application of DOE.

4. Describe how you personally could apply control charting and DOE techniques at work or at home.

30

Understanding the Creation of Full and Fractional Factorial 2^k DOEs

This is the second of six chapters on design of experiment (DOE). The last chapter provided a background for the power of wisely applied DOE. This chapter provides the basic understanding of full and fractional factorial DOEs, which is necessary for effective design creation and execution, which is described as part of the project define–measure–analyze–improve–control (P-DMAIC) roadmap steps shown in Appendix Section D.1. This chapter provides a conceptual explanation of two-level factorial experiments. It uses a nonmanu-facturing example to illustrate the application of the techniques.

It should be noted that the described DOE designs are not in "standard order." This was done to avoid possible confusion with the unique Tables M and N. Breyfogle (2003) Appendix Table D.5 illustrates the standard order and compares a standard order design to that determined from Table M.

30.1 IEE Application Examples: DOE

- *Transactional 30,000-foot-level metric*: An IEE project was to reduce days sales outstanding (DSO) for an invoice. Wisdom of the organization and passive analysis led the creation of a DOE experiment that considered factors: size of order (large versus small), calling back within a week after mailing invoice (Yes versus No), prompt paying customer (Yes versus No), origination department (from passive analysis: least DSO versus highest DSO average), stamping "past due" on envelope (Yes versus No).

- *Transactional and manufacturing 30,000-foot-level metric*: An IEE project was to improve customer satisfaction for a product or service. Wisdom of the organization and passive analysis led to the creation of a DOE experiment that considered factors: type of service purchased (A versus B), size of order (large versus small), department that sold service (from passive analysis: best versus worst), and experience of person selling/delivering service (experienced versus new).
- *Manufacturing 30,000-foot-level metric – critical dimension*: An IEE project was to improve the process capability/performance metric of a plastic part's diameter from an injection-molding machine. Wisdom of the organization and passive analysis led to the creation of a DOE experiment that considered factors are temperature (high versus low), pressure (high versus low), hold time (long versus short), raw material (high side of tolerance versus low side of tolerance), machine (from passive analysis: best performing versus worst performing), and operator (from passive analysis: best versus worst).
- *Manufacturing 30,000-foot-level metric – defect rate*: An IEE project was to improve the process capability/performance metric for the daily defect rate of a printed circuit board assembly diameter of a plastic part from an injection-molding machine. Wisdom of the organization and passive analysis led to the creation of a DOE experiment that considered factors: board complexity (complicated versus less complicated), manufacturing line (*A* versus *B*), processing temperature (high versus low), solder type (new versus current), and operator (*A* versus *B*).
- *Product DFIEE/DFSS – DOE guard-band test*: An IEE project was to improve the process capability/performance metric for the number of notebook computer design problems uncovered during the product's life. A DOE test procedure assessing product temperature was added to the test process, where factors and their levels would be various features of the product. Each trial computer configuration would experience, while operational, an increase in temperature

until failure occurs. The temperature at failure would be the response for the DOE, as measured with temperature sensing devices that are placed on various components within computer. Wisdom of the organization and passive analysis led to the creation of a DOE experiment that considered factors: hard drive size (large versus small), speed of processor (fast versus slow), design (new versus old), test case (high stress on machine processing versus low stress on machine processing), and modem (high speed versus low speed).

- *Product DFIEE/DFSS – DOE set-up time validation test*: An IEE project was to improve the process capability/performance metric for the number of daily problem phone calls received within a call center. Passive analysis indicates product setup was the major source of calls for existing products/services. A DOE test procedure assessing product setup time was added to the test process for new products. Wisdom of the organization and passive analysis led to the creation of a DOE experiment that considered factors: features of products or services, where factors and their levels would be various features of the product/service, along with various operator experience, included as a factor special setup instruction sheet in box (sheet included versus no sheet included).

30.2   Conceptual Explanation: Two-Level Full Factorial Experiments and Two-Factor Interactions

This section discusses two-level full factorial experiment designs. The next section illustrates why fractional factorial design matrices "work."

When executing a full factorial experiment, a response is achieved for all combinations of factor levels. The three-factor experiment design in Table 30.1 is a two-level full factorial experiment. For analyzing three factors, eight trials are needed (i.e., $2^3=8$) to address all assigned combinations of the factor levels. The +/– notation illustrates the high/low level of the factors. When a trial is performed, the factors are set to the noted +/– limits (levels), and a response value is then noted for the trial.

In this experiment design, each factor is executed at its high and low level an equal number of times. Note that there are an equal number of plus and minus signs in each column. The best

Table 30.1: Two-Level Full Factorial Experiment Design

| Trial Number | Factor Designation | | | Experiment Response |
	A	B	C	
1	+	+	+	x_1
2	+	+	−	x_2
3	+	−	+	x_3
4	+	−	−	x_4
5	−	+	+	x_5
6	−	+	+	x_6
7	−	−	+	x_7
8	−	−	−	x_8

estimate factor effects can be assessed by noting the difference in the average outputs of the trials. The calculation of this number for the factor A effect is

$$[(\bar{x}_{[A^+]}) - (\bar{x}_{[A^-]})] = \frac{x_1 + x_2 + x_3 + x_4}{4} - \frac{x_5 + x_6 + x_7 + x_8}{4}$$

The result is an estimate of the average response change from the high to the low level of A. The other factor effects can be calculated in a similar fashion.

Interaction effects are a measurement of factor levels "working together" to affect a response; for example, a product's performance degrades whenever temperature is high in conjunction with low humidity. In addition to the main effects, all interaction effects can be assessed given these eight trials with three factors, as shown in Table 30.2. "Interaction columns" can be generated in the matrix by multiplying the appropriate columns together and noting the resultant sign using conventional algebraic rules. In this table the third trial sign, in the AB column, for example, is determined by multiplying the A sign (+) by the B sign (−) to achieve an AB sign (−).

Two-factor interaction effects are noted similarly. For the AB interaction, the best estimate of the effect can be determined from

$$[(\bar{x}_{[AB^+]}) - (\bar{x}_{[AB^-]})] = \frac{x_1 + x_2 + x_7 + x_8}{4} - \frac{x_3 + x_4 + x_5 + x_6}{4}$$

A question of concern in a factorial experiment is whether the calculated effects are large enough to be considered statistically significant. In other words, we need to determine whether the result

Table 30.2: Full Factorial Experiment Design with Interaction Considerations

	Factors and Interactions							Experiment
Trial No.	A	B	C	AB	BC	AC	ABC	Response
1	+	+	+	+	+	+	+	x_1
2	+	+	−	+	−	−	−	x_2
3	+	−	+	−	−	+	−	x_3
4	+	−	−	−	+	−	+	x_4
5	−	+	+	−	+	−	−	x_5
6	−	+	−	−	−	+	+	x_6
7	−	−	+	+	−	−	+	x_7
8	−	−	−	+	+	+	−	x_8

of the two previous calculations is a large number relative to differences caused by experimental error.

If a two-factor interaction is found statistically significant, more information about the interaction is shown, using a plot as shown in Figure 30.1. From this plot, it is noted that there are four combinations of the levels of the AB factors (AB levels: ++, +−, −+, and −). To make the interaction plot, the average value for each of these combinations is first calculated [e.g., AB = ++ effect is $(x_1 + x_2)/2$]. The averages are then plotted. In this plot, A^-B^+ yields a high-output response, while A^-B^- yields a low-output response. The levels of these factors interact to affect the output level.

If there is no interaction between factors, the lines on an interaction plot will be parallel. The overall effect initially determined for the interaction ($\bar{x}_{[AB^+]} - \bar{x}_{[AB^-]}$) is a measure of the lack of parallelism of the lines.

30.3   Conceptual Explanation: Saturated Two-Level DOE

When many factors are considered, full factorials can yield a very large test sample size, whereas a saturated fractional factorial can require a much reduced sample size. For example, an eight-trial saturated fractional factorial experiment can assess seven two-level factors, while it would take 128 trials as a full factorial.

The basic saturated fractional factorial experiment design is illustrated in Table 30.3. The calculated interaction columns give the levels of four additional factors, making the total number of two-level factor considerations seven in eight trials.

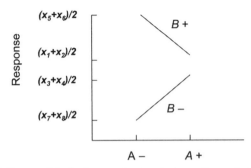

Figure 30.1: A two-factor interaction plot.

Table 30.3: Saturated Fractional Factorial Experiment: Eight Trials, Seven Factors

	Factors and Interactions							
Trial No.	A	B	C	D AB	E BC	F AC	G ABC	Experiment Response
1	+	+	+	+	+	+	+	x_1
2	+	+	−	+	−	−	−	x_2
3	+	−	+	−	−	+	−	x_3
4	+	−	−	−	+	−	+	x_4
5	−	+	+	−	+	−	−	x_5
6	−	+	−	−	−	+	+	x_6
7	−	−	+	+	−	−	+	x_7
8	−	−	−	+	+	+	−	x_8

The disadvantage of this saturated fractional factorial experiment is the confounding of two-factor interaction effects and main effects. There is confounding of the AB interaction and the main effect D. However, there is also confounding of factor D and other two-factor interactions, because of the introduction of the additional factors D, E, F, and G.

Because each column can now have more than one meaning, it is assigned a number, which is called *contrast column number* (see Tables Ml to M5 and N1 to N3).

Table 30.4: Example Output from Table 30.3 Design

Trail Number	A	B	Experiment Response
1	+	+	500
2	+	−	0
3	+	−	0
4	+	+	500
5	−	+	500
6	−	−	0
7	−	−	0
8	−	+	500

It may be hard for the reader to believe that all main effect information of seven two-level factors can be obtained in only eight trials. There may be a concern that the significance of one factor could affect the decision about another factor. To address this concern, assume that E is the only statistically significant factor and that there are no interactions. The question of concern, for example, is whether factor E can affect the decision of whether factor A is statistically significant.

A subset of the matrix from Table 30.3 is shown in Table 30.4 with output that was designed to make factor E very significant. The A and E factor mean effects are

$$
\begin{aligned}
\bar{x}_{[E^+]} - \bar{x}_{[E^-]} &= \frac{x_1 + x_4 + x_5 + x_8}{4} - \frac{x_2 + x_3 + x_6 + x_7}{4} \\
&= \frac{500 + 500 + 500 + 500}{4} \\
&\quad - \frac{0 + 0 + 0 + 0}{4} = 500 \\
\bar{x}_{[A^+]} - \bar{x}_{[A^-]} &= \frac{x_1 + x_2 + x_3 + x_4}{4} - \frac{x_5 + x_6 + x_7 + x_8}{4} \\
&= \frac{500 + 0 + 0 + 500}{4} \\
&\quad - \frac{500 + 0 + 0 + 500}{4} = 0
\end{aligned}
$$

This example illustrates that even though factor E was very significant, this significance did not affect our decision about the nonsignificance of factor A. Like factor A, factors B, C, D, F, and G, can similarly be shown to be not significant.

The purpose of this example is to illustrate that a main effect will not be confounded with another main effect in this seven-factor, eight-trial experiment design. However, the experimenter must be aware that an interaction (e.g., *BC*) could be making factor *E* appear significant even though factors *B* and *C* individually were not found significant.

30.4   Example 30.1: Applying DOE Techniques to a Nonmanufacturing Process

This example gives an overview of the thought process involved in setting up a DOE experiment and illustrates the application of these techniques. Consider that a high-school administration wants to reduce absenteeism of students in high school.

Several factors can affect school absenteeism. These factors, perhaps identified in a brainstorming session, include the following:

- *Student*: age, gender, ethnic background, and so forth
- *School*: location, teacher, class, and so forth
- *Time*: day of week, class period, and so forth

Consider how you might approach the problem if you were a consultant commissioned to assist with this effort. A typical approach would be to regress factors on the response to determine which factors significantly affect the output. A regression approach might indicate that there was a difference in the amount of absenteeism depending on the gender of the student. Consider what should now be done with the system to reduce absenteeism. Difficult, isn't it? The information from this experiment might be interesting to report in the news media, but suggesting what should be done differently to reduce absenteeism, given this information, would be pure conjecture.

There are several problems with a pure regression approach. First, regression only observes the factors and levels of factors that occur naturally in the system; for example, it would not detect that an increase in pressure beyond normal operating conditions could dramatically improve product quality. Second, it does not assess new factors; for example, a call back program. Third, the conclusion could be happenstance; for example, the phase of the moon might look significant within a regression model because some other factor had a monthly cycle.

After an initial regression assessment, consider using a DOE approach with the following factor designations *A-G:*

A: Day of the week
B: Call back when absent
C: School
D: Class period
E: Mentor if missed a great deal
F: Contract if already missed many classes
G: Gender of the student

Consider what two fundamental differences exist between these factors. Some factors are observations while other factors are improvement possibilities. Day of the week, school, class period, and gender of student are observations, while call back when absent, assignment of a mentor if class is missed often, and contract if a great many classes have already been missed but there are improvement possibilities. Normally, a student would fail if he or she missed more than a certain number of days. This "contract" improvement possibility would offer the student a second chance if he or she agreed to attend all classes during the remaining portion of the semester.

Choose now how to address the levels for each factor. The tendency is to assign many levels to each factor, but this could add much complexity to the experiment. We should always ask whether the additional level is helpful for addressing the problem at hand: determining what should be done to reduce student absenteeism. Consider the number of trials that would be needed if the following levels were assigned to each factor:

A: Day of the week: Monday versus Friday.
B: Call back when absent: Yes versus No
C: School: Locations 1, 2, 3, 4
D: Class period: 1, 2, 3
E: Mentor if missed a great deal: Yes versus No
F: Contract if already missed many classes: Yes versus No
G: Gender of student: Male versus Female

The total number of combinations for a full factorial is ($2 \times 2 \times 4 \times 3 \times 2 \times 2 \times 2 = 384$). This number of trials is impossible for many situations. To reduce the number of trials for the full factorial, consider altering the number of levels to two. To do this, consider the question at hand. Perhaps it can be satisfactorily addressed, for example, by choosing only two schools: the one with the best attendance record and the other with the worst attendance record. A two-level assessment would reduce the number of trials to $2^7 = 128$ trials for a full factorial design. This could be further reduced to 64, 32, 16, or 8 trials using a fractional factorial structure. For fractional DOEs, the alternatives of 64, 32, 16, or 8 trials give varying resolution of factor information. Resolution is related to the management of two-factor interactions. Two-factor interactions may or may not be confounded (aliased) with each other or main effects. To illustrate a two-factor interaction, consider that there was a difference between absenteeism caused by day of the week (Friday versus Monday) and call-back program (Yes versus No), so that the call-back program was much more effective in reducing absenteeism on Friday, perhaps because students would be corrected by parent after weekend calls.

When reducing the number of factors to two-levels, quantitative factors such as pressure would be modeled as a linear relationship. For qualitative factors such as suppliers, schools, operators, or machines, consider choosing the sources that represent the extremes.

For purposes of illustration, consider initially only three of the two-level factors:

- Day of week: Monday versus Friday
- Call back when absent: Yes versus No
- School: 1 versus 2

Eight trials can assess all possible combinations of the levels of three factors (i.e., $2^3 = 8$).

The factors and levels could have the following designation:

	Level	
Factor	–	+
A: Day of week	Friday	Monday
B: Call back when absent	Yes	No
C: School	1	2

One experiment design and response approach could be to select randomly 800 students from two schools. Students are then randomly placed into one of the eight trial categories, 100 students in each trial). The total number of days absent from each category for the 100 students is the response for the analysis.

This approach offers some advantages over a more traditional regression analysis. New factors are assessed that could improve the process, such as a call-back program. Effects from happenstance occurrences are lessened. The eight-trial combinations are as follows:

	Factor Designation			
Trial Number	A	B	C	Response
1	+	+	+	x_1
2	+	+	–	x_2
3	+	–	+	x_3
4	+	–	–	x_4
5	–	+	+	x_5
6	–	+	–	x_6
7	–	–	+	x_7
8	–	–	–	x_8

While considering trial 2, the response would be the total absenteeism of 100 students on Monday with no call back for school 1. We also note from the initial design matrix that there are four levels for each factors for the experiment; that is, four trials had C at a "+" level and four trials had A at a "–" level. The effect for a factor would be the average for that factor at the "+" level minus the average for that factor at the "–" level.

Consider that this experiment yielded the following results. (These data were created so that there was an interaction between factors A and B.)

	Factor Designation			
Trial Number	A	B	C	Response
1	+	+	+	198
2	+	+	–	203
3	+	–	+	169
4	+	–	–	172
5	–	+	+	183
6	–	+	–	181
7	–	–	+	94
8	–	–	–	99

The estimated main effects are

A: Day of week	+46.25
B: Call back when absent	+57.75
C: School	–2.75

By observation, the magnitude of the school effect seems small. The sign of the other two factors indicates which level of the factor is best. In this case, lower numbers are best; hence Friday and call back is best. However, this model does not address the interaction.

As mentioned earlier, a two-factor interaction causes a lack of parallelism between the two lines in a two-factor interaction plot. When sample data are plotted, the lines typically will not be exactly parallel. The question for a practitioner is whether the degree of out-of-parallelism between two lines from an interaction plot is large enough to be considered originating from a true interaction as opposed to chance. This issue is addressed through the calculation of an interaction effect.

An interaction contrast column is created by multiplying the level designations of all main effect contrast columns to create new contrast columns of pluses and minuses:

	Factor Designation							
Trial Number	A	B	C	AB	BC	AC	ABC	Response
1	+	+	+	+	+	+	+	x_1
2	+	+	−	+	−	−	−	x_2
3	+	−	+	−	−	+	−	x_3
4	+	−	−	−	+	−	+	x_4
5	−	+	+	−	+	−	−	x_5
6	−	+	−	−	−	+	+	x_6
7	−	−	+	+	−	−	+	x_7
8	−	−	−	+	+	+	−	x_8

Again, there are four plusses and four minuses in each contrast column. The magnitude of the effect from an interaction contrast column (e.g., AB) relative to other contrast column effects can be used to assess the likelihood of an interaction. Hence, all possible two-factor interaction plots do not need to be plotted. Only those two-factor interactions that are thought to be sufficiently large need to be plotted.

Entering our trial responses in this format yields the following:

	Factor Designation							
Trial Number	A	B	C	AB	BC	AC	ABC	Response
1	+	+	+	+	+	+	+	198
2	+	+	−	+	−	−	−	203
3	+	−	+	−	−	+	−	169
4	+	−	−	−	+	−	+	172

5			−	+	+	−	+	−	−	183
6			−	+	−	−	−	+	+	181
7			−	−	+	+	−	−	+	94
8			−	−	−	+	+	+	−	99

The interaction effects are determined in a similar fashion to main effects. For example, the *AB* interaction is determined as follows: $(198 + 203 + 94 + 99)/4 - (169 + 172 + 183 + 181)/4 = -27.75$. The following summarizes these results for all main effects and interactions:

A:	Day of week	46.25 (Friday is best)
B:	Call back when absent	57.75 (call back is best)
C:	School	−2.75 (not significant)
AB:	Day*call back	27.75 (significant)
BC:	Call back*school	1.25 (not significant)
AC:	Day*school	−1.25 (not significant)
ABC:	Day*call back*school	−2.25 (not significant)

This summary indicates that the *A*, *B*, and *AB* effects are large relative to the other effects, which are presumed to be the result of experimental error. That is, the magnitude of the day*call back interaction looks significant. We cannot talk about "day of the week" and "call back" without talking about the two-factor interaction. A two-factor interaction plot shows which factor levels are most beneficial. A reduction of this table to create an *AB* interaction plot is

Trial Number	A	B	AB	Response
1	+	+	+	198
2	+	+	+	203
3	+	−	−	169
4	+	−	−	172
5	−	+	−	183
6	−	+	−	181
7	−	−	+	94
8	−	−	+	99

A plot of the average of the four response combinations for *AB* (i.e., *AB* = ++, *AB* = −+, *AB* = +−, and *AB* = −−) shown in Figure 30.2 shows out-of-parallelism of the two lines. The plot indicates that the call-back program helps more on Friday than on Monday. A call back when a student is absent on Friday results in a reduction in

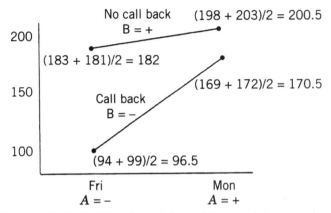

Figure 30.2: Call back and day of the week interaction.

absenteeism. The call-back program for absenteeism on Monday does not appear to reduce absenteeism.

To illustrate how the magnitude of an effect helps assess the out-of-parallelism of a two-factor interaction plot, let us examine the appearance of an interaction that is not thought to be significant (e.g., AC). A subset of the contrast columns to combine for the interaction plot is as follows:

Trial Number	A	C	AC	Response
1	+	+	+	198
2	+	−	−	203
3	+	+	+	169
4	+	−	−	172
5	−	+	−	183
6	−	−	+	181
7	−	+	−	94
8	−	−	+	99

	Experiment			Plot Positions		
	A	C		A		C
1	+	+	198	$(198 + 169)/2 =$		183
3	+	+	169	+	+	
2	+	−	203	$(203 + 172)/2 =$		187
4	+	−	172	+	−	
5	−	+	183	$(183 + 94)/2 =$		138
7	−	+	94	−	+	
6	−	−	181	$(181 + 99)/2 =$		140
8	−	−	99	−	−	

Figure 30.3 shows a plot of these two lines, which are parallel: no interaction is apparently present.

To restate the strategy for two-factor interaction assessments, the effects of two-factor interaction column contrasts are used to determine if interactions are statistically significant. Two-factor interaction plots are used to get a picture of what factor levels are best.

Reflecting again on the differences between this strategy and a regression approach, we were able to identify what should be done differently and to quantify the effects. We can also think about how to modify the current call-back method to improve the effect on Mondays.

The number of trials can increase dramatically if we follow a similar procedure for an increased number of factors. For example, if we similarly assess seven (not three) two-level factors, the resulting number of trials are 128 (2^7 = 128). Consider now the addition of four factors to our original design with the noted levels:

A: Day of the week: Friday versus Monday
B: Call back when absent: Yes versus No
C: School: Locations 1 versus 2
D: Class period: 1 versus 2
E: Mentor if missed a great deal: Yes versus No
F: Contract if already missed many classes: Yes versus No
G: Gender: Male versus Female

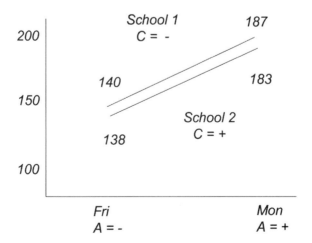

Figure 30.3 Interaction plot where factor interaction is not significant.

A 128-trial seven-factor experiment contains very high factor interactions. It also contains three-factor, four-factor, five-factor, six-factor, and seven-factor. Normally, we assume that any interactions above two are small, if they exist at all; hence, we do not need this many trials. A fractional DOE is an alternative to a full factorial DOE.

Consider again the eight-trial two-level full factorial design with all interactions. An assignment of the four additional factors to the interaction contrast columns yields the following:

| | Factor Designation | | | | | | | |
Trial Number	*A*	*B*	*C*	*D*	*E*	*F*	*G*	Response
1	+	+	+	+	+	+	+	x_1
2	+	+	−	+	−	−	−	x_2
3	+	−	+	−	−	+	−	x_3
4	+	−	−	−	+	−	+	x_4
5	−	+	+	−	+	−	−	x_5
6	−	+	−	−	−	+	+	x_6
7	−	−	+	+	−	−	+	x_7
8	−	−	−	+	+	+	−	x_8

This seven-factor, eight-trial two-level factorial saturated design minimizes sample size, assesses main factor information, and confounds two-factor interactions with main effects. A summary of the main and two-factor interaction effects are as follows:

A:	Day of week (1 versus 2)	46.25 (Friday is best)
B:	Call back (Yes versus No)	57.75 (Call back is best)
C:	School (1 versus 2)	–2.75 (not significant)
D:	Class period (1 versus 2)	27.75 (significant)
E:	Mentor (Yes versus No)	1.25 (not significant)
F:	Contract (Yes versus No)	–1.25 (not significant)
G:	Gender (Male versus Female)	–2.25 (not significant)

From the analysis of main effects, the expectation now for factor *D* is that class period 2 has more absenteeism than class period 1 (about 27.75 days in a semester for 100 students). Strategies discussed later will address concerns that two-factor interaction confounding with main effects will distort conclusions.

The example above illustrates a nonmanufacturing example of DOE techniques. For eight trials the extremes discussed are as follows:

- Three two-level factors (full factorial)
- Seven two-level factors (saturated factorial)

For eight trials, the confounding of two-factor interactions is as follows:

- Three two-level factors (full factorial): all interactions are determined
- Seven two-level factors (saturated factorial): two-factor interactions are confounded with main effects

For eight trials, the resolution designation is as follows:

- Three two-level factors (full factorial): V^+
- Seven two-level factors (saturated factorial): III

However, there are other choices for the number of factors in eight trials instead of three or seven factors. There could be four, five, or six two-level factors examined in eight trials. This additional number of factors can lead to other resolution levels besides III and V^+. Resolution IV designs confound two-factor interactions with each other but not with main effects. Resolution V designs do not confound two-factor interactions with other two-factor interactions or with main effects. Table M shows various resolution alternatives, number of factors for 8, 16, 32, and 64 trials, and design matrices.

30.5 Exercises

1. Create a 16-trial full factorial where the factors have two levels. Determine the contrast columns for all interactions and list them with the factorial design. Comment on the frequency of the plusses and minuses in each column.
2. Explain the setup of a DOE for a nonmanufacturing situation.

31

P-DMAIC: Improve
Phase – Planning 2^k DOEs

31.1 P-DMAIC Roadmap Component

The graphic in this section highlights the project define–measure–analyze–improve–control (P-DMAIC) roadmap steps (see Appendix Section D.1) that are described in this chapter. Appendix E contains the tollgate check sheets for this and other phases.

This is the third of six chapters on design of experiment (DOE). The first chapter in this series provided a background for the power of wisely applied DOE, while the last chapter gave a basic understanding of full and fractional factorial DOEs.

Executing a DOE is not difficult, but time and resources can be wasted if the experiment is not setup *wisely*. This chapter discusses thoughts to consider when setting up a DOE.

31.2 Initial Thoughts When Setting Up a DOE

One major obstacle in implementing an efficient DOE test strategy is that the initial problem definition may not imply that a DOE is appropriate, when in fact it is the best alternative.

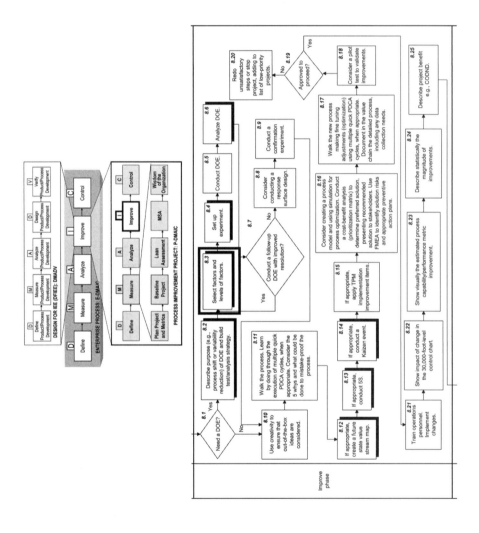

It is often most effective to combine DOE statistical methods with the skills of experts in a field of concern. Because of their structure, DOE techniques are conducive to evaluating in one experiment a collection of agreed-on conditions determined by team brainstorming sessions. This team management strategy tool can be dramatically more efficient than one-at-a time experiments conducted by many individuals independently.

When designing an experiment, it is most important first to agree on a clear set of objectives and criteria. An IEE practitioner needs to consider historical information and ask detailed questions before deciding the details of an experiment. Brainstorming and cause-and-effect diagram techniques can help with collecting this information.

The IEE practitioner should strive to identify all relevant sources of information on factors, their levels, and ranges. Factors that are believed to be important need to be included in an experiment design to produce meaningful results. Factor effects that are not of primary interest in an experiment should be held constant or blocked (as described later). In addition, the sequence of experiment trials should be randomized to reduce the risk of an unknown or unexpected occurrence jeopardizing accurate conclusions. Care should be exercised to ensure that there is minimal error in the measurements for each trial.

After an experiment is determined, its structure is conducive to an individual or team presentation to management and other organizations. The proposed factors, levels of factors, and outputs in the experiment can be presented in a fashion that makes the test strategy easily understood. Perhaps this presentation will provoke a constructive critique that results in a better implementation strategy.

31.3 Experiment Design Considerations

This volume describes unreplicated two-level fractional factorial design matrices from Tables M1 to M5. Other experiment design matrices are also available in tabular form in other books, journals, or computer programs. The basic experiment design strategy suggested in this volume is also applicable to many of these design matrix alternatives.

To most people it seems appropriate to have factors with many levels, which can make an experiment become very cumbersome and unreasonable to conduct. Reducing the number of factor levels and listing associated assumptions can change an experiment's feasibility dramatically.

The next task is to determine what resolution is desired. I often suggest a single replication of a 2^k design, which is sometimes called an *unreplicated factorial*. There is no internal estimate of error (i.e., pure error). One approach for the analysis of unreplicated factorials is to assume that high-order interactions are negligible and to combine mean squares to estimate error. A justification for this is the *sparsity of effects principle*, which states the following: Main effects dominate most systems and low-order interactions, and most high-order interactions are negligible.

In addition, many experiment design considerations fall into two general classifications. The first type needs to optimize a process or help give direction toward a basic problem's resolution, while the second type needs to consider how a product will perform under various situations relative to meeting a specification.

Factor interaction considerations may be more important for the first type of classification than for the second type. In the second type, a continuous response may have many factors that are statistically significant, but if the product is well within criterion, additional analysis may not be necessary. If the statistically significant factor information will not lead to a cost reduction or a reduction in manufacturing variability, the experimenter should avoid analysis paralysis and move on to the next problem/investigation.

In a fractional factorial experiment, there often is a higher probability of problems from unconscious experimental bias or data collection techniques that introduce large amounts of error than from a 16-trial DOE being too of small of sample size. Good techniques can reduce these problems. First, the sequence in which the experimental trials are performed should be random. Second, external nuisance factors may need to be blocked to avoid confusion between them and experimental factor effects.

Note that for some factors, randomization may be very difficult to implement. Whenever the experiment is not randomized, care must be taken to consider that a bias could be the real reason that a factor is statistically significant.

At the end of a DOE, a confirmation experiment should be performed to quantify and confirm the magnitude of statistically significant effects more accurately. A comparison test may, for example, be appropriate to compare the old design with new design considerations that were found statistically significant within the experiment.

The following is a checklist of items to consider when designing a two-level DOE. Note that both a team brainstorming session and historical information should be considered when addressing these issues.

- List the objectives of the experiment. Consider whether the intent of the DOE is the understanding of factor mean effects or variability reduction.
- List the assumptions.
- List factors that might be considered in the experiment.
- Choose factors and their levels to consider in the experiment.
- List what other factors will not be evaluated in the experiment and will be held constant.
- Reduce many-level factors to two-level factors.
- Choose the number of trials and resolution of the experiment.
- Determine if any of the factors will need to be blocked.
- If possible, change attribute-response considerations to continuous-response considerations.
- Determine if any design center points will be used to check for curvature.
- Choose a fractional factorial design.
- Determine if trials will be replicated or repeated.
- Choose a sample size for the number of repetitions per trial and the number of replications needed. Adjust number of trials and experiment resolution as needed.
- Determine a random order trial sequence to use.
- Determine what can be done to minimize experimental error.
- Plan a follow-up experiment strategy (e.g., a higher resolution follow-up experiment or confirmation experiment).
- Plan the approach to be used for the analysis.

The difference between the approximation model and the truth is sometimes referred to as lack-of-fit or model bias. Two approaches historically used to protect from lack of fit is to include special runs for detection (e.g., addition of center points) and decreasing the range of settings, where this second approach does not quantify the amount of lack of fit.

Design efficiency is the amount of information per trial in relationship to a model. Efficiency and the lack-of-fit protection compete. When a design maximizes efficiency, there is not room for the detection of lack of fit; that is, we are implying that the model is adequate.

I prefer DOE matrices that have two-levels, where two-factor interactions will be managed. This leads to designs that have 2^n trials, where n is an integer (e.g., 4, 8, 16, 32, and 64). A resolution III design for these trial alternatives is considered a screening design. There are other DOE experiment options such as Plackett–Burman designs. These designs offer additional trial alternatives such as 12, 20, 24, 38, 36, 40, 44, and 48 trials; that is, $4(i)$ trials where i is an integer and the number of trials is not 2^n. Plackett–Burman designs loose information about where the two-factor interactions are confounded. DOE Taguchi Methodologies offer other design alternatives that contain more than two-levels; for example, L9 and L27, which have 9 and 27 trials for three levels of the factors. These design alternatives which can have several levels also do not address two-factor interactions.

31.4   Sample Size Considerations for a Continuous Response Output DOE

Breyfogle (2003) Appendix Section D1 discusses a mathematical method for determining a sample size to use when conducting a DOE. However, over the years I have found the following procedure and rationale satisfactory for many industrial experiments that have a continuous response output, where the DOE is to assess the significance of mean effects of a response. Note that this discussion does not address sample size issues when the focus of the experiment is to understand and reduce the variability of a response (see Chapter 33).

Many industry experiments can be structured so that they have either 16 or 32 trials, normally with no trial replication and only two-level factor considerations. However, if trials are "cheap" and time is not an issue, more trials are better.

The following discussion illustrates the logic behind this conclusion. With two-level experiment designs, advantages are achieved relative to two-factor interaction assessments when the number of trials are 2^n (i.e., those containing the number of trials in Tables M1 to M5), where n is a whole number. This will then yield 2, 4, 8, 16, 32, 64, 128, ... trial experiment design alternatives. Experiments with 2, 4, and 8 trials are in general too small to give adequate confidence in the test results. Experiments with

64 and higher numbers of trials are usually too expensive. Also, when larger experiments require much manual data collection, the person responsible for this work may become fatigued, causing sloppy data collection. Sloppy data collection can cause high experimental error, which can mask factors that have a relatively small but important effect on the response. In addition, any individual trial mistake that goes undetected can jeopardize the accuracy of all conclusions. Sixteen- and 32-trial DOEs are a more manageable size and can usually address the number of factors of interest with sufficient accuracy. Consider also that a series of shorter tests that give quick feedback can sometimes be more desirable than one long test.

It is perhaps more important than getting a large sample size to do everything possible to achieve the lowest possible measurement error. Often experimental error can be reduced by simple operator awareness. For an individual experiment, there is typically a trade-off between the number of factors, number of trials, experiment resolution, and number of possible follow-up experiments.

A 16-trial experiment may appear to be "too much testing" to someone who has not been introduced to design experiment concepts. An eight-trial experiment, still much better than a one-at-a-time strategy, can be a more viable alternative.

31.5   Experiment Design Considerations: Choosing Factors and Levels

The specific situations to which a DOE is being applied will affect how factors and levels are chosen. In a manufacturing environment, data analysis may subject the best factors and levels to use in an experiment to relate key process input variables to key process output variables. In development, there may be little data to give direction, so that a DOE may be begun without much previous data analysis However, in both cases, a major benefit of the DOE structure is that it gives teams direct input into the selection of factors and the levels of factors.

Factor levels also can take different forms. Levels can be quantitative or qualitative. When the factor takes on one of many different values, for example, the temperature input in a manufacturing process step, this describes a quantitative level, while qualitative levels take on categorical values (e.g., material *x* versus material *y*). The results obtained from the described two-level manual DOE analysis techniques are similar. However, the effect from two levels of a quantitative factor can be used to interpolate an output response for other magnitudes of the factor, assuming that a linear relationship exists between the two-level factors.

There is often a strong desire to conduct an initial DOE with factors that have more than two levels. Initial experiments that have more than two levels can add much unnecessary time, expense, and complexity to the testing process. Before beginning a multilevel experiment, the question should be asked: Why increase the levels of a factor beyond two? When we analyze the response to this question, the initial reasons for having more than two levels often disappear.

In some situations, this transition down from many-level to two-level considerations can require much thought. For example, instead of considering how a process operates at three temperatures, an experiment could first be conducted only at the tolerance extremes of temperature. If there were concerns that the end-condition levels of the factor have similar effects and the midpoint showed a statistically significant difference, one tolerance extreme versus a nominal condition could be used in an initial experiment. If this factor is still considered important after the first experiment, the second tolerance extreme can be addressed in another experiment in conjunction with the nominal condition or another factor-level setting. When the number of factors is not large, a response surface design may be an appropriate alternative.

If a factor has many levels (e.g., four supplier sources), perhaps previous knowledge can be used to choose the two extreme scenarios in the initial experiment considerations, realizing that there is a trade-off between the risk of making a wrong decision relative to the selection of suppliers and the implications of a larger sample size. If there appears to be a difference between these two levels, additional investigation of the other levels may then be appropriate.

When only two levels are considered, the possibility of nonlinearity may raise concern. It is generally best to consider a multiple experiment DOE approach initially and then to use mathematical modeling during the analysis. Curvature can be checked by the addition of center points. If curvature exists in the region of concern, this can be quantified later through another experiment that is setup using response surface methods and evolutionary operation (EVOP) techniques. It is sometimes better to reduce the differences between levels in one experiment so that the response between levels can be approximately modeled as a linear relationship.

There may be concern that there is a difference between three machines where machine is one factor in the test. One of the main purposes for conducting a DOE is to identify improvement opportunities through structured choices. Other techniques treated in this volume are useful for determining and describing differences between such factors as machines, suppliers, and operators. To create a DOE, consider initially identifying the best and worst machine and using these as levels for the machine factor. This approach could lead to an interaction, which could end up determining why the best machine is getting more desirable results.

Another situation that might arise is one factor can either perform at high tolerance, perform at low tolerance, or be turned off. If we take this factor as initially described into consideration, we are forced to consider its levels as qualitative because one of the levels is "off." In addition to the added complexity of a three-level experiment, this initial experiment design does not permit us to model the expected response directly at different "on" settings within the tolerance extremes.

To address this situation better, consider two experiment designs in which each experiment considers each factor at two levels. The first experiment leads to a 16-trial experiment where the two levels of the factor are the tolerance extremes when the factor is "on." The "off" factor condition is then considered by the addition of eight trials to the initial design. The other factor settings for a given trial in the "off" level setting are similar to those used at either the high or low factor setting for the "on" experiment design. This results in 24 total trials, which should be executed in random order.

After collecting the responses from the 24 trials, the data can be analyzed using several approaches. Three simple techniques are as follows. First, 16 trials, where the described factor level is quantitative, can be analyzed separately. If this factor is found to have statistical significance, the model equation can be used to predict the response at other settings besides tolerance extremes. Second, the eight trials for the "off" level can be analyzed in conjunction with the appropriate eight trials from the 16 trials that give a DOE matrix. This analysis will test the significance of the "on" versus "off" levels of this factor. Third, analyze the data collectively using multiple regression analysis techniques.

31.6   Experiment Design Considerations: Factor Statistical Significance

For DOEs, continuous outputs, as opposed to attribute outputs, are desired. A typical DOE conclusion statement might be "Voltage is significant at a level of 0.05." If voltage were a two-level factor in the experiment, this statement means that a response is affected by changing the voltage from one level to another, and there is an α risk of 0.05 that this statement is not true. Statements can also be made about the amount of change in output that is expected between levels of factors. For example, a "best estimate" for a statistically significant factor might be the following: A shift from the high tolerance level of the voltage factor to its low tolerance level will cause an average output timing change of 4 milliseconds (msec).

The next chapter discusses methods for testing for factor significance given an estimate for error. If a factor is statistically significant (i.e., we reject the null hypothesis that the factor levels equally affect the response) the statement is made with a α risk of being wrong. However, the inverse is not true about factors not found to be statistically significant. In other words, there is *not* a α risk of being wrong when these factors are *not* found to be statistically-significant. The reason for this is that the second statement has a β risk; that is, not rejecting the null hypothesis, which is a function of the sample size and δ magnitude. Breyfogle (2003) Appendix Section D1 discusses an approach where the sample size of a factorial experiment is made large enough to address the β risk of not rejecting the null hypothesis when it is actually false.

31.7   Experiment Design Considerations: Experiment Resolution

Full factorial designs are used to assess all possible combinations of the factor levels under consideration. These designs provide information about all possible interactions of the factor levels. For example, a full factorial experiment consisting of seven two-level factors will require 128 trials ($2^7=128$). It will provide information about all possible interactions, including whether all seven factors work in conjunction to affect the output (defined as a seven-factor interaction), as well as information about lower-factor interactions (i.e., any combination of 6, 5, 4, 3, and 2 factors).

In many situations, three-factor and higher interaction effects can be considered small relative to the main effects and two-factor interaction effects. Therefore, interactions higher than two can often be ignored. In such cases, a smaller number of trials are needed to assess the same number of factors. A DOE can assess factors with various resolutions (see instructions in Table M1). A resolution V design evaluates the main effects and two-factor interactions independently. A resolution IV design evaluates main effects and confounded or mixed-up two-factor interactions; that is, there is aliasing of the two-factor interactions. A resolution III design evaluates the main effects, which are confounded with the two-factor interactions. Tables M1 to M5 will later be used to give test alternatives for each of these resolutions. Plackett and Burman (1946) give other resolution III design alternatives, but the way in which two-factor interactions are confounded with main effects is often complicated.

31.8   Blocking and Randomization

Many experiments can inadvertently give results that are biased. For example, error can occur in the analysis of experimental data if no consideration is given during the execution of an experiment to the use of more than one piece of equipment, operator, and/or test days. Blocking is a means of handling nuisance factors so that they do not distort the analysis of the factors that are of interest.

Consider, for example, that the experiment design in Table 30.3 is conducted sequentially in the numeric sequence shown over a two-day period (trials 1–4 on day 1 and trials 5–8 on day 2). Consider that, unknown to the test designer, humidity conditions affect the process results dramatically. As luck would have it, the weather conditions changed, and it started raining very heavily on the second day. Results from the experiment would lead the experimenter to believe that factor A was very statistically significant because this factor was + on the first day and − on the second day, when, in fact, the humidity conditions caused by the rain were the real source of significance.

There are two approaches to avoid this unplanned confounding: In the first approach, the experimental trials are randomized. This should always be the goal. If this were done for the above scenario, the differences between days would not affect our decision about factor significance, and the variability between day differences would show up as experimental error. Another approach is to block the experimental trials. This is a better approach for factors that we do not want to consider within our model but that could affect our results (e.g., operators, days, machines, ovens, etc.).

An application example for blocking in Table 30.3 is that "day" could have been blocked using the *ABC* interaction column. The trial numbers 1, 4, 6, and 7 could then be performed in random sequence the first day, while the other four trials could be exercised in random sequence on the second day. If the block on "day" was shown to be statistically significant, then the conclusion would be that something changed from day 1 to day 2. However, the specific cause of the difference may not be understood to the experimenter from a basic data analysis. More importantly, this confounding would not affect decisions made about the other factors of interest.

High-factor interaction contrast columns can be used for the assignment of blocks when there are only two-level blocks to consider, as described earlier. However, care must be exercised when there are more than two levels in a block. Consider that four ovens are to be used in an experiment. Undesirable confounding can result if two high-factor interaction contrast columns are arbitrarily chosen to describe the trials that will use each of the ovens (i.e., – – = oven 1, – + = oven 2, + – = oven 3, and + + = oven 4). Commercially available computer statistical packages often offer various blocking alternatives.

Blocking reduces the number of factor you can use in a DOE since it uses one of the contrast columns.

31.9   Curvature Check

In a two-level experiment design, linearity is assumed between the factor level extremes. When factors are from a continuous scale, or a quantitative factor, (e.g., factor *A* is an adjustment value that can take on any value from 1 to 10, as opposed to discrete levels, or a qualitative factor such as supplier 1 versus supplier 2), a curvature check can be made to evaluate the validity of this assumption by adding center points to the design matrix.

To illustrate this procedure, the average of the four response trials for a 2^2 full factorial (i.e., – –, + –, – +, and + +) can be compared to the average of the trials that were taken separately at the average of levels of each of the factor extremes. The difference between these two numbers can then be compared to see if there is a statistically significant difference in their magnitudes, in which case a curvature exists. In lieu of a manual approach, some computer programs can perform a statistical check for curvature. The examples discussed in this chapter do not have trials setup to make a curvature check, but this topic will be addressed in the response surface chapter.

Center points may not be appropriate in a design

- If the design has more than one or two factors that are qualitative.
- If a technical assessment indicates that the difference between the high- and low-factor levels is not large enough for curvature detection.
- If it is unlikely that curvature could be detected because the magnitude of experimental error is not small and not many center points can economically be run.
- If economic and time constraints indicate that the number of additional trials needed beyond a factorial design to be able to detect curvature is prohibitive.

31.10 Applying IEE

Many "what ifs" can be made about experimental designs proposed by others. A good way to overcome challenges is to bring potential challenging parties and/or organizations into a brainstorming session when planning DOEs. One of the main benefits of a DOE is that the selection of factors and levels of factors is the ideal topic for a brainstorming session. Better designs typically result from this activity. In addition, there will be more buy-in to the basic strategy and results when they become available.

When planning a DOE, write down the options. For example, consider whether suppliers should be considered a controlled or noise factor within the design (see Chapter 33). Also, consider the cost of doing nothing; a DOE may not be the right thing to do.

When planning the execution of a DOE where experimental trials are expensive, it might be advantageous to begin with trials that are the least expensive and evaluate the trial results as they occur. These findings might give direction to a solution before all trials are completed.

31.11   Exercises

1. The position of the leads on an electronic component is important for getting a satisfactory solder mount of the component to an electronic printed circuit board. There is concern that an electronic tester of the component function is bending the component leads. To monitor physical changes from tester handling, the leads from a sample of components are noted before and after handling.

    (a) Create a plan for implementing a DOE that assesses what should be done differently to reduce the amount of bending on each component. Consider the selection of measurement response, selection of factors, and results validation.

    (b) Create a plan that could be used in the future for a similar machine setup.

2. A machine measures the peel-back force necessary to remove the packaging for electrical components. The tester records an output force that changes as the packaging is separated. The process was found to be incapable of consistently meeting specification limits. The average peel-back force needed to be reduced.

    (a) Create a DOE plan to determine what should be done to improve the process capability/performance metric.

    (b) Create a plan that the company could use in the future to setup similar equipment to avoid this type of problem.

3. Half of the trials for an experiment need to be conducted on Monday, while the remaining trials need to be conducted on Tuesday. Describe what should be done to avoid potential changes from Monday to Tuesday affecting conclusions about the other factors.

4. Create a list of items that is important for a successful DOE and another list of things that can go wrong with a DOE.

5. In Example 28.2, a multiple regression analysis created a best subset model from the consideration of four input factors. Plan the factors and the levels of the factors for a DOE, given that the desired throughput is to be at least 25. A new design is also to be considered within the DOE, along with plant location. Maximum acceptable ranges for the input variables are

A: 6–9
B: 1–5
C: 3–4
D: 135–180
E: Design (old versus new)
F: Plant (location 1 versus location 2)

32

P-DMAIC – Improve Phase: Design and Analysis of 2^k DOEs

32.1   P-DMAIC Roadmap Component

This is the fourth of six chapters on design of experiment (DOE). The first chapter in this series provided a background for the power of wisely applied DOE. The second chapter gave a basic understanding of full and fractional factorial DOEs, The last chapter discussed thoughts when setting up a DOE, as applicable in the P-DMAIC improve phase or elsewhere.

This chapter describes design alternatives and analysis techniques for conducting a DOE. Tables M1 to M6 in the appendix can be used to create test trials easily. These design patterns are similar to those created by many statistical software packages. The graphic in this section highlights the P-DMAIC roadmap steps (see Appendix Section D.1) that are described in this chapter. Appendix E contains the tollgate check sheets for this and other phases.

The advantage of explaining the creation of test cases using these tables is that the practitioner gains quick understanding of the concept of design resolution. A good understanding of this concept enables the practitioner to create better experiment designs.

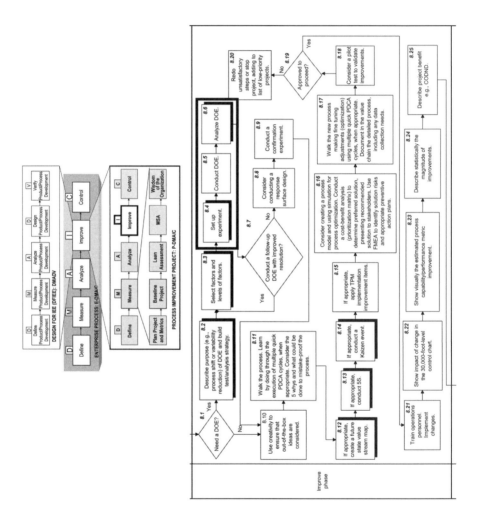

32.2 Two-Level DOE Design Alternatives

It was illustrated above how a saturated fractional factorial experiment design could be created from a full factorial design. However, there are other alternatives between full and saturated designs, which can give differing resolutions to the experiment design. The question of concern is how to match the factors to the interaction columns so that there is minimal confounding (e.g., of main effects and two-factor interactions).

Tables Ml to M5 manages this issue by providing the column selections for the practitioner, while Tables NI to N3 describe the confounding with two-factor interaction. Another alternative to the manual creation of a test design using these tables is to create the design using a statistical software package. However, as described earlier, the novice to DOE techniques gains knowledge quickly by using these tables initially.

Table 32.1 and Table Ml indicate test possibilities for 4, 8, 16, 32, and 64 two-level factor designs with resolution V+, V, IV, and III. To illustrate the use of these tables, consider the eight-trial test alternatives that are shown. If an experiment has three two-level factors and is conducted in eight trials, all combinations are executed; it is a full factorial. This test alternative is shown in the table as 3 (number of factors) at the intersection of the V+ column (full factorial) and the row designation 8 (number of trials).

Table 32.1: Number of Two-Level Factor Considerations Possible for Various Full and Fractional Factorial Design Alternatives in Table M

Number of Trials	Experiment Resolution			
	V+	V	IV	III
4	2			3
8	3		4	5–7
16	4	5	6–8	9–15
32	5	6	7–16	17–31
64	6	7–8	9–32	33–63

where resolution is defined as

V+: Full two-level factorial.
  V: All main effects and two-factor interactions are unconfounded with either main effects or two-factor interactions.
 IV: All main effects are unconfounded by two-factor interactions. Two-factor interactions are confounded with each other.
 III: Main effects confounded with two-factor interactions.

Consider now an experiment in which there are seven factors in eight trials. Table 32.1 shows that it is a resolution III design, which confounds two-factor interactions and main effects. For example, the significance of a contrast could technically be caused by a main effect such as *D,* its aliased interaction *AB,* or other aliased interactions. In a resolution III test, technically a screening design, the experimenter normally initially assumes that the *D* level is statistically significant and then confirms/rejects this theory through a confirmation experiment. This table shows that designs with five, six, or seven factors in eight trials produce a resolution III design.

Table 32.1 also shows that a resolution IV design is possible for accessing four two-level factors in eight trials. In this test, there is no confounding of main effects and two-factor interaction effects, but two-factor interaction effects are confounded with each other. This table also shows resolution V experiment-design alternatives where there is no confounding either of the main effects with two-factor interaction effects, or of two-factor interaction effects with each other. This is possible in a test of five factors in 16 trials.

The next section shows how the experiment trials noted in Table 32.1 can be obtained from Table M.

32.3 Designing a Two-Level Fractional Experiment Using Tables M and N

This section explains the method used to create two-level full and fractional factorial design alternatives from Tables M1 to M5. The confounding structure of these designs is shown in Tables N1 to N3. These designs may look different from the two-level design matrices suggested in other books, but they are actually very similar. Diamond (1989) describes the creation of these matrices from the Hadamard matrix. I have taken the 4, 8, 16, 32, and 64 designs from this work and put the designs into the tabular format shown in Tables M1 to M5.

In Tables M1 to M5, the rows of the matrix define the trial configurations. Sixteen rows mean that there will be 16 trials. The columns are used to define the two-level states of the factors for each trial, where the level designations are + or −. Step-by-step descriptions for creating an experiment design using these tables are provided in Table M1.

After the number of factors, resolution, and number of trials are chosen, a design can then be determined from the tables by choosing columns from left to right using those identified by an asterisk (*) and the numbers sequentially in the header, until the number of columns equals the number of factors in the experiment. The contrast column numbers are then assigned sequential alphabetic characters from left to right. These numbers from the original matrix are noted and cross-referenced with Tables N1 to N3, if information is desired about two-factor interactions and two-factor interaction confounding.

32.4   Determining Statistically Significant Effects and Probability Plotting Procedure

Analysis of variance (ANOVA) techniques have traditionally been used to determine the significant effects in a factorial experiment. The t-test for assessing significance gives the same results as ANOVA techniques but can be more appealing because the significance assessment is made against the magnitude of the effect, which has more physical meaning than a mean-square value, and would be calculated using ANOVA.

DOE techniques are often conducted with a small number of trials to save time and resources. Experimental trials are often not replicated, which leads to no knowledge about pure experimental error. Other analysis methods are then needed. One approach is to use nonsignificant interaction terms (or nonsignificant main effect terms) to estimate error for these significance tests. A method is needed to identify the terms that can be combined to estimate experimental error.

This method is an alternative to a formal significance test in which a probability plot of the contrast column effects is created. For the two-level factorial designs included in this volume, a contrast column effect, Δ, can be determined from the equation

$$\Delta = \left(\sum_{i=1}^{n_{high}} \frac{x_{high\ i}}{n_{high}} \right) - \left(\sum_{i=1}^{n_{low}} \frac{x_{low\ i}}{n_{low}} \right)$$

where $x_{high\ i}$ and $x_{low\ i}$ are the response values of each of the i responses from the total of n_{high} and n_{low} trials, for high (+) and low (−) factor-level conditions, respectively. A plot of the absolute values of the contrast column effects is an alternative plotting approach (i.e., a half-normal probability plot).

Main effect or interaction effect is said to be statistically significant if its magnitude is large relative to the other contrast column effects. When the plot position of an effect is beyond the bounds of a "straight line" through the "nonsignificant" contrast column effects, this effect is thought to be statistically significant. Because this is not a rigorous approach, there can be differences of opinions as to whether some effects are really statistically significant.

Statistical computer programs are available to create this effects probability plot, along with an effects Pareto chart. When no error term exists, these programs sometime use Lenth's method (1989) to display the unstandardized effects, with an accompanying significance assessment.

The contrast columns not believed significant in an effects probability plot and Pareto chart analysis will then be combined to create an estimate of experimental error for a significance test of the other model main effects and two-factor interactions. During the selection of terms for this analysis, I suggest exercising care when using the Lenth's computer-generated probability calculations for unreplicated designs that have no experimental error terms in the model. I have seen cases when significant terms using Lenth's Pareto limits cut-offs did not seem appropriate and other cases when nonsignificant terms seemed appropriate for the model build.

A few things that I consider when selecting terms for this reduced-model analysis from the fractional factorial design effects are

- Large visual transitions from an overall effects probability plot straight line indicate that a contrast column or columns is large relative to other lesser-effect magnitudes. The main effects or interactions in these contrast columns are then considered large relative to the other magnitudes, which are considered to be caused by experimental error. Keep in mind that the magnitude of the effects is important in this selection, not whether the effect is positive or negative.
- For resolution IV and III designs, I observe the following when examining high to low ordered ranking of the Pareto chart effects:
  - When the design has several contrast columns that only have two-factor interactions, I look for a transition in this ranking from main effects, with perhaps a few interactions, to a string of two factor interactions. The beginning of the string of two-factor interactions is an indication to

me where the lower contrast column magnitudes can be considered to constitute the error term of the model. The rationale for this is that, in general, two-factor interaction terms are less likely to occur than main effects.

- In a resolution III design analysis, when main effects are high in a ranking of effects, I look for their interactions to see if they are high in the overall Pareto-chart-effect ranking. When doing this, consideration needs to be made to the aliasing of two-factor interaction effects that may be present in the design. The rationale for this is that two-factor interactions usually have one or more of their factor effects that are significant.

32.5 Modeling Equation Format for a Two-Level DOE

If an experimenter has a situation where "lower is always better" or "higher is always better," the choice of the statistically significant factor levels to use either in a conformation or follow-up experiment may be obvious, after some simple data analyses. However, in some situations a mathematical model is needed for the purpose of estimating the response as a function of the factor-level considerations.

For a seven-factor two-level test, the modeling equation, without interaction terms, would initially take the form

$$y = b_0 + b_1 x_1 + b_2 x_2 + b_3 x_3 + b_4 x_4 + b_5 x_5 + b_6 x_6 + b_7 x_7$$

where y is the response and b_0 would be the average of all the trials. In this equation, b_1 to b_7 are half of the calculated effects of the factors x_1 (factor A) to x_7 (factor G), noting that x_1 to x_7 would take on values of -1 or $+1$.

The reader should not confuse the x_1 to x_7 nomenclature used in this equation with the output response nomenclature shown previously (e.g., in Table 30.1).

The model resulting from the experimental responses shown in Table 30.4 would be

$$y = 250 + 0(x_1) + 0(x_2) + 0(x_3) + 0(x_4) + 250(x_5) + 0(x_6) + 0(x_7)$$

Because b_5 is the E factor or x_5 factor consideration coefficient, it would have a value of 250. This equation would reduce to $y = 250 + 250(x_5)$. We then note that when factor E is high (i.e., $x_5 = 1$), the response y is equal to 500 and when E is low (i.e., $x_5 = -1$) the response y is equal to zero.

This equation form assumes that the factor levels have a linear relationship with the response. Center points may have been included in the basic experiment design to check this assumption. The results from one or more two-level DOEs might lead a practitioner from considering many factors initially to considering a few factors that may need to be analyzed further using response surface techniques.

Interaction terms in a model are added as the product of the factors, as illustrated in the equation

$$y = b_0 + b_1 x_1 + b_2 x_2 + b_{12} x_1 x_2$$

If an interaction term is found statistically significant, the hierarchy rule states that all main factors and lower interaction terms that are a part of the statistically significant interaction should be included in the model.

32.6   Example 32.1: A Resolution V DOE

The settle-out time of a stepper motor was a critical item in the design of a document printer. The product development group proposed a change to the stepping sequence algorithm that they believed would improve the settle-out characteristics of the motor. Note that this wording is typical in industry. Both specification vagueness and engineering change evaluation exist.

One approach to this problem would be to manufacture several motors and monitor their settle-out time. If we assume that these motors are a random sample, a confidence interval on the average settle-out characteristics of the motor could then be determined. Another approach could also be to determine the percentage of population characteristics by using probability plotting techniques. However, the original problem did not mention any specification. One could also object that the sample would not necessarily be representative of future product builds.

What the development organization was really proposing was an improved design. This could lead one to perform a comparison test between the old design and new design, perhaps conducted as a paired comparison test. Because several adjustments and environmental conditions could affect this comparison, test conditions for making this comparison would have to be determined. A DOE addresses this question and can often provide more information than just "between algorithm effects."

Consider that a team brainstorming technique was conducted to determine which factors would be considered in the experiment relative to the response, i.e., motor settle-out time. The resulting factor assignments and associated levels were as follows:

		Levels	
Factors and Their Designations		(−)	(+)
A: Motor temperature	(mot_temp)	Cold	Hot
B: Algorithm	(algor)	Current design	Proposed redesign
C: Motor adjustment	(mot_adj)	Low tolerance	High tolerance
D: External adjustment	(ext_adj)	Low tolerance	High tolerance
E: Supply voltage	(sup_volt)	Low tolerance	High tolerance

The development and test group team agreed to evaluate these five two-level factors in a resolution V design. This factorial design is sometimes called a half-fraction since 16 trials of the 32 full factorial trials are evaluated. It can also be given the designation of 2^{5-1} since

$$\tfrac{1}{2}\,(2^5) = 2^{-1}\,2^5 = 2^5\,2^{-1} = 2^{5-1}$$

Table 32.1 (or instructions on Table M1) shows that 16 test trials are needed to get this resolution with the five two-level factors. Table 32.2 illustrates the procedure for extracting the design matrix trials from Table M3. Table 32.3 shows the resulting resolution V design matrix with trial response outputs. From Table N, it is noted for this design that all the contrast columns contain either a main or two-factor interaction effect. There are no contrast columns with three-factor and higher interactions that could be used to estimate experimental error.

Table 32.2: Fractional Factorial Experiment Design Creation

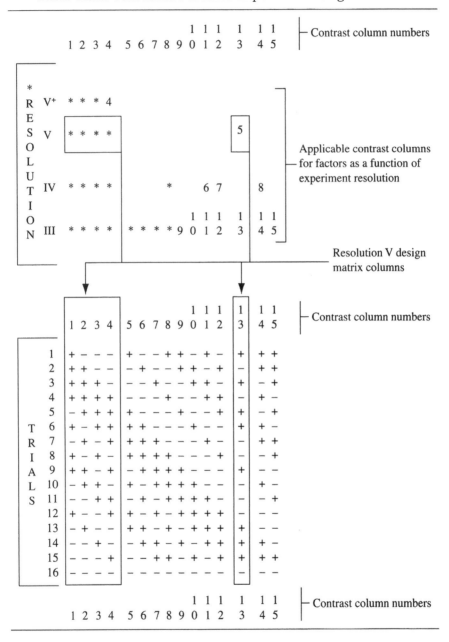

Table 32.3: Test Design with Trial Responses

	A	B	C	D	E	
			Number of Trial Input Factors			Output timing
	mot_temp	algor	mot_adj	ext_adj	sup_volt	(msec)
1	+	−	−	−	+	5.6
2	+	+	−	−	−	2.1
3	+	+	+	−	+	4.9
4	+	+	+	+	−	4.9
5	−	+	+	+	+	4.1
6	+	−	+	+	+	5.6
7	−	+	−	+	−	1.9
8	+	−	+	−	−	7.2
9	+	+	−	+	+	2.4
10	−	+	+	−	−	5.1
11	−	−	+	+	−	7.9
12	+	−	−	+	−	5.3
13	−	+	−	−	+	2.1
14	−	−	+	−	+	7.6
15	−	−	−	+	+	5.5
16	−	−	−	−	−	5.3
	1	2	3	4	13 ──┐	Table M3 contrast column numbers

From this experimental design it is noted that trial 5, for example, would be exercised with:

$$\begin{aligned}
\text{Mot\_temp } (–) &= \text{cold temperature} \\
\text{algor } (+) &= \text{proposed redesign} \\
\text{mot\_adj } (+) &= \text{high tolerance} \\
\text{ext\_adj } (+) &= \text{high tolerance} \\
\text{sup\_volt } (+) &= \text{high tolerance}
\end{aligned}$$

The interaction assignment associated with each contrast column number noted from Table N is

1	2	3	4	5	6	7	8	9	10	11	12	13	14	15
*A	*B	*C	*D	AB	BC	CD	ABD	AC	BD	ABC	BCD	ABCD	ACD	AD
						CE			DE	AE	*E	BE		

We note that all the contrast columns have either a two-factor interaction or main-effect consideration. It should also be noted that the factors are highlighted with an asterisk (*) and that the higher-order terms which were used to generate the design are also shown.

A probability plot of the effects from the contrast columns is shown in Figure 32.1. The normal score for each data point is shown in this plot. The data points can be related to percentage values through the Z Table (i.e. Table A). A Pareto chart of these contrast column effects created from a computer program is also shown in Figure 32.2, with an $\alpha = 0.05$ decision line. When the magnitude of an effect is beyond this line, this factor is thought to be statistically significant. However, the significance decision in these two charts is estimated since the design there is no estimation for error. These charts alone should not be used to select the final model; however, from these plots, it is quite apparent that we expect that factors B and C will later be found significant.

This plot suggests that we should now build a model using only factors *B* and *C* with no two-factor interaction terms. However, in this type of situation, I prefer first to examine a model with all the main effects. The results of this analysis are as follows:

```
Fractional Factorial Fit

Estimated Effects and Coefficients for resp (coded units)
```

Term	Effect	Coef	StDev Coef	T	P
Constant		4.844	0.1618	29.95	0.000
mot_temp	-0.187	-0.094	0.1618	-0.58	0.575
algor	-2.812	-1.406	0.1618	-8.69	0.000
mot_adj	2.138	1.069	0.1618	6.61	0.000
ext_adj	-0.288	-0.144	0.1618	-0.89	0.395
sup_volt	-0.238	-0.119	0.1618	-0.73	0.480

```
Analysis of Variance for resp (coded units)
```

Source	DF	Seq SS	Adj SS	Adj MS	F	P
Main Effects	5	50.613	50.613	10.1226	24.18	0.000
Residual Error	10	4.186	4.186	0.4186		
Total	15	54.799				

```
Unusual Observations for resp
```

Obs	resp	Fit	StDev Fit	Residual	St Resid
6	5.60000	6.96250	0.39621	-1.36250	-2.66R

R denotes an observation with a large standardized residual

The *P* value from this analysis again indicates that factors *B* and *C*, algor and mot_adj, have a high degree of statistical significance, and the other factors are not significant; i.e., their *P* values are not equal to or less than .05. Let's now examine an analysis of the model where only the two statistically significant terms are evaluated.

```
Fractional Factorial Fit

Estimated Effects and Coefficients for resp (coded units)
```

Term	Effect	Coef	StDev Coef	T	P
Constant	4.844	0.1532		31.61	0.000
algor	-2.812	-1.406	0.1532	-9.18	0.000
mot_adj	2.137	1.069	0.1532	6.98	0.000

```
Analysis of Variance for resp (coded units)
```

Source	DF	Seq SS	Adj SS	Adj MS	F	P
Main Effects	2	49.9163	49.9163	24.9581	66.44	0.000
Residual Error	13	4.8831	4.8831	0.3756		
Lack of Fit	1	0.9506	0.9506	0.9506	2.90	0.114
Pure Error	12	3.9325	3.9325	0.3277		
Total	15	54.7994				

```
Unusual Observations for resp
```

Obs	resp	Fit	StDev Fit	Residual	St Resid
6	5.60000	7.31875	0.26539	-1.71875	-3.11R

R denotes an observation with a large standardized residual

This second analysis is a reduction from five model factors to two. In this second analysis residual error is now broken down into lack of fit and pure error. Pure error is represented by replicates since the differences between observed responses are caused by random variation. During model term reduction when a resulting lack-of-fit *P* value is less than the selected α level, the term that was removed from the model should be retained. Our model reduction did not have this issue.

In this output, effect represents the difference from going to two levels of a factor. The sign indicates direction. For example, the effect -2.812 estimates that the proposed algorithm reduces the settle-out time of the selection motor by 2.812 msec (on average). Figure 32.3 shows these factor effects graphically. If

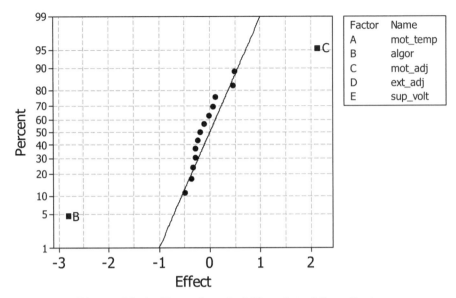

Figure 32.1: Normal probability plot of the effects.

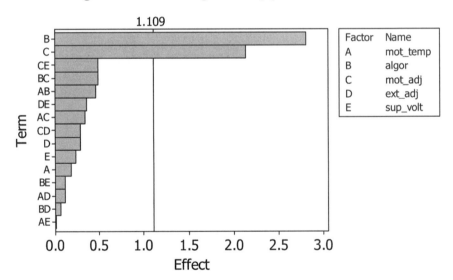

Lenth's PSE = 0.43125

Figure 32.2: Pareto chart of the effects. Lenth's PSE level equals 0.05.

we accept this model and these data, we can create from the coefficients the following estimated mean response model:

$$\text{Motor settleout time} = 4.844 - 1.406(\text{algorithm}) + 1.069(\text{Motor Adjustment})$$

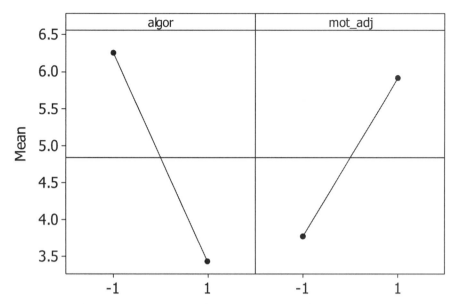

Figure 32.3: Main effect plots of significant factors.

where the coded values used in the equation are algorithm = –1 (current design), algorithm = +1 (proposed redesign), motor adjustment = –1 (low tolerance), and motor adjustment = +1 (high tolerance).

The accuracy of these significance tests and best estimate assessments depend on the accuracy of the assumption that the errors are normal and independently distributed with mean zero and constant but unknown variance. These assumptions are not generally exact, but it is wise to ensure that there are not any large deviations from them. Violations of some basic assumptions can be investigated by examining the residuals of the model. The residual for each trial is the difference between the trial output and the model prediction value. If these assumptions are valid, the data have balanced scatter and no patterns. If there is much deviation from the assumptions, a data normalizing transformation may be necessary to get a more accurate significance test.

The statistical software package output of the data indicates that there is an unusual observation. Table 32.4 shows the residuals and predicted values for each trial. The residual plots of these data in Figure 32.4 and Figure 32.5 are consistent with this computer software package analysis in showing that observation 6 does not fit the model well. Consider now that we

Table 32.4: Experimental Data with Model Predictions and Residuals

Trial No.	mot_temp	algor	mot_adj	ext_adj	sup_volt	resp	Fits	Residuals
1	1	-1	-1	-1	1	5.6	5.18125	0.41875
2	1	1	-1	-1	-1	2.1	2.36875	-0.26875
3	1	1	1	-1	1	4.9	4.50625	0.39375
4	1	1	1	1	-1	4.9	4.50625	0.39375
5	-1	1	1	1	1	4.1	4.50625	-0.40625
6	1	-1	1	1	1	5.6	7.31875	-1.71875
7	-1	1	-1	1	-1	1.9	2.36875	-0.46875
8	1	-1	1	-1	-1	7.2	7.31875	-0.11875
9	1	1	-1	1	1	2.4	2.36875	0.03125
10	-1	1	1	-1	-1	5.1	4.50625	0.59375
11	-1	-1	1	1	-1	7.9	7.31875	0.58125
12	1	-1	-1	1	-1	5.3	5.18125	0.11875
13	-1	1	-1	-1	1	2.1	2.36875	-0.26875
14	-1	-1	1	-1	1	7.6	7.31875	0.28125
15	-1	-1	-1	1	1	5.5	5.18125	0.31875
16	-1	-1	-1	-1	-1	5.3	5.18125	0.11875

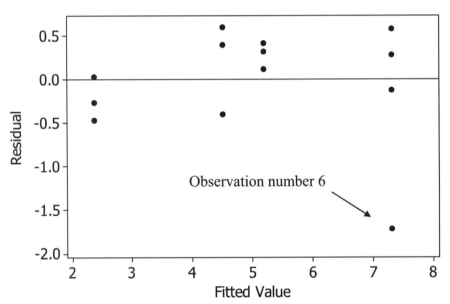

Figure 32.4: Residuals versus fitted values.

examined our data and concluded that there was something wrong with observation 6. A computer analysis of the data without this data point yields the following computer analysis results:

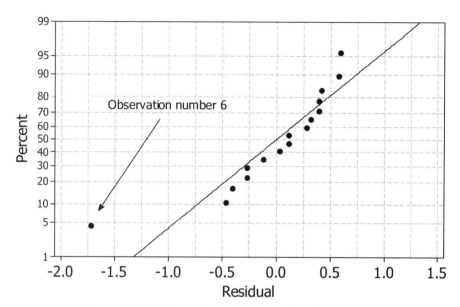

Figure 32.5: Normal probability plot of residuals.

Fractional Factorial Fit

Estimated Effects and Coefficients for resp (coded units)

Term	Effect	Coef	StDev Coef	T	P
Constant	4.976	0.08364	59.49	0.000	
algor	-3.077	-1.538	0.08364	-18.39	0.000
mot_adj	2.402	1.201	0.08364	14.36	0.000

Analysis of Variance for resp (coded units)

Source	DF	Seq SS	Adj SS	Adj MS	F	P
Main Effects	2	52.9420	52.9420	26.4710	254.67	0.000
Residual Error	12	1.2473	1.2473	0.1039		
Lack of Fit	1	0.2156	0.2156	0.2156	2.30	0.158
Pure Error	11	1.0317	1.0317	0.0938		
Total	14	54.1893				

This model does not indicate any unusual observations, which is consistent with the residual plots in Figures 32.6 and 32.7. For this model and these data we can create from the coefficients the estimated mean response model of

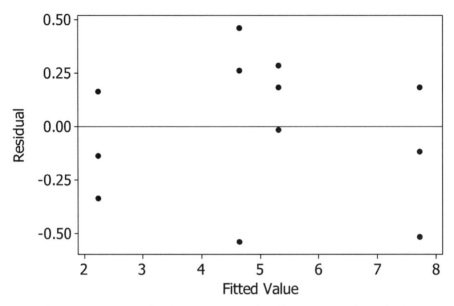

Figure 32.6: Residuals versus Fitted Values (Second Analysis).

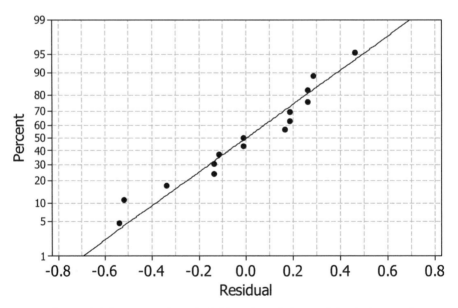

Figure 32.7: Normal probability plot of the residuals (second
analysis).

$$\text{Motor Settleout Time} = 4.976 - 1.538(\text{algorithm})$$
$$+ 1.201(\text{Motor Adjustment})$$

the coefficients of which are slightly different from those of the previous model.

The initial purpose of the experiment was to determine whether a new algorithm should be used to move a stepper motor. The answer to this question is yes; the new algorithm can be expected to improve the motor settle-out time by approximately 2.81 msec. We have also learned that the motor adjustment can also affect settle-out time.

A couple of additional steps can be useful for addressing questions beyond the initial problem definition and for putting the data in better form for presentation. Dissecting and presenting the data in a clearer form can have hidden benefits that may be useful in reducing overall product costs. These additional considerations may point to a tolerance that should be tightened to reduce overall manufacturing variability, resulting in fewer customer failures and/or complaints. Another possibility is that a noncritical tolerance may be increased, causing another form of cost reduction.

In this experiment, the settle-out time was shown to be affected by motor adjustment in addition to algorithm level; a +1 level of motor adjustment on the average increases the settle-out time by 2.1 msec. To understand this physical effect better, determine from the raw data the mean values for the four combinations of algorithm (algor) and motor adjustment (mot__adj):

New algorithm	Motor adjustment low tolerance	2.125
New algorithm	Motor adjustment high tolerance	4.75
Old algorithm	Motor adjustment low tolerance	5.425
Old algorithm	Motor adjustment high tolerance	7.075

Assuming that the decision is made to convert to the new algorithm, a settle-out time of about 4.75 msec with the +1 level of the motor adjustment is expected. This time should be about 2.12 msec with the –1 level of that factor, i.e., a settle-out time difference of 2.25 msec. It would be better if the motor adjustment factor could always be adjusted near the low tolerance; however, the cost to achieve this could be large.

Let's now illustrate what I call a DOE collective response capability assessment (DCRCA). In this study we evaluate the overall response of the DOE to specification limits. Figure 32.8 shows a probability plot of all the data from the 16 trials. This type of plot

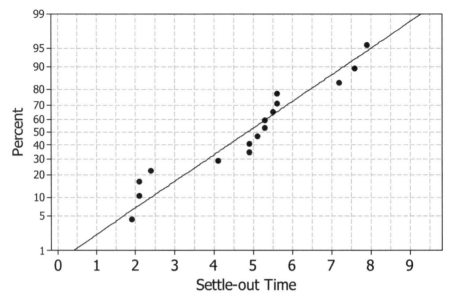

Figure 32.8: DCRCA of settle-out time.

can be very useful when attempting to project how a new process would perform relative to specification limits. If the levels of the DOE factors were chosen to be the tolerance extremes for the new process and the response was the output of the process, this probability plot gives an overall picture of how we expect the process to perform later relative to specification limits. The percentage of occurrence would provide only a very rough picture of what might occur in the future since the data that were plotted are not random future data from the process, noting again that there are no historical data from which a future assessment can be made.

This DCRCA plot can be useful in a variety of situations; however, in this example, our future process would not experience the two algorithm extremes. Only one of the two algorithms would be used when setting up the process. Because of this and the understanding that motor adjustment is also statistically significant, I have chosen to create a DCRCA plot by specific factor levels, as shown in Figure 32.9. This probability plot shows the four scenarios and provides a clearer understanding of alternatives. This plot clearly indicates that combination 4 is superior. The outlier data point from the previous analysis (lowest value for situation 1) again does not appear to fit the model as well as the other data points.

Similarly, using the means and standard deviation values from each of the four combinations, the probability density function

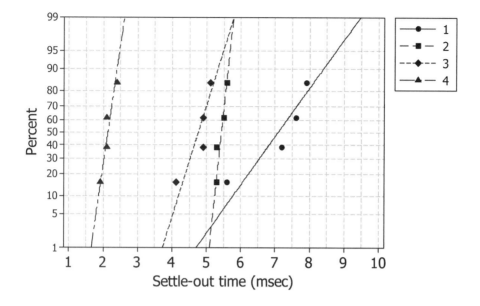

1: Algorithm = − (old)   motor adj = +

2: Algorithm = − (old)   motor adj = −

3: Algorithm = + (new) motor adj = +

4: Algorithm = + (new) motor adj = −

Figure 32.9: DCRCA of the four combinations of algorithm
and motor adjustment.

shown in Figure 32.10 gives a graphical sizing illustrating the
potential effects in another format. Care needs to be exercised
when drawing specific conclusions from these graphs because they
only indicate trends from the calculated estimates and do not represent a random sample of a population with such characteristics.

The experimenter's next step depends on the settle-out time
requirements for the product design. If a settle-out time less than
15 msec, for example, presents no chance of causing a machine
failure, the best decision may be simply to accept the new algorithm with no special considerations about the motor adjustment. However, to obtain additional safety factors for unknown
variabilities, such as motor-to-motor differences, a tightening of the motor adjustment tolerance toward the low tolerance
should perhaps be considered. If, however, the settle-out time

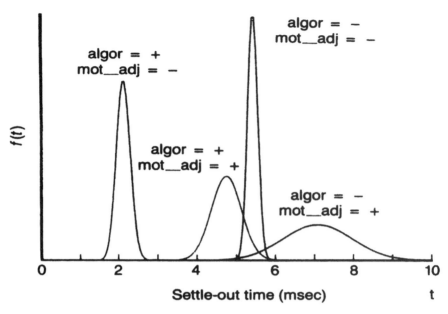

Figure 32.10: PDF "sizing" of the four combinations of algorithm and
motor adjustment.

requirement were less than 6 msec, for example, then another experiment seems appropriate to assess other factors along with the
other statistically significant factor, motor adjustment, in order
to reduce this variability. Perhaps a further extremity below the
current low tolerance level could be considered.

A confirmation experiment should be considered before
utilizing the information from a DOE within a manufacturing or
transactional process. For the previous example, a comparison
experiment might be appropriate using several motors (e.g., 10),
where the settle-out time characteristics of old algorithm/motor
adj = +1 is compared to new algorithm/motor adj = −1. In addition to statistically comparing mean and variance of the two situations, probability plots of the timings for the 10 "new" and "old"
motors could be very enlightening.

32.7   DOE Alternatives

This section provides examples of DOE experiment alternatives for
16 trial tests. Three examples will be illustrated that have different

resolutions for 16 trials. The confounding of main effects and interactions will be discussed. Situation X will be a five-factor 16-trial
experiment, situation Y will be an eight-factor 16-trial experiment,
and Situation Z will be a 15-factor 16-trial experiment. Table 32.5
shows how these designs can be determined from Table M3.

Situation X, which has five factors in 16 trials, is a resolution
V design. From Table 32.5, we note that the design uses contrast
columns 1, 2, 3, 4 and 13. From Table N1, we can determine
the aliasing structure of the 15 contrast columns for this design
to be

1	2	3	4	5	6	7	8
A	B	C	D	AB	BC	CD CE	ABD

9	10	11	12	13	14	15
AC	BD	ABC DE	BCD AE	ABCD E	ACD BE	AD

We note from this summary that all contrast columns have either no more than one main effect or one two-factor interaction.

Table 32.5: DOE Matrix Alternatives

This is a characteristic of a resolution V design. The first row of the contrast column indicates how it was created. Because this is a 16-trial design, four columns are needed to create the 15 contrast columns, i.e., the first columns *A*, *B*, *C*, and *D*. Each of the remaining contrast columns is a multiple of these first four contrast columns and may include a minus one multiple. For example, contrast column 13 is the multiple of *A* x *B* x *C* x *D*. For this design, the fifth factor *E* was placed in the 13 contrast column. The result of this is the other two-factor interaction combinations that contain *E*; e.g., contrast column 12 has a pattern which is the multiple of *A* times *E*.

When conducting an analysis (probability plot or *t*-test), we are assessing the magnitude of each contrast column relative to error. If a two-factor interaction contrast column is large relative to error, our conclusion is that an interaction exists. We would then create a two-factor interaction plot to determine which set of conditions is most advantageous for our particular situation. In the model equation for a balanced design, one-half of the effect would be the coefficient of the multiple of the two factor levels.

Situation *Y*, which has eight factors in 16 trials, is a resolution IV design. From Table 32.5, we note that the design uses contrast columns 1, 2, 3, 4, 8, 11, 12, and 14. From Table N2, we can determine the aliasing structure of the 15 contrast columns for this design to be

1	2	3	4	5	6	7	8
*A	*B	*C	*D	AB	BC	CD	ABD
		DE	AF	EF	*E		
		CF	DG	BG			
		GH	EH	AH			

9	10	11	12	13	14	15
AC	BD	ABC	BCD	ABCD	ACD	AD
BF	AE	*F	*G	CE	*H	BE
EG	CG			DF		FG
DH	FH			AG		CH
				BH		

We note from this summary that all contrast columns have either one main effect or two-factor interactions. This is a characteristic of a resolution IV design. If the design has less than eight factors, the inappropriate two-factor interactions are not considered part of the aliasing structure. If, for example, there were only seven factors, i.e., *A, B, C, D, E, F,* and *G,* two-factor interactions with *H* would make no sense; e.g., *CH* in contrast column 15.

Situation *Z*, which has fifteen factors in 16 trials, is a resolution III design. From Table 32.5, we note that the design uses all the contrast columns. From Table N3, we can determine the aliasing structure of the 15 contrast columns for this design to be

1	2	3	4	5	6	7	8
*A	*B	*C	*D	AB	BC	CD	ABD
BE	AE	BF	CG	*E	*F	*G	DE
CI	CF	DG	EH	DH	EI	FJ	*H
HJ	DJ	AI	BJ	FI	GJ	HK	AJ
FK	IK	EK	FL	CK	AK	BL	GK
LM	GL	JL	KM	GM	DL	EM	IL
GN	MN	HM	IN	LN	HN	AN	CM
DO	HO	NO	AO	JO	MO	IO	FN
							BO

9	10	11	12	13	14	15
AC	BD	ABC	BCD	ABCD	ACD	AD
EF	FG	CE	DF	EG	AG	BH
*I	AH	AF	BG	CH	FH	GI
BK	*J	GH	HI	IJ	DI	EJ
HL	CL	BI	CJ	DK	JK	KL
JM	IM	*K	*L	AL	EL	FM
DN	KN	DM	AM	*M	BM	CN
GO	EO	JN	EN	BN	*N	*O
BO			LO	KO	FO	CO

We note from this summary that these contrast columns have main effects confounded with two-factor interactions. This is a characteristic of a resolution III design. This particular design is a saturated design because it has 15 factors in 16 trials.

An experiment with enough trials to address all interaction concerns is desirable, but the costs of performing such a test may be prohibitive. Instead, experimenters may consider fewer factors. This would lead to less confounding of interactions but yields no information about the factors not considered within the experiment.

Concerns about missing statistically significant factors during an initial experiment of reasonable size can be addressed by using a multi-experiment test strategy. A screening experiment, perhaps 25% of the resource allotment for the total experimental effort, should "weed out" small effects so that more detailed information can be obtained about the large effects and their interactions through a higher-resolution experiment. A resolution III or IV design can be used for a screening experiment.

There are situations where an experimenter would like a resolution III or IV design but yet manage a "few" two-factor interactions. This is achievable by using Tables Ml to M5 and N1 to N3 collectively when designing an experiment. When using Tables Ml to M5, if there are columns remaining above the number of main effect assignments, these columns can be used for interaction assignments. This is done by using Tables N1 to N3 to assign the factor designations so that the interactions desired appear in the open columns. It should be noted that in Tables NI to N3 the lower tabular interaction considerations are dropped if they are not possible in the experiment. For example, an *AO* interaction should be dropped from the list of confounded items if there is no *O* main effect in the design.

Much care needs to be exercised when using this pretest interaction assignment approach because erroneous conclusions can result if a statistically significant interaction was overlooked when setting up the experiment. This is especially true with resolution III experiment designs. When interaction information is needed, it is best to increase the number of trials to capture this information. The descriptive insert to Table Ml is useful, for example, for determining the resolution that is obtainable for six two-level factors when the test size is increased to 32 or 64 trials.

Even though there is much confounding in a resolution III design, interaction information can sometimes be assessed when technical information is combined with experimental results. For example, if factors *A*, *B*, and *E* are statistically significant, one might suspect that a two-factor interaction is prevalent. It is possible that a two-factor interaction does not contain statistically significant main effects, for example, an "X" pattern on a two-factor interaction plot, but this occurs rarely. From the above aliasing pattern we note that factor *E* is confounded with the *AB* interaction, factor *A* is confounded with *BE*, and factor *B* is confounded with *AE*. For this situation we might plot all three interactions during the analysis to see if any of the three makes any technical sense. This could give us additional insight during a follow-up experiment.

32.8   Example 32.2: A DOE Development Test

The techniques of DOE are often related to process improvement. This example presents a method that can be used in the development process to assess how well a design performs.

Consider that a computer manufacturer determines that "no trouble found (NTF)" is the largest category of returns that they get from their customers. For this category of problem, a customer had a problem and returned the system; however, the manufacturer could not duplicate the problem; hence the category description NTF. This manufacturer did some further investigation to determine that there was a heat problem in the system. Whenever a system heated up, circuit timing would start to change and eventually cause a failure. When the system cooled down, the failure mode disappeared.

A fix for the problem in manufacturing would be very difficult because the problem was design related. Because of this, it was determined to focus on this potential problem in the design process so that new products would not exhibit similar problems. A test was desired that could check the current design before first customer shipment.

The problem description is a new computer design that can fail whenever module temperature exceeds a value that frequently occurs in a customer environment with certain hardware configurations and software applications. The objective is to develop a strategy that identifies both the problem and risk of failure early in the product development cycle.

Computers can have different configurations depending upon customer preferences. Some configurations are probably more likely to cause failure than others. Our direction will be first to identify the worst-case configuration using DOE techniques and then stress a sample of these configured machines to failure to determine the temperature guardband.

From a brainstorming session, the following factors and levels were chosen

	Level	
Factor	−1	1
System type	New	Old
Processor speed	Fast	Slow
Hard-drive size	Large	Small
Card	No card	1 card

Memory module   2 extra   0 extra
Test case   Test case 1   Test case 2
Battery state   Full charge   Charging

Table 32.6 shows the design selected. Temperature was measured at three different positions within the product. An analysis of the data for processor temperature yielded the following mean temperature model:

Processor temperature (est.) = 73.9 + 3.3(system type)
− 3.5 (processor speed) − 0.9(memory module) − 0.8(test case)

Consider that we want to determine the configuration that causes the highest temperature and to estimate the mean component temperature at this configuration. From the modeling equation for the processor, the mean overall temperature is 73.9°. Temperature is higher for some configurations. For example, the processor module temperature would increase 3.3° if system type were at the +1 level, i.e., old system type. The worst case levels and temperatures are

Average	73.9
System type = 1 (old)	3.3
Processor speed = −1 (fast)	3.5
Memory module = −1 (2 extra)	0.9
Test_case = −1 (test case 1)	0.8
Total	82.4

Table 32.6: DOE Results

Trial	System Type	Processor Speed	Hard Drive Size	Card	Memory module	Test case	Battery state	Temp. Processor	Temp. Hard Drive Case	Temp. Video Chip
1	-1	-1	-1	-1	-1	-1	-1	76	58.5	72.8
2	1	1	-1	-1	-1	1	-1	73.7	63.3	71.3
3	-1	-1	1	-1	-1	1	1	73.8	67.2	75.2
4	1	1	1	-1	-1	-1	1	74.8	58.3	73.2
5	1	-1	-1	1	-1	1	1	81.3	66.2	70.9
6	-1	1	-1	1	-1	-1	1	67	56.1	69.1
7	1	-1	1	1	-1	-1	-1	84.1	61.1	69.7
8	-1	1	1	1	-1	1	-1	67.5	63.6	71.7
9	1	-1	-1	-1	1	-1	1	79.4	58.2	65.5
10	-1	1	-1	-1	1	1	1	65.6	62.3	69.6
11	1	-1	1	-1	1	1	-1	78.7	59.2	68.1
12	-1	1	1	-1	1	-1	-1	68.6	61.3	71.5
13	-1	-1	-1	1	1	1	-1	71.6	64.6	74.5
14	1	1	-1	1	1	-1	-1	73.7	56.8	69.8
15	-1	-1	1	1	1	-1	1	74.4	64.2	74.2
16	1	1	1	1	1	1	1	72.3	57.4	69.5

In this model, we need to note that mean temperature is modeled as a function of various configurations. Product-to-product variability has a distribution around an overall mean. If the mean temperature of a configuration is close to an expected failure temperature, additional product-to-product evaluation is needed.

We now have to select a worst-case configuration to evaluate further. In this model, we note that the new system type has a lower temperature than the old system type. Because we are most interested in new products, we would probably limit additional evaluations to this area. We also need to consider that failure from temperature might be more sensitive in other areas of the product, e.g., hard drive.

The model created from the DOE experiment is a mean temperature model. For any configuration we would expect product-to-product temperature variability as shown in Figure 32.11. However, we would not expect all products to fail at a particular temperature because of the variability of electrical characteristics between assemblies and other factors. Hence there would be another distribution that describes temperature at failure because of this variability of product parameters. The difference between these distributions would be the margin of safety for a machine, as shown in Figure 32.12, where the zero value for temperature is an expected customer ambient temperature. This figure indicates that roughly 5% of the products would fail when the internal operating

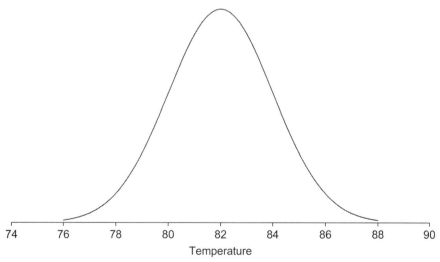

Figure 32.11: Potential product-to-product processor temperature variability.

temperatures of the worst-case configured machines reach a steady-state temperature; i.e., approximately 5% of the area of the curve is below the zero value, which is ambient temperature.

We need next to build a plan that estimates this margin of safety for temperature. One approach would be to select randomly a sample of machines that have a worst-case configuration. This sample could then be placed in a temperature chamber. The chamber could initially be set below the normal ambient temperature chosen. All machines would then be exercised continually with an appropriate test case. After the machines reach their normal internal operating temperature, the chamber temperature would then be gradually increased. Chamber temperature is then documented when each machine fails. Ambient temperature is subtracted from these temperatures at failure for each of the products under test. A normal probability plot of these data can yield the percentage value shown conceptually in Figure 32.12. The resulting percentage is an estimate of the margin of safety for temperature. This information can help determine whether changes are needed.

32.9   Fold-Over Designs

Consider the situation in which a resolution III experiment is conducted. After looking at the results, the experimenters wished that they had initially conducted a resolution IV experiment

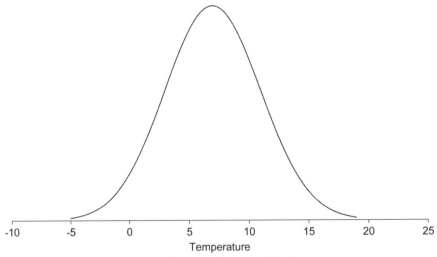

Figure 32.12: Product design margin for temperature.

because they were concerned about the confounding of two-factor interactions with the main effect.

A technique called fold-over can be used to create a resolution IV design from a resolution III design. To create a fold-over design, simply include with the original resolution III design a second DOE with all the signs reversed. This fold-over process can be useful in the situation where the experimenter has performed a resolution III design initially and now wishes to remove the confounding of the main and two-factor interaction effects.

32.10   Applying IEE

I have found that sorting DOE experiment trials by level of response can be an effective tool when looking at the data given by traditional statistical analyses for the purpose of gaining additional insight. Diamond (1989) refers to this approach as "analysis of goodness." This method may help identify factors or combination of factors that affect the response but do not show significance in a formal analysis. In addition, this approach can lead to the identification of a bad data point that distorted the formal statistical analysis. Conclusions from this type of evaluation need further consideration in a follow-up confirmation experiment.

Practitioners sometimes do not consider the amount of "hidden" information that might be included in data obtained from a DOE, even when no factors are found statistically significant. It is obvious that if no factors are found to be statistically significant and a problem still exists, it may be helpful to consider having another brainstorming session to determine other factors to consider and/or how the measurement technique might be improved to give a more reliable response in another experiment. There are situations when looking at the trial response data can be very enlightening. Consider the following:

- If all the response data are "good," then perhaps the experimenter is done with the specific task at hand.
- A ranking of DOE trials according to the level of a response can sometimes yield additional insight into other important interaction possibilities.
- If much of the response data are "bad" but a few trials were especially "good," unusual setup or other conditions should be investigated for these good trials so that these conditions might be mimicked.

- If factors with levels consistent with those used in the manufacturing process were not found to be statistically significant, these tolerances might be relaxed as part of a cost reduction effort.
- A probability plot of the raw experiment data could be useful for showing pictorially the variability of the overall response when the factors vary within the levels set in the DOE.
- A "sizing" for the process capability/performance metric could be made from the raw data information.

Often the output from a DOE is only considered at one point in time, but in many applications a DOE can be considered a part of a process improvement effort. This was illustrated in Example 32.2, where a DOE was part of a process to estimate temperature design margin for a product design. If we consider the creation of product as an output to a development and test process, we could track the design margin over time for similar product vintages. This tracking could indicate whether (and what) changes might be needed in the development process. Example metrics that could be tracked in this matter are electromagnetic emission levels, acoustic emissions, and electrostatic discharge levels.

It is important not only to decide upon an efficient test strategy, but also for the experimenter and team to become involved in the data collection. If this is not done, the data might be faulty because of a misunderstanding, which can lead to erroneous conclusions and/or a waste of resources.

Confirmation experiments should be used to assess the validity and to quantify the benefits of changes resulting from DOE activities. It is always a good practice to document the results of experimental work and to present the benefits in monetary terms so that others, including all levels of management, can appreciate the results. This work will make the justification of similar efforts in the future much easier.

The structure of the examples described in this chapter along with the following robust DOE chapter could be used as a powerful approach to achieve what Taguchi calls parameter design and tolerance design experiments. In a parameter design, effort is given to determine optimum factor settings for a desired response. After these settings are determined, effort is then given to determine the acceptable tolerances (i.e., tolerance design) for key factors so that the desired output will later be achieved in production even considering variation from noise factors; i.e., those that are not controllable. Breyfogle (2003) describes several unique

DOE set-ups and analyses that address these along with other design considerations.

32.11 Exercises

1. A five-factor two-level, 16-trial DOE design is needed.
   (a) List the experimental trials in nonrandom order.
   (b) List the main and two-factor interaction effects in each contrast column.
   (c) Note the experiment resolution and explain what this level of resolution means.
   (d) Describe possible applications of this experiment to both a manufacturing problem and a service problem. Include potential responses and factors.
2. A seven-factor two-level, 16-trial DOE design is needed.
   (a) List the experimental trials in nonrandom order.
   (b) List the main and two-factor interaction effects in each contrast column.
   (c) Note the experiment resolution and describe what this level of resolution means.
3. An 11-factor two-level, 16-trial DOE design is needed.
   (a) List the experimental trials in nonrandom order.
   (b) List the main and two-factor interaction effects in each contrast column.
   (c) Note the experiment resolution and explain what this level of resolution means.
4. A factorial design is needed to assess 10 factors.
   (a) Create a two-level, 16-trial factorial design matrix.
   (b) Note the experiment resolution and explain what this level of resolution means.
   (c) Describe any main or two-factor interaction aliasing with the AB interaction.
   (d) If this is the first experiment intended to fix a problem, note the percentage of resources often suggested for this type of experiment.
   (e) Suggest a procedure for determining the factors and levels of factors to use in the experiment.
   (f) Consider that the analysis indicated the likelihood of a C^*D interaction. Draw a conceptual two-factor interaction plot where $C=+$ and $D=-$ yielded a high value, while the other combinations yielded a low value.

5. The resources for an experiment are limited to 16 trials. There are 14-factors (factor designations are A-N); however, there is concern about the interaction of the temperature and humidity factors. Describe an appropriate assignment of the temperature and humidity factors.
6. Create an eight-trial un-replicated two-level DOE. List the trials in the sequence planned for investigation.
   (a) Include the effects of four factors: A–150 to 300; B–0.2 to 0.8; C–22 to 26; D–1200 to 1800.
   (b) Add five center points.
   (c) Your manager insists that the best combination is when $A = 150$, $B = 0.8$, $C = 26$, and $D = 1800$. If the above design does not contain this combination, make adjustments so that this combination will occur in the experiment.
7. Conduct a DOE analysis of the processor temperature data in Example 32.2. Recreate the model and list/record any assumptions.
8. Conduct an analysis of the hard-drive case temperature response shown in Example 32.2. Create a model. List any assumptions or further investigation needs.
9. Conduct an analysis of the video chip temperature response shown within example 32.2. Create a model. List any assumptions or further investigation needs.
10. Analyze the following DOE data:

A	B	C	D	E	Response
-1	-1	-1	-1	1	38.9
1	-1	-1	-1	-1	35.3
-1	1	-1	-1	-1	36.7
1	1	-1	-1	1	45.5
-1	-1	1	-1	-1	35.3
1	-1	1	-1	1	37.8
-1	1	1	-1	1	44.3
1	1	1	-1	-1	34.8
-1	-1	-1	1	-1	34.4
1	-1	-1	1	1	38.4
-1	1	-1	1	1	43.5
1	1	-1	1	-1	35.6
-1	-1	1	1	1	37.1
1	-1	1	1	-1	33.8
-1	1	1	1	-1	36.0
1	1	1	1	1	44.9

(a) Determine if there are any outlier data points. Comment on the techniques used to make the assessment.

(b) Determine what factors, if any, are statistically significant and to what significance level.

(c) Determine if there are any two-factor interactions. Determine and illustrate the combinations from any interactions that give the greatest results.

(d) Write a model equation with the statistically significant terms.

(e) If B high (i.e., +) were 30 volts and B low (i.e., –) were 40 volts, determine from the model equation the expected output at 32 volts if all other factors are set to nominal conditions.

11. A machine needs to be improved. A DOE was planned with factors temperature 1, speed, pressure, material type, and temperature 2. Create a 16-trial DOE. Fabricate data so that there is a pressure and speed interaction. Analyze the data and present results.

12. A DOE was created to obtain an understanding of how a color response could be minimized with reduced variability in the response. Analyze the data for the purpose of determining the optimum settings. Describe any questions you would like to ask someone who is technically familiar with the process.

Run Order	Film Thickness	Dry Time	Delay	Test Spots	Door Openings	Oven Position	Centrifuge	Shake	Response
1	1	1	1	1	1	1	1	1	0.13
2	−1	−1	1	−1	1	1	1	−1	0.07
3	−1	1	1	1	1	−1	−1	−1	0.26
4	−1	1	−1	1	−1	1	1	−1	0.31
5	1	−1	−1	1	1	−1	1	−1	0.19
6	1	1	1	−1	−1	−1	1	−1	0.25
7	−1	1	1	−1	−1	1	−1	1	0.3
8	1	−1	−1	−1	−1	1	1	1	0.11
9	1	−1	1	−1	1	−1	−1	1	0.11
10	−1	−1	−1	1	1	1	−1	1	0.24
11	1	−1	1	1	−1	1	−1	−1	0.14
12	1	1	−1	−1	1	1	−1	−1	0.19

13	−1	−1	1	1	−1	−1	1	1	0.25
14	1	1	−1	1	−1	−1	−1	1	0.27
15	−1	1	−1	−1	1	−1	1	1	0.34
16	−1	−1	−1	−1	−1	−1	−1	−1	0.16

13. Three factors (A, B, and C) were evaluated within one DOE, where each factor was evaluated at high and low levels. Document the null and alternative hypotheses that would be considered for each factor within the DOE. Upon completion of the experiment, the level of significance for each factor was

    Factor A: p = .04
    Factor B: p = .37
    Factor C: p = .97

    Using hypothesis statement terminology, describe the results of this experiment relative to a desired significance level of .05.

14. Create a five-factor, 16-trial DOE. Randomly generate data such that there is an AB interaction. Analyze the data.
    (a) Describe the trial setup for the standard order trial number one.
    (b) Create the random data such that there is a *AB* interaction.
    (c) Analyze the DOE and describe results.
    (d) Describe an IEE scenario where such a situation could have occurred in your business.

15. Consider that the response from all factors of a 16-trial five-factor DOE was not significant; however, we did not know that. Also, for some unknown reason that there was a dramatic linear increase in the response output for each of the 16 trials. Conduct a DOE analysis for a randomized and nonrandomized design, where the response for trial 1 and 16 is: 0.99, 2.0094, 2.9804, 3.9901, 5.0045, 5.9935, 7.0031, 8.0107, 8.9809, 9.9994, 11.0072, 12.0046, 12.9991, 14.0137, 15.0061, 16.006 (i.e., trial 1 response is 0.99 and trial 16 response is 16.006). Note the generation of this data is from summing the trial number (i.e., from 1 to 16) with a random error of mean zero and standard deviation of .01.

(a) Create a 16-trial, five-factor DOE with nonrandomized trials. Consider the above responses for the trials from 1 to 16. Analyze the data.

(b) Create a 16-trial, five-factor DOE with randomized trials. Consider the above responses for the trials from 1 to 16. Analyze the data.

(c) Comment on the significance of factors for the nonrandom 16-trial, five-factor DOE.

(d) Comment on the significance of factors for the random 16-trial, five-factor DOE.

(e) Give your general comments.

16. Consider that the response from all factors of a 16-trial five-factor DOE was not significant; however, we did not know that. In addition, the experiment was going to have half its trials executed on one day and the other half on another day, where for some unknown reason that there was a dramatic shift in the response output between the two days. Conduct a DOE analysis for a nonrandomized, blocked, and randomized design. The response for trial 1 and 16 is the following: 102.134, 101.719, 99.673, 104.333, 102.98, 102.584, 105.285, 103.539, 83.952, 94.299, 96.272, 93.523, 92.902, 85.158, 78.719, 90.014. (i.e., trial 1 response is 102.134 and trial 16 response is 90.014). Note the random generation of this data is where one set of eight trials had a mean of 100 mean and standard deviation of 5, while the other set of eight trials had a mean of 90 and standard deviation of 5.

(a) Create a 16-trial, five-factor DOE with nonrandomized trials. Consider the above responses for the trials from 1 to 16. Analyze the data.

(b) Create a 16-trial, five-factor DOE with blocked trials. Consider the above responses for the trials from 1 to 16. Analyze the data.

(c) Create a 16-trial, five-factor DOE with random trials. Consider the above responses for the trials from 1 to 16. Analyze the data.

(d) Comment on the significance of factors for the nonrandom 16-trial, five-factor DOE.

(e) Comment on the significance of factors for the blocked 16-trial, five-factor DOE.

(f) Comment on the significance of factors for the random 16-trial, five-factor DOE.

(g) Conduct an analysis of the blocked trials with five-factor DOE. Note the experimental error value used for significance tests (i.e., adjust MS value for residual error).

(h) Conduct an analysis of the random trials with five-factor DOE. Note the experimental error value used for significance tests.

(i) Compare the experimental error value of the blocked experiment to the random trial experiment. Comment on the difference.

(j) Give your general comments.

33

P-DMAIC – Improve Phase: Robust DOE

33.1 P-DMAIC Roadmap Component

This is the fifth of six chapters on design on experiment (DOE). The first chapter in this series provided a background for the power of wisely applied DOE. The second chapter gave a basic understanding of full and fractional factorial DOEs, The third chapter discussed thoughts when setting up a DOE, as applicable in the project define–measure–analyze–improve–control (P-DMAIC) improve phase or elsewhere. The last chapter described design alternatives and analysis techniques for conducting a DOE.

The experiment procedures proposed by Genichi Taguchi (Taguchi and Konishi, 1987; Ross, 1988) have provoked both acclaim and criticism. Some nonstatisticians like the practicality of the techniques, while statisticians have noted problems that can lead to erroneous conclusions. However, most statisticians will agree that Taguchi has increased the visibility of DOE. In addition, most statisticians and engineers will probably agree with Taguchi that more direct emphasis should have been given in the past to the reduction of process variability and of cost in product design and manufacturing processes.

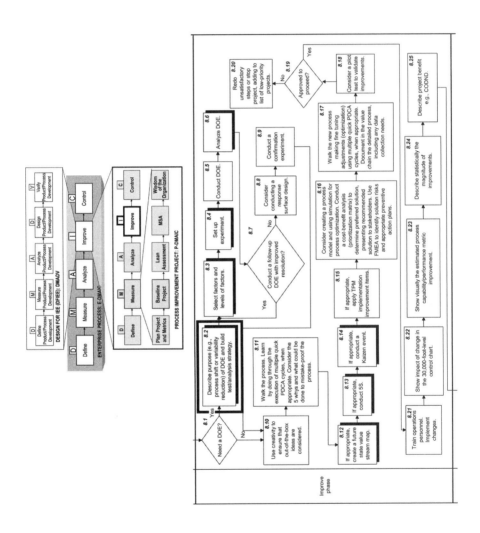

I will use the term robust *DOE* to describe the IEE implementation of key points from the Taguchi philosophy. Robust DOE is an extension of previously discussed DOE design techniques that focus not only on mean factor effects but also on expected response variability differences from the levels of factors. Robust DOE offers us a methodology where focus is given to create a process or product design that is robust or desensitized to inherent noise input variables.

This chapter explains a brief overview of the basic Taguchi philosophy as it relates to the concepts discussed in this volume. The loss function is also discussed, along with an approach that can be used to reduce variability in the manufacturing process. In addition, the analysis of 2^k residuals is discussed for assessing potential sources of variability reduction. The graphic in this section highlights the P-DMAIC roadmap steps (see Appendix D) that are described in this chapter. Appendix E contains the tollgate check sheets for this and other phases.

33.2   IEE Application Examples: Robust DOE

- *Transactional 30,000-foot-level metric*: An IEE project was to reduce days sales outstanding (DSO) for an invoice. Wisdom of the organization and passive analysis led the creation of a robust DOE experiment that considered factors: size of order (large versus small), calling back within a week after mailing invoice (Yes versus No), prompt paying customer (Yes versus No), origination department (from passive analysis: least DSO versus highest DSO average), and stamping "past due" on envelope (Yes versus No). The DSO time for 10 transactions for each trial will be recorded. The mean and logarithm of standard deviation for these responses will be analyzed in the robust DOE.

- *Manufacturing 30,000-foot-level metric*: An IEE project was to improve the process capability/performance metric for the diameter of a plastic part from an injection-molding machine. Wisdom of the organization and passive analysis led to the creation of a DOE experiment that considered factors: temperature (high versus low), pressure (high versus low), hold time (long versus short), raw material (high versus. low side of tolerance), and machine (from passive analysis:

best performing versus worst performing), and operator (from passive analysis: best versus worst). The diameter for 10 parts manufactured for each trial will be recorded. The mean and logarithm of standard deviation for these responses will be analyzed in the robust DOE.

- *Product DFIEE*: An IEE project was to improve the process capability/performance metric for the number of daily problem phone calls received within a call center. Passive analysis indicated that product setup was the major source of calls for existing products/services. A DOE test procedure assessing product setup time was added to the test process for new products. Wisdom of the organization and passive analysis led to the creation of a DOE experiment that considered factors: features of products or services, where factors and their levels would be various features of the product/service, including as a factor special setup instruction sheet in box (sheet included versus no sheet included). The setup time for three operators was recorded for each trial. The mean and logarithm of standard deviation for these responses will be analyzed in the robust DOE.

33.3   Test Strategies

Published Taguchi (Taguchi and Konishi, 1987) "orthogonal arrays and linear graphs" contain both two- and three-level experiment design matrices. In general, I prefer a basic two-level factor strategy for most experiments, with follow-up experiments to address additional levels of a factor or factors. The response surface techniques described in Chapter 34 could also be used, in some cases, as part of that follow-up effort.

The basic two-level Taguchi design matrices are equivalent to those in Table M (Breyfogle, 1989e), where there are n trials with $n-1$ contrast column considerations for the two-level designs of 4, 8, 16, 32, and 64 trials. Table N contains the two-factor interaction confounding for the design matrices found in Table M.

One suggested Taguchi test strategy consists of implementing one experiment (which can be rather large) with a confirmation experiment. Taguchi experiment analysis techniques do not normally dwell on interaction considerations that are not anticipated before the start of test. If care is not taken during contrast column selection when choosing the experiment design matrix, an unnecessary or a messy interaction confounding structure may result, which can lead the experimenter to an erroneous conclusion (Box *et al.*, 1988).

This volume suggests first considering what initial experiment resolution is needed and is manageable with the number of two-level factors that are present. If a resolution is chosen that does not directly consider interactions, some interaction concerns can be managed by using the techniques described earlier. After this first experiment analysis, one of several actions may next be appropriate, depending on the results. First, the test may yield dramatic conclusions that answer the question of concern. For this situation, a simple confirmation experiment would be appropriate. The results from another experiment may lead testers to plan a follow-up experiment that considers other factors in conjunction with those factors that appear statistically significant. Still another situation may suggest a follow-up experiment of statistically significant factors at a higher resolution for interaction considerations.

If interactions are not managed properly in an experiment, again confusion and erroneous action plans can result. In addition, the management of these interactions is much more reasonable when three-level factors are not involved in the design.

33.4 Loss Function

The loss function is a contribution of Genichi Taguchi (Taguchi, 1978). This concept can bridge the language barrier between upper management and those involved in the technical details. Upper management better understands money, whereas those involved in the technical arena better understand product variability. Classical experiment design concepts do not directly translate the reduction of process variability into economical considerations understood by all management.

The loss function describes the loss that occurs when a process does not produce a product that meets a target value. Loss is minimized when there is "no variability," and the "best" response is achieved in all areas of the product design.

Traditionally, manufacturing has considered all parts that are outside specification limits to be equally nonconforming and all

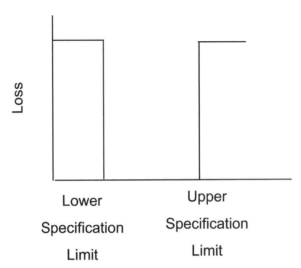

Figure 33.1: Traditional method of interpreting manufacturing limits.

parts within specification equally conforming. The loss function associated with this way of thinking is noted in Figure 33.1.

In the Taguchi approach, loss relative to the specification limit is not assumed to be a step function. To understand this point, consider whether it is realistic, for example, to believe that there is no exposure of having any problems (i.e., loss) when a part is barely within the specification limit, and that the maximum loss level is appropriate whenever the part is barely outside these limits. Most people would agree that this is not normally true.

Taguchi addresses variability in the process using a loss function. The loss function can take many forms. A common form is the quadratic loss function

$$L = k(y - m)^2$$

where L is the loss associated with a particular value of the independent variable y. The specification nominal value is m, while k is a constant depending on the cost and width of the specification limits. Figure 33.2 graphically illustrates this loss function. When this loss function is applied to a situation, more emphasis will be given toward achieving the target as opposed to just meeting specification limits. This type of philosophy encourages, for example, a television manufacturer to strive continually to manufacture routinely products that have a very high quality picture, that is, a nominal specification value, as opposed to accepting and distributing a quality level that is "good enough."

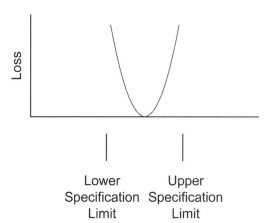

Figure 33.2: Taguchi loss function.

As described earlier, process tracking over time at the 30,000-foot-level is to first establish predictability and then if the process is predictable, provide a prediction statement. For a predictable process, a probability plot provides a gap analysis of how well the specification needs are being met. An improvement in this process capability/performance metric is analogous to an improvement in the process loss function.

33.5   Example 33.1: Loss Function

Given that the cost of scrapping a part is $10.00 when it deteriorates from a target by ±0.50 mm, the quadratic loss function given m (the nominal value) of 0.0 is

$$\$10.00 = k(0.5 - 0.0)^2$$

Hence,

$$k = 10.00/0.25 = \$40.00 \text{ per mm}^2 \text{ (i.e., } \$25,806 \text{ per in.}^2)$$

This loss function then becomes

$$L = 40(y - 0)^2$$

The loss function can yield different conclusions from decisions based on classical "goal post" specification limits. For example, a different decision can result relative to frequency of maintenance for a tool that wears in a manufacturing process. In addition, this loss function can help make economic decisions to determine whether the expense to implement a new process that can yield a tighter tolerance should be implemented.

33.6   Analyzing 2^k Residuals for Sources of Variability Reduction

A study of residuals from a single replicate of a 2^k design can give insight into process variability, because residuals can be viewed as observed values of noise or error (Box and Meyer, 1986; Montgomery, 1997). When the level of a factor affects variability, a plot of residuals versus the factor levels will indicate more variability of the residuals at one factor level than at the other level.

The magnitude of contrast column dispersion effects in the experiment can be tested by calculating

$$F_i^* = \ln \frac{s^2(i^+)}{s^2(i^-)} \qquad i = 1, 2, \ldots, n$$

where n is the number of contrast columns for an experiment. Also, the standard deviation of the residuals for each group of signs in each contrast column is designated as $s^2(i^-)$ and $s^2(i^+)$. This statistic is approximately normally distributed if the two variances are equal. A normal probability plot of the dispersion effects for the contrast columns can be used to assess the significance of a dispersion effect.

33.7   Example 33.2: Analyzing 2^k Residuals for Sources of Variability Reduction

The present defect rate of a process producing internal panels for commercial aircraft is too high (5.5 defects per panel). A four-factor, 16-trial, 2^k-single replicate design was conducted and yielded the results shown in Table 33.1 for a single press load (Montgomery, 1997).

Table 33.1: Experiment Design and Results

Trial	A	B	C	D	Response		Factors		Level −	Level +
1	−1	−1	−1	−1	5.0	A	Temperature	295	325
2	1	−1	−1	−1	11.0	B	Clamp time	7	9
3	−1	1	−1	−1	3.5	C	Resin flow	10	20
4	1	1	−1	−1	9.0	D	Closing time	15	30
5	−1	−1	1	−1	0.5				
6	1	−1	1	−1	8.0				
7	−1	1	1	−1	1.5				
8	1	1	1	−1	9.5				
9	−1	−1	−1	1	6.0				
10	1	−1	−1	1	12.5				
11	−1	1	−1	1	8.0				
12	1	1	−1	1	15.5				
13	−1	−1	1	1	1.0				
14	1	−1	1	1	6.0				
15	−1	1	1	1	5.0				
16	1	1	1	1	5.0				

A normal probability plot of the factor effects in Figure 33.3 indicates that factors A and C are statistically significant. From this analysis we conclude that lower temperature (A) and higher resin flow (C) would decrease the frequency of panel defects.

However, careful analysis of the residuals gives other insight. For a model containing factors A and C, no abnormalities were shown from a normal probability plot of the residuals, but a plot of the residuals versus each of factors (A, B, C, and D) yielded the pattern shown in Figure 33.4 for B. The B factor was not shown to affect the average number of defects per panel, but appears to be very important in its effect on process variability. It appears that a low clamp time results in less variability in the average number of defects per panel.

The magnitude of the B contrast column dispersion effect in the experiment is

$$F_B^* = \ln \frac{s^2(B^+)}{s^2(B^-)} = \frac{(2.72)^2}{(0.82)^2} = 2.39$$

Table 33.2 shows the result of this dispersion effect calculation for all contrast columns. The normal probability plot of these

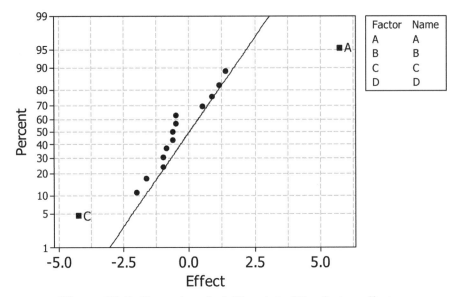

Figure 33.3: Normal probability plot of the factor effects.

contrast column dispersion effects in Figure 33.5 clearly confirms our early observation of the importance of the *B* factor with respect to process dispersion.

33.8 Robust DOE Strategy

Most practitioners of statistical techniques agree with Taguchi that it is important to reduce variability in the manufacturing process. To do this, Taguchi suggests using an inner and outer array (i.e., DOE design structure), to address the issue. The inner array addresses the items that can be controlled (e.g., process speed), while the outer array addresses factors that cannot necessarily be controlled (e.g., ambient temperature and humidity). For an inner-array DOE all trials of the outer array would be conducted.

To analyze the multiple-response trial data, Taguchi converted the trial data to a signal-to-noise ratio, which Box *et al.* (1988) showed can yield debatable results. He describes a better approach where both the trial mean and logarithm of the standard deviation are each analyzed as a separate trial response. With this approach, different factors could be found significant relative to variability reduction and mean response shifts.

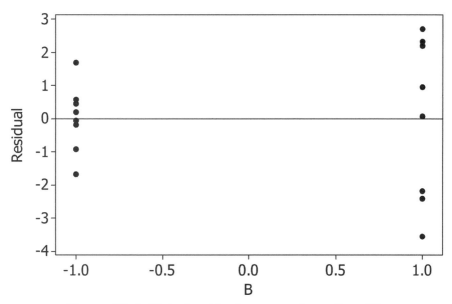

Figure 33.4: Plot of residuals versus clamp time (*B*).

Table 33.2: Calculation of Dispersion Effects

Trial	A	B	C	D	AB	AC	BC	ABC	AD	BD	-ABD	CD	ACD	BCD	ABCD	Residual
1	-	-	-	-	+	+	+	-	+	+	-	+	-	-	+	-0.94
2	+	-	-	-	-	-	+	+	-	+	+	+	+	-	-	-0.69
3	-	+	-	-	-	+	-	+	+	-	+	+	-	+	-	-2.44
4	+	+	-	-	+	-	-	-	-	-	-	+	+	+	+	-2.69
5	-	-	+	-	+	-	-	+	+	+	-	-	+	+	-	-1.19
6	+	-	+	-	-	+	-	-	-	+	+	-	-	+	+	0.56
7	-	+	+	-	-	-	+	-	+	-	+	-	+	-	+	-0.19
8	+	+	+	-	+	+	+	+	-	-	-	-	-	-	-	2.06
9	-	-	-	+	+	+	+	-	-	-	-	+	+	+	-	0.06
10	+	-	-	+	-	-	+	+	+	-	-	-	-	+	+	0.81
11	-	+	-	+	-	+	-	+	-	+	-	-	+	-	+	2.06
12	+	+	-	+	+	-	-	-	+	+	+	-	-	-	-	3.81
13	-	-	+	+	+	-	-	+	-	-	+	+	-	-	+	-0.69
14	+	-	+	+	-	+	-	-	+	-	-	+	+	-	-	-1.44
15	-	+	+	+	-	-	+	-	-	+	-	+	-	+	-	3.31
16	+	+	+	+	+	+	+	+	+	+	+	+	+	+	+	-2.44
$s(i^+)$	2.25	2.72	1.91	2.24	2.21	1.81	1.80	1.80	2.05	2.28	1.97	1.93	1.52	2.09	1.61	
$s(i^-)$	1.85	0.82	2.20	1.55	1.86	2.24	2.26	2.24	1.93	1.61	2.11	1.58	2.16	1.89	2.33	
F_i^*	0.39	2.39	-0.29	0.74	0.35	-0.43	-0.45	-0.44	0.13	0.69	-0.14	0.40	-0.71	0.20	-0.74	

The DOE designs included in this volume can be used to address reducing manufacturing variability with the inner/outer array experimentation strategy. To do this, simply categorize the factors listed into controllable and noncontrollable factors. The controllable factors can be fit into a design structure similar to those illustrated in the previous chapters on DOE, while

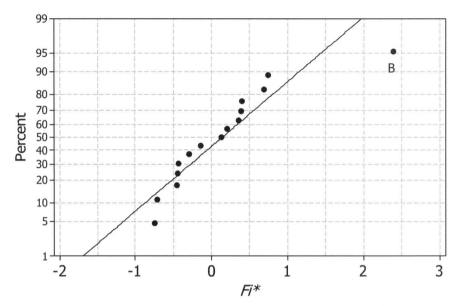

Figure 33.5: Normal probability plot of the dispersion effects.

the noncontrollable factors would be set to levels determined by another DOE design. As described earlier, all the noncontrollable factor experimental design trials would be performed for each trial of the controllable factor experimentation design. Note, however, that in using this inner/outer experimentation strategy a traditional design of 16 trials might now contain a total of 64 trials if the outer experiment design contains four-test trials.

Both mean and standard deviation value can now be obtained for each trial and analyzed independently. The trial responses can be directly analyzed using the DOE procedures described above. The standard deviation, or variance, for each trial should be given a logarithm transformation to normalize standard deviation data.

If the Taguchi philosophy of using an inner and outer array were followed in the design of the stepper motor DOE, the temperature factor would probably be considered in an outer array matrix. This could be done, perhaps along with other parameters, remembering that the mean value needs to be optimized, that is, minimized to meet this particular test objective, in addition to minimizing variability.

A practitioner is not required to use the inner/outer array experiment design approach when investigating the source of variability. It may be appropriate, for example, to construct an experiment design where each trial is repeated and, in addition to the mean trial response, the variance or standard deviation between repetitions is considered a trial response. Data may need a log transformation. The sample size for each trial repetition needs to be large enough so that detection of the magnitude of variability differences is possible. If the number of repetitions is small, the range in response repetitions can yield a better estimate than the variance.

33.9   Example 33.3: Robust Inner/Outer Array DOE to Reduce Scrap and Downtime

A process has very high downtime (Viswanathan, 2005). Scrap is excessive and production efficiency is low from a particular finish weld cell. This problem source is the result of tin/zinc plating thickness inconsistency and variation. The team believes that there is a strong relationship between the thickness and composition variation plating to welding parameters of current, heat, gun pressure, and impulses. A DOE was to assess how to maximize weld strength, that is, nugget size measured through destructive testing, and to minimize variability in weld process.

Table 33.3 lists DOE controllable and noise factors and their levels. The table also contains the eight outer array responses for each trial, along with the calculated mean trial response, standard deviation trial response, and natural logarithm of the trail standard deviation response.

A Pareto chart of the DOE effects from the natural log of standard deviation trial responses is shown in Figure 33.6, along with mean trial responses. From this analysis, it appears that a *BD* interaction significantly affects the natural log standard deviation response. This analysis also indicates that both a *BD* interaction and *C* significantly affect the mean response. The following significance tests support these conclusions.

```
Factorial Fit: LnStdDevResp versus Current, Impulses

Estimated Effects and Coefficients for LnStdDevResp
(coded units)

Term             Effect    Coef  SE Coef     T       P
Constant                -0.0358  0.06674  -0.54   0.601
Current         -0.8203 -0.4101  0.06674  -6.15   0.000
```

```
Impulses              -0.7733 -0.3867  0.06674  -5.79  0.000
Current*Impulses-0.6733 -0.3366  0.06674  -5.04  0.000


S = 0.266956       PRESS = 1.52033
R-Sq = 88.97%      R-Sq(pred) = 80.39%      R-Sq(adj) = 86.21%


Factorial Fit: MeanResp versus Current, Heat, Impulses


Estimated Effects and Coefficients for MeanResp (coded
units)


Term                    Effect     Coef SE Coef       T      P
Constant                         3.6083 0.07165  50.36  0.000
Current                1.2878   0.6439 0.07165   8.99  0.000
Heat                   0.5841   0.2920 0.07165   4.08  0.002
Impulses               1.1206   0.5603 0.07165   7.82  0.000
Current*Impulses -0.5050  -0.2525 0.07165  -3.52  0.005


S = 0.286611   R-Sq = 93.95%    R-Sq(adj) = 91.76%
```

The residual analysis in Figure 33.7 seems to indicate that there could be less variability in the response when the magnitude of the response is at the lowest level. For the mean response, the residuals seem well behaved.

If there are significant factors in both the log/ln standard deviation model and mean model, it is most desirable first to select factor levels that minimize response variability. These factor levels are then used in the mean effect model to determine the other significant factors levels that best achieve the desired target response.

The interaction plot of the *BD* standard deviation response and mean response interactions are shown in Figure 33.8. Since the response levels are easier to interpret, an interaction plot of standard deviation was created rather than the log standard deviation.

From the log standard deviation plot, we would prefer operational levels of Impulse = 2 and current = 83 (i.e., *B* = +1 and *D* = +1), since a low standard deviation is most desirable. From the mean plot, we would also select the operational levels of Impulse = 2 and current = 83 (i.e., *B* = +1 and *D* = +1), since the largest strength is most desirable.

Table 33.3: Factor Levels and Responses for Weld Cell DOE

Signal Factors

Factor	Low	High
Heat	6	8
Current %	77	83
Pressure	19	23
Impulses	1	2

Noise Factors

Factor	Low	High
Plating Thickness	(10-15) microns	>= 20 microns
Plating Composition	(20-25%) Zn	>= 26 % Zn
Electrode	used	new

	N1	N2	N3	N4	N5	N6	N7	N8
Tip wear	+	+	+	+	-	-	-	-
Plating thickness	+	+	-	-	+	+	-	-
Plating composition	+	-	+	-	+	-	+	-

Trials	Gun Pressure	Current	Heat	Impulses	N1	N2	N3	N4	N5	N6	N7	N8	MeanResp	StdDevResp	LnStdDevResp
1	19	77	6	1	2.19	3.32	3.17	2.16	0.01	1.47	0.01	1.48	1.72625	1.25613	0.22803
2	19	77	6	2	5.08	4.7	3.89	4.17	0.01	3.46	4.75	2.64	3.58750	1.64577	0.49821
3	19	83	8	1	4.85	4.63	4.26	5.68	2.02	5.05	5.49	3.6	4.44750	1.18384	0.16876
4	19	83	8	2	4.5	5.28	5.12	4.75	4.77	4.71	4.61	4.83	4.82125	0.25848	-1.35293
5	19	77	8	1	3.29	3.56	3.46	3.78	0.01	1.41	3.97	2.7	2.77250	1.37855	0.32103
6	19	77	8	2	4.14	4.48	4.28	5.88	1.79	4.49	4.88	2.87	4.10125	1.25107	0.22400
7	19	83	6	1	4.54	4.16	4.11	3.55	0.9	4.77	4.83	2.34	3.65000	1.37317	0.31712
8	19	83	6	2	4.53	4.82	4.53	5.04	4.28	4.61	4.61	4.55	4.62125	0.22465	-1.49319
9	23	77	8	1	2.37	4.3	3.98	3.56	0.01	0.01	3.77	0.01	2.25125	1.93793	0.66162
10	23	77	8	2	3.94	4.93	4.29	4.95	3.07	4.17	4.29	2.01	3.95625	0.98400	-0.01613
11	23	83	6	1	3.42	4.3	4.1	5.09	0.85	3.8	3.43	0.53	3.19000	1.63463	0.49141
12	23	83	6	2	4.53	4.67	4.68	4.98	3.72	4.62	4.8	3.48	4.43500	0.53612	-0.62339
13	23	77	6	1	1.8	3.33	3.77	3.08	0.01	0.01	2.84	0.01	1.85625	1.62695	0.48671
14	23	77	6	2	3.79	5.4	4.05	4.7	1.45	3.87	4.44	0.01	3.46375	1.80591	0.59106
15	23	83	8	1	4.57	4.32	4.06	5.42	2.75	6.54	4.65	3.61	4.49000	1.14113	0.13202
16	23	83	8	2	3.82	4.21	4.25	4.42	4.5	4.39	4.88	4.43	4.36250	0.29894	-1.20752

Figure 33.6: Ln standard deviation and mean response Pareto chart of the effects.

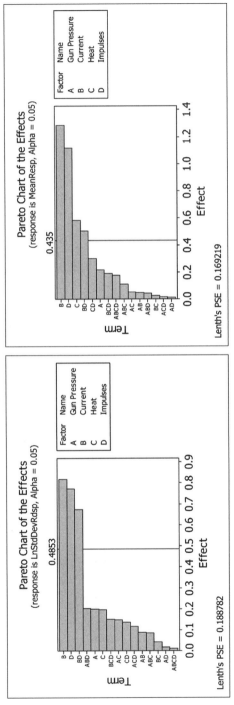

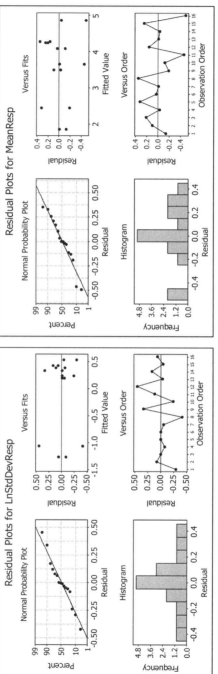

Figure 33.7: Residual analyses of ln standard deviation response and mean response analyses.

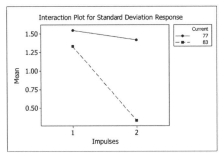

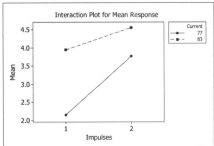

Figure 33.8: Interaction plot of standard deviation and mean responses.

A factor *C* main effects plot is shown in Figure 33.9 for the response mean. Since a higher strength is better, from this plot we conclude that it is best that heat = 8 (i.e., *C* = +1). From the analysis output above, our mean response best estimate is

$$\text{MeanResp} = 3.6083 + 0.6439(\text{Current}) + 0.2920(\text{Heat})$$
$$+ 0.5603(\text{Impulses}) - 0.2525(\text{Current*Impulses})$$

Substitution yields an estimated mean response of

$$\text{MeanResp} = 3.6083 + 0.6439(+1) + 0.2920(+1) + 0.5603(+1)$$
$$- 0.2525(+1*+1) = 4.852$$

We note that the following two trials were conducted at the selected conditions.

Trial	Gun Pressure	Current	Heat	Impulses	N1	N2	N3	N4	N5	N6	N7	N8
4	19	83	8	2	4.5	5.28	5.12	4.75	4.77	4.71	4.61	4.83
16	23	83	8	2	3.82	4.21	4.25	4.42	4.5	4.39	4.88	4.43

Since these values are taken at extreme noise conditions, these data are not a random sample of what we would expect in the future. Because of this, a collective analysis of these data could provide what might be considered a somewhat pessimistic view of the future.

A probability plot of this data is shown in Figure 33.10. This plot provides another picture beyond the overall mean response estimate noted above. This picture not only provides a mean estimate but also addresses what variability could be expected from the process.

One should consider that these estimates provide only a rough picture of what the process could produce. Other factors not

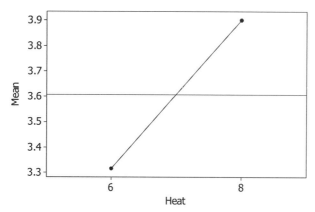

Figure 33.9: Main effects plot of the mean response.

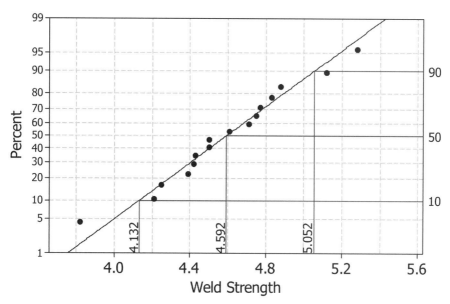

Figure 33.10: Probability plot of data at factor levels that were indicated to be the best.

controlled in this experiment could also impact future performance. However, if the lower strengths noted in this plot are well within what is needed from the process, then we should feel good. If the lower values are not well within the needed strengths, then we would conclude that more work is needed.

If the technical team concludes from the analysis that the projected nugget strength level is sufficiently large to improve the overall process defect rates, a confirmation experiment should be conducted at the selected settings to confirm the experiment conclusions.

33.10   Applying IEE

The mechanics of implementing some of the Taguchi concepts discussed in other books are questionable, but Taguchi has gotten management's attention on the importance of using DOE techniques. He has also shown the importance of reducing variability. DOE concepts with standard deviation as a response can be used to improve the process capability/performance metric of a process. An assessment of residuals in a 2^k design can help identify sources for the reduction of variability.

33.11   Exercises

1. Reconsider how the following situation, which was presented in Exercise 31.1, could be conducted using a DOE centered on the reduction of variability. The position of the leads on an electronic component is important to get a satisfactory solder mount of the component to an electronic printed circuit board. There is concern that, in manufacturing, an electronic tester of the component function is bending the component leads. To monitor physical changes from tester handling, the leads from a sample of components are examined and noted before and after the tester.
    (a) Create a plan for implementing a DOE that assesses what should be done differently to reduce the amount of bending on each component. Consider the selection of measurement response, selection of factors, and results validation.
    (b) Create a plan that could be used in the future for a similar machine setup.
2. Reconsider how the following situation, presented as an exercise, could be conducted using a DOE centered on the reduction of variability: A machine measures the peel-back force necessary to remove the packaging for electrical components. The tester records an output force that changes as the packaging is separated. The process was found not

capable of consistently meeting specification limits. The average peel-back force needed to be reduced.

(a) Create a DOE plan to determine what should be done to improve the process capability/performance metric.

(b) Create a plan that the company could use in the future to setup similar equipment to avoid this type of problem.

3. A manufacturing process has 15 controllable and 3 uncontrollable factors that could affect the output of a process.

(a) Create an inner/outer array test plan if the three uncontrollable factors are ambient temperature, humidity, and barometric pressure.

(b) Describe difficulties that may be encountered when conducting the experiment.

4. Early in development, three prototype automobiles were used to estimate average miles per gallon. The net average of the three vehicles over 20,000 miles was reported to management. Suggest what might be done differently if the objective of the test was to understand the characteristics of the vehicles better relative to sensitivity of different operators.

5. Explain robust DOE setup alternatives for Exercise 29.2.

34

P-DMAIC – Improve Phase: Response Surface Methodology, Evolutionary Operation, and Path of Steepest Ascent

34.1 P-DMAIC Roadmap Component

The last five of the six chapters on design on experiment (DOE) described the application of DOE to the project define–measure–analyze–improve–control (P-DMAIC) roadmap, design for Integrated Enterprise Excellence (DFIEE), and elsewhere. The 2^k DOE techniques described in these chapters consider that there is a linear relationship between factor levels. However, there are situations where the response between factor levels is not linear. In this sixth chapter on DOE, response surface methodology (RSM) is described as a technique to address this situation.

RSM determines how a response is affected by a set of quantitative variables/factors over some specified region. This information, for example, can be used to optimize the settings of a process to give a maximum or minimum response. Knowledge of the response surface can help in choosing settings for a process so that day-to-day variations typically found in a manufacturing environment will have a minimal affect on the degradation of product quality.

For a given number of variables, response surface analysis techniques require more trials than the two-level DOEs; hence, the number

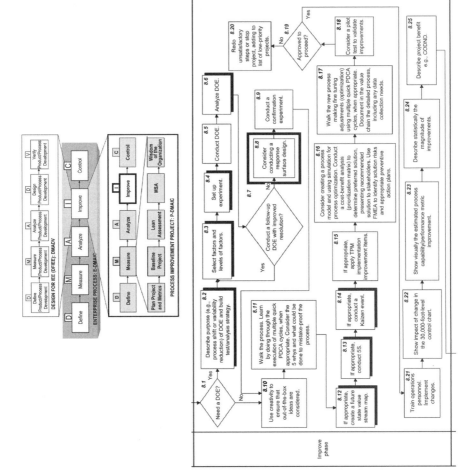

of variables considered in an experiment may first need to be reduced through either technical considerations or a prior DOE.

This chapter explains how to apply central composite rotatable and Box–Behnken designs for determining the response surface analysis of variables, along with evolutionary operation (EVOP). The graphic in this section highlights the P-DMAIC roadmap steps (see Appendix Section D.1) that are described in this chapter. Appendix E contains the tollgate check sheets for this and other phases.

34.2   Modeling Equations

The previous five DOE chapters covered two-level DOE experimentation that considered main effects and interaction effects. For these designs, the response was assumed to be linear between the levels considered for the factors. The general approach of investigating factor extremes addresses problems expediently with a minimal number of test trials. This form of experimentation is adequate in itself for solving many types of problems, but there are situations in which a response needs to be optimized as a function of the levels of a few input factors/variables. This chapter focuses on such situations.

The prediction equation for a two-factor linear main-effect model without the consideration of interactions takes the form

$$y = b_0 + b_1 x_1 + b_2 x_2$$

where y is the response, b_0 is the y-axis intercept, and (b_1, b_2) are the coefficients of the factors. For a balanced experiment design with factor-level considerations for x_1 and x_2, respectively equal to -1 and $+1$, the b_1 and b_2 coefficients equate to one-half of the effect and b_0 is the average of all the responses. For a given set of experimental data, computer programs can determine these coefficients by such techniques as least-squares regression.

If there is an interaction consideration, the equation model would then take the form

$$y = b_0 + b_1 x_1 + b_2 x_2 + b_{12} x_1 x_2$$

The number of terms in the equation represents the minimum number of experimental trials needed to determine the model. For example, the equation above has four terms; a minimum of four trials is needed to calculate the coefficients. The two-level DOE significance tests discussed in previous chapters were to determine which of the coefficient estimates were large enough to have a statistically significant affect on the response (y) when changed from a low (-1) level to a high ($+1$) level.

Center points can be added to the two-level DOE design to test for linearity of the model. When using a regression program on the coded effects, the DOE levels should take on symmetrical values around zero (i.e., -1 and $+1$). To determine if the linearity assumption is valid, the average response of the center points can be compared to the overall average of the two-level DOE experiment trials.

If the first-degree polynomial approximation does not fit the process data, a second-degree polynomial model may adequately describe the curvature of the response surface as a function of the input factors. For two-factor considerations, this model takes the form

$$y = b_0 + b_1 x_1 + b_2 x_2 + b_{11} x_1^2 + b_{22} x_2^2 + b_{12} x_1 x_2$$

34.3 Central Composite Design

To determine the additional coefficients of a second-degree polynomial, additional levels of the variables are needed between the endpoint levels. An efficient test approach to determine the coefficients of a second-degree polynomial is to use a central composite design. Figure 34.1 shows this design for the two-factor situation.

An experiment design is said to be rotatable if the variance of the predicted response at some point is a function only of the distance of the point from the center. The central composite

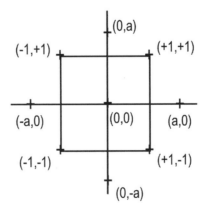

Figure 34.1: Central composite design for two factors.

design is made rotatable when $[a = (F)^{1/4}]$, where F is the number of points used in the factorial part of the design. For two factors $F = 2^2 = 4$; hence $a = (4)^{1/4} = 1.414$. A useful property of the central composite design is that the additional axial points can be added to a two-level DOE design as additional trials after the curvature is detected from initial experimental data.

With a proper number of center points, the central composite design can be made so that the variance of the response at the origin is equal to the variance of the response at unit distance from the origin (i.e., a uniform precision design). This characteristic in the uniform precision design is important because it gives more protection against bias in the regression coefficients than does the orthogonal design, due to the presence of third-degree and higher terms in the true surface. Table 34.1 shows the parameters needed to achieve a uniform precision design as a function of the number of variables in the experiment. From this table, for example, a design assessing five variables along with all two-factor interactions plus the curvature of all variables would be that shown in Table 34.2. Data are then analyzed using regression techniques to determine the output response surface as a function of the input variables.

Cornell (1984), Montgomery (1997), and Box et al. (1978) discuss analytical methods to determine maximum points on the response surface using the canonical form of the equation. The coefficients of this equation can be used to describe the shape of the surface (ellipsoid, hyperboloid, etc.). An alternative approach is to understand the response surface by using a computer contour plotting program, as illustrated in the next example. Determining the particular contour plot may help determine/ change process factors to yield a desirable/improved response output with minimal day-to-day variation. It is important to high-

Table 34.1: Uniform Precision Central Composite Rotatable Designs

Number of Variables	Number of Factorial Trials	Number of Axial Trials	Number of Center Trials	a	Total Number of Trials
2	4	4	5	1.4142	13
3	8	6	6	1.6820	20
4	16	8	7	2.0000	31
5	16	10	6	2.0000	32
6	32	12	9	2.3780	53
7	64	14	14	2.8280	92

Table 34.2: Response Surface Design Matrix for Five Variables

A	B	C	D	E		
+1	−1	−1	−1	+1		
+1	+1	−1	−1	−1		
+1	+1	+1	−1	+1		
+1	+1	+1	+1	−1		
−1	+1	+1	+1	·+1		
+1	−1	+1	+1	+1		
−1	+1	−1	+1	−1		Fractional factorial design from
+1	−1	+1	−1	−1		Table M3
+1	+1	−1	+1	+1		
−1	+1	+1	−1	−1		
−1	−1	+1	+1	−1		
+1	−1	−1	+1	−1		
−1	+1	−1	−1	+1		
−1	−1	+1	−1	+1		
−1	−1	−1	+1	+1		
−1	−1	−1	−1	−1		
−2	0	0	0	0		
+2	0	0	0	0		
0	−2	0	0	0		
0	+2	0	0	0		
0	0	−2	0	0		Axial trials
0	0	+2	0	0		with levels
0	0	0	−2	0		consistent
0	0	0	+2	0		with
0	0	0	0	−2		Table 33.1
0	0	0	0	+2		
0	0	0	0	0		
0	0	0	0	0		
0	0	0	0	0		Center point trials
0	0	0	0	0		consistent with
0	0	0	0	0		Table 33.1
0	0	0	0	0		

light that the response surface shape is a function of the model selected, which is not necessarily the same as the data. A residual review is important to ensure that lack of fit is not significant.

Creating a contour representation for the equation derived from an RSM can give direction for a follow-up experiment using an evolutionary operation (EVOP) or direction of steepest ascent strategy (described later in this chapter).

Table 34.3: Responses in Central Composite Design

Natural Variables		Coded Variables		Yield	Viscosity	Molecular weight
u_1	u_2	x_1	x_2	y_1	y_2	y_3
80	170	-1	-1	76.5	62	2940
80	180	-1	1	77.0	60	3470
90	170	1	-1	78.0	66	3680
90	180	1	1	79.5	59	3890
85	175	0	0	79.9	72	3480
85	175	0	0	80.3	69	3200
85	175	0	0	80.0	68	3410
85	175	0	0	79.7	70	3290
85	175	0	0	79.8	71	3500
92.07	175	1.414	0	78.4	68	3360
77.93	175	-1.414	0	75.6	71	3020
85	182.07	0	1.414	78.5	58	3630
85	167.93	0	-1.414	77.0	57	3150

34.4 Example 34.1: Response Surface Design

A chemical engineer desires to determine the operating conditions that maximize the yield of a process. An earlier two-level factorial experiment of several considerations indicated that reaction time and reaction temperature were the parameters that should be optimized. A central composite design was chosen and yielded the responses shown in Table 34.3 (Montgomery, 1997). A second-degree model can be fitted using the natural levels of the variables (e.g., time = 80) or the coded levels (e.g., time = –1). A statistical analysis of yield in terms of the coded variables is as follows.

```
Response Surface Regression

The analysis was done using coded variables.

Estimated Regression Coefficients for y1 (yield)

Term                  Coef        StDev            T          P
Constant            79.940      0.11909      671.264      0.000
v1 (time)            0.995      0.09415       10.568      0.000
v2 (temperature)     0.515      0.09415        5.472      0.001
v1*v1               -1.376      0.10098      -13.630      0.000
v2*v2               -1.001      0.10098       -9.916      0.000
v1*v2                0.250      0.13315        1.878      0.103

S = 0.2663       R-Sq = 98.3%       R-Sq(adj) = 97.0%
```

```
Analysis of Variance for y1

Source            DF  Seq SS   Adj SS   Adj MS        F     P
Regression         5 28.2467  28.2467  5.64934    79.67 0.000
  Linear           2 10.0430  10.0430  5.02148    70.81 0.000
  Square           2 17.9537  17.9537  8.97687   126.59 0.000
  Interaction      1  0.2500   0.2500  0.25000     3.53 0.103
Residual Error 7     0.4964   0.4964  0.07091
  Lack-of-Fit    3   0.2844   0.2844  0.09479     1.79 0.289
  Pure Error     4   0.2120   0.2120  0.05300
Total             12 28.7431
```

A statistical analysis of yield in terms of natural variables is as follows:

```
Response Surface Regression

The analysis was done using natural variables.

Estimated Regression Coefficients for y1 (yield)

Term                     Coef       StDev           T         P
Constant             -1430.69     152.851      -9.360     0.000
u1 (time)                7.81       1.158       6.744     0.000
u2 (temperature)        13.27       1.485       8.940     0.000
u1*u1                   -0.06       0.004     -13.630     0.000
u2*u2                   -0.04       0.004      -9.916     0.000
u1*u2                    0.01       0.005       1.878     0.103

S = 0.2663   R-Sq = 98.3%      R-Sq(adj) = 97.0%

Analysis of Variance for y1

Source            DF  Seq SS   Adj SS   Adj MS        F     P
Regression         5 28.2467  28.2467  5.64934    79.67 0.000
  Linear           2 10.0430   6.8629  3.43147    48.39 0.000
  Square           2 17.9537  17.9537  8.97687   126.59 0.000
  Interaction      1  0.2500   0.2500  0.25000     3.53 0.103
Residual Error 7     0.4964   0.4964  0.07091
  Lack-of-Fit    3   0.2844   0.2844  0.09479     1.79 0.289
  Pure Error     4   0.2120   0.2120  0.05300
Total             12 28.7431
```

From this analysis, the second-degree model in terms of the coded levels of the variables is

$$\hat{y} = 79.940 + 0.995v_1 + 0.515v_2 - 1.376v_1^2 + 0.250v_1v_2 - 1.001v_2^2$$

This equates to an equation for the natural levels of

$$\hat{y} = -1430.69 + 7.81u_1 + 13.27u_2 - 0.06u_1^2 + 0.01u_1u_2 - 0.04u_2^2$$

These equations will yield the same response value for a given input data state. The advantage of using the coded levels is that the importance of each term can be compared somewhat by looking at the magnitude of the coefficients because the relative magnitude of the variable levels is brought to a single unit of measure.

When projections are made from a response surface, it is important that the model fit the initial data satisfactorily. Erroneous conclusions can result when there is lack of fit. The residuals versus order plot in Figure 34.2 indicate that something could have changed over time or the trials were not conducted randomly. The experimenter should work to understand why this residual shift occurred. I will ignore this shift for the purpose of this example analysis.

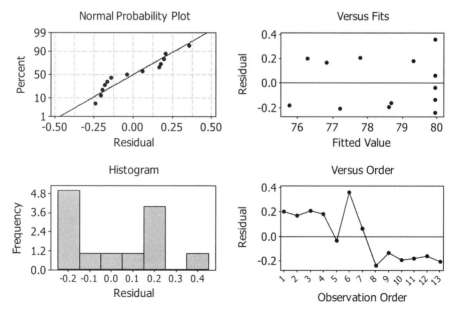

Figure 34.2: Residual analysis of the response surface model.

The computer analysis did not indicate that there was lack of fit; hence, the second-degree polynomial model is accepted. The natural form of this polynomial equation is shown as a contour plot in Figure 34.3 and as a response surface plot in Figure 34.4. From these plots, we could conclude that yield is maximized with a processing time of about 87.5 and a temperature of 177 degrees.

34.5   Box-Behnken Designs

When estimating the first- and second-order terms of a response surface, Box and Behnken (1960) give an alternative to the central composite design approach. They present a list of 10 second-order rotatable designs covering 3, 4, 5, 6, 7, 9, 10, 11, 12, and 16 variables. However, in general, Box–Behnken designs are not always rotatable nor are they block orthogonal.

One reason that an experimenter may choose this design over a central composite design is physical test constraints. This design requires only three levels of each variable, as opposed to five for the central composite design. Figure 34.5 shows the test points for this design approach given three design variables.

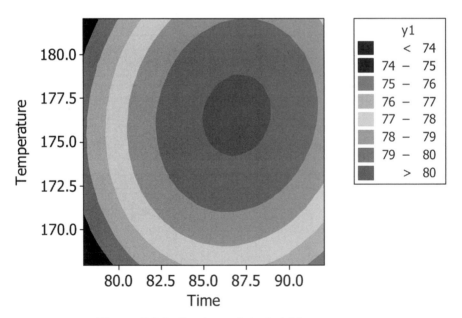

Figure 34.3: Contour plot of yield response.

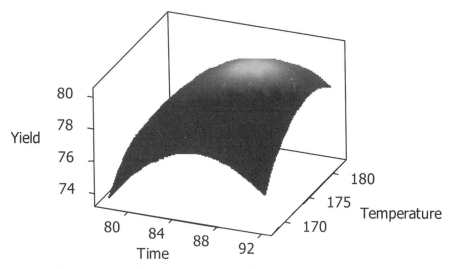

Figure 34.4: Response surface plot of the yield response.

Experiment Trials

x	y	z
+1	+1	0
+1	−1	0
−1	+1	0
−1	−1	0
+1	0	+1
+1	0	−1
−1	0	+1
−1	0	−1
0	+1	−1
0	+1	+1
0	−1	−1
0	−1	+1
0	0	0
0	0	0
0	0	0

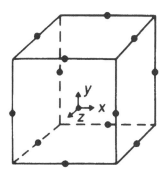

Figure 34.5: Box–Behnken design space for three factors.

34.6   Additional Response Surface Design Considerations

When no linear relationship exists between the regressors, they are said to be orthogonal. For these situations, the following inferences can be made relatively easily:

- Estimation and/or prediction
- Identification of relative effects of regressor variables
- Selection of a set of variables for the model

However, conclusions from the analysis-of-response surface designs may be misleading because of dependencies between the regressors. When near-linear dependencies exist between the regressors, multicollinearity is said to be prevalent. Additional books [e.g., Montgomery and Peck (1982)] discuss diagnostic procedures for this problem (e.g., variance inflation factor) along with other procedures used to understand better the output from regression analyses (e.g., detecting influential observations).

Additional book design alternatives to the central composite and Box–Behnken designs are discussed in Cornell (1984), Montgomery (1997), and Khuri and Cornell (1987). "Algorithm" designs can also be applied to nonmixture problems, as discussed in Wheeler (1989), where, as described earlier, algorithm designs are "optimized" to fit a particular model (e.g., linear or quadratic), with a given set of factor considerations.

34.7   Evolutionary Operation

Evolutionary operation (EVOP) is an analytical approach targeted at securing data from a manufacturing process where process conditions are varied in a planned factorial structure from one lot to another without jeopardizing the manufactured product. It is an ongoing mode of utilizing the operation of a full-scale process so that information on ways to improve the process is generated from simple experiments while production continues. Analytical techniques are then used to determine what process changes to make for product improvement (Box *et al.*, 1978).

As DOEs explained earlier, it is typically desirable to include as many factors as possible in each design, keeping the factors studied to runs ratio as high as possible. However, the circumstances when conducting an EVOP are different. Box *et al.* (1978) provide the following suggestions when conducting an EVOP:

- Because the signal-to-noise ratio must be kept low, a large number of runs is usually necessary to reveal the effects of changes.
- However, these are manufacturing runs that must be made anyway and result in very little additional cost.
- In the manufacturing environment things need to be simple, and usually it is practical to vary only two or three factors in any given phase of the investigation.
- In these circumstances it makes sense to use replicated 2^2 or 2^3 factorial designs, often with an added center point.
- As results become available, averages and estimates of effects are continually updated and displayed on an information board as a visual factory activity in the area under investigation.
- The information board must be located where the results are visible to those responsible for running the process.
- In consultation with an EVOP committee, the process supervisor uses the information board as a guide for better process conditions.

Figure 34.6 illustrates how an EVOP over time can be used to maximize the response from a process. One can also use this approach to identify a minimum.

34.8   Example 34.2: EVOP

A study was conducted to decrease the cost per ton of a product in a petrochemical plan (Jenkins, 1969, Box *et al.*, 1978). For one stage of the investigation, two variables believed important:

1. Reflux ratio of a distillation column
2. Ratio of recycle flow to purge flow

Changes to the magnitude of the input variables were expected to cause transients, which would subside in about 6 hours.

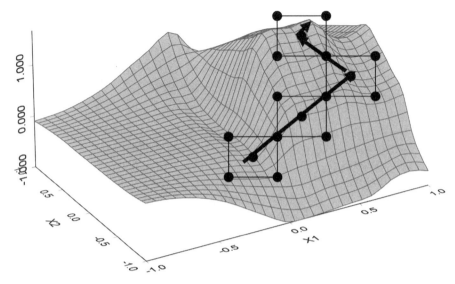

Figure 34.6: EVOP illustration.

Measurements for the study would be made during an additional 18 hours of steady operation.

Figure 34.7 shows the posting at the end of each of the three phases, where the recorded response was the average cost per ton recorded to the nearest unit. The design was a 2^2 factorial with a center point. Phase I results are the averages of five cycle replications. Upon completion of Phase I, it was believed that sufficient evidence existed to justify a move to the lower reflux ratio and higher recycle/purge ratio in Phase II. The five cycles from phase II suggested that this move did lower costs as expected, while further suggesting assessing even higher values of recycle/purge ratio assessment in Phase III. Phase III was terminated after four cycles with the conclusion that the lowest cost of approximately £80 was achieved when the reflux ratio was close to 6.3 and the recycle/purge ratio was about 8.5.

The cost for the described 4.5 month program was £6,000, which resulted in a per ton cost reduction from £92 to £80. This annualized savings was £100,000.

34.9   Path of Steepest Ascent

An alternative process response improvement strategy, which is similar to EVOP, is the path of steepest ascent (or descent).

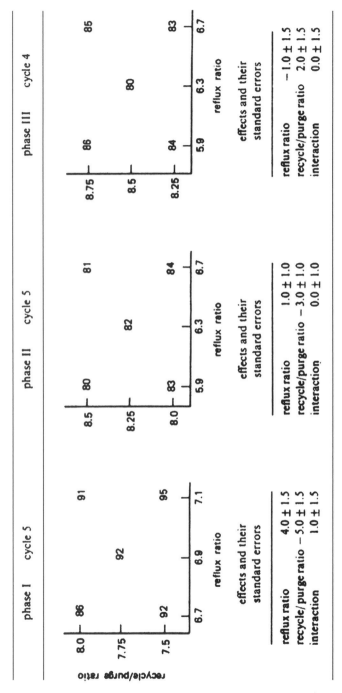

Figure 34.7: Appearance of the information board at the end of Phases I, II, and III, petrochemical plant data. Response is average cost per ton. (from Box et al., 1978)

A point of initiation for this strategy is a model that was built around current operating conditions. This equation may consist of several DOE-determined terms.

Experiments are then conducted along the direction of steepest ascent (or descent) until there is no response improvement. At the point of no response improvement, another DOE is conducted with center points for determining a new search direction. This new steepest ascent search direction is perpendicular to the contours determined by the model.

34.10   Applying IEE

If there are several response outputs to the trials, it may be necessary to compromise the optimum solution for each response to get an overall optimization. Several response outputs can be collectively weighted to yield a combined response output for consideration.

An overall implementation strategy for continuous-response variables can be first to implement a linear model design (i.e., a two-level DOE design with center points). The center points are used to determine if there is adequate fit. If the model does not fit well and an "optimum" response is needed, then additional trials can be added in consideration of higher-order model terms (e.g., second-order polynomial). After the initial test, factor considerations that were not found important can be removed to make the response surface experiment more manageable in size.

Wheeler (1989) explains that "boldness" should be used when choosing the levels of the variables so that the desired maximum or minimum is likely to be contained within the response surface design. When building a response surface, a basic strategy is first to choose bold factor levels consistent with a simple model and then make lack-of-fit tests. If the model does not fit, additional trials can then be added to the original design consistent with the variable levels needed to add higher-order terms.

An evaluation of the magnitude of the center points relative to the end points of the DOE factors may indicate that the initial selection of the magnitude of the variables did not have enough "boldness" to contain the optimum value. The surface outside these bounds can be quite different from the extrapolated value. A multiexperiment response surface test strategy may be needed to evaluate possible process improvements outside the bounds initially considered in the experiment. The variable levels to consider in the next experiment can be determined by evaluating the data collectively to gain insight to improved setting-level opportunities.

34.11 Exercises

1. Create a three-factor central composite response surface design.
2. Create a three-factor Box–Behnken response surface design.
3. Conduct a response surface analysis of the viscosity response shown in Table 34.3.
4. Conduct a response surface analysis of the molecular weight response shown in Table 34.3.
5. Estimate the factor levels that provides minimum response variability and a target response of –225.4.
   (a) From a DOE screening experiment, determine the factors that affect the variability and level of the response.
   (b) For a mean and variability response, report significant main effects and anticipated interactions (note aliasing and any expected interactions), coefficients, and probability levels of significance.
   (c) Describe any normalizing transformations that were made.
   (d) Residuals appear OK? If no, what looks abnormal?
   (e) Describe interaction plot(s), if appropriate.
   (f) Was curvature detected at a significance level of 0.05?
   (g) State what would be an appropriate next step.

A	B	C	D	E	F	G	Resp1	Resp2	Resp3	Resp4	Resp5	Resp6
-50	-50	-50	-50	-50	-50	-50	-814.866	-911.429	-757.525	-877.659	-871.279	-691.62
50	-50	-50	-50	50	-50	50	-923.652	-770.285	-791.542	-910.083	-291.823	-770.107
-50	50	-50	-50	50	50	-50	-614.77	-629.43	-628.662	-575.584	-574.077	-611.724
50	50	-50	-50	-50	50	50	-671.898	-676.625	-670.538	-671.963	-669.673	-662.667
-50	-50	50	-50	50	50	50	-718.413	-744.531	-740.161	-646.816	-864.791	-595.448
50	-50	50	-50	-50	50	-50	-764.504	-697.616	-675.269	-717.71	-883.121	-801.096
-50	50	50	-50	-50	-50	50	-673.61	-650.662	-655	-664.414	-667.198	-672.649
50	50	50	-50	50	-50	-50	-576.64	-655.001	-594.191	-490.848	-538.363	-674.21
-50	-50	-50	50	-50	50	50	584.388	499.651	603.93	490.904	649.868	659.415
50	-50	-50	50	50	50	-50	651.262	487.689	639.81	553.888	802.873	677.499
-50	50	-50	50	50	-50	50	856.533	758.568	781.775	837.735	876.88	791.1
50	50	-50	50	-50	-50	-50	666.75	669.369	671.794	661.524	659.906	660.748
-50	-50	50	50	50	-50	-50	694.033	761.279	473.826	563.263	501.567	670.232
50	-50	50	50	-50	-50	50	783.333	523.841	476.405	609.384	551.995	395.443
-50	50	50	50	-50	50	-50	668.198	676.076	676.003	675.054	675.107	665.707
50	50	50	50	50	50	50	858.678	759.765	835.597	825.815	707.877	733.607
0	0	0	0	0	0	0	-4.143	-9.439	61.809	6.102	27.588	-2.96
0	0	0	0	0	0	0	-10.364	32.956	58.522	41.227	21.99	-21.215
0	0	0	0	0	0	0	-60.184	-26.985	68.451	46.318	-34.91	21.244
0	0	0	0	0	0	0	51.97	-16.723	-40.027	-1.263	19.428	22.084
0	0	0	0	0	0	0	-57.056	63.327	-33.522	-13.556	-3.288	-10.696

6. Estimate the factor levels that provide minimum response variability and a target response of –225.4 using the concepts presented in this chapter.
   (a) For a mean and variability response, report significant main effects and anticipated interactions (note aliasing and any expected interactions), coefficients, and probability levels of significance.
   (b) State whether any normalizing transformation(s) was made.
   (c) State whether residuals appear OK or describe a specific problem that might exist.
   (d) Create appropriate main effect and interaction plots.
   (e) State the level of the factor(s) that are expected to produce the lowest response variability and achieve a target of –225.4. Determine from equation – optimizer may give different answer.
   (f) Describe the factors as thought they were from a manufacturing and then transactional example, where the seven factors are either discrete or continuous.

Factor B	Factor D	Factor E	Factor F	Resp1	Resp2	Resp3	Resp4	Resp5	Resp6	mean
–50	–50	–50	–50	–873.724	–478.643	–543.776	–655.846	–859.184	–588.57	–666.624
50	–50	–50	–50	–667.395	–670.003	–671.432	–659.291	–672.129	–676.834	–669.514
–50	50	–50	–50	531.035	680.444	575.947	537.035	483.445	632.135	573.34
50	50	–50	–50	669.033	656.288	662.453	660.856	652.405	672.425	662.243
–50	–50	50	–50	–751.88	–724.222	–841.998	–649.25	–867.207	–648.563	–747.187
50	–50	50	–50	–584.83	–494.933	–572.491	–431.981	–504.795	–411.061	–500.015
–50	50	50	–50	971.562	743.094	684.184	575.698	815.739	824.89	769.195
50	50	50	–50	968.191	868.199	639.672	761.527	705.493	509.592	742.112
–50	–50	–50	50	–735.274	–684.618	–892.137	–808.403	–932.478	–727.096	–796.668
50	–50	–50	50	–662.422	–666.906	–659.876	–678.508	–669.149	–661.069	–666.322
–50	50	–50	50	408.254	293.365	341.397	603.878	474.086	517.653	439.772
50	50	–50	50	666.417	676.946	683.261	681.286	660.393	661.072	671.563
–50	–50	50	50	–582.655	–850.046	–562.155	–662.435	–812.654	–792.489	–710.406
50	–50	50	50	–680.142	–390.91	–593.206	–536.641	–547.56	–612.014	–560.079
–50	50	50	50	595.33	453.946	684.9	741.366	813.686	599.151	648.063
50	50	50	50	943.193	716.024	821.613	718.613	785.299	808.312	798.842

35

P-DMAIC – Improve Phase: Innovation and Creativity

35.1 P-DMAIC Roadmap Component

The project define–measure–analyze–improve–control (P-DMAIC) analyze phase tools and the improve phase design on experiment (DOE) and response surface methodology (RSM) tools described in the last six chapters provide a structured framework for compiling information. These analyses often provided sufficient direction to an obvious improvement solution. For example, a statistical difference between operator performance led to a consistent well-followed best-practice procedure or a DOE led to the refinement of machine settings. However, in other cases, a solution is not so obvious. In these cases, information gained from the above passive and proactive analyses can be combined with creativity and innovation concepts. These creativity tools are also applicable in the E-DMAIC analyze and improve phases when determining enterprise direction for improving satellite-level metrics. The graphic in this section highlights the P-DMAIC roadmap steps (see Appendix Section D.1) that are described in this chapter. Appendix E contains the tollgate check sheets for this and other phases. The chapter touches on some creativity-generating concepts.

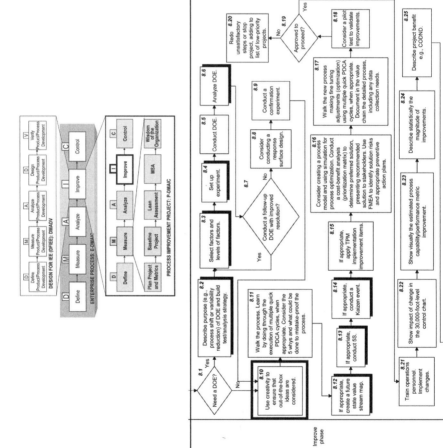

Creativity is a process of creating unusual associations among mental objects. Invention is a result of creative problem solving. Creativity can sometime result when there is an association of the right combination of objects. One frequently described example of association effect of the right objects is the exhaustive search by Thomas Edison during the development of a durable filament for a light bulb. In other cases, the objects are known, but an unusual association type becomes creative. An example of this is the creation of music from a fixed set of notes.

Creativity facilitates the success of brainstorming and allows out-of-the-box ideas and solutions to be considered. Without an emphasis on creativity, most improvement teams find only evolutionary improvements and conventional causes. It is the creativity that increases the chance of finding unconventional causes and revolutionary improvements.

Many team exercises are available to enhance creative behavior. With respect to process improvement efforts, the best ones focus on breaking the conventional paradigms. This can be done by starting the brainstorming of causes or solutions by setting a ground rule that some current policy(s) or current barrier(s) does not exist. The benefit of this method is that it may generate a cause or solution that is so revolutionary that the organization will set aside the barrier or policy to allow the process improvement to occur.

Another common method to spur greater creativity is to perform a creativity exercise with the team before the tools that benefit from greater creativity, such as brainstorming and solution selection. These may be simple exercises such as connecting the nine dots in a square without lifting your pencil (there are at least three ways) or making multiple patterns with straws.

Another stimulus for creative thought is provided in the article "A Modern Parable" (Callandra, 1968). The question is how do you measure the height of a tall building using a barometer? This question has led to the creation of a list of more than 40 different methods. The methods extend from the simple physics-based pressure measurement to geometric-based methods using shadows or perspective, to everyone's favorite which is to use bribery by offering to give the barometer to the building superintendent if he or she will tell you the building height. This 10-minute discussion will generate laughs and creativity, but it also provides a lead in to a discussion on unspoken paradigms and their hidden inhibitions on creativity.

35.2   Alignment of Creativity with IEE

From a how-to create perspective, Jones (1999) states that to encourage creativity we need to put ourselves in the place of most potential which gives us insight to process improvement or breakthrough improvements. Jones lists nine points for creativity:

1. Creativity is the ability to look at the ordinary and see the extraordinary.
2. Every act can be a creative one.
3. Creativity is a matter of perspective.
4. There is always more than one right answer.
5. Re-frame problems into opportunities.
6. Don't be afraid to make mistakes.
7. Break the pattern.
8. Train your technique.
9. You've got to really care.

The IEE approach described in this series of volumes aligns with these points. IEE creates an environment that encourages the implementation of creative solutions that align with the needs of the business. Satellite-level metrics can track overall value to an organization both from a financial and customer point of view. A closer view of the value from processes can then be obtained from operational and project 30,000-foot-level metrics. Creativity activities are then to be a very integral part of the IEE project execution roadmap.

This IEE implementation process is a procedure for creating an environment where we put ourselves in the place of the most potential for the execution of projects that create value for the organization and its customers. One example of this occurrence: A colleague of mine executed in two stages a DOE that I had designed for him because a new assembly factor was not available. The first stage had the old assembly, while the second stage had a new assembly. An analysis of this DOE indicated that the statistically significant difference between the two types of assemblies was large. I raised suspicion about the execution of this experiment when a follow-up experiment did not indicate significance of this factor. On further investigation, my colleague discovered that the first test had been executed using a different procedure for mounting the machine. My colleague was very apologetic about his oversight. I indicated that this was a blessing in disguise since this uncovered a testing problem we would later have within manufacturing. From this test we discovered, before production start-up, that the test fixture yielded an erroneous response relative to how a customer experiences the machine function. Through the execution of this DOE, we put ourselves in "a place of most potential" for discovery/creativity.

35.3 Creative Problem Solving

Teams might find that a less rigid creative approach to solving problems yields the best solutions (Teamwork, 2002). With this *association of ideas* approach, one needs to understand the factors that make creative thinking work best. Through this process, imagination feeds off memory and knowledge, resulting in one idea leading to another.

This creative thinking process is dependent on the execution of the following factors within the process:

- *Suspend judgment*: An open mind is an important contributor to the success of this process.
- *Self-assessment*: It may be helpful for team members to conduct a self-evaluation of their tendency to cling to dogmatic ideas and opinions so that they can better assess how much work they need to do in this area.
- *Develop a positive attitude*: We need to develop an attitude that all ideas are good ideas.
- *Use checklists*: All ideas should be written down. This sends the message that all ideas are good. It also ensures that nothing is forgotten.
- *Be self-confident*: Great ideas often can initially be ridiculed. Be self-confident in ideas that are different from the traditional approach.
- *Encourage others*: The fuel for creativity is praise and encouragement.

Five steps to solving problems creatively are:

1. *Orientation*: Set the stage for a productive session.
2. *Preparation and analysis*: Gather facts without getting into too much detail. Research for successful past solutions to problems that are similar.

3. *Brainstorming*: Conduct a brainstorming session where many ideas are created.

4. *Incubation*: Disperse the group for a period of time to let ideas grow. This time period could be a lunch break or a good-night's sleep.

5. *Synthesis and verification*: Construct a whole out of the ideas generated by brainstorming. To stimulate this process, the team might create a list of the desirable and undesirable qualities of the solutions. Another approach is to synthesize ideas through the creation of an outline or grouping of ideas together with similar ideas assigned to the same group. Relationships between these groups can then be mapped out.

35.4   Inventive Thinking as a Process

In this volume, we suggest creating and using processes wherever possible. The purpose of this section is to present some background information that might be used to initiate the creation of a more rigorous inventive process within organizations.

System inventive thinking is a problem-solving methodology developed in Israel and inspired by the Russian TRIZ methodology. Innovations were added that simplified the learning and application of the problem-solving methodology. These included the closed-world diagram, the qualitative-change graph, the particles method (an improvement on "smart little people" of the TRIZ method), and a simplified treatment of the solution techniques (which the Israelis call "tricks"). Whereas TRIZ stresses the use of databases of effects, the Israeli method stresses making the analyst an independent problem solver (Sickafus, 1997).

Structured inventive thinking (SIT) is a modified version of the Israeli systematic inventive thinking problem-solving methodology. The methodology, sometimes referenced in the 8D problem-solving methodology, develops creative solutions to technical problems that are conceptual. The problem solver focuses on the essence of the problem. The method efficiently overcomes psychological barriers to creative thinking, enabling the discovery of inventive solutions.

Unified structured inventive thinking (USIT) was developed by Sickafus (1997) when teaching an elementary form of SIT at Ford Motor Company in Dearborn, Michigan.

35.5 TRIZ

TRIZ states that some design problems may be modeled as technical contradiction. Creativity is required when attempts to improve some functional attributes lead to deterioration of other functional attributes. Design problems associated with a pair of functional contradiction can be solved by making trade-offs or by overcoming the obstacle. TRIZ stresses that an ideal design solution overcomes the conflict, as opposed to making a trade-off.

Problems can be grouped into those with generally known solutions and those with unknown solutions. Solutions to problems come in levels:

- *Standard*: uses methods well known in the profession.
- *Improvement*: uses methods from inventor's own industry and technology (improves an existing system).
- *Within existing paradigm*: uses methods from other fields and technologies (improves an existing system).
- *Outside existing paradigm*: uses little-known and understood physical effects (physics, chemistry, and geometry).
- *Discovery*: goes beyond contemporary scientific knowledge (e.g., utilizes a new science).

Those problems with known solutions can usually be solved by currently available information. Those with no known solution are called inventive problems. These problems often contain contradictory requirements.

TRIZ is the Russian acronym that means *The Theory of inventive problem solving*. Genrich Altshuller, a Russian mechanical engineer is credited with the creation of TRIZ. While analyzing patents for the Russian Navy, Altshuller noticed patterns in the inventive process, which he developed into a set of inventive tools and techniques for solving problems.

Instead of classifying patents by industry, such as automotive or aerospace, Altshuller removed the subject matter to uncover the problem-solving process. Altshuller found that often the same problems had been solved over and over again using one of only four fundamental inventive principles (e.g., transformation of properties, self-service, do it in reverse, and nesting).

Altshuller also classified engineering system development into eight laws:

1. *Law of completeness of the system*: Systems derive from synthesis of separate parts into a functional system.
2. *Law of energy transfer in the system*: Shaft, gears, magnetic fields, charged particles, which are the heart of many inventive problems.
3. *Law of increasing ideality*: Function is created with minimum complexity, which can be considered a ratio of system usefulness to its harmful effects. The ideal system has the desired outputs with no harmful effects (i.e., no machine, just the function(s)).
4. *Law of harmonization*: Transferring energy more efficiently.
5. *Law of uneven development of parts*: Not all parts evolve at the same pace. The least will limit the overall system.
6. *Law of transition to a super system*: Solution system becomes subsystem of larger system.
7. *Law of transition from macro to micro*: Using physically smaller solutions (e.g., electronic tubes to chips).
8. *Law of increasing substance-field involvement*: Viewing and modeling systems as composed of two substances interacting through a field.

Most effective solutions come from resolving contradictions without compromise. When improving some part or characteristic of our system causes deterioration in another that is contradiction. Altshuller states that invention surmounts the contradiction by moving both characteristics in a favorable direction. For example, to increase the capacity of an air conditioner, we can increase weight, price, and power consumed. However, a better solution is the use of a new technology that improves efficiency and capacity.

Altshuller thought that if only later inventors had knowledge of earlier work, solutions could have been discovered more quickly and efficiently. His approach was to use the principle of abstraction to map the problems to categories of solutions outside of a particular field of study. Conflict can be resolved through the *Principle of Abstraction*; that is, classification of problems in order to map the problems to categories of solutions.

To solve a problem, probably some feature or parameter has been selected for change to improve the process feature of the problem. TRIZ describes these basic approaches through a list of standard features such as waste of time, force, speed, and shape.

TRIZ facilitates the solution process through abstraction. Problems are stated in terms of a conflict between two attributes (e.g., parts, characteristics, functions, and features). This allows seeing generic solutions that may already be documented in other industries or fields of study. This also allows for a better search in the global patent collection. The Web site www.SmarterSolutions.com/triz provides tools to facilitate the TRIZ execution process.

35.6   Six Thinking Hats

Complexity is the biggest enemy of thinking since it leads to confusion. Six Thinking Hats is a technique developed by DeBono (1999) to help clarify and simplify thinking so that it is more enjoyable and effective. Six Thinking Hats simplifies thinking by permitting a thinker to cope with one thing at a time. The thinker is able to deal with logic, emotions, information, hope, and creativity individually. Emphasis is given in the Six Hats method to "what can be" rather than simply "what is." Focus is given to determining a way forward, not on who is right or wrong.

Western thinking focuses on "what is," as determined by analysis, judgment, and argument, while many world cultures, if not most, regard argument as aggressive, personal, and nonconstructive. Instead of judging our way forward, what is needed is a system that helps determine "what can be," not just "what is." Six Hats provides this system through parallel thinking, where everyone at any moment is looking at a situation from the same direction.

In Six Hats, the colors white, red, black, yellow, green, and blue describe hat colors and its role descriptions, which are to be used at various times (e.g., during a meeting). Each hat color is related to the following function:

- White Hat: White is neutral and objective; hence, the white hat objective is facts and figures.
- Red Hat: Red suggests anger, range, and emotions; hence, the red hat provides emotional view.
- Black Hat: Black is somber and serious; hence, the black hat provides caution and carefulness by providing idea weaknesses.
- Yellow Hat: Yellow is sunny and positive; hence, the yellow hat provides optimism, covering hope, and positive thinking.
- Green Hat: Green is grass, vegetation, and abundant and fertile growth; hence, the green hat indicates creativity and generation of new ideas.

- Blue Hat: Blue is cool and the sky color, which is above all else; hence, the blue hat concern is with control, the organization thinking process, and other hat usage.

Two basic ways to use hats are to singly request a thinking type or as a meeting sequence for subject exploration or problem solving. A single use might lead to the statement: I think we need some green hat thinking here. Meeting sequence can involve two, three, four, or more hats.

Meeting sequence can be evolving or preset. In the evolving sequence, hat topic selections are chosen during the meeting; in preset sequence, hat topic sequence is setup under a blue hat at the meeting's beginning. Preset sequences are suggested until experience is gained in Six Hats facilitation.

Some basic Six Hats meeting protocols are as follows:

- The chairperson or facilitator wears a blue hat and maintains hat-meeting discipline.
- There is no need to use every hat.
- Hats can be used several times during a meeting.
- Group members must stay with current hat.
- Initial time allotment for most hats is 1 minute for each attendee; that is, five attendees would mean 5 minutes.
- Blue hat is always used at both meeting beginning and end.
- There is no one right hat sequence to follow; however, some sequences are appropriate for exploration, problem solving, and dispute settlement.

The white hat is about information. White hat becomes a discipline for encouraging the thinker to clearly separate fact from extrapolations or interpretations.

The red hat provides the opportunity to express feelings and intuition with no need for explanation or justification; for example, I feel that the idea has potential. This hat considers both ordinary emotions and complex judgments such as a hunch and intuition. Emotions do not need to be logical or consistent.

The black hat is logical thinking that addresses caution and survival. Black Hat Thinking may highlight procedural errors but is not argumentative and must not be allowed to degenerate into argument. The black hat addresses the questions: What will happen if we take this action? What are the potential problems? What can go wrong? How will people react? Do we have the resources? Will it continually be profitable? In assessment, the black hat can address whether we should proceed with the suggestion. In the design processes, the black hat addresses weaknesses that need to be overcome.

The yellow hat is positive and constructive thinking with optimism, which focuses people to seek out value. Under this hat the thinker deliberately sets out to find whatever benefit there might be in a suggestion; such as, if we invest heavily in promoting this product, we should have success on our hands. Suggestions can be prefixed with the words proven, very likely, good chance, even chance, possible, or remote.

The green hat presents new ideas, concepts, perceptions, or possibilities. The green hat incorporates lateral thinking, which is pattern switching in an asymmetric patterning system. Lateral thinking helps the thinker cut across patterns instead of just following them. A key component of lateral thinking is movement where we use an idea for its forward effect. Provocation is an important part of green hat thinking and is symbolized by the word po. Provocation is used to take us out of usual thinking patterns.

The blue hat is like the orchestra conductor. The blue hat is typically worn by the facilitator or session leader. When wearing the blue hat, we think about the subject exploration, not the subject. The blue hat thinker can make comments on meeting observations; for example, we are spending too much time arguing about this point. Let us just note it down as a point on which there are conflicting views. The first blue hat indicates purpose of meeting, definition of the situation, what we want to achieve, and plan for hat sequence. The final blue hat indicates what was achieved: conclusion, design, solution, and next steps.

35.7   Innovation Creation Process

Innovation is the act of introducing something new, which can involve both radical and incremental change to products, services, or processes. Often the goal of innovation is considered to be problem solving. Innovation problem solving can lead to the creation of a new opportunity; i.e., the development of a new product (innovation) leads to increased revenue (problem) or resolves a customer need (problem). Innovation can lead to a process enhancement that reduces a process defective rate; i.e., a process enhancement (innovation) leads to the reduction of a defective rate (problem).

To be most effective, a rational problem-solving/opportunity-creation approach blends analytics with creativity. However, an execution structure for this blending is often lacking, which can lead to much inefficiency and ineffectiveness, resulting in a solution that is far from optimal.

This section describes the execution of a six-step innovation creation process (ICP), which adds structure to this overall blending process, without stifling the creation of innovation opportunities. Steps for this ICP event are:

1. Environmental Analysis
2. Problem Description
3. Assumptions
4. Generating Alternatives
5. Evaluation and Choice
6. Implementation Plan

ICP has several potential IEE applications. An ICP event can occur in the E-DMAIC analyze phase for project identification and scoping, P-DMAIC improve phase for solution determination, or DFIEE/DFSS for product/process design definition/creation. The Enterprise Improvement Plan (EIP) system described in the Volume 2 provides a framework for organizational ICP E-DMAIC execution.

Steps 1–3 create a foundation for the generation of ideas in step 4. Highlights for each step from the viewpoint of P-DMA-IC execution are (Volume 2 describes ICP execution from an E-DMAIC point of view):

1. Environmental Analysis: Compile project execution work that has been executed to date in a presentation format. The presentation should address all appropriate project execution checklist items (see Appendix Table E.1); e.g., stakeholder analysis, 30,000-foot-level base line metric, MSA results, Lean assessment, wisdom of the organization summary, passive analysis summary, and DOE analyses. This compiling of previous P-DMAIC work can provide valuable information that can serve as the foundation for an innovatively developed problem solution.

2. Problem Description: Compiled information from the environmental analysis step can be used to provide more information about the previously-created project problem description, which the ICP event is to address.

3. Assumptions: Listing current and future factor condition assumptions can be beneficial when generating solution alternatives and the prioritization of these alternatives;

however, care must be exercised not to set boundaries that are too restrictive.

4. Generating Alternatives: This step is the most creative stage of ICP. This step is to use information from the previous steps to help formulate useful options. The creative-idea-generation techniques described in previous sections of this chapter can help generate more solution alternatives than could otherwise be derived.

5. Evaluation and Choice: Decision making needs a systematic evaluation of alternatives against existing criteria and goals. Key to this rational-process step is to determine possible outcomes from various alternatives and how they would impact 30,000-foot-level and satellite-level metrics. A cause-and-effect matrix and/or nominal group technique (NGT) can be used as part of the evaluation process.

6. Implementation Plan: After there is a clear idea of what is desired and a plan to accomplish the results, action needs to be taken. However, the best solution still may not be obvious. For this situation, a plan-do-check-act (PDCA) implementation, as described in the next chapter, may be the most appropriate approach for structurally gaining problem-solution-generation knowledge.

The dynamics of executing an ICP event in a team environment can take many forms. I will now provide an accelerated ICP event execution option. In this process, the team lead for this process compiles a rough-cut at putting together background information before the team begins their collective work. This generic process can be especially beneficial when team members work remotely to each other. The basic process for accelerated ICP execution is:

1. The team lead works with individuals or groups independently to create a first-pass presentation document that summarizes the results from ICP steps 1–3; i.e., the previous P-DMAIC work. This document could build upon previous project report-outs.

2. He/she sends the first-pass ICP document with instructions that every team member is to read the document at least one day before an ICP team event. The document is sent ahead of time so that each team member has time to read the information and let the concepts settle in their mind for idea percolation.

3. Each team member is instructed to take notes in the first-pass document before a team meeting on what they think should be changed or added to each ICP step.

4. During the ICP team meeting event, the team lead or a facilitator uses a computer projector to display the first-pass ICP 6-step document.

5. Using a projector, the team lead walks through each ICP document step, making team agreed-to changes for steps 1–3. Team members are to use their pre-meeting notes when providing inputs; however, team members can also provide additional thoughts that could have been generated because of meeting comments from others.

6. ICP step 4 is to contain a listing of brainstorming ideas or alternatives generated by the team. Classical brainstorming work in this step needs to follow traditional rules; i.e., there is no inappropriate idea and all ideas are recorded. The ICP document provides a media for listing all idea alternatives. At this point in the ICP event TRIZ or other creative idea development tools can used to help stimulate thought.

7. Ideas prioritization in ICP step 5 can be done using any-one of several approaches. An affinity diagram can be a useful tool for the categorization and then prioritization of ideas. With this approach, ideas are printed out so that each idea is recorded on a small sheet of paper, which is taped to the wall. The team would then move ideas around in typical affinity diagram fashion creating a few natural groupings. NGT or a cause-and-effect matrix could be used for affinity diagram category prioritization. Nominal group technique could be used to prioritize ideas within categories.

8. The above steps can be completed in one or two team meetings. Upon completion of the above accelerated ICP team actions, the team lead can then compile the information in a prioritization format for distribution to each team member.

9. A follow-up team meeting can be used to formulate an implementation plan; i.e., step 6.

The above described generic accelerated ICP process is not appropriate for all situation and teams. Teams need to decide the best execution approach for their situation.

35.8   Exercises

1. Describe your place of most creativity; for example, showering or shaving, while commuting to work, while falling asleep or waking up, during a boring meeting, during leisure time, during exercising, on waking up in the middle of the night, while listening to an inspirational speaker, or while performing nonmental tasks.
2. Describe what you might do to stimulate creativity for yourself and your team.

36

P-DMAIC – Improve Phase: Lean Tools and the PDCA Cycle

36.1 P-DMAIC Roadmap Component

The last chapter described the use of creativity tools. This chapter's progression through the improve phase of the P-DMAIC roadmap leads to the Lean tool applications for solution development. The previously described creativity techniques can be blended with the described Lean methodologies to develop a unique and much improved system.

The graphic in this section highlights the P-DMAIC roadmap steps (see Appendix Section D.1) that are described in this chapter. Appendix E contains the tollgate check sheets for this and other phases. When considering Lean tools in the measure phase as part of the P-DMAIC roadmap, Table 14.1 summarized Lean principles. The same principles apply in the improve phase of the roadmap. This chapter describes a how-to system that integrates Lean tools for process improvement. In this phase, activities that fell into the major or some categories of the Lean assessment matrix of Table 14.2 provide direction for improvement efforts.

In Chapter 14, future state value stream mapping, along with current value stream mapping, was described. The P-DMAIC roadmap shown in Appendix Section D.1 includes current value

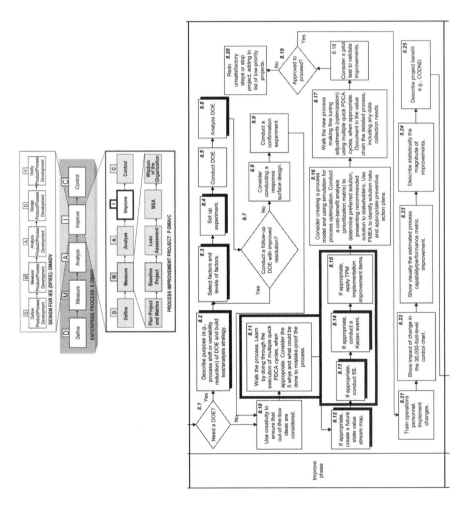

stream mapping as a tool in the consider-lean-tools drill down of the measure phase. In the P-DMAIC roadmap, future state value stream mapping is described as a tool that could be used in the improve phase.

Deming's plan–do–check–act (PDCA), or plan–do–study–act (PDSA), cycle is included in this chapter as a model that can be very beneficial when a solution is not obvious and knowledge needs to be gained through an iterative process. This chapter also describes kaizen event integration into the improve phase of the P-DMAIC roadmap. This focused team-based, learn-by-doing methodology for making improvement should be considered when executing P-DMAIC projects. An effective orchestrated kaizen event can speed the completion and effectiveness of a project. The creativity tools described in the previous chapter can provide the vehicle for stimulating thought on what should be done to improve the system as part of this overall process.

5S (sort, straighten, shine, standardize, and sustain) is included in this phase since a basic housekeeping improvement strategy may be needed as part of the project's execution. This chapter also includes the improve topics of kanban, load leveling, continuous flow, total productive maintenance (TPM), and changeover reduction.

It is important to note that these techniques are not just applicable to manufacturing but also to transactional processes. For example, work in progress (WIP) is not restricted to part count. WIP at each process step could be the number of insurance claims passing through a process. The concept of layouts for cells does need to be restricted to a physical layout but could also apply to IT solutions and file structure.

The why-why or five whys technique described earlier can be very beneficial to identify opportunities for improvement.

36.2   Learning by Doing

Lean emphases the learning by doing approach, where process improvement team members consist of those who are most closely associated with adding value to the product. These improvement team activities are to be facilitated by an experienced teacher who uses the Socratic method of learning, where a dialog of questions leads to an agree-to solution. This is a very powerful methodology that should be strongly considered for every project, where implementation can take the form of a kaizen event. In IEE, it is suggested that other experts be included in this process improvement team.

Gemba is the workplace where value is added. A key Lean concept is using "try-storm," at the Gemba, rather than conducting an improvement brainstorming session that is physically removed from the workplace. To illustrate this approach, consider the creation of a new work cell. At Gemba, a trained facilitator might lead the team in modeling the new work cell using cardboard equipment mockups. Boxes would be moved around until the best layout is determined.

Before beginning this effort, it is important that all team members understand waste and its implication. Before redesigning a cell, teams can benefit from an identification-waste examination

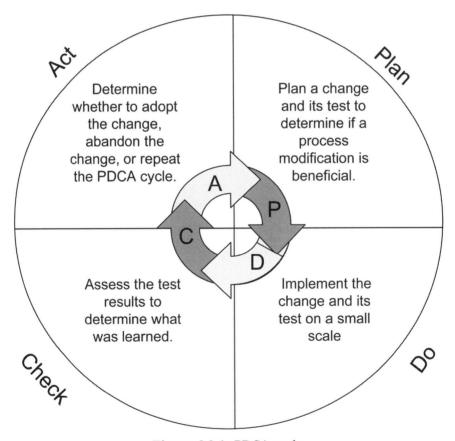

Figure 36.1: PDCA cycle.

of other business areas. This experience can help teams create a cell redesigns that minimizes waste.

36.3   Plan-Do-Check-Act (PDCA)

The four-step process of PDCA, as illustrated in Figure 36.1, is also known as the Deming cycle, Shewhart cycle, or plan-do-study-act (PDSA). Dr. Edwards Deming popularized PDCA, which he later modified to PDSA, since "study" better described his intended action than "check."

In an IEE project execution, passive data analyses, and/or a DOE can directly lead to a long-lasting solution. However, there are situations when a solution is not obvious and knowledge needs to be gained through an over-time iterative fine-tuning process. For this type situation, a solution can be developed through reiteratively executing the PDCA cycle. When used in the improvement phase of P-DMAIC, assessment of change in the 30,000-foot-level project response can be considered part of the PDCA check step.

The PDCA process can also be used for solution development to an E-DMAIC improve-phase BPIE. This application situation might not have a direct link to a key performance 30,000-foot-level metric. However, general consensus could be that real-time process improvement is needed for a particular business area, which can indirectly affect another key business metric. For this situation, an individual or a team could undertake the PDCA structure for making improvement. The PDCA could also be used in DIEE for process development.

The PDCA execution model steps, which can used in the improve phases of P-DMAIC or E-DMAIC and DIEE process development, is

Plan: Plan a change and its test to determine if a process modification is beneficial.

Do: Implement the change and its test on a small scale.

Check or study: Assess the test results to determine what was learned. Describe what went right, what went wrong, and how well the change worked. A 30,000-foot-level control chart and a hypothesis test can provide a quantitative assessment of how the change impacted the process output.

Act: Determine whether to adopt the change, abandon the change, or repeat the PDCA cycle. A termination decision is appropriate when no significant value is anticipated through the execution of additional PDCA cycles. It can be appropriate to either abort or repeat the PDCA cycle when the evaluated change would create adherence issues or no/minimal improvements were observed. A repeat of the PDCA cycle would be appropriate when the amount of improvement was not as much as desired but additional change enhancements opportunities have been identified. When objectives are met, the process needs to be standardized. In IEE, agreed-to process enhancements are to be documented in the organization's E-DMAIC value chain.

The power of PDCA is in its apparent simplicity and inductive logic utilization. While being relative easy to understand, it can be difficult to accomplish on a on-going basis due to the analytical difficulty in judging tested hypotheses on the basis of measured results.

36.4   Standard Work and Standard Operating Procedures

A process' work combination is the blending of materials, process operations, people, and technology. In Lean, standard operations are the most efficient work combination created by the organization.

Standards are not rigid. Standards should address the aspects of work time, operational sequence, and WIP. Standards are applicable in both repetitive and nonrepetitive work such as design, maintenance, service, and management, whereas the development of the best and safest approach is a participative effort.

The value chain, as part of an overall E-DMAIC system, can be the best repository for process documentation. With an E-DMAIC value-chain system, documented procedures and process-step flow steps, along with its interconnections and dependencies, can be made readily available to users of the process.

Hall (1998) presents three stages of standardization. The first stage is when a plan or drawing describes the outcome with no plan to get there. With this stage there generally is a high level of variation and there is a need for inspectors. The second stage is when there are standardized processes. For this situation variance is reduced by following standardized methods to achieve the outcome using tools such as process control and poke-yoke.

The third stage is standardized predictive methods where a high level of consistency is achieved directly from the design using standardized processes that work the first time with no need for prototype, test, or special tools. Very few companies and processes are at the third stage.

As part of a measure phase lean assessment, this volume previously described the use of a standardized work chart and combination work table to describe existing process workflow. In the improve phase, this information along with wisdom-of-the-organization findings and analyze phase results can be used as inputs to the creation of a new, improved standardized work chart and standard operations combination chart. The tools describe in this chapter can be very instrumental in the development of these new procedures.

36.5 One-Piece Flow

One-piece flow describes the sequence of activities through a process one unit at a time. For example, an insurance claim might be considered a single unit. In contrast, batch processing handles activities on a large number of transactions at one time—sending them together as a group through each operational step.

One-piece flow advantages, which could positively impact a project's 30,000-foot-level manufacturing and transactional metrics include

- Manufacturing
  - Reduced customer order to shipment times
  - Reduction of WIP
  - Early detection of defects and errors
  - Increased flexibility for customer product/transaction demands
  - Reduced operating costs through the exposure and elimination of nonvalue-added work waste
- Transactional
  - Reduced response time to customer requests
  - Reduced manpower requirements to meet customer demand
  - Early detection of bottlenecks and problem transactions
  - Identification of cross training the workforce to handle workforce availability
  - Policy issues that slow processing; for example, batch reviews or overnight IT processing

A project process improvement could be a work flow change that reduces batch size or changes from batch processing to single-piece flow

36.6   Poka-Yoke (Mistake Proofing)

In the E-DMAIC roadmap analyze phase, Jidoka or autonomation was described, where Jidoka is a term used in Lean meaning automation with a human touch. As was noted earlier, Jidoka applies the following four principles:

- Detect the abnormality
- Stop
- Fix or correct the immediate condition
- Investigate the root cause and install a countermeasure

A *poka-yoke* (pronounced POH-kah YOH-kay) device is a mechanism that goes hand-in-hand with Jidoka. Poka-yoke either prevents a mistake from occurring or makes a mistake obvious at a glance. Shigeo Shingo at Toyota as an industrial engineer was credited with creating and formalizing zero quality control (ZQC), an approach that relies heavily on poka-yoke (i.e., mistake proofing or error proofing).

To understand a poka-yoke application, consider an operator who creates customized assemblies from small bins in front of him. One approach to the task would be to give the operator a list of parts to assemble, taking the parts as needed from the bins. This approach can lead to assembly errors by the operator. He might forget either to include a part or add parts that are not specified. A poka-yoke solution might be to include lights on all bins. When the operator is to create a new assembly, the bins that contain the specified parts for the assembly light up. The operator then systematically removes one part from each bin and places it in front of him. He does this until one part has been removed from each bin. He knows that their assembly is complete when no parts remain in front of him.

Poke-yoke offers solutions to organizations that experience frequent discrepancies in the packaging of their products; for example, someone forgot to include the instructions or a mounting screw. Poke-yoke devices can be much more effective than simple demands on workers to "be more careful."

Many poka-yokes exist in transactional processes today. Consider the use of lookup lists used in software data entry, limits on going to the next screen if all the data is not provided, and automatic spelling checkers for documents.

Improvement focus should always be given to what can be done to mistake proof the process, as opposed to inspecting quality into the produced product. Steps for poke-yoke execution are

- Describe the potential defect
- Identify where the defect is likely to occur
- Analyze process steps
- Identify errors that may contribute to the defect
- Apply why-why or five whys analysis to determine root causes
- With the team, identify mistake proofing strategies
- Verify efficiency of the mistake proofing actions

36.7 Visual Management

Visual management can address both visual display and visual control. Visual displays present information, while visual control focuses on action needs. Information needs address items such as schedules, standard work, quality, and maintenance. Visual control can address whether a production line is running according to plan and highlights problems.

In both manufacturing and transactional processes, visual management systems can encompass the following items and are illustrated in Figure 36.2.

Visual management techniques include

- Manufacturing
    - Display boards in public area showing processes in use or unavailable for use
    - Lights on machines showing status (red = unavailable, Yellow = available but not in use, Green = in use
    - Business/performance metrics posted in public areas, showing throughput and quality performance in a common format
- Transactional
    - Status board in public area showing personnel availability
    - In and out boxes in public area showing queues and backlogs
    - Pegboard showing who has what job with tags or markers
    - Status boards in public areas reporting error rates and cycle time performance in a common format

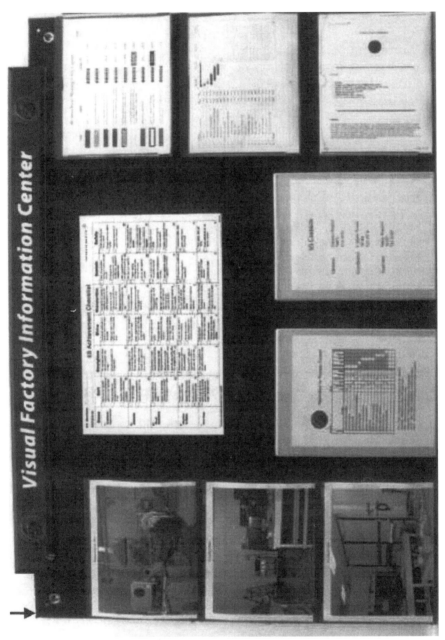

Figure 36.2: Visual factory illustration.

Visual management organizations can
- improve quality through error prevention, detection, and resolution
- increase workplace efficiency
- improve workplace safety
- reduce total costs

In IEE, visual management can include the posting and readily availability of 30,000-foot-level metrics and 50-foot-level metrics, along with standard operating procedures availability. The 5S process described in the next session can facilitate the creation of organization visual management systems.

36.8   5S Method

The primary reason for 5S should be is the creation of standardized work. 5S offers a basic housekeeping discipline for both the shop floor and office, which contains the following steps: sort, straighten, shine, standardize, and sustain.

5S should be considered in two ways. It could be considered an everyday continuous improvement activity for individuals and small groups. Or, it could be considered as a KPIV that should impact a 30,000-foot-level project/operational metric. When the 30,000-foot-level metric indicates lead time, quality, or safety issues, 5S should be considered as an execution strategy. The sustain portion of 5S should be part of the control phase within a DMAIC roadmap. Activities for each of these steps are

1. *Sort*: Clearly distinguish the needed from the unneeded tools, supplies, and material. Tag items (see Figure 36.3) if not used within a month, unnecessary to perform job, broken or not useable, or insufficient for intended purpose.
   - *Manufacturing*: On a sheet of paper list all red-tagged items. Remove the red-tagged items and place them in an identified red-tag storage area. All items are to be reviewed by supervisor and initialed, if approved for removal.
   - *Transactional*: Put a piece of colored adhesive tape on all desktop, shelves and cabinets items. Items that are found to be used multiple times a day, mark with one color and keep them on the desktop. Items used a few

```
┌─────────────────────────────────────────────────┐
│                    RED TAG                       │
│                                                  │
│   Category:    1. Tools & supplies        □      │
│                2. Raw material            □      │
│                3. WIP                     □      │
│                4. Finished goods          □      │
│                5. Other                   □      │
│                                                  │
│   Item & Number: _____│
│   Quantity: _____ Due Date: _____ │
│   Scrap: _____ Transfer: _____ Rejected: ____│
│   Explanation: _____│
│                                                  │
└─────────────────────────────────────────────────┘
```

Figure 36.3: Red tag example.

times a week are labeled with a second color and put onto shelves. Items only used infrequently are labeled with a third color and are put in cabinets or moved to a public shared area. After a reasonable time, list the items names by color and standardize similar work area locations.

2. *Straighten:* All items in the work area have a marked place and a place exists for everything to allow for easy and immediate retrieval.

    –   Organize remaining items in work area by usage. Daily usage items to be labeled on a shadow board. Weekly usage items to be placed in a labeled drawer. Monthly usage items to be under work station or in a cabinet and labeled with pictures and text.

    –   In a transactional process, this involves the use of desk caddies to hold daily tools and supplies. This is equivalent to a shadow board, if all are the same at equivalent work stations. Label drawers, shelves, and cabinets with the contents so that they are easily found.

3. *Shine:* The work area is cleaned and straightened regularly as you work.

    –   Determine what needs to be done to create a visually attractive workplace. Clean work station. Plan weekly 10-minute cleaning maintenance for area.

- *Manufacturing illustration*: Clean tools and machines/painting if necessary. Sweep/mop floor. Tighten loose fittings. Create specific cleaning instructions for work environment, including which cleaning supplies to use and where. Add maintenance items to monthly schedule.
- *Transactional illustration*: Enforcing a clean desk policy during the workday and at the end of the day. Keep up on maintenance such as painting, adequate power outlets, and bundling cables so that order is kept.

4. *Standardize*: Work method, tools, and identification markings are standard and recognizable throughout the factory. 5S methods are applied consistently in a uniform and disciplined manner.

  - *Identify source for waste*: Look at your job to see where debris is created. Check for debris during course of your job, determining whether machine is producing any debris. Often method is needed to identify source of dirt or waste. Create discipline or the individual becomes source for waste.
  - *Manufacturing illustration*: Check machine for oil leaks; standardize maintenance. Check for debris during course of job. Check for broken yet functional switches that need repair.
  - *Transactional illustration*: Use work checklists to evaluate documents or service tasks to ensure that everyone follows the same procedure. This checklist procedure may be self checks or peer reviews.

5. *Sustain*: 5S is a regular part of work and continuous actions are taken to improve work. Established procedures are maintained by checklist. After cleaning an area, we all can identify with frustration after some period of time of not being able to find something.

  - Clean and maintenance checklist should be developed. Without discipline we have nothing.
  - *Create a checklist*: List tagged items removed from work station, list remaining items and location, document steps of cleaning process, and list action items for preventative maintenance.

5S should be considered in two ways

  - As an everyday continuous improvement activity for both individuals and small groups.

    –   As a KPIV that should impact our 30,000-foot-level project/operational metrics.

Bicheno (2004) describes 5S as: sort–simplify–sweep–standardize – sustain. Offered are the following illustrative applications:

- *Inventory*: Sort—Throw out all dead and excessive stock; Simplify—Arrange in the best positions; Sweep—Regularly review dated stock and ABC category changes; Standardize — footprint; Sustain—audit ABC.
- *Suppliers*: Sort—Select the best two suppliers in each category, scrapping the rest; Simplify—Cut all wasteful, duplicate transactions; Sweep—Improve supplier performance supplier association; Standardize—Milkrounds, payments; Sustain—Audit performance.
- *Computer systems*: Sort—Delete all dead files and applications; Simplify—Arrange files in logical folders, hierarchies; Sweep—Clear out inactive files regularly; Standardize— Systems, formats; Sustain—audit perform and response.
- *Costing systems*: Sort—Do you need all those costs and variances? Prune them; Simplify—cut transactions. Review report frequency. Incorporate overhead directly; Sweep—Audit the use made of costing reports and transaction size/frequency; Standardize—Adopt reporting standards; Sustain— Review and reduce.

An application example is multiple marketing reps' keeping track of their own quotes with their own system. Less waste would be generated if they standardized on one system or better yet used a common system.

36.9   Kaizen Event

The Japanese word *kaizen* literally means continuous improvement. The hallmark of a kaizen event is its empowerment of people fostering their creativity. Through the work of Taiichi Ohno, the Toyota production system (TPS) has become synonymous with the implementation of kaizen events, embodying the philosophy and applying the principles. Some companies use a kaizen event or kaizen blitz to fix specific problem or workflow issue within their organization. IEE integrates with this activity through 30,000-foot-level metrics, where a kaizen event is created when there is a need to improve a particular aspect of the business, as identified by this metric, and a kaizen event is a tool that can be used to accomplish this. Rother and Shook (1999) describe two kinds of kaizen events. A process kaizen event addresses the elimination of waste, which has a focus at the front lines, while a flow kaizen event addresses value stream improvements, which has focus from senior management.

Kaizen events and the TPS are based on quantitative analysis. Ohno said, "At our factory, we start our kaizen efforts by looking at the way our people do their work, because it doesn't cost anything." A starting point for the identification of waste can be the study of the motion. In the late 19th and early 20th century, Frederick W. Taylor set the foundation for industrial engineering. The initial objectives were to set work standards by quantifying times and motions of the routine tasks performed by workers, which gave a basis for compensation. This resulted in a method according to which work could be analyzed and wasted motion eliminated. The scientific management approach was broadly adopted but was perceived by many as inhumane, although Taylor did respect the worker and undoubtedly intended the system to benefit both the employer and employee.

Taylor's primary tool of time study remains a basis tool for kaizen events. The difference between Taylor's original implementation and the implementation of today is the source of inputs to work methods (i.e., process). Taylor's work standards were set by the standards department with no worker input, but now kaizen events provide the worker with both the opportunity and means to find better ways to do his or her job.

Abraham Maslow was American psychologist noted for his proposal of hierarchy of human needs. A list hierarchy from lowest to highest is physiological safety, belongingness and love, esteem, self-actualization. Maslow describes self-actualization as an individual's development to their fullest or the growth process of what is already within them. Kaizen events have been described as a new manifestation of achievement motivation. The implementation of IEE involves not only good quantitative measurements but also humanism.

The management styles of Taylor and Maslow, once thought to be opposite, can share common ground with a kaizen event approach (Cheser, 1994).

The generic steps when conducting a kaizen event follow. Appropriate modifications are made to these steps when executing an IEE project execution.

1. Prepare and train the team
2. Analyze present methods
3. Brainstorm, test, and evaluate ideas
4. Implement and evaluate improvements
5. Present results and follow-up

The following should be considered for these steps:

1. During event preparation, identify problem cells and select the cell that will be given focus. This work should have been done in the early stages of the IEE project execution roadmap. Assemble the team. If necessary, conduct training on muda (waste), standardized work, and continuous flow.
2. The team analyzes during and after training the cell in action using a videotape. The team then analyzes the video to determine material flow, lead time, cell layout, process waste, and other vital measurements. During this time they can generate a standardized work and work combination table. The team needs to record the current number of operations over time and defect rates. Photographs should be used to document the kaizen event.
3. The overall team is divided into smaller groups to discuss ways to improve the cell using the compiled work cell analysis statistics. Groups then test potential improvement tactics on the work cell, assessing their impact. The results from tested ideas are shared with other group team members. This keeps other groups from making similar mistakes and provides new idea inspiration. This cycle of brainstorming, testing, and evaluating may be performed many times before desired results are achieved.
4. After team has developed its plan for achieving results from the kaizen event, a maintenance request is generated, if necessary, where modifications are fully described so that management can authorize the changes. Improvements are made to the work cell and its processes. All personnel are trained in the new process by the kaizen event team members. After implementation, the improvements are monitored. Process is revideotaped and restandardized. Results are measured. Items that require additional time to be put into effect are placed on a 30-day list. Team is formed to ensure their completion.
5. Team members write up all improvement items. Teams are to compile results determining monetary savings, improved space utilization, and time reductions. Team

members present to top management, making commitment to complete outstanding items. Management recognizes the team, making suggestions for the future. Thirty-day action items are implemented by the team. Final results are compiled. The process may be restarted.

36.10   Kanban

A business system that creates work or a product, before it is ordered or needed by the customer (could be the next step in a process) is called a push system. If there is no mechanism to keep the WIP below some level that is consistent with the customer demand, work output can become excessive, which can lead to many problems including finished goods storage in the manufacturing case or excessive work and rework in a transactional case.

In *pull* systems, products and transactions are created at a pace that matches customer demand. Kanbans are used to buffer variations in customer or next process step demands. A most familiar form of kanban is implementation is American-style supermarkets. In these supermarkets, each product has a short-term buffer, where its replenishment from a regional distribution facility is triggered when the item is scanned at checkout. When the distribution center receives the replenishment signal, an order to the supplier is triggered for a replenishment of the distribution center. The kanban is the signal that occurs when the product is scanned.

In supermarkets a customer can get (1) what is needed, (2) at the time needed, and (3) in the amount needed (Ohno, 1988). Compared to Japan's traditional turn-of-the-century (i.e., 1900) merchandising methods such as peddling medicines door to door, going around to customers to take orders, and hawking wares, America's supermarket system is more rational. From the seller's viewpoint, labor is not wasted carrying items that may not sell, while the buyer does not have to worry about whether to buy extra items.

The Japanese word kanban refers to the pulling of product through a production process (i.e., a pull system). The intent of kanban is to signal a preceding process that the next process needs parts/material. In the supermarket example, an order is only placed with the originating supplier after an item is sold to the final customer.

A bottleneck is a system constraint. In a pull system, the bottleneck should be used to set the pace for the entire production line. Buffers in high-volume manufacturing serve to balance the line. It is important that such operations receive the necessary supplies in a timely basis and that poorly sequenced work does not interfere with the process completion. Pull systems address what the external and internal customer needs when they want it. Through this, WIP is reduced.

A simple kanban managed transaction system is when the transactional process manager does not let any new work start until a transaction is completed and provided to the customer.

Rules to consider when operating an effective kanban:

- Manufacturing Rules
  - No withdrawal of parts is to occur without a kanban where subsequent processes are to withdraw only what is needed.
  - Defective parts are not to be used for later processes.
  - Preceding processes are to produce only the exact quantity of parts withdrawn by successive processes.
  - Variability in the demand process should be minimized.
  - A lack of available product to pull or an inability of the next step to pull product triggers a shift in resources to balance the work flow.
- Transactional Rules
  - No transaction is worked until the next process step pulls a transaction into their area.
  - Working ahead is not allowed.
  - If the customer demand rate increases, then all process steps increase their throughput equally.
  - If an error or mistake is found, it is corrected or restarted before other work is started at that operation. This transaction is not considered as a completion unless it is corrected.
  - A lack of available work to pull or an inability of the next step to pull work triggers a shift in resources to balance the work flow.

If production requirements drop off, the process must be slowed down. An increase in production requirements is addressed through overtime and process improvement activities within the IEE discipline.

Kanban can dramatically improve a process that produces few defects or errors within work areas. However, if there are work areas that have high defect rates (i.e., a hidden factory), the system can become "starved" for work. Kanban systems do not work well when there are high defect rates. This defect problem could be avoided by integrating kanban with an IEE measurement and improvement system since both statistical (e.g., DOE) and nonstatistical analytical tools could help reduce defect rates.

Kanban can be the relay signal between supplier and customer. Kanban signals can be generated by lights, colored balls down a tube, or a computer network. A food market can know when to stock by keeping track of product-volume sold through a UPC barcode system. A stock person responds to a product pull by replenishing the prescribed number using first-in-first-out product restocking. The supplier knows to the volume of product to supply because of the kanban system.

One simple equation to determine a kaizen number is:

$$\text{Kanban number} = \frac{\text{Process lead time}}{\text{Takt time} \times \text{Container quantity}} + X \text{ Factor}$$

where X factor is a management confidence gage that is affected by

- Changeover time variations
- Management safety stock; for example, bad weather for shipments
- Lot size withdrawal; for example, customer may change the amount of daily withdrawal from their weekly order
- Customer variation; that is, customer ordering may have a lot of variability

36.11 Demand Management

The system works best when there is a uniform flow of work within the system. The policies of a company should encourage stability. Unfortunately, this does not often happen. For example, the reward system for product sales might encourage a spike in customer demands at the end of each month. This can lead to supply chain amplification in the form of inaccurate product forecast when these signals are read incorrectly. Accounting procedures can also encourage management to produce excess inventory or excess overtime in order to make the number on which they are evaluated look better.

Supply chain improvements can be expected when lead times are reduced, which would improve forecasting accuracy, and there is supply-chain information sharing that leads to agreement-to uniform schedules.

Another improvement opportunity is to change internal policies, which impact demand volume. For example, consider an end-of-the-month/quarter sales-target bonus policy, which results in the sales department giving temporary price concessions so that they meet their monthly or quarter sales targets. This policy could be a candidate for change, since the sales-force reward policy can be causing a manufacturing demand peak that leads to much overtime and quality issues.

36.12   Heijunka

Heijunka (Hey-Joon-Kah) is a traditional Lean scheduling methodology for environments that contain a repetitive mix of products or family of products. Heijunka is a kanban card postbox system that is usually at the pacemaker process. A Heijunka box provides process level scheduling/pacing, schedule visibility, and early problem highlighting.

In a transactional environment, this would be accomplished by keeping a balanced mix of easy and difficult transactions or daily mix of transaction types that match the customer demand for each transaction. It is the opposite of batch processing groups of similar transactions and then switching to another type.

Leveled production is customer order averaging so that small sequenced cycles produce the required volume and product mix. In a Heijunka box customer monthly or weekly volume demands can be leveled into daily demands.

Pull systems and Heijunka work well hand-in-hand. However, system improvement may be needed for success (e.g., quick changeover). When the visual system indicates a problem, prompt identification and correction are absolutely essential.

Figure 36.4 illustrates a Heijunka box that levels out customer work order into smaller quantities of work order information or pitch, which equates to

$$\text{Pitch} = \text{Takt time x Box Quantity}$$

Figure 36.5 provides a sample Heijunka calculation.

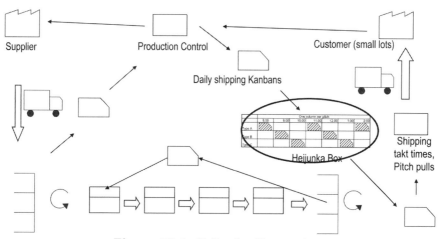

Figure 36.4: Heijunka illustration.

	One column per pitch							
	8:00	9:00	10:00	11:00	1:00	2:00	3:00	4:00
Type A								
Type B								
Type C								

Order		
Total Quantity = 16		
Type A	Type B	Type C
10	4	2

$$\text{Cards per slot} = \frac{\text{Total cards}}{\text{Number of slots}} = \frac{16}{8} = 2 \text{ cards per time slot}$$

- 1st level largest quantity, filling balance with other cards

$$\frac{10 \text{ Type A}}{8 \text{ time slots}} = 1 \text{ card/time slot with 2 remainder}$$

	One column per pitch							
	8:00	9:00	10:00	11:00	1:00	2:00	3:00	4:00
Type A	2 cards	1 card	1 card	1 card	2 cards	1 card	1 card	1 card
Type B								
Type C								

- 2nd level by the next largest quantity (Type C)
- 3rd level the remaining type (Type B): Put into slots to balance out

	One column per pitch							
	8:00	9:00	10:00	11:00	1:00	2:00	3:00	4:00
Type A	2 cards	1 card	1 card	1 card	2 cards	1 card	1 card	1 card
Type B		1 card		1 card		1 card		1 card
Type C			1 card				1 card	

Figure 36.5: Heijunka example calculation.

The ideal situation is the maintenance of smooth or leveled production processing with minimal fluctuation. Leveling should be processed by both product type and volume. Complex assembly processes may have to be leveled by product families with the aid of a computer. When visual system indicates that a problem exists, prompt identification and correction are essential.

36.13   Continuous Flow and Cell Design

The disadvantages of traditional batch production as illustrated in Figure 36.6 are large WIP, large conveyance time for parts, large lead time, and large liability for defect; for example, all WIP if detected at last process step. Batching occurs in a transactional situation when groups of transactions collect in an in or out box and then are moved to the next process step in a group or they wait for an overnight computer update before processing further.

Small lot production removes the walls from batch production, reduces WIP, lead times, and conveyance, if the product is allowed to move between steps in the same small groups, as illustrated in Figure 36.7. Small lot production can be challenging in a transactional environment because the resource that does the work also moves the transaction and they are probably rewarded for work time, not transportation time. Resistance to stopping batch process for this environment is usually high since it typically can take the same time to move one transactions as it would to move 10. It can be impossible, however, to balance task durations for machine operations with this push system, since one operator can spend a great deal of time waiting and inventory can build up at a station.

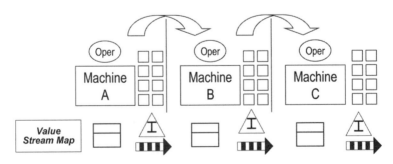

Figure 36.6: Batch flow.

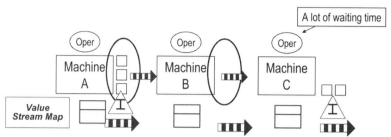

Figure 36.7: Small lot flow.

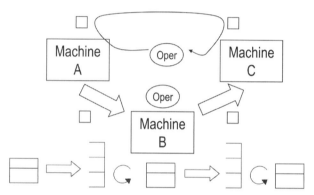

Figure 36.8: Cellular flow.

U-shaped cell, as illustrated in Figure 36.8 offers balanced operator processing time to takt time. Figure 36.9 illustrates how one operator can now handle more than one machine depending on individual machine lead times' relationship to takt time.

Within U-shaped layouts, employees are cross-functionally trained and move with changing cell layouts. These layouts provide the benefit that one person can control WIP. In addition, the close proximity of workers enhances communications, there can be quick defective part detection, and work load adjustments can be made for volume changes.

This form of cell layout can be more difficult to implement in manufacturing than for transactional processes. In manufacturing, many processes have been built around the use of high volume capital equipment, while in a transactional process which is built around people. The transactional use of a work cell involves co-locating multiple small groups of the resources needed to

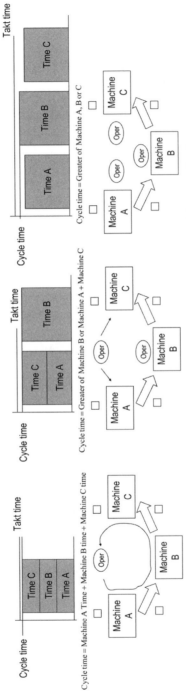

Figure 36.9: Operator utilization in cell with varying machine cycle times.

process a transaction. The barrier to this work model is a business strategy to have people work to organizational structure based on keeping same skilled personnel in the same department, which limits the ability to manage cross functional work groups.

Advantages of cells over a single high capacity process are multiple lower capacity equipment may be less costly, a single failure will not stop production, and each cell always works at full capacity. The last item is important relative to workforce management. In a large process, work rate slows with the takt time can result in workers becoming accustomed to working slower. In the cellular flow model, cells can be added or dropped to match takt time requirements. With cellular flow, workers can always work at the same rate.

36.14 Changeover Reduction

Let's consider a 30,000-foot-level metric (Y variable or KPOV) that has a lead time reduction goal. For this situation, we would consider a Lean tool application, since one major objective of Lean is the reduction of lead time. To achieve this, the size of batches often needs reduction which creates a focus for reducing changeover times; that is, time from the last piece of one batch to the first piece of the next batch.

Changeover time can have several components; for example, internal when a machine is stopped and external which involves preparation. Other types of changeovers are manufacturing line changeover, maintenance operations, vehicle/aircraft loading/unloading, and office operations. The classic changeover is, of course, the grand prix pit stop! It is important not only to reduce the mean changeover time, but also reduce its variability using a standardized process.

Within Shingo's classic single-minute exchange of die (SMED), internal and external activities are classified within a flowchart of the changeover. It is desirable to move internal activities to external activities when possible. This permits more uptime of the machine since the maximum amount of preparation is accomplished before the machine is stopped. Example applications for the improvement of external activities are placing tools on carts near the die and using color codes to avoid confusion. Example applications for the improvement of internal activities are quick-change nuts and the standardization of activities.

This issue addresses a problem that is pervasive but also unrecognized in the transactional work environment. Every interruption of a worker, every meeting, every change in tasking causes a work changeover. Does anyone believe that there is a loss in productive time when one task is stopped before it is done and another is started? Of course, we need to put one away, pick up the new task and review it to see where we should start. This concept of a changeover time penalty in the transactional environment is often unrecognized.

Consider recording and plotting on a visible run chart all changeover times, asking for improvement suggestions.

The classic over methodology is (Bicheno, 2004):

- Identify and classify internal and external activities. Make a video?
- Separate internal activities from external activities. External or preparation activities should be maximized. Cut or reduce waste activities such as movement, fetching tools, filling in forms.
- Try to convert internal activities to external (e.g., by pre-hearting a die).
- Use engineering on the remaining internal activities. There are many tricks, from quick release nuts to constant platform shims, to multiple hole connections all in one. Both Shingo and McIntosh are excellent source of ideas.
- Finally, minimize external activity time. This is because in small batch production there may be insufficient time to prepare for the changeover during a batch run.

36.15   Total Productive Maintenance (TPM)

As implementation programs with a company, Lean and TPM have similarities. The TPM description within this section describes TPM and its linkage to an overall IEE implementation strategy.

TPM is productive maintenance carried out by all employees through small group activities. Like TQC, which is company-wide total quality control, TPM is equipment maintenance performed on a company-wide basis (Nakajima, 1998).

Sources for the scheduled downtime of a machine are maintenance, breaks, and lunch. Sources for unscheduled downtime include machine breakdown, setup time, and part shortages. Equipment needs to be available and to function properly when needed. TPM emphasizes not only prevention but also improvement in productivity. To achieve these goals, we need the participation of both experts and operators with a feeling of ownership for this process.

Focus is given within TPM to eliminate the obstacles to the effectiveness of equipment. These *six big losses* can be broken down into three categories:

- Downtime
  1. *Equipment failure* from breakdowns
  2. *Setup and adjustment* from die changes, etc
- Speed Losses
  3. *Idling and minor stoppages* due to abnormal sensor operation, etc
  4. *Reduced speed* due to discrepancies between the design and actual operational speed
- Defect
  5. *Process defects in process* due to scrap and reworks
  6. *Reduced yield* from machine startup to stable/predictable production

from an equipment point of view:
  - Load time and operating time are impacted by losses numbered 1 and 2
  - Net operating time is impacted by losses numbered 3 and 4.
  - Valuable operating time is impacted by losses numbered 5 and 6

Metrics within TPM could be tracked at the 30,000-foot-level, where improvement projects are initiated when the metrics are not satisfactory. The highest level TPM metric is overall equipment effectiveness (Nakajina, 1988), which is determined through the relationship:

$$\text{Overall equipment effectiveness} = \text{Availability} \\ \times \text{Performance efficiency} \\ \times \text{Rate of quality products}$$

where the downtime loss metric (loss 1 from equipment failure and loss 2 from setup and adjustment) is

$$\text{Availability} = \frac{\text{operation time}}{\text{loading time}} = \frac{\text{loading time} - \text{downtime}}{\text{loading time}}$$

and the speed loss metric (loss 3 from idling and minor stoppages and loss 4 from reduced speed) is performance efficiency, where

$$\text{Performance efficency} = \frac{\text{ideal cycle time} \times \text{processed amount}}{\text{operating time}} \times 100$$

and the defect loss metric (loss 5 from defects in process and loss 6 from reduced yield) is rate of quality products, where

$$\text{Rate} = \frac{\text{processed amount} - \text{defect amount}}{\text{processed amount}} \times 100$$

Based on experience (Nakajima, 1998), the ideal conditions are

- *Availability*: greater than 90%
- *Performance efficiency*: greater than 95%
- *Rate of quality products*: greater than 99%.

Therefore, the ideal *overall equipment effectiveness* should be

$$0.90 \times 0.95 \times 0.99 \times 100 = 85 + \%$$

Overall demands and constraints of the system need to be considered when selecting IEE projects that affect these metrics.

The three stages of TPM development and steps within each stage are (Nakajima, 1998):

- Preparation
  1. Announce top management decision to introduce TPM
  2. Launch education and campaign to introduce TPM
  3. Create organizations to promote TPM
  4. Establish basic TPM policies and goals
  5. Formulate master plan for TPM development
- Preliminary implementation
  6. Hold TPM kick-off
- TPM implementation:
  7. Improve effectiveness of each piece of equipment
  8. Develop an autonomous maintenance program
  9. Develop a scheduled maintenance program for the maintenance department
  10. Conduct training to improve operation and maintenance skills

11. Develop early equipment management program
12. Perfect TPM implementation and raise TPM levels

The infrastructure of IEE and TPM has some similarities. However, within IEE there is an additional emphasis on how best to track the organization statistically over time, where measures are to be in alignment with the needs of the business.

As part of a lower-level view of processes, some TPM measures could be appropriate. Another application of TPM is within the execution of an IEE project where the project situation suggests the application of a unique TPM tool.

36.16   Applying IEE

Six Sigma is a project-based methodology led by trained black belts and green belts who work with teams that consist of area experts and those who are involved in the day-to-day operations. Lean zealots often believe that their hands-on-doing kaizen event methodology works better than a project based Six Sigma approach led black belts and green belts. Some people believe that Six Sigma project execution generally takes longer, but is more sustainable than most Lean kaizen events. Lean Six Sigma is to combine the methodologies; however, it has been my experience that deployments don't generally truly integrate the tool applications.

IEE truly integrates the strengths of both tool sets at both the project execution (P-DMAIC) and enterprise level (E-DMAIC). In IEE, emphasis is given so that the right Six Sigma or Lean tool is used at the right time relative to the true business needs; that is, 30,000-foot-level metric improvement objective that is in true alignment with business needs.

36.17   Exercises

1. Total productive maintenance addresses equipment effectiveness. How do the three parts of TPM; Availability, Performance Efficiency, and Rate of Quality Products relate to overall organizational capacity?

2. What are the workforce issues that can be avoided by
    using a series of small capacity cellular production centers
    in contrast to a large capacity single production line if the
    customer demand (Takt time) is fluctuating at values less
    than the overall capacity?

37

P-DMAIC – Improve Phase: Selecting, Implementing, and Demonstrating Project Improvements

37.1   P-DMAIC Roadmap Component

The last chapter described the integration of Lean improvement tools within the project define–measure–analyze–improve–control (P-DMAIC) roadmap. This chapter describes the selection and demonstration of process improvement. Similar to the cause-and-effect matrix, the largest totals from a solution selection matrix gives direction on which of the multiple solution alternatives appears best.

The graphic in this section highlights the P-DMAIC roadmap steps (see Appendix Section D.1) that are described in this chapter. Appendix E contains the tollgate check sheets for this and other phases. An IEE project report-out is to include demonstrated results; i.e., 30,000-foot-level metric report-out that describes the response improvement along with a statistical and visual improvement representation and financial benefits. The examples in this chapter illustrate some of the points and thought process from an IEE execution.

In addition to timely project completion, presentation effectiveness is essential to convey project status, analyses, and result to others. Appendix C highlight four presentation focus areas: be in earnest, vocal variety, make it persuasive, and speak with knowledge.

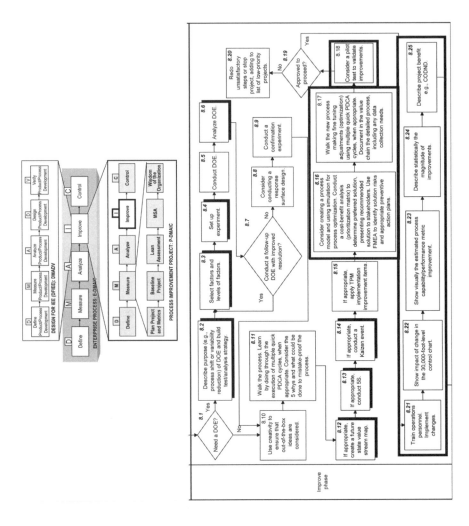

37.2   Process Modeling and Simulation in the Improve Phase

Process modeling was earlier described as an option in the P-DMAIC wisdom of the organization measure phase to gain insight to improvement opportunities. Use of process modeling in the improve phase can provide insight assessment for various what-if scenarios, which can be used to determine the effectiveness of these opportunities. Figure 37.1 illustrates some of the options that are available as inputs to the model, along with an example output.

The staffing, or resources, used to perform each activity can be added to the model

The time, or duration, to perform each activity can be added to the model

Schedules, duration of simulation, etc. defined by unique "scenarios" can be included

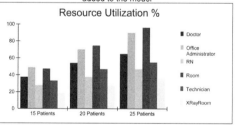

Processes can be simulated for various scenarios, generating analysis reports

Figure 37.1: Process modeling input and output alternatives.

A process model can provide

- Process performance animation
- Quantified cycle and waiting times
- Identified bottlenecks, capacity constraints, and costs
- Effectiveness determination of various improvement options

37.3   Solution Selection and Pugh Matrices

Table 37.1 shows an example solution selection matrix.

Table 37.1: Solution Selection and Pugh Matrices

Solution Selection Matrix					
	Effectivness of Solution to fix problem	*Benefits other areas*	*Short Time to implement*	*Low Cost of Solution*	<<<<Decision Criteria
	10	*6*	*8*	*2*	<<<<<<<Importance
----- Process input -----	--------- Correlation of Input to Output ---------				--------- Total ---------
Lost time in transport					
Mechanical transport	*6*	*1*	*3*	*1*	*92*
Move work locations	*9*	*1*	*6*	*6*	*156*
Hire faster person	*3*	*1*	*3*	*6*	*72*
Current method/No change	*1*	*1*	*9*	*9*	*106*
Step 2 takes too long					
Training & SOP improvement	*3*	*6*	*6*	*6*	*126*
Re-distribute work load	*9*	*6*	*9*	*9*	*216*
Automate the step	*9*	*1*	*3*	*1*	*122*
Current method/No change	*1*	*1*	*9*	*9*	*106*
Low quality Product					
Training and SOP usage	*3*	*6*	*6*	*6*	*126*
Mistake proofing (template)	*9*	*1*	*6*	*9*	*162*
Increased quality feedback (operator self inspection)	*6*	*3*	*6*	*3*	*132*
Current method/No change	*1*	*1*	*9*	*9*	*106*

Pugh Matrix Method				
	Current	Solution 1	Solution 2	Solution 3
Reduction in Defects (30,000-foot-level metric)	*	+	+	+
Lead time reduction	*	*	-	+
Reduce operating expenses	*	+	*	+
Resources required to implement	*	*	*	*
Cost to implement	*	+	-	-
Complete by due date	*	-	+	-
Number of (+)	0	3	2	3
Number of (-)	0	1	2	2
Total score	0	2	0	1
* = no benefit to current method + = beneficial to current method - = not as beneficial as current method Choose solution 1 because of higher total score				

The following guidelines should be considered when creating the matrix:

1. Do not duplicate weight values. Try to spread them from 1 to 10.
2. Try to limit the columns from 2 to 5. More than 5 causes too much averaging and the tool looses some power in discrimination.
3. All columns must be independent.
4. Always evaluate solutions for their effectiveness to fix the project problem. Also consider solution cost (lower is better), solution implementation time (shorter is better), and the ability to improve other organizational aspects (more is better).
5. Consider allowing more than one solution to be adopted. This is advantageous when the most effective solution will take a long period to implement, but there is a solution of medium effectiveness with is relatively low cost and quite quick. Get a quick gain and then a permanent improvement comes later.
6. Consider using a modified Pugh Matrix in place of a standard decision matrix. This includes the current process as a 0 with all the solutions scored as + or – based on their effect on the decision criteria being better or worse than current methods.

37.4   Walking the New Process and Value-Chain Documentation

If at all possible, the new process should undergo a step-by-step walk through. Often many optimization refinements can be uncovered using multiple quick plan–do–study–act (PDSA) cycles during this process refinement step.

On completion of the detailed process, new procedure documentation can be made in the value chain utilizing swim lanes, drill downs, value stream maps, and attachment documents. This value chain procedural standardization should be an integral part of initial and ongoing process-user training.

37.5 Pilot Testing

As improvements are identified and evaluated, there may be some out-of-the-box ideas chosen. Many times the organization will then require more than a statistical estimation of the gain as enough evidence to approve the implementation. In these cases, it is beneficial to execute a pilot test of the solution recommendations.

Pilot testing provides the following benefits:

1. Allows the business to provide indisputable evidence of the identified cause and effect relationship and the solution effectiveness.
2. Allows the business to experience the solution without fully committing to the change.
3. Allows the business to better understand the impacts and to obtain feedback from customers and other down stream process participants.

Additional reasons to consider a pilot test are

1. Reduces the risk of potentially unrecognized problems and failures.
2. Increases organizational buy in if there is only marginal support for the change.
3. Provides information to validate Cost of Doing Nothing Differently (CODND) estimates.
4. Provides one more PDSA cycle to optimize the solutions.

Pilot test considerations are

1. Select neither the worst nor the best area to use in the pilot.
2. Choose an area with advocates of the solution.
3. Ensure the current process is stable and predictable before initiating the pilot test.
4. Choose the pilot size to be large enough to validate the solution, but small enough to manage.
5. Identify a time period to execute the pilot test so that there are limited nonstandard events; that is, no atypical product mix changes and where the extraneous factors can be held constant.

6. Establish clear guidelines for the pilot test. These must include triggers to end the pilot if the process output deviates significantly from expectation (i.e., risk reduction).
7. Success of the pilot test must include two facets of the solution:
   (a) *Implementation effectiveness*: The training, briefing, and documentation were adequate.
   (b) *30,000-foot-level metric impact*: The pilot test performance must improve the 30,000-foot-level metric.

Pilot test planning considerations are

1. Pilot the full implementation plan rather than just the process changes:
   (a) Provide process oversight as if it was a full implementation. Do not provide additional oversight to assist during the pilot execution because it may invalidate the evaluation of the implementation efforts.
   (b) Ensure the process operators have the skills and knowledge to be successful with the pilot? If not, include what they will need in the implementation effort.
   (c) Ensure the documentation used for the proposed pilot is sufficient for training process operators on the new procedures. If not, correct it before the pilot test initiates.
   (d) Determine the best way to introduce the new procedures or pilot process to those that will have to perform it.
   (e) Determine when and how will the training be conducted?
2. Brief all participants as if it was a typical process change.
3. Determine all the additional data collection efforts that will be maintained during the pilot. This should include down stream processes to ensure that any changes in their quality or performance are quickly identified.
4. Consider a failure mode and effects analysis (FMEA) to fully evaluate the risk to the process and business during the pilot to reduce risk. Implement a specific plan to mitigate problems if they arise due to the pilot test.

Execute the pilot test under typical business conditions.

At the end of the pilot test period,

1. Restore the process to the original state.
2. Review collected data and interview the pilot test participants to determine the positive and negative aspects of the test.
3. Create an action plan to improve the implementation plan to mitigate or remove problems identified during the pilot test.
4. Determine if the implementation plan changes will require a second pilot test. If so, repeat the entire pilot test with a new set of participants.

When the pilot test is determined to be acceptable,

1. Report to organizational leadership on the pilot test results.
2. Schedule full implementation.

37.6   Process Change Implementation Training and Project Validation

When transitioning to the new process, there needs to be sufficient detailed planning so that implemented changes create as little disruption as possible to current work.

Initial and futures users of the process need adequate training. When user training includes the organizational value chain with its associated procedures and metrics, process users gain insight to how their work integrates with the big picture. When appropriate, specific self-paced training can also be linked to value-chain-process steps.

Completed projects need to:

- Demonstrate their impact to a 30,000-foot-level metric.
- Show visually the estimated process capability/performance metric improvement.
- Describe statistically the magnitude of improvements.
- Describe project benefit (e.g., CODND).

The following examples illustrate this project-benefit-identification process. The next chapter will describe control mechanisms to maintain project gain.

37.7   Example 37.1: Sales Quoting Process

The following example shows how the IEE approach can be applied to the quoting process within the sales function (Enck, 2002). This application illustrates how nonmanufacturing or transactional processes within a business can greatly benefit from IEE. Transactional business activities do not manufacture a household product; however, as seen in the example below, these activities typically have greater visibility to the customer than many manufactured products.

Company ABC is a small electronic components supplier. It makes plastic connectors which are used by computer manufacturers and hi-tech internet hardware providers. One particular product line had been floundering for a number of months. The company has been facing a weak market for the past 6 months with sales at 50% of forecast. It has been losing sales of existing products and has been winning a low percentage of new product requests. The managers responsible for this product line met with a black belt to determine whether IEE could help them improve their situation within the current market and prepare for the future.

At first, the discussion focused around product quality and delivery time which were both poor due to a recent change in manufacturing sites. To make sure they were considering the entire value stream, the team studied a flowchart of the supply chain from high level, as shown in Figure 37.2.

From the supply chain map it became clear that the first opportunity to lose potential customers existed in all of the transactional interactions that took place before the customer placed an order. After a quote request, the sale could be lost due to the quote's taking too long, inability to meet specifications, price, or long manufacturing lead times. After making some phone calls, the team determined that the quoting lead times, which were expected to be hours, were in fact days. The team decided to work on quoting and manufacturing lead times in parallel. This example covers the quoting process.

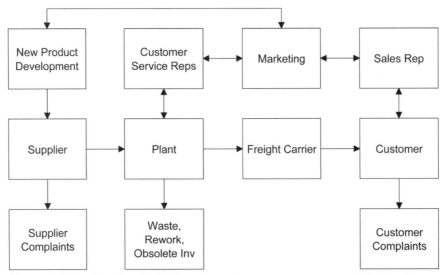

Figure 37.2: Supply chain flowchart for component assembly business.

The number of customers lost to long lead times was not known. However, after talking to some customers, the team made a decision that the lead time needed to be less than two days. The customers they spoke with indicated that competitors were quoting within one day, and, if they did not have their quote within one or two days, customers felt that the company did not have its act together.

To understand the current process, a baseline control chart of 30 quote times was produced; one quote was randomly sampled per day during the previous 30 days, as shown in Figure 37.3 [the chart creation data is later shown in Table 37.2 as "1(baseline)"]. Next, the team developed a time-value map of the quoting process to identify the high potential areas for reducing the quoting time, as shown in Figure 37.4.

It was clear from the time-value diagram that the outsource manufacturing was the reason for the long quote times. The quoting specialists had often complained that the outsource manufacturer delayed their quoting process. However, they were never able to get management within their company or the outsource company to work on the process. The time-value diagram was sent to management at both companies. Within a week, the black belt's team had a meeting with the chief operating officer (COO) and with the managers responsible for quoting at the outsource manufacturer.

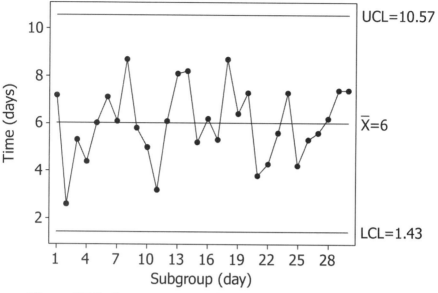

Figure 37.3: Customer quote time – baseline 30,000-foot-level control chart.

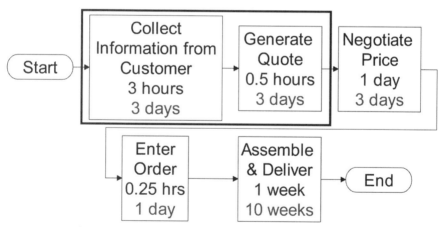

Figure 37.4: Quoting process time-value diagram.

At that meeting, they created as is and future state flowcharts for the quoting process, as shown in Figure 37.5. Management at both companies was amazed at the convoluted process for quoting. The current quoting process evolved in the rush to get the process established when the outsourcing company was first

As Is Process Map

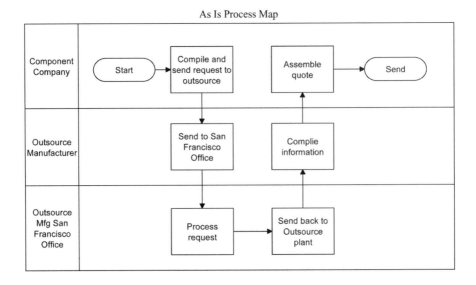

Future State Process Map

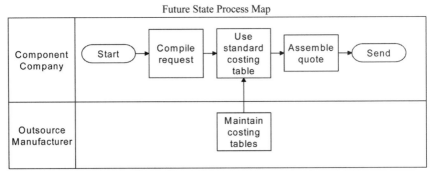

Figure 37.5: As-is and future-state process map.

contracted to do the work. The team that selected the outsource manufacturer focused on its manufacturing abilities. Once the contract was signed, the marketing people realized that the costing information resided in San Francisco so that the process was setup with the agreement that the cost requests would be answered within one day. Once the business started, people on both ends were scrambling to keep up with their daily activities along with the new costing requirements, and the process was not capable of meeting the one-day agreement.

With the support of the COO of the outsourcing company, the future state quoting process was implemented within two weeks. The plan was to use randomly sample quotes during the next several days to verify that the process had improved. The proposed improvement was made after this time. Figures 37.6–37.8 can be used to evaluate the improvements after 10 days of implementation. The data for the creation of these figures and analyses is shown in Table 37.2.

These figures indicate that there is an improvement in the average quoting times. A statistical comparison of the old and new process mean quote time yielded:

```
Two-sample T for Quote Time

Stage            N      Mean      StDev     SE Mean
1 (Baseline)    30      6.00      1.56         0.28
2 (Current)     10      1.640     0.151        0.048
```

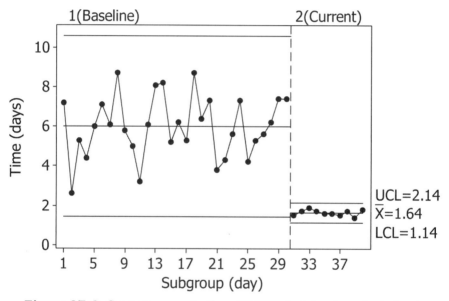

Figure 37.6: Customer quote time 30,000-foot-level control chart, baseline, and improvement.

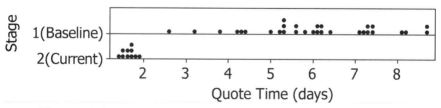

Figure 37.7: Customer quote time – before and after change dot plot illustration.

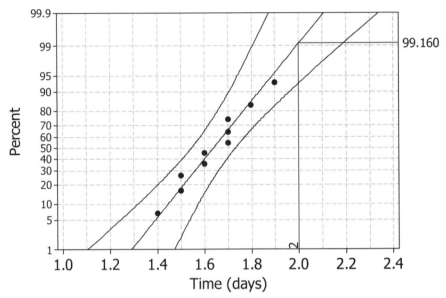

Figure 37.8: Process capability/performance metric for new quote time, maximum likelihood estimates with 95% confidence interval.

Table 37.2: Sales quote process baseline and current times after process improvement

Day	Quote Time	Stage	Day	Quote Time	Stage	Day	Quote Time	Stage	Day	Quote Time	Stage
1	7.2	1(Baseline)	11	3.2	1(Baseline)	21	3.8	1(Baseline)	31	1.5	2(Current)
2	2.6	1(Baseline)	12	6.1	1(Baseline)	22	4.3	1(Baseline)	32	1.7	2(Current)
3	5.3	1(Baseline)	13	8.1	1(Baseline)	23	5.6	1(Baseline)	33	1.9	2(Current)
4	4.4	1(Baseline)	14	8.2	1(Baseline)	24	7.3	1(Baseline)	34	1.7	2(Current)
5	6.0	1(Baseline)	15	5.2	1(Baseline)	25	4.2	1(Baseline)	35	1.6	2(Current)
6	7.1	1(Baseline)	16	6.2	1(Baseline)	26	5.3	1(Baseline)	36	1.6	2(Current)
7	6.1	1(Baseline)	17	5.3	1(Baseline)	27	5.6	1(Baseline)	37	1.5	2(Current)
8	8.7	1(Baseline)	18	8.7	1(Baseline)	28	6.2	1(Baseline)	38	1.7	2(Current)
9	5.8	1(Baseline)	19	6.4	1(Baseline)	29	7.4	1(Baseline)	39	1.4	2(Current)
10	5.0	1(Baseline)	20	7.3	1(Baseline)	30	7.4	1(Baseline)	40	1.8	2(Current)

```
Difference = mu (1(Baseline)) - mu (2(Current))
Estimate for difference:  4.360
95% CI for difference:  (3.771, 4.949)
T-Test of difference = 0 (vs not =):
T-Value = 15.11  P-Value = 0.000  DF = 30
```

The process control chart showed a new level of process performance around a mean of 1.6 days. The dot plot is a simple way to convey the capability of the new quoting process relative to the old quoting system. The probability plot can be used to estimate the percentage of time that the quotes will be made within two days; that is, best estimate is that this will occur 99% of the time.

While there was still some work to be done on this process, the black belt and the team had essentially achieved their objective of reducing the quoting time to less than 2 days. The process owners (marketing and sales) agreed to make sure that all quotes would be made in less than 2 days while the black belt moved on to other more pressing problems within the organization.

Some people might view this as a problem that should easily have been fixed by management and was not in need of an IEE project. This argument would miss the point that IEE not only provides a process to improve business but also provides a methodology to help better manage business. Businesses have so many problems that not all can be addressed at any given time. IEE provides a way to assess the important business processes and decide what needs to be worked on and how to fix it. In other words, IEE provides a means to help management structure and improve their management activities.

In this particular example, the company broadened its view of the problem and picked problems to work on, given the data that was available. There are certainly many other improvement opportunities within this quoting process. However, this project focused on the high potential areas, which is what businesses need to do to increase their effectiveness.

There was a tremendous improvement in the quoting process as a result of this project. This transaction is very important because it is seen by the customer long before any product is purchased and can cause the loss of customers, who would ordinarily prefer your product, just because they had a poor quoting experience. The team decided that this quoting process was a core competence that had to exist to survive. This project, as with many other transactional projects, can certainly provide large opportunities in increasing sales and reducing costs for any type of company.

37.8 Example 37.2: Sales Quote Project

This example contains highlights from a project execution report-out. Describe the overall project thought process and accompanying metrics. The project included the application of Lean tools.

A company's customer satisfaction survey indicated that potential customers were dissatisfied with quote turnaround time. A project was created to improve customer satisfaction by reducing the quote turnaround time and inside sales representatives' (IFS) work load.

The current quote-time data was rounded to whole-number daily increments (See Table 37.3). This data recording is not in increments as fine as we would like, which results in a less than ideal 30,000-foot-level control chart; for example, bound by lower recording of one day, which transforms to a logarithm transformation of zero. Still the IEE 30,000-foot-level project baseline metric provides a reasonable estimate that is easy to understand.

Figure 37.9 contains both an estimate for process centering (50% frequency of occurrence level) and variability (80% frequency of occurrence); that is, the response time for the inside sales quote turnaround process is predictable with an estimated process capability/performance metric of 2.1 days median response with an 80% frequency of occurrence of 0.96–4.40 days. It needs to be highlighted that the Anderson Darling (AD) test will reject granular data even if it fits the distribution. This data set distribution fit was accepted for that reason even with a *p*-value less than .05.

For this project, information flow is described in Figure 37.10, the floor plan is shown in Figure 37.11, and the current value stream map is shown in Figure 37.12.

Table 37.3: Sales Quote Project, Baseline and Current Quote Times

Subgroup (Day)	Days	Stage	Subgroup (Day)	Days	Stage	Subgroup (Day)	Days	Stage	Subgroup (Day)	Days	Stage	Subgroup (Day)	Days	Stage
1	2	1(Baseline)	22	4	1(Baseline)	43	5	1(Baseline)	64	7	1(Baseline)	85	0.15	2(Current)
2	3	1(Baseline)	23	2	1(Baseline)	44	1	1(Baseline)	65	2	1(Baseline)	86	0.09	2(Current)
3	4	1(Baseline)	24	3	1(Baseline)	45	2	1(Baseline)	66	3	1(Baseline)	87	0.13	2(Current)
4	6	1(Baseline)	25	2	1(Baseline)	46	3	1(Baseline)	67	2	1(Baseline)	88	0.69	2(Current)
5	4	1(Baseline)	26	3	1(Baseline)	47	2	1(Baseline)	68	1	1(Baseline)	89	0.77	2(Current)
6	1	1(Baseline)	27	1	1(Baseline)	48	2	1(Baseline)	69	1	1(Baseline)	90	0.63	2(Current)
7	1	1(Baseline)	28	1	1(Baseline)	49	2	1(Baseline)	70	1	1(Baseline)	91	0.7	2(Current)
8	1	1(Baseline)	29	3	1(Baseline)	50	1	1(Baseline)	71	0.09	2(Current)	92	0.19	2(Current)
9	1	1(Baseline)	30	3	1(Baseline)	51	3	1(Baseline)	72	0.15	2(Current)	93	0.15	2(Current)
10	1	1(Baseline)	31	5	1(Baseline)	52	3	1(Baseline)	73	0.15	2(Current)	94	0.08	2(Current)
11	4	1(Baseline)	32	2	1(Baseline)	53	3	1(Baseline)	74	0.08	2(Current)	95	0.04	2(Current)
12	1	1(Baseline)	33	4	1(Baseline)	54	2	1(Baseline)	75	0.16	2(Current)	96	0.08	2(Current)
13	2	1(Baseline)	34	3	1(Baseline)	55	2	1(Baseline)	76	0.84	2(Current)	97	0.77	2(Current)
14	2	1(Baseline)	35	8	1(Baseline)	56	2	1(Baseline)	77	0.72	2(Current)	98	0.17	2(Current)
15	1	1(Baseline)	36	1	1(Baseline)	57	2	1(Baseline)	78	0.08	2(Current)	99	0.17	2(Current)
16	1	1(Baseline)	37	2	1(Baseline)	58	2	1(Baseline)	79	0.08	2(Current)	100	0.11	2(Current)
17	6	1(Baseline)	38	2	1(Baseline)	59	1	1(Baseline)	80	0.07	2(Current)	101	0.68	2(Current)
18	2	1(Baseline)	39	2	1(Baseline)	60	1	1(Baseline)	81	0.18	2(Current)	102	0.17	2(Current)
19	5	1(Baseline)	40	1	1(Baseline)	61	1	1(Baseline)	82	0.01	2(Current)	103	0.1	2(Current)
20	3	1(Baseline)	41	1	1(Baseline)	62	2	1(Baseline)	83	0.74	2(Current)	104	0.14	2(Current)
21	3	1(Baseline)	42	1	1(Baseline)	63	6	1(Baseline)	84	0.1	2(Current)			

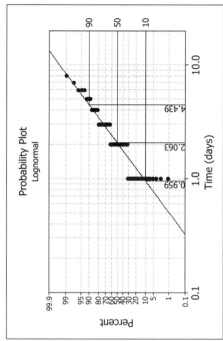

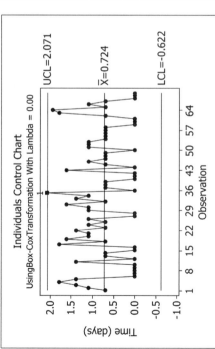

Predictable process with an approximate median of 2.1 days and 80% frequency of occurrence between 0.96 and 4.40 days

Figure 37.9: Project 30,000-foot-level base-line metric for inside sales quote turnaround time.

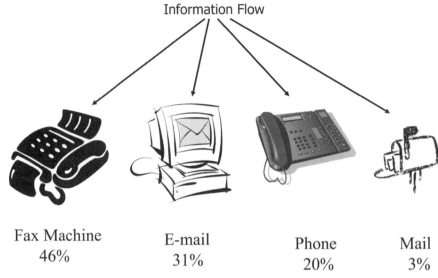

Information Flow

Fax Machine   E-mail   Phone   Mail
46%   31%   20%   3%

Figure 37.10: Information flow.

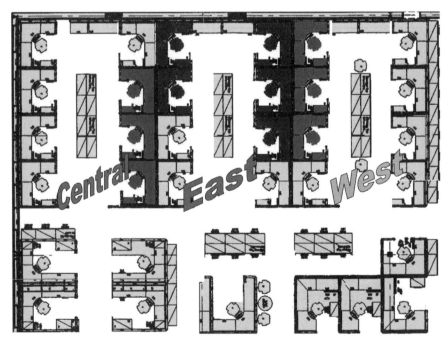

Floor Plan Before

Figure 37.11: Initial flow plan and responsibilities.

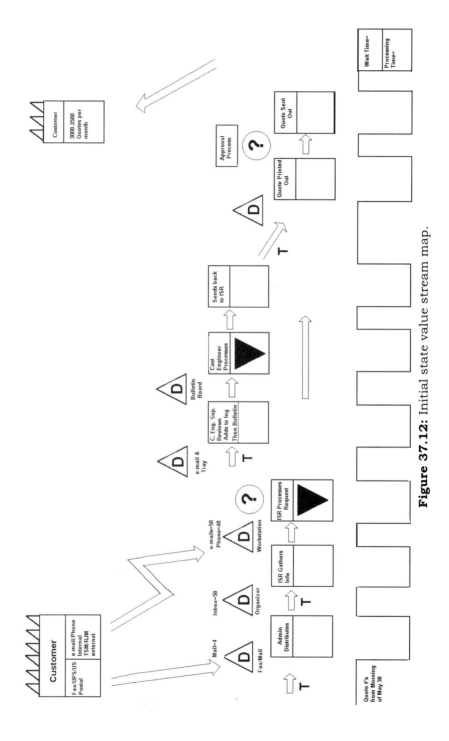

Figure 37.12: Initial state value stream map.

A wisdom-of-the-organization assessment for long lead time quotes yielded the cause-and-effect diagram and corresponding cause-and-effect matrix assessment shown in Figure 37.13. The highest ranked cause was too many tasks for the inside sales representative (ISR).

This led to a week-long collection of data where ISRs checked off the task that was being performed at 35 random times per day. A check sheet from this analysis is shown in Figure 37.14, along with a Pareto chart of the results. From a process point of view, the large amount of time spent on expedites and the small amount of time spent on quote follow-ups is not desirable.

Current cycle times measured by time observations were:

Task	Process Cycle Time
Request For Quote	5.4 min/Line Item
Quote Follow-Up	10 min
Orders	9.5 min/Line Item
ATR's	35 min
Expedites	20.3 min/Line Item
Credit/Debit	13.7 min

From a regional job description subdivision, this work led to revamping of work cell responsibilities and expectations, as described in Figure 37.15, where a description for each task is

Quotes/follow-up

- Same day turnaround and processing of quotes
- Status of quote communication to customer and management
- Quote track to completion
- Follow-up with customers on receipt of quote
- Close order through quote follow-up
- Report weekly follow-up hit rate in dollars

Order Expedites

- Same day entry of orders
- Expedite communications turnaround in 24 hours or sooner, if needed
- Proactive communications of late orders to customer
- Identify key parts numbers and customers for tracking of repeat business to close
- Process returns and credits

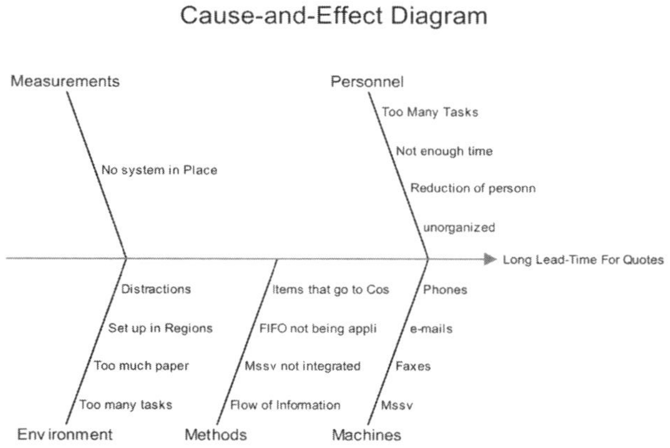

Cause and Effect Matrix	Key Process Output Variables (KPOV's)				
	Quote Turn-around Time	Customer Satisfaction	ISR Load	Paper Handling	Results
Ranking ——→	10	10	5	5	
1. Too Many tasks for an I.S.R	10	10	10	10	300
2. Flow of Information	10	9	10	9	285
3. Reduction of Personnel (30%)	10	5	10	3	215
4. Large number of faxes	9	3	9	10	215
5. Unorganized Behaviors	9	3	9	9	210
6. FIFO not being applied	10	9	0	0	190
7. Distractions(phones, e-mails, etc..)	3	5	9	9	170
8. Items that go to costing	10	3	3	5	170
9. Mssv not easily integrated	3	3	5	3	100
10. No measurement system in place	3	0	1	0	35
11. I.S.R's are set up in regions	0	0	5	0	25
Total					1915

Figure 37.13: Wisdom-of-the-organization inputs.

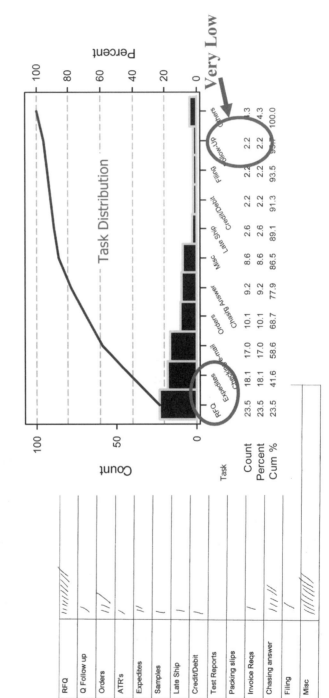

Figure 37.14: Data collection and ranking of wisdom-of-the-organization inputs.

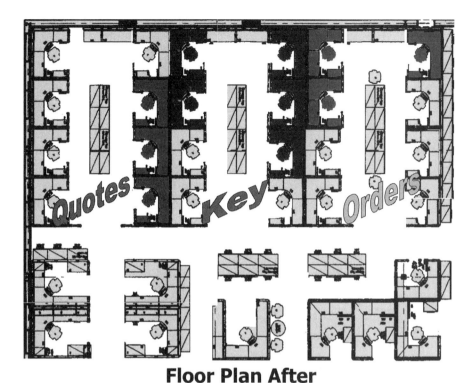

Floor Plan After

Figure 37.15: Reconfigured work cells and responsibilities.

Key accounts

- Handle all inquiries for key accounts from order, expedites, quotes, returns, etc.
- Strategically analyze results monthly and report orders and shipment activities for each month; that os, forecasts and demand pull
- Proactively close new business and repeat business

The resulting value stream map is shown in Figure 37.16. The 30,000-foot-level change impact from the process change is shown in Figure 37.17. The resulting process capability/performance metric is then shown in Figure 37.18. From these plots the process capability/performance metric estimation is

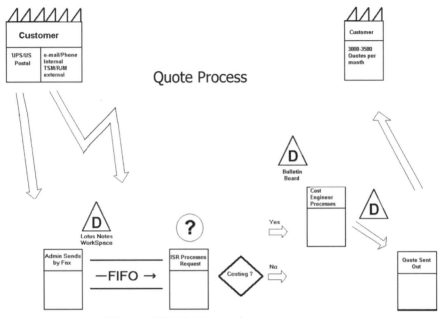

Figure 37.16: New value stream map.

- *Initial*: median of 2.1 days with 80% frequency of occurrence of 0.96–4.4 days
- *New*: median of 0.18 days with 80% frequency of occurrence of 0.05–0.72 days

The gap in the Figure 37.18 probability plot indicates that there are two distributions. This gap relates to quotes going overnight (e.g., 0–8 hours or 16–24 hours). As an alternative, one could consider converting to work hours. However, for this example, since a vast majority of completed transactions for the new process are within the 1-day criterion, a more accurate estimate is not justifiable.

The "fence posting" of plotted points in the probability plot occurred because of the measurement resolution, which affected calculated probability values. If visually the best estimate line seems to fit the data, I typically will go ahead and use the best estimate line estimates for determining the process capability/performance metric, even though the Anderson Darling statistic may be less than .05.

The company that implemented this change experienced benefits. The Inside Sales Department in this company processes during 34,000 quotes a year. During the past year, they have

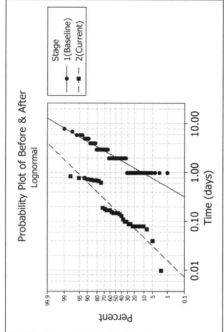

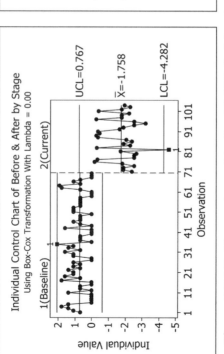

Figure 37.17: Change impact to the 30,000-foot-level project metric (sales quote turn-around processing time).

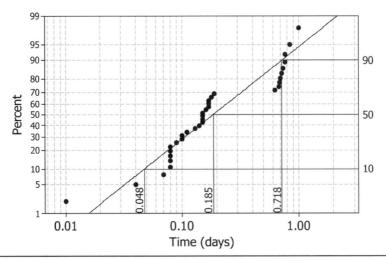

Predictable process (from previous individuals control chart) with an
approximate median of 0.2 days and 80% frequency of occurrence
between 0.05 and 0.70 days

Figure 37.18: Estimated process capability/performance metric of
inside sales quote turn around after the change from a lognormal
probability plot.

had a 30% reduction in workforce. The quote turnaround project
resulted in a lead-time measured in hours instead of days. The
projected savings were calculated at $43,800 per year. In reality,
the benefits were probably a lot higher in that the problems would
have been worse with the initial process due to the major staff reduction that was experienced. If the savings from the sales force
reduction were included in the financial benefit of the project, the
project benefits would have been much larger.

This project also identified many other potential projects in
the inside-sales function such as cycle time reduction, customer
feedback survey, and reduction of keystroke defects.

37.9   Example 37.3: Sales Personnel Scorecard/
Dashboard and Data Analyses

This example illustrates an IEE alternative to traditional score-
card/dashboard reporting and analyses described in Chapter 1.
More specifically, this example focuses on alternatives to the
charting described in Figures 1.1 to 1.3 for the Table 37.4 data.

In this example, this scorecard/dashboard creation process is compared to traditional scorecard/dashboard annual or quarter calendar-based statement reporting. Chapters 12 and 13 described the mechanics of creating satellite-level/30,000-foot-level control charts and formulating process capability/performance statements for a variety of situations.

As was noted earlier, the Figure 1.1 to 1.3 charts report formats typically lead to *stories* about the past. The chart presentation format will dictate the presented *story* type. For example, the calendar

Table 37.4: Sales Scorecard/Dashboard Data

Month Count	Year	Month	Revenue	Sales Person	Stage	Month Count	Year	Month	Revenue	Sales Person	Stage	Month Count	Year	Month	Revenue	Sales Person	Stage	Month Count	Year	Month	Revenue	Sales Person	Stage
1	1	1	34969	1	1	10	1	10	83161	5	1	20	2	8	81508	4	1	30	3	6	50595	3	1
1	1	1	88135	2	1	11	1	11	49674	1	1	20	2	8	69549	5	1	30	3	6	32913	4	1
1	1	1	51123	3	1	11	1	11	57223	2	1	21	2	9	95727	1	1	30	3	6	81762	5	1
1	1	1	50845	4	1	11	1	11	55203	3	1	21	2	9	62510	2	1	31	3	7	35650	1	1
1	1	1	131719	5	1	11	1	11	77731	4	1	21	2	9	88725	3	1	31	3	7	58252	2	1
2	1	2	54926	1	1	11	1	11	65248	5	1	21	2	9	19078	4	1	31	3	7	129721	3	1
2	1	2	157637	2	1	12	1	12	2000	1	1	21	2	9	147451	5	1	31	3	7	100734	4	1
2	1	2	95178	3	1	12	1	12	110131	2	1	22	2	10	101962	1	1	31	3	7	116974	5	1
2	1	2	69030	4	1	12	1	12	29210	3	1	22	2	10	53754	2	1	32	3	8	106538	1	1
2	1	2	117008	5	1	12	1	12	1200	4	1	22	2	10	96651	3	1	32	3	8	89405	2	1
3	1	3	42623	1	1	12	1	12	84348	5	1	22	2	10	54919	4	1	32	3	8	53907	3	1
3	1	3	93521	2	1	13	2	1	101319	1	1	22	2	10	120358	5	1	32	3	8	85316	4	1
3	1	3	63296	3	1	13	2	1	61193	2	1	23	2	11	38956	1	1	32	3	8	135957	5	1
3	1	3	53634	4	1	13	2	1	59790	3	1	23	2	11	39521	2	1	33	3	9	16504	1	1
3	1	3	90716	5	1	13	2	1	23991	4	1	23	2	11	125041	3	1	33	3	9	51972	2	1
4	1	4	53981	1	1	13	2	1	104281	5	1	23	2	11	74804	4	1	33	3	9	18991	3	1
4	1	4	67017	2	1	14	2	2	161092	1	1	23	2	11	83914	5	1	33	3	9	44125	4	1
4	1	4	85399	3	1	14	2	2	28392	2	1	24	2	12	48009	1	1	33	3	9	94590	5	1
4	1	4	69865	4	1	14	2	2	56699	3	1	24	2	12	100034	2	1	34	3	10	84307	1	1
4	1	4	152789	5	1	14	2	2	62438	4	1	24	2	12	111232	3	1	34	3	10	62449	2	1
5	1	5	57628	1	1	14	2	2	99260	5	1	24	2	12	68673	4	1	34	3	10	84446	3	1
5	1	5	47585	2	1	15	2	3	79160	1	1	24	2	12	102650	5	1	34	3	10	63752	4	1
5	1	5	21212	3	1	15	2	3	32581	2	1	25	3	1	75178	1	1	34	3	10	103945	5	1
5	1	5	41716	4	1	15	2	3	62689	3	1	25	3	1	102110	2	1	35	3	11	99710	1	2
5	1	5	78185	5	1	15	2	3	87080	4	1	25	3	1	80236	3	1	35	3	11	108526	2	2
6	1	6	95744	1	1	15	2	3	111742	5	1	25	3	1	40957	4	1	35	3	11	93391	3	2
6	1	6	3936	2	1	16	2	4	98524	1	1	25	3	1	103049	5	1	35	3	11	104531	4	2
6	1	6	62703	3	1	16	2	4	46928	2	1	26	3	2	49872	1	1	35	3	11	106597	5	2
6	1	6	32950	4	1	16	2	4	80334	3	1	26	3	2	45034	2	1	36	3	12	79179	1	2
6	1	6	96591	5	1	16	2	4	50350	4	1	26	3	2	71657	3	1	36	3	12	110223	2	2
7	1	7	79108	1	1	16	2	4	107349	5	1	26	3	2	61589	4	1	36	3	12	108309	3	2
7	1	7	94614	2	1	17	2	5	56133	1	1	26	3	2	113439	5	1	36	3	12	57019	4	2
7	1	7	106464	3	1	17	2	5	53586	2	1	27	3	3	103052	1	1	36	3	12	126439	5	2
7	1	7	46893	4	1	17	2	5	54897	3	1	27	3	3	52918	2	1	37	4	1	61433	1	2
7	1	7	110152	5	1	17	2	5	88038	4	1	27	3	3	130968	3	1	37	4	1	130435	2	2
8	1	8	64376	1	1	17	2	5	95695	5	1	27	3	3	21527	4	1	37	4	1	107330	3	2
8	1	8	27319	2	1	18	2	6	46721	1	1	27	3	3	145602	5	1	37	4	1	106640	4	2
8	1	8	47222	3	1	18	2	6	32251	2	1	28	3	4	78929	1	1	37	4	1	118398	5	2
8	1	8	63039	4	1	18	2	6	74020	3	1	28	3	4	34991	2	1	38	4	2	65322	1	2
8	1	8	121866	5	1	18	2	6	71424	4	1	28	3	4	98408	3	1	38	4	2	80393	2	2
9	1	9	105821	1	1	18	2	6	103391	5	1	28	3	4	77927	4	1	38	4	2	119582	3	2
9	1	9	22965	2	1	19	2	7	88761	1	1	28	3	4	131056	5	1	38	4	2	104869	4	2
9	1	9	57262	3	1	19	2	7	67731	2	1	29	3	5	56053	1	1	38	4	2	97565	5	2
9	1	9	56388	4	1	19	2	7	36421	3	1	29	3	5	51731	2	1	39	4	3	113024	1	2
9	1	9	95788	5	1	19	2	7	3010	4	1	29	3	5	46524	3	1	39	4	3	122048	2	2
10	1	10	83282	1	1	19	2	7	101091	5	1	29	3	5	82588	4	1	39	4	3	143169	3	2
10	1	10	48811	2	1	20	2	8	30112	1	1	29	3	5	64808	5	1	39	4	3	102895	4	2
10	1	10	57556	3	1	20	2	8	34052	2	1	30	3	6	45440	1	1	39	4	3	109127	5	2
10	1	10	1088	4	1	20	2	8	78787	3	1	30	3	6	68631	2	1						

boundaries in the Figure 1.3 bar-chart reporting format will surely lead to adjacent-month and previous yearly-month comparisons. Consider how accurate is a year-based reporting if something changed during the year? For example, if there was a fundamental sales process change in July, then we would be including old information with the latest information when examining annualized data in a pie chart. Wouldn't it be better to first identify if and when a change occurred and then either compare new to old process responses, or describe what is happening most recently?

Consider also, which interests us the most: the past or the future? Most often the response to this question is "the future." Reporting individual up-and-down historical movement or arbitrary-time-based comparisons do not provide insight to future process-output expectations, assuming that the process experiences no dramatic positive or negative change. However, if we could somehow estimate the future and we then do not like the resulting prediction, we gain insight to improvement focus opportunities; that is, the metric improvement needs pull for process improvement project creation. What is next described is an IEE metric reporting alternative that provides insight that these forms of reporting do not.

Figure 37.19 (part B) describes the results of a business area drill down of the gross revenue satellite-level metric. From this 30,000-foot-level scorecard/dashboard reporting analysis, we are able to identify a process shift in October 2003. This was when a team made a change and they could now see the impact from this change by the shift in the 30,000-foot-level control chart. The process reached an improved performance level, where the noted predictability statement reflects the past 5 months of stability.

The following IEE scorecard/dashboard metric reporting process will be used when analyzing the data:

1. Assess process predictability.
2. When the process is considered predictable, formulate a prediction statement for the latest region of stability. The usual reporting format for this statement is
   (a) When there is a specification requirement: nonconformance percentage or defects per million opportunities (DPMOs)
   (b) When there are no specification requirements: median response and 80% frequency of occurrence rate.

Interpretation of Figure 37.19 (Part B) using this process:

1. The individuals control chart of the mean sales from the five salespersons indicates that the between subgroup mean response shifted and established a new level of predictive performance in October 2003. The individuals control chart of log standard deviation indicates that the between subgroup variability differences by salesperson shifted and established a new level of predictive performance in October 2003.

2. From the probability plot of individual salesperson monthly revenue, a prediction statement for the new level of process performance is that the approximate expected salesperson's performance will be mean monthly revenue of $103,000 and 80% frequency of occurrence by month of $76,000 to $130,000; that is, 80% of all individual monthly sales performances is expected to be between these two estimates.

Since October 2003, this process has been experiencing common cause variability. These are best estimates of the performance of this process. If this process response is not satisfactory, something needs to be done to improve the process (i.e., a pull for project creation).

Figure 1.1 was included in Figure 37.19 (Part A) for illustrative purposesto compare IEE 30,000-foot-level metric reporting against one form of traditional performance measures reporting. The reader should compare this report-out format to other options shown in Figures 1.2 and 1.3.

For example, consider the month–year bar chart reporting format illustrated in Figure 1.3. I suspect that the stories typically conveyed from a Figure 1.3 report-out format would be quite different from the conclusions presented during an IEE performance metrics report-out. The stories that are conveyed from traditional reporting can often lead to resource-draining activities that have little value. For example, Joe might be told to investigate why September revenues are down when this reported value was from common-cause variation, not a special-cause condition.

I should point out that all data for this illustration were randomly generated, where the only process special cause occurrence was the process shift that occurred on October 2003. That is, except for this shift, all data up-and-down movements were what we could expect from common-cause variability.

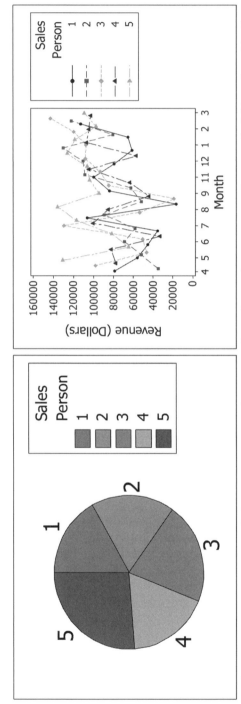

Figure 37.19: (Part A) Drill down to generated revenue from five salespersons, where probability plot of individual salesperson revenue (see Part B) is from the last 5 months of stability.

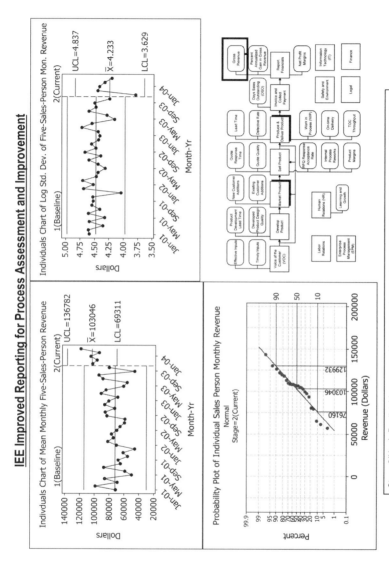

Figure 37.19: (Part B) Drill down to generated revenue from five salespersons, where probability plot of individual salesperson revenue is from the last 5 months of stability.

In Figure 37.19, we note that the estimated mean monthly revenue for the five salespersons is $103,046. Five times this mean response is greater than $500,000 mean monthly goal. Hence, our scorecard/dashboard prediction statement indicates that with the current process we expect to meet in the future the sales goals for the five salesmen. This statement also implies that any new higher goal for these five salesmen would require additional process change.

It should also be highlighted that when a process change does not occur on January 1 of a year, there will always be some bridging of old and new process levels with annual reporting. This phenomenon does not occur with IEE reporting, since process capability/performance metric statements can be made at any point in time during the year.

> ... when process input comparisons are assessed over an arbitrary interval such as annual, conclusions about the impact of these inputs can be distorted.

In addition, when process input comparisons are assessed over an arbitrary interval such as annual, conclusions about the impact of these inputs can be distorted. To illustrate this, consider the pie chart in Figure 1.1, which compared monthly salesperson revenue for the past 12 months. From this chart, it appears that salesperson number five contributed more revenue than the other salesmen. I will now illustrate an IEE approach to make these assessments using both visualization and hypothesis statements in regions of stability.

An E-DMAIC analysis was to test the hypothesis that generated monthly sales from the five salesmen were equal. Instead of making an annual or some other arbitrary timeframe comparison, it is better to make comparisons within stable/predictable regions; for example, something could have changed between regions of stability. Figure 37.20 shows a dot plot visualization and a statistical analysis, which indicates a statistically significant difference in mean stage response. Because of this, each stage was analyzed separately.

Figures 37.21 and 37.22 show visualization and statistical analysis for both Stage 1 (Baseline) and Stage 2 (Current). The marginal plot in each figure gives a visual representation of not only mean responses but also the accompanying variability that each salesperson is delivering. In the analysis of means (ANOM) in these figures five hypothesis tests are present; that is, the mean of each salesperson was compared to the overall mean. When a plotted mean value in an ANOM plot is beyond one of the two horizontal decision lines, significance is stated at the charted risk probability, 0.05 in this case.

From the Figure 37.21 before change analysis [i.e., Stage 1 (Baseline)], it appears that salesperson number five generated significantly larger revenue than the other salespersons. It appears that this larger revenue shifted the overall to a level that salesperson number two and four were significantly lower than the overall mean.

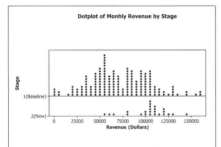
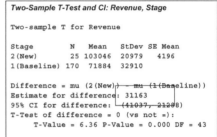

Conclusion: Significant difference in monthly sales personnel revenue. A per person best estimate for amount of monthly increased revenue is $31,200 (95% confidence interval of $21,300 and $41,000).

Figure 37.20: Visually and statistically comparing Stage 1 with Stage 2 mean monthly salesperson revenue.

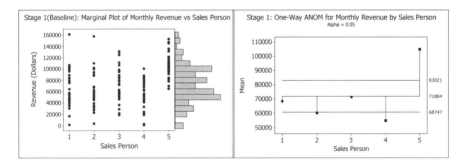

Stage 1(Baseline)
Observation: From the ANOM mean plot, it is noted that some sales person's mean revenue plot points are beyond the two horizontal decision lines.
Conclusion: Some sales person's mean monthly generated revenue was significantly different than the overall monthly mean. That is, there is reason to believe that some of the graphically-illustrated marginal plot means are different from the overall mean.

Figure 37.21: Stage 1: Mean monthly revenue visualization and statistical analysis by salesperson.

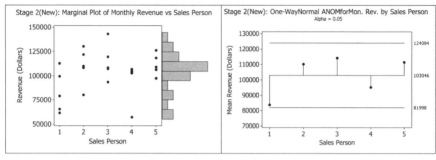

Stage 2(New)
Observation: From the ANOM mean plot, it is noted that no sales person mean revenue plot point is beyond the two horizontal decision lines.
Conclusion: There was no significant difference in any sales person's mean monthly generated revenue from the overall monthly mean. That is, we have no reason to believe that the graphically-illustrated marginal plot differences in means are what might be expect from sampling variability.

Figure 37.22: Stage 2: Mean monthly revenue visualization and statistical analysis by salesperson.

From the after change Figure 37.22 analyses [i.e., Stage 2 (Current)], no salesperson mean revenue could be shown statistically different from the overall mean. It was noted that between Stage 1 (Baseline) and Stage 2(Current) a project had changed the sales process of salespersons 1, 2, 3, and 4 to be consistent with the most successful salesperson (i.e., number 5).

The reader should compare the thought process and conclusions from this analysis to the stories that would have been created from Figures 1.1 to 1.3.

37.10   Exercises

1. You are to report the performance of a business process that you have implemented an improvement. There are many methods you could choose to show the change. Assuming the metric has continuous data and a specification, how would you present the information?

2. You are to report the performance of a business process you have implemented an improvement. There are many methods you could choose to show the change. Assuming the metric has attribute data (yield). How would you present the information?

3. You are to report the performance of a business process you have implemented an improvement. There are many methods you could choose to show the change. Assuming the metric has continuous data and no specification limits, how would you present the information?

PART VI
Improvement Project Roadmap: Control Phase

This part of this volume describes control plan implementation, along with other DMAIC tools. Project success at one point in time does not necessarily mean that the changes will stick after the project leader moves on to another project. Because of this, the control phase is included in define–measure–analyze–improve–control (DMAIC).

Included in this part of the volume is the setting of process input variable tolerances, 50-foot-level control, and pre-control charting.

38

P-DMAIC—Control Phase: Active Process Control

38.1 P-DMAIC Roadmap Component

In the enterprise define-measure-analyze-improve-control (E-DMAIC) roadmap measure phase, focus was given to tracking high-level 30,000-foot-level process outputs so that typical process input fluctuations that could affect the process' response level are considered common cause variability sources. When compiling an overall process capability/performance metric, the collection of common cause variability would then be used to assess whether the process delivers an adequate response relative to both internal and external customer needs. If this collective response is not satisfactory relative to these needs, an overall system process improvement project could be created as part of the E-DMAIC improve phase; that is, pull for project creation by business metric improvement need.

In the project define-measure-analyze-improve-control (P-DMAIC) roadmap measure phase, focus was given in the measure phase to describe the project baseline metric that was to be improved. One roadmap measure phase output was wisdom of the organization inputs on potential causes for the inadequate baseline metric performance.

The analyze phase presented a systematic approach for passively investigating various hypotheses for the purpose of gaining

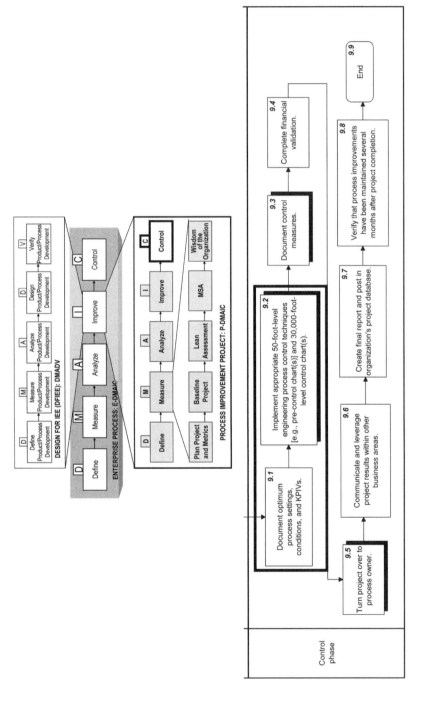

insight to what might be done differently to improve. The improve phase of the roadmap provided a proactive assessment system through DOE, plus an integration of creating thinking and Lean improvement methodologies. In addition, as part of the improve phase the last chapter described selecting and demonstrating project improvements.

This chapter progresses into the control phase in the area of active process control. The graphic in this section highlights the P-DMAIC roadmap steps (see Appendix D) that are described in this chapter. Appendix E contains the tollgate check sheets for this and other phases.

38.2   Process Improvements and Adjustments

As a process improvement strategy, we have suggested that both nonstatistical and statistical analysis techniques be used to gain insight to what might be done to improve the system. Improvements from this work could involve significantly changing the overall process or input variable levels. This management practice can have dramatic benefits over a commonly used practice of managing process *Y*s against organizational goals. As described earlier, this latter form of management can lead to the Enron effect.

Dr. Deming illustrated the increase in variability from process tweaking using a funnel. In this experiment, someone drops a marble though a funnel that is held waist high with the objective of impacting a targeted mark on the floor. The marble's impact point on the floor is marked. Before dropping the next marble, the experimenter is to then move the funnel to another position that compensates for the distance that the marble missed the target. For example, if the marble impacted the floor approximately one inch to the right of the target, the funnel should be moved approximately one inch to the left before dropping the next marble. After several marbles are dropped using this process, the impact scatter of markings is noted.

The experimenter now moves to a different position in the room and drops a similar number of marbles without readjusting the funnel after every shot. The impact scatter is again noted after several shots. A comparison of this shot pattern to the first shot pattern will show that the initial funnel adjustment procedure (i.e., process tweaking) leads to a larger shot pattern scatter (i.e., more process variability).

This situation is not different for an incapable process that is tweaked whenever the process has an observation that is outside its specification limits. This adjustment procedure can make the process variability worse so that the process has more defects from these adjustments than it would have without the adjustments.

However, there are situations where the Xs of a process need active management control so that a more desired Y response level is achieved. This is called engineering process control (EPC). This need occurs when a response is autocorrelated to previous responses. For this situation, random scatter does not exist over time and there are up and down cyclic trends in the data.

To illustrate, consider a 30,000-foot-level, nontransformed, individual-value control chart that is predictable. If we were required to provide a point estimate prediction for the next time period, we would pick the average response or the centerline of the control chart over the region of the chart's predictability (e.g., 23 months). However, if we were given the same requirement for the stock market's Dow Jones Industrial Average (DJIA), we could not make such a next-day prediction since the stock market is autocorrelated; that is, tomorrow's output is dependent more on its closing value today than on an average historical value. With no other information, our best estimate for tomorrow's DJIA closing value is today's closing value, that is, not, for example, the average value during last year.

If we want to improve the overall response of data that can experience auto-correlation from various input variation/levels, we need to have an input "knob" that can be adjusted to make this compensation. For the US Federal Reserve Board Chairman, interest rate is the knob used to control his observed economic indicator response levels.

This type of situation also occurs in business processes when process noise input levels change sufficiently to adversely affect the process's response levels relative to fulfilling customer requirements. To maintain a satisfactory response level, a timely adjustment procedure is needed so that there is minimal impact to the 30,000-foot-level process response. Various situations where this occurs are

- The number of people wanting to check-out in a grocery store can differ as a function of times of day and days of the week. Management needs to address this in staffing its check-outs.

- The frequency of calls in a call center can differ as a function of times of day and days of the week. Management needs to address this in staffing the call center.
- A grinding wheel wears. The wheel needs periodic redressing so that the desired grinding dimension is maintained.
- A titanium sheet of metal is chemically pickled using acid to change locally a sheet's thickness. Periodically, the acid needs replenishing to adjust for its depletion over time.

It is important to highlight that in all the above situations we had a "knob to adjust" and we knew how much adjustment was needed for a given *Y* response level adjustment. This is not the same as the production of a part that is not meeting specifications where only vague instructions are available about what adjustments should be made to process controllable input levels.

This chapter describes the application of exponentially weighted moving average (EWMA) an EPC and pre-control techniques to the above active process control needs.

38.3   IEE Application Examples: Engineering Process Control (EPC)

- *Transactional 30,000-foot-level metric:* An IEE project to improve days sales outstandings (DSOs) identified a key process input variable (KPIV) to the process as being the importance of calling customers in a timely fashion to ensure that they received the company's invoice. An automatic feedback system was created to notify the appropriate person in the company to make contact to ensure that the invoice was received.

38.4   Control of Process Input Variables

It would be great if all processes could be designed so that they are mistake proof and that input noise to the process does not affect the response. If this were the case, we would not need process metrics. Unfortunately, this is not typically the situation.

For those in the quality profession, the thought of process control typically generates thoughts about statistical control charting. Traditionally the approach for control charting has been to select a chart type from those described in Figure 10.1. The selected chart is then to be used by operations in real time to determine when a process is out of control, that is, experiences special cause conditions, for the purpose of making corrective action to the process.

As described earlier, generated control charting signals depend on the sampling techniques and can lead to the wrong activities if care is not exercised. It has been my real-world experience that control charts are typically not as useful a tool for operations to make timely adjustments to out-of-control processes as they are claimed to be. It seems that control charts are most often examined by the Quality department after the fact.

The 30,000-foot-level control chart can be used to identify process change. However, these charts are not useful for timely intervention and are not focusing on specific components of the overall process or inputs to these processes.

Nonetheless, the nature of some processes requires timely adjustments to maintain a satisfactory performance at the 30,000-foot-level (e.g., a part's dimension after extrusion). What is most desirable is that an input variable is identified so that it can be tracked frequently at the 50-foot-level (e.g., process temperature), so that appropriate timely adjustments can be made if this input variable drifts to an unacceptable level. Because these systems often have autocorrelated data, it can be beneficial to have a system to make adjustments when specification limits are approached. However, it is very important that the system is very capable of consistently delivering a response that is desirable before using this procedure; otherwise, the tweaking problems previously described can occur. It has been suggested that pre-control (described later in this chapter) are only applicable if the current process spread of six standard deviations covers less than 88% of the tolerance range (Traver, 1985).

Through the passive analyses and proactive DOE assessment techniques, acceptable input tolerances can be determined. The following section illustrates how this can be accomplished through a regression analysis.

38.5   Realistic Tolerances

Consider that the IEE methods presented earlier identified a critical key process output variable (KPOV) and then characterized

KPIVs. Consider also that mistake proofing methods were not found effective. We would like to then create a system to control the process inputs, which are continuous.

We can track process inputs through automation or manual techniques. This tracking can involve monitoring or control. Often we only monitor KPOVs because we are unable to control process inputs. But for situations where we are knowledgeable of KPIVs characteristics that affect the process and we can control these inputs, we have the opportunity of improving the process capability/performance metric.

When the KPIV to KPOV relationship is understood, the establishment of optimum levels for KPIVs can be accomplished through the following approach, which is exemplified in Figure 38.1:

1. Identify the target and specification for a critical KPOV.
2. Select from previous IEE activities KPIVs that have been shown to affect the KPOV.
3. Explain what has been learned from previous IEE activities (e.g., the DOE activities) about the levels of each KPIV that is thought to yield an optimum KPOV response.
4. Plot the relationship between each KPIV and the KPOV on an *X-Y* plot describing not only the best-fit line but also the

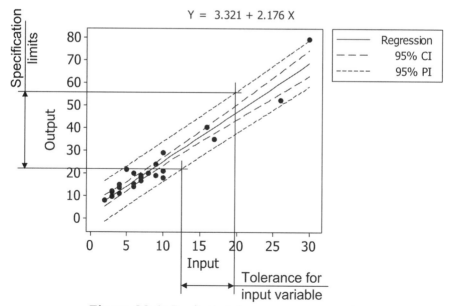

Figure 38.1: Realistic tolerance assessment.

95% prediction interval bounds. An approach to do this is to create 30 samples over the range of the KPIVs thought to optimize the KPOV. Plot then the relationship of each KPIV to the KPOV using statistical software to determine the 95% prediction bounds for individual points. When creating these relationships, consider not only the effect from each KPIV but also the simultaneous impact of other KPIVs.

5. Draw two parallel lines horizontally from the specification bounds of the KPOV to the upper and lower prediction limits.
6. Draw two parallel lines vertically from the intersection of the previously drawn lines and the prediction limits.
7. Determine the maximum tolerance permitted for the each KPIV by observing the *x*-axis intersection points of the two vertical lines.
8. Compare the determined KPIV tolerance to existing operating levels.
9. Implement changes to the standard operating procedures as required, documenting changes in the FMEA and control plan.

38.6   EWMA and EPC

Under the Shewhart model for control charting, it is assumed that the mean is constant. Also, errors are to be normal, independent, with zero mean and constant variance σ^2. This assumption is not true in many situations. EWMA techniques offer an alternative based on exponential smoothing, sometimes called geometric smoothing.

The computation of EWMA as a filter is done by taking the weighted average of past observations with progressively smaller weights over time. EWMA has flexibility of computation through the selection of a weight factor and can use this factor to achieve balance between older data and more recent observations.

EWMA techniques can be combined with EPC to indicate when a process should be adjusted. Application examples for EWMA with EPC include the monitoring of parts produced by a tool that wears and needs periodic sharpening, adjustment, or replacement.

Consider a sequence of observations Y_1, Y_2, Y_3, ..., Y_t. We could examine these data using any of the following procedures, with the differences noted:

- Shewhart: no weighting of previous data.
- CUSUM: equal weights for previous data (Reference: *Implementing Six Sigma*, 2nd edition).
- Moving average: weight, for example, the five most recent responses equally as an average.
- EWMA: weight the most recent reading the highest and decrease weights exponentially for previous readings.

A Shewhart, CUSUM, or moving average control chart for these variables data, would all be based on the model

$$Y_t = \eta + m_t$$

where the expected value of the observations $E(Y_t)$ is a constant η and m_t is $NID(0, \sigma_m^2)$. For the Shewhart model, the mean and variance are both constant, with independent errors. Also with the Shewhart model, the forecast for the next observation or average of observations is the centerline of the chart (η_0).

An EWMA is retrospective when plotted under Shewhart model conditions. It smoothes the time trace, thereby reducing the role of noise which can offer insight into what the level of the process might have been, which can be helpful when identifying special causes. Mathematically, for $0 < \lambda < 1$ this can be expressed as

$$EWMA = \hat{Y}_{s,t} = \lambda Y_t + \theta \hat{Y}_{s,t-1} \quad \text{where} \quad \theta = (1 - \lambda)$$

This equation can be explained as follows: At time t, the smoothed value of the response equals the multiple of lambda times today's observation plus theta times yesterday's smoothed value. A more typical plotting expression for this relationship is

$$EWMA = \hat{Y}_{t+1} = \hat{Y}_t + \lambda e_t \quad \text{where} \quad e_t = Y_t - \hat{Y}_t$$

This equation can be explained briefly. The predicted value for tomorrow equals the predicted value of today plus a "depth of memory parameter" (λ) times the difference between the observation and the current day's prediction. For plotting convenience, EWMA is often put one unit ahead of Y_t. Under certain conditions, as described later, EWMA can be used as a forecast.

The three sigma limits for a EWMA control chart are

$$\pm 3\sigma_{EWMA} = \sqrt{\lambda / (2 - \lambda)} [\pm 3\sigma_{Shewhart}]$$

When there are independent events, an EWMA chart with λ = 0.4 yields results almost identical to the combination of Western Electric rules, where the control limits are exactly half of those from a Shewhart chart (Hunter, 1989).

The underlying assumptions for a Shewhart model are often not true in reality. Expected values are not necessarily constant, and data values are not necessarily independent. A EWMA model does not have this limitation. A EWMA can be used to model processes that have linear or low-order time trends, cyclic behavior, and a response that is a function of an external factor, nonconstant variance, and autocorrelated patterns.

Though EWMA with EPC has applicability to active process control, the tool does not seem to be used very frequently. *Implementing Six Sigma*, 2nd edition (Breyfogle 2003a), includes an illustrative example of the application of EWMA and EPC.

38.7 Pre-control Charts

Pre-control charts, sometimes called stoplight control, monitors test units by classifying them into one of three groups (green, yellow, or red), as illustrated in Figure 38.2. From a small sample, the number of green, yellow, and red units observed determines when to stop and adjust the process. Since its initial proposal, at least three different versions of pre-control have been suggested. This chapter discusses the classical and two-stage process.

Classical pre-control refers to the original method proposed. Two-stage pre-control involves taking an additional sample if initial sample results are ambiguous.

The schemes of pre-control are defined by their group classification, decision, and qualification procedures. The setup or qualification procedure defines the required results of an initial sampling scheme to determine if pre-control is appropriate for the situation. For all three of these options, a process passes qualification if five consecutive green units are observed. Differences between the three versions of pre-control are most substantial in their methods of group classification. Classical and two-stage pre-control base the classification of units on specification limits.

After qualification or setup, a unit is classified as green if its quality characteristic is within the central half of the tolerance range or control chart limits. A yellow unit has a quality

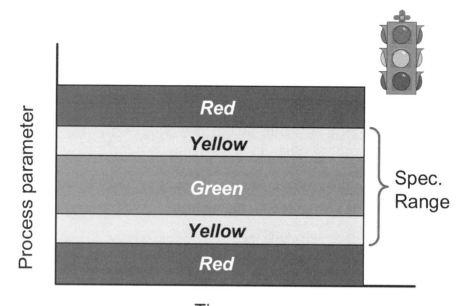

Time

Figure 38.2: Pre-control chart.

characteristic within the remaining tolerance range. A red unit has a quality characteristic that is outside the tolerance range for a classical or two-stage pre-control chart.

38.8 Pre-control Setup (Qualification Procedure)

Before conducting classical or two-stage pre-control on a "running" basis, a setup needs to be passed. A unit is classified as green if its quality characteristic is within the central half of the tolerance range. A yellow unit has a quality characteristic within the remaining tolerance. A red unit has a quality characteristic that is outside the tolerance range. The setup rules are as follows (Shainin and Shainin, 1989):

Setup. OK to run when five pieces in a row are green:

    A. If one yellow, restart count.

    B. If two yellows in a row, adjust.

    C. Return to setup after adjustment, tool change, new operator, or material.

38.9   Classical Pre-control Charts

With classical pre-control charts, a unit is classified as green if its quality characteristic is within the central half of the tolerance range. A yellow unit has a quality characteristic within the remaining tolerance range. A red unit has a quality characteristic that is outside the tolerance range.

When the setup or qualification rules are satisfied, the following rules are applied (Shainin and Shainin, 1989):

Running. Sample two consecutive pieces, A and B:

> A. If A is green, continue to run.
>
> B. If A is yellow, check B.
>
> C. If A and B are yellow, stop.
>
> D. If A or B is red, stop.

Average six sample pairs between consecutive adjustment:

Average Time between Process Adjustments	Sampling Interval
8 hours	Every 80 minutes
4 hours	Every 40 minutes
2 hours	Every 20 minutes
1 hour	Every 10 minutes

38.10   Two-Stage Pre-control Chart

The two-stage pre-control chart has the same red, yellow, and green rules as classical pre-control. With the two-stage pre-control chart, when the setup or qualification rules are satisfied, the following rules are applied (Steiner, 1997):
Sample two consecutive parts.

- If either part is red, stop process and adjust.
- If both parts are green, continue operation.
- If either or both of the parts are yellow, continue to sample up to three more units. Continue operation if the combined

sample contains three green units, and stop the process if three yellow units or a single red unit is observed.

The advantage of the more complicated decision procedure for two-stage over classical pre-control chart is that decision errors are less likely. However, the disadvantage is that, on the average, large sample sizes are needed to make decisions about the state of the process.

38.11   Example 38.1: EPC During Store Checkout

As a 30,000-foot-level voice of the customer metric, the time from entering a store's checkout line to the beginning of checkout was considered acceptable if this time was between 2 and 15 minutes. The upper value of 15 minutes was considered the maximum tolerable time from a customer frustration point of view, while the lower value of 2 was determined by the store; that is, they did not want to have excess checkers and also wanted customers to spend some time in the line since this increased the probability that they might buy an additional item in the check-out line.

A study was conducted where the average number of people in all checkout lines was recorded for a sample of customers entering the check-out line. This value was paired with how long it took before initiation of the customer's check-out. Results from this study are shown in Table 38.1.

Demand for checking out varies throughout the day and differs by day of the week. Create a management plan to shift employees between check-out duty and other in-store tasks.

An analysis of the realistic tolerance fitted-line plot yielded an acceptable tolerance of 1.9 to 3.7 people in the check-out line, as shown in Figure 38.3. A plan could then be setup where the average number of people in the check-out lines would be tracked using a pre-control chart that had specification limits of 1.9 to 3.7 people. The assignment and re-assignment of checkers would follow pre-control chart rules.

A technology implementation solution was being considered where a high-positioned camera could count and average the number of people at check-out every 3–5 minutes and electronically notify employees of their task re-assignments.

Table 38.1: Checkout Study

Test Number	1	2	3	4	5	6	7	8	9	10
Avg. No. People	6.6	0.9	0.4	7.6	6	6.5	8.3	1.8	4.6	6.3
Wait Time	17.1	1.3	0.7	23.9	17.3	22.1	27.9	5.3	12.4	18.9

Test Number	11	12	13	14	15	16	17	18	19	20
Avg. No. People	1.9	9	6.4	0.1	9.8	8.7	8.6	2.1	0.7	4.5
Wait Time	2.1	28.7	19.2	0.8	28.7	24.4	24.9	4.4	2.6	14.5

Test Number	21	22	23	24	25	26	27	28	29	30
Avg. No. People	3.5	9.4	4.3	4.7	0.8	1.2	3.2	7.3	8.2	3.7
Wait Time	13.4	31.3	11.8	13.4	3.5	4.4	8.4	22.3	23.9	11.4

Test Number	31	32	33	34	35	36	37	38	39	40
Avg. No. People	5	0.2	9.6	1.5	7.1	5.9	2.5	6.1	4.9	2.7
Wait Time	17.1	0.1	24.8	4.7	19.3	16.2	8.6	17.1	13.7	7.3

Test Number	41	42	43	44	45	46	47	48	49	50
Avg. No. People	1	7.7	5.4	4.1	6.7	10	2.2	7.4	9.1	0.6
Wait Time	6.8	23.3	17.2	9.9	20.8	27.4	7.8	21.5	29.4	0.5

Test Number	51	52	53	54	55	56	57	58	59	60
Avg. No. People	3.4	1.7	7.9	8.1	3.1	8.8	1.6	9.7	7	1.3
Wait Time	10.6	6.4	25.9	23.9	13.6	29.7	3.4	28.2	20.8	0.9

Test Number	61	62	63	64	65	66	67	68	69	70
Avg. No. People	5.6	2	7.2	5.8	2.9	2.8	8	5.2	2.4	8.9
Wait Time	17.8	3.5	21.3	20.7	8.1	11.0	22.5	14.4	5.8	30.0

Test Number	71	72	73	74	75	76	77	78	79	80
Avg. No. People	5.3	5.1	4	1.4	4.8	9.2	8.5	6.9	7.5	3.9
Wait Time	15.9	13.4	10.9	1.4	14.5	24.0	27.3	20.2	18.4	12.9

Test Number	81	82	83	84	85	86	87	88	89	90
Avg. No. People	3.3	7.8	4.2	3.6	9.5	0.3	5.5	3.8	6.8	5.7
Wait Time	13.3	24.9	11.3	8.1	28.3	1.2	15.5	13.1	17.2	19.1

Test Number	91	92	93	94	95	96	97	98	99	100
Avg. No. People	9.9	1.1	8.4	2.3	6.2	2.6	9.3	0.5	4.4	3
Wait Time	25.3	5.4	25.8	6.7	17.0	6.2	24.6	5.9	13.0	9.8

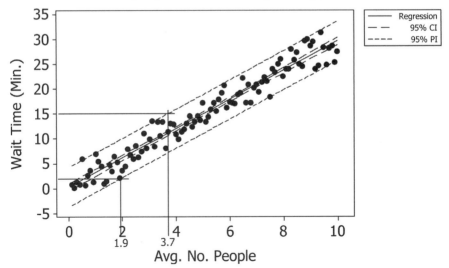

Figure 38.3: Determining KPIV tolerance.

38.12 Exercises

1. A manufacturing process produces quality products whenever a grinding wheel is well maintained. Describe how the techniques in this chapter could be used to maintain this process.

2. A manufacturing process produces sheet metal, which has a tightly toleranced thickness requirement. The processes consistently produces quality product whenever the bath for an etching process step has the correct level of acid. Describe how the techniques in this chapter could be used to maintain this process.

39

P-DMAIC – Control Phase: Control Plan and Project Completion

39.1 P-DMAIC Roadmap Component

The last chapter describes active control. This chapter describes the control plan and project completion. The graphic in this section highlights the project define–measure–analyze–improve–control (P-DMAIC) roadmap steps (see Appendix Section D.1) that are described in this chapter. Appendix E contains the tollgate check sheets for this and other phases.

39.2 Control Plan: Is and Is Nots

A control plan offers a systematic approach for process control and identifying/resolving issues. It offers a troubleshooting guide for process owners through its documented response plan. A good control plan strategy is a means to

- Reduce process tampering.
- Provide a vehicle for the initiation/implementation of process improvement activities.

985

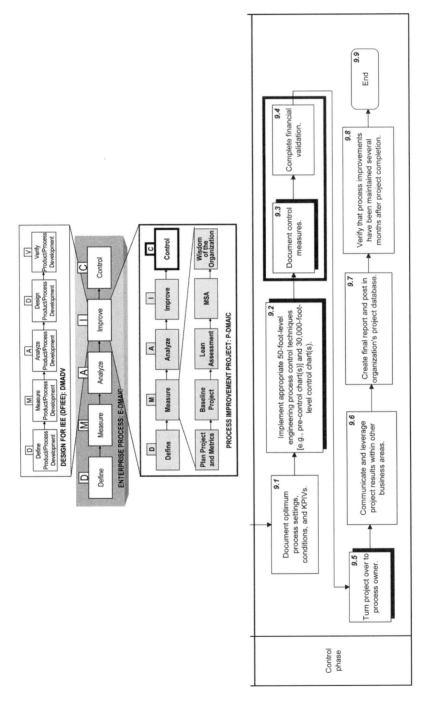

- Describe the training needs for standard operating procedures.
- Document maintenance schedule requirements.

Control plans should reduce the amount of firefighting and save money through fire preventive actions; however, often control plans are not set to the optimum conditions, as illustrated in Figure 39.1. Excessive controls cause unnecessary expense, and a lack of controls can lead to expensive problems.

A control plan is *not a*

- way to establish excessive and unnecessary controls.
- plan to add inspection or audits.
- list of next steps of a project.
- way to create more documents or a bureaucracy.
- way get the organization to address a pet peeve.
- way to create more cost, additional lead time, or customer issues.
- set of ambiguous or vague instructions with no owners.
- firefighting tool.

> A control plan offers a systematic approach for process control and identifying/resolving issues. It offers a troubleshooting guide for process owners through its documented response plan.

39.3   Controlling and Error-Proofing Processes

Earlier I used a go-to-school/work process to describe input-process-output (IPO). In this section, the following statements were made to describe process inputs.

> If we examine the inputs to our process, there are both controllable inputs and uncontrollable or noise inputs. A controllable input might be setting the alarm clock, while an uncontrollable input is whether someone had an accident on our route that affected our travel time.

The setting of the alarm is indeed a controllable variable as I described it. However, what we really want is an alarm to sound at a certain point in time for us to get out of bed so that we can

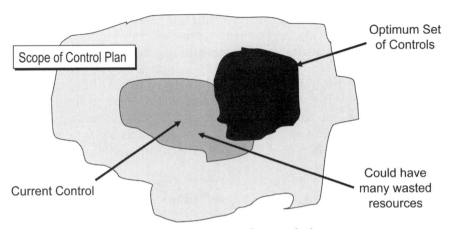

Figure 39.1: Scope of control plan.

leave the house on time, which in turn should get us to work/school on time.

The question of concern is whether this process is mistake proof. An failure mode and effects analysis (FMEA) of this process would indicate that it is not. For example, we might forget to set the alarm, the power to an electric alarm clock might be interrupted during the night, or we might turn off the alarm clock and go back to sleep.

If key process input variable (KPIV) levels are subject to errors, this can be a very large detriment to achieving a consistent system response output over time. To make our process more mistake proof, we might purchase two clocks, one electric and the other battery operated, which are placed on the opposite side of the room from the bed so that we have to get up to turn off the clocks. However, we still have the exposure of forgetting to set the alarm clock. Perhaps this is where a technology solution would be appropriate; for example, a 7-day programmable clock for wake-up times could reduce the risk of this error type.

Similarly, it is important to control KPIVs within organizational systems. However, this control mechanism can be more difficult when many people are involved in the process. Because of this, we create a control plan that documents this low-level, but important, activity; making the control mechanism as mistake proof as possible.

The tracking of KPIVs at the 50-foot-level involves frequent sampling and reporting so that changes to input levels are quickly detected. Timely corrective action can then be made following the procedure documented in the reaction plan of the control plan. This timely resolution of important process input issues minimizes exposure to an unsatisfactory impact to the process 30,000-foot-level KPOV.

39.4   Control Plan Creation

As described in the E-DMAIC phase, a control plan is a written document created to ensure that processes are run so that products or services meet or exceed customer requirements at all times. In IEE, created or modified control plans during a P-DMAIC project are to have linkage to the controls in E-DMAIC.

A control plan should be a living document with both additions and deletions of controls based on experience from the process. A control plan may need approval of the procuring organization(s). A control plan is an extension of the control column of an FMEA. The FMEA is an important source for the identification of KPIVs that are included within a control plan. Other sources for the identification of KPIVs are process maps, cause-and-effect matrices, multivariable studies, regression analysis, DOE and IEE project execution findings.

The traditional focus of a control plan has been to offer a systematic approach for finding and resolving out-of-control conditions. It can offer a troubleshooting guide for operators through its documented reaction plan. A good control plan strategy should reduce process tampering, provide a vehicle for the initiation/implementation of process improvement activities, describe the training needs for standard operating procedures, and document maintenance schedule requirements. Control plans should reduce the amount of firefighting and save money through fire preventive actions.

A control plan should be created from the knowledge gained from other IEE phases and utilize mistake proofing as much as possible. KPIVs considerations should include monitoring procedures, frequency of verification, and selection of optimum targets/specifications. Uncontrollable noise inputs' considerations should include their identification, control procedures, and robustness of the system to the noise. Standard operating procedure issues include documentation, ease-of-use, applicability, utilization, updating, and training. Maintenance procedure issues include identification of critical components, scheduling frequency, responsibility, training, and availability of instructions.

AIAG (1995a) lists three types of control plans: prototype, prelaunch, and production. A prototype control plan is a description of measurements, material, and performance tests that are to occur during the building of prototypes. A prelaunch control plan is a description of measurements, material, and performance tests that are to occur after prototype and before normal production. A Production control plan is a comprehensive documentation of product/process characteristics, process controls, tests, and measurement systems occurring during normal production.

39.5 AIAG Control Plan: Entries

This section describes the control plan format used in the automobile industry. This section was included to stimulate thought on the creation of appropriate control plan entries for other transactional and manufacturing applications. Entries from tables presented in this section and Table 3.2 can aid with the formulation of IEE value-chain linkage control plans for a variety of situations.

Categories that AIAG (1995a) includes in a control plan as part of advanced product quality planning (APQP) are noted below. The general control plan layout is shown in Table 39.1, where the term "characteristics" in the table means a distinguishing feature, dimension, or property of a process or its output (product) on which continuous response or attribute data can be collected.

Header Information

1. *Control plan type*: Prototype, prelaunch, production.
2. *Control plan number*: A tracking number, if applicable.
3. *Part number/latest change*: Number to describe the system, subsystem, or component that is to be controlled, along with any revision number.
4. *Part name or description*: Name and description of the product or process that is to be controlled.
5. *Supplier/plant*: Name of company and appropriate division, plant, or department that is preparing the control plan.

Table 39.1: Control Plan Entry

Part/Process Number	Process Name/Operation Description	Machine, Device, Jig, Tools for Mfg.	Characteristics			Special Char. Class	Methods					
			No.	Product	Process		Product/Process Specification/Tolerance	Evaluation/Measurement Technique	Sample		Control Method	Reaction Plan
									Size	Freq.		
⑮	⑯	⑰	⑱	⑲	⑳	㉑	㉒	㉓			㉕	㉖

Header Information ① 1 to 14

Methods ㉔   Sample ㉔

6. *Supplier code*: Procurement organization identification number.
7. *Key contact and phone*: Name and contact information for primary person who responsible for control plan.
8. *Core team*: Names and contact information for those responsible for preparing the control plan and its latest revision.
9. *Supplier/plant approval date*: If required, obtain approval from responsible facility.
10. *Date (original)*: Date the original control plan was compiled.
11. *Date (revision)*: Date of latest update to the control plan.
12. *Customer engineering approval and date*: If required, obtain the approval of the responsible engineer.
13. *Customer quality approval and date*: If required, obtain approval of supplier quality representative.
14. *Other approvals and dates*: If required, obtain approvals.

Line by Line Items

15. *Part or process number*: Usually referenced from process flow chart. When there are multiple assembled parts, list individual part numbers.
16. *Process name/operation description*: All steps in the manufacturing of a system, subsystem, or component, which are described in a process flow diagram. This line entry contains the process/operation name that best describes the activity that is addressed.
17. *Machine, device, jig, tools for manufacturing*: Identification of the processing equipment for each described operation; for example, machine, device, jig, or other tools for manufacturing.
18. *Number characteristic*: Cross-reference number from which all applicable documents can be referenced (e.g., FMEA).
19. *Product characteristic*: Features or properties of a part component or assembly that are described on drawings or other primary engineering information. All special characteristics need to be listed in the control plan, while other product characteristics for which process controls are routinely tracked during normal operations may be listed.
20. *Process characteristic*: Process characteristics are the process-input variables that have a cause-and-effect relationship with the identified product characteristics. A process

characteristic can only be measured at the time it occurs. The core team should identify process characteristics for which variation must be controlled to minimize product variation. There could be one or more process characteristics listed for each product characteristic. In some processes, one process characteristic may affect several product characteristics.

21. *Special characteristic classification*: Customers may use unique symbols to identify important characteristics such as those affecting safety, compliance with regulations, function, fit, or appearance. These characteristics can be determined (e.g., critical, key, safety, or significant).

22. *Product/process specification/tolerance*: Sources can include various engineering documents such as drawings, design reviews, material standard, computer-aided design data, manufacturing, and/or assembly requirements.

23. *Evaluation/measurement technique*: Identifies measurement system that is used. Could include gages, fixtures, tools, and/or test equipment that is required to measure the part/process/manufacturing equipment. An analysis of linearity, reproducibility, repeatability, stability, and accuracy of the measurement system should be completed before relying on a measurement system, where improvements are made as applicable.

24. *Sample size and frequency*: Identifies sample size and frequency when sampling is required.

25. *Control method*: Contains a brief description of how the operation will be controlled, including applicable procedure numbers. The described control method should be based on the type of process and an effective analysis of the process. Examples of operational controls are inspection, mistake proofing, and sampling plans. Descriptions should reflect the planning and strategy that is being implemented in the process. Elaborate control procedures typically reference a procedure or procedure number. Control methods should be continually evaluated for their effectiveness in controlling the process. Significant changes in the process should lead to an evaluation of the control method.

26. *Reaction plan*: Specifies the corrective actions that are necessary to avoid producing nonconforming products or operating out of control (i.e., having an unpredictable process). The people closest to the process should normally be responsible for the actions. This could be the operator, jobsetter, or supervisor, who is clearly designated in the plan. Provisions should be made for documenting reactions.

Suspect and nonconforming products must be clearly identified and quarantined, and disposition made by the responsible person who is designated in the reaction plan. Sometimes this column will make reference to a specific reaction plan number, identifying the responsible person.

Example control plan entries using this format are shown in Table 39.2.

A control plan checklist is noted below (AIAG, 1995a). Any negative comment is to have an associated comment and/or action required along with responsible part and due date.

1. Were the above control plan methods used in preparing the control plan?
2. Have all known customer concerns been identified to facilitate the selection of special product/process characteristics?
3. Are all special product/process characteristics included in the control plan?
4. Were the appropriate FMEA techniques used to prepare the control plan?
5. Are material specifications that require inspection identified?
6. Are incoming material and component packaging issues addressed?
7. Are engineering performance-testing requirements identified?
8. Are required gages and test equipment available?
9. If required, has there been customer approval?
10. Are gage methods compatible between supplier and customer?

The above guidelines are consistent with the basic IEE method. However, I would suggest including 30,000-foot-level key process output variables (KPOVs) wherever appropriate. IEE project results can have a major influence in the details of the control plan as they currently exist in an organization.

39.6 Project Completion

Before a project is complete, the process owner needs to agree to the conclusions of the IEE project and be willing to take over any responsibilities resulting from the project. Organizations need to establish a process for this transfer of ownership.

One approach to accomplish this transfer is that the black belt schedules and then leads a project turnover meeting. If the project owner accepts the project, the black belt works with the owner to finalize the presentation slides. The process owner and project team then present the results. However, if the process owner rejects the project results/conclusions, the process owner, black belt and champion need to discuss the project. If they agree to continue the project, agreement needs to be reached as to what specifics need to be addressed within the DMAIC procedure. Other options for this meeting are that the project be redefined or placed on hold.

Other items that also need to be addressed are

- To maximize gains, a process needs to be established that leverages the results of a project to other areas of the business. A communication process needs to be established between organizations.
- Organizations need to encourage the documentation of projects so that others can understand and use the information learned. A repository needs to be established for storing project information so that others can easily research and learn from the project findings.
- Organizations need to check after some period of time to insure that project gains are sustained after the project is completed.

39.7 Applying IEE

IEE complements the traditional approach that creates control plans. Processes that are well established and have no problems using their existing control procedures would not be a good IEE process improvement project candidate. However, processes that are experiencing problems can be the target of IEE work, if these processes impact the organizational 30,000-foot-level and satellite-level scorecard/dashboard metrics. Results from this IEE work can then directly impact the control plan for this process.

Organizations should consider having discussions with HR about the policy of including control-planning items as specific items into employee performance plans, where measurements are assessed as a 30,000-foot-level scorecard/dashboard metric.

Table 39.2: Example Control Plan Entries [AIAGc].

Header Information

Part/Process Number	Process Name/Operation Description	Machine, Device, Jig, Tools for Mfg	No.	Characteristics Product	Characteristics Process	Special Char. Class	Product/Process Specification/Tolerance	Evaluation/Measurement Technique	Sample Size	Sample Freq.	Control Method	Reaction Plan
3	Plastic injection molding	Mach No. 1-5	18	Appearance		*	Free of blemishes	Visual inspecton	100%	Continuous	100% insp	Notify supervisor
				No blemishes			Flowlines	1st piece buy-off			Check sheet	Adjust/re-check
						*	Sink marks	1st piece buy-off			Check sheet	Adjust/re-check
		Machine No. 1-5	19	Mounting hole loc.			Hole "X" location	Fixture #10	1st piece	Buy-off per run	Check sheet	Adjust/re-check
							25 +/- 1mm		5 pcs	Hr	x-bar & R chart	Quarnantine and adjust
		Machine No 1-5	20	Dimension		*	Gap 3 +/- .5 mm	Fixture #10	1st piece	Buy-off per run	Check sheet	Adjust and recheck
		Fixture #10	21	Perimenter fit		*	Gap 3 +/- .5mm	Check gap to fixture 4 locations	5 pcs	Hr	x-bar & R chart	Quarantine and adjust
		Machine No 1-5	22		Set-up of mold machine		See attached set-up card	Review of set-up card and machine settings	Each set-up		1st piece buy-off	Adjust and reset machine
											Inspector verifies setting	

Header Information

Part/Process Number	Process Name/Operation Description	Machine, Device, Jig, Tools for Mfg.	Characteristics			Special Char. Class	Product/Process Specification/Tolerance	Methods				Reaction Plan
			No.	Product	Process			Evaluation/Measurement Technique	Sample		Control Method	
									Size	Freq.		
3	Soldering connections	Wave solder machine		Wave solder height		*	2.0 +/- 0.25mc	Sensor continuity check	100%	Continuous	Automated inspection (error proofing)	Adjust and retest
					Flux concentration		Standard #302B	Test sampling lab environment	1 pc	4 hours	x-MR chart	Segregate and retest

Header Information

Part/Process Number	Process Name/Operation Description	Machine, Device, Jig, Tools for Mfg.	Characteristics			Special Char. Class	Product/Process Specification/Tolerance	Methods				Reaction Plan
			No.	Product	Process			Evaluation/Measurement Technique	Sample		Control Method	
									Size	Freq.		
4	Form metal bracket	Stamping die (13-19)	6	Hole			Presence of hole	Light beam/light sensor	100%	ongoing	Automated inspection (error proofing)	Segregate and replace hole punch

Header Information

Part/Process Number	Process Name/Operation Description	Machine, Device, Jig, Tools for Mfg.	Characteristics			Special Char. Class	Product/Process Specification/Tolerance	Methods				Reaction Plan
			No.	Product	Process			Evaluation/Measurement Technique	Sample		Control Method	
									Size	Freq.		
30	Broach internal spline	Acme Broach B-752		Yoke			Pitch dia. .7510 .7525	Visual comparator	1st pc	buy-off per run	Set-up sheet	Repair tool and recheck
								Special dial indicator T-0375	2 pcs	each shift	Tool control check sheet	Contain parts, replace tool and recheck

39.8   P-DMAIC Summary

The E-DMAIC section of this volume provided insight to how organizations can benefit from knowledge-centered activity (KCA) in an IEE system and create a long-lasting Level Five System. This P-DMAIC section provided a detailed project improvement execution roadmap that had a true integration of Lean with Six Sigma tools. Additional articles/information about IEE and how-to-obtain more information about the subprocess roadmap drill downs (i.e., shaded process steps) are described at www. SmarterSolutions.com.

39.9   Exercises

1. In Example 28.3, a multiple regression model was created for lead time. Create a specification for the KPIV "D," given a lead time that was to be between 460 and 500, treating the other factors as noise.
2. Reference Exercise 14.5 to identify potential control plan items. Assume that the IEE change noted involved sampling several parts daily to ensure that the now "very capable" process relative to quality did not drift. With the new process only one dimension was determined to be a potential problem for this process, which has very large daily volume. Considering that the quality process improvement change involved the identification of a KPIV when machining parts; that is, it was determined that the speed at which a part is machine should be between certain limits (not normally a problem but could occur).

   (a) Consider what control plan item and action plan would assess the overall process production rate at a high level.
   (b) Consider what control plan item and action plan would assess the sampling and inspection of one-part daily from a high-level perspective.
   (c) Consider what control plan item and action plan would address the KPIV, machine speed.

PART VII
Appendix

Appendix A: Infrastructure

A.1 Roles and Responsibilities

IEE roles and responsibilities build upon the structure of traditional Lean Six Sigma deployments. This organizational structure includes:

- *Executive*
  - Motivates others towards a common vision
  - Sets the standard, demonstrate the behaviors
  - Uses satellite-level and 30,000-foot-level scorecard/dashboard metrics
  - Asks the right questions
  - Uses IEE tools in day-to-day operations
  - Is visible
  - Gives a short presentation for each IEE training wave
  - Attends project completion presentations conducted by IEE team
  - Stays involved
- *Measurements and Improvements Function (Steering Team)*
  - Same as executive roles and responsibilities, plus
  - Develops project selection criteria
  - Sets policies for accountability for project results

- Develops policies for financial evaluation of project benefits
- Establishes internal and external communication plan
- Identifies effective training and qualified trainers
- Develops human resource policies for IEE roles
- Determines computer hardware and software standards
- Sets policies for team reward and recognition
- Identifies high potential candidates for IEE roles
- *Champion*
  - Removes barriers to success
  - Develops incentive programs with executive team
  - Communicates and executes the IEE vision
  - Determines project selection criteria with executive team
  - Identifies and prioritize projects
  - Question methodology and project improvement recommendations
  - Verifies completion of phase deliverables
  - Drives and communicates results
  - Approves completed projects
  - Leverages project results
  - Rewards and recognizes team members
- *Master black belt*
  - Functions as change agents
  - Conducts and oversees IEE training
  - Coaches black belts/green belts
  - Leverages projects and resources
  - Formulates project selection strategies with steering team
  - Communicates the IEE vision
  - Motivates others toward a common vision
  - Approves completed projects
- *Black belt*
  - Leads change
  - Communicates the IEE vision
  - Leads the team in the effective utilization of the IEE Methodology
  - Selects, teaches, and uses the most effective tools
  - Develops a detailed project plan
  - Schedules and leads team meetings
  - Oversees data collection and analysis
  - Sustains team motivation and stability
  - Delivers project results
  - Tracks and reports milestones and tasks

- Calculates project savings
- Interfaces between Finance and Information Management (IM)
- Monitors critical success factors and prepare risk abatement plans
- Prepares and presents executive level presentations
- Completes 4–6 projects per year
- Communicates the benefit of the project to all associated with the process
- *Green belt: Similar to black belt except that the green belt typically*
  - Addresses projects that are confined to their functional area
  - Has less training than black belts
  - Leads improvement projects as a part-time job function
- *Yellow belt*
  - Supports black belt and green belt project execution as a team member
  - Offers suggestions for improving day-to-day work and measurement systems
- *Sponsor*
  - Functions as change agents
  - Removes barriers to success
  - Ensures that process improvements are implemented and sustained
  - Obtains necessary approval for any process changes
  - Communicates the IEE vision
  - Aids in selecting team members
  - Maintains team motivation and accountability

A.2 Reward and Recognition

When building an IEE infrastructure, reward and recognition need to be addressed. Lessons learned from past Six Sigma and Lean Six Sigma deployments can be very beneficial.

Successful implementations have developed special reward and recognition systems. The following list summarizes the black belt recognition program for one company. Note that this plan does not mention rewarding others in the Six Sigma work (Snee *et al.*, 2003):

- *Base Pay*
  - Potential increase at time of selection
  - Retain current salary grade
  - Normal group performance review and merit pay
- *Incentive Compensation*
  - Special plan for black belts
  - Target award at 15% of base pay
  - Performance rating on 0–150% scale
  - Measured against key project objectives
  - Participation ends at end of black belt assignment

Another company's plan is more complete in that it includes the recognition of green belts, master black belts, champions, and other team members.

- *Black belt Selection* – Receive Six Sigma pin
- *Black belt certification* – $5,000 certification bonus plus plaque
- *Black belt project completion*
  - $500 to $5,000 in cash or stock options for first project
  - Plaque with project name engraved for first and subsequent projects
- *Black belt Six Sigma activity awards*
  - Recognize efforts and achievements during projects with individual and team awards – Cash, tickets, dinners, shirts, etc.
- *Green belt recognition*
  - Similar to black belt recognition
  - No certification bonus
- *Project team member recognition*
  - Similar to black belt and green belt recognitions
  - No certification awards
- *Annual Six Sigma celebration event*
  - Presentation of key projects
  - Dinner reception with senior leadership

It should be noted that all rewards need not be monetary. Peer and management recognition such as opportunity for project presentation is a greater reward than money. The most appropriate plan is company dependent; that is, what will work for one company or individual will not necessarily work for another.

Appendix B: Six Sigma Metric and Article

B.1   Sigma Quality Level

The purpose of this section is to provide a basic understanding of sigma quality level so that the reader can understand the methodology. IEE discourages the use of sigma quality level metric at both the enterprise and project execution level; however, the reader needs a basic understanding since the term can arise in conversations with other Six Sigma practitioners. I will reference a failure rate unit of parts per million (ppm); however, DPMO could be used instead of ppm.

The sigma level (i.e., sigma quality level) sometimes used as a measurement within a Six Sigma program, includes a $\pm 1.5\sigma$ value to account for "typical" shifts and drifts of the mean. This sigma quality level relationship is not linear. In other words, a percentage unit improvement in ppm defect rate does not equate to the same percentage improvement in the sigma quality level.

Figure B.1 shows the sigma quality level associated with various services, considering the 1.5σ shift of the mean. From this figure, we note that the sigma quality level of most services is about four sigma, while world class is considered six. A goal of IEE implementation is continually to improve processes and become world class.

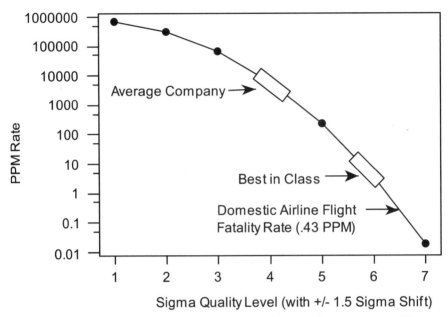

Figure B.1: Implication of the sigma quality level. Parts per million
(PPM) rate for part or process step.

Figures B.2, B.3, and B.4 illustrate various aspects of a normal
distribution as it applies to Six Sigma measures and the implication of the 1.5σ shift. Figure B.2 illustrates the basic measurement concept of Six Sigma and frequency of nonconformance.
Figure B.3 shows the frequency of nonconformance in ppm
units, if the data were centered within these limits and had various standard deviations. Figure B.4 extends Figure B.3 to non-
central data relative to specification limits, where the data mean
is shifted by 1.5σ. Figure B.5 shows the relationship of ppm defect
rates versus sigma quality level for a centered and 1.5σ shifted
process, along with a quantification for the amount of improvement needed to change a sigma quality level. Table L has a finer
conversion of ppm rates to sigma quality level values.

A metric that describes how well a process meets requirements
is process capability. A Six Sigma quality level process can be
translated to C_p and C_{pk} process capability indices of 2.0 and 1.5,
respectively. A basic Six Sigma program goal might then be to
produce at least 99.99966% quality at the process step and part
level within an assembly. This would result in no more than 3.4
defects per million parts or process steps when allowing for a
mean process shift of 1.5σ.

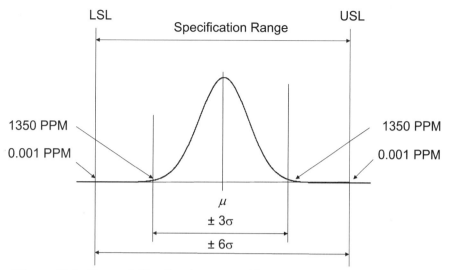

Figure B.2: Normal distribution curve illustrates the three sigma and six sigma parametric conformance rates.

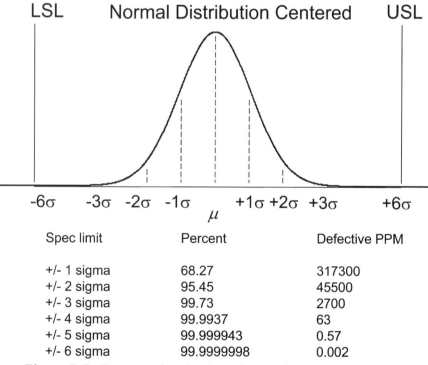

Spec limit	Percent	Defective PPM
+/- 1 sigma	68.27	317300
+/- 2 sigma	95.45	45500
+/- 3 sigma	99.73	2700
+/- 4 sigma	99.9937	63
+/- 5 sigma	99.999943	0.57
+/- 6 sigma	99.9999998	0.002

Figure B.3: Between the six sigma limits of a centered normal distribution, only two devices per billion fail to meet the specification target.

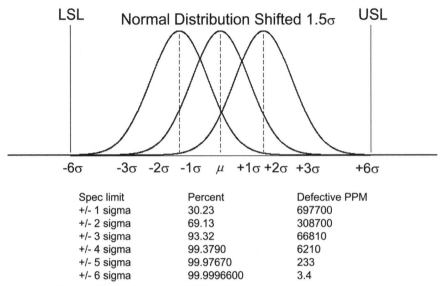

Figure B.4: A 1.5σ shift leads to a 3.4 ppm failure rate.

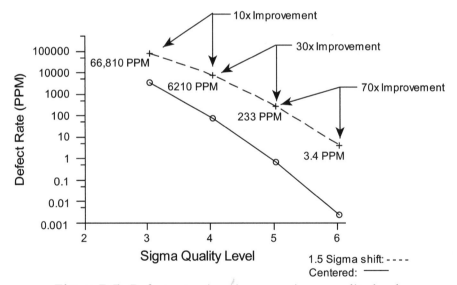

Figure B.5: Defect rates (ppm) versus sigma quality level.

Consider the following example: On the average, one defect occurred on an assembly, which contained 40 parts and four process steps. Using Figure B.5, one could conclude that the assembly is being manufactured at a four sigma quality level since the calculated DPMO rate is $(^1/_{160})(1 \times 10^6) \approx 6250$.

B.2 Article: Individuals Control Chart and Data Normality

This section is from a January 24, 2004 article (Breyfogle, 2004c), with some modifications.

Purpose

The purpose of this paper is to illustrate that individuals control charts are not robust to non-normally distributed data. An alternate control charting approach is presented along with a procedure to describe process capability/performance reporting in terms that are easy to understand and visualize.

Application Example

In the accounts receivable department, invoices are sent to customers for payment. The difference between payment date and due date often follow a lognormal distribution. The following data could be considered a random selection of one invoice daily for 1000 days, where payment due date for the invoice was subtracted from its payment-receive date (e.g., a value of 10 indicates that an invoice payment was 10 days late).

Analysis

One thousand points were randomly generated in Minitab from a lognormal distribution with a location parameter of 2, a scale parameter of 1.0, and a threshold of 0. A histogram of the data yielded the plot shown in Figure B.6. A normal probability plot of the data is shown in Figure B.7. From this figure, we statistically reject the null hypothesis of normality technically because of the low P value and physically since the normal probability plotted data does not follow a straight line.

A lognormal probability plot of the data is shown in Figure B.8. From this Figure, we statistically fail to reject the null hypothesis of the data being from a lognormal distribution since the P value is not below our criteria of 0.05 and physically since the lognormal probability plotted data tends to follow a straight line.

If the individuals control chart is robust to the non-normality of data, an individuals control chart of the randomly generated data

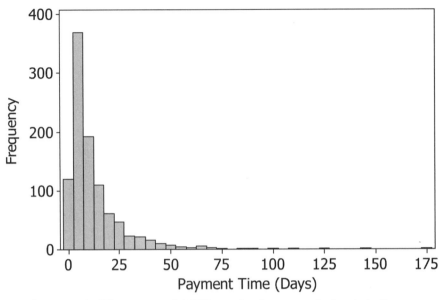

Figure B.6: Histogram of 1000 randomly generated points from a lognormal distribution.

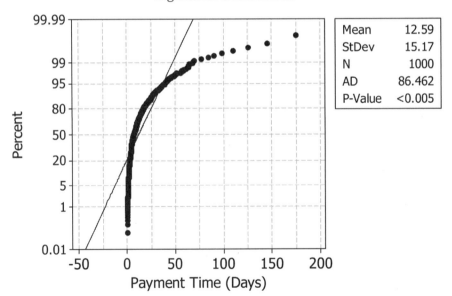

Figure B.7: Normal probability plot of the data.

should be in statistical control. Figure B.9 shows an individuals plot of the randomly generated data.

The individuals control chart in Figure B.9 shows many out of control points beyond the upper control limit (UCL). In addition, the

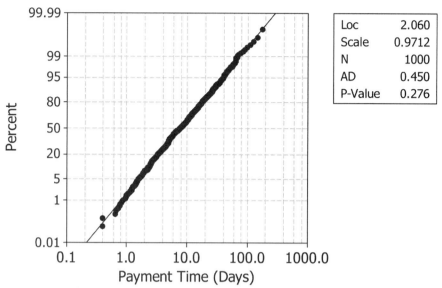

Figure B.8: Lognormal probability plot of the data.

individuals control chart shows a physical lower boundary of 0 for the data, which is well within the lower control limit (LCL) of −21.2. We would like to see a random scatter pattern within the control limits, which is not prevalent in the individuals control chart.

Figure B.10 shows a control chart using a Box–Cox transformation with a lambda value of 0, the appropriate normalizing

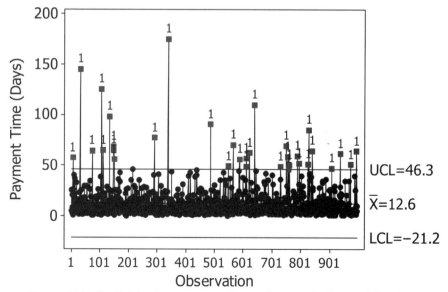

Figure B.9: Individuals non-transformed control chart of the data.

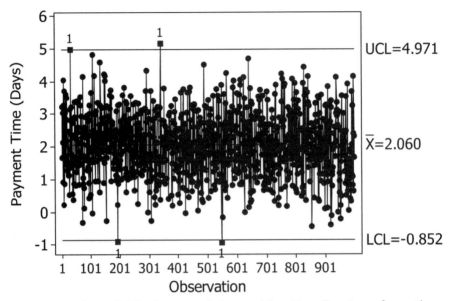

Figure B.10: Individuals control chart with a Box–Cox transformation lambda value of 0.

transformation for lognormally distributed data. The control chart in Figure B.10 is much better behaved than the control chart in Figure B.9. Almost all 1000 points in the individuals control chart are in statistical control.

A very descriptive estimate for the process capability/performance metric for this process, when no specification exists, is shown in Figure B.11.

From Figure B.11, a best estimate process capability/performance metric output for the process is 80% of all invoices are paid between 2.3 and 27.2 days beyond the due date, with a median of 7.8 days.

Conclusions

If data are not from a normal distribution, an individuals control chart can generate many false signals. When no specifications exist, a best estimate for the 80% frequency of occurrence rate along with median response is an easy-to-understand description that conveys what the process is expected produce in terms that everyone can visualize.

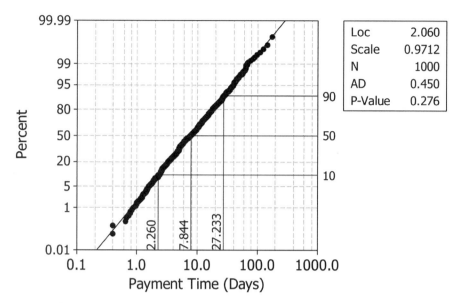

Figure B.11: Lognormal plot of data with 80% frequency of occurrence rate.

Reference

Implementing Six Sigma: Smarter Solutions using Statistical Methods, 2nd edn, F. W. Breyfogle III, Wiley, 2003.

Appendix C: Creating Effective Presentations

We have all attended stimulating presentations as well as those at the other side of the pendulum. Everyone wants to deliver effective presentations; however, presentations often do not effectively convey the desired message. Leadership effectiveness is dependent upon presentation skills. The understanding and acceptance of a project is often directly linked to presentation skills.

Toastmasters International (www.toastmasters.org) provides a great worldwide system for improving presentation skills through local clubs. Delivered Toastmasters' speeches focus on a number of areas that are part of an effective presentation. In this appendix, I will highlight four of these focus areas: be in earnest, employ vocal variety, make it persuasive, and speak with knowledge (Toastmasters International, 1990).

C.1 Be In Earnest

A successful speech is one made in earnest, radiating conviction, and sincerity. The presentation should strongly advocate your viewpoint. Presentations need to be natural but forceful, where there is a combination of thought and strong feeling.

The audience is giving their time to listen. The presenter owes them more than an exercise in words. When an audience is convinced that your subject has meaning to you, then they will listen and consider your viewpoint.

Any natural nervousness should be directed toward two objects: yourself and your topic. Your self-energy direction can be used to add excitement to your personality. The audience will see your enthusiasm and be sympathetic to your cause. Energy direction to the topic means using nervous energy as a motivating force to thoroughly research the topic. Full mastery of subject helps with speaking confidence. There is nothing to be nervous about when you demonstrate understanding of topic and stimulate audience enthusiasm. Cato the Elder's directive to budding orators still holds true: *Rem tene, verba sequentur* (Grasp hold of the matter; the words will follow).

Have a definite point of view. Prepare protest, appeal, or call for action that promotes your viewpoint. The presentation purpose should affect your choice of using supporting materials (e.g., facts and illustrations). The speech needs to be adapted to the audience, speaking to their interest. Plan your introduction to awaken the audience, so that they become interested in the subject. Show timeliness and relevance to them.

The body of the talk should identify the source of concern and how the problem can be solved. Final conclusions should bring understanding to the audience and sympathy to your side (i.e., the audience should now be ready to support your convictions).

Practice is very important, preferably with the aid of someone who will give helpful feedback. Try several different illustrations and lines of reasoning to determine which is most appropriate. Think clearly about the approach that you will use. Take everything out that is not supportive. Become excited about the topic, using large graphics to illustrate your point for each main idea.

Slides should be an aid to listener understanding, rather than a support for your presentation. Avoid reading visual aid content to the audience. Slides should never come between you and your audience. Involve listeners from the very beginning of the talk. The first sentence should awaken them and make them want to listen.

Maintain eye contact with the audience and carry through in earnest. Windup on a strong appeal note. Assume that you have sold the audience on your position. Have true conviction in what you say, showing your true beliefs.

C.2   Employ Vocal Variety

Psychologist Albert Mehrabian has shown that the listener is five times more likely to be influenced by voice than by the speaker's spoken word. The speaker's voice should be loud enough to be clearly heard, articulated enough to be understood, expressive enough to be interesting, and pleasing enough to be enjoyable.

A good speaking voice maintains a balance between extremes of:

- *Volume*: Varied to add emphasis or dramatic impact.
- *Pitch*: Conscious effort to be conversational.
- *Rate*: Most effective rate is 125–160 words per minute. Vary rate to reflect mode changes and to add emphasis.
- *Sound Quality*: Think friendliness, confidence, and desire. Relax to remove tension from voice.

Characteristics of a good speaking voice are:

- *Pleasant Tone*: Conveys sense of friendliness.
- *Natural*: Reflects true personality and sincerity.
- *Vitality*: Force and strength impression, even when not loud.
- *Shades of Meaning*: Variety in tone and emotion.
- *Easily Heard*: Proper volume and clear articulation.

To train your voice listen closely to the way you speak and concentrate on improvement. Rehearse until you've mastered the voices you'll use during the speech. Find a place where you can be alone so that you can practice without inhibitions or interruptions. Make an honest effort to bring your voice out of a monotone, while not overdoing it. Vary pitch, volume, and quality of your voice – especially rate of speech.

Don't forget gestures and other body language. Consider using a tape or video recorder, continuing to practice until satisfied. Replay of a recording may be an initial surprise, but this is closer to what the audience hears/sees, than what you hear yourself say. Apply the voice techniques developed during rehearsal.

Speak with enthusiasm. Use a wide variety of vocal styles, but don't speak so rapidly that your audience cannot follow your presentation. Let the context of your speech be the motivation for voice change. Provide reflection, sincerity when sincere, and humor when amused. Include pauses for the audience to catch up, taking moderately deep breaths and vary your voice to match words and gestures. Speak clearly and project your voice so that all can hear.

C.3 Make It Persuasive

One essential leadership quality is to persuade; that is, to get people to understand, accept, and act on your ideas. Effective persuasion is a valuable service, since it gives needed information for key decisions and arouses emotional reactions that create actions.

The 19th-century preacher Lyman Beecher called persuasion "logic on fire." For people to adopt new beliefs or change those they hold, they need rational appeal that gives logical justification for believing, emotional arousal, and trust in the message source. The Greek philosopher Aristotle referred to these as fact, emotion, and credibility. To persuade, you must phrase the appeal in terms of the audience's self-interest, not yours. You need to show them the benefits, as one would with advertising.

Aristotle said "The fool tells me his reasons: the wise man persuades me with my own." People need a persuasive message but at the same time need to be wary of it; hence, the speaker needs to establish trust and respect to gain credibility. Here again, Cato the Elder's definition of an orator, *bonus vir, dicendi peritus* (a good man, skilled in speaking), shows what an audience seeks in a speaker. Audience members must view you as someone with whom they can identify; that is, someone who has similar needs and interest (they cannot dislike, distrust, or think you are phony) and who is credible (convinced of the validity and value of your viewpoint).

The approach which you use to convey a persuasive message depends on your audience and their attitudes toward the subject. Consider:

- Their position within the organization
- Information they already have on the subject
- Importance of issue to them

Consider their viewpoint position: favorable, undecided, or opposed. Analyze your audience to determine the purpose of your speech.

- Are you reinforcing a position?
- Are you creating a new attitude?
- Are you attempting to change their beliefs?

What results do you seek? The persuasive approach depends on your objective.

- *If the audience agrees*: Your goal is to reinforce and strengthen the agreement. It may not be necessary to present both sides, but if some listeners have been exposed to other points of view, you may bring those up. Your task may be to bring passive belief up to active commitment.
- *If audience is neutral or apathetic*: Your primary objective is to convince listeners that the issues presented directly affect them and are important to them. For this situation, show how the problem relates to them and their lives. After showing the relevance, present possible solutions, demonstrating why yours is the best. It is best to show your solution first and then to dispose of major counter arguments, concluding with a position restatement.
- *If the audience opposes your view*: Simply strive to have listeners recognize the merits of your position and reconsider their own views. For this situation, you need to reduce confrontation between your view and that of the audience. Begin by establishing common ground, leading back to indisputable facts on which you and they agree. Present your message fairly, not trampling on others' feelings.

The motivated sequence, developed by Professor Alan H. Monroe, has a five-step speech structure that presents the following normal thought pattern:

1. *Attention*: The opening statement should seize the audience's attention toward the topic; for example, a physician's opening statement that three out of five people in this room will die of heart disease will certainly grab the audience's attention.
2. *Need*: State the need. This may include facts, examples, and illustrations that describe a need and build a logical foundation for a solution which you will present.
3. *Satisfaction*: Present your solution to fulfill the need or solve the problem. Support your position with evidence, overcoming any objections, or opposing solutions.

4. *Visualization*: Draw a picture of future conditions, intensifying audience commitment to your position. Can be positive, showing what happens if adopted, or negative, showing what happens if not adopted. You can also present both positive and negative pictures. Be vivid, using strong imagery.

5. *Action*: Turn agreement and commitment into positive action or fixed attitude. The speech should achieve a final purpose, a final reaction to what you want from the audience.

Few people are persuaded by logic alone. During your speech, work on building strong audience rapport and positive feeling toward your cause. Show listeners that their self-interest, along with your proposal, coincide with noble motives. Focus squarely on their needs, keeping in mind the more basic need, the stronger emotional response.

The emotional aspect should reach its peak at your conclusion. The feeling that a speech generates is what people will remember, not the dazzling logic presented.

Prepare and send-out the agenda ahead of the meeting. Prepare and then rehearse with an audience. If possible, carefully select the presentation location (i.e., where the action is). Be entertaining, but at least be interesting! Clearly spell out the objectives and expectations.

Make use of visuals such as graphs and charts whenever possible. Know these visual aids well, and use language familiar to your audience. Make careful use of hand-outs, distributing them at the end of the presentation end or e-mail them following the presentation. Ask for immediate engagement and action. Respect the time of your audience. Maintain consistent and continuous communication (i.e., one time is not enough).

C.4   Inspire Your Audience

You want to deliver an uplifting or inspirational talk. You want to challenge people to embrace noble motives to achieve the highest potential.

You need to organize thoughts and beliefs which you and audience share, putting together a dynamic speech that is inspirational. Think back to great speeches delivered by inspirational leaders. During the US Constitutional Convention in 1789, there was much division of opinion. In this time of turmoil, George Washington said, "If we offer to the people something of which we ourselves do not approve, how can we afterward defend our work? Let us raise a standard to which the wise and honest may gladly repair. The event is in the hands of God."

Members looked at each other in shame. They then, with determination, resumed work and produced the US Constitution, often considered one of the greatest documents in history. To be effective, an inspirational speech cannot be superficial. You must exhibit the qualities of leadership; that is, you must relate to the listeners and have sufficient insight to show them a better way. Talks that are highly demanding call for dignity, excellence in style, and emotional rapport with the audience.

A speech should follow four essential precepts of leadership:

- *Be confident*: Don't raise questions or express doubt.
- *Be forceful*: Show enthusiasm and vitality. Use body language to demonstrate conviction. Paint vivid word pictures.
- *Be positive*: Bold statements telling the audience what they should do will stir them to action. Criticizing them or making excuses for what they have failed to do will not inspire.
- *Be definite*: Give clear and specific illustrations and conclusions.

A speech goal is to accurately sense the mood of the occasion and to express that mood with originality and depth. A speech should contain illustrations and thoughts that captivate the imagination of the audience, putting life into a talk. An inspirational speech meets the members of the audience where they are at the moment, expressing the mood and feelings of the listeners in stirring words, moving them to a higher plane.

Build your talk out of the occasion on which you are presenting. You need to have a feeling for the audience and their expectations. Look inside yourself as a representative of the group, considering what you would want to hear and what you already know and what you could contribute in a presentation.

It is okay to channel the feeling of the audience members into a different direction from what they expect, as long as their basic mood or beliefs are not challenged. You may strive to improve the quality of the audience members' feelings, replacing selfish motives with more generous ones. After audience members accept you as one of them, they will accept and be grateful for your attempts to lift them to a more noble level.

Just as the content of your talk is determined by the occasion, delivery must also be appropriate for the mood, be it thoughtful, enthusiastic, mournful, or exalted. Emphasize your agreement with the audience, using phrases that include "we" and "us." The presentation should be a powerful expression of what you really are. The speech should be controlled and confident, while showing sincerity and enthusiasm. Give audience members reason to respect your balanced judgment and deep understanding. Rely heavily on illustrations and examples, making your audience feel what you feel. Choose words carefully, aiming so that people not only hear the message but also feel it as well.

Appendix D: P-DMAIC Execution Roadmap and Selected Drill Downs

D.1 P-DMAIC Execution Roadmap

The next three pages provide the high-level IEE project execution roadmap described in this volume. The beginning section of many chapters includes the IEE roadmap (shown below) with a bold box around the roadmap phase, which has implementation details described in the chapter. In addition, this beginning section will also include the corresponding phase swim lane from the project execution roadmap; e.g., define phase of the 9-phase roadmap that is shown later in this section.

The sequence of Part II–Part VI chapters in this volume follows the basic sequence of project execution steps. Tools are listed sequentially in the project execution roadmap but need not be exercised sequentially.

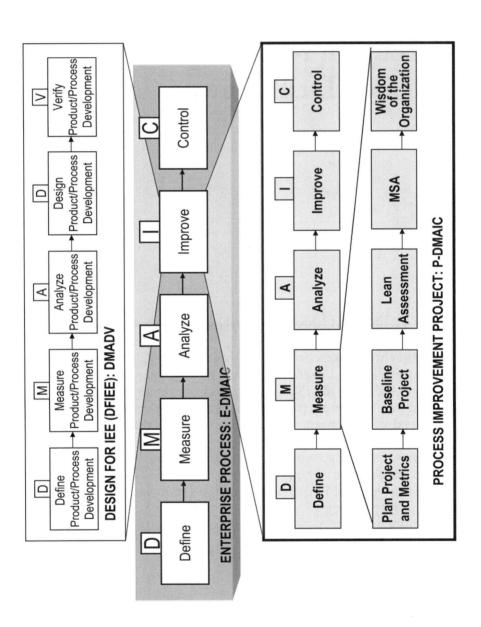

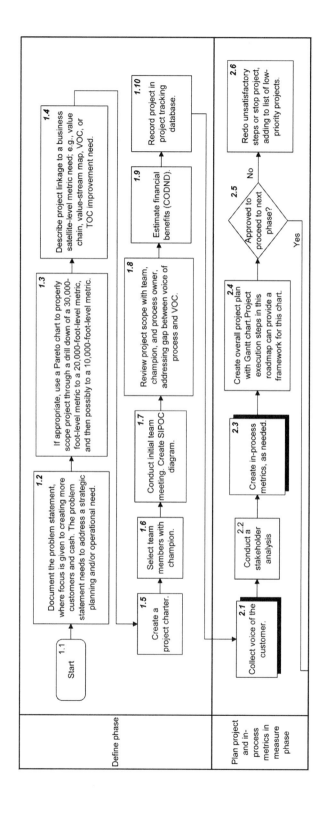

Define phase

1.1 Start

1.2 Document the problem statement, where focus is given to creating more customers and cash. The problem statement needs to address a strategic planning and/or operational need.

1.3 If appropriate, use a Pareto chart to properly scope project through a drill down of a 30,000-foot-level metric to a 20,000-foot-level metric, and then possibly to a 10,000-foot-level metric.

1.4 Describe project linkage to a business satellite-level metric need; e.g., value chain, value-stream map, VOC, or TOC improvement need.

1.5 Create a project charter.

1.6 Select team members with champion.

1.7 Conduct initial team meeting. Create SIPOC diagram.

1.8 Review project scope with team, champion, and process owner, addressing gap between voice of process and VOC.

1.9 Estimate financial benefits (CODND).

1.10 Record project in project tracking database.

Plan project and in-process metrics in measure phase

2.1 Collect voice of the customer.

2.2 Conduct a stakeholder analysis

2.3 Create in-process metrics, as needed.

2.4 Create overall project plan with Gantt chart. Project execution steps in this roadmap can provide a framework for this chart.

2.5 Approved to proceed to next phase?

No

Yes

2.6 Redo unsatisfactory steps or stop project, adding to list of low-priority projects.

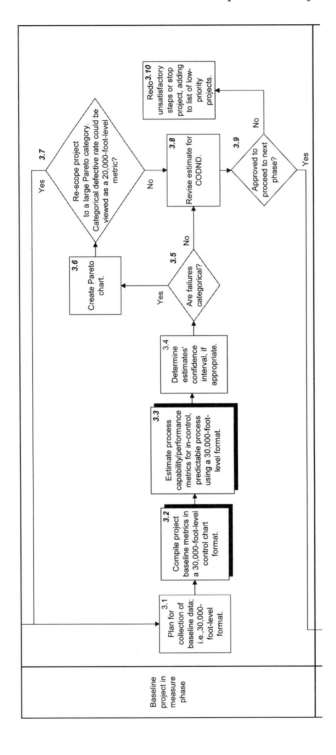

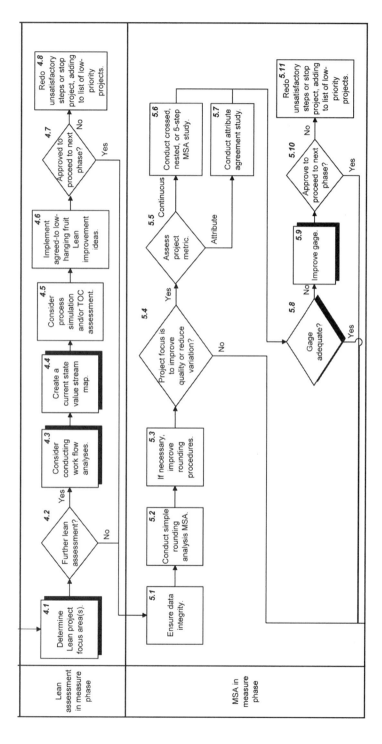

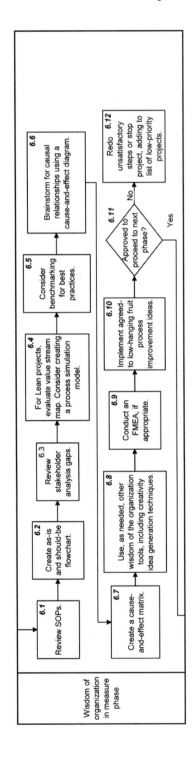

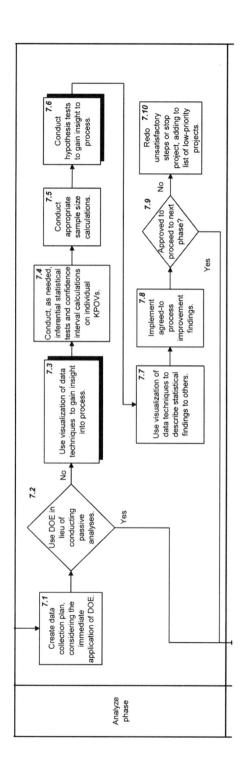

Analyze phase

7.1 Create data collection plan, considering the immediate application of DOE.

7.2 Use DOE in lieu of conducting passive analyses.

No — 7.3 Use visualization of data techniques to gain insight into process.

Yes

7.4 Conduct, as needed, inferential statistical tests and confidence interval calculations on individual KPOVs.

7.5 Conduct appropriate sample size calculations.

7.6 Conduct hypothesis tests to gain insight to process.

7.7 Use visualization of data techniques to describe statistical findings to others.

7.8 Implement agreed-to process improvement findings.

7.9 Approved to proceed to next phase?

No

Yes

7.10 Redo unsatisfactory steps or stop project, adding to list of low-priority projects.

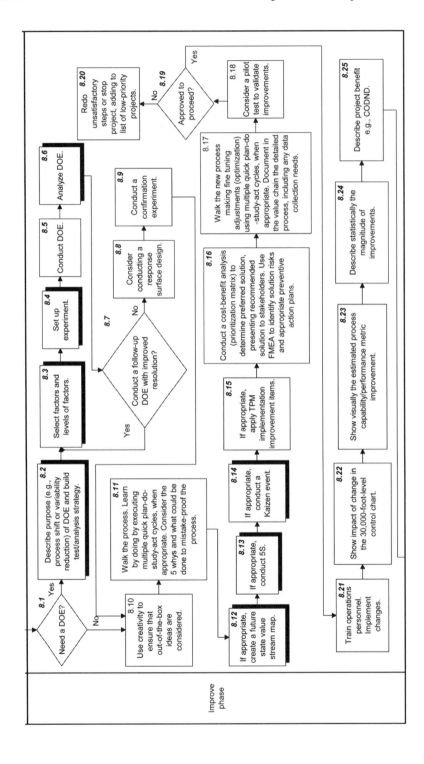

Improve phase

8.1 Need a DOE?

8.2 Describe purpose (e.g., process shift or variability reduction) of DOE and build test/analysis strategy.

8.3 Select factors and levels of factors.

8.4 Set up experiment.

8.5 Conduct DOE.

8.6 Analyze DOE.

8.7 Conduct a follow-up DOE with improved resolution?

8.8 Consider conducting a response surface design.

8.9 Conduct a confirmation experiment.

8.10 Use creativity to ensure that out-of-the-box ideas are considered.

8.11 Walk the process. Learn by doing by executing multiple quick plan-do-study-act cycles, when appropriate. Consider the 5 whys and what could be done to mistake-proof the process.

8.12 If appropriate, create a future state value stream map.

8.13 If appropriate, conduct 5S.

8.14 If appropriate, conduct a Kaizen event.

8.15 If appropriate, apply TPM implementation improvement items.

8.16 Conduct a cost-benefit analysis (prioritization matrix) to determine preferred solution, presenting recommended solution to stakeholders. Use FMEA to identify solution risks and appropriate preventive action plans.

8.17 Walk the new process making fine tuning adjustments (optimization) using multiple quick plan-do-study-act cycles, when appropriate. Document in the value chain the detailed process, including any data collection needs.

8.18 Consider a pilot test to validate improvements.

8.19 Approved to proceed?

8.20 Redo unsatisfactory steps or stop project, adding to list of low-priority projects.

8.21 Train operations personnel. Implement changes.

8.22 Show impact of change in the 30,000-foot-level control chart.

8.23 Show visually the estimated process capability/performance metric improvement.

8.24 Describe statistically the magnitude of improvements.

8.25 Describe project benefit e.g., CODND.

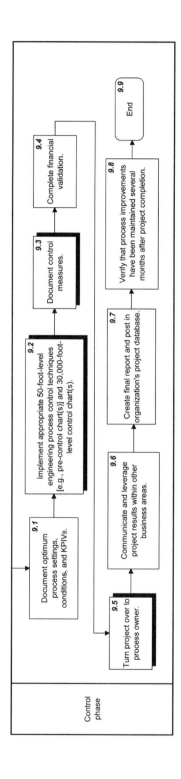

D.2   P-DMAIC Execution Roadmap Drill Down: In-Process Metrics Decision Tree

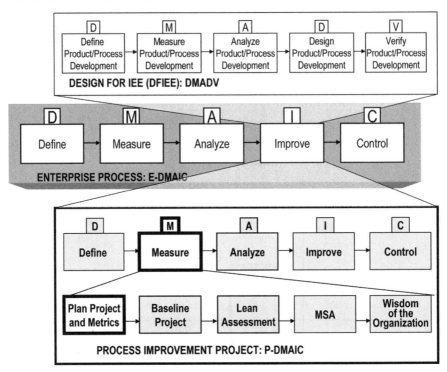

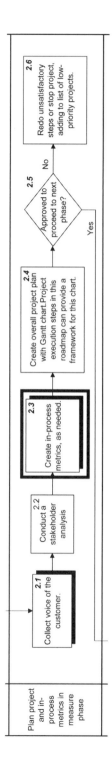

Step 2.2 drilldown is described in Figure D.1

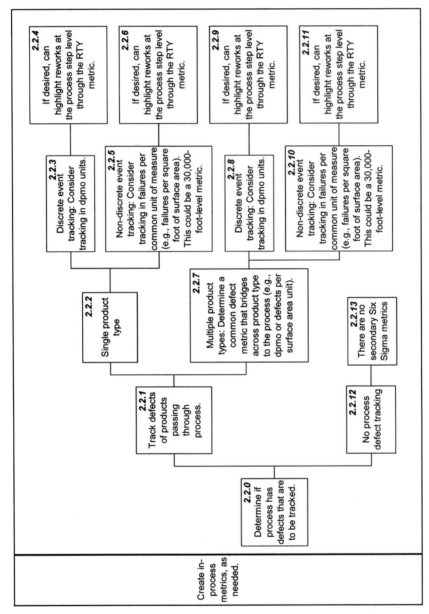

Figure D.1: In-process metrics decision tree. Drill down of step 2.2 of P-DMAIC execution roadmap.

D.3   P-DMAIC Execution Roadmap Drill Down: Baseline Project

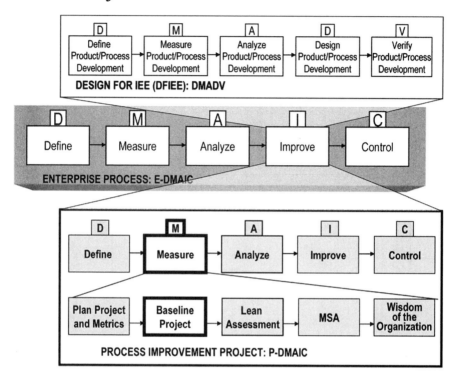

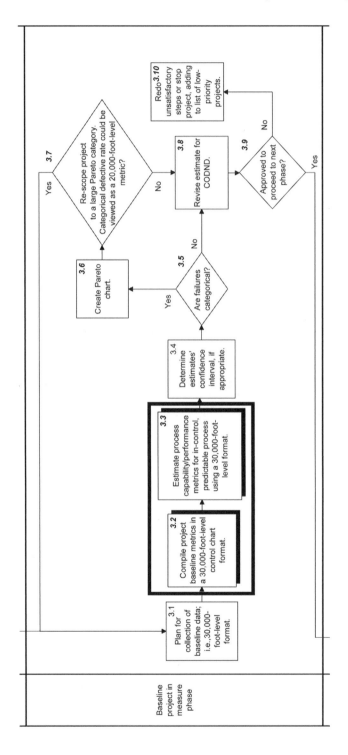

Figures D.2 and D.3 contain the drill downs of steps 3.2 and 3.3, which are described in Chapters 12 and 13. These techniques are also applicable for value chain metrics in E-DMAIC.

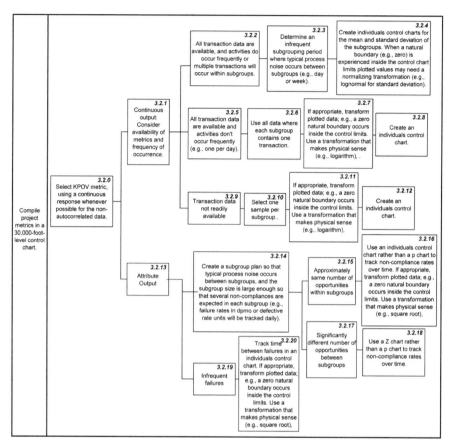

Figure D.2: Measure phase drill down of P-DMAIC execution roadmap step 3.2, which compiles project baseline metrics in 30,000-foot-level format.

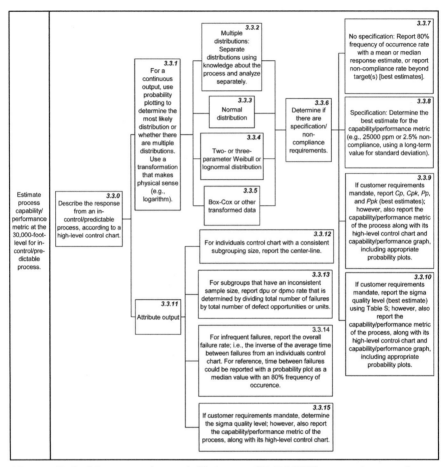

Figure D.3: Measure phase drill down of P-DMAIC execution roadmap step 3.3, which estimates process capability/performance metrics for in-control, predictable process using a 30,000-foot-level format.

D.4   P-DMAIC Execution Roadmap Drill Down: Visualization of Data and Hypothesis Decision Tree

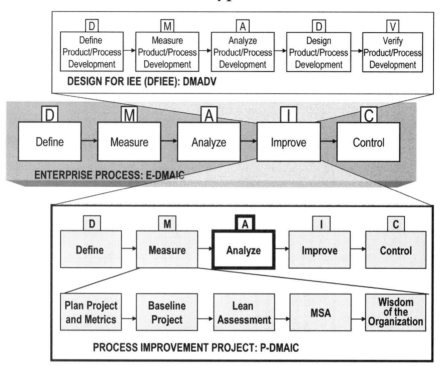

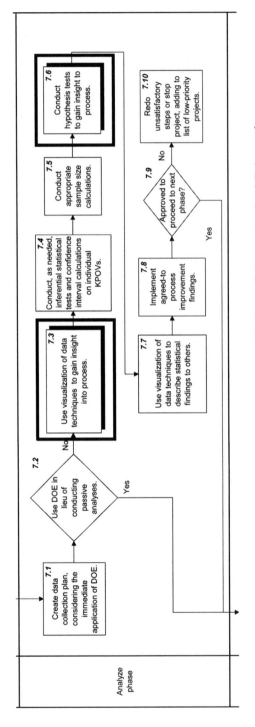

Figure D.4 contains the drill down of step 7.3, while Figure D.5 contains the drill down of step 7.6. The drill-down methodologies also apply at the enterprise analyze phase.

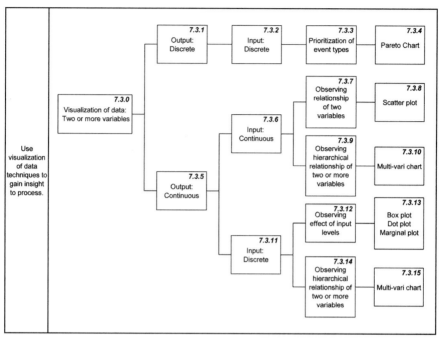

Figure D.4: Analyze phase drill down of P-DMAIC execution roadmap step 7.3, visualization of data.

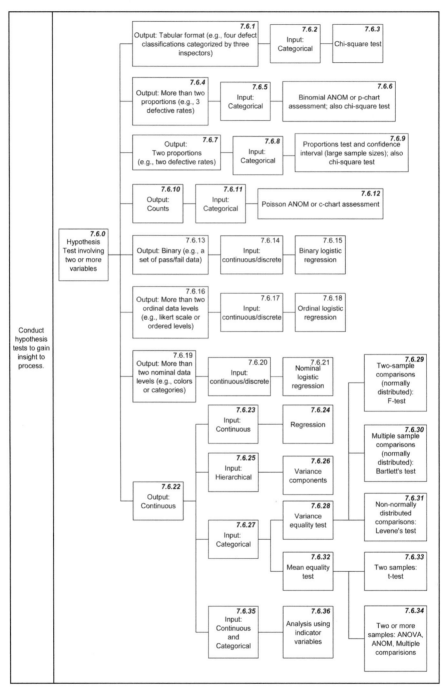

Figure D.5: Analyze phase drill down of P-DMAIC execution roadmap step 7.6, hypothesis tests.

Appendix E: P-DMAIC Execution Tollgate Check Sheets

Tables E.1 through E.9 describe the P-DMAIC execution check sheets.

Table E.1: P-DMAIC Define Phase Check Sheet

Description	Questions	Yes/No NA
Define Phase Check Sheet		
Tool/Methodology		
Project selection	Is the project aligned with a company goal and current needs?	
	Is this the best project to be working on at this time?	
COPQ/CODND	Was a rough estimate of COPQ/CODND used to determine potential benefits?	
	Is there agreement on how hard/soft financial benefits will be determined?	
Problem Statement	KPOV primary and secondary metrics are defined and quantifiable?	
	KPOV links to customer requirements and business goals?	
	Impact is quantified based on process data?	
	Data source and measurement method are indicated?	
	No stated or predetermined solutions?	
	Outlines scope of the project?	
Project description	Completed a gap analysis of what the customer/stakeholder of the process needs versus what the process is delivering?	
	Completed a goal statement with measurable targets?	
	Created an SIPOC which includes the primary customer and key requirements of the process?	
	Completed a visual representation of what high-level value chain metric is to be improved by the project?	
	Completed an EIP visual representation of how the project aligns with the organization's goals?	
Project charter	Are the roles and goals of the team clear to all members and upper management?	
	Has the team reviewed and accepted the charter?	
	Is the project scoped sufficiently?	
Communication plan	Is there a communication plan for communicating project status and results to appropriate levels of the organization?	
	Has the project been recorded in an IEE database?	
Team		
Resources	Does the team include cross-functional members/process experts?	
	Are all team members motivated and committed to the project?	
	Is the process owner supportive of the project?	
	Is the champion supportive of the project?	
	Has a kickoff team meeting been held?	
Next Phase		
Approval to proceed	Did the team adequately complete the above steps?	
	What is the detailed plan for the Measure Phase?	
	Are barriers to success identified and planned for?	

Table E.2: P-DMAIC – Measure Plan Project and Metrics Check Sheet

Description	Questions	Yes/No NA
Measure Phase: Plan Project and Metrics Check Sheet		
Tool/Methodology		
KPOV	Are the primary and secondary key process output variables clearly defined?	
	Were the most appropriate metrics chosen in order to give insight into the process (continuous vs. attribute)?	
	Were continuous data used when available?	
In process metrics	Are any in process metrics such as DPMO and RTY going to be used?	
Financial metrics	Has it been finalized with Finance how financial benefits will be calculated?	
	Does the project include any cost avoidance, improved efficiency, improved customer satisfaction or other soft money considerations?	
Voice of the customer/stakehoder	Did the team identify key internal and external customers/stakeholders of the project process?	
	Did the team speak with customers/stakeholders of the project process?	
	Has input from a stakerholders analysis been included in the project description and scope?	
	Has a stakeholder gap analysis been completed?	
Project plan	Are project milestones identified?	
	Is the project time line reasonable and acceptable?	
Team		
Resources	Are team members and key stakeholders identified and engaged?	
	Are all team members motivated and committed to the project?	
	Is the process owner committed to the project?	
Next Phase		
Approval to proceed	Did the team adequately complete the above steps?	
	Has the project database been updated and communication plan followed?	
	Is there a detailed plan for baselining the project?	
	Are barriers to success identified and planned for?	
	Is the team tracking with the project schedule?	
	Have schedule revisions been approved?	

Table E.3: P-DMAIC – Measure Phase: Baseline Project
Check Sheet

Measure Phase: Baseline Project Check Sheet		
Description	**Questions**	**Yes/No NA**
Tool/Methodology		
30,000-foot-level control chart	Were project metrics compliled in a 30,000-foot-level control chart with an infrequent subgrouping/sampling plan so that typical process noise occurs between subgroups?	
	Was historical data used when initiating the 30,000-foot-level control charts?	
	Is the 30,000-foot-level control chart now being updated regularly?	
	Is the process in control/predictable?	
	Have special-cause issues been resolved?	
Process capability/performance metric	If specification limits exist for a continuous response KPOV, was the process capability/performance metric estimated as a frequency of occurrence percentage or ppm of non-compliance?	
	If data are attribute, has the process capability been shown as the centerline of a 30,000-foot-level control chart, if the subgroup sizes are equal?	
Probability plot/ dot plot	If KPOV response is continuous, were probability plots and/or dot plots used to show process capability/performance metric?	
	Was the appropriate probability plot used?	
	Are the data normally distributed?	
	If there is more than one distribution, were the data separated for further analysis?	
Pareto chart	If KPOV data are classified by failure type, was a Pareto chart used to prioritize failure types?	
Data collection	Has the team collected and reviewed the current standard operating procedures?	
	Are the data you are using good and truly representative of the process?	
	Do you know how much data you will need?	
	Is your data collection plan satisfactory to all stakeholders?	
COPQ/CODND	Now that the process capability/performance metric has been determined, given the refined COPQ/CODND estimate, is this still the right project to work on?	
Team		
Resources	Are all team members motivated and committed to the project?	
	Is there a plan for executive management to interface with the team to keep motivation alive and commitment visible?	
	Does process owner understand and agree with baselining?	
Next Phase		
Approval to proceed	Did the team adequately complete the above steps?	
	Has the project database been updated and communication plan followed?	
	Is the team considering Lean Tools?	
	Have barriers to success been identified and resolved?	
	Is the team tracking with the project schedule?	
	Have schedule revisions been approved?	

Table E.4: P-DMAIC – Measure Phase: Lean Assessment Check Sheet

Measure Phase: Lean Assessment Check Sheet		
Description	**Questions**	**Yes/No NA**
Tool/Methodology		
Lean tools	Is the KPOV a Lean metric, like cycle time or inventory?	
	Are you addressing the *workplace* as a Lean project focus area, i.e., workplace organization, standardized work, and/or visual presentation?	
	Are you addressing *people* as a Lean project focus area, i.e., people utilization or quality at the source?	
	Are you addressing the *system* as a Lean project focus area, i.e., tool reliability, cellular flow, batch reduction/elimination, or pull vs. push systems?	
Standardized work chart, combination work table, logic flow diagram, and/or time value diagram	Have you conducted a work flow analysis; i.e., walked the process (documenting elements and work layout in a standardized work chart), created a combination work table for work element timings, created a logic flow diagram, and/or created a time-value diagram?	
Value stream map	Have you created a current state value-stream map?	
Assessment	Were any process improvements made?	
	If so, were they statistically verified with the appropriate hypothesis test?	
	Did you describe the change over time on a 30,000-foot-level control chart?	
	Did you calculate and display the change in the process capability/performance metric?	
	Have you documented and communicated the improvements?	
	Have you summarized the benefits and annualized financial benefits?	
Team		
Resources	Are all team members motivated and committed to the project?	
	Is process owner committed to the project?	
Next Phase		
Approval to proceed	Did the team adequately complete the above steps?	
	Has the project database been updated and communication plan followed?	
	Should an MSA be conducted for this project?	
	Is the team tracking with the project schedule?	
	Have schedule revisions been approved?	
	Are barriers to success identified and planned for?	

Table E.5: P-DMAIC – Measure Phase: Measurement Systems
Analysis Check Sheet

Measure Phase: Measurement Systems Analysis Check Sheet		
Description	**Questions**	**Yes/No NA**
Tool/Methodology		
Data integrity	Is there a common operational definition for the data being collected that reflects the needs of the customer?	
	Are the recorded data representative of the actual process?	
	Have appropriate steps been taken to error-proof the data collection process?	
Gage R&R	Was a Gage R&R needed?	
	If so, is the Measurement System satisfactory?	
	If the Measurement System was not satisfactory, have improvements been implemented to make it capable, or has the data collection plan been revised?	
Assessment	Were any process improvements made?	
	If so, were they statistically verified with the appropriate hypothesis test?	
	Was the change over time described on a 30,000-foot-level control chart?	
	Was any change in the process capability/performance metric calculated and displayed?	
	Were improvements documented and communicated?	
	Have the annualized financial benefits been summarized?	
Team		
Resources	Are all team members motivated and committed to the project?	
	Is process owner supportive of MSA?	
Next Phase		
Approval to proceed	Did the team adequately complete the above steps?	
	Has the project database been updated and communication plan followed?	
	Is there a detailed plan for collecting Wisdom of the Organization?	
	Are barriers to success identified and planned for?	
	Is the team tracking with the project schedule?	
	Have schedule revisions been approved?	

Table E.6: P-DMAIC: Measure Phase: Wisdom of the Organization
Check Sheet

Measure Phase: Wisdom of the Organization Check Sheet		
Tool/Methodology	**Questions**	**Yes/No NA**
Process flowchart and stakeholder analysis	Was a should-be and as-is process map created at the appropriate level of detail?	
	Does the flowchart address critical suppliers, stakeholders, and end customer needs?	
	Are the results from a stakeholder analysis gap being considered?	
Cause-and-effect diagram	Was a brainstorming session held with a cross-functional team to collect the Wisdom of the Organization inputs?	
Cause-and-effect matrix	Were the results of the cause-and-effect diagram prioritized with the C&E Matrix?	
	Were there any "low-hanging-fruit" opportunities that can be fixed immediately?	
FMEA	Was an FMEA conducted with resulting action items?	
Assessment	Were any process improvements made?	
	If so, were they statistically verified with the appropriate hypothesis test?	
	Was any change over time described in a 30,000-foot-level control chart?	
	Was any change in the process capability/performance metric calculated and displayed?	
	Have any improvements been documented and communicated?	
	Have benefits and annualized financial savings been document?	
Team		
Resources	Are all team members motivated and committed to the project?	
	Does the process owner agree with the major outcomes that came from wisdom of the organization assessment?	
Next Phase		
Approval to proceed	Did the team adequately complete the above steps?	
	Has the project database been updated and communication plan followed?	
	Should this project proceed to the Analyze Phase?	
	Is there a detailed plan for the Analyze Phase?	
	Are barriers to success identified and planned for?	
	Is the team tracking with the project schedule?	
	Have schedule revisions been approved?	

Table E.7: P-DMAIC: Analyze Phase Check Sheet

Description	Questions	Yes/No NA
Analyze Phase Check Sheet		
Tool/Methodology		
Box plots, marginal plots, and multi-vari charts	Was the appropriate visualization of data technique used in order to gain process insight to the process?	
Pareto charts	If data are discrete, were Pareto Charts used to drill down to the KPIVs?	
Chi Square p-chart/u-chart (and/or ANOM)	If input data and output data are both discrete, was a chi-square test used to test for statistical significance and a p-chart or ANOM analysis (u-chart or ANOM analysis for count data) used to assess individual difference from the overall mean?	
Scatter Plots	If data are continuous, were scatter plots used to display the relationship between KPIVs and a KPOV?	
Comparison tests	Were statistical significance tests used to gain process insight?	
Variance components	If output data were continuous and inputs are hierarchical, was variance components considered to gain insight?	
Regression analysis	For continuous input and output data, was regression analysis used to compare the relationship between inputs and the output(s)?	
ANOVA / ANOM, Bartlett's /Levene's test	For discrete KPIVs and continuous KPOV data, was the appropriate tool used to compare populations for the different levels of KPIVs?	
Assessment	Were any process improvements made?	
	If so, were they statistically verified with the appropriate hypothesis test?	
	Was any change over time shown on a 30,000-foot-level control chart?	
	Was any change in the process capability/performance metric calculated and displayed?	
	Were improvements documented and communicated?	
	Were benefits and annualized financial savings documented?	
Team		
Resources	Are all team members motivated and committed to the project?	
	Does the process owner understand and support the major conclusions from the analyze phase?	
	Is the champion ready to remove potential obstacles to the upcoming changes?	
Next Phase		
Approval to proceed	Did the team adequately complete the above steps?	
	Has the project database been updated and a communication plan followed?	
	Is DOE needed?	
	If so, should this project proceed to the Improve Phase?	
	Is there a detailed plan for the Improve Phase?	
	Has the team considered improvements to both the process mean and process variation?	
	Are barriers to success identified and planned for?	
	Is the team tracking with the project schedule?	
	Have schedule revisions been approved?	

Table E.8: P-DMAIC: Improve Phase Check Sheet

	Improve Phase Check Sheet	
Descriptions	**Questions**	**Yes/No NA**
Tool/Methodology		
DOE	Was the DOE carefully planned, selecting the appropriate factors, levels, and response (mean and variance)?	
	Was appropriate randomization used?	
	Were results analyzed appropriately to determine KPIVs?	
	Is a follow-up DOE necessary?	
	Is Response Surface Methodology needed?	
	Was a confirmation experiment conducted?	
Improvement strategies	Was a future state value stream map created?	
	Were innovation techniques used to determine potential solutions?	
	Was PDCA used to determine a solution?	
	Was 5S, a kaizen event, or TPM used to facilitate improvements?	
Mistake-proofing	Were mistake-proofing options considered?	
Improvement recommendations	Are improvement recommendations well thought out?	
	Do improvement recommendations address the KPIVs determined in the Analyze Phase?	
	Is there an action plan for implementation of improvements with accountabilities and deadlines specified?	
Assessment	Were any process improvements made?	
	If so, were they statistically verified with the appropriate hypothesis test?	
	Was change over time described in a 30,000-foot-level control chart?	
	Was change in the process capability/performance metric calculated and displayed?	
	Have improvements been documented and communicated?	
	Have benefits and annualized financial savings been determined?	
Team		
Team members	Are all team members motivated and committed to the project?	
Process owner	Does the process owner support the recommended improvements?	
Champion	Is champion ready to step in to promote the proposed changes, if needed and appropriate?	
Next Phase		
Approval to proceed	Did the team adequately complete the above steps?	
	Has the project database been updated and communication plan followed?	
	Should this project proceed to the Control Phase?	
	Is there a detailed plan for the Control Phase?	
	Are barriers to success identified and planned for?	
	Is the team tracking with the project schedule?	
	Have schedule revisions been approved?	

Table E.9: P-DMAIC: Control Phase Check Sheet

Description	Questions	Yes/No NA
Control Phase Check Sheet		
Tool/Methodology		
Process map /SOPs/FMEA	Were process changes and procedures documented with optimum process settings?	
Control charts	Were appropriate control charts created at the 50-foot-level and 30,000-foot-level?	
	Was the appropriate control chart used for the input variable data type?	
	Is the sampling plan sufficient?	
	Is a plan in place to maintain the appropriate 30,000-foot-level control charts using this metric and the process capability/performance metrics as operational metrics?	
	Has the responsibility for process monitoring been assigned?	
	Is there a reaction plan for out-of-control conditions?	
	Have the 30,000-foot-level and 50-foot-level control metrics been assigned to the appropriate person's performance plan?	
Control plan	Are all items in the control plan sufficiently documented?	
Assessment	Were any process improvements made?	
	If so, were they statistically verified with the appropriate hypothesis test?	
	Was change over time described in a 30,000-foot-level control chart?	
	Was change in the process capability/performance metric calculated and displayed?	
	Have improvements been documented and communicated?	
	Have benefits and annualized financial savings been summarized?	
Communications plan	Has the project been handed off to the process owner?	
	Are the changes to the process and improvements being communicated appropriately throughout the organization?	
	Is there a plan to leverage project results to other areas of the business?	
Team		
Resources	Were all contributing members of the team acknowledged and thanked?	
	Has the project success been celebrated?	
	Is the process owner ready to take ownership of the project sustainment effort?	
Change management	Has the team considered obstacles to making this change last?	
Next Phase		
Final approval and closure	Is there a detailed plan to monitor KPIV and KPOV metrics over time to ensure that change is sustained?	
	Have all action items and project deliverables been completed?	
	Has a final project report been approved?	
	Was the project certified and the financial benefits validated?	
	Has the project database been updated?	

Appendix F: *Implementing Six Sigma* (Breyfogle 2003) Supplemental Material

Supplemental techniques are described in *Implementing Six Sigma*, 2nd edition. These techniques are described in the following chapters or appendices.

Chapter/Appendix	Chapter and Topics
1	**Six Sigma Overview and IEE Implementation**
	Traditional approach to the deployment of statistical methods
	Six sigma benchmarking study
2	**Voice of the customer and the IEE define phase**
	Voice of the customer
	A survey methodology to identify customer needs
	Goal setting and measurements
	Scorecard
3	**Measurements and the IEE measure phase**

	4	**Process flowcharting/process mapping**
	5	**Basic tools**
		Interrelationship digraph (ID)
		Process decision program chart (PDPC)
	6	**Probability**
		Multiple events
		Multiple event relationships
		Bayes' theorem
	7	**Overview of distributions and statistical processes**
		An overview of the application of distributions
		Hazard rate
		Non-homogeneous poisson process (NHPP)
		Homogeneous poisson process (HPP)
	8	**Probability and hazard plotting**
		Hazard plots
	9	**Six sigma measurements**
		Converting defect rates (DPMO or ppm) to sigma quality level units
		Six sigma relationships
		Process cycle time
		Yield
		Z variable equivalent
		Defects per million opportunities (DPMO)
		Normalized yield and Z value for benchmarking
		Six sigma assumptions
	10	**Basic control charts**
		AQL (acceptable quality level) sampling can be deceptive
		Median charts
	11	**Process capability and process performance**

	Example 43.18: IEE project: qualification of supplier's production process and on-going certification
44	**Lean and its integration with IEE**
45	**Integration of theory of constraints (TOC) with six sigma**
46	**Manufacturing applications and a 21-step integration of the tools**
	21-step integration of the tools: manufacturing processes
47	**Service/transactional applications and a 21-step integration of the tools**
	Measuring and improving service/transactional processes
	21-step integration of the tools: service/transactional processes
48	**DFSS overview and tools**
	DMADV
	Using previously-described methodologies within dfss
	Design for x (dfx)
49	**Product DFSS**
	Measuring and improving development processes
	21-step integration of the tools: product DFSS
	Example 49.1: notebook computer development
50	**Process DFSS**
	21-step integration of the tools: process DFSS
51	**Change management**
52	**Project management and financial analysis**
53	**Team effectiveness**
54	**Creativity**

Appendix G: Reference Tables

Table A: Area Under the standardized Normal Curve.

TABLE A Area Under the Standardized Normal Curve

Z	.00	.01	.02	.03	.04	.05	.06	.07	.08	.09
0.0	.5000	.4960	.4920	.4880	.4840	.4801	.4761	.4721	.4681	.4641
0.1	.4602	.4562	.4522	.4483	.4443	.4404	.4364	.4325	.4286	.4247
0.2	.4207	.4168	.4129	.4090	.4052	.4013	.3974	.3936	.3897	.3859
0.3	.3821	.3783	.3745	.3707	.3669	.3632	.3594	.3557	.3520	.3483
0.4	.3446	.3409	.3372	.3336	.3300	.3264	.3228	.3192	.3156	.3121
0.5	.3085	.3050	.3015	.2981	.2946	.2912	.2877	.2843	.2810	.2776
0.6	.2743	.2709	.2676	.2643	.2611	.2578	.2546	.2514	.2483	.2451
0.7	.2420	.2389	.2358	.2327	.2296	.2266	.2236	.2206	.2177	.2148
0.8	.2119	.2090	.2061	.2033	.2005	.1977	.1949	.1922	.1894	.1867
0.9	.1841	.1814	.1788	.1762	.1736	.1711	.1685	.1660	.1635	.1611
1.0	.1587	.1562	.1539	.1515	.1492	.1469	.1446	.1423	.1401	.1379
1.1	.1357	.1335	.1314	.1292	.1271	.1251	.1230	.1210	.1190	.1170
1.2	.1151	.1131	.1112	.1093	.1075	.1056	.1038	.1020	.1003	.0985
1.3	.0968	.0951	.0934	.0918	.0901	.0885	.0869	.0853	.0838	.0823
1.4	.0808	.0793	.0778	.0764	.0749	.0735	.0721	.0708	.0694	.0681
1.5	.0668	.0655	.0643	.0630	.0618	.0606	.0594	.0582	.0571	.0559
1.6	.0548	.0537	.0526	.0516	.0505	.0495	.0485	.0475	.0465	.0455
1.7	.0446	.0436	.0427	.0418	.0409	.0401	.0392	.0384	.0375	.0367
1.8	.0359	.0351	.0344	.0336	.0329	.0322	.0314	.0307	.0301	.0294
1.9	.0287	.0281	.0274	.0268	.0262	.0256	.0250	.0244	.0239	.0233
Z	**.00**	**.01**	**.02**	**.03**	**.04**	**.05**	**.06**	**.07**	**.08**	**.09**
2.0	.0228	.0222	.0217	.0212	.0207	.0202	.0197	.0192	.0188	.0183
2.1	.0179	.0174	.0170	.0166	.0162	.0158	.0154	.0150	.0146	.0143
2.2	.0139	.0136	.0132	.0129	.0125	.0122	.0119	.0116	.0113	.0110
2.3	.01072	.01044	.01017	.00990	.00964	.00939	.00914	.00889	.00866	.00842
2.4	.00820	.00798	.00776	.00755	.00734	.00714	.00695	.00676	.00657	.00639
2.5	.00621	.00604	.00587	.00570	.00554	.00539	.00523	.00508	.00494	.00480
2.6	.00466	.00453	.00440	.00427	.00415	.00402	.00391	.00379	.00368	.00357
2.7	.00347	.00336	.00326	.00317	.00307	.00298	.00289	.00280	.00272	.00264
2.8	.00256	.00248	.00240	.00233	.00226	.00219	.00212	.00205	.00199	.00193
2.9	.00187	.00181	.00175	.00169	.00164	.00159	.00154	.00149	.00144	.00139
Z	**0**	**0.1**	**0.2**	**0.3**	**0.4**	**0.5**	**0.6**	**0.7**	**0.8**	**0.9**
3	.00135	.968E-03	.687E-03	.483E-03	.337E-03	.233E-03	.159E-03	.108E-03	.723E-04	.481E-04
4	.317E-04	.207E-04	.133E-04	.854E-05	.541E-05	.340E-05	.211E-05	.130E-05	.793E-06	.479E-06
5	.287E-06	.170E-06	.996E-07	.579E-07	.333E-07	.190E-07	.107E-07	.599E-08	.332E-08	.182E-08
6	.987E-09	.530E-09	.282E-09	.149E-09	.777E-10	.402E-10	.206E-10	.104E-10	.523E-11	.260E-11

Note 1: The same information can be obtained from Tables B and C; however, this table format is different.

Note 2: The tabular value corresponds to Z where is the value of probability associated with the distribution area pictorially reprsented as

1063

Table B: Probability Points of the Normal Distribution: Single Sided
(Variance Known)

α or β	U	α or β	U
0.001	3.090	0.100	1.282
0.005	2.576	0.150	1.036
0.010	2.326	0.200	0.842
0.015	2.170	0.300	0.524
0.020	2.054	0.400	0.253
0.025	1.960	0.500	0.000
0.050	1.645	0.600	-0.253

Note 1: The same information can be obtained from Table A; however, this table format is different.

Note 2: In this text the tabular value corresponds to U_α, where α is the value of probability associated with the distribution area pictorially represented as

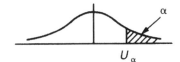

Source: Diamond (1989).

Table C: Probability Points of the Normal Distribution: Double Sided
(Variance Known)

α only	U	α only	U
0.001	3.291	0.100	1.645
0.005	2.807	0.150	1.440
0.010	2.576	0.200	1.282
0.015	2.432	0.300	1.036
0.020	2.326	0.400	0.842
0.025	2.241	0.500	0.675
0.050	1.960	0.600	0.524

Note 1: The same information can be obtained from Table A; however, this table format is different.

Note 2: In this text the tabular value corresponds to U_α, where α is the value of probability associated with the distribution area pictorially represented as

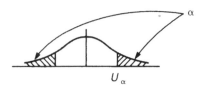

Source: Diamond (1989).

Table D: Probability Points of the t Distribution: Single Sided

ν	.40	.30	.20	.10	.050	.025	.010	.005	.001	.0005
1	.325	.727	1.376	3.078	6.314	12.71	31.82	63.66	318.3	636.6
2	.289	.617	1.061	1.886	2.920	4.303	6.965	9.925	22.33	31.60
3	.277	.584	.978	1.638	2.353	3.182	4.541	5.841	10.22	12.94
4	.271	.569	.941	1.533	2.132	2.776	3.747	4.604	7.173	8.610
5	.267	.559	.920	1.476	2.015	2.571	3.365	4.032	5.893	6.859
6	.265	.553	.906	1.440	1.943	2.447	3.143	3.707	5.208	5.959
7	.263	.549	.896	1.415	1.895	2.365	2.998	3.499	4.785	5.405
8	.262	.546	.889	1.397	1.860	2.306	2.896	3.355	4.501	5.041
9	.261	.543	.883	1.383	1.833	2.262	2.821	3.250	4.297	4.781
10	.260	.542	.879	1.372	1.812	2.228	2.764	3.169	4.144	4.587
11	.260	.540	.876	1.363	1.796	2.201	2.718	3.106	4.025	4.437
12	.259	.539	.873	1.356	1.782	2.179	2.681	3.055	3.930	4.318
13	.259	.538	.870	1.350	1.771	2.160	2.650	3.012	3.852	4.221
14	.258	.537	.868	1.345	1.761	2.145	2.624	2.977	3.787	4.140
15	.258	.536	.866	1.341	1.753	2.131	2.602	2.947	3.733	4.073
16	.258	.535	.865	1.337	1.746	2.120	2.583	2.921	3.686	4.015
17	.257	.534	.863	1.333	1.740	2.110	2.567	2.898	3.646	3.965
18	.257	.534	.862	1.330	1.734	2.101	2.552	2.878	3.611	3.922
19	.257	.533	.861	1.328	1.729	2.093	2.539	2.861	3.579	3.883
20	.257	.533	.860	1.325	1.725	2.086	2.528	2.845	3.552	3.850
21	.257	.532	.859	1.323	1.721	2.080	2.518	2.831	3.527	3.819
22	.256	.532	.858	1.321	1.717	2.074	2.508	2.819	3.505	3.792
23	.256	.532	.858	1.319	1.714	2.069	2.500	2.807	3.485	3.767
24	.256	.531	.857	1.318	1.711	2.064	2.492	2.797	3.467	3.745
25	.256	.531	.856	1.316	1.708	2.060	2.485	2.787	3.450	3.725
26	.256	.531	.856	1.315	1.706	2.056	2.479	2.779	3.435	3.707
27	.256	.531	.855	1.314	1.703	2.052	2.473	2.771	3.421	3.690
28	.256	.530	.855	1.313	1.701	2.048	2.467	2.763	3.408	3.674
29	.256	.530	.854	1.311	1.699	2.045	2.462	2.756	3.396	3.659
30	.256	.530	.854	1.310	1.697	2.042	2.457	2.750	3.385	3.646
40	.255	.529	.851	1.303	1.684	2.021	2.423	2.704	3.307	3.551
50	.255	.528	.849	1.298	1.676	2.009	2.403	2.678	3.262	3.495
60	.254	.527	.848	1.296	1.671	2.000	2.390	2.660	3.232	3.460
80	.254	.527	.846	1.292	1.664	1.990	2.374	2.639	3.195	3.415
100	.254	.526	.845	1.290	1.660	1.984	2.365	2.626	3.174	3.389
200	.254	.525	.843	1.286	1.653	1.972	2.345	2.601	3.131	3.339
500	.253	.525	.842	1.283	1.648	1.965	2.334	2.586	3.106	3.310
∞	.253	.524	.842	1.282	1.645	1.960	2.326	2.576	3.090	3.291

Note: In this text the tabular value corresponds to $t_{\alpha;\nu}$, where ν is the number of degrees of freedom and α is the value of probability associated with the distribution area pictorially represented as

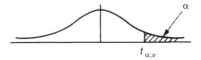

Source: Pearson and Hartley (1958). Parts of the table are also taken from Table III of Fisher and Yates (1953).

Table E: Probability Points of the t Distribution: Double Sided

Degrees of Freedom	Probability of a Larger Value, Sign Ignored								
	0.500	0.400	0.200	0.100	0.050	0.025	0.010	0.005	0.001
1	1.000	1.376	3.078	6.314	12.706	25.452	63.657		
2	.816	1.061	1.886	2.920	4.303	6.205	9.925	14.089	31.598
3	.765	.978	1.638	2.353	3.182	4.176	5.841	7.453	12.941
4	.741	.941	1.533	2.132	2.776	3.495	4.604	5.598	8.610
5	.727	.920	1.476	2.015	2.571	3.163	4.032	4.773	6.859
6	.718	.906	1.440	1.943	2.447	2.969	3.707	4.317	5.959
7	.711	.896	1.415	1.895	2.365	2.841	3.499	4.029	5.405
8	.706	.889	1.397	1.860	2.306	2.752	3.355	3.832	5.041
9	.703	.883	1.383	1.833	2.262	2.685	3.250	3.690	4.781
10	.700	.879	1.372	1.812	2.228	2.634	3.169	3.581	4.587
11	.697	.876	1.363	1.796	2.201	2.593	3.106	3.497	4.437
12	.695	.873	1.356	1.782	2.179	2.560	3.055	3.428	4.318
13	.694	.870	1.350	1.771	2.160	2.533	3.012	3.372	4.221
14	.692	.868	1.345	1.761	2.145	2.510	2.977	3.326	4.140
15	.691	.866	1.341	1.753	2.131	2.490	2.947	3.286	4.073
16	.690	.865	1.337	1.746	2.120	2.473	2.921	3.252	4.015
17	.689	.863	1.333	1.740	2.110	2.458	2.898	3.222	3.965
18	.688	.862	1.330	1.734	2.101	2.445	2.878	3.197	3.922
19	.688	.861	1.328	1.729	2.093	2.433	2.861	3.174	3.883
20	.687	.860	1.325	1.725	2.086	2.423	2.845	3.153	3.850
21	.686	.859	1.323	1.721	2.080	2.414	2.831	3.135	3.819
22	.686	.858	1.321	1.717	2.074	2.406	2.819	3.119	3.792
23	.685	.858	1.319	1.714	2.069	2.398	2.807	3.104	3.767
24	.685	.857	1.318	1.711	2.064	2.391	2.797	3.090	3.745
25	.684	.856	1.316	1.708	2.060	2.385	2.787	3.078	3.725
26	.684	.856	1.315	1.706	2.056	2.379	2.779	3.067	3.707
27	.684	.855	1.314	1.703	2.052	2.373	2.771	3.056	3.690
28	.683	.855	1.313	1.701	2.048	2.368	2.763	3.047	3.674
29	.683	.854	1.311	1.699	2.045	2.364	2.756	3.038	3.659
30	.683	.854	1.310	1.697	2.042	2.360	2.750	3.030	3.646
35	.682	.852	1.306	1.690	2.030	2.342	2.724	2.996	3.591
40	.681	.851	1.303	1.684	2.021	2.329	2.704	2.971	3.551
45	.680	.850	1.301	1.680	2.014	2.319	2.690	2.952	3.520
50	.680	.849	1.299	1.676	2.008	2.310	2.678	2.937	3.496
55	.679	.849	1.297	1.673	2.004	2.304	2.669	2.925	3.476

Degrees of Freedom	Probability of a Larger Value, Sign Ignored								
	0.500	0.400	0.200	0.100	0.050	0.025	0.010	0.005	0.001
60	.679	.848	1.296	1.671	2.000	2.299	2.660	2.915	3.460
70	.678	.847	1.294	1.667	1.994	2.290	2.648	2.899	3.435
80	.678	.847	1.293	1.665	1.989	2.284	2.638	2.887	3.416
90	.678	.846	1.291	1.662	1.986	2.279	2.631	2.878	3.402
100	.677	.846	1.290	1.661	1.982	2.276	2.625	2.871	3.390
120	.677	.845	1.289	1.658	1.980	2.270	2.617	2.860	3.373
∞	.6745	.8416	1.2816	1.6448	1.9600	2.2414	2.5758	2.8070	3.2905

Note: In this text the tabular value corresponds to $t_{\alpha;\nu}$, where ν is the number of degrees of freedom and α is the value of probability associated with the distribution area, pictorially represented as

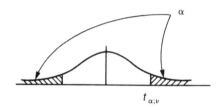

Source: Snedecor and Cochran (1989).

Table F: Probability Points of the Variance Ratio (F Distribution)

Probability Point	ν_2	Numerator (ν_1)																		
		1	2	3	4	5	6	7	8	9	10	12	15	20	24	30	40	60	120	α
0.1	1	39.9	49.5	53.6	55.8	57.2	58.2	58.9	59.4	59.9	60.2	60.7	61.2	61.7	62.0	62.3	62.5	62.8	63.1	63.3
0.05		161	199	216	225	230	234	237	239	241	242	244	246	248	249	250	251	252	253	254
0.01		4052	4999	5403	5625	5764	5859	5928	5982	6022	6056	6106	6157	6209	6235	6261	6287	6313	6339	6366
0.1	2	8.53	9.00	9.16	9.24	9.29	9.33	9.35	9.37	9.38	9.39	9.41	9.42	9.44	9.45	9.46	9.47	9.47	9.48	9.49
0.05		18.5	19.0	19.2	19.2	19.3	19.3	19.4	19.4	19.4	19.4	19.4	19.4	19.4	19.5	19.5	19.5	19.5	19.5	19.5
0.01		98.5	99.0	99.2	99.2	99.3	99.3	99.4	99.4	99.4	99.4	99.4	99.4	99.4	99.5	99.5	99.5	99.5	99.5	99.5
0.1	3	5.54	5.46	5.39	5.34	5.31	5.28	5.27	5.25	5.24	5.23	5.22	5.20	5.18	5.18	5.17	5.16	5.15	5.14	5.13
0.05		10.1	9.55	9.28	9.12	9.01	8.94	8.89	8.85	8.81	8.79	8.74	8.70	8.66	8.64	8.62	8.59	8.57	8.55	8.53
0.01		34.1	30.8	29.5	28.7	28.2	27.9	27.7	27.5	27.3	27.2	27.1	26.9	26.7	26.6	26.5	26.4	26.3	26.2	26.1
0.1	4	4.54	4.32	4.19	4.11	4.05	4.01	3.98	3.95	3.94	3.92	3.90	3.87	3.84	3.83	3.82	3.80	3.79	3.78	3.76
0.05		7.71	6.94	6.59	6.39	6.26	6.16	6.09	6.04	6.00	5.96	5.91	5.86	5.80	5.77	5.75	5.72	5.69	5.66	5.63
0.01		21.2	18.0	16.7	16.0	15.5	15.2	15.0	14.8	14.7	14.5	14.4	14.2	14.0	13.9	13.8	13.7	13.7	13.6	13.5
0.1	5	4.06	3.78	3.62	3.52	3.45	3.40	3.37	3.34	3.32	3.30	3.27	3.24	3.21	3.19	3.17	3.16	3.14	3.12	3.10
0.05		6.61	5.79	5.41	5.19	5.05	4.95	4.88	4.82	4.77	4.74	4.68	4.62	4.56	4.53	4.50	4.46	4.43	4.40	4.36
0.01		16.3	13.3	12.1	11.4	11.0	10.7	10.5	10.3	10.2	10.1	9.89	9.72	9.55	9.47	9.38	9.29	9.20	9.11	9.02
0.1	6	3.78	3.46	3.29	3.18	3.11	3.05	3.01	2.98	2.96	2.94	2.90	2.87	2.84	2.82	2.80	2.78	2.76	2.74	2.72
0.05		5.99	5.14	4.76	4.53	4.39	4.28	4.21	4.15	4.10	4.06	4.00	3.94	3.87	3.84	3.81	3.77	3.74	3.70	3.67
0.01		13.7	10.9	9.78	9.15	8.75	8.47	8.26	8.10	7.98	7.87	7.72	7.56	7.40	7.31	7.23	7.14	7.06	6.97	6.88
0.1	7	3.59	3.26	3.07	2.96	2.88	2.83	2.78	2.75	2.72	2.70	2.67	2.63	2.59	2.58	2.56	2.54	2.51	2.49	2.47
0.05		5.59	4.74	4.35	4.12	3.97	3.87	3.79	3.73	3.68	3.64	3.57	3.51	3.44	3.41	3.38	3.34	3.30	3.27	3.23
0.01		12.2	9.55	8.45	7.85	7.46	7.19	6.99	6.84	6.72	6.62	6.47	6.31	6.16	6.07	5.99	5.91	5.82	5.74	5.65
0.1	8	3.46	3.11	2.92	2.81	2.73	2.67	2.62	2.59	2.56	2.54	2.50	2.46	2.42	2.40	2.38	2.36	2.34	2.32	2.29
0.05		5.32	4.46	4.07	3.84	3.69	3.58	3.50	3.44	3.39	3.35	3.28	3.22	3.15	3.12	3.08	3.04	3.01	2.97	2.93
0.01		11.3	8.65	7.59	7.01	6.63	6.37	6.18	6.03	5.91	5.81	5.67	5.52	5.36	5.28	5.20	5.12	5.03	4.95	4.86
0.1	9	3.36	3.01	2.81	2.69	2.61	2.55	2.51	2.47	2.44	2.42	2.38	2.34	2.30	2.28	2.25	2.23	2.21	2.18	2.16
0.05		5.12	4.26	3.86	3.63	3.48	3.37	3.29	3.23	3.18	3.14	3.07	3.01	2.94	2.90	2.86	2.83	2.79	2.75	2.71
0.01		10.6	8.02	6.99	6.42	6.06	5.80	5.61	5.47	5.35	5.26	5.11	4.96	4.81	4.73	4.65	4.57	4.48	4.40	4.31

df	α																				
10	0.1	2.06	2.08	2.11	2.13	2.16	2.18	2.20	2.24	2.28	2.32	2.35	2.38	2.41	2.46	2.52	2.61	2.73	2.92	3.28
	0.05	2.54	2.58	2.62	2.66	2.70	2.74	2.77	2.84	2.91	2.98	3.02	3.07	3.14	3.22	3.33	3.48	3.71	4.10	4.96
	0.01	3.91	4.00	4.08	4.17	4.25	4.33	4.41	4.56	4.71	4.85	4.94	5.06	5.20	5.39	5.64	5.99	6.55	7.56	10.0
11	0.1	1.97	2.00	2.03	2.05	2.08	2.10	2.12	2.17	2.21	2.25	2.27	2.30	2.34	2.39	2.45	2.54	2.66	2.86	3.23
	0.05	2.40	2.45	2.49	2.53	2.57	2.61	2.65	2.72	2.79	2.85	2.90	2.95	3.01	3.09	3.20	3.36	3.59	3.98	4.84
	0.01	3.60	3.69	3.78	3.86	3.94	4.02	4.10	4.25	4.40	4.54	4.63	4.74	4.89	5.07	5.32	5.67	6.22	7.21	9.65
12	0.1	1.90	1.93	1.96	1.99	2.01	2.04	2.06	2.10	2.15	2.19	2.21	2.24	2.28	2.33	2.39	2.48	2.61	2.81	3.18
	0.05	2.30	2.34	2.38	2.43	2.47	2.51	2.54	2.62	2.69	2.75	2.80	2.85	2.91	3.00	3.11	3.26	3.49	3.89	4.75
	0.01	3.36	3.45	3.54	3.62	3.70	3.78	3.86	4.01	4.16	4.30	4.39	4.50	4.64	4.82	5.06	5.41	5.95	6.93	9.33
13	0.1	1.85	1.88	1.90	1.93	1.96	1.98	2.01	2.05	2.10	2.14	2.16	2.20	2.23	2.28	2.35	2.43	2.56	2.76	3.14
	0.05	2.21	2.25	2.30	2.34	2.38	2.42	2.46	2.53	2.60	2.67	2.71	2.77	2.83	2.92	3.03	3.18	3.41	3.81	4.67
	0.01	3.17	3.25	3.34	3.43	3.51	3.59	3.66	3.82	3.96	4.10	4.19	4.30	4.44	4.62	4.86	5.21	5.74	6.70	9.07
14	0.1	1.80	1.83	1.86	1.89	1.91	1.94	1.96	2.01	2.05	2.10	2.12	2.15	2.19	2.24	2.31	2.39	2.52	2.73	3.10
	0.05	2.13	2.18	2.22	2.27	2.31	2.35	2.39	2.46	2.53	2.60	2.65	2.70	2.76	2.85	2.96	3.11	3.34	3.74	4.60
	0.01	3.00	3.09	3.18	3.27	3.35	3.43	3.51	3.66	3.80	3.94	4.03	4.14	4.28	4.46	4.69	5.04	5.56	6.51	8.86
15	0.1	1.76	1.79	1.82	1.85	1.87	1.90	1.92	1.97	2.02	2.06	2.09	2.12	2.16	2.21	2.27	2.36	2.49	2.70	3.07
	0.05	2.07	2.11	2.16	2.20	2.25	2.29	2.33	2.40	2.48	2.54	2.59	2.64	2.71	2.79	2.90	3.06	3.29	3.68	4.54
	0.01	2.87	2.96	3.05	3.13	3.21	3.29	3.37	3.52	3.67	3.80	3.89	4.00	4.14	4.32	4.56	4.89	5.42	6.36	8.68
16	0.1	1.72	1.75	1.78	1.81	1.84	1.87	1.89	1.94	1.99	2.03	2.06	2.09	2.13	2.18	2.24	2.33	2.46	2.67	3.05
	0.05	2.01	2.06	2.11	2.15	2.19	2.24	2.28	2.35	2.42	2.49	2.54	2.59	2.66	2.74	2.85	3.01	3.24	3.63	4.49
	0.01	2.75	2.84	2.93	3.02	3.10	3.18	3.26	3.41	3.55	3.69	3.78	3.89	4.03	4.20	4.44	4.77	5.29	6.23	8.53
17	0.1	1.69	1.72	1.75	1.78	1.81	1.84	1.86	1.91	1.96	2.00	2.03	2.06	2.10	2.15	2.22	2.31	2.44	2.64	3.03
	0.05	1.96	2.01	2.06	2.10	2.15	2.19	2.23	2.31	2.38	2.45	2.49	2.55	2.61	2.70	2.81	2.96	3.20	3.59	4.45
	0.01	2.65	2.75	2.83	2.92	3.00	3.08	3.16	3.31	3.46	3.59	3.68	3.79	3.93	4.10	4.34	4.67	5.18	6.11	8.40
18	0.1	1.66	1.69	1.72	1.75	1.78	1.81	1.84	1.89	1.93	1.98	2.00	2.04	2.08	2.13	2.20	2.29	2.42	2.62	3.01
	0.05	1.92	1.97	2.02	2.06	2.11	2.15	2.19	2.27	2.34	2.41	2.46	2.51	2.58	2.66	2.77	2.93	3.16	3.55	4.41
	0.01	2.57	2.66	2.75	2.84	2.92	3.00	3.08	3.23	3.37	3.51	3.60	3.71	3.84	4.01	4.25	4.58	5.09	6.01	8.29
19	0.1	1.63	1.67	1.70	1.73	1.76	1.79	1.81	1.86	1.91	1.96	1.98	2.02	2.06	2.11	2.18	2.27	2.40	2.61	2.99
	0.05	1.88	1.93	1.98	2.03	2.07	2.11	2.16	2.23	2.31	2.38	2.42	2.48	2.54	2.63	2.74	2.90	3.13	3.52	4.38
	0.01	2.49	2.58	2.67	2.76	2.84	2.92	3.00	3.15	3.30	3.43	3.52	3.63	3.77	3.94	4.17	4.50	5.01	5.93	8.18

ν_2	Probability Point	1	2	3	4	5	6	7	8	9	10	12	15	20	24	30	40	60	120	α
20	0.1	2.97	2.59	2.38	2.25	2.16	2.09	2.04	2.00	1.96	1.94	1.89	1.84	1.79	1.77	1.74	1.71	1.68	1.64	1.61
	0.05	4.35	3.49	3.10	2.87	2.71	2.60	2.51	2.45	2.39	2.35	2.28	2.20	2.12	2.08	2.04	1.99	1.95	1.90	1.84
	0.01	8.10	5.85	4.94	4.43	4.10	3.87	3.70	3.56	3.46	3.37	3.23	3.09	2.94	2.86	2.78	2.69	2.61	2.52	2.42
21	0.1	2.96	2.57	2.36	2.23	2.14	2.08	2.02	1.98	1.95	1.92	1.87	1.83	1.78	1.75	1.72	1.69	1.66	1.62	1.59
	0.05	4.32	3.47	3.07	2.84	2.68	2.57	2.49	2.42	2.37	2.32	2.25	2.18	2.10	2.05	2.01	1.96	1.92	1.87	1.81
	0.01	8.02	5.78	4.87	4.37	4.04	3.81	3.64	3.51	3.40	3.31	3.17	3.03	2.88	2.80	2.72	2.64	2.55	2.46	2.36
22	0.1	2.95	2.56	2.35	2.22	2.13	2.06	2.01	1.97	1.93	1.90	1.86	1.81	1.76	1.73	1.70	1.67	1.64	1.60	1.57
	0.05	4.30	3.44	3.05	2.82	2.66	2.55	2.46	2.40	2.34	2.30	2.23	2.15	2.07	2.03	1.98	1.94	1.89	1.84	1.78
	0.01	7.95	5.72	4.82	4.31	3.99	3.76	3.59	3.45	3.35	3.26	3.12	2.98	2.83	2.75	2.67	2.58	2.50	2.40	2.31
23	0.1	2.94	2.55	2.34	2.21	2.11	2.05	1.99	1.95	1.92	1.89	1.85	1.80	1.74	1.72	1.69	1.66	1.62	1.59	1.55
	0.05	4.28	3.42	3.03	2.80	2.64	2.53	2.44	2.37	2.32	2.27	2.20	2.13	2.05	2.00	1.96	1.91	1.86	1.81	1.76
	0.01	7.88	5.66	4.76	4.26	3.94	3.71	3.54	3.41	3.30	3.21	3.07	2.93	2.78	2.70	2.62	2.54	2.45	2.35	2.26
24	0.1	2.93	2.54	2.33	2.19	2.10	2.04	1.98	1.94	1.91	1.88	1.83	1.78	1.73	1.70	1.67	1.64	1.61	1.57	1.53
	0.05	4.26	3.40	3.01	2.78	2.62	2.51	2.42	2.36	2.30	2.25	2.18	2.11	2.03	1.98	1.94	1.89	1.84	1.79	1.73
	0.01	7.82	5.61	4.72	4.22	3.90	3.67	3.50	3.36	3.26	3.17	3.03	2.89	2.74	2.66	2.58	2.49	2.40	2.31	2.21
25	0.1	2.92	2.53	2.32	2.18	2.09	2.02	1.97	1.93	1.89	1.87	1.82	1.77	1.72	1.69	1.66	1.63	1.59	1.56	1.52
	0.05	4.24	3.39	2.99	2.76	2.60	2.49	2.40	2.34	2.28	2.24	2.16	2.09	2.01	1.96	1.92	1.87	1.82	1.77	1.71
	0.01	7.77	5.57	4.68	4.18	3.86	3.63	3.46	3.32	3.22	3.13	2.99	2.85	2.70	2.62	2.54	2.45	2.36	2.27	2.17
26	0.1	2.91	2.52	2.31	2.17	2.08	2.01	1.96	1.92	1.88	1.86	1.81	1.76	1.71	1.68	1.65	1.61	1.58	1.54	1.50
	0.05	4.23	3.37	2.98	2.74	2.59	2.47	2.39	2.32	2.27	2.22	2.15	2.07	1.99	1.95	1.90	1.85	1.80	1.75	1.69
	0.01	7.72	5.53	4.64	4.14	3.82	3.59	3.42	3.29	3.18	3.09	2.96	2.82	2.66	2.58	2.50	2.42	2.33	2.23	2.13
27	0.1	2.90	2.51	2.30	2.17	2.07	2.00	1.95	1.91	1.87	1.85	1.80	1.75	1.70	1.67	1.64	1.60	1.57	1.53	1.49
	0.05	4.21	3.35	2.96	2.73	2.57	2.46	2.37	2.31	2.25	2.20	2.13	2.06	1.97	1.93	1.88	1.84	1.79	1.73	1.67
	0.01	7.68	5.49	4.60	4.11	3.78	3.56	3.39	3.26	3.15	3.06	2.93	2.78	2.63	2.55	2.47	2.38	2.29	2.20	2.10
28	0.1	2.89	2.50	2.29	2.16	2.06	2.00	1.94	1.90	1.87	1.84	1.79	1.74	1.69	1.66	1.63	1.59	1.56	1.52	1.48
	0.05	4.20	3.34	2.95	2.71	2.56	2.45	2.36	2.29	2.24	2.19	2.12	2.04	1.96	1.91	1.87	1.82	1.77	1.71	1.65
	0.01	7.64	5.45	4.57	4.07	3.75	3.53	3.36	3.23	3.12	3.03	2.90	2.75	2.60	2.52	2.44	2.35	2.26	2.17	2.06

Numerator (ν_1)

ν_2	α																			
29	0.1	2.89	2.50	2.28	2.15	2.06	1.99	1.93	1.89	1.86	1.83	1.78	1.73	1.68	1.65	1.62	1.58	1.55	1.51	1.47
	0.05	4.18	3.33	2.93	2.70	2.55	2.43	2.35	2.28	2.22	2.18	2.10	2.03	1.94	1.90	1.85	1.81	1.75	1.70	1.64
	0.01	7.60	5.42	4.54	4.04	3.73	3.50	3.33	3.20	3.09	3.00	2.87	2.73	2.57	2.49	2.41	2.33	2.23	2.14	2.03
30	0.1	2.88	2.49	2.28	2.14	2.05	1.98	1.93	1.88	1.85	1.82	1.77	1.72	1.67	1.64	1.61	1.57	1.54	1.50	1.46
	0.05	4.17	3.32	2.92	2.69	2.53	2.42	2.33	2.27	2.21	2.16	2.09	2.01	1.93	1.89	1.84	1.79	1.74	1.68	1.62
	0.01	7.56	5.39	4.51	4.02	3.70	3.47	3.30	3.17	3.07	2.98	2.84	2.70	2.55	2.47	2.39	2.30	2.21	2.11	2.01
40	0.1	2.84	2.44	2.23	2.09	2.00	1.93	1.87	1.83	1.79	1.76	1.71	1.66	1.61	1.57	1.54	1.51	1.47	1.42	1.38
	0.05	4.08	3.23	2.84	2.61	2.45	2.34	2.25	2.18	2.12	2.08	2.00	1.92	1.84	1.79	1.74	1.69	1.64	1.58	1.51
	0.01	7.31	5.18	4.31	3.83	3.51	3.29	3.12	2.99	2.89	2.80	2.66	2.52	2.37	2.29	2.20	2.11	2.02	1.92	1.80
60	0.1	2.79	2.39	2.18	2.04	1.95	1.87	1.82	1.77	1.74	1.71	1.66	1.60	1.54	1.51	1.48	1.44	1.40	1.35	1.29
	0.05	4.00	3.15	2.76	2.53	2.37	2.25	2.17	2.10	2.04	1.99	1.92	1.84	1.75	1.70	1.65	1.59	1.53	1.47	1.39
	0.01	7.08	4.98	4.13	3.65	3.34	3.12	2.95	2.82	2.72	2.63	2.50	2.35	2.20	2.12	2.03	1.94	1.84	1.73	1.60
120	0.1	2.75	2.35	2.13	1.99	1.90	1.82	1.77	1.72	1.68	1.65	1.60	1.54	1.48	1.45	1.41	1.37	1.32	1.26	1.19
	0.05	3.92	3.07	2.68	2.45	2.29	2.18	2.09	2.02	1.96	1.91	1.83	1.75	1.66	1.61	1.55	1.50	1.43	1.35	1.25
	0.01	6.85	4.79	3.95	3.48	3.17	2.96	2.79	2.66	2.56	2.47	2.34	2.19	2.03	1.95	1.86	1.76	1.66	1.53	1.38
∞	0.1	2.71	2.30	2.08	1.94	1.85	1.77	1.72	1.67	1.63	1.60	1.55	1.49	1.42	1.38	1.34	1.30	1.24	1.17	1.00
	0.05	3.84	3.00	2.60	2.37	2.21	2.10	2.01	1.94	1.88	1.83	1.75	1.67	1.57	1.52	1.46	1.39	1.32	1.22	1.00
	0.01	6.63	4.61	3.78	3.32	3.02	2.80	2.64	2.51	2.41	2.32	2.18	2.04	1.88	1.79	1.70	1.59	1.47	1.32	1.00

Note: The tabular value corresponds to $F_{\alpha; \nu_1; \nu_2}$, where ν_1 is the number of degrees of freedom of the larger value in the numerator, ν_2 is the number of degrees of freedom of the smaller value in the denominator, and α is the value of probability associated with the distribution area pictorially represented as

Source: Table V of Fisher and Yates (1953), with permission. (The labeling reflects the nomenclature used in this text.)

Table G: Cumulative Distribution of Chi-Square

Degrees of Freedom	Probability of a Greater Value												
	0.995	0.990	0.975	0.950	0.900	0.750	0.500	0.250	0.100	0.050	0.025	0.010	0.005
1	...	...	...	...	0.02	0.10	0.45	1.32	2.71	3.84	5.02	6.63	7.88
2	0.01	0.02	0.05	0.10	0.21	0.58	1.39	2.77	4.61	5.99	7.38	9.21	10.60
3	0.07	0.11	0.22	0.35	0.58	1.21	2.37	4.11	6.25	7.81	9.35	11.34	12.84
4	0.21	0.30	0.48	0.71	1.06	1.92	3.36	5.39	7.78	9.49	11.14	13.28	14.86
5	0.41	0.55	0.83	1.15	1.61	2.67	4.35	6.63	9.24	11.07	12.83	15.09	16.75
6	0.68	0.87	1.24	1.64	2.20	3.45	5.35	7.84	10.64	12.59	14.45	16.81	18.55
7	0.99	1.24	1.69	2.17	2.83	4.25	6.35	9.04	12.02	14.07	16.01	18.48	20.28
8	1.34	1.65	2.18	2.73	3.49	5.07	7.34	10.22	13.36	15.51	17.53	20.09	21.96
9	1.73	2.09	2.70	3.33	4.17	5.90	8.34	11.39	14.68	16.92	19.02	21.67	23.59
10	2.16	2.56	3.25	3.94	4.87	6.74	9.34	12.55	15.99	18.31	20.48	23.21	25.19
11	2.60	3.05	3.82	4.57	5.58	7.58	10.34	13.70	17.28	19.68	21.92	24.72	26.76
12	3.07	3.57	4.40	5.23	6.30	8.44	11.34	14.85	18.55	21.03	23.34	26.22	28.30
13	3.57	4.11	5.01	5.89	7.04	9.30	12.34	15.98	19.81	22.36	24.74	27.69	29.82
14	4.07	4.66	5.63	6.57	7.79	10.17	13.34	17.12	21.06	23.68	26.12	29.14	31.32
15	4.60	5.23	6.27	7.26	8.55	11.04	14.34	18.25	22.31	25.00	27.49	30.58	32.80
16	5.14	5.81	6.91	7.96	9.31	11.91	15.34	19.37	23.54	26.30	28.85	32.00	34.27
17	5.70	6.41	7.56	8.67	10.09	12.79	16.34	20.49	24.77	27.59	30.19	33.41	35.72
18	6.26	7.01	8.23	9.39	10.86	13.68	17.34	21.60	25.99	28.87	31.53	34.81	37.16
19	6.84	7.63	8.91	10.12	11.65	14.56	18.34	22.72	27.20	30.14	32.85	36.19	38.58
20	7.43	8.26	9.59	10.85	12.44	15.45	19.34	23.83	28.41	31.41	34.17	37.57	40.00

ν													
21	8.03	8.90	10.28	11.59	13.24	16.34	20.34	24.93	29.62	32.67	35.48	38.93	41.40
22	8.64	9.54	10.98	12.34	14.04	17.24	21.34	26.04	30.81	33.92	36.78	40.29	42.80
23	9.26	10.20	11.69	13.09	14.85	18.14	22.34	27.14	32.01	35.17	38.08	41.64	44.18
24	9.89	10.86	12.40	13.85	15.66	19.04	23.34	28.24	33.20	36.42	39.36	42.98	45.56
25	10.52	11.52	13.12	14.61	16.47	19.94	24.34	29.34	34.38	37.65	40.65	44.31	46.93
26	11.16	12.20	13.84	15.38	17.29	20.84	25.34	30.43	35.56	38.89	41.92	45.64	48.29
27	11.81	12.88	14.57	16.15	18.11	21.75	26.34	31.53	36.74	40.11	43.19	46.96	49.64
28	12.46	13.56	15.31	16.93	18.94	22.66	27.34	32.62	37.92	41.34	44.46	48.28	50.99
29	13.12	14.26	16.05	17.71	19.77	23.57	28.34	33.71	39.09	42.56	45.72	49.59	52.34
30	13.79	14.95	16.79	18.49	20.60	24.48	29.34	34.80	40.26	43.77	46.98	50.89	53.67
40	20.71	22.16	24.43	26.51	29.05	33.66	39.34	45.62	51.80	55.76	59.34	63.69	66.77
50	27.99	29.71	32.36	34.76	37.69	42.94	49.33	56.33	63.17	67.50	71.42	76.15	79.49
60	35.53	37.48	40.48	43.19	46.46	52.29	59.33	66.98	74.40	79.08	83.30	88.38	91.95
70	43.28	45.44	48.76	51.74	55.33	61.70	69.33	77.58	85.53	90.53	95.02	100.42	104.22
80	51.17	53.54	57.15	60.39	64.28	71.14	79.33	88.13	96.58	101.88	106.63	112.33	116.32
90	59.20	61.75	65.65	69.13	73.29	80.62	89.33	98.64	107.56	113.14	118.14	124.12	128.30
100	67.33	70.06	74.22	77.93	82.36	90.13	99.33	109.14	118.50	124.34	129.56	135.81	140.17

Note: In this text the tabular value corresponds to $\chi^2_{\alpha;\nu}$, where ν is the number of degrees of freedom and α is the value of probability associated with the distribution area pictorially represented as

Source: Snedecor and Cochran (1989).

Table H: Generic Percent Plot Positions (F_i) for Probability Plotting

$$[F_i = 100(i - 0.5)/n]$$

Ranking Number i	Sample Size (n)												
	1	2	3	4	5	6	7	8	9	10	11	12	13
1	50.0	25.0	16.7	12.5	10.0	8.3	7.1	6.3	5.6	5.0	4.5	4.2	3.8
2		75.0	50.0	37.5	30.0	25.0	21.4	18.8	16.7	15.0	13.6	12.5	11.5
3			83.3	62.5	50.0	41.7	35.7	31.3	27.8	25.0	22.7	20.8	19.2
4				87.5	70.0	58.3	50.0	43.8	38.9	35.0	31.8	29.2	26.9
5					90.0	75.0	64.3	56.3	50.0	45.0	40.9	37.5	34.6
6						91.7	78.6	68.8	61.1	55.0	50.0	45.8	42.3
7							92.9	81.3	72.2	65.0	59.1	54.2	50.0
8								93.8	83.3	75.0	68.2	62.5	57.7
9									94.4	85.0	77.3	70.8	65.4
10										95.0	86.4	79.2	73.1
11											95.5	87.5	80.8
12												95.8	88.5
13													96.2

Sample Size (n)

Ranking Number i	14	15	16	17	18	19	20	21	22	23	24	25	26
1	3.6	3.3	3.1	2.9	2.8	2.6	2.5	2.4	2.3	2.2	2.1	2.0	1.9
2	10.7	10.0	9.4	8.8	8.3	7.9	7.5	7.1	6.8	6.5	6.3	6.0	5.8
3	17.9	16.7	15.6	14.7	13.9	13.2	12.5	11.9	11.4	10.9	10.4	10.0	9.6
4	25.0	23.3	21.9	20.6	19.4	18.4	17.5	16.7	15.9	15.2	14.6	14.0	13.5
5	32.1	30.0	28.1	26.5	25.0	23.7	22.5	21.4	20.5	19.6	18.8	18.0	17.3
6	39.3	36.7	34.4	32.4	30.6	28.9	27.5	26.2	25.0	23.9	22.9	22.0	21.2
7	46.4	43.3	40.6	38.2	36.1	34.2	32.5	31.0	29.5	28.3	27.1	26.0	25.0
8	53.6	50.0	46.9	44.1	41.7	39.5	37.5	35.7	34.1	32.6	31.3	30.0	28.8
9	60.7	56.7	53.1	50.0	47.2	44.7	42.5	40.5	38.6	37.0	35.4	34.0	32.7
10	67.9	63.3	59.4	55.9	52.8	50.0	47.5	45.2	43.2	41.3	39.6	38.0	36.5
11	75.0	70.0	65.6	61.8	58.3	55.3	52.5	50.0	47.7	45.7	43.8	42.0	40.4
12	82.1	76.7	71.9	67.6	63.9	60.5	57.5	54.8	52.3	50.0	47.9	46.0	44.2
13	89.3	83.3	78.1	73.5	69.4	65.8	62.5	59.5	56.8	54.3	52.1	50.0	48.1
14	96.4	90.0	84.4	79.4	75.0	71.1	67.5	64.3	61.4	58.7	56.3	54.0	51.9
15		96.7	90.6	85.3	80.6	76.3	72.5	69.0	65.9	63.0	60.4	58.0	55.8
16			96.9	91.2	86.1	81.6	77.5	73.8	70.5	67.4	64.6	62.0	59.6
17				97.1	91.7	86.8	82.5	78.6	75.0	71.7	68.8	66.0	63.5
18					97.2	92.1	87.5	83.3	79.5	76.1	72.9	70.0	67.3
19						97.4	92.5	88.1	84.1	80.4	77.1	74.0	71.2
20							97.5	92.9	88.6	84.8	81.3	78.0	75.0
21								97.6	93.2	89.1	85.4	82.0	78.8
22									97.7	93.5	89.6	86.0	82.7
23										97.8	93.8	90.0	86.5
24											97.9	94.0	90.4
25												98.0	94.2
26													98.1

Table I: Exact Critical Values for Use of the Analysis of Means. Source, Nelson (1983), with permission of ASQ.

DF		Exact Critical Values $h_{0.10}$ for the Analysis of Means Significance Level = 0.10 Number of Means, k																	DF
	3	4	5	6	7	8	9	10	11	12	13	14	15	16	17	18	19	20	
3	3.16																		3
4	2.81	3.10																	4
5	2.63	2.88	3.05																5
6	2.52	2.74	2.91	3.03															6
7	2.44	2.65	2.81	2.92	3.02														7
8	2.39	2.59	2.73	2.85	2.94	3.02													8
9	2.34	2.54	2.68	2.79	2.88	2.95	3.01												9
10	2.31	2.50	2.64	2.74	2.83	2.90	2.96	3.02											10
11	2.29	2.47	2.60	2.70	2.79	2.86	2.92	2.97	3.02										11
12	2.27	2.45	2.57	2.67	2.75	2.82	2.88	2.93	2.98	3.02									12

TABLE I *(Continued)*

Exact Critical Values $h_{0.10}$ for the Analysis of Means
Significance Level = 0.10
Number of Means, k

DF	3	4	5	6	7	8	9	10	11	12	13	14	15	16	17	18	19	20	DF
13	2.25	2.43	2.55	2.65	2.73	2.79	2.85	2.90	2.95	2.99	3.03								13
14	2.23	2.41	2.53	2.63	2.70	2.77	2.83	2.88	2.92	2.96	3.00	3.03							14
15	2.22	2.39	2.51	2.61	2.68	2.75	2.80	2.85	2.90	2.94	2.97	3.01	3.04						15
16	2.21	2.38	2.50	2.59	2.67	2.73	2.79	2.83	2.88	2.92	2.95	2.99	3.02	3.05					16
17	2.20	2.37	2.49	2.58	2.65	2.72	2.77	2.82	2.86	2.90	2.93	2.97	3.00	3.03	3.05				17
18	2.19	2.36	2.47	2.56	2.64	2.70	2.75	2.80	2.84	2.88	2.92	2.95	2.98	3.01	3.03	3.06			18
19	2.18	2.35	2.46	2.55	2.63	2.69	2.74	2.79	2.83	2.87	2.90	2.94	2.96	2.99	3.02	3.04	3.06		19
20	2.18	2.34	2.45	2.54	2.62	2.68	2.73	2.78	2.82	2.86	2.89	2.92	2.95	2.98	3.00	3.03	3.05	3.07	20
24	2.15	2.32	2.43	2.51	2.58	2.64	2.69	2.74	2.78	2.82	2.85	2.88	2.91	2.93	2.96	2.98	3.00	3.02	24
30	2.13	2.29	2.40	2.48	2.55	2.61	2.66	2.70	2.74	2.77	2.81	2.84	2.86	2.89	2.91	2.93	2.96	2.98	30
40	2.11	2.27	2.37	2.45	2.52	2.57	2.62	2.66	2.70	2.73	2.77	2.79	2.82	2.85	2.87	2.89	2.91	2.93	40
60	2.09	2.24	2.34	2.42	2.49	2.54	2.59	2.63	2.66	2.70	2.73	2.75	2.78	2.80	2.82	2.84	2.86	2.88	60
120	2.07	2.22	2.32	2.39	2.45	2.51	2.55	2.59	2.62	2.66	2.69	2.71	2.74	2.76	2.78	2.80	2.82	2.84	120
∞	2.05	2.19	2.29	2.36	2.42	2.47	2.52	2.55	2.59	2.62	2.65	2.67	2.69	2.72	2.74	2.76	2.77	2.79	∞

Exact Critical Values $h_{0.05}$ for the Analysis of Means
Significance Level = 0.05
Number of Means, k

DF	3	4	5	6	7	8	9	10	11	12	13	14	15	16	17	18	19	20	DF
3	4.18																		3
4	3.56	3.89																	4
5	3.25	3.53	3.72																5
6	3.07	3.31	3.49	3.62															6
7	2.94	3.17	3.33	3.45	3.56														7
8	2.86	3.07	3.21	3.33	3.43	3.51													8
9	2.79	2.99	3.13	3.24	3.33	3.41	3.48												9
10	2.74	2.93	3.07	3.17	3.26	3.33	3.40	3.45											10
11	2.70	2.88	3.01	3.12	3.20	3.27	3.33	3.39	3.44										11
12	2.67	2.85	2.97	3.07	3.15	3.22	3.28	3.33	3.38	3.42									12
13	2.64	2.81	2.94	3.03	3.11	3.18	3.24	3.29	3.34	3.38	3.42								13
14	2.62	2.79	2.91	3.00	3.08	3.14	3.20	3.25	3.30	3.34	3.37	3.41							14
15	2.60	2.76	2.88	2.97	3.05	3.11	3.17	3.22	3.26	3.30	3.34	3.37	3.40						15

TABLE I *(Continued)*

Exact Critical Values $h_{0.05}$ for the Analysis of Means
Significance Level = 0.05
Number of Means, k

DF	3	4	5	6	7	8	9	10	11	12	13	14	15	16	17	18	19	20	DF
16	2.58	2.74	2.86	2.95	3.02	3.09	3.14	3.19	3.23	3.27	3.31	3.34	3.37	3.40					16
17	2.57	2.73	2.84	2.93	3.00	3.06	3.12	3.16	3.21	3.25	3.28	3.31	3.34	3.37	3.40				17
18	2.55	2.71	2.82	2.91	2.98	3.04	3.10	3.14	3.18	3.22	3.26	3.29	3.32	3.35	3.37	3.40			18
19	2.54	2.70	2.81	2.89	2.96	3.02	3.08	3.12	3.16	3.20	3.24	3.27	3.30	3.32	3.35	3.37	3.40		19
20	2.53	2.68	2.79	2.88	2.95	3.01	3.06	3.11	3.15	3.18	3.22	3.25	3.28	3.30	3.33	3.35	3.37	3.40	20
24	2.50	2.65	2.75	2.83	2.90	2.96	3.01	3.05	3.09	3.13	3.16	3.19	3.22	3.24	3.27	3.29	3.31	3.33	24
30	2.47	2.61	2.71	2.79	2.85	2.91	2.96	3.00	3.04	3.07	3.10	3.13	3.16	3.18	3.20	3.22	3.25	3.27	30
40	2.43	2.57	2.67	2.75	2.81	2.86	2.91	2.95	2.98	3.01	3.04	3.07	3.10	3.12	3.14	3.16	3.18	3.20	40
60	2.40	2.54	2.63	2.70	2.76	2.81	2.86	2.90	2.93	2.96	2.99	3.02	3.04	3.06	3.08	3.10	3.12	3.14	60
120	2.37	2.50	2.59	2.66	2.72	2.77	2.81	2.84	2.88	2.91	2.93	2.96	2.98	3.00	3.02	3.04	3.06	3.08	120
∞	2.34	2.47	2.56	2.62	2.68	2.72	2.76	2.80	2.83	2.86	2.88	2.90	2.93	2.95	2.97	2.98	3.00	3.02	∞

Exact Critical Values $h_{0.01}$ for the Analysis of Means

Significance Level = 0.01

Number of Means, k

DF	3	4	5	6	7	8	9	10	11	12	13	14	15	16	17	18	19	20	DF
3	7.51																		3
4	5.74	6.21																	4
5	4.93	5.29	5.55																5
6	4.48	4.77	4.98	5.16															6
7	4.18	4.44	4.63	4.78	4.90														7
8	3.98	4.21	4.38	4.52	4.63	4.72													8
9	3.84	4.05	4.20	4.33	4.43	4.51	4.59												9
10	3.73	3.92	4.07	4.18	4.28	4.36	4.43	4.49											10
11	3.64	3.82	3.96	4.07	4.16	4.23	4.30	4.36	4.41										11
12	3.57	3.74	3.87	3.98	4.06	4.13	4.20	4.25	4.31	4.35									12
13	3.51	3.68	3.80	3.90	3.98	4.05	4.11	4.17	4.22	4.26	4.30								13
14	3.46	3.63	3.74	3.84	3.92	3.98	4.04	4.09	4.14	4.18	4.22	4.26							14
15	3.42	3.58	3.69	3.79	3.86	3.92	3.98	4.03	4.08	4.12	4.16	4.19	4.22						15
16	3.38	3.54	3.65	3.74	3.81	3.87	3.93	3.98	4.02	4.06	4.10	4.14	4.17	4.20					16
17	3.35	3.50	3.61	3.70	3.77	3.83	3.89	3.93	3.98	4.02	4.05	4.09	4.12	4.14	4.17				17
18	3.33	3.47	3.58	3.66	3.73	3.79	3.85	3.89	3.94	3.97	4.01	4.04	4.07	4.10	4.12	4.15			18
19	3.30	3.45	3.55	3.63	3.70	3.76	3.81	3.86	3.90	3.94	3.97	4.00	4.03	4.06	4.08	4.11	4.13		19
20	3.28	3.42	3.53	3.61	3.67	3.73	3.78	3.83	3.87	3.90	3.94	3.97	4.00	4.02	4.05	4.07	4.09	4.12	20
24	3.21	3.35	3.45	3.52	3.58	3.64	3.69	3.73	3.77	3.80	3.83	3.86	3.89	3.91	3.94	3.96	3.98	4.00	24
30	3.15	3.28	3.37	3.44	3.50	3.55	3.59	3.63	3.67	3.70	3.73	3.76	3.78	3.81	3.83	3.85	3.87	3.89	30
40	3.09	3.21	3.29	3.36	3.42	3.46	3.50	3.54	3.58	3.60	3.63	3.66	3.68	3.70	3.72	3.74	3.76	3.78	40
60	3.03	3.14	3.22	3.29	3.34	3.38	3.42	3.46	3.49	3.51	3.54	3.56	3.59	3.61	3.63	3.64	3.66	3.68	60
120	2.97	3.07	3.15	3.21	3.26	3.30	3.34	3.37	3.40	3.42	3.45	3.47	3.49	3.51	3.53	3.55	3.56	3.58	120
∞	2.91	3.01	3.08	3.14	3.18	3.22	3.26	3.29	3.32	3.34	3.36	3.38	3.40	3.42	3.44	3.45	3.47	3.48	∞

Table J: Factors for Constructing Variables Control Charts

Observations in Sample n	Chart for Averages — Factors for Control Limits			Chart for Averages — Factors for Central Line		Chart for Standard Deviations — Factors for Control Limits				Chart for Ranges — Factors for Central Line		d_3	Chart for Ranges — Factors for Control Limits			
	A	A_2	A_3	c_4	$1/c_4$	B_3	B_4	B_5	B_6	d_2	$1/d_2$	d_3	D_1	D_2	D_3	D_4
2	2.121	1.880	2.659	0.7979	1.2533	0	3.267	0	2.606	1.128	0.8865	0.853	0	3.686	0	3.267
3	1.732	1.023	1.954	0.8862	1.1284	0	2.568	0	2.276	1.693	0.5907	0.888	0	4.358	0	2.574
4	1.500	0.729	1.628	0.9213	1.0854	0	2.266	0	2.088	2.059	0.4857	0.880	0	4.698	0	2.282
5	1.342	0.577	1.427	0.9400	1.0638	0	2.089	0	1.964	2.326	0.4299	0.864	0	4.918	0	2.114
6	1.225	0.483	1.287	0.9515	1.0510	0.030	1.970	0.029	1.874	2.534	0.3946	0.848	0	5.078	0	2.004
7	1.134	0.419	1.182	0.9594	1.0423	0.118	1.882	0.113	1.806	2.704	0.3698	0.833	0.204	5.204	0.076	1.924
8	1.061	0.373	1.099	0.9650	1.0363	0.185	1.815	0.179	1.751	2.847	0.3512	0.820	0.388	5.306	0.136	1.864
9	1.000	0.337	1.032	0.9693	1.0317	0.239	1.761	0.232	1.707	2.970	0.3367	0.808	0.547	5.393	0.184	1.816
10	0.949	0.308	0.975	0.9727	1.0281	0.284	1.716	0.276	1.669	3.078	0.3249	0.797	0.687	5.469	0.223	1.777
11	0.905	0.285	0.927	0.9754	1.0252	0.321	1.679	0.313	1.637	3.173	0.3152	0.787	0.811	5.535	0.256	1.744
12	0.866	0.266	0.886	0.9776	1.0229	0.354	1.646	0.346	1.610	3.258	0.3069	0.778	0.922	5.594	0.283	1.717
13	0.832	0.249	0.850	0.9794	1.0210	0.382	1.618	0.374	1.585	3.336	0.2998	0.770	1.025	5.647	0.307	1.693
14	0.802	0.235	0.817	0.9810	1.0194	0.406	1.594	0.399	1.563	3.407	0.2935	0.763	1.118	5.696	0.328	1.672
15	0.775	0.223	0.789	0.9823	1.0180	0.428	1.572	0.421	1.544	3.472	0.2880	0.756	1.203	5.741	0.347	1.653
16	0.750	0.212	0.763	0.9835	1.0168	0.448	1.552	0.440	1.526	3.532	0.2831	0.750	1.282	5.782	0.363	1.637
17	0.728	0.203	0.739	0.9845	1.0157	0.466	1.534	0.458	1.511	3.588	0.2787	0.744	1.356	5.820	0.378	1.622
18	0.707	0.194	0.718	0.9854	1.0148	0.482	1.518	0.475	1.496	3.640	0.2747	0.739	1.424	5.856	0.391	1.608
19	0.688	0.187	0.698	0.9862	1.0140	0.497	1.503	0.490	1.483	3.689	0.2711	0.734	1.487	5.891	0.403	1.597
20	0.671	0.180	0.680	0.9869	1.0133	0.510	1.490	0.504	1.470	3.735	0.2677	0.729	1.549	5.921	0.415	1.585
21	0.655	0.173	0.663	0.9876	1.0126	0.523	1.477	0.516	1.459	3.778	0.2647	0.724	1.605	5.951	0.425	1.575
22	0.640	0.167	0.647	0.9882	1.0119	0.534	1.466	0.528	1.448	3.819	0.2618	0.720	1.659	5.979	0.434	1.566
23	0.626	0.162	0.633	0.9887	1.0114	0.545	1.455	0.539	1.438	3.858	0.2592	0.716	1.710	6.006	0.443	1.557
24	0.612	0.157	0.619	0.9892	1.0109	0.555	1.445	0.549	1.429	3.895	0.2567	0.712	1.759	6.031	0.451	1.548
25	0.600	0.153	0.606	0.9896	1.0105	0.565	1.435	0.559	1.420	3.931	0.2544	0.708	1.806	6.056	0.459	1.541

For $n > 25$

$$A = \frac{3}{\sqrt{n}}, A_3 = \frac{3}{c_4\sqrt{n}}, c_4 \approx \frac{4(n-1)}{4n-3}, B_3 = 1 - \frac{3}{c_4\sqrt{2(n-1)}}, B_4 = 1 + \frac{3}{c_4\sqrt{2(n-1)}}, B_5 = c_4 - \frac{3}{\sqrt{2(n-1)}}, B_6 = c_4 + \frac{3}{\sqrt{2(n-1)}}$$

Source: Montgomery (1985), with permission.

Table K: Poisson Distribution Factors

Decimal Confidence Level (c)	Poisson Distribution Confidence Factor B — Number of Failures (r)											
	0	1	2	3	4	5	6	7	8	9	10	
.999	6.908	9.233	11.229	13.062	14.794	16.455	18.062	19.626	21.156	22.657	24.134	.001
.99	4.605	6.638	8.406	10.045	11.604	13.108	14.571	16.000	17.403	18.783	20.145	.01
.95	2.996	4.744	6.296	7.754	9.154	10.513	11.842	13.148	14.435	15.705	16.962	.05
.90	2.303	3.890	5.322	6.681	7.994	9.275	10.532	11.771	12.995	14.206	15.407	.10
.85	1.897	3.372	4.723	6.014	7.267	8.495	9.703	10.896	12.078	13.249	14.411	.15
.80	1.609	2.994	4.279	5.515	6.721	7.906	9.075	10.232	11.380	12.519	13.651	.20
.75	1.386	2.693	3.920	5.109	6.274	7.423	8.558	9.684	10.802	11.914	13.020	.25
.70	1.204	2.439	3.616	4.762	5.890	7.006	8.111	9.209	10.301	11.387	12.470	.30
.65	1.050	2.219	3.347	4.455	5.549	6.633	7.710	8.782	9.850	10.913	11.974	.35
.60	0.916	2.022	3.105	4.175	5.237	6.292	7.343	8.390	9.434	10.476	11.515	.40
.55	0.798	1.844	2.883	3.916	4.946	5.973	7.000	8.021	9.043	10.064	11.083	.45
.50	0.693	1.678	2.674	3.672	4.671	5.670	6.670	7.669	8.669	9.669	10.668	.50
.45	0.598	1.523	2.476	3.438	4.406	5.378	6.352	7.328	8.305	9.284	10.264	.55
.40	0.511	1.376	2.285	3.211	4.148	5.091	6.039	6.991	7.947	8.904	9.864	.60
.35	0.431	1.235	2.099	2.988	3.892	4.806	5.727	6.655	7.587	8.523	9.462	.65
.30	0.357	1.097	1.914	2.764	3.634	4.517	5.411	6.312	7.220	8.133	9.050	.70

Decimal Conf. Level (c)	1	2	3	4	5	6	7	8	9	10	11
.75	0.288	0.961	1.727	2.535	3.369	4.219	5.083	5.956	6.838	7.726	8.620
.80	0.223	0.824	1.535	2.297	3.090	3.904	4.734	5.576	6.428	7.289	8.157
.85	0.162	0.683	1.331	2.039	2.785	3.557	4.348	5.154	5.973	6.802	7.639
.90	0.105	0.532	1.102	1.745	2.432	3.152	3.895	4.656	5.432	6.221	7.021
.95	0.051	0.355	0.818	1.366	1.970	2.613	3.285	3.981	4.695	5.425	6.169
.99	0.010	0.149	0.436	0.823	1.279	1.786	2.330	2.906	3.508	4.130	4.771
.999	0.001	0.045	0.191	0.429	0.740	1.107	1.521	1.971	2.453	2.961	3.492

Number of Failures (r)

Poisson Distribution Confidence Factor A

Applications of Table K

Total test time: $T = B_{r,c}/\rho_a$ for $\rho \le \rho_a$, where ρ_a is a failure rate criterion, r is allowed number of test failures, and c is a confidence factor.

Confidence interval statements (time-terminated test); $\rho \le B_{r,c}/T \quad \rho \ge A_{r,c}/T$

Examples: 1 failure test for a 0.0001 failures/hour criterion (i.e., 10,000-hr MTBF)

95% confidence test: Total test time = 47,440 hr (i.e., 4.744/0.001)

5 failures in a total of 10,000 hr

95% confident: $\rho \le 0.0010513$ failures/hour (i.e., 10,513/10,000)

95% confident: $\rho \ge 0.0001970$ failures/hour (i.e., 1,970/10,000)

90% confidence: $0.0001970 \le \rho \le 0.0010513$

Table L: Conversion Between PPM and Sigma Level

+/− Sigma Level at Spec. Limit*	Percent within Spec.: Centered Distribution	Defective ppm: Centered Distribution	Percent within Spec.: 1.5 Sigma Shifted Distribution	Defective ppm: 1.5 Sigma Shifted Distribution
1	68.2689480	317310.520	30.232785	697672.15
1.1	72.8667797	271332.203	33.991708	660082.92
1.2	76.9860537	230139.463	37.862162	621378.38
1.3	80.6398901	193601.099	41.818512	581814.88
1.4	83.8486577	161513.423	45.830622	541693.78
1.5	86.6385542	133614.458	49.865003	501349.97
1.6	89.0401421	109598.579	53.886022	461139.78
1.7	91.0869136	89130.864	57.857249	421427.51
1.8	92.8139469	71860.531	61.742787	382572.13
1.9	94.2567014	57432.986	65.508472	344915.28
2	95.4499876	45500.124	69.122979	308770.21
2.1	96.4271285	35728.715	72.558779	274412.21
2.2	97.2193202	27806.798	75.792859	242071.41
2.3	97.8551838	21448.162	78.807229	211927.71
2.4	98.3604942	16395.058	81.589179	184108.21
2.5	98.7580640	12419.360	84.131305	158686.95
2.6	99.0677556	9322.444	86.431323	135686.77
2.7	99.3065954	6934.046	88.491691	115083.09
2.8	99.4889619	5110.381	90.319090	96809.10
2.9	99.6268240	3731.760	91.923787	80762.13
3	99.7300066	2699.934	93.318937	66810.63
3.1	99.8064658	1935.342	94.519860	54801.40
3.2	99.8625596	1374.404	95.543327	44566.73
3.3	99.9033035	966.965	96.406894	35931.06
3.4	99.9326038	673.962	97.128303	28716.97
3.5	99.9534653	465.347	97.724965	22750.35
3.6	99.9681709	318.291	98.213547	17864.53
3.7	99.9784340	215.660	98.609650	13903.50
3.8	99.9855255	144.745	98.927586	10724.14
3.9	99.9903769	96.231	99.180244	8197.56
4	99.9936628	63.372	99.379030	6209.70
4.1	99.9958663	41.337	99.533877	4661.23
4.2	99.9973292	26.708	99.653297	3467.03
4.3	99.9982908	17.092	99.744481	2555.19
4.4	99.9989166	10.834	99.813412	1865.88
4.5	99.9993198	6.802	99.865003	1349.97
4.6	99.9995771	4.229	99.903233	967.67
4.7	99.9997395	2.605	99.931280	687.20
4.8	99.9998411	1.589	99.951652	483.48
4.9	99.9999040	0.960	99.966302	336.98
5	99.9999426	0.574	99.976733	232.67

+/− Sigma Level at Spec. Limit*	Percent within Spec.: Centered Distribution	Defective ppm: Centered Distribution	Percent within Spec.: 1.5 Sigma Shifted Distribution	Defective ppm: 1.5 Sigma Shifted Distribution
5.1	99.9999660	0.340	99.984085	159.15
5.2	99.9999800	0.200	99.989217	107.83
5.3	99.9999884	0.116	99.992763	72.37
5.4	99.9999933	0.067	99.995188	48.12
5.5	99.9999962	0.038	99.996831	31.69
5.6	99.9999979	0.021	99.997933	20.67
5.7	99.9999988	0.012	99.998665	13.35
5.8	99.9999993	0.007	99.999145	8.55
5.9	99.9999996	0.004	99.999458	5.42
6	99.9999998	0.002	99.999660	3.40

*Sometimes referred to as sigma level or sigma quality level when considering process shift.

Table M.1: Two-Level Full and Fractional Factorial Designs,
4 Trials

TABLE M1   Two-Level Full and Fractional Factorial Designs, 4 Trials

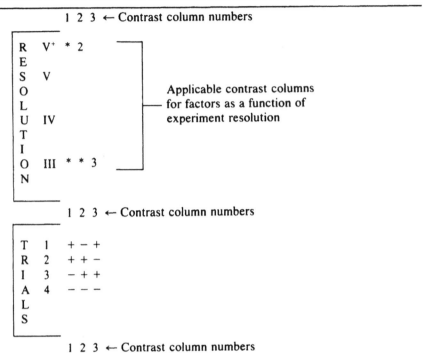

1 2 3 ← Contrast column numbers

R	V⁺	* 2
E		
S	V	
O		
L		
U	IV	
T		
I		
O	III	* * 3
N		

Applicable contrast columns
for factors as a function of
experiment resolution

1 2 3 ← Contrast column numbers

T	1	+ − +
R	2	+ + −
I	3	− + +
A	4	− − −
L		
S		

1 2 3 ← Contrast column numbers

Instructions for Tables M1–M5: Creating a Two-Level Factorial Test Design Matrix[a]

---

1. Choose for the given number of two-level factors a table (i.e., M1–M5) such that the number of test trials yields the desired resolution, which is defined to be the following:

V^+: **Full two-level factorial.**

V: **All main effects and two-factor interactions are not confounded with other main effects or two-factor interactions.**

IV: **All main effects are not confounded with two-factor interactions. Two-factor interactions are confounded with each other.**

III: **Main effects confounded with two-factor interactions.**

The maximum number of factors for each trial matrix resolution is noted in the following:

Number of Trials	Experiment Resolution			
	V^+	V	IV	III
4	2			3
8	3		4	5–7
16	4	5	6–8	9–15
32	5	6	7–16	17–31
64	6	7–8	9–32	33–63

2. Look at the row of asterisks and numerics within the selected table corresponding to the desired resolution.

3. Begin from the left identifying columns designated by either an asterisk or numeric until the number of selected contrast columns equals the number of factors.

4. Record, for each contrast column identified within step number three, the level states for each trial. Columns are included only if they have the asterisk or numeric resolution designator. A straightedge can be helpful to align the contrast numbers tabulated within the columns.

---

[a] See Example 30.1.

Table M.2: Two-Level Full and Fractional Factorial Designs,
8 Trials

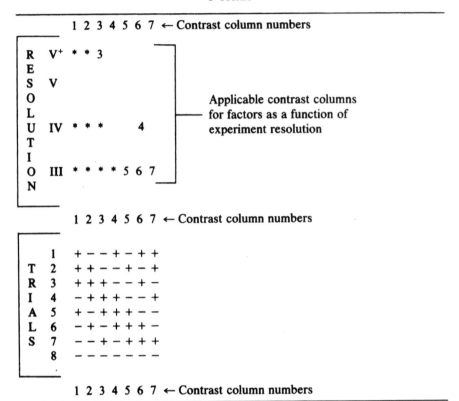

1 2 3 4 5 6 7 ← Contrast column numbers

R	V+	*	*	3				
E								
S	V							
O								
L								
U	IV	*	*	*		4		
T								
I								
O	III	*	*	*	*	5	6	7
N								

Applicable contrast columns
for factors as a function of
experiment resolution

1 2 3 4 5 6 7 ← Contrast column numbers

		1	2	3	4	5	6	7
T	1	+	−	−	+	−	+	+
R	2	+	+	−	−	+	−	+
I	3	+	+	+	−	−	+	−
A	4	−	+	+	+	−	−	+
L	5	+	−	+	+	+	−	−
S	6	−	+	−	+	+	+	−
	7	−	−	+	−	+	+	+
	8	−	−	−	−	−	−	−

1 2 3 4 5 6 7 ← Contrast column numbers

a Table usage instructions are noted following Table M1.
The 8, 16, 32, and 64 trial matrices in Tables M2–M5 were created from a computer program described by Diamond (1989).

Table M.3: Two-Level Full and Fractional Factorial Designs, 16 Trials

		1	2	3	4	5	6	7	8	9	1 0	1 1	1 2	1 3	1 4	1 5	
																	← Contrast column numbers

R E S O L U T I O N	V⁺	*	*	*	4											
	V	*	*	*	*						5					
	IV	*	*	*	*			*		6	7		8			
	III	*	*	*	*	*	*	*	*	*	9	1 0	1 1	1 2	1 3	1 4	1 5

Applicable contrast columns for factors as a function of experiment resolution

	1	2	3	4	5	6	7	8	9	1 0	1 1	1 2	1 3	1 4	1 5	
																← Contrast column numbers

TRIALS		1	2	3	4	5	6	7	8	9	10	11	12	13	14	15
	1	+	−	−	−	+	−	−	+	+	−	+	−	+	+	+
	2	+	+	−	−	−	+	−	−	+	+	−	+	−	+	+
	3	+	+	+	−	−	−	+	−	−	+	+	−	+	−	+
	4	+	+	+	+	−	−	−	+	−	−	+	+	−	+	−
	5	−	+	+	+	+	−	−	−	+	−	−	+	+	−	+
	6	+	−	+	+	+	+	−	−	−	+	−	−	+	+	−
	7	−	+	−	+	+	+	+	−	−	−	+	−	−	+	+
	8	+	−	+	−	+	+	+	+	−	−	−	+	−	−	+
	9	+	+	−	+	−	+	+	+	+	−	−	−	+	−	−
	10	−	+	+	−	+	−	+	+	+	+	−	−	−	+	−
	11	−	−	+	+	−	+	−	+	+	+	+	−	−	−	+
	12	+	−	−	+	+	−	+	−	+	+	+	+	−	−	−
	13	−	+	−	−	+	+	−	+	−	+	+	+	+	−	−
	14	−	−	+	−	−	+	+	−	+	−	+	+	+	+	−
	15	−	−	−	+	−	−	+	+	−	+	−	+	+	+	+
	16	−	−	−	−	−	−	−	−	−	−	−	−	−	−	−

	1	2	3	4	5	6	7	8	9	1 0	1 1	1 2	1 3	1 4	1 5	
																← Contrast column numbers

a Table usage instructions are noted following Table M1.

Table M.4: Two-Level Full and Fractional Factorial Designs, 32 Trials

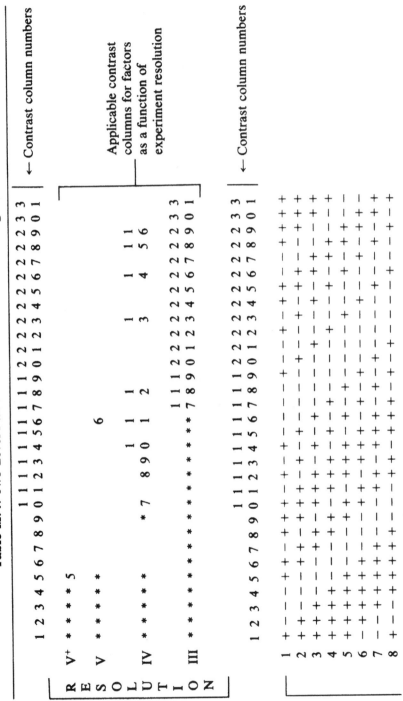

TRIALS	1	2	3	4	5	6	7	8	9	10	11	12	13	14	15	16	17	18	19	20	21	22	23	24	25	26	27	28	29	30	31
9	+	+	−	−	+	+	+	+	+	−	−	−	+	+	−	+	+	+	−	+	−	+	−	−	−	−	+	−	−	+	−
10	−	+	+	−	−	+	+	+	+	+	−	−	−	+	+	−	+	+	+	−	+	−	+	−	−	−	−	+	−	−	+
11	+	−	+	+	−	−	+	+	+	+	+	−	−	−	+	+	−	+	+	+	−	+	−	+	−	−	−	−	+	−	−
12	−	+	−	+	+	−	−	+	+	+	+	+	−	−	−	+	+	−	+	+	+	−	+	−	+	−	−	−	−	+	−
13	−	−	+	−	+	+	−	−	+	+	+	+	+	−	−	−	+	+	−	+	+	+	−	+	−	+	−	−	−	−	+
14	+	−	−	+	−	+	+	−	−	+	+	+	+	+	−	−	−	+	+	−	+	+	+	−	+	−	+	−	−	−	−
15	−	+	−	−	+	−	+	+	−	−	+	+	+	+	+	−	−	−	+	+	−	+	+	+	−	+	−	+	−	−	−
16	−	−	+	−	−	+	−	+	+	−	−	+	+	+	+	+	−	−	−	+	+	−	+	+	+	−	+	−	+	−	−
17	−	−	−	+	−	−	+	−	+	+	−	−	+	+	+	+	+	−	−	−	+	+	−	+	+	+	−	+	−	+	−
18	−	−	−	−	+	−	−	+	−	+	+	−	−	+	+	+	+	+	−	−	−	+	+	−	+	+	+	−	+	−	+
19	+	−	−	−	−	+	−	−	+	−	+	+	−	−	+	+	+	+	+	−	−	−	+	+	−	+	+	+	−	+	−
20	−	+	−	−	−	−	+	−	−	+	−	+	+	−	−	+	+	+	+	+	−	−	−	+	+	−	+	+	+	−	+
21	+	−	+	−	−	−	−	+	−	−	+	−	+	+	−	−	+	+	+	+	+	−	−	−	+	+	−	+	+	+	−
22	−	+	−	+	−	−	−	−	+	−	−	+	−	+	+	−	−	+	+	+	+	+	−	−	−	+	+	−	+	+	+
23	+	−	+	−	+	−	−	−	−	+	−	−	+	−	+	+	−	−	+	+	+	+	+	−	−	−	+	+	−	+	+
24	+	+	−	+	−	+	−	−	−	−	+	−	−	+	−	+	+	−	−	+	+	+	+	+	−	−	−	+	+	−	+
25	+	+	+	−	+	−	+	−	−	−	−	+	−	−	+	−	+	+	−	−	+	+	+	+	+	−	−	−	+	+	−
26	−	+	+	+	−	+	−	+	−	−	−	−	+	−	−	+	−	+	+	−	−	+	+	+	+	+	−	−	−	+	+
27	+	−	+	+	+	−	+	−	+	−	−	−	−	+	−	−	+	−	+	+	−	−	+	+	+	+	+	−	−	−	+
28	+	+	−	+	+	+	−	+	−	+	−	−	−	−	+	−	−	+	−	+	+	−	−	+	+	+	+	+	−	−	−
29	−	+	+	−	+	+	+	−	+	−	+	−	−	−	−	+	−	−	+	−	+	+	−	−	+	+	+	+	+	−	−
30	−	−	+	+	−	+	+	+	−	+	−	+	−	−	−	−	+	−	−	+	−	+	+	−	−	+	+	+	+	+	−
31	−	−	−	+	+	−	+	+	+	−	+	−	+	−	−	−	−	+	−	−	+	−	+	+	−	−	+	+	+	+	+
32	−	−	−	−	−	−	−	−	−	−	−	−	−	−	−	−	−	−	−	−	−	−	−	−	−	−	−	−	−	−	−

← Contrast column numbers

[a] Table usage instructions are noted following Table M1.

Table M.5: Two-Level Full and Fractional Factorial Designs, 64 Trials

TRIALS	1	2	3	4	5	6	7	8	9	10	11	12	13	14	15	16	17	18	19	20	21	22	23	24	25	26	27	28	29	30	31	32	33	34	35	36	37	38	39	40	41	42	43	44	45	46	47	48	49	50	51	52	53	54	55	56	57	58	59	60	61	62	63
9	−	+	−	+	+	+	+	+	−	−	−	−	−	+	−	−	−	+	+	−	−	+	−	+	−	+	+	+	−	+	−	+	−	−	+	+	−	−	+	−	−	+	−	+	+	−	+	+	+	−	+	+	−	−	+	+	−	+	+	−	+	−	+
10	+	−	+	−	+	+	+	+	+	−	−	−	−	+	−	−	−	+	+	−	−	+	−	+	−	+	+	+	−	+	−	−	+	+	+	−	−	+	+	−	−	+	−	+	+	−	+	+	+	−	+	+	+	−	+	+	−	+	+	−	+	+	−
11	−	+	−	+	−	+	+	+	+	+	+	−	+	−	−	−	+	−	−	−	+	−	−	+	−	+	−	+	−	+	+	+	+	−	+	−	−	+	+	+	−	+	−	−	+	−	+	−	+	−	+	−	+	+	−	+	+	+	+	+	−	+	+
12	−	+	−	+	−	+	+	+	+	+	+	−	+	−	−	−	+	−	−	−	+	−	−	+	−	+	−	+	−	+	+	+	+	−	+	−	−	+	+	+	−	+	−	−	+	−	+	−	+	−	+	−	+	+	−	+	+	+	+	+	−	+	+
13	+	+	−	+	−	−	+	+	+	+	−	+	−	−	−	−	−	+	−	−	+	+	−	−	+	−	−	+	−	+	−	+	−	+	+	−	+	−	+	+	−	−	+	+	+	−	+	−	−	+	+	+	−	+	+	+	+	+	−	+	+	−	−
14	−	+	+	−	+	−	+	−	+	+	+	+	+	+	−	+	+	−	−	−	+	−	−	+	−	−	+	+	−	+	−	+	+	−	+	+	−	+	−	+	+	+	−	−	+	−	+	−	+	−	+	−	+	−	+	+	−	+	+	+	−	+	−
15	−	−	+	+	−	+	−	+	−	+	+	+	+	−	+	+	−	−	+	−	−	−	+	−	+	−	−	+	−	+	−	−	+	+	+	−	+	+	−	+	−	+	+	−	+	−	+	−	+	+	−	−	+	+	+	−	+	−	−	+	−	+	+
16	+	−	−	+	+	−	+	−	+	+	−	+	+	+	+	+	+	+	−	+	−	−	−	−	+	+	−	−	+	+	−	+	−	+	+	−	+	−	−	+	+	−	+	−	+	−	−	+	+	+	+	−	+	−	+	−	+	+	+	−	+	+	+
17	+	+	−	+	+	−	+	+	−	+	−	+	−	+	−	+	−	−	−	+	−	−	−	−	+	+	+	−	+	+	−	+	−	+	+	−	+	−	−	+	+	−	+	−	+	−	−	+	+	+	+	−	+	−	+	−	+	+	+	−	+	−	+
18	−	+	+	−	+	−	+	−	+	+	+	+	+	+	+	−	−	−	+	−	+	−	−	−	−	+	+	+	+	−	−	+	+	−	−	+	−	+	−	+	−	−	+	+	+	−	−	+	+	−	+	−	+	−	+	+	−	+	+	−	+	+	+
19	+	−	+	+	−	+	+	−	+	−	+	+	+	+	+	+	+	−	−	−	−	+	−	−	−	+	+	−	+	−	+	−	+	−	+	−	+	+	+	−	−	+	−	−	+	−	+	+	−	+	−	−	+	+	+	−	+	−	+	+	+	+	+
20	+	+	−	+	−	+	+	−	−	−	+	−	+	+	−	−	+	+	+	+	+	−	+	−	−	−	+	−	+	−	+	−	+	−	−	+	−	+	+	−	+	−	−	+	+	−	+	−	−	+	−	+	+	−	+	−	+	+	−	+	−	+	+
21	+	+	+	−	+	+	−	−	+	+	+	+	+	+	+	+	−	−	−	+	+	+	−	−	−	+	+	−	−	−	+	−	−	+	−	+	−	+	+	+	−	+	−	−	+	−	+	+	−	+	−	−	+	+	+	−	+	−	−	+	−	+	+
22	−	+	+	−	+	+	−	+	−	+	+	+	+	+	+	−	−	−	+	−	+	−	+	−	−	−	+	−	+	−	+	−	+	−	−	+	+	+	−	+	−	+	−	−	+	+	−	+	−	+	−	−	+	+	+	−	−	+	+	−	+	+	+
23	+	−	+	+	−	+	−	+	−	+	+	+	+	+	+	−	+	−	−	−	+	+	−	−	+	−	+	+	−	−	+	−	+	−	−	+	−	+	+	+	−	−	+	−	+	−	+	+	−	−	+	−	+	+	−	+	+	−	−	+	+	−	+
24	+	+	−	+	+	−	+	−	+	−	+	+	+	−	+	+	+	+	+	+	−	−	−	−	+	−	−	+	−	−	−	+	−	+	+	+	−	+	−	−	+	−	+	−	−	+	+	+	+	−	+	−	+	−	−	+	+	+	−	−	+	+	−
25	−	+	+	−	+	+	+	−	+	+	−	+	−	+	−	−	+	−	+	−	+	+	+	+	+	−	−	−	+	−	−	−	+	−	−	+	+	−	−	+	+	−	−	+	+	−	+	−	−	+	+	+	−	+	−	−	+	+	+	−	+	−	+
26	+	−	+	+	+	−	+	+	−	+	+	−	+	−	+	−	−	+	+	+	+	+	+	−	−	−	−	−	−	+	−	−	−	+	+	−	−	+	+	−	−	−	+	+	+	−	−	+	+	−	+	−	+	−	−	+	+	+	−	+	−	+	−
27	−	+	−	+	+	−	+	+	−	+	+	−	+	+	−	+	−	+	+	−	+	−	+	+	+	+	−	−	−	−	−	−	+	−	−	−	+	−	−	−	+	−	+	−	+	+	−	−	+	+	+	−	+	+	+	−	−	+	+	+	−	−	+
28	−	−	+	+	−	+	+	+	−	+	+	+	+	+	−	+	−	+	+	−	−	−	−	−	−	−	+	−	−	+	−	−	+	−	+	−	−	−	+	+	+	+	−	+	−	+	+	+	−	−	+	+	−	−	+	+	−	+	+	−	−	+	+
29	+	−	−	+	−	+	+	+	−	+	+	+	−	−	+	−	+	−	+	+	+	+	+	−	−	+	−	−	−	−	+	−	−	−	+	+	−	+	−	−	−	+	−	+	+	+	−	+	+	−	−	+	−	−	+	−	−	+	+	+	−	−	+
30	−	+	−	+	−	+	+	−	+	+	+	−	+	+	−	+	+	−	−	+	−	+	−	+	−	+	+	+	+	+	+	−	−	−	−	−	+	−	−	−	+	−	−	−	+	+	−	−	+	−	+	−	+	+	+	+	−	+	−	−	+	+	+
31	−	−	+	−	+	−	+	+	+	+	−	+	+	−	+	+	−	−	+	+	−	−	+	−	+	−	+	+	+	+	+	+	−	−	−	−	+	−	−	−	+	−	−	−	+	+	−	−	+	−	+	−	+	+	+	+	−	+	−	−	−	+	+
32	+	−	−	+	−	−	+	−	+	+	+	+	+	+	+	−	+	+	−	−	−	+	+	−	−	−	−	+	−	−	−	−	−	+	−	−	−	−	+	−	−	−	−	+	−	+	−	−	+	+	−	+	+	−	+	+	−	+	−	−	−	+	+

Contrast

R E S O L U T I O N

V⁺
V
IV
III

Contrast

33
34
35
36
37
38
39
40
41
42

T R I A L S

43 44 45 46 47 48 49 50 51 52 53 54 55 56 57 58 59 60 61 62 63 64

Contrast 1 2 3 4 5 6 7 8 9 10 11 12 13 14 15 16 17 18 19 20 21 22 23 24 25 26 27 28 29 30 31 32 33 34 35 36 37 38 39 40 41 42 43 44 45 46 47 48 49 50 51 52 53 54 55 56 57 58 59 60 61 62 63

[a] Table usage instructions are noted following Table M1.

Table N.1: Two-Factor Interaction Confounding in the Contrast Columns of the Tables M.1–M.5 Resolution V Fractional Factorial Designs

4 Trials

1	2	3
*A	*B	AB

8 Trials

Not Applicable

16 Trials

1	2	3	4	5	6	7	8	9	10	11	12	13	14	15
*A	*B	*C	*D	AB	BC	CD	ABD	AC	BD	ABC	BCD	ABCD	ACD	AD
							CE			DE	AE	*E	BE	

32 Trials

1	2	3	4	5	6	7	8	9	10	11	12	13	14	15	16	17	18	19	20	21
*A	*B	*C	*D	*E	AC	BD	CE	ACD	BDE	AE	ABC	BCD	CDE	ACDE	ABCDE	ABDE	ABE	AB	BC	CD
														BF	*F	CF				

22	23	24	25	26	27	28	29	30	31
DE	ACE	ABCD	BCDE	ADE	ABCE	ABD	BCE	AD	BE
		EF	AF		DF				

64 Trials

1	2	3	4	5	6	7	8	9	10	11	12	13	14	15	16	17	18	19	20	21
*A	*B	*C	*D	*E	*F	AB	BC	CD	DE	EF	ABF	AC	BD	CE	DF	ABE	BCF	ABCD	BCDE	CDEF
																		*G		

22	23	24	25	26	27	28	29	30	31	32	33	34	35	36	37	38	39	40	41	42
ABDEF	ACEF	ADF	AE	BF	ABC	BCD	CDE	DEF	ABEF	ACF	AD	BE	CF	ABD	BCE	CDF	ABDE	BCEF	ABCDF	ACDE
GH	*H				DG	AG				EH				CG					FG	

43	44	45	46	47	48	49	50	51	52	53	54	55	56	57	58	59	60	61	62	63
BDEF	ABCEF	ACDF	ADE	BEF	ABCF	ACD	BDE	CEF	ABDF	ACE	BDF	ABCE	BCDF	ABCDE	BCDEF	ABCDEF	ACDEF	ADEF	AEF	AF
GH	*H	BH				BG		AH		FH				EG				DH	CH	

---

[a] The higher-order terms were used when generating the design. Main effects are denoted by an asterisk.

Table N.2: Two-Factor Interaction Confounding in the Contrast Columns of the Tables M.1–M.5 Resolution IV Fractional Factorial Designs

8 Trials

1	2	3	4	5	6	7
*A	*B	*C	AB	BC	ABC	AC
			CD	AD	*D	BD

16 Trials

1	2	3	4	5	6	7	8	9	10	11	12	13	14	15
*A	*B	*C	*D	AB	BC	CD	ABD	AC	BD	ABC	BCD	ABCD	ACD	AD
				DE	AF	EF	*E	BF	AE	*F	*G	CE	*H	BE
				CF	DG	BG		EG	CG			DF		FG
				GH	EH	AH		DH	FH			AG		CH
												BH		

32 Trials

1	2	3	4	5	6	7	8	9	10	11	12	13	14	15	16	17	18	19	20	21
*A	*B	*C	*D	*E	AC	BD	CE	ACD	BDE	AE	ABC	BCD	CDE	ACDE	ABCDE	ABDE	ABE	AB	BC	CD
					DF	EG	GI	*F	*G	FJ	*H	*I	*J	EF	*K	AG	*L	CH	AH	AF
					BH	FH	DJ			IK				GH		HJ		FI	DI	BL
					GK	CI	HL			BL				AJ		CK		JK	GJ	EJ
					EM	KM	AM			CM				BK		DL		EL	LM	KL
					JN	LN	FN			DN				IL		IM		GN	KN	MN
					IO	AO	KO			GO				DM		BN		DO	FO	HO
					LP	JP	BP			HP				CN		EO		MP	EP	GP
														OP		FP				

22	23	24	25	26	27	28	29	30	31
DE	ACE	ABCD	BCDE	ADE	ABCE	ABD	BCE	AD	BE
BG	*M	BF	CG	*N	FG	*O	*P	CF	DG
CJ		DH	EI		EH			HI	IJ
HK		AI	BJ		DK			GL	FK
FM		EK	AK		CL			JM	AL
AN		JL	FL		BM			EN	HM
LO		GM	HN		IN			BO	NO
IP		CO	MO		JO			KP	CP
		NP	DP		AP				

64 Trials

#	Code	Members
1	•A	
2	•B	
3	•C	
4	•D	
5	•E	
6	•F	
7	AB	FG EH CL JO IP DQ ST MX VY UZ Ra Kb Nc de Wf
8	BC	FI AL DM GP ER KT QX NY WZ Ha Sb Vc Od Je Uf
9	CD	BM EN KP LQ FS GT JU AX RY OZ Va Ib Hc Wd ef
10	DE	BM CN FO HQ MR TU AV BY SZ Xa Wb Lc Id Pe KJ
11	EF	GH DO JQ IR NS LU KV BW CZ Pa Yb Tc Md Xe Af
12	ABF •G	
13	AC	GI BL FP MQ HR KS NV UW DX Ea Tb Yc Jd Oe ZJ
14	BD	GK CM AQ NR IS PT HV OW LX EY Fb ac Zd Ue Jf
15	CE	HL DN BR OS JT GU IW VX MY FZ Aa Qc bd Ke Pf
16	DF	HJ AK IM EO GQ CS LT PX WY NZ Bb Uc Rd ae Vf
17	ABE •H	
18	BCF •I	
19	ABCD	IK DL AM HN CQ GS FT OU RV BX JZ Ya Pb Ec We df
20	BCDE	EM BN IO JP DR KU LV SW HX CY Qa Zb Ac Fd Ge Tf
21	CDEF	JL FN CO ES HT QU PV MW IY DZ Ka Rb Gc Bd Ae Xf
22	ABDEF •J	
23	ACEF	HI JM KN EP GR BU
24	ADF •K	
25	AE	BH KO LR IU DV GW
26	BF	AG CI LP KQ MS JV
27	ABC •L	
28	BCD •M	
29	CDE •N	
30	DEF •O	
31	ABEF	EG FH DI OQ PR NT
32	ACF •P	
33	AD	FK LM BQ PS IT EV
34	BE	AH JK MN CR PU QV
35	CF	BI GL NO AP DS QT
36	ABD •Q	
37	BCE •R	
38	CDF •S	
39	ABDE	DH FJ LN GO EQ SU
40	BCEF	EI MO HP FR AU TV
41	ABCDF •T	
42	ACDE	IJ HM AN OP QR CV

	SV		NX	EW					CU		JW	FW	HU				BV	CW		TW
	LW		QY	TX					AW		CX	DY	RW				KW	JX		EX
	OX		PZ	OY					KY		HY	IZ	KX				RX	SY		LY
	TY		Ca	RZ					LZ		Na	La	EZ				AY	BZ		KZ
	AZ		Jb	Ua					Ia		Gb	Ob	Mb				TZ	Ga		Da
	Fa		Mc	Db					Vb		Rc	Xc	Jc				Ma	Nb		Ub
	bc		Td	Nd					Sc		Ud	Sd	Yd				Cc	Kc		Bc
	Qd		Se	ce					Xd		Ze	Te	Ve				Pd	Dd		Gd
	De		Ff	Hf					Me		Of	Gf	af				Ie	Qe		Fe
	Cf								Bf								bf	If		Sf
43	44	45	46	47	48	49	50	51	52	53	54	55	56	57	58	59	60	61	62	63
BDEF	ABCEF	ACDF	ADE	BEF	ABCF	ACD	BDE	CEF	ABDF	ACE	BDF	ABCE	BCDF	ABCDE	BCDEF	ABCDEF	ACDEF	ADEF	AEF	AF
AJ	*U	CK	*V	*W	CG	*X	*Y	*Z	DG	*a	*b	CH	DI	*d	*d	CJ	*e	BJ	*f	BG
HK		GM			AI				EJ			EL	KL			GN		EK		DK
IN		DP			FL				BK			NQ	FM			LO		AO		IL
BO		IQ			KM				HO			AR	PQ			KR		NP		CP
RS		JR			JN				MP			JS	OR			HS		RT		MT
GV		AS			BP				FQ			OT	BS			ET		MU		RU
DW		BT			QS				LS			FU	AT			DU		FV		OV
UX		FX			DT				CT			MV	UV			IV		QW		HW
FY		UY			EU				NU			PW	NW			WX		GY		SX
MZ		VZ			HZ				VW			XY	GX			PY		XZ		JY
Ta		Oa			Wa				IX			GZ	YZ			QZ		Sa		Za
Eb		Lb			Xb				Ab			Ba	Ja			ab		Hb		Qb
Pc		Wc			Oc				Zc			Dc	Cb			Fc		Ic		cd
Cd		Hd			Vd				ad			Kd	Ed			Ad		Ld		Ne
Le		Ee			Ye				Re			be	He			Be		Ce		Ef
Qf		Nf			Rf				Yf			If	cf			Mf		Df		

[a] The higher-order terms were used when generating the design. Main effects are denoted by an asterisk.

Table N.3: Two-Factor Interaction Confounding in the Contrast Columns of the Tables M.1–M.5 Resolution III Fractional Factorial Designs

8 Trials

1	2	3	4	5	6	7
*A	*B	*C	AB	BC	ABC	AC
BD	AD	BE	*D	*E	CD	DE
EF	CE	DF	CF	AF	AE	BF
CG	FG	AG	EG	DG	*F	*G
					BG	

16 Trials

1	2	3	4	5	6	7	8	9	10	11	12	13	14	15
*A	*B	*C	*D	AB	BC	CD	ABD	AC	BD	ABC	BCD	ABCD	ACD	AD
BE	AE	BF	CG	*E	*F	*G	DE	EF	FG	CE	DF	EG	AG	BH
CI	CF	DG	EH	DH	EI	FJ	*H	*I	AH	AF	BG	CH	FH	GI
HJ	DJ	AI	BJ	FI	GJ	HK	AJ	BK	*J	GH	HI	IJ	DI	EJ
FK	IK	EK	FL	CK	AK	BL	GK	HL	CL	BI	CJ	DK	JK	KL
LM	GL	JL	KM	GM	DL	EM	IL	JM	IM	*K	*L	AL	EL	FM
GN	MN	HM	IN	LN	HN	AN	CM	DN	KN	DM	AM	*M	BM	CN
DO	HO	NO	AO	JO	MO	IO	FN	GO	EO	JN	EN	BN	*N	*O
							BO							

32 Trials

1	2	3	4	5	6	7	8	9	10	11	12	13	14	15	16	17	18	19	20	21
*A	*B	*C	*D	*E	AC	BD	CE	ACD	BDE	AE	ABC	BCD	CDE	ACDE	ABCDE	ABDE	ABE	AB	BC	CD
CF	DG	AF	BG	CH	*F	*G	*H	DF	EG	FH	BF	CG	DH	EI	FJ	AJ	BK	CL	AL	AI
EK	FL	EH	FI	GJ	DI	EJ	FK	*I	*J	*K	GI	HJ	IK	JL	KM	GK	HL	IM	DM	BM
NO	OP	GM	HN	AK	HK	IL	JM	GL	HM	IN	*L	*M	*N	AN	BO	LN	MO	NP	JN	EN
JQ	KR	PQ	QR	IO	BL	CM	DN	KN	LO	MP	JO	KP	AO	*O	*P	CP	DQ	ER	OQ	KO

Left block:

PR	GT	*U	HV	SX	WZ	Qa	Lb	Jc	Fd		Ye
FS	*T	GU	RW	VY	PZ	Ka	Ib	Ec	Xd		He
*S	FT	QV	UX	OY	JZ	Ha	Db	Wc	Gd		Ke
*R	ES	PU	TW	NX	IY	GZ	Ca	Vb	Fc	Jd	Ae
*Q	DR	OT	SV	MW	HX	FY	BZ	Ua	Eb	Ic	de
CQ	NS	RU	LV	GW	EX	AY	TZ	Da	Hb	cd	Ie
BP	MR	QT	KU	FV	DW	SY	CZ	Ga	bc	Hd	Xe
LQ	PS	JT	EU	CV	RX	BY	FZ	ab	Gc	Wd	Me
OR	IS	DT	BU	QW	AX	EY	Za	Fb	Vc	Ld	Ne
NQ	HR	CS	AT	PV	DX	YZ	Ea	Ub	Kc	Md	We
GQ	BR	OU	CW	XY	DZ	Ta	Jb	Lc	Vd		Se
FP	AQ	NT	BV	WX	CY	SZ	Ia	Kb	Uc	Rd	De
EO	MS	AU	VW	BX	RY	HZ	Ja	Tb	Qc	Cd	Pe
LR	UV	AW	QX	GY	IZ	Sa	Pb	Bc	Od		Te
KQ	TU	PW	FX	HY	RZ	Oa	Ab	Nc	Sd		Ve
JP	ST	OV	EW	GX	QY	NZ	Mb	Rc	Ud		ae
RS	NU	DV	FW	PX	MY	La	Qb	Tc	Zd		Be
MT	CU	EV	OW	LX	KZ	Pa	Sb	Yc	Ad		Je
LS	BT	DU	NV	KW	JY	OZ	Ra	Xb	Id		ce
AS	CT	MU	JV	IX	NY	QZ	Wa	Hc	bd		Ee
BS	LT	IU	HW	MX	PY	VZ	Gb	ac	Dd		Re

Right block:

22	23	24	25	26	27	28	29	30	31
DE	ACE	ABCD	BCDE	ADE	ABCE	ABD	BCE	AD	BE
BJ	EF	FG	GH	HI	IJ	AG	BH	CI	DJ
CN	AH	BI	CJ	DK	EL	JK	KL	LM	MN
FO	CK	DL	EM	FN	GO	FM	GN	HO	IP
LP	DO	AM	BN	CO	DP	HP	IQ	JR	AR
QS	GP	EP	AP	BQ	CR	EQ	FR	GS	KS
HU	MQ	HQ	FQ	GR	HS	DS	ET	FU	HT
*V	RT	NR	IR	JS	KT	IT	JU	KV	GV
IW	IV	SU	OS	PT	QU	LU	MV	NW	LW
TY	*W	JW	TV	AV	BW	NV	SW	TX	OX
AZ	JX	*X	KX	UW	VX	CX	DY	EZ	UY
Xa	UZ	KY	*Y	LY	MZ	WY	XZ	Ya	Fa
Rb	Ba	Va	LZ	*Z	*a	Na	Aa	Bb	Zb
Mc	Yb	Cb	Wb	Ma	Nb	*b	Ob	Pc	Cc
Kd	Sc	Zc	Dc	Xc	Ac	Oc	*c	*d	Qd
Ge	Nd	Td	ad	Ed	Yd	Bd	Pd	Qe	*e
	Le	Oe	Ue	be	Fe	Ze	Ce		

64 Trials

	1	2	3	4	5	6	7	8	9	10	11	12	13	14	15	16	17	18	19	20	21
	*A	*B	*C	*D	*E	*F	AB	BC	CD	DE	EF	ABF	AC	BD	CE	DF	ABE	BCF	ABCD	BCDE	CDEF
	BG	AG	BH	CI	DJ	EK	*G	*H	*I	*J	*K	*L	GH	HI	IJ	JK	EG	FH	GI	HJ	IK
	CM	CH	DI	EJ	FK	GL	HM	GM	HN	IO	JP	KQ	GH	HI	IJ	JK	KL	LM	MN	NO	OP
	PX	DN	AM	BN	CO	DP	EQ	IN	JO	KP	LQ	MR	DI	MS	LR	OU	KL	LM	MN	NO	*U
	EY	QY	EO	FP	GQ	HR	IS	FR	GS	HT	IU	JV	NS	OT	NT	QV	*Q	*R	*S	*T	TZ
	LZ	FZ	RZ	Sa	AY	BZ	Ca	JT	KU	LV	MW	NX	KW	LX	PU	QV	PV	QW	RX	SY	UZ
	Ha	Ma	Ga	Hb	Tb	Uc	Vd	Aa	Bb	Cc	Dd	Ee	OY	PZ	MY	AX	RW	SX	TY	UZ	Va
	Sb	Ib	Nb	Oc	Ic	Jd	Ke	Db	Ec	Fd	Ge	Hf	Ba	Cb	Qa	NZ	BY	CZ	Da	Eb	Fc
	Dg	Tc	Jc	Kd	Pd	Qe	Rf	We	Xf	Yg	Zh	Ai	Ff	Gg	Dc	Rb	Oa	Pb	Qc	Rd	Cd
	Qh	Eh	Ud	Ve	Le	Mf	Ng	Lf	Mg	Nh	Oi	Pj	Ig	Jh	Gg	Ed	Sc	Td	Ue	Vf	Se
	fi	Ri	Fi	Ag	Wf	Xg	Ng	Sg	Th	Ui	Vj	Wk	ai	Hf?	Ki	Ii	Fe	Gf	Hg	Ih	Wg
	Nj	gj	Sj	Gj	Bh	Ci	Dj	Oh	Pi	Qj	Rk	Sl	Pj	Aj	Bk	Lj	Ah	Bi	Cj	Dk	Ji
	cp	Ok	hk	Tk	Ul	Vm	Wn	Zi	aj	bk	cl	dm	Wk	ck	dl	Cl	Jj	Kk	Ll	Mm	El
	Vq	dq	Pl	il	jm	kn	lo	Ek	Fl	Gm	Hn	Io	Sl	Rl	Sm	em	Mk	Nl	Om	Pn	Nn
	nr	Wr	er	Qm	Rn	So	Tp	Kn	Lo	Mp	Nq	Or	Tm	Un	Zn	Tn	Dm	En	Fo	Gp	Qo
	Ls	os	Xs	Yr	gt	hu	iv	Xo	Yp	Zq	ar	bs	en	fo	Vo	ao	fn	go	hp	iq	Hq
	Ji	mt	pt	fs	Zu	av	bw	mp	nq	or	ps	qt	Jp	Kq	gp	Wp	Uo	Vp	Wq	Xr	jr
	eu	Ku	nu	qu	pv	sw	ix	Uq	Vr	Ws	Xt	Yu	Ps	Qt	Lr	hq	bp	cq	dr	es	Ys
	Rv	fv	Lv	ov	Nx	Oy	ry	jw	kx	ly	mz	na	ct	du	Ru	Ms	Yr	Zs	at	bu	ft
	Iw	Sw	gw	Mw	by	jz	Pz	cx	dy	ez	fa	gβ	ru	sv	Sv	Sv	js	is?	Zs	cs	bu
	mx	Jx	Tx	hx	Vz	Wa	ka	uy	vz	wa	xβ	yy	Zv	aw	fw	fw	Ou	Av	Pv	lu	mv
	Wy	ny	Ky	Uy	Ma	Nβ	Xβ	sz	tα	uβ	vy	wδ	Dw	Ex	bx	ux	Tw	Ux	Bw	Ow	Rx
	Oa	Xz	oz	Lz	qβ	rγ	Oγ	Qα	Rβ	Sγ	Tδ	Uε	oβ	FB	Fy	cy	gx	hy	Vy	Cx	Dy
	zβ	PB	Ya	pα	aγ	bδ	sδ	IB	JB?	md?	oε	Ve	hγ	Pγ	Aα	cγ	vy	wz	iz	Wz	Xa
	kγ	αγ	Qγ	ZB	Se	Tζ	Oγ	Yγ	Zδ	nδ	oε	ws	zδ	iδ	Gγ	Bβ	dz	ea	ja	Vy	kβ
	oδ	βδ	Bδ	Rδ	gζ	pθ	sδ	Pδ	Oε	RZ	Rζ	Ue	xε	αε	qδ	Hδ	Ha	ca	xα	ja	zγ
	Tε	pε	me	γε	oη	tι	Uη	dζ	uζ	Rζ	Sη	pζ	xε	αε	jε	rε	Cy	le	β	yβ	hδ
	Tζ	Uζ	qζ	nζ	sθ	Yκ	ζθ	dζ	Qε	ν?	Sη	cη	qη	yζ	BK	rε	le	IB	γ	gy	Lε
	Uθ	ηθ	Vη	rη	Xι	AA	qι	Vθ	uζ	vη	wθ	Tθ	dθ	Wη	zη	γη	sζ	Dδ	Jy	Kδ	Bζ
	dι	Vι	θι	Wθ	Xκ	*?	ukκ	τη	eη	gι	gι	cη	Uι	rθ	Xθ	αθ	sζ	Fζ	Eε	Aε	Gη
	Kκ	eκ	bκ	uι	kA	rκ	ZA	dζ	Oε	Xκ	gι	xι	yκ	Vκ	sι	Yι	εη	εη	Kη	Lθ	Aθ
	FA	LA	WA	XA	kA	AA	vA	vA	sA	uλ	YA	BA	iA	zA	WA	gA	βA	aA	uθ	νι	Mι

22 ABDEF	23 ACEF	24 ADF	25 AE	26 BF	27 ABC	28 BCD	29 CDE	30 DEF	31 ABEF	32 ACF	33 AD	34 BE	35 CF	36 ABD	37 BCE	38 CDF	39 ABDE	40 BCEF	41 ABCDF	42 ACDE
JL	KM	LN	AE	BF	CG	DH	EI	FJ	GK	HL	IM	JN	KO	DG	EH	FI	GJ	HK	IL	JM
PQ	QR	AP	MO	AL	AH	BI	CJ	DK	EL	FM	GN	HO	IP	AN	BO	CP	DQ	ER	FS	GT
*V	*W	RS	BQ	NP	BM	CN	DO	EP	FQ	GR	HS	AQ	BR	LP	MQ	NR	OS	PT	QU	RV
Ua	Vb	*X	ST	CR	OQ	PR	QS	RT	SU	TV	UW	IT	JU	JQ	KR	LS	MT	NU	OV	PW
Wb	Xc	Wc	*Y	TU	DS	AS	BT	CU	DV	EW	FX	VX	WY	CS	DT	EU	FV	GW	HX	IY
Gd	He	Yd	Xd	*Z	UV	ET	FU	GV	HW	IX	JY	GY	HZ	KV	LW	MX	NY	OZ	Pa	Qb
De	Ef	lf	Ze	Ye	*a	VW	WX	XY	YZ	Za	ab	KZ	La	XZ	Ya	Zb	ac	bd	ce	Ac
Tf	Ug	Fg	Jg	af	Zf	*b	*c	*d	*e	*f	*g	bc	cd	la	Jb	Kc	Ld	Me	Nf	df
Xh	Yi	Vh	Gh	Kh	bg	ag	bh	ci	dj	Ai	Bj	*h	Af	Mb	Nc	Od	Pe	Qf	Rg	Og
Kj	Lk	Zj	Wi	Hi	Li	ch	di	ej	fk	ek	fl	Ck	*i	de	ef	fg	gh	hi	ij	sh
Fm	Gn	Ml	ak	Xj	ij	Mj	Nk	Ol	Pm	gl	hm	in	DI	Bg	Ch	Di	Ej	Fk	Gl	jk
Oo	Pp	Ho	Nm	bl	Yk	Jk	Kl	Lm	Mn	Qn	Ro	Sp	hm	*j	*k	*l	*m	*n	*o	Hm
Rp	Sq	Qq	Ip	On	cm	Zl	am	bn	co	No	Op	Pq	jo	Em	Fn	Go	Hp	Iq	Jr	*p
Aq	Br	Tr	Rr	Jq	Po	dn	eo	fp	gq	dp	eq	fr	Tq	io	jp	kq	lr	Ar	Bs	Ks
Ir	Js	Cs	Us	Ss	Kr	Qp	Ap	Bq	Cr	hr	is	ji	Qr	kp	lq	mr	ns	ms	nt	Ci
ks	lt	Kt	Di	Vt	Tt	Ls	Rq	Sr	Ts	Ds	Et	Fu	gs	Ur	Vs	As	Bt	ot	pu	ou
Zl	au	mu	Lu	Eu	Wu	Uu	Mt	Nu	Au	Ut	Vu	Wv	ku	Rs	Sr	Wt	Xu	Cu	Dv	qv
gu	hv	bv	nv	Mv	Fv	Xv	Vv	Ww	Ov	Bv	Cw	Dx	Gv	ht	iu	Tu	Uv	Yv	Zw	Ew
cv	dw	iw	bv	ow	Nw	Gw	Yw	Zx	Xx	Pw	Qx	Ry	Xw	lv	mw	jv	kw	Vw	Wx	Xy
nw	ox	ex	cw	dx	px	Ox	Hx	ty	ay	Yy	Zz	aα	Ey	Hw	Ix	nx	Ax	Lz	my	ax
Sy	Ay	py	jx	ky	ey	qy	Py	Qz	Jz	bz	ca	dβ	Sz	Yx	Zy	Jy	oy	By	Cz	nz
Ez	Tz	Bz	fy	gz	lz	fz	rz	sα	Ra	Ka	Lβ	Mγ	bβ	Fz	Ga	az	Kz	pz	qa	Dα
Yβ	Fa	Ua	qz	rα	ha	mα	gα	Hβ	tβ	Sβ	Tγ	Uδ	eγ	Ta	Uβ	Hβ	ba	La	Mβ	rβ
lγ	Zγ	Gβ	Cα	Dβ	sβ	iβ	nβ	oγ	iγ	uγ	vδ	wε	Nδ	cγ	Aγ	Vγ	Iγ	cβ	dγ	Nγ
aδ	mδ	aδ	Vβ	Wγ	Eγ	τγ	jγ	kδ	pδ	jδ	kε	lζ	Vε	fδ	dδ	Bδ	Wδ	Jδ	Aδ	eδ
ie	Bε	nε	Hγ	Iδ	Xδ	Fδ	uδ	vε	lε	qε	rζ	sη	xζ	Oε	gε	eε	Ce	Xe	Ke	Bε
Mζ	jζ	χκ	be	cζ	Je	Ye	Ge	Hζ	wζ	mζ	nη	oθ	mη	Wζ	Pζ	hζ	fζ	Dζ	Yζ	Lζ
Cη	Nη	kη	oζ	pη	dη	Kζ	Zζ	aη	Iη	xη	yθ	zι	tθ	yη	Xη	Qη	iη	gη	Eη	Zη
Hθ	Dθ	Oθ	δη	eθ	qθ	eθ	Lη	Mθ	bθ	Jθ	Kι	Lκ	pι	nθ	zθ	Yθ	Rθ	jθ	hθ	Fθ
Bι	lι	Eι	lθ	mι	ζι	rι	fι	Aι	Nι	cι	dκ	eλ	aκ	uι	oι	aι	Zι	Sι	kι	iι
Nκ	Cκ	Jκ	Pι	Qκ	nκ	πκ	sκ	gκ	Bκ	Oκ	PA		MA	qκ	vκ	pκ	Bκ	aκ	Tκ	lκ
xλ	OA	DA	Fκ	GA	RA	oλ	θλ	τλ	hλ	CA		eλ		βλ	rλ	wλ	qλ	γλ	bλ	UA

43 BDEF	44 ABCEF	45 ACDF	46 ADE	47 BEF	48 ABCF	49 ACD	50 BDE	51 CEF	52 ABDF	53 ACE	54 BDF	55 ABCE	56 BCDF	57 ABCDE	58 BCDEF	59 ABCDEF	60 ACDEF	61 ADEF	62 AEF	63 AF
KN	LO	MP	NQ	BK	CL	AI	BJ	CK	GP	EM	FN	GO	HP	IQ	JR	KS	LT	MU	AK	BL
HU	IV	JW	KX	OR	AR	DM	EN	FO	EV	AO	BP	CQ	DR	ES	FT	GU	AU	BV	NV	OW
AV	BW	CX	DY	LY	PS	BS	CT	DU	TW	HQ	IR	JS	KT	AT	BU	CV	HV	IW	CW	DX
SW	TX	UY	VZ	EZ	MZ	QT	RU	SV	BX	FW	GX	HY	IZ	LU	MV	NW	DW	EX	JX	KY
QX	RY	SZ	Ta	Wa	Fa	Na	Ob	AW	Qd	UX	VY	WZ	Xa	Ja	Kb	Lc	OX	PY	FY	GZ
JZ	Ka	Lb	Mc	Ub	Xb	Gb	Hc	Pc	Je	CY	DZ	Ea	Fb	Yb	Zc	ad	Md	Ad	QZ	Ra
Rc	Sd	Te	Uf	Nd	Vc	Yc	Zd	Id	bf	Re	Sf	Tg	Yh	Gc	Hd	Ie	be	Ne	Be	Cf
Bd	Ce	Df	Eg	Ae	Oe	Wd	Xe	ae	Zg	Kf	Lg	Mh	Ni	Vi	Wj	Xk	Jf	cf	dg	Pg
eg	fh	gi	hj	Vg	Bf	Pf	Qg	YY	Si	cg	dh	ei	fj	Oj	Pk	Ql	Yl	Kg	Lh	eh
Ph	Qi	Rj	Sk	Fh	Wh	Cg	Dh	Rh	Fj	ah	bi	cj	dk	gk	hl	im	Rm	Zm	an	Mi
Ti	Uj	Vk	Wl	ik	Gi	Xi	Yj	Ei	al	Tj	Uk	Ak	Bl	el	fm	gn	jn	Sn	To	bo
kl	Im	Al	Bm	Tl	jl	Hj	Ik	Zk	Km	Gk	HI	Vl	Wm	Cm	Dn	Eo	Fp	ko	lp	Up
In	An	mn	no	Xm	Um	km	Am	Jl	Co	bm	cn	Im	Jn	Xn	Yo	Zp	aq	ip	jq	mq
*q	Jo	Bo	Cp	Cn	Yn	Vn	ln	Bn	np	Ln	Mo	do	Ao	Ko	Lp	Mq	Nr	Gq	Hr	kr
Lt	*r	Kp	Lq	op	Do	Zo	Wo	mo	Yq	Dp	Eq	Np	ep	Bp	Cq	Dr	Es	br	cs	ls
Du	Mu	*s	*t	Dq	pq	Ep	ap	Xp	cr	oq	pr	Fr	Oq	jq	gr	hs	it	Os	Pt	dt
pv	Ev	Nv	Ow	Mr	Er	qr	Fq	bq	Hs	Zr	as	qs	Gs	Pr	Qs	Rt	Su	Ft	Gu	Qu
rw	qw	Fw	Gx	*u	Ns	Fs	rs	Gr	tu	ds	et	bt	rt	Ht	Iu	Jv	Kw	ju	kv	Hv
Fx	sx	rx	sy	Px	*v	Ot	Gt	st	Iv	It	Ju	fu	cu	su	tv	uw	vx	Tv	Uw	lw
by	Gy	ty	uz	Hy	Qy	*w	Pu	Hu	Rw	uv	vw	Kv	gv	dv	ew	fx	gy	Lx	My	Vx
Yz	cz	Hz	Ia	tz	Iz	Rz	*x	Qv	*z	Jw	Kx	wx	Lw	hw	ix	jy	kz	wy	xz	Nz
oα	Za	da	eβ	va	ua	Ja	Sa	*y	Aβ	Sx	Ty	Ly	xy	Mx	Ny	Oz	Pa	hz	iα	ya
Eβ	pβ	aβ	bγ	JB	wβ	vβ	Kβ	Tβ	Uγ	*α	Az	Uz	Mz	yz	za	aβ	βγ	QB	iβ	jβ
sγ	Fγ	qγ	rδ	fγ	Kγ	xγ	wγ	Lγ	Mδ	Bγ	*β	Ba	Va	Na	Oβ	Pγ	Qδ	γδ	mβ	nγ
Oδ	tδ	Gδ	He	cδ	gδ	Lδ	yδ	xδ	ye	Vδ	Cδ	*γ	Cβ	Wβ	Xγ	Yδ	Zε	Re	Rγ	Sδ
fε	Pε	uε	vζ	sε	dε	he	Me	ze	aζ	Ne	We	De	*δ	Dγ	Eδ	Fε	Ze	aζ	δε	eε
Cζ	gζ	Qζ	Rη	Iζ	iζ	eζ	iζ	Nζ	Oη	zζ	Oζ	Xζ	Eζ	*ε	*ζ	*η	Gζ	Hη	Sζ	Tη
Mη	Dη	hη	iθ	wη	Jη	uη	fη	jη	kθ	βη	αη	Pη	Yη	Fη	Aη	Bθ	Bη	Cθ	bη	cθ
aθ	Nθ	Eθ	Fι	Sθ	xθ	Kθ	vθ	gθ	hι	Pθ	γθ	ββ	Qθ	Zθ	Gθ	Gι	*θ	*ι	Iθ	Jι
Gι	bι	Oι	Pκ	jι	Tι	yι	Lι	wι	xκ	lι	Qι	δ	γ	Rι	aι	Hλ	Cι	Dκ	Dι	Eκ
jκ	Hκ	cκ	dλ	Gκ	kκ	Uκ	zκ	Mκ	NA	iκ	mκ	Rx	εκ	δκ	Sκ	bκ	Iκ	Dκ	*κ	*λ
mλ	kλ	lλ		Qλ	HA	IA	VA	aA		yA	jA	nA	SA	ζA	eA	TA	cA	JA	EA	*A

[a] The higher-order terms were used when generating the design. Main effects are denoted by an asterisk.

List of Acronyms and Symbols

Some symbols used locally in this volume are not shown.

$A_{r;c}$	Factor from the Poisson distribution that is tabulated in Table K
ABC	Activity Based Costing
AD	Anderson Darling (statistic)
AFR	Average failure rate
AHP	Analytical hierarchy process
AIAG	Automotive Industry Action Group
ANOM	Analysis of means
ANOVA	Analysis of variance
APQP	Advanced product quality planning
AQL	Accept quality level
AQP	Advanced quality planning
ARL	Average run length
ASQ	American Society for Quality (Previously ASQC, American Society for Quality Control)
ASTM	American Society for Testing and Materials
AV	Appraiser variation
A_t	Acceleration test factor
BB	Black belt

1105

$B_{r;c}$ Factor from the Poisson distribution tabulated in Table K

b Weibull distribution shape parameter (slope of a Weibull probability plot); a parameter used in the NHPP with Weibull intensity model

BOK Body of knowledge

BPIEs Business process improvement events

c Confidence factor used in Table K

c chart Control chart for nonconformities

°C Celsius temperature

CCD Central composite Design

CI Confidence interval

CL Centerline in an control chart

CDF Cumulative distribution function

CFM Continuous flow manufacturing

CAP Change acceleration process

CEO Chief executive officer

CFO Chief financial officer

C_p Capability index (AIAG, 1995b) – does not address process centering within specification limits

C_{pk} Capability index (AIAG, 1995b) – addresses process centering within specification limits

cP Centipoise (measure of fluid viscosity)

CPM Critical path method

CRM Customer Relationship Management

CUSUM Cumulative sum (control chart approach)

C&E Cause-and-Effect (Diagram)

C/O Changeover

CODND Cost of doing nothing differently

COPQ Cost of poor quality

C/T Cycle time

CTC Critical to cost

CTD Critical to delivery

CTP Critical to process

CTQ Critical to quality

DCP Data collection plan

DCRCA DOE collective response capability assessment

df Degrees of freedom

DFA Design for assembly (Example of DFX)

DFIEE Design for Integrated Enterprise Excellence

DFLSS Design for Lean Six Sigma

DFM Design for manufacturability (Example of DFX)

DFMEA Design failure mode and effects analysis

DFSS	Design for Six Sigma
DFX	Design for X or a characteristic (e.g., DFA or DFM)
DMAIC	Define–measure–analyze–improve–control
DMADV	Define–measure–analyze–design–verify
DOA	Dead on arrival
DOE	Design of experiments
DPMO	Defects per million opportunities
DPU	Defects per unit
DSO	Days sales outstanding
DSS	Decision support system
8D	8 Disciplines
e	2.71828
EBIDA	Earnings before interest, depreciation, and amortization
ECMM	Enterprise cascading measurement methodology
EDA	Exploratory data analysis
E-DMAIC	Enterprise process DMAIC (roadmap)
EIP	Enterprise improvement plan
EPE	Every part every (batch size) (e.g., EPE day)
EPM	Enterprise process management
EPRO	Event probability (logistic regression)
ERA	Emergency response action
ERP	Enterprise process resource planning
EVOP	Evolutionary operation
ERP	Enterprise process Resource Planning
EWMA	Exponentially Weighted Moving Average
$\exp(x)$	$= e^x = (2.71828...)^x$
°F	Fahrenheit temperature
F_0	Test criterion value from the F distribution (Table F)
$F_{a,v1;v2}$	Value from the F distribution for α risk and v_1 and v_2 degrees of freedom (Table F)
F_i	Probability plot positions determined from Table H
FIFO	First-in-first-out
FG	Finished goods
FIT	Failures in time
FMEA	Failure mode and effects analysis
FR	Functional requirement
FT	Fault tree
FV	Future value
$F(x)$	Describes the CDF where the independent variable is x
$f(x)$	Describes the PDF where the independent variable is x

GAAP	Generally Accepted Accounting Principles
Gage R&R	Gage repeatability and reproducibility
GB	Green belt
GDT	Geometric dimensioning and tolerancing
GLM	General linear modeling
H_0	Null hypothesis
H_a	Alternative hypothesis
HPP	Homogeneous Poisson process
HR	Human resources
ICA	Interim containment action
ICP	Innovation creation process
IEE	Integrated Enterprise (process) Excellence
in.	Inches
ImR chart	Individuals control chart and moving range chart (Same as *XmR* chart)
IPO	Input-process-output
JIT	Just-in-time
K	Temperature in degrees Kelvin ($273.16 + °C$); Boltzmann's constant
k	Characteristic life or scale parameter in the Weibull distribution
KCA	Knowledge-centered activity
KTS	Knowledge-transfer sessions
KPIV	Key process input variables
KPOV	Key process output variables
LCL	Lower control limit
LDL	Lower decision level (in ANOM)
L/T	Lead time
ln	$\log_e = \log_{2.718}$
log	$\log_{10}$
min	Minutes, minimum
MBA	Master of business administration
MBB	Master black belt
ML	Maximum likelihood
MP	Maintenance prevention
mph	Miles per hour
MR	Moving range
MRP	Material requirements planning
MS	Mean square
MSA	Measurement systems analysis
msec	Milliseconds
MTBF	Mean time between failures

Mu	Greek letter μ, which often symbolizes the mean of a population
N/A	Not applicable
n	Sample size
ndc	Number of distinct categories, in measurement systems analysis
np (chart)	Control chart of number of nonconforming items
NGT	Nominal group technique
NHPP	Non-homogeneous Poisson process
NID(0,σ^2)	Modeling errors are often assumed to be normally and independently distributed with mean zero and a constant but unknown variance
NIST	National Institute of Standards and Technology
NPV	Natural process variation, net present value
NTF	No trouble found
OC	Operating characteristic (curve)
OEM	Original equipment manufacturer (customers)
ORT	Ongoing reliability test
p (chart)	Control chart of fraction nonconforming
PCA	Permanent corrective actions
PDCA	Plan-do-check-act
PDF	Probability density function
P-DMAIC	Project DMAIC (roadmap)
PDSA	Plan-do-study-act
PERT	Program evaluation and review technique
PFMEA	Process failure mode and effects analysis
PI	Prediction interval
P&L	Profit and loss
PPAP	Production part approval process
PP&E	Plant property and equipment
ppm	Parts per million (defect rate)
P	Probability
PM	Preventive maintenance, productive maintenance, performance measurement
P_p	Performance index (AIAG, 1995b); calculated using long-term standard deviation
P_{pk}	Performance index (AIAG, 1995b); calculated using long-term standard deviation
Prob	Probability
PV	Part Variation, Present value
QFD	Quality function deployment
RFQ	Request for quotation

ROI	Return on investment
RQL	Reject quality level
R	Range
RM	Raw material
RMR	Rejected material review
RPN	Risk priority number (in FMEA)
RO	Results orchestration
RSM	Response surface methodology
RTY	Rolled throughput yield
r	Number of failures, correlation coefficient
R^2	Coefficient of determination
$r(t)$	System failure rate at time (t) for the NHPP model
s	Standard deviation of a sample
S&A	Sales and administration
SBU	Strategic business unit
SIPOC	Supplier–input–process–output–customer
SIT	Structured inventive thinking
SMART	See glossary
SME	Subject matter expert
SMED	Single-minute exchange of die
SOD	Severity, occurrence, and detection (used in FMEA)
SOP	Standard operating procedure
SPC	Statistical process control
Spec	Specification (limit)
SS	Sum of squares
Std. dev.	Standard deviation
SWOT	Strengths, weaknesses, opportunities, and threats
S^4	Smarter Six Sigma Solutions
T	Total test time used in Table K
t	Time
TOC	Theory of constraints
TPM	Total productive maintenance
TPS	Toyota production system
TQC	Total quality control
TQM	Total quality management
t_0	Test criterion value from the t distribution (Tables D or E)
T_q	$q\%$ of the population is expected to be below this value for a population
TRIZ	Teoriya Resheniya Izobretatelskikh Zadatch (Theory of problem solving)

$t_{\alpha;\nu}$	Value from the t distribution for α risk and ν degrees of freedom (Tables D and E)
UCL	Upper control limit
UDL	Upper decision level (ANOM)
U_0	Test criterion value from the normal distribution (Table B or C)
U_α	Value from the normal distribution for α risk (Table B or C)
U_β	Value from the normal distribution for β risk (Table B or C)
u (chart)	Control chart of number of nonconformities per unit
USIT	Unified structured inventive thinking
VA time	Value-added time
VIF	Variance inflation factor
VOC	Voice of the customer
VOP	Voice of the process
WIP	Work in progress, Work in process
XmR (chart)	Control chart of individual and moving range measurements
x_0	Three-parameter Weibull distribution location parameter
$\bar{x}$	Mean of a variable x
$\bar{x}$ chart	Control chart of means (i.e., $\bar{x}$ chart)
$\tilde{x}$	Median of variable x
YB	Yellow belt
ZD	Zero defects
Z_α	Normal distribution value for α risk (Table A)
α	Alpha, risk of rejecting the null hypothesis erroneously
β	Beta, risk of not rejecting the null hypothesis erroneously
Δ	Delta, effect of contrast column
δ	Delta, an acceptable amount of uncertainty
θ	Theta, the parameter in the exponential distribution equation (mean of the distribution)
λ	Lambda, hazard rate; intensity term in the NHPP equation
μ	Mu, population true mean
$\hat{\mu}$	Estimate of population mean
ν	Nu, degrees of freedom
ρ	Rho, actual failure rate of population, correlation coefficient between two variables

ρ_a	A single failure rate test criterion
ρ_t	The highest failure rate that is to be exhibited by the samples in a time-terminated test before a "pass test" statement can be given
ρ_1	Higher failure rate (failures/unit time) involving β risk in Poisson sequential testing (typically assigned equality to failure rate criterion ρ_a)
ρ_0	Lower failure rate (failures/unit time involving α risk in Poisson sequential testing
ρ_α	Used when calculating sample size for a fixed length test; the failure rate at which a is to apply
ρ_β	Used when calculating sample size for a fixed length test; the failure rate at which β is to apply
Σ	Mathematical summation
σ	Sigma, population standard deviation
$\hat{\sigma}$	Estimate of population standard deviation
$\chi^2_{\alpha;i}$	Chi-square value from the chi-square distribution for α risk and ν degrees of freedom (Table G)
χ^2_o	Test criterion value from the chi-square distribution (Table G)
$\|\ \|$	Mathematical symbol used to denote the absolute value of a quantity

Glossary

Abscissa: The coordinate representing the distance from the y axis in a two-dimensional plot.

Acceptable quality level (AQL): The maximum proportion of defective units in a sampling plan that can be considered satisfactory as the process average.

Accuracy: The closeness of agreement between an observed value and the accepted reference value (AIAG, 2002).

Active experimentation: Experiments are conducted where variable levels are changed to assess their impact on responses.

Activity Based Costing (ABC): Technique for businesses to understand the components and drivers of overhead costs. Through ABC, organizations can more realistically assign indirect overhead costs to products or services.

Advanced quality planning (AQP) or Advanced product quality planning (APQP): The act of ensuring that a new product or service will meet customer expectations.

Alias: *See* Confounded.

Affinity diagram: A methodology by which a team can organize and summarize the natural grouping from a large number of ideas and issues.

Alpha (α) risk: Risk of rejecting the null hypothesis erroneously. Also called type I error or producer's risk.

Alternative hypothesis (H_a): *See* Hypothesis testing.

Analysis of goodness: The ranking of DOE trials according to the level of a response. An attempt is then made to identify factors or combination of factors that potentially affects the response.

Analysis of means (ANOM): A statistical procedure to compare the means of individual groups to the grand mean.

Analysis of variance (ANOVA): A statistical procedure for analyzing the differences in the means of two or more groups.

Anderson Darling (Statistic): Measures how well data follow a distribution. A smaller statistic indicates a better distribution fit. Statistic is used to compare competing distribution fits.

Appraiser variation (AV): The variation in average measurements of the same part between different appraisers using the same measuring instrument and method in a stable environment. AV is one of the common sources of measurement system variation that results from difference in operator skill or technique using the same measurement system. Appraiser variation is commonly assumed to be the reproducibility error associated with a measurement; this is not always true (see Reproducibility).

Attribute data (Discrete data): The presence or absence of some characteristic in each device under test (e.g., proportion nonconforming in a pass/fail test).

Attribute screen: A test procedure that screens compliant parts from non-compliant parts.

Autocorrelation: In time series analyses, correlation between values and previous values of the same series.

Average: A location parameter; frequently the arithmetic mean.

Average run length (ARL): The average number of points required before an out-of-control process condition is indicated.

Balanced (design): A design in which each factor appears an equal number of times.

Balanced scorecard (The): The balanced scorecard (Kaplan and Norton, 1992) tracks business organizational functions in the areas of financial, customer, and internal business process and learning & growth. In this system, an organization's vision and strategy is also to lead to the cascading of objectives, measures, targets, and initiatives throughout the organization. This volume describes issues with this system and an alternative IEE system that overcomes these shortcomings.

Bar charts: Horizontal or vertical bars that graphically illustrate the magnitude of multiple situations.

Baseline: Beginning information from which a response change is assessed.

Bathtub curve: A curve used to describe the life cycle of a system/device as a function of usage. When the curve has its initial downward slope, the failure rate is decreasing with usage. This is the early-life region where manufacturing problems are typically encountered. The failure rate is constant during the flat part of the curve. When the curve begins sloping upward, the failure rate is increasing with usage. This region describes wear-out of a product.

Benchmarking: A discovery process for determining what is the best practice or performance within your company, a competitor, or another industry.

Beta (β) risk: Chance of not rejecting the false null hypothesis; also called type II error or consumer's risk.

Bias: The difference between the observed average of measurements (trials under repeatability conditions) and a reference value; historically referred to as accuracy. Bias is evaluated and expressed at a single point with the operating range of the measurement system. (AIAG, 2002)

Bimodal distribution: A distribution that is a combination of two different distributions resulting in two distinct peaks.

Binomial distribution: A distribution that is useful to describe discrete variables or attributes that have two possible outcomes: for example, a pass/fail proportion test, heads/tails outcome from flipping a coin, defect/no defect present.

Black belts (BBs): Process improvement Six Sigma and IEE practitioners who typically receive four weeks of training over four months. It is most desirable that black belts are dedicated resources; however, many organizations utilize part-time resources. During training, black belt trainees lead the execution of a project that has in-class report-outs and critiques. Between training sessions black belt trainees should receive project coaching, which is a very important for their success. They are expected to deliver high quality report-outs to peers, champions, and executives. Upon course completion, black belts are expected to continue delivering financial beneficial projects; for example, 4–6 projects per year with financial benefits of $500,000–$1,000,000. Black belts can mentor green belts.

Black box: Describes a system where the interior operations are not known.

Blocking: For experiments it may be necessary or desirable to divide the experimental units into smaller, more homogeneous groups. These groups are call blocks.

Boldness: The term used to describe the choosing of the magnitude of the variable levels to use within a response surface design. The concept suggests that the magnitudes of variables should be large enough to capture the minimum and maximum responses of the process under test.

Bootstrapping: A re-sampling technique that provides a simple but effective methodology to describe the uncertainty associated with a summary statement without concern about details of complexity of the chosen summary or exact distribution from which data are calculated.

Bottleneck: The slowest operation in a chain of operations; it will pace the output of the entire line.

Bottom Line: The final profit or loss that a company experiences at the end of a given period of time.

Box-Cox transformation: A general approach for transforming data to a normal distribution, where values (Y) are transformed to the power of λ (i.e., Y^λ).

BPIE: *See* Business process improvement event system.

Brainstorming: Consensus-building among experts about a problem or issue using group discussion.

Business Process Improvement Event (BPIE) System: A system for identifying and timely resolving reoccurring problems.

The resolution for these issues could lead to a simple agree-to procedure change, a DMADV design project, or P-DMAIC process improvement project.

Calibration: A set of operations that establishes, under specified conditions, the relationship between a measuring device and a traceable standard of known reference value and uncertainty. Calibration may also include steps to detect, correlate, report, or eliminate by adjustment any discrepancy in accuracy of the measuring device being compared. (AIAG, 2002)

Calipers: An instrument consisting of a pair of movable, curved legs fastened together at one end. It is used to measure the thickness or diameter of something. There are both inside and outside calipers.

Canonical form: A transformed form of a response surface equation to a new coordinate system so that the origin is at the maximum, minimum, or saddle point and the axis of the system is parallel to the principal axis of the fitted quadratic response surface.

Capability/performance metric: *See* Process capability/performance metric.

Capability, Process: See Process capability.

Categorical variables: Represent types of data which may be divided into groups. Examples of categorical variables are race, gender, age group, and educational level. While the latter two variables may also be considered in a numerical manner by using exact values for age and highest grade completed, it is often more informative to categorize such variables into a relatively small number of groups.

Cause-and-effect diagram (C&E diagram): This technique, sometimes called an Ishikawa diagram or fishbone diagram, is useful in problem solving using brainstorming sessions. With this technique, possible causes from such sources as materials, equipment, methods, and personnel are typically identified as a starting point to begin discussion.

Cell: A grouping of data that, for example, comprises a bar in a histogram.

Censored datum: The sample has not failed at a usage or stress level.

Central composite rotatable design: A type of response surface experiment design.

Central limit theorem: The means of samples from a population will tend to be normally distributed around the population mean.

Certification: A test to determine whether, for example, a product is expected to meet or be better than its failure rate criterion.

Champions: Executive-level managers who are responsible for managing and guiding the Lean Six Sigma or IEE deployment and its projects.

Changeover is the time from the last piece of one batch to the first piece of the next batch.

Characteristic life (k): A parameter that is contained in the Weibull distribution. In a reliability test, the value of this parameter equates to the usage when 63.2% of the devices will fail.

Checks sheets: Sheets that are use do systematically record and compile data from historical or current observations.

Chi-square test: The proper statistical name is the chi-square test of independence. This is different from the chi-square goodness of fit test, which has a different purpose. The only similarity is that the chi-square statistic is used for estimating significance. This volume uses the term chi-square test to describe a chi-square test of independence.

Class variables: Factors that have discrete levels.

Coded levels: Regression analysis of factorial or response surface data can be performed where the levels are described in the natural levels of the factors (e.g., 5.5 and 4.5 V) or the coded levels of the factors (e.g., −1 and +1).

Coefficient: *See* Regression analysis.

Coefficient of determination (R^2): The square of the correlation coefficient. Values for R^2 describe the percentage of variability accounted for by the model. For example, $R^2 = 0.8$ indicates that 80% of the variability in the data is accounted for by the model.

Coefficient of variation: A measure of dispersion where standard deviation is divided by the mean and is expressed as a percentage.

Collins three circles: 1. What can you do to be the best in the world? 2. What drives your economic engine? 3. What are you deeply passionate about? (Collins, 2001)

Common cause: Natural or random variation that is inherent in a process over time, affecting every outcome of the process. If a process is in-control, it has only common cause variation and can be said to be predictable. When a process experiences common cause variability but does not meet customer needs it can be said that the process is not capable. Process or input variable change is needed to improve this situation; (i.e., this is metric is creating a pull for project creation).

Concurrent engineering: An approach to the development of new products where the product and its associated processes, such as manufacturing, distribution, and service, are all developed in parallel.

Confidence interval: The region containing the limits or band of a parameter with an associated confidence level that the bounds are large enough to contain the true parameter value. The bands can be single-sided to describe an upper/lower limit or double-sided to describe both upper and lower limits.

Confounded: Two factor effects that are represented by the same comparison are aliases of one another (i.e., different names for the same computed effect). Two effects that are aliases of one another are confounded, or confused, with one another. Although the word *confounded* is commonly used to describe aliases between factorial effects and block effects, it can more generally be used to describe any effects that are aliases of one another.

Consumer's risk: *See* Beta (β) risk.

Contingency tables: If each member of a sample is classified by one characteristic into S classes, and by a second characteristic into R classes, the data may be presented by a contingency table with S rows and R columns. Statistical independence of characteristics can also be determined by contingency tables.

Continuous data (Variables data): Data that can assume a range of numerical responses on a continuous scale, as opposed to data that can assume only discrete levels.

Continuous distribution: A distribution used in describing the probability of a response when the output is continuous (see Response).

Continuous data response: *See* Response.

Continuous flow manufacturing (CFM): Within CFM, operations and machines are efficiently used to build parts. Non-value added activities in the operation are eliminated. Flexibility is a substitute for work-in-process inventory. A product focus is established in all areas of operation.

Contrast column effects: The effect in a contrast column, which might have considerations that are confounded.

Control chart: A procedure used to track a process with time for the purpose of determining if common or special causes exist.

Control: *In control* or predictable is used in process control charting to indicate when the chart shows that there are no indicators that the process is not predictable.

Corrective action: Process of resolving problems.

Correlation coefficient (r): A statistic that describes the strength of a relationship between two variables is the sample correlation coefficient. A correlation coefficient can take values between -1 and $+1$. A -1 indicates perfect negative correlation, while a $+1$ indicates perfect positive correlation. A zero indicates no correlation.

Cost of doing nothing differently (CODND): To keep IEE from appearing as a quality initiative, I prefer to reference the Six Sigma metric COPQ as the cost of doing nothing differently (CODND), which has even broader costing implications than COPQ. In this volume, I make reference to the CODND.

Cost of poor quality (COPQ): Traditionally, cost of quality issues have been given the broad categories of internal failure costs, external failure costs, appraisal costs, and prevention costs. See Glossary description for cost of doing nothing differently. Within Six Sigma, COPQ addresses the cost of not performing work correctly the first time or not meeting customer's expectations.

Covariate: A quantitative variable that can be included within an ANOVA model. This may be a variable where the level is measured but not controlled as part of the design. For this situation, when the covariate is entered into the model, the error variance would be reduced. A covariate may also be a quantitative variable where its levels were controlled as part of the experiment. For both situations, the statistical model contains a coefficient for the covariate, which would be interpreted as a predictor in a regression model.

Cumulative distribution function (CDF) [$F(x)$]: The calculated integral of the PDF from minus infinity to x. This integration takes on a characteristic "percentage less than or percentile" when plotted against x.

Cumulative sum (CUSUM) (control chart): An alternative control charting technique to Shewhart control charting. CUSUM control charts can detect small process shifts faster than Shewhart control charts can.

Customer: Someone for whom work or a service is performed. The end user of a product is a customer of the employees within a company that manufactures the product. There are also internal customers in a company. When an employee does work or performs a service for someone else in the company, the person who receives this work is a customer of this employee.

CUSUM: *See* Cumulative sum (CUSUM) (control chart).

Cycle Time: Frequency that a part/product is completed by process. Also, time it takes for operator to go through work activities before repeating the activities. In addition, cycle time can be used to quantify customer order to delivery time.

Dashboard: See Scorecard.

Days Sales Outstanding (DSO): In general, the average number of days it takes to collect revenue after a sale has been made. In this volume, DSO is considered to be the number of days beyond the due date that a payment is to be received (i.e., for an invoice 3 indicates that payment was received three days late) while −2 indicates receipt was 2 days early.

Discrete data: Discrete data are based on counts. Only a finite number of values are possible, and the values cannot be subdivided meaningfully (e.g., the number of parts damaged in shipment).

DOE-collective-response-capability-assessment (DCRCA): Consider a DOE where the factors were chosen to be the tolerance extremes for a new process and the response was the output of the process. Consider also that there were no historical data that could be used to make a process capability/performance metric statement for the process. A probability plot of the DOE responses can give an overall picture of how we expect the process to perform later, relative to specification limits or other desired conformance targets. This type of plot can be very useful when attempting to project how a new process would perform relative to specification limits (i.e., a DCRCA assessment). The percentage of occurrence provides only a very rough picture of what might occur in the future since the data that were plotted are not random future data from the process.

Dead on arrival (DOA): A product that does not work the first time it is used or tested. The binomial distribution can often be used to evaluate DOA scenarios statistically (i.e., it works or does not work).

Decision tree: A graphical decision-making tool that integrates for a defined problem both uncertainties and cost with the alternatives to decide on the *best* alternative.

Defect: A nonconformity or departure of a quality characteristic from its intended level or state.

Defective: A nonconforming item that contains at least one defect or having a combination of several imperfections, causing the unit not to satisfy intended requirements.

Deming, Dr. W. Edwards: As an American statistician, Dr. Deming is known for his top management teachings in Japan after World War II. Dr. Deming made a significant contribution to Japan becoming renown for its high-quality, innovative products.

Descriptive statistics: Descriptive statistics help pull useful information from data, whereas probability provides among other things a basis for inferential statistics and sampling plans.

Design for X (DFX): Examples of DFX (Dodd, 1992) are design for assembly, design for performance, design for ergonomics, design for manufacturability, design for quality, design for recyclability, design for redesign, design for reliability, design for maintainability, design for serviceability, and design for test. Example nomenclature is DFA for design for assembly.

Degrees of freedom (*df* or v): Number of measurements that are independently available for estimating a population parameter. For a random sample from a population, the number of degrees of freedom is equal to the sample size minus one.

Delphi technique: A method of *predicting* the future by surveying experts in the area of concern.

Design of experiments (DOE): A structured experiment where the response effects of several factors are studied at one time.

Design for Integrated Enterprise Excellence (DFIEE): A process used when developing new products/services, processes, or information technology (IT) projects. This development is to be efficient and effective with a focus on up front understanding of customer requirements. IEE uses a DMADV process for DFIEE execution.

DFIEE: *See* Design for Integrated Enterprise Excellence.

Discrete data (Attribute data): The presence or absence of some characteristic in each device under test (e.g., proportion non-conforming in a pass/fail test).

Discrete distribution: A distribution function that describes the probability for a random discrete variable.

Discrete random variable: A random variable that can only assume discrete values.

Discrimination (of a measurement system): Alias smallest readable unit, discrimination is the measurement resolution, scale limit, or smallest detectable unit of the measurement device and standard. It is an inherent property of gage design and reported as a unit of measurement or classification. The number of data categories is often referred to as the discrimination ratio (not to be confused with the discrimination ratio used in Poisson sequential testing) since it describes how many classifications can be reliably distinguished given the observed process variation (AIAG, 2002).

Distinct data categories: The number of data classifications (NDC) or categories that can be reliably distinguished, determined by the effective resolution of the measurement system and part variation from the observed process for a given application. (AIAG, 2002)

Distribution: A pattern that is followed from a random sample from a population. Described normal, Weibull, Poisson, binomial, and lognormal distributions are applicable to the modeling of various industrial situations.

DMAIC: Define–measure–analyze–improve–control Six Sigma roadmap.

DMADV: Define–measure–analyze–design–verify DFSS and DFIEE roadmap.

DNA rules: DNA is the material, inside the nucleus of cells, which carries genetic information. The scientific name for DNA is deoxyribonucleic acid. DNA rules describe the basic building blocks of a system (e.g., IEE DNA rules).

Dot plot: A plot of symbols that represent individual observations from a batch of data.

Double-sided test: A statistical consideration whereby, for example, an alternative hypothesis is that the mean of a population is not equal to a criterion value. *See* single-sided test.

DPMO: When using the non-conformance rate calculation of defects per million opportunities (DPMO), one first needs to describe what the opportunities for defects are in the process; for example, the number of components and solder joints when manufacturing printed circuit boards. Next, the number of defects is periodically divided by the number of opportunities to determine the DMPO rate.

Drill down: To drill down is to transition from general category information to more specific details by moving through a hierarchy.

Early-life failures: *See* Bathtub curve.

E-DMAIC (Roadmap): An IEE enterprise define–measure–analyze–improve–control roadmap contains among other things a value chain measurement and analysis system where metric improvement needs can pull for project creation.

Effect: The main effect of a factor in a two-level factorial experiment is the mean difference in responses between the two levels of the factor, which is averaged over all levels of the other factors.

Efficiency: A concept due to R. A. Fisher, who said that one estimator is more efficient than another if it has a smaller variance. Percentage efficiency is 100 times the ratio of the variance of the estimator with minimum variance to the variance of the estimator in question.

Engineering process control (EPC): In industries such as chemical processing, oil refining, and the food/beverage industry automated process controls can make adjustments depending upon characteristics of incoming raw material. In these systems analog signals from sensors and meters can be transmitted to computers which cause appropriate real time process pressure or temperature adjustment. However, EPC techniques do not require automation and can apply to transactional environments. EPC techniques can be used to determine when to adjust the number of people working in a call center or a grocery store checkout line depending upon current demand. EPC technique can be applied to determine when to redress a grinding wheel that experiences wear or add acid to a chemical etching process that depletes over time.

Enron effect: At the beginning of the 21st century, the executive management style in Enron and other companies led to the downfall of these companies and to executives' spending time behind bars. In Enron, executive management had to do whatever it took to meet prescribed numbers. Enron lacked metrics that gave a true picture of what was happening. This resulted in a smoke-and-mirror system which had integrity issues relative to the handling of business challenges. In addition, this system encouraged executive management to have no respect for either the financial or the general well-being of others inside and outside the company. I make reference to the result of this management style as the Enron effect.

Enterprise cascading measurement methodology (ECMM): A system where meaningful measurements are statistically tracked over time at various functional levels of the business. This leads to a cascading and alignment of important metrics throughout the organization.

Enterprise improvement plan (EIP): A project drill-down strategy that follows: goal–strategies–high potential area–projects.

Enterprise process define-measure-analyze-improve-control: See E-DMAIC (Roadmap).

Enterprise process management (EPM): Rather than having a governance model that addresses initiatives as separate entities, in IEE a value chain EPM function can be created that orchestrates this system. The EPM function is responsible for integrating, overseeing, and improving the execution of these processes, utilizing an E-DMAIC roadmap.

EPM: *See* Enterprise process management.

Error (experimental): Ambiguities during data analysis caused from such sources as measurement bias, random measurement error, and mistake.

Error proofing: See Mistake proofing.

Escape: Failure of a control system that allowed advancement of a product or service that was sub-standard.

Evolutionary operation (EVOP): An analytical approach whereby process conditions are changed structurally in a manufacturing process, for example, using a DOE matrix for the purpose of analytically determining changes to make for product improvement.

Exploratory data analysis (EDA): The examination of the appearance of data for the purpose of gaining insight to the development of a theory of cause-and-effect.

Experimental error: Variations in the experimental response under identical test conditions; also called residual error.

Factorial experiment: *See* Full factorial experiment and Fractional factorial experiment.

Factors: Variables that are studied at different levels in a designed experiment.

Failure: A device is said to fail when it no longer performs its intended function satisfactorily.

Failure mode and effects analysis (FMEA): Analytical approach directed toward problem prevention through the prioritization of potential problems and their resolution. Opposite of fault-tree analysis.

Failure rate: Failures/unit time or failures/units of usage, that is, 1/MTBF. Sample failure rates are: 0.002 failures/hour, 0.0003 failures/auto miles traveled, 0.01 failures/1000 parts manufactured. Failure rate criterion (ρ_a) is a failure rate value that is not to be exceeded in a product. Tests to determine if a failure rate criterion is met can be fixed or sequential in duration. With fixed-length test plans, the test design failure rate (ρ_t) is the sample failure rate that cannot be exceeded in order to certify the criterion (ρ_a) at the boundary of the desired confidence level. With sequential test plans, failure rates ρ_1 and ρ_0 are used to determine the test plans.

Fault tree analysis: A schematic picture of possible failure modes and associated probabilities. A fault tree analysis is opposite of failure mode and effects analysis.

50-foot-level: Low-level tracking of a key process input variable; for example, process temperature when manufacturing plastic parts or daily salesperson activity. This type of chart can involve frequent sampling to make sure that the desired input level is maintained over time. Tracking at the 50-foot-level can lead to the timely detection and resolution of problems or undesirable drifts in input levels so that the 30,000-foot-level metric for product/service quality, timeliness, and other metrics is not jeopardized.

Firefighting: The practice of giving much focus to fixing the problems of the day/week. The usual corrective actions taken in fire-fighting, such as tweaking a stable/predictable process, do not create any long-term fixes and may actually cause process degradation.

Fixed-effects model: A factorial experiment where the levels of the factors are specifically chosen by the experimenter, as opposed to a random effects or components-of-variance model.

Flow chart: A graphical process representation using boxes as process steps with connection arrows.

Fold-over designs: Resolution IV designs can be created from resolution III designs by the process of fold-over. To fold-over a resolution III design, simply add to the original DOE design matrix a second DOE design matrix, often with all the signs reversed.

Force field analysis: Representation of the conflicting forces in an organization which are supporting and driving toward a solution and those which are restraining progress.

Fractional factorial experiment: Design of experiments (DOE) strategy that assesses several factors/variables simultaneously in one test, where only a partial set of all possible combinations of factor levels is tested to identify important factors more efficiently. This type of test is much more efficient than a traditional one-at-a-time test strategy.

Full factorial experiment: Factorial experiment where all combinations of factor levels are tested.

Gage: Any device used to obtain measurements. The term is frequently used to refer specifically to shop floor devices, including go/no-go devices.

Gage blocks are precision standards used for calibrating other measuring devices.

Gage repeatability and reproducibility (R&R) study: The evaluation of measuring instruments to determine capability to yield a precise response. Gage repeatability is the variation in measurements, considering one part and one operator. Gage reproducibility is the variation between operators measuring one part.

Gantt chart: A bar chart that shows activities as blocks over time. A block's beginning and end correspond to the beginning and end date of the activity.

Gemba: The workplace, where value is added. A manager's office is not considered to be gemba.

General linear modeling (GLM): A statistical procedure for univariate analysis of variance with balanced/unbalanced designs, analysis of covariance, and regression.

Goodness-of-fit tests: A type of test to compare an observed frequency distribution with a theoretical distribution like the Poisson, binomial or normal. *See* Lack of fit.

Go/no-go: A technique often used in manufacturing whereby a device is tested with a gage that evaluates the device against its upper/lower specification limit. A decision is made that the device either meets or does not meet the criterion. Go/no-go gages provide a rapid means of giving a pass/fail assessment to whether a part is beyond a conformance limit.

Governance, corporate: The system by which business corporations are directed and controlled. The corporate governance structure specifies the distribution of rights and responsibilities among different participants in the corporation, such as, the board, managers, shareholders and other stakeholders, and spells out the rules and procedures for making decisions on corporate affairs. By doing this, it also provides the structure through which the company objectives are set, and the means of attaining those objectives and monitoring performance. Organization for Economic Cooperation and Development (OECD) April 1999.

Green belts (GBs): Part-time practitioners who typically receive two weeks of training over two months. Their primary focus is on projects that are in their functional area. The inference that someone becomes a green belt before a black belt should not be made. Business and personal needs/requirements should influence the decision whether someone becomes a black belt or green belt. If someone's job requires a more in-depth skill set, such as the use of DOE, then the person should be trained as a black belt. Also, at deployment initiation black belt training should be conducted first so that this additional skill set can be used when coaching others.

Groupthink: The tendency where highly cohesive groups can lose their critical evaluative capabilities (Janis, 1971).

Half-normal probability plot: A normal probability plot where the absolute data measurements are plotted.

Hard savings: Savings that directly impact the bottom line.

Hazard rate (λ): The probability that a device will fail between times x and $x + dx$, after it has survived time (usage) x (i.e., a conditional probability of failure given survival to that time). At a given point in time, the hazard rate and instantaneous failure rate are equivalent.

Hidden factory: Reworks within an organization that have no value and are often not considered within the metrics of a factory.

Histogram: A frequency diagram in which bars proportionally in area to the class frequencies are erected on the horizontal axis. The width of each section corresponds to the class interval of the variate.

Homogeneous Poisson process (HPP): A model that considers that failure rate does not change with time.

Hoshin kanri: Japanese name for policy deployment. Used by some Lean companies to guide their operations strategy.

Hypergeometric distribution: A distribution of a discrete variate usually associated with sampling without replacement from a finite population.

Hypothesis: A tentative statement, which has a possible explanation to some event or phenomenon. Hypotheses are not a theoretical statement. Instead, hypotheses are to have a testable statement, which might include a prediction.

Hypothesis testing: Consists of a null hypothesis (H_0) and alternative hypothesis (H_a) where, for example, a null hypothesis indicates equality between two process outputs and an alternative hypothesis indicates non-equality. Through a hypothesis test, a decision is made whether to reject a null hypothesis or not reject a null hypothesis. When a null hypothesis is rejected, there is α risk of error. Most typically, there is no risk assignment when we fail to reject the null hypothesis. However, an appropriate sample size could be determined so that failure to reject the null hypothesis is made with β risk of error.

IEE: *See* Integrated enterprise excellence.

IEE scorecard/dashboard metric reporting process:
1. Assess process predictability.
2. When the process is considered predictable, formulate a prediction statement for the latest region of stability. The usual reporting format for this statement is:
   (a) When there is a specification requirement: nonconformance percentage or defects per million opportunities (DPMO)
   (b) When there are no specification requirements: median response and 80% frequency of occurrence rate

IEE Workout: See Workout (IEE).

Indifference quality level (IQL): Quality level is somewhere between AQL and RQL in acceptance sampling.

Individuals control chart: A control chart of individual values where between-subgroup variability affects the calculated upper and lower control limits; that is, the width between the upper and lower control limits increases when there is more between subgroup variability. When plotted individuals chart data is within the upper and lower control limits and there are no patterns, the process is said to be stable/predictable and typically referenced as an in control process. In IEE, this common cause state is referenced as a predictable process. Control limits are independent of specification limits or targets.

Inner array: The structuring in a Taguchi-style DOE the factors that can be controlled in a process (as opposed to an outer array).

In control: The description of a process where variation is consistent over time (i.e., only common causes exist). The process is predictable.

Inferential statistics: From the analysis of samples, we can make statements about the population's using inferential statistics. That is, properties of the population are inferred from the analysis of samples.

Information technology: Computer systems and applications, which involves development, installation, and/or implementation.

Infrequent subgrouping/sampling: Traditionally, rational subgrouping issues involve the selection of samples that yield relatively homogeneous conditions within the subgroup for a small region of time or space, perhaps five in a row. For an $\overline{x}$ and R chart, the within-subgroup variation defines the limits of the control chart on how much variation should exist between the subgroups. For a given situation, a differing subgrouping/sampling methodology can dramatically affect the measured variation within subgroups, which in turn affects the width of the control limits. For the high-level metrics of IEE, we want infrequent subgrouping/sampling so that short-term variations caused by KPIV perturbations are viewed as common cause variability; that is, typical process variability is to occur between subgroups in an individuals control chart. This type of control chart can reduce the amount of firefighting in an organization. However, this does not mean that a problem does not exist within the process. When process capability/performance metric improvements are needed for these metrics, we can initiate an IEE project (i.e., IEE projects are pulled into the system) as they are needed by the metrics.

Integrated Enterprise (process) Excellence (IEE, I double E): A roadmap for the creation of an enterprise process system in which organizations can significantly improve both customer satisfaction and their bottom line. IEE is a structured approach that guides organizations through the tracking and attainment of organizational goals. IEE goes well beyond traditional Lean Six Sigma and the balanced scorecard methods. IEE integrates enterprise process measures and improvement methodologies with tools such as Lean and Theory of constraints (TOC) in a never-ending pursuit of excellence. IEE becomes an enabling framework, which integrates, improves, and aligns with other initiatives such as Total Quality Management (TQM), ISO 9000, Malcolm Baldrige Assessments, and the Shingo Prize. IEE is the organizational orchestration that moves toward the achievement goal of the three Rs of Business; that is, everyone is doing the Right things and doing them Right at the Right time.

Intensity function: A function that was used to describe failure rate as a function of time (usage) in the NHPP.

Interaction: A description for the measure of the differential comparison of response for each level of a factor at each of the several levels of one or more other factors.

Interrelationship digraph (ID): A methodology that permits systematic identification, analysis, and classification of cause-and-effect relationships. From these relationships, teams can focus on key drivers or outcomes to determine effective solutions.

Inventory turns: The number of times that a company's inventory cycles or turns over per year.

ISO 9000: The International Organization for Standardization (ISO) series of developed and published standards. The intent of these standards is to define, establish, and maintain an effective quality assurance system in both manufacturing and service industries.

IT: *See* Information technology.

Jidoka (autonomation): A term used in Lean meaning automation with a human touch. This approach applies the following four principles: detect the abnormality, stop, fix or correct the immediate condition, and investigate the root cause and install a countermeasure.

Jim Collin's three circles: See Collin's three circles.

Just-in-time (JIT): An inventory management strategy where manufacturing material and component needs are immediately fulfilled by the supplier.

Kaikaku: Radical improvement.

Kaizen: Continuous incremental improvement.

Kaizen event or blitz: An intense short-term project that gives focus to improve a process. Substantial resources are committed during this event (e.g., Operators, Engineering, Maintenance, and others are available for immediate action). A facilitator directs the event, which usually includes training followed by analysis, design, and area rearrangement.

KPIV (Key Process Input Variable): Factors within a process correlated to an output characteristic(s) important to the internal or external customer. Optimizing and controlling these is vital to the improvement of the KPOV.

KPOV (Key Process Output Variable): Characteristic(s) of the output of a process that are important to the customer. Understanding what is important to the internal and external customer is essential to identifying KPOVs.

Knowledge-centered activity (KCA): A term used that means striving to obtain knowledge wisely and utilize it wisely.

Lack of fit: A value determined by using one of many statistical techniques stating probabilistically whether data can be shown not to fit a model. Lack of fit is used to assess the goodness-of-fit of a model to data. See residual error.

Lambda plot: A technique to determine a normalizing transformation for data.

Law of physics: A physical law or a law of nature that is considered true.

Lean: Improving operations and the supply chain with an emphasis on the reduction of wasteful activities such as waiting, transportation, material hand-offs, inventory, and overproduction.

Least squares: A method used in regression to estimate the equation coefficients and constant so that the sum of squares of the differences between the individual responses and the fitted model is a minimized.

Lead time: Time for one piece to move through a process or a value stream. Lean time can also describe the setup time to start a process.

Levels: The settings of factors in a factorial experiment (e.g., high and low levels of temperature).

Level Five System: Jim Collins (2001) describes in *Good to Great* a level five leader as someone who is not only great when he is leading an organization but the organization remains great after the person is no longer affiliated with the organization. I describe the level-five-leader-created legacy as being a *Level Five System*.

Linearity: The condition of being represented by a first order model.

Location parameter (x_0): A parameter in the three-parameter Weibull distribution that equates to the minimum value for the distribution.

Logic pass/fail response: *See* Response.

Logit (transformation): A type of data transformation sometimes advantageous in factorial analysis when data have an upper and lower bound restriction (e.g., 0–1 proportion defective).

Loss function: A continuous Taguchi function that measures the cost implications of product variability.

Malcolm Baldrige Award: An award that recognizes yearly up to five companies that demonstrate outstanding quality management systems. The award, started in 1986, would later become known as the Malcolm Baldrige National Quality Improvement Act which was created under the direction of ASQ and the National Institute of Standards and Technology. The Act established a national award that recognizes total quality management in American industry.

Main distribution: The main distribution is centered around an expected value of strengths, while a smaller freak distribution describes a smaller set of substandard products that are produced by random occurrences in a manufacturing process.

Main effect: An estimate of the effect of a factor measured independently of other factors.

Mallows C_p Statistic: A value used to determine the smallest number of parameters that should be used when building a model. The number of parameters corresponding to the minimum of this statistic is the minimum number of parameters to include during the model-building process.

Master black belts (MBBs): Black belts who have undertaken two weeks of advanced training and have a proven track record delivering results through various projects and project teams. They should be a dedicated resource to the deployment. Before they train, master black belts need to be certified in the material that they are to deliver. Their responsibilities include coaching black belts, monitoring team progress, and assisting teams when needed.

Maximum likelihood estimator (MLE): Maximum likelihood estimates are calculated through maximizing the likelihood function. For each set of distribution parameters, the likelihood function describes the chance that the true distribution has the parameters based on the sample.

Mean: The mean of a sample ($\bar{x}$) is the sum of all the responses divided by the sample size. The mean of a population (μ) is the sum of all responses of the population divided by the population·size. In a random sample of a population, ($\bar{x}$) is an estimate of μ of the population.

Mean square: Sum of squares divided by degrees of freedom.

Mean time between failures (MTBF): A term that can be used to describe the frequency of failures in a reparable system with a constant failure rate. MTBF = 1/failure rate.

Measurement systems: The complete process of obtaining measurements. This includes the collection of equipment, operations, procedures, software, and personnel that affects the assignment of a number to a measurement characteristic.

Measurement systems analysis: *See* Gage repeatability and reproducibility (R&R).

Measurement system error: The combined variation due to gage bias, repeatability, reproducibility, stability and linearity (AIAG, 2000).

Median: For a sample, the number that is in the middle when all observations are ranked in magnitude. For a population, the value at which the cumulative distribution function is 0.5.

Metric: a measurement that quantifies a particular characteristic.

Metrology: The Greek root of the word means "measurement science." That portion of measurement science used to provide, maintain, and disseminate a consistent set of units; to provide support for the enforcement of equity in trade by weights and measurement laws; or to provide data for quality control in manufacturing (Simpson, 1981).

Micrometer calipers: Calipers with a finely-threaded screw of definite pitch with a head graduated to show how much the screw has been moved in or out.

Mil: Unit of linear measurement equivalent to one thousandth of an inch.

Milk rounds: An application illustration is when a vehicle collects parts from several suppliers during an established route that starts and ends at the plant.

Mini kaizen: Recognizes that the best expert for a job is the person who does the job. Everyone is encouraged to make small improvements that are within their power to implement. The collection of thousands of small improvements have can have a major impact. Its implementation requires both conscious and sub-conscious day-to-day and minute-by-minute thinking about improvements by all employees. Required also is that these employees possess this type of thinking skills.

Mistake-proofing: A structured approach for process or design creation so that specific mistakes will not occur or which makes a mistake obvious at a glance (i.e., error-proofing or poke-yoke).

Mixture experiments: Variables are expressed as proportions of the whole and sum to unity. Measured responses are assumed to depend only on the proportions of the ingredients and not on the amount of the mixture.

Multicollinearity: When there exists near-linear dependencies between regressors, the problem of multicollinearity is said to exist. *See* Variance inflation factor (VIF).

Multimodal distribution: A combination of more than one distribution that has more than one distinct peak.

Multi-vari chart: A chart that is constructed to display the variation within units, between units, between samples, and between lots.

Natural tolerances of a process: Three standard deviations on either side of the mean.

Nested data: An experiment design where the trials are not fully randomized sets. In lieu of full randomization, trials are structured so that some factor considerations are randomized within other factor considerations.

Nonconformance: Failure to meet specification requirement.

Nominal group technique (NGT): A voting procedure to expedite team consensus on relative importance of problems, issues, or solutions.

Non-homogenous Poisson process (NHPP) with Weibull intensity: A mathematical model that can often be used to describe the failure rate of a reparable system that has a decreasing, constant, or increasing rate.

Non-reparable device: A term used to describe something that is discarded after it fails to function properly. Examples of a non-reparable device are a tire, spark plug, and the water pump in an automobile (if it is not rebuilt after a failure).

Nonreplicable testing: Destructive testing AIAG (2002).

Nonstationary process: A process with a level and variance that can grow without limit.

Normal distribution: A bell-shaped distribution that is often useful to describe various physical, mechanical, electrical, and chemical properties.

Null hypothesis (H_0): *See* Hypothesis testing.

Optical comparator: device to evaluate a part through the enlargement of its image.

One-at-a-time experiment: An individual tries to fix a problem by making a change and then executing a test. Depending on the findings, something else may need to be tried. This cycle is repeated indefinitely.

One piece flow: The production or procurement of one unit at a time, as opposed to large lots.

One-sided test: *See* Single-sided test.

One-way analysis of variance: *See* single-factor analysis of variance.

Ordinal: Possesses natural ordering.

Ordinate: The coordinate representing the distance from the x axis in a two-dimensional plot.

Orming model: Tuckman (1965) described the four stages of team development as forming, storming, norming, and performing. These stages are often referenced as the orming model.

Orthogonal: An experimental design is call orthogonal if observed variates or linear combinations of them are independent.

Outlier: A data point that does not fit a model because of an erroneous reading or some other abnormal situation.

Outer array: The structuring in a Taguchi-style DOE the factors that cannot be controlled in a process, as opposed to an inner array.

Out of control: Control charts exhibit special-cause conditions. The process is not predictable.

Pacemaker: The point in the overall process where Lean production is schedules.

Pareto chart: A graphical technique used to quantify problems so that effort can be expended in fixing the "vital few" causes, as opposed to the "trivial many." Named after Vilfredo Pareto (born 1848), an Italian economist.

Pareto principle: Eighty percent of the trouble comes from 20% of the problems (i.e., the vital few problems).

Part variation (PV): Related to measurement systems analysis, PV represents the expected part-to-part and time-to-time variation for a stable process (AIAG, 2002).

Pass/fail functional test: A test strategy described to determine whether a failure will occur given that the response is a logic pass/fail situation. *See* Response.

Passive analysis: In IEE and a traditional DMAIC, most Six Sigma tools are applied in the same phase. However, the term passive analysis is often used in IEE to describe the analyze phase, where process data are observed passively (i.e., with no process adjustments) in an attempt to find a causal relationship between input and output variables. It should be noted that improvements can be made in any of the phases. If there is "low-hanging fruit" identified during a brainstorming session in the measure phase, this improvement can be made immediately, yielding a dramatic improvement to the 30,000-foot-level output metric.

Path of steepest ascent: A methodology used to maximize the response of a process. A point of initiation for this strategy is a model built around current operating conditions, which can have several DOE-determined terms. Experiments are then conducted along the direction of steepest ascent (or descent) until there is no response improvement. At the point of no response improvement, another DOE is conducted with center points for determining a new search direction. This new steepest ascent search direction is perpendicular to the contours determined by the model.

Paynter chart: In this chart, increments of time (e.g., months) are on the horizontal axis. In the vertical axis there are customer problem classifications. At the intersection of the horizontal and vertical axes, the number of problem classification occurrences for the time period is noted.

P-DMAIC (Roadmap): An IEE project define–measure–analyze–improve–control roadmap for improvement project execution, which contains a true integration of Six Sigma and Lean tools.

Percent (%) R&R: The percentage of process variation related to the measurement system for repeatability and reproducibility.

Performance, Process: *See* Process performance.

Plan-do-check-act (PDCA) or Plan-do-study-act (PDSA): PDCA is frequently referred to as the Deming cycle or Shewhart cycle. The check step can be replaced by a study step; that is, PDSA. PDCA has the following components: Plan – Recognize a need for change then establish objectives and process for delivering desired results; Do – Implement change that is to be assessed; Check – study results and identify lessons learned; Act – Use lessons learned to take appropriate action. If change was not satisfactory repeat the process.

Point estimate: An estimate calculated from sample data without a confidence interval.

Poisson distribution: A discrete probability distribution where the probability of a number of events occurring in a fixed period of time has an average rate and is independent of the time since the last event. A distribution that is useful, for example, to design reliability tests, where the failure rate is considered to remain constant as a function of usage.

Population: Statistically a population is a group of data from a single distribution. In a practical sense, a population could also be considered to be a segment or a group of data from a single source or category. In the process of explaining tools and techniques, multiple populations may be discussed as originating from different sources, locations, or machines.

Precision: The net effect of discrimination, sensitivity, and repeatability over the operating range (size, range, and time) of the measurement system. In some organizations, precision is used interchangeably with repeatability. In fact, precision is most often used to describe the expected variation of repeated measurements over the range of measurement; that range may be size or time. The use of the more descriptive component terms is generally preferred over the term *precision* (AIAG, 2002).

Predictable: The control limits in a control chart are calculated from the data. Specifications in no way affect the control limits. This chart is a statement of the voice of the process (VOP) relative to whether the process is considered in statistical control or not (i.e., stable or not). Since people often have difficulty in understanding what *in control* means), I prefer to use the term *predictable* instead of *in control*.

Predictable process: A stable, controlled process where variation in outputs is only caused by natural or random variation in the inputs or in the process itself.

Prediction Interval: Describes a likely range for a single new observation at a specified predictor setting.

Preventive action: An action that is taken to eliminate from reoccurrence a potential nonconformity cause or other undesirable situation.

Proactive Testing: In IEE and a traditional DMAIC, most Six Sigma tools are applied in the same phase. The descriptive term proactive testing is often used within IEE to describe the improve phase. The reason for this is that within the improve DMAIC phase design of experiments (DOE), tools are typically used. In DOE you can make many adjustments to a process in a structured fashion, observing/analyzing the results collectively (i.e., proactively testing to make a judgment). It should be noted that improvements can be made in any of the phases. If there is low- hanging fruit identified during a brainstorming session in the measure phase, this improvement can be made immediately, yielding a dramatic improvement to the 30,000-foot-level output metric.

Probability (P): A numerical expression for the likelihood of an occurrence.

Probability density function (PDF) [$f(x)$]: A mathematical function that can model the probability density reflected in a histogram.

Probability plot: Data are plotted on a selected probability plot coordinate system to determine if a particular distribution is appropriate (i.e., the data plot as a straight line) and to make statements about percentiles of the population. The plot can be used to make prediction statements about stable/predictable processes.

Problem solving: The process of determining the cause from a symptom and then choosing an action to improve a process or product.

Process: A method to make or do something that involves a number of steps; a mathematical model such as the HPP (homogeneous Poisson process).

Process capability indices (C_p and C_{pk}): C_p is a measurement of the allowable tolerance spread divided by the actual 6σ data spread. C_{pk} has a similar ratio to that of C_p, except that this ratio considers the shift of the mean relative to the central specification target.

Process capability: AIAG (1995b) definition for the variables data case is 6σ range of a process's inherent variation; for statistically stable processes, where σ is usually estimated by $\overline{R}/d_2$. For the attribute data case, it is usually defined as the average proportion or rate of defects or defectives (e.g., center of an attribute control chart). The Boethe (1997) definition is: "Process capability is broadly defined as the ability of a process to satisfy consumer expectations."

Process capability/performance metric: IEE uses the term process capability/performance metric to describe a process's predictive output in terms that everyone can understand. The process to determine this metric is:
1. An infrequent subgrouping/sampling plan is determined so that the typical variability from process input factors occurs between subgroups (e.g., subgroup by day, week, or month).
2. The process is analyzed for predictability using control charts.
3. For the region of predictability, the non-compliant proportion or parts per million (ppm) are estimated and reported. If there are no specifications, the estimated median response and 80% frequency of occurrence are reported.

Process cycle efficiency: The amount of value-added process time divided by total lead time.

Process performance: The AIAG (1995b) definition is the 6σ range of a process's total variation, where σ is usually estimated by s, the sample standard deviation.

Process flow diagram (chart): Path of steps of work used to produce or do something.

Producer's risk: *See* Alpha (α) risk.

Project define-measure-analyze-improve-control: See P-DMAIC (Roadmap).

Pull: A Lean term that results in an activity when a customer or down-stream process step requests the activity. A homebuilder that builds houses only when an agreement is reached on the sale of the house is using a pull system. *See* push.

Pull for project creation: This term is derived from the Lean term, pull. An IEE deployment objective is that performance metric ownership is assigned through the business value chain, where metric tracking is at the 30,000-foot-level. In the E-DMAIC process, the enterprise is analyzed as a whole to determine what performance metrics need improvement and by how much so that whole-organizational goals can be met. These metric improvement needs would then create a pull for project creation. *See* push for project creation.

Pure error: See residual error.

Push: A Lean term that results in an activity that a customer or down-stream process step has not specifically requested. This activity can create excessive waste and/or inventory. A homebuilder that builds houses on the speculation of sale is using a push system. If the house does not sell promptly upon completion, the homebuilder has created excess inventory for his company, which can be very costly. *See* pull.

Push for project creation: This term is derived from the Lean term, push. Lean Six Sigma deployments are to create and execute projects that are to be beneficial to the business. However, when assessing the typical Lean Six Sigma project selection process we note that either a deployment steering committee or some level of management selects projects from a list that they and others think are important. For this type of deployment, for example, there is often a scurry to determine a project to work on during training. I refer this system as a push for project creation; that is, people are hunting for projects because they need to get certified or whatever. With this deployment system, there can be initial successes since agree-to low hanging fruit projects can often be readily identified and provide significant benefits; however, it has been my experience that this system of project determination is not typically long lasting. After some period of time, people have a hard time defining and/or agreeing to what projects should be undertaken. In addition, this project creation system does not typically look at the system as a whole when defining projects to undertake. This system of project selection can lead to suboptimization, which could be detrimental enterprise as a whole. Finally, this Lean Six Sigma deployment system typically creates a separate function entity that manages the deployment, which is separate from operational scorecards and functional units. In time, people in these functions can be very visible on the corporate radar screen when downsizing forces occur or their in a change in executive management, even thought the function has been claiming much past success. *See* pull for project creation.

***P* value or *P*:** The significance level for a term in a model.

Qualitative factor: A factor that has categorical levels. For example, product origination where the factor levels are supplier A, supplier B, and supplier C.

Quantitative factor: A factor that is continuous. For example, a product can be manufactured with a process temperature factor between 50°C and 80°C.

Quality function deployment (QFD): A technique that is used, for example, to get the voice of the customer in the design of a product.

Radar chart: A chart that is sometimes called a spider chart. The chart is a two-dimensional chart of three or more quantitative variables represented on axes originating from the same point.

Randomizing: A statistical procedure used to avoid bias possibilities as the result of influence of systematic disturbances, which are either known or unknown.

Random: Having no specific pattern.

Random effects (or components of variance) model: A factorial experiment where the variance of factors is investigated, as opposed to a fixed effects model.

Range: For a set of numbers, the absolute difference between the largest and smallest value.

Ranked sample values: Sample data that are listed in order relative to magnitudes.

Reference value: A measurand value that is recognized and serves as an agreed-upon reference or master value for comparisons. This can be: a theoretical or established value based on scientific principles; an assigned value based on some national or international organization; a consensus value based on collaborative experimental work under the auspices of a scientific or engineering group; or, for a specific application, an agreed-upon value obtained using an accepted reference method. A reference value is consistent with the definition of a specific quantity and is accepted, sometimes by convention, as appropriate for a given purpose. Other terms used synonymously with reference value are accepted reference value, accepted value, conventional value, conventional true value, assigned value, best estimate of the value, master value, and master measurement (AIAG, 2002).

Regression analysis: Data collected from an experiment are used to quantify empirically through a mathematical model the relationship that exists between the response variable and influencing factors. In a simple linear regression model, $y = b_0 + b_1 x + \varepsilon$, x is the regressor, y is the expected response, b_0 and b_1 are coefficients, and ε is random error.

Regressor: *See* Regression analysis.

Reject quality level (RQL): The level of quality that is considered unsatisfactory when developing a test plan.

Reliability: The proportion surviving at some point in time during the life of a device. Can also be a generic description of tests which are conducted to evaluate failure rates.

Reparable system: A system that can be repaired after experiencing a failure.

Repeatability: The variability resulting from successive trials under defined conditions of measurement. Often referred to as equipment variation (EV); however, this can be a misleading term. The best term for repeatability is *within*-system variation when the conditions of measurement are fixed and defined (i.e., fixed part, instrument, standard, method, operator, environment, and assumptions). In addition to within-equipment variation, repeatability will include all within variation from the conditions in the measurement error model. (AAIG, 2002)

Replication: Test trials that are made under identical conditions.

Reproducibility: The variation in the average of measurements caused by a normal condition(s) of change in the measurement process. Typically, it has been defined as the variation in average measurements of the same part between different appraisers (operators) using the same measurement instrument and method in a stable environment. This is often true for manual instruments influenced by the skill of the operator. It is not true, however, for measurement processes (i.e., automated systems), where the operator is not a major source of variation. For this reason, reproducibility is referred to as the average variation *between*-systems or *between*-conditions of measurement. (AIAG, 2002)

Residuals: In an experiment, the differences between experimental responses and predicted values that are determined from a model.

Residual error: Also call experimental error. An ANOVA output can list residual error as having a pure error and lack-of-fit component. Pure error is represented by replicates since the differences between observed responses are caused by random variation. During model term reduction when a resulting lack-of-fit P value is less than the selected α level, the term that was removed from the model should be retained.

Resolution III: A DOE where main effects and two-factor interaction effects are confounded.

Resolution IV: A DOE where the main effects and two-factor interaction effects are not confounded; however, two-factor interaction effects are confounded with each other.

Resolution V: A DOE where all main effects and two-factor interaction effects are not confounded with other main effects or two-factor interaction effects.

Resolution V+: Full factorial designed experiment.

Response: Three described outputs are continuous (variables), attribute (discrete), and logic pass/fail. A response is said to be continuous if any value can be taken between limits (e.g., 2, 2.0001, and 3.00005). A response is said to be attribute if the evaluation takes on a pass/fail proportion output; for example, 999 out of 1000 sheets of paper on the average can be fed through a copier without a jam. In this series of volumes, a response is considered to be logic pass/fail if combinational considerations are involved that are said always to cause an event either to pass or fail; for example, a computer display design will not work in combination with a particular keyboard design and software package.

Response surface methodology (RSM): The empirical study of relationships between one or more responses and input variable factors. The technique is used to determine the *best* set of input variables to optimize a response and/or gain a better understanding of the overall system response.

Risk priority number (RPN): Product of severity, occurrence, and detection rankings within an FMEA. The ranking of RPN prioritizes design concerns; however, issues with a low RPN still deserve special attention if the severity ranking is high.

Rolled throughput yield (RTY): For a process that has a series of steps, RTY is the product of yields for each step.

Robust: A description of a procedure that is not sensitive to deviations from some of its underlying assumptions.

Robust DOE: A DOE strategy where focus is given within the design to the reduction of variability.

Root cause analysis: A study to determine the reason for a process nonconformance. Removal or correction of the root cause eliminates future nonconformance from this source.

Rotatable: A term used in response surface designs. A design is said to be rotatable if the variance of the predicted response at some point is a function of only the distance of the point from the center.

Run: A group of consecutive observations either all greater than or all less than some value.

Run (control chart): A consecutive number of points, for example, that are consistently decreasing, increasing, or on one side of the central line in a control chart.

Run chart: A time series plot permits the study of observed data for trends or patterns over time, where the *x*-axis is time and the *y*-axis is the measured variable.

Run-in: A procedure to put usage on a machine within the manufacturing facility for the purpose of capturing early-life failures before shipment. *See* Screen (in manufacturing).

Sample: A selection of items from a population.

Sampling distribution: A distribution obtained from a parent distribution by random sampling.

Sample size: The number of observations made or the number of items taken from a population.

Sarbanes-Oxley (SOX): This legislation act was created in 2002 partly in response to the Enron and WorldCom financial scandals. SOX protects shareholder and the public from enterprise process accounting errors and from fraudulent practices. In addition, it also ensures a degree of consistency in access to and reporting of information that could impact the value of a company's stock.

Satellite-level: Used to describe a high-level IEE business metric that has infrequent subgrouping/sampling so that short-term variations, which are caused by typical variation from key process input variables, will result in control charts that view these as common-cause variabilty. This metric has no calendar boundaries and the latest region of stability can be used to provide a predictive statement for the future.

Scale parameter: *See* Characteristic life (*k*).

Scatter plot: A plot to assess the relationship between two variables. A scatter plot is sometimes called a scatterplot or a scatter diagram.

Scorecard: A scorecard helps manage an organization's performance through the optimization and alignment of organizational units, business processes, and individuals. A scorecard can also provide goals and targets, which is to help individuals understand their organizational contribution. Scorecards span the operational, tactical and strategic business aspects and decisions. A dashboard displays information so that an enterprise can be run effectively. A dashboard organizes and presents information in a format that is easy to read and to interpret. In this series of volumes, I make reference to the IEE performance measurement as either a scorecard or scorecard/dashboard.

Screening experiment: A first step of a multiple factorial experiment strategy, where the experiment assesses primarily the significance of main effects. Two-factor interactions are normally considered in the experiments that follow a screening experiment. Screening experiments should typically consume only 25% of the monies that are allotted for the total experiment effort to solve a problem.

Screen (in manufacturing): A process step in the manufacturing process that is used to capture marginal product performance problems before the product is shipped to a customer. A burn-in or run-in test is a test that could be considered a screen for an electro-mechanical device.

Sensei: Teacher or mentor.

Sensitivity: Smallest input signal that results in a detectable (discernible) output signal for a measurement device. An instrument should be at least as sensitive as its unit of discrimination. Sensitivity is determined by inherent gage design and quality, in-service maintenance, and operating condition. Sensitivity is reported in units of measurement (AIAG, 2002).

Shape parameter (*b*): A parameter used in the Weibull distribution that describes the shape of the distribution and is equal to the slope of a Weibull probability plot.

Shewhart control chart: Dr. Shewhart is credited with developing the standard control chart test based on 3σ limits to separate the steady component of variation from assignable causes.

Shingo prize: Established in 1988, the prize promotes awareness of Lean manufacturing concepts and recognizes United States, Canada, and Mexico companies that achieve world-class manufacturing status. The philosophy is that world-class business performance may be achieved through focused core manufacturing and business process improvements.

Sigma: The Greek letter (σ) that is often used to describe the standard deviation of a population.

Sigma level or sigma quality level: A quality that is calculated by some to describe the capability of a process to meet specification. Some have stated that a six sigma quality level equates to a 3.4 ppm rate, while others have reported this same value in dpmo units. Pat Spagon from Motorola University prefers to distinguish between sigma as a measure of spread and sigma used in sigma quality level (Spagon, 1998).

Significance: A statistical statement indicating that the level of a factor causes a difference in a response with a certain degree of risk of being in error.

Single-factor analysis of variance ANOVA: One-way analysis of variance with two levels (or treatments) that is to determine if there is a statistically significant difference between level effects.

Single-sided test: A statistical consideration where, for example, an alternative hypothesis is that the mean of a population is less than a criterion value. *See* double-sided test.

SIPOC (supplier–input–process–output–customer): A tool that describes the events from trigger to delivery at the targeted process. Provides a snapshot of workflows, where the process aspect of the diagram consists of only 4–7 blocks.

Six Sigma: A term coined by Motorola that emphasizes the improvement of processes for the purpose of reducing variability and making general improvements. GE in the mid-1990's expanded the scope of Six Sigma so that it became a project based selection and execution system with a support infrastructure, where project were to have organizational benefits.

SMART goals: Not everyone uses the same letter descriptors for SMART. My preferred descriptors are italicized in the following list: S: *specific*, significant, stretching; M: *measurable*, meaningful, motivational; A: agreed upon, attainable, achievable, acceptable, action-oriented, *actionable*; R: realistic, *relevant*, reasonable, rewarding, results-oriented; T: *time-based*, timely, tangible, trackable.

Smarter Six Sigma Solutions (S⁴): Term used to describe the *wise* and often unique application of statistical techniques to create meaningful measurements and effective improvements.

Smarter Six Sigma Solutions assessment (S⁴ assessment): A term introduced in Breyfogle (2003a). The methodology uses statistically-based concepts while determining the *best* question to answer from the point of view of the customer. Assessment is made to determine if the right measurements and the right actions are being conducted. This includes noting that there are usually better questions to ask to protect the customer than "What sample do I need?" or "What one thing should I do next to fix this problem?", (i.e., a one-at-a-time approach). IEE resolution may involve putting together what often traditionally are considered separated statistical techniques in a smart fashion to address various problems.

Socratic Method: A method that uses dialect for philosophical inquiry. Typically, at any point in time, it involves two speakers where the discussion is led by one person and the other agrees to certain assumptions put forward for his/her acceptance or rejection. Socratic dialog happens when two people seek to answer a question through reflecting and thinking. This dialog starts from the concrete, asking all sorts of questions until details are uncovered, which serves as a platform for making more general judgments.

Soft savings: Savings that do not directly impact the financial statement as do hard savings. Possible soft savings' categories are cost avoidance, lost profit avoidance, productivity improvements, profit enhancement, and other intangibles.

Soft skills: A person who effectively facilitates meetings and works well with other people has good soft skills.

Space (functional): A description of the range of factor levels that describe how a product will be used in customer applications.

Span time: Cycle time for specific task.

Special cause: Variation in a process from a cause that is not an inherent part of that process. That is, it's not a common cause.

Specification: A criterion that is to be met by a part or product.

Stability: Refers to both statistical stability of measurement process and measurement stability over time. Both are vital for a measurement system to be adequate for its intended purpose. Statistical stability implies a predictable, underlying measurement process operating within common-cause variation.

Stakeholders: Those people or organizations who is not directly involved with project work but are affected its success or can influence its results. Example stakeholders are process owners, managers affected by the project, and people who work in the studied process. Stakeholders also include internal departments, which support the process, finance, suppliers, and customers.

Standard deviation (σ, s): A mathematical quantity that describes the variability of a response. It equals the square root of variance. The standard deviation of a sample (s) is used to estimate the standard deviation of a population (σ).

Standard error: The square root of the variance of the sampling distribution of a statistic.

Stationary process: A process with an ultimate constant variance.

Statistical process control (SPC): The application of statistical techniques in the control of processes. SPC is often considered a subset of SQC, where the emphasis in SPC is on the tools associated with the process but not on product acceptance techniques.

Statistical quality control (SQC): The application of statistical techniques in the control of quality. SQC includes the use of regression analysis, tests of significance, acceptance sampling, control charts, distributions, and so on.

Stem-and-leaf diagram: Constructed much like a tally column for creating a histogram, except that the last digit of the data value is recorded in the plot instead of a tally mark.

Stock options: A stock option is a specific type of option with a stock as the underlying instrument (i.e., the security that the value of the option is based on). A contract to buy is known as a call contract, while a contract to sell is known as a put contract.

Stories: An explanation for the up-and-down from previous quarter or yearly scorecard/dashboard metrics. This is not dissimilar to a nightly stock market report of the previous day's activity, where the television or radio reporter gives a specific reason for even small market movements. This form of reporting provides little, if any, value when it comes to making business decisions for a data-driven company.

Stratified random sampling: Samples can be either from random sampling with replacement or random sampling without replacement. In addition, there are more complex forms of sampling such as stratified random sampling. For this form of sampling, a certain number of random samples are drawn and analyzed from divisions to the population space.

Stress test: A test of devices outside usual operating conditions in an attempt to find marginal design parameters.

Structured inventive thinking (SIT): A method of developing creative solutions to technical problems that are conceptual. Focus is given to the essence of the problem by the problem solver. The method is designed to efficiently overcome psychological barriers to creative thinking, enabling the discovery of inventive solutions. This is a modified version of the Israeli systematic inventive-thinking, problem-solving methodology. The methodology is sometimes referenced in the 8D problem-solving methodology.

Supermarket: An inventory of parts that are controlled for the production scheduling of an upstream process.

Subcause: In a cause-and-effect diagram, the specific items or difficulties that are identified as factual or potential causes of the problem.

Subgrouping: Traditionally, rational subgrouping issues involve the selection of samples that yield relatively homogeneous conditions within the subgroup for a small region of time or space, perhaps five in a row. Hence, the within-subgroup variation defines the limits of the control chart on how much variation should exist between the subgroups. For a given situation, differing subgrouping/sampling methodologies can dramatically affect the measured variation within subgroups, which in turn affects the width of the control limits. For the high-level metrics of IEE, we want infrequent subgrouping/sampling so that typical short-term KPIV perturbations are viewed as common-cause variabiltiy. A 30,000-foot-level individuals control chart, which is created with infrequent subgrouping/sampling, can reduce the amount of firefighting in an organization. However, this does not mean that a problem does not exist within the process. IEE describes approaches to view the process capability/performance metric, or how well the process meets customer specifications or overall business needs. When improvements are needed to a process capability/performance metric, we can create an IEE project that focuses on this need (i.e., IEE projects are pulled for creation when metric improvements are needed).

Sum of squares (SS): The summation of the squared deviations relative to zero, to level means, or the grand mean of an experiment.

Swim lane flowchart: A swim lane is a rectangular flowchart region for the placement of activities. Parallel rectangular regions form swim lanes that can be used to describe, for example, task-completion activities within and cross functional boundaries; (e.g., departments in an organizational).

System: Devices that collectively perform a function. In this volume, systems are considered reparable, where a failure is caused by failure of a device(s). System failure rates can either be constant or change as a function of usage (time). See Breyfogle (2003).

System inventive thinking: A problem-solving methodology developed in Israel and inspired by a Russian methodology called TRIZ. Innovations were added that simplified the learning and application of the problem- solving methodology. These included the closed-world diagram, the qualitative-change graph, the particles method (an improvement on "smart little people" of the TRIZ method), and a simplified treatment of the solution techniques which the Israelis call "tricks". Whereas TRIZ stresses the use of databases of effects, the Israeli method stresses making the analyst an independent problem solver (Sickafus, 1997).

Taguchi philosophy: This volume supports G. Taguchi's basic philosophy of reducing product/process variability for the purpose of improving quality and decreasing the loss to society; however, the procedures used to achieve this objective are often different.

Takt Time: Customer demand rate (e.g., available work time per shift divided by customer demand rate per shift).

Tensile strength: Obtained by dividing the maximum load a part can withstand before fracture by the original cross-sectional area of the part.

Test coverage: The percent of possible combinations of group sizes (e.g., 3) evaluated in a pass/fail functional test (e.g., for a given test) there might be 90% test coverage of the levels of three-factor combinational considerations.

Test performance ratio (ρ): For a reliability test using the Poisson distribution, the ratio of the sample failure rate to the criterion (ρ_t / ρ_a).

Test: Assessment of whether an item meets specified requirements by subjecting the item to a set of physical, environmental, chemical, or operating actions/conditions.

The balanced scorecard: See Balanced scorecard (the).

Theory of constraints (TOC): Constraints can be broadly classified as being internal resource, market, or policy. The outputs of a system are a function of the whole system, not just individual processes. System performance is a function of how well constraints are identified and managed. When we view our system as a whole, we realize that the output is a function of the weakest link. The weakest link of the system is the constraint. If care is not exercised, we can be focusing on a subsystem that, even though improved, does not impact the overall system output. We need to focus on the orchestration of efforts so that we optimize the overall system, not individual pieces. Unfortunately, organization charts lead to workflow by function, which can result in competing forces within the organization. With TOC, systems are viewed as a whole and work activities are directed so that the whole system performance measures are improved.

Three Rs of business: Everyone doing the Right things and doing them Right at the Right time.

30,000-foot-level: A Six Sigma KPOV, CTQ, or Y variable response that is used in IEE to describe a high-level project or operation metric that has infrequent subgrouping/sampling so that short-term variations, which might be caused by typical KPIV swings, will result in charts that view these perturbations as common cause variability. It is not the intent of the 30,000-foot-level control chart to provide timely feedback for process intervention and correction, as traditional control charts do. Representative 30,000-foot-level metrics are lead time, inventory, defective rates, and a critical part dimension. There can be a drill down to a 20,000-foot-level metric if there is an alignment (e.g., the largest product defect type). A 30,000-foot-level individuals control chart can reduce the amount of firefighting in an organization when used to report operational metrics. As a business metric, 30,000-foot-level reporting can lead to more efficient resource utilization and less playing games with the numbers.

Throughput, TOC: The rate of generating money in an organization. This is a financial value-add metric which equates to revenues minus variable costs.

Time-line chart: Identification of the specific start, finish, and amount of time required to complete an activity.

Time-value diagram: A Lean tool that can describe a process or series of process steps from concept to launch to production, order to delivery to disposition, or raw materials to customer receipt to disposal. It consists of steps that add value to a product. Within Lean, steps are eliminated that do not add value, where a product can be tangible or intangible.

Titration: The process of determining how much of a substance is in a known volume of a solution by measuring the volume of a solution of known concentration added to produce a given reaction.

TOC: *See* Theory of constraints.

TOC throughput: *See* Throughput, TOC.

Total quality management (TQM): A management program, which worked on continuous product/service improvements through workforce involvement.

Toyota production system (TPS): Toyota developed techniques that focus on adding value and reducing waste through setup, lead time, and lot size reduction. The term has become synonymous with Lean manufacturing.

TQM: *See* Total quality management.

Treatment: *See* Levels.

Trend chart: Shows data trends over time. A trend chart is sometimes called a run chart.

Trial: One of the factor combinations in an experiment.

TRIZ: (pronounced "trees") TRIZ is a problem-solving methodology invented by Henry Altshuller in the former Soviet Union in 1947. TRIZ is a Russian acronym for the theory of solving inventive problems (Sickafus, 1997).

t test: A statistical test that utilizes tabular values from the *t* distribution to assess, for example, whether two population means are different.

20,000-foot-level: A cascading of a 30,000-foot-level metric, which still has infrequent subgrouping/sampling. A 20,000-foot-level metric could be the tracking of the largest defect from a 30,000-foot-level metric. Another 20,000-foot-level metric could be the cascading of a corporate on-time delivery 30,000-foot-level metric to one site's on-time delivery performance.

Type I error: *See* Alpha (α) risk.

Type II error: *See* Beta (β) risk.

Type III error: Answering the wrong question.

Two-sided test: *See* Double-sided test.

Uncensored data: All sample data have failed or have a reading.

Uncertainty (δ): An amount of change from a criterion that is considered acceptable. The parameter is used when considering β risk in sample size calculation.

Unified Structured Inventive Thinking (USIT): Sickafus (1997) describes the process, which evolved from the structured inventive thinking (SIT) process, which is referenced sometimes as part of the 8D problem-solving process (see Breyfogle, 2003a).

Uniform precision design: A type of central composite response surface design where the number of center points is chosen so that there is more protection against bias in the regression coefficients.

Unimodal: A distribution that has one peak.

Usage: During a life test, the measure of time on test. This measurement could, for example, be in units of power-on hours, test days, or system operations.

Validation: Proof after implementation of an action over time that the action does what is intended. See Verification.

Value-added (VA) time: The execution time for the work elements for which a customer is willing to pay.

Value chain: Describes in flowchart fashion both primary and support organizational activities and their accompanying 30,000-foot-level or satellite-level metrics. Example primary activity flow is develop product – market product – sell product – produce product – invoice/collect payments – report satellite-level metrics. Example support activities include IT, finance, HR, labor relations, safety & environment, and legal.

Value stream mapping: At Toyota, value stream mapping is known as "material and information flow mapping." In the Toyota production system, current and future states/ideal states are depicted by practitioners when they are developing plans to install Lean systems. Attention is given to establishing flow, eliminating waste, and adding value. Toyota views manufacturing flows as material, information, and people/process. The described value stream mapping covers the first two of these three items (Rother and Shook, 1999).

Variables data (Continuous data): Data that can assume a range of numerical responses on a continuous scale, as opposed to data that can assume only discrete levels.

Variables: Factors within a designed experiment.

Variance (Finance): Difference between actual and budget.

Variance (Statistical) [σ^2, s^2]: A measure of dispersion of observations based upon the mean of the squared deviations from the arithmetic mean.

Variance inflation factor (VIF): A calculated quantity for each term in a regression model that measures the combined effect of the dependencies among the regressors on the variance of that term. One or more large VIFs can indicate multicollinearity.

Variate: A random variable that has a numerical value defined for a given sample space.

Validation is proof after implementation of an action over time and that the action does what is intended. *See* verification.

Verification: The act of establishing and documenting whether processes, items, services, or documents conform to a specified requirement. Verification is proof before implementation that an action does what is intended. *See* validation.

Visual factory: Management by sight. Visual factory involves the collection and display of real-time information to the entire workforce at all times. Work cell bulletin boards and other easily-seen media might report information about orders, production schedules, quality, delivery performance, and financial health of business.

Voice of the customer (VOC): The identification and prioritization of true customer needs and requirements, which can be accomplished through focus groups, interviews, data analyses, and other methods.

Voice of the process (VOP): A quantification of what the process delivers. A voice of the process to voice of the customer needs assessment can identify process improvement focus areas (e.g., a 30,000-foot-level assessment indicates an 11% delivery-time non-conformance rate).

Waste: Seven elements to consider for the elimination of muda, a Japanese term for waste, are correction, overproduction, processing, conveyance, inventory, motion, and waiting.

Wear-out failures: *See* Bathtub curve.

Weibull distribution: This distribution has a density function that has many possible shapes. The two-parameter distribution is described by the shape parameter *(b)* and the location parameter *(k)*. This distribution has an x-intercept value at the low end of the distribution that approaches zero (i.e., zero probability of a lower value). The three-parameter distribution has, in addition to the other parameters, the location parameter (x_0), which is the lowest x-intercept value.

Weibull slope (*b*): *See* Shape parameter (*b*).

WIP: A general description for inventory that is being processed within an operation or is awaiting another operation.

Work in process (WIP): *See* WIP.

Work in progress (WIP): *See* WIP.

Workout (IEE): An IEE workout is a week-long concentrated effort to build the E-DMAIC framework (i.e., a kaizen event to create the E-DMAIC framework). Typically on Monday there is a one-day executive workshop, which among other things describes IEE and its structure. On Tuesday through Wednesday the facilitator works with an IEE in-house technical team and others to build the E-DMAIC framework with its process drilldowns. On Friday, a two-hour report out of the customization of the E-DMAIC system, as described on Monday, is presented to the executive team that attended the Monday session. This presentation will include, among other things, a comparison of a sample of their 30,000-foot-level metric report outs with their current reporting methods. After the week-long session, the workout facilitator will continue work with the IEE in-house technical team to continually refine their E-DMAIC system.

Yellow belts (YBs): Process improvement team members who typically receive three-days of training, which helps them in the effectiveness of their participation in project execution such as data collection, identifying voice of the customer, and team meetings.

References

Affourtit, B. B. (1986), Statistical Process Control (SPC) Implementation Common Misconceptions, *Proc. 39th Ann. Qual. Cong.*, American Society for Quality Control, pp. 440–445.

AIAG (1995a), *Advanced Product Quality Planning (APQP) and Control Plan Reference Manual*, Chrysler Corporation, Ford Motor Company, General Motors Corporation.

AIAG (1995b), *Statistical Process Control (SPC) Reference Manual*, Third edition, Chrysler Corporation, Ford Motor Company, General Motors Corporation.

AIAG (2001), *Potential Failure Mode and Effects Analysis (FMEA) Reference Manual*, Chrysler Corporation, Ford Motor Company, General Motors Corporation.

AIAG (2002), Automotive Industry Action Group, *Measurement Systems Analysis (MSA) Reference Manual*, Third edition, Chrysler Corporation, Ford Motor Company, General Motors Corporation.

Altshuller, G. (1998), *40 Principles: TRIZ Keys to Technical Innovation*, Technical Innovation Center, Worcester, MA.

Altshuller, G. (2001), *And Suddenly the Inventor Appeared: TRIZ, the Theory of Inventive Problem Solving*, Technical Innovation Center, Inc. Worcester, MA.

American Society for Quality (1983), *Glossary and Tables for Statistical Quality Control*, ASQ, Milwaukee, WI.

APQC (2001), *Benchmarking Study: Deploying Six Sigma to Bolster Business Processes and the Bottom Line*, APQC, Houston, TX.

ASQ (2002), *Certified Six Sigma Black Belt Body of Knowledge Brochure*, ASQ, Milwaukee, WI.

Austin, (2004), http://www.ci.austin.tx.us/budget/eperf/index.cfm.

Babich, P. (2005), *Hoshin Handbook*, Third edition, Total Quality Engineering. Poway, CA.

Berger, R. W., Donald, W. B., Ahmad, K. E., and Walker, H. F. (2002), *The Certified Quality Engineer Handbook*, ASQ, Milwaukee, WI.

Bicheno, J. (2004), *The New Lean Tool Box: Towards Fast, Flexible Flow*, Production and Inventory Control, Systems and Industrial Engineering Books, Buckingham, England.

Bierman, H. Jr. (1992), *Capital Budgeting in 1992*.

Box, G. E. P., Hunter, W. G., and Hunter, S. J. (1978), *Statistics for Experimenters*, Wiley, New York.

Brassard, M., and Ritter, D. (1994), *The Memory Jogger II*, GOAL/QPC, MA.

Breyfogle, F. W., Gomez, D. McEachron, N., Millham, E., and Oppenheim, A. (1991), A Design and Test Roundtable – Six Sigma: Moving Towards Perfect Products, *IEEE Design and Test of Computers*, Los Alamitos, CA, June, pp. 88–89.

Breyfogle, F. W. (1992), Process Improvement with Six Sigma, *Wescon/92 Conference Record*, Western Periodicals Company, Ventura, CA, pp. 754–756.

Breyfogle, F. W. (1992), *Statistical Methods for Testing, Development, and Manufacturing*, Wiley, Hoboken, NJ.

Breyfogle, F. W., Cupello, J. M., and Meadows, B (2001a) *Managing Six Sigma: A Practical Guide to Understanding, Assessing, and Implementing the Strategy that Yields Bottom-Line Success,* Wiley, New York.

Breyfogle, F. W., Enck, D., Flories, P., and Pearson, T. (2001b), *Wisdom on the Green: Smarter Six Sigma Business Solutions,* Smarter Solutions, Inc., Austin, TX.

Breyfogle, F. W. (2003a), *Implementing Six Sigma: Smarter Solutions® using Statistical Methods,* Second edition, Wiley, Hoboken, NJ.

Breyfogle., F. W. (2003b), "Control Charting at the 30,000-foot-level: Separating special-cause events from common-cause variability," *Quality Progress,* November pp. 67–70.

Breyfogle, F. W. (2004a), "Starting a Six Sigma Initiative," *Six Sigma, Ask the Expert,* http://www.isixsigma.com/library/content/ask-05.asp.

Breyfogle, F. W. (2004b), "Control Charting at the 30,000-foot-level, Part 2," *Quality Progress,* Nov. pp. 85–87.

Breyfogle, F. W., and Arvind, S. (2004b), *Lean Six Sigma in Sickness and in Health,* Smarter Solutions, Inc., Austin, TX.

Breyfogle, F. W. (2004c), *XmR Control Charts and Data Normality,* February 15, 2004, www.smartersolutions.com/pdfs/XmRControlChartDataNormality.pdf.

Breyfogle, F. W. (2005a), "21 Common Problems (and What To Do About Them)," *Six Sigma Forum Magazine,* pp. 35–37.

Breyfogle, F. W. (2005b), "Control Charting at the 30,000-foot-level, Part 3," *Quality Progress, 3.4 per Million Series,* November. pp. 66–70.

Breyfogle, F. W. (2006), "Control Charting at the 30,000-foot-level, Part 4," *Quality Progress, 3.4 per Million Series,* November. pp. 59–62.

Breyfogle, F. W. (2008a), *Integrated Enterprise Excellence Volume I – The Basics: Four Golfing Buddies Going Beyond Lean Six Sigma and the Balanced Scorecard,* Bridgeway Books, Austin, TX.

Breyfogle, F. W. (2008b), *Integrated Enterprise Excellence Volume II – Business Deployment: A Leaders' Guide for Going Beyond Lean Six Sigma and the Balanced Scorecard,* Bridgeway Books, Austin, TX.

Breyfogle, F. W. (2008c), *Integrated Enterprise Excellence Volume III – Improvement Project Execution: A Management and Black Belt Guide for Going Beyond Lean Six Sigma and the Balanced Scorecard*, Bridgeway Books, Austin, TX.

Breyfogle, F. W. (2008d), *The Integrated Enterprise Excellence System: An Enhanced Approach to Balanced Scorecards, Strategic Planning and Business Improvement*, Bridgeway Books, Austin, TX.

Brush, G. G. (1988), *How to Choose the Proper Sample Size,* American Society for Quality Control, Milwaukee, WI.

Callandra, A. (1968), "A Modern Parable," *Saturday Review*, December 21.

Cheser, R. (1994), Kaizen is More than Continuous Improvement, *Quality Progress*, pp. 23–25.

Collins, Jim (2001), *Good to Great: Why Some Companies Make the Leap. and Others Don't*, HarperCollins Publishers Inc., New York, NY.

Conover, W. J. (1980), *Practical Nonparametric Statistics*, Second edition, Wiley.

Cowley, M., and Domb, E. (1997), *Beyond Strategic Vision: Effective Corporate Action with Hoshin Planning*, Elsevier, Burlington, MA.

Cunningham, J. E., and Fiume, O. J. (2003), *Real Numbers: Management Accounting in a Lean Organization*, Managing Times Press, Durham, NC.

Davenport, T. H., and Harris, J. G. *Competing on Analytics: The New Science of Winning*, Harvard Business School Publishing Corp., Boston, MA.

De Bono, E. (1999), *Six Thinking Hats*, Little, Brown and Company, New York.

Deming, W. E. (1982), *Quality, Productivity and Competitive Position,* MIT Center for Advanced Engineering Study, Cambridge, MA.

Deming, W. E. (1986), *Out of the Crisis*, Massachusetts Institute of Technology, Cambridge, MA.

Dettmer, H. W. (1995), Quality and the Theory of Constraints, *Quality Progress*, April, 77–81.

Diamond, W. J. (1989), *Practical Experiment Designs for Engineers and Scientists*, Van Nostrand Reinhold, New York.

Dodd, C. W. (1992), Design for "X", *IEEE Potentials*, October, pp. 44–46.

Draper, N. R., and Smith, H. (1966), *Applied Regression Analysis*, Wiley, New York.

Drucker, P. F. (1954), *The Practice of Management*, Peter F. Drucker.

Enck, D. (2002), contributed Sections 15.20, 15.22, and 37.3.

Emerald Hills Strategy (2004) http://www.emeraldhillsstrategy.com/dashboard.html.

Ferrel, E. B. (1958), *Plotting Experimental Data on Normal or Lognormal Probability Paper* 15(1), pages 12–15.

Fiume, O. J. (2006), "Management Accounting for Lean Businesses," Connecticut Quality Council Presentation, October 4.

Foxconn (2006), Foxconn Strategy, http://www.foxconn.com/about/strategy.asp.

Goldratt, E. M. (1992), *The Goal*, Second edition, North River Press, New York.

Grove, A. S. (1999), *Only the Paranoid Survive*, Currency.

Hall, R. W. (1998), "Standard Work: Holding the Gains," Target, Forth Quarter, pp. 13–19.

Hambrick, D. C., and Fredrickson, J. W. (2001), *Are you sure you have a strategy?* Academy of Management Executive, 15(4).

Hamel, G., and Prahalad, C. K. (1994), "Competing for the Future," *Harvard Business Review*, July–August.

Harry, M. J. (1994), *The Vision of Six Sigma: Tools and Methods for Breakthrough*, Sigma Publishing Company, Phoenix, AZ.

Hauser, J. R., and Clausing, D. (1988), The House of Quality, *Harvard Business Review,* May–June, pp. 63–73.

Higgins, J. M. (1994), *101 Creative Problem Solving Techniques: The Handbook of New Ideas for Business*," New Management Publishing Company, Winter Park, FL.

Hunter, J. S. (1986), The Exponentially Weighted Moving Average, *J. Qual. Technol.*, 18: 203–210.

Hunter, J. S. (1995), Just What Does and EWMA Do? (Part 2), *ASQ Statistics Division Newsletter, Fall* 16(1): 4–12.

Jackson, T. L., *Hoshin Kanri for the Lean Enterprise*, Productivity Press, NY.

Janis, I. (1971), Groupthink *Psychology Today*, June.

John, P. W. M. (1990), *Statistical Methods in Engineering and Quality Assurance*, John Wiley and Sons, Hoboken, NJ.

Johnson, R. B., and Melicher, R. W. (1982), Financial Management, Fifth edition, Allyn and Bacon, Inc., Boston.

Juran, J. M., and Blanton Godfrey, A. (1999), *Juran's Quality Control Handbook*, Fifth edition, McGraw-Hill, New York.

Kano, N., Seraku, N., Takashashi, F., and Tsuji, S. (1984), Attractive Quality and Must be Quality, *Nippon QC Gakka*, 12th annual meeting, 14(2): 39–48.

Kaplan, R. S., and Norton, D. P. (1992), "The Balanced Scorecard – Measures that Drive Performance," *Harvard Business Review*, January–February.

Kaplan, S. (1996), *An Introduction to TRIZ: The Russian Theory of Inventive Problem Solving*, Ideation International, www.ideationtriz.com.

Kaplan, R. S., and Norton, D. P. (1996), *The Balanced Scorecard*, Harvard Business School Press, Boston.

Kelly, J. (2006), *CEO Firings at a Record Pace so far This Year: Leaders Are Getting Pushed Aside as Boards, Wary Of Enron-Type Problems, Become more Vigilant*, Bloomberg News, Austin American Statesman, October 1, 2006.

Kotter, J. P. (1995), Leading Change: Why Transformation Efforts Fail, *Harvard Business Review*, Product Number 4231.

Laney, D. B. (1997), *Control Charts for Attributes Without Distributional Assumptions*, BellSouth, Birmingham, AL.

Lenth, R.V. (1989), "Quick and Easy Analysis of Unreplicated Factorials," *Technometrics*, 31, 469–473.

Lloyd, M. E. (2005), *Krispy Kreme Knew Early of Slowing Sales, Suit Says*, Austin American Statesman, Business Briefing, Dow Jones Newswire, January 4, 2005.

MacInnes, R. L. (2002), *The Lean Enterprise process Memory Jogger*, GOAL/QPC, Salem, NH.

Mallows, C. L. (1973), Some Comments on *C(p)*, *Technometrics*, 15(4): 666–675.

McIntosh, R. I., Culley, S. J., Mileham, A. R., and Owen, G. W. (2001), *Improving Changeover Performance*, Butterworth Heinemann, London.

Minitab (2007), *Minitab Statistical Software*, Release 15, State College, PA.

Montgomery, D. C. (1985), *Introduction to Statistical Quality Control*, Wiley, New York.

Montgomery, D. C. (1997), *Design and Analysis of Experiments*, Wiley, New York.

Montgomery, D. C., and Peck, F. A. (1982), *Introduction to Linear Regression Analysis*, Wiley, New York.

Nakajima, S. (1988), *Introduction to TPM: Total Productive Maintenance*, Productivity Press, Portland, OR.

Nelson, L. S. (1983), Exact Critical Values for Use with the Analysis of Means, *Journal of Quality Technology*, 15(1): 40–42.

Nelson, L. S. (1993), Personal communication during critique *of Statistical Methods for Testing, Development, and Manufacturing*, Wiley, New York.

Nelson, L. S. (1999a), Personal feedback from the First edition of *Implementing Six Sigma*.

Nelson, L. S. (1999b), Notes on the Shewhart Control Chart, *JQT*, Vol 31, No 1, January.

Ohno, T., *Toyota Production System: Beyond Large-Scale Production*, Productivity Press, 1988.

Petruno, Tom (2006), *Options Inquiries Smell of Scandal*, Austin American Statesman, Business & Personal Finance, Los Angeles Times Article, July 16, 2006.

Quality Council of Indiana (2002), *CSSSBB Primer Solution Text*, Quality Council of Indiana.

Quickbase (2006), https://www.quickbase.com/help/chart.

Rother, M., and Shook, J. (1999), *Learning to See: Value Stream Mapping to Create Value and Eliminate Muda*. Brookline, M.A.: The Lean Enterprise Institute, www.lean.org, 617-871-2900.

Scholtes, P. R. (1988), *The Team Handbook: How to Use Teams to Improve Quality*, Joiner Associates, Madison, WI.

Schonberger, R. (1987), "Frugal Manufacturing", *Harvard Business Review*.

Seder, L. A. (1950), Diagnosis with Diagrams – Part I, Industrial Quality Control, VI(4): 11–19.

Senge P. M. (1990), *The Fifth Discipline: The Art and Practice of the Learning Organization*, Doubleday/Current, New York.

Shainin, D., and Shainin, P. (1989), PRE-Control versus $\bar{x}$ and R Charting: Continuous or Immediate Quality Improvement? *Qual. Eng.*, 1(4): 419–429.

Shingo, S. (1985), *SMED*, Productivity Press, Portland, OR.

Six Sigma Study Guide (2002), Engineering Software, Inc. See more information about this product at www.smartersolutions. com. This study guide randomly generates test questions with a solution.

Snee, R. D., and Hoerl, R. W. *Leading Six Sigma: A Step-by-Step Guide Based on Experience with GE and other Six Sigma Companies*, Prentice Hall, 2003.

Spear, S. J., and Bowen, H. K. (1999), "Decoding the DNA of the Toyota Production System," *Harvard Business Review*, September.

Sporting News (1989), July 3: 7.

Strategosinc (2006), http://www.strategosinc.com/just_in_time. htm.

Thurm, S. (2007), "Now, It's Business By Data, but Numbers Still Can't Tell Future," *Wall Street Journal*, July 23, B1.

Toastmasters International (1990), *Communication and Leadership Program*, Mission Viejo, CA.

US Department of Interior (2003), *OMB and Bureau Scorecard Actions: Getting to Green*, http://www.doi.gov/ppp/scorecard. html.

Viswanathan A. (2005), *Robust DOE example.*

Vitalentusa (2006), http://www.vitalentusa.com/learn/6-sigma_vs_kaizen_1.php.

Western Electric (1956), *Statistical Quality Control Handbook,* Western Electric Co., Newark, NJ.

Wheeler, B. (1989), *E-CHIP™ Course Text,* ECHIP Inc., Hockessin, DE.

Wheeler, D. J. (1996), Charts for Rare Events, *Quality Digest,* December.

Wheeler, D. J. (1997), Personal communication with Lloyd Nelson, which was referenced in Nelson (1999b).

Wheeler, S. G. (1990), Personal communications.

Womack, J. P., and Jones, D.T., *Lean Thinking,* Simon & Schuster, 1996.

Womack, J. P., Jones, D. T., and Roos, D., *The Machine that Changed the World,* Harper Perennial, 1990.

Wortman, B., (1990), *The Quality Engineer Primer,* Quality Council of Indiana, Terre Haute, IN.

Index